Correlation Guide for *Ways of the World,* Third Edition

For the AP® Course

Find a complete correlation guide to the AP® World History Key Concepts, Learning Objectives, and Historical Thinking Skills at **highschool.bfwpub.com/strayer3e.**

About the Cover Image

Opening of the First Railway Station in Japan (Shimbashi Station, Tokyo), 19th century (print), Anonymous / Private Collection / Bridgeman Images

The cover image depicts the opening in 1872 of the first commercial railway line in Japan, some sixty-eight years after the earliest steam locomotive took to the rails in Britain. This image evokes several central processes (or themes) in world history that recur repeatedly in *Ways of the World.* One of them is technological diffusion, as innovations in one place spread widely to distant locations. Long before the discovery of steam power and its subsequent adoption throughout the world, other technological innovations — horse collars and saddles, ironworking, gunpowder, and printing, for example — had found a place in societies far removed from their points of origin. A second and related theme is cross-cultural interaction. The opening of this railway station in 1872 followed directly from Japan's encounter with American naval forces in 1853. Such interactions — between Egyptians and Nubians, Greeks and Persians, Chinese and Indians, Muslims and Christians — have long been among the chief motors of transformation throughout the human journey. You can learn more about Japan's modernization in "The Japanese Difference: The Rise of a New East Asian Power" on page 852.

Ways of the World

A Global History with Sources

FOR THE AP® COURSE

Ways of the World
A Global History with Sources

ROBERT W. STRAYER

The College at Brockport: State University of New York

ERIC W. NELSON

Missouri State University

THIRD EDITION

Bedford/St. Martin's
Boston • New York

For BFW & Bedford/St. Martin's

Vice President, Editorial, Macmillan Higher Education Humanities: Edwin Hill

Publisher for High School: Ann Heath

Sponsoring Editor: Janie Pierce-Bratcher

Senior Production Editor: Christina M. Horn

Senior Media Producer: Michelle Camisa

Production Manager: Joe Ford

Marketing Manager: Julie Comforti

Marketing Assistant: Nont Pansringarm

Production Assistant: Erica Zhang

Copy Editor: Jennifer Brett Greenstein

Indexer: Leoni Z. McVey

Cartography: Mapping Specialists, Ltd.

Photo Researcher: Bruce Carson

Director of Rights and Permissions: Hilary Newman

Senior Art Director: Anna Palchik

Text Design: Joyce Weston/Lisa Buckley

Cover Design: William Boardman

Cover Art: Opening of the First Railway Station in Japan (Shimbashi Station, Tokyo), 19th century (print), Anonymous/Private Collection/Bridgeman Images

Composition: Jouve

Printing and Binding: RR Donnelley and Sons

Manufactured in the United States of America.

1 2 3 4 5 6   20 19 18 17 16

For information, write: BFW Publishers, One New York Plaza, Suite 4500, New York, NY 10004
socialstudies@bfwpub.com

ISBN 978-1-319-02272-3

To lovers of history,
young, old, and in-between:
may we all learn what we need
from the past

About the Authors

ROBERT W. STRAYER (Ph.D., University of Wisconsin) brings wide experience in world history to the writing of *Ways of the World*. His teaching career began in Ethiopia, where he taught high school world history for two years as part of the Peace Corps. At the university level, he taught African, Soviet, and world history for many years at the State University of New York–College at Brockport, where he received the Chancellor's Awards for Excellence in Teaching and for Excellence in Scholarship. In 1998 he was visiting professor of world and Soviet history at the University of Canterbury in Christchurch, New Zealand. Since moving to California in 2002, he has taught world history at the University of California, Santa Cruz; California State University, Monterey Bay; and Cabrillo College. He is a longtime member of the World History Association and served on its Executive Committee. He has also participated in various AP® World History gatherings, including two years as a reader. His publications include *Kenya: Focus on Nationalism*, *The Making of Mission Communities in East Africa*, *The Making of the Modern World*, *Why Did the Soviet Union Collapse?*, and *The Communist Experiment*.

ERIC W. NELSON (D.Phil., Oxford University) is a professor of history at Missouri State University. He is an experienced teacher who has won a number of awards, including the Governor's Award for Teaching Excellence in 2011 and the CASE and Carnegie Foundation for the Advancement of Teaching Professor of the Year Award for Missouri in 2012. He is currently Faculty Fellow for Engaged Learning, developing new ways to integrate in-class and online teaching environments. His publications include *The Legacy of Iconoclasm: Religious War and the Relic Landscape of Tours, Blois and Vendôme* and *The Jesuits and the Monarchy: Catholic Reform and Political Authority in France*.

About the Contributors

BARBARA BRUN-OZUNA, Paschal High School, Texas
Author of *Multiple-Choice Practice Questions*

Barbara is a teacher and academic coordinator with nineteen years of experience. She is an AP® World History Consultant and AP® Exam Table Leader. She has trained new AP® readers and has helped to develop rubrics for past AP® World History Exams. She teaches in Fort Worth, Texas, where she has developed and implemented three district-wide AP® courses.

JOSEPH (JAY) HARMON, Houston Christian High School, Texas
Author of *AP® Exam Tips* and *Document-Based Practice Questions*

Jay has taught AP® World History, AP® U.S. History, and AP® European History. He has been a member of the AP® World History Test Development Committee, a consultant to the College Board, and has led AP® history workshops in the United States, England, Germany, and Panama. Jay's Web site harmonhistory.com/apwh has helped many a new teacher prepare for the rigors of teaching AP® World History. He is currently the Social Studies Department chair at his school in Houston, Texas.

DAVE NEUMANN, California State University, Long Beach
Author of *AP® Historical Thinking Skills: A Primer*

Dave is the Site Director of The History Project and an award-winning high school history teacher with experience in the AP® World History and AP® U.S. History courses. He has worked with pre-service elementary and secondary teachers and has organized numerous one-day and week-long workshops for teachers at all grade levels. He has published many articles in education journals and presented at dozens of conferences and workshops. Dave has written test items for AP® World History, the Praxis World History Exam, and the SAT World History Subject Test Study Guide. He also coauthored the Tenth-Grade Course Description for the California Department of Education's Framework for History–Social Science.

JAMES SABATHNE, Hononegah High School, Illinois
Author of *Short-Answer* and *Long-Essay Practice Questions*

James teaches AP® World History and AP® U.S. History in Rockton, Illinois. He serves on the College Board AP® U.S. History Curriculum Development and Assessment Committee and is a table leader for AP® U.S. History. James has presented at the AP® Annual Conference, scored essays at district-wide table readings, authored AP® exam questions, and coordinated a district-wide implementation of DBQ essay formative assessments.

Brief Contents

Contents

5 Society and Inequality in Eurasia/North Africa, 600 B.C.E.–600 C.E.   191

PART THREE

An Age of Accelerating Connections, 600 C.E.–1450

7 Commerce and Culture, 600–1450

8 China and the World: East Asian Connections, 600–1300   323

9 The Worlds of Islam: Afro-Eurasian Connections, 600–1450   363

10 The Worlds of Christendom: Contraction, Expansion, and Division, 600–1300

11   Pastoral Peoples on the Global Stage: The Mongol Moment, 1200–1450

12   The Worlds of the Fifteenth Century

To the Student

Dear readers of AP® World History:

A warm greeting to all of you about to embark on the AP® World History course from the two of us (Robert Strayer and Eric Nelson) who have written this book to guide you through this journey.

We hope that you open this book with a sense of anticipation and even excitement. You are embarking on a remarkable excursion through the history of our species, a history that you are part of and destined to contribute to in the years ahead. It is hard to imagine a more interesting or relevant subject to study than world history.

At the same time, world history can be intimidating—to students, teachers, and textbook writers alike. You may feel that you know little enough of U.S. history, let alone the history of China, India, Africa, the Islamic world, Europe, and Latin America. How are you supposed to take in the mass of information about all of the peoples and places contained in a world history course? If you've thought about it, you may well feel a bit overwhelmed by what awaits you.

> " You are embarking on a remarkable excursion through the history of our species, a history that you are part of and destined to contribute to in the years ahead.

If it is any comfort, you might want to know that the authors of your textbook also feel some anxiety about the daunting task of world history. We are aware that every sentence we write rests on an enormous body of historical research and that historians disagree about almost everything important. So we worry about getting it right. That's why the creation of this book has involved input from dozens of teachers, professors, and scholars who are real experts in particular areas of world history. We have benefited greatly from their criticisms and suggestions.

Beyond accurate information and reasonable interpretations of that information, we also struggle with the even greater problem of putting it all together in some coherent fashion. After all, the potential subject matter of world history is nothing less than everything human, as well as the natural environment in which human beings have made their history. This inclusive scope of world history gives it a certain grandeur, for we seek to tell the story of humankind as a whole from the beginning to the present. Such a story allows you to see yourself, your aspirations, your difficulties, your values, your time and place—in short, your life—in the largest possible setting. In a word, it offers a grand perspective.

BUT this appealing feature of world history is also the source of its greatest difficulty—telling a story that makes sense and hangs together. How can we meaningfully present the planet's many and distinct peoples and their intersections with one another within a single book? How can you possibly embrace the entirety of the human journey in a single course in a single year, while keeping up with the rest of your life as well? What prevents world history from bogging down in unending facts about various civilizations or cultures, from losing the forest for the trees, from suggesting that history is just "one thing after another"?

> **World history is NOT the history of everything; rather, it is highly selective.**

We have sought to cope with this fundamental dilemma of world history—the tension between inclusion and coherence—in several ways. First, we have kept our discussions brief. Despite the seemingly hefty size of this book, its story line or narrative is succinct and straightforward, and the book also includes a large number of documents and images. If you think there's a lot here, you should see what we left out. Whole libraries have been written about the American Revolution, for example, while we summarize its global significance in about two pages. The benefit of such brevity is that *Ways of the World* will not overwhelm you or dominate the course. It also allows for more creativity from your teachers, giving them the opportunity to mix and match textbook, primary sources, and other materials in their own unique ways.

Furthermore, a "themes and cases" approach also contributes to telling a meaningful story. You will find that most chapters are organized in terms of broad themes that are illustrated with a limited number of specific examples. This keeps you focused on the big pictures of world history without drowning you in endless detail. In practice, world history is NOT the history of everything; rather, it is highly selective.

This selectivity favors context over mere information. Every historical character, event, process, culture, or civilization takes on richer significance when it finds a place in some larger framework or context. Thus the American Revolution takes on new meaning when it is viewed in the context of other revolutions in France, Latin America, Russia, and China. Those of us who practice world history as teachers or textbook authors are seldom specialists in the particulars of what we study and teach. Neither we nor your teachers have really mastered the history of the world. Rather, we are "specialists of the whole" and your guide in contextual thinking. In short, for students and teachers of world history, nothing stands alone; context is everything. That is the perspective which *Ways of the World* seeks to convey.

In doing so, we have chosen to highlight three such contexts. We call them the "three Cs" of world history: change/continuity, comparison, and connection. They occur repeatedly throughout the book.

The first "C" emphasizes large-scale **change**, both within and especially across major regions of the world. Examples include:

- The breakthrough to agriculture and the emergence of "civilization"
- The rise and transformation of universal religions: Buddhism, Christianity, and Islam
- The linking of Eastern and Western hemispheres following the voyages of Columbus
- The Industrial Revolution
- The evolution of globalization

The flip side of change, of course, is **continuity**, implying a focus on what has persisted over long periods of time. While civilizations have changed dramatically during many centuries, some of their essential features—cities, states, patriarchy, and class inequality, for example—have long endured.

The second "C" involves frequent **comparison** in which we bring several regions or cultures into our field of vision at the same time. It encourages reflection both on the common elements of the human experience and on their many variations. Such comparisons are pervasive throughout the book, informing both the chapter discussions and many of the book's features. For example, we examine the difference between:

> 66 In short, for students and teachers of world history, nothing stands alone; context is everything.

- The Agricultural Revolution in the Eastern and Western hemispheres
- The beginnings of Buddhism and the early history of Christianity and Islam
- Various expressions of patriarchy and slavery
- European and Asian empires
- The Chinese and the Japanese response to European intrusion
- The Russian and Chinese revolutions

Many of the primary source features are also broadly comparative or cross-cultural. For example, a document-based feature in Chapter 11 explores understandings of the Mongols from the perspective of Persians, Russians, Europeans, and the Mongols themselves. Likewise, an image-based feature in Chapter 15 uses art and architecture to examine various expressions of Christianity in Reformation Europe, colonial Bolivia, seventeenth-century China, and Mughal India. World history is relentlessly comparative.

The final "C" emphasizes **connections**, networks of communication and exchange that linked neighboring and more distant peoples to one another. For world historians, "no man [and no culture] is an island, entire of itself" as the English poet John Donne put it. And so cross-cultural interactions assume a prominent place in this text and are treated as one of the major motors of historical transformation. Such connections are addressed in nearly every chapter and in many *Ways of the World* features. Examples include:

- The clash of the ancient Greeks and the Persians
- Long-distance commercial networks, such as the famous Silk Roads that long linked the Afro-Eurasian world
- The numerous cross-cultural encounters spawned by the spread of Islam
- The Atlantic slave trade, joining Europe, Africa, and the Americas in a tragic transcontinental commercial system
- The growth of a genuinely global economy and culture

So can you do it, this daunting enterprise that is world history? Absolutely yes—but not easily. Like all AP® courses, this one asks you to undertake college-level work. This, you might know, is a college-level textbook, widely used in many colleges and universities across the country. You will be required not only to read it, but to question it, to argue with it, and certainly not to regard it as the last word. You will, of course, assimilate a fair amount of new information, but, of far greater importance, you will be asked to make use of that information—to answer provocative questions, to explain why changes occur, to make frequent comparisons, to assess the impact of encounters with strangers, to evaluate documents and images for how they illuminate the past.

You are embarking on a challenging and rewarding journey that many students of your age and grade level have completed successfully before you. Our book is designed to help and guide you on this journey with a wide array of tools.

- Guided Reading Questions
- Succinct summaries in graphic form
- AP® Exam Tips
- Numerous maps and images
- Main point reminders
- AP® Exam Practice Questions

Your teacher will also provide important guidance throughout the process, and working collaboratively with your fellow students can greatly enhance your learning.

Finally, we expect that your encounter with world history can be engaging, absorbing, exhilarating, and, yes, fun. Really, you'd have to work very hard to make world history boring and mere drudgery. You will encounter much that is new; you will listen in, or perhaps eavesdrop, on conversations from the past; you will be witness to the triumphs and the tragedies of the human journey; you will hopefully gain some sense of your own kinship with people of long ago as well as an awareness of how you differ from them; you will gain some perspective on your own moment in history and your own life. In all of this, your mind will surely be stretched, and if you are willing, your heart will be touched as well. What more might you ask from an AP® course?

With all good wishes for the adventure that awaits you,

Robert Strayer

La Selva Beach, California, Summer 2015

Eric Nelson

Springfield, Missouri, Summer 2015

How to Get the Most from This Program

Start Smart!

Notice that this book is organized into six parts. **These parts align with the six time periods established by the College Board for the AP® World History course.** Each part and chapter of this text is structured around a common set of features designed to convey the rich story of humankind while helping you develop the skills required to realize success on the AP® World History exam. Follow these steps to begin exploring history.

Ways of the World Part	AP® World History Time Periods	% Tested
ONE	to c. 600 B.C.E.	5%
TWO	c. 600 B.C.E.–c. 600 C.E.	15%
THREE	c. 600 C.E.–c. 1450	20%
FOUR	c. 1450–c. 1750	20%
FIVE	c. 1750–c. 1900	20%
SIX	c. 1900–present	20%

AP® HISTORICAL THINKING SKILLS   HTS-11

Creating and Supporting an Argument

The final step in historical thinking is learning to formulate and communicate your own conclusions about the past. The word *argument* reminds us that any attempt to explain the past requires interpretation, since our understanding of the past is limited by distance from the events we study and the incomplete evidence that has survived. Earlier you learned about how historians make arguments; now you'll practice making your own. Arguing means making a logical case for your interpretation of a particular historical question or controversy.

Argumentation

Argumentation is a complex, sophisticated skill that will develop with practice over the course of the school year. Your teacher will likely employ various methods to help you develop this skill, from oral discussions to writing/journaling activities to practicing AP®-style document-based questions. Argumentation includes five components. *First*, a historical argument is a response to a particular debate or question, so forming an argument begins with identifying and framing a question. If you are responding to a prompt or a question posed by your teacher or a textbook, you have to understand the question itself and make sure your response clearly addresses that question. Framing the question means placing it in historical or historiographic context; therefore, often you will need to determine whether the question is part of a historical debate and, if so, what the sides are and where your response fits within that debate. You will also want to explain the significance of the question—what's at stake or why the question matters. *Second*, you need to articulate your argument in a clear, concise, compelling way that directly responds to the prompt. Teachers typically identify this argument as your thesis—a short

FIVE STEPS TO ARGUMENTATI...

1. Frame a question.
2. Form an argument/
3. Examine/analyze ev
4. Display historical th skills.
5. Examine/explain relationships in evidence.

Before you begin reading the text, review **AP® Historical Thinking Skills: A Primer**. This section provides tips on reading this college-level text, suggestions for analyzing what you read, and recommendations for synthesizing the information and writing a cohesive argument—all skills you must demonstrate on the AP® exam. Getting these insights at the beginning of the course will help you study more thoughtfully and efficiently.

Put Things in Context

THE BIG PICTURE

TURNING POINTS IN EARLY
WORLD HISTORY

Human beings have long been inveterate storytellers. Those who created our
myths, legends, fairy tales, oral traditions, family sagas, and more have sought to
distill meaning from experience, to explain why things turned out as they did,
and to provide guidance for individuals and communities. Much the same might
be said of modern historians. They too tell stories—about individuals, communities, nations, and, in the case of world history, of humankind as a whole.
Those stories seek to illuminate the past, to provide context for the present,
and, very tentatively, to offer some indication about possible futures. All tellers
of stories—ancient and modern alike—have to decide at what point to begin
their accounts and what major turning points in those nar[...]
For world historians seeking to tell the story of "all und[...]
Chinese put it, four major "beginnings," each of them a[...]
process, have charted the initial stages of the human journey.

Begin your study in each part by
reading the **Big Picture** essay as an
overview of what you will study in
that time period.

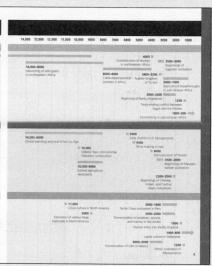

Refer as often as needed to
the **Landmarks** timeline at the
beginning of each part. These
timelines provide a chronological overview of key events and
processes in that particular part
of the book.

UNDERSTANDING AP® THEMES IN PART ONE

Technological and Environmental Transformations

Corresponding to Period 1 of the AP® course outline, Part One of this text
constitutes just 5 percent of the exam but lays the groundwork for your
study of world history and the themes you will encounter within it. In this
part, we will chart the course of human history from its earliest migrations,
which colonized the entire planet, to the emergence of the First Civilizations, which flourished from around 3500 B.C.E. to 600 B.C.E. This immense
period of time encompasses most of the human journey and is characterized
by three major global transformations: the initial colonization of the earth by
humans, the advent of agricultural societies, and, much later, the emergence
of the city- and state-based societies that we refer to as civilizations. These
three long-term processes reshaped humankind in any number of ways:

- Our relationships to the natural order
- Our understanding of the world
- Our systems of maintaining order
- Our methods for addressing conflicts
- Our techniques of survival and making a living
- Our social organizations and ways of relating to one another
- The range of our interactions with those beyond our own communities

The chart on the opposite page provides an overview of the AP® World
History themes you will encounter in this part. While this list is by no means
exhaustive, it offers threads that are significant for the time period and
important for your course studies. As you read the following chapters, pay
close attention to these five themes. Also watch for AP® Exam Tips throughout the text to assist you in your coursework and exam preparation.

Identify the important
forces shaping each period
and make connections
between chapters in
**Understanding AP®
Themes**, located at the
beginning of each part

Read with a Purpose

achievements of humankind and yet people within them have often sought to escape the constraints, artificiality, hierarchies, and other discontents of civilized living.

So what exactly are these civilizations that have generated such ambivalent responses among their inhabitants? When, where, and how did they first arise in human history? What changes did they bring to the people who lived within them? Why might some people criticize or seek to escape from them?

As historians commonly use the term, "civilization" represents a new and particular type of human society, made possible by the immense productivity of the Agricultural Revolution. Such societies encompassed far larger populations than any earlier form of human community and for the first time concentrated some of those people in sizable cities. Both within and beyond these cities, people were organized and controlled by states whose leaders could use force to compel obedience. Profound differences in economic function, skill, wealth, and status sharply divided the people of civilizations, making them far less equal and subject to much greater oppression than had been the case in earlier Paleolithic communities, agricultural villages, pastoral societies, or chiefdoms. Pyramids, temples, palaces, elaborate sculptures, written literature, and complex calendars, as well as more elaborate class and gender hierarchies, slavery, and large-scale warfare — all of these have been among the cultural products of civilization.

> Preview the **Seeking the Main Point** question at the beginning of each chapter to focus your attention on an important chapter theme.

SEEKING THE MAIN POINT

What distinguished "civilizations" from earlier Paleolithic and Neolithic societies?

Something New: The Emergence of Civilizations

AP® EXAM TIP

Know the definition of "civilization."

Like agriculture, civilization was a global phenomenon, showing up independently in seven major locations scattered around the world during the several millennia after 3500 B.C.E. and in a number of other smaller expressions as well (see Map 2.1). In the long run of human history, these civilizations — small breakthroughs to a new way of life — gradually absorbed, overran, or displaced people practicing other ways of living. Over the next 5,000 years, civilization, as a unique kind of human community, gradually encompassed ever-larger numbers of people and extended over ever-larger territories, even as particular civilizations rose, fell, revived, and changed.

Introducing the First Civilizations

Guided Reading Question

■ CHANGE
When and where did the First Civilizations emerge?

The earliest of these civilizations emerged around 3500 B.C.E. to 3000 B.C.E. in three places. One was the "cradle" of Middle Eastern civilization, expressed in the many and competing city-states of Sumer in southern Mesopotamia (located in present-day Iraq). Much studied by archeologists and historians, Sumerian civilization likely gave rise to the world's earliest written language, which was used initially by officials to record the goods received by various temples. Almost simultaneously, the Nile River valley in northeastern Africa witnessed the emergence

> Refer to the **Guided Reading Questions** for help focusing on what's important.

> Look for **Snapshot** boxes that offer succinct glimpses of particular themes, regions, or time periods, thus adding some trees to the forest of world history.

ZOOMING IN

Ishi, the Last of His People

In late August of 1911, an emaciated and nearly naked man, about fifty years old, staggered into the corral of a slaughterhouse in northern California. As it turned out, he was the last member of his people, a gathering and hunting group known as the Yahi, pushed into extinction by the intrusion of more powerful farming, herding, and "civilized" societies. It was a very old story, played out for over 10,000 years since the Agricultural Revolution placed Paleolithic cultures on the defensive, inexorably eroding their presence on the earth. The tragic story of this individual allows us to put a human face on that enormous and largely unrecorded process.

Within a few days, this bedraggled and no doubt bewildered man was taken into the care of several anthropologists from the University of California, who brought him to a museum in San Francisco, where he lived until his death from tuberculosis in 1916.

Ishi.

They called him Ishi, "person" in his native because he was unwilling to provide them with his actual name. In his culture it was inappropriate to reveal one's name, especially to strangers.

In the mid-nineteenth century, the Yahi consisted of about 300 to 400 people living in a rugged and mountainous area of northern California. There they hunted, fished, gathered acorns, and otherwise provided for themselves in a fashion familiar to gathering and hunting peoples the world over. But the 1849 California gold rush brought a massive influx of American settlers, miners, and farmers that quickly pushed the Yahi to the edge of extinction. Yahi raiding and resistance was met by massacres at the hands of local militia and vigilantes, who were only too glad to "clean up the Indians," killing and scalping

photo: Courtesy of The Bancroft Library, University of California, Berkeley

> While this text focuses on the big picture of world history, you can find close examinations of particular people, places, and events in the **Zooming In** features.

human population, as the greater productivity of agriculture was able to support much larger numbers. An early agricultural settlement uncovered near Jericho in present-day Israel probably had 2,000 people, a vast increase in the size of human communities compared to much smaller Paleolithic bands. On a global level, scholars estimate that the world's population was about 6 million around 10,000 years ago, before the Agricultural Revolution got under way, and shot up to some 50 million by 5,000 years ago and 250 million by the beginning of the Common Era. Here was the real beginning of the human dominance over other forms of life on the planet.

That dominance was reflected in major environmental transformations. In a growing number of places, forests and grasslands became cultivated fields and grazing lands. Human selection modified the genetic composition of numerous plants and animals. In parts of the Middle East, within a thousand years after the beginning of agriculture, villages were abandoned when soil erosion and

> Read and take notes on the **AP® Exam Tips** to learn important concepts and develop skills that will help you succeed on the AP® exam.

Think Like a Historian

Your AP® World History exam will require you to read, think, and write about primary sources. Review the **Working with Evidence** feature at the end of each chapter to practice reading, thinking, and writing about primary documents.

WORKING WITH EVIDENCE

Indus Valley Civilization

In most accounts of the First Civilizations, Egypt and Mesopotamia hold center stage. And yet the civilization of the Indus River valley was much larger, and its archeological treasures have been equally impressive, though clearly distinctive. This civilization flourished around 2000 B.C.E., about a thousand years later than its better-known counterparts in the Middle East and Northeast Africa. By 1700 B.C.E., Indus Valley civilization was in decline, as the center of Indian or South Asian civilization shifted gradually eastward

Read the **Chapter Review**, study the terms, and answer Big Picture questions to put your identification, analysis, and speculation skills to work.

Answer the **Practicing AP® Historical Thinking** questions to apply what you have learned in the chapter.

But if agriculture provided humankind with the power to dominate nature, it also, increasingly, enabled some people to dominate others. This was not immedi-... ...usand years, and much longer in some places, ...munities retained elements of the social equality ... Slowly, though, many of the resources released ...mulated in the hands of a few. Rich and poor, ...en, slaves and free people—these distinctions, ...history, took shape most extensively in highly ...ch generated a substantial economic surplus. ...differences, for better or worse, became a major ...al societies known to us as "civilizations." ...make among various kinds of human commu-...ples, pastoral societies, agricultural village com-munities, chiefdoms, civilizations—do not represent hard-and-fast differences, but lie on a continuum. Many gathering and hunting societies were nomadic, but some became sedentary; many agricultural and pastoral peoples continued to enrich their diets with foods hunted, gathered, or fished; the line between chiefdoms and civilizations is not always obvious. Such terms are useful for identifying variations in human history, but lived experience is usually messier and less clear than our tidy concepts.

PRACTICING AP® HISTORICAL THINKING

What was revolutionary about the Agricultural Revolution?

REFLECTIONS

The Uses of the Paleolithic

Even when it is about the distant past, history is also about those who tell it in the present. We search the past, always, for our own purposes. For example, modern people were long inclined to view their Paleolithic or gathering and hunting ancestors as primitive or superstitious, unable to exercise control over nature, and ignorant of its workings. Such a view was, of course, a kind of self-congratulation, designed to highlight the "progress" of modern humankind. It was a way of saying, "Look how far we have come."

In more recent decades, however, growing numbers of people, disillusioned with modernity, have looked to the Paleolithic era for material with which to criti-...ary life. Feminists have found in gathering ...er-equal society and religious thinking that ...hat encouragingly suggested that patriarchy ...vironmentalists have sometimes identified ...quely in tune with the natural environment ...e nutritionists have advocated a "Paleolithic ...suited to our physiology. Critics of modern

materi... which ... hierarc... explosi... ered nor... pathological. All of these uses of the Paleolithic have been a way of asking, "What have we lost in the mad rush to modernity, and how can we recover it?"

Both those who look with disdain on Paleolithic "backwardness" and those who praise, often quite romantically, its simplicity and equality seek to use these ancient people for their own purposes. In our efforts to puzzle out the past, all of us—historians and students of history very much included—stand somewhere. None of us can be entirely detached when we view the past, but this is not neces-sarily a matter for regret. What we may lose in objectivity, we gain in passionate involvement with the historical record and with the many men and women who have inhabited it. Despite its remoteness from us in time and manner of living, the Paleolithic era resonates still in the twenty-first century, reminding us of our kin-ship with these distant people and the significance of that kinship to finding our own way in a very different world.

Chapter Review

What's the Significance?

Venus figurines, 14; 23
Dreamtime, 15
Clovis culture, 18
megafaunal extinction, 18
Austronesian migrations, 19
"the original affluent society," 22
shamans, 23
trance dance, 24
Paleolithic settling down, 24
Göbekli Tepe, 25

Fertile Crescent, 28; 32
teosinte, 34
diffusion, 36
Bantu migration, 37
Ishi, 38
Banpo, 40
"secondary products revolution," 41
pastoral societies, 41
Çatalhüyük, 43
chiefdoms, 44

Big Picture Questions

1. In what ways did various Paleolithic societies differ from one another, and how did they change over time?
2. The Agricultural Revolution marked a decisive and progressive turning point in human history. What evidence might you offer to support this claim, and how might you argue against it?
3. How did early agricultural societies differ from those of the Paleolithic era?
4. Was the Agricultural Revolution inevitable? Why did it occur so late in the story of humankind?
5. In what different ways did human beings relate to the natural world during the early and long phases of our history explored in the chapter?

Read the **Reflections** essays for examples of how to use your developing historical thinking skills to answer provocative questions about the unfolding of the human story.

Practice for the AP® Exam

Multiple-Choice Questions

Use the chart below and your knowledge of world history to answer questions 1–3.

Agricultural Breakthroughs

LOCATION	DATES (B.C.E.)	PLANTS	ANIMALS
Southwest Asia (Fertile Crescent)	9000–7000	barley, wheat, lentils, figs	goats, sheep, cattle, pigs
China	6500–5000	rice, millet, soybeans	pigs, chickens, water buffalo
Saharan and sub-Saharan Africa	3000–2000	sorghum, millet, yams, teff	cattle (perhaps 8000 B.C.E.)
Highland New Guinea	7000–4000	taro, bananas, yams, sugarcane	—
Andes region	3000–2000	potatoes, quinoa, manioc	llamas, alpacas, guinea pigs
Mesoamerica	3000–2000	maize, squash (perhaps 7000 B.C.E.), beans	turkeys
Eastern woodlands of North America	2000–1000	sunflowers, goosefoot, sumpweed	—

> Test yourself at the end of each part by answering the **AP® Exam Practice Questions**. These are the types of questions you'll see on the AP® exam.

1. Which of the following could be considered the oldest domesticated plant?
   a. Potatoes
   b. Rice
   c. Squash
   d. Sunflowers

2. Based on the information provided, which of these is the most likely conclusion that can be drawn regarding domestication?
   a. All animals were domesticated at the same time as plants.
   b. Every region domesticated plants and animals before 5000 B.C.E.
   c. Inhabitants of the New Guinea highlands relied solely on vegetarian diets since they had no domesticated animals.
   d. Cattle were among the earliest domesticated animals.

3. Based on the information provided, what conclusions can be drawn about the development of agriculture?
   a. Agriculture init[iated in] specific areas th[at ...] innovation.
   b. Agriculture init[iated ...] widespread tec[...]
   c. Agriculture init[iated ...] rise of civilizati[...]
   d. Agriculture dev[eloped ...] out of Africa.

95-a

> Find more practice questions in the accompanying **Strive for a 5** study and prep guide. You can also study when and where you want with **edaptext**—our easy-to-use, flexible e-book.

Short-Answer Question

Question 4 refers to the passage below.

"From the point of view of the lives of women, the Neolithic period is perhaps the most important phase of prehistory.... It is likely that at the end of the Paleolithic ..., women enjoyed equality with men. They probably collected as much, if not more, of the food eaten by the community and derived equal status from their contribution.... [W]omen almost certainly "invented" agriculture as well as many of the concomitant skills and tools which go to make crop agriculture possible and profitable.... But between then and now ... the status of women has been drastically reduced, and in many areas farming has become a predominately male preserve....As the balance of work changed from part hunting, part crop cultivation and tending a small number of animals to an economy dependent on mixed farming, so the roles and duties of women and men may have shifted....[I]t was in the later Neolithic, when men began to take over most agricultural work, that the social status of women declined."

   Margaret Ehrenberg, historian, *Women in Prehistory*, 1989

4. Answer parts A, B, and C.
   A. Identify and explain how ONE specific historical development prior to 600 B.C.E. could be used to support one of Ehrenberg's assertions in the passage above.
   B. Identify and explain how ANOTHER specific historical development prior to 600 B.C.E. could be used to support one of Ehrenberg's assertions in the passage above.
   C. Identify and explain how ONE specific historical development prior to 600 B.C.E. could be used to challenge one of Ehrenberg's assertions in the passage above.

Document-Based Question

Directions: *Question 5 refers to the following documents. You will likely need to flip back and forth between these documents to answer the question adequately. Use scrap pieces of paper or sticky notes to tab these documents. When answering the question, refer to the "Advice for Responding to a DBQ" on the inside of the back cover.*

5. Using the following documents from this textbook and your knowledge of world history, compare and contrast images that humans made of themselves in the era before c. 600 B.C.E.

DOCUMENT	PAGE	DOCUMENT NAME
1	35	The Statues of Ain Ghazal
2	40	Nok Culture
3	58	Raherka and Mersankh
4	79	Olmec Head
5	93	Man from Mohenjo Daro

Long-Essay Question

When answering the following question, refer to the "Advice for Responding to an LEQ" on the inside of the back cover.

6. Using specific examples, compare and contrast the political systems in agricultural chiefdoms and First Civilizations, analyzing reasons for the similarities and differences.

Maps

Features

Zooming In

Snapshot

Working with Evidence

At the end of each chapter of *Ways of the World* is a set of primary sources called **Working with Evidence** that represent the kind of evidence that historians use in drawing their conclusions about the past. In addition, there are primary source activities surrounded by a distinctive and sophisticated pedagogy of self-grading exercises called **Thinking through Sources** available only in LaunchPad, the interactive course space for this book. (For more information about Launch-Pad, visit **highschool.bfwpub.com**, or to arrange a demo, contact us at **socialstudies @bfwpub.com**.) Some of the primary sources are written—inscriptions, letters, diaries, law codes, official records, sacred texts, and much more. Others are visual—paintings, sculptures, engravings, photographs, posters, cartoons, buildings, and artifacts. Collectively they provide an opportunity for you to practice the work of historians in a kind of guided "history laboratory." In working with this evidence, you are "doing history," much as students conducting lab experiments in chemistry or biology courses are "doing science."

Since each feature explores a theme of the chapter, the chapter narrative itself provides a broad context for analyzing these sources. Furthermore, brief introductions to each feature and to each document or image offer more specific context or background information, while questions provide specific elements to look for as you examine each source. Other more integrative questions offer a focus for using those sources together to probe larger historical issues. What follows are a few more specific suggestions for assessing these raw materials of history.

Working with Written Sources

Written sources or documents are the most common type of primary source that historians use. Analysis of documents usually begins with the basics:

- Who wrote the document?
- When and where was it written?
- What type of document is it (for example, a letter to a friend, a political decree, an exposition of a religious teaching)?

Sometimes the document itself will provide answers to these questions. On other occasions, you may need to rely on the introductions.

Once these basics have been established, a historian is then likely to consider several further questions, which situate the document in its particular historical context:

- Why was the document written, for what audience, and under what circumstances?

- What point of view does it reflect? What other views or opinions is the document arguing against?

Inspiration and intention are crucial factors that shape the form and content of a source. For instance, one might examine a document differently depending on whether it was composed for a private or a public readership, or whether it was intended to be read by a small elite or a wider audience.

Still another level of analysis seeks to elicit useful information from the document.

- What material in the document is believable, and what is not?
- What might historians learn from this document?
- What can the document tell us about the individual who produced it and the society from which he or she came?

In all of this, historical imagination is essential. Informed by knowledge of the context and the content of the document, your imagination will help you read it through the eyes of its author and its audience. You should ask yourself: how might this document have been understood at the time it was written? But in using your imagination, you must take care not to read into the documents your own assumptions and understandings. It is a delicate balance, a kind of dance that historians constantly undertake. Even documents that contain material that historians find unbelievable can be useful, for we seek not only to know what actually happened in the past but also to grasp the world as the people who lived that past understood it. And so historians sometimes speak about reading documents "against the grain," looking for meanings that the author might not have intended to convey.

While each source must be read and understood individually, historians typically draw their strongest conclusions when they analyze a number of such sources together. The document features in *Ways of the World* are designed to explore sets of primary sources that address a central theme of the chapter by drawing on several related texts. In the documents for Chapter 11, for example, you can reflect on the Mongol Empire by reading several accounts written by Mongols themselves and several others composed by Russian or Persian victims of Mongol aggression. And in Chapter 22, you will encounter a debate among Muslims about the relationship between their faith and the modern world, with positions ranging from those that advocate the removal of Islam from public life to those that seek to embed Islamic law in the social and cultural fabric of their countries.

Working with Visual Sources

Visual sources derive from the material culture of the past—religious icons or paintings that add to our understanding of belief systems, a family portrait that provides insight into presentations of self in a particular time and place, a building or sculpture that reveals how power and authority were displayed in a specific empire. These kinds of evidence represent another category of primary source material that historians can use to re-create and understand the past. But such visual sources can be even more difficult to interpret than written documents. The ideas that animated the creators of particular images or artifacts are often not obvious. Nor are the meanings they conveyed to those who viewed or used them. The lovely images from the Indus River valley civilization contained in the visual sources feature for Chapter 2, for example, remain enigmatic although still engaging to twenty-first-century viewers.

Despite the difficulties of interpretation, visual sources can provide insights not offered by written documents. Various images of the Buddha shown in Chapter 4 effectively illustrate how the faith that he initiated changed as it spread beyond India to other parts of Asia. And the posters from Mao Zedong's China in Chapter 21 convey an immediate emotional sense about the meanings attached to communism at the time, at least to its supporters. Indeed, for preliterate societies, such as those described in Chapter 1, archeological and artistic evidence is almost all that remains of their history.

To use visual sources, we must try as best we can to see these pieces of evidence through the eyes of the societies that produced them and to decode the symbols and other features that imbue them with meaning. Thus context is, if anything, even more crucial for analyzing visual evidence than it is for documents. Understanding scenes from the life of Muhammad, featured in Chapter 9, depends heavily on some knowledge of Islamic history and culture. And the images in Chapter 16, illustrating various perceptions of the French Revolution, require some grasp of the unfolding of that enormous upheaval.

A set of basic questions, similar to those you would ask about a written document, provides a starting point for analyzing visual sources:

- When and where was the image or artifact created?
- Who made the image or artifact? Who paid for or commissioned it? For what audience(s) was it intended?
- Where was the image or artifact originally displayed or used?

Having established this basic information about the image or artifact, you may simply want to describe it, as if to someone who had never seen it before.

- If the source is an image, who or what is depicted? What activities are shown? How might you describe the positioning of figures, their clothing, hairstyles, and other visual cues?
- If the source is an object or building, how would you describe its major features?

Finally, you will want to take a stab at more interpretive issues, making use of what you know about the context in which the visual source was created.

- What likely purpose or function did the image or artifact serve?
- What message(s) does it seek to convey?
- How could it be interpreted differently depending on who viewed or used it?

- What are the meanings of any symbols or other abstract features in the visual source?
- What can the image or artifact tell us about the society that produced it and the time period in which it was created?

Beyond analyzing particular images or objects, you will be invited to draw conclusions from sets of related visual sources that address a central theme in the chapter. What can you learn, for example, about the life of Chinese elites from the visual sources in Chapter 8? And what do the images in the Working with Evidence feature of Chapter 15 disclose about the reception of Christianity in various cultural settings?

Primary sources—documentary and visual alike—are the foundation for all historical accounts. To read only secondary sources, such as textbooks or articles, is to miss much of the flavor and texture of history as it was actually experienced by people in the past. But immersing yourself in the documents and visual sources presented here allows you to catch a glimpse of the messiness, the ambiguity, the heartaches, and the achievements of history as it was lived.

Using these sources effectively, however, is no easy task. In fact, the work of historians might well be compared with that of Sisyphus, the ancient Greek king who, having offended the gods, was condemned to eternally roll a large rock up a mountain, only to have it ceaselessly fall back down. Like Sisyphus, historians work at a mission that can never be completely successful—to recapture the past before it is lost forever in the mists of time and fading memory. The evidence available is always partial and fragmentary. Historians and students of history alike are limited and fallible, for we operate often at a great distance—in both time and culture—from those we are studying. And we rarely agree on important matters, divided as we are by sex, nationality, religion, race, and values, all of which shape our understandings of the past.

Despite these challenges, scholars and students alike have long found their revisiting of the past a compelling project—intensely interesting, personally meaningful, and even fun—particularly when working with "primary" or "original" sources, which are the building blocks of all historical accounts. Such sources are windows into the lives of our ancestors, though these windows are often smudged and foggy. We hope that working with the evidence contained in these sources will enrich your own life as you listen in on multiple conversations from the past, eavesdropping, as it were, on our ancestors.

AP® Historical Thinking Skills

A Primer

DAVE NEUMANN

Director, The History Project
California State University, Long Beach

Students and adults alike often grumble that history is just a bunch of facts to memorize. While it's true that studying history requires data, information, and facts, that's not the essence of what history is. History is a way of understanding the world by learning about the past. It is an interpretive reconstruction of the past based on several skills. Advanced Placement (AP®) World History requires students to demonstrate an understanding of these skills. This primer will help you develop the historical thinking skills needed to succeed in your AP® World History class and exam, as well as improve the critical thinking, reading, and writing skills that will be useful in college and in your future career.

Historical Thinking Skills for World History

The AP® World History curriculum introduces you to nine thinking skills in four categories, representing the ways historians talk about the past. These skills are sometimes described as "habits of mind." This useful phrase should remind you that a skill needs to be practiced repeatedly until it becomes second nature. Because practice is an integral part of learning to think historically, the sections below include exercises to help you develop these "habits of mind." Like shooting free throws, rehearsing dance moves, or playing scales, historical thinking skills need to be exercised regularly until you can use them easily and almost effortlessly.

While all historians use the skills described here, world historians use them in distinctive ways. That's because world history deals with a much larger region (often the entire globe) and a much longer period of time (thousands of years) than United States history or even European history. Thus, while the AP® United

States History and AP® European History courses employ these very same skills, in AP® World History you will practice historical thinking from a very broad point of view. And even though we discuss each skill separately below, these skills overlap in many ways. For example, you can't make a historical argument without also evaluating evidence. So as you develop one historical thinking skill, you'll also be learning other skills at the same time.

Analyzing Historical Sources and Evidence

To start, historians make arguments about the past based on evidence, which is categorized as either primary or secondary sources. A *primary source* is something produced in the time period you are studying. In contrast, a *secondary source* is a text written about that time period, usually something a historian writes long after the fact. Secondary sources result from scholarly research of primary sources. Effective historical thinking requires the ability to analyze primary sources—reading carefully for the author's point of view and purpose, the format of the document, and its context—as well as to analyze the ways historians create interpretations (secondary sources) based on their own use of primary-source evidence. Until now, you might have thought of your school textbooks as conveyors of facts and truths, but by definition, the narrative of this book—that is, the portions written by Drs. Robert Strayer and Eric Nelson—is in fact a secondary source with which you might disagree. To do so, you would use historical thinking skills in order to question their interpretation of primary sources.

> " Historians make arguments about the past based on evidence, which is categorized as either primary or secondary sources.

Analyzing Evidence: Content and Sourcing— Primary Sources

Traditionally, primary sources have consisted overwhelmingly of written sources. In fact, historians used to refer to any time before the invention of writing as "prehistory." In the last few decades, however, historians have moved well beyond relying exclusively on written primary sources. Historians now use paintings, photographs, architecture, artifacts, and so on, as well as evidence from other fields of knowledge. For example, scientific and medical information informs historians about the role that disease played throughout history. And since no historian can be an expert in every field, they also make use of the secondary-source scholarship of specialists who have studied materials such as ancient DNA or pottery shards in their own concentrated studies.

In assessing primary sources, you need to begin with a careful examination of the source itself. But you also have to pay attention to the broader *context* of the source. Primary sources are creations from a particular time and place, often created for someone else, so determining the author, purpose, and audience of a source is essential to your understanding of it. It is often helpful to distinguish between primary sources that people in the past intentionally preserved (like government records) and those things that accidentally survived (such as materials in ancient trash heaps).

The following questions will help you examine primary sources:

- *Context:* How does the time and place of this document's creation help you understand the document better?
  - What beliefs and/or practices of the time might make this document more understandable?
  - What important events might this document relate to?

- *Author:* How does information about the author's position, identity, or experience help you to assess his or her point of view or perspective?
  - What is the author's *position*—occupation, authority, status?
  - What is the author's *identity*—race, class, gender, age?
  - What is the author's *experience*—education or training?

- *Purpose and Audience:* Given the information above, what inference(s) can you make about the author's purpose in creating this document?
  - What might the author be trying to get his or her audience to think or to do? Why?
  - If the author's original purpose in writing differs from your own reasons for reading the document historically, how do you read between the lines to determine useful evidence?

- *Document:* How does information about the document help you assess its usefulness or limitations?
  - Is the document public or private?
  - Is the document formal or informal?
  - Is the author knowledgeable or unknowledgeable about this subject?
  - Does the author have a favorable or unfavorable view of the subject?
  - Does the audience have a close or distant relationship to the author?
  - Is the audience an inferior or a superior of the author?

When examining sources, you should consider:

- Context
- Author/Point of View
- Purpose/Audience
- Document/Format

EXERCISE   Read pages 580–82 to acquire information to use as context in examining the document by Mughal emperor Jahangir on pages 590–92. Use the questions above to guide your examination of the document.

Interpretation—Secondary Sources

Historians interpret both primary and secondary sources, evaluating points of view and considering context to create their own interpretations. By analyzing different historical interpretations, you will see how historical interpretations change over time.

Formulating a historical argument requires making inferences from evidence. For example, most scholars agree that the adoption of agriculture about 11,000 years ago marked the beginning of a major world historical development. But because this development preceded writing, our only evidence comes from archeology and anthropology. Consequently, historians disagree about whether agriculture led to permanent settlement in a particular location—or vice versa.

Not surprisingly, the background of a particular historian (gender, nationality, political philosophy, time of writing, etc.) often shapes the way he or she interprets the past. In many cases, knowing something about the context of a historian can help you understand his or her argument better—in the same way that understanding the context of the author of a primary source helps you understand the primary source. Sometimes, this information can help you identify the prejudices or limitations of a particular interpretation.

For example, in the early 1960s a British historian claimed that Africa had no history until Europeans took over the continent. Subsequent scholarship has shown this conclusion to be quite false, and we can assume that this historian's context as a citizen of an imperial nation writing during the era of decolonization influenced his outlook. About the same time, American scholars developed an influential model of modernization for "third world" countries. Later scholars have argued that this model oversimplified the world by assuming all countries would grow economically the same way the United States had.

You can't simply assume, however, that because a scholar has a particular background he or she will make a certain argument. There are far too many exceptions for such a rule. Instead, begin by finding out what you can about a scholar's background and then develop a hunch about how this background *might* shape his or her views. Then, as you read the scholar's argument, carefully look for evidence that the author actually makes the kinds of arguments you anticipated. If you don't find such evidence, discard your hunch.

EXERCISE   On pages 26–28, how do Drs. Strayer and Nelson explain the emergence of agriculture? What inferences do they make?

Making Historical Connections

The second category of historical thinking skills reflects the ways historians make sense of the past by placing details and particulars in some larger framework. For example, we understand historical events and processes by comparing them to related events and processes to see how they're similar and different (such as examining how patriarchy—a term you will learn well in AP® World History—manifested in cultures). Second, historians recognize that they can only really understand historical evidence, including artifacts, photographs, speeches, and historical narratives (secondary sources), when they know something about their context, that is, the time and place when they came into existence.

> "The second category of historical thinking skills reflects the ways historians make sense of the past by placing details and particulars in some larger framework.

Comparison

Comparisons help world historians understand how one development in the past was similar to or different from another development, and in this way determine what was distinctive. For example, through comparative study, scholars have concluded that empires that developed over the last 2,000 years share key features. First, rulers have to legitimize their rule through religious or ideological traditions. Second, they have to maintain political unity by dealing with people on the peripheries of the empire. Finally, since empires develop by conquering other groups of people, their leaders have to deal with ethnic diversity among their subjects and the tensions this diversity can cause.

But while these patterns hold true for all empires, each one addresses these challenges in its own way. The Ottoman Empire justified its rule through Turkish tradition as well as Islamic belief. Its leaders rewarded loyal elites on the margins of their empire through tax breaks. And they dealt with minorities by creating the *millet* system (whereby Ottoman subjects were divided into religious communities, each ruled by its religious leaders). Through the tool of comparison, we understand how Ottoman rulers handled common problems in unique ways.

As you develop this skill, practice comparing two states that existed at the same time, like the Ottoman and Mughal empires. You can also compare the same state at two different points in time. For example, how was government in Song China similar to—and different from—government in Tang China? Be sure that the two things you're comparing are relatively similar, or else comparing doesn't make much sense.

EXERCISE Look at the authors' comparison of Atlantic empires on pages 563–64 and determine what makes a comparison of these empires useful. How are these empires basically alike? Why are they alike? What key features do the authors say are different? Why are they different?

Contextualization

Historians know that just as historical events make more sense when they're studied alongside similar events, any event can be understood only in *context*. Context refers to the historical circumstances surrounding a particular event. World historians look for major global developments in any era to help determine context. Also, in the same way that they conceptualize causation at different scales, they typically think in terms of two levels of context: an *immediate* (or short-term) context and a *broad* (or long-term) context.

The easiest way to begin thinking about context is to figure out when a particular event took place (or when a particular document was created). Then brainstorm the major developments of the era. Ask yourself, "How might these larger events have shaped this event (or document)?"

For example, when reading the Turkish leader Mustafa Kemal Atatürk's "Speech to the General Congress of the Republican Party" on page 1013, note that it was written in 1927. What were the major *immediate* geopolitical developments at this point of the twentieth century? World War I had recently ended when he made this speech, which is likely to be crucial for understanding the speech. The war accelerated nationalist ideologies and calls for national self-determination, which are crucial for understanding what Atatürk is concerned about. The *broad* context of nationalism and liberal republicanism form the background that help explain Atatürk's leadership.

EXERCISE Look at "Working with Evidence: Representing the French Revolution" on pages 730–34. What *immediate* developments in the French Revolution inspired these illustrations? How does the *broad* context of European developments in the modern period help you understand these illustrations?

Synthesis

Some complex historical developments can be grasped only by examining multiple elements separately, then pulling them all together. Synthesis is a complex skill that challenges you to draw a variety of evidence, themes, and/or patterns together into a coherent understanding. To synthesize, you may need to draw on evidence outside the field of history, particularly from the social sciences: archeology, anthropology, economics, sociology, and so on. Or you might need to apply insights from historical evidence in one historical period to developments in another period, or to a similar development in another region. This is a variation on the skill of comparison.

> "Synthesis is a complex skill that challenges you to draw a variety of evidence, themes, and/or patterns together into a coherent understanding.

EXERCISE   The beginnings of agriculture roughly 11,000 years ago brought major changes to human societies that adopted it. But agricultural techniques have not remained static since their original invention. Trace major changes in Western Christendom's agriculture (pages 428–31), in the growth of sugar plantations (pages 622–24), and in the "Green Revolution" of the late twentieth century (pages 1053–54). Write a sentence that summarizes the economic and social impact of changes in agricultural technology.

Chronological Reasoning

Our third historical thinking category, chronological reasoning, means thinking logically about how and why the world changes—or, sometimes, stays the same—over time. While all fields of knowledge offer arguments based on evidence or make comparisons, historians are uniquely concerned about the past and its relationship to the present. How is the world different now than it was 50 years ago, 500 years ago, or 5,000 years ago? Why did the world change? Why have some aspects of the world remained relatively the same over long periods of time? On what basis do historians simplify the long and complicated past by breaking it into smaller eras?

Causation

Causation has to do with explanations about how or why changes take place in world history. Sometimes there is an obvious connection between an event and its consequence, like a cue ball striking the eight ball and making it move. Some events seem fairly straightforward: the attack on Pearl Harbor prompted President Roosevelt to ask Congress for a declaration of war against Japan. But even this seemingly simple example is more complex. Why did Japan attack the United States? What role did the American embargo on the sale of oil have on Japan's decision? Why did the United States enact this embargo? All of these other events took place just a few years before the Pearl Harbor attack. If we go even further back, we'll see the ways European imperialism, the Meiji Restoration, and early-twentieth-century Japanese expansion help explain the Pearl Harbor attack.

As this example shows, you will need to pay attention to both short-term and long-term factors to understand the causes (and effects) of historical events. Also, just as there were many factors behind the Japanese decision to bomb Pearl Harbor, most examples of historical causation involve multiple causes. Historical causation also involves large processes, unintended consequences, and contingencies, as the following chart describes.

> " Chronological reasoning means thinking logically about how and why the world changes, or stays the same, over time.

Historical causation involves...

Multiple causes	Most events or developments, such as the Japanese attack on Pearl Harbor, occur from a combination of factors, not just one.
Large processes	Many changes take place through major processes that are larger than any one person. For example, urbanization is a complex set of changes resulting from the actions of countless different individuals.
Unintended causes	Many changes take place accidentally, like the large-scale deaths of Native Americans during the Columbian exchange due to diseases Europeans weren't aware they were carrying.
Contingency	Events are not preordained, and history could have turned out differently. This is known as contingency. Because we read major events in history already knowing their outcome, we have a tendency to think they were bound to happen, but that is not the case. The initial Spanish conquest of the Incas was very precarious, for example, and early on the Spanish might have been defeated.

You can begin to develop the skill of determining causation by asking yourself, what reasons explain this development? When you encounter a significant change in world history and you identify immediate causes, you should then zoom your analytical lens out to look for longer-term factors.

EXERCISE   One major controversy in world history regarding causation has to do with why Western Europe industrialized in the nineteenth century—and China didn't. How do Drs. Strayer and Nelson explain the causes of British industrialization on pages 744–45? Which of the types of explanations from the box above do they use in their explanation?

Patterns of Continuity and Change over Time

As is probably becoming evident, historians are interested in both historical changes and persisting patterns, or *continuities*. Change is usually easier to detect; for example, when one empire overthrows another, that event often becomes part of the historical record. But some things stay relatively the same for long periods of time. Continuity (such as a network of trade that remains in existence for hundreds of years) is typically less dramatic than change and thus often harder to spot.

What counts as continuity depends on the scale of time you're working with. For example, if we only look at the twentieth century, the emergence of the Soviet Union represents an important political development. However, if we examine Russia's history since the formation of Kievan Rus in the ninth century, the Soviet era looks more like a modern variation of a longer pattern of autocratic rule.

When historians talk about continuity, they're not implying that a particular pattern applied to everyone in the world or even in a particular region. Nor are they claiming that a particular pattern included absolutely no change or variation. For example, agricultural production has been continuous for thousands of years, but there are exceptions to this broad statement: on the one hand, some people have continued to be foragers; on the other hand, methods of farming have changed substantially with technology. So the continuity of agriculture is a generalization but not a completely unchanging pattern or a pattern that applies to everyone on the planet.

To work on developing this skill, look for places in your textbook where the authors directly indicate that a historical pattern persisted over time and explain *why* that pattern persisted. Conversely, if the authors focus on change in world history, you can still find continuity by inference, since few things ever change completely. So when you read about a new development, ask yourself what *didn't* change. For example, while Buddhism became popular after its introduction into China, Confucianism remained an important force in Chinese culture.

> " Historians are interested in both historical changes and persisting patterns, or *continuities*.

EXERCISE   Look at the authors' discussion of "The World of Islam as a New Civilization" on pages 391–96. What language do they use to convey that they are talking about patterns of continuity?

Periodization

Periodization refers to the ways that historians break the past into separate periods of time. Historians look for major turning points in history—places where the world looked very different *before* some event than it did *after*—to decide how to break the past into chunks. They then give a label to each period to convey the key characteristics and developments of that era.

NOTE   In this text, you will find two different abbreviations for the word *circa*. Circa means "around" or "approximately" when referring to a date. The authors use **ca.** uniformly throughout their narrative and in part and chapter titles. The College Board uses **c.** in the AP® World History Curriculum Framework, so you will see **c.** here in *AP® Historical Thinking Skills: A Primer* and again at the end of each part in the *AP® Exam Practice Questions*. Don't be confused—**ca.** and **c.** mean the same thing.

Because the past is complex, any attempt to create eras and give those eras labels can provoke disagreement, particularly when talking about a subject as vast as world history. Periods are, after all, constructed by historians and reflect the particular context in which they are writing. Some world historians, for example, argue for a major division at 1000 C.E., which would highlight the beginning point of the growing importance of nomadic peoples in the period between 1000 and 1450. Others prefer to maintain a single period from about 600 to 1450, since they don't think nomadic empires significantly interrupted a larger period of Afro-Eurasian contact. These disagreements often carry over into the classroom. The AP® World History course used to include a break at 1914, instead of the current course's break at 1900. The older periodization made World War I a major turning point. Pushing the period back to the beginning of the twentieth century in 1900 places the war in the context of other important contemporary developments, including those less focused on Europe, such as the rise of nationalist movements among colonial peoples.

As you become familiar with periodization, pay attention to the chapter you're in, noting the major time period and thinking about what the different labels for that era say about the main "story" of that era. Keep in mind that these labels may differ among your teacher, your textbook, or the AP® World History Curriculum Framework.

> **EXERCISE** Compare the authors' periodization in Parts One through Six to the College Board's historical periodization. How do the time periods in the part titles compare to those in the AP® World History Curriculum Framework? What explains these differences?

Ways of the World with Sources, **Third Edition**	**AP® World History Curriculum Framework**
Part One: First Things First: Beginnings in History, to 600 B.C.E.	Period 1: Technological and Environmental Transformations, to c. 600 B.C.E.
Part Two: Second-Wave Civilizations in World History, 600 B.C.E.–600 C.E.	Period 2: Organization and Reorganization of Human Societies, c. 600 B.C.E. to 600 C.E.
Part Three: An Age of Accelerating Connections, 600 C.E.–1450	Period 3: Regional and Transregional Interactions, c. 600 C.E. to c. 1450
Part Four: The Early Modern World, 1450–1750	Period 4: Global Interactions, c. 1450 to c. 1750
Part Five: The European Moment in World History, 1750–1900	Period 5: Industrialization and Global Integration, c. 1750 to c. 1900
Part Six: The Most Recent Century, 1900–present	Period 6: Accelerating Global Change and Realignments, c. 1900 to Present

Creating and Supporting an Argument

The final step in historical thinking is learning to formulate and communicate your own conclusions about the past. The word *argument* reminds us that any attempt to explain the past requires interpretation, since our understanding of the past is limited by distance from the events we study and the incomplete evidence that has survived. Earlier you learned about how historians make arguments; now you'll practice making your own. Arguing means making a logical case for your interpretation of a particular historical question or controversy.

Argumentation

Argumentation is a complex, sophisticated skill that will develop with practice over the course of the school year. Your teacher will likely employ various methods to help you develop this skill, from oral discussions to writing/journaling activities to practicing AP®-style document-based questions. Argumentation includes five components. *First*, a historical argument is a response to a particular debate or question, so forming an argument begins with identifying and framing a question. If you are responding to a prompt or a question posed by your teacher or a textbook, you have to understand the question itself and make sure your response clearly addresses that question. Framing the question means placing it in historical or historiographic context; therefore, often you will need to determine whether the question is part of a historical debate and, if so, what the sides are and where your response fits within that debate. You will also want to explain the significance of the question—what's at stake or why the question matters. *Second*, you need to articulate your argument in a clear, concise, compelling way that directly responds to the prompt. Teachers typically identify this argument as your thesis—a short, explicit statement of your interpretation that appears near the beginning of your written response. *Third*, your argument or thesis needs to be substantiated by evidence, which may include both facts and information from lecture, textbook, or secondary texts, as well as your analysis of primary sources. *Fourth*, you need to frame your argument through the use of one or more historical thinking skills, like causation or comparison. Often, the wording of a question or prompt will provide some direction about the appropriate historical skill(s) to employ

Finally, the fifth step of argumentation is to convince your reader by using multiple, divergent, and sometimes-contradictory pieces of evidence. In working with evidence, particularly primary sources, you have to explain the relationship between this evidence—including corroborating facts and resolving contradictions—while clearly showing how the evidence supports your thesis. Effective historical writing balances nuance and clarity, as you recognize the complexity

FIVE STEPS TO ARGUMENTATION

1. Frame a question.
2. Form an argument/thesis.
3. Examine/analyze evidence.
4. Display historical thinking skills.
5. Examine/explain relationships in evidence.

of historical questions (including interpretations that diverge from your own) while still making a clear, succinct argument. "Creating and Supporting a Historical Argument" is a culminating skill that reflects your ability to analyze evidence and draw on the other historical thinking skills—comparison, contextualization, synthesis, causation, continuity and change, and periodization—to provide your own compelling understanding of key world history questions.

Getting the Most out of Reading World History

Active reading means reading for meaning. The big challenges of reading relate to length and detail, and the topic of world history has quite a lot of both. But if you understand the "big picture," you can read much more quickly and effectively, which helps address the challenge of length. At the same time, recognizing the main ideas allows you to see when specific information is provided to illustrate those big ideas; this helps address the challenge of detail. The three stages of reading described below will help you understand the big picture when reading this and other college-level texts.

Pre-reading

When approaching an informational text, it is helpful to spend a few minutes pre-reading the material. During the pre-reading stage, you are simply getting prepared for what you will be reading. This involves two steps. First, try to determine chronology, theme(s), and region(s). Do this by looking at chapter dates, the part or unit that includes that chapter (keeping in mind that not all books are divided into units/parts), the chapter that came before and the one that comes next, and the chapter title. Note that the next main section of a chapter may not describe something that happened later in time, but it may instead reflect a different theme about the same time and place. Second, try to determine the major changes, comparisons, and connections discussed in the chapter by scanning the section titles, images and captions (maps, charts, photos, etc.), and any pedagogical tools included (chronologies, key terms, document headnotes, review questions, exam tips, etc.). Also, skim the introduction to the chapter—usually reading the topic sentences of this section is sufficient.

EXERCISE   Let's practice by pre-reading Chapter 1: First Peoples; First Farmers: Most of History in a Single Chapter, to 4000 B.C.E. Chapter 1 is in Part One, which is introduced on pages 2–9. Scan the part opener and, without writing anything down, answer the following questions:

- *Chronology:* Looking at page 2, what is the chronology of Part One? Why might there be an ending date but no starting date? Now glance at the timeline on pages 8–9. How much time does this part cover? Why so much? See pages 6–7 for a clear explanation of the time span of this part.

- *Theme:* What is Part One all about? What are the three big topics in this part, indicated by the bold headings on pages 3–5? Turn to page 5, where "The Revolution of Farming and Herding" is discussed. Read the three topic sentences in this section. What is this section of Chapter 1 going to be about? Why is the topic important? Why is it part of "Beginnings in History"? Based on your reading of the contents list on page 2, what chapter comes after this one? How do the chapters fit together?

- *Region:* Does Part One focus on particular regions or larger global processes? How do you know?

Again, there's no need to write this down. The point right now is just to get a clear idea of the "big picture" of the part where this chapter appears. Now turn to the chapter itself and answer these similar questions:

- *Chronology:* According to the title on page 11, what time period does the chapter cover? Turn to the chart on page 13. Based on the title of the chapter, can you figure out why the chapter begins and ends when it does?

- *Theme:* Look at the title and the chapter contents listed on page 11. What is the chapter about? What are the major topics of the chapter? Now flip through the images in the chapter, maps included. What else do they tell you about the chapter that you haven't learned already?

- *Region:* Maps often provide a key to the regional focus of a chapter. Based on the map on pages 30–31, what part of the world does the portion of the chapter on agriculture address? Would you consider this chapter more "global" or "regional"?

At this point, you haven't read the chapter, and you haven't taken a single note. But by spending five minutes pre-reading the chapter, you already have a good idea what the chapter is about. By taking this time, you'll be able to read with a clear focus, saving yourself a lot of time as you read more efficiently. Now that you have a good idea of the "big picture," you're ready to begin actually reading the text.

During Reading

As you read chapters of this text, remember that reading is an active process — so stay focused. The meaning will become clear only as you work at it. The authors have intentionally written an organized textbook and want you to be able to follow along, so take advantage of the clues provided, especially titles and headings.

Active readers use four skills to understand texts: *questioning, clarifying, summarizing*, and *predicting*. These steps don't have to happen in a particular order. In fact, once you become comfortable with them, they'll pop up in your mind independently without much effort on your part, perhaps several at the same time. That's when you know that they've truly become habits of mind. Use these skills along with note taking to get the most out of your reading.

Questioning

Historians look at the world in a particular way, and we usually organize our writing around the historical thinking skills discussed above: cause and effect, comparison, interpretation, and so forth. By questioning, you can identify these patterns. For every chapter of this book, you want to find out the major subject. The easiest way to do this is to ask the "reporter questions": Who? What? Where? When? Why?

1. *Who* is the chapter about? History texts are almost always about people. Is the focus an individual? A social group? A political entity?
2. *What* does the section say about this person or group? Texts usually describe some major event or pattern. Did these people do something important? Did something happen to them?
3. *Where* did the subject being described take place? Physical location is often crucial in history. Does this location help make sense of the subject in some way?
4. *When* did the events take place? Like physical location, chronology forms part of the historical context that makes events understandable. Does the text describe something unfolding over a very short period or a longer one? Are there crucial events that came before that make the description understandable?
5. *Why* did the event or pattern being described take place—and why does it matter? Whether talking about a dramatic development or a continuity that endured for a long period of time, historians always attempt to understand what led to it. What reasons does the text provide for the event or pattern? How is the significance of the development explained?

Clarifying

Are there any words you don't understand? If they're crucial for making sense of the passage, can you define them using the glossary included on this text's book companion Web site, a dictionary, or another outside source? If there are any sentences you don't understand, do they become clearer as you reread them or as you read on in the text?

When it comes to vocabulary, use good judgment. Is the word crucial for understanding the passage? If not, read right past it. If it is a crucial word, you may need to look it up in a dictionary. Before you take the time to look it up, however, check that it hasn't been defined already for you in the text.

When a longer passage throws you off, usually clearing up difficult vocabulary will help make the passage clearer. If it doesn't, simply reread the sentence a few times (slowly!). If you're still unclear, back up—usually to the beginning of the paragraph—and try again. The most common way skilled readers get clarification is simply by rereading.

Summarizing

A summary is a brief review of the "big picture" of a particular section or chapter. After reading, briefly explain what each chapter is about in one sentence, being sure your summary answers all five questions from the "Questioning" section above.

Predicting

Based on your reading of an entire section or chapter, what do you think will come next in the text? How do you know? You may think predicting what's coming next is a waste of time, but it's a really good test of how well you understand the flow of the text. If you're in a car with your family going to visit your grandmother, you probably know the route to get there. If your mother takes an unanticipated turn, it alerts you that something is different from what you were expecting— and prompts you to ask why. So if your prediction based on reading is wildly off, it may alert you to the fact that your previous idea of the "big picture" of the section was off for some reason. You might need to back up and reread a section, or you might at least move forward with a better sense of where the author is going.

Note Taking

Of course, simply reading the text is not sufficient. You'll never remember everything that's important unless you take notes. Students experience many pitfalls when taking notes. You should write notes only *after* you understand what you have read. Actively *question, clarify, summarize,* and *predict* in your head (or out loud) as you read each chapter; then go back through the subsections and take brief notes representing the key ideas of that section.

Brief is generally better: don't wear yourself out on the notes themselves. Find some consistent abbreviations for frequent words and use symbols. For example, use an up arrow to indicate growth, a flat arrow to indicate cause/effect, an "=" to indicate a definition, and so on. Don't write everything; ask yourself if a particular point is a main idea or just an example. If you own your textbook, make annotations in the margins. If not, get a stack of sticky notes and place them in the margins for your comments.

Find a link to these glossaries at highschool .bfwpub.com/strayer3e:

- AP® World History Glossary
- Academic Glossary
- Glosarios en Español

EXERCISE   Let's practice these four skills with the section titled "Break-throughs to Agriculture" on pages 26–28.

- *Questioning:* The title is a key to this section. You should finish this section knowing (1) who was involved in the breakthrough to agriculture, (2) what the agricultural revolution was, (3) where (broadly) agriculture developed, (4) when the Agricultural Revolution took place, and (5) why agriculture emerged—and why it matters (that is, why historians often consider the development of agriculture "revolutionary").

- *Clarifying:* Important words like "Neolithic" and "domestication" are defined in the text itself, but how about "Paleolithic"? If there are any sentences you don't understand, do they become clearer as you reread them or as you read on in the text?

- *Summarizing:* Briefly explain what this section is about in one sentence—being sure your summary answers all five questions from the "Questioning" section above.

- *Predicting:* Based on the section you've just read, what do you think will come next in the text? How do you know?

Now that you know what this section is about, what brief comments are worth writing down in your notes?

Post-reading

Reflecting on what you've read places information you've just learned into long-term memory. Post-reading involves doing the same kind of summarizing you've done section by section, but now for the entire chapter. In essence, it is a summary of your summaries. While it might seem enough to summarize the chapter verbally, writing down key ideas helps you remember them a week or a month later. Read through the notes that you've taken for the chapter, particularly the summary of each section. Then, using no more than fifty words, try to write a master summary of the entire chapter that captures the key idea of each section of the chapter, as well as the chapter as a whole.

EXERCISE   Write a master summary of the portion of Chapter 1 you have just read.

Writing about World History

This skills primer began by introducing you to the patterns of thinking you need to really understand history. The next section pointed out ways to be smart about reading your textbook. This third and final section turns to the writing skills you need to develop for the AP® World History course and exam. Our focus now shifts from *receiving* input to *providing* output: you will learn how to share your understanding of historical thinking skills through writing. We will begin by addressing components that apply to all the writing tasks you'll encounter.

To successfully demonstrate what you know, you have to answer the question that has been asked. This sounds simple, but many students get in trouble on the exam by failing to address the prompt in front of them. Every prompt contains several elements, and you need to pay attention to all of them as you plan your response to the prompt:

- A periodization or date range expressed in years. Obviously, you need to be sure your response addresses this era. One of the most common problems in student essays on the exam is providing historical information from the wrong era.

- A task expressed as the main verb of the prompt: *compare, describe, explain, analyze,* and so forth. Pay attention to this task verb, as these tasks are not the same.

- A subject, expressed in two important types of nouns. A *proper noun* refers to a specific historical entity: Confucianism, the Mali Empire, the Silk Road. A *common noun* typically refers to a historical concept: a key historical idea (monotheism, nationalism) or process (diffusion of culture, expansion of empire). Sometimes this process is limited in time, but often it is a pattern that occurs repeatedly in world history. The subjects are drawn directly from the topics in the AP® World History Thematic Learning Objectives.

- A historical thinking skill. Each question will ask you to demonstrate your understanding of at least one skill from the first three categories: Analyzing Historical Sources and Evidence, Making Historical Connections, and Chronological Reasoning. So you may have to evaluate a historian's argument, make a historical comparison, explain continuity and change over time, or discuss a particular periodization issue.

Short-Answer Questions

The main issue to note about the short-answer section of the AP® exam is how quickly you need to respond to the writing tasks. You have to answer four questions in 50 minutes, which means that you have 12½ minutes per question, on average, to understand the question, brainstorm your response, and then write your answer. This task does *not* require that you form a thesis or create distinct paragraphs. It is a brief response to a very focused question.

Long-Essay Question

The Long-Essay Question (LEQ) and the Document-Based Question (DBQ) share many defining features. The following notes apply to both the LEQ and the DBQ, while a separate section includes specific suggestions for the DBQ.

First, every essay needs to have a specific, focused *thesis* that makes an argument addressing the prompt. It doesn't matter how strong your content knowledge and historical skills are if you can't communicate clearly what you know. Your thesis should be as brief as possible, while still addressing the complexity of the topic. If you explicitly respond to each of the prompt elements clearly and accurately, you will have a strong thesis—and you'll be on your way to a persuasive essay.

Second, every essay needs to be organized into distinct paragraphs. The number of paragraphs depends on the complexity of the prompt. Typically, however, two body paragraphs won't be sufficient to address the topic thoroughly. What's most important is that you clearly announce the point you're going to make in each paragraph through a *topic sentence* that effectively covers the subject of the paragraph. Any content in the paragraph that doesn't support the topic sentence doesn't belong there.

Third, every essay requires you to make use of *evidence* to support your claims. The type of evidence also differs depending on the type of essay. The Document-Based Question (DBQ) requires you to reference each of the documents included with the question, but both the DBQ and the Long Essay require you to draw on relevant outside knowledge of the subject. And in each case, you will need to place the essay question in appropriate *historical context*.

Finally, you need to demonstrate your mastery of *synthesis*. You will do this by explaining how your argument relates to one of the following: a similar development in another part of the world or in a different era, a different course theme than the theme the question addresses (for example, if the question explicitly addresses economic developments, you may want to talk about the cultural consequences of this development), or another discipline (for example, how a historical political structure relates to government and politics, how anthropology sheds light on a particular form of economic organization, or how art history explains the meaning or significance of a particular painting).

While many of these writing suggestions would apply equally to essays in other academic subjects, the essay types on the AP® World History exam are all geared to the concerns of history. Each type of essay requires the use of the historical thinking skills discussed above, often in combination with one another. For example, every essay requires you to discuss the *historical context* of the subject you're writing about and to *appropriately use relevant evidence*.

Document-Based Question Essay

The Document-Based Question, or DBQ, essay is a defining and culminating feature of the AP® History exam. Of all the essays, this one tends to make students the most anxious. But much of this anxiety is misplaced. Once you understand the DBQ, you will feel less worried about it and may even come to find it your favorite type of essay. Unlike the other two essays, in which you have to call on your memory to provide all the evidence, the documents in the DBQ form the basic evidence you need to use. You also have your "Five Steps to Argumentation" to assist in organizing your essay. You're already more prepared than you think!

To do well on a DBQ, you need to use all, or all but one, of the documents included in the question. In addition, you must go beyond the content of the documents in order to set the context, make a clear argument, and analyze the documents properly. Using documents as evidence requires the sophisticated analysis skills we discussed in the section on "Analyzing Historical Sources and Evidence." This means that you have to consider the perspective or point of view of the documents. Every primary source—textual, visual, or statistical—was created for a specific purpose. This doesn't mean the author had an agenda, though sometimes that is the case. But even if the author didn't have an agenda, every document is limited and imperfect in the information it provides. Use the questions included on page HTS-3 in the "Analyzing Evidence: Content and Sourcing—Primary Sources" section to interrogate each document and then consider the limitations of each document before writing your DBQ. Then be sure to incorporate these insights about document limitations into the essay itself to make your essay more analytical.

Consider the example of a photo depicting indentured servants on a nineteenth-century sugar plantation. Students tend to view a document like this as a straightforward factual record. After all, we often hear that "pictures don't lie." But someone took the picture for a particular purpose and the individuals are posed. So it's worth asking *why* someone wanted this picture taken. What purpose would this picture serve? Since it's posed, what's left out of it? How might it misrepresent—or represent in a very limited way—the realities of the indentured experience?

You also need to corroborate your documents. That means thinking about how the documents relate to each other. Since the documents in a DBQ don't directly refer to each other, you have to use your deductive skills to see connections. This requirement relates to a distinctive task of the DBQ: you need to organize the evidence from the documents into several categories, usually at least three. The categories are sometimes stated or implied in the prompt, but you'll often have to call on your knowledge of world history and the content of the documents themselves to determine what categories (and how many) make sense. Please note that you can use the same document multiple times, so that often gives you flexibility in coming up with categories.

Many students feel anxious about having to write the AP® World History essays. But once you become familiar with the elements of each prompt and know how to address these prompts effectively, you'll realize there's no reason to be stressed about this. In fact, you should feel confident as you approach the writing portion of the test. The essay section gives you a lot of freedom to demonstrate what you know in an open-ended way. And if you've been thinking historically, reading the text with that lens, and sharing your ideas in class, you may begin to look forward to the opportunity to show how developed your historical thinking skills have become.

Prologue
From Cosmic History to Human History

History books in general, and world history textbooks in particular, share something in common with those Russian nested dolls in which a series of carved figures fit inside one another. In much the same fashion, all historical accounts take place within some larger context, as stories within stories unfold. Individual biographies and histories of local communities, particularly modern ones, occur within the context of one nation or another. Nations often find a place in some more encompassing civilization, such as the Islamic world or the West, or in a regional or continental context such as Southeast Asia, Latin America, or Africa. And those civilizational or regional histories in turn take on richer meaning when they are understood within the even broader story of world history, which embraces humankind as a whole.

In recent decades, some world historians have begun to situate that remarkable story of the human journey in the much larger framework of both cosmic and planetary history, an approach that has come to be called "big history." It is really the "history of everything" from the big bang to the present, and it extends over the enormous, almost unimaginable timescale of some 13.7 billion years, the current rough estimate of the age of the universe.[1]

Guided Reading Question

■ CHANGE
What have been the major turning points in the pre-human phases of "big history"?

The History of the Universe

To make this vast expanse of time even remotely comprehensible, some scholars have depicted the history of the cosmos as if it were a single calendar year (see Snapshot). On that cosmic calendar, most of the action took place in the first few milliseconds of January 1. As astronomers, physicists, and chemists tell it, the universe that we know began in an eruption of inconceivable power and heat. Out of that explosion of creation emerged matter, energy, gravity, electromagnetism, and the "strong" and "weak" forces that govern the behavior of atomic nuclei. As gravity pulled the rapidly expanding cosmic gases into increasingly dense masses, stars formed, with the first ones lighting up around 1 to 2 billion years after the big bang, or the end of January to mid-February on the cosmic calendar.

Hundreds of billions of stars followed, each with its own history, though following common patterns. They emerge, flourish for a time, and then collapse and die. In their final stages, they sometimes generate supernovae, black holes, and pulsars—phenomena at least as fantastic as the most exotic of earlier creation stories. Within the stars, enormous nuclear reactions gave rise to the elements that are

SNAPSHOT   The History of the Universe as a Cosmic Calendar[2]

Big bang	January 1	13.7 billion years ago
Stars and galaxies begin to form	End of January/ mid-February	12 billion years ago
Milky Way galaxy forms	March/early April	10 billion years ago
Origin of the solar system	September 9	4.7 billion years ago
Formation of the earth	September 15	4.5 billion years ago
Earliest life on earth	Late September/ early October	4 billion years ago
Oxygen forms on earth	December 1	1.3 billion years ago
First worms	December 16	658 million years ago
First fish, first vertebrates	December 19	534 million years ago
First reptiles, first trees	December 23	370 million years ago
Age of dinosaurs	December 24–28	329–164 million years ago
First human-like creatures	December 31 (late evening)	2.7 million years ago
First agriculture	December 31: 11:59:35	12,000 years ago
Birth of the Buddha/ Greek civilization	December 31: 11:59:55	2,500 years ago
Birth of Jesus	December 31: 11:59:56	2,000 years ago
Aztec and Inca empires	December 31: 11:59:59	500 years ago

reflected in the periodic table known to all students of chemistry. Over eons, these stars came together in galaxies, such as our own Milky Way, which probably emerged in March or early April, and in even larger structures called groups, clusters, and superclusters. Adding to the strangeness of our picture of the cosmos is the recent and controversial notion that perhaps 90 percent or more of the total mass of the universe is invisible to us, consisting of a mysterious and mathematically predicted substance known to scholars only as "dark matter."

The contemplation of cosmic history has prompted profound religious or philosophical questions about the meaning of human life. For some, it has engendered a sense of great insignificance in the face of cosmic vastness. In disputing the earth- and human-centered view of the cosmos, long held by the Catholic Church, the eighteenth-century French thinker Voltaire wrote: "This little globe, nothing more than a point, rolls in space like so many other globes; we are lost in this immensity."[3] Nonetheless, human consciousness and our awareness of the mystery of this immeasurable universe render us unique and generate for many people feelings of awe, gratitude, and humility that are almost religious. As tiny but knowing observers of this majestic cosmos, we have found ourselves living in a grander home than ever we knew before.

The History of a Planet

For most of us, one star, our own sun, is far more important than all the others, despite its quite ordinary standing among the billions of stars in the universe and its somewhat remote location on the outer edge of the Milky Way galaxy. Circling that star is a series of planets, formed of leftover materials from the sun's birth. One of those planets, the third from the sun and the fifth largest, is home to all of us. Human history — our history — takes place not only on the earth but also as part of the planet's history.

That history began with the emergence of the entire solar system about two-thirds of the way through the history of the universe, some 4.7 billion years ago, or early September on the cosmic calendar. Geologists have learned a great deal about the history of the earth: the formation of its rocks and atmosphere; the movement of its continents; the collision of the tectonic plates that make up its crust; and the constant changes of its landscape as mountains formed, volcanoes erupted, and erosion transformed the surface of the planet. All of this has been happening for more than 4 billion years and continues still.

The most remarkable feature of the earth's history — and so far as we know unrepeated elsewhere — was the emergence of life from the chemical soup of the early planet. It happened rather quickly, only about 600 million years after the earth itself took shape, or late September on the cosmic calendar. Then for some 3 billion years, life remained at the level of microscopic single-celled organisms. According to biologists, the many species of larger multicelled creatures — all of the flowers, shrubs, and trees as well as all of the animals of land, sea, and air — have evolved in an explosive proliferation of life-forms over the past 600 million years, or since mid-December on the cosmic calendar. The history of life on earth has, however, been periodically punctuated by massive die-offs, at least five of them, in which very large numbers of animal or plant species have perished. The most widespread of these "extinction events," known to scholars as the Permian mass extinction, occurred around 250 million years ago and eliminated some 96 percent of living species on the planet. That catastrophic diminution of life-forms on the planet has been associated with massive volcanic eruptions, the release of huge quantities of carbon dioxide and methane into the atmosphere, and a degree of global warming that came close to extinguishing all life on the planet. Much later, around 65 million years ago, another such extinction event decimated about 75 percent of plant and animal species, including what was left of the dinosaurs. It too, some scientists believe, involved another wave of volcanic eruptions and drastic climate change, exacerbated this time by the impact of a huge asteroid, perhaps six miles in diameter, which landed near the Yucatán peninsula off the coast of southern Mexico. Many scholars believe we are currently in the midst of a sixth extinction event, driven, like the others, by major climate change, but which, unlike the others, is the product of human actions.

So life on earth has been and remains both fragile and resilient. Within these conditions, every species has had a history as its members struggled to find resources, cope with changing environments, and deal with competitors. Egocentric creatures that we are, however, human beings have usually focused their history books and history courses entirely on a single species—our own, *Homo sapiens*, humankind. On the cosmic calendar, *Homo sapiens* is an upstart primate whose entire history occurred in the last few minutes of December 31. Almost all of what we normally study in history courses—agriculture, writing, civilizations, empires, industrialization—took place in the very last minute of that cosmic year. The entire history of the United States occurred in the last second.

Yet during that very brief time, humankind has had a career more remarkable and arguably more consequential for the planet than any other species. At the heart of human uniqueness lies our amazing capacity for accumulating knowledge and skills. Other animals learn, of course, but for the most part they learn the same things over and over again. Twenty-first-century chimpanzees in the wild master the same skills as their ancestors did a million years ago. But the exceptional communication abilities provided by human language allow us to learn from one another, to express that learning in abstract symbols, and then to pass it on, cumulatively, to future generations. Thus we have moved from stone axes to lasers, from spears to nuclear weapons, from "talking drums" to the Internet, from grass huts to the pyramids of Egypt, the Taj Mahal of India, and the skyscrapers of modern cities.

This extraordinary ability has translated into a human impact on the earth that is unprecedented among all living species.[4] Human populations have multiplied far more extensively and have come to occupy a far greater range of environments than has any other large animal. Through our ingenious technologies, we have appropriated for ourselves, according to recent calculations, some 25 to 40 percent of the solar energy that enters the food chain. We have recently gained access to the stored solar energy of coal, gas, and oil, all of which have been many millions of years in the making, and we have the capacity to deplete these resources in a few hundred or a few thousand years. Other forms of life have felt the impact of human activity, as numerous extinct or threatened species testify. Human beings have even affected the atmosphere and the oceans as carbon dioxide and other emissions of the industrial age have warmed the climate of the planet in ways that broadly resemble the conditions that triggered earlier extinction events. Thus human history has been, and remains, of great significance, not for ourselves alone, but also for the earth itself and for the many other living creatures with which we share it.

The History of the Human Species . . . in a Single Paragraph

The history of our species has occupied roughly the last 250,000 years, conventionally divided into three major phases, based on the kind of technology that was most widely practiced. The enormously long Paleolithic age, with its gathering and hunting way of life, accounts for 95 percent or more of the time that humans have occupied the planet. People utilizing a stone-age Paleolithic technology initially settled every major landmass on the earth and constructed the first human societies (see Chapter 1). Then beginning about 12,000 years ago with the first Agricultural Revolution, the domestication of plants and animals increasingly became the primary means of sustaining human life and societies. In giving rise to agricultural villages and chiefdoms, to pastoral communities depending on their herds of animals, and to state- and city-based civilizations, this agrarian way of life changed virtually everything and fundamentally reshaped human societies and their relationship to the natural order. Finally, around 1750 a quite sudden spurt in the rate of technological change, which we know as the Industrial Revolution, began to take hold. That vast increase in productivity, wealth, and human control over nature once again transformed almost every aspect of human life and gave rise to new kinds of societies that we call "modern."

Here then, in a single paragraph, is the history of humankind—the Paleolithic era, the agricultural era, and, most recently and briefly, the modern industrial era. Clearly this is a big picture perspective, based on the notion that the human species as a whole has a history that transcends any of its particular and distinctive cultures. That perspective—known variously as planetary, global, or world history—has become increasingly prominent among those who study the past. Why should this be so?

Why World History?

Not long ago—in the mid-twentieth century, for example—virtually all college-level history courses were organized in terms of particular civilizations or nations. In the United States, courses such as Western Civilization or some version of American History served to introduce students to the study of the past. Since then, however, a set of profound changes has pushed much of the historical profession in a different direction.

The world wars of the twentieth century, revealing as they did the horrendous consequences of unchecked nationalism, persuaded some historians that a broader view of the past might contribute to a sense of global citizenship. Economic and cultural globalization has highlighted both the interdependence of the world's peoples and their very unequal positions within that world. Moreover, we are aware as never before that our problems—whether they involve economic well-being, global warming, disease, or terrorism—respect no national boundaries. To many

Guided Reading Question

■ CHANGE
Why has world history achieved an increasingly prominent place in American education in recent decades?

thoughtful people, a global present seemed to call for a global past. Furthermore, as colonial empires shrank and new nations asserted themselves on the world stage, these peoples also insisted that their histories be accorded equivalent treatment with those of Europe and North America. An explosion of new knowledge about the histories of Asia, Africa, and pre-Columbian America erupted from the research of scholars around the world. All of this has generated a "world history movement," reflected in college and high school curricula, in numerous conferences and specialized studies, and in a proliferation of textbooks, of which this is one.

This world history movement has attempted to create a global understanding of the human past that highlights broad patterns cutting across particular civilizations and countries, while acknowledging in an inclusive fashion the distinctive histories of its many peoples. This is, to put it mildly, a tall order. How is it possible to encompass within a single book or course the separate stories of the world's various peoples? Surely it must be something more than just recounting the history of one civilization or culture after another. How can we distill a common history of humankind as a whole from the distinct trajectories of particular peoples? Because no world history book or course can cover everything, what criteria should we use for deciding what to include and what to leave out? Such questions have ensured no end of controversy among students, teachers, and scholars of world history, making it one of the most exciting fields of historical inquiry.

Change, Comparison, and Connection: The Three Cs of World History

Despite much debate and argument, one thing is reasonably clear: in world history, nothing stands alone. Every event, every historical figure, every culture, society, or civilization gains significance from its inclusion in some larger context. Most world historians would probably agree on three such contexts that define their field of study. Each of those contexts confronts a particular problem in our understanding of the past.

The first context in which the particulars of world history can be situated is that of **change** over time. In world history, it is the "big picture" changes—those that affect large segments of humankind—that are of greatest interest. How did the transition from a gathering and hunting economy to one based on agriculture take place? How did cities, empires, and civilizations take shape in various parts of the world? What lay behind the emergence of a new balance of global power after 1500, one that featured the growing prominence of Europe on the world stage? What generated the amazing transformations of the "revolution of modernity" in recent centuries? How did the lives of women change as a result of industrialization?

A focus on change provides an antidote to a persistent tendency of human thinking that historians call "essentialism." A more common term is "stereotyping." It refers to our inclination to define particular groups of people with an unchanging or essential set of characteristics. Women are nurturing; peasants are conservative;

Americans are aggressive, Hindus are religious. Serious students of history soon become aware that every significant category of people contains endless divisions and conflicts and that those human communities are constantly in flux. Peasants may often accept the status quo, except of course when they rebel, as they frequently have. Americans have experienced periods of isolationism and withdrawal from the world as well as times of aggressive engagement with it. Things change.

But some things persist, even if they also change. We should not allow an emphasis on change to blind us to the continuities of human experience. A recognizably Chinese state has operated for more than 2,000 years. Slavery and patriarchy persisted as human institutions for thousands of years until they were challenged in recent centuries, and in various forms they exist still. The teachings of Buddhism, Christianity, and Islam have endured for centuries, though with endless variations and transformations.

A second major context that operates constantly in world history books and courses is that of **comparison**. Whatever else it may be, world history is a comparative discipline, seeking to identify similarities and differences in the experience of the world's peoples. What is the difference between the development of agriculture in the Middle East and in Mesoamerica? Was the experience of women largely the same in all patriarchal societies? What did the Roman Empire and Han dynasty China have in common? Why did the Industrial Revolution and a modern way of life evolve first in Western Europe rather than somewhere else? What distinguished the French, Russian, and Chinese revolutions from one another? What different postures toward modernity emerged within the Islamic world? Describing and, if possible, explaining such similarities and differences are among the major tasks of world history. Comparison, then, is a recurring theme in this book, with expressions in every chapter.

Comparison has proven an effective tool in efforts to counteract Eurocentrism, the notion that Europeans or people of European descent have long been the primary movers and shakers of the historical process. That notion arose in recent centuries when Europeans were in fact the major source of innovation in the world and did for a time exercise something close to world domination. This temporary preeminence decisively shaped the way Europeans thought and wrote about their own histories and those of other people. In their own eyes, Europeans alone were progressive people, thanks to some cultural or racial superiority. Everyone else was to some degree stagnant, backward, savage, or barbarian. The unusual power of Europeans allowed them for a time to act on those beliefs and to convey such ways of thinking to much of the world. But comparative world history sets European achievements in a global and historical context, helping us to sort out what was distinctive about the development of Europe and what similarities it bore to other major regions of the world. Puncturing the pretensions of Eurocentrism has been high on the agenda of world history.

A third context that informs world history involves the interactions, encounters, and **connections** among different and often distant peoples. World history is less about what happened within particular civilizations or cultures than about the processes and outcomes of their meetings with one another. Focusing on cross-cultural connections—whether those of conflict or more peaceful exchange—represents an effort to counteract a habit of thinking about particular peoples, states, or cultures as self-contained or isolated communities. Despite the historical emergence of many separate and distinct societies, none of them developed alone. Each was embedded in a network of relationships with both near and more distant peoples.

Moreover, these cross-cultural connections did not begin with Columbus. The Chinese, for example, interacted continuously with the nomadic peoples on their northern border; generated technologies that diffused across all of Eurasia; transmitted elements of their culture to Japan, Korea, and Vietnam; and assimilated a foreign religious tradition, Buddhism, which had originated in India. Though clearly distinctive, China was not a self-contained or isolated civilization.

The growing depth and significance of such cross-cultural relationships, known now as globalization, has been a distinguishing feature of the modern era. The voyages of Columbus brought the peoples of the Eastern and Western hemispheres into sustained contact for the first time with enormous global consequences. Several centuries later, Europeans took advantage of their industrial power to bring much of the world temporarily under their control. The new technologies of the twentieth century have intertwined the economies, societies, and cultures of the world's peoples more tightly than ever before. During the past five centuries, the encounter with strangers, or at least with their ideas and practices, was everywhere among the most powerful motors of change in human societies. Thus world history remains always alert to the networks, webs, and cross-cultural encounters in which particular civilizations or peoples were enmeshed.

Changes, comparisons, and connections—all of them operating on a global scale—represent three contexts or frameworks that can help us bring some coherence to the multiple and complex stories of world history. They will recur repeatedly in the pages that follow.

A final observation about this account of world history: *Ways of the World*, like all other world history textbooks, is radically unbalanced in terms of coverage. The first chapter, for example, takes on some 95 percent of the human story, well over 200,000 years of our history. By contrast, the last century alone occupies four entire chapters. In fact, the six major sections of the book deal with progressively shorter time periods, in progressively greater detail. This imbalance owes much to the relative scarcity of information about earlier periods of our history. But it also reflects a certain "present mindedness," for we look to history, always, to make sense of our current needs and circumstances. And in doing so, we often assume that more recent events have a greater significance for our own lives in the here and now than those that occurred in more distant times. Whether you agree with this assumption or not, you will have occasion to ponder it as you consider the many and various "ways of the world" that have emerged in the course of the human journey and as you contemplate their relevance for your own journey.

Review

What's the Significance?

big history, PRO-1

cosmic calendar, PRO-1

the three C's, PRO-6

comparative world history, PRO-7

Big Picture Questions

1. How do modern notions of the immense size and age of the universe affect your understanding of human history?
2. What examples of comparison, connection, and change in world history would you like to explore further as your course unfolds?
3. In what larger contexts might you place your own life history?

Next Steps: For Further Study

David Christian, Cynthia Stokes Brown, and Craig Benjamin, *Big History: Between Nothing and Everything* (2013). A thoughtful survey of the emerging field of "big history" by three of its leading practitioners.

Ross E. Dunn, ed., *The New World History: A Teacher's Companion* (2000). A collection of articles dealing with the teaching of world history.

Patrick Manning, *Navigating World History: Historians Create a Global Past* (2003). An up-to-date overview of the growth of world history, the field's achievements, and the debates within it.

J. R. McNeill and William H. McNeill, *The Human Web: A Bird's-Eye View of World History* (2003). An approach to world history that emphasizes the changing webs of connection among human communities.

Heidi Roupp, ed., *Teaching World History in the Twenty-First Century: A Resource Book* (2010). A practical resource book for the teaching of world history.

"World History Matters," http://worldhistorymatters.org/. A point of entry to many world history Web sites, featuring numerous images and essays.

Ways of the World

A Global History with Sources

PART ONE

FIRST THINGS FIRST

Beginnings in History
to 600 B.C.E.

Contents

TURNING POINTS IN EARLY WORLD HISTORY

Human beings have long been inveterate storytellers. Those who created our myths, legends, fairy tales, oral traditions, family sagas, and more have sought to distill meaning from experience, to explain why things turned out as they did, and to provide guidance for individuals and communities. Much the same might be said of modern historians. They too tell stories—about individuals, communities, nations, and, in the case of world history, of humankind as a whole. Those stories seek to illuminate the past, to provide context for the present, and, very tentatively, to offer some indication about possible futures. All tellers of stories—ancient and modern alike—have to decide at what point to begin their accounts and what major turning points in those narratives to highlight. For world historians seeking to tell the story of "all under Heaven," as the Chinese put it, four major "beginnings," each of them an extended historical process, have charted the initial stages of the human journey.

> **AP® EXAM TIP**
>
> The historical events in Part One make up 5 percent of the AP® World History exam.

The Emergence of Humankind

Ever since Charles Darwin, most scholars have come to view human beginnings in the context of biological change on the planet. In considering this enormous process, we operate on a timescale quite different from the billions of years that mark the history of the universe and of the earth. According to archeologists and anthropologists, the evolutionary line of descent leading to *Homo sapiens* diverged from that leading to chimpanzees, our closest primate relatives, some 5 million to 6 million years ago, and it happened in eastern and southern Africa. There, perhaps twenty or thirty different species emerged, all of them members of the Homininae (or hominid) family of human-like creatures. What they all shared was bipedalism, the ability to walk upright on two legs. In 1976, the archeologist Mary Leakey uncovered in what is now Tanzania a series of footprints of three such hominid individuals, preserved in cooling volcanic ash about 3.5 million years ago. Two of them walked side by side, perhaps holding hands.

Over time, these hominid species changed. Their brains grew larger, as evidenced by the size of their skulls. About 2.3 million years ago, a hominid creature known as *Homo habilis* began to make and use simple stone tools. Others

3

started to eat meat, at least occasionally. By 1 million years ago, some hominid species, especially *Homo erectus*, began to migrate out of Africa, and their remains have been found in various parts of Eurasia. This species is also associated with the first controlled use of fire.

Eventually all of these earlier hominid species died out, except one. *Homo sapiens*, ourselves. With a remarkable capacity for symbolic language that permitted the accumulation and transmission of learning, we too emerged first in Africa and quite recently, probably no more than 250,000 years ago (although specialists constantly debate these matters). For a long time, all of the small number of *Homo sapiens* lived in Africa, but sometime after 100,000 years ago, they too began to migrate out of Africa onto the Eurasian landmass, then to Australia, and ultimately into the Western Hemisphere and the Pacific islands. The great experiment of human history had begun.

The Globalization of Humankind

Today, every significant landmass on earth is occupied by human beings, but it was not always so. A mere half million years ago our species did not exist, and only 100,000 years ago that species was limited to Africa and numbered, some scholars believe, fewer than 10,000 individuals. These ancient ancestors of ours, rather small in stature and not fast on foot, were armed with a very limited technology of stone tools with which to confront the multiple dangers of the natural world. But then, in perhaps the most amazing tale in all of human history, they moved from this very modest and geographically limited role in the scheme of things to a worldwide and increasingly dominant presence. What kinds of societies, technologies, and understandings of the world accompanied, and perhaps facilitated, this globalization of humankind?

The phase of human history during which these initial migrations took place is known to scholars as the Paleolithic era. The word "Paleolithic" literally means the "old stone age," but it refers more generally to a food-collecting or gathering, hunting, and fishing way of life, before agriculture allowed people to grow food or raise animals deliberately. Paleolithic cultures operated within natural ecosystems, while creatively manipulating the productive capacities of those systems to sustain individual lives and societies. Lasting until roughly 11,000 years ago, and in many places much longer, the Paleolithic era represents over 95 percent of the time that human beings have inhabited the earth, although it accounts for only about 12 percent of the total number of people who have lived on the planet. It was during this time that *Homo sapiens* colonized the world, making themselves at home in every environmental setting, from the frigid Arctic to the rain forests of Central Africa and Brazil, in mountains, deserts, and plains. It was an amazing achievement, accomplished by no other large species. Accompanying this global migration were slow changes in the technological tool kits of early humankind as well as early attempts to impose meaning on the world through art, ritual, religion, and stories. Although often neglected by historians and history textbooks, this long period of the human experience merits greater attention and is the focus of the initial sections of Chapter 1.

The Revolution of Farming and Herding

In 2015, almost all of the world's 7.3 billion people lived from the food grown on farms and gardens and from domesticated animals raised for their meat, milk, or eggs. But before 11,000 years ago, no one survived in this fashion. Then, repeatedly and fairly rapidly, at least in world history terms, human communities in parts of the Middle East, Asia, Africa, and the Americas began the laborious process of domesticating animals and selecting seeds to be planted. This momentous accomplishment represents another "first" in the human story. After countless millennia of relying on the gathering of wild foods and the hunting of wild animals, why and how did human societies begin to practice farming and animal husbandry? What changes to human life did this new technology bring with it?

This food-producing revolution, also considered in Chapter 1, surely marks the single most significant and enduring transformation of the human condition and of human relationships to the natural world. Now our species learned to exploit and manipulate particular organisms, both plant and animal, even as we created new and simplified ecosystems. The entire period from the beginning of agriculture to the Industrial Revolution around 1750 might be considered a single phase of the human story—the age of agriculture—calculated now on a timescale of millennia or centuries rather than the more extended periods of earlier eras. Although the age of agriculture was far shorter than the immense Paleolithic era that preceded it, farming and raising animals allowed for a substantial increase in human numbers and over many centuries an enduring transformation of the environment. Forests were felled, arid lands irrigated, meadows plowed, and mountains terraced. Increasingly, the landscape reflected human intentions and actions.

In the various beginnings of food production lay the foundations for some of the most enduring divisions within the larger human community. Much depended on the luck of the draw—on the climate and soils, on the various wild plants and animals that were available for domestication. Everywhere communities worked within their environments to develop a consistent supply of food. Some relied primarily on single crops, while others cultivated several crops that collectively met their needs. Root crops such as potatoes were prominent in the Andes, while tree crops such as bananas were important in Africa and grain crops such as wheat, rice, or corn prevailed elsewhere. Many communities engaged heavily in small or large animal husbandry, but others, especially in the Americas, did not. In some regions, people embraced agriculture on a full-time basis, but many more agricultural communities, at least initially, continued to rely in part on gathering, hunting, or fishing for their dietary needs. These various approaches led to a spectrum of settlement patterns from sedentary villages to fully nomadic communities, and many in between. In general, the most mobile of these societies were those of pastoralists, who depended heavily on their herds of domesticated animals for survival. Such communities, which usually thrived in more arid environments where farming was difficult, had to move frequently, often in regular seasonal patterns, to secure productive pasturelands for their animals. However, not all were fully nomadic, because in some regions pastoralists were able to combine permanent settlements with seasonal migration of animals to grazing areas. Thus the Agricultural Revolution fostered a wide variety of adaptations to the natural environment and an equally wide range of social organizations.

The Turning Point of Civilization

The most prominent and powerful human communities to emerge from this Agricultural Revolution were those often designated as "civilizations," more complex societies that were based in bustling cities and governed by formal states. Virtually all of the world's people now live in such societies, so that states and cities have come to seem almost natural. In world history terms, however, their appearance is a rather recent phenomenon. Not until several thousand years *after* the beginning of agriculture did the first cities and states emerge, around 3500 B.C.E. Well after 1000 C.E., substantial numbers of people still lived in communities without any state or urban structures. Nonetheless, people living in state- and city-based societies or civilizations have long constituted the most powerful and innovative human communities on the planet. They gave rise to empires of increasing size, to enduring cultural and religious traditions, to new technologies, to sharper class and gender inequalities, to new conceptions of masculinity and femininity, and to large-scale warfare.

For all these reasons, civilizations have featured prominently in accounts of world history, sometimes crowding out the stories of other kinds of human communities. The earliest civilizations, which emerged in at least seven separate locations between 3500 and 600 B.C.E., have long fascinated professional historians and lovers of history everywhere. What was their relationship to the Agricultural Revolution? What new ways of living did they bring to the experience of humankind? These are the questions that inform Chapter 2.

Time and World History

Reckoning time is central to all historical study, for history is essentially the story of change over time. Recently it has become standard in the Western world to refer to dates prior to the birth of Christ as B.C.E. (before the Common Era), replacing the earlier B.C. (before Christ) usage. This convention is an effort to become less Christian-centered and Eurocentric in our use of language, although the chronology remains linked to the birth of Jesus. Similarly, the time following the birth of Christ is referred to as C.E. (the Common Era) rather than A.D. (*Anno Domini*, Latin for "year of the Lord"). Dates in the more distant past are designated in this book as BP ("before the present," by which scholars mean 1950, the dawn of the nuclear age) or simply as so many "years ago." Of course, these conventions are only some of the many ways that human societies have charted time, and they reflect the global dominance of Europeans in recent centuries. But the Chinese frequently dated important events in terms of the reign of particular emperors, while Muslims created a new calendar beginning with Year 1, marking Muhammad's forced relocation from Mecca to Medina in 622 C.E. As with so much else, the maps of time that we construct reflect the cultures in which we have been born and the historical experience of our societies.

World history frequently deals with very long periods of time, often encompassing many millennia or centuries in a single paragraph or even in a single sentence. Such quick summaries may sometimes seem to flatten the texture of historical experience, minimizing the immense complexities and variations of human life and dismissing the rich and distinctive flavor of individual lives. Yet this very drawback of world history permits its greatest contribution to our understanding—perspective, context, a big picture framework in which we can situate the particular events, societies, and individual experiences that constitute the historical record. Such a panoramic outlook on the past allows us to discern patterns and trends that may be invisible from the viewpoint of a local community or a single nation. In the narrative that follows, there will be plenty of particulars—events, places, people—but always embedded in some larger setting that enriches their significance.

Landmarks in World History (to ca. 600 B.C.E.) *(All dates are B.C.E.)*

	27,000	26,000	25,000	24,000	23,000	22,000	21,000	20,000	19,000	18,000	17,000	16,000	15,000

AFRICA

◄ **250,000–200,000**
Emergence of *Homo sapiens*

◄ **100,000–70,000**
Earliest evidence of human symbolic behavior

◄ **100,000–60,000**
Human migration out of Africa into Eurasia

16,000–9000
Development of distinctive regional cultures

EURASIA

◄ **70,000**
Human entry into Asia

◄ **45,000**
Human entry into Europe

◄ **35,000**
Earliest female figurines from Germany

30,000–15,000
Paleolithic cave art in Europe

■ **25,000**
Extinction of Neanderthals

THE AMERICAS AND PACIFIC OCEANIA

◄ **60,000–40,000**
Human entry into Australia

◄ **30,000**
Extinction of large mammals in Australia

30,000–15,000
Human entry into the Americas

14,000 13,000 12,000 11,000 10,000 9000 8000 7000 6000 5000 4000 3000 2000 1000

4000
Domestication of donkey
in northeastern Africa

3500–3000
Beginnings of
Egyptian civilization

14,000–8000
Harvesting of wild grains
in northeastern Africa

8000–4000
Cattle-based pastoral
societies in Africa

3400–3200
Nubian kingdom
of Ta-Seti

3000–1000
Agricultural breakthroughs
in sub-Saharan Africa

3000–2000
Beginning of Bantu migrations

1259
Treaty ending conflict between
Egypt and the Hittites

1000–500
Ironworking in sub-Saharan Africa

6000
Early chiefdoms in Mesopotamia

5400
Wine making in Iran

14,000–8000
Global warming and end of last Ice Age

4000
Domestication of horses

10,000
Göbekli Tepe: monumental
Paleolithic construction

3500–3000
Beginnings of Mesopo-
tamian civilization

10,000–8000
Earliest agricultural
revolutions

2200–2000
Beginnings of Chinese,
Indian, and Central
Asian civilizations

11,000
Clovis culture in North America

3000–1800
Norte Chico civilization in Peru

9000
Extinction of various large
mammals in North America

3000–2000
Domestication of potatoes, quinoa,
and manioc in the Andes

1500
Human entry into Pacific Oceania

1400–800
Lapita culture in Melanesia

4000–3000
Domestication of corn in Mexico

1200
Olmec civilization in
Mesoamerica

9

UNDERSTANDING AP® THEMES
IN PART ONE

Technological and Environmental Transformations

Corresponding to Period 1 of the AP® course outline, Part One of this text constitutes just 5 percent of the exam but lays the groundwork for your study of world history and the themes you will encounter within it. In this part, we will chart the course of human history from its earliest migrations, which colonized the entire planet, to the emergence of the First Civilizations, which flourished from around 3500 B.C.E. to 600 B.C.E. This immense period of time encompasses most of the human journey and is characterized by three major global transformations: the initial colonization of the earth by humans, the advent of agricultural societies, and, much later, the emergence of the city- and state-based societies that we refer to as civilizations. These three long-term processes reshaped humankind in any number of ways:

- Our relationships to the natural order
- Our understandings of the world
- Our systems of maintaining order
- Our methods for addressing conflicts
- Our techniques of survival and making a living
- Our social organizations and ways of relating to one another
- The range of our interactions with those beyond our own communities

The chart on the opposite page provides an overview of the AP® World History themes you will encounter in this part. While this list is by no means exhaustive, it offers threads that are significant for the time period and important for your course studies. As you read the following chapters, pay close attention to these five themes. Also watch for AP® Exam Tips throughout the text to assist in your coursework and exam preparation.

Environment	Cultures	State Building	Economies	Social Structures
Initial human migrations	Paleolithic religions	Political life in pre-state societies	Gathering/hunting technologies and economies	Paleolithic egalitarianism; ex.: among the San and Aboriginal Australians
Paleolithic environmental transformations	Stories from the Australian Dreamtime	Emergence of chiefdoms	Breakthroughs to agricultural economies	Sedentary life among gathering/hunting peoples
Global warming and the Agricultural Revolution	Connections between religion and politics in the First Civilizations	State building in the First Civilizations	Comparing Agricultural Revolutions; ex.: in Mesopotamia and Mesoamerica	Agricultural village life: gender, age, and kin
Environmental effects of agricultural societies	Outlooks on the afterlife in Egypt and Mesopotamia	Comparing political life in ancient Egypt and Mesopotamia	Globalization of agriculture and resistance to it	Pastoral societies
Environmental basis of pastoralism	Cultural diffusion in the ancient world; ex.: Egyptian influence in Nubia, Crete, and Greece	Flowering of an Egyptian empire	Agriculture and technological innovations	Emergence of urban life
Environmental effects of First Civilizations	Art in the Indus Valley civilizations	Sumerian incorporation into Akkadian, Babylonian, and Assyrian empires	Emergence of pastoral economies	Class structures of early civilizations
Environment and culture in Egypt and Mesopotamia	Writing in the earliest civilizations	Hittite invasion of Egypt and Babylonia	Conflicts between pastoral and agricultural peoples	The evolution of patriarchy
		Diplomatic relations of Egypt and Mesopotamia	Agriculture: setting the stage for civilization	Consent and coercion in maintaining highly unequal societies
			Long-distance trade among ancient Afro-Eurasian civilizations	

First Peoples; First Farmers

Most of History in a Single Chapter
to 4000 B.C.E.

"We do not want cattle, just wild animals to hunt and water that we can drink."[1] That was the view of Gudo Mahiya, a prominent member of the Hadza people of northern Tanzania, when he was questioned in 1997 about his interest in a settled life of farming and cattle raising. The Hadza represent one of the very last peoples on earth to continue a way of life that was universal among humankind until 10,000 to 12,000 years ago. In 2014, only about 1,300 Hadza survived, and of these just several hundred still made a living by hunting game, collecting honey, digging up roots, and gathering berries and fruit. Those few lived in quickly assembled grass huts located in small mobile camps averaging eighteen people and moved frequently around their remote region, following animal migrations. Almost certainly, their way of life is doomed, as farmers, cattle herders, governments, missionaries, and now tourists push them toward extinction. The likely disappearance of their culture is among the final chapters of a very long story in which gathering, hunting, and fishing peoples have been unsuccessfully on the defensive against more numerous and powerful neighbors for 10,000 years.

Nonetheless, that way of life sustained humankind for more than 95 percent of the time that our species has inhabited the earth. During countless centuries, human beings successfully adapted to a wide variety of environments without benefit of deliberate farming or animal husbandry. Instead, our early ancestors wrested a livelihood by gathering wild foods such as berries, nuts, roots, and grain; by scavenging dead animals; by hunting live animals; and by

---

Paleolithic Art   The rock art of gathering and hunting peoples has been found in Africa, Europe, Australia, and elsewhere. This image from the San people of southern Africa represents aspects of their outer life in the form of wild animals and hunters with bows as well as the inner life of their shamans during a trance, reflected in the elongated figures with both human and animal features.

fishing. Known to scholars as "gathering and hunting" peoples, they were foragers or food collectors rather than food producers. Because they used stone rather than metal tools, they also have been labeled "Paleolithic," or "Old Stone Age," peoples.

Then, around 12,000 years ago, an enormous transformation began to unfold as a few human societies—in Eurasia, Africa, and the Americas alike—started to practice the deliberate cultivation of plants and the domestication of animals. This Agricultural or Neolithic (New Stone Age) Revolution marked a technological breakthrough of immense significance, with implications for every aspect of human life. This chapter, then, dealing with the long Paleolithic era and the initial transition to an agricultural way of life, represents most of human history—everything, in fact, before the advent of urban-based civilizations, which began around 5,500 years ago.

And yet history courses and history books often neglect this long phase of the human journey and instead choose to begin the story with the early civilizations of Egypt, Mesopotamia, China, and elsewhere. Some historians identify "real history" with writing and so dismiss the Paleolithic and Neolithic eras as largely unknowable because their peoples did not write. Others, impressed with the rapid pace of change in human affairs in more recent times, assume that nothing much of real significance happened during the long Paleolithic era—and that no change meant no history.

But does it make sense to ignore the first 200,000 years or more of human experience? Although written records are absent, scholars have learned a great deal about Paleolithic and Neolithic peoples through their material remains: stones and bones, fossilized seeds, rock paintings and engravings, and much more. Archeologists, biologists, botanists, demographers, linguists, and anthropologists have contributed much to our growing understanding of gathering and hunting peoples and early agricultural societies. Furthermore, the achievements of Paleolithic peoples—the initial settlement of the planet, the creation of the earliest human societies, the beginnings of reflection on the great questions of life and death—surely deserve our attention. And the breakthrough to agriculture arguably represents the single most profound transformation of human life in all of history. The changes wrought by our early ancestors, though far slower than those of more recent times, were extraordinarily rapid in comparison to the transformation experienced by any other species. Those changes were almost entirely cultural or learned, rather than the product of biological evolution, and they provided the foundation on which all subsequent human history was constructed. Our grasp of the human past is incomplete—massively so—if we choose to disregard the Paleolithic and Neolithic eras.

SEEKING THE MAIN POINT

What arguments does this chapter make for paying serious attention to human history before the coming of "civilization"?

Out of Africa: First Migrations

The first 150,000 years or more of human experience was an exclusively African story. Around 200,000 to 250,000 years ago, in the grasslands of eastern and southern Africa, *Homo sapiens* first emerged, following in the footsteps of many other hominid or human-like species before it. Time and climate have erased much of the record

A MAP OF TIME   (All dates B.P.: Before the Present)

250,000–200,000	Earliest *Homo sapiens* in Africa
100,000–80,000	Beginnings of migration out of Africa
70,000	Human entry into eastern Asia
60,000–40,000	Human entry into Australia (first use of boats)
45,000	Human entry into Europe
30,000	Extinction of large mammals in Australia
30,000–15,000	Human entry into the Americas
30,000–17,000	Cave art in Europe
25,000	Extinction of Neanderthals
16,000–10,000	End of last Ice Age (global warming)
12,000–10,000	Earliest agricultural revolutions
11,000	Extinction of large mammals in North America
After 8,000	First chiefdoms in Mesopotamia
6,000–5,000	Beginning of domestication of corn in southern Mexico
3,500–1,000	Austronesian migration to Pacific islands and Madagascar
1,000–800	Human entry into New Zealand (last major region to receive human settlers)

of these early people, and Africa has witnessed much less archeological research than have other parts of the world. Nonetheless, scholars have turned up evidence of distinctly human behavior in Africa long before its appearance elsewhere. Africa, almost certainly, was the place where the "human revolution" occurred, where "culture," defined as learned or invented ways of living, became more important than biology in shaping behavior.

What kinds of uniquely human activity show up in the early African record?[2] In the first place, human beings began to inhabit new environments within Africa— forests and deserts—where no hominids had lived before. Accompanying these movements of people were technological innovations of various kinds: stone blades and points fastened to shafts replaced the earlier hand axes; tools made from bones appeared, and so did grindstones. Evidence of hunting and fishing, not just the scavenging of dead animals, marks a new phase in human food collection. Settlements were planned around the seasonal movement of game and fish. Patterns of exchange over a distance of almost 200 miles indicate larger networks of human communication. The use of body ornaments, beads, and pigments such as ochre as well as possible planned burials suggests the kind of social and symbolic behavior that has characterized human activity ever since. The earliest evidence for this kind of human activity comes from the Blombos Cave in South Africa, where excavations in 2008 uncovered a workshop for the processing of ochre dating to around 100,000 years ago, well before such behavior surfaced elsewhere in the world.

Then, sometime between 100,000 and 60,000 years ago, human beings began their long trek out of Africa and into Eurasia, Australia, the Americas, and, much later, the islands of the Pacific (see Map 1.1). In occupying the planet, members of our species accomplished the remarkable feat of learning to live in virtually every environmental setting on earth, something that no other large animal had done; and they did it with only stone tools and a gathering and hunting technology to aid them. Furthermore, much of this long journey occurred during the difficult climatic conditions of the last Ice Age (at its peak around 20,000 years ago), when thick ice sheets covered much of the Northern Hemisphere. The Ice Age did give these outward-bound human beings one advantage, however: the amount of water frozen in northern glaciers lowered sea levels around the planet, creating land bridges among various regions that were separated after the glaciers melted. Britain was then joined to Europe; eastern Siberia was connected to Alaska; and parts of what is now Indonesia were linked to mainland Southeast Asia.

Into Eurasia

Human migration out of Africa led first to the Middle East and from there westward into Europe about 45,000 years ago and eastward into Asia. Among the most carefully researched areas of early human settlement in Eurasia are those in southern France and northern Spain. Colder Ice Age climates around 20,000 years ago apparently pushed more northerly European peoples southward into warmer regions. There they altered their hunting habits, focusing on reindeer and horses, and developed new technologies such as spear throwers and perhaps the bow and arrow as well as many different kinds of stone tools. Most remarkably, they also left a record of their world in hundreds of cave paintings, depicting bulls, horses, and other animals, brilliantly portrayed in colors of red, yellow, brown, and black. Images of human beings, impressions of human hands, and various abstract designs sometimes accompanied the cave paintings.

Farther east, archeologists have uncovered still other remarkable Paleolithic adaptations to Ice Age conditions. Across the vast plains of Central Europe, Ukraine, and Russia, new technologies emerged, including bone needles, multilayered clothing, weaving, nets, storage pits, baskets, and pottery. Partially underground dwellings constructed from the bones and tusks of mammoths compensated for the absence of caves and rock shelters. All of this suggests that some of these people had lived in more permanent settlements, at least temporarily abandoning their nomadic journeys. Associated with these Eastern European peoples were numerous female figurines, the oldest of which was uncovered in 2008 in Germany and dated to at least 35,000 years ago. Carved from stone, antlers, mammoth tusks, or, occasionally, baked clay, these so-called Venus figurines depict the female form, often with

AP® EXAM TIP

Global migration patterns of early humans are an important concept in world history. Also see the map on pages 16–17.

Guided Reading Question
....
■ CHANGE
What was the sequence of human migration across the planet?

AP® EXAM TIP

The ways humans have interacted with their environments are a key theme on the AP® exam.

exaggerated breasts, buttocks, hips, and stomachs. Similar figurines have been found all across Eurasia, raising any number of controversial questions. Does their widespread distribution suggest a network of human communication and cultural diffusion over a wide area? If so, did they move from west to east or vice versa? What do they mean in terms of women's roles and status in Paleolithic societies?

Into Australia

Early human migration to Australia, perhaps 60,000 years ago, came from Indonesia and involved another first in human affairs—the use of boats. Over time, people settled in most regions of this huge continent, though quite sparsely. Scholars estimate the population of Australia at about 300,000 in 1788, when the first Europeans arrived. Over tens of thousands of years, the

Australian Rock Art
This Australian rock painting utilized the distinctive Aboriginal X-ray style, showing the internal bones and organs. The largest and main figure at the top is a Creation Ancestor known as Namondjok. To the right is Namarrgon, or Lightning Man, who generates the tremendous lightning storms that occur during the rainy season. The arc around his body represents the lightning, while the axes on his head, elbow, and feet are used to split the dark clouds, creating thunder and lightning. The female figure beneath Namondjok is Barrginj, the wife of Lightning Man, while the people below her, elaborately dressed, are perhaps on their way to a ceremony. (Aboriginal rock painting from the Kakadu National Park/Werner Forman Archive/Bridgeman Images)

peoples of Australia developed perhaps 250 languages; learned to collect a wide variety of bulbs, tubers, roots, seeds, and cereal grasses; and became proficient hunters of large and small animals, as well as birds, fish, and other marine life. A relatively simple technology, appropriate to a gathering and hunting economy, sustained Australia's Aboriginal people into modern times. When outsiders arrived in the late eighteenth century, Aboriginals still practiced that ancient way of life, despite the presence of agriculture in nearby New Guinea.

Accompanying Aboriginals' technological simplicity and traditionalism was the development of an elaborate and complex outlook on the world, known as the Dreamtime. (See Working with Evidence, page 49, for more on the Dreamtime.) Expressed in endless stories, in extended ceremonies, and in the evocative rock art of the continent's peoples, the Dreamtime recounted the beginning of things: how ancestral beings crisscrossed the land, creating its rivers, hills, rocks, and waterholes; how various peoples came to inhabit the land; and how they related to animals and to one another. In this view of the world, everything in the natural order was a vibration, an echo, a footprint of these ancient happenings, which linked the current inhabitants intimately to particular places and to timeless events in the past.

The journeys of the Dreamtime's ancestral beings reflect the networks of migration, communication, and exchange that linked the continent's many Paleolithic

Map 1.1   The Global Dispersion of Humankind

With origins in Africa perhaps 250,000 years ago, members of our species (*Homo sapiens*) have migrated to every environmental setting on the planet over the past 100,000 years.

EUROPE
(45,000 years ago)

ASIA

(70,000 years ago)

(100,000 years ago)

PACIFIC OCEAN

AFRICA

Equator

(3,500 years ago)

(1,500 years ago)

(40,000–60,000 years ago)

AUSTRALIA

INDIAN OCEAN

(1,000 years ago)
NEW ZEALAND

Ice sheet (20,000 years ago)
Land bridges (20,000 years ago)
Human expansion (dates for earliest human occupation)

ANTARCTICA

peoples. Far from living as isolated groups, they had long exchanged particular stones, pigments, materials for ropes and baskets, wood for spears, feathers and shells for ornaments, and an addictive psychoactive drug known as *pituri* over distances of hundreds of miles. Songs, dances, stories, and rituals likewise circulated. Precisely how far back in time these networks extend is difficult to pinpoint, but it seems clear that Paleolithic Australia, like ancient Europe, was both many separate worlds and, at the same time, one loosely connected world.

Into the Americas

The earliest settlement of the Western Hemisphere occurred much later than that of Australia, for it took some time for human beings to penetrate the frigid lands of eastern Siberia, which was the jumping-off point for the move into the Americas. Experts continue to argue about precisely when the first migrations occurred (somewhere between 30,000 and 15,000 years ago), about the route of migration (by land across the Bering Strait or by sea down the west coast of North America), about how many separate migrations took place, and about how long it took to penetrate to the tip of South America. Some DNA evidence suggests a possible separate migration by sea from Pacific Polynesia.

Whenever the earliest migrations occurred, one of the first clearly defined and widespread cultural traditions in the Americas is associated with people who made a distinctive projectile point, known to archeologists as a Clovis point. Scattered all over North America, Clovis culture first emerged around 13,000 years ago and spread rapidly across much of North America. Scattered bands of Clovis people ranged over this huge area, camping along rivers, springs, and waterholes, where large animals congregated. Although they certainly hunted smaller animals and gathered many wild plants, Clovis men show up in the archeological record most dramatically as hunters of very large mammals, such as mammoths and bison. Killing a single mammoth could provide food for many weeks or, in cold weather, for much of the winter. The wide distribution of Clovis point technology suggests yet again a regional pattern of cultural diffusion and at least indirect communication over a large area.

Then, rather abruptly, by roughly 11,000 years ago, all trace of the Clovis culture disappeared from the archeological record at about the same time that many species of large animals, including the mammoth and several species of horses and camels, also became extinct. Did the Clovis people hunt these animals to extinction and then vanish themselves as their source of food disappeared? Or did the drier climate that came with the end of the Ice Age cause this megafaunal extinction? Experts disagree, but what happened next was the creation of a much greater diversity of cultures as people adapted to this new situation in various ways. Hunters on the Great Plains continued to pursue bison, which largely avoided the fate of the mammoths. Others learned to live in the desert, taking advantage of seasonal plants and smaller animals, while those who lived near the sea, lakes, or streams drew on local fish and birds. Many peoples of the Americas retained their gathering and

AP® EXAM TIP

It is important that you understand the concept of "diffusion," including cultural, technological, and biological diffusion.

hunting way of life into modern times, while others became farmers and, in a few favored regions, later developed cities and large-scale states.

Into the Pacific

The last phase of the great human migration to the ends of the earth took place in the Pacific Ocean and was distinctive in many ways. In the first place, it occurred quite recently, jumping off only about 3,500 years ago from the Bismarck and Solomon Islands near New Guinea as well as from the islands of the Philippines. It was everywhere a waterborne migration, making use of oceangoing canoes and remarkable navigational skills, and it happened very quickly and over a huge area of the planet. Speaking Austronesian languages that trace back to southern China, these oceanic voyagers had settled every habitable piece of land in the Pacific basin within about 2,500 years. Other Austronesians had sailed west from Indonesia across the Indian Ocean to settle the island of Madagascar off the coast of eastern Africa. This extraordinary process of expansion made the Austronesian family of languages the most geographically widespread in the world and Austronesian trading networks, reaching some 5,000 miles from western Indonesia to the mid-Pacific, the most extensive. With the occupation of Aotearoa (New Zealand) and Rapa Nui (Easter Island) around 1000 to 1200 C.E., the initial human settlement of the planet was finally complete (see Map 1.2).

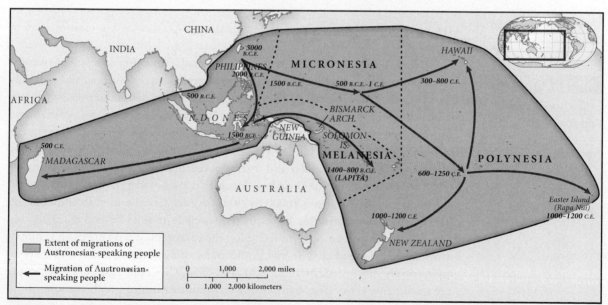

Map 1.2 Migration of Austronesian-Speaking People
People speaking Austronesian languages completed the human settlement of the earth quite recently as they settled the islands of the vast Pacific and penetrated the Indian Ocean to Madagascar, off the coast of southeast Africa.

Guided Reading Question

■ COMPARISON
How did Austronesian migrations differ from other early patterns of human movement?

In contrast with all of the other initial migrations, these Pacific voyages were undertaken by agricultural people who carried both domesticated plants and animals in their canoes. Both men and women made these journeys, suggesting a deliberate intention to colonize new lands. Virtually everywhere they went, two developments followed. One was the creation of highly stratified societies or chiefdoms, of which ancient Hawaiian society is a prime example. In Hawaii, an elite class of chiefs with political and military power ruled over a mass of commoners. The other development involved a profound ecological impact of this initial intrusion into a pristine environment: extensive deforestation and the quick extinction of many species of animals, especially large flightless birds such as the *moa* of New Zealand, which largely vanished within a century of human arrival. (See Chapter 6, pages 258–62, for more on the historical development of Pacific Oceania.)

The Ways We Were

During their long journeys across the earth, Paleolithic people created a multitude of separate and distinct societies, each with its own history, culture, language, identity, stories, and rituals, but the limitations of a gathering and hunting technology using stone tools imposed some commonalities on these ancient people. Based on the archeological record and on observations of gathering and hunting peoples that still existed in recent centuries, scholars have sketched out some of the common features of these early societies.

The First Human Societies

AP® EXAM TIP

Take good notes on the features of Paleolithic societies.

Above all else, these Paleolithic societies were small, consisting of bands of twenty-five to fifty people, in which all relationships were intensely personal and normally understood in terms of kinship. The available technology permitted only a very low population density and ensured an extremely slow rate of population growth. Some scholars speculate that this growth was dramatically interrupted around 70,000 years ago by an enormous volcanic eruption on the island of Sumatra in present-day Indonesia, resulting in a cooler and drier global climate and causing human numbers to drop to some 10,000 or less. From that point of near extinction, world population grew slowly to 500,000 by 30,000 years ago and then to 6 million by 10,000 years ago.[3] Paleolithic bands were seasonally mobile or nomadic, moving frequently and in regular patterns to exploit the resources of wild plants and animals on which they depended. The low productivity of a gathering and hunting economy normally did not allow the production of much surplus, and because people were on the move so often, transporting an accumulation of goods was out of the question.

All of this resulted in highly egalitarian societies, lacking the many inequalities of wealth and power that came later with agricultural and urban life. With no formal chiefs, kings, bureaucrats, soldiers, nobles, or priests, Paleolithic men and women were perhaps freer of human tyranny and oppression than any subsequent kind of human society, even if they were more constrained by the forces of nature. Without specialists, most people possessed the same set of skills, although male and female tasks often differed sharply. The male role as hunter, especially of big game, perhaps gave rise to one of the first criteria of masculine identity: success in killing large animals.

Relationships between women and men usually were far more equal than in later societies. As the primary food gatherers, women provided the bulk of the family's sustenance. One study of the San people, a surviving gathering and hunting society in southern Africa, found that plants, normally gathered by women, provided 70 percent of the diet, while meat, hunted by men, accounted for just 30 percent. This division of labor underpinned what anthropologist Richard Lee called "relative equality between the sexes with no-one having the upper hand." Among the San, teenagers engaged quite freely in sex play, and the concept of female virginity was apparently unknown, as were rape, wife beating, and the sexual double standard. Although polygamy was permitted, most marriages were in fact monogamous because women strongly resisted sharing a husband with another wife. Frequent divorce among very young couples allowed women to leave unsatisfactory marriages easily. Lee found that longer-term marriages seemed to be generally fulfilling and stable. Both men and women expected a satisfying sexual relationship, and both occasionally took lovers, although discreetly.[4]

When the British navigator and explorer Captain James Cook first encountered the gathering and hunting peoples of Australia in 1770, he described them, perhaps a little enviously, in this way:

> They live in a Tranquillity which is not disturb'd by the Inequality of Conditions: The Earth and sea of their own accord furnishes them with all things necessary for life, they covet not Magnificent houses, Household-stuff. . . . In short they seem'd to set no value upon any thing we gave them. . . . They think themselves provided with all the necessarys of Life.[5]

The Europeans who settled permanently among such people some twenty years later, however, found a society in which physical competition among men was expressed in frequent one-on-one combat and in formalized but bloody battles. It also meant recurrent, public, and quite brutal

Native Australians
A small number of Aboriginal Australians maintained their gathering and hunting way of life well into the twentieth century. Here an older woman shows two young boys how to dig for honey ants, a popular food. (© Bill Bachman/Alamy)

beatings of wives by their husbands.[6] And some Aboriginal myths sought to explain how men achieved power over women. Among the San, frequent arguments about the distribution of meat or the laziness or stinginess of particular people generated conflict, as did rivalries among men over women. Richard Lee identified twenty-two murders that had occurred between 1920 and 1955 and several cases in which the community came together to conduct an execution of particularly disruptive individuals. More generally, recent studies have found that in Paleolithic societies some 15 percent of deaths occurred through violence at the hands of other people, a rate far higher than in later civilizations, where violence was largely monopolized by the state.[7] Although sometimes romanticized by outsiders, the relative equality of Paleolithic societies did not always ensure a utopia of social harmony.

Like all other human cultures, Paleolithic societies had rules and structures. A gender-based division of labor usually cast men as hunters and women as gatherers. Values emphasizing reciprocal sharing of goods resulted in clearly defined rules about distributing the meat from an animal kill. Various rules about incest and adultery governed sexual behavior, while understandings about who could hunt or gather in particular territories regulated economic activity. Leaders arose as needed to organize a task such as a hunt, but without conferring permanent power on individuals.

Economy and the Environment

For a long time, modern people viewed their gathering and hunting ancestors as primitive and impoverished, barely eking out a living from the land. In more recent decades, anthropologists studying contemporary Paleolithic societies—those that survived into the twentieth century—began to paint a different picture. They noted that gathering and hunting people frequently worked fewer hours to meet their material needs than did people in agricultural or industrial societies and so had more leisure time. One scholar referred to them as "the original affluent society," not because they had so much but because they wanted or needed so little.[8] Nonetheless, life expectancy was low, probably little more than thirty-five years on average. Life in the wild was surely dangerous, and dependency on the vagaries of nature rendered it insecure as well.

But Paleolithic people also acted to alter the natural environment substantially. The use of deliberately set fires to encourage the growth of particular plants certainly changed the landscape and in Australia led to the proliferation of fire-resistant eucalyptus trees at the expense of other plant species. In many ecosystems, especially small ones like Pacific islands, the arrival of humans resulted in the rapid extinction of some native plants and animals. Other hominid, or human-like, species, such as the Neanderthals in Europe or "Flores man," discovered in 2003 in Indonesia, also perished after living side by side with *Homo sapiens* for millennia.

Whether their disappearance occurred through massacre, interbreeding, peaceful competition, or something unrelated to the human presence, ultimately they did not survive the rise of humankind. Thus the biological environment inhabited by gathering and hunting peoples was not wholly natural but was shaped in part by their own hands.

The Realm of the Spirit

The religious or spiritual dimension of Paleolithic culture has been hard to pin down, because bones and stones tell us little about what people thought, art is subject to many interpretations, and the experience of contemporary gathering and hunting peoples may not reflect the distant past. Clear evidence exists, however, for a rich interior life. The presence of rock art deep inside caves and far from living spaces suggests a "ceremonial space" separate from ordinary life. The extended rituals of contemporary Australian Aboriginals, which sometimes last for weeks, confirm this impression, as do numerous and elaborate burial sites found throughout the world. No full-time religious specialists or priests led these ceremonies, but part-time shamans (people believed to be especially skilled at dealing with the spirit world) emerged as the need arose. Such people sometimes entered an altered state of consciousness or a trance while performing the ceremonies, often with the aid of psychoactive drugs.

Precisely how Paleolithic people understood the nonmaterial world is hard to reconstruct, and speculation abounds. Linguistic evidence from ancient Africa suggests a variety of understandings: some Paleolithic societies were apparently monotheistic; others saw several levels of supernatural beings, including a creator deity, various territorial spirits, and the spirits of dead ancestors; still others believed in an impersonal force suffused throughout the natural order that could be accessed by shamans during a trance dance.[9] The prevalence of Venus figurines and other symbols all across Europe has convinced some, but not all, scholars that Paleolithic religious thought had a strongly feminine dimension, embodied in a Great Goddess and concerned with the regeneration and renewal of life.[10] Many gathering and hunting peoples likely developed a cyclical view of time derived from recurring natural cycles: sunrise and sunset; changing seasons; the phases of the moon; patterns of female fertility—birth, menstruation, pregnancy, new birth—and, of course, life, death, and new life. These understandings of the cosmos, which saw endlessly repeated patterns of regeneration and disintegration, differed from later Western views, which saw time moving in a straight line toward some predetermined goal. Nor did Paleolithic people make sharp distinctions between the material and spiritual worlds, for they understood that animals, rocks, trees, mountains, and much more were animated by spirit or possessed souls of their own. Earlier scholars sometimes dubbed such views as "animistic" and regarded them as "primitive" or "simple" in comparison to later literate religions. More recent

The Willendorf Venus
Less than four and a half inches in height and dating to about 25,000 years ago, this female figure, which was found near the town of Willendorf in Austria, has become the most famous of the many Venus figurines. Certain features— the absence of both face and feet, the coils of hair around her head, the prominence of her breasts and sexual organs—have prompted much speculation among scholars about the significance of these intriguing carvings. (Naturhistorisches Museum, Vienna, Austria/ Ali Meyer/Bridgeman Images)

SNAPSHOT   Paleolithic Era in Perspective

	Paleolithic Era (from 10,000 to 250,000 years ago)	Agricultural Era (from 200 to 10,000 years ago)	Modern Industrial Era (since 1800)
Duration of each era, as a percentage of 250,000 years[11]	96%	4%	0.08%
Percentage of people who lived, out of 80 billion total	12%	68%	20%
Percentage of years lived in each era (reflects changing life expectancies)	9%	62%	29%

accounts generally avoid the term, preferring to focus on the specifics of particular religious traditions rather than some overall evolutionary scheme.

Settling Down: The Great Transition

Though glacially slow by contemporary standards, changes in Paleolithic cultures occurred over time as people moved into new environments, as populations grew, as climates altered, and as different human groups interacted with one another. For example, all over the Afro-Eurasian world after 25,000 years ago, a tendency toward the miniaturization of stone tools is evident, analogous perhaps to the miniaturization of electronic components in the twentieth century. Known as micro-blades, these smaller and more refined spear points, arrowheads, knives, and scrapers were carefully struck from larger cores and often mounted in antler, bone, or wooden handles. Another important change in the strategies of Paleolithic people involved the collection of wild grains, which represented a major addition to the food supply beyond the use of roots, berries, and nuts. This innovation originated in northeastern Africa around 16,000 years ago.

But the most striking and significant change in the lives of Paleolithic peoples occurred as the last Ice Age came to an end between 16,000 and 10,000 years ago. What followed was a general global warming, though one with periodic fluctuations and cold snaps. Unlike the contemporary global warming, generated by human activity and especially the burning of fossil fuels, this ancient warming phase was a wholly natural phenomenon, part of a long cycle of repeated heating and cooling characteristic of the earth's climatic history. Plants and animals that had struggled

Guided Reading Question
....

■ CHANGE
Why did some Paleolithic peoples abandon earlier, more nomadic ways and begin to live a more settled life?

in the Ice Age climate now flourished and increased their range, providing a much richer and more diverse environment for many human societies. Under these improved conditions, human populations grew, and some previously nomadic gathering and hunting communities, but not all of them, found it possible to settle down and live in more permanent settlements or villages. These societies were becoming both larger and more complex, and it was less possible to simply move away if trouble struck. Settlement also meant that households could store and accumulate goods to a greater degree than previously. Because some people were more energetic, more talented, or luckier than others, the thin edge of inequality gradually began to wear away the egalitarianism of Paleolithic communities.

Changes along these lines emerged in many places. Paleolithic societies in Japan, known as Jomon, settled down in villages by the sea, where they greatly expanded the number of animals, both land and marine, that they consumed. They also created some of the world's first pottery, along with dugout canoes, paddles, bows, bowls, and tool handles, all made from wood. A similar pattern of permanent settlement, a broader range of food sources, and specialized technologies is evident in parts of Scandinavia, Southeast Asia, North America, and the Middle East between 12,000 and 4,000 years ago. In Labrador, longhouses accommodating 100 people appear in the archeological record. Far more elaborate burial sites in many places testify to the growing complexity of human communities and the kinship systems that bound them together. Separate cemeteries for dogs suggest that humankind's best friend was also our first domesticated animal friend. Some of the most stunning and unexpected achievements of such sedentary Paleolithic people come from the archeological complex of Göbekli Tepe (goh-BEHK-lee TEH-peh) in southeastern Turkey, described more fully in the Zooming In feature on page 26.

Studies of more recent gathering and hunting societies, which were able to settle permanently in particular resource-rich areas, show marked differences from their more nomadic counterparts. Among the Chumash of southern California, for example, early Spanish settlers found peoples who had developed substantial and permanent structures accommodating up to seventy persons; hereditary political elites; elements of a market economy, including the use of money and private ownership of some property; and the beginnings of class distinctions.

This process of settling down among gathering and hunting peoples—and the changes that followed from it—marked a major turn in human history, away from countless millennia of nomadic journeys by very small communities. It also provided the setting within which the next great transition would occur. Growing numbers of men and women, living in settled communities, placed a much greater demand on the environment than did small bands of people on the move. Therefore, it is perhaps not surprising that among the innovations that emerged in some of these more complex gathering and hunting societies was yet another way for increasing the food supply—agriculture.

PRACTICING AP® HISTORICAL THINKING

How do you understand the significance of the long Paleolithic era in the larger context of world history?

Göbekli Tepe: Monumental Construction before Agriculture

Perhaps the most stunning archeological discovery of recent decades comes from the site known as Göbekli Tepe, or "potbelly hill," in southeastern Turkey, which has been under excavation since the mid-1990s. Dating to almost 12,000 years ago, this twenty-five-acre complex currently consists of about 200 massive limestone pillars, some as tall as eighteen feet and weighing as much as fifty tons. Carved in a T shape, perhaps to represent human beings with arms outstretched, they were arranged in a set of walled circles or rings. Five such circles have been unearthed so far, with another twenty or so awaiting excavation. Gracefully carved wild animals—gazelles, snakes, boars, foxes, lions, scorpions, vultures—decorate the pillars. Göbekli Tepe was probably a ceremonial or religious site, for little evidence of long-term human habitation has been found. Dubbed "the world's oldest temple," it likely attracted worshippers or pilgrims from many miles around and

Göbekli Tepe.

may well have served as a place of ritual burials, although no actual graves have yet been found.

The most amazing feature of Göbekli Tepe involves those who constructed it, for they were clearly gathering and hunting peoples, living at least part of the year in settled villages. No evidence of agriculture or domesticated animals has emerged. Rather, the tens of thousands of animal bone fragments found at the site suggest that those who built the complex dined on wild gazelles, pigs, sheep, deer, vultures, and ducks, as well as wild plants native to the area. Thus Göbekli Tepe represents a kind of monumental construction long associated only with agricultural societies and civilizations, forcing scholars to rethink their understanding of the late Paleolithic era.

photo: Vincent J. Musi/National Geographic Creative

Breakthroughs to Agriculture

AP® EXAM TIP

The Agricultural Revolution and its effects are important concepts on the AP® exam.

The chief feature of the long Paleolithic era—and the first human process to operate on a global scale—was the initial settlement of the earth. Then, beginning around 12,000 years ago, a second global pattern began to unfold—agriculture. The terms "Neolithic (New Stone Age) Revolution" and "Agricultural Revolution" both refer to the deliberate cultivation of particular plants as well as the taming and breeding of particular animals. Thus a whole new way of life gradually replaced the earlier practices of gathering and hunting in most parts of the world. Although it took place over centuries and millennia, the coming of agriculture represented a genuinely revolutionary transformation of human life all across the planet and provided the foundation for almost everything that followed: growing populations, settled villages, animal-borne diseases, horse-drawn chariot warfare, cities, states, empires, civilizations, writing, literature, and much more.

How did such pre-agricultural peoples with only the simplest of stone tools carve, transport, and erect such enormous structures? What kind of social organization facilitated their remarkable achievement? What did this complex mean to those who created it? Since stones and bones tell us little about these matters, many mysteries remain.

Although Göbekli Tepe was the product of pre-agricultural peoples, the process of its construction may well have played a role in the breakthrough to farming in this region. Klaus Schmidt, the chief archeologist at the site for many years, argued that the need for food to supply those who built and maintained this massive religious complex may well have triggered the development of agriculture in the area. Certainly, some of the earliest domesticated wheat has been located just twenty miles away and at roughly the same date. If this connection holds, it suggests that the

Carved lion on a stone pillar at Göbekli Tepe.

human impulse to worship collectively played a significant role in generating the epic transformation of the Agricultural Revolution.

Scholars have long believed that large-scale construction, settled village life, and institutional religion were generated by agricultural societies. The finds at Göbekli Tepe and elsewhere now suggest that these achievements may have figured in the creation of those farming communities. Perhaps they were precursors to agriculture rather than products of it.

Questions: In what ways has Göbekli Tepe forced historians to rethink earlier views? How does this archeological discovery affect your own understanding of the Paleolithic era?

photo: © Vincent J. Musi/National Geographic Society/Corbis

Among the most revolutionary aspects of the age of agriculture was a new relationship between humankind and other living things, for now men and women were not simply using what they found in nature but actively changing nature as well. They were consciously "directing" the process of evolution. The actions of farmers in the Americas, for example, transformed corn from a plant with a cob of an inch or so to one measuring about six inches by 1500. Later efforts more than doubled that length. Farmers everywhere stamped the landscape with a human imprint in the form of fields with boundaries, terraced hillsides, irrigation ditches, and canals. Animals too were transformed as selective breeding produced sheep that grew more wool, cows that gave more milk, and chickens that laid more eggs than their wild counterparts.

This was "domestication"—the taming, and the changing, of nature for the benefit of humankind—but it created a new kind of mutual dependence. Many domesticated plants and animals could no longer survive in the wild and relied on

AP® EXAM TIP

Pay close attention to the domestication of plants and animals and their effects on societies.

human action or protection to reproduce successfully. Similarly, farmers and herders became dependent on their domesticated plants and animals, for as their populations grew, those larger numbers could no longer sustain themselves in the older gathering, hunting, and fishing fashion. From an outside point of view, it might well seem that corn and cows had tamed human beings, using people to ensure their own survival and growth as a species, as much as the other way around. In many agricultural communities, however, gathering, hunting, and fishing did not quickly disappear, but long continued to supplement agriculture and animal husbandry as food sources. Even in modern industrial societies, hunting continues as a sport, gathering wild mushrooms and berries persists as an enjoyable pastime, and fishing for both profit and pleasure remains a widespread activity. In such ways, the original human style of living resonates still, even in the twenty-first century.

A further revolutionary aspect of the agricultural age is summed up in the term "intensification." It means getting more for less, in this case more food and resources—far more—from a much smaller area of land than was possible with a gathering and hunting technology. More food meant more people. Growing populations in turn required an even more intensive exploitation of the environment. And so was launched the continuing human effort to "subdue the earth" and to "have dominion over it," as the biblical story in Genesis recorded God's command to Adam and Eve.

Common Patterns

Perhaps the most extraordinary feature of the Neolithic or Agricultural Revolution was that it occurred, separately and independently, in many widely scattered parts of the world: the Fertile Crescent of Southwest Asia, several places in sub-Saharan Africa, China, Southeast Asia, New Guinea, Mesoamerica, the Andes, and eastern North America (see Map 1.3). Even more remarkably, all of this took place at roughly the same time (at least as measured by the 250,000-year span of human history on the planet)—between 12,000 and 4,000 years ago. These facts have generated many questions with which historians have long struggled. Why was the Agricultural Revolution so late in the history of humankind? What was unique about the period after 10,000 B.C.E. that may have triggered or facilitated this vast upheaval? In what different ways did the Agricultural Revolution take shape in its various locations? How did it spread from its several points of origin to the rest of the earth? And what impact did it have on the making of human societies?

It is no accident that the Agricultural Revolution coincided with the end of the last Ice Age, a process of global warming that began some 16,000 years ago. By about 11,000 years ago, the Ice Age was over, and climatic conditions similar to those of our own time generally prevailed. This was but the latest of some twenty-five periods of glaciation and warming that have occurred over the past several million years of the earth's history and that are caused by minor periodic changes in the earth's orbit around the sun. The end of the last Ice Age, however, coincided with the migration of *Homo sapiens* across the planet and created new conditions that made agriculture more possible in some areas, even as rising sea levels inundated other regions (see Map 1.1). Combined perhaps with active hunting by human societies, climate change in some places helped to push into extinction various species of large mammals on which Paleolithic people had depended, thus adding to the pressure to find new food sources. The warmer, wetter, and more stable conditions, particularly in the tropical and temperate regions of the earth, also permitted the flourishing of more wild plants, especially cereal grasses, which were the ancestors of many domesticated crops. What climate change took away with one hand, it apparently gave back with the other.

Over their long history, gathering and hunting peoples had already developed a deep knowledge of the natural world and, in some cases, the ability to manage it actively. They had learned to make use of a large number of plants and to hunt and eat both small and large animals, creating what archeologists call a "broad-spectrum diet." In the Middle East, people had developed sickles for cutting newly available wild grain, baskets to carry it, mortars and pestles to remove the husk, and storage pits to preserve it. Peoples of the Amazon and elsewhere had learned to cut back some plants to encourage the growth of their favorites. Native Australians had built elaborate traps in which they could capture, store, and harvest large numbers of eels.

In hindsight, much of this looks like a kind of preparation for agriculture. Because women in particular had long been intimately associated with collecting wild plants, they were the likely innovators who led the way to deliberate farming, with men perhaps taking the lead in domesticating animals. Clearly the knowledge and technology necessary for agriculture were part of a longer process involving more intense human exploitation of the earth. Nowhere was agriculture an overnight invention.

Using such technologies, and benefiting from the global warming at the end of the last Ice Age, gathering and hunting peoples in various resource-rich areas were able to settle down and establish more permanent villages, abandoning their nomadic ways and more intensively exploiting the local area. In settling down, however, they found themselves now required to support growing populations. Evidence for increasing human numbers around the world during this period of global warming has persuaded some scholars that agriculture was a response to the need for additional food, perhaps even a "food crisis." Such conditions surely motivated people to experiment and to innovate in an effort to increase the food supply. Clearly, many of the breakthroughs to agriculture occurred only *after* gathering and hunting peoples had already grown substantially in numbers and had established a sedentary way of life.

AP® EXAM TIP

You should know the features and contributions of gathering and hunting peoples.

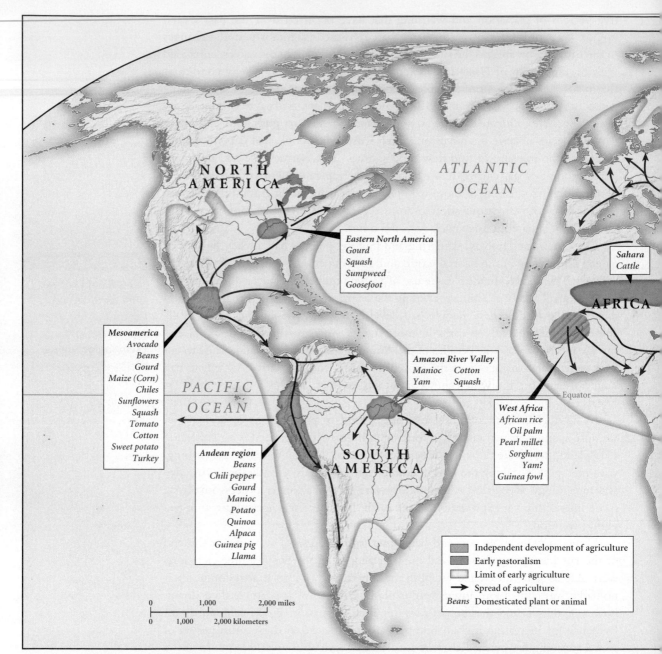

Map 1.3   The Global Spread of Agriculture and Pastoralism

From ten or more separate points of origin, agriculture spread to adjacent areas, eventually encompassing almost all of the world's peoples.

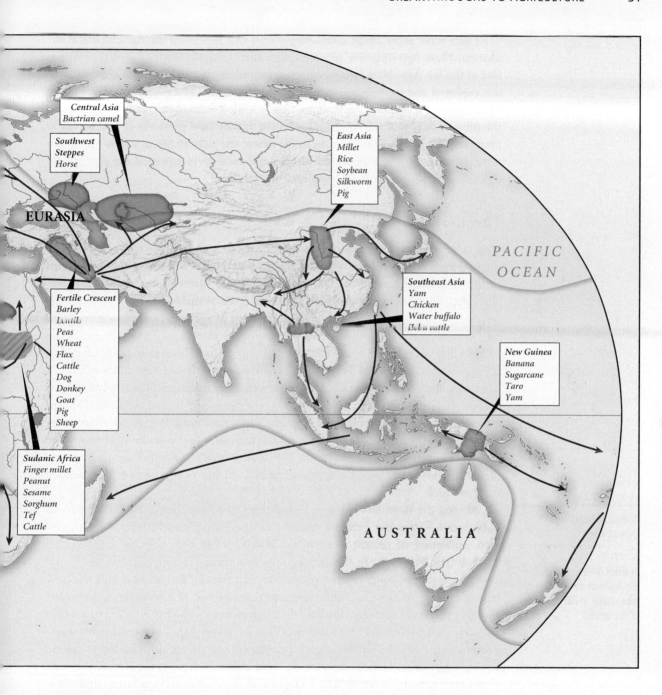

Central Asia
Bactrian camel

Southwest
Steppes
Horse

East Asia
Millet
Rice
Soybean
Silkworm
Pig

EURASIA

Fertile Crescent
Barley
Lentils
Peas
Wheat
Flax
Cattle
Dog
Donkey
Goat
Pig
Sheep

PACIFIC
OCEAN

Southeast Asia
Yam
Chicken
Water buffalo
Zebu cattle

New Guinea
Banana
Sugarcane
Taro
Yam

Sudanic Africa
Finger millet
Peanut
Sesame
Sorghum
Tef
Cattle

AUSTRALIA

These were some of the common patterns that facilitated the Agricultural Revolution. New opportunities appeared with the changed climatic conditions at the end of the Ice Age. New knowledge and technology emerged as human communities explored and exploited that changed environment. The disappearance of many large mammals, growing populations, newly settled ways of life, and fluctuations in the process of global warming—all of these represented pressures or incentives to increase food production and thus to minimize the risks of life in a new era. From some combination of these opportunities and incentives emerged the profoundly transforming process of the Agricultural Revolution.

Variations

This new way of life initially operated everywhere with a simple technology—the digging stick or hoe. Plows were developed much later. But the several transitions to this hoe-based agriculture, commonly known as horticulture, varied considerably, depending on what plants and animals were available locally. For example, potatoes were found in the Andes region, but not in Africa or Asia; wheat and wild pigs existed in the Fertile Crescent, but not in the Americas. Furthermore, of the world's 200,000 plant species, only several hundred have been domesticated, and in more recent centuries just five of these—wheat, corn, rice, barley, and sorghum—have supplied more than half of the calories that sustain human life. Only fourteen species of large mammals have been successfully domesticated, of which sheep, pigs, goats, cattle, and horses have been the most important. Because they are stubborn, nervous, solitary, or finicky, many animals simply cannot be readily domesticated. Thus the kind of Agricultural Revolution that unfolded in particular places depended very much on what happened to be available locally; in short, it depended on sheer luck.

Guided Reading Question

■ COMPARISON
In what different ways did the Agricultural Revolution take shape in various parts of the world?

Among the most favored areas—and the first to experience a full Agricultural Revolution—was the Fertile Crescent, an area sometimes known as Southwest Asia, consisting of present-day Iraq, Syria, Israel/Palestine, Jordan, and southern Turkey (see Map 1.4). In this region, an extraordinary variety of wild plants and animals capable of domestication provided a rich array of species on which the now largely settled gathering and hunting people could draw. What triggered the transition to agriculture remains a much-debated question. Some have argued that a cold and dry spell between 11,000 and 9500 B.C.E., a very rapid but temporary interruption in the general process of global warming, was the stimulus for the transition to farming. Larger settled populations, now threatened with the loss of the wild plants and animals on which they had come to depend, found a solution in domestication, either during or soon after this cold and dry period passed. Figs were apparently the first cultivated crop, dating to about 9400 B.C.E. In the millennium or so that followed, wheat, barley, rye, peas, lentils, sheep, goats, pigs, and cattle all came under human control, providing the foundation for the world's first agricultural societies.

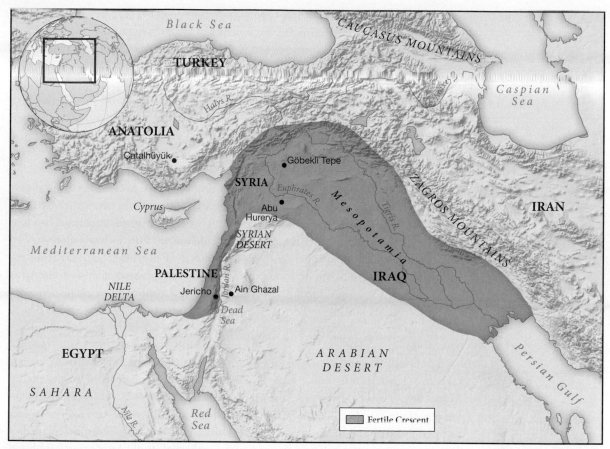

Map 1.4 The Fertile Crescent

Located in what is now called the Middle East, the Fertile Crescent was the site of many significant processes in early world history, including a major breakthrough to agriculture and later the development of one of the First Civilizations.

Archeological evidence suggests that the transition to a fully agricultural way of life in parts of this region took place quite quickly, within as few as 500 years. Signs of that transformation included large increases in the size of settlements, which now housed as many as several thousand people. In these agricultural settings, archeologists have found major innovations: the use of sun-dried mud bricks; the appearance of monuments or shrine-like buildings; displays of cattle skulls; more elaborate human burials, including the removal of the skull; and more sophisticated tools, such as sickles, polished axes, and awls. From this point on, global climate remained remarkably stable, when compared to sharp variations of earlier times, which proved to be a great advantage for settled life and agricultural development.

At roughly the same time, or perhaps a bit later, another process of domestication was unfolding on the African continent in the eastern part of what is now the

Sahara in present-day Sudan. Between 10,000 and 5,000 years ago, scholars tell us that there was no desert in this region, which received more rainfall than currently, had extensive grassland vegetation, and was "relatively hospitable to human life."[12] It seems likely that cattle were domesticated in this region about 1,000 years before they were separately brought under human control in the Middle East and India. At about the same time, the donkey was also domesticated in northeastern Africa near the Red Sea and spread from there into Southwest Asia, even as the practice of raising sheep and goats moved in the other direction. In terms of farming, the African pattern again was somewhat different. Unlike the Fertile Crescent, where a number of plants were domesticated in a small area, sub-Saharan Africa witnessed the emergence of several widely scattered farming practices. Sorghum, which grows well in arid conditions, was the first grain to be "tamed" in the eastern Sahara region. In the highlands of Ethiopia, teff, a tiny, highly nutritious grain, as well as enset, a relative of the banana, came under cultivation. In the forested region of West Africa, yams, oil palm trees, okra, and the kola nut (used as a flavoring for cola drinks) emerged as important crops. The scattered location of these domestications generated a less productive agriculture than in the more favored and compact Fertile Crescent, but a number of African domesticates—sorghum, castor beans, gourds, millet, the donkey—subsequently spread to enrich the agricultural practices of Eurasian peoples.

Yet another pattern of agricultural development took shape in the Americas. Like the Agricultural Revolution in Africa, the domestication of plants in the Americas occurred separately in a number of locations—in the coastal Andean regions of western South America, in Mesoamerica, in the Mississippi River valley, and perhaps in the Amazon basin. Surely the most distinctive common feature of these regions was the relative absence of animals that could be domesticated. Of the fourteen major species of large mammals that have been brought under human control, just two, the llama and alpaca, existed in the Western Hemisphere, and only in the Andes region, where they proved enormously useful for food, fiber, and transportation. Without goats, sheep, pigs, cattle, or horses, the peoples of the Americas lacked sources of protein, manure (for fertilizer), and power (to draw plows or pull carts, for example) that were widely available to societies in the Afro-Eurasian world. Because they could not depend on domesticated animals for meat, many agricultural peoples in the Americas relied more on hunting and fishing than did peoples in the Eastern Hemisphere. Europe too lacked most of the animals that could be readily domesticated, but it was geographically closer to areas that had them and so could borrow from neighboring regions. Farmers in the Americas could not.

While the Americas lacked the cereal grains that were widely available in Afro-Eurasia, they had maize or corn, first domesticated in southern Mexico by 4000 to 3000 B.C.E. Unlike the cereal grains of the Fertile Crescent, which closely resemble their wild predecessors, the ancestor of corn, a mountain grass called teosinte (tee-

AP® EXAM TIP

You should still be taking notes on how the Neolithic Revolution developed around the world. Be sure to note differences as well as similarities.

The Statues of Ain Ghazal
Among the largest of the early agricultural settlements investigated by archeologists is that of Ain Ghazal, located in the modern state of Jordan. Inhabited from about 7200 to 5000 B.C.E., in its prime it was home to some 3,000 people, who lived in multi-roomed stone houses; cultivated barley, wheat, peas, beans, and lentils; and herded domesticated goats. These remarkable statues, around three feet tall and made of limestone plaster applied to a core of bundled reeds, were among the most startling finds at that site. Did they represent heroes, gods, goddesses, or ordinary people? No one really knows. (Courtesy, Department of Antiquities of Jordan [DoA]/Photo by John Tsantesi, Courtesy, Dr. Gary O. Rollefson)

uh-SIHN-tee), looks nothing like what we now know as corn or maize. Thousands of years of selective adaptation were required to develop a sufficiently large cob and number of kernels to sustain a productive agriculture, an achievement that one geneticist has called "arguably man's first, and perhaps his greatest, feat of genetic engineering."[13] Thus while Middle Eastern societies quite rapidly replaced their gathering and hunting economy with agriculture, that process took several thousand years in Mesoamerica. Beyond maize, Native American farmers domesticated squash, beans, potatoes, sunflowers, quinoa, pigweed, and goosefoot, which were harvested on a large scale.

Another difference in the unfolding of the Agricultural Revolution lay in the north/south orientation of the Americas, which required agricultural practices to move through, and adapt to, quite distinct climatic and vegetation zones if they were to spread. The east/west axis of North Africa / Eurasia meant that agricultural innovations could spread more rapidly because they were entering roughly similar environments. Thus corn, beans, and squash, which were first domesticated in Mesoamerica, took several thousand years to travel the few hundred miles from their Mexican homeland to the southwestern United States and another thousand years or more to arrive in eastern North America. The llama, guinea pig, quinoa, and potato, which were domesticated in the Andean highlands, never reached Mesoamerica.

The Globalization of Agriculture

From the various places where it originated, agriculture spread gradually to much of the rest of the earth, although for a long time it coexisted with gathering and hunting ways of life, even as it eroded and diminished those cultures. Broadly speaking, this extension of farming occurred in two ways. The first, known as diffusion, refers to the gradual spread of agricultural techniques, and perhaps of the plants and animals themselves, but without the extensive movement of agricultural people. Neighboring groups exchanged ideas and products in a down-the-line pattern of communication. A second process involved the slow colonization or migration of agricultural peoples as growing populations pushed them outward. Often this meant the conquest, absorption, or displacement of the earlier gatherers and hunters, along with the spread of the languages and cultures of the migrating farmers. In many places, both processes took place.

Triumph and Resistance

Some combination of diffusion and migration underpinned the spread of agriculture to new regions, and the adoption of farming practices was at times accompanied by the spread of languages as well. For instance, between 6500 and 4000 B.C.E. the agricultural package of Southwest Asia spread into Europe, Central Asia, Egypt, and North Africa. In the case of Europe, the adoption of agriculture was accompanied by the spread into the region of Indo-European languages, which had originated further east in Anatolia or, as some scholars suggest, in the area north of the Black and Caspian Seas. In a similar process, the Chinese farming system moved into Southeast Asia and elsewhere, and with it a number of related language families developed. India received agricultural influences from the Middle East, Africa, and China alike. Within Africa, the development of agricultural societies in the southern half of the continent is associated with the migration of peoples speaking one or another of the some 400 Bantu languages. Beginning from what is now southern Nigeria or Cameroon around 3000 B.C.E., Bantu-speaking people moved east and south over the next several millennia, taking with them their agricultural, cattle-raising, and, later, ironworking skills, as well as their languages. The Bantus generally absorbed, killed, or drove away the indigenous Paleolithic peoples or exposed them to animal-borne diseases to which they had no immunities. A similar process brought agricultural Austronesian-speaking people, who originated in southern China, to the Philippine and Indonesian islands, with similar consequences for their earlier inhabitants. Later, Austronesian speakers carried agriculture to the uninhabited islands of the Pacific and to Madagascar off the coast of southeastern Africa (see Map 1.2, page 19).

The globalization of agriculture was a prolonged process, lasting 10,000 years or more after its first emergence in the Fertile Crescent, but it did not take hold everywhere. The Agricultural Revolution in highland New Guinea, for example, generated a number of domesticated plants including yams, taro, bananas, and sugarcane. But while these spread to parts of Island Southeast Asia, they did not pass to the nearby peoples of Australia, who remained steadfastly committed to gathering and hunting ways of life. The people of the west coast of North America, arctic regions, and southwestern Africa also maintained their gathering and hunting economies into the modern era. A very few, such as the Hadza, described at the beginning of this chapter, practice it still in vanishing numbers.

Bantu Migrations

Some of those who resisted the swelling tide of agriculture lived in areas unsuitable to farming, such as harsh desert or arctic environments; others lived in regions of particular natural abundance, so they felt little need for agriculture. Such societies found it easier to resist agriculture if they were not in the direct line of advancing, more powerful farming people. But many of the remaining gathering and hunting peoples knew about agricultural practices from nearby neighbors, suggesting that they quite deliberately chose to resist it in favor of the freer life of their Paleolithic ancestors.

Nonetheless, by the beginning of the Common Era, the global spread of agriculture had reduced gathering and hunting peoples to a small and dwindling minority of humankind. If that process meant "progress" in certain ways, it also claimed many victims as the relentlessly expanding agricultural frontier slowly destroyed gathering and hunting societies. Whether this process occurred through the peaceful diffusion of new technologies, through intermarriage, through disease, or through the violent displacement of earlier peoples, the steady erosion of this ancient way of life has been a persistent thread of the human story over the past 10,000 years. The final chapters of that long story are being written in our own times. (See Zooming In, page 38, for a recent example of this process.) After the Agricultural Revolution, the future, almost everywhere, lay with the farmers and herders and with the distinctive societies that they created.

The Culture of Agriculture

What did that future look like? In what ways did societies based on the domestication of plants and animals differ from those rooted in a gathering and hunting economy? In the first place, the Agricultural Revolution led to an increase in

Guided Reading Question

■ CHANGE
What changes did the Agricultural Revolution bring in its wake?

ZOOMING **IN**

Ishi, the Last of His People

In late August of 1911, an emaciated and nearly naked man, about fifty years old, staggered into the corral of a slaughterhouse in northern California. As it turned out, he was the last member of his people, a gathering and hunting group known as the Yahi, pushed into extinction by the intrusion of more powerful farming, herding, and "civilized" societies. It was a very old story, played out for over 10,000 years since the Agricultural Revolution placed Paleolithic cultures on the defensive, inexorably eroding their presence on the earth. The tragic story of this individual allows us to put a human face on that enormous and largely unrecorded process.

Within a few days, this bedraggled and no doubt bewildered man was taken into the care of several anthropologists from the University of California, who brought him to a museum in San Francisco, where he lived until his death from tuberculosis in 1916.

Ishi.

They called him Ishi, which means "person" in his native language, because he was unwilling to provide them with his own given name. In his culture, it was highly inappropriate to reveal one's name, especially to strangers.

In the mid-nineteenth century, the Yahi consisted of about 300 to 400 people living in a rugged and mountainous area of northern California. There they hunted, fished, gathered acorns, and otherwise provided for themselves in a fashion familiar to gathering and hunting peoples the world over. But the 1849 California gold rush brought a massive influx of American settlers, miners, and farmers that quickly pushed the Yahi to the edge of extinction. Yahi raiding and resistance was met by massacres at the hands of local militias and vigilantes, who were only too glad to "clean up the Indians," killing and scalping

photo: Courtesy of The Bancroft Library, University of California, Berkeley

AP® EXAM TIP

Demographic (population) patterns over time are important.

human population, as the greater productivity of agriculture was able to support much larger numbers. An early agricultural settlement uncovered near Jericho in present-day Israel probably had 2,000 people, a vast increase in the size of human communities compared to much smaller Paleolithic bands. On a global level, scholars estimate that the world's population was about 6 million around 10,000 years ago, before the Agricultural Revolution got under way, and shot up to some 50 million by 5,000 years ago and 250 million by the beginning of the Common Era. Here was the real beginning of the human dominance over other forms of life on the planet.

That dominance was reflected in major environmental transformations. In a growing number of places, forests and grasslands became cultivated fields and grazing lands. Human selection modified the genetic composition of numerous plants and animals. In parts of the Middle East, within a thousand years after the beginning of settled agricultural life, some villages were abandoned when soil erosion and hundreds. One such massacre in 1865 likely killed Ishi's father, while the young Ishi, his mother, and a few others escaped.

By 1870, Ishi's community had dwindled to fifteen or sixteen people, who lived in an even more inaccessible region of their homeland. In these desperate circumstances, traditional gender roles blurred, even as they undertook great efforts to conceal their presence. To avoid making footprints when traveling, they jumped from rock to rock; they ground acorns on smooth stones rather than on more obvious hollowed-out rocks and carefully camouflaged their thatched dwellings and campfires. By 1894, this tiny Yahi community numbered only five people: Ishi, his mother, his sister or cousin, and an older man and woman.

Then in 1908, a group of American surveyors came across a naked Ishi harpooning fish in the river, and a few days later they found the tiny settlement that sheltered the remaining Yahi. Only Ishi's aged mother was present, hidden under a pile of skins and rags. They did not harm her, but they took away every movable item— tools, food, baskets, bows and arrows—as souvenirs. Ishi returned to carry his mother away and she soon died. He never saw his sister/cousin or the others again. For some time, then, Ishi lived absolutely alone, until he stumbled into the slaughterhouse on August 29, 1911, his hair burned short in a Yahi sign of mourning.

In his new home in the museum, Ishi became something of a media sensation, willingly demonstrating his skills for visitors—starting a fire and fashioning tools and weapons of stone and bone, but refusing to make baskets, because it was women's work. Actively cooperating with anthropologists who sought to document the culture of his people, he took them on a hunt one summer, teaching them how to track and kill deer and to process the meat on the spot. All who met him remarked on his gentleness and kindness, his love of company, his delight in children, and his fondness for laughing and joking. Alfred Kroeber, the primary anthropologist involved with Ishi, observed, "He was the most patient man I ever knew . . . without trace of self-pity or of bitterness to dull the purity of his cheerful enduringness."[14]

Questions: What accounts for the ability of Ishi's people to survive into the twentieth century? What emotional or moral posture toward Ishi's life seems most appropriate? What perspective does it lend to the larger story of the gradual erosion of gathering and hunting societies the world over?

deforestation led to declining crop yields, which could not support mounting populations. The advent of more intensive agriculture associated with city-based civilizations only heightened this human impact on the landscape.

Human life too changed dramatically in farming communities, and not necessarily for the better. Farming involved hard work and more of it than in many earlier gathering and hunting societies. The remains of early agricultural people show some deterioration in health—more tooth decay, malnutrition, and anemia; a shorter physical stature; and diminished life expectancy. Living close to animals subjected humans to new diseases—smallpox, flu, measles, chicken pox, malaria, tuberculosis, rabies—while living in larger communities generated epidemics for the first time in human history. Furthermore, relying on a small number of plants or animals rendered early agricultural societies vulnerable to famine, in case of crop failure, drought, or other catastrophes. The advent of agriculture bore costs as well as benefits.

AP® EXAM TIP

Be able to compare features of agricultural peoples with those of gathering and hunting peoples.

Agriculture also imposed constraints on human communities. Some Paleolithic people had settled in permanent villages, but most agricultural people did so, as farming usually required a settled life. A good example of an early agricultural settlement comes from northern China, one of the original independent sources of agriculture, where the domestication of rice, millet, pigs, and chickens gave rise to settled communities by about 7,000 years ago. In 1953, workers digging the foundation for a factory uncovered the remains of an ancient village, now called Banpo, near the present-day city of Xian. Millet, pigs, and dogs had been domesticated, but diets were supplemented with wild plants, animals, and fish. Some forty-five houses covered with thatch laid over wooden beams provided homes to perhaps 500 people. More than 200 storage pits permitted the accumulation of grain, and six kilns and pottery wheels enabled the production of various pots, vases, and dishes, many decorated with geometric designs and human and animal images. A large central space suggests an area for public religious or political activity, and a trench surrounding the village indicates some common effort to defend the community.

Early agricultural villages such as Banpo reveal another feature of the age of agriculture—an explosion of technological innovation. Mobile Paleolithic peoples had little use for pots, but such vessels were essential for settled societies, and their creation and elaboration accompanied agriculture everywhere. So too did the weaving of textiles, made possible by collecting the fibers of domesticated plants (cotton and flax, for example) and raising animals such as sheep. Evidence for the invention of looms of several kinds dates back to 7,000 years ago, and textiles, some elaborately decorated, show up in Peru, Switzerland, China, and Egypt. Like agriculture itself, weaving was a technology in which women were probably the primary innovators. It was a task that was compatible with child-rearing responsibilities, which virtually all human societies assigned primarily to women. Another technology associated with the Agricultural Revolution was metallurgy. The working of gold and copper, then bronze, and, later, iron became part of the jewelry-, tool-, and weapon-making skill set of humankind. The long "stone age" of human technological history was coming to an end, and the age of metals was beginning.

Nok Culture

The agricultural and iron-using Nok culture of northern Nigeria in West Africa generated a remarkable artistic tradition of terra-cotta, or fired-clay, figures depicting animals and, especially, people. This one dates to somewhere between 600 B.C.E. and 600 C.E. Some scholars have dubbed this and many similar Nok sculptures "thinkers." Does it seem more likely that this notion reflects a present-day sensibility or that it is an insight into the mentality of the ancient artist who created the image? (Musée du Quai Branly/Scala/Art Resource, NY)

A further set of technological changes, beginning around 4000 B.C.E., has been labeled the "secondary products revolution."[15] These technological innovations involved new uses for domesticated animals, beyond their meat and hides. Agricultural people in parts of Europe, Asia, and Africa learned to milk their animals, to harvest their wool, and to enrich the soil with their manure. Even more important, they learned to ride horses and camels and to hitch various animals to plows and carts. Because these animals did not exist in the Americas, this revolutionary new source of power and transportation was available only in the Eastern Hemisphere.

Finally, the Agricultural Revolution presented to humankind the gift of wine and beer, often a blessing, sometimes a curse. As barley, wheat, rice, and grapes were domesticated, their potential for generating alcoholic beverages soon became apparent. Evidence for wine making in the mountains of present-day northwestern Iran dates to around 5400 B.C.E., though its expense rendered it an elite beverage for millennia. Chinese wine making can be traced to around 4000 B.C.E. Drunken debauchery and carousing among the aristocracy prompted an unsuccessful effort by one Chinese ruler around 1046 B.C.E. to outlaw the beverage. The precise origins of beer are unclear, but its use was already quite widespread in the Middle East by 4000 B.C.E., when a pictogram on a seal from Mesopotamia showed two figures using straws to drink beer from a large pottery jar. Regarded as a gift from the gods, beer, like bread, was understood in Mesopotamia as something that could turn a savage into a fully human and civilized person.[16] In the Americas, an alcoholic beverage known as *chicha* had been produced from maize, manioc, honey, and various fruits from ancient times and was the drink of choice in the Inca court.

Social Variation in the Age of Agriculture

The resources generated by the Agricultural Revolution opened up vast new possibilities for the construction of human societies, but they led to no single or common outcome. Differences in the natural environment, the encounter with strangers, and, sometimes, deliberate choices gave rise to several distinct kinds of societies early on in the age of agriculture, all of which have endured into modern times.

Pastoral Societies

One variation of great significance grew out of the difference between the domestication of plants and the domestication of animals. Many societies made use of both, but in regions where farming was difficult or impossible — arctic tundra, certain grasslands, and deserts — some people came to depend far more extensively on their animals, such as sheep, goats, cattle, horses, camels, or reindeer. Animal husbandry was a "distinct form of food-producing economy," relying on the products of animals.[17] Those animals could turn grass or waste products into meat, fiber, hides, and milk; they were useful for transport and warfare; and they could walk to market. Known as herders, pastoralists, or nomads, peoples largely dependent on their

Guided Reading Question

....

■ COMPARISON

What different kinds of societies emerged out of the Agricultural Revolution?

The Domestication of Animals
Although farming often gets top billing in discussions of the Neolithic Revolution, the raising of animals was equally important, for they provided meat, pulling power, transportation (in the case of horses and camels), and manure. Animal husbandry also made possible pastoral societies, which were largely dependent on their domesticated animals. This rock art painting from the Sahara (now southeastern Algeria) dates to somewhere around 4000 B.C.E. and depicts an early pastoral community. The white ovals represent a group of huts. (Fresco from Tassili n'Ager, Algeria, Henri Lhote Collection/ Musée de l'Homme, Paris, France/Erich Lessing/Art Resource, NY)

domesticated animals emerged most prominently in Central Asia, the Arabian Peninsula, the Sahara, and parts of eastern and southern Africa. What they had in common was mobility, for they moved seasonally as they followed the changing patterns of the vegetation necessary as pasture for their animals. Some lived a nomadic existence of constant seasonal movement, but for others it was possible to combine permanent settlements in lowland areas and the movement of animals to more mountainous pasturelands in the summer.

The particular animals central to pastoral economies differed from region to region. The domestication of horses by 4000 B.C.E. and the mastery of horseback-riding skills several thousand years later enabled the growth of pastoral peoples all across the steppes of Central Asia by the first millennium B.C.E. Although organized primarily in kinship-based clans or tribes, these nomads periodically created powerful military confederations, which played a major role in the history of Eurasia for thousands of years. In the Inner Asian, Arabian, and Saharan deserts, domesticated camels made possible the human occupation of forbidding environments. (See Zooming In: The Arabian Camel, Chapter 7, page 302.) The grasslands south of the Sahara and in parts of eastern Africa supported cattle-raising pastoralists. In the Americas, llamas and alpacas were tremendously important in the economy of Andean civilizations, but only in a few pockets in the Andes did human communities rely as heavily on their domesticated animals as did the pastoral peoples of the Afro-Eurasian world.

The relationship between nomadic herders and their farming neighbors has been one of the enduring themes of Afro-Eurasian history. Frequently, it was a relationship of conflict, as pastoral peoples, unable to produce their own agricultural products, were attracted to the wealth and sophistication of agrarian societies and sought access to their richer grazing lands as well as their food crops and manufactured products. The biblical story of the deadly rivalry between two brothers— Cain, a "tiller of the ground," and Abel, a "keeper of sheep"—reflects this ancient conflict, which persisted well into modern times. But not all was conflict between pastoral and agricultural peoples. The more peaceful exchange of technologies, ideas, products, and people across the ecological frontier of pastoral and agricultural societies also served to enrich and to change both sides. In the chapters that follow, we will encounter pastoral societies repeatedly, particularly as they interact with neighboring agricultural and "civilized" peoples.

Within pastoral communities, the relative equality of men and women, characteristic of most Paleolithic societies, persisted, perhaps because women's work was so essential. Women were centrally involved in milking animals, in processing that milk, and in producing textiles such as felt, which was widely used in Central Asia for tents, beds, rugs, and clothing. Among the Saka pastoralists in what is now Azerbaijan, women rode horses and participated in battles along with men. A number of archeological sites around the Black Sea have revealed high-status women buried with armor, swords, daggers, and arrows. In the Xinjiang region of western China, still other women were buried with the apparatus of healers and shamans, strongly suggesting an important female role in religious life.

Agricultural Village Societies

For thousands of years, people practiced agriculture using digging sticks or hoes, rather than plows, and even after plows came into use, many societies continued with hoe-based or horticultural farming. Most such hoe-based agricultural peoples lived in settled villages such as those of Banpo or Jericho, but to varying degrees they continued to augment their agricultural livelihood with gathering, hunting, and fishing. They also retained much of the social and gender equality of gathering and hunting communities, as they continued to do without kings, chiefs, bureaucrats, or aristocracies.

An example of this type of social order can be found at Çatalhüyük (cha-TAHL-hoo-YOOK), a very early agricultural village in southern Turkey, which flourished between 7400 and 6000 B.C.E. A careful excavation of the site revealed a population of several thousand people who buried their dead under their houses and then filled the houses with dirt and built new ones on top, layer upon layer. No streets divided the houses, which were constructed adjacent to one another. People moved about the village on adjoining rooftops, from which they entered their homes. Despite the presence of many specialized crafts, few signs of inherited social inequality have surfaced. Nor is there any indication of male or female dominance, although men were more closely associated with hunting wild animals and women with plants and agriculture. "Both men and women," concludes one scholar, "could carry out a series of roles and enjoy a range of positions, from making tools to grinding grain and baking to heading a household."[18]

In many horticultural villages, women's critical role as farmers as well as their work in the spinning and weaving of textiles no doubt contributed to a social position of relative equality with men. Some such societies traced their descent through the female line and practiced marriage patterns in which men left their homes to live with their wives' families. Archeologist Marija Gimbutas has highlighted the prevalence of female imagery in the art of early agricultural societies in Europe and

AP® EXAM TIP

The AP® exam typically features questions about interactions between pastoral communities and agricultural communities and the role these interactions played in conveying culture, disease, and technology.

Anatolia, which has suggested to her a widespread cult of the Goddess, focused on "the mystery of birth, death and the renewal of life."[19] But early agriculture did not produce identical gender systems everywhere. Some societies practiced patrilineal descent and required a woman to live in the household of her husband. Grave sites in early Eastern European farming communities reveal fewer adult females than males, indicating perhaps the practice of female infanticide. Some early written evidence from China suggests a long-term preference for male children. These variations in practice suggest that gender roles were likely determined more by cultural preference than by any biological need for a sexual division of labor and power.

In all of their diversity, many village-based agricultural societies flourished well into the modern era, usually organizing themselves in terms of kinship groups or lineages, which incorporated large numbers of people well beyond the immediate or extended family. Such a system provided the framework within which large numbers of people could make and enforce rules, maintain order, and settle disputes without going to war. In short, the lineage system performed the functions of government, but without the formal apparatus of government, and thus did not require kings or queens, chiefs, or permanent officials associated with a state organization. Despite their democratic qualities and the absence of centralized authority, village-based lineage societies sometimes developed modest social and economic inequalities. Elders could exploit the labor of junior members of the community and sought particularly to control women's reproductive powers, which were essential for the growth of the lineage. People with special knowledge, skills, or experience could achieve higher status and greater influence. Among the Igbo of southern Nigeria well into the twentieth century, "title societies" enabled men and women of wealth and character to earn a series of increasingly prestigious "titles" that set them apart from other members of their community, although these honors could not be inherited. Lineages also sought to expand their numbers, and hence their prestige and power, by incorporating war captives or migrants in subordinate positions, sometimes as slaves.

Given the frequent oppressiveness of organized political power in human history, agricultural village societies represent an intriguing alternative to the states, kingdoms, and empires so often highlighted in the historical record. They pioneered the human settlement of vast areas; adapted to a variety of environments; maintained a substantial degree of social and gender equality; created numerous cultural, artistic, and religious traditions; and interacted continuously with their neighbors.

AP® EXAM TIP

Note the features of early agricultural villages and chiefdoms.

Chiefdoms

In other places, agricultural village societies came to be organized politically as chiefdoms, in which inherited positions of power and privilege introduced a more distinct element of inequality, but unlike later kings, chiefs could seldom use force

Cahokia
Pictured here in an artist's reconstruction, Cahokia (near St. Louis, Missouri) was the center of an important agricultural chiefdom around 1100 C.E. See Chapter 6 for details. (Cahokia Mounds State Historic Site, Illinois. Painting by Lloyd K. Townsend)

to compel the obedience of their subjects. Instead, chiefs relied on their generosity or gift giving, their ritual status, or their personal charisma to persuade their followers. The earliest such chiefdoms seem to have emerged in the Tigris-Euphrates river valley called Mesopotamia (present-day Iraq), sometime after 6000 B.C.E., when temple priests may have organized irrigation systems and controlled trade with nearby societies.

Many chiefdoms followed in all parts of the world, and the more recent ones have been much studied by anthropologists. For example, chiefdoms emerged everywhere in the Pacific islands, which had been colonized by agricultural Polynesian peoples. Chiefs usually derived from a senior lineage, tracing their descent to the first son of an imagined ancestor. With both religious and secular functions, chiefs led important rituals and ceremonies, organized the community for warfare, directed its economic life, and sought to resolve internal conflicts. They collected tribute from commoners in the form of food, manufactured goods, and raw materials. These items in turn were redistributed to warriors, craftsmen, religious specialists, and other subordinates, while chiefs kept enough to maintain their prestigious positions and imposing lifestyle. In North America as well, a remarkable series of chiefdoms emerged in the eastern woodlands, where an extensive array of large earthen mounds testify to the organizational capacity of these early societies. The largest of them, known as Cahokia, flourished around 1100 C.E.

Thus the Agricultural Revolution radically transformed both the trajectory of the human journey and the evolution of life on the planet. This epic process granted to one species, *Homo sapiens*, a growing power over many other species of plants and animals and made possible an increase in human numbers far beyond what a gathering and hunting economy could support.

But if agriculture provided humankind with the power to dominate nature, it also, increasingly, enabled some people to dominate others. This was not immediately apparent, and for several thousand years, and much longer in some places, agricultural villages and pastoral communities retained elements of the social equality that had characterized Paleolithic life. Slowly, though, many of the resources released by the Agricultural Revolution accumulated in the hands of a few. Rich and poor, chiefs and commoners, landowners and dependent peasants, rulers and subjects, dominant men and subordinate women, slaves and free people—these distinctions, so common in the record of world history, took shape most extensively in highly productive agricultural settings, which generated a substantial economic surplus. There the endless elaboration of such differences, for better or worse, became a major feature of those distinctive agricultural societies known to us as "civilizations."

The distinctions that historians make among various kinds of human communities—gathering and hunting peoples, pastoral societies, agricultural village communities, chiefdoms, civilizations—do not represent hard-and-fast differences, but lie on a continuum. Many gathering and hunting societies were nomadic, but some became sedentary; many agricultural and pastoral peoples continued to enrich their diets with foods hunted, gathered, or fished; the line between chiefdoms and civilizations is not always obvious. Such terms are useful for identifying variations in human history, but lived experience is usually messier and less clear than our tidy concepts.

> **PRACTICING AP® HISTORICAL THINKING**
>
> What was revolutionary about the Agricultural Revolution?

REFLECTIONS

The Uses of the Paleolithic

Even when it is about the distant past, history is also about those who tell it in the present. We search the past, always, for our own purposes. For example, modern people were long inclined to view their Paleolithic or gathering and hunting ancestors as primitive or superstitious, unable to exercise control over nature, and ignorant of its workings. Such a view was, of course, a kind of self-congratulation, designed to highlight the "progress" of modern humankind. It was a way of saying, "Look how far we have come."

In more recent decades, however, growing numbers of people, disillusioned with modernity, have looked to the Paleolithic era for material with which to criticize, rather than celebrate, contemporary life. Feminists have found in gathering and hunting peoples a much more gender-equal society and religious thinking that featured the divine feminine, qualities that encouragingly suggested that patriarchy was neither inevitable nor eternal. Environmentalists have sometimes identified peoples in the distant past who were uniquely in tune with the natural environment rather than seeking to dominate it. Some nutritionists have advocated a "Paleolithic diet" of wild plants and animals as well suited to our physiology. Critics of modern materialism and competitive capitalism have been delighted to discover societies in which values of sharing and equality predominated over those of accumulation and hierarchy. Still others have asked, in light of the long Paleolithic era, whether the explosive population and economic growth of recent centuries should be considered normal or natural. Perhaps they are better seen as extraordinary, possibly even pathological. All of these uses of the Paleolithic have been a way of asking, "What have we lost in the mad rush to modernity, and how can we recover it?"

Both those who look with disdain on Paleolithic "backwardness" and those who praise, often quite romantically, its simplicity and equality seek to use these ancient people for their own purposes. In our efforts to puzzle out the past, all of us—historians and students of history very much included—stand somewhere. None of us can be entirely detached when we view the past, but this is not necessarily a matter for regret. What we may lose in objectivity, we gain in passionate involvement with the historical record and with the many men and women who have inhabited it. Despite its remoteness from us in time and manner of living, the Paleolithic era resonates still in the twenty-first century, reminding us of our kinship with these distant people and the significance of that kinship to finding our own way in a very different world.

Chapter Review

What's the Significance?

Venus figurines, 14; 23

Dreamtime, 15

Clovis culture, 18

megafaunal extinction, 18

Austronesian migrations, 19

"the original affluent society," 22

shamans, 23

trance dance, 23

Paleolithic settling down, 24

Göbekli Tepe, 25

Fertile Crescent, 28; 32

teosinte, 34

diffusion, 36

Bantu migration, 37

Ishi, 38

Banpo, 40

"secondary products revolution," 41

pastoral societies, 41

Çatalhüyük, 43

chiefdoms, 44

Big Picture Questions

1. In what ways did various Paleolithic societies differ from one another, and how did they change over time?

2. The Agricultural Revolution marked a decisive and progressive turning point in human history. What evidence might you offer to support this claim, and how might you argue against it?

3. How did early agricultural societies differ from those of the Paleolithic era?

4. Was the Agricultural Revolution inevitable? Why did it occur so late in the story of humankind?

5. In what different ways did human beings relate to the natural world during the early and long phases of our history explored in the chapter?

Next Steps: For Further Study

Elizabeth Wayland Barber, *Women's Work: The First 20,000 Years* (1994). Explores the role of women in early technological development, particularly textile making.

Peter Bellwood, *First Farmers: The Origins of Agricultural Societies* (2005). An up-to-date account of the Agricultural Revolution, considered on a global basis.

David Christian, *This Fleeting World: A Short History of Humanity* (2008). A lovely essay by a leading world historian, which condenses parts of his earlier *Maps of Time* (2004).

Steven Mithen, *After the Ice: A Global Human History, 20,000–5000 B.C.* (2004). An imaginative tour of world archeological sites during the Agricultural Revolution.

Lauren Ristvet, *In the Beginning* (2007). A brief account of human evolution, Paleolithic life, the origins of agriculture, and the First Civilizations, informed by recent archeological discoveries.

Fred Spier, *Big History and the Future of Humanity* (2011). An effort to place human history in the context of cosmic, geological, and biological history with a focus on the growth of complexity.

Mark B. Tauger, *Agriculture in World History* (2011). An overview of the origins and significance of farming on a global scale.

"The Agricultural Revolution," http://www.youtube.com/watch?v=Yocja_N5s1I. An eleven-minute animated survey from John Green's *Crash Course World History* series.

"Prehistoric Art," http://witcombe.sbc.edu/ARTHprehistoric.html#general. An art history Web site with a wealth of links to Paleolithic art around the world.

WORKING WITH EVIDENCE

Stories of the Australian Dreamtime

The Aboriginal, or native, peoples of Australia have lived on their island/ continent for tens of thousands of years, and until the arrival of Europeans in the late eighteenth century, they practiced a gathering and hunting way of life. These peoples have persisted into the twenty-first century as a small minority in modern Australia, and a dwindling few of them still practice their ancient culture. Over an enormously long period of time, these peoples developed an elaborate body of myths, legends, and stories that gave expression to an Aboriginal cosmology, or understanding of the world. Known collectively as the Dreamtime, these stories served to anchor the landscape and its human and animal inhabitants to distant events and mythical ancestors.

In this cosmology, long before humans appeared, ancestral beings emerged from the earth and traversed the land. Their places of emergence became waterholes or caves; their journeys gave rise to rivers and gorges; trees grew where their digging sticks were stuck in the ground; plants arose from their footsteps. In Aboriginal thinking, the numerous rock paintings that dot the landscape were not the product of human hands but the continuing presence, image, or shadow of these ancestral beings.

A contemporary Aboriginal artist, Semon Deeb, explains:

> Around the beginning the Ancestral Beings rose from the folds of the earth and stretching up to the scorching sun they called, "I am!" As each Ancestor sang out their name, "I am Snake," "I am Honey Ant," they created the most sacred of their songs. Slowly they began to move across the barren land naming all things and thus bringing them into being. Their words forming verses as the Ancestors walked about, they sang mountains, rivers and deserts into existence. Wherever they went, their songs remained, creating a web of Songlines over the Country. As they travelled the Ancestors hunted, ate, made love, sang and danced leaving a trail of Dreaming along the songlines. Finally at the end of their journey the Ancestral Beings sang "back into" the earth where they can be seen as land formations, sleeping.[20]

Transmitted orally and changing over time, numerous Dreamtime stories have been collected and set down in writing over the past two centuries. The tales presented here illustrate these Aboriginal efforts to give meaning and shape to their experience.

Source 1.1
Understanding Creation

People everywhere have sought to understand the beginnings of things and through doing so to frame human life in some larger and more meaningful context. In this and other stories from Australia, creation occurred in the Dreamtime, or the "time before time," when ancient ancestral beings brought into existence the latent possibilities of a world that was frozen or asleep. Then they disappeared when their work was finished. But they remained present in the sun, moon, and stars, in the features of the landscape, in the animals of the world, or in paintings on the walls of rock faces.

- How might you compare this creation story with the biblical account in Genesis?

- How much of a difference does it make that both male and female figures participated in creation?

- What is the relationship between Yhi and Baiame in creating and sustaining the world? Do they play equal roles, or is one superior to the other?

- In what ways are human beings and other living creatures made aware of their connection to the spirit world?

Yhi Brings Life to the World
(oral tradition recorded in twentieth century)

In the beginning the world lay quiet, in utter darkness. There was no vegetation, no living or moving thing on the bare bones of the mountains. No wind blew across the peaks. There was no sound to break the silence.

The world was not dead. It was asleep, waiting for the soft touch of life and light. Undead things lay asleep in icy caverns in the mountains. Somewhere in the immensity of space Yhi [a sun goddess of light and creation] stirred in her sleep, waiting for the whisper of Baiame, the Great Spirit [a creator deity, Sky Father], to come to her.

Then the whisper came, the whisper that woke the world. Sleep fell away from the goddess like a garment falling to her feet. Her eyes opened and the darkness was dispelled by their shining. . . .

The Nullarbor Plain was bathed in a radiance that revealed its sterile wastes.

Yhi floated down to earth and began a pilgrimage that took her far to the west, to the east, to north, and south. Where her feet rested on the ground, there the earth leaped in ecstasy. Grass, shrubs, trees, and flowers sprang from it, lifting themselves towards the radiant source of light. Yhi's tracks crossed and recrossed until the whole earth was clothed with vegetation.

Her first joyous task completed, Yhi, the sun goddess, rested on the Nullarbor Plain, looked around her, and knew that the Great Spirit was pleased with the result of her labour.

"The work of creation is well begun," Baiame said, "but it has only begun. The world is full of beauty, but it needs dancing life to fulfill its destiny. Take your light into the caverns of earth and see what will happen."

Yhi rose and made her way into the gloomy spaces beneath the surface. There were no seeds there to spring to life at her touch. Harsh shadows lurked behind the light. Evil spirits shouted, "No, no, no," until the caverns vibrated with voices that boomed and echoed in the darkness. The shadows softened. Twinkling points of light sparkled in an opal mist. Dim forms stirred restlessly.

"Sleep, sleep, sleep," the evil spirits wailed, but the shapes had been waiting for the caressing warmth of the sun goddess. Filmy wings opened, bodies raised themselves on long legs. . . . Soon Yhi was surrounded by myriads of insects, creeping, flying, swarming from every dark corner. . . . They followed her out into the world, into the sunshine, into the embrace of the waiting grass and leaves and flowers. . . . There was work for the insects to do in the world, and time for play, and time to adore the goddess.

"Caves in the mountains, the eternal ice," whispered Baiame. Yhi sped up the hill slopes. . . . She disappeared into the caverns, chilled by the black ice that hung from the roofs and walls. . . . [There her light awakened snakes, reptiles, birds, and many other animals.] Birds and animals gathered round her, singing in their own voices, racing down the slopes, choosing homes for themselves, drinking in a new world of light, colour, sound, and movement.

"It is good. My world is alive," Baiame said.

Yhi took his hand and called in a golden voice to all the things she had brought to life. "This is the land of Baiame. It is yours forever, to enjoy. Baiame is the Great Spirit. He will guard you and listen to your requests. I have nearly finished my work, so you must listen to my words."

"I shall send you the seasons of summer and winter—summer with warmth which ripens fruit ready for eating, winter for sleeping while the cold winds sweep through the world and blow away the refuse of summer. These are changes that I shall

send you . . . , the creatures of my love. Soon I shall leave you and live far above in the sky. When you die your bodies will remain here, but your spirits will come to live with me."

She rose from the earth and dwindled to a ball of light in the sky, and sank slowly behind the western hills. All living things sorrowed, and their hearts were filled with fear, for with the departure of Yhi darkness rushed back into the world.

Long hours passed, and sorrow was soothed by sleep. Suddenly there was a twittering of birds, for the wakeful ones had seen a glimmer of light in the east. It grew stronger and more birds joined in until there came a full-throated chorus as Yhi appeared in splendour and flooded the plains with the morning light.

One by one the birds and animals woke up, as they have done every morning since the first dawn. After the first shock of darkness they knew that day would succeed night, that there would always be a new sunrise and sunset, giving hours of daylight for work and play, and night for sleeping.

The river spirit and the lake spirit grieve most of all when Yhi sinks to rest. They long for her warmth and light. They mount up into the sky, striving with all their might to reach the sun goddess. Yhi smiles on them and they dissolve into drops of water which fall back upon the earth as rain and dew, freshening the grass and the flowers and bringing new life.

One last deed remained to be done, because the dark hours of night were frightening for some of the creatures. Yhi sent the Morning Star to herald her coming each day. Then, feeling sorry for the star in her loneliness, she gave her Bahloo, the Moon, for her husband. A sigh of satisfaction arose from the earth when the white moon sailed majestically across the sky, giving birth to myriads of stars, making a new glory in the heavens.

Source: "Yhi Brings Life to the World," in A. W. Reed, *Aboriginal Stories of Australia* (Chatsworth, New South Wales: New Holland Publishers, 1980), 11–14.

Source 1.2
Understanding the Significance of Animals

The platypus is a semi-aquatic mammal that lays eggs, has fur, and sports a duck-like bill, a beaver-like tail, and otter-like feet. A spur on its rear foot delivers poisonous venom. Aboriginal Australians have long revered this rather strange and eclectic creature and have considered killing it taboo. A widely told story explains Aboriginal thinking about the platypus. Here is one version of that story.

- To what social problems might this story respond? What social meaning might it carry for a land of many small societies and interacting peoples?

- Does this tale bear something of universal human wisdom, or is it a more distinctly Aboriginal Australian story?

The Platypus
(oral tradition recorded in twentieth century)

In the Dreamtime all the creatures on earth thought that they belonged to the most important group of creatures. Each group had their own special meetings. . . . The animals thought that they were the most special because they had fur on their bodies and could run across the land. The birds thought that they were even more special because they could fly and lay eggs. And the water creatures thought that they were even more special still because they could swim and explore all the water-ways on earth and because "there is more water than land anyway," they said.

But then someone in each group remembered that shy Platypus belong to no group at all and each one of them resolved to ask Platypus to join their own Very Special Group. . . . [In response to each of these requests,] Platypus asked them to come back after he had thought about their offer.

Now Platypus asked his friends and family whose group he should join, but no one could help him. . . . After thinking hard about it for some time, Platypus called all the animals and bird and water creatures to his place. They all gathered around, all wondering which group Platypus would join. Platypus came out of his home, climbed a log and when all the creatures were quiet, Platypus spoke. "Thank you all for coming today. I have decided not to join any group at all."

All the creatures were shocked. "You have to join someone's group," they cried.

"Please listen," said Platypus patiently. "Everyone is special in their own special way, and I don't have to join any group to prove that. After all, I have a bit of animal in me because of my fur and because I like running across the land, but I have a bit of bird in me too, because my wife lays eggs and we both have beaks. And if that's not enough, I also have a bit of water creature in me because my home is near the water's edge, and I like swimming and exploring the underwater world. So you see, I don't have to join any special group to be special. But it's not only me — every one of us has something that makes us special in our own very special way."

All the creatures agreed and from that time onwards, Platypus has been considered very wise and very special indeed.

Source: Pauline McLeod, *Aboriginal Art and Stories* (Carlingford, New South Wales: Intechnics, 1994), http://trove.nla.gov.au/work/11650463?q&versionId=45880979.

Source 1.3
Understanding Men and Women

No theme in human history and human interactions is more universal than the relationship of men and women. Many Aboriginal stories seek to justify the superiority of men, while hinting at the possibility of an earlier time when women had the upper hand and implying that they might challenge male authority once again.

- What does this story suggest about the relationships between women and men? Does it support or undermine notions of gender equality among Paleolithic peoples?

- What was the source of Mutjinga's power? How does the story explain her abuse of that power?

- What aspects of a gathering and hunting way of life are reflected in this tale? What elements of Dreamtime cosmology appear in the story?

The Man-Eater: The Mutjinga Myth
(oral tradition recorded in twentieth century)

In the Dreamtime, in the land of the Murinbata people, a great river flowed from the hills through a wide plain to the sea. As it is today, the land then was rich with much fish and game. From the river rose at one place a series of high hills, where lived an old woman named Mutjinga, a woman of power. She it was who called the invisible spirits to her side with secret incantations that none other knew. She was a *kirman*, leader of the ceremonies in which the people sang and danced the exploits of the totemic beings so their spirits would be pleased and would bring food in its season and many children for the people. In those days, all the things in the world had both a physical form that could be touched, seen, and felt, and a spirit form, which was invisible. When living things died, their spirits went to a secret cave where they remained until it was time for them to be born again. Mutjinga was caretaker of this cave. Only she knew where it was. In the cave, she kept the sacred totems to which the spirits returned.

Mutjinga could speak with the spirits. Because she had this power, she could do many things which the men could not. She could send the spirits to frighten away game, to waylay people at night, or to cause a child to be born without life. The men feared the power of Mutjinga and did not consort with her. They called upon her to lead their dances and teach them songs, but none came to sit by her fire.

Mutjinga became lonely and sent for her young granddaughter to keep her company. Mutjinga and the girl gathered bulbs and nuts and caught small game, but Mutjinga found no satisfaction in this food, for she craved the flesh of men. . . .

[*The story then recounts how Mutjinga dug a hole and covered it with branches in order to trap unsuspecting hunters. Magically turning herself into a goanna (a lizard), she appeared to hunters, led them to their deaths in the hole, and then ate them. This fate befell even the younger brother of her granddaughter, despite the girl's unsuccessful efforts to save him. He too was killed and partially eaten, while Mutjinga kept the rest of his body in a nearby stream.*]

The next morning, the little girl was at her early chores when she saw two men coming up the hillside. As she watched, recognition lit her face and she turned toward Mutjinga.

"It is my father and brother who come. Please do not harm them," she implored.

"I crave their flesh. If you trick me again I shall eat you, as well as your father and brother," Mutjinga warned. "This time I shall wait beside you until the men appear so you cannot deceive me."

The men approached the fire, paid their respects to the old woman, and greeted the child warmly. "Daughter, have you seen your brother who came hunting this way yesterday?" the father asked.

Mutjinga hastened to reply for the child. "No, we have not seen him," she said. "It is too bad, for nearby are many goanna holes. There is a large goanna right there," and she pointed to the hole where she kept the club.

"I thirst. First give me water," said the father.

"There is cold water in the stream," the little girl told him as she pointed down the hill.

The two men walked through the bush to the stream. As the father bent to drink, he saw the leg of his elder son, which Mutjinga had weighted down in the water with a large rock. At once he understood.

"The old woman will kill us unless we kill her first," he said to his younger son, and the two men returned to the fire.

"The goanna went into the tall grass," Mutjinga told them when they appeared. "Leave your spears and light a fire to burn the grass. This will drive the goanna out, and when it runs toward its hole, you can kill it with your spears."

The men went to fire the grass. As soon as they were out of sight, the father said, "Son, climb this tree and watch the old woman closely. She works powerful magic."

This the son did, and he saw Mutjinga speak the magic words. She repeated them twice. He watched as the woman and the girl changed into goannas. From the limb of the tree, he observed the larger goanna chase the smaller one into the bush. Soon great billows of smoke were rising from the burning grass. The small goanna scuttled from the bush, its companion nipping at its heels. They ran past the hunters and disappeared down the hole.

"Get the spears," the father commanded and ran toward the hole. Just as the son returned, spears in hand, the ground beneath the father gave way and he plunged through. Waiting at the bottom was Mutjinga, club raised for the kill. But the son hurled his spear and Mutjinga fell bleeding to the ground.

The father seized her roughly. "Say the magic words that will release my daughter or we shall kill you," he threatened.

Painfully Mutjinga did as she was bidden. The daughter changed into her human form and the two men and the girl climbed from the hole.

"Daughter, show us the secret cave where the spirits are hidden," said the father, "and teach us the magic words you have learned from the old woman. We shall take the spirits to another place, and we shall have the power."

And so it was. The father took the totems from that place and hid them in another cave. He became the *kirman*, the song leader, and he taught the people the sacred dances and ceremonies. To him they brought their problems and he judged between them when they quarreled. And to this day, the men have kept the power.

Source: Louis A. Allen, *Time Before Morning* (New York: Thomas Y. Crowell, 1975), 145–48.

Source 1.4

Understanding Death

Death marks the end of a life, but an awareness of death shapes much of the living of our lives. And so humans everywhere have sought to understand death, with an eye perhaps to avoiding or delaying it. In the Australian Dreamtime, the immortal ancestor Purukapali was responsible for the introduction of death into the world. The story that follows is one version of this event.

- How does this story account for the entry of death into human life?

- What responses to death are suggested in the story?

- Does such a story carry any meaning to modern people of the twenty-first century?

How Death Came: The Purukapali Myth

(oral tradition recorded in twentieth century)

In the pleasant land of the Tiwi people, Purukapali lived with his wife, Bima, and their infant son, Djinini. This was in the earliest days when spirits became men and death had not yet come to the earth. In their camp also lived Purukapali's younger brother, Tjapara, strong and handsome. Many times the brothers stalked wallaby together, but most often it was Purukapali who carried game into the camp and received the women's praise.

Tjapara had no wife and he hungered for Bima. One morning after the brothers had returned from the hunt, Bima rose and placed the sleeping Djinini beside her husband, who was skinning a slain wallaby.

"I go find yams," she said. "Guard the child. He will sleep now and will have my milk when I return."

She picked up a net bag and walked off into the bush. Tjapara watched her swinging hips and said, "I saw shellfish at the shore. I will go gather them," and he strode off toward the beach, leaving Purukapali with the sleeping child.

As soon as he was well out of sight, Tjapara quickly circled back through the bush and came upon Bima as she bent over her digging stick. Softly he crept upon her and clasped her from behind.

"Lie with me," he urged.

Only a moment did the wife of Purukapali resist. Then the long hours slipped quickly by. In the camp the child cried for his mother's milk. Still the couple tarried. From the camp came the faint voice of Purukapali calling his wife. Bima started to rise, but Tjapara was still eager. "Soon," he said and pulled her toward him.

Now the Sun Woman carried her torch to the horizon and the shadows grew long. Again the voice of Purukapali sounded, angry and stricken. Bima rose to answer, but Tjapara placed his hand over her mouth.

"We must go bathe, or Purukapali will know we have lain together," he said.

The two went to a hidden cove and entered the water. They played together in the coolness and ate some crabs they found near the shore. This was Tjapara's favorite food. But Purukapali's angry voice again reached their hearing. The frightened Bima took her net bag and hurried to camp. She found Djinini on the grass, cold and still. Death had come to him in the early darkness. Bima lifted the child and pressed him to her breast.

Now Purukapali turned on his wife. "He was hungry. He cried for you and you did not come. Now he is gone from us and will not return," said the father, and he wrested the dead infant from Bima's arms.

Bima began to moan and beat her breast. "I am a bad woman, for I let my son die," she cried.

Hearing this, great anger came to Purukapali. Still holding his dead son, he turned on Bima and began to beat her with his freed hand. As she bent before his blows, Tjapara stepped from the bush and thrust himself between the couple.

"Give the child to me, brother, and I will bring him back to life in three days," he said.

But Bima lashed out at Tjapara in despair. "You killed him!" she accused, "for you would not let me go."

Now did Purukapali understand. Still holding fast to the child, he picked up a forked fighting stick and attacked. "You, too, shall die!" he screamed at his brother.

Tjapara refused to run and begged again for the child. But Purukapali threw the stick in response and struck his brother in the eye. "You will die as the baby died," he shouted. In his excitement, Purukapali dropped the lifeless body of Djinini.

Half blinded, Tjapara fought back. Soon the two men were locked in combat. Blood gushed from Tjapara's gouged eye and from the gashes on his face. He began to weaken.

Now Bima picked up Djinini and held him out to her husband. "Take the child you loved so dearly," she pleaded. "Do not kill your brother."

Her plea went unheard as Purukapali again hurled his killing stick. Tjapara fled to a tall tree and frantically began to climb. When he reached the top limb, he let out a great shout and leaped into the sky, rising higher and higher until he reached the moon.

Purukapali returned to camp and took Djinini's body in his arms. "I shall die with my son," he announced to the Tiwi people. "And all who now live also shall die."

Then he danced the first ceremony of death and sang of the events that led to it. "This shall be your pukamani ceremony," he decreed, "and you shall dance it to remember those who die." Purukapali wrapped his son in paperbark, walked backward into the sea, and disappeared. As he sank beneath the surface, a whirlpool formed which marks the spot to this day.

Bima lived on, but grief soon made her haggard and old. She too wandered about the camp, complaining in a shrill voice until she, too, died. Her spirit lived on as the curlew bird, which still flits and cries mournfully about the beaches.

Tjapara became the Moon Man. He can be seen in the night sky, his face marked by the bruises and wounds that Purukapali inflicted. He still feels Purukapali at his heels, for he never ceases his restless journey. Hungry from his travels, he gorges on crabmeat, growing rounder and fatter each day until he has feasted so much he falls sick. His wasting body is the waning moon. Each month he dies, but after three days he comes back to life and begins his journey once again. His loneliness is over, for he has found many wives, the planets, who accompany him on his journey across the sky.

So death comes to the people of earth, the Tiwi say, but always life returns.

Source: Louis A. Allen, *Time Before Morning* (New York: Thomas Y. Crowell Company, 1975), 215–19.

DOING HISTORY

Stories of the Australian Dreamtime

1. **Considering human commonality and diversity:** The study of world history highlights both the common humanity of people from all times and places as well as the vast differences that have separated particular cultures from one another. How might these texts serve to illustrate both of these perspectives?

2. **Linking documents and text narrative:** How do these documents support or amplify the narrative account of the Paleolithic era in Chapter 1? How might they challenge or contradict that narrative?

3. **Considering the relationship of technology and culture:** How might the gathering and hunting technology of these Australian peoples have shaped their cultural understandings as expressed in these sources? In what ways might cultural expression, as a product of human imagination, have developed independently of their technology? Does it make sense to evaluate technology as more or less "advanced"? Should culture be assessed in the same way?

4. **Pondering relevance:** How might these stories from a very different time and place speak to us in the modern world of the twenty-first century? Or are they only of historical interest?

5. **Thinking about sources:** How does the fact that these stories were only committed to writing over the past two centuries affect their usefulness as historical sources?

CHAPTER 2

First Civilizations

Cities, States, and Unequal Societies
3500 B.C.E.–600 B.C.E.

"Sometimes the weight of civilization can be overwhelming. The fast pace . . . the burdens of relationships . . . the political strife . . . the technological complexity—it's enough to make you dream of escaping to a simpler life more in touch with nature."[1] Found on the Web site of an organization called Mother Nature Network, this expression of discontent with modernity reflects the perspectives of the back-to-the-land movement that began in the mid-1960s as an alternative to the pervasive materialism of modern life. Growing numbers of urban dwellers, perhaps as many as a million in North America, exchanged their busy city lives for a few acres of rural land and a very different way of living.

This urge to "escape from civilization" has long been a central feature in modern life. It found expression in Henry David Thoreau's musings on his sojourn at Walden Pond. It is also a major theme in Mark Twain's famous novel *The Adventures of Huckleberry Finn*, in which the restless and rebellious Huck resists all efforts to "sivilize" him by fleeing to the freedom of life on the river. In addition, it is a large part of the "cowboy" image in American culture, and it permeates environmentalist efforts to protect the remaining wilderness areas of the country. Nor has this impulse been limited to modern societies and the Western world. The ancient Chinese teachers of Daoism likewise urged their followers to abandon the structured and demanding world of urban and civilized life and to immerse themselves in the eternal patterns of the natural order. It is a strange paradox that we count the creation of civilizations among the major

Raherka and Mersankh   Writing was among the defining features of civilizations almost everywhere. In ancient Egyptian civilization, the scribes who possessed this skill enjoyed both social prestige and political influence. This famous statue shows Raherka, an "inspector of the scribes" during Egypt's Fifth Dynasty (ca. 2350 B.C.E.), in an affectionate pose with his wife, Mersankh.

achievements of humankind and yet people within them have often sought to escape the constraints, artificiality, hierarchies, and other discontents of civilized living.

So what exactly are these civilizations that have generated such ambivalent responses among their inhabitants? When, where, and how did they first arise in human history? What changes did they bring to the people who lived within them? Why might some people criticize or seek to escape from them?

As historians commonly use the term, "civilization" represents a new and particular type of human society, made possible by the immense productivity of the Agricultural Revolution. Such societies encompassed far larger populations than any earlier form of human community and for the first time concentrated some of those people in sizable cities. Both within and beyond these cities, people were organized and controlled by states whose leaders could use force to compel obedience. Profound differences in economic function, skill, wealth, and status sharply divided the people of civilizations, making them far less equal and subject to much greater oppression than had been the case in earlier Paleolithic communities, agricultural villages, pastoral societies, or chiefdoms. Pyramids, temples, palaces, elaborate sculptures, written literature, and complex calendars, as well as more elaborate class and gender hierarchies, slavery, and large-scale warfare—all of these have been among the cultural products of civilization.

SEEKING THE MAIN POINT

What distinguished "civilizations" from earlier Paleolithic and Neolithic societies?

Something New: The Emergence of Civilizations

AP® EXAM TIP

Know the definition of "civilization."

Like agriculture, civilization was a global phenomenon, showing up independently in seven major locations scattered around the world during the several millennia after 3500 B.C.E. and in a number of other smaller expressions as well (see Map 2.1). In the long run of human history, these civilizations—small breakthroughs to a new way of life—gradually absorbed, overran, or displaced people practicing other ways of living. Over the next 5,000 years, civilization, as a unique kind of human community, gradually encompassed ever-larger numbers of people and extended over ever-larger territories, even as particular civilizations rose, fell, revived, and changed.

Introducing the First Civilizations

Guided Reading Question

■ CHANGE

When and where did the First Civilizations emerge?

The earliest of these civilizations emerged around 3500 B.C.E. to 3000 B.C.E. in three places. One was the "cradle" of Middle Eastern civilization, expressed in the many and competing city-states of Sumer in southern Mesopotamia (located in present-day Iraq). Much studied by archeologists and historians, Sumerian civilization likely gave rise to the world's earliest written language, which was used initially by officials to record the goods received by various temples. Almost simultaneously, the Nile River valley in northeastern Africa witnessed the emergence

A MAP OF TIME (All dates B.C.E.)

3500–3000	Beginnings of Mesopotamian, Egyptian, and Norte Chico civilizations
3400–3200	Nubian kingdom of Ta-Seti
3200–2350	Period of independent Sumerian city-states
2663–2195	Old Kingdom Egypt (high point of pharaoh's power and pyramid building)
2200–2000	Beginnings of Chinese, Indus Valley, and Central Asian (Oxus) civilizations
2070–1600	Xia dynasty in China (traditionally seen as first dynasty of Chinese history)
After 2000	*Epic of Gilgamesh* compiled
1900–1500	Babylonian Empire
1792–1750	Reign of Hammurabi
1700	Abandonment of Indus Valley cities
1550–1064	New Kingdom Egypt
1200	Beginnings of Olmec civilization
760–660	Kush conquest of Egypt
586	Babylonian conquest of Judah
By 500	Egypt and Mesopotamia incorporated into Persian Empire

of Egyptian civilization, famous for its pharaohs and pyramids, as well as a separate civilization known as Nubia, farther south along the Nile. Unlike the city-states of Sumer, Egyptian civilization took shape as a unified territorial state in which cities were rather less prominent. Later in this chapter, we will compare these two First Civilizations in greater detail.

Less well known and only recently investigated by scholars was a third early civilization that was developing along the central coast of Peru from roughly 3000 B.C.E. to 1800 B.C.E., at about the same time as the civilizations of Egypt and Sumer. This desert region received very little rainfall, but it was punctuated by dozens of rivers that brought the snowmelt of the adjacent Andes Mountains to the Pacific Ocean. Along a thirty-mile stretch of that coast and in the nearby interior, a series of some twenty-five urban centers emerged in an area known as Norte Chico, the largest of which was Caral, in the Supe River valley. (See Zooming In: Caral, a City of Norte Chico, page 64.)

Norte Chico was a distinctive civilization in many ways. Its cities were smaller than those of Mesopotamia and show less evidence of economic specialization. The

AP® EXAM TIP

Names, places, and dates of development of the First Civilizations are "must know" information. Review the map on pages 62–63 for a visual interpretation.

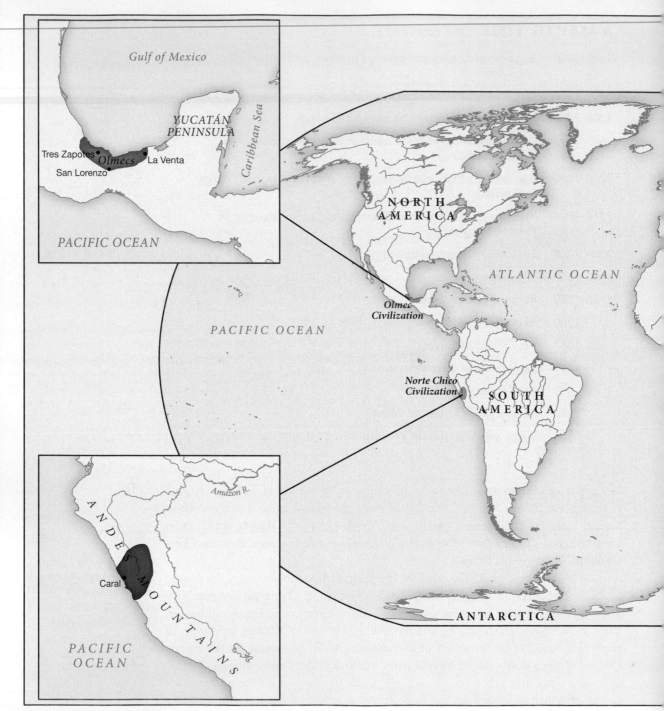

Map 2.1   First Civilizations

Seven First Civilizations emerged independently in locations scattered across the planet, all within a few thousand years, from 3500 to 1000 B.C.E.

Caral, a City of Norte Chico

In early 2001, published reports of archeological excavations at a site called Caral set off a firestorm of amazed commentary in both academic circles and the popular media. And no wonder! Archeologists had uncovered, about fourteen miles inland from the coast of Peru, an urban center dating to the time of the Egyptian pyramids, around 2600 B.C.E., far earlier than any previously known urban settlements in the Americas. Thus Egyptian and Mesopotamian claims to the status of "First Civilizations" were now joined by those of Peru.

Most obviously impressive about Caral was its elaborate and monumental architecture. One of its six pyramids stood sixty feet tall and occupied an area the size of four football fields. Circular sunken plazas, temples, an amphitheater, stairways, and many residential spaces, including apartment-style complexes, likewise emerged from the excavations. Stones collected in grass-woven mesh bags became part of the retaining walls that supported these structures. An intricate irrigation system funneled water from the nearby Supe River to agricultural fields.

Stonework at Caral.

Smaller finds at the site convey something about ordinary life in Caral. A clay figure with long hair, a colorful costume, and a decorative necklace suggested a shaman, who served as an intermediary between the gods and humans at Caral. The skeleton of a baby, wrapped in layers of fine cloth, had been carefully buried with a necklace of stone beads. Dozens of beautifully carved flutes and cornets made of condor, pelican, deer, and llama bones revealed an instrumental musical tradition. A *quipu*, consisting of knotted cords and later widely used by the Incas for accounting purposes, pointed to an element of cultural continuity in the Andes region that spanned over 4,000 years.

Archeologists also discovered remains of plants that enhanced sexual performance, as well as hallucinogenic drugs, long used in the Andes and elsewhere in religious ceremonies. A possible hint about Caral's religious outlook derives from a drawing etched on a gourd, which shows a sharp-toothed figure wearing a hat and holding long sticks or rods in each hand. It clearly resembles

photo: © Peruvian National Institute/epa/Corbis

economy was based to an unusual degree on an extremely rich fishing industry in anchovies and sardines along the coast. These items apparently were exchanged for cotton, essential for fishing nets, as well as food crops such as squash, beans, and guava, all of which were grown by inland people in the river valleys using irrigation agriculture. Unlike Egyptian and Mesopotamian societies, this Peruvian civilization did not rest on grain-based farming; its people did not develop pottery or writing; and few sculptures, carvings, or drawings have been uncovered so far. Archeologists have, however, found a 5,000-year-old *quipu* (a series of knotted cords, later used extensively by the Inca for accounting purposes), which some scholars have suggested may have been an alternative form of writing or symbolic communication. Furthermore, the cities of Norte Chico lacked defensive walls, and archeologists have discovered little evidence of warfare, such as burned buildings and mutilated corpses. Norte Chico apparently "lighted a cultural fire" in the Andes and estab-the Staff God prevalent in later Andean civilizations. And the remains of a young man found in a ceremonial place suggest the possibility of human sacrifice.

Nor was Caral an isolated instance of urban living. More than twenty other related sites in the river valleys of the area make up what scholars are now calling the Norte Chico civilization. Caral and other inland cities had close relationships with coastal communities, exchanging their agricultural products such as cotton, beans, squash, and sweet potatoes for sardines and anchovies, whose bones have been found in abundance in Caral. Goods from as far away as present-day Ecuador, the high Andes, and rain forests that lay to the east suggest a network of wider relationships.

But what was missing from Caral has proved equally intriguing. Grain-based agriculture, pottery, metallurgy, and writing—all features of urban life in Egypt and Mesopotamia—were noticeably absent in Caral. Do we therefore need to revisit the criteria for defining a "First Civilization"? Warfare too apparently played little role in Caral, as no walls, fortresses, weapons, or signs of violent

The bone flutes found at Caral.

destruction have appeared in the archeological record. Does this mean that Caral uniquely enjoyed "a thousand years of peace," as one of the lead excavators suggested? Was trade rather than warfare the stimulus to creating a complex society? Perhaps so, but it is early in the study of this distinctive civilization. We may want to remember that Maya civilization was once viewed as a peaceful society of stargazing people devoted to religious and intellectual pursuits, until scholars discovered unmistakable evidence for bloodletting rituals and violent conflict among its various city-states. The past may not change, but our understanding of it is in constant flux.

Questions: In what ways do recent discoveries at Caral invite reconsideration of Andean civilization and of the history of the earliest civilizations generally? What do you find most surprising about Caral?

lished a pattern for the many Andean civilizations that followed—Chavín, Moche, Wari, Tiwanaku, and Inca.[2]

Somewhat later, at least four additional First Civilizations made their appearance. In the Indus and Saraswati river valleys of what is now Pakistan, a remarkable civilization arose during the third millennium B.C.E. By 2000 B.C.E., it embraced a far larger area than Mesopotamia, Egypt, or coastal Peru and was expressed primarily in its elaborately planned cities. All across this huge area, common patterns prevailed: standardized weights, measures, architectural styles, even the size of bricks. As elsewhere, irrigated agriculture provided the economic foundation for the civilization, and a written language, thus far undeciphered, provides evidence of a literate culture for the few.

Unlike its Middle Eastern counterparts, the Indus Valley civilization apparently generated no palaces, temples, elaborate graves, kings, or warrior classes. In short, the archeological evidence provides little indication of a political hierarchy or centralized state. This absence of evidence has sent scholars scrambling to provide an explanation for the obvious specialization, coordination, and complexity that the Indus Valley civilization exhibited. A series of small republics, rule by priests, an early form of the caste system—all of these have been suggested as alternative mechanisms of integration in this first South Asian civilization. Although no one knows for sure, the possibility that the Indus Valley may have housed a sophisticated civilization without a corresponding state has excited the imagination of scholars. (See Working with Evidence: Indus Valley Civilization, page 91.)

Whatever its organization, the local environmental impact of the Indus Valley civilization, as in many others, was heavy and eventually undermined its ecological foundations. Repeated irrigation increased the amount of salt in the soil and lowered crop yields. The making of mud bricks, dried in ovens, required an enormous amount of wood for fuel, generating large-scale deforestation and soil erosion. Thus environmental degradation contributed significantly to the abandonment of these magnificent cities by about 1700 B.C.E. Thereafter, they were largely forgotten, until their rediscovery by archeologists in the twentieth century. Nonetheless, many features of this early civilization—ceremonial bathing, ritual burning, yoga positions, bulls and elephants as religious symbols, styles of clothing and jewelry—continued to nourish the later civilization of the Indian subcontinent. In fact they persist into the present.[3]

The early civilization of China, dating to perhaps 2200 B.C.E., was very different from that of the Indus Valley. The ideal—if not always the reality—of a centralized state was evident from the days of the Xia (shyah) dynasty (2070–1600 B.C.E.), whose legendary monarch Wu organized flood control projects that "mastered the waters and made them to flow in great channels." Subsequent dynasties—the Shang (1600–1046 B.C.E.) and the Zhou (JOH) (1046–771 B.C.E.)—substantially enlarged the Chinese state, erected lavish tombs for their rulers, and buried thousands of human sacrificial victims to accompany them in the next world. By the Zhou dynasty, a distinctive Chinese political ideology had emerged, featuring a ruler, known as the Son of Heaven. This monarch served as an intermediary between heaven and earth and ruled by the Mandate of Heaven only so long as he governed with benevolence and maintained social harmony among his people. An early form of written Chinese has been discovered on numerous oracle bones, which were intended to predict

Shang Dynasty Bronze
This bronze tiger, created around 1100 B.C.E., illustrates Chinese skill in working with bronze and the mythological or religious significance of the tiger as a messenger between heaven and the human world. (© Asian Art & Archeology, Inc./Corbis)

the future and to assist China's rulers in the task of governing. Like Egypt, China has experienced an impressive continuity of identity as a distinct civilization from its earliest expression into modern times.

Central Asia was the site of yet another First Civilization. In the Oxus or Amu Darya river valley and nearby desert oases (what is now northern Afghanistan and southern Turkmenistan), a quite distinctive and separate civilization took shape very quickly after 2200 B.C.E. Within two centuries, a number of substantial forti- fied centers had emerged, containing residential compounds, artisan workshops, and temples, all surrounded by impressive walls and gates. Economically based on irrigation agriculture and stock raising, this Central Asian or Oxus civilization had a distinctive cultural style, expressed in its architecture, ceramics, burial techniques, seals, and more, though it did not develop a literate culture. Evidence for an aris- tocratic social hierarchy comes from depictions of gods and men in widely differ- ing dress performing various functions from eating at a banquet to driving chariots to carrying heavy burdens. Visitors to this civilization would have found occasional goods from China, India, and Mesopotamia, as well as products from pastoral nomads of the steppe land and the forest dwellers of Siberia. According to a leading historian, this Central Asian civilization was the focal point of a "Eurasian-wide sys- tem of intellectual and commercial exchange."[4] Compared to Egyptian and Meso- potamian civilizations, however, it had a relatively brief history, for by 1700 B.C.E., it had faded away as a civilization, at about the same time as a similar fate befell its Indus Valley counterpart. Its cities were abandoned and apparently forgotten until their resurrection by archeologists in the twentieth century. And yet its influence persisted, as elements of this civilization's cultural style show up much later in Iran, India, and the eastern Mediterranean world.

A final First Civilization, known as the Olmec, took shape around 1200 B.C.E. along the coast of the Gulf of Mexico near present-day Veracruz in southern Mex- ico. Based on an agricultural economy of maize, beans, and squash, Olmec cities arose from a series of competing chiefdoms and became ceremonial centers filled with elaborately decorated temples, altars, pyramids, and tombs of rulers. The most famous artistic legacy of the Olmecs lay in some seventeen colossal basalt heads, weighing twenty tons or more. Recent discoveries suggest that the Olmecs may well have created the first written language in the Americas by about 900 B.C.E. Sometimes regarded as the "mother civilization" of Mesoamerica, Olmec civiliza- tion generated cultural patterns—mound building, artistic styles, urban planning, a game played with a rubber ball, ritual sacrifice, and bloodletting by rulers—that spread widely throughout the region and influenced subsequent civilizations, such as the Maya and Teotihuacán.

Beyond these seven First Civilizations, other smaller civilizations also flour- ished. Lying south of Egypt in the Nile Valley, an early Nubian civilization (3400– 3200 B.C.E.) known as Ta-Seti was clearly distinctive and independent of its north- ern neighbor, although Nubia was later involved in a long and often contentious relationship with Egypt. Likewise in China, a large city known as Sanxingdui, rich

AP® EXAM TIP

The AP® exam may expect you to know that regional trade existed even in the earliest civilizations.

in bronze sculptures and much else, arose separately but at the same time as the more well-known Shang dynasty. As a new form of human society, civilization was beginning its long march toward encompassing almost all of humankind by the twentieth century. At the time, however, these breakthroughs to new forms of culture and society were small islands of innovation in a sea of people living in much older ways.

The Question of Origins

The first question that historians ask about almost everything is "How did it get started?" Scholars of all kinds—archeologists, anthropologists, sociologists, and historians—have been arguing about the origins of civilization for a very long time, with no end in sight. Amid all the controversy, one thing seems reasonably clear: civilizations had their roots in the Agricultural Revolution. That is the reason they appeared so late in the human story, for only an agricultural technology permitted human communities to produce sufficient surplus to support large populations and the specialized or elite minorities who did not themselves produce food. But not all agricultural societies or chiefdoms developed into civilizations, so something else must have been involved. It is the search for this "something else" that has provoked such great debate among scholars.

Some historians have emphasized the need to organize large-scale irrigation projects as a stimulus for the earliest civilizations, but archeologists have found that the more complex water control systems appeared long after states and civilizations had already been established. Alternatively, perhaps states responded to the human need for order as larger and more diverse populations grew up in particular localities. Others have suggested that states were useful in protecting the privileges of favored groups. Warfare and trade have figured in still other explanations for the rise of civilizations. Geography surely played a role as well, for civilizations often took shape in biologically rich and productive environments such as wetlands, estuaries, and river basins. Anthropologist Robert Carneiro combined several of these factors in a thoughtful approach to the question.[5] He argued that a growing density of population, producing more congested and competitive societies, was a fundamental motor of change, especially in areas where rich agricultural land was limited, either by geography (oceans, deserts, mountains) or by powerful neighboring societies. Such settings provided incentives for innovations, such as irrigation or plows that could produce more food, because opportunities for territorial expansion were not readily available. But circumscribed environments with dense populations also generated intense competition among rival groups, which led to repeated warfare. A strong and highly organized state was a decided advantage in such competition. Because losers could not easily flee to new lands, they were absorbed into the winner's society as a lower class. Successful leaders of the winning side emerged as elites with an enlarged base of land, a class of subordinated workers, and a powerful state at their disposal—in short, a civilization.

Guided Reading Question

■ CHANGE
What accounts for the initial breakthroughs to civilization?

AP® EXAM TIP

Understand historians' debates over the causes and effects of major developments in world history. See Reflections on page 89 for more insights.

Although such a process was relatively rapid by world history standards, it took many generations, centuries, or perhaps millennia to evolve. It was, of course, an unconscious undertaking in which the participants had little sense of the long-term outcome as they coped with the practical problems of life on a day-to-day basis. What is surprising, though, is the rough similarity of the outcome in many widely separated places from about 3500 B.C.E. to the beginning of the Common Era.

However they got started (and much about this is still guesswork), the First Civilizations, once established, represented a very different kind of human society than anything that came before. All of them were based on highly productive agricultural economies. Various forms of irrigation, drainage, terracing, and flood control enabled these early civilizations to tap the food-producing potential of their regions more intensively. All across the Afro-Eurasian hemisphere, though not in the Americas, animal-drawn plows and metalworking greatly enhanced the productivity of farming. Ritual sacrifice, sometimes including people, accompanied the growth of civilization, and the new rulers normally served as high priests, their right to rule legitimated by association with the sacred.

AP® EXAM TIP

You must know common features of early civilizations.

An Urban Revolution

It was the resources from agriculture that made possible one of the most distinctive features of the First Civilizations—cities. What would an agricultural villager have made of Uruk, ancient Mesopotamia's largest city? Uruk had walls more than twenty feet tall and a population around 50,000 in the third millennium B.C.E. The city's center, visible for miles around, was a stepped pyramid, or ziggurat, topped with a temple (see the photo on page 77). Inside the city, this village visitor would have found other temples as well, serving as centers of ritual performance and as places for the redistribution of stored food. Numerous craftspeople labored as masons, copper workers, and weavers and in many other specialties, while bureaucrats helped administer the city. It was, surely, a "vibrant, noisy, smelly, sometimes bewildering and dangerous, but also exciting place."[6] Here is how the *Epic of Gilgamesh*, Mesopotamia's ancient epic poem, describes the city:

AP® EXAM TIP

The characteristics of cities as well as their emergence, growth, and decline are important concepts throughout the AP® course.

Come then, Enkidu, to ramparted Uruk,
Where fellows are resplendent in holiday clothing,
Where every day is set for celebration,
Where harps and drums are played.
And the harlots too, they are fairest of form,
Rich in beauty, full of delights,
Even the great gods are kept from sleeping at night.[7]

Equally impressive to a village visitor would have been the city of Mohenjo Daro (moe-hen-joe DAHR-oh), which flourished along the banks of the Indus River around 2000 B.C.E. With a population of perhaps 40,000, Mohenjo Daro and

Guided Reading Question

■ CHANGE
What was the role of cities in the early civilizations?

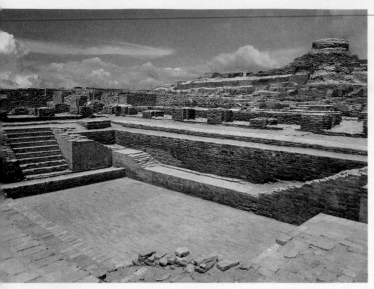

Mohenjo Daro
Flourishing around 2000 B.C.E., Mohenjo Daro was by far the largest city of the Indus Valley civilization, covering more than 600 acres. This photograph shows a small part of that city as it has been uncovered by archeologists during the past century. The large watertight tank or pool, shown in the foreground, probably offered bathers an opportunity for ritual purification. (View of the Great Bath/Luca Tettoni/Bridgeman Images)

its sister city of Harappa featured large, richly built houses of two or three stories, complete with indoor plumbing, luxurious bathrooms, and private wells. Streets were laid out in a grid-like pattern, and beneath the streets ran a complex sewage system. Workers lived in row upon row of standardized two-room houses. Grand public buildings, including what seems to be a huge public bath, graced the city, while an enormous citadel was surrounded by a brick wall some forty-five feet high.

Even larger, though considerably later, was the Mesoamerican city of Teotihuacán (tay-uh-tee-wah-KAHN), located in the central valley of Mexico. It housed perhaps 200,000 people in the middle of the first millennium C.E. Broad avenues, dozens of temples, two huge pyramids, endless stone carvings and many bright frescoes, small apartments for the ordinary, palatial homes for the wealthy—all of this must have seemed another world for a new visitor from a distant village. In shopping for obsidian blades, how was she to decide among the 350 workshops in the city? In seeking relatives, how could she find her way among many different compounds, each surrounded by a wall and housing a different lineage? And what would she make of a neighborhood composed entirely of Maya merchants from the distant coastal lowlands?

Cities, then, were central to most of the First Civilizations, though to varying degrees. They were political/administrative capitals; they functioned as centers for the production of culture, including art, architecture, literature, ritual, and ceremony; they served as marketplaces for both local and long-distance exchange; and they housed most manufacturing activity. Everywhere they generated a unique kind of society, compared to earlier agricultural villages or Paleolithic camps. Urban society was impersonal, for it was no longer possible to know everyone. Relationships of class and occupation emerged alongside those of kinship and village loyalty. Most notably, the degree of specialization and inequality far surpassed that of all preceding human communities.

The Erosion of Equality

Among the most novel features of early urban life, at least to our imaginary village visitor, was the amazing specialization of work outside of agriculture—scholars, officials, merchants, priests, and artisans of all kinds. In ancient Mesopotamia, even scribes were subdivided into many categories: junior and senior scribes, temple scribes and royal scribes, scribes for particular administrative or official functions. None of these people, of course, grew their own food; they were supported by the highly productive agriculture of farmers.

Hierarchies of Class

Alongside the occupational specialization of the First Civilizations lay their vast inequalities—in wealth, status, and power. As ingenuity and technology created more productive economies, the greater wealth now available was everywhere piled up rather than spread out. Early signs of this erosion of equality were evident in the more settled and complex gathering and hunting societies and in agricultural chiefdoms, but the advent of urban-based civilizations multiplied and magnified these inequalities many times over, as the more egalitarian values of earlier cultures were everywhere displaced. This transition represents one of the major turning points in the social history of humankind.

As the First Civilizations took shape, inequality and hierarchy soon came to be regarded as normal and natural. Upper classes everywhere enjoyed great wealth in land or salaries, were able to avoid physical labor, had the finest of everything, and occupied the top positions in political, military, and religious life. Frequently, they were distinguished by the clothing they wore, the houses they lived in, and the manner of their burial. Early Chinese monarchs bestowed special robes, banners, chariots, weapons, and ornaments on their regional officials, and all of these items were graded according to the officials' precise location in the hierarchy. In Mesopotamia, the punishments prescribed in the famous Code of Hammurabi (hahm-moo-RAH-bee) depended on social status. A free-born commoner who struck a person of equal rank had to pay a small fine, but if he struck "a man who is his superior, he [would] receive 60 strokes with an oxtail whip in public." Clearly, class had consequences.

In all of the First Civilizations, free commoners represented the vast majority of the population and included artisans of all kinds, lower-level officials, soldiers and police, servants, and, most numerous of all, farmers. It was their surplus production—appropriated through a variety of taxes, rents, required labor, and tribute payments—that supported the upper classes. At least some of these people were aware of, and resented, these forced extractions and their position in the social hierarchy. Most Chinese peasants, for example, owned little land of their own and worked on plots granted to them by royal or aristocratic landowners. An ancient poem compared the exploiting landlords to rats and expressed the farmers' vision of a better life:

> Large rats! Large rats!
> Do not eat our spring grain!
> Three years have we had to do with you.
> And you have not been willing to think of our toil.

AP® EXAM TIP

You need to know about the development of and characteristics of different classes of people, or "social hierarchies," in early civilizations.

Guided Reading Question

■ CHANGE
In what ways was social inequality expressed in early civilizations?

We will leave you,
And go to those happy borders.
Happy borders, happy borders!
Who will there make us always to groan?[8]

At the bottom of social hierarchies everywhere were slaves. Evidence for slavery dates to well before the emergence of civilization and was clearly present in some gathering and hunting societies and early agricultural communities. But the practice of "people owning people" flourished on a larger scale in the urban- and state-based societies of civilizations. Female slaves, captured in the many wars among rival Mesopotamian cities, were put to work in large-scale semi-industrial weaving enterprises, while males helped to maintain irrigation canals and construct ziggurats. Others worked as domestic servants in the households of their owners. In all of the First Civilizations, slaves—derived from prisoners of war, criminals, and debtors—were available for sale; for work in the fields, mines, homes, and shops of their owners; or on occasion for sacrifice. From the days of the earliest civilizations until the nineteenth century, slavery was everywhere an enduring feature of these more complex societies.

Its practice in ancient times, however, varied considerably from place to place. Egypt and the Indus Valley civilizations initially had far fewer slaves than did Mesopotamia, which was highly militarized. Later, the Greeks of Athens and the Romans employed slaves far more extensively than did the Chinese or Indians (see Chapter 5). Furthermore, most ancient slavery differed from the type of slavery practiced in the Americas during recent centuries: in the early civilizations, slaves were not a primary agricultural labor force; many children of slaves could become free people; and slavery was not associated primarily with "blackness" or with Africa.

War and Slavery
This Mesopotamian victory monument, dating to about 2200 B.C.E., shows the Akkadian ruler Naram-Sin crushing his enemies. Prisoners taken in such wars were a major source of slaves in the ancient world. (Musée du Louvre, Paris, France/Bridgeman Images)

Hierarchies of Gender

No division of human society has held greater significance for the lives of individuals than those of sex and gender. Sex describes the obvious biological differences between males and females. More important to historians, however, has been gender, which refers to the many and varied ways that cultures have assigned meaning to those sexual differences. To be gendered as masculine or feminine defines the roles and behavior considered appropriate for men and women in every human community. At least since the emergence of the First Civilizations, and in some cases even earlier, gender systems have been patriarchal, meaning that women have been subordinate to men in the family and in society generally. The inequalities of gender, like those of class, decisively shaped the character of the First Civilizations and those that followed.

The patriarchal ideal regarded men as superior to women and sons preferable to daughters. Men had legal and property rights unknown to most women. Public life in general was associated with masculinity, which defined men as rulers, warriors, scholars, and heads of households. Women's roles—both productive and reproductive—took place in the home, mostly within a heterosexual family, where women were defined largely by their relationship to a man: as a daughter, wife, mother, or widow. Frequently men could marry more than one woman and claim the right to regulate the social and sexual lives of the wives, daughters, and sisters in their families. Widely seen as weak but feared as potentially disruptive, women required both the protection and control of men.

But the reality of the lives of men and women did not always correspond to these ideals. Most men, of course, were far from prominent and exercised little power, except perhaps over the women and children of their own families. Gender often interacted with class to produce a more restricted but privileged life for upper-class women, who were largely limited to the home and the management of servants or slaves. By contrast, the vast majority of women always had to be out in public, working in the fields, tending livestock, buying and selling in the streets, or serving in the homes of their social superiors. A few women also operated in roles defined as masculine, acting as rulers, priests, and scholars, while others pushed against the limits and restrictions assigned to women. But most women no doubt accepted their assigned roles, unable to imagine anything approaching gender equality, even as most men genuinely believed that they were protecting and providing for their women.

The big question for historians lies in trying to explain the origins of this kind of pervasive patriarchy. Clearly it was neither natural nor of long standing. For millennia beyond measure, gathering and hunting societies had developed gender systems without the sharp restrictions and vast inequalities that characterized civilizations. Early farming societies, those using a hoe or digging stick for cultivation, continued the relative gender equality that had characterized Paleolithic peoples. What was it, then, about civilization that seemed to generate a more explicit and restrictive patriarchy? One approach to answering this question highlights the role of a new and more intensive form of agriculture, involving the use of animal-drawn plows and the keeping and milking of large herds of animals. Unlike earlier farming practices that relied on a hoe or digging stick, plow-based agriculture meant heavier work, which men were better able to perform. Taking place at a distance from the village, this new form of agriculture was perhaps less compatible with women's primary responsibility for child rearing and food preparation. Furthermore, the growing population of civilizations meant that women were more often pregnant and thus more deeply involved in child care than before. Hence, in plow-based

AP® EXAM TIP

Patriarchy is an important recurring theme across place and time throughout the AP® course.

Guided Reading Question

■ CHANGE

In what ways have historians tried to explain the origins of patriarchy?

AP® EXAM TIP

As you begin developing your essay-writing skills, use these paragraphs as an example of an essay that includes a lot of specific information.

communities, men took over most of the farming work, and the status of women declined correspondingly, even though their other productive activities—weaving and food preparation, for example—continued. "As women were increasingly relegated to secondary tasks," writes archeologist Margaret Ehrenberg, "they had fewer personal resources with which to assert their status."[9] In much of Africa, all of the agricultural areas of the Americas, and parts of Southeast Asia, hoe-based farming persisted and with it, arguably, less restrictive lives for women.

Women have long been identified not only with the home but also with nature, for they are central to the primordial natural process of reproduction. But civilization seemed to highlight culture, or the human mastery of nature, through agriculture, monumental art and architecture, and creation of large-scale cities and states. Did this mean, as some scholars have suggested, that women were now associated with an inferior dimension of human life (nature), while men assumed responsibility for the higher order of culture?[10]

A further aspect of civilization that surely contributed to patriarchy was warfare. While earlier forms of human society certainly experienced violent conflict, large-scale military clashes with professionally led armies were a novel feature of almost all of the First Civilizations, and female prisoners of war often were the first slaves. With military service largely restricted to men, its growing prominence in the affairs of civilizations enhanced the values, power, and prestige of a male warrior class and cemented the association of masculinity with organized violence and with the protection of society, especially its women.

Private property and commerce, central elements of the First Civilizations, may also have helped to shape early patriarchies. Without sharp restrictions on women's sexual activity, how could a father be certain that family property would be inherited by his offspring? In addition, the buying and selling associated with commerce were soon applied to male rights over women, as female slaves, concubines, and wives were exchanged among men.

AP® EXAM TIP

Societies' expectations for what men and women are supposed to do or be (that is, "gender roles") are an important theme throughout this course.

Patriarchy in Practice

Whatever the precise origins of patriarchy, women's subordination permeated the First Civilizations, marking a gradual change from the more equal relationships of men and women within agricultural villages or Paleolithic bands. By the second millennium B.C.E. in Mesopotamia, various written laws codified and sought to enforce a patriarchal family life that offered women a measure of paternalistic protection while insisting on their submission to the unquestioned authority of men. Central to these laws was the regulation of female sexuality. A wife caught sleeping with another man might be drowned at her husband's discretion, whereas he was permitted to enjoy sexual relations with his female servants, though not with another man's wife. Divorce was far easier for the husband than for the wife. Rape was a serious offense, but the injured party was primarily the father or the husband of the victim, rather than the violated woman herself. While wealthy women might own and operate their own businesses or act on behalf of their powerful husbands, they too saw themselves as dependent. "Let all be well with [my husband]," prayed one such wife, "that I may prosper under his protection."[11]

Furthermore, women in Mesopotamian civilization were sometimes divided into two sharply distinguished categories. Under an Assyrian law code that was in effect between the fifteenth and eleventh centuries B.C.E., respectable women, those under the protection and sexual control of one man, were required to be veiled when outside the home, whereas nonrespectable women, such as slaves and prostitutes, were forbidden to wear veils and were subject to severe punishment if they presumed to cover their heads.

Finally, in some places, the powerful goddesses of earlier times were gradually relegated to the home and hearth. They were replaced in the public arena by dominant male deities, who now were credited with the power of creation and fertility and viewed as the patrons of wisdom and learning. This "demotion of the goddess," argued historian Gerda Lerner, found expression in the Hebrew Scriptures, in which a single male deity, Yahweh (YAH-way), alone undertakes the act of creation without any participation of a female counterpart. Yet this demotion did not occur always or everywhere; in Mesopotamia, for example, the prominent goddess Inanna, or Istar, long held her own against male gods and was regarded as a goddess of love and sexuality as well as a war deity. In a hymn to Inanna dating to around 2250 B.C.E., the poet and priestess Enheduanna declared: "It is her game to speed conflict and battle, untiring, strapping on her sandals."

Thus expressions of patriarchy varied among the First Civilizations. Egypt, while clearly patriarchal, afforded its women greater opportunities than did most other First Civilizations. In Egypt, women were recognized as legal equals to men, able to own property and slaves, to administer and sell land, to make their own wills, to sign their own marriage contracts, and to initiate divorce. Moreover, married women in Egypt were not veiled as they were at times in Mesopotamia. Royal women occasionally exercised significant political power, acting as regents for their young sons or, more rarely, as queens in their own right. Clearly, though, this was seen as abnormal, for Egypt's most famous queen, Hatshepsut (r. 1472–1457 B.C.E.), was sometimes portrayed in statues as a man, dressed in male clothing and sporting the traditional false beard of the pharaoh.

The Rise of the State

What, we might reasonably ask, held ancient civilizations together despite the many tensions and complexities of urban living and the vast inequalities of civilized societies? Why did they not fly apart amid the resentments born of class and gender hierarchies? The answer, in large part, lay in yet another distinctive feature of the First Civilizations—states. Organized around particular cities or larger territories, early states were headed almost everywhere by kings, who employed a variety of ranked officials, exercised a measure of control over society, and defended against

Guided Reading Question

■ COMPARISON
How did Mesopotamian and Egyptian patriarchy differ from each other?

AP® EXAM TIP
The AP® exam frequently includes questions about the common features and functions of early states.

external enemies. To modern people, the state is such a familiar reality that we find it difficult to imagine life without it. Nonetheless, it is a quite recent invention in human history, with the state replacing, or at least supplementing, kinship as the basic organizing principle of society and exercising far greater power than earlier chiefdoms. But the power of central states in the First Civilizations was limited and certainly not "totalitarian" in the modern sense of that term. The temple and the private economy rivaled and checked the power of rulers, and most authority was local rather than directed from the capital.

Coercion and Consent

Yet early states in Mesopotamia, Egypt, China, Mesoamerica, and elsewhere were influential, drawing their power from various sources, all of which assisted in providing cohesion for the First Civilizations. One basis of authority lay in the recognition that the complexity of life in cities or densely populated territories required some authority to coordinate and regulate the community. Someone had to organize the irrigation systems of river valley civilizations. Someone had to direct efforts to defend the city or territory against aggressive outsiders. Someone had to adjudicate conflicts among the many different peoples, unrelated to one another, who rubbed elbows in the streets of early cities. The state, in short, solved certain widely shared problems and therefore had a measure of voluntary support among the population. For many people, it was surely useful.

The state, however, was more useful for some people than for others, for it also served to protect the privileges of the upper classes, to require farmers to give up a portion of their product to support city-dwellers, and to demand work on large public projects such as pyramids and fortifications. If necessary, state authorities had the ability, and the willingness, to use force to compel obedience. An Egyptian document described what happens to a peasant unable to pay his tax in grain:

> Now the scribe lands on the shore. He surveys the harvest. Attendants are behind him with staffs, Nubians with clubs. One says [to the peasant], "Give grain." There is none. He is beaten savagely. He is bound, thrown into a well, submerged head down. His wife is bound in his presence. His children are in fetters. His neighbors abandon them and flee.[12]

Such was the power of the state, as rulers accumulated the resources to pay for officials, soldiers, police, and attendants. This capacity for violence and coercion marked off the states of the First Civilizations from earlier chiefdoms, whose leaders had only persuasion, prestige, and gifts to back up their authority. But as states increasingly monopolized the legitimate right to use violence, rates of death from interpersonal violence declined as compared to earlier nonstate communities.[13]

Force, however, was not always necessary, for the First Civilizations soon generated ideas suggesting that state authority as well as class and gender inequalities were normal, natural, and ordained by the gods. Rulers in many places were

Guided Reading Question

■ CHANGE
What were the sources of state authority in the First Civilizations?

AP® EXAM TIP

Expect to see AP® exam questions on how kings of early states—and kings throughout history—used religion to back up their claims to power.

thought to be morally responsible for the care of their subjects, especially in times of crisis or catastrophe. Kingship everywhere was associated with the sacred. Ancient Chinese kings were known as the Son of Heaven, and only they or their authorized priests could perform the rituals and sacrifices necessary to keep the cosmos in balance, thus preventing war, pestilence, and natural disaster. Mesopotamian rulers were thought to be the stewards of their city's patron gods. Their symbols of kingship—crown, throne, scepter, mace—were said to be of divine origin, sent to earth when the gods established monarchy. Egyptians, most of all, invested their pharaohs with divine qualities. Rulers claimed to embody all the major gods of Egypt, and their supernatural power ensured the regular flooding of the Nile and the defeat of the country's enemies.

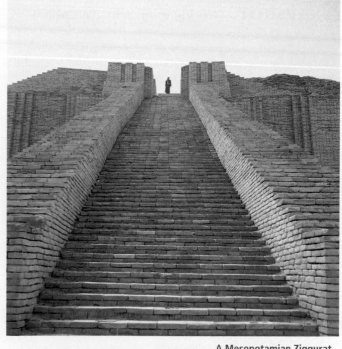

A Mesopotamian Ziggurat
This massive ziggurat/temple to the Mesopotamian moon god Nanna was built around 2100 B.C.E. in the city of Ur. The solitary figure standing atop the staircase illustrates the size of this huge structure. (© Richard Ashworth/Robert Harding World Imagery/Corbis)

But if religion served most often to justify unequal power and privilege, it might also on occasion be used to restrain, or even undermine, the established order. Hammurabi claimed that his law code was inspired by Marduk, the chief god of Babylon, and was intended to "bring about the rule of righteousness in the land, to destroy the wicked and the evil-doers; so that the strong should not harm the weak."[14] Another Mesopotamian monarch, Urukagina from the city of Lagash, claimed authority from the city's patron god for reforms aimed at ending the corruption and tyranny of a previous ruler. In China during the Western Zhou dynasty (1046–771 B.C.E.), emperors ruled by the Mandate of Heaven, but their bad behavior could result in the removal of that mandate and their overthrow.

Writing and Accounting

A further support for state authority lay in the remarkable invention of writing. It was a powerful and transforming innovation, regarded almost everywhere as a gift from the gods, while people without writing often saw it as something magical or supernatural. Distinctive forms of writing emerged in most of the First Civilizations (see Snapshot, page 78), sustaining them and their successors in many ways. Literacy defined elite status and conveyed enormous prestige to those who possessed it. For Egyptians, a scribe earned a kind of immortality through his writing, for it persisted long after his death. Because it can be learned, writing also provided a means for some commoners to join the charmed circle of the literate. Writing as propaganda, celebrating the great deeds of the kings, was prominent, especially

SNAPSHOT   Writing in Ancient Civilizations

Most of the early writing systems were logophonetic, using symbols to designate both whole words and particular sounds or syllables. Chinese characters, which indicated only words, were an exception. None of the early writing systems employed alphabets.

Location	Type	Initial Use	Example	Comment
Sumer	Cuneiform: wedge-shaped symbols on clay tablets representing objects, abstract ideas, sounds, and syllables	Records of economic transactions, such as temple payments and taxes	bird	Regarded as the world's first written language; other languages such as Babylonian and Assyrian were written with Sumerian script
Egypt	Hieroglyphs ("sacred carvings"): a series of signs that denote words and consonants (but not vowels or syllables)	Business and administrative purposes; later used for religious inscriptions, stories, poetry, hymns, and mathematics	rain, dew, storm	For everyday use, less formal systems of cursive writing (known as hieratic and demotic) were developed
Andes	Quipu: a complex system of knotted cords in which the color, length, type, and location of knots conveyed mostly numerical meaning	Various accounting functions; perhaps also used to express words	numerical data (possibly in codes), words, and ideas	Widely used in the Inca Empire; recent discoveries place quipus in Caral some 5,000 years ago
Indus River Valley	Some 400 pictographic symbols representing sounds and words, probably expressing a Dravidian language currently spoken in southern India	Found on thousands of clay seals and pottery; probably used to mark merchandise	6 fish	As yet undeciphered
China	Oracle bone script: pictographs (stylized drawings) with no phonetic meaning	Inscribed on turtle shells or animal bones; used for divination (predicting the future) in the royal court of Shang dynasty rulers	horse	Direct ancestor of contemporary Chinese characters
Olmec	Signs that represent sounds (syllables) and words; numbering system using bars and dots	Used to record the names and deeds of rulers and shamans, as well as battles and astronomical data	jaguar	Structurally similar to later Mayan script; Olmec calendars were highly accurate and the basis for later Meso-american calendars

among the Egyptians and later among the Maya. A hymn to the pharaoh, dating to about 1850 B.C.E., extravagantly praised the Egyptian ruler:

> He has come unto us . . . and has given peace to the two Riverbanks
> and has made Egypt to live; he hath banished its suffering;
> he has caused the throat of the subjects to breathe
> and has trodden down foreign countries;
> he has delivered them that were robbed; he has come unto us, that we may
>   [nurture up?] our children and bury our aged ones.[15]

In Mesopotamia and elsewhere, writing served an accounting function, recording who had paid their taxes, who owed what to the temple, and how much workers had earned. Thus it immensely strengthened bureaucracy. Complex calendars indicated precisely when certain rituals should be performed. Writing also gave weight and specificity to orders, regulations, and laws. Hammurabi's famous law code, while correcting certain abuses, made crystal clear that fundamental distinctions divided men and women and separated slaves, commoners, and people of higher rank.

Once it had been developed, writing, like religion, proved hard to control and operated as a wild card in human affairs. It gave rise to literature and philosophy, to astronomy and mathematics, and, in some places, to history, often recording what had long been oral traditions. On occasion, the written word proved threatening, rather than supportive, to rulers. China's so-called First Emperor, Qin Shihuangdi (r. 221–210 B.C.E.), allegedly buried alive some 460 scholars and burned their books when they challenged his brutal efforts to unify China's many warring states, or so his later critics claimed (see Chapter 3). Thus writing became a major arena for social and political conflict, and rulers have always sought to control it.

The Grandeur of Kings

Yet another source of state authority derived from the lavish lifestyle of elites, the impressive rituals they arranged, and the imposing structures they created. Everywhere, kings, high officials, and their families lived in luxurious palaces or homes, dressed in splendid clothing, bedecked themselves with the loveliest jewelry, and were attended by endless servants. Their deaths triggered elaborate burials, of which the pyramids of the Egyptian pharaohs were perhaps the most ostentatious. Monumental palaces, temples, ziggurats, pyramids, and statues conveyed the imposing power of the state and its elite rulers. The Olmec civilization of Mesoamerica (1200–400 B.C.E.) erected enormous human heads,

Olmec Head
This colossal statue, some six feet high and five feet wide, is one of seventeen such carvings, dating to the first millennium B.C.E., that were discovered in the territory of the ancient Olmec civilization. Thought to represent individual rulers, each of the statues has a distinct and realistically portrayed face. (© Danny Lehman/Corbis)

more than ten feet tall and weighing at least twenty tons, carved from blocks of basalt and probably representing particular rulers. Somewhat later, the Maya Temple of the Great Jaguar, towering 154 feet tall, was the most impressive among many temples, pyramids, and palaces that graced the city of Tikal. All of this must have seemed overwhelming to common people in the cities and villages of the First Civilizations.

Comparing Mesopotamia and Egypt

A productive agricultural technology, city living, distinct class and gender inequalities, the emerging power of states—all of these were common features of First Civilizations across the world and also of those that followed. Still, these civilizations were not everywhere the same, for differences in political organization, religious beliefs and practices, the role of women, and much more gave rise to distinctive traditions. Nor were they static. Like all human communities, they changed over the centuries. Finally, these civilizations did not exist in complete isolation, for they participated in networks of interactions with near and sometimes more distant neighbors. In looking more closely at two of these First Civilizations—Mesopotamia and Egypt—we can catch a glimpse of the differences, changes, and connections that characterized early civilizations.

Environment and Culture

The civilizations of both Mesopotamia and Egypt grew up in river valleys and depended on their rivers to sustain a productive agriculture in otherwise-arid lands. Those rivers, however, were radically different. At the heart of Egyptian life was the Nile, "that green gash of teeming life," which rose predictably every year to bring the soil and water that nurtured a rich Egyptian agriculture. The Tigris and Euphrates rivers, which gave life to Mesopotamian civilization, also rose annually, but "unpredictably and fitfully, breaking man's dikes and submerging his crops"[16] (see Map 2.2). Furthermore, an open environment without serious obstacles to travel made Mesopotamia far more vulnerable to invasion than the much more protected space of Egypt, which was surrounded by deserts, mountains, seas, and cataracts. For long periods of its history, Egypt enjoyed a kind of "free security" from external attack that Mesopotamians clearly lacked.

But does the physical environment shape the human cultures that develop within it? Most historians are reluctant to endorse any kind of determinism, especially one suggesting that "geography is destiny," but in the case of Mesopotamia and Egypt, it is hard to deny some relationship between the physical setting and culture.

Mesopotamia's location within a precarious, unpredictable, and often-violent environment arguably contributed to an outlook suggesting that humankind was caught in an inherently disorderly world, subject to the whims of capricious and

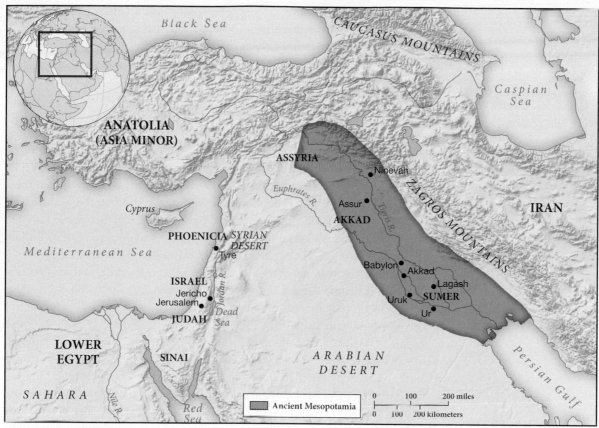

Map 2.2   Mesopotamia

After about 1,000 years of independent and competitive existence, the city-states of Sumer were incorporated into a number of larger imperial states based in Akkad, Babylon, and then Assyria.

quarreling gods, and faced death without much hope of a blessed life beyond. A Mesopotamian poet complained: "I have prayed to the gods and sacrificed, but who can understand the gods in heaven? Who knows what they plan for us? Who has ever been able to understand a god's conduct?" One character in the famous *Epic of Gilgamesh* declared: "When the gods created man, they allotted to him death, but life they retained in their own keeping."

By contrast, elite literate culture in Egypt, developing in a more stable, predictable, and beneficent environment, produced a rather more cheerful and hopeful outlook on the world. The rebirth of the sun every day and of the river every year seemed to assure Egyptians that life would prevail over death. The amazing pyramids, constructed during Egypt's Old Kingdom (2663–2195 B.C.E.), reflected the firm belief that at least the pharaohs and other high-ranking people could successfully make the journey to eternal life in the Land of the West. Incantations for the dead describe an afterlife of abundance and tranquillity that Gilgamesh could only

AP® EXAM TIP

The interactions between humans and the physical environments in which they lived are featured throughout this course.

have envied. Over time, larger groups of people, beyond the pharaoh and his entourage, came to believe that they too could gain access to the afterlife if they followed proper procedures and lived a morally upright life. Thus Egyptian civilization not only affirmed the possibility of eternal life but also expanded access to it.

If the different environments of Mesopotamia and Egypt shaped their societies and cultures, those civilizations, with their mounting populations and growing demand for resources, likewise had an impact on the environment.[18] The *Epic of Gilgamesh* inscribed in mythology the deforestation of Mesopotamia. When the ruler Gilgamesh sought to make for himself "a name that endures" by building walls, ramparts, and temples, he required much timber. But to acquire it, he had first to kill Humbaba, appointed by the gods to guard the forests. The epic describes what happened next: "Then there followed confusion. . . . Now the mountains were moved and all the hills, for the guardian of the forest was killed. They attacked the cedars. . . . So they pressed on into the forest . . . and while Gilgamesh felled the first of the trees of the forest, Enkidu [the friend of Gilgamesh] cleared their roots as far as the banks of Euphrates."[19]

In Sumer (southern Mesopotamia), such deforestation and the soil erosion that followed from it sharply decreased crop yields between 2400 and 1700 B.C.E. Also contributing to this disaster was the increasing salinization of the soil, a long-term outcome of intensive irrigation. By 2000 B.C.E., there were reports that "the earth turned white" as salt accumulated in the soil. As a result, wheat was largely replaced by barley, which is far more tolerant of salty conditions. This ecological deterioration clearly weakened Sumerian city-states, facilitated their conquest by foreigners, and shifted the center of Mesopotamian civilization permanently to the north.

Egypt, by contrast, created a more sustainable agricultural system, which lasted for thousands of years and contributed to the remarkable continuity of its civilization. Whereas Sumerian irrigation involved a complex and artificial network of canals and dikes that led to the salinization of the soil, its Egyptian counterpart was much less intrusive, simply regulating the natural flow of the Nile. Such a system avoided the problem of salty soils, allowing Egyptian agriculture to emphasize wheat production, but it depended on the general regularity and relative gentleness of the Nile's annual flooding. On occasion, that pattern was interrupted, with serious consequences for Egyptian society. An extended period of low floods between 2250 and 1950 B.C.E. led to sharply reduced agricultural output, large-scale starvation, the loss of livestock, and, consequently, social upheaval and political disruption. Nonetheless, Egypt's ability to work *with* its more favorable natural environment enabled a degree of stability and continuity that proved impossible in Sumer, where human action intruded more heavily into a less benevolent natural setting.

Cities and States

Politically as well as culturally and environmentally, Mesopotamian and Egyptian civilizations differed sharply. For its first thousand years (3200–2350 B.C.E.), Mesopotamian civilization, located in the southern Tigris-Euphrates region known as

AP® EXAM TIP

The *Epic of Gilgamesh* is an important example of early written stories.

Sumer, was organized in a dozen or more separate and independent city states. Each city-state was ruled by a king, who claimed to represent the city's patron deity and who controlled the affairs of the walled city and surrounding rural area. Quite remarkably, some 80 percent of the population of Sumer lived in one or another of these city-states, making Mesopotamia the most thoroughly urbanized society of ancient times. The chief reason for this massive urbanization, however, lay in the great flaw of this system, for frequent warfare among these Sumerian city-states caused people living in rural areas to flee to the walled cities for protection. With no overarching authority, rivalry over land and water often led to violent conflict.

These conflicts, together with environmental devastation, eventually left Sumerian cities vulnerable to outside forces, and after about 2350 B.C.E., stronger peoples from northern Mesopotamia conquered Sumer's warring cities, bringing an end to the Sumerian phase of Mesopotamian civilization. First the Akkadians (2350–2000 B.C.E.), and later the Babylonians (1900–1500 B.C.E.) and the Assyrians (900–612 B.C.E.), created larger territorial states or bureaucratic empires that encompassed all or most of Mesopotamia. Periods of political unity now descended upon this First Civilization, but it was unity imposed from outside.

Egyptian civilization, by contrast, began its history around 3100 B.C.E., with the merger of several earlier states or chiefdoms into a unified territory that stretched some 1,000 miles along the Nile. For an amazing 3,000 years, the Egypt of the pharaohs maintained its unity and independence, though with occasional interruptions. A combination of wind patterns that made it easy to sail south along the Nile and a current flowing north facilitated communication, exchange, unity, and stability within the Nile Valley. Here was a record of political longevity and continuity that the Mesopotamians and many other ancient peoples could not replicate. An Egyptian territorial state and cultural identity persist still in northeastern Africa.

Cities in Egypt were less important than in Mesopotamia, although political capitals, market centers, and major burial sites gave Egypt an urban presence as well. Most people lived in agricultural villages along the river rather than in urban centers, perhaps because Egypt's greater security made it less necessary for people to gather in fortified towns. The focus of the Egyptian state resided in the pharaoh, believed to be a god in human form. He alone ensured the daily rising of the sun and the annual flooding of the Nile. All of the country's many officials served at his pleasure, and access to the afterlife lay in proximity to him and burial in or near his towering pyramids.

This image of the pharaoh and his role as an enduring symbol of Egyptian civilization persisted over the course of three millennia, but the realities of Egyptian political life did not always match the ideal, as the Zooming In feature on Paneb so vividly illustrates (see page 84). By 2400 B.C.E., the power of the pharaoh had diminished, as local officials and nobles, who had been awarded their own land and were able to pass their positions on to their sons, assumed greater authority. When changes in the weather resulted in the Nile's repeated failure to flood properly around 2200 B.C.E., the authority of the pharaoh was severely discredited, and Egypt dissolved for several centuries into a series of local principalities.

Paneb, an Egyptian Troublemaker

The life of Paneb (ca. thirteenth century B.C.E.) illuminates an underside of Egyptian life rather different from the images of order and harmony portrayed in much of ancient Egyptian art and literature.[20] Paneb was born into a family and a village of tomb workers—people who quarried, sculpted, and painted the final resting places of the pharaohs and other elite figures at a time when royal pyramids were no longer being constructed. Granted generous allowances of grain, beer, fish, vegetables, firewood, and clothing, tomb workers represented a prestigious occupation in ancient Egypt.

Paneb was apparently orphaned as a youngster and raised by another tomb-working family, that of the childless Neferhotep, a foreman of the tomb workers' crew who brought his adopted son into the profession. But Paneb quarreled violently with Neferhotep, on one occasion smashing the door to his house and threatening to kill him.

As an adult, Paneb married and sired a large family of eight or nine children. He also indulged in numerous

Paneb worshipping a coiled cobra representing the goddess Meretseger, patron deity of the burial grounds in Thebes, where Paneb worked.

affairs with married women and was involved in at least one rape. One of his lovers was the wife of a man with whom Paneb had grown up in Neferhotep's home; the couple subsequently divorced, a frequent occurrence in ancient Egypt. In another case, Paneb seduced both a married woman and her daughter and shared the sexual favors of the daughter with his son Aapehty. It is not difficult to imagine the tensions that such behavior created in a small, close-knit village.

When Paneb's adoptive father, Neferhotep, died—he was perhaps murdered—Paneb succeeded him as workplace foreman, thus incurring the lifelong hostility of Neferhotep's brother, Amennakht, who felt he had better claim to the job. What turned the tide in Paneb's favor was his "gift" of five servants, made to the vizier, the pharaoh's highest official, who was responsible for such appointments. To add insult to Amennakht's injury, those servants had belonged to Neferhotep himself.

Even when centralized rule was restored around 2000 B.C.E., the pharaohs never regained their old power and prestige. Kings were now warned that they too would have to account for their actions at the Day of Judgment. Nobles no longer sought to be buried near the pharaoh's pyramid but instead created their own more modest tombs in their own areas. Osiris, the god of the dead, became increasingly prominent, and all worthy men, not only those who had been close to the pharaoh in life, could aspire to immortality in his realm.

Interaction and Exchange

Although Mesopotamia and Egypt represented separate and distinct civilizations, they interacted frequently with each other and with both near and more distant

While such bribes were common practice in obtaining promotions, it was Paneb's use of his position as foreman of the tomb workers' crew that got him into ever-deeper trouble. He actively harassed his rival Amennakht, preventing him and his family from using the small chapel in which workers celebrated the festivals of their gods. He quarreled with the foreman of another work crew, saying, "I'll attack you on the mountain and I'll kill you." Such angry outbursts led to frequent fighting and gained Paneb a reputation for brutality.

Paneb also exploited his position as foreman to his own advantage. He used—or stole—expensive tools given to the work crew for his own purposes. He ordered members of his work crew to do personal work for him—making a bed that he then sold to a high official, feeding his oxen, weaving baskets for his personal use, and preparing and decorating his own tomb, using materials pilfered from the royal tombs he was charged with constructing. On one occasion he stole the covering of a royal chariot, and another time he entered a royal tomb, drank the wine intended for the pharaoh's afterlife, and in an act of enormous disrespect—even blasphemy—actually sat on the sarcophagus containing the embalmed body of the ruler.

Although Paneb was rebuked from time to time by high officials, his bad behavior continued. "He could

not stop his clamor," according to an official document. At some point, Paneb's son publicly denounced his father's sexual escapades. But the final straw that broke his career came from Amennakht, Paneb's longtime rival. He apparently had had enough and drew up a long list of particulars detailing Paneb's crimes. That document, from which our knowledge of Paneb largely derives, has survived. It concluded in this fashion:

> He is thus not worthy of this position. For truly, he seems well, [but] he is like a crazy person. And he kills people to prevent them from carrying out a mission of the Pharaoh. See, I wish to convey knowledge of his condition to the vizier.

The outcome of this complaint is unclear, for Paneb subsequently disappears from the historical record, and a new foreman was appointed in his place. It was not, however, Amennakht.

Questions: Since most of the evidence against Paneb comes from his archrival, how much weight should historians grant to that account? How might the story appear if written from Paneb's viewpoint? What perspectives on the Egypt of his time does Paneb's career disclose? How do those perspectives differ from more conventional and perhaps idealized understandings?

neighbors. Even in these ancient times, the First Civilizations were embedded in larger networks of commerce, culture, and power. None of them stood alone.

The early beginnings of Egyptian civilization illustrate the point. Its agriculture drew upon wheat and barley, which likely reached Egypt from Mesopotamia, as well as gourds, watermelon, domesticated donkeys, and cattle, which came from the Sudan to the south. The practice of "divine kingship" probably derived from the central or eastern Sudan, where small-scale agricultural communities had long viewed their rulers as sacred and buried them with various servants and officials. From this complex of influences, the Egyptians created something distinct and unique, but that civilization had roots in both Africa and Southwest Asia.

Furthermore, once they were established, both Mesopotamia and Egypt carried on long-distance trade, mostly in luxury goods destined for the elite. Sumerian

Guided Reading Question

■ CONNECTION
In what ways were Mesopotamian and Egyptian civilizations shaped by their interactions with near and distant neighbors?

merchants had established seaborne contact with the Indus Valley civilization as
early as 2300 B.C.E., while Indus Valley traders and their interpreters had taken up
residence in Mesopotamia. Other trade routes connected it to Anatolia (present-
day Turkey), Egypt, Iran, and Afghanistan. During Akkadian rule over Mesopotamia, a Sumerian poet described its capital of Agade:

> In those days the dwellings of Agade were filled with gold,
> its bright-shining houses were filled with silver,
> into its granaries were brought copper, tin, slabs of
> lapis lazuli [a blue gemstone], its silos bulged at the sides . . .
> its quay where the boats docked were all bustle.[21]

All of this and more came from far away.

Egyptian trade likewise extended far afield. Beyond its involvement with the
Mediterranean and the Middle East, Egyptian trading journeys extended deep into
Africa, including Nubia, south of Egypt in the Nile Valley, and Punt, along the East
African coast of Ethiopia and Somalia. One Egyptian official described his return
from an expedition to Nubia: "I came down with three hundred donkeys laden
with incense, ebony, . . . panther skins, elephant tusks, throw sticks, and all sorts of
good products."[22] What most intrigued the very young pharaoh who sent him,
however, was a dancing dwarf who accompanied the expedition back to Egypt.

Along with trade goods went cultural influence from the civilizations of Mesopotamia and Egypt. Among the smaller societies of the region to feel this influence
were the Hebrews. Their sacred writings, recorded in the Old Testament, showed
the influence of Mesopotamia in the "eye for an eye" principle of their legal system
and in the story of a flood that destroyed the world. The Phoenicians, who were
commercially active in the Mediterranean basin from their homeland in present-
day Lebanon, also were influenced by Mesopotamian civilization. They venerated

Egypt and Nubia
By the fourteenth century B.C.E., Nubia was a part of an Egyptian empire. This wall painting shows Nubian princes
bringing gifts or tribute, including rings and bags of gold, to Huy, the Egyptian viceroy of Nubia. The mural comes
from Huy's tomb. (© The Trustees of the British Museum/Art Resource, NY)

Asarte, a local form of the Mesopotamian fertility goddess Istar. They also adapted the Sumerian cuneiform method of writing to a much easier alphabetic system, which later became the basis for Greek and Latin writing. Various Indo-European peoples, dispersing probably from north-central Anatolia, also incorporated Sumerian deities into their own religions as well as bronze metallurgy and the wheel into their economies. When their widespread migrations carried them across much of Eurasia, they took these Sumerian cultural artifacts with them.

Egyptian cultural influence likewise spread in several directions. Nubia, located to the south of Egypt in the Nile Valley, not only traded with its more powerful neighbor but also was subject to periodic military intervention and political control from Egypt. Skilled Nubian archers were actively recruited for service as mercenaries in Egyptian armies. They often married Egyptian women and were buried in Egyptian style. All of this led to the diffusion of Egyptian culture in Nubia, expressed in building Egyptian-style pyramids, worshipping Egyptian gods and goddesses, and making use of Egyptian hieroglyphic writing. Despite this cultural borrowing, Nubia remained a distinct civilization, developing its own alphabetic script, retaining many of its own gods, developing a major ironworking industry by 500 B.C.E., and asserting its political independence whenever possible. The Nubian kingdom of Kush, in fact, invaded Egypt in 760 B.C.E. and ruled it for about 100 years. (See Zooming In: Piye, Kushite Conqueror of Egypt, Chapter 6, page 236.)

In the Mediterranean basin, clear Egyptian influence is visible in the art of Minoan civilization, which emerged on the island of Crete about 2500 B.C.E. More controversial has been the claim by historian Martin Bernal in a much publicized book, *Black Athena* (1987), that ancient Greek culture—its art, religion, philosophy, and language—drew heavily upon Egyptian as well as Mesopotamian precedents. His book lit up a passionate debate among scholars. To some of his critics, Bernal seemed to undermine the originality of Greek civilization by suggesting that it had Afro-Asian origins. His supporters accused the critics of Eurocentrism. Whatever its outcome, the controversy surrounding Bernal's book served to focus attention on Egypt's relationship to black Africa and to the world of the Mediterranean basin.

Influence was not a one-way street, however, as Egypt and Mesopotamia likewise felt the impact of neighboring peoples. Pastoral peoples, speaking Indo-European languages and living in what is now southern Russia, had domesticated the horse by perhaps 4000 B.C.E. and later learned to tie that powerful animal to wheeled carts and chariots. This new technology provided a fearsome military potential that enabled various chariot-driving peoples, such as the Hittites, to threaten ancient civilizations. Based in Anatolia, the Hittites sacked the city of Babylon in 1595 B.C.E. Several centuries later, conflict between the Hittites and Egypt over control of Syria resulted in the world's first written peace treaty. But chariot technology was portable, and soon both the Egyptians and the Mesopotamians incorporated it into their own military forces. In fact, this powerful military innovation, together with the knowledge of bronze metallurgy, spread quickly and widely, reaching China by 1200 B.C.E. There it enabled the creation of a strong Chinese state ruled by the Shang dynasty.

AP® EXAM TIP

Questions about early forms of weaponry and transportation have been known to appear on the AP® exam.

Black Sea

ANATOLIA
(ASIA MINOR)

Tigris R.

SYRIA

Euphrates R.

Aegean Sea

Crete

Cyprus

Mediterranean Sea

PALESTINE

Jericho

Dead Sea

LOWER EGYPT

Giza

Memphis

SINAI PENINSULA

ARABIA

Akhetaten
(Tell el-Amarna)

Nile R.

UPPER EGYPT

Thebes

SAHARA

Aswan

Red Sea

First Cataract

Second Cataract

Third Cataract

Kerma

NUBIA

Fourth Cataract

Fifth Cataract

Napata

Meroë

Sixth Cataract

Hittite empire

Map 2.3   An Egyptian Empire

During the New Kingdom period after 1550 B.C.E., Egypt became for several centuries an empire, extending its political control southward into Nubia and northward into Palestine and Syria.

All of these developments provide evidence of at least indirect connections across parts of the Afro-Eurasian landmass in ancient times. Even then, no civilization was wholly isolated from larger patterns of interaction.

In Egypt, the centuries following 1650 B.C.E. witnessed the migration of foreigners from surrounding regions and conflict with neighboring peoples, shaking the sense of security that this Nile Valley civilization had long enjoyed. It also stimulated the normally complacent Egyptians to adopt a number of technologies pioneered earlier in Asia, including the horse-drawn chariot; new kinds of armor, bows, daggers, and swords; improved methods of spinning and weaving; new musical instruments; and olive and pomegranate trees. Absorbing these foreign innovations, Egyptians went on to create their own empire, both in Nubia and in the eastern Mediterranean regions of Syria and Palestine. By 1500 B.C.E., the previously self-contained Egypt became for several centuries an imperial state bridging Africa and Asia, ruling over substantial numbers of non–Egyptian peoples (see Map 2.3). It also became part of an international political system that included the Babylonian and later Assyrian empires of Mesopotamia as well as many other peoples of the region. Egyptian and Babylonian rulers engaged in regular diplomatic correspondence, referred to one another as "brother," exchanged gifts, and married their daughters into one another's families. Or at least they tried to. While Babylonian rulers were willing to send their daughters to Egypt, the Egyptians were exceedingly reluctant to return the favor, claiming that "from ancient times the daughter of the king of Egypt has not been given to anyone." To this rebuff, the disappointed Babylonian monarch replied: "You are a king and you can do as pleases you. . . . Send me [any] beautiful woman as if she were your daughter. Who is to say this woman is not the daughter of the king?"[23]

"Civilization": What's in a Word?

In examining the cultures of ancient Mesopotamia and Egypt, we are worlds away from life in agricultural villages or Paleolithic camps. Much the same holds for those of the Indus Valley, Central Asia, China, Mesoamerica, and the Andes. Strangely enough, historians have been somewhat uncertain as to how to refer to these new forms of human community. Following common practice, we have called them "civilizations," but scholars have reservations about the term for two reasons. The first is its implication of superiority. In popular usage, "civilization" suggests refined behavior, a "higher" form of society, something unreservedly positive. The opposite of "civilized"—"barbarian," "savage," or "uncivilized"—is normally understood as an insult implying inferiority. That, of course, is precisely how the inhabitants of many civilizations have viewed outsiders, particularly those neighboring peoples living without the alleged benefit of cities and states.

Modern assessments of the First Civilizations reveal a profound ambiguity about these new, larger, and more complex societies. On the one hand, these civilizations have given us inspiring art, profound reflections on the meaning of life, more productive technologies, increased control over nature, and the art of writing—all of which have been cause for celebration. On the other hand, as anthropologist Marvin Harris noted, "human beings learned for the first time how to bow, grovel, kneel, and kowtow."[24] Massive inequalities, state oppression, slavery, large-scale warfare, the subordination of women, and epidemic disease also accompanied the rise of civilization, generating discontent, rebellion, and sometimes the urge to escape. This ambiguity about the character of civilizations has led some historians to avoid the word, referring to early Egypt, Mesopotamia, and other regions instead as complex societies, urban-based societies, state-organized societies, or some other more neutral term.

A second reservation about using the term "civilization" derives from its implication of solidity—the idea that civilizations represent distinct and widely shared identities with clear boundaries that mark them off from other such units. It is unlikely, however, that many people living in Mesopotamia, Norte Chico, or ancient China felt themselves part of a shared culture. Local identities defined by occupation, clan affiliation, village, city, or region were surely more important for most people than those of some larger civilization. At best, members of an educated upper class who shared a common literary tradition may have felt themselves part of some more inclusive civilization, but that left out most of the population. Moreover, unlike modern nations, none of the earlier civilizations had definite borders. Any identification with that civilization surely faded as distance from its core region increased. Finally, the line between civilizations and other kinds of societies is not always clear. Just when does a village or town become a city? At what point does a chiefdom become a state? Scholars continue to argue about these distinctions.

Given these reservations, should historians discard the notion of civilization? Maybe so, but this book continues to use it both because it is so deeply embedded in our way of thinking about the world and because no alternative concept has achieved widespread acceptance for making distinctions among different kinds of human communities. But it is important to recall that historians use "civilization" as a purely descriptive term, referring to a particular and distinctive type of human society—one with cities and states—without implying any judgment or assessment, any sense of superiority or inferiority. Furthermore "civilization" serves to define broad cultural patterns in particular geographic regions—Mesopotamia, the Peruvian coast, or China, for example—even though many people living in those regions may have been more aware of differences and conflicts than of those commonalities.

Chapter Review

What's the Significance?

Big Picture Questions

1. How does historians' use of the term "civilization" differ from popular usage? How do you use it?
2. "Civilizations were held together largely by force." Do you agree with this assessment, or were there other mechanisms of integration as well?
3. How did the various First Civilizations differ from one another?
4. **Looking Back:** To what extent did civilizations represent "progress" in comparison with earlier Paleolithic and Neolithic societies? And in what ways did they constitute a setback for humankind?

Next Steps: For Further Study

Cyril Aldred, *The Egyptians* (1998). A brief account from a widely recognized expert.

Jonathan M. Kenoyer, *Ancient Cities of the Indus Valley Civilization* (1998). A thorough and beautifully illustrated study by a leading archeologist of the area.

Samuel Noah Kramer, *History Begins at Sumer* (1981). A classic account of Sumerian civilization, filled with wonderful stories and anecdotes.

David B. O'Connor, *Ancient Nubia: Egypt's Rival in Africa* (1994). An overview of this ancient African civilization, with lovely illustrations based on a museum exhibit.

Christopher A. Pool, *Olmec Archeology and Early Mesoamerica* (2007). A scholarly and up-to-date account of the earliest civilization in Mesoamerica.

Robert Thorp, *China in the Early Bronze Age: Shang Civilization* (2006). An accessible and scholarly account of early Chinese civilization informed by recent archeological discoveries.

The British Museum, "Ancient Egypt," http://www.ancientegypt.co.uk/menu.html. An interactive exploration of Egyptian civilization.

"The Indus Civilization," http://www.harappa.com/har/har0.html. Hundreds of vivid pictures and several brief essays on the Indus Valley civilization.

WORKING WITH EVIDENCE

Indus Valley Civilization

In most accounts of the First Civilizations, Egypt and Mesopotamia hold center stage. And yet the civilization of the Indus River valley was much larger, and its archeological treasures have been equally impressive, though clearly distinctive. This civilization flourished around 2000 B.C.E., about a thousand years later than its better-known counterparts in the Middle East and Northeast Africa. By 1700 B.C.E., Indus Valley civilization was in decline, as the center of Indian or South Asian civilization shifted gradually eastward to the plains of the Ganges River. In the process, all distinct memory of the earlier Indus Valley civilization vanished, to be rediscovered only in the early twentieth century as archeologists uncovered its remarkable remains. Here is yet another contrast with Egypt and Mesopotamia, where conscious memory of earlier achievements persisted long after those civilizations had passed into history.

Among the most distinctive elements of Indus Valley civilization were its cities, of which Mohenjo Daro and Harappa were the largest and are the most thoroughly investigated. Laid out systematically on a grid pattern and clearly planned, they were surrounded by substantial walls made from mud bricks of a standardized size and interrupted by imposing gateways. Inside the walls, public buildings, market areas, large and small houses, and craft workshops stood in each of the cities' various neighborhoods. Many houses had indoor latrines, while wide main streets and narrow side lanes had drains to carry away polluted water and sewage. (See page 70 for an image of a ritual bathing pool in Mohenjo Daro.)

The images that follow are drawn from archeological investigations of the Indus Valley civilization and offer us a glimpse of its achievements and unique features. Since its written language was limited in extent and has not yet been deciphered, scholars have been highly dependent on its physical remains for understanding this First Civilization.

In many ancient and more recent societies, seals have been used for imprinting an image on a document or a product. Such seals have been among the most numerous artifacts found in the Indus Valley cities. They often carried the image of an animal—a bull, an elephant, a crocodile, a buffalo, or even a mythic creature such as a unicorn—as well as a title or inscription in a still-undeciphered script. Thus the seals were accessible to an illiterate worker loading goods on a boat as well as to literate merchants or officials. Particular

91

seals may well have represented a specific clan, a high official, a particular business, or a prominent individual. Unicorn seals have been the most numerous finds and were often used to make impressions on clay tags attached to bundled goods, suggesting that their owners were involved in trade or commerce. Because bull seals, such as the one shown in Source 2.1, were rarer, their owners may have been high-ranking officials or members of a particularly powerful clan. The bull, speculates archeologist Jonathan Kenoyer, "may symbolize the leader of the herd, whose strength and virility protects the herd and ensures the procreation of the species, or it may stand for a sacrificial animal."[25] Indus Valley seals, as well as pottery, have been found in Mesopotamia, indicating an established trade between these two First Civilizations.

- How might a prominent landowner, a leading official, a clan head, or a merchant make use of such a seal?

- What meaning might you attach to the use of animals as totems or symbols of a particular group or individual?

- Notice the five characters of the Indus Valley script at the top of the seal. Do a little research on the script with an eye to understanding why it has proved so difficult to decipher.

De Agostini Picture Library/A. Dagli Orti/Bridgeman Images

Source 2.1 A Seal from the Indus Valley

The most intriguing features of Indus Valley civilization involve what is missing, at least in comparison with ancient Egypt and Mesopotamia. Archeologists have found no grand temples or palaces; no elite burial places filled with great wealth; no images of warfare, conquest, or the seizing of captives; no monuments to celebrate powerful rulers. These absences have left scholars guessing about the social and political organization of this civilization. Kenoyer has suggested that the great cities were likely controlled not by a single ruler, but by "a small group of elites, comprised of merchants, landowners, and ritual specialists."[26]

Source 2.2, a statue seven inches tall and found in Mohenjo Daro, likely depicts one of these elite men.

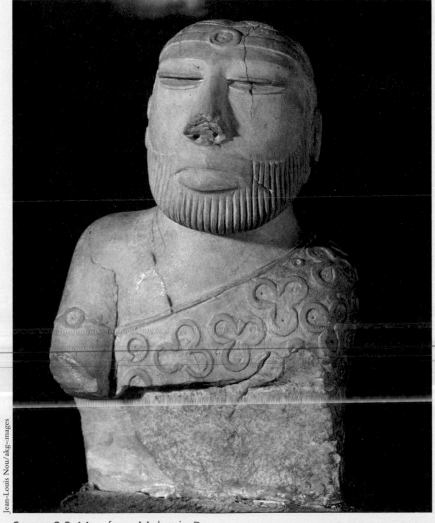

Jean-Louis Nou/akg-images

Source 2.2 Man from Mohenjo Daro

- What specific features of the statue can you point out?
- What possible indication of elite status can you identify?
- What overall impression does the statue convey?

Limited archeological evidence suggests that some urban women played important social and religious roles in the Indus Valley civilization. Figurines of women or goddesses are more common than those of men. Women, apparently, were buried near their mothers and grandmothers, while men were not interred with their male relatives. The great variety of clothing, hairstyles, and decorations displayed on female figurines indicates considerable class, ethnic, and perhaps individual variation.

Among the most delightful discoveries in the Indus Valley cities is the evocative statue shown in Source 2.3. It is about four inches tall and dates to

National Museum of India, New Delhi, India/Bridgeman Images

Source 2.3 Dancing Girl

around 2500 B.C.E. This young female nude is known generally as the "danc
ing girl." Cast in bronze using a sophisticated "lost wax" method, this statue
provides evidence for a well-developed copper/bronze industry. The figure
herself was portrayed in a dancer's pose, her hair gathered in a bun and her
left arm covered with bangles and holding a small bowl. Both her arms and
legs seem disproportionately long. She has been described variously as a queen,
a high-status woman, a sacred temple dancer, and a tribal girl. Although no
one really knows her precise identity, she has evoked wide admiration and
appreciation. Mortimer Wheeler, a famous British archeologist, described her
as "a girl perfectly, for the moment, perfectly confident of herself and the
world." American archeologist Gregory Possehl, also active in the archeology
of the Indus Valley civilization, commented, "We may not be certain that she
was a dancer, but she was good at what she did and she knew it."[27]

- What features of this statue may have provoked such observations?

- How do you react to this statue? What qualities does the figure evoke?

- What does Source 2.3 suggest about views of women, images of female
  beauty, and attitudes about sexuality and the body?

DOING HISTORY

Indus Valley Civilization

1. **Using art as evidence:** What can we learn about Indus Valley civilization from these visual sources? How does our level of understanding of
   this civilization differ from that of Egypt and Mesopotamia, where plentiful written records are available?

2. **Considering accessibility:** Do you find the art of civilizations, such
   as that of the Indus Valley, more accessible to modern people than artistic products of earlier eras? Is it possible to speak of artistic "progress"
   or "development," or should we be content with simply noticing
   differences?

3. **Comparing representations of people:** Notice the various ways that
   human figures were portrayed in the images shown in Chapters 1 and 2,
   both those in the chapter narrative and in the Working with Evidence
   section. How might you define those differences? Can you identify
   changes from the Paleolithic to the Neolithic eras and then to the age of
   First Civilizations? How are gender differences represented in these images?

4. **Seeking further evidence:** What additional kinds of archeological
   discoveries would be helpful in furthering our understanding of Indus
   Valley civilization?

Multiple-Choice Questions

Use the chart below and your knowledge of world history to answer questions 1–3.

Agricultural Breakthroughs

LOCATION	DATES (B.C.E.)	PLANTS	ANIMALS
Southwest Asia (Fertile Crescent)	9000–7000	barley, wheat, lentils, figs	goats, sheep, cattle, pigs
China	6500–5000	rice, millet, soybeans	pigs, chickens, water buffalo
Saharan and sub-Saharan Africa	3000–2000	sorghum, millet, yams, teff	cattle (perhaps 8000 B.C.E.)
Highland New Guinea	7000–4000	taro, bananas, yams, sugarcane	—
Andes region	3000–2000	potatoes, quinoa, manioc	llamas, alpacas, guinea pigs
Mesoamerica	3000–2000	maize, squash (perhaps 7000 B.C.E.), beans	turkeys
Eastern woodlands of North America	2000–1000	sunflowers, goosefoot, sumpweed	—

1. Which of the following could be considered the oldest domesticated plant?

a. Potatoes

b. Rice

c. Squash

d. Sunflowers

2. Based on the information provided, which of these is the most likely conclusion that can be drawn regarding domestication?

a. All animals were domesticated at the same time as plants.

b. Every region domesticated plants and animals before 5000 B.C.E.

c. Inhabitants of the New Guinea highlands relied solely on vegetarian diets since they had no domesticated animals.

d. Cattle were among the earliest domesticated animals.

3. Based on the information provided, what conclusions can be drawn about the development of agriculture?

a. Agriculture initially developed in a few specific areas through independent innovation.

b. Agriculture initially developed through widespread technological diffusion.

c. Agriculture initially developed after the rise of civilizations.

d. Agriculture developed as humans migrated out of Africa.

Short-Answer Question

Question 4 refers to the passage below.

"From the point of view of the lives of women, the Neolithic period is perhaps the most important phase of prehistory.... It is likely that at the end of the Paleolithic ..., women enjoyed equality with men. They probably collected as much, if not more, of the food eaten by the community and derived equal status from their contribution.... [W]omen almost certainly "invented" agriculture as well as many of the concomitant skills and tools which go to make crop agriculture possible and profitable.... But between then and now ... the status of women has been drastically reduced, and in many areas farming has become a predominately male preserve.... As the balance of work changed from part hunting, part crop cultivation and tending a small number of animals to an economy dependent on mixed farming, so the roles and duties of women and men may have shifted.... [I]t was in the later Neolithic, when men began to take over most agricultural work, that the social status of women declined."

Margaret Ehrenberg, historian, *Women in Prehistory*, 1989

4. Answer parts A, B, and C.
   A. Identify and explain how ONE specific historical development prior to 600 B.C.E. could be used to support one of Ehrenberg's assertions in the passage above.
   B. Identify and explain how ANOTHER specific historical development prior to 600 B.C.E. could be used to support one of Ehrenberg's assertions in the passage above.
   C. Identify and explain how ONE specific historical development prior to 600 B.C.E. could be used to challenge one of Ehrenberg's assertions in the passage above.

Document-Based Question

Directions: *Question 5 refers to the following documents. You will likely need to flip back and forth between these documents to answer the question adequately. Use scrap pieces of paper or sticky notes to tab these documents. When answering the question, refer to the "Advice for Responding to a DBQ" on the inside of the back cover.*

5. Using the following documents from this textbook and your knowledge of world history, compare and contrast images that humans made of themselves in the era before c. 600 B.C.E.

DOCUMENT	PAGE	DOCUMENT NAME
1	35	The Statues of Ain Ghazal
2	40	Nok Culture
3	58	Raherka and Mersankh
4	79	Olmec Head
5	93	Man from Mohenjo Daro

Long-Essay Question

When answering the following question, refer to the "Advice for Responding to an LEQ" on the inside of the back cover.

6. Using specific examples, compare and contrast the political systems in agricultural chiefdoms and First Civilizations, analyzing reasons for the similarities and differences.

PART TWO

SECOND-WAVE CIVILIZATIONS IN WORLD HISTORY

600 B.C.E.–600 C.E.

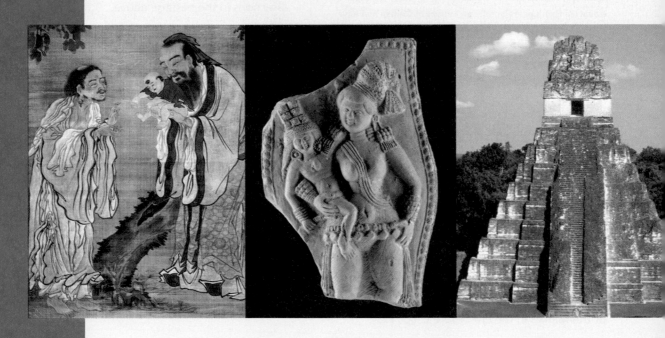

Contents

AFTER THE FIRST CIVILIZATIONS: WHAT CHANGED AND WHAT DIDN'T?

Studying world history has much in common with using the zoom lens of a camera. Sometimes, we pull the lens back to get a picture of the broadest possible panorama. At other times, we zoom in a bit for a middle-range shot, or even farther for a close-up of some particular feature of the historical landscape. Students of world history soon become comfortable with moving back and forth among these several perspectives.

AP® EXAM TIP

The historical events in Part Two make up 15 percent of the AP® World History exam.

As we bid farewell to the First Civilizations, we will take the opportunity to pull back the lens and look broadly, and briefly, at the entire age of agricultural civilizations, a period from about 3500 B.C.E., when the earliest of the First Civilizations arose, to about 1750 C.E., when the first Industrial Revolution launched a new and distinctively modern phase of world history. During these more than 5,000 years, the most prominent large-scale trend was the globalization of civilization as this new form of human community increasingly spread across the planet, encompassing more people and larger territories.

The first wave of that process, addressed in Chapter 2, was already global in scope, with expressions in Asia, Africa, and the Americas. Those First Civilizations generated the most impressive and powerful human societies created thus far, but they proved fragile and vulnerable as well. The always-quarreling city-states of ancient Mesopotamia had long ago been absorbed into the larger empires of Babylon and Assyria. By the middle of the second millennium B.C.E., the Indus Valley, Central Asian, and Norte Chico civilizations had collapsed or faded away. Egypt too fell victim to a series of foreign invaders during the first millennium B.C.E., including the forces of Nubia, Assyria, Alexander the Great, and the Roman Empire. The end of Olmec civilization around 400 B.C.E. has long puzzled historians, for it seems that the Olmecs themselves razed and then abandoned their major cities even as their civilizational style spread to neighboring peoples. About the same time, China's Zhou dynasty kingdom fragmented into a series of competing states.

Even though these First Civilizations broke down, there was no going back. Civilization as a form of human community proved durable and resilient as well as periodically fragile. Thus, in the millennium between 600 B.C.E. and 600 C.E., new or enlarged urban-centered and state-based societies emerged to replace the First Civilizations in the Mediterranean basin, the Middle East, India,

China, Mesoamerica, and the Andes. Furthermore, smaller expressions of civilization began to take shape elsewhere—in Ethiopia and West Africa, in Japan and Indonesia, in Vietnam and Cambodia. In short, the development of civilization was becoming a global process.

Many of these second-wave civilizations likewise perished, as the collapse of the Roman Empire, Han dynasty China, and the Maya cities reminds us. They were followed by yet a third wave of civilizations, from roughly 600 to 1450 C.E. (see Part Three). Some of them represented the persistence or renewal of older patterns, as in the case of China, for example, while elsewhere—such as in Western Europe, Russia, Japan, and West Africa—newer civilizations emerged, all of which borrowed heavily from their more-established neighbors. The largest of these, Islamic civilization, incorporated a number of older centers of civilization, Egypt and Mesopotamia, for example, under the umbrella of a new religion. Thus the globalization of civilization continued apace. So too did the interaction of civilizations with one another and with the gathering and hunting peoples, agricultural village societies, and pastoral communities who were their neighbors.

Continuities in Civilization

As this account of the human journey moves into the second and third waves of civilization, the question arises as to how they differed from the first ones. From a panoramic perspective, the answer is "not much." States and empires rose, expanded, and collapsed with a tiresome regularity. It is arguable, however, that little fundamental change occurred amid these constant fluctuations. Monarchs continued to rule most of the new civilizations; women remained subordinate to men in all of them; a sharp divide between the elite and everyone else persisted almost everywhere, as did the practice of slavery.

Furthermore, no technological or economic breakthrough occurred to create new kinds of human societies as the Agricultural Revolution had done earlier or as the Industrial Revolution would do much later. Landowning elites had little incentive to innovate, for they benefited enormously from simply expropriating the surplus that peasant farmers produced. Nor would peasants have any reason to invest much effort in creating new forms of production when they knew full well that any gains they might generate would be seized by their social superiors. Merchants, who often were risk takers, might have spawned innovations, but they usually were dominated by powerful states and were viewed with suspicion and condescension by more prestigious social groups.

Many fluctuations, repetitive cycles, and minor changes characterize this long era of agricultural civilization, but no fundamental or revolutionary transformation of social or economic life took place. The major turning points in human history had occurred earlier with the emergence of agriculture and the birth of the First Civilizations and would occur later with the breakthrough of industrialization.

Changes in Civilization

While this panoramic perspective allows us to see the broadest outlines of the human journey, it also obscures much of great importance that took place during the second and third waves of the age of agrarian civilization. If we zoom in a bit more closely, significant changes emerge, even if they did not result in a thorough transformation of human life. Population, for example, grew more rapidly than ever before during this period, as the Snapshot illustrates. Even though the overall trend was up, important fluctuations interrupted the pattern, especially during the first millennium C.E., when little overall growth took place. Moreover, the rate of growth, though rapid in comparison with Paleolithic times, was quite slow if we measure it against the explosive expansion of recent centuries, when human numbers quadrupled in the twentieth century alone. This modest and interrupted pattern of population growth during the age of agrarian civilization reflected the absence of any fundamental economic breakthrough, which could have supported much larger numbers.

Another change lies in the growing size of the states or empires that structured civilizations. The Roman, Persian, Indian, and Chinese empires of second-wave civilizations, as well as the Arab, Mongol, and Inca empires of the third wave, all dwarfed the city-states of Mesopotamia and the Egypt of the pharaohs. Each of these empires brought together in a single political system a vast diversity

SNAPSHOT   World Population during the Age of Agricultural Civilization[1]

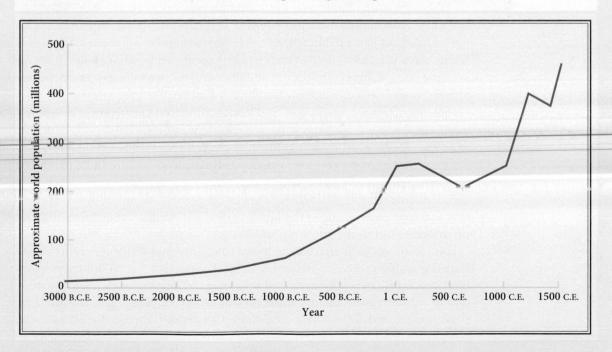

of peoples. Even so, just to keep things in perspective, as late as the seventeenth century C.E., only one-third of the world's landmass was under the control of any state-based system, although these societies now encompassed a considerable majority of the world's people.

The rise and fall of these empires likewise represented very consequential changes to the people who experienced them. In the course of its growth, the Roman Empire utterly destroyed the city of Carthage in North Africa, with the conquerors allegedly sowing the ground with salt so that nothing would ever grow there again. Similar bloodshed and destruction accompanied the creation of other much-celebrated states. Their collapse also had a dramatic impact on the lives of their people. Scholars have estimated that the large population of Maya civilization shrank by some 85 percent in less than a century as that society dissolved around 840 C.E. It is difficult to imagine the sense of trauma and bewilderment associated with a collapse of this magnitude.

Second- and third-wave civilizations also generated important innovations in many spheres. Those in the cultural realm have been perhaps the most widespread and enduring. Distinctive "wisdom traditions"—the great philosophical/religious systems of Confucianism and Daoism in China; Hinduism and Buddhism in India; Greek rationalism in the Mediterranean; and Judaism, Zoroastrianism, Christianity, and Islam in the Middle East—have provided the moral and spiritual framework within which most of the world's peoples have sought to order their lives and define their relationship to the mysteries of life and death. All of these philosophical and religious systems are the product of second- and third-wave civilizations.

Although no technological breakthrough equivalent to the Agricultural or Industrial Revolution took place during this time, more modest innovations considerably enhanced human potential for manipulating the environment. China was a primary source of such technological change, though by no means the only one. "Chinese inventions and discoveries," wrote one prominent historian, "passed in a continuous flood from East to West for twenty centuries before the scientific revolution."[2] They included piston bellows, the drawloom, silk-handling machinery, the wheelbarrow, a better harness for draft animals, the crossbow, iron casting, the iron-chain suspension bridge, gunpowder, firearms, the magnetic compass, paper, printing, and porcelain. India pioneered the crystallization of sugar and techniques for the manufacture of cotton textiles. Roman technological achievements were particularly apparent in construction and civil engineering—the building of roads, bridges, aqueducts, and fortifications—and in the art of glassblowing.

Nor were social hierarchies immune to change and challenge. India's caste system grew far more elaborate over time. Roman slaves and Chinese peasants on occasion rose in rebellion. Some Buddhist and Christian women found a measure of autonomy and opportunities for leadership and learning in the monastic communities of their respective traditions. Gender systems too fluctuated in the intensity with which women were subordinated to men. Generally women were less restricted in the initial phase of a civilization's development and during times of disruption, while patriarchy limited women more sharply as a civilization matured and stabilized.

A further process of change following the end of the First Civilizations lay in the emergence of far more elaborate, widespread, and dense networks of communication and exchange that connected many of the world's peoples to one another. Many of the technologies mentioned here diffused widely across large areas, as did the religious and cultural traditions of second- and third-wave civilizations. Long-distance trade routes represented another form of transregional interaction. Caravan trade across northern Eurasia, seaborne commerce within the Indian Ocean basin, the exchange of goods across the Sahara, river-based commerce in the eastern woodlands of North America, various trading networks radiating from Mesoamerica—all of these carried goods, and sometimes disease, technology, culture, and religion as well. In the early centuries of the Common Era, for example, Southeast Asia attracted distant merchants and some settlers from both China and India, bringing Confucianism, Hinduism, and Buddhism to various parts of that vast region. Disease also increasingly linked distant human communities. According to the famous Greek historian Thucydides, a mysterious plague "from parts of Ethiopia above Egypt" descended on Athens in 430 B.C.E., decimating the city.[3]

In all of these ways, the world became quite different from what it had been in the age of the First Civilizations, even though fundamental economic and social patterns had not substantially changed.

The first three chapters of Part Two focus in a thematic fashion on the Eurasian / North African civilizations of the second-wave era (600 B.C.E.–600 C.E.), which hosted the vast majority of the world's population, some 80 percent or more. Chapter 3 introduces them by examining and comparing their political frameworks and especially the empires (great or terrible, depending on your point of view) that took shape in most of them. Far more enduring than their empires were the cultural or religious traditions that second-wave civilizations generated. These are examined, also comparatively, in Chapter 4. The social life of these civilizations, expressed in class, caste, slavery, and gender relationships, also varied considerably, as Chapter 5 spells out. In Chapter 6, the historical spotlight turns to inner Africa, the Americas, and Pacific Oceania during the second-wave era, asking whether their histories paralleled Eurasian patterns or explored alternative possibilities.

In recalling this second-wave phase of the human journey, we will have occasion to compare the experiences of its various peoples, to note their remarkable achievements, to lament the tragedies that befell them and the suffering to which they gave rise, and to ponder their continuing power to fascinate us still.

Landmarks in World History (ca. 600 B.C.E.–ca. 600 C.E.)

| 700 B.C.E. | 600 B.C.E. | 500 B.C.E. | 400 B.C.E. | 300 B.C.E. | 200 B.C.E. | 100 B.C.E. |

ASIA

7th century B.C.E.
Zoroaster

326–185 B.C.E.
Mauryan Empire in India

6th–5th centuries B.C.E.
Confucius and Laozi in China

553–330 B.C.E.
First Persian Empire
(Achaemenid dynasty)

566–486 B.C.E.
Buddha in India

By 400 B.C.E.
Upanishads compiled as philosophical
expression of Hinduism

332–326 B.C.E.
Alexander the Great's conquest
of Persian Empire

EUROPE AND THE MEDITERRANEAN BASIN

800–500 B.C.E.
Hebrew prophets

750–336 B.C.E.
Era of Greek city-states

73 B.C.E.
Spartacus
slave
rebellion

509 B.C.E.
Founding of Roman Republic

490–480 B.C.E.
Greco-Persian Wars

336–323 B.C.E.
Reign and conquests of
Alexander the Great

469–432 B.C.E.
Socrates, Plato, Aristotle

AFRICA

730 B.C.E.
Nubian conquest of Egypt

300 B.C.E.–100 C.E.
Kingdom of Meroë in upper Nile Valley

300 B.C.E.–900 C.E.
Niger Valley civilization

THE AMERICAS

900–200 B.C.E.
Chavín religious movement
in Peru

400 B.C.E.
Decline of Olmec
civilization

200 B.C.E.–400 C.E.
Hopewell "mound-building" culture

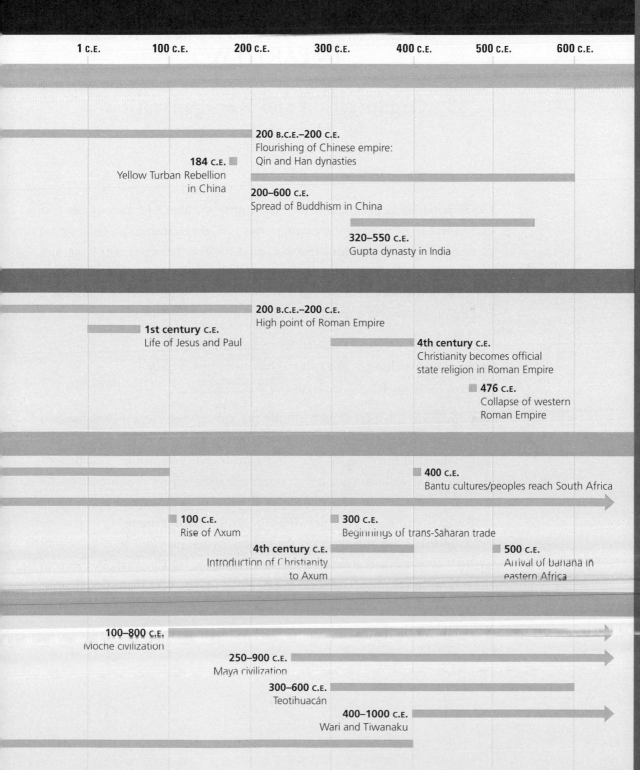

1 C.E.   100 C.E.   200 C.E.   300 C.E.   400 C.E.   500 C.E.   600 C.E.

200 B.C.E.–200 C.E.
Flourishing of Chinese empire:
Qin and Han dynasties

184 C.E.
Yellow Turban Rebellion
in China

200–600 C.E.
Spread of Buddhism in China

320–550 C.E.
Gupta dynasty in India

200 B.C.E.–200 C.E.
High point of Roman Empire

1st century C.E.
Life of Jesus and Paul

4th century C.E.
Christianity becomes official
state religion in Roman Empire

476 C.E.
Collapse of western
Roman Empire

400 C.E.
Bantu cultures/peoples reach South Africa

100 C.E.
Rise of Axum

300 C.E.
Beginnings of trans-Saharan trade

4th century C.E.
Introduction of Christianity
to Axum

500 C.E.
Arrival of banana in
eastern Africa

100–800 C.E.
Moche civilization

250–900 C.E.
Maya civilization

300–600 C.E.
Teotihuacán

400–1000 C.E.
Wari and Tiwanaku

103

UNDERSTANDING AP® THEMES
IN PART TWO

Organization and Reorganization
of Human Societies

Corresponding to Period 2 of the AP® course outline, Part Two of this text constitutes 15 percent of the exam. In this part, we examine the millennium of second-wave civilizations that occurred roughly between 600 B.C.E. and 600 C.E. We will explore first the major civilizations of Eurasia and North Africa (Chinese, Indian, Persian, and Mediterranean) using a thematic approach. For example, we will consider the following:

- The construction of imperial states in Chapter 3
- Prominent religious and cultural traditions in Chapter 4
- Patterns of social organization in Chapter 5

And finally, in Chapter 6 we examine the second-wave era in sub-Saharan Africa, the Americas, and Pacific Oceania, with special emphasis on social and political alternatives to city- and state-based civilizations. Throughout Part Two, you will see repeated references to the reciprocal influence of the natural order and human activity as well as the economic structures of particular civilizations and the networks of linkage among them.

As in Part One, the chart on the opposite page provides an overview of the AP® World History themes you will encounter in this part. As you read the following chapters, continue to pay close attention to these five themes. Also watch for AP® Exam Tips throughout the text to assist in your course-work and exam preparation.

Environment	Cultures	State Building	Economies	Social Structures
Greek geography and environmental effects of Greek civilization	Cross-cultural perceptions in the ancient world	Eurasian empires of the second-wave era ■ Persian ■ Greek (Alexander) ■ Roman: from republic to empire ■ Chinese empires (Qin and Han) ■ Indian empires (Mauryan and Gupta)	Persian commercial networks and agricultural systems	Empires and the definition of masculinity
Environmental effects of Roman and Chinese civilizations	Chinese cultural traditions: Legalist, Confucian, Daoist		Chinese agriculture, metallurgy, and landowning patterns	Class in China
African landscapes and environmental limitations of agriculture	Evolution of Indian religious thought		Economic condition of Chinese peasants	Caste in India
Environmental diversity in Mesoamerica and the Andes	Birth and spread of Buddhism		Merchants and state authorities in China	Class and citizenship in Athens
Maya environmental engineering	Artistic representations of the Buddha	City-states: Greek, Niger Valley, Maya, Teotihuacán	Economic functions of caste in India	Slavery in the Roman world
Ecological degradation: its role in the collapse of Maya civilization and the Roman Empire	The Greek intellectual tradition and the spread of Greek culture in the Hellenistic era	Greco-Persian Wars	Indian commercial and cultural network in the Indian Ocean region	Patriarchy ■ Evolution in China and Roman world ■ Athens/Sparta comparison ■ Variations in Oceania
"Verticality" in Wari and Tiwanaku	Greco-Roman cultural synthesis and the attractions of Roman culture	Peloponnesian Wars	Slave labor systems in the Roman world	Cities without states in West Africa
Geography and continental variation	Art and architecture in Pompeii	Vietnamese resistance to China	Pastoralism in Afro-Eurasia and its absence in the Americas	Female rulers in Meroë
Iron making and deforestation in Meroë	Cultural interaction in the Kushan Empire	Chinese relationships with northern "barbarians"	Economic specialization in the Niger Valley	Urban life in Teotihuacán
The environment of Pacific Oceania and human impact on it	Monotheisms of the Middle East: Judaism and Zoroastrianism	Slave rebellion in the Roman Empire	Axumite trade relationships	Social variation among Bantu-speaking peoples
Ecological collapse in Rapa Nui	The rise and spread of Christianity	Meroitic and Axumite empires	Patterns of economic and cultural exchange in North America	Social differences in Oceania
	Chavín religious movement	Wari and Tiwanaku states	Wari and Tiwanaku agriculture compared	
	Moche art	Chiefdoms in Bantu Africa, the Americas, and Oceania	Ritualized economic exchange in Oceania	
	Spread of Bantu culture			
	Mana and tapu in Oceania			

CHAPTER 3

State and Empire in Eurasia/North Africa

600 B.C.E.–600 C.E.

Empires and Civilizations in Collision: The Persians and the Greeks
The Persian Empire
The Greeks
Collision: The Greco-Persian Wars
Collision: Alexander and the Hellenistic Era
Comparing Empires: Roman and Chinese
Rome: From City-State to Empire
China: From Warring States to Empire
Consolidating the Roman and Chinese Empires
The Collapse of Empires
Intermittent Empire: The Case of India
Reflections: Enduring Legacies of Second-Wave Empires
Zooming In: Trung Trac: Resisting the Chinese Empire
Zooming In: The Kushan Empire
Working with Evidence:
Perceptions of Outsiders in the Ancient World

Are We Rome? It was the title of a thoughtful book, published in 2007, asking what had become a familiar question in the early twenty-first century: "Is the United States the new Roman Empire?"[1] With the collapse of the Soviet Union by 1991 and the subsequent U.S. invasions of Afghanistan and Iraq, some commentators began to make the comparison. The United States' enormous multicultural society, its technological achievements, its economically draining and over-stretched armed forces, its sense of itself as unique and endowed with a global mission, its concern about foreigners penetrating its borders, its apparent determination to maintain military superiority—all of this invited comparison with the Roman Empire. Supporters of a dominant role for the United States argued that Americans must face up to their responsibilities as "the undisputed master of the world" as the Romans did in their time. Critics warned that the Roman Empire became overextended abroad and corrupt and dictatorial at home and then collapsed, suggesting that a similar fate may await the U.S. empire. Either way, the point of reference was an empire that had passed into history some 1,500 years earlier, a continuing reminder of the significance of the distant past to our contemporary world. In fact, for at least several centuries, that empire has been a source of metaphors and "lessons" about personal morality, corruption, political life, military expansion, and much more.

Even in a world largely critical of empires, they still excite the imagination of historians and readers of history alike. The earliest ones show up in the era of the First Civilizations when Akkadian, Babylonian, and Assyrian empires encompassed the city-states of Mesopotamia and established an enduring imperial tradition in the Middle East.

Terra-Cotta Archer Part of the immense funerary complex constructed for the Chinese ruler Qin Shihuangdi, this kneeling archer represents the military power that reunified a divided China under the Qin dynasty in 221 B.C.E.

105

Egypt became an imperial state when it temporarily ruled Nubia and the lands of the eastern Mediterranean. Following in their wake were many more empires, whose rise and fall have been central features of world history for the past 4,000 years.

But what exactly is an empire? At one level, empires are simply states, political systems that exercise coercive power. The term, however, is normally reserved for larger and more aggressive states, those that conquer, rule, and extract resources from other states and peoples. Thus empires have generally encompassed a considerable variety of peoples and cultures within a single political system, and they have often been associated with political or cultural oppression. Frequently, empires have given political expression to a civilization or culture, as in the Chinese and Persian empires. But civilizations have also flourished without a single all-encompassing state or empire, as in the competing city-states of Mesopotamia, Greece, and Mesoamerica or the many rival states of post-Roman Europe. In such cases, civilizations were expressed in elements of a common culture rather than in a unified political system.

The Eurasian empires of the second-wave era—those of Persia, Greece under Alexander the Great, Rome, China during the Qin (chihn) and Han dynasties, and India during the Mauryan (MORE-yuhn) and Gupta dynasties—shared a set of common problems. Would they seek to impose the culture of the imperial heartland on their varied subjects? Would they rule conquered people directly or through established local authorities? How could they extract the wealth of empire in the form of taxes, tribute, and labor while maintaining order in conquered territories? And, no matter how impressive they were at their peak, they all sooner or later collapsed, providing a useful reminder to their descendants of the fleeting nature of all human projects.

Why have these and other empires been of such lasting fascination to both ancient and modern people? Perhaps in part because they were so big, creating a looming presence in their respective regions. Their armies and their tax collectors were hard to avoid. Maybe also because they were so bloody. The violence of conquest easily grabs our attention, and certainly all of these empires were founded and sustained at a great cost in human life. The collapse of these once-powerful states is likewise intriguing, for the fall of the mighty seems somehow satisfying, perhaps even a delayed form of justice. The study of empires also sets off by contrast those times and places in which civilizations have prospered without an enduring imperial state.

But empires have also commanded attention simply because they were important. While the political values of recent times have almost universally condemned empire building, very large numbers of people—probably the majority of humankind before the twentieth century—have lived out their lives in empires, where they were often governed by rulers culturally different from themselves. These imperial states brought together people of quite different traditions and religions and so stimulated the exchange of ideas, cultures, and values. Despite their violence, exploitation, and oppression, empires also imposed substantial periods of

AP® EXAM TIP

You must know the definition of "empire" as well as the names, places, and contributions of these empires.

A MAP OF TIME

750–336 B.C.E.	Era of Greek city-states
553–330 B.C.E.	Persian Achaemenid Empire
509 B.C.E.	Founding of the Roman Republic
500–221 B.C.E.	Chinese age of warring states
490 and 480 B.C.E.	Major battles between Persians and Greeks
479–429 B.C.E.	Golden Age of Athens
431–404 B.C.E.	Peloponnesian War
336–323 B.C.E.	Reign of Alexander the Great
326–184 B.C.E.	India's Mauryan dynasty empire
221–206 B.C.E.	China's Qin dynasty empire
206 B.C.E.–220 C.E.	China's Han dynasty empire
200 B.C.E.–200 C.E.	High point of Roman Empire
1st century B.C.E.	Transition from republic to empire in Rome
184 C.E.	Yellow Turban Rebellion in China
220 C.E.	Collapse of Chinese Han dynasty
320–550 C.E.	India's Gupta dynasty empire
5th century C.E.	Collapse of western Roman Empire

AP® EXAM TIP

You need to know when the empires featured in this chapter rose and fell.

peace and security, which fostered economic and artistic development, commercial exchange, and cultural mixing. In many places, empire also played an important role in defining masculinity, as conquest generated a warrior culture that gave particular prominence to the men who created and ruled those imperial states.

SEEKING THE MAIN POINT

How might you assess—both positively and negatively—the role of empires in the history of the second wave era?

Empires and Civilizations in Collision: The Persians and the Greeks

The millennium between 600 B.C.E. and 600 C.E. in North Africa and Eurasia witnessed the flowering of second-wave civilizations in the Mediterranean world, the Middle East, India, and China. For the most part, these distant civilizations did not directly encounter one another, as each established its own political system, cultural values, and ways of organizing society. A great exception to that rule lay in the Mediterranean world and in the Middle East, where the emerging Persian Empire and Greek civilization, physically adjacent to each other, experienced a centuries-long interaction and clash. It was one of the most consequential cultural encounters of the ancient world. (For another example of contact among second-wave empires, see the Zooming In feature on the Kushan Empire, page 128.)

The Persian Empire

In 500 B.C.E., the largest and most impressive of the world's empires was that of the Persians, an Indo-European people whose homeland lay on the Iranian plateau just north of the Persian Gulf. Living on the margins of the earlier Mesopotamian civilization, the Persians under the Achaemenid (ah-KEE-muh-nid) dynasty (553–330 B.C.E.) constructed an imperial system that drew on previous examples, such as the Babylonian and Assyrian empires, but far surpassed them all in size and splendor. Under the leadership of the famous monarchs Cyrus (r. 557–530 B.C.E.) and Darius (r. 522–486 B.C.E.), Persian conquests quickly reached from Egypt to India, encompassing in a single state some 35 to 50 million people, an immensely diverse realm containing dozens of peoples, states, languages, and cultural traditions (see Map 3.1).

The Persian Empire centered on an elaborate cult of kingship in which the monarch, secluded in royal magnificence, could be approached only through an elaborate ritual. When the king died, sacred fires all across the land were extinguished, Persians were expected to shave their hair in mourning, and the manes of horses were cut short. Ruling by the will of the great Persian god Ahura Mazda (uh-HOORE-uh MAHZ-duh), kings were absolute monarchs, more than willing to crush rebellious regions or officials. Interrupted on one occasion while he was with his wife, Darius ordered the offender, a high-ranking nobleman, killed, along with his entire clan. In the eyes of many, Persian monarchs fully deserved their effusive title — "Great king, King of kings, King of countries containing all kinds of men, King in this great earth far and wide." Darius himself best expressed the authority of the Persian ruler when he observed, "What was said to them by me, night and day, it was done."[2]

But more than conquest and royal decree sustained the empire. An effective administrative system placed Persian governors, called *satraps* (SAY-traps), in each of the empire's twenty-three provinces, while lower-level officials were drawn from local authorities. A system of imperial spies, known as the "eyes and ears of the King," represented a further imperial presence in the far reaches of the empire. A general policy of respect for the empire's many non-Persian cultural traditions also cemented the state's authority. Cyrus won the gratitude of the Jews when in 539 B.C.E. he allowed those exiled in Babylon to return to their homeland and rebuild their temple in Jerusalem (see Chapter 4, pages 166–67). In Egypt and Babylon, Persian kings took care to uphold local religious cults in an effort to gain the support of their followers and officials. The Greek historian Herodotus commented that "there is no nation which so readily adopts foreign customs. They have taken the dress of the Medes and in war they wear the Egyptian breastplate.

AP® EXAM TIP

You will be expected to know at least one of the three Persian empires. The Achaemenid is the most famous.

Guided Reading Question

■ COMPARISON

How did Persian and Greek civilizations differ in their political organization and values?

AP® EXAM TIP

Note these examples of how empires were governed, or their "imperial administration." Examples continue on page 109.

Map 3.1   The Persian Empire

At its height, the Persian Empire was the largest in the world. It dominated the lands of the First Civilizations in the Middle East and was commercially connected to neighboring regions.

As soon as they hear of any luxury, they instantly make it their own."[3] (See more on Herodotus's perceptions of Persia in Working with Evidence, Source 3.1, page 137.) For the next 1,000 years or more, Persian imperial bureaucracy and court life, replete with administrators, tax collectors, record keepers, and translators, provided a model for all subsequent regimes in the region, including, later, those of the Islamic world.

The infrastructure of empire included a system of standardized coinage, predictable taxes levied on each province, and a newly dug canal linking the Nile with the Red Sea, which greatly expanded commerce and enriched Egypt. A "royal road," some 1,700 miles in length, facilitated communication and commerce across this vast empire. Caravans of merchants could traverse this highway in three months, but agents of the imperial courier service, using a fresh supply of horses every twenty-five to thirty miles, could carry a message from one end of the road to another in a week or two. Herodotus was impressed. "Neither snow, nor rain, nor heat, nor darkness of night," he wrote, "prevents them from accomplishing the task proposed to them with utmost speed." And an elaborate underground irrigation

Persepolis
The largest palace in Persepolis, the Persian Empire's ancient capital, was the Audience Hall. The emperor officially greeted visiting dignitaries at this palace, which was constructed around 500 B.C.E. This relief, which shows a lion attacking a bull and Persian guards at attention, adorns a staircase leading to the Audience Hall. (Giraudon/Bridgeman Images)

system sustained a rich agricultural economy in the semi-arid conditions of the Iranian plateau and spread from there throughout the Middle East and beyond.

Elaborate imperial centers, particularly Susa and Persepolis, reflected the immense wealth and power of the Persian Empire. Palaces, audience halls, quarters for the harem, monuments, and carvings made these cities into powerful symbols of imperial authority. Materials and workers alike were drawn from all corners of the empire and beyond. Inscribed in the foundation of Persepolis was Darius's commentary on what he had set in motion: "And Ahura Mazda was of such a mind, together with all the other gods, that this fortress [should] be built. And [so] I built it. And I built it secure and beautiful and adequate, just as I was intending to."[4]

The Greeks

AP® EXAM TIP

You should know the features and roles of cities throughout the course.

It would be hard to imagine a sharper contrast than that between the huge and centralized Persian Empire, governed by an absolute and almost unapproachable monarch, and the small competing city-states of classical Greece, which allowed varying degrees of popular participation in political life. Like the Persians, the Greeks were an Indo-European people whose early history drew on the legacy of the First Civilizations. The classical Greece of historical fame emerged around 750 B.C.E. as a new civilization and flourished for about 400 years before it was incorporated into a succession of foreign empires. During that relatively short period, the civilization of Athens and Sparta, of Plato and Aristotle, of Zeus and Apollo took shape and collided with its giant neighbor to the east.

Calling themselves Hellenes, the Greeks created a civilization that was distinctive in many ways, particularly in comparison with that of the Persians. The total population of Greece and the Aegean basin was just 2 million to 3 million, a fraction of that of the Persian Empire. Furthermore, Greek civilization took shape on a small peninsula, deeply divided by steep mountains and valleys. Its geography certainly contributed to the political shape of that civilization, which found expression not in a Persian-style empire, but in hundreds of city-states or small settlements (see Map 3.2). Most were quite modest in size, with between 500 and 5,000 male

Map 3.2   Classical Greece

The classical civilization of Greece was centered on a small peninsula of southeastern Europe, but Greek settlers planted elements of that civilization along the coasts of the Mediterranean and Black seas.

citizens. But Greek civilization, like its counterparts elsewhere, also left a decisive environmental mark on the lands it encompassed. Smelting metals such as silver, lead, copper, bronze, and iron required enormous supplies of wood, leading to deforestation and soil erosion. Plato declared that the area around Athens had become "a mere relic of the original country. . . . All the rich soil has melted away, leaving a country of skin and bone."[5]

Each of these city-states was fiercely independent and in frequent conflict with its neighbors, yet they had much in common, speaking the same language and worshipping the same gods. Every four years they temporarily suspended their continual conflicts to participate together in the Olympic Games, which had begun

Guided Reading Question

■ CHANGE

How did semidemocratic governments emerge in some of the Greek city-states?

in 776 b.c.e. But this emerging sense of Greek cultural identity did little to overcome the endemic political rivalries of the larger city-states, including Athens, Sparta, Thebes, and Corinth, among many others.

Like the Persians, the Greeks were an expansive people, but their expansion took the form of settlement in distant places rather than conquest and empire. Pushed by a growing population, Greek traders in search of iron and impoverished Greek farmers in search of land stimulated a remarkable emigration. Between 750 and 500 b.c.e., the Greeks established settlements all around the Mediterranean basin and the rim of the Black Sea. Settlers brought Greek culture, language, and building styles to these new lands, even as they fought, traded, and intermarried with their non-Greek neighbors.

The most distinctive feature of Greek civilization, and the greatest contrast with Persia, lay in the extent of popular participation in political life that occurred within at least some of the city-states. It was the idea of "citizenship," of free people managing the affairs of state, of equality for all citizens before the law, that was so unique. A foreign king, observing the operation of the public assembly in Athens, was amazed that male citizens as a whole actually voted on matters of policy: "I find it astonishing," he noted, "that here wise men speak on public affairs, while fools decide them."[6] Compared to the rigid hierarchies, inequalities, and absolute monarchies of Persia and other ancient civilizations, the Athenian experiment was remarkable. This is how one modern scholar defined it:

> Among the Greeks the question of who should reign arose in a new way. Previously the most that had been asked was whether one man or another should govern and whether one alone or several together. But now the question was whether all the citizens, including the poor, might govern and whether it would be possible for them to govern as citizens, without specializing in politics. In other words, should the governed themselves actively participate in politics on a regular basis?[7]

The extent of participation and the role of "citizens" varied considerably, both over time and from city to city. Early in Greek history, only wealthy and well-born men had the rights of full citizenship, such as speaking and voting in the assembly, holding public office, and fighting in the army. Gradually, men of the lower classes, mostly small-scale farmers, also obtained these rights. At least in part, this broadening of political rights was associated with the growing number of men able to afford the armor and weapons that would allow them to serve as hoplites, or infantrymen, in the armies of the city-states. In many places, strong but benevolent rulers known as tyrants emerged for a time, usually with the support of the poorer classes, to challenge the prerogatives of the wealthy. Sparta—famous for its extreme forms of military discipline and its large population of helots, conquered people who lived in slave-like conditions—vested most political authority in its Council of Elders. The council was composed of twenty-eight men over the age of sixty, derived from the wealthier and more influential segment of society, who served for life and provided political leadership for Sparta.

AP® EXAM TIP

Use the discussion on these pages of similarities and differences between the Persians and Greeks to develop your skills in writing comparative essays.

It was in Athens that the Greek experiment in political participation achieved its most distinctive expression. Early steps in this direction were the product of intense class conflict, leading almost to civil war. A reforming leader named Solon emerged in 594 B.C.E. to push Athenian politics in a more democratic direction, breaking the hold of a small group of aristocratic families. Debt slavery was abolished, access to public office was opened to a wider group of men, and all citizens were allowed to take part in the Assembly. Later reformers such as Cleisthenes (KLEYE-sthuh-nees) and Pericles extended the rights of citizens even further. By 450 B.C.E., all holders of public office were chosen by lot and were paid, so that even the poorest could serve. The Assembly, where all citizens could participate, became the center of political life.

Athenian democracy, however, was different from modern democracy. It was direct, rather than representative, democracy, and it was distinctly limited. Women, slaves, and foreigners, together far more than half of the population, were wholly excluded from political participation. Nonetheless, political life in Athens was a world away from that of the Persian Empire and even from that of many other Greek cities.

Collision: The Greco-Persian Wars

In recent centuries, many writers and scholars have claimed classical Greece as the foundation of Western or European civilization. But the ancient Greeks themselves looked primarily to the East—to Egypt and the Persian Empire. In Egypt, Greek scholars found impressive mathematical and astronomical traditions on which they built. And Persia represented both an immense threat and later, under Alexander the Great, an opportunity for Greek empire building.

If ever there was an unequal conflict between civilizations, surely it was the collision of the Greeks and the Persians. The confrontation between the small and divided Greek cities and Persia, the world's largest empire, grew out of their respective patterns of expansion. A number of Greek settlements on the Anatolian seacoast, known to the Greeks as Ionia, came under Persian control as that empire extended its domination to the west. In 499 B.C.E., some of these Ionian Greek cities revolted against Persian domination and found support from Athens on the Greek mainland. Outraged by this assault from the remote and upstart Greeks, the Persians, twice in ten years (490 and 480 B.C.E.), launched major military expeditions to punish the Greeks in general and Athens in particular. Against all odds and all expectations, the Greeks held them off, defeating the Persians on both land and sea.

Though no doubt embarrassing, their defeat on the far western fringes of the empire had little effect on the Persians. However, it had a profound impact on the Greeks and especially on Athens, whose forces had led the way to victory. Beating the Persians in battle was a source of enormous pride for Greece. Years later, elderly Athenian men asked one another how old they had been when the Greeks triumphed in the momentous Battle of Marathon in 490 B.C.E. In their view, this

Guided Reading Question

■ CONNECTION

What were the consequences for both sides of the encounter between the Persians and the Greeks?

victory was the product of Greek freedoms because those freedoms had motivated men to fight with extraordinary courage for what they valued so highly. It led to a Western worldview in which Persia represented Asia and despotism, whereas Greece signified Europe and freedom. Thus was born the notion of an East/West divide, which has shaped European and North American thinking about the world into the twenty-first century.

The Greek victory also radicalized Athenian democracy, for it had been men of the poorer classes who had rowed their ships to victory and who were now in a position to insist on full citizenship. The fifty years or so after the Greco-Persian Wars were not only the high point of Athenian democracy but also the Golden Age of Greek culture. During this period, the Parthenon, that marvelous temple to the Greek goddess Athena, was built; Greek theater was born from the work of Aeschylus, Sophocles, and Euripides; and Socrates was beginning his career as a philosopher and an irritant in Athens.

But Athens's Golden Age was also an era of incipient empire. In the Greco-Persian Wars, Athens had led a coalition of more than thirty Greek city-states on the basis of its naval power, but Athenian leadership in the struggle against Persian aggression had spawned an imperialism of its own. After the war, Athenian efforts to solidify Athens's dominant position among the allies led to intense resentment and finally to a bitter civil war (431–404 B.C.E.), with Sparta taking the lead in defending the traditional independence of Greek city-states. In this bloody conflict, known as the Peloponnesian War, Athens was defeated, while the Greeks exhausted themselves and magnified their distrust of one another. Thus the way was open to their eventual takeover by the growing forces of Macedonia, a frontier kingdom on the northern fringes of the Greek world. The glory days of the Greek experiment were over, but the spread of Greek culture was just beginning.

Collision: Alexander and the Hellenistic Era

The Macedonian takeover of Greece, led by its king, Philip II, finally accomplished by 338 B.C.E. what the Greeks themselves had been unable to achieve—the political unification of Greece, but at the cost of much of the prized independence of its various city-states. It also set in motion a second round in the collision of Greece and Persia as Philip's son, Alexander, prepared to lead a massive Greek expedition against the Persian Empire. Such a project appealed to those who sought vengeance for the earlier Persian assault on Greece, but it also served to unify the fractious Greeks in a war against their common enemy.

The story of this ten-year expedition (333–323 B.C.E.), accomplished while Alexander was still in his twenties, has become the stuff of legend (see Map 3.3). Surely it was among the greatest military feats of the ancient world in that it created a Greek empire from Egypt and Anatolia in the west to Afghanistan and India in the east. In the process, the great Persian Empire was thoroughly defeated; its capital, Persepolis (per-SEP-uh-lis), was looted and burned; and Alexander was hailed as

Guided Reading Question

■ CONNECTION
What changes did Alexander's conquests bring in their wake?

Map 3.3   Alexander's Empire and Successor States

Alexander's conquests, though enormous, did not long remain within a single empire, for his generals divided them into three successor states shortly after his death. This was the Hellenistic world within which Greek culture spread.

the "king of Asia." In Egypt, Alexander, then just twenty-four years old, was celebrated as a liberator from Persian domination, was anointed as pharaoh, and was declared by Egyptian priests to be the "son of the gods." Arrian, a later Greek historian, described Alexander in this way:

> His passion was for glory only, and in that he was insatiable. . . . Noble indeed was his power of inspiring his men, of filling them with confidence, and in the moment of danger, of sweeping away their fear by the spectacle of his own fearlessness.[8]

Alexander died in 323 B.C.E., without returning to Greece, and his empire was soon divided into three kingdoms, ruled by leading Macedonian generals.

From the viewpoint of world history, the chief significance of Alexander's amazing conquests lay in the widespread dissemination of Greek culture during what historians call the Hellenistic era (323–30 B.C.E.). Elements of that culture, generated

AP® EXAM TIP

Take good notes on the cultural effects of Hellenism, discussed here and in Chapter 4.

Alexander the Great
This mosaic of Alexander on horseback comes from the Roman city of Pompeii. It depicts the Battle of Issus (333 B.C.E.), in which Greek forces, although considerably outnumbered, defeated the Persian army, led personally by Emperor Darius III. (Museo Archeologico Nazionale, Naples, Italy/De Agostini Picture Library/G. Nimatallah/Bridgeman Images)

in a small and remote Mediterranean peninsula, now penetrated the lands of the First Civilizations—Egypt, Mesopotamia, and India—resulting in one of the great cultural encounters of the ancient world.

The major avenue for the spread of Greek culture lay in the many cities that Alexander and later Hellenistic rulers established throughout the empire. Complete with Greek monuments, sculptures, theaters, markets, councils, and assemblies, these cities attracted many thousands of Greek settlers serving as state officials, soldiers, or traders. Alexandria in Egypt—the largest of these cities, with half a million people—was an enormous cosmopolitan center where Egyptians, Greeks, Jews, Babylonians, Syrians, Persians, and many others rubbed elbows. A harbor with space for 1,200 ships facilitated long-distance commerce. Greek learning flourished thanks to a library of some 700,000 volumes and the Museum, which sponsored scholars and writers of all kinds.

From cities such as these, Greek culture spread. From the Mediterranean to India, Greek became the language of power and elite culture. The Indian monarch Ashoka published some of his decrees in Greek, while an independent Greek state was established in Bactria in what is now northern Afghanistan. The attraction of many young Jews to Greek culture prompted the Pharisees to develop their own school system, as this highly conservative Jewish sect feared for the very survival of Judaism. (See Zooming In: The Kushan Empire, page 128, for Greek influence on this Central Asian kingdom.)

Cities such as Alexandria were very different from the original city-states of Greece, both in their cultural diversity and in the absence of the independence so valued by Athens and Sparta. Now they were part of large conquest states ruled by Greeks: the Ptolemaic (TOL-uh-MAY-ik) empire in Egypt and the Seleucid empire in Persia. These were imperial states, which, in their determination to preserve order, raise taxes, and maintain the authority of the monarch, resembled the much older empires of Mesopotamia, Egypt, Assyria, and Persia. Macedonians and Greeks, representing perhaps 10 percent of the population in these Hellenistic kingdoms, were clearly the elite and sought to keep themselves separate from non-Greeks. In Egypt, different legal systems for Greeks and native Egyptians maintained this separation. An Egyptian agricultural worker complained that because he was an Egyptian, his supervisors despised him and refused to pay him.[9] Periodic rebellions expressed resentment at Greek arrogance, condescension, and exploitation. But the separation between the Greeks and native populations was by no means complete, and a fair amount of cultural interaction and blending occurred. Alexander himself had taken several Persian princesses as his wives and actively encouraged intermarriage between his troops and Asian women. In both Egypt and Mesopotamia, Greek rulers patronized the building of temples to local gods and actively supported their priests. A growing number of native peoples were able to become Greek citizens by obtaining a Greek education, speaking the language, dressing appropriately, and assuming Greek names. In India, Greeks were assimilated into the hierarchy of the caste system as members of the Kshatriya (warrior) caste, while in Bactria a substantial number of Greeks converted to Buddhism, including one of their kings, Menander. A school of Buddhist art that emerged in the early centuries of the Common Era depicted the Buddha in human form for the first time, but in Greek-like garb with a face resembling the god Apollo. (See Working with Evidence, Source 4.2, page 186.) Clearly, not all was conflict between the Greeks and the peoples of the East.

In the long run, much of this Greek cultural influence faded as the Hellenistic kingdoms that had promoted it weakened and vanished by the first century B.C.E. While it lasted, however, it represented a remarkable cultural encounter, born of the collision of two empires and two second-wave civilizations. In the western part of that Hellenistic world, Greek rule was replaced by that of the Romans, whose empire, like Alexander's, also served as a vehicle for the continued spread of Greek culture and ideas.

Comparing Empires: Roman and Chinese

While the adjacent civilizations of the Greeks and the Persians collided, two other empires were taking shape—the Roman Empire on the far western side of Eurasia and China's imperial state on the far eastern end. They flourished at roughly the same time (200 B.C.E.–200 C.E.); they occupied a similar area (about 1.5 million square miles); and they encompassed populations of a similar size (50 to 60 million). They were the giant empires of their time, shaping the lives of close to half of the world's population. Unlike the Greeks and the Persians, the Romans and the Chinese were only dimly aware of each other and had almost no direct contact. Historians, however, have seen them as fascinating variations on an imperial theme and have long explored their similarities and differences.

Rome: From City-State to Empire

The rise of empires is among the perennial questions that historians tackle. Like the Persian Empire, that of the Romans took shape initially on the margins of the civilized world and was an unlikely rags-to-riches story. Rome began as a small and impoverished city-state on the western side of central Italy in the eighth century

AP® EXAM TIP

The AP® exam has included questions about political, social, and/or economic connections between the Roman and Chinese empires in this era.

AP® EXAM TIP

Know the reasons for the rise of empires in the classical era.

AP® EXAM TIP

You should know differences in the features and dates of the Roman Republic and the Roman Empire.

B.C.E. According to legend, the city was so weak that Romans were reduced to kidnapping neighboring women to maintain its population. In a transformation of epic proportions, Rome subsequently became the center of an enormous imperial state that encompassed the Mediterranean basin and included parts of continental Europe, Britain, North Africa, and the Middle East.

Originally ruled by a king, around 509 B.C.E. Roman aristocrats threw off the monarchy and established a republic in which the men of a wealthy class, known as patricians, dominated. Executive authority was exercised by two consuls, who were advised by a patrician assembly, the Senate. Deepening conflict with the poorer classes, called plebeians (plih-BEE-uhns), led to important changes in Roman political life. A written code of law offered plebeians some protection from abuse; a system of public assemblies provided an opportunity for lower classes to shape public policy; and a new office of tribune, who represented plebeians, allowed them to block unfavorable legislation. Romans took great pride in this political system, believing that they enjoyed greater freedom than did many of their more autocratic neighbors. The values of the republic—rule of law, the rights of citizens, the absence of pretension, upright moral behavior, keeping one's word—were later idealized as "the way of the ancestors."

With this political system and these values, the Romans launched their empire-building enterprise, a prolonged process that took more than 500 years (see Map 3.4). It began in the 490s B.C.E. with Roman control over its Latin neighbors in central Italy and over the next several hundred years encompassed most of the Italian peninsula. Between 264 and 146 B.C.E., victory in the Punic Wars with Carthage, a powerful empire with its capital in North Africa, extended Roman control over the western Mediterranean, including Spain, and made Rome a naval power. Subsequent expansion in the eastern Mediterranean brought the ancient civilizations of Greece, Egypt, and Mesopotamia under Roman domination. Rome also expanded into territories in Southern and Western Europe, including present-day France and Britain. By early in the second century C.E., the Roman Empire had reached its maximum extent. Like classical Greece, that empire has been associated with Europe. But in its own time, elites in North Africa and Southwest Asia likewise claimed Roman identity, and the empire's richest provinces were in the east.

No overall design or blueprint drove the building of empire, nor were there any precedents to guide the Romans. What they created was something wholly new—an empire that encompassed the entire Mediterranean basin and beyond. It was a piecemeal process, which the Romans invariably saw as defensive. Each addition of territory created new vulnerabilities, which could be assuaged only by more conquests. For some, the growth of empire represented opportunity. Poor soldiers hoped for land, loot, or salaries that might lift their families out of poverty. The well-to-do or well-connected gained great estates, earned promotions, and sometimes achieved public acclaim and high political office. The wealth of long-established societies in the eastern Mediterranean (Greece and Egypt, for example) beckoned, as did the resources and food supplies of the less developed regions, such

Guided Reading Question

■ CHANGE

How did Rome grow from a single city to the center of a huge empire?

Map 3.4   The Roman Empire

At its height in the second century C.E., the Roman Empire incorporated the entire Mediterranean basin, including the lands of the Carthaginian Empire, the less developed region of Western Europe, the heartland of Greek civilization, and the ancient civilizations of Egypt and Mesopotamia.

AP® EXAM TIP

Knowledge of maps of empires throughout world history is critical. In fact, a clear understanding of every map in this text is essential. Be sure you know how to read the maps and understand the information they convey.

as Western Europe. There was no shortage of motivation for the creation of the Roman Empire.

Although Rome's central location in the Mediterranean basin provided a convenient launching pad for empire, it was the army, "well-trained, well-fed, and well-rewarded," that built the empire.[10] Drawing on the growing population of Italy, that army was often brutal in war. Carthage, for example, was utterly destroyed; the city was razed to the ground, and its inhabitants were either killed or sold into slavery. Nonetheless, Roman authorities could be generous to former enemies. Some were granted Roman citizenship; others were treated as allies and allowed to maintain their local rulers. As the empire grew, so too did political

Queen Boudica
This statue in London commemorates the resistance of the Celtic people of eastern Britain against Roman rule during a revolt in 60–61 C.E., led by Queen Boudica. A later Roman historian lamented that "all this ruin was brought upon the Romans by a woman, a fact which in itself caused them the greatest shame." (Daniel Boulet, photographer)

AP® EXAM TIP

Gender roles—the expectations for how men and women should act and interact in societies—are an important concept in this course.

forces in Rome that favored its continued expansion and were willing to commit the necessary manpower and resources.

Centuries of empire building and the warfare that made it possible had an impact on Roman society and values. That vast process, for example, shaped Roman understandings of gender and the appropriate roles of men and women. Rome was becoming a warrior society in which the masculinity of upper-class male citizens was defined in part by a man's role as a soldier and a property owner. In private life, this translated into absolute control over his wife, children, and slaves, including the theoretical right to kill them without interference from the state. This ability of a free man and a Roman citizen to act decisively in both public and private life lay at the heart of ideal male identity. A Roman woman could participate proudly in this warrior culture by bearing brave sons and inculcating these values in her offspring.

Strangely enough, by the early centuries of the Common Era the wealth of empire, the authority of the imperial state, and the breakdown of older Roman social patterns combined to offer women in the elite classes a less restricted life than they had known in the early centuries of the republic. Upper-class Roman women had never been as secluded in the home as were their Greek counterparts, and now the legal authority of their husbands was curtailed by the intrusion of the state into what had been private life. The head of household, or *pater familias*, lost his earlier power of life and death over his family. Furthermore, such women could now marry without transferring legal control to their husbands and were increasingly able to manage their own finances and take part in the growing commercial economy of the empire. According to one scholar, Roman women of the wealthier classes gained "almost complete liberty in matters of property and marriage."[11] At the other end of the social spectrum, Roman conquests brought many thousands of women as well as men into the empire as slaves, who were often brutally treated and subject to the whims of their masters (see Chapter 5, pages 203–8).

The relentless expansion of empire raised yet another profound question for Rome: could republican government and values survive the acquisition of a huge empire? The wealth of empire enriched a few, enabling them to acquire large estates and many slaves, while pushing growing numbers of free farmers into the cities and poverty. Imperial riches also empowered a small group of military leaders—

Marius, Sulla, Pompey, Julius Caesar—who recruited their troops directly from the ranks of the poor and whose fierce rivalries brought civil war to Rome during the first century B.C.E. Traditionalists lamented the apparent decline of republican values—simplicity, service, free farmers as the backbone of the army, the authority of the Senate—amid the self-seeking ambition of the newly rich and powerful. When the dust settled from the civil war, Rome was clearly changing, for authority was now vested primarily in an emperor, the first of whom was Octavian, later granted the title of Augustus (r. 27 B.C.E.–14 C.E.), which implied a divine status for the ruler. The republic was history; Rome had become an empire and its ruler an emperor.

But it was an empire with an uneasy conscience, for many felt that in acquiring an empire, Rome had betrayed and abandoned its republican origins. Augustus was careful to maintain the forms of the republic—the Senate, consuls, public assemblies—and referred to himself as "first man" rather than "king" or "emperor," even as he accumulated enormous personal power. And in a bow to republican values, he spoke of the empire's conquests as reflecting the "power of the Roman people" rather than of the Roman state. Despite this rhetoric, he was emperor in practice, if not in name, for he was able to exercise sole authority, backed up by his command of a professional army. Later emperors were less reluctant to flaunt their imperial prerogatives.

During the first two centuries C.E., this empire in disguise provided security, grandeur, and relative prosperity for the Mediterranean world. In 155 C.E., Aelius Aristides, one of the empire's Greek subjects from the west coast of Anatolia and himself a Roman citizen, expressed this perspective as he praised the empire to the sky in front of the emperor Antonius:

> Everywhere you have made citizens all those who are the more accomplished, noble and powerful people, even if they retain their native affinities. . . . No envy walks in your empire. . . . There has arisen a single harmonious government which has embraced all men. . . . And the whole inhabited world, as it were attending a national festival, has laid aside . . . the carrying of weapons. . . . Now it is possible for both Greek and barbarian to travel easily wherever he wishes.[12]

This was the *pax Romana*, the Roman peace, the era of imperial Rome's greatest extent and greatest authority.

China: From Warring States to Empire

About the same time, on the other side of Eurasia, another huge imperial state was in the making—China. Here, however, the task was understood differently. It was not a matter of creating something new, as in the case of the Roman Empire, but of restoring something old. As one of the First Civilizations, a Chinese state had emerged as early as 2200 B.C.E. and under the Xia, Shang, and Zhou dynasties had grown progressively larger. By 500 B.C.E., however, this Chinese state was in shambles. Any earlier unity vanished in an "age of warring states," featuring the endless rivalries of seven competing kingdoms.

To many Chinese, this was a wholly unnatural and unacceptable condition, and rulers in various states vied to reunify China. One of them, known to history as Qin Shihuangdi (chihn shee-HUANG-dee) (i.e., Shihuangdi from the state of Qin), succeeded brilliantly. The state of Qin had already developed an effective bureaucracy, subordinated its aristocracy, equipped its army with iron weapons, and enjoyed rapidly rising agricultural output and a growing population. It also had adopted a political philosophy called Legalism, which advocated clear rules and harsh punishments as a means of enforcing the authority of the state. With these resources, Shihuangdi (r. 221–210 B.C.E.) launched a military campaign to reunify China and in just ten years soundly defeated the other warring states. Believing that he had created a universal and eternal empire, he grandly named himself Shihuangdi, which means the "first emperor." Unlike Augustus, he showed little ambivalence about empire. Subsequent conquests extended China's boundaries far to the south into the northern part of Vietnam, to the northeast into Korea, and to the northwest, where the Chinese pushed back the nomadic pastoral people of the steppes. (See Zooming In: Trung Trac, page 124, for an example of resistance to Chinese expansion.) Although the boundaries fluctuated over time, Shihuangdi laid the foundations for a unified Chinese state, which has endured, with periodic interruptions, to the present (see Map 3.5).

Building on earlier precedents, the Chinese process of empire formation was far more compressed than the centuries-long Roman effort, but it was no less dependent on military force and no less brutal. Scholars who opposed Shihuangdi's policies were executed and their books burned. Aristocrats who might oppose his centralizing policies were moved physically to the capital. Hundreds of thousands of laborers were recruited to construct the Great Wall of China, designed to keep out northern "barbarians," and to erect a monumental mausoleum as the emperor's final resting place. More positively, Shihuangdi imposed a uniform system of weights, measures, and currency and standardized the length of axles for carts and the written form of the Chinese language.

As in Rome, the creation of the Chinese empire had domestic repercussions, but they were brief and superficial compared to Rome's transition from republic to empire. The speed and brutality of Shihuangdi's policies ensured that his own Qin dynasty did not last long, and it collapsed unmourned in 206 B.C.E. The Han dynasty that followed (206 B.C.E.–220 C.E.) retained the centralized features of Shihuangdi's creation, although it moderated the harshness of his policies, adopting a milder and moralistic Confucianism in place of Legalism as the governing philosophy of the state. It was Han dynasty rulers who consolidated China's imperial state and established the political patterns that lasted into the twentieth century.

Guided Reading Question

■ COMPARISON
Why was the Chinese empire able to take shape so quickly, while that of the Romans took centuries?

AP® EXAM TIP

You should know political features of the Qin dynasty.

Map 3.5   Classical China
The brief Qin dynasty brought unity to the heartland of Chinese civilization, and the much longer Han dynasty extended its territorial reach south toward Vietnam, east to Korea, and west into Central Asia. To the north lay the military confederacy of the nomadic Xiongnu.

Consolidating the Roman and Chinese Empires

Once established, these two huge imperial systems shared a number of common features. Both, for example, defined themselves in universal terms. The Roman writer Polybius spoke of bringing "almost the entire world" under the control of Rome, while the Chinese state was said to encompass "all under heaven." Both of them invested heavily in public works—roads, bridges, aqueducts, canals, protective walls—all designed to integrate their respective domains militarily and commercially.

Furthermore, Roman and Chinese authorities both invoked supernatural sanctions to support their rule. By the first century C.E., Romans began to regard their deceased emperors as gods and established a religious cult to bolster the authority of living rulers. It was the refusal of early Christians to take part in this cult that provoked their periodic persecution by Roman authorities.

AP® EXAM TIP

The ways emperors built and maintained power in the classical era is an important concept in AP® World History.

Guided Reading Question

■ EXPLANATION
Why were the Roman and Chinese empires able to enjoy long periods of relative stability and prosperity?

Trung Trac: Resisting the Chinese Empire

Empires have long faced resistance from people they conquer and never more fiercely than in Vietnam, which was incorporated into an expanding Chinese empire for over a thousand years (111 B.C.E.–939 C.E.). Among the earliest examples of Vietnamese resistance to this occupation was that led around 40 C.E. by Trung Trac and her younger sister Trung Nhi,

Trung Trac and Trung Nhi.

daughters in an aristocratic, military family. Trung Trac married a prominent local lord, Thi Sach, who was a vocal opponent of offensive Chinese policies—high taxes, even on the right to fish in local rivers; required payoffs to Chinese officials; and the imposition of Chinese culture on the Vietnamese. In response to this opposition, the Chinese governor of the region ordered Thi Sach's execution.

This personal tragedy provoked Trung Trac to take up arms against the Chinese occupiers, and she quickly gained a substantial following among peasants and aristocrats alike. Famously addressing some 30,000 soldiers, while dressed in full military regalia rather than the expected mourning clothes, she declared to the assembled crowd:

> Foremost I will avenge my country.
> Second I will restore the Hung lineage.
> Third I will avenge the death of my husband.
> Lastly I vow that these goals will be accomplished.

Within months, her forces had captured sixty-five towns, and, for two years, they held the Chinese at bay, while Trung Trac and Trung Nhi ruled a briefly independent state as co-queens. Chinese sources referred to Trung Trac as a "ferocious warrior." During their rule, the sisters eliminated the hated tribute taxes imposed by the Chinese and sought to restore the authority of Vietnamese aristocrats. A large military force, said to number some 80,000, counted among its leaders thirty-six female "generals," including the Trung sisters' mother.

Soon, however, Chinese forces overwhelmed the rebellion, and Trung Trac's support faded. Later Vietnamese records explained the failure of the revolt as a consequence of its female leadership. In traditional Vietnamese accounts, the Trung sisters committed suicide, jumping into a nearby river, as did a number of their followers.

Although the revolt failed, it lived on in stories and legends to inspire later Vietnamese resistance to invaders—Chinese, French, Japanese, and American alike. Men were reminded that women had led this rebellion. "What a pity," wrote a thirteenth-century Vietnamese historian, "that for a thousand years after this, the men of our land bowed their heads, folded their arms, and served the northerners [Chinese]."[13] To this day, temples, streets, and neighborhoods bear the name of the Trung sisters, and a yearly celebration in their honor coincides with International Women's Day. Usually depicted riding on war elephants and wielding swords, these two women also represent the more fluid gender roles then available to some Vietnamese women in comparison to the stricter patriarchy prevalent in China.

Question: How might you imagine the reactions to the Trung sisters' revolt from Chinese officials; Vietnamese aristocrats; Vietnamese peasants, both male and female; and later generations of Vietnamese men and women?

photo: CPA Media

In China, a much older tradition had long linked events on Earth with the invisible realm called "Heaven." In this conception, Heaven was neither a place nor a supreme being, but rather an impersonal moral force that regulated the universe. Emperors were called the Son of Heaven and were said to govern by the Mandate of Heaven so long as they ruled morally and with benevolence. Peasant rebellions, "barbarian" invasions, or disastrous floods were viewed as signs that the emperor had ruled badly and had thus lost the Mandate of Heaven. Among the chief duties of the emperor was the performance of various rituals thought to maintain the appropriate relationship between Heaven and Earth. What moral government meant in practice was spelled out in the writings of Confucius and his followers, which became the official ideology of the empire (see Chapter 4).

Both of these second-wave civilizations also absorbed a foreign religious tradition — Christianity in the Roman world and Buddhism in China — although the process unfolded somewhat differently. In the case of Rome, Christianity was born as a small sect in a remote corner of the empire. Aided by the *pax Romana* and Roman roads, the new faith spread slowly for several centuries, particularly among the poor and lower classes. Women were prominent in the leadership of the early Church, as were a number of more well-to-do individuals from urban families. After suffering intermittent persecution, Christianity in the fourth century C.E. obtained state support from emperors who hoped to shore up a tottering empire with a common religion, and thereafter the religion spread quite rapidly.

In the case of China, by contrast, Buddhism came from India, far beyond the Chinese world. It was introduced to China by Central Asian traders and received little support from Han dynasty rulers. In fact, the religion spread only modestly among Chinese until after the Han dynasty collapsed (220 C.E.), when it appealed to people who felt bewildered by the loss of a predictable and stable society. Not until the Sui (sway) dynasty emperor Wendi (r. 581–604 C.E.) reunified China did the new religion gain state support, and then only temporarily. Buddhism thus became one of several alternative cultural traditions in a complex Chinese mix, while Christianity, though divided internally, ultimately became the dominant religious tradition throughout Europe (see Chapters 8 and 10).

The Roman and Chinese empires also had a different relationship to the societies they governed. Rome's beginnings as a small city-state meant that Romans, and even Italians, were always a distinct minority within the empire. The Chinese empire, by contrast, grew out of a much larger cultural heartland, already ethnically Chinese. Furthermore, as the Chinese state expanded, especially to the south, it actively assimilated the non-Chinese, or "barbarian," people. In short, they became Chinese, culturally, linguistically, and through intermarriage in physical appearance as well. Many Chinese in modern times are in fact descended from people who at one point or another were not Chinese at all.

The Roman Empire offered a different kind of assimilation to its subject peoples. Gradually and somewhat reluctantly, the empire granted Roman citizenship to various individuals, families, or whole communities for their service to the empire

AP® EXAM TIP

You must know the significance of China's Mandate of Heaven.

AP® EXAM TIP

Take good notes on the development and spread of religions during the classical era, both here and in Chapter 4.

or in recognition of their adoption of Roman culture. In 212 C.E., Roman citizenship was bestowed on almost all free people of the empire. Citizenship offered clear advantages—the right to hold public office, to serve in the Roman military units known as legions, to wear a toga, and more—but it conveyed a legal status, rather than cultural assimilation, and certainly did not erase other identities, such as being Greek, Egyptian, or a citizen of a particular city.

Various elements of Roman culture—its public buildings, its religious rituals, its Latin language, its style of city life—were attractive, especially in Western Europe, where urban civilization was something new. In the eastern half of the empire, however, things Greek retained tremendous prestige. Many elite Romans in fact regarded Greek culture—its literature, philosophy, and art—as superior to their own and proudly sent their sons to Athens for a Greek education. To some extent, the two blended into a mixed Greco-Roman tradition, which the empire served to disseminate throughout the realm. Other non-Roman cultural traditions—such as the cult of the Persian god Mithra or the compassionate Egyptian goddess Isis, and, most extensively, the Jewish-derived religion of Christianity—also spread throughout the empire. Nothing similar occurred in Han dynasty China, except for Buddhism, which established a modest presence, largely among foreigners. Chinese culture experienced little competition from older, venerated, or foreign traditions. It was widely recognized across much of East Asia—in Japan, Korea, and Vietnam, for example—as the model to which others should conform.

Language served these two empires in important but contrasting ways. Latin, an alphabetic language depicting sounds, gave rise to various distinct languages—Spanish, Portuguese, French, Italian, Romanian—whereas Chinese did not. Chinese characters, which represented words or ideas more than sounds, were not easily transferable to other languages. Written Chinese, however, could be understood by all literate people, no matter which spoken dialect of the language they used. Thus Chinese, more than Latin, served as an instrument of elite assimilation. For all of these reasons, the various peoples of the Roman Empire were able to maintain their separate cultural identities far more than was the case in China.

Politically, both empires established effective centralized control over vast regions and huge populations, but the Chinese, far more than the Romans, developed an elaborate bureaucracy to hold the empire together. The Han emperor Wudi (r. 141–87 B.C.E.) established an imperial academy for training officials for an emerging bureaucracy with a curriculum based on the writings of Confucius. This was the beginning of a civil service system, complete with examinations and selection by merit, which did much to integrate the Chinese empire and lasted into the early twentieth century. Roman administration was a somewhat ramshackle affair, relying more on regional aristocratic elites and the army to provide cohesion. Unlike the Chinese, however, the Romans developed an elaborate body of law, applicable equally to all people of the realm, dealing with matters of justice, property, commerce, and family life. Chinese and Roman political development thus generated

AP® EXAM TIP

You could see an AP® exam question on the functions of China's bureaucracy over time—especially the examination system.

different answers to the question of what made for good government. For those who inherited the Roman tradition, it was good laws, whereas for those in the Chinese tradition, it was good men.

Finally, both Roman and Chinese civilizations had marked effects on the environment in various ways. The Roman poet Horace complained of the noise and smoke of the city and objected to the urban sprawl that extended into the adjacent fertile lands. Roman mining operations, the smelting of metals, its large-scale agriculture, and its growing population—all of this led to extensive deforestation and consequent soil erosion. The shortage of wood in the heartland of the empire led to the relocation of some ceramic workshops to Gaul, where timber was more plentiful. Lead pollution, derived from the smelting of lead ores in open furnaces and from lead water pipes and cooking pots, shows up in the bones of Roman burials and in bones found as far away as Greenland, where studies of the icecap indicate that lead in the atmosphere increased during Roman times. Here is perhaps the earliest example of international atmospheric pollution.

Large-scale Chinese ironworking during the Han dynasty likewise contributed to substantial urban air pollution, while a rapidly growing and dense population practicing intensive agriculture stripped the North China plain of its ancient forest cover, causing sufficient soil erosion to turn the Hwang-ho River its characteristic yellow-brown color. What had been known simply as "the River" now became the Yellow River, which frequently flooded with devastating results and over many centuries dramatically changed course. In addition, as China expanded north and west into the steppe lands of the pastoral peoples, military/agricultural colonies of Chinese farmers turned pasturelands into farmlands, plowing up long-established sod. When the Chinese state subsequently grew weaker or actually collapsed, such farms were abandoned, wind erosion took hold, and deserts emerged.[14]

The Collapse of Empires

Empires rise, and then, with some apparent regularity, they fall, and in doing so, they provide historians with one of their most intriguing questions: what causes the collapse of these once-mighty structures? In China, the Han dynasty empire came to an end in 220 C.E.; the traditional date for the final disintegration of the Roman Empire is 476 C.E., although a process of decline had been under way for several centuries. In the Roman case, however, only the western half of the empire collapsed, while the eastern part, subsequently known as the Byzantine Empire, maintained the tradition of imperial Rome for another thousand years.

Despite these differences, a number of common factors have been associated with the end of these imperial states. At one level, they both simply got too big, too overextended, and too expensive to be sustained by the available resources, and no fundamental technological breakthrough was available to enlarge these resources. Furthermore, the growth of large landowning families with huge estates and political

AP® EXAM TIP

The internal and external reasons for the fall of the classical empires is "must know" information for the AP® exam.

ZOOMING IN

The Kushan Empire

Often lost among the giant second-wave empires of Persia, Macedonia/ Greece, Rome, China, and India is the story of a smaller empire—that of the Kushan people—whose Central Asian state interacted directly or indirectly with all the others. At its height during the first two centuries of the Common Era, the Kushan Empire, according to one recent account, "created stable conditions at the heart of Central Asia, allowing for the great flowering of trans-Eurasian mercantile and cultural exchange that occurred along the Silk Roads."[15]

The Kushans, originally a pastoral nomadic people from an area around Dunhuang at the far western edge of China, had migrated in the early centuries B.C.E. to the region that now makes up northwestern India, Pakistan, Afghanistan, and Tajikistan, where they established a sizable and prosperous empire linked to the Silk Road trading network. It was a remarkably cosmopolitan place, illustrating the mixing and blending of many cultural

A pendant from the Kushan Empire.

traditions. Since parts of this empire had earlier been ruled by Alexander the Great and his Greek successors (see pages 114–17), classical Mediterranean culture was a prominent element of Kushan life. The Kushans used the Greek alphabet to write their official language, which was derived from India. Roman bronze and glassware items have been found in Kushan merchant warehouses, and scholars suspect that Roman gold coins, used to pay for Eastern imports, were melted down and recast as Kushan coins. From the other end of Eurasia, Kushans imported Chinese lacquer goods, and on at least one occasion, Kushan military forces clashed with those of an expanding Han dynasty China. The greatest of the Kushan rulers, Kanishka (r. ca. 127–153 C.E.), styled himself "Great King, King of Kings, Son of God," a title that had both Persian and Chinese precedents.

photo: Victoria & Albert Museum/V&A Images/Art Resource, NY

clout enabled them to avoid paying taxes, turned free peasants into impoverished tenant farmers, and diminished the authority of the central government. In China, such conditions led to a major peasant revolt, known as the Yellow Turban Rebellion, in 184 C.E. (see Chapter 5, pages 197–98).

Rivalry among elite factions created instability in both empires and eroded imperial authority. In China, persistent tension between castrated court officials (eunuchs) loyal to the emperor and Confucian-educated scholar-bureaucrats weakened the state. In the Roman Empire between 235 and 284 C.E., some twenty-six individuals claimed the title of Roman emperor, only one of whom died of natural causes. In addition, epidemic disease ravaged both societies, though more extensively in the Roman world. The population of the Roman Empire declined by 25 percent in the two centuries following 250 C.E., a demographic disaster that meant diminished production, less revenue for the state, and fewer men available for the defense of the empire's long frontiers.

Religiously, the Kushan Empire was a diverse and apparently tolerant place. Hindu devotional cults as well as Buddhism flourished, and evidence of Persian Zoro-astrian religious practice is found on many Kushan coins, which depict the ruler conducting a sacrifice over a fire altar. It was in the Kushan realm that the earliest human representations of the Buddha were sculpted, and often with distinctly Greek features. (See Working with Evidence, Source 4.2, page 186.) Despite these outside influences, Kushan artists recalled their nomadic past as they depicted their rulers in typical steppe nomadic style: on horseback, wearing loose trousers, heavy boots, and knee-length robes.

A Kushan pendant dating to the fourth century C.E., shown opposite, illustrates the cultural blending so characteristic of Kushan life. It features Hariti, originally a fearsome Hindu goddess who abducted and killed children, feeding their flesh to her own offspring. But in an encounter with the Buddha, Hariti repented and was transformed into a compassionate protector of children. Here she is depicted holding in her right hand a lotus blossom, a prominent Buddhist symbol; her left hand holds another lotus flower supporting a flask or cornu-copia overflowing with pomegranates (symbolizing

food and abundance). According to local mythology, the Buddha had offered Hariti pomegranates (often said to resemble human flesh) as a substitute for the children she was devouring.

While the content of this pendant is thoroughly Indian and Buddhist, its representation of Hariti was probably modeled after the Greek goddess Tyche (TEE-chee), also portrayed holding a cornucopia. Furthermore, her short tunic worn with a belt was likewise of Greek or Hellenistic origin. And the border of pearls and stylized flowers that surround the image derives from Persia.

During the time of the Kushan Empire, Central Asia, so often regarded as a backwater in recent centuries, was a place where the political, cultural, and economic influences of all the Eurasian civilizations overlapped and intermingled. For those several centuries, the Kushan Empire was at the center of an interacting world.

Questions: How does the Kushan Empire challenge impressions that second-wave civilizations of Eurasia existed in isolation from one another? Why do you think the Kushan artist who created this pendant chose to weave together so many distinct cultural strands?

Historians have often linked the collapse of empires with environmental factors as well, more often with reference to Rome than to Han dynasty China. Consider-able fluctuations in the climate after about 250 C.E. led to drought in the third century, cold and wet conditions in the fourth, and increased rainfall and cooler temperatures in the fifth, all of which generated substantial soil erosion and declin-ing agricultural productivity. The North African breadbasket of the empire suffered from serious salinization and increasingly desert-like conditions. The extent to which such factors contributed to the collapse of the Roman Empire remains a point of dispute among scholars.

To these mounting internal problems was added a growing threat from nomadic or semi-agricultural peoples occupying the frontier regions of both empires. The Chinese had long developed various ways of dealing with the Xiongnu and other nomadic people to the north—building the Great Wall to keep them out, offering them trading opportunities at border markets, buying them off with lavish gifts,

AP® EXAM TIP

A major theme in AP® World History is the interaction be-tween humans and the environment.

Guided Reading Question

■ CHANGE

What internal and external factors contributed to the collapse of the Roman and Chinese empires?

Meeting of Attila and Pope Leo I
Among the "barbarian" invaders of the Roman Empire, none were more feared than the Huns, led by the infamous Attila. In a celebrated meeting in 452 C.E., Pope Leo I persuaded Attila to spare the city of Rome and to withdraw from Italy. This seventeenth-century Spanish painting records one view of that remarkable meeting. (Mural in church, El Hospital de Los Venerables, Seville, Spain/© Islandstock/Alamy)

contracting marriage alliances with nomadic leaders, and conducting periodic military campaigns against them. But as the Han dynasty weakened in the second and third centuries C.E., such peoples more easily breached the frontier defenses and set up a succession of "barbarian states" in north China. Culturally, however, many of these foreign rulers gradually became Chinese, encouraging intermarriage, adopting Chinese dress, and setting up their courts in Chinese fashion.

A weakening Roman Empire likewise faced serious problems from Germanic-speaking peoples living on its northern frontier. Growing numbers of these people began to enter the empire in the fourth century C.E.—some as mercenaries in Roman armies and others as refugees fleeing the invasions of the ferocious Huns, who were penetrating Europe from Central Asia. Once inside the declining empire, various Germanic groups established their own kingdoms, at first controlling Roman emperors and then displacing them altogether by 476 C.E. Unlike the nomadic groups in China, who largely assimilated Chinese culture, Germanic kingdoms in Europe developed their own ethnic identities—Visigoths, Franks, Anglo-Saxons, and others—even as they drew on Roman law and adopted Roman Christianity. Far more than in China, the fall of the western Roman Empire produced a new culture, blending Latin and Germanic elements, which provided the foundation for the hybrid civilization that would arise in Western Europe.

The collapse of empire meant more than the disappearance of centralized government and endemic conflict. In post-Han China and post-Roman Europe, it also

AP® EXAM TIP

You should know the effects that various invaders had on the decline and fall of classical empires.

meant the decline of urban life, a contracting population, less area under cultivation, diminishing international trade, and vast insecurity for ordinary people. It must have seemed that civilization itself was unraveling.

The most significant difference between the collapse of empire in China and that in the western Roman Empire lay in what happened next. In China, after about 350 years of disunion, disorder, frequent warfare, and political chaos, a Chinese imperial state, similar to that of the Han dynasty, was reassembled under the Sui (589–618 C.E.), Tang (618–907), and Song (960–1279) dynasties. Once again, a single emperor ruled; a bureaucracy selected by examinations governed; and the ideas of Confucius informed the political system. Such a Chinese empire persisted into the early twentieth century, establishing one of the most continuous political traditions of any civilization in world history.

The story line of European history following the end of the western Roman Empire was very different indeed. No large-scale, centralized, imperial authority encompassing all of Western Europe has ever been successfully reestablished there for any length of time. The memory of Roman imperial unity certainly persisted, and many subsequently tried unsuccessfully to re-create it. But most of Western Europe dissolved into highly decentralized political systems involving nobles, knights and vassals, kings with little authority, various city-states in Italy, and small territories ruled by princes, bishops, or the pope. From this point on, Europe would be a civilization without an encompassing imperial state.

From a Chinese point of view, Western Europe's post-Roman history must seem an enormous failure. Why were Europeans unable to reconstruct something of the unity of their classical empire, while the Chinese clearly did? Surely the greater cultural homogeneity of Chinese civilization made that task easier than it was amid the vast ethnic and linguistic diversity of Europe. The absence in the Roman legacy of a strong bureaucratic tradition also contributed to European difficulties, whereas in China the bureaucracy provided some stability even as dynasties came and went. The Chinese also had in Confucianism a largely secular ideology that placed great value on political matters in the here and now. The Roman Catholic Church in Europe, however, was frequently at odds with state authorities, and its "otherworldliness" did little to support the creation of large-scale empires. Finally, Chinese agriculture was much more productive than that of Europe, and for a long time its metallurgy was more advanced.[16] These conditions gave Chinese state builders more resources to work with than were available to their European counterparts.

Intermittent Empire: The Case of India

Among the second-wave civilizations of Eurasia, empire loomed large in Persian, Mediterranean, and Chinese history, but it played a rather less prominent role in Indian history. In the Indus River valley flourished the largest of the First Civilizations, embodied in exquisitely planned cities such as Harappa but with little evidence of any central political authority (see Chapter 2). The demise of this early civilization by 1500 B.C.E. was followed over the next thousand years by the creation of a new civilization based farther east, along the Ganges River on India's northern plain. That process has occasioned considerable debate, which has focused on the role of the Aryans, a pastoral Indo-European people long thought to have invaded and destroyed the Indus Valley civilization and then created the new one along the Ganges. More recent research questions this interpretation. Did the Aryans invade suddenly, or did they migrate slowly into the Indus River valley? Were they already there as a part of the Indus Valley population? Was the new civilization largely the work of Aryans, or did it evolve gradually from Indus Valley culture? Scholars have yet to reach agreement on any of these questions.[17]

However it occurred, by 600 B.C.E. what would become the second-wave civilization of South Asia had begun to take shape across northern India. Politically, that civilization emerged as a fragmented collection of towns and cities, some small republics governed by public assemblies, and a number of regional states ruled by kings. An astonishing range of ethnic, cultural, and linguistic diversity also characterized this civilization, as an endless variety of peoples migrated into India from Central Asia across the mountain passes in the northwest. These features of Indian civilization—political fragmentation and vast cultural diversity—have informed much of South Asian history throughout many centuries, offering a sharp contrast to the pattern of development in China. What gave Indian civilization a recognizable identity and character was neither an imperial tradition nor ethno-linguistic commonality, but rather a distinctive religious tradition, known later to outsiders as Hinduism, and a unique social organization, the caste system. These features of Indian life are explored further in Chapters 4 and 5.

Nonetheless, empires and emperors were not entirely unknown in India's long history. Northwestern India had been briefly ruled by the Persian Empire and then conquered by Alexander the Great. These Persian and Greek influences helped stimulate the first and largest of India's short experiments with a large-scale political system, the Mauryan Empire (326–184 B.C.E.), which encompassed all but the southern tip of the subcontinent (see Map 3.6).

The Mauryan Empire was an impressive political structure, equivalent to the Persian, Chinese, and Roman empires, though not nearly as long-lasting. With a population of perhaps 50 million, the Mauryan Empire boasted a large military force, reported to include 600,000 infantry soldiers, 30,000 cavalry, 8,000 chariots, and 9,000 elephants. A civilian bureaucracy featured various ministries and a large contingent of spies to provide the rulers with local information. A famous treatise called the *Arthashastra* (*The Science of Worldly Wealth*) articulated a pragmatic, even amoral, political philosophy for Mauryan rulers. It was, according to one scholar, a book that showed "how the political world does work and not very often stating how it ought to work, a book that frequently discloses to a king what calculating

Guided Reading Question

■ COMPARISON
Why were centralized empires so much less prominent in India than in China?

AP® EXAM TIP

Be prepared to compare the features of classical empires, like those of India, Rome, and China in this era.

and sometimes brutal measures he must carry out to preserve the state and the common good."[18] The state also operated many industries—spinning, weaving, mining, shipbuilding, and armaments. This complex apparatus was financed by taxes on trade, on herds of animals, and especially on land, from which the monarch claimed a quarter or more of the crop.

Mauryan India is perhaps best known for one of its emperors, Ashoka (r. 268–232 B.C.E.), who left a record of his activities and his thinking in a series of edicts carved on rocks and pillars throughout the kingdom. Ashoka's conversion to Buddhism and his moralistic approach to governance gave his reign a different tone than that of China's Shihuangdi or Greece's Alexander the Great, who, according to legend, wept because he had no more worlds to conquer. Ashoka's legacy to modern India has been that of an enlightened ruler, who sought to govern in accord with the religious values and moral teachings of Hinduism and Buddhism.

Despite their good intentions, these policies did not long preserve the empire, which broke apart soon after

Map 3.6   **Empire in South Asia**
Large-scale empires in the Indian subcontinent were less frequent and less enduring than those in China. Two of the largest efforts were those of the Mauryan and Gupta dynasties.

Ashoka's death. About 600 years later, a second brief imperial experiment, known as the Gupta Empire (320–550 C.E.), took shape. Faxian, a Chinese Buddhist traveler in India at the time, noted a generally peaceful, tolerant, and prosperous land, commenting that the ruler "governs without decapitation or corporal punishment." Free hospitals, he reported, were available to "the destitute, crippled and diseased," but he also noticed "untouchables" carrying bells to warn upper-caste people of their polluting presence.[19] Culturally, the Gupta era witnessed a flourishing of art, literature, temple building, science, mathematics, and medicine, much of it patronized by rulers. Indian trade with China also thrived, and elements of Buddhist and Hindu culture took root in Southeast Asia (see Chapter 7). Indian commerce reached as far as the Roman world. A Germanic leader named Alaric laid siege to Rome in 410 C.E., while demanding 3,000 pounds of Indian pepper to spare the city.

AP® EXAM TIP

On the AP® exam, the Mauryan and Gupta empires are often combined.

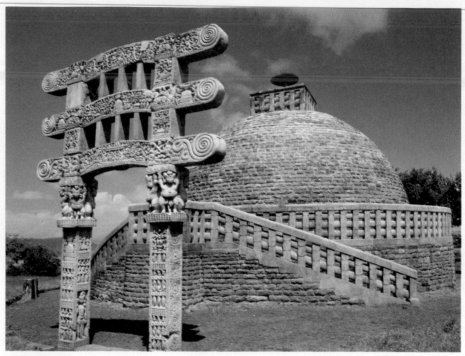

The Great Stupa
The Great Stupa of Sanchi, the oldest stone building in India, was commissioned by Ashoka in the third century B.C.E. to house precious relics of the Buddha. (© Luca Tettoni/Bridgeman Images)

Thus India's political history resembled that of Western Europe after the collapse of the Roman Empire far more than that of China or Persia. Neither imperial nor regional states commanded the kind of loyalty or exercised the degree of influence that they did in other second-wave civilizations. India's unparalleled cultural diversity surely was one reason, as was the frequency of invasions from Central Asia, which repeatedly smashed emerging states that might have provided the nucleus for an all-India empire. Finally, India's social structure, embodied in a caste system linked to occupational groups, made for intensely local loyalties at the expense of wider identities (see Chapter 5).

Nonetheless, a frequently vibrant economy fostered a lively internal commerce and made India the focal point of an extensive network of trade in the Indian Ocean basin. In particular, its cotton textile industry long supplied cloth throughout the Afro-Eurasian world. Strong guilds of merchants and artisans provided political leadership in major towns and cities, and their wealth supported lavish temples, public buildings, and religious festivals. Great creativity in religious matters generated Hindu and Buddhist traditions that later penetrated much of Asia. Indian mathematics and science, especially astronomy, were also impressive; Indian

AP® EXAM TIP

Take notes on the Indian Ocean trade network, both here and in Chapter 7.

scientists plotted the movements of stars and planets and recognized quite early that the earth was round. Clearly, the absence of consistent imperial unity did not prevent the evolution of a lasting civilization.

Enduring Legacies of Second-Wave Empires

The second-wave empires discussed in this chapter have long ago passed into history, but their descendants have kept them alive in memory, for they have proved useful, even in the twentieth and early twenty-first centuries. Those empires have provided legitimacy for contemporary states, inspiration for new imperial ventures, and abundant warnings and cautions for those seeking to criticize more recent empires. For example, in bringing communism to China in the twentieth century, the Chinese leader Mao Zedong compared himself to Shihuangdi, the unifier of China and the brutal founder of its Qin dynasty. Reflecting on his campaign against intellectuals in general and Confucianism in particular, Mao declared to a Communist Party conference: "Emperor Qin Shihuang was not that outstanding. He only buried alive 460 Confucian scholars. We buried 460 thousand Confucian scholars. . . . To the charge of being like Emperor Qin, of being a dictator, we plead guilty."[20]

In contrast, modern-day Indians, who have sought to present their country as a model of cultural tolerance and nonviolence, have been quick to link themselves to Ashoka and his policies of inclusiveness. When the country became independent from British colonial rule in 1947, India soon placed an image of Ashoka's Pillar on the new nation's currency.

In the West, it has been the Roman Empire that has provided a template for thinking about political life. Many in Great Britain celebrated their own global empire as a modern version of the Roman Empire. If the British had been "civilized" by Roman rule, then surely Africans and Asians would benefit from falling under the control of the "superior" British. Likewise, to the Italian fascist dictator Benito Mussolini, his country's territorial expansion during the 1930s and World War II represented the creation of a new Roman Empire. Most recently, the United States' dominant role in the world has prompted the question, are the Americans the new Romans?

Historians frequently cringe as politicians and students use (and perhaps misuse) historical analogies to make their case for particular points of view in the present. But we have little else to go on except history in making our way through the complexities of contemporary life, and historians themselves seldom agree on the "lessons" of the past. Lively debate about the continuing relevance of these ancient empires shows that although the past may be gone, it surely is not dead.

AP® EXAM TIP

Study this essay about the long-term effects of the classical empires for insights into writing comparison essays that contain specific examples.

Chapter Review

What's the Significance?

Persian Empire, 100

Athenian democracy, 112

Greco-Persian Wars, 113

Alexander the Great, 114

Hellenistic era, 115

Augustus, 121

pax Romana, 121

Qin Shihuangdi, 122

Han dynasty, 122

Trung Trac, 124

Kushan Empire, 128

Mauryan Empire, 132

Ashoka, 133

Big Picture Questions

1. What common features can you identify in the empires described in this chapter? In what ways did they differ from one another? What accounts for those differences?

2. Are you more impressed with the "greatness" of empires or with their destructive and oppressive features? Why?

3. Do you think that these second-wave empires hold "lessons" for the present, or are contemporary circumstances sufficiently unique as to render the distant past irrelevant?

4. **Looking Back:** How do these empires of the second-wave civilizations differ from the political systems of the First Civilizations?

Next Steps: For Further Study

Jane Burbank and Frederick Cooper, *Empires in World History* (2010). A fascinating account by two major scholars of the imperial theme across the world. Chapter 2 compares the Roman and Chinese empires.

Arthur Cotterell, *The First Emperor of China* (1988). A biography of Shihuangdi.

Christopher Kelley, *The Roman Empire: A Very Short Introduction* (2006). A brief, up-to-date, and accessible account of the Roman achievement.

Cullen Murphy, *Are We Rome? The Fall of an Empire and the Fate of America* (2007). A reflection on the usefulness and the dangers of comparing the Roman Empire to the present-day United States.

Sarah Pomeroy et al., *Ancient Greece* (1999). A highly readable survey of Greek history by a team of distinguished scholars.

Romila Thapar, *Ashoka and the Decline of the Mauryas* (1961). A classic study of India's early empire builder.

Illustrated History of the Roman Empire, http://www.roman-empire.net. An interactive Web site with maps, pictures, and much information about the Roman Empire.

The Story of Han Dynasty, episode 1, http://www.youtube.com/watch?v=9U45tvzxP74. The first episode of a Chinese TV series dramatizing the founding of the Han dynasty, with English subtitles.

WORKING WITH EVIDENCE

Perceptions of Outsiders in the Ancient World

The peoples of ancient Eurasia did not live in splendid isolation from one another. Nor did they inhabit the kind of deeply interconnected and globalized world that the past century has created. But through war, commerce, the migration of peoples, the spread of religions, and sheer geographic proximity, some of those peoples became sharply aware of one another.

Thus the Greeks went to war with Persia, and a few of them visited or lived in Egypt. Romans derived their much-beloved pepper from India and some silk from China, while facing those they regarded as "barbarians" in the European lands to the north of their imperial boundaries. For many centuries, the Chinese too had to deal with their own "barbarians" beyond the Great Wall, even as Chinese Buddhist pilgrims sought out the sources of their faith in India. These are but a few of the cross-cultural encounters that helped to shape histories of ancient peoples.

Such encounters with strangers have long been an important motor of change in human history, as foreign ideas, diseases, goods, technologies, and military challenges required adjustment in established ways of living. Here, however, we are more interested in the perceptions or understandings of outsiders that arose from these interactions, mental images of life beyond the familiar confines of one's own culture. How do we understand those who are "other" than ourselves? What distortions arise as we ponder those outside our circle? How can the "other" provide opportunities to question or critique one's own society? The documents that follow provide three examples of this process from the ancient world.

Source 3.1

A Greek Historian on Persia and Egypt

Born to a wealthy Greek family in Asia Minor, Herodotus (ca. 485–425 B.C.E.) came of age when the wars between the Greeks and Persians were still recent memories. He devoted much of his life to recording the history of that great conflict in a series of books known as *The Histories*. In doing so, he pretty much invented for the Western world the craft of history as a systematic and connected narrative based on research. As a man of means, he was able to travel widely in the Persian Empire, Egypt, Syria, Babylon, Sicily, and Italy, making notes of what he saw and collecting stories, myths, and oral recollections along the way. The selection that follows contains some of his personal impressions of Persia and Egypt.

■ What cultural differences does Herodotus notice between Greek ways of living and those of Persia and Egypt?

■ What posture does Herodotus take toward these differences? He does refer to Persians as "barbarians," but at the time that term may have meant simply "non-Greek," without the implication of "savage" or "uncivilized" that it later acquired. Does he express a critical view of the Persians and Egyptians or a more positive understanding?

■ What parts of these accounts might be helpful to historians seeking to describe life in ancient Persia or Egypt? What might a historian learn about Greek culture itself from these descriptions?

HERODOTUS

The Histories

Mid-Fifth Century B.C.E.

On Persians

The customs that I know the Persians follow are these. They have no images of the gods and no temples or altars; they consider the use of them a sign of foolishness. This comes, I think, from their not believing the gods to have the same nature as human beings, as the Greeks imagine. The Persians' practice is to climb to the tops of the highest mountains to offer sacrifices to Zeus, the Greek name for the chief god of the universe. The Persians use this god's name to refer to the whole extent of the sky. They also sacrifice to the sun and moon, to the earth, to fire, to water, and to the winds. . . .

The Persians offer sacrifice to these gods in the following way: They do not construct an altar, light a fire, or pour a libation, and there is no flute music, no wearing of garlands, and no consecrated barley cake. The person who wishes to sacrifice brings the victim to a spot of ground that is pure from ritual pollution and there calls upon the name of the god for whom the sacrifice is meant. It is usual to have one's turban encircled with a wreath, most commonly of myrtle. The sacrificer is not allowed to pray for blessings on himself alone, but he prays for the welfare of the king and of the whole Persian people, among whom he is necessarily included. He cuts the [animal] victim in pieces, and having boiled the meat, he lays it out on the softest grass that he can find, clover in particular. When everything is ready, one of the mages [priests] comes forward and chants a hymn, which they say describes the origins of the gods. . . . After a short time, the sacrificer carries the meat of the victim away with him to use as he likes.

Of all the days in the year, the one they celebrate the most is their birthday. It is customary to serve much more food on that day than usual. The richer Persians have an ox, a horse, a camel, and an ass roasted whole for the meal; poorer people cook smaller kinds of cattle. They eat relatively few main courses but many extra courses, which they serve a few dishes at a time. For this reason, the Persians say that the Greeks leave a meal hungry because they have nothing worth mentioning served to them as an extra after the meats and that if the Greeks did have extra courses served, they would never stop eating. The Persians love wine and drink large amounts of it. . . .

When they meet another person in the street, you can tell if the people meeting are of equal status by the following indication: If they are, instead of speaking, they kiss each other on the lips. In the case where one is a little inferior to the other, the kiss is given on the cheek. Where the difference of rank is great, the inferior lies down on the ground in front of the superior. . . . The farther away other peoples live, the less the Persians respect them. The reason is that they regard themselves as very greatly superior in all respects to the rest of humanity, believing that other peoples' excellence is directly proportional to how close they live to Persia. . . .

No one so readily adopts foreign customs as the Persians. For this reason, they wear clothing like that of the Medes, considering it superior to their own. In war, they wear Egyptian armor to protect their chests. As soon as they hear of any luxury from any country, they instantly make it their own. In particular, they learned from the Greeks to have sex with adolescent boys. Each man has several wives and an even greater number of concubines.

In terms of manliness, manly courage on the battlefield is the greatest proof, with fathering many sons the second greatest. . . . They carefully educate their sons from the age of five to the age of twenty in only three subjects: riding horses, shooting arrows, and speaking the truth. Until boys are five, they are not allowed to come into the sight of their fathers, but instead spend their time with the women. They do this so that if the child dies young, the father will not be saddened at losing him.

I praise this custom and the following one too. The king does not put anyone to death for a single instance of wrong-doing, and no Persian inflicts an extreme penalty on a slave for a single instance of wrong-doing.

I can say all these things about the Persians with complete certainty, relying on my own personal knowledge.

On Egyptians

Concerning Egypt itself I am going to say a great deal because there is no country that possesses so many amazing things or has such a large number of buildings and monuments that defy description. Not only is the climate different from that of the rest of the world and the rivers unlike any other rivers, but the people also, in the majority of their ways and customs, exactly reverse what the rest of humanity usually does. The women there participate in the markets and in trade, while the men sit at home weaving on a loom. And while the rest of the world works the woof up the warp while weaving, the Egyptians work it down. The women also carry loads on their shoulders, while the men carry them on their heads. They eat their food out-of-doors in the streets, but they withdraw into their houses to go to the bathroom, explaining that what is shameful but necessary should be done in private, but that which has nothing shameful about it should be done openly. A woman cannot serve as a priest, either for a god or a goddess, but men are priests for both. Sons are not required to support their parents unless they choose to do so, but daughters must, whether they want to or not.

In other countries, the priests have long hair, but in Egypt their heads are shaved. In other lands, it is customary for close relatives while mourning their dead to cut their hair short. The Egyptians, who shave their hair the rest of the time, let their beards and the hair on their heads grow long when a relative dies. All other people live their lives separate from animals, but the Egyptians always have animals living with them. Others make barley and wheat their food; it is a disgrace to do so in Egypt, where the grain they live on is spelt, which some call *zea* [a distinct form of wheat, sometimes known as emmer]. They knead dough with their feet, but they mix clay, and even pick up dung, with their hands. They are the only people in the world, except for those who learned it from them, to use circumcision. . . . When they write or do math, they move their hand from right to left, instead of writing from left to right, like the Greeks. They insist that their method is "right-handed" and therefore dexterous, but that the Greeks' method is "left-handed" and awkward. They have two quite different kinds of writing, one of which is called sacred, the other "of the people."

They are excessively religious, far beyond any other peoples. . . . They drink out of bronze cups,

which they clean every day. They wear linen clothes, which they are especially careful to have always freshly washed. They practice circumcision for the sake of cleanliness, considering it better to be clean than attractive.

Source: Herodotus, *The Histories*, 1:131–37, 140; 2:35–37, in Thomas R. Martin, ed., *Herodotus and Sima Qian: The First Great Historians of Greece and China* (Boston: Bedford/St. Martin's, 2010), 46–51.

Source 3.2
A Roman Historian on the Germans

Occupying much of Central Europe north of the Roman Empire, ancient Germanic-speaking peoples were never a single "nation" but rather a collection of tribes, clans, and chiefdoms. They were regarded by the Romans as barbarians, though admired and feared for their military skills. These Germanic peoples were famously described by Tacitus (56–117 C.E.), a Roman official and well-known historian. Tacitus himself had never visited the lands of the people he describes; rather, he relied on earlier written documents and interviews with merchants and soldiers who had traveled and lived in the region. Unlike Herodotus, he wrote about people who lived without the states and cities characteristic of civilizations.

■ What can we learn from Tacitus's account about the economy, politics, society, and culture of the Germanic peoples of the first century C.E.?

■ Which statements of Tacitus might you regard as reliable, and which are more suspect? Why?

■ Why did Tacitus regard Germanic peoples as distinctly inferior to Romans? How might he have responded to the idea that these people would play a major role in the collapse of the Roman Empire several centuries later?

■ Modern scholars have argued that Tacitus used the Germanic peoples to criticize aspects of his own Roman culture. What evidence might support this point of view?

■ What differences might you notice between Herodotus's description of neighboring civilizations and Tacitus's discussion of an agricultural village society?

TACITUS

Germania

First Century C.E.

The Germans themselves I should regard as aboriginal, and not mixed at all with other races through immigration or intercourse. . . . [W]ho would leave Asia, or Africa, or Italy for Germany, with its wild country, its inclement skies, its sullen manners and aspect, unless indeed it were his home? In their ancient songs, their only way of remembering or recording the past, they celebrate an earthborn god, Tuisco, and his son Mannus, as the origin of their race, as their founders. . . .

The tribes of Germany are free from all taint of intermarriages with foreign nations, and they appear as a distinct, unmixed race, like none but themselves. Hence, too, the same physical peculiarities throughout so vast a population. All have fierce blue eyes, red hair, huge frames, fit only for a sudden exertion. They are less able to bear laborious work. Heat and thirst they cannot in the least endure; to cold and hunger their climate and their soil inure them. . . .

They choose their kings by birth, their generals by merit. These kings have not unlimited or arbitrary power, and the generals do more by example than by authority. . . . But to reprimand, to imprison, even to flog, is permitted to the priests alone, and that not as a punishment, or at the general's bidding, but, as it were, by the mandate of the god whom they believe to inspire the warrior. . . . And what most stimulates their courage is that their squadrons or battalions, instead of being formed by chance or by a fortuitous gathering, are composed of families and clans. Close by them, too, are those dearest to them, so that they hear the shrieks of women, the cries of infants. . . .

Tradition says that armies already wavering and giving way have been rallied by women who, with earnest entreaties and bosoms laid bare, have vividly represented the horrors of captivity, which the Germans fear with such extreme dread on behalf of their women. . . . They even believe that the female sex has a certain sanctity and prescience, and they do not despise their counsels, or make light of their answers. . . .

Mercury is the deity whom they chiefly worship, and on certain days they deem it right to sacrifice to him even with human victims. . . .

Augury and divination by lot no people practice more diligently. . . . In public questions the priest of the particular state, in private the father of the family, invokes the gods, and, with his eyes toward heaven, takes up each piece [of a small tree branch] three times, and finds in them a meaning according to the mark previously impressed on them. . . .

When they go into battle, it is a disgrace for the chief to be surpassed in valor, a disgrace for his followers not to equal the valor of the chief. And it is an infamy and a reproach for life to have survived the chief, and return from the field. To defend, to protect him, to ascribe one's own brave deeds to his renown, is the height of loyalty. The chief fights for victory; his vassals fight for their chief. . . . Feasts and entertainments, which though inelegant, are plentifully furnished, are their only pay. The means of this bounty come from war or rapine. Nor are they as easily persuaded to plough the earth and to wait for the year's produce as to challenge an enemy and earn the honor of wounds. Nay, they actually think it tame and stupid to acquire by the sweat of toil what they might win by their blood.

Whenever they are not fighting, they pass much of their time in hunting, and still more in idleness, giving themselves up to sleep and to feasting, the bravest and the most warlike doing nothing, and surrendering the management of the household of the home, and of the land, to the women, the old men, and all the weakest members of the family. . . . It is the custom of the states to bestow by voluntary and individual contribution on the chief a present of cattle or of grain, which, while accepted as a compliment, supplies their wants. They are particularly delighted by gifts from neighboring tribes . . . such as choice steeds, heavy armor, trappings, and neckchains. We have now taught them to accept money also.

It is well known that the nations of Germany have no cities, and that they do not even tolerate closely contiguous dwellings. They live scattered and apart, just as a spring, a meadow, or a wood has attracted them. Their villages they do not arrange in our fashion, . . . but every person surrounds his dwelling with an open space, either as a precaution against the disasters of fire, or because they do not know how to build. No use is made by them of stone or tile; they employ timber for all purposes, rude masses without ornament or attractiveness. . . .

They all wrap themselves in a cloak which is fastened with a clasp, or, if this is not forthcoming, with a thorn, leaving the rest of their persons bare. . . . They also wear the skins of wild beasts. . . .

Their marriage code, however, is strict, and indeed no part of their manners is more praiseworthy. Almost alone among barbarians they are content with one wife, except a very few among them. . . . Lest the woman should think herself to stand apart from aspirations after noble deeds and from the perils of war, she is reminded by the ceremony which inaugurates marriage that she is her husband's partner in toil and danger, destined to suffer and to dare with him alike both in peace and in war. . . .

Very rare for so numerous a population is adultery, the punishment of which is prompt, and in the husband's power. Having cut off the hair of the adulteress and stripped her naked, he expels her from the house in the presence of her kinfolk, and then flogs her through the whole village. The loss of chastity meets with no indulgence; neither beauty, youth, nor wealth will procure the culprit a husband.

No one in Germany laughs at vice, nor do they call it the fashion to corrupt and to be corrupted. . . . To limit the number of their children or to destroy any of their subsequent offspring is accounted infamous, and good habits are here more effectual than good laws elsewhere. . . .

It is the duty among them to adopt the feuds as well as the friendships of a father or a kinsman. These feuds are not implacable; even homicide is expiated by the payment of a certain number of cattle and of sheep, and the satisfaction is accepted by the entire family, greatly to the advantage of the state, since feuds are dangerous in proportion to a people's freedom. . . .

[S]laves are not employed after our manner with distinct domestic duties assigned to them, but each one has the management of a house and home of his own. The master requires from the slave a certain quantity of grain, of cattle, and of clothing, as he would from a tenant, and this is the limit of subjection. All other household functions are discharged by the wife and children. . . .

Of lending money on interest and increasing it by compound interest they know nothing—a more effectual safeguard than if it were prohibited.

Land proportioned to the number of inhabitants is occupied by the whole community in turn, and afterward divided among them according to rank. A wide expanse of plains makes the partition easy. They till fresh fields every year, and they have still more land than enough; . . . corn [wheat] is the only produce required from the earth.

Source: Alfred John Church and William Jackson Brodribb, *The Agricola and Germania of Tacitus* (London: Macmillan, 1877), 87ff.

Source 3.3
A Chinese Historian on the Xiongnu

During the time of the Han dynasty, the Chinese historian and high official Sima Qian (ca. 145–86 B.C.E.), like his Roman counterpart Tacitus, had occasion to observe and describe neighboring "barbarian" peoples and their history.

In Sima Qian's case, those people were the Xiongnu, pastoral nomads living to the north of China's Great Wall. China's fluctuating relationship with these peoples, involving war, trade, exchange of ambassadors, and periodic treaties, are described more fully in Chapter 8 (see pages 334–35). While the Chinese generally felt enormously superior to such "uncivilized" people, they were compelled on occasion to accommodate the military prowess of the Xiongnu. The following excerpts from Sima Qian's enormous history of ancient China illustrate his understanding of these people, who long represented a mirror through which the Chinese defined their image of themselves.

■ Based on this document and what you know about Chinese life, what aspects of Xiongnu culture would likely appear most different or distasteful to Sima Qian?

■ What purpose does the story about Maodun serve in this account?

■ What can you infer about the relationship between China and the Xiongnu from the letter of Emperor Wen? How do you imagine he and Sima Qian felt about that letter?

SIMA QIAN
Records of the Grand Historian
ca. 100 B.C.E.

The ancestor of the Xiongnu descended from the ruler of the Xia dynasty, whose name was Qun Wei. From before the time of Emperors [of the third millennium B.C.E.], there have been barbarians . . . living in northern uncivilized areas and wandering around herding animals. They herd mainly horses, cattle, and sheep, but also some unusual animals, such as camels, donkeys, mules, and wild horses. . . . They move around looking for water and pasture and have no walled settlements or permanent housing. They do not farm, but they do divide their land into separate holdings under different leaders. They have no writing, and all contracts are verbal. When their children can ride a sheep, they begin to use bows and arrows to shoot birds and rodents. When they are older, they shoot foxes and rabbits for food. In this way, all the young men are easily able to become archers and serve as cavalry. It is their custom when times are easy to graze their animals and hunt with the bow

for their living, but when hard times come, they take up weapons to plunder and raid. This is their innate nature. Their long-range weapons are bows and arrows; they use swords and spears in close combat. When they have the advantage in battle, they advance, but if not, they retreat, since there is no shame in running away. They are only concerned with self-interest, knowing nothing of proper behavior or justice.

Everyone, including the chiefs, eats the meat of their domesticated animals and wears clothing of hides and coats of fur. The men who are in their prime eat the fattiest and best food, while the elderly eat what is left over, since the Xiongnu treasure the strong and healthy but place little value on the weak and old. When his father dies, a son marries his stepmother, and when brothers die, the surviving brothers marry their widows. They have personal names but no family names or additional names. . . .

[*Then Sima Qian relates a story about how Maodun became the Xiongnu ruler in 209 B.C.E.*]

Maodun had arrows made that whistled in flight and trained his men to shoot their bows as they were riding. He ordered, "He who does not shoot where my whistling arrow hits will be executed!" He then went out hunting birds and animals, and if any of his men failed to shoot at what he shot at with his whistling arrow, he immediately beheaded them. Next, he shot a whistling arrow at his own favorite horse. Some of his men hesitated, not daring to shoot the horse. Maodun beheaded them. A little later, he used a whistling arrow to shoot at his favorite wife. Again, some of his men, perhaps because they were afraid, did not dare to shoot. Once more, Maodun beheaded them. Later, he went hunting with his men and shot his father's best horse. All his men shot it, too. Then Maodun knew that he could rely on his troops. Accompanying Touman [Maodun's father] on a hunting trip, he shot a whistling arrow at his father. All his followers shot where the whistling arrow struck and killed the chief. Next, Maodun murdered his stepmother, his younger brother, and all the senior officers who refused to follow his commands. So Maodun made himself the chief [in 209 B.C.E.].

At the start of the year, their leaders hold a small gathering at the chief's location. By the fifth month, a large meeting takes place at Longcheng, during which they offer sacrifices to their ancestors Heaven and Earth, and the gods and spirits. In the fall, when the horses are fat, they hold another large meeting in the Dai forest. There they count up the number of persons and animals. According to their law, anyone who pulls out his sword one foot from its scabbard receives the death penalty, while those convicted of theft have their property confiscated. They punish minor crimes by whipping and major ones by execution. Nobody is held in confinement for more than ten days, and no more than a handful of men are in jail in the entire nation. At dawn the chief rises to worship the sun as it rises, and at night he does the same to the moon. . . . When a ruler dies, his favorite ministers and concubines must follow him in death,

and they often number in the hundreds or even thousands. . . .

Whenever they start some action, they track the stars and the moon. They launch attacks at the full moon and pull back their army when the moon wanes. Following a battle, they award a jug of wine to those who have cut off the heads of enemies, and they are allowed to keep the plunder that they have seized. They make slaves of any prisoners of war. Therefore, when they make war, each warrior works for his own profit. They are very skilled at using decoy soldiers to trick opponents to their destruction. As soon as they see the enemy, they go after their booty like a flock of birds hungry for prey, but when they are defeated they disperse and evaporate. . . . Anyone who brings back a fallen comrade's body from the battlefield is given all the dead man's property. . . .

[*In describing the fluctuating relationship between the Chinese and the Xiongnu, Sima Qian quotes a letter written from the Chinese emperor Wen in 162 B.C.E. to the Xiongnu.*]

"The emperor respectfully asks about the health of the chief of the Xiongnu. Your ambassadors . . . have brought us two horses. We accept them with respect.

In accordance with what the previous emperor decreed the chief of the Xiongnu was to command the region north of the Great Wall where men shoot arrows from their bows, while we were to rule the region south of the wall, where the people live in houses and wear hats and sashes. Under this arrangement, the multitudes of inhabitants of these areas would get their food and clothing by farming, weaving, or hunting, fathers and sons would live side by side, rulers and officials would both be safe, and no one would act violently or rebel. We have heard, however, that a number of evil and deluded men, whose greed for wealth has overcome them, have forsaken justice and broken our peace treaty, paying no heed to what will happen to the multitudes of inhabitants and destroying the harmony that has been in place between the rulers of our two lands.

This, however, is now past history. You said in your [earlier] letter to me that, since our two nations have been brought together again in peace and our two rulers are again in agreement, you want to rest your army and let your horses graze, so that there may be prosperity and happiness for generation upon generation, and so that we can begin again to exist peacefully and harmoniously. We enthusiastically agree with what you said. The sagely wise man, it is said, renews himself every day, reforming and starting over again so that the elderly can rest and the young can mature, with each one keeping his life secure and living out the span of time that Heaven bestows on him. As long as we and the chief of the Xiongnu join together to walk this path, obeying the will of Heaven and having mercy on the people, granting the benefits of peace to generations without end, then no one in the entire world will fail to benefit. Our two great nations, the Han and the Xiongnu, exist next to one another. Since the Xiongnu live in the north, where the country is cold and the severe frosts arrive early in the year, we have ordered our imperial officials to send annually to the chief of the Xiongnu a specified amount of grain, yeast, gold, silk cloth, thread, fiber stuffing for clothing, and other items.

The world currently is experiencing a secure peace, and our peoples are undisturbed. We and the chief of the Xiongnu must be like their parents. When we look back at the past, we recognize that the plans of our officials came to nothing as a result of minor things and insignificant causes. Nothing of this sort deserves to overturn the concord existing between brothers."

Source: Sima Qian, *The Records of the Historian*, chap. 110 in Thomas R. Martin, ed., *Herodotus and Sima Qian: The First Great Historians of Greece and China* (Boston: Bedford/St. Martin's, 2010), 129–33, 136–37.

DOING HISTORY

Perceptions of Outsiders in the Ancient World

1. **Making comparisons:** How might you compare the perceptions of outsiders in these three accounts? Did the authors notice the same features of these societies? Did they focus more on what was exotic or different rather than on what may have been familiar? Did they adopt a similar posture toward the peoples they were describing? Were they simply reporting what they observed or were they making judgments as well?

2. **Describing the "uncivilized":** Both Tacitus and Sima Qian wrote about peoples living beyond the boundaries of "civilization." To what extent did they describe these peoples in a similar fashion?

3. **Relating encounters and observations:** How might the actual relationships between the observers and the observed peoples affect the writers' perceptions of those peoples?

CHAPTER 4

Culture and Religion in Eurasia/North Africa

600 B.C.E.–600 C.E.

In September of 2009, Kong Dejun returned to China from her home in Great Britain. The occasion was a birthday celebration for her ancient ancestor Kong Fuzi, or Confucius, born 2,560 years earlier. Together with some 10,000 other people—descendants, scholars, government officials, and foreign representatives—Kong Dejun attended ceremonies at the Confucian Temple in Qufu, the hometown of China's famous sage. "I was touched to see my ancestor being revered by people from different countries and nations," she said.[1] What made this celebration remarkable was that it took place in a country still ruled by the Communist Party, which had long devoted enormous efforts to discrediting Confucius and his teachings. In the view of communist China's revolutionary leader, Mao Zedong, Confucianism was associated with class inequality, patriarchy, feudalism, superstition, and all things old and backward. But the country's ancient teacher and philosopher had apparently outlasted its revolutionary hero, for now the Communist Party claims Confucius as a national treasure and has established over 300 Confucian Institutes to study his writings. He appears in TV shows and movies, even as many anxious parents offer prayers at Confucian temples when their children are taking the national college entrance exams.

Buddhism and Daoism (DOW-i'zm) have also experienced something of a revival in China, as thousands of temples, destroyed during the heyday of communism, have been repaired and reopened. Christianity too has grown rapidly since the death of Mao in 1976. Here are reminders, in a Chinese context, of the continuing appeal of cultural traditions forged long ago. Those traditions are among the most enduring legacies that second-wave civilizations have bequeathed to the modern world.

China's Cultural Traditions In this idealized painting, attributed to the Chinese artist Wang Shugu (1649–1730), the Chinese teacher Confucius presents a baby Buddha to the Daoist master Laozi. The image illustrates the assimilation of a major Indian religion into China as well as the generally peaceful coexistence of these three traditions.

AP® EXAM TIP

Expect questions on the AP® exam about the formation, beliefs, and effects of religions and philosophies that developed in the classical era (ca. 600 B.C.E.–ca. 600 C.E.).

In the several centuries surrounding 500 B.C.E., something quite remarkable happened all across Eurasia. More or less simultaneously, in China, India, the Middle East, and Greece, there emerged cultural traditions that have spread widely, have persisted in various forms into the twenty-first century, and have shaped the values and outlooks of most people who have inhabited the planet over the past 2,500 years. But we do well to remember that alongside these larger and more extensive cultural systems flourished a multitude of locally embedded and orally transmitted religious traditions. Within the major civilizations, these so-called "little traditions" interacted constantly with the "great traditions," and in societies that lay beyond the zone of civilization, such as those in Aboriginal Australia, they linked living human beings to the land, to the vegetable and animal worlds, to their ancestors, and to the gods or spirits that inhabited everything. (See, for example, the Aboriginal Dreamtime stories in Working with Evidence, Chapter 1, page 49, and the discussion of ancient African religious beliefs in Chapter 6, pages 254–55.) Here, however, the spotlight falls on those spiritual or religious traditions that emerged from the civilizations of the second-wave era.

In China, it was the time of Confucius and Laozi (low-ZUH), whose teachings gave rise to Confucianism and Daoism, respectively. In India, a series of religious writings known as the Upanishads gave expression to the classical philosophy of what we know as Hinduism, while a religious reformer, Siddhartha Gautama (sih-DHAR-tuh GOW-tau-mah), set in motion a separate religion known later as Buddhism. In the Middle East, a distinctively monotheistic religious tradition appeared. It was expressed in Zoroastrianism, derived from the teachings of the Persian prophet Zarathustra (zar-uh-THOO-struh), and in Judaism, articulated in Israel by a number of Jewish prophets such as Amos, Jeremiah, and Isaiah. Later, this Jewish religious outlook became the basis for both Christianity and Islam. Finally, in Greece, a rational and humanistic tradition found expression in the writings of Socrates, Plato, Aristotle, and many others.

These cultural traditions differed greatly. Chinese and Greek thinkers focused more on the affairs of this world and credited human rationality with the power to understand that reality. Indian, Persian, and Jewish intellectuals, by contrast, explored the unseen realm of the Divine and the relationship of God or the gods to human life. All these traditions sought an alternative to an earlier polytheism, in which the activities of various gods and spirits explained what happened in this world. These gods and spirits had generally been seen as similar to human beings, though much more powerful. Through ritual and sacrifice, men and women might placate the gods or persuade them to do human bidding. In contrast, the new cultural traditions of the second-wave era sought to define a single source of order and meaning in the universe, some moral or religious realm, sharply different from and higher than the sphere of human life. The task of humankind, according to these new ways of thinking, was personal moral or spiritual transformation—often expressed as the development of compassion—by aligning with that higher order.[2] These enormously rich and varied traditions have collectively posed the great questions of human life and society that have haunted and inspired much of humankind ever

A MAP OF TIME

800–400 B.C.E.	Upanishads composed
9th–6th centuries B.C.E.	Hebrew prophets (Amos, Hosea, Micah, Isaiah)
ca. 7th–6th centuries B.C.E.	Life of Zarathustra
600–300 B.C.E.	Emergence of Greek rationalism
6th–5th centuries B.C.E.	Life of Buddha, Confucius, Laozi
586–539 B.C.E.	Jewish exile in Babylon
558–330 B.C.E.	Achaemenid dynasty in Persia; state support for Zoroastrianism
500–221 B.C.E.	Age of warring states in China
469–399 B.C.E.	Life of Socrates
221–206 B.C.E.	Qin dynasty in China
Early 1st century C.E.	Life of Jesus
10–65 C.E.	Life of Paul
4th century C.E.	Christianity becomes state religion of Roman Empire, Armenia, Axum

since. They also defined and legitimated the hierarchies of class and gender that distinguished the various second-wave civilizations from one another.

Why did these traditions all emerge at roughly the same time? Here we encounter an enduring issue of historical analysis: What is the relationship between ideas and the circumstances in which they arise? Are ideas generated by particular political, social, and economic conditions? Or are they the product of creative human imagination independent of the material environment? Or do they derive from some combination of the two? In the case of these cultural traditions, many historians have noted the tumultuous social changes that accompanied their emergence. An iron-age technology, available since roughly 1000 B.C.E., made possible more productive economies and more deadly warfare. Growing cities, increased trade, the prominence of merchant classes, the emergence of new states and empires, new contacts among civilizations — all of these disruptions, occurring in already-literate societies, led thinkers to question older outlooks and to come up with new solutions to fundamental questions. What is the purpose of life? How should human society be ordered? What is the relationship between human life in this world and the moral or spiritual realms that lie beyond or within? But precisely why various societies developed their own distinctive answers to these questions remains elusive — a tribute, perhaps, to the unpredictable genius of human imagination.

AP® EXAM TIP

You should know when and where each of the major belief systems developed.

SEEKING THE MAIN POINT

Fundamentally, religions are basically alike. Does the material of this chapter support or challenge this idea?

China and the Search for Order

As one of the First Civilizations, China had a tradition of state building that historians have traced back to around 2000 B.C.E. or earlier. When the Zhou dynasty took power in 1122 B.C.E., the notion of the Mandate of Heaven had already taken root, as had the idea that the normal and appropriate condition of China was one of political unity. By the eighth century B.C.E., the authority of the Zhou dynasty and its royal court had substantially weakened, and by 500 B.C.E. any unity that China had earlier enjoyed was long gone. What followed was a period (500–221 B.C.E.) of chaos, growing violence, and disharmony that became known as the age of warring states (see Chapter 3, pages 121–22).

During these dreadful centuries of disorder and turmoil, a number of Chinese thinkers began to consider how order might be restored, how the apparent tranquillity of an earlier time could be realized again. From their reflections emerged classical cultural traditions of Chinese civilization.

The Legalist Answer

AP® EXAM TIP

The political and cultural effects of Legalism in China over time are important concepts for this course.

Guided Reading Question
....
■ COMPARISON
What different answers to the problem of disorder arose in classical China?

One answer to the problem of disorder—though not the first to emerge—was a hardheaded and practical philosophy known as Legalism. To Legalist thinkers, the solution to China's problems lay in rules or laws, clearly spelled out and strictly enforced through a system of rewards and punishments. "If rewards are high," wrote Han Fei, one of the most prominent Legalist philosophers, "then what the ruler wants will be quickly effected; if punishments are heavy, what he does not want will be swiftly prevented."[3] Legalists generally entertained a rather pessimistic view of human nature. Most people, they believed, were stupid and shortsighted. Only the state and its rulers could act in their long-term interests. Doing so meant promoting farmers and soldiers, the only two groups in society who performed essential functions, while suppressing merchants, aristocrats, scholars, and other classes regarded as useless.

Legalist thinking provided inspiration and methods for the harsh reunification of China under Shihuangdi and the Qin dynasty (221–206 B.C.E.), but the brutality of that short dynasty thoroughly discredited Legalism (see Chapter 3, page 122). Although its techniques and practices played a role in subsequent Chinese statecraft, few philosophers or rulers ever again openly advocated its ideas as the sole guide for Chinese political life. The Han and all subsequent dynasties drew instead on the teachings of China's greatest sage—Confucius.

The Confucian Answer

Born to an aristocratic family in the state of Lu in northern China, Confucius (551–479 B.C.E.) was both learned and ambitious. Believing that he had found the key to solving China's problem of disorder, he spent much of his adult life seeking a politi-

SNAPSHOT Thinkers and Philosophies of the Second-Wave Era

Person	Date	Location	Religion/Philosophy	Key Ideas
Zoroaster	7th century B.C.E. (?)	Persia (present-day Iran)	Zoroastrianism	Single High God; cosmic conflict of good and evil
Hebrew prophets (such as Isaiah, Amos, Jeremiah)	9th–6th centuries B.C.E.	Eastern Mediterranean/Palestine/Israel	Judaism	Transcendent High God; covenant with chosen people; social justice
Anonymous writers of Upanishads	800–400 B.C.E.	India	Brahmanism/Hinduism	Brahman (the single impersonal divine reality); karma; rebirth; goal of liberation (moksha)
Confucius	6th–5th centuries B.C.E.	China	Confucianism	Social harmony through moral example; secular outlook; importance of education; family as model of the state
Mahavira	6th century B.C.E.	India	Jainism	All creatures have souls; purification through non-violence; opposed to caste
Siddhartha Gautama	6th–5th centuries B.C.E.	India	Buddhism	Suffering caused by desire/attachment; end of suffering through modest and moral living and meditation practice
Laozi, Zhuangzi	6th–3rd centuries B.C.E.	China	Daoism	Withdrawal from the world into contemplation of nature; simple living; end of striving
Socrates, Plato, Aristotle	5th–4th centuries B.C.E.	Greece	Greek rationalism	Style of persistent questioning; secular explanation of nature and human life
Jesus	Early 1st century C.E.	Palestine/Israel	Christianity	Supreme importance of love based on intimate relationship with God; at odds with established authorities
Saint Paul	1st century C.E.	Palestine/Israel/eastern Roman Empire	Christianity	Christianity as a religion for all; salvation through faith in Jesus Christ

cal position from which he might put his ideas into action. But no such opportunity came his way. Perhaps it was just as well, for it was as a thinker and a teacher that Confucius left a profound imprint on Chinese history and culture and also on other East Asian societies, such as Korea's and Japan's. After his death, his students collected his teachings in a short book called the *Analects*, and later scholars elaborated and commented endlessly on his ideas, creating a body of thought known as Confucianism.

The Confucian answer to the problem of China's disorder was very different from that of the Legalists. Not laws and punishments, but the moral example of superiors was the Confucian key to a restored social harmony. For Confucius, human society consisted primarily of unequal relationships: the father was superior to the son; the husband to the wife; the older brother to the younger brother; and, of course, the ruler to the subject. If the superior party in each of these relationships behaved with sincerity, benevolence, and genuine concern for others, then the inferior party would be motivated to respond with deference and obedience. Harmony then would prevail. As Confucius put it, "The relation between superiors and inferiors is like that between the wind and the grass. The grass must bend when the wind blows across it." Thus, in both family life and in political life, the cultivation of *ren*—translated as human-heartedness, benevolence, goodness, nobility of heart—was the essential ingredient of a tranquil society.

But how were these humane virtues to be nurtured? Believing that people have a capacity for improvement, Confucius emphasized education as the key to moral betterment. He prescribed what we might call a broad liberal arts education emphasizing language, literature, history, philosophy, and ethics, all applied to the practical problems of government. Ritual and ceremonies were also important, for they conveyed the rules of appropriate behavior in the many and varying circumstances of life. For the "superior person," or "gentleman" in Confucian terms, this process of improvement involved serious personal reflection and a willingness to strive continuously to perfect his moral character.

Guided Reading Question

■ DESCRIPTION

Why has Confucianism been defined as a "humanistic philosophy" rather than a supernatural religion?

AP® EXAM TIP

The political and cultural effects of Confucianism are among the most important concepts in all of China's long history. Evidence continues on page 153.

Filial Piety

The long-enduring social order that Confucius advocated began at home with unquestioning obedience and the utmost respect for parents and other senior members of the family. This Qing dynasty woodcut illustrates the proper filial relationship between father and son in a variety of circumstances. (Chinese colored woodcut, Qing Dynasty [1644–1912]/Private Collection/Roland and Sabrina Michaud/akg-images)

Such ideas left a deep mark on Chinese culture. The discrediting of Legalism during the Qin dynasty opened the door to the adoption of Confucianism as the official ideology of the Chinese state, to such an extent that Confucianism became almost synonymous with Chinese culture. As China's bureaucracy took shape during and after the Han dynasty, Confucianism became the central element of the educational system, which prepared students for the examinations required to gain official positions. In those examinations, candidates were required to apply the principles of Confucianism to specific situations that they might encounter in office. Thus generation after generation of China's male elite was steeped in the ideas and values of Confucianism.

Family life had long been central to Chinese popular culture, expressed in the practice of ancestor veneration, including visiting the graves of the deceased, presenting them with offerings, and erecting commemorative tablets and shrines in their honor. In Confucian thinking, the family became a model for political life, a kind of miniature state. Filial piety, the honoring of one's ancestors and parents, was both an end in itself and a training ground for the reverence due to the emperor and state officials.

Confucian views of the family were rigidly patriarchal and set the tone for defining the lives of women and men alike. Those views were linked to a hierarchical understanding of the cosmos in which an inferior and receptive earth was in balance with the superior and creative principle of Heaven. But these were gendered concepts, with Heaven associated with things male and earth with those female. Thus the subordinate and deferential position of women in relation to men was rooted in the structure of the cosmos itself. What this meant for women was spelled out by a somewhat later woman writer, Ban Zhao (bahn jow) (45–116 C.E.), in a famous work called *Lessons for Women*.

> Let a woman modestly yield to others. . . . Always let her seem to tremble and to fear. . . . Then she may be said to humble herself before others. . . . To guard carefully her chastity . . . , to choose her words with care . . . , to wash and scrub filth away . . . , with whole-hearted devotion to sew and to weave, to love not gossip and silly laughter, in cleanliness and order to prepare the wine and food for serving guests; [these] may be called the characteristics of womanly work.[4]

Ban Zhao called for greater attention to education for young girls, not because they were equal to boys, but so that a young woman might be better prepared to serve her husband. Education for boys, on the other hand, enabled them to more effectively control their wives.

Corresponding Confucian virtues for ideal men were contained in the paired concepts of *wen* and *wu*, both limited largely to males. The superior principle of wen referred to the refined qualities of rationality, scholarship, and literary and artistic abilities, while wu focused attention on physical and martial achievements. Thus men alone, and superior men at that, were eligible for the civil service exams

AP® EXAM TIP

The Confucian-based exam system, the concept of filial piety, and Confucian gender roles are all vital to understanding China's history.

that led to political office and high prestige, while military men and merchants occupied a distinctly lower position in a male social hierarchy.[5]

Beyond defining gender expectations, Confucianism also placed great importance on history, for the ideal good society lay in the past. Confucian ideas were reformist, perhaps even revolutionary, but they were consistently presented as an effort to restore a past golden age. Those ideas also injected a certain democratic element into Chinese elite culture, for the great sage had emphasized that "superior men" and potential government officials were those of outstanding moral character and intellectual achievement, not simply those of aristocratic background. Usually only young men from wealthy families could afford the education necessary for passing examinations, but on occasion villagers could find the resources to sponsor one of their bright sons, potentially propelling him into the stratosphere of the Chinese elite while bringing honor and benefit to the village itself.

Confucian values clearly justified the many inequalities of Chinese society, but they also established certain expectations for the superior parties in China's social hierarchy. Thus emperors should keep taxes low, administer justice, and provide for the material needs of the people. Those who failed to govern by the moral norms of Confucian values forfeited the Mandate of Heaven and invited upheaval and their replacement by another dynasty. Likewise, husbands should deal kindly with their wives and children, lest they invite conflict and disharmony in the family.

Finally, Confucianism marked Chinese elite culture by its secular, or nonreligious, character. Confucius did not deny the reality of gods and spirits. In fact, he advised people to participate in family and state rituals "as if the spirits were present," and he believed that the universe had a moral character with which human beings should align themselves. But the thrust of Confucian teaching was distinctly this-worldly and practical, concerned with human relationships, effective government, and social harmony. Asked on one occasion about his view of death and the spirits, Confucius replied that because we do not fully understand this life, we cannot possibly know anything about the life beyond. Members of the Chinese elite generally acknowledged that magic, the gods, and spirits were perhaps necessary for the lower orders of society, but educated people, they argued, would find them of little help in striving for moral improvement and in establishing a harmonious society.

The Daoist Answer

No civilization has ever painted its cultural outlook in a single color. As Confucian thinking became generally known in China, a quite different school of thought also took shape. Known as Daoism, it was associated with the legendary figure Laozi, who, according to tradition, was a sixth-century B.C.E. archivist. He is said to have penned a short poetic volume, the *Daodejing* (DOW-DAY-JIHNG) (*The Way and Its Power*), before vanishing in the wilderness to the west of China on his water buffalo. Daoist ideas were later expressed in a more explicit fashion by the philosopher Zhuangzi (369–286 B.C.E.).

AP® EXAM TIP

You should understand the importance of Confucian-based social hierarchies in East Asia.

AP® EXAM TIP

Take good notes on the basic concepts of Daoism and their effects on East Asian cultures. Know contributions of belief systems to art and architecture, such as the painting on the opposite page, which was inspired by Daoist teachings.

In many ways, Daoist thinking ran counter to that of Confucius, who had emphasized the importance of education and earnest striving for moral improvement and good government. The Daoists ridiculed such efforts as artificial and useless, claiming that they generally made things worse. In the face of China's disorder and chaos, Daoists urged withdrawal into the world of nature and encouraged behavior that was spontaneous, individualistic, and natural. Whereas Confucius focused on the world of human relationships, the Daoists turned the spotlight on the immense realm of nature and its mysterious unfolding patterns. "Confucius roams within society," the Chinese have often said. "Laozi wanders beyond."

The central concept of Daoist thinking is *dao*, an elusive notion that refers to the way of nature, the underlying and unchanging principle that governs all natural phenomena. The dao "moves around and around, but does not on this account suffer," wrote Laozi in the *Daodejing*. "All life comes from it. It wraps everything with its love as in a garment, and yet it claims no honor, for it does not demand to be lord. I do not know its name and so I call it the Dao, the Way, and I rejoice in its power."[6]

Amid the world of civilization, so highly valued by Confucius, the Daoists yearned for an earlier time, "an age of perfect virtue" that had been disrupted by Confucian striving for something better. Then, according to one Daoist master, "there were no paths and ramps on the mountains and no boats upon the bridges. . . . There were vast numbers of animals and grasses, and trees reached their natural growth. Wild animals could be taken for walks on leashes, and one could climb up to the nests of magpies and other birds." Such a vision of human harmony with nature contrasted sharply with the Confucian outlook, which urged "the development of a world of culture from a nature experienced as hostile." To Confucians, humankind "disposes over the world of [wild] things, tames wild animals, and brings cowed vermin under his control."[7] Thus individual Daoists often fled to the mountains, where they might experience the dao in union with nature. Li Po, a much-acclaimed Chinese poet of the eighth century, expressed a Daoist sensibility in this short poem:

> The birds have vanished into the sky,
> And now the last cloud drains away.

Guided Reading Question

■ COMPARISON
How did the Daoist outlook differ from that of Confucianism?

Chinese Landscape Paintings
Focused largely on mountains and water, Chinese landscape paintings were much influenced by the Daoist search for harmony with nature. Thus human figures and buildings were usually eclipsed by towering peaks, waterfalls, clouds, and trees. This thirteenth-century ink-on-silk painting illustrates that sensibility. The poem at the top reads: "Night rains cleansed the capital's suburban farms, / Morning sun brightens the emperor's city; / People work happily in a good year, / Dancing and singing they cross a path in the field." (*Singing and Dancing*, Southern Song Period [960–1279], [ink and watercolor on silk], Ma Yuan [1190–1235]/Palace Museum, Beijing, China/Bridgeman Images)

We sit together, the mountain and me,
until only the mountain remains.[8]

Applied to human life, Daoism invited people to withdraw from the world of political and social activism, to disengage from the public life so important to Confucius, and to align themselves with the way of nature. It meant simplicity in living, small self-sufficient communities, limited government, and the abandonment of education and active efforts at self-improvement. "Give up learning," declares the *Daodejing*, "and put an end to your troubles." The flavor of the Daoist approach to life is evident in this passage from the *Daodejing*, describing a small and simple society:

Though there were individuals with the abilities of ten or a hundred men,
there should be no employment of them . . . ;
Though they had boats and carriages, they should have no occasion to ride in them;
though they had buff coats and sharp weapons, they should have no occasion to
use them.
I would make the people return to the use of knotted cords (instead of written
characters).
They should think their (coarse) food sweet; their (plain) clothes beautiful;
their (poor) dwellings places of rest;
and their common (simple) ways sources of enjoyment.
There should be a neighbouring state within sight . . . ,
but I would make the people . . . not have any intercourse with it.[9]

Like Confucianism, the Daoist perspective viewed family life as central to Chinese society, though the element of male/female hierarchy was downplayed in favor of complementarity and balance between the sexes.

Despite its various differences with the ideas of Confucianism, the Daoist perspective was widely regarded by elite Chinese as complementing rather than contradicting Confucian values (see the chapter-opening image on page 146). Such an outlook was facilitated by the ancient Chinese concept of *yin* and *yang*, which expressed a belief in the unity of opposites (see figure).

The Yin Yang Symbol

Thus a scholar-official might pursue the Confucian project of "government by goodness" during the day, but upon returning home in the evening or following his retirement, he might well behave in a more Daoist fashion—pursuing the simple life, reading Daoist philosophy, practicing Daoist meditation and breathing exercises, or enjoying landscape paintings in which tiny human figures are dwarfed by the vast peaks and valleys of the natural world (see image on page 155). Daoism also shaped the culture of ordinary people as it entered popular religion. This kind of Daoism sought to tap the power of the dao for practical uses and came to include magic, fortune-telling, and the search for immortality. It also on occasion provided an ideology for peasant uprisings, such as the Yellow Turban Rebellion (184–204 C.E.), which imagined a utopian society without the oppression of governments and landlords (see Chapter 5, pages 197–98). In its many and varied forms, Daoism, like Confucianism, became an enduring element of the Chinese cultural tradition.

Cultural Traditions of Classical India

The cultural development of Indian civilization was far different from that of China. Whereas Confucianism paid little attention to the gods, spirits, and speculation about religious matters, Indian elite culture embraced the Divine and all things spiritual with enthusiasm and generated elaborate philosophical visions about the nature of ultimate reality. But the Indian religious tradition—later called Hinduism—differed from other world religions as well. Unlike Buddhism, Christianity, or Islam, Hinduism had no historical founder; rather, it grew up over many centuries along with Indian civilization. Although it later spread into Southeast Asia, Hinduism was not a missionary religion seeking converts, but was, like Judaism, associated with a particular people and territory.

In fact, "Hinduism" was never a single tradition at all, and the term itself derived from outsiders—Greeks, Muslims, and later the British—who sought to reduce the infinite variety of Indian cultural patterns into a recognizable system. From the inside, however, Hinduism dissolved into a vast diversity of gods, spirits, beliefs, practices, rituals, and philosophies. This endlessly variegated Hinduism served to incorporate into Indian civilization the many diverse peoples who migrated into or invaded the South Asian peninsula over many centuries and several millennia. Its ability to accommodate this diversity gave India's cultural development a distinctive quality.

AP® EXAM TIP

Pay attention to these comparisons of major Eurasian belief systems as you develop your skills in writing comparative essays.

South Asian Religion: From Ritual Sacrifice to Philosophical Speculation

Despite the fragmentation and variety of Indian cultural and religious patterns, an evolving set of widely recognized sacred texts provided some commonality. The earliest of these texts, known as the Vedas (VAY-duhs), were collections of poems, hymns, prayers, and rituals. Compiled by priests called Brahmins, the Vedas were for centuries transmitted orally and were reduced to writing in Sanskrit around 600 B.C.E. In the Vedas, historians have caught fleeting glimpses of Indian civilization in its formative centuries (1500–600 B.C.E.). Those sacred writings tell of small competing chiefdoms or kingdoms, of sacred sounds and fires, of numerous gods, rising and falling in importance over the centuries. They also suggest a clearly patriarchal society, but one that afforded upper-class women somewhat greater opportunities than they later enjoyed. Vedic women participated in religious sacrifices, sometimes engaged in scholarship and religious debate, were allowed to wear the sacred thread that symbolized ritual purity in the higher castes, and could on occasion marry a man of their own choosing. The Vedas described as well the elaborate ritual sacrifices that Brahmin priests required. Performing these sacrifices and rituals with great precision enabled the Brahmins to acquire enormous power and wealth, sometimes exceeding even that of kings and warriors. But Brahmins also generated growing criticism, as ritual became mechanical and formal and as Brahmins required heavy fees to perform them.

AP® EXAM TIP

You should know examples of writings from major belief systems in world history, such as the Vedas and the Upanishads (see page 158).

Guided Reading Question

■ CHANGE

In what ways did the religious traditions of South Asia change over the centuries?

From this dissatisfaction arose another body of sacred texts, the Upanishads (oo-PAHN-ee-shahds). Composed by largely anonymous thinkers between 800 and 400 B.C.E., these were mystical and highly philosophical works that sought to probe the inner meaning of the sacrifices prescribed in the Vedas. In the Upanishads, external ritual gave way to introspective thinking, which expressed in many and varied formulations the central concepts of philosophical Hinduism that have persisted into modern times. Chief among them was the idea of Brahman, the World Soul, the final and ultimate reality. Beyond the multiplicity of material objects and individual persons and beyond even the various gods themselves lay this primal unitary energy or divine reality infusing all things, similar in some ways to the Chinese notion of the dao. This alone was real; the immense diversity of existence that human beings perceived with their senses was but an illusion.

The fundamental assertion of philosophical Hinduism was that the individual human soul, or *atman*, was in fact a part of Brahman. Beyond the quest for pleasure, wealth, power, and social position, all of which were perfectly normal and quite legitimate, lay the effort to achieve the final goal of humankind — union with Brahman, an end to our illusory perception of a separate existence. This was *moksha* (MOHK-shuh), or liberation, compared sometimes to a bubble in a glass of water breaking through the surface and becoming one with the surrounding atmosphere.

Achieving this exalted state was held to involve many lifetimes, and the notion of *samsara*, or rebirth/reincarnation, became a central feature of Hindu thinking. Human souls migrated from body to body over many lifetimes, depending on one's actions. This was the law of *karma*. Pure actions, appropriate to one's station in life, resulted in rebirth in a higher social position or caste. Thus the caste system of distinct and ranked groups, each with its own duties, became a register of spiritual progress. Birth in a higher caste was evidence of "good karma," based on actions in a previous life, and offered a better chance to achieve moksha, which brought with it an end to the painful cycle of rebirth.

If Hinduism underpinned caste, it also legitimated and expressed India's gender system. As South Asian civilization crystallized during the second-wave era, its patriarchal features tightened. Women were increasingly seen as "unclean below the navel," forbidden to learn the Vedas, and excluded from public religious rituals. The Laws of Manu, probably composed in the early centuries of the Common Era, described a divinely ordained social order and articulated a gender system whose ideals endured for a millennium or more. It taught that all embryos were basically male and that only weak semen generated female babies. It advocated child marriage for girls to men far older than themselves. "A virtuous wife," the Laws proclaimed, "should constantly serve her husband like a god" and should never remarry after his death. In a famous prescription similar to that of Chinese and other patriarchal societies, the Laws declared: "In childhood a female must be subject to her father; in youth to her husband; when her lord is dead to her sons; a woman must never be independent."[10]

AP® EXAM TIP

Know the basic teachings of the major Eurasian belief systems, like reincarnation in Hinduism.

AP® EXAM TIP

Take good notes on the social and political effects of India's caste system, both here and in Chapter 5.

Hindu Ascetics
Hinduism called for men in the final stage of life to leave ordinary ways of living and withdraw into the forests to seek spiritual liberation, or moksha. Here, in an illustration from an early thirteenth-century Indian manuscript, a holy man explores a text with three disciples in a secluded rural setting. (Musée des Arts Asiatiques—Guimet, Paris, France/© RMN–Grand Palais/Art Resource, NY)

And yet some aspects of Hinduism served to empower women. Sexual pleasure was considered a legitimate goal for both men and women, and its many and varied techniques were detailed in the *Kamasutra*. Many Hindu deities were female, some life-giving and faithful, others, like Kali, fiercely destructive. Women were particularly prominent in the growing devotional cults dedicated to particular deities, where neither gender nor caste was an obstacle to spiritual fulfillment.

A further feature of Hindu religious thought lay in its provision of different paths to the ultimate goal of liberation, or moksha. Various ways to this final release, appropriate to people of different temperaments, were spelled out in Hindu teachings. Some might achieve moksha through knowledge or study; others by means of detached action in the world, doing one's work without regard to consequences; still others through passionate devotion to some deity or through extended meditation practice. Such ideas—carried by Brahmin priests and wandering ascetics or holy men, who had withdrawn from ordinary life to pursue their spiritual development—became widely known throughout India.

The Buddhist Challenge

About the same time as philosophical Hinduism was emerging, another movement took shape that soon became a distinct and separate religious tradition—Buddhism. Unlike Hinduism, this new faith had a historical founder, Siddhartha Gautama (ca. 566–ca. 486 B.C.E.), a prince from a small north Indian state. According to Buddhist tradition, the prince had enjoyed a sheltered and delightful youth but was shocked to his core upon encountering old age, sickness, and death. Leaving family and fortune behind, he then set out on a six-year spiritual quest, finally achieving insight, or "enlightenment," at the age of thirty-five. For the rest of his life, he taught what he had learned and gathered a small but growing community whose members came to see him as the Buddha, the Enlightened One, a human being who had awakened.

Guided Reading Question

....

■ COMPARISON

In what ways did Buddhism reflect Hindu traditions, and in what ways did it challenge them?

"I teach but one thing," the Buddha said, "suffering and the end of suffering." To the Buddha, suffering or sorrow—experiencing life as imperfect, impermanent, and unsatisfactory—was the central and universal feature of human life. Widely known to Buddhists as *dukkha*, this kind of suffering derived from desire or craving for individual fulfillment, from attachment to that which inevitably changes, particularly to the notion of a core self or ego that is uniquely and solidly "me." The cure for this "dis-ease" lay in living a modest and moral life combined with meditation practice. Those who followed the Buddhist path most fully could expect to achieve enlightenment, or *nirvana*, a virtually indescribable state in which individual identity would be "extinguished" along with all greed, hatred, and delusion. With the pain of unnecessary suffering finally ended, the enlightened person would experience an overwhelming serenity, even in the midst of difficulty, as well as an immense loving-kindness, or compassion, for all beings. It was a simple message, elaborated endlessly and in various forms by those who followed the Buddha.

Much of the Buddha's teaching reflected the Hindu traditions from which it sprang. The idea that ordinary life is an illusion, the concepts of karma and rebirth, the goal of overcoming the incessant demands of the ego, the practice of meditation, the hope for final release from the cycle of rebirth—all of these Hindu elements found their way into Buddhist teaching. In this respect, Buddhism was a simplified and more accessible version of Hinduism.

Other elements of Buddhist teaching, however, sharply challenged prevailing Hindu thinking. Rejecting the religious authority of the Brahmins, the Buddha ridiculed their rituals and sacrifices as irrelevant to the hard work of dealing with one's suffering. Nor was he much interested in abstract speculation about the creation of the world or the existence of God, for such questions, he declared, "are not useful in the quest for holiness; they do not lead to peace and to the direct knowledge of *nirvana*." Individuals had to take responsibility for their own spiritual development with no help from human authorities or supernatural beings. It was a path of intense self-effort, based on personal experience. The Buddha also challenged the inequalities of a Hindu-based

Classic Indian Buddha

This sixth-century C.E. image of the Buddha from eastern India shows a classical representation of the great teacher. The Buddha's right hand with palm facing the viewer indicates reassurance, or "have no fear." The partially webbed fingers are among the *lakshanas*, or signs of a Buddha image, that denote the Buddha's unique status. So too is the knot on the top of his head, symbolizing enlightenment. The elongated earlobes remind the viewer that earlier in his life the Buddha wore heavy and luxurious earrings, while his partially closed and downcast eyes and his bare feet indicate detachment from the world. (Standing Buddha, India [probably Bihar]. Gupta period. Late 6th–early 7th century. Bronze. H. 18½ x 6⅛ in. [47.0 × 15.6 cm.]. Hands: Diam. 5⅝ in. [14.3 cm.]. Purchase, Florance Waterbury Bequest, 1969 [69.222]. Photo: Bruce White. The Metropolitan Museum of Art, New York, NY, USA/Image copyright © Metropolitan Museum of Art/Image source: Art Resource, NY) caste system, arguing that neither caste position nor gender was a barrier to enlightenment. The possibility of "awakening" was available to all.

But when it came to establishing a formal organization of the Buddha's most devoted followers, the prevailing patriarchy of Indian society made itself felt. Buddhist texts recount that the Buddha's foster mother, Prajapati Gotami, sought to enter the newly created order of monks but was repeatedly refused admission by the Buddha himself. Only after the intervention of the Buddha's attendant, Ananda, did he relent and allow women to join a separate order of nuns. Even then, these nuns were subjected to a series of rules that clearly subordinated them to men. Male monks, for example, could officially admonish the nuns, but the reverse was forbidden. Such policies reflected a particular strain of Buddhist thinking that viewed women as a distracting obstacle to male enlightenment.

Nonetheless, thousands of women flocked to join the Buddhist order of nuns, where they found a degree of freedom and independence unavailable elsewhere in Indian society. Buddhist nuns delighted in the relative freedom of their order, where they largely ran their own affairs, were forbidden to do household chores, and devoted themselves wholly to the search for "awakening," which many apparently achieved. A nun named Mutta declared: "I am free from the three crooked things: mortar, pestle, and my crooked husband. I am free from birth and death and all that dragged me back."[11]

Gradually, Buddhist teachings found an audience in India. Buddhism's egalitarian message appealed especially to lower-caste groups and to women. The availability of its teaching in the local language of Pali, rather than the classical Sanskrit, made it accessible. Establishing monasteries and stupas (commemorative monuments containing relics of the Buddha) on the site of neighborhood shrines to earth spirits or near a sacred tree linked the new religion to local traditions. The most dedicated followers joined monasteries, devoting their lives to religious practice and spreading the message among nearby people. (See Zooming In: Nalanda, page 162.) State support during the reign of Ashoka (r. 268–232 B.C.E.) (see Chapter 3, page 133) likewise helped the new religion gain a foothold in India as a distinct tradition separate from Hinduism.

As Buddhism spread, both within and beyond India, differences in understanding soon emerged, particularly as to how nirvana could be achieved or, in a common Buddhist metaphor, how to cross the river to the far shore of enlightenment. The Buddha had taught a rather austere doctrine of intense self-effort, undertaken most actively by monks and nuns who withdrew from society to devote themselves fully to the quest. This early version of the new religion, known as Theravada (Teaching of the Elders), portrayed the Buddha as an immensely wise teacher and model, but certainly not divine. It was more psychological than religious, a set of practices rather than a set of beliefs. The gods, though never completely denied, played little role in assisting believers in their search for enlightenment. In short, individuals were on their own in crossing the river. Each person had to row his or her own boat. Clearly, this was not for everyone.

AP® EXAM TIP

You should know basic differences and similarities between Hinduism and Buddhism.

Guided Reading Question

■ COMPARISON
What is the difference between the Theravada and Mahayana expressions of Buddhism?

AP® EXAM TIP

Be able to give examples of factors that attract people to belief systems.

Nalanda, India's Buddhist University

Nalanda, a village in the Bihar region of northeastern India, has a storied past in the world of Buddhism, for tradition has it that the Buddha himself visited on several occasions and the Mauryan dynasty emperor Ashoka built a temple there. But the village came to a wider prominence much later during the fifth century C.E. when a huge monastic complex, dedicated to Buddhist learning, began to take shape. Many have viewed it as the world's first university. With eight separate compounds, ten temples, many meditation halls and classrooms, and numerous sculptures, Nalanda was a stunning architectural achievement.

Patronized by the emperors of India's Gupta dynasty and later rulers, Nalanda was supported by the dedicated revenue from 100 or more villages in the region and operated under state supervision. Students, numbering in the many thousands, lived in dormitories and were taught by hundreds of instructors. Scholars and students alike came to Nalanda from all over the Buddhist world and

One of the many temples in the Nalanda complex.

beyond—China, Korea, Japan, Tibet, Indonesia, Persia, and Central Asia. Many spent a few years in Indonesia or elsewhere to improve their Sanskrit before moving on to the highly prestigious Nalanda center. There they had access to a huge library occupying three buildings, one of them a nine-story structure, housing endless books and manuscripts.

If the student body was international, the curriculum was likewise inclusive. While focused on distinctly Buddhist writings, students also studied Hindu sacred texts, Sanskrit grammar, logic, astronomy, medicine, and philosophy. Numerous Buddhist images were joined by those representing Hindu deities. Nalanda was a cosmopolitan place of lively discussion and controversy among rival schools of thought.

Visitors from the more remote regions of the Buddhist world were stunned at what they witnessed at

photo: Votive stupa of the principal temple of Site III/Giraudon/Bridgeman Images

AP® EXAM TIP

Major belief systems often divided and subdivided across time and place. One example is the development of Theravada and Mahayana Buddhism.

By the early centuries of the Common Era, a modified form of Buddhism called Mahayana (mah-huh-YAH-nah) (Great Vehicle) had taken root in parts of India, proclaiming that help was available for the strenuous voyage. Buddhist thinkers developed the idea of *bodhisattvas* (BOH-dih-SAT-vuhs), spiritually developed people who postponed their own entry into nirvana to assist those who were still suffering. The Buddha himself became something of a god, and both earlier and future Buddhas were available to offer help. Elaborate descriptions of these supernatural beings, together with various levels of Heavens and Hells, transformed Buddhism into a popular religion of salvation. Furthermore, religious merit, leading to salvation, might now be earned by acts of piety and devotion, such as contributing to the support of a monastery, and that merit might be transferred to others. This was the Great Vehicle, allowing far more people to make the voyage across the river. (See Working with Evidence, page 183, for the evolution of Buddhism reflected in images.)

Nalanda. In the seventh century C.E., the Chinese Buddhist monk Xuanzang recorded some of his impressions:

> Ten thousand monks always lived there, both hosts and guests. They studied Mahayana [Buddhist] teachings and the doctrines of the eighteen schools, as well as worldly books such as the [Hindu] Vedas. They also learned about works on logic, grammar, medicine, and divination. . . . Lectures were given at more than a hundred places in the monastery every day, and the students studied diligently without wasting a single moment. As all the monks who lived there were men of virtue, the atmosphere in the monastery was naturally solemn and dignified. For more than seven hundred years since its establishment, none of the monks had committed any offence.[12]

Xuanzang's comments about the "solemn and dignified" atmosphere of Nalanda may have been a little exaggerated, for reports of dice and board games, tumbling, shooting marbles, sword play, and even performances by dancing girls cast a somewhat different picture. Students apparently will be students.

Turkish Muslim invasions of India around 1200 badly damaged Nalanda; many monks were killed, others fled to Tibet or Nepal, and the library was burned. A Tibetan visitor in 1235 found a much-reduced Nalanda with only seventy students and one ninety-year-old teacher. The subsequent closure of Nalanda was part of a more general process by which Buddhism largely vanished within India. Even the name of Nalanda was apparently forgotten, as the area came to be called Bargaon. But the scholarship of Nalanda had enriched both Indian science and Buddhist learning and practice in Tibet, China, and elsewhere. In late 2013, the Dalai Lama paid tribute to the Nalanda tradition: "The name Nalanda was very familiar to me as the source of the tradition we follow in Tibet. First we memorize the root text, then study it word by word and then debate it with our fellow students to penetrate the depths of its meaning."[13]

The spectacular ruins of Nalanda began to be excavated in the nineteenth century when India was a British colony. And in 2014, a new, revived, and modern Nalanda University, now a secular institution, welcomed students for the first time, some 1,500 years after the opening of the original Nalanda complex.

Questions: What is most striking to you about Nalanda? How might the experiences of its students compare to your university experience? In what ways did Nalanda's influence stretch beyond India's borders and persist even after its collapse?

Hinduism as a Religion of Duty and Devotion

Strangely enough, Buddhism as a distinct religious practice ultimately died out in the land of its birth as it was reincorporated into a broader Hindu tradition, but it spread widely and flourished, particularly in its Mahayana form, in other parts of Asia. Buddhism declined in India perhaps in part because the mounting wealth of monasteries and the economic interests of their leading figures separated them from ordinary people. Competition from Islam after 1000 C.E. also played a role. But the most important reason for the waning of Buddhism in India was the growth during the first millennium C.E. of a new kind of popular Hinduism, which the masses found more accessible than the elaborate sacrifices of the Brahmins or the philosophical speculations of intellectuals. Expressed in the widely known epic poems called the *Mahabharata* (mah-hah-BAH-rah-tah) and the *Ramayana*, this revived Hinduism indicated more clearly that action in the world and the detached performance of caste duties might also provide a path to liberation. It was perhaps a response to the challenge of Buddhism.

In the much-beloved Hindu text known as the Bhagavad Gita (BUH-guh-vahd GEE-tuh), the troubled warrior-hero Arjuna is in anguish over the necessity of killing his kinsmen as a decisive battle approaches. But he is assured by his charioteer Lord Krishna, an incarnation of the god Vishnu, that performing his duty as a warrior, and doing so selflessly without regard to consequences, is an act of devotion that would lead to "release from the shackles of repeated rebirth." This was not an invitation to militarism, but rather an affirmation that ordinary people, not just Brahmins, could also find spiritual fulfillment by selflessly performing the ordinary duties of their lives: "The man who, casting off all desires, lives free from attachments, who is free from egoism, and from the feeling that this or that is mine, obtains tranquility." Withdrawal and asceticism were not the only ways to moksha.

Also becoming increasingly prominent was yet another religious path—the way of devotion to one or another of India's many gods and goddesses. Beginning in south India and moving northward, this *bhakti* (BAHK-tee) (worship) movement involved the intense adoration of and identification with a particular deity through songs, prayers, and rituals. By far the most popular deities were Vishnu, the protector and preserver of creation who was associated with mercy and goodness, and Shiva, a god representing the Divine in its destructive aspect, but many others also had their followers. This form of Hindu expression sometimes pushed against the rigid caste and gender hierarchies of Indian society by inviting all to an adoration of the Divine. After all, Krishna in the Bhagavad Gita had declared that "those who take shelter in Me, though they be of lower birth—women, vaishyas [merchants] and shudras [workers]—can attain the supreme destination."

The proliferation of gods and goddesses, and of their bhakti cults, occasioned very little friction or serious religious conflict. "Hinduism," writes a leading scholar, "is essentially tolerant, and would rather assimilate than rigidly exclude."[14] This capacity for assimilation extended to an already-declining Buddhism, which for many people had become yet another cult worshipping yet another god. The Buddha in fact was incorporated into the Hindu pantheon as the ninth incarnation of Vishnu. By 1000 C.E., Buddhism had largely disappeared as a separate religious tradition within India.

Thus a constantly evolving and enormously varied South Asian religious tradition had been substantially transformed. An early emphasis on ritual sacrifice gave way to that of philosophical speculation, devotional worship, and detached action in the world. In the process, that tradition had generated Buddhism, which became the first of the great universal religions of world history, and then had absorbed that new faith back into the fold of an emerging popular Hinduism.

Toward Monotheism: The Search for God in the Middle East

Paralleling the evolution of Chinese and Indian cultural traditions was the movement toward a distinctive monotheistic religious outlook in the Middle East, which found expression in Persian Zoroastrianism and in Judaism. Neither of these religions themselves spread very widely, but the monotheism that they nurtured became the basis for both Christianity and Islam, which have shaped so much of world history over the past 2,000 years. Amid the proliferation of gods and spirits that had long characterized religious life throughout the ancient world, monotheism—the idea of a single supreme deity, the sole source of all life and being—was a radical cultural innovation. That conception created the possibility of a universal religion, open to all of humankind, but it could also mean an exclusive and intolerant faith.

AP® EXAM TIP

You should be able to point out similarities and differences between the monotheistic religions in this section and the other major belief systems discussed in this chapter.

Zoroastrianism

During the glory years of the powerful Persian Empire, a new religion arose to challenge the polytheism of earlier times. Tradition dates its Persian prophet, Zarathustra (Zoroaster to the Greeks), to the sixth or seventh century B.C.E., although some scholars place him hundreds of years earlier. Whenever he actually lived, his ideas took hold in Persia and received a degree of state support during the Achaemenid dynasty (558–330 B.C.E.). Appalled by the endemic violence of recurring cattle raids, Zarathustra recast the traditional Persian polytheism into a vision of a single unique god, Ahura Mazda, who ruled the world and was the source of all truth, light, and goodness. This benevolent deity was engaged in a cosmic struggle with the forces of evil, embodied in an equivalent supernatural figure, Angra Mainyu. Ultimately this struggle would be decided in favor of Ahura Mazda, aided by the arrival of a final savior who would restore the world to its earlier purity and peace. At a day of judgment, those who had aligned with Ahura Mazda would be granted new resurrected bodies and rewarded with eternal life in Paradise. Those who had sided with evil and the "Lie" (which found expression as greed, wrath, and envy) were condemned to everlasting punishment. Zoroastrian (zohr-oh-ASS-tree-ahn) teaching thus placed great emphasis on the free will of humankind and the necessity for each individual to choose between good and evil.

The Zoroastrian faith achieved widespread support within the Persian heartland, although it also found adherents in other parts of the empire, such as Egypt, Mesopotamia, and Anatolia. But it never became an active missionary religion and did not spread widely beyond the region. Alexander the Great's invasion of the Persian Empire and the subsequent Greek-ruled Seleucid dynasty (330–155 B.C.E.) were disastrous for Zoroastrianism, as temples were plundered, priests slaughtered, and sacred writings burned. But the new faith managed to survive this onslaught

Guided Reading Question

■ CONNECTION
What aspects of Zoroastrianism and Judaism subsequently found a place in Christianity and Islam?

Zoroastrian Fire Altar
Representing the energy of the creator god Ahura Mazda, the fire altar became an important symbol of Zoroastrianism and was often depicted on Persian coins in association with images of Persian rulers. This particular coin dates from the third century C.E. (© AAAC/Topham/The Image Works)

and flourished again during the Parthian (247 B.C.E.–224 C.E.) and Sassanid (224–651 C.E.) dynasties. It was the arrival of Islam and an Arab empire that occasioned the final decline of Zoroastrianism in Persia, although a few believers fled to India, where they became known as Parsis ("Persians"). The Parsis have continued their faith into present times.

Like Buddhism, the Zoroastrian faith vanished from its place of origin, but unlike Buddhism, it did not spread beyond Persia in a recognizable form. Some elements of the Zoroastrian belief system, however, did become incorporated into other religious traditions. The presence of many Jews in the Persian Empire meant that they surely became aware of Zoroastrian ideas. Many of those ideas—including the conflict of God and an evil counterpart (Satan); the notion of a last judgment and resurrected bodies; and a belief in the final defeat of evil, the arrival of a savior (Messiah), and the remaking of the world at the end of time—found a place in an evolving Judaism. Some of these teachings, especially the concepts of Heaven and Hell, later became prominent in those enormously influential successors to Judaism—Christianity and Islam.[15] Thus the Persian tradition of Zoroastrianism continued to echo well beyond its disappearance in the land of its birth.

Judaism

AP® EXAM TIP

You should know the basic tenets of Judaism and its political and social effects on world history.

Guided Reading Question

■ DESCRIPTION
What was distinctive about the Jewish religious tradition?

While Zoroastrianism emerged in the greatest empire of its time, Judaism, the Middle East's other ancient monotheistic tradition, was born among one of the region's smaller and, at the time, less significant peoples—the Hebrews. Their traditions, recorded in the Hebrew scriptures, tell of an early migration from Mesopotamia to Canaan under the leadership of Abraham. Those same traditions report that a portion of these people later fled to Egypt, where they were first enslaved and then miraculously escaped to rejoin their kinfolk in Palestine. There, around 1000 B.C.E., they established a small state, which soon split into two parts—a northern kingdom called Israel and a southern state called Judah.

In a region politically dominated by the large empires of Assyria, Babylon, and Persia, these tiny Hebrew communities lived a precarious existence. Israel was conquered by Assyria in 722 B.C.E., and many of its inhabitants were deported to distant regions, where they assimilated into the local culture. In 586 B.C.E., the kingdom of Judah likewise came under Babylonian control, and its elite class was shipped off to exile. "By the rivers of Babylon," wrote one of their poets, "there we sat down, yea, we wept, when we remembered Zion [Jerusalem]." It was in Babylonian exile that these people, now calling themselves Jews, retained and renewed their cultural identity, and later a small number were able to return to their homeland. A large part of that identity lay in their unique religious ideas. It was in creating that religious tradition, rather than in building a powerful empire, that this small people cast a long shadow in world history.

Ancient Israel

From their unique historical memory of exodus from Egypt and exile in Babylon, the Hebrews evolved over many centuries a distinctive conception of God. Unlike the peoples of Mesopotamia, India, Greece, and elsewhere—all of whom populated the invisible realm with numerous gods and goddesses—Jews found in their God, whom they called Yahweh (YAH-way), a powerful and jealous deity, who demanded their exclusive loyalty. "Thou shalt have no other gods before me"—this was the first of the Ten Commandments. It was a difficult requirement, for as the Hebrews turned from a pastoral life to agriculture, many of them were attracted by the fertility gods of neighboring peoples. Their neighbors' goddesses were also attractive, offering a kind of spiritual support that the primarily masculine Yahweh could not. Foreign deities also entered Hebrew culture through royal treaty obligations with nearby states. Thus the emerging Hebrew conception of the Divine was not quite monotheism, for the repeated demands of the Hebrew prophets to turn away from other gods show that those deities remained real for many Jews. Over time, however, the priesthood that supported the one-god theory triumphed. The Jews came to understand their relationship to Yahweh as a contract or a covenant. In return for their sole devotion and obedience to God's laws, Yahweh would consider the Jews his chosen people, favoring them in battle, causing them to grow in numbers, and bringing them prosperity and blessing.

Unlike the bickering, arbitrary, polytheistic gods of Mesopotamia or ancient Greece, who were associated with the forces of nature and behaved in quite human fashion, Yahweh was increasingly seen as a lofty, transcendent deity of utter holiness and purity, set far above the world of nature, which he had created. But unlike the impersonal conceptions of ultimate reality found in Daoism and Hinduism, Yahweh was encountered as a divine person with whom people could actively communicate. He also acted within the historical process, bringing the Jews out of Egypt or using foreign empires to punish them for their disobedience.

Furthermore, for some, Yahweh was transformed from a god of war, who ordered his people to "utterly destroy" the original inhabitants of the Promised Land, to a god of social justice and compassion for the poor and the marginalized, especially in the passionate pronouncements of Jewish prophets such as Amos and Isaiah. The prophet Isaiah describes Yahweh as rejecting the empty rituals of his chosen but sinful people: "What to me is the multitude of your sacrifices, says the Lord. . . . Wash yourselves, make yourselves clean, . . . cease to do evil, learn to do good; seek justice; correct oppression; defend the fatherless; plead for the widow."[16]

Here was a distinctive conception of the Divine—singular, transcendent, personal, ruling over the natural order, engaged in history, and demanding social justice and moral righteousness above sacrifices and rituals. This set of ideas sustained a separate Jewish identity in both ancient and modern times, and it was this understanding of God that provided the foundation on which those later Abrahamic faiths of Christianity and Islam were built.

Jewish understanding of the natural world likewise informed all three religious traditions. The Jewish scriptures pronounced the world of nature as real and positively valued, not simply an illusion or a distraction from spiritual concerns, as in some versions of Hindu or Buddhist thinking. The first chapter of Genesis ends with God's review of his creation: "And God saw everything that he had made, and behold it was very good." Moreover, the material world disclosed or revealed something of the divine mystery. The writer of the Psalms affirmed that "the heavens declare the glory of God and the firmament shows his handiwork." Much later, the Quran echoed this understanding: "There are signs in the creation of the heavens and the earth, and in the alternation of night and day for people of understanding." Finally, Jewish tradition made human beings the stewards of creation. They were to "have dominion . . . over all the earth," even as Adam and Eve in the Garden of Eden were instructed "to till it and keep it." The Jewish teacher named Jesus affirmed this view of the world in the famous Lord's prayer: "Thy kingdom come, on earth as it is in heaven."

The Cultural Tradition of Classical Greece: The Search for a Rational Order

Unlike the Jews, the Persians, or the civilization of India, Greek thinkers of the second-wave era generated no lasting religious tradition of world historical importance. The religion of these city-states brought together the unpredictable, quarreling, and lustful gods of Mount Olympus, secret fertility cults, oracles predicting the future, and the ecstatic worship of Dionysus, the god of wine. The distinctive feature of the classical Greek cultural tradition was the willingness of many Greek intellectuals to abandon this mythological framework, to affirm that the world was a physical reality governed by natural laws, and to assert that human rationality could both understand these laws and work out a system of moral and ethical life as well. In separating science and philosophy from conventional religion, the Greeks developed a way of thinking that bore some similarity to the secularism of Confucian thought in China.

Precisely why Greek thought evolved in this direction is hard to say. Perhaps the diversity and incoherence of Greek religious mythology presented its intellectuals with a challenge to bring some order to their understanding of the world. Greece's geographic position on the margins of the great civilizations of Mesopotamia, Egypt, and Persia certainly provided intellectual stimulation. Furthermore, the growing role of law in the political life of Athens possibly suggested that a similar regularity also underlay the natural order.

Guided Reading Question

....

■ DESCRIPTION
What are the distinctive features of the Greek intellectual tradition?

The Greek Way of Knowing

The foundations of this Greek rationalism emerged in the three centuries between 600 and 300 B.C.E., coinciding with the flourishing of Greek city-states, especially Athens, and with the growth of its artistic, literary, and theatrical traditions. The enduring significance of Greek thinking lay not so much in the answers it provided to life's great issues, for the Greeks seldom agreed with one another, but rather in its way of asking questions. Their emphasis on argument, logic, and the relentless questioning of received wisdom; their confidence in human reason; their enthusiasm for puzzling out the world without much reference to the gods—these were the defining characteristics of the major Greek thinkers.

The great exemplar of this approach to knowledge was Socrates (469–399 B.C.E.), an Athenian philosopher who walked about the city engaging others in conversation about the good life. He wrote nothing, and his preferred manner of teaching was not the lecture or exposition of his own ideas but rather a constant questioning of the assumptions and logic of his students' thinking. Concerned always to puncture the pretentious, he challenged conventional ideas about the importance of wealth and power in living well, urging instead the pursuit of wisdom and virtue. He was critical of Athenian democracy and on occasion had positive things to say about Sparta, the great enemy of his own city. Such behavior brought him into conflict with city authorities, who accused him of corrupting the youth of Athens and sentenced him to death. At his trial, he defended himself as the "gadfly" of Athens, stinging its citizens into awareness. To any and all, he declared, "I shall question, and examine and cross-examine him, and if I find that he does not possess virtue, but says he does, I shall rebuke him for scorning the things that are most important and caring more for what is of less worth."[17]

The earliest of the classical Greek thinkers, many of them living on the Ionian coast of Anatolia, applied this rational and questioning way of knowing to the world of nature. For example, Thales, drawing on Babylonian astronomy, predicted an eclipse of the sun and argued that the moon simply reflected the sun's light. He was also one of the first Greeks to ask about the fundamental nature of the universe and came up with the idea that water was the basic stuff from which all else derived, for it existed as solid, liquid, and gas. Others argued in favor of air or fire or some combination. Democritus suggested that atoms, tiny "uncuttable" particles, collided in various configurations to form visible matter. Pythagoras believed that beneath the chaos and complexity of the visible world lay a simple, unchanging mathematical order. What these thinkers had in common was a commitment to a rational and nonreligious explanation for the material world.

Such thinking also served to explain the functioning of the human body and its diseases. Hippocrates and his followers came to believe that the body was composed of four fluids, or "humors," which caused various ailments when out of proper balance. He also traced the origins of epilepsy, known to the Greeks as "the sacred disease," to simple heredity: "It appears to me to be nowise more divine nor more

AP® EXAM TIP

You should know the effects of Greek approaches to science and logic.

The Death of Socrates
Condemned to death by an Athenian jury, Socrates declined to go into exile, voluntarily drank a cup of poison hemlock, and died in 399 B.C.E. in the presence of his friends. The dramatic scene was famously described by Plato and much later was immortalized on canvas by the French painter Jacques-Louis David in 1787. (*The Death of Socrates*, 1787. Oil on canvas, 51 x 77¼ in. [129.5 x 196.2 cm.]. Catharine Lorillard Wolfe Collection, Wolfe Fund, 1931 [31.45]./The Metropolitan Museum of Art, New York, NY, USA/Image copyright © The Metropolitan Museum of Art/Image source: Art Resource, NY)

sacred than other diseases, but has a natural cause . . . like other afflictions."[18] A similar approach informed Greek thinking about the ways of humankind. Herodotus, who wrote about the Greco-Persian Wars, explained his project as an effort to discover "the reason why they fought one another." This assumption that human reasons lay behind the conflict, not simply the whims of the gods, was what made Herodotus a historian in the modern sense of that word. Ethics and government also figured importantly in Greek thinking. Plato (429–348 B.C.E.) famously sketched out in *The Republic* a design for a good society. It would be ruled by a class of highly educated "guardians" led by a "philosopher-king." Such people would be able to penetrate the many illusions of the material world and to grasp the "world of forms," in which ideas such as goodness, beauty, and justice lived a real and unchanging existence. Only such people, he argued, were fit to rule.

Aristotle (384–322 B.C.E.), a student of Plato and a teacher of Alexander the Great, represents the most complete expression of the Greek way of knowing, for he wrote or commented on practically everything. With an emphasis on empirical observation, he cataloged the constitutions of 158 Greek city-states, identified hundreds of species of animals, and wrote about logic, physics, astronomy, the weather, and much else besides. Famous for his reflections on ethics, he argued that "virtue" was a product of rational training and cultivated habit and could be learned. As to government, he urged a mixed system, combining the principles of monarchy, aristocracy, and democracy.

The Greek Legacy

The rationalism of the Greek tradition was clearly not the whole of Greek culture. The gods of Mount Olympus continued to be a reality for many people, and the ecstatic songs and dances that celebrated Dionysus, the god of wine, were anything but rational and reflective. The death of Socrates at the hands of an Athenian jury showed that philosophy could be a threat as well as an engaging pastime. Nonetheless, Greek rationalism, together with Greek art, literature, and theater, persisted long after the glory days of Athens were over. Alexander's empire and that of the Romans facilitated the spread of Greek culture within the Mediterranean basin and beyond, and not a few leading Roman figures sent their children to be educated in Athens at the Academy, which Plato had founded. An emerging Christian theology was expressed in terms of Greek philosophical concepts, especially those of Plato. Even after the western Roman Empire collapsed, classical Greek texts were preserved in the eastern half, known as the Byzantine Empire or Byzantium.

In the West, however, direct access to Greek texts was far more difficult in the chaotic conditions of post-Roman Europe, and for centuries Greek scholarship was neglected in favor of distinctly Christian writers. Much of that legacy was subsequently rediscovered after the twelfth century C.E. as European scholars gained access to classical Greek texts. From that point on, the Greek legacy has been viewed as a central element of an emerging "Western" civilization. It played a role in formulating an updated Christian theology, in fostering Europe's Scientific Revolution, and in providing a point of departure for much of European philosophy.

Long before this European rediscovery, the Greek legacy had also entered the Islamic world. Systematic translations of Greek works of science and philosophy into Arabic, together with Indian and Persian learning, stimulated Muslim thinkers and scientists, especially in the fields of medicine, astronomy, mathematics, geography, and chemistry. It was in fact largely from Arabic translations of Greek writers that Europeans became reacquainted with the legacy of classical Greece, especially during the twelfth and thirteenth centuries. Despite the many centuries that have passed since the flourishing of ancient Greek culture, that tradition has remained, especially in the West, an inspiration for those who celebrate the powers of the human mind to probe the mysteries of the universe and to explore the equally challenging domain of human life.

> **AP® EXAM TIP**
>
> Know the effects of the spread of Greek culture throughout Afro-Eurasia over time.

The Birth of Christianity ... with Buddhist Comparisons

About 500 years after the time of Confucius, the Buddha, Zarathustra, and Socrates, a young Jewish peasant/carpenter in the remote province of Judaea in the Roman Empire began a brief three-year career of teaching and miracle working before he got in trouble with local authorities and was executed. In one of history's most unlikely stories, the life and teachings of that obscure man, barely noted in the historical records of the time, became the basis of the world's second great universal religion, after Buddhism. This man, Jesus of Nazareth, and the religion of Christianity that grew out of his brief career, had a dramatic impact on world history, similar to and often compared with that of India's Siddhartha Gautama, the Buddha.

The Lives of the Founders

The family background of the two teachers could hardly have been more different. Gautama was born to royalty and luxury, whereas Jesus was a rural or small-town worker from a distinctly lower-class family. But both became spiritual seekers, mystics in their respective traditions, who claimed to have personally experienced another and unseen level of reality. Those powerful religious experiences provided the motivation for their life's work and the personal authenticity that attracted their growing band of followers.

Both were "wisdom teachers," challenging the conventional values of their time, urging the renunciation of wealth, and emphasizing the supreme importance of love or compassion as the basis for a moral life. The Buddha had instructed his followers in the practice of *metta*, or loving-kindness: "Just as a mother would protect her only child at the risk of her own life, even so, let [my followers] cultivate a boundless heart towards all beings."[19] In a similar vein during his famous Sermon on the Mount, Jesus told his followers: "You have heard that it was said 'Love your neighbor and hate your enemy,' but I tell you 'Love your enemies and pray for those who persecute you.'"[20] Both Jesus and the Buddha called for the personal transformation of their followers, through "letting go" of the grasping that causes suffering, in the Buddha's teaching, or "losing one's life in order to save it," in the language of Jesus.[21]

Despite these similarities, there were also some differences in their teachings and their life stories. Jesus inherited from his Jewish tradition an intense devotion to a single personal deity with whom he was on intimate terms, referring to him as Abba ("papa" or "daddy"). According to the New Testament, the miracles he performed reflected the power of God available to him as a result of that relationship. The Buddha's original message, by contrast, largely ignored the supernatural, involved no miracles, and taught a path of intense self-effort aimed at ethical living and mindfulness as a means of ending suffering. Furthermore, Jesus' teachings had a sharper social and political edge than did those of the Buddha. Jesus spoke more clearly on

---

Guided Reading Question

■ COMPARISON

How would you compare the lives and teachings of Jesus and the Buddha? In what different ways did the two religions evolve after the deaths of their founders?

AP® EXAM TIP

Pay attention to these comparisons of Jesus and Siddhartha Gautama as you develop your skills as an essay writer.

behalf of the poor and the oppressed, directly criticized the hypocrisies of the powerful, and deliberately associated with lepers, adulterous women, and tax collectors, all of whom were regarded as "impure." These actions reflected his lower-class background, the Jewish tradition of social criticism, and the reality of Roman imperial rule over his people, none of which corresponded to the Buddha's experience. Finally, Jesus' public life was very brief, probably less than three years, compared to more than forty years for the Buddha. His teachings had so antagonized both Jewish and Roman authorities that he was crucified as a political rebel. The Buddha's message was apparently less threatening to the politically powerful, and he died a natural death at age eighty.

The Spread of New Religions

Neither Jesus nor the Buddha had any intention of founding a new religion; rather, they sought to revitalize the traditions from which they had come. Nonetheless, Christianity and Buddhism soon emerged as separate religions, distinct from Judaism and Hinduism, proclaiming their messages to a much wider and more inclusive audience. In the process, both teachers were transformed by their followers into gods. According to many scholars, Jesus never claimed divine status, seeing himself as a teacher or a prophet, whose close relationship to God could be replicated by anyone. The Buddha likewise viewed himself as an enlightened but fully human person, an example of what was possible for all who followed the path. But in Mahayana Buddhism, the Buddha became a supernatural being who could be worshipped and prayed to and was spiritually available to his followers. Jesus also soon became divine in the eyes of his early followers, such as Saint Paul and Saint John. According to one of the first creeds of the Church, he was "the Son of God, Very God of Very God," while his death and resurrection made possible the forgiveness of sins and the eternal salvation of those who believed.

The transformation of Christianity from a small Jewish sect to a world religion began with Saint Paul (10–65 C.E.), an early convert whose missionary journeys in the eastern Roman Empire led to the founding of small Christian communities that included non-Jews. The Good News of Jesus, Paul argued, was for everyone, and Gentile (non-Jewish) converts need not follow Jewish laws or rituals such as circumcision. In one of his many letters to these new communities, later collected as part of the New Testament, Paul wrote, "There is neither Jew nor Greek . . . neither slave nor free . . . neither male nor female, for you are all one in Christ Jesus."[22]

Despite Paul's egalitarian pronouncement, early Christianity, like Buddhism, offered a mix of opportunities and restrictions for women. Jesus himself had interacted easily with a wide range of women, and they had figured prominently among his followers. Some scholars have argued that Mary Magdalene was a part of his inner circle.[23] And women played leadership roles in the "house churches" of the first century C.E. Nonetheless, some New Testament writings counseled women to "be subject to your husbands" and declared that "it is shameful for a woman to

AP® EXAM TIP

You should know that Buddhism and Christianity developed out of earlier belief systems, Hinduism and Judaism, respectively.

Guided Reading Question

■ CHANGE

In what ways was Christianity transformed in the five centuries following the death of Jesus?

speak in church." Men were identified with the role of Christ himself, for "the husband is head of the wife as Christ is head of the Church."[24] It was not long before male spokesmen for the faith had fully assimilated older and highly negative views of women. As daughters of Eve, they were responsible for the introduction of sin and evil into the world and were the source of temptation for men. On the other hand, Jesus' mother, Mary, soon became the focus of a devotional cult; women were among the martyrs of the early Church; and growing numbers of Christian women, like their Buddhist counterparts, found a more independent space in the monasteries, even as the official hierarchy of the Church became wholly male.

AP® EXAM TIP

As with other world religions, you should know the factors that attracted followers to Christianity across place and time.

Nonetheless, the inclusive message of early Christianity was one of the attractions of the new faith as it spread very gradually within the Roman Empire during the several centuries after Jesus' death (see Map 4.1). The earliest converts were usually lower-stratum people—artisans, traders, and a considerable number of women—mostly from towns and cities, while a scattering of wealthier, more prominent, and better-educated people subsequently joined the ranks of Christians. The spread of the faith was often accompanied by reports of miracles, healings, and the casting out of demons—all of which were impressive to people thoroughly accustomed to seeing the supernatural behind the events of ordinary life. Christian communities also attracted converts by the way their members cared for one another. In the middle of the third century C.E., the Church in Rome supported 154 priests (of whom 52 were exorcists) and some 1,500 widows, orphans, and destitute people.[25] By 300 C.E., perhaps 10 percent of the Roman Empire's population (some 5 million people) identified themselves as Christians.

Although Christians in the West often think of their faith as a European-centered religion, during the first six centuries of the Christian era, most followers of Jesus lived in the non-European regions of the Roman Empire—North Africa, Egypt, Anatolia, Syria—or outside the empire altogether in Arabia, Persia, Ethiopia, India, and China. Saint Paul's missionary journeys had established various Christian communities in the Roman province of Asia—what is now Turkey—and also in Syria, where the earliest recorded Christian church building was located. The Syrian Church also developed a unique liturgy with strong Jewish influences and a distinctive musical tradition of chants and hymns. The language of that liturgy was neither Greek nor Latin, but Syriac, a Semitic tongue closely related to Aramaic, which Jesus spoke.

From Syria, the faith spread eastward into Persia, where it attracted a substantial number of converts, many of them well educated in the sciences and medicine, by the third century C.E. Those converts also encountered periodic persecution from the Zoroastrian rulers of Persia and were sometimes suspected of political loyalty to the Roman Empire, Persia's longtime enemy and rival. To the north of Syria on the slopes of the Caucasus Mountains, the Kingdom of Armenia became the first place where rulers adopted Christianity as a state religion. In time, Christianity

Map 4.1   The Spread of Early Christianity and Buddhism

In the five centuries after the birth of Jesus, Christianity found converts from Spain to northeast Africa, the Middle East, Central Asia, and India. In the Roman Empire, Axum, and Armenia, the new religion enjoyed state support as well. Subsequently, Christianity took root solidly in Europe and after 1000 C.E. in Russia as well. Meanwhile, Buddhism was spreading from its South Asian homeland to various parts of Asia, even as it was weakening in India itself.

became—and remains to this day—a central element of Armenian national identity. A distinctive feature of Armenian Christianity involved the ritual killing of animals at the end of the worship service, probably a continuation of earlier pre-Christian practices.

Syria and Persia represented the core region of the Church of the East, distinct both theologically and organizationally from the Latin Church focused on Rome and an emerging Eastern Orthodox Church based in Constantinople. Its missionaries took Christianity even farther to the east. By the fourth century, and perhaps much earlier, a well-organized Church had taken root in southern India, which later gained tax privileges and special rights from local rulers. In the early seventh century, a Persian monk named Alopen initiated a small but remarkable Christian experiment in China, described more fully in Chapter 10. A modest Christian presence in Central Asia was also an outgrowth of this Church of the East.

Perpetua, Christian Martyr

"The blood of the martyrs," declared the Christian writer Tertullian, "is the seed of the church." Few of those martyrs, whose stories so inspired the persecuted converts of the early Christian centuries, could match that of Perpetua, a young woman whose prison diary provides a highly personal account of her arrest and trial.[26]

Born in 181 C.E. in the North African city of Carthage, Perpetua hailed from an upper-class Roman family and was quite well educated, literate in Latin and probably Greek, and acquainted with Roman philosophical writings. By the time she entered the historical record at age twenty-two, she had given birth to a son, had lost her husband to either death or abandonment, and had recently begun to study Christianity, becoming part of a small but growing group of educated people who were turning toward the new faith. Coinciding with her conversion was a wave of persecutions ordered by the Roman emperor Septimus Severus, also of North

Perpetua.

African descent and a devotee of the Egyptian cult of Isis and Osiris. Severus sought to forbid new conversions rather than punish long-established Christians. In line with this policy, in 203 C.E., the hard-line governor of the region ordered the arrest of Perpetua along with four others—two slaves, one of them a woman named Felicitas who was eight months pregnant, and two free men. Before she was taken to the prison, however, Perpetua decisively confirmed her commitment to Christianity by accepting baptism.

Once in the "dark hole" of the prison, Perpetua was terrified. It was crowded and stiflingly hot, and she was consumed with anxiety for her child. Several fellow Christians managed to bribe the prison guards to permit Perpetua to nurse her baby son. Reunited with her child, she found that "my prison had suddenly

photo: Detail from vault mosaic, Archbishop's Palace, Ravenna, Italy/Scala/ Art Resource, NY

In other directions as well, Christianity spread from its Palestinian place of origin. By the time Muhammad was born in 570, a number of Arabs had become Christians. One of them, in fact, was among the first to affirm Muhammad as an authentic prophet. A particularly vibrant center of Christianity developed in Egypt, where tradition holds that Jesus' family fled to escape persecution by King Herod. Egyptian priests soon translated the Bible into the Egyptian language known as Coptic, and Egyptian Christians pioneered various forms of monasticism. By 400 C.E., hundreds of monasteries, cells, and caves dotted the desert, inhabited by reclusive monks dedicated to their spiritual practices. Increasingly, the language, theology, and practice of Egyptian Christianity diverged from that of Rome and Constantinople, giving expression to Egyptian resistance against Roman or Byzantine oppression. To the west of Egypt, a Church of North Africa furnished a number of the intellectuals of the early Church, including Saint Augustine, as well as many become a palace, so that I wanted to be there rather than anywhere else."

A few days later, Perpetua's deeply distressed non-Christian father arrived for a visit, hoping to persuade his only daughter to recant her faith and save her life and the family's honor. It was a heartbreaking encounter. "Daughter," he said, "have pity on my grey head. . . . Do not abandon me to be the reproach of men. Think of your brothers, think of your mother and your aunt, think of your child, who will not be able to live once you are gone. Give up your pride! You will destroy all of us! None of us will ever be able to speak freely again if anything happens to you." Firm in her faith, Perpetua refused his entreaties, and she reported that "he left me in great sorrow."

On the day of her trial, with her distraught father in attendance, the governor Hilarianus also begged Perpetua to consider her family and renounce her faith by offering a sacrifice to the emperor. Again she refused and together with her four companions was "condemned to the beasts," a humiliating form of execution normally reserved for the lower classes. Although she was now permanently separated from her child, she wrote, "We returned to the prison in high spirits." During her last days in the prison, Perpetua and the others were treated "more humanely" and were allowed to visit with family and friends, as the head of the jail was himself a Christian.

But then, on the birthday of the emperor, this small band of Christians was marched to the amphitheater, "joyfully as though they were going to heaven," according to an eyewitness account. After the prisoners strenuously and successfully resisted dressing in the robes of pagan priests, the three men were sent into the arena to contend with a boar, a bear, and a leopard. Then it was the turn of the women, Perpetua and the slave Felicitas, who had given birth only two days earlier. When a mad cow failed to kill them, a soldier was sent to finish the work. As he approached Perpetua, he apparently hesitated, but as an eyewitness account put it, "she took the trembling hand of the young gladiator and guided it to her throat." Appended to her diary was this comment from an unknown observer: "It was as though so great a woman, feared as she was by the unclean spirit, could not be dispatched unless she herself were willing."

Questions: How might you understand the actions and attitudes of Perpetua? Is her experience accessible to people living in a largely secular modern society?

Christian martyrs to Roman persecution. (See Zooming In: Perpetua, above.) Here and elsewhere, the coming of Christianity provoked not only hostility from Roman political authorities but also tensions within families. The North African Carthaginian writer Tertullian (160–220 C.E.), known as the "father of Latin Christianity," described the kind of difficulties that might arise between a Christian wife and her "pagan" husband:

> She is engaged in a fast; her husband has arranged a banquet. It is her Christian duty to visit the streets and the homes of the poor; her husband insists on family business. She celebrates the Easter Vigil throughout the night; her husband expects her in his bed. . . . She who has taken a cup at Eucharist will be required to take of a cup with her husband in the tavern. She who has foresworn idolatry must inhale the smoke arising from the incense on the altars of the idols in her husband's home.[27]

Further south in Africa, Christianity became during the fourth century the state religion of Axum, an emerging kingdom in what is now Eritrea and Ethiopia (see Chapter 6). This occurred at about the same time as both Armenia and the Roman Empire officially endorsed Christianity. In Axum, a distinctively African expression of Christianity took root with open-air services, the use of drums and stringed instruments in worship, and colorful umbrellas covering priests and musicians from the elements. Linked theologically and organizationally to Coptic Christianity in Egypt, the Ethiopian Church used Ge'ez, a local Semitic language and script, for its liturgy and literature.

In the Roman world, the strangest and most offensive feature of the new faith was its exclusive monotheism and its antagonism to all other supernatural powers, particularly the cult of the emperors. Christians' denial of these other gods caused them to be tagged as "atheists" and was one reason behind the empire's intermittent persecution of Christians during the first three centuries of the Common Era. All of that ended with Emperor Constantine's conversion in the early fourth century C.E. and with growing levels of state support for the new religion in the decades that followed.

Roman rulers sought to use an increasingly popular Christianity as glue to hold together a very diverse population in a weakening imperial state. Constantine and his successors thus provided Christians with newfound security and opportunities. The emperor Theodosius (r. 379–395 C.E.) enforced a ban on all polytheistic ritual sacrifices and ordered the temples that practiced them closed. Christians, by contrast, received patronage for their buildings, official approval for their doctrines, suppression of their rivals, prestige from imperial recognition, and, during the late fourth century, the proclamation of Christianity as the official state religion. All of this set in motion a process by which the Roman Empire, and later all of Europe, became overwhelmingly Christian. At the time, however, Christianity was expanding at least as rapidly to the east and south as it was to the west. In 500, few observers could have predicted that the future of Christianity would lie primarily in Europe rather than in Asia and Africa.

The spread of Buddhism in India was quite different from that of Christianity in the Roman Empire. Even though Ashoka's support gave Buddhism a considerable boost, it was never promoted to the exclusion of other faiths. Ashoka sought harmony among India's diverse population through religious tolerance rather than uniformity. The kind of monotheistic intolerance that Christianity exhibited in the Roman world was quite foreign to Indian patterns of religious practice. Although Buddhism subsequently died out in India as it was absorbed into a reviving Hinduism, no renewal of Roman polytheism occurred, and Christianity became an enduring element of European civilization. Nonetheless, Christianity did adopt some elements of religious practice from the Roman world, including, perhaps, the cult of saints and the dating of the birth of Jesus to the winter solstice. In both cases, however, these new religions spread widely beyond their places of origin. Buddhism provided a network of cultural connections across much of Asia, while Christianity during its early centuries established an Afro-Eurasian presence.

Institutions, Controversies, and Divisions

As Christianity spread within the Roman Empire and beyond, it developed a hier-archical organization, with patriarchs, bishops, and priests—all men—replacing the house churches of the early years, in which women played a more prominent part. At least in some places, however, women continued to exercise leadership and even priestly roles, prompting Pope Gelasius in 494 to speak out sharply against those who encouraged women "to officiate at the sacred altars, and to take part in all matters imputed to the offices of the male sex, to which they do not belong."[28] In general, though, the exclusion of women from the priesthood established a male-dominated clergy and a patriarchal church, which has lasted into the twenty-first century.

The emerging Christian movement was, however, anything but unified. Its immense geographic reach, accompanied by inevitable differences in language, cul-ture, and political regime, ensured that a single focus for Christian belief and prac-tice was difficult to achieve. Doctrinal differences also tore at the unity of Chris-tianity and embroiled church authorities in frequent controversy about the nature of Jesus (was he human, divine, or both?), his relationship to God (equal or infe-rior?), and the always-perplexing concept of the Trinity (God as Father, Son, and Holy Spirit). There was debate as well about what writings belonged in the official New Testament, as dozens of letters, gospels, poems, and songs circulated among the early Christian communities. A series of church councils—at Nicaea (325 C.E.), Chalcedon (451 C.E.), and Constantinople (553 C.E.), for example—sought to define an orthodox, or correct, position on these and other issues, declaring those who disagreed as *anathema* and expelling them from the Church. Thus Egyptian Christians, for example, held to the unorthodox position called Monophysite. This view, that Jesus had a single divine nature simply occupying a human body, expressed resistance to domination from Rome or Constantinople, which held that Jesus was both fully human and fully divine. Likewise, the Church of the East adopted Nesto-rianism, another unorthodox view that emphasized the human side of Jesus' nature and distinguished its theology from the Latin and Eastern Orthodox Churches.

Beyond these theological debates, political and cultural differences generated division even among the orthodox. The bishop of Rome gradually emerged as the dominant leader, or pope, of the Church in the western half of the empire, but his authority was sharply contested in the East. This division contributed to the later split between the Latin, or Roman Catholic, and the Greek, or Eastern Orthodox, branches of Christendom, a division that continues to the present (see Chapter 10). Thus the Christian world of 500 C.E. was not only geographically extensive but also politically and theologically very diverse and highly fragmented.

Buddhists too clashed over various interpretations of the Buddha's teachings, and a series of councils failed to prevent the division between Theravada, Maha-yana, and other approaches. A considerable proliferation of different sects, prac-tices, teachings, and meditation techniques subsequently emerged within the Bud-dhist world, but these divisions generally lacked the "clear-cut distinction between

AP® EXAM TIP

The methods of leadership within Christianity—as well as in all major belief systems—are important concepts.

AP® EXAM TIP

You should know factors that led to divisions within major belief systems, as seen in this example.

'right' and 'wrong' ideas" that characterized conflicts within the Christian world.[29] Although Buddhist states and warrior classes (such as the famous samurai of Japan) sometimes engaged in warfare, religious differences among Buddhists seldom provided the basis for the bitterness and violence that often accompanied religious conflict within Christendom. Nor did Buddhists develop the kind of overall religious hierarchy that characterized Christianity, although communities of monks and nuns, organized in monasteries, created elaborate rules to govern their internal affairs.

PRACTICING AP® HISTORICAL THINKING

How might you understand the appeal of Buddhism and Christianity as opposed to the more rationalist approaches of Greek and Confucian philosophy?

REFLECTIONS

Religion and Historians

To put it mildly, religion has always been a sensitive subject, and no less so for historians than for anyone else. Throughout human history, the vast majority of people have simply assumed the existence of an unseen realm, that of the gods, the spirits, the sacred, or the Divine. They further accepted the capacity of human beings, guided often by tradition, ritual, or religious authority, to align themselves with that other world. But more recently, as an outgrowth of the Scientific Revolution and the European Enlightenment, some have challenged those assumptions, arguing that the only realities worth considering are those that can be accessed with the techniques of science and our five senses. This situation has generated various tensions or misunderstandings between historians and religious practitioners because modern secular historians, whatever their personal beliefs, can rely only on evidence available in this world.

One of these tensions involves the question of change. Most religions present themselves as timeless revelations from the beyond, partaking of eternity or at least reflecting ancient practice. In the eyes of historians, however, the religious aspect of human life changes as much as any other. The Hindu tradition changed from a religion of ritual and sacrifice to one of devotion and worship. Buddhism became more conventionally religious, with an emphasis on the supernatural, as it evolved from Theravada to Mahayana forms. A male-dominated hierarchical Christian Church, with its pope, bishops, priests, and state support, was very different from the small house churches that suffered persecution by imperial authorities in the early Christian centuries. The implication—that religions are largely a human phenomenon—has been troublesome to some believers.

Historians, on the other hand, have sometimes been uncomfortable in the face of claims by believers that they have actually experienced a divine reality, and therein lies a second problem. How could such experiences be verified, when even the biographical details for Buddha and Jesus are difficult to prove by the standards of historians? Certainly, modern historians are in no position to validate or refute the spiritual claims of these teachers, but we need to take them seriously. Although we will never know precisely what happened to the Buddha as he sat in meditation in northern India or what transpired when Jesus spent forty days in the wilderness, clearly those experiences changed the two men and motivated their subsequent actions. Later, Muhammad likewise claimed to have received revelations from God in the caves outside Mecca. Millions of the followers of these religious leaders have also acted on the basis of what they perceived to be an encounter with the Divine or the unseen. This interior dimension of human experience, though difficult to grasp with any precision and impossible to verify, has been a significant mover and shaper of the historical process.

Yet a third problem arises from debates within particular religious traditions about which group most accurately represents the "real" or authentic version of the faith. Historians usually refuse to take sides in such disputes. They simply notice with interest that most human cultural traditions generate conflicting views, some of which become the basis for serious conflict in societies.

Reconciling personal religious convictions with the perspectives of modern historical scholarship is no easy task. At the very least, all of us can appreciate the immense human effort that has gone into the making of religious traditions, and we can acknowledge the enormous significance of these traditions in the unfolding of the human story. They have shaped the meanings that billions of people over thousands of years have attached to the world they inhabit. These religious traditions have justified the vast social inequalities and oppressive states of human civilizations, but they have also enabled human beings to endure the multiple sufferings that attend human life, and on occasion they have stimulated reform and rebellion. And the religions born in second-wave civilizations have guided much of humankind in our endless efforts to penetrate the mysteries of the world beyond and of the world within.

Chapter Review

What's the Significance?

Big Picture Questions

1. Is a secular outlook on the world an essentially modern phenomenon, or does it have precedents in the second-wave era?
2. "Religion is a double-edged sword, both supporting and undermining political authority and social elites." How would you support both sides of this statement?
3. How would you define the appeal of the religious/cultural traditions discussed in this chapter? To what groups were they attractive, and why?
4. Imagine that you were a Roman Christian traveler in the Eurasian world of 500 C.E. writing home about your encounter with other religious traditions. What similarities and differences might you notice? What might you appreciate in those traditions? And what might you find appalling?
5. **Looking Back:** What relationships can you see between the political dimensions of second-wave civilizations described in Chapter 3 and their cultural or religious aspects discussed in this chapter?

Next Steps: For Further Study

Karen Armstrong, *The Great Transformation* (2006). A comparative and historical study of the major religions by a well-known scholar.

Robert N. Bellah, *Religion in Human Evolution: From the Paleolithic to the Axial Age* (2011). An impressive but controversial account of the origins of religion in general and those of second-wave civilizations in particular.

Peter Brown, *The Rise of Western Christendom* (2003). A history of the first 1,000 years of Christianity, cast in a global framework.

Huston Smith, *An Illustrated World's Religions* (1994). A sympathetic account of major world religions, beautifully illustrated, by a prominent scholar of comparative religion.

Arthur Waley, *Three Ways of Thought in Ancient China* (1983). A classic work, first published more than half a century ago, about the major philosophies of old China.

Jonathan S. Walters, *Finding Buddhists in Global History* (1998). A brief account that situates Buddhism in a world history framework.

BBC, "Religions," http://www.bbc.co.uk/religion/religions/. A succinct introduction to the history, beliefs, and practices of many of the world's religious traditions.

Bridging World History, "Early Belief Systems," http://www.learner.org/courses/worldhistory/unit_main_5 .html. A thoughtful Web site that explores the origins of the religious impulse and many of the traditions covered in this chapter.

WORKING WITH EVIDENCE

Representations of the Buddha

Buddhism derived from a single individual, Siddhartha Gautama, born in northern India, probably in the sixth century B.C.E. The son of royalty, the young Siddhartha enjoyed a splendid but sheltered upbringing encased in luxury, and his father spared no effort to protect the child from anything painful or difficult. At the age of sixteen, he was married to a beautiful cousin, Yasodhara, who bore him a son thirteen years later. Buddhist tradition tells us that while riding beyond the palace grounds, this curious and lively young man encountered human suffering in the form of an old man, a sick person, and a corpse. Shattered by these revelations of aging, illness, and death, Siddhartha determined to find the cause of such sufferings and a remedy for them. And so, at the age of twenty-nine and on the very day his son was born, the young prince left his luxurious life as well as his wife and child, shed his royal jewels, cut off his hair, and set off on a quest for enlightenment. This act of severing his ties to the attachments of ordinary life is known in Buddhist teaching as the Great Renunciation.

What followed were six years of spiritual experimentation that finally led Siddhartha to an ancient fig tree in northern India, now known as the Bodhi (enlightenment) tree. There, Buddhist sources tell us, he began a forty-nine-day period of intensive meditation that ended with an almost indescribable experience of spiritual realization. Now he was the Buddha, the man who had awakened. For the next forty years, he taught what he had learned, setting in motion the cultural tradition of Buddhism. Over many centuries, the religion evolved as it grew in numbers and intersected with various cultures throughout Asia, including those of China, Japan, Tibet, Korea, and Vietnam.

For almost five centuries after his death, which likely took place in the early fifth century B.C.E., artists represented the Buddha as an empty throne, a horse with no rider, a tree, a wheel, or in some other symbolic way, while largely shunning any depiction of him in human form. Among the most widespread of those early symbolic representations of the Buddha were images of his footprints. Found throughout Buddhist Asia, such footprints indicated the Buddha's spiritual presence and served as a focus for devotion or contemplation. They also reminded his followers that since he had passed into nirvana, he could not be physically present. One Buddhist text declared that those who looked on those footprints "shall be freed from the bonds of error, and conducted upon the Way of Enlightenment."[30]

Permission courtesy of John Eskenazi, photo courtesy of AC Cooper

Source 4.1 Footprints of the Buddha

Source 4.1 shows a footprint image from northwestern India dating probably from the second century C.E. and containing a number of Buddhist symbols. In the center of each footprint is a *dharmachakra*, a wheel-like structure that had long symbolized the Buddha's teaching. Here, it surrounds a lotus flower, representing the Buddha's purity. Near the heel is a three-pronged emblem known as a *triratna*. It symbolizes the three things in which Buddhists can take refuge: the Buddha himself, his teaching, and the *sangha* (the Buddhist community). This particular footprint image also includes in the bottom corners two *yakshis*, Indian female earth spirits suggesting fertility. The position of their hands conveys a respectful greeting.

■ Why might artists have been reluctant to portray the human figure of the Buddha?

■ Why might the wheel serve as an effective symbol of the Buddha's message?

- What does the inclusion of the yakshis add to the message of this image?
- What overall religious message might this footprint convey to those who gazed on it?

By the first century C.E., the impulse to depict the Buddha in human form had surfaced, with some of the earliest examples coming from the region of South Asia known as Gandhara in what is now northern Pakistan and eastern Afghanistan (see Map 3.3, page 115). That area had been a part of the empire of Alexander the Great and his Hellenistic successors from about 322 B.C.E. to 50 B.C.E. and had developed commercial ties to the Roman Empire as well. These early images of the Buddha reflect this Greco-Roman influence, depicting him with a face similar to that of the Greek god Apollo, dressed in a Roman-style toga, and with curly hair characteristic of the Mediterranean region.

Source 4.2, from India of the second or third century C.E., depicts in Gandhara style a famous scene from the life of the Buddha—his temptation by the demon Mara and Mara's seductive daughters while meditating under the Bodhi tree.

- How are Mara and his daughters, shown on the right, portrayed in this relief?
- What attitude characterizes the Buddha, shown on the left and surrounded by attendants?
- Why might Greco-Roman cultural influence have stimulated physical representations of the Buddha?
- What larger meaning might the Buddha's followers take from this story?

By the time of India's Gupta dynasty (320–550 C.E.), the Greco-Roman influence of the Gandhara style was fading, replaced by more completely Indian images of the Buddha, which became the "classic" model, shown on page 160. Yet, as the message of the Buddha gained a mass following and spread across much of Asia, some of its early features—rigorous and time-consuming meditation practice, a focus on monks and nuns withdrawn from ordinary life, the absence of accessible supernatural figures able to provide help and comfort—proved difficult for many converts. And so the religion adapted. A new form of the faith, Mahayana Buddhism, offered greater accessibility, a spiritual path available to a much wider range of people beyond the monks and ascetics, who were the core group in early Buddhism.

In most expressions of Mahayana Buddhism, enlightenment (or becoming a Buddha) was available to everyone; it was possible within the context of ordinary life, rather than a monastery; and it might occur within a single lifetime rather than over the course of many lives. While Buddhism had

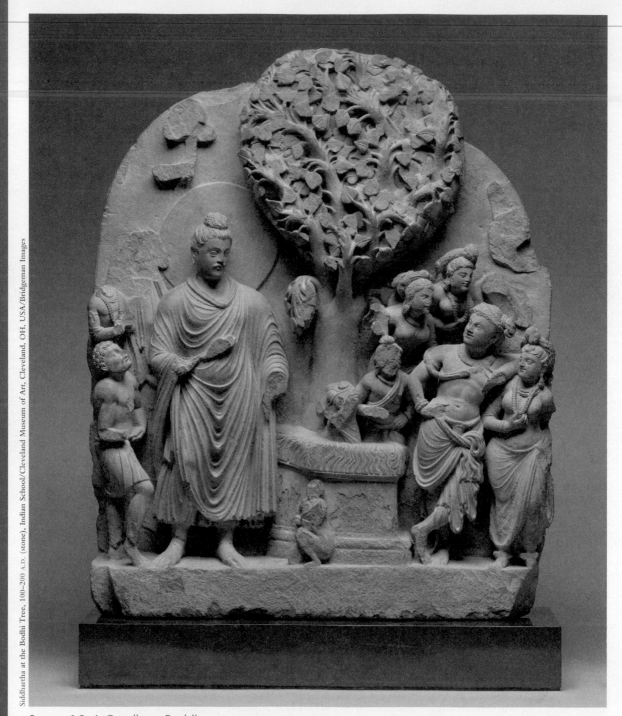

Siddhartha at the Bodhi Tree, 100–200 A.D. (stone), Indian School/Cleveland Museum of Art, Cleveland, OH, USA/Bridgeman Images

Source 4.2 A Gandhara Buddha

originally put a premium on spiritual wisdom, leading to liberation from rebirth and the achievement of nirvana, Mahayana expressions of the faith emphasized compassion—the ability to feel the sorrows of other people as if they were one's own. This compassionate religious ideal found expression in the notion of bodhisattvas, fully enlightened beings who postponed their own final liberation in order to assist a suffering humanity. They were spiritual beings, intermediaries between mortal humans and the Buddhas, whose countless images in sculpture or painting became objects of worship and sources of comfort and assistance to many Buddhists.

Across the world of Asian Mahayana Buddhism, the most widely popular of the many bodhisattva figures was that of Avalokitesvara, known in China as Guanyin and in Japan as Kannon. This Bodhisattva of Compassion, often portrayed as a woman or with distinctly feminine characteristics, was known as "the one who hears the cries of the world." Calling on him or her for assistance, devotees could be rescued from all kinds of danger and distress. Women, for example, might petition for a healthy child. Moral transformation too was possible. According to the *Lotus Sutra*, a major Mahayana text, "Those who act under the impulse of hatred will, after adoring the Bodhisattva Avalokitesvara, be freed from hatred."

Among the most striking of the many representations of this bodhisattva are those that portray him or her with numerous heads, with which to hear the many cries of a suffering humanity, or with multiple arms to aid them. Source 4.3 provides an illustration of such a figure, a gilded wooden statue from Korea dating to the tenth or eleventh century C.E.

- What elements of Buddhist imagery can you identify in this statue?

- To whom might such an image appeal? And why?

- Some scholars have identified similarities between the Bodhisattva of Compassion and the Virgin Mary in the Christian tradition. What common elements and what differences can you identify?

Beyond providing numerous bodhisattvas, Mahayana Buddhism also populated the spiritual universe with various Buddhas in addition to the historical Buddha. One of these is the Maitreya Buddha, or the Buddha of the future, predicted to appear when the teachings of the historical Buddha have been lost or forgotten. In China, this Buddha of the future was sometimes portrayed as the "laughing Buddha," a fat, smiling, contented figure, said to be modeled on a tenth-century monk named Budai, who wandered the country merrily spreading happiness and good cheer, while evoking contentment and abundance. Source 4.4 illustrates this Chinese Maitreya Buddha together with some of his disciples in a carving, dating to the tenth through fourteenth centuries, in China's Feilai Feng caves.

Source 4.3 A Bodhisattva of Compassion: Avalokitesvara with a Thousand Arms

- How does this Buddha image differ, both physically and in its religious implications, from the other Buddhas already discussed in this feature?

- Why might this image be appealing to some Buddhists, and why might others take exception to it?

- In what ways does this figure represent an adaptation of Buddhist imagery to Chinese culture? Consider what you know about Confucian and Daoist postures to the world.

© Nazima Kowail/Corbis

Source 4.4 The Chinese Maitreya Buddha

DOING HISTORY

Representations of the Buddha

1. **Tracing change:** What transformations in Buddhist belief and practice are disclosed in these images?

2. **Identifying cultural adaptation:** What evidence do these images provide about the blending of Buddhism into a variety of cultural settings?

3. **Understanding the growth of Buddhism:** What do these images suggest about the appeal of Buddhism to growing numbers of people across Asia?

4. **Considering cultural boundaries:** To what extent are these images meaningful to people outside the Buddhist tradition? In what ways do they speak to universal human needs or desires? What is specifically Buddhist or Asian about them?

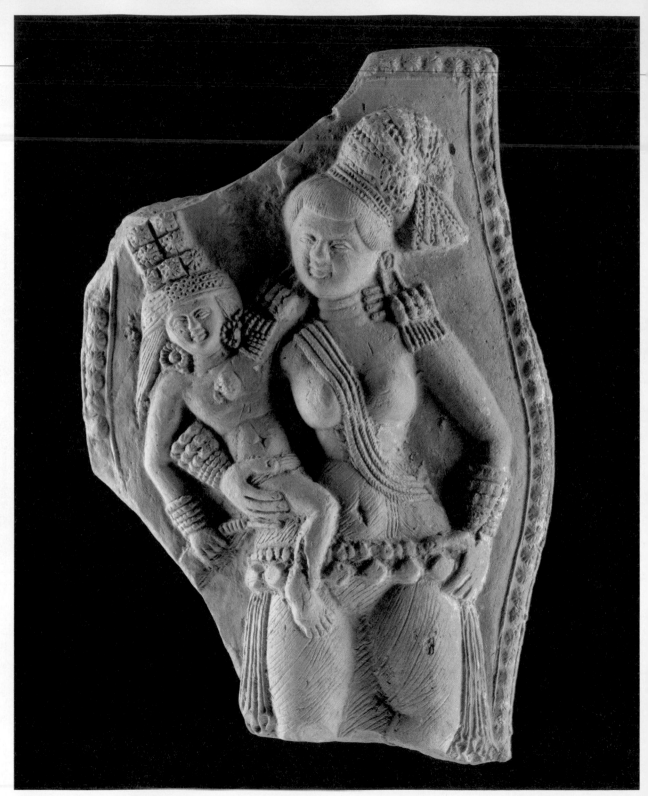

CHAPTER 5

Society and Inequality in Eurasia/North Africa

600 B.C.E.–600 C.E.

"Caste has no impact on life today," declared Chezi K. Ganesan in 2010.[1] Certainly, Mr. Ganesan's low-caste background as a Nadar, ranking just above the "untouchables," has had little impact on the career of this prosperous high-tech businessman, who shuttles between California's Silicon Valley and the city of Chennai in southern India. Yet his grandfather could not enter Hindu temples, and until the mid-nineteenth century, the women of his caste, as a sign of their low status, were forbidden to cover their breasts in the presence of Brahmin men. But if caste has proven no barrier to Mr. Ganesan, it remains significant for many others in contemporary India. Personal ads for those seeking a marriage partner in many online services often indicate an individual's caste as well as other personal data. Affirmative action programs benefiting low-caste Indians have provoked great controversy and resentment among some upper-caste groups. The brutal murder of an entire Dalit, or "untouchable," family in 2006 sparked much soul-searching in the Indian media. So while caste has changed in modern India, it has also persisted. Both the changes and the persistence have a long history.

The most recent 250 years of world history have called into question social patterns long assumed to be natural and permanent. The French, Russian, and Chinese revolutions challenged and destroyed ancient monarchies and class hierarchies; the abolitionist movement of the nineteenth century attacked slavery, largely unquestioned for millennia; the women's movement has confronted long and deeply held patriarchal assumptions about the proper

---

Mother and Child   Mothers and their children have been at the core of social life everywhere and a prominent theme of many artistic traditions. This lovely statue comes from the Sunga dynasty, which flourished in northeastern India from about 185 to 73 B.C.E., after the collapse of the Mauryan Empire.

relationship between the sexes; and Mahatma Gandhi, during India's struggle for independence in the twentieth century, sought to raise the status of "untouchables," referring to them as Harijan, or "children of God." Nevertheless, caste, class, patriarchy, and even slavery have certainly not vanished from human society, even now. During the era of second-wave civilizations in Eurasia, these patterns of inequality found expressions and generated social tensions that endured well beyond that era.

As Chapter 3 pointed out, millions of individual men and women inhabiting the civilizations of Eurasia and North Africa lived within a political framework of states or empires. They also occupied a world of ideas, religions, and values that derived both from local folkways and from the teaching of the great religious or cultural traditions of these civilizations, as described in Chapter 4. In this chapter, we explore the social arrangements of these civilizations—relationships between rich and poor, powerful and powerless, slaves and free people, and men and women. Those relationships shaped the daily lives and the life chances of everyone and provided the foundation for political authority as well as challenges to it.

Like the First Civilizations, those of the second-wave era were sharply divided along class lines, and they too were patriarchal, with women clearly subordinated to men in most domains of life. In constructing their societies, however, these second-wave civilizations differed substantially from one another. Chinese, Indian, and Mediterranean civilizations provide numerous illustrations of the many and varied ways in which these peoples organized their social lives. The assumptions, tensions, and conflicts accompanying these social patterns provided much of the distinctive character and texture that distinguished these diverse civilizations from one another.

SEEKING THE MAIN POINT

To what extent were the massive inequalities of second-wave civilizations generally accepted, and in what ways were they resisted or challenged?

Society and the State in China

Chinese society was unique in the ancient world in the extent to which it was shaped by the actions of the state. Nowhere was this more apparent than in the political power and immense social prestige of Chinese state officials, all of them male. For more than 2,000 years, these officials, bureaucrats acting in the name of the emperor both in the capital and in the provinces, represented the cultural and social elite of Chinese civilization. This class had its origins in the efforts of early Chinese rulers to find administrators loyal to the central state rather than to their own families or regions. Philosophers such as Confucius had long advocated selecting such officials on the basis of merit and personal morality rather than birth or wealth. As the Han dynasty established its authority in China around 200 B.C.E., its rulers required each province to send men of promise to the capital, where they were examined and chosen for official positions on the basis of their performance.

A MAP OF TIME

470–400 B.C.E.	Life of Aspasia in Athens
124 B.C.E.	Imperial academy for training Chinese officials established
1st century B.C.E.	Poetry of Buddhist nuns set to writing
73 B.C.E.	Spartacus slave rebellion in Italy
1–200 C.E.	Laws of Manu prescribing proper social behavior in India
Early 1st century C.E.	Reforming emperor Wang Mang in power in China
45–116 C.E.	Life of Ban Zhao in China
79 C.E.	Eruption of Mount Vesuvius destroys Pompeii
184 C.E.	Yellow Turban Rebellion in China
After 221 C.E.	Loosening of restrictions on elite Chinese women as Han dynasty collapsed
After 500 C.E.	Slavery replaced by serfdom in Roman world
690–705 C.E.	Empress Wu reigned in China

An Elite of Officials

Over time, this system of selecting administrators evolved into the world's first professional civil service. In 124 B.C.E., Emperor Wu Di established an imperial academy where potential officials were trained as scholars and immersed in texts dealing with history, literature, art, and mathematics, with an emphasis on Confucian teachings. By the end of the Han dynasty, it enrolled some 30,000 students, who were by then subjected to a series of written examinations to select officials of various grades. Private schools in the provinces funneled still more aspiring candidates into this examination system, which persisted until the early twentieth century. In theory open to all men, this system in practice favored those whose families were wealthy enough to provide the years of education required to pass even the lower-level exams. Proximity to the capital and family connections to the imperial court also helped in gaining a position in this highest of Chinese elites. Nonetheless, village communities or a local landowner might sponsor the education of a bright young man from a commoner family, enabling him to enter the charmed circle of officialdom. One rags-to-riches story told of a pig farmer who became an adviser to the emperor himself. Thus the examination system provided a modest measure of social mobility in an otherwise quite hierarchical society.

Guided Reading Question

■ DESCRIPTION
How would you characterize the social hierarchy of China during the second-wave era?

AP® EXAM TIP

The roles of Confucian scholars, which lasted into the twentieth century, represent a major continuity in Chinese history.

In later dynasties, that system grew even more elaborate and became an enduring and distinguishing feature of Chinese civilization. During the Tang dynasty, the famous poet and official Po Chu-I (772–846 C.E.) wrote a poem titled "After Passing the Examination," which shows something of the fame and fortune that awaited an accomplished student as well as the continuing loyalty to family and home that ideally marked those who succeeded:

> For ten years I never left my books,
> I went up . . . and won unmerited praise.
> My high place I do not much prize;
> The joy of my parents will first make me proud.
> Fellow students, six or seven men,
> See me off as I leave the City gate.
> My covered coach is ready to drive away;
> Flutes and strings blend their parting tune.
> Hopes achieved dull the pains of parting;
> Fumes of wine shorten the long road. . . .
> Shod with wings is the horse of him who rides
> On a Spring day the road that leads to home.[2]

Those who made it into the bureaucracy entered a realm of high privilege and great prestige. Senior officials moved about in carriages and were bedecked with robes, ribbons, seals, and headdresses appropriate to their rank. Even lower officials who served in the provinces rather than the capital were distinguished by their polished speech, their cultural sophistication, and their urban manners as well as their political authority. Proud of their learning, they were the bearers, and often the makers, of Chinese culture. "Officials are the leaders of the populace," stated an imperial edict of 144 B.C.E., "and it is right and proper that the carriages they ride in and the robes that they wear should correspond to the degrees of their dignity."[3] Some of these men, particularly in times of political turmoil, experienced tension between their official duties and their personal inclination toward a more withdrawn life of reflective scholarship. (See Zooming In: Ge Hong, page 196.)

The Landlord Class

AP® EXAM TIP

Be sure you understand social hierarchy and its roles throughout China's history, as well as in all major civilizations.

Most officials came from wealthy families, and in China wealth meant land. When the Qin dynasty unified China by 210 B.C.E., most land was held by small-scale peasant farmers. But by the first century B.C.E., the pressures of population growth, taxation, and indebtedness had generated a class of large landowners as impoverished peasants found it necessary to sell their lands to more prosperous neighbors. This accumulation of land in sizable estates was a persistent theme in Chinese history and one that was frequently, though not very successfully, opposed by state authorities. Landlords of such large estates were often able to avoid paying taxes, thus decreasing state revenues and increasing the tax burden for the remaining peasants. In some cases, they could also mount their own military forces that might challenge the authority of the emperor.

One of the most dramatic state efforts to counteract the growing power of large landowners is associated with Wang Mang, a high court official of the Han dynasty who usurped the emperor's throne in 8 C.E. and immediately launched a series of startling reforms. A firm believer in Confucian good government, Wang Mang saw his reforms as re-creating a golden age of long ago in which small-scale peasant farmers represented the backbone of Chinese society. Accordingly, he ordered the great private estates to be nationalized and divided up among the landless. Government loans to peasant families, limits on the amount of land a family might own, and an end to private slavery were all part of his reform program, but these measures proved impossible to enforce. Opposition from wealthy landowners, nomadic invasions, poor harvests, floods, and famines led to the collapse of Wang Mang's reforms and his assassination in 23 C.E.

Large landowning families, therefore, remained a central feature of Chinese society, although the fate of individual families rose and fell as the wheel of fortune raised them to great prominence or plunged them into poverty and disgrace. As a class, they benefited both from the wealth that their estates generated and from the power and prestige that accompanied their education and their membership in the official elite. The term "scholar-gentry" reflected their twin sources of privilege. With homes in both urban and rural areas, members of the scholar-gentry class lived luxuriously. Multi-storied houses, the finest of silk clothing, gleaming carriages, private orchestras, high-stakes gambling—all of this was part of the life of China's scholar-gentry class.

Peasants

Throughout the long course of China's civilization, the vast majority of its population consisted of peasants, living in small households representing two or three generations. Some owned enough land to support their families and perhaps even sell something on the local market. Many others could barely survive. Nature, the state, and landlords combined to make the life of most peasants extremely vulnerable. Famines, floods, droughts, hail, and pests could wreak havoc without warning. State authorities required the payment of taxes, demanded about a month's labor every year on various public projects, and conscripted young men for military service. During the Han dynasty, growing numbers of impoverished and desperate peasants had to sell

Chinese Peasants
For many centuries, the normal activities of Chinese peasant farmers included plowing, planting, and threshing grain, as shown in this painting from China's Song dynasty (960–1279 C.E.). (Mogao Caves, Dunhuang, Gansu Province, China/ Bridgeman Images)

Ge Hong, a Chinese Scholar in Troubled Times

Had Ge Hong lived at a different time, he might have pursued the life of a Confucian scholar and civil servant, for he was born to a well-established aristocratic family in southern China. But when he entered the world in 283 C.E., the times were clearly out of joint. The Han dynasty, which had given China four centuries of relative peace and prosperity, had fragmented into a number of competing states. Nomadic peoples invaded and ruled the northern parts of the country. Coups and rebellions were frequent. Many northern Chinese fled south to escape the chaos. The life of Ge Hong illustrates how these larger historical circumstances shaped the life of a single individual.[4]

Ge Hong's family directly experienced the disorder when the family library was destroyed during the repeated wars of the time. Furthermore, the family patriarch, Ge Hong's father, died when the young boy was only thirteen years old, an event that brought hardship and a degree of impoverishment to the family. Ge Hong reported later in his autobiography that he had to "walk long distances to borrow books" and that he cut and

A solitary scholar in China, such as Ge Hong sought to become.

sold firewood to buy paper and brushes. Nonetheless, like other young men of his class, he received a solid education, reading the classic texts of Confucianism along with history and philosophy.

At about the age of fourteen or fifteen, Ge Hong began to study with the aged Daoist master Zheng Yin. He had to sweep the floor and perform other menial chores for the master while gaining access to rare and precious texts of the esoteric and alchemical arts aimed at creating the "gold elixir" that could promote longevity and transcendence. Withdrawal into an interior life, reflected in both Daoist and Buddhist thought, had a growing appeal to the elite classes of China in response to the political disturbances and disorder of public life. It was the beginning of a life-long quest for Ge Hong.

And yet the Confucian emphasis on office holding, public service, and moral behavior in society persisted,

photo: *Scholar Walking with a Staff in a Landscape*, Qing Dynasty [ink and color on silk], Chinese School/Saint Louis Art Museum, Saint Louis, Missouri, USA/Bridgeman Images

Guided Reading Question

■ CHANGE
What class conflicts disrupted Chinese society?

AP® EXAM TIP

Throughout history, most people lived at the bottom of society, like these peasants in China.

out to large landlords and work as tenants or sharecroppers on their estates, where rents could run as high as one-half to two-thirds of the crop. Other peasants fled, taking to a life of begging or joining gangs of bandits in remote areas.

An eighth-century C.E. Chinese poem by Li Shen reflects poignantly on the enduring hardships of peasant life:

The cob of corn in springtime sown
In autumn yields a hundredfold.
No fields are seen that fallow lie:
And yet of hunger peasants die.

sending Ge Hong into a series of military positions. Here too was a reflection of the disordered times of his life, for in more settled circumstances, young elite men would have disdained military service, favoring a career in the civil bureaucracy. Thus in 303, at the age of twenty, he organized and led a small group of soldiers to crush a local rebellion, later reporting that he alone among military leaders prevented his troops from looting the valuables of the enemy. For his service, he received the title of "wave conquering general" and 100 bolts of cloth. "I was the only one," he wrote, "to distribute it among my officers, soldiers, and needy friends." At several other points in his life as well, Ge Hong accepted official appointments, some of them honorary and others more substantive.

But his heart lay elsewhere, as he yearned for a more solitary and interior life. "Honor, high posts, power, and profit are like sojourning guests," he wrote in his memoir. "They are not worth all the regret and blame, worry and anxiety they cause." Thus he spent long periods of his life in relative seclusion, refusing a variety of official positions. "Unless I abandon worldly affairs," he asked, "how can I practice the tranquil Way?" To Ge Hong, withdrawal was primarily for the purpose of seeking immortality, "to live as long as heaven and earth," a quest given added urgency no doubt by the chaotic world of his own time. In his writings, he explored various techniques for enhancing *qi*, the vital energy that sustains all life, including breathing exercises, calisthenics, sexual practices, diet, and herbs. But it was the search for alchemically generated elixirs, especially those containing liquid gold and cinnabar (derived from mercury), that proved most compelling to Ge Hong. Much to his regret, he lacked the resources to obtain and process these rare ingredients.

However, Ge Hong did not totally abandon the Confucian tradition and its search for social order, for he argued in his writings that the moral virtues advocated by China's ancient sage were a necessary prerequisite for attaining immortality. And he found a place in his philosophy also for the rewards and punishments of Legalist thinking. Thus he sought to reconcile the three major strands of Chinese thought—Confucianism, Daoism, and Legalism—even as he acknowledged that his practices were "always ill-suited to the times."

Ge Hong spent the last years of his life on the sacred mountain of Luofu in the far south of China, continuing his immortality research until he died in 343 at the age of sixty. When his body was lifted into its coffin, contemporaries reported that it was "exceedingly light as if one were lifting empty clothing."[5] They concluded from this that Ge Hong had in fact achieved transcendence, joining the immortals in everlasting life, as he had so fervently hoped.

Question: In what ways did the larger conditions of China shape the life of Ge Hong?

As at noontide they hoe their crops,
Sweat on the grain to earth down drops.
How many tears, now many a groan,
Each morsel on thy dish did mould![6]

Such conditions provoked periodic peasant rebellions, which have punctuated Chinese history for over 2,000 years. Toward the end of the second century C.E., wandering bands of peasants began to join together as floods along the Yellow River and resulting epidemics compounded the misery of landlessness and poverty. What emerged was a massive peasant uprising known as the Yellow Turban Rebellion

Yellow Turban Rebellion

Han Empire, ca. 100 B.C.E.
Area of Yellow Turban Rebellion

because of the yellow scarves the peasants wore around their heads. That movement, which swelled to about 360,000 armed followers by 184 C.E., found leaders, organization, and a unifying ideology in a popular form of Daoism. Featuring supernatural healings, collective trances, and public confessions of sin, the Yellow Turban movement looked forward to the "Great Peace"—a golden age of equality, social harmony, and common ownership of property. Although the rebellion was suppressed by the military forces of the Han dynasty, the Yellow Turban and other peasant upheavals devastated the economy, weakened the state, and contributed to the overthrow of the dynasty a few decades later. Repeatedly in Chinese history, such peasant movements, often expressed in religious terms, registered the sharp class antagonisms of Chinese society and led to the collapse of more than one ruling dynasty.

Merchants

Peasants were oppressed in China and certainly exploited, but they were also honored and celebrated in the official ideology of the state. In the eyes of the scholar-gentry, peasants were the solid productive backbone of the country, and their hard work and endurance in the face of difficulties were worthy of praise. Merchants, however, did not enjoy such a favorable reputation in the eyes of China's cultural elite. They were widely viewed as unproductive, making a shameful profit from selling the work of others. Stereotyped as greedy, luxury loving, and materialistic, merchants stood in contrast to the presumed frugality, altruism, and cultured tastes of the scholar-gentry. They were also seen as a social threat, as their ill-gained wealth impoverished others, deprived the state of needed revenues, and fostered resentments.

Such views lay behind periodic efforts by state authorities to rein in merchant activity and to keep them under control. Early in the Han dynasty, merchants were forbidden to wear silk clothing, ride horses, or carry arms. Nor were they permitted to sit for civil service examinations or hold public office. State monopolies on profitable industries such as salt, iron, and alcohol limited merchant opportunities. Later dynasties sometimes forced merchants to loan large sums of money to the state. Despite this active discrimination, merchants frequently became quite wealthy. Some tried to achieve a more respectable elite status by purchasing landed estates or educating their sons for the civil service examinations. Many had backdoor relationships with state officials and landlords who found them useful and were not averse to profiting from business connections with merchants, despite their unsavory reputation.

Class and Caste in India

India's social organization shared certain broad features with that of China. In both civilizations, birth determined social status for most people; little social mobility was available for the vast majority; sharp distinctions and great inequalities characterized social life; and religious or cultural traditions defined these inequalities as natural, eternal, and ordained by the gods. Despite these similarities, the organization, flavor, and texture of ancient Indian society were distinctive compared to almost all other civilizations. These unique aspects of Indian society have long been embodied in what we now call the caste system, a term that comes from the Portuguese word *casta*, which means "race" or "purity of blood." That social organization emerged over thousands of years and in some respects has endured into modern times.

Caste as Varna

The origins of the caste system are at best hazy. An earlier idea—that caste evolved from a racially defined encounter between light-skinned Aryan invaders and the darker-hued native peoples—has been challenged in recent years, but no clear alternative theory has emerged. Perhaps the best we can say at this point is that the distinctive social system of India grew out of the interactions among South Asia's immensely varied cultures together with the development of economic and social differences among these peoples as the inequalities of "civilization" spread throughout the Ganges River valley and beyond. Notions of race, however, seem less central to the growth of the caste system than those of economic specialization and of culture.

Guided Reading Question

■ DESCRIPTION

What set of ideas underlies India's caste-based society?

Caste in India

This 1947 photograph from *Life* magazine illustrates the "purity and pollution" thinking that has long been central to the ideology of caste. It shows a high-caste landowner carefully dropping wages wrapped in a leaf into the outstretched hands of his low-caste workers. By avoiding direct physical contact with them, he escapes the ritual pollution that would otherwise ensue. (Margaret Bourke-White/ The LIFE Picture Collection/Getty Images)

Whatever the precise origins of the caste system, by around 500 B.C.E., the idea that society was forever divided into four ranked classes, or *varnas*, was deeply embedded in Indian thinking. Everyone was born into and remained within one of these classes for life. At the top of this hierarchical system were the Brahmins, priests whose rituals and sacrifices alone could ensure the proper functioning of the world. They were followed by the Kshatriya class, warriors and rulers charged with protecting and governing society. Next was the Vaisya class, originally commoners who cultivated the land. These three classes came to be regarded as pure Aryans and were called the "twice-born," for they experienced not only a physical birth but also formal initiation into their respective varnas and status as people of prestigious Aryan descent. Far below these twice-born in the hierarchy of varna groups were the Sudras, native peoples incorporated into the margins of Aryan society in very subordinate positions. Regarded as servants of their social betters, they were not allowed to hear or repeat the Vedas or to take part in Aryan rituals. So little were they valued that a Brahmin who killed a Sudra was penalized as if he had killed a cat or a dog.

According to varna theory, these four classes were formed from the body of the god Purusha and were therefore eternal and changeless. Although these divisions are widely recognized in India even today, historians have noted considerable social flux in ancient Indian history. Members of the Brahmin and Kshatriya groups, for example, were frequently in conflict over which ranked highest in the varna hierarchy, and only slowly did the Brahmins emerge clearly in the top position. Although theoretically purely Aryan, both groups absorbed various tribal peoples as Indian civilization expanded. Tribal medicine men or sorcerers found a place as Brahmins, while warrior groups entered the Kshatriya varna. The Vaisya varna, originally defined as cultivators, evolved into a business class with a prominent place for merchants, while the Sudra varna became the domain of peasant farmers. Finally a whole new category, ranking lower even than the Sudras, emerged in the so-called untouchables, men and women who did the work considered most unclean and polluting, such as cremating corpses, dealing with the skins of dead animals, and serving as executioners. (See Snapshot, opposite.)

Caste as Jati

As the varna system took shape in India, another set of social distinctions also arose, based largely on occupations. In India as elsewhere, urban-based civilization gave rise to specialized occupations, many organized in guilds that regulated their own affairs in a particular region. Over time, these occupationally based groups, known as *jatis*, blended with the varna system to create India's unique caste-based society.

The many thousands of jatis became the primary cell of India's social life beyond the family or household, but each of them was associated with one of the great classes (varnas). Thus Brahmins were divided into many separate jatis, or subcastes,

AP® EXAM TIP

It is important to note that all major religions had connections with politics and social hierarchies.

Guided Reading Question

■ COMPARISON
What is the difference between varna and jati as expressions of caste?

SNAPSHOT   Social Life and Duty in Classical India

Much personal behavior in classical India, at least ideally, was regulated according to caste. Each caste was associated with a particular color, with a part of the body of the god Purusha, and with a set of duties.

Caste (Varna)	Color/Symbolism	Part of Purusha	Duties
Brahmin	white/spirituality	head	priests, teachers
Kshatriya	red/courage	shoulders	warriors, rulers
Vaisya	yellow/wealth	thighs	farmers, merchants, artisans
Sudra	black/ignorance	feet	labor
Untouchables (outside of the varna system; thus no color and not associated with Purusha)	—	—	polluted labor

Beyond caste, behavior was ideally defined in terms of four stages of life, at least for the first three varna groups. Each new stage was marked by a *samskara*, a ritual initiating the person into this new phase of life.

Stage of Life	Duties
Student	Boys live with a teacher (guru); learn Sanskrit, rituals, Vedas; practice obedience, respect, celibacy, nonviolence.
Householder	Marriage and family; men practice caste-based career/occupation; women serve as wives and mothers, perform household rituals and sacrifices, actively support children and elders.
Retirement	Both husband and wife withdraw to the forests following birth of grandchildren; diminished household duties; greater focus on spiritual practice; sex permitted once a month.
Wandering ascetic	Only for men (women return to household); total rejection of ordinary existence; life as wandering hermit without shelter or possessions; caste becomes irrelevant; focus on achieving moksha and avoiding future rebirth.

as were each of the other varnas as well as the untouchables. In a particular region or village, each jati was ranked in a hierarchy known to all, from the highest of the Brahmins to the lowest of the untouchables. Marriage and eating together were permitted only within an individual's own jati. Each jati was associated with a particular set of duties, rules, and obligations, which defined its members' unique and separate place in the larger society. Brahmins, for example, were forbidden to eat meat, while Kshatriyas were permitted to do so. Upper-caste women covered their breasts, while some lower-caste women were forbidden this privilege as a sign of their subordination. "It is better to do one's own duty badly than another's well"— this frequently quoted saying summed up the underlying idea of Indian society. With its many separate, distinct, and hierarchically ranked social groups, Indian society was quite different from that of China or the Greco-Roman world. It was also unique in the set of ideas that explained and justified that social system. Foremost among them was the notion of ritual purity and pollution applied to caste groups. Brahmins or other high-caste people who came in contact with members of lower castes, especially those who cleaned latrines, handled corpses, or butchered and skinned dead animals, were in great danger of being polluted, or made ritually unclean. Thus untouchables were forbidden to use the same wells or to enter the temples designated for higher-caste people. Sometimes they were required to wear a wooden clapper to warn others of their approach. A great body of Indian religious writing defined various forms of impurity and the ritual means of purification.

A further support for this idea of inherent inequality and permanent difference derived from emerging Hindu notions of *karma*, *dharma*, and rebirth. Being born into a particular caste was generally regarded as reflecting the good or bad deeds (karma) of a previous life. Thus an individual's prior actions were responsible for his or her current status. Any hope for rebirth in a higher caste rested on the faithful and selfless performance of one's present caste duties (dharma) in this life. Doing so contributed to spiritual progress by subduing the relentless demands of the ego. Such teachings, like that of permanent impurity, provided powerful sanctions for the inequalities of Indian society. So too did the threat of social ostracism, because each jati had the authority to expel members who violated its rules. No greater catastrophe could befall a person than this, for it meant the end of any recognized social life and the loss of all social support.

As caste restrictions tightened, it became increasingly difficult—virtually impossible—for individuals to raise their social status during their lifetimes. However, another kind of upward mobility enabled entire jatis, over several generations, to raise their standing in the local hierarchy of caste groups. By acquiring land or wealth, by adopting the behaviors of higher-caste groups, by finding some previously overlooked "ancestor" of a higher caste, a particular jati might slowly be redefined in a higher category. India's caste system was in practice rather more fluid and changing than the theory of caste might suggest.

India's social system thus differed from that of China in several ways. It gave priority to religious status and ritual purity (the Brahmins), whereas China elevated political officials to the highest of elite positions. The caste system divided Indian society into vast numbers of distinct social groups; China had fewer, but broader, categories of society—scholar-gentry, landlords, peasants, merchants. Finally, India's caste society defined these social groups far more rigidly than in China and provided even less opportunity for social mobility.

AP® EXAM TIP

Be prepared to compare different methods of social control across place and time, like in China and India.

The Functions of Caste

This caste-based social structure shaped India's emerging civilization in various ways. Because caste (jati) was a very local phenomenon, rooted in particular regions or villages, it focused the loyalties of most people on a quite restricted territory and weakened the appeal or authority of larger all-Indian states. This localization is one reason that India, unlike China, seldom experienced an empire that encompassed the entire subcontinent (see Chapter 3, pages 131–35). Caste, together with the shared culture of a diverse Hinduism, provided a substitute for the state as an integrative mechanism for Indian civilization. It offered a distinct and socially recognized place for almost everyone. In looking after widows, orphans, and the destitute, jatis provided a modest measure of social security and support. Even the lowest-ranking jatis had the right to certain payments from the social superiors whom they served.

Furthermore, caste represented a means of accommodating the many migrating or invading peoples who entered the subcontinent. The cellular, or honeycomb, structure of caste society allowed various peoples, cultures, and traditions to find a place within a larger Indian civilization while retaining something of their unique identity. The process of assimilation was quite different in China, where it meant becoming Chinese ethnically, linguistically, and culturally. Finally, India's caste system facilitated the exploitation of the poor by the wealthy and powerful. The multitude of separate groups into which it divided the impoverished and oppressed majority of the population made class consciousness and organized resistance across caste lines much more difficult to achieve.

> **PRACTICING AP® HISTORICAL THINKING**
>
> How did India's caste system differ from China's class system?

Slavery: The Case of the Roman Empire

Beyond the inequalities of class and caste lay those of slavery, a social institution with deep roots in human history, extending into the Paleolithic era of gathering and hunting peoples. Some have suggested that the early domestication of animals provided a model for enslaving people. Certainly, slave owners have everywhere compared their slaves to tamed animals. Aristotle, for example, observed that the ox is "the poor man's slave." War, patriarchy, and the notion of private property, all of which accompanied the First Civilizations, also contributed to the growth of slavery. Large-scale warfare generated numerous prisoners, and everywhere in the ancient world capture in war meant the possibility of enslavement. Early records suggest that women captives were the first slaves, usually raped and then enslaved as concubines, whereas male captives were killed. Patriarchal societies, in which men sharply controlled and perhaps even "owned" women, may have suggested the possibility of using other people, men as well as women, as slaves. The class inequalities of early civilizations, which were based on great differences in privately owned property, also made it possible to imagine people owning other people.

> **AP® EXAM TIP**
>
> Know the theories about the origins of slavery.

Slavery and Civilization

Guided Reading Question

■ COMPARISON

How did the inequalities of slavery differ from those of caste?

Whatever its precise origins, slavery generally meant ownership by a master, the possibility of being sold, working without pay, and the status of an "outsider" at the bottom of the social hierarchy. For most, it was a kind of "social death,"[7] for slaves usually lacked any rights or independent personal identity recognized by the larger society. By the time Hammurabi's law code casually referred to Mesopotamian slavery (around 1750 B.C.E.), it was already a long-established tradition in the region and in all the First Civilizations. Likewise, virtually all subsequent civilizations—in the Americas, Africa, and Eurasia—practiced some form of slavery.

Slave systems throughout history have varied considerably. In some times and places, such as ancient Greece and Rome, a fair number of slaves might be emancipated in their own lifetimes, through the generosity or religious convictions of their owners, or to avoid caring for them in old age, or by allowing slaves to purchase their freedom with their own funds. In some societies, the children of slaves inherited the status of their parents, while in others, such as the Aztec Empire, they were considered free people. Slaves likewise varied considerably in the labor they were required to do, with some working for the state in high positions, others performing domestic duties in their owner's household, and still others toiling in fields or mines in large work gangs.

The second-wave civilizations of Eurasia differed considerably in the prominence and extent of slavery in their societies. In China, it was a minor element, amounting to perhaps 1 percent of the population. Convicted criminals and their families, confiscated by the government and sometimes sold to wealthy private individuals, were among the earliest slaves in Han dynasty China. In desperate circumstances, impoverished or indebted peasants might sell their children into slavery. In southern China, teenage boys of poor families could be purchased by the wealthy, for whom they served as status symbols. Chinese slavery, however, was never very widespread and did not become a major source of labor for agriculture or manufacturing.

In India as well, people could fall into slavery as criminals, debtors, or prisoners of war and served their masters largely in domestic settings, but religious writings and secular law offered, at least in theory, some protection for slaves. Owners were required to provide adequately for their slaves and were forbidden to abandon them in old age. According to one ancient text, "A man may go short himself or stint his wife and children, but never his slave who does his dirty work for him."[8] Slaves in India could inherit and own property and earn money in their spare time. A master who raped a slave woman was required to set her free and pay compensation. The law encouraged owners to free their slaves and allowed slaves to buy their freedom. All of this suggests that Indian slavery was more restrained than that of other ancient civilizations. Nor did Indian civilization depend economically on slavery, for most work was performed by lower-caste, though free, men and women.

The Making of Roman Slavery

In sharp contrast to other second-wave civilizations, slavery played an immense role in the Mediterranean, or Western, world. Although slavery was practiced in Chinese, Indian, and Persian civilizations, in the Greco-Roman world society was based on slavery. By a conservative estimate, classical Athens alone was home to perhaps 60,000 slaves, or about one-third of the total population. In Athens, ironically, the growth of democracy and citizenship was defined and accompanied by the simultaneous growth of slavery on a mass scale. The greatest of the Greek philosophers, Aristotle, developed the notion that some people were "slaves by nature" and should be enslaved for their own good and for that of the larger society.

"The ancient Greek attitude toward slavery was simple," writes one modern scholar. "It was a terrible thing to become a slave, but a good thing to own a slave."[9] Even poor households usually had at least one or two female slaves, providing domestic work and sexual services for their owners. Although substantial numbers of Greek slaves were granted freedom by their owners, they usually did not become citizens or gain political rights. Nor could they own land or marry citizens, and particularly in Athens they had to pay a special tax. Their status remained "halfway between slavery and freedom."[10]

Practiced on an even larger scale, slavery was a defining element of Roman society. By the time of Christ, the Italian heartland of the Roman Empire had some 2 to 3 million slaves, representing 33 to 40 percent of the population.[11] Not until the modern slave societies of the Caribbean, Brazil, and the southern United States was slavery practiced again on such an enormous scale. Wealthy Romans could own many hundreds or even thousands of slaves. One woman in the fifth century C.E. freed 8,000 slaves when she withdrew into a life of Christian monastic practice. Even people of modest means frequently owned two or three slaves. In doing so, they confirmed their own position as free people, demonstrated their social status, and expressed their ability to exercise power. Slaves and former slaves also might be slave owners. One freedman during the reign of Augustus owned 4,116 slaves at the time of his death. (See Working with Evidence, page 220, for more on Roman society viewed through the lens of Pompeii.)

Guided Reading Question

■ COMPARISON

How did Greco-Roman slavery differ from that of other classical civilizations?

Roman Slavery

This Roman mosaic from the third century C.E. shows the slave Myro serving a drink to his master, Fructus. (Bardo Museum, Tunis, Tunisia/Gianni Dagli Orti/The Art Archive at Art Resource, NY)

The vast majority of Roman slaves had been prisoners captured in the many wars that accompanied the creation of the empire. In 146 B.C.E., following the destruction of the North African city of Carthage, some 55,000 people were enslaved en masse. From all over the Mediterranean basin, men and women were funneled into the major slave-owning regions of Italy and Sicily. Pirates also furnished slaves, kidnapping tens of thousands and selling them to Roman slave traders on the island of Delos. Roman merchants purchased still other slaves through networks of long-distance commerce extending to the Black Sea, the East African coast, and northwestern Europe. The supply of slaves also occurred through natural reproduction, as the children of slave mothers were regarded as slaves themselves. Such "home-born" slaves had a certain prestige and were thought to be less troublesome than those who had known freedom earlier in their lives. Finally, abandoned or exposed children could legally become the slave of anyone who rescued them.

Unlike American slavery of later times, Roman practice was not identified with a particular racial or ethnic group. Egyptians, Syrians, Jews, Greeks, Gauls, North Africans, and many other people found themselves alike enslaved. From within the empire and its adjacent regions, an enormous diversity of people were bought and sold at Roman slave markets.

Like slave owners everywhere, Romans regarded their slaves as "barbarians"—lazy, unreliable, immoral, prone to thieving—and came to think of certain peoples, such as Asiatic Greeks, Syrians, and Jews, as slaves by nature. Nor was there any serious criticism of slavery in principle, although on occasion owners were urged to treat their slaves in a more benevolent way. Even the triumph of Christianity within the Roman Empire did little to undermine slavery, for Christian teaching held that slaves should be "submissive to [their] masters with all fear, not only to the good and gentle, but also to the harsh."[12] In fact, the New Testament used the metaphor of slavery to describe the relationship of believers to God, styling them as "slaves of Christ," while Saint Augustine (354–430 C.E.) described slavery as God's punishment for sin. Thus slavery was deeply embedded in the religious thinking and social outlook of elite Romans.

Similarly, slavery was entrenched throughout the Roman economy. No occupation was off-limits to slaves except military service, and no distinction existed between jobs for slaves and those for free people. Frequently they labored side by side. In rural areas, slaves provided much of the labor force on the huge estates, or *latifundia*, which produced grain, olive oil, and wine, mostly for export, much like the later plantations in the Americas. There they often worked chained together. In the cities, slaves worked in their owners' households, but also as skilled artisans, teachers, doctors, business agents, entertainers, and actors. In the empire's many mines and quarries, slaves and criminals labored under brutal conditions. Slaves in the service of the emperor provided manpower for the state bureaucracy, maintained temples and shrines, and kept Rome's water supply system functioning.

Trained in special schools, they also served as gladiators in the violent spectacles of Roman public life. Female slaves usually served as domestic servants but were also put to work in brothels, served as actresses and entertainers, and could be used sexually by their male owners. Thus slaves were represented among the highest and most prestigious occupations and in the lowest and most degraded.

Slave owners in the Roman Empire were supposed to provide the necessities of life to their slaves. When this occurred, slaves may have had a more secure life than was available to impoverished free people, who had to fend for themselves, but the price of this security was absolute subjection to the will of the master. Beatings, sexual abuse, and sale to another owner were constant possibilities. Lacking all rights in the law, slaves could not legally marry, although many contracted unofficial unions. Slaves often accumulated money or possessions, but such property legally belonged to their masters and could be seized at any time. If a slave murdered his master, Roman law demanded the lives of all of the victim's slaves. When one Roman official was killed by a slave in 61 C.E., every one of his 400 slaves was condemned to death. For an individual slave, the quality of life depended almost entirely on the character of the master. Brutal owners made life a living hell. Benevolent owners made life tolerable and might even grant favored slaves their freedom or permit them to buy that freedom. As in Greece, manumission of slaves was a widespread practice, and in the Roman Empire, unlike in Greece, freedom was accompanied by citizenship.

Roman slaves, like their counterparts in other societies, responded to enslavement in many ways. Most, no doubt, did what was necessary to survive, but there are recorded cases of Roman prisoners of war who chose to commit mass suicide rather than face the horrors of slavery. Others, once enslaved, resorted to the "weapons of the weak"—small-scale theft, sabotage, pretending illness, working poorly, and placing curses on their masters. Fleeing to the anonymous crowds of the city or to remote rural areas prompted owners to post notices in public places, asking for information about their runaways. Catching runaway slaves became an organized private business. Occasional murders of slave owners made masters conscious of the dangers they faced. "Every slave we own is an enemy we harbor" ran one Roman saying.[13]

On several notable occasions, the slaves themselves rose in rebellion. The most famous uprising occurred in 73 B.C.E. when a slave gladiator named Spartacus led seventy other slaves from a school for gladiators in a desperate bid for freedom that mushroomed into a huge uprising. (See Zooming In: The Spartacus Slave Revolt, page 208, for a more detailed account.) Nothing on the scale of Spartacus's rebellion occurred again in the Western world of slavery until the Haitian Revolution of the 1790s. But Haitian rebels sought the creation of a new society free of slavery altogether. None of the Roman slave rebellions, including that of Spartacus, had any such overall plan or goal. The rebels simply wanted to escape

AP® EXAM TIP

Know examples of slave rebellions and their effects.

The Rebellion of Spartacus

The Spartacus Slave Revolt

Despite the prominence of slavery in ancient civilizations, large-scale slave revolts were rare. One of the most impressive began in the Roman Empire during the summer of 73 B.C.E. when around seventy slaves escaped from a gladiator school at Capua, about 125 miles south of Rome. Grabbing knives and skewers from the kitchen on their way out, this small band of men, who had been trained to fight to the death for the entertainment of spectators, established a stronghold on nearby Mount Vesuvius and chose as their leader Spartacus, described by the historian Sallust as "a man of immense bodily strength and spirit."[14] The defeat of Roman forces sent to seize them encouraged other slaves and some free men to join the rebellion. Their numbers eventually swelled to as many as 120,000 men, women, and children at the height of the uprising, reflecting the large number of slaves employed on the great estates of southern Italy.

Roman authorities became increasingly concerned when Spartacus and his followers began to manufacture

The death of Spartacus, 71 B.C.E.

their own weapons and to organize into a more coherent military force, which defeated in turn several hurriedly assembled Roman armies and plundered the rich farming region of Campania. The fortunes of the rebels peaked in 72 B.C.E. when they briefly threatened Rome itself. Both sides treated their opponents brutally. The Greek historian Appian reported that Spartacus ordered the sacrifice of 300 Roman prisoners in honor of the slain rebel leader Crixus, while another historian claimed that Spartacus staged gladiatorial games using 400 captives. When the revolt was finally suppressed, captured rebel slaves received similarly brutal treatment from the Roman authorities.

Fearful for the safety of the capital, the Roman authorities acted decisively. They appointed Marcus Licinius Crassus, a rich and ambitious Roman aristocrat

Roman slavery. Although rebellions created a perpetual fear in the minds of slave owners, slavery itself was hardly affected.

Comparing Patriarchies

Social inequality was embedded not only in the structures of class, caste, and slavery, but also in the gender systems of second-wave civilizations, as the patriarchies of the First Civilizations (see Chapter 2, pages 72–75) were replicated and elaborated in those that followed. Until quite recently, women's subordination in all civilizations has been so widespread and pervasive that historians have been slow to recognize that gender systems had a history, changing over time. New agricultural technologies, the rise or decline of powerful states, the incorporation of world religions, interaction with culturally different peoples—all of these developments and

and military commander, to lead eight Roman legions, totaling perhaps 40,000 troops, against Spartacus and his rebels. Crassus cornered the slave army in the far south of Italy, and Spartacus soon realized that his followers faced a fight to the death. According to the historian Appian, he advertised their precarious situation to his troops by crucifying a Roman soldier "as a visual reminder to his own men of what would happen to them if they did not win."[15] Rather than be captured, Spartacus and the slaves with him chose to make a last stand. The Greek historian Plutarch reports that Spartacus killed his horse in front of his troops to show that he had no intention of fleeing, and led his forces in a final desperate engagement with Crassus's army. Even the most hostile of later historians recounted that Spartacus died bravely during the battle, even if some claimed that his body was never found. For those that survived, a terrible vengeance followed as some 6,000 captured rebel slaves were nailed to crosses along the Appian Way, between Capua, where the rebellion began, and Rome. These crucified prisoners, spaced some thirty-five to forty yards apart for over a hundred miles, provided a clear warning to all others who contemplated rebellion.

Spartacus's revolt had little lasting effect on the society in which he lived. No further large-scale revolts took place in the Roman Empire, and Rome continued its economic system based on slave labor. Moreover, the rebellion occasioned little historical comment until the eighteenth century. However, over the past two and a half centuries, a number of groups have embraced Spartacus, casting him as an inspirational leader of the downtrodden who resisted injustice and subjugation. Marxists, socialists, and nationalists have all found something to admire in Spartacus and his rebellion. In the United States, Spartacus entered the popular imagination due in no small part to the success of the 1960 epic film *Spartacus*, starring Kirk Douglas as the rebel leader fighting against the odds to free the oppressed. While there is no historical evidence that Spartacus ever intended to abolish slavery or fundamentally reform Roman society, in modern times his heroic, if ultimately failed, quest for freedom has been recovered from the past, becoming for many an inspirational symbol of just resistance to oppression. In such ways, the past continues to resonate in the present.

Questions: What can Spartacus's revolt tell us about the nature of the slave system in the Roman Empire? How might you account for the renewed interest in Spartacus over the past two and a half centuries?

more generated significant change in understandings of what was appropriate masculine and feminine behavior. Most often, patriarchies were lighter and less restrictive for women in the early years of a civilization's development and during times of upheaval, when established patterns of male dominance were disrupted.

Furthermore, women were often active agents in the histories of their societies, even while largely accepting their overall subordination. As the central figures in family life, they served as repositories and transmitters of their peoples' culture. Some were able to occupy unorthodox and occasionally prominent positions outside the home as scholars, religious functionaries, managers of property and participants in commerce, and even as rulers or military leaders. In Britain, Egypt, and Vietnam, for example, women led efforts to resist their countries' incorporation into the Roman or Chinese empires. (See Zooming In: Trung Trac, page 124, and the statue of Boudica, page 120.) Both Buddhist and Christian nuns carved out

AP® EXAM TIP

Be prepared to offer examples of how women functioned in patriarchal societies.

small domains of relative freedom from male control. But these changes or challenges to male dominance occurred within a patriarchal framework, and nowhere did they evolve out of or beyond that framework. Thus a kind of "patriarchal equilibrium" ensured the long-term persistence of women's subordination despite fluctuations and notwithstanding various efforts to redefine gender roles or push against gendered expectations.[16]

Nor was patriarchy everywhere the same. Restrictions on women were far sharper in urban-based civilizations than in those pastoral or agricultural societies that lay beyond the reach of cities and empires. The degree and expression of patriarchy also varied from one civilization to another, as the discussion of Mesopotamia and Egypt in Chapter 2 illustrated. And within particular civilizations, elite women both enjoyed privileges and suffered the restrictions of seclusion in the home to a much greater extent than their lower-class counterparts whose economic circumstances required them to operate in the larger social arena. China provides a fascinating example of how patriarchy changed over time, while the contrasting patriarchies of Athens and Sparta illustrate clear variations even within the much smaller world of Greek civilization.

A Changing Patriarchy: The Case of China

As Chinese civilization took shape during the Han dynasty, elite thinking about gender issues became more explicitly patriarchal, more clearly defined, and linked to an emerging Confucian ideology. Long-established patterns of thinking in terms of pairs of opposites were now described in gendered and unequal terms. The superior principle of *yang* was viewed as masculine and related to Heaven, rulers, strength, rationality, and light, whereas *yin*, the lower feminine principle, was associated with the earth, subjects, weakness, emotion, and darkness. Thus female inferiority was seen as permanent and embedded in the workings of the universe.

What this view meant more practically was spelled out repeatedly over the centuries in various Confucian texts. Two notions in particular summarized the ideal position of women, at least in the eyes of elite male writers. The adage "Men go out, women stay in" emphasized the public and political roles of men in contrast to the domestic and private domain of women. A second idea, known as the "three obediences," emphasized a woman's subordination first to her father, then to her husband, and finally to her son. "Why is it," asked one text, "that according to the rites the man takes his wife, whereas the woman leaves her house [to join her husband's family]? It is because the *yin* is lowly, and should not have the initiative; it proceeds to the *yang* in order to be completed."[17]

The Chinese woman writer and court official Ban Zhao (45–116 C.E.) observed that the ancients had practiced three customs when a baby girl was born. She was placed below the bed to show that she was "lowly and weak," required always to "humble herself before others." Then she was given a piece of broken pottery to play with, signifying that "her primary duty [was] to be industrious." Finally, her

AP® EXAM TIP

Generally speaking, patriarchy became stronger in China as each dynasty's government strengthened. Knowledge of this pattern may help you on the AP® exam.

Guided Reading Question

■ CHANGE

In what ways did the expression of Chinese patriarchy change over time, and why did it change?

Chinese Women Musicians
This tenth-century rendering by the painter Gu Hongzhong shows these upper-class women serving as musicians for a high official of a Tang dynasty emperor. It was titled *The Night Revels of Han Xizai*. The painter was apparently sent by the emperor to spy on the suspicious behavior of the minister, who in various tellings was suspected of either rebellion or undignified activity. (Beijing Palace Museum, Imperial Palace [Forbidden City], Beijing, China/Werner Forman/Art Resource, NY)

birth was announced to the ancestors with an offering to indicate that she was responsible for "the continuation of [ancestor] worship in the home."[18]

Yet such notions of passivity, inferiority, and subordination were not the whole story of women's lives in ancient China. A few women, particularly the wives, concubines, or widows of emperors, were able on occasion to exercise considerable political authority. Several others led peasant rebellions. In doing so, they provoked much antifemale hostility on the part of male officials, who understood governance as a masculine task and often blamed the collapse of a dynasty or natural disasters on the "unnatural" and "disruptive" influence of women in political affairs. Others, however, praised women of virtue as wise counselors to their fathers, husbands, and rulers and depicted them positively as active agents.

Within her husband's family, a young woman was clearly subordinate as a wife and daughter-in-law, but as a mother of sons, she was accorded considerable honor for her role in producing the next generation of male heirs to carry on her husband's lineage. When her sons married, she was able to exercise the significant authority of a mother-in-law. Furthermore, a woman, at least in the upper classes, often brought with her a considerable dowry, which was regarded as her own property and gave her some leverage within her marriage. Women's roles in the production of textiles, often used to pay taxes or to sell commercially, made a woman's

Chinese Women at Work
For a long time, the spinning and weaving of cloth were part of women's domestic work in China. In this detail from a Ming dynasty vase, women are shown weaving silk. (Detail from a ceramic vase, Chinese School, Ming Dynasty [1368–1644]/Goleston Palace, Tehran, Iran/Giraudon/Bridgeman Images)

labor quite valuable to the family economy. And a man's wife was sharply distinguished from his concubines, for she was legally mother to all her husband's children. Furthermore, peasant women could hardly follow the Confucian ideal of seclusion in the home, as their labor was required in the fields. Thus women's lives were more complex and varied than the prescriptions of Confucian orthodoxy might suggest.

Much changed in China following the collapse of the Han dynasty in the third century C.E. Centralized government vanished amid much political fragmentation and conflict. Confucianism, the main ideology of Han China, was discredited, while Daoism and Buddhism attracted a growing following. Pastoral and nomadic peoples invaded northern China and ruled a number of the small states that had replaced the Han government. These new conditions resulted in some loosening of the strict patriarchy of Han dynasty China over the next five or six centuries.

The cultural influence of nomadic peoples, whose women were far less restricted than those of China, was noticed, and criticized, by more Confucian-minded male observers. One of them lamented the sad deterioration of gender roles under the influence of nomadic peoples:

> In the north of the Yellow river it is usually the wife who runs the household. She will not dispense with good clothing or expensive jewelry. The husband has to settle for old horses and sickly servants. The traditional niceties between husband and wife are seldom observed, and from time to time he even has to put up with her insults.[19]

Others criticized the adoption of nomadic styles of dress, makeup, and music. By the time of the Tang dynasty (618–907), writers and artists depicted elite women as capable of handling legal and business affairs on their own and on occasion riding horses and playing polo, bareheaded and wearing men's clothing. Tang legal codes even recognized a married daughter's right to inherit property from her family of birth. Such images of women were quite different from those of Han dynasty China.

A further sign of a weakening patriarchy and the cause of great distress to advocates of Confucian orthodoxy lay in the unusual reign of Empress Wu (r. 690–705 C.E.), a former high-ranking concubine in the imperial court, who came to power amid much palace intrigue and was the only woman ever to rule China with the title of emperor. With the support of China's growing Buddhist establishment, Empress Wu governed despotically, but she also consolidated China's civil service examination system for the selection of public officials and actively patronized scholarship and the arts. Some of her actions seem deliberately designed to elevate the position of women. She commissioned the biographies of famous women, decreed that the mourning period for mothers be made equal to that for fathers, and ordered the creation of a Chinese character for "human being" that suggested the process of birth flowing from one woman without a prominent male role. Her reign was brief and unrepeated.

The growing popularity of Daoism provided new images of the feminine and new roles for women. Daoist texts referred to the *dao* as "mother" and urged the traditionally feminine virtues of yielding and passive acceptance rather than the male-oriented striving of Confucianism. Daoist sects often featured women as priests, nuns, or reclusive meditators, able to receive cosmic truth and to use it for the benefit of others. A variety of female deities from Daoist or Buddhist traditions found a place in Chinese village religion, while growing numbers of women found an alternative to family life in Buddhist monasteries. None of this meant an end to patriarchy, but it does suggest some change in the tone and expression of that patriarchy. However, during the Song dynasty that followed, a more restrictive patriarchy reemerged. (See Chapter 8.)

Contrasting Patriarchies: Athens and Sparta

The patriarchies of second-wave civilizations not only fluctuated over time but also varied considerably from place to place. Nowhere is this variation more apparent than in the contrasting cases of Athens and Sparta, two of the leading city-states of Greek civilization (see Map 3.2, page 111). Even within this small area, the opportunities available to women and the restrictions imposed on them differed substantially. Although Athens has been celebrated as a major expression of democracy and rationalism, its posture toward women was far more restrictive than that of the highly militaristic and much less democratic Sparta.

In the several centuries between about 700 and 400 B.C.E., as the free male citizens of Athens moved toward unprecedented participation in political life, the city's women experienced growing limitations. They had no role whatsoever in the Assembly, the councils, or the juries of Athens, which were increasingly the focus of life for free men. In legal matters, women had to be represented by a guardian, and court proceedings did not even refer to them by name, but only as someone's wife or mother.

Greek thinkers, especially Aristotle, provided a set of ideas that justified women's exclusion from public life and their general subordination to men. According to Aristotle, "A woman is, as it were, an infertile male. She is female in fact on account of a kind of inadequacy." That inadequacy lay in her inability to generate

Guided Reading Question

■ COMPARISON

How did the patriarchies of Athens and Sparta differ from each other?

A Woman of Athens
This grave stele from about 400 B.C.E. marked the final resting place of Hegeso, a wealthy Athenian woman, shown in the women's quarter of a Greek home examining her jewelry, perhaps for the last time, while attended by her slave. The domestic setting of this grave marker contrasts with that common for men, which usually showed them as warriors in a public space. (National Archeological Museum, Athens, Greece/Marie Mauzy/Art Resource, NY)

AP® EXAM TIP

Be absolutely sure you can compare societies across place and time.

sperm, which contained the "form" or the "soul" of a new human being. Her role in the reproductive process was passive, providing a receptacle for the vital male contribution. Compared often to children or domesticated animals, women were associated with instinct and passion and lacked the rationality to take part in public life. "It is the best for all tame animals to be ruled by human beings," wrote Aristotle. "In the same way, the relationship between the male and the female is by nature such that the male is higher, the female lower, that the male rules and the female is ruled."[20]

As in China, elite Athenian women were expected to remain inside the home, except perhaps for religious festivals or funerals. Even within the home, women's space was quite separate from that of men. Although poorer women, courtesans, and prostitutes had to leave their homes to earn money, collect water, or shop, ideal behavior for upper-class women meant assigning these tasks to slaves or to men and involved a radical segregation of male and female space. "What causes women a bad reputation," declared Andromache, a female character in the Greek playwright Euripides' *The Trojan Women*, "is not remaining inside."

Within the domestic realm, Athenian women were generally married in their midteens to men ten to fifteen years older than themselves. Their main function was the management of domestic affairs and the production of sons who would become active citizens. These sons were expected to acquire a literate education, while their sisters were normally limited to learning spinning, weaving, and other household tasks. The Greek writer Menander exclaimed: "Teaching a woman to read and write? What a terrible thing to do! Like feeding a vile snake on more poison." Nor did women have much economic power. Although they could own personal property obtained through dowry, gifts, or inheritance, land was usually passed through male heirs. By law, women were forbidden to buy or sell land and could negotiate contracts only if the sum involved was valued at less than a bushel of barley.

There were exceptions, although rare, to the restricted lives of upper-class Athenian women, the most notable of which was Aspasia (ca. 470–400 B.C.E.). She was born in the Greek city of Miletus, on the western coast of Anatolia, to a wealthy family that believed in educating its daughters. As a young woman, Aspasia found her way to Athens, where her foreign birth gave her somewhat more free-dom than was normally available to the women of that city. She soon attracted the attention of Pericles, Athens's leading political figure. The two lived together as husband and wife until Pericles' death in 429 B.C.E., although they were not officially married. Treated as an equal partner by Pericles, Aspasia proved to be a learned and witty conversationalist who moved freely in the cultured circles of Athens. Her foreign birth and her apparent influence on Pericles provoked crit-ics to suggest that she was a *hetaera*, a professional, educated, high-class entertainer and sexual companion, similar to a Japanese geisha. Although little is known about Aspasia, a number of major Athenian writers commented about her, both posi-tively and negatively. She was, by all accounts, a rare and remarkable woman in a city that offered little opportunity for individuality or achievement to its female population.

The evolution of Sparta differed in many ways from that of Athens. Early on, Sparta solved the problem of feeding a growing population not by creating over-seas colonies as did many Greek city-states, but by conquering its immediate neigh-bors and reducing them to a status of permanent servitude, not far removed from slavery. Called helots, these dependents far outnum-bered the free citizens of Sparta and represented a permanent threat of rebellion. Solving this problem shaped Spartan society decisively. Sparta's answer was a militaristic regime, constantly ready for war to keep the helots in their place. To maintain such a system, all boys were removed from their families at the age of seven to be trained by the state in military camps, where they learned the ways of war. There they remained until the age of thirty. The ideal Spartan male was a warrior, skilled in battle, able to endure hardship, and willing to die for his city. Mothers are said to have told their sons departing for battle to "come back with your shield . . . or on it." Although economic equality for men was the ideal, it was never completely realized in practice. And unlike Athens, political power was exercised primarily by a small group of wealthy men.

This militaristic and far-from-democratic system had implications for women that, strangely enough, offered them greater freedoms and fewer restric-tions. As in many warrior societies, their central task was reproduction—bearing warrior sons for Sparta. To strengthen their bodies for childbearing, girls were encouraged to take part in sporting events—running, wrestling, throwing the discus and javelin,

A Girl of Sparta
This figurine portrays a young female Spartan athlete or runner. Compare her clothing with that worn by Hegeso in the photo opposite. (The British Museum, London, UK/Bridgeman Images)

even driving chariots. At times, women and men alike competed in the nude before mixed audiences. Their education, like that of boys, was prescribed by the state, which also insisted that newly married women cut their hair short, unlike adult Greek women elsewhere. Thus Spartan women were not secluded or segregated, as were their Athenian counterparts.

Furthermore, Spartan young women, unlike those of Athens, usually married men of their own age, about eighteen years old, thus putting the new couple on a more equal basis. Marriage often began with a trial period to make sure the new couple could produce children, with divorce and remarriage readily available if they could not. Because men were so often away at war or preparing for it, women exercised much more authority in the household than was the case in Athens.

It is little wonder that the freedom of Spartan women appalled other Greeks, who believed that it undermined good order and state authority. Aristotle complained that the more egalitarian inheritance practices of Spartans led to their women controlling some 40 percent of landed estates. In Sparta, he declared, women "live in every sort of intemperance and luxury" and "the [male] rulers are ruled by women." Plutarch, a Greek writer during the heyday of the Roman Empire, observed critically that "the men of Sparta always obeyed their wives." The clothing worn by Spartan women to give them greater freedom of movement seemed immodest to other Greeks.

Nonetheless, in another way, Sparta may have been more restrictive than Athens and other Greek city-states, particularly in its apparent prohibition of homosexuality. At least, this was the assertion of the Athenian writer Xenophon (427–355 B.C.E.), who stated that Sparta's legendary founder Lycurgus "caused lovers to abstain from sexual intercourse with boys."[21] Elsewhere, however, homoerotic relationships were culturally approved and fairly common for both men and women, although this did not prevent their participants from entering heterosexual marriages as well. The ideal homosexual relationship—between an older man and a young adolescent boy—was viewed as limited in time, for it was supposed to end when the boy's beard began to grow. Unlike contemporary Western societies where sexuality is largely seen as an identity, ancient Greek society viewed sexual choice more casually and as a matter of taste.

Sparta clearly was a patriarchy, with women serving as breeding machines for its military system and lacking any formal role in public life, but it was a lighter patriarchy than that of Athens. The joint efforts of men and women seemed necessary to maintain a huge class of helots in permanent subjugation. Death in childbirth was considered the equivalent of death in battle, for both contributed to the defense of Sparta, and both were honored alike. In Athens, on the other hand, growing freedom and democracy were associated with the strengthening of the male-dominated, property-owning household, and within that household, the cornerstone of Athenian society, men were expected to exercise authority. Doing so required increasingly severe limitations and restrictions on the lives of women.

REFLECTIONS: WHAT CHANGES? WHAT PERSISTS? 217

Together, the cases of Athens and Sparta illustrate how the historical record appears in a different light when viewed through the lens of gender. Athens, so celebrated for its democracy and philosophical rationalism, offered little to its women, whereas Sparta, often condemned for its militarism and virtual enslavement of the helots, provided a somewhat wider scope for the free women of the city.

What Changes? What Persists?

So what is more impressive in human history—the innovations and changes or the enduring patterns and lasting features? At the level of personal history, most people have no doubt noticed the brevity and transience of life, marked as it is by childhood, coming of age, marriage, the birth of children, illness, decline, and death. Every culture has developed rituals to honor these changes. And yet we also recognize some enduring sense of self across the span of a life, some continuity, at least in memory, between the child and the elder.

Beyond our individual histories, however, our perception of change or continuity in the wider arenas of life surely depends on when we are living. During the long Paleolithic and Neolithic eras, few people were aware of major changes in the larger patterns of life. Of course, change happened: nomadic peoples settled down in villages; agriculture developed; cities arose; states and empires took shape; class structures evolved; patriarchy emerged more sharply defined. But few of these changes occurred quickly enough to be noticeable in a single lifetime. It is among the great contributions of world history to call attention to transformations of which we might otherwise be unaware. In the modern era, and certainly in our own time, the pace of change has dramatically accelerated. We have come to value, celebrate, expect, and promote change in ways that many of our distant—and not so distant—ancestors would find unimaginable.

What might we say about the balance of change and persistence in the era of second-wave civilizations? Clearly, there was much that was new, even if those innovations had roots in earlier times. The Greek conquest of the Persian Empire under the leadership of Alexander the Great was both novel and unexpected. The Roman Empire encompassed the entire Mediterranean basin in a single political system for the first time. Buddhism and Christianity emerged as new, distinct, and universal religious traditions, although both bore the marks of their origin in Hindu and Jewish religious thinking, respectively. The collapse of dynasties, empires, and civilizations long thought to be solidly entrenched—the Chinese and Roman, for example—must surely have seemed to people of the time to be something fearfully new.

But much that was created in the second-wave era—particularly its social and cultural patterns—has demonstrated an impressive continuity throughout many

AP® EXAM TIP

You must be able to write an essay on continuity and change over time. This discussion is a good introduction to such essays.

centuries, even if it also changed in particular ways over time. China's scholar-gentry class retained its prominence throughout the ups and downs of changing dynasties into the twentieth century. India's caste-based social structure still endures as a way of thinking and behaving for hundreds of millions of men and women on the South Asian peninsula. Although slavery gave way to serfdom in post-Roman Europe, it was widely practiced in the Islamic world and massively extended in Europe's American colonies after 1500. In various expressions, slavery remained an important and largely unquestioned feature of all civilizations until the nineteenth century, and in a few places it still exists. Patriarchy, with its assumptions of male superiority and dominance, has surely been the most fundamental, long-lasting, and taken-for-granted feature of all civilizations. Not until recent centuries have those assumptions effectively been challenged, and even so, patriarchy has continued to shape the lives and the thinking of the vast majority of humankind. And many hundreds of millions of people in the twenty-first century still honor or practice religious and cultural traditions begun during the second-wave era.

Persistence and change alike have long provided the inextricable warp and woof of both individual experience and historical study. Each of us no doubt ponders the tension between them in our own lives. Untangling their elusive relationship has figured prominently in the task of historians and has contributed much to the enduring fascination of historical study.

Chapter Review

What's the Significance?

Wang Mang, 195

China's scholar-gentry class, 195

Ge Hong, 196–97

Yellow Turban Rebellion, 197–98

caste as *varna* and *jati*, 199–202

"ritual purity" in Indian social practice, 202

Greek and Roman slavery, 203–8

Spartacus, 208

patriarchy, 208–17

the "three obediences," 210–11

Empress Wu, 212

Aspasia and Pericles, 214

helots, 215–17

Big Picture Questions

1. What might an observant Chinese traveler from the Han dynasty era find surprising or offensive in India or the Greco-Roman world? What similarities might he or she notice?

2. Why do you think slavery was so much more prominent in Greco-Roman civilization than in India or China?

3. What philosophical, religious, or cultural ideas served to legitimate the class and gender inequalities of second-wave civilizations?

4. What changes in the patterns of social life in second-wave civilizations can you identify? What accounts for these changes?

5. **Looking Back:** Cultural and social patterns of civilizations seem to endure longer than the political framework of states and empires. What evidence from Chapters 3, 4, and 5 might support this statement? How might you account for this phenomenon? Is there evidence that could support a contrary position?

Next Steps: For Further Study

Jeannine Auboyer, *Daily Life in Ancient India* (2002). A social history of ancient India, with a focus on caste, ritual, religion, and art.

Sue Blundell, *Women in Ancient Greece* (1999). A well-written academic study, with occasional humorous stories and anecdotes.

Keith Bradley, *Slavery and Society at Rome* (1994). A scholarly but very readable account of slavery in the Roman Empire.

Michael Lowe, *Everyday Life in Early Imperial China* (1968). A vivid description of social life during the Han dynasty.

Merry Weisner-Hanks, *Gender in History* (2001). A thoughtful overview by a leading scholar in both women's history and world history.

"The Indian Caste System: An Introduction," http://www.youtube.com/watch?v=Oh_xvKLhZHg. A brief BBC documentary on the beginnings of caste in India.

"Women in World History," http://chnm.gmu.edu/wwh/index.html. Documents, reviews, and lesson plans for learning and teaching about women's history in a global context.

WORKING WITH EVIDENCE

Pompeii as a Window on the Roman World

> You could hear the shrieks of women, the wailing of infants, and the shouting of men; some were calling their parents, others their children or their wives, trying to recognize them by their voices. People bewailed their own fate or that of their relatives, and there were some who prayed for death in their terror of dying. Many besought the aid of the gods, but still more imagined there were no gods left, and that the universe was plunged into eternal darkness for evermore.[22]

Written by a prominent Roman known as Pliny the Younger, this eyewitness account details reactions to the volcanic eruption of Mount Vesuvius, located on the southwestern side of the Italian peninsula, on August 24, 79 C.E. That eruption buried the nearby city of Pompeii, located about 150 miles south of Rome, but it also preserved the city, frozen in time, until archeologists began to uncover it in the mid-eighteenth century (see Map 3.4, page 119). Now substantially excavated, Pompeii is an archeological and historical treasure, offering a unique window into the life of a Roman city during the first century C.E.

As this city of perhaps 20,000 people emerged from layers of ash, it stood revealed as a small but prosperous center of commerce and agriculture, serving as a point of entry for goods coming to southern Italy by sea. Pompeii also hosted numerous vineyards, production facilities for wine and olive oil, and a fisheries industry. In addition, the city was a tourist destination for well-to-do Romans. The houses of the wealthy were elegant structures, often built around a central courtyard, and were decorated with lovely murals displaying still-life images, landscapes, and scenes from Greek and Roman mythology. An inscription found on the threshold of one house expressed the entrepreneurial spirit of the town: "Gain is pure joy."[23]

Laid out in a grid pattern with straight streets, the city's numerous public facilities included a central bathing/swimming pool, some twenty-five street fountains, various public bathhouses, and a large food market as well as many bars and small restaurants. More than thirty brothels, often featuring explicit erotic art, offered sexual services at relatively inexpensive prices. One inscription, apparently aimed at local tourists, declared: "If anyone is looking for some tender love in this town, keep in mind that here all the girls are very

Source 5.1 Terentius Neo and His Wife

Museo Archeologico Nazionale, Naples, Italy/Roger-Viollet, Paris, France/Bridgeman Images

Source 5.2 A Pompeii Banquet

friendly." Graffiti too abounded, much of it clearly sexual. Here are three of the milder examples: "Atimetus got me pregnant"; "Sarra, you are not being very nice, leaving me all alone like this"; and "If anyone does not believe in Venus, they should gaze at my girlfriend."[24]

The preserved art of Pompeii, especially the wall paintings, provides a glimpse into the social life of that city. Most of that art, of course, catered to and reflected the life of the more prosperous classes. Source 5.1 shows a portrait of Terentius Neo, a prominent businessman and magistrate (an elected public official), and his unnamed wife. He is wearing a toga and holding a papyrus scroll, while she wears a tunic and is holding to her lips a stylus, used for writing on the wax covered wooden tablet that she carries. Her hair is styled in a fashion popular in the mid-first century.

■ What significance do you attribute to the absence in the painting's title of a name for the woman?

■ What do you think the artist is trying to convey by highlighting the literacy of this couple?

■ What overall impression of these two people and their relationship to each other does this painting suggest?

Terentius Neo and his wife were no doubt served by slaves in their home, as slave owning was common in the Roman world, particularly among the upper classes. In the streets and homes of urban areas, slaves and free people mingled quite openly. Roman slavery was not distinguished by race, and the outward signs of urban slavery were few, especially for those practicing professions. Such a couple no doubt gave and attended banquets similar to the one depicted in Source 5.2, where well-to-do guests reclined on padded couches while slaves served them food and drink. Dancers, acrobats, and singers often provided entertainment at such events, which provided an occasion for elites to impress others with their lavish display of wealth and generosity.

■ What signs of social status are evident in this painting?

■ How are slaves, shown here in the foreground, portrayed? See also the mosaic of a slave and master on page 205.

The lives of the less exalted appear infrequently in the art of Pompeii, but the images in Source 5.3 provide some entrée into their world. These are frescoes painted on the wall of a *caupona*, an inn or tavern catering to the lower classes. The first image shows Myrtale, a prostitute, kissing a man, while the caption above reads: "I don't want to, with Myrtale." In the second image, a

Source 5.3 Scenes in a Pompeii Tavern

Museo Archeologico Nazionale, Naples, Italy/Photos: Fotografica Foglia/Scala/Art Resource, NY

female barmaid serves two customers with a large jug and a cup, while they compete for her attention. In the third image, two men playing dice are arguing.

- Why do you think a tavern owner might have such paintings in his place of business?

- What might we learn about tavern life from these images?

- What roles did women play in the tavern?

- What differences do you notice between these paintings and those depicting the lives of the upper classes?

The excavated ruins of Pompeii have much to tell us about the religious as well as the social life of the Roman world in the first century C.E., before Christianity had spread widely. Based on ritual observance rather than doctrine or theology, Roman religious practice sought to obtain the favor of the gods as a way of promoting success, prosperity, and good fortune. A core expression of the diverse and eclectic world of Roman religion was the imperial cult. In Pompeii, a number of temples were dedicated to one or another of the deified emperors, employing together a large cadre of priests and priestesses. Linked to the imperial cult were temples devoted to the traditional Greco-Roman gods such as Apollo, Venus, and Jupiter.

Probably more important to ordinary people were their *lararia* (household shrines), often a niche in the wall that housed paintings or sculptures of *lares* (guardian spirits or deities believed to provide protection within the home). Families offered gifts of fruit, cakes, and wine to these spirits, and the lararia were the focal point for various sacrifices and rituals associated with birth, marriage, and death. Source 5.4 shows one of these shrines, uncovered in the home of a well-to-do freedman (former slave) named Vetti. Protecting the family from external danger were two lares, standing on either side of the lararium and holding their drinking horns. In the center was the *genius*, the spirit of the male head of household. Dressed in a toga and offering a sacrifice, this spirit embodied the character of the man, especially his procreative powers, and so guaranteed many children for the household. The snake at the bottom represented still other benevolent guardian spirits of the family in a fashion very different from Christian symbolism of the snake.

- Why might such a shrine and the spirits it accommodated be more meaningful for many people than the state-approved cults?

- What significance might you find in the temple-like shape of the lararium?

In addition to the official cults and the veneration of household gods, by the first century C.E. a number of newer traditions, often called "mystery

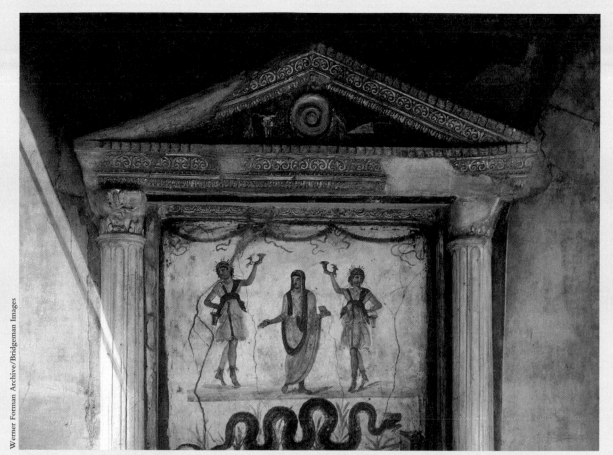

Werner Forman Archive/Bridgeman Images

Source 5.4 A Domestic Shrine

religions," were spreading widely in the Roman Empire. Deriving from the eastern realm of the empire and beyond (Greece, Egypt, and Persia, for example), these mystery religions illustrate the kinds of cultural exchange that took place within the empire. They offered an alternative to the official cults, for they were more personal, emotional, and intimate, usually featuring a ritual initiation into sacred mysteries, codes of moral behavior, and the promise of an afterlife. Among the most popular of these mystery cults in Pompeii was that of Isis, an Egyptian goddess who restored her husband/brother, Osiris, to life and was worshipped as a compassionate protector of the downtrodden.

Another mystery cult, this one of Greek origin, was associated with Dionysus, a god of wine, ecstasy, and poetic inspiration, who was especially popular with women. Often associated with drunkenness, trance states, wild dancing, and unrestrained sexuality, the cult of Dionysus encouraged at least

Werner Forman Archive/Bridgeman Images

Source 5.5 Mystery Religions: The Cult of Dionysus

the temporary abandonment of conventional inhibitions and social restrictions as initiates sought union with Dionysus. A series of wall paintings on a Pompeii building known as the Villa of Mysteries depicts the process of initiation into the cult of Dionysus, perhaps in preparation for marriage.

Source 5.5 shows a particularly dramatic phase of that initiation in which a woman is ritually whipped, while a naked devotee dances ecstatically with a pair of cymbals above her head and a companion holds a rod of phallic symbolism sacred to Dionysus. In any such process of religious initiation, the initiate undergoes a series of trials or purifications in which he or she "dies" symbolically, achieves mystical union with the god, and is "reborn" into the new community of the cult.

- What aspects of the initiation process are visible in this image?

- How might you understand the role of whipping in the initiation process? How would you interpret the relationship of the initiate and the woman on whose lap she is resting her head?

- In what way is sexual union, symbolized by the rod, significant in the initiation?

- Why do you think Roman authorities took action against these mystery religions, even as they did against Christianity?

- What did the mystery cults of Isis or Dionysus provide that neither the state cults nor household gods might offer?

DOING HISTORY

Pompeii as a Window on the Roman World

1. **Characterizing Pompeii:** What does the art of Pompeii, as reflected in these sources, tell us about the social and religious life of this small Roman city in the first century C.E.?

2. **Noticing class differences:** What class or social distinctions are apparent in these visual sources?

3. **Identifying gender roles:** What do these sources suggest about the varied lives and social roles of women and men in Pompeii?

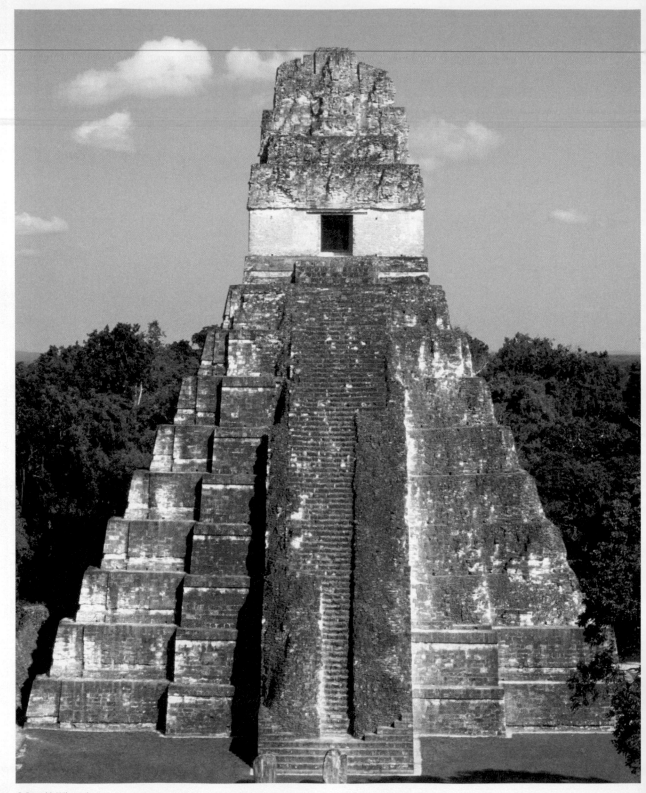

CHAPTER 6

Commonalities and Variations

Africa, the Americas, and Pacific Oceania
600 B.C.E.–1200 C.E.

In early 2010, Bolivian president Evo Morales was inaugurated for his second term in office, the only person from the country's Native American population ever elected to that post since independence from Spain in 1825. The day before the official ceremony in the capital of La Paz, Morales traveled to Tiwanaku (tee-wah-NAH-coo), the center of an impressive empire that had flourished in the Andean highlands between 400 and 1000 C.E., long before either the Incas or the Spanish ruled the area. There he sought to link himself and his administration to this ancient culture, a symbol of Bolivian nationalism and indigenous pride. On his arrival, Morales was ritually cleansed with holy water and herbs and dressed in a llama wool robe. After offerings were made to Pachamama, an Andean earth goddess, and to Tata Inti, the Inca sun god, Morales was invested with symbols of both kingship and spiritual leadership, thus joining political and religious sources of authority. Proclaiming a new multinational state, Morales declared: "Gone forever is the colonial state, which allowed the looting of our natural resources, and gone also is the discriminatory [against native peoples] colonial state."[1] This recent ceremony provides a reminder that memories of American second-wave civilizations remained alive and were available for mobilizing political support and legitimating political authority in the very different circumstances of the early twenty-first century.

For many people, the second-wave era evokes most vividly the civilizations of Eurasia—the Greeks and the Romans, the Persians and the Chinese, and the Indians of South Asia—yet those were not the only civilizations of that era. During this period, the

---

The Maya Temple of the Great Jaguar in Tikal   Located in the Maya city of Tikal in present-day Guatemala, this temple was constructed in the eighth century C.E. and excavated by archeologists in the late nineteenth century. It served as the tomb of the Tikal ruler Jasaw Chan K'awiil I (682–734). Some 144 feet tall, it was topped by a three-room temple complex and a huge roofcomb showing the ruler on his throne. Carved on a wooden beam inside the temple is an image of the ruler protected by a huge jaguar, along with illustrations of his military victories.

Mesoamerican Maya and the Andean Tiwanaku thrived, as did several civilizations in sub-Saharan Africa, including Meroë (MER-oh-ee), Axum (AHK-soom), and the Niger River valley. Furthermore, those peoples who did not organize themselves around cities or states likewise had histories of note and alternative ways of constructing their societies, although they are often neglected in favor of civiliza-

SEEKING THE MAIN POINT

To what extent did the histories of Africa and the Americas parallel those of Eurasia? In what ways did they forge new or different paths?

tions. This chapter explores the histories of the varied peoples of Africa, the Americas, and Pacific Oceania during this phase of world history. On occasion, those histories will extend some centuries beyond the chronological boundaries of the second-wave era in Eurasia because patterns of historical development around the world did not always coincide precisely.

Continental Comparisons

At the broadest level, human cultures evolved in quite similar fashion around the world. All, of course, were part of that grand process of human migration that initially peopled the planet. Beginning in Africa, that vast movement of humankind subsequently encompassed Eurasia, Australia, the Americas, and Pacific Oceania. Almost everywhere, gathering, hunting, and fishing long remained the sole basis for sustaining life and society. Then, on the three supercontinents—Eurasia, Africa, and the Americas—the momentous turn of the Agricultural Revolution took place independently and in several distinct areas of each landmass (see Chapter 1). That revolutionary transformation of human life subsequently generated, in particularly rich agricultural environments of all three regions, those more complex societies that we know as civilizations, featuring cities, states, monumental architecture, and great social inequality (see Chapter 2). In these ways, the historical trajectory of the human journey has a certain unity and similarity across quite distinct continental regions. These commonalities provide the foundation for a genuinely global history of humankind. At the beginning of the Common Era, that trajectory had generated a total world population of about 250 million people, substantially less than the current population of the United States alone. By modern standards, it was still a sparsely populated planet.

Guided Reading Question

■ COMPARISON
What similarities and differences are noticeable among the three major continents of the world?

The world's human population was then distributed very unevenly across the three giant continents, as the Snapshot on page 232 indicates. Eurasia was then home to more than 85 percent of the world's people, Africa about 10 percent, the Americas around 5 percent, and Oceania less than 1 percent. That unevenness in population distribution, a pattern that has persisted to the present, is part of the reason why world historians focus more attention on Eurasia than on these other regions. Here lies one of the major differences among the continents.

There were others as well. The absence of most animals capable of domestication meant that few pastoral societies developed in the Americas, and only in pockets of the Andes Mountains based on the herding of llamas and alpacas. No animals

A MAP OF TIME

1400–800 B.C.E.	Lapita culture in Oceania
900–200 B.C.E.	Chavín religious movement in Peruvian Andes
730 B.C.E.	Nubian conquest of Egypt
300 B.C.E.–100 C.E.	Kingdom of Meroë in upper Nile Valley
300 B.C.E.–900 C.E.	Niger Valley civilization in West Africa
200 B.C.E.–400 C.E.	Hopewell "mound-building" culture in U.S. eastern woodlands
1st–8th centuries C.E.	Flourishing of Axum (East Africa) and Moche (coastal Peru) civilizations; spread of Bantu-speaking people in eastern and southern Africa
250–900 C.E.	Classical Maya civilization
300–600	Flourishing of Teotihuacán
4th century	Introduction of Christianity to Axum
400–1000	Tiwanaku and Wari in the Andes
860–1130	Chaco culture in U.S. Southwest
900–1250	Cahokia
After 1000	Flourishing of Tonga trading network
1100–1600	Saudeleur dynasty on island of Pohnpei
1200	Initial settlement of New Zealand

were available in the Americas to pull plows or carts or to be ridden into combat. Africa too lacked wild sheep, goats, chickens, horses, and camels, but its proximity to Eurasia meant that these animals, once domesticated, became widely available to African peoples. Metallurgy in the Americas was likewise far less developed than in Eurasia and Africa, where iron tools and weapons played such an important role in economic and military life. In the Americas, writing was limited to the Mesoamerican region and was most highly developed among the Maya, whereas in Africa it was confined to the northern and northeastern parts of the continent. In Eurasia, by contrast, writing emerged elaborately in many regions. Furthermore, civilizations in Africa and the Americas were fewer in number and generally smaller than those of Eurasia, and larger numbers of people in those two continents lived outside the confines of any civilization in communities that did not feature cities and states.

A final continental comparison distinguishes the history of Africa from that of the Americas. Geography placed Africa adjacent to Eurasia, while it separated the Americas from both Africa and Eurasia. This has meant that parts of Africa frequently

AP® EXAM TIP

You should remember that interactions between humans and their environment are a key theme in this course.

AP® EXAM TIP

Be able to define and describe the processes of "demographics" throughout world history.

SNAPSHOT Continental Population in the Second-Wave Era and Beyond

(Note: Population figures for such early times are merely estimates and are often controversial among scholars. Percentages do not always total 100 percent due to rounding.[2])

	Eurasia	Africa	North America	Central/South America	Australia/ Oceania	Total World
Area (in square miles and as percentage of world total)						
	21,049,000 (41%)	11,608,000 (22%)	9,365,000 (18%)	6,880,000 (13%)	2,968,000 (6%)	51,870,000
Population (in millions and as percentage of world total)						
400 B.C.E.	127 (83%)	17 (11%)	1 (0.7%)	7 (5%)	1 (0.7%)	153
10 C.E.	213 (85%)	26 (10%)	2 (0.8%)	10 (4%)	1 (0.4%)	252
200 C.E.	215 (84%)	30 (12%)	2 (0.8%)	9 (4%)	1 (0.4%)	257
600 C.E.	167 (80%)	24 (12%)	2 (1%)	14 (7%)	1 (0.5%)	208
1000 C.E.	195 (77%)	39 (15%)	2 (0.8%)	16 (6%)	1 (0.4%)	253
1500	329 (69%)	113 (24%)	4.5 (0.9%)	53 (11%)	3 (0.6%)	477
1750	646 (83%)	104 (13%)	3 (0.4%)	15 (1.9%)	3 (0.4%)	771
2013	5,041 (70.4%)	1,110 (15.5%)	355 (5%)	617 (8.6%)	38 (0.5%)	7,162

interacted with Eurasian civilizations. In fact, Mediterranean North Africa was long part of a larger zone of Afro-Eurasian interaction. Ancient Egyptian civilization was certainly in contact with Crete, Syria, and Mesopotamia and provided inspiration for the Greeks. The entire North African coastal region was incorporated into the Roman Empire and used to produce wheat and olives on large estates with slave labor. Christianity spread widely across North Africa, giving rise to some of the early Church's most famous martyrs and theologians. The Christian faith found an even more permanent foothold in the lands now known as Ethiopia.

Arabia, located between Africa and Asia, was another point of contact with a wider world for African peoples. The arrival of the domesticated camel, probably from Arabia, generated a pastoral way of life among some of the Berber peoples of the western Sahara during the first three centuries C.E. A little later, camels also made possible trans-Saharan commerce, which linked interior West Africa to the world of Mediterranean civilization. Over many centuries, the East African coast was a port of call for Egyptian, Roman, and Arab merchants, and that region subsequently became an integral part of Indian Ocean trading networks. The transoceanic voyages of Austronesian-speaking sailors from Southeast Asia brought various food crops of that region, bananas for example, to Madagascar and from there to the East African mainland. The Americas and Oceania, by contrast, developed almost wholly apart from this Afro-Eurasian network until that separation was breeched by the voyages of Columbus from 1492.

To illustrate the historical developments of the second-wave era beyond Eurasia / North Africa, this chapter examines first the civilizations that emerged in sub-Saharan Africa and the Americas. Then our historical spotlight turns to several regions on both continents as well as the islands of the Pacific that remained outside the zone of civilization, reminding us that the histories of many peoples took shape without the cities, states, and empires that were so prominent within that zone.

Civilizations of Africa

When historians refer to Africa in premodern times, they are speaking generally of a geographic concept, a continental landmass, and not a cultural identity. Certainly few, if any, people living on the continent at that time thought of themselves as Africans. Like Eurasia or the Americas, Africa hosted numerous separate societies, cultures, and civilizations with vast differences among them as well as some interaction between them.

Many of these differences grew out of the continent's environmental variations. Small regions of Mediterranean climate in the northern and southern extremes, large deserts (the Sahara and the Kalahari), even larger regions of savanna grasslands, tropical rain forest in the continent's center, highlands and mountains in eastern Africa — all of these features, combined with the continent's enormous size, ensured endless variation among Africa's many peoples. Africa did, however, have one distinctive environmental feature: bisected by the equator, it was the most tropical of the world's three supercontinents. While some regions, such as highland Ethiopia, sustained very productive agriculture, elsewhere a variety of factors generated lower crop yields and diminished soil fertility. These included heavy but sometimes-erratic rainfall frequently followed by long dry seasons and the leaching of nutrients from often very ancient soils. Climatic conditions also spawned numerous disease-carrying insects and parasites, which have long created serious health problems in many parts of the continent. It was within these environmental constraints that African peoples made their histories. In several distinct regions of the continent — the upper Nile Valley, northern Ethiopia/Eritrea, and the Niger River valley — small civilizations flourished during the second-wave era, while others followed later. A further African civilization falling partly within this time period grew up along the East African coast in conjunction with Indian Ocean commerce. Known as Swahili civilization, it is treated in greater detail in Chapter 7.

AP® EXAM TIP

Expect the AP® exam to ask you to identify political, social, and economic connections between major regions.

Meroë: Continuing a Nile Valley Civilization

Guided Reading Question

■ CONNECTION
How did the history of Meroë and Axum reflect interaction with neighboring civilizations?

In the Nile Valley south of Egypt lay the lands of Nubian civilization, almost as old as Egypt itself. Over many centuries, Nubians both traded and fought with Egypt, and on one occasion the Nubian Kingdom of Kush conquered Egypt and ruled it for a century. (See Zooming In: Piye, page 236.) While borrowing heavily from Egypt, Nubia remained a distinct and separate civilization. As Egypt fell increasingly under foreign control, Nubian civilization came to center on the southern city of Meroë (MER-oh-ee), where it flourished between 300 B.C.E. and 100 C.E. (see Map 6.1).

Politically, the Kingdom of Meroë was governed by an all-powerful and sacred monarch, a position held on at least ten occasions by women, governing alone or as co-rulers with a male monarch. Unlike the female pharaoh Hatshepsut in Egypt, who was portrayed in male clothing, Meroë queens appeared in sculptures as women and with a prominence and power equivalent to their male counterparts. In accordance with ancient traditions, such rulers were buried along with a number of human sacrificial victims. The city of Meroë and other urban centers housed a wide variety of economic specialties—merchants, weavers, potters, and masons, as well as servants, laborers, and slaves. The smelting of iron and the manufacture of iron tools and weapons were especially prominent industries. The rural areas surrounding Meroë were populated by peoples who practiced some combination of herding and farming and paid periodic tribute to the ruler. Rainfall-based agriculture was possible in Meroë, and consequently farmers were less dependent on irrigation. This meant that the rural population did not need to concentrate so heavily near the Nile as was the case in Egypt.

The wealth and military power of Meroë derived in part from extensive long-distance trading connections, to the north via the Nile and to the east and west by means of camel caravans. Its iron weapons and cotton cloth, as well as its access to gold, ivory, tortoiseshells, and ostrich feathers, gave Meroë a reputation for great riches in the world of northeastern Africa and the Mediterranean. The discovery in Meroë of a statue of the Roman emperor Augustus, probably seized during a raid on Roman Egypt,

A Bracelet from Meroë
This gold bracelet, dating to about 100 B.C.E., illustrates the skill of Meroë's craftsmen as well as the kingdom's reputation as one of the wealthiest states of the ancient world. The bracelet's depiction of a seated Hathor, a popular Egyptian goddess, shows the influence of Egyptian culture in Nubia. (Bracelet with an image of Hathor, from Pyramid B, Gebel Barkal, Nubia, Meroitic Period, 250–100 B.C. [gold and enamel], Nubian/Museum of Fine Arts, Boston, Massachusetts, USA/Harvard University–Boston Museum of Fine Arts Expedition/Bridgeman Images)

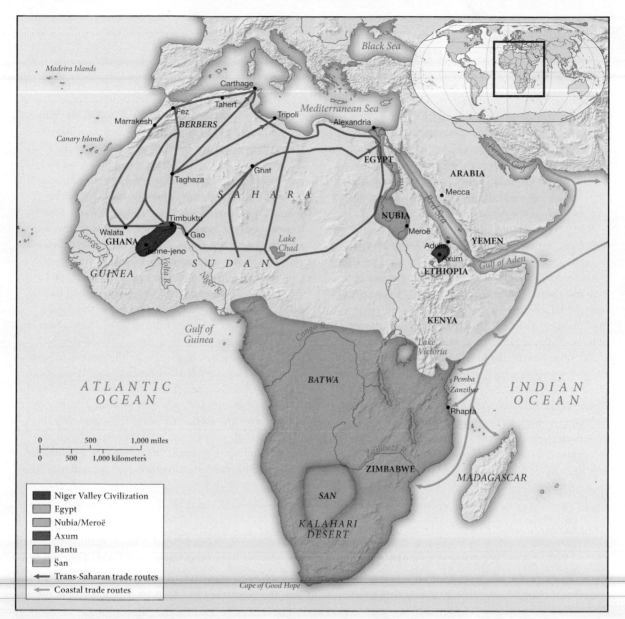

Map 6.1   Africa in the Second-Wave Era

During the second-wave era, older African civilizations such as Egypt and Nubia persisted and changed, while new civilizations emerged in Axum and the Niger River valley. South of the equator, the process of Bantu expansion created many new societies and identities.

testifies to contact with the Mediterranean world. Culturally, Meroë seemed to move away from the heavy Egyptian influence of earlier times. A local lion god, Apedemek, grew more prominent than Egyptian deities such as Isis and Osiris, while the use of Egyptian-style writing declined as a new and still-undeciphered Meroitic script took its place.

Piye, Kushite Conqueror of Egypt

During the eighth century B.C.E., a remarkable reversal took place in northeastern Africa. The ancient Kingdom of Kush in the southern Nile Valley, long under the control of Egypt, conquered its former ruler and governed it for a century. The primary agent of that turnabout was Piye, a Kushite ruler (r. 752–721 B.C.E.), who recorded his great victory in a magnificent inscription that provides some hints about his own personality and outlook on the world.[3]

The very beginning of the inscription discloses Piye's self-image, for he declares himself a "divine emanation, living image of Atum," the Egyptian creator-god closely connected to kingship. Like most of the Kushite elite, Piye had thoroughly assimilated much of Egyptian culture and religion, becoming perhaps "more Egyptian than the Egyptians."[4] Even the inscription was written in hieroglyphic Egyptian and in the style of earlier pharaohs. Who better then to revive an Egypt that, over the past several centuries, had become hopelessly fragmented and that also had neglected the worship of Amun? Thus Piye's conquest reflected the territorial ambitions of Kush's "Egyptianized" rulers, a sense of divinely inspired mission to set things right in Egypt, and the opportunity presented by the sorry state of Egyptian politics.

If we are to believe the inscription, Piye went to war reluctantly and only in response to requests from various Egyptian "princes, counts, and generals." Furthermore, he was careful to pay respect to the gods all along the way. After celebrating the new year in 730 B.C.E., Piye departed from his capital of Napata and made an initial stop in Thebes, a southern Egyptian city already controlled by Kushite forces. There he took part in the annual Opet Festival, honoring Amun, his wife Mut (Egypt's mother goddess), and their offspring Khonsu, associated with the moon. Moving north, Piye then laid siege to Hermopolis, located in middle Egypt. From a high tower, archers poured arrows into the city and "slingers" hurled stones, "slaying people among them daily," according to the inscription. Soon the city had become "foul to the nose," and its ruler, Prince Namlot, prepared for surrender. He sent his wife and daughter, lying on their bellies, to plead with the women in Piye's entourage, begging them to intercede with Piye, which they did. Grandly entering the city, Piye went first to the temple of the chief god, where he offered sacrifices of "bulls, calves and fowl." To establish his authority, he then "entered every chamber of [Namlot's] house, his treasury and his magazines." Piye pointedly ignored the women of Namlot's harem when they greeted him "in

In the centuries following 100 C.E., the Kingdom of Meroë declined, in part because of deforestation caused by the need for wood to make charcoal for smelting iron. Furthermore, as Egyptian trade with the African interior switched from the Nile Valley route to the Red Sea, the resources available to Meroë's rulers diminished and the state weakened. The effective end of the Meroë phase of Nubian civilization came with the kingdom's conquest in the 340s C.E. by the neighboring and rising state of Axum. In the centuries that followed, three separate Nubian states emerged, and Coptic (Egyptian) Christianity penetrated the region. For almost a thousand years, Nubia was a Christian civilization, using Greek as a liturgical language and constructing churches in Coptic or Byzantine fashion. After 1300 or so, political division, Arab immigration, and the penetration of Islam eroded this Christian civilization, and Nubia became part of the growing world of Islam (see Chapter 10).

the manner of women." Yet in the stable, he was moved by the suffering of the horses. He seized Namlot's possessions for his treasury and assigned his enemy's grain to the temple of Amun.

And so it went as Piye moved northward. Many cities capitulated without resistance, offering their treasure to the Kushites. Presenting himself as a just and generous conqueror, Piye declared that "not a single one has been slain therein, except the enemies who blasphemed against the god, who were dispatched as rebels." However, it was a different story when he arrived outside the major north Egyptian city of Memphis, then ruled by the Libyan chieftain Tefnakht. There "a multitude of people were slain" before Tefnakht was induced to surrender. He sent an envoy to Piye to deliver an abject and humiliating speech: "Be thou appeased! I have not beheld thy face for shame; I cannot stand before thy flame, I tremble at thy might." The city was ritually cleansed; proper respect was paid to the gods, who confirmed Piye's kingship; and tribute was collected. Soon all resistance collapsed, and Piye,

The stele of Piye, showing Piye to the right of the seated god Amun, receiving the surrender of his Egyptian enemies, while below defeated rulers prostrate themselves before him.

once ruler of a small Kushite kingdom, found himself master of all Egypt.

And then, surprisingly, he departed, leaving his underlings in charge and his sister as the high priestess and wife of Amun in Thebes. His ships "were laden with silver, gold, copper, clothing, and everything of the Northland, every product of Syria, and all sweet woods of God's Land [Egypt]. His majesty sailed up-stream, with glad heart." Never again did Piye set foot in Egypt, preferring to live out his days in his native country, where he was buried in an Egyptian-style pyramid. But he had laid the foundation for a century of Kushite rule in Egypt, reunifying that ancient country, reinvigorating the cult of Amun, and giving expression to the vitality of an important African civilization.

Questions: How did Piye understand himself and his actions in Egypt? How might ancient Egyptians or modern historians view his conquests?

photo: James Henry Breasted, *The Piankhi Stela, Ancient Records of Egypt* (Chicago, 1906), Part IV, 816ff/Visual Connection Archive

Axum: The Making of a Christian Kingdom

If Meroë represented the continuation of an old African/Nubian civilization, Axum marked the emergence of a new one. (For various accounts about or from Axum, see Working with Evidence: Axum and the World, page 265.) Axum lay in the Horn of Africa, in what is now Eritrea and northern Ethiopia (see Map 6.1). Its economic foundation was a highly productive agriculture that used a plow-based farming system, unlike most of the rest of Africa, which relied on the hoe or digging stick. Axum's agriculture generated substantial amounts of wheat, barley, millet, and teff, a highly nutritious grain unique to that region. By 50 C.E. or so, a substantial state had emerged, stimulated by its participation in the rapidly increasing Red Sea and Indian Ocean commerce, which was itself a product of growing Roman demand for Indian pearls, textiles, and especially pepper. At Adulis, then the largest

AP® EXAM TIP

The development and spread of Christianity is a key element in this course.

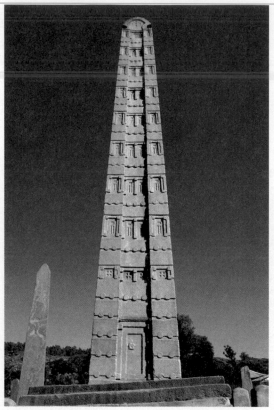

The Columns of Axum
Dating to the time when Axum first encountered Christianity (300–500 C.E.), this column, measuring some seventy-nine feet tall, probably served as a funeral monument for the kingdom's ancient rulers. (McPhoto/ZAD/age fotostock)

port on the East African coast, a wide range of merchants sought the products of the African interior — animal hides, rhinoceros horn, ivory, obsidian, tortoiseshells, and slaves. Taxes on this trade provided a major source of revenue for the Axumite state and the complex society that grew up within it. Thus the decline of Meroë and the rise of Axum were both connected to changing patterns of long-distance commerce.

The interior capital city, also known as Axum, was a center of monumental building and royal patronage for the arts. The most famous structures were huge stone obelisks, which most likely marked royal graves. Some of them were more than 100 feet tall and at the time were the largest structures in the world hewn from a single piece of rock. The language used at court, in the towns, and for commerce was Ge'ez, written in a script derived from South Arabia. The Axumite state exercised a measure of control over the mostly Agaw-speaking people of the country through a loose administrative structure focusing on the collection of tribute payments. To the Romans, Axum was the third major empire within the world they knew, following their own and the Persian Empire.

Through its connections to Red Sea trade and the Roman world, particularly Egypt, Axum was introduced to Christianity in the fourth century C.E. Its monarch at the time, King Ezana, adopted the new religion about the same time as Constantine did in the Roman Empire. Early in his reign, the kingdom's coins featured images of gods derived from southern Arabia, while by the end, they were inscribed with the Christian cross. Supported by royal authority, Christianity took root in Axum, linking that kingdom religiously to Egypt, where a distinctive Christian Church known as Coptic was already well established. (See Chapter 4, page 176, and Chapter 10, page 414.) Although Egypt subsequently became largely Islamic, reducing its Christian community to a small minority, Christianity maintained a dominant position in the mountainous terrain of highland Ethiopia and in the early twenty-first century still represents the faith of perhaps 60 percent of the country's population.

During the fourth through the sixth centuries C.E., Axum mounted a campaign of imperial expansion that took its forces into the Kingdom of Meroë and across the Red Sea into Yemen in South Arabia. By 571, the traditional date for the birth of Muhammad, an Axumite army, including a number of African war elephants, had reached the gates of Mecca, but it was a fairly short-lived imperial venture. The next several centuries were ones of decline for the Axumite state, owing partly to environmental changes, such as soil exhaustion, erosion, and deforestation, brought about by intensive farming. Equally important was the rise of Islam, which altered trade routes and diminished the revenue available to the Axumite state. Its last coins were struck in the early seventh century. When the state revived several centuries later, it was centered farther south on the Ethiopian plateau. In this new location, there emerged the Christian Church and the state that present-day Ethiopia has inherited, but the link to ancient Axum was long remembered and revered.

With their long-distance trading connections, urban centers, centralized states, complex societies, monumental architecture, written languages, and imperial ambitions, both Meroë and Axum paralleled on a smaller scale the major features of the second-wave civilizations of Eurasia. Furthermore, both were in direct contact with the world of Mediterranean civilizations. Across the continent in West Africa, a rather different civilization took shape.

Along the Niger River: Cities without States

The middle stretches of the Niger River in West Africa witnessed the emergence of a remarkable urbanization (see Map 6.1, page 235). A prolonged dry period during the five centuries after 500 B.C.E. brought growing numbers of people from the southern Sahara into the fertile floodplain of the middle Niger in search of more reliable access to water. Accompanying them were their domesticated cattle, sheep, and goats; their agricultural skills; and their ironworking technology. Over many centuries (roughly 300 B.C.E.–900 C.E.), the peoples of this region created a distinctive city-based civilization. The most fully studied of the urban clusters that grew up along the middle Niger was the city of Jenne-jeno (jihn-AY jihn-OH), which at its high point probably housed more than 40,000 people.

AP® EXAM TIP

Know the features of the West African kingdoms, including their resources and major trade cities.

Among the most distinctive features of the Niger Valley civilization was the apparent absence of a corresponding state structure. Unlike the cities of Egypt, China, the Roman Empire, or Axum, these middle Niger urban centers were not encompassed within some larger imperial system. Nor were they like the city-states of ancient Mesopotamia, in which each city had its own centralized political structure, embodied in a monarch and his accompanying bureaucracy. According to a leading historian of the region, they were "cities without citadels," complex urban centers that apparently operated without the coercive authority of a state, for archeologists have found in their remains few signs of despotic power, widespread warfare, or deep social inequalities.[6] In this respect, these urban centers resemble the early cities of Norte Chico or the Indus Valley civilization, where likewise little archeological evidence of centralized state structures has been found (see Chapter 2).

Guided Reading Question

■ DESCRIPTION
How does the experience of the Niger Valley challenge conventional notions of "civilization"?

In place of such hierarchical organization, Jenne-jeno and other cities of the region emerged as clusters of economically specialized settlements surrounding a larger central town. The earliest and most prestigious of these specialized occupations was iron smithing. Working with fire and earth (ore) to produce this highly useful metal, the smiths of the Niger Valley were both feared and revered. Archeologist

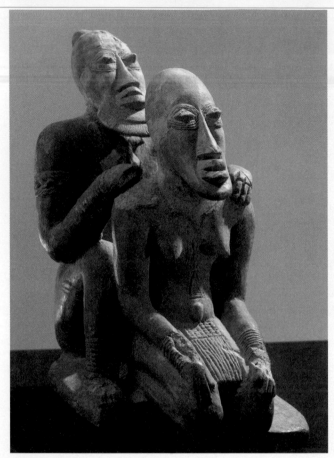

Terra-Cotta Statue from Jenne-jeno
The artistic tradition of Niger Valley civilization includes a number of terra-cotta couples, reflecting perhaps the emphasis on the separate but complementary roles of men and women in much of African thought. This statue and others like it date to sometime after the twelfth century and may express the resistance of an indigenous tradition to the growing penetration of Islam. (Entwistle Gallery, London, UK/ Werner Forman/Art Resource, NY)

Roderick McIntosh, a leading figure in the excavation of Jenne-jeno, argued that "their knowledge of the transforming arts—earth to metal, insubstantial fire to the mass of iron—was the key to a secret, occult realm of immense power and immense danger."[6]

Other specializations followed. Villages of cotton weavers, potters, leather workers, and griots (praise-singers who preserved and recited the oral traditions of their societies) grew up around the central towns. Gradually these urban artisan communities became occupational castes, whose members passed their jobs and skills to their children and could marry only within their own group. In the surrounding rural areas, as in all urban-based civilizations, farmers tilled the soil and raised their animals, but specialization also occurred in food production as various ethnic groups focused on fishing, rice cultivation, or some other agricultural pursuit. At least for a time, these middle Niger cities represented an African alternative to an oppressive state, which in many parts of the world accompanied an increasingly complex urban economy and society. A series of distinct and specialized economic groups shared authority and voluntarily used the services of one another, while maintaining their own identities through physical separation.

Accompanying this unique urbanization, and no doubt stimulating it, was a growing network of indigenous West African commerce. The middle Niger floodplain supported a rich agriculture and contained clay for pottery, but it lacked stone, iron ore, salt, and fuel. This scarcity of resources was the basis for a long-distance commerce that operated by boat along the Niger River and overland by donkey to the north and south. Iron ore from more than 50 miles away, copper from mines 200 miles distant, gold from even more distant sources, stones and salt from the Sahara—all of these items have been found in Jenne-jeno, exchanged no doubt for grain, fish, smoked meats, iron implements, and other staples. Jenne-jeno itself was an important transshipment point in this commerce, in which goods were transferred from boat to donkey or vice versa. By the 500s C.E., there is evidence of an even wider commerce, and at least indirect contact, from Mauritania in the west to present-day Mali and Burkina Faso in the east.

In the second millennium C.E., new historical patterns developed in West Africa (see Chapter 7). A number of large-scale states or empires emerged in the region—Ghana, Mali, and Songhay, among the most well-known. At least partially responsible for this development was the flourishing of a camel-borne trans-Saharan commerce, previously but a trickle across the great desert. As West Africa became more firmly connected to North Africa and the Mediterranean, Islam penetrated the region, marking a gradual but major cultural transformation. All of this awaited West Africa in later centuries, submerging, but not completely eliminating, the decentralized city life of the Niger Valley.

Civilizations of Mesoamerica

Westward across the Atlantic Ocean lay an altogether separate world, later known as the Americas. Although geography encouraged some interaction between African and Eurasian peoples, the Atlantic and Pacific oceans ensured that the cultures and societies of the Western Hemisphere operated in a world apart from their Afro-Eurasian counterparts. Nor were the cultures of the Americas stimulated by the kind of fruitful interaction among their own peoples that played such an important role in the Eastern Hemisphere. Nothing similar to the contact between Egypt and Mesopotamia, or Persia and the Greeks, or the extensive communication along the Silk Road trading network, enriched the two major centers of civilization in the Americas—Mesoamerica and the Andes—which had little if any direct contact with each other.

AP® EXAM TIP

Pay close attention to these explanations of differences between the rise of civilizations in Afro-Eurasia and the Americas.

Another geographic feature that distinguished these centers of civilization from those in the Afro-Eurasian world was their rugged mountainous terrain. Sharp changes in the landscape ascending from sea level to summit gave rise to an enormous range of microclimates as well as great ecological and biological diversity. Arid coastal environments, steamy lowland rain forests, cold and windy highland plateaus cut by numerous mountains and valleys—all of this was often encompassed in a relatively small area. Such conditions contributed to substantial linguistic and ethnic diversity and to the development of many distinct and competing cities, chiefdoms, and states. It also meant that states, and sometimes individual families, sought "vertical integration," an effort to control a variety of ecological zones where a number of different crops and animals could flourish.

Finally, the remarkable achievements of early American civilizations and cultures occurred without the many large domesticated animals or ironworking technologies that were so important throughout the Eastern Hemisphere. In the Andes, an important exception to this generalization involved the domestication of the llama and alpaca, which offered food, fiber, and transport for the civilizations of that region and in a few places provided for a time the basis for largely pastoral communities.

Accounts of pre-Columbian American societies often focus primarily on the Aztec and Inca empires (see Chapter 12), yet these impressive creations, flourishing in the fifteenth and early sixteenth centuries, were but the latest in a long line

AP® EXAM TIP

You must know the location and features of the Mesoamerican and Andean civilizations in the classical era.

AP® EXAM TIP

Although civilizations around the world rose and fell at different times, they shared many features. Understanding the time frames of major movements is using the historical skill of periodization.

of civilizations that preceded them in Mesoamerica and the Andes, respectively. These two regions housed the vast majority of the population of the Americas. Here the historical spotlight focuses on the long period following the First Civilizations of the Olmecs and Norte Chico but preceding the Aztecs and Incas, roughly 500 B.C.E. to 1300 C.E.

The region housing Mesoamerican civilizations stretched from central Mexico to northern Central America. Despite its environmental and ethnic diversity, Mesoamerica was also a distinct region, bound together by elements of a common culture. Its many peoples shared an intensive agricultural technology devoted to raising maize, beans, chili peppers, and squash. They prepared maize in a distinctive and highly nutritious fashion and based their economies on market exchange. They practiced religions featuring a similar pantheon of male and female deities, understood time as a cosmic cycle of creation and destruction, practiced human sacrifice, and constructed monumental ceremonial centers. Furthermore, they employed a common ritual calendar of 260 days and hieroglyphic writing, and they interacted frequently among themselves. During the first millennium B.C.E., for example, the various small states and chiefdoms of the region, particularly the Olmec, exchanged a number of luxury goods used to display social status and for ritual purposes—jade, serpentine, obsidian tools, ceramic pottery, shell ornaments, stingray spines, and turtle shells. As a result, aspects of Olmec culture, such as artistic styles, temple pyramids, the calendar system, and rituals involving human sacrifice, spread widely throughout Mesoamerica and influenced many of the civilizations that followed.

The Maya: Writing and Warfare

Among Mesoamerican civilizations, none has attracted more attention than that of the Maya. Scholars have traced the beginnings of the Maya people to ceremonial centers constructed as early as 2000 B.C.E. in present-day Guatemala and the Yucatán region of Mexico (see Map 6.2). During the first millennium B.C.E., a number of substantial urban centers with concentrated populations and monumental architecture had emerged in the region. In northern Guatemala, for example, the archeological site of El Mirador was home to tens of thousands of people, a pyramid/temple said by some to be the largest in the world, and a stone-carved frieze depicting the Maya creation story known as the Popul Vuh.

But it was during a later phase of Maya civilization, between 250 and 900 C.E., that their most well-known

Map 6.2   Civilizations of Mesoamerica
During the second-wave era, Maya civilization and the large city of Teotihuacán represented the most prominent features of Mesoamerican civilization.

cultural achievements emerged. Intellectuals, probably priests, developed a mathematical system that included the concept of zero and place notation and was capable of complex calculations. They combined this mathematical ability with careful observation of the night skies to plot the cycles of planets, to predict eclipses of the sun and the moon, to construct elaborate calendars, and to calculate accurately the length of the solar year. The distinctive art of the Maya elite was likewise impressive to later observers.

Accompanying these intellectual and artistic achievements was the creation of the most elaborate writing system in the Americas, which used both pictographs and phonetic or syllabic elements. Carved on stone and written on bark paper or deerskin books, Mayan writing recorded historical events, masses of astronomical data, and religious or mythological texts. Temples, pyramids, palaces, and public plazas abounded, graced with painted murals and endless stone carving. It is not surprising that early scholars viewed Maya civilization somewhat romantically as a peaceful society led by gentle stargazing priest-kings devoted to temple building and intellectual pursuits.

The economic foundations for these cultural achievements were embedded in an "almost totally engineered landscape."[7] The Maya drained swamps, terraced hillsides, flattened ridgetops, and constructed an elaborate water-management system. Much of this underpinned a flourishing agriculture, which supported a very rapidly growing and dense population by 750 C.E. This agriculture sustained substantial elite classes of nobles, priests, merchants, architects, and sculptors, as well as specialized artisans producing pottery, tools, and cotton textiles. And it was sufficiently productive to free a large labor force for work on the many public structures that continue to amaze contemporary visitors.

The earlier romantic view of Maya civilization changed as scholars realized that its many achievements took place within a highly fragmented political system of city-states, local lords, and regional kingdoms with no central authority, with frequent warfare, and with the extensive capture and sacrifice of prisoners. The larger political units of Maya civilization were densely populated urban and ceremonial centers, ruled by powerful kings and on a few occasions queens. They were divine rulers or "state shamans" able to mediate between humankind and the supernatural. One of these cities, Tikal (tee-KAHL), contained perhaps 50,000 people, with another 50,000 or so in the surrounding countryside, by 750 C.E. (See the chapter-opening photo, page 228, of a temple from Tikal.) Some of these city-states had imperial ambition, but none succeeded in creating a unified Maya empire. Various centers of Maya civilization rose and fell; fluctuating alliances among them alternated with periods of sporadic warfare; ruling families intermarried; the elite classes sought luxury goods from far away—jade, gold, shells, feathers from exotic birds, cacao—to bolster their authority and status. In its political dimensions, Maya civilization more closely resembled the competing city-states of ancient Mesopotamia or classical Greece than the imperial structures of Rome, Persia, or China.

AP® EXAM TIP

Know the main features of the Maya civilization.

Guided Reading Question

■ COMPARISON
With what Eurasian civilizations might the Maya be compared?

But large parts of that imposing civilization collapsed with a completeness and finality rare in world history. Clearly, this was not a single or uniform phenomenon, as flourishing centers of Maya civilization persisted in the northern Yucatán, and many Maya survived to fight the Spanish in the sixteenth century. But in the southern regions where the collapse was most complete, its outcomes were devastating. In less than a century following the onset of a long-term drought in 840, the population of the low-lying southern heartland of the Maya dropped by 85 percent or more as famine, epidemic, and fratricidal warfare reaped a horrific toll. It was a catastrophe from which there was no recovery. Elements of Maya culture survived in scattered settlements, but the great cities were deserted, and large-scale construction and artistic work ceased. The last date inscribed in stone corresponds to 909 C.E. As a complex civilization, the Maya had passed into history.

Explaining this remarkable demise has long kept scholars guessing, with recent accounts focusing on ecological and political factors. Rapid population growth after 600 C.E. pushed total Maya numbers to perhaps 5 million or more and soon outstripped available resources, resulting in deforestation and the erosion of hillsides. Under such conditions, climate change in the form of prolonged droughts in the 800s may well have placed unbearable pressures on Maya society. Political disunity and endemic rivalries, long a prominent feature of Maya civilization, prevented a coordinated and effective response to the emerging catastrophe. Warfare in fact became more frequent as competition for increasingly scarce land for cultivation became sharper. Rulers dependent on ritual splendor for their legitimacy competed to mount ever more elaborate temples, palaces, and pageants, requiring more labor and taxes from their subjects and tribute from their enemies. Whatever the precise explanation, the Maya collapse, like that of the Romans and others, illustrates the fragility of civilizations, whether they are embodied in large empires or organized in a more decentralized fashion.

Teotihuacán: The Americas' Greatest City

At roughly the same time as the Maya flourished in the southern regions of Mesoamerica, the giant city of Teotihuacán (tay-uh-tee-wah-KAHN) was also thriving further north in the Valley of Mexico. Begun around 150 B.C.E. and apparently built to a plan rather than evolving haphazardly, the city came to occupy about eight square miles and by 550 C.E. had a population variously estimated between 100,000 and 200,000. It was by far the largest urban complex in the Americas at the time and one of the six largest in the world. Beyond this, much about Teotihuacán is unknown, such as its original name, the language of its people, the kind of government that ordered its life, and the precise function of its many deities.

Physically, the city was enormously impressive, replete with broad avenues, spacious plazas, huge marketplaces, temples, palaces, apartment complexes, slums, waterways, reservoirs, drainage systems, and colorful murals. Along the main north/south boulevard, now known as the Street of the Dead, were the grand homes of

AP® EXAM TIP

You should be able to compare the features and functions of major classical-era cities, such as Teotihuacán and Jenne-jeno in this chapter.

Guided Reading Question

■ CONNECTION
In what ways did Teotihuacán shape the history of Mesoamerica?

Teotihuacán
Taken from the summit of the Pyramid of the Moon, this photograph looks down the famous Avenue of the Dead to the Pyramid of the Sun in the upper left. (Alison Wright/Science Source)

the elite, the headquarters of state authorities, many temples, and two giant pyramids. One of them, the Pyramid of the Sun, had been constructed over an ancient tunnel leading to a cave and may well have been regarded as the site of creation itself, the birthplace of the sun and the moon. At the Temple of the Feathered Serpent, archeologists have found the remains of some 200 people, their hands and arms tied behind them; they were the apparently unwilling sacrificial victims meant to accompany the high-ranking persons buried there into the afterlife.

Off the main avenues in a grid-like pattern of streets lay thousands of residential apartment compounds, home to the city's commoners, each with its own kitchen area, sleeping quarters, courtyards, and shrines. In these compounds, perhaps in groups of related families or lineages, lived many of the farmers who tilled the lands outside the city. Thousands of Maya specialists — masons, leather workers, potters, construction laborers, merchants, civil servants — also made their homes in these apartments. So too did skilled makers of obsidian blades, who plied their trade in hundreds of separate workshops, generating products that were in great demand throughout Mesoamerica. At least two small sections of the city were reserved exclusively for foreigners.

Buildings, both public and private, were decorated with mural paintings, sculptures, and carvings. Many of these works of art display abstract geometric and stylized images. Others depict gods and goddesses, arrayed in various forms — feathered serpents, starfish, jaguars, flowers, and warriors. One set of murals shows happy

AP® EXAM TIP
You should know that monumental architecture was a common feature in civilizations around the world in the classical era.

people cavorting in a paradise of irrigated fields, playing games, singing, and chasing butterflies, which were thought to represent the souls of the dead. Another, however, portrays dancing warriors carrying elaborate curved knives, to which were attached bleeding human hearts.

The art of Teotihuacán, unlike that of the Maya, has revealed few images of self-glorifying rulers or individuals. Nor did the city have a tradition of written public inscriptions as the Maya did, although a number of glyphs or characters indicate at least a limited form of writing. One scholar has suggested that "the rulers of Teotihuacán might have intentionally avoided the personality cult of the dynastic art and writing" so characteristic of the Maya.[8] Perhaps those rulers constituted an oligarchy or council of high-ranking elites rather than a single monarch.

However it was governed, Teotihuacán cast a huge shadow over Mesoamerica, particularly from 300 to 600 C.E. A core region of perhaps 10,000 square miles was administered directly from the city itself, while tribute was no doubt exacted from other areas within its broader sphere of influence. At a greater distance, the power of Teotihuacán's armies gave it a presence in the Maya heartland more than 600 miles to the east. At least one Maya city, Kaminaljuyú in the southern highlands, was completely taken over by the Teotihuacán military and organized as a colony. In Tikal, a major lowland Maya city, in the year 378 C.E., agents of Teotihuacán apparently engineered a coup that placed a collaborator on the throne and turned the city for a time into an ally or a satellite. Elsewhere—in the Zapotec capital of Monte Albán, for example—murals show unarmed persons from Teotihuacán engaged in what seem to be more equal diplomatic relationships.

At least some of this political and military activity was no doubt designed to obtain, either by trade or by tribute, valued commodities from afar—food products, cacao beans, tropical bird feathers, honey, salt, medicinal herbs. The presence in Teotihuacán of foreigners, perhaps merchants, from the Gulf Coast and Maya lowlands, as well as much pottery from those regions, provides further evidence of long-distance trade. Moreover, the sheer size and prestige of Teotihuacán surely persuaded many, all across Mesoamerica, to imitate the architectural and artistic styles of the city. Thus, according to a leading scholar, "Teotihuacán meant something of surpassing importance far beyond its core area."[9] Almost a thousand years after its still-mysterious collapse around 650 C.E., the great metropolis was dubbed Teotihuacán, the "city of the gods," by the peoples of the Aztec Empire.

Civilizations of the Andes

Yet another and quite separate center of civilization in the Americas lay in the dramatic landscape of the Andes. Bleak deserts along the coast supported human habitation only because they were cut by dozens of rivers flowing down from the mountains, offering the possibility of irrigation and cultivation. The offshore waters of the Pacific Ocean also provided an enormously rich marine environment with an endless supply of seabirds and fish. The Andes themselves, a towering mountain chain

AP® EXAM TIP

Study similarities and differences between the city-state of Teotihuacán and those in Greece in the classical era.

with many highland valleys, afforded numerous distinct ecological niches, depending on altitude. Andean societies generally sought access to the resources of these various environments through colonization, conquest, or trade—seafood from the coastal regions; maize and cotton from lower-altitude valleys; potatoes, quinoa, and pastureland for their llamas in the high plains; tropical fruits and coca leaves from the moist eastern slope of the Andes and the arid western slope as well (see Map 6.3).

The most well-known of the civilizations to take shape in this environment was that of the Incas, which encompassed practically the entire region, some 2,500 miles in length, in the fifteenth century. Yet the Incas represented only the most recent and the largest in a long history of civilizations in the area.

The coastal region of central Peru had in fact generated one of the world's First Civilizations, known as Norte Chico, dating back to around 3000 B.C.E. (see Chapter 2). During the two millennia between roughly 1000 B.C.E. and 1000 C.E., a number of Andean civilizations rose and passed away. Because none of them had developed writing, historians are largely dependent on archeology for an understanding of these civilizations.

Map 6.3   Civilizations of the Andes

No single civilization dominated the Andes region during the second-wave era. Rather, a number of religious movements, states, and empires rose and fell before the entire region was encompassed by the Inca Empire in the fifteenth century.

Chavín: A Pan-Andean Religious Movement

In both the coastal and highland regions of Peru, archeologists have uncovered numerous local ceremonial centers or temple complexes, dating to between 2000 and 1000 B.C.E. Then around 900 B.C.E., one of them, situated in the Andean highlands at a village called Chavín (cha-BEEN) de Huántar, became the focus of a religious movement that soon swept through both coastal and highland Peru, aided by its strategic location on trade routes to both the coastal region to the west and the Amazon rain forest to the east.

By perhaps 750 B.C.E., this small center had become a town of 2,000 to 3,000 people, with clear distinctions between an elite class, who lived in stone houses, and ordinary people, with adobe dwellings. An elaborate temple complex included numerous galleries, hidden passageways, staircases, ventilation shafts, drainage canals, and distinctive carvings. Chavín artwork suggests influences from both the desert coastal region and the rain forests. Major deities were represented as jaguars, crocodiles, and snakes, all of them native to the Amazon basin. Shamans or priests likely made use of the San Pedro cactus, native to the Andes Mountains, employing its

AP® EXAM TIP

Be aware of the location and some features of the Chavin civilization.

Guided Reading Question

■ CONNECTION
What kind of influence did Chavín exert in the Andes region?

hallucinogenic properties to penetrate the supernatural world. Some of the fantastic artwork of this civilization—its jaguar-human images, for example—may well reflect the visions of these religious leaders.

Over the next several centuries, this blended religious movement proved attractive across much of Peru and beyond, as Chavín-style temple architecture, sculpture, pottery, religious images, and painted textiles were widely imitated within the region. Chavín itself became a pilgrimage site and perhaps a training center for initiates. Although some evidence suggests violence and warfare, no Chavín "empire" emerged. Instead, a widespread religious cult, erected on the back of a trading network, provided for the first time and for several centuries a measure of economic and cultural integration to much of the Peruvian Andes.

Moche: A Civilization of the Coast

By 200 B.C.E., the pan-Andes Chavín cult had faded, replaced by a number of regional civilizations. Among them, Moche (MOH-chee) civilization clearly stands out. Dominating a 250-mile stretch of Peru's northern coast and incorporating thirteen river valleys, the Moche people flourished between about 100 and 800 C.E. Their economy was rooted in a complex irrigation system, requiring constant maintenance, which funneled runoff from the Andes into fields of maize, beans, and squash and acres of cotton, all fertilized by rich bird droppings called guano. Moche fishermen also harvested millions of anchovies from the bountiful Pacific.

Politically, Moche was governed by warrior-priests, some of whom lived atop huge pyramids, the largest of which was constructed from 143 million sun-dried bricks. There shaman-rulers, often under the influence of hallucinogenic drugs, conducted ancient rituals that mediated between the world of humankind and that of the gods. They also presided over the ritual sacrifice of human victims, drawn from their many prisoners of war, which became central to the politico-religious life of the Moche. Images on Moche pottery show a ruler attired in a magnificent feather headdress and seated on a pyramid, while a parade of naked prisoners marches past him. Other scenes of decapitation and dismemberment indicate the fate that awaited those destined for sacrifice. For these rulers, the Moche world was apparently one of war, ceremony, and diplomacy.

The immense wealth of this warrior-priest elite and the exquisite artistry of Moche craftsmen are reflected in the elaborate burials accorded the rulers. (See Zooming In: The Lord of Sipan and the Lady of Cao, page 250.) In the absence of written texts, these artistic products are the most accessible aspect of Moche life, and much of what scholars know about the Moche world derives from the superb skill of its craftspeople, such as metalworkers, potters, weavers, and painters. Face masks, figures of animals, small earrings, and other jewelry items, many plated in gold, display amazing technical abilities and a striking artistic sensibility. Decorating Moche ceramic pottery are naturalistic portraits of noble lords and rulers and images from the life of common people, including the blind and the sick. Battle scenes show

AP® EXAM TIP

Be sure you know features of the Moche civilization.

Guided Reading Question

■ DESCRIPTION
What features of Moche life characterize it as a civilization?

warriors confronting their enemies with raised clubs. Erotic encounters between men and women and gods making love to humans likewise represent common themes, as do grotesque images of the many Moche gods and goddesses. Much of this, of course, reflects the culture of the Moche elite. We know much less about the daily life of the farmers, fishermen, weavers, traders, construction workers, and servants whose labor made that elite culture possible.

These cultural achievements, however, rested on fragile environmental foundations, for the region was subject to drought, earthquakes, and occasional torrential rains associated with El Niño episodes (dramatic changes in weather patterns caused by periodic warming of Pacific Ocean currents). During the sixth century C.E., some combination of these forces caused extended ecological disruption, which seriously undermined Moche civilization. In these circumstances, the Moche were vulnerable to aggressive neighbors and possibly to internal social tensions as well. By the end of the eighth century C.E., that civilization had passed into history.

Wari and Tiwanaku: Empires of the Interior

Far more than the Moche and other coastal civilizations, the interior empires of Wari (wah-ree) and Tiwanaku provided a measure of political integration and cultural commonality for the entire Andean region. Growing out of ancient settlements, these two states flourished between 400 and 1000 C.E., Wari in the northern highlands and Tiwanaku to the south. Both were centered in large urban capitals, marked by monumental architecture and stratified populations numbering in the tens of thousands. Both governments collected surplus food in warehouses as an insurance against times of drought and famine.

But neither state controlled a continuous band of territory. Adapting to their vertical environment, both empires established colonies at lower elevations on the eastern and western slopes of the Andes as well as throughout the highlands, seeking access to resources such as seafood, maize, chili peppers, cocoa, hallucinogenic plants, obsidian, and feathers from tropical birds. Caravans of llamas linked distant centers, allowing the exchange and redistribution of goods, while the religious prestige and ceremonial power of the capital city provided further integration. Cultural influences from the center, such as styles of pottery and textiles, spread well beyond the regions of direct political control. Similar religious symbols and images prevailed in both places, including the ancient Andean Staff God, a deity portrayed with a staff in each hand. Versions of this image have been found in Norte Chico, Chavín, and Moche sites as well, suggesting a long-term continuity in the religious culture of the Andean region.

But Wari and Tiwanaku were hardly carbon copies of each other. Wari's agriculture employed an elaborate system of hillside terracing and irrigation, using snowmelt from the Andes. A seventeenth-century Jesuit missionary thought the hillsides of the Wari region "were covered with flights of stairs." Tiwanaku's highly productive farming economy, by contrast, utilized a "raised field" system in which artificially

Guided Reading Question

■ **DESCRIPTION**
What was the significance of Wari and Tiwanaku in the history of Andean civilization?

The Lord of Sipan and the Lady of Cao

In the mid- to late third century C.E., a prominent man of Moche society died in what is now Peru. We do not know his name, for a written language was not a part of Moche life. But since archeologists uncovered his final resting place in 1987, scholars have learned a great deal about him and about his culture. He was five feet four inches in height, relatively tall for his time and place, and was somewhere around forty years of age. The condition of his teeth and bones suggests that he ate a well-balanced diet and probably performed little physical labor during his life. The cause of his death is unclear, but scholars think that he may well have died of an epidemic disease during a severe famine.

The Moche ruler in the center of the grave, dating to about 250 C.E., was about forty years old when he died and, at five feet four inches, was quite tall for the time.

Much more obvious is his high social status, for which he has been dubbed the Lord of Sipan, named for the town in Peru where the archeological site is located. Laid to rest in the official and ceremonial finery he likely donned in life, the Lord of Sipan was bedecked in gold. He wore a huge gold crescent headdress, a gold face mask, two necklaces with gold and silver beads in the shape of oversized peanuts, and gold earspools exquisitely inlaid with turquoise; he had a gold warrior's shield on his back and a golden scepter in his hand. Hundreds of pots contained food and drink, while 451 ceremonial objects also accompanied the burial. Guarding the entrance to his tomb was the skeleton of a man with his feet cut off, presumably to prevent him from leaving his post. Buried with the Lord of Sipan were six other individuals: a young child (perhaps his own?); two robust men (perhaps ritually sacrificed warriors?); and three young women (perhaps his wives?). A dog, claimed by local traditions to guide the dead into the afterworld, and two llamas also attended the lord in death. In its archeological significance and its material splendor, this burial site has been compared to that of Tutankhamen, the young pharaoh of Egypt. (See the photo of his burial site above.)

Clearly, the Lord of Sipan was a very high-ranking member of Moche's highly stratified society. Such lords received food from their subjects, some of which they passed on to lesser lords, and they had access to the rare and prestigious objects created for them by Moche's

photo: © Karl Heinz Raach/laif/Redux

AP® EXAM TIP

You should know the general effects of the fall of empires in the classical era, like political fragmentation, discussed here.

elevated planting surfaces in swampy areas were separated by small irrigation canals. Tiwanaku, furthermore, has become famous for its elaborately fitted stone walls and buildings, while Wari's tombs and temples were built of fieldstone set in mud mortar and covered with smooth plaster. Cities in the Wari region seemed built to a common plan and linked to the capital by a network of highways, which suggests a political system more tightly controlled from the center than in Tiwanaku.[10]

Despite these differences and a 300-mile common border, little overt conflict or warfare occurred between Wari and Tiwanaku. In areas where the two peoples lived near one another, they apparently did not mingle much. They each spoke their own language, wore different clothing, furnished their homes with distinctive goods, and looked to their respective capital cities for inspiration.

immensely skillful artisans. Various objects in the tomb correspond closely to images on Moche pottery and temples of prisoners being slaughtered and a warrior-priest collecting and drinking their blood. Perhaps the Lord of Sipan was one such warrior-priest.

At the time the Lord of Sipan came to light, it was widely assumed that the ruling elite of Moche society was all

Object found in the tomb of the Lady of Cao.

male. Then in 2005, another remarkable burial site was uncovered, containing the intact body of a young woman who had died in childbirth around 450 c.e. while still in her twenties. Now known as the Lady of Cao, she had been carefully wrapped in hundreds of yards of cotton strips, wore long braided hair, and bore numerous tattoos of snakes, crabs, and spiders on her arms and legs. Accompanying her was a huge collection of elaborate grave goods indicating great wealth: fifteen elaborate necklaces, gold sewing needles, weaving tools, beautiful jewelry, and a vessel depicting a nursing mother. But beyond these feminine objects were more surprising signs of real power. Her nose rings featured designs of men wielding war clubs and heads being pecked by condors. Two copper and wood staffs, symbols of authority, were entombed with her, as well as many weapons, including

two massive war clubs and twenty-three spear throwers. "The war clubs are clear symbols not only of combat but of power," declared one member of the archeological team.[11]

So was the Lady of Cao a local ruler in her own right or simply a woman from an elite family? The case for her political and religious role has been strengthened by the subsequent discovery of eight more burials of prominent Moche women. One of them contained a tall silver goblet, very similar to those depicted in Moche artistic scenes of ritual sacrifice and the consumption of blood. Some scholars suggest that Moche society was highly decentralized, with men in positions of authority in some communities and women in others. Thus the Lord of Sipan and the Lady of Cao, though living several hundred years apart, may have played equivalent roles in Moche society.

Questions: What do we learn about Moche society from these two figures? If you could interview these individuals, what would you want to ask them? What might be inferred from these burials about Moche understandings of the afterlife?

photo: © EFE/Zuma Press

In the several centuries following 1000 c.e., both civilizations collapsed, their impressive cities permanently abandoned. What followed was a series of smaller kingdoms, one of which evolved into the Inca Empire that gave to Andean civilization a final and spectacular expression before all of the Americas was swallowed up in European empires from across the sea. The Incas themselves clearly drew on the legacy of Wari and Tiwanaku, adopting aspects of their imperial models and systems of statecraft, building on the Wari highway system, and utilizing similar styles of dress and artistic expression. Such was the prestige of Tiwanaku centuries after its collapse that the Incas claimed it as their place of origin.

PRACTICING AP® HISTORICAL THINKING

What features common to all civilizations can you identify in the civilizations of Africa and the Americas? What distinguishing features give each of them a distinctive identity?

Alternatives to Civilization

World historians are frequently occupied, sometimes almost preoccupied, with civilizations, and understandably so, since those urban and state-based communities were clearly the most powerful, expansive, and innovative societies, later embracing almost the entire population of the planet. And yet it is useful to remind ourselves that other ways of organizing human communities evolved alongside civilizations, and they too made history. Two such regions were Africa south of the equator and North America. They shared environments that featured plenty of land and relatively few people compared to the greater population densities and pressure on the land that characterized many civilizations. And a third was Pacific Oceania, where small numbers of people navigated a sea covering about one-third of the world's surface, settled the mostly tiny specks of land that rose above the surface of that ocean, and created there a remarkable range of human communities.

Bantu Africa: Cultural Encounters and Social Variation

AP® EXAM TIP

Be sure you know the migrations of the Bantus over time, their way of life, and their contributions to the cultures of the regions of sub-Saharan Africa.

In the vast region of Africa south of the equator, the most significant development during the second-wave era involved the accelerating movement of Bantu-speaking peoples, cultures, and technologies into the enormous subcontinent. That process had begun many centuries earlier, probably around 3000 B.C.E., from a homeland region in what are now southeastern Nigeria and the Cameroons. Over the long run, some 400 distinct but closely related languages emerged, known collectively as Bantu. By the first century C.E., agricultural peoples speaking Bantu languages and now bearing an ironworking technology had largely occupied the forest regions of equatorial Africa, and at least a few of them had probably reached the East African coast. In the several centuries that followed, they established themselves quite rapidly in most of eastern and southern Africa (see Map 6.1, page 235), introducing immense economic and cultural changes to a huge region of the continent.

Bantu expansion was not a conquest or invasion such as that of Alexander the Great; nor was it a massive and self-conscious migration like that of Europeans to the Americas in more recent times. Rather, it was a slow movement of peoples, perhaps a few extended families at a time. And sometimes Bantu expansion was less a movement of people than the diffusion of new patterns of living involving language, root crops, grains, sheep and cattle, pottery styles, and ironworking technology. In this way, already-established communities could "become Bantu" without the wholesale migration of outsiders. Taken as a whole, these processes brought to Africa south of the equator a measure of cultural and linguistic commonality, marking it as a distinct region of the continent.

That movement of individuals and cultural patterns also generated numerous situations that required decisions about how to respond to new peoples, ideas, and technologies. Among those encounters, none was more significant than that between the agricultural Bantu and the gathering and hunting peoples who earlier occupied this region of Africa. Their interaction was part of a long-term global phenomenon in which farmers largely replaced foragers as the dominant people on the planet (see Chapter 1).

In these encounters, Bantu-speaking farmers had various advantages. One was numerical, as agriculture generated a more productive economy, enabling larger numbers to live in a smaller area than was possible with a gathering and hunting way of life. A second advantage was a greater immunity to animal-borne disease, acquired by prolonged exposure to both parasitic and infectious illnesses common to farming and herding societies. Foraging peoples lacked that immunity, and many quickly succumbed when they encountered the agricultural newcomers. A third advantage was iron, so useful for tools and weapons, which accompanied Bantu expansion in its interactions with peoples still operating with stone-age technology. Thus gathering and hunting peoples were displaced, absorbed, or largely eliminated in most parts of Africa south of the equator—but not everywhere.

In the rain forest region of Central Africa, the foraging Batwa (Pygmy) people, at least some of them, became "forest specialists" who produced honey, wild game, elephant products, animal skins, and medicinal barks and plants, all of which entered regional trading networks in exchange for the agricultural products of their Bantu neighbors. Some also adopted Bantu languages, thus becoming Bantu linguistically, while maintaining a gathering and hunting lifestyle and a separate identity.

Bantu-speaking peoples themselves also changed as they encountered different environments and peoples. In the drier climate of East Africa, the yam-based agriculture of the West African Bantu homeland was unable to support their growing numbers, so Bantu farmers increasingly adopted grains as well as domesticated sheep and cattle from the already-established people of the region. They also enriched their agriculture by acquiring a variety of food crops from Southeast Asia—coconuts, sugarcane, and especially bananas—which were brought to East Africa by Indonesian Malay sailors and immigrants early in the first millennium C.E. This agricultural package and its associated ironworking technology then spread throughout the vast area of eastern and southern Africa, probably reaching present-day South Africa by 400 C.E. Some newly "Bantuized" areas incorporated musical traditions, linguistic patterns, and kinship systems derived from the earlier inhabitants. From these interactions a common set of cultural and social practices diffused widely across Bantu Africa. One prominent historian described these practices:

> [They encompassed] in religion, the centrality of ancestor observances; in philosophy, the problem of evil understood as the consequence of individual malice or of the failure to honor one's ancestors; in music, an emphasis on polyrhythmic performance with drums as the key instrument; in dance, a new form of expression in which a variety of prescribed body movements took preference over footwork; and in agriculture, the pre-eminence of women as the workers and innovators.[12]

All of this became part of the common culture of Bantu-speaking Africa.

As Bantu-derived patterns of living became established in Africa south of the equator during the thousand or so years between 500 and 1500 C.E., a wide variety

Guided Reading Question

■ CONNECTION

In what ways did the process of Bantu expansion stimulate cross-cultural interaction?

of quite distinct societies and cultures took shape. Some societies—in present-day Kenya, for example—organized themselves without any formal political specialists at all. Instead, they made decisions, resolved conflicts, and maintained order by using kinship structures or lineage principles supplemented by age grades, which joined men of a particular generation together across various lineages. Elsewhere, lineage heads who acquired a measure of personal wealth, or who proved skillful at mediating between the local spirits and the people, might evolve into chiefs with a modest political authority. In several areas, such as the region around Lake Victoria or present-day Zimbabwe, larger and more substantial kingdoms evolved. Along the East African coast after 1000 C.E., dozens of rival city-states linked the African interior with the commerce of the Indian Ocean basin (see Chapter 7, pages 291–93).

Many societies in the Bantu-speaking world developed gender systems that were markedly less patriarchal than those of established urban-based civilizations. Male ironworkers in the Congo River basin, for example, sought to appropriate the power and prestige of female reproductive capacity by decorating their furnaces with clay breasts and speaking of their bellows as impregnating the furnaces. Among the Luba people of Central Africa, male rulers operated in alliance with powerful women, particularly spirit mediums, who were thought to contain the spirit of the king. Only a woman's body was considered sufficiently strong to acquire this potent and dangerous presence. Luba art represented female ancestors as "keepers of secret royal knowledge." And across a wide area of south-central Africa, a system of "gender parallelism" associated female roles with village life (child care, farming, food preparation, making pots, baskets, and mats), while masculine identity revolved around hunting and forest life (fishing, trapping, collecting building materials and medicinal plants). It was a complementary or "separate but equal" definition of gender roles.[13]

In terms of religion, Bantu practice in general placed less emphasis on a High or Creator God, who was viewed as remote and largely uninvolved in ordinary life, and focused instead on ancestral or nature spirits. The power of dead ancestors might be accessed through rituals of sacrifice, especially of cattle. Supernatural power deriving from ancient heroes, ancestors, or nature spirits also resided in charms, which could be activated by proper rituals and used to control the rains, defend the village, achieve success in hunting, or identify witches. Belief in witches was widespread, reflecting the idea that evil or misfortune was the work of malicious people. Diviners, skilled in penetrating the unseen world, used dreams, visions, charms, or trances to identify the source of misfortune and to prescribe remedies. Was a particular illness the product of broken taboos, a dishon-

A Female Luba Ancestral Statue
Representations of powerful women, often ancestral figures, were frequent in the wood carvings of the Bantu-speaking Luba people of Central Africa. Many of them showed women touching their breasts, a gesture signifying devotion, respect, and the holding of secret knowledge. (Scala/Art Resource, NY)

ored ancestor, an unhappy nature spirit, or a witch? Was a remedy to be found in a cleansing ceremony, a sacrifice to an ancestor, the activation of a charm, or the elimination of a witch?[14]

Unlike the major monotheistic religions, with their "once and for all" revelations from God through the Christian Bible or the Muslim Quran, Bantu religious practice was predicated on the notion of "continuous revelation"—the possibility of constantly receiving new messages from the world beyond through dreams, visions, or trance states. Moreover, unlike Buddhism, Christianity, or Islam, Bantu religions were geographically confined, intended to explain, predict, and control local affairs, with no missionary impulse or inclination toward universality.

North America: Ancestral Pueblo and Mound Builders

If the Americas played host to civilizations, cities, and empires in Mesoamerica and the Andes, they also housed various alternative forms of human community during the second-wave era and beyond. Arctic and subarctic cultures, the bison hunters of the Great Plains, the complex and settled communities of the Pacific coast of North America, nomadic bands living in the arid regions of southern South America—all of these represent the persistence of gathering and hunting ways of living.

Even more widespread—in the eastern woodlands of the United States, Central America, the Amazon basin, the Caribbean islands—were societies sustained by village-based agriculture. Owing to environmental or technological limitations, it was a less intensive and productive agriculture than in Mesoamerica or the Andes and supported usually much smaller populations (see Map 6.4 and Map 12.5, page 523). These peoples too made their own histories, changing in response to their unique environments, their interactions with outsiders, and their own visions of the world. The Anasazi of the southwestern United States, now called the Ancestral Pueblo, and the mound-building cultures of the eastern woodlands provide two illustrations from North America.

The southwestern region of North America, an arid land cut by mountain ranges and large basins, first acquired maize from its place of origin in Mesoamerica during the second millennium B.C.E., but it took roughly 2,000 years for that crop, later supplemented by beans and squash, to become the basis of a settled agricultural way of living. In a desert region, farming was risky, and maize had to be gradually adapted to the local environment. Not until around 600 to 800 C.E. did permanent village life take hold widely. People then lived in pit houses with floors sunk several feet below ground level. Some settlements had only a few such homes, whereas others contained twenty-five or more. By 900 C.E., many of these villages also included kivas, much larger pit structures used for ceremonial purposes, which symbolized the widespread belief that humankind emerged into this world from another world below. Individual settlements were linked to one another in local trading networks and sometimes in wider webs of exchange that brought them buffalo hides, copper, turquoise, seashells, macaw feathers, and coiled baskets from quite distant locations.

AP® EXAM TIP
You should be aware of the characteristics of societies in North America in the classical era.

Guided Reading Question

■ COMPARISON
In what ways were the histories of the Ancestral Pueblo and the Mound Builders similar to each other, and how did they differ?

Map 6.4   North America in the Second-Wave Era

A sparsely populated North America hosted a number of semi-sedentary agricultural societies as well as various gathering and hunting peoples rather than the "civilizations" characteristic of Mesoamerica and the Andes.

These processes of change—growing dependence on agriculture, increasing population, more intensive patterns of exchange—gave rise to larger settlements and adjacent aboveground structures known as pueblos. The most spectacular of these took shape in Chaco canyon in what is now northwestern New Mexico. There, between 860 and 1130 C.E., five major pueblos emerged. This Chaco Phenomenon encompassed 25,000 square miles and linked some seventy outlying settlements to the main centers. The population was not large, perhaps as few as 5,000 people, although experts continue to debate the issue. The largest of these towns, or "great houses," Pueblo Bonito, stood five stories high and contained more than 600 rooms and many kivas. Hundreds of miles of roads, up to forty feet wide, radiated out from Chaco, likewise prompting much debate among scholars. Without wheeled carts or large domesticated animals, such an elaborate road system seems unnecessary for ordinary trade or travel. Did the roads represent, as some scholars speculate, a "sacred landscape which gave order to the world," joining its outlying communities to a "Middle Place," an entrance perhaps to the underworld?[15]

Among the Chaco elite were highly skilled astronomers who constructed an observatory of three large rock slabs situated so as to throw a beam of light across a spiral rock carving behind it at the summer solstice. By the eleventh century, Chaco also had become a dominant center for the production of turquoise ornaments, which became a major item of regional commerce, extending as far south as Mesoamerica. Not all was sweetness and light, however. Warfare, internal conflict, and occasional cannibalism (a matter of much controversy among scholars) apparently increased in frequency as an extended period of drought in the half century following 1130 brought this flourishing culture to a rather abrupt end. By 1200, the great houses had been abandoned and their inhabitants scattered in small communities that later became the Pueblo peoples of more recent times.

Unlike the Chaco region in the southwest, the eastern woodlands of North America and especially the Mississippi River valley hosted an independent Agricultural Revolution. By 2000 B.C.E., many of its peoples had domesticated local plant species, including sumpweed, goosefoot, some gourds and squashes, and a form of artichoke. Sunflowers, originally domesticated in Mesoamerica, also found a place in diets of eastern woodland peoples. These few plants, however, were not sufficient to support a fully settled agricultural village life; rather, they supplemented diets derived from gathering and hunting without fundamentally changing that ancient way of life. Such peoples created societies distinguished by arrays of large earthen mounds, found all over the United States east of the Mississippi, prompting archeologists to dub them the Mound Builders. The earliest of these mounds date to around 2000 B.C.E., but the most elaborate and widespread took shape between 200 B.C.E. and 400 C.E., commonly called the Hopewell culture, after an archeological site in Ohio.

Several features of the Hopewell culture have intrigued archeologists. Particularly significant are the striking burial mounds and geometric earthworks, sometimes covering areas equivalent to several city blocks, and the wide variety of artifacts found within them—smoking pipes, human figurines, mica mirrors, flint blades, fabrics, and jewelry of all kinds. The mounds themselves were no doubt the focus of elaborate burial rituals, but some of them were aligned with the moon with such precision as to mark lunar eclipses. Developed most elaborately in the Ohio River valley, Hopewell-style earthworks, artifacts, and ceremonial pottery have also been found throughout the eastern woodlands region of North America. Hopewell centers in Ohio contained mica from the Appalachian Mountains, volcanic glass from Yellowstone, conch shells and a few sharks' teeth from the Gulf of Mexico, and copper from the Great Lakes. All of this suggests a large "Hopewell Interaction Sphere," linking this entire region in a loose network of exchange, as well as a measure of cultural borrowing of religious ideas and practices.[16]

The next and most spectacular phase in the history of these mound-building peoples took shape as corn-based agriculture, derived ultimately but indirectly from Mexico, gained ground in the Mississippi valley after 800 C.E., allowing larger populations and more complex societies to emerge. The dominant center was Cahokia, near present-day St. Louis, Missouri, which flourished from about 900 to 1250 C.E. Its central mound, a terraced pyramid of four levels, measured 1,000 feet long by 700 feet wide, rose more than 100 feet above the ground, and occupied fifteen acres. It was the largest structure north of Mexico, the focal point of a community numbering 10,000 or more people, and the center of a widespread trading network (see an artist's reconstruction of Cahokia on page 45).

Evidence from burials and from later Spanish observers suggests that Cahokia and other centers of this Mississippi culture were stratified societies with a clear elite and with rulers able to mobilize the labor required to build such enormous structures. One high-status male was buried on a platform of 20,000 shell beads, accompanied by 800 arrowheads, sheets of copper and mica, and a number of sacrificed men and women nearby.[17] Well after Cahokia had declined and was abandoned, sixteenth-century Spanish and French explorers encountered another such chiefdom among the Natchez people, located in southwestern Mississippi. Paramount chiefs, known as Great Suns, dressed in knee-length fur coats and lived luxuriously in deerskin-covered homes. An elite class of "principal men" or "honored peoples" clearly occupied a different status from commoners, sometimes referred to as "stinkards." These sharp class distinctions were blunted by the requirement that upper-class people, including the Great Suns, had to marry "stinkards."

The military capacity of these Mississippi chiefdoms greatly impressed European observers, as this Spanish account indicates:

> The next day the cacique [paramount chief] arrived with 200 canoes filled with men, having weapons, . . . the warriors standing erect from bow to stern, holding bows and arrows. . . . [F]rom under the canopy where the chief man was, the course was directed and orders issued to the rest. . . . [W]hat with the awnings, the plumes, the shields, the pennons, and the number of people in the fleet, it appeared like a famous armada of galleys.[18]

Here then, in the eastern woodlands of North America, were peoples who independently generated a modest Agricultural Revolution, assimilated corn and beans from distant sources, developed increasingly complex chiefdoms, and created monumental structures, new technologies, and artistic traditions. Beyond the separate societies that emerged within this large area, scholars have noticed some similarities in artifacts, symbols, ceremonies, mythologies, and artistic styles, many of which seem related to marking the status of elites. A horned serpent, sometimes depicted with wings, and various animal-god representations were widely shared symbols, though the meaning of these symbols no doubt changed as they entered new cultural environments. Dubbed the Southeast Ceremonial Complex, the loose networks of connection that generated these similarities grew outward from Cahokia for several centuries after 1200 or so, continuing earlier patterns of interaction associated with the Hopewell cultural region. While no linguistic, cultural, or political unity emerged from these relationships, they testify to a measure of exchange, borrowing, and cultural adaptation across an enormous region of North America.

Pacific Oceania: Peoples of the Sea

The peoples of Pacific Oceania, like those of Bantu Africa and North America, created enduring human communities without the large cities, states, and empires so prominent in civilizations. But the ecological setting for these historical journeys was distinctive, for they took place on the islands of the immense Pacific: a few larger territories, such as New Guinea and New Zealand, as well as thousands of much smaller islands, many of them specks in the sea, barely visible from space (see Map 6.5). New Guinea had been settled for perhaps 50,000 years, initially at a time when it was connected to Australia by a land bridge. But the rest of Oceania was the last part of the world to receive human settlers, who began arriving from Island Southeast Asia only about 3,500 years ago (see Chapter 1, pages 19–20). By 1200 C.E., they had achieved a presence on every habitable piece of land throughout this enormous region. It was, as one historian summarized the process, "the greatest maritime expansion known to history."[19]

The settlers' arrival, however, produced an enormous and sometimes devastating environmental impact as humans entered and disrupted bountiful but fragile ecosystems, especially as their populations grew. Referring to some of the early settlers

Map 6.5   Pacific Oceania
Covering about one-third of the world's surface, the Pacific Ocean encompasses thousands of islands, which were home to many distinct societies but also constituted a cultural region that shared numerous commonalities and connections.

in Melanesia during the first millennium B.C.E., Pacific historian Ian Campbell wrote: "They hunted, gathered, and fished profligately, and burnt large tracts of previously undisturbed forests."[20] In New Zealand, initially settled much later, around 1200 C.E., human hunting largely eliminated the huge flightless *moa* bird within a century. Archeologists have discovered the remains of some 90,000 moa at a single butchery. A similar impact occurred in Hawaii and elsewhere as smaller birds fell victim to the rats, pigs, and dogs introduced by the settlers. Resource depletion, deforestation, and soil erosion followed, no doubt contributing to the abandonment of at least several dozen islands, as their inhabitants found themselves forced to flee or perish. Rapa Nui (Easter Island) in easternmost Polynesia had come almost to the point of ecological collapse by the time Europeans arrived in the eighteenth century, as much of its tree cover had vanished and many bird species had likewise disappeared. Human activity had surely contributed to this outcome with overhunting, overfishing, and the cutting down of forests. But Polynesian rats, whether introduced accidentally or intentionally by the original settlers to the island, were at least equally responsible, as their numbers exploded and they devoured the seeds of the palm trees.[21]

Another change occasioned by growing populations lay in increased social complexity on some of the most densely populated islands. One example comes from the Micronesian island of Pohnpei, where an urban complex, constructed from stone and coral, served as the ceremonial, administrative, and burial center of a powerful Saudeleur dynasty that governed the island for several centuries. Probably emerging in the tenth century, this impressive urban center, later dubbed by Europeans the "Venice of the Pacific," contained numerous seawalls and canals, over ninety small artificial islands, marketplaces, and a large tomb and funerary complex. However, local legends tell of increasingly despotic rulers whose oppressive policies triggered a revolt by lower-ranking chiefs.

The Polynesian Tonga Islands witnessed yet another example of growing social complexity. By the fourteenth century, powerful rulers, known as Tu'i Tonga, stood at the head of a royal court including many wives and concubines, various relatives, ceremonial attendants, prisoners of war, and specialized craftsmen such as carvers, navigators, and fishermen. The court collected and redistributed food and various gifts to lesser chiefs, who then did the same for their followers. The widespread military and commercial influence of Tonga in the central Pacific has led some scholars to regard it as an incipient empire, while others view it as a tributary network or a system of economic interdependence.

Given the vast distances separating these island societies, considerable diversity among them is hardly surprising. And yet they also participated in the making of a single cultural region with numerous commonalities and connections. Many of their cultural and dietary similarities derive from their common origin in Island Southeast Asia and ultimately from southern China as well as from a common Pacific environment. Variations developed from the adaptation of this shared heritage to the distinctive environment of particular islands—large or small, tropical or semitropical, sea-level coastal terrain or mountainous interior, uninhabited or containing established societies as in New Guinea. The relative isolation of these societies, as well as periodic contact with near and more distant neighboring islands, also shaped their histories.

Linguistically, the peoples of Oceania, despite their small numbers, have spoken hundreds of different languages, over 100 on the small island chain of Melanesian Vanuatu alone. But almost all of them are members of the Austronesian family of languages, whose speakers also include those of Malaysia, Indonesia, and Madagascar. New Guinea, however, is a different story, with well over 1,000 languages, most of which are part of the Papuan language family, derived from its much earlier settlement. Similarly, Pacific islanders everywhere practiced the art of body decoration called *tatau* (which became "tattoo" in English), but particularly in Polynesia each archipelago developed distinctive designs, reflecting its unique identity.

This pattern of diversity and unity found other expression as well, both among the three major regions of Melanesia, Micronesia, and Polynesia and within them. In economic life, for example, these people of the sea drew heavily on the ocean as a major source of food, while its shells were used as currency and tools. But they were also farmers, raising pigs, dogs, and fowl, while everywhere cultivating taro, a starchy root vegetable. Other crops—yams, sweet potatoes, breadfruit, coconut palms—were cultivated variously as availability and conditions allowed.

In political and social life, Oceanic societies were generally organized as chiefdoms, but with considerable variation. On small islands, chiefs and priests could hardly be distinguished from anyone else, while village councils, operating by consensus, made decisions. In parts of Melanesia, so-called "big men," or locally influential individuals, exercised authority through ceremony, feasts, and gift giving. Elsewhere, societies were more stratified and authority more centralized. In New Zealand, the Maori people distinguished among chiefly families, commoners, and slaves derived from prisoners of war. Frequent warfare among its chiefdoms prevented greater political unity. In Hawaii and Tonga, by contrast, elaborate social hierarchies emerged with powerful rulers who had hundreds or even thousands of warriors at their disposal.

Women everywhere in ancient Oceania were considered dangerous and polluting, especially during menstruation and childbirth, and were isolated at those times. However, gender roles differed substantially from place to place. In Melanesia, women were more actively involved in food production, but in Polynesia their labor was directed more toward the making of mats and cloth. Throughout Polynesia, women were accorded high status, and women of chiefly families could exercise considerable power through their male relatives. Melanesian women, by contrast, were more sharply subordinated to men than their counterparts in other regions of Oceania.

Religious life in Oceania was pragmatic, designed to protect against harm and to manipulate the spirits or gods in one's favor. It found expression in two pervasive concepts: *mana* and *tapu*. Mana was a spiritual energy or power, associated especially with chiefs and demonstrated by remarkable actions or great success. To maintain the purity of mana, ritual restriction or prohibitions known as tapu (which came into English as "taboo") served to make someone or something sacred or elevated far above the ordinary. Throughout Polynesia, only a particular official could handle the chief's food or his possessions. A Maori chief in New Zealand could not allow even his shadow to fall on food, for doing so made it forbidden to all others. Hawaiians prostrated themselves on the ground before their major chiefs. Since

The Moai of Rapa Nui
The most iconic artistic representations of Polynesian culture are these huge stone figures called *moai*. Carved from volcanic rock on the island of Rapa Nui sometime between 1200 and 1600, they are thought to depict sacred ancestors or clan chiefs. Around 1,000 of them were quarried and carved, and hundreds were somehow transported up to eight miles to stand on stone platforms near the coast. The largest reached some thirty-three feet tall and weighed over eighty tons. (Ken Welsh/Bridgeman Images)

violating a tapu could result in death, religion provided supernatural sanctions for political authorities and social elites, as it has in so many other societies. While much of this was common across all of Pacific Oceania, the gods, ghosts, ancestors, and spirits differed considerably, as did the role of priests or shamans as well as the associated rituals and artistic expression of religious life.

Despite the distances between these island societies, they were not wholly isolated from one another. Networks of exchange and communication—both regional and at a greater distance—allowed for some interaction among the various peoples of Oceania. Between roughly 1400 and 800 B.C.E., the spread of a distinctive pottery style known as Lapita throughout Melanesia and as far as Tonga and Samoa suggests a widespread pattern of exchange involving both commercial and ceremonial elements. During this time, obsidian from the island of New Britain off the northeastern coast of New Guinea had a distribution that extended over 4,000 miles from Borneo in Island Southeast Asia to Fiji in eastern Melanesia.

In western Micronesia, another system of exchange arose in the Caroline Island chain, with a particular focus on the island of Yap. It involved trade in commodities such as sea turtles, coconuts, and breadfruit; permission to fish near neighboring islands; and promises of refuge and shelter in times of famine. But it was also a set of tributary relationships in which the high-ranking island of Yap periodically received payments such as woven cloth, various coconut products, mats, and shells from islands of lesser rank up to 1,200 miles farther east. In return, the subordinates received gifts from Yap that exceeded the value of their tribute: wood for canoes, flint stone, food, and powdered turmeric, used as a skin paste and in coming-of-age rituals. Cast in terms of a parent-child relationship between Yap and the other islands, the whole system was supported by fears of powerful Yapese sorcery capable of generating great storms, should the required tribute not be forthcoming. Such trading circuits often contained an elaborate ceremonial element in which the exchange of noneconomic items—bracelets, necklaces, feathers, or shells—served to display status, to cement bonds of mutual assistance across great distances, and to confirm relationships of dominance and submission. Small island societies were invariably vulnerable and limited in resources; such networks of exchange provided insurance for their survival.

Polynesian networks of exchange also flourished in the centuries after 1000 C.E., with Tonga at the center of a system linked by trade with Samoa and Fiji. Finely woven Samoan mats were highly valued for displaying prestige, and large logs from Fiji were prized for the huge canoes that could be carved from them for Tonga's impressive warships. From the far eastern edge of Polynesia, sailors had apparently reached the coast of South America, from which they returned with sweet potatoes and bottle gourds. Taking hold in Rapa Nui, those domesticates from the Americas then entered Polynesian voyaging networks and found their way to Hawaii, New Zealand, and elsewhere, becoming a major food source.

Linked to Asia by their distant origins and to the Americas by the slender thread of the sweet potato, the peoples of Pacific Oceania lived largely, but not entirely, in a world apart from the rest of humankind.

AP® EXAM TIP

Pay attention to the networks that connected peoples in the Pacific Ocean regions during the classical era.

Deciding What's Important:
Balance in World History

Among the perennial problems that teachers and writers of world history confront is sorting through the vast record of times past and choosing what to include and what to leave out. A related issue involves the extent to which particular peoples or civilizations will be treated. Should the Persians get as much space as the Greeks? Does Africa merit equal treatment with Eurasia? Where do the Americas fit in the larger human story? What, in short, are the criteria for deciding what is important in recalling the history of the human venture?

One standard might be duration. Should ways of living that have endured for longer periods of time receive greater attention than those of lesser length? If historians followed only this criterion, then the Paleolithic era of gathering, hunting, and fishing societies should occupy 90 percent or more of any world history text. On the other hand, perhaps change is more important than continuity. If so, then something new merits more space than something old. Thus we pay attention to both agriculture and civilizations because they represent significant turning points in human experience. Population provides yet another principle for determining inclusion. That, of course, is the reason that Eurasia / North Africa, with over 80 percent of the world's population, is addressed in three chapters of this section, whereas inner Africa, the Americas, and Pacific Oceania together receive just one chapter. There is also the related issue of range of influence. Buddhism, Christianity, and Islam spread more widely and shaped the lives of more people than did the religions of the Maya or the Bantu-speaking peoples of Africa. Do they therefore deserve more extended treatment? Still another factor involves the availability of evidence. In this respect, Eurasia generated far more written records than either Africa or the Americas did, and therefore its history has been investigated far more thoroughly.

A final possible criterion involves the location of the historian and his or her audience. Those who have recently developed world history as a field of study have vigorously sought to counteract a Eurocentric telling of the human story. Still, is there anything inherently wrong with an account of world history that is centered on one's own people? When I taught history in an Ethiopian high school in the mid-1960s, I was guided by an Afrocentric curriculum, which focused first on Ethiopian history, then on Africa as a whole, and finally on the larger world. Might a world historian from the Middle East, for example, legitimately strike a somewhat different balance in the treatment of various civilizations than someone writing for a largely Western audience or for Chinese readers?

Any account of the world's past will mix and match these criteria in various and contested ways. Among historians, there exists neither a consensus about this question nor any formula to ensure a "proper" balance. You may want to consider whether the balance struck in this chapter, this section, and the book as a whole is appropriate or somehow out of line.

AP® EXAM TIP

Be aware of historical debates over the meanings of important events and peoples throughout world history.

Chapter Review

What's the Significance?

Meroë, 234–36

Piye, 236–37

Axum, 237–39

Niger Valley civilization,
    239–41

Maya civilization, 242–44

Teotihuacán, 244–46

Chavín, 247–48

Moche, 248–49

Wari and Tiwanaku, 249–51

Bantu expansion, 252–55

Chaco Phenomenon, 256

Mound Builders / Cahokia,
    256–58

Pohnpei, 260

Tonga, 260

mana and *tapu*, 261

Yap, 262

Big Picture Questions

1. "The particular cultures and societies of Africa, the Americas, and Pacific Oceania discussed in this chapter developed largely in isolation." What evidence would support this statement, and what might challenge it?

2. How do you understand areas of the world, such as Bantu Africa, North America, and Pacific Oceania, that did not generate "civilizations"? Do you see them as "backward," as moving slowly toward civilization, or as simply different?

3. How did Africa's proximity to Eurasia shape its history? And how did America's separation from the Eastern Hemisphere affect its development?

4. **Looking Back:** "The histories of Africa and the Americas during the second-wave era largely resemble those of Eurasia." Do you agree with this statement? Explain why or why not.

Next Steps: For Further Study

Christopher Ehret, *The Civilizations of Africa* (2002). An overview of African history before 1800 by a prominent scholar.

Brian M. Fagan, *Ancient North America* (2005). A prominent archeologist's account of North American history.

Steven R. Fischer, *A History of the Pacific Islands* (2013). A recent account of the history of Pacific Oceania from ancient times to the present.

Eric Gilbert and Jonathan T. Reynolds, *Africa in World History* (2004). An accessible account of African history set in a global context.

Guy Gugliotta, "The Maya: Glory and Ruin," *National Geographic* (August 2007). A beautifully illustrated account of the rise and fall of Maya civilization.

Charles C. Mann, *1491: New Revelations of the Americas before Columbus* (2005). A journalist's thoughtful account, delightfully written, of the controversies surrounding the history of the Americas before 1492.

Ancient Africa's Black Kingdoms, http://www.homestead.com/wysinger/ancientafrica.html. A Web site exploring the history of Nubia.

Maya Adventure, http://www.smm.org/sln/ma. A collection of text and pictures about the Maya, past and present.

Maya Videos, http://www.history.com/topics/maya/videos/the-mayans. A series of brief video depictions of Maya history and culture from the History channel.

WORKING WITH EVIDENCE

Axum and the World

In the world of ancient African history, Axum has occupied a unique position in several ways (see Map 6.1, page 235, and pages 237–39). It is one of the few places in Africa, outside of Egypt, for which considerable documentary evidence exists. Some of the written sources—royal inscriptions and coins, for example—derive from within Axum itself, while others come from Greco-Roman and Christian visitors. Furthermore, after the rise of Islam, Axum—and its Ethiopian successor state—was the major surviving outpost of a Christian tradition that had earlier spread widely across northern and northeastern Africa. Finally, Axum has demonstrated an impressive cultural and religious continuity. Even after the decline of the Axumite Empire by the eighth century C.E., the city of Axum remained a major pilgrimage site for Christians, while Ethiopian kings into the twentieth century were crowned there.[22] The documents that follow offer a series of windows on this African kingdom.

Source 6.1
A Guidebook to the World of Indian Ocean Commerce

The earliest documentary reference to Axum was composed during the first century C.E. in an anonymous text known as *The Periplus of the Erythraean Sea*. Likely written by a sea captain from Roman-controlled Egypt, the *Periplus* offers a guide to the places and conditions that merchants might encounter as they traversed the Red Sea and the East African coast while on their way to India.

- According to this text, why is the Axumite port of Adulis significant?

- What evidence does the *Periplus* provide about Axum's cultural and economic ties to the larger world?

- Based on the list of imports and exports, how would you describe Axum's role in the international commerce of the first century C.E.?

- How might Axum's participation in long-distance trade have stimulated and sustained its growth as an empire?

The Periplus of the Erythraean Sea
First Century C.E.

Below Ptolemais of the Hunts [near modern Port Sudan on the Red Sea] . . . there is Adulis, a port established by law. . . . Before the harbor lies the so-called Mountain Island, about two hundred stadia sea-ward [1 stadium = ⅛ mile] from the very head of the bay, with the shores of the mainland close to it on both sides. Ships bound for this port now anchor here because of attacks from the land. . . . Opposite Mountain Island, on the mainland twenty stadia from shore, lies Adulis, a fair-sized village, from which there is a three-days' journey to Coloe, an inland town and the first market for ivory. From that place to the city of the people called Axumites there is a five days' journey more; to that place all the ivory is brought from the country beyond the Nile . . . and thence to Adulis. Practically the whole number of elephants and rhinoceros that are killed live in the places inland, although at rare intervals they are hunted on the seacoast even near Adulis. Before the harbor of that market-town, out at sea on the right hand, there lie a great many little sandy islands called Alalaei, yielding tortoise-shell, which is brought to market there by the Fish-Eaters.

And about eight hundred stadia beyond there is another very deep bay, with a great mound of sand piled up at the right of the entrance; at the bottom of which the opsian [obsidian] stone is found, and this is the only place where it is produced. These places . . . are governed by Zoscales [an Axumite ruler], who is miserly in his ways and always striving for more, but otherwise upright, and acquainted with Greek literature.

There are imported into these places undressed cloth made in Egypt for the Berbers; robes from Arsinoe [an Egyptian port]; cloaks of poor quality dyed in colors; double-fringed linen mantles; many articles of flint glass, and others of murrhine [used for making Roman vases] made in Diospolis [Thebes in Egypt]; and brass, which is used for ornament and in cut pieces instead of coin; sheets of soft copper, used for cooking utensils and cut up for bracelets and anklets for the women; iron, which is made into spears used against the elephants and other wild beasts, and in their wars. Besides these, small axes are imported, and adzes and swords; copper drinking-cups, round and large; a little coin [Roman money] for those coming to the market [probably foreign merchants living in Adulis]; wine of Laodicea and Italy, not much; olive oil, not much; for the king, gold and silver plate made after the fashion of the country, and for clothing, military cloaks, and thin coats of skin, of no great value. Likewise from the district of Ariaca [in western India] across this sea, there are imported Indian iron, and steel, and Indian cotton cloth; . . . and girdles, and coats of skin and mallow-colored cloth, and a few muslins, and colored lac [a resinous secretion of an insect, used in the form of shellac]. There are exported from these places ivory, and tortoise-shell and rhinoceros-horn. The most from Egypt is brought to this market from the month of January.

Source: Wilfred H. Schoff, trans. and ed., *The Periplus of the Erythraean Sea* (New York: Longman, Green, 1912), secs. 4–6.

Source 6.2
The Making of an Axumite Empire

At its high point in the mid-fourth century C.E., Axum ruled an empire stretching from Meroë in the upper Nile Valley, across much of what is now Eritrea and Ethiopia, and incorporating parts of southern Arabia on the opposite side of the Red Sea. Source 6.2 comes from an Axumite inscription written in Greek on a stone throne adorned with figures of the Greek gods Hercules and Mercury. Commissioned by an unknown Axumite monarch, the inscription dates probably from the second or third century C.E. It was copied and then published in the sixth century by Cosmas, a Greek merchant born in Alexandria, Egypt, who had become a monk. This text describes some of the conquests that generated the Axumite Empire.

- What internal evidence from the document itself dates it prior to Axum's acceptance of Christianity?

- How would you describe the point of view from which the document was written?

- What techniques of imperial control does the document reveal?

- How might you account for the obvious Greek influence that is apparent in the inscription?

- How would you describe the religious or ideological underpinnings of this empire? Why might the Axumite ruler who commissioned this inscription single out Ares, Zeus, and Poseidon for special attention?

Inscription on a Stone Throne
Second or Third Century C.E.

Having after this with a strong hand compelled the nations bordering on my kingdom to live in peace, I made war upon the following nations, and by force of arms reduced them to subjection. I warred first with the nation of Gaze [Axum, probably in an internal struggle for power], then with Agame and Sigye, and having conquered them, I exacted the half of all that they possessed. . . . [*There follows a long list of other peoples that this ruler conquered.*]

I proceeded next against the Tangaltae, who adjoin the borders of Egypt; and having reduced them I made a footpath giving access by land into Egypt from that part of my dominions. Next I reduced Annine and Metine—tribes inhabiting precipitous mountains. My arms were next directed against the Sesea nation. These had retired to a high mountain difficult of access; but I blockaded the mountain on every side, and compelled them to come down and surrender. I then selected for myself the best of their young men and their women, with their sons and daughters and all besides that

they possessed. The tribes of Rhausi I next brought to submission: a barbarous race spread over wide waterless plains in the interior of the frankincense country. [Advancing thence toward the sea,] I encountered the Solate, whom I subdued, and left with instructions to guard the coast.

All these nations, protected though they were by mountains all but impregnable, I conquered, after engagements in which I was myself present. Upon their submission I restored their territories to them, subject to the payment of tribute. Many other tribes besides these submitted of their own accord, and became likewise tributary. And I sent a fleet and land forces against the Arabitae and Cinaedocolpitae who dwelt on the other side of the Red Sea [southern Arabia], and having reduced the sovereigns of both, I imposed on them a land tribute and charged them to make traveling safe both by sea and by land. . . .

I first and alone of the kings of my race made these conquests. For this success I now offer my thanks to my mighty god, Ares [the Greek god of warfare and slaughter], who begat me, and by whose aid I reduced all the nations bordering on my own country. . . . Of these expeditions, some were conducted by myself in person, and ended in victory, and the others I entrusted to my officers. Having thus brought all the world under my authority to peace, I came down to Adulis and offered sacrifice to Zeus [chief god of the Greek pantheon], and to

Ares, and to Poseidon [Greek god of the sea], whom I entreated to befriend all who go down to the sea in ships. Here also I reunited all my forces, and setting down this Chair [throne] in this place, I consecrated it to Ares in the twenty-seventh year of my reign.

Source: J. W. McCrindle, trans. and ed., *The Christian Topography of Cosmas, an Egyptian Monk* (London: Hakluyt Society, 1897), 59–66.

Source 6.3

The Coming of Christianity to Axum

The introduction of Christianity in the mid-fourth century C.E. represented a major change in the cultural history of Axum. It meant that Axum would be more closely aligned to Christian Egypt and Byzantium than to South Arabia, from which many of its earlier cultural traditions had derived. Source 6.3 relates the story of the coming of Christianity to Axum. It was written by Rufinus (345–410 C.E.), a Christian monk and writer who was born in Italy but spent much of his life in Jerusalem, where he heard this story from those who had taken part in it. Note that Greco-Roman writers of this time used "India" to refer vaguely to East Africa and southern Arabia as well as the South Asian peninsula.

- According to this document, by what means was Christianity introduced to Axum? What do you think was the relative importance of Frumentius and Aedesius, as opposed to Roman merchants living in Axum?

- Why do you think the Axumite royal family was so receptive to this foreign religion? How might the story differ if told from the ruling family's perspective?

- How does the fact that this document was written by outsiders shape the emphasis of the story?

RUFINUS

On the Evangelization of Abyssinia

Late Fourth Century C.E.

A certain philosopher Metrodorus is said to have penetrated the more remote parts of India in order to study their world and investigate its regions. Meropius, a philosopher from Tyre, was motivated by his example and decided to go to India for similar reasons. Two little boys went with

him. He had been educating them in the liberal arts because they were his relatives. The younger boy was named Aedesius, the older Frumentius.

During the journey the things Meropius studied and learned nourished his mind. Then, while headed home, the philosopher's ship had to land because the travelers needed water or some other necessities. Where they landed the barbarians had a custom of cutting the throats of all Romans they found among them whenever neighboring nations announced that their treaties with the Romans were broken. The barbarians attacked the philosopher's ship. They killed him and all with him likewise. But the little boys they found studying and doing their reading under a tree. The barbarians spared the boys out of pity and led them to their king [the ruler of Axum].

The king made Aedesius his cup bearer. But he trusted Frumentius to be his accountant and scribe because he understood that the boy had a sharp mind and wisdom. From then on the king honored and loved them both. When the king died, he left as his successor his wife, who had a little son. He granted the boys, now young men, free opportunity to do whatever they wanted. And the queen, as if she trusted no one in the kingdom more, humbly asked them to share in taking care of the kingdom with her until her son was a young man. She especially wanted Frumentius to help because he had enough wisdom to direct a kingdom, while Aedesius displayed only a pure faith and sober mind.

While this was happening as well as during the time Frumentius directed the government of the kingdom, he carefully began to inquire — for God moved his mind and spirit — whether there were any Christians among the Roman merchants. And he gave the greatest power to these Christians and advised them to make meeting places in every part of the country so that they could congregate in them for prayer in the Roman manner. Moreover, he himself did the same to a much greater degree, and so encouraged others, motivated them with favor and benefits, offered whatever might be useful, supplied land for buildings and other necessi-

ties, and acted in every way to grow the Christian seed in the kingdom.

When the royal child for whom Aedesius and Frumentius were taking care of the kingdom became a young man, their task was fulfilled and they faithfully handed over everything to him. Then they returned again to our world [the Roman Empire], even though the queen and her son delayed their journey and asked them to remain.

While Aedesius hurried to Tyre to visit his parents and relatives, Frumentius went to Alexandria, saying that it was not right to hide the work of the Lord. As such, he presented everything as it had happened to the Bishop [Athanasius] and advised him to provide some worthy man whom he might send as a bishop to the churches built in the barbarian land and their already large number of Christians.

Then in truth Athanasius . . . after he readily and attentively considered Frumentius' words and deeds, said in a council of the priests, "What other man will we find who can achieve such things and in whom the spirit of God is as in you, Frumentius?" Athanasius made Frumentius a priest and ordered him to return with the grace of God to the place from which he had come. And when he had gone out as a bishop to India, they say that so much virtuous grace was given to him by God that miracles were worked through him and a countless number of barbarians was converted to the faith. From then on, Christian peoples and churches were created in the regions of India, and a clerical hierarchy was instituted. We know these things happened not by the report of common people, but because Aedesius himself, the former companion of Frumentius and later made a priest of Tyre, related them.

Source: *The Church History of Rufinus of Aquileia*, book 10, sections 9 and 10. Translation from Latin by Edward M. Gutting, Missouri State University.

Source 6.4
Axum and the Gold Trade

The foundations of the Axumite state lay not only in its military conquests and its adoption of a new religion but also in its economic ties to the larger world. Among these ties was its reputation as a major source of gold for the

Roman Empire. Source 6.4 describes the distinctive fashion in which Axumite traders obtained the gold from the African peoples living on the margins of the Axumite state. The author, Cosmas (see Source 6.2, page 266), was involved in this trade.

■ How would you define the pattern of exchange described in this document? Was it state-directed trade, private enterprise, or both? To what problems of cross-cultural interaction was it a response?

■ Who, if anyone, had the upper hand in this trade? Was it conducted between politically equal parties?

■ What purposes did this trade serve for the people who mined and "sold" the gold?

■ Beyond the peaceful trade for gold described here, what other purposes did this region serve for Axum?

COSMAS
The Christian Topography
Sixth Century C.E.

The country known as that of Sasu is itself near the ocean . . . in which there are many gold mines. The King of the Axumites accordingly, every other year, through the governor of Agau, sends thither special agents to bargain for the gold, and these are accompanied by many other traders— upwards, say, of five hundred—bound on the same errand as themselves. They take along with them to the mining district oxen, lumps of salt, and iron, and when they reach its neighborhood, they make a halt at a certain spot and form an encampment, which they fence round with a great hedge of thorns. Within this they live, and having slaughtered the oxen, cut them in pieces, and lay the pieces on the top of the thorns, along with the lumps of salt and the iron. Then come the natives bringing gold in nuggets like peas, and lay one or two or more of these upon what pleases them— the pieces of flesh or the salt or the iron, and then they retire to some distance off. Then the owner of the meat approaches, and if he is satisfied he takes the gold away, and upon seeing this, its owner comes and takes the flesh or the salt or the iron. If, however, he is not satisfied, he leaves the gold, when the native, seeing that he has not taken it, comes and either puts down more gold, or takes up what he had laid down, and goes away. Such is the mode in which business is transacted with the people of that country, because their language is different and interpreters are hardly to be found.

The time they stay in that country is five days more or less, according as the natives, more or less readily coming forward, buy up all their wares. On the journey homeward they all agree to travel well-armed, since some of the tribes through whose country they must pass might threaten to attack them from a desire to rob them of their gold. The space of six months is taken up with this trading expedition, including both the going and the returning. In going they march very slowly, chiefly because of the cattle, but in returning they quicken their pace lest on the way they should be overtaken by winter and its rains. For the sources of the river Nile lie somewhere in these parts, and in winter, on account of the heavy rains, the numerous rivers which they generate obstruct the path of the traveler. The people there have their winter at the time we have our summer . . . and during the three months the rain falls in torrents, and makes a multitude of rivers all of which flow into the Nile.

The facts which I have just recorded fell partly under my own observation and partly were told me by traders who had been to those parts. . . .

For most of the slaves which are now found in the hands of merchants who resort to these parts are taken from the tribes of which we speak. As for the Semenai, where . . . there are snows and ice, it is to that country the King of the Axumites expatriates anyone whom he has sentenced to be banished.

Source: J. W. McCrindle, trans. and ed., *The Christian Topography of Cosmas, an Egyptian Monk* (London: Hakluyt Society, 1897), 52–54, 67.

DOING HISTORY

Axum and the World

1. **Assessing sources:** How does each of these documents reflect the distinctive perspective of its author? What different perspectives can you notice between those documents written from within Axum and those written by outsiders? How did the particular social role that each author represents (missionary, monarch, merchant) affect his view of Axum?

2. **Considering external influences:** Based on these documents, how would you describe Axum's various relationships with the world beyond its borders? How did its geographic location shape those relationships? (See Map 6.1, page 235.) In what ways did those external connections influence Axum's historical development? From another perspective, how did Axum actively assimilate foreign influences or deliberately take advantage of opportunities that came from outside?

3. **Explaining the rise and significance of Axum:** How might you account for the flourishing of Axum? What was the religious and military significance of Axum within the region?

4. **Comparing civilizations:** In what ways might Axum be viewed as a smaller-scale version of the second-wave civilizations of Eurasia? In what ways did it differ from them?

5. **Seeking further evidence:** What else would you like to know about Axum? If you could uncover one additional document, what would you want it to reveal?

Multiple-Choice Questions

Questions 1 and 2 refer to the poem below by the Chinese poet Li Shen, from the eighth century C.E.

> The cob of corn in springtime sown
> In autumn yields a hundredfold.
> No fields are seen that fallow lie:
> And yet of hunger peasants die.
> As at noontide they hoe their crops,
> Sweat on the grain to earth down drops.
> How many tears, how many a groan,
> Each morsel on thy dish did mould!*

1. What does the poem infer happens to the peasants' crops?
   a. The crops become moldy and inedible.
   b. There is more grain than the peasants can eat.
   c. The fields are empty because of poor weather.
   d. The crops are taken from the peasants.

2. This poem is about Chinese peasants, but in what way could it be about any agrarian society?
   a. Peasants were well provided for by the rest of society.
   b. Peasants were at the top of most social hierarchies.
   c. Peasant labor provided food that allowed the rest of society to eat.
   d. Most peasants owned their own farmland.

Short-Answer Question

3. Answer parts A, B, and C.
   A. Briefly explain ONE important similarity between social systems in Rome and Han China in the period from c. 200 B.C.E. to c. 200 C.E.
   B. Briefly explain ONE important difference between social systems in Rome and Han China in the period from c. 200 B.C.E. to c. 200 C.E.
   C. Briefly explain ONE factor that accounts for the difference that you indicated in part B.

*Li Shen, "Old Style," Selected Poems from T'ang Dynasty, accessed May 15, 2014, http://www.shigeku.org/xlib/lingshidao/hanshi/tang1.htm.

Document-Based Question

Directions: Question 4 refers to the following documents. You will likely need to flip back and forth between these documents to answer the question adequately. Use scrap pieces of paper or sticky notes to tab these documents. When answering the question, refer to the "Advice for Responding to a DBQ" on the inside of the back cover.

4. Using the following documents from this textbook and your knowledge of world history, analyze beliefs about women's roles in societies in the classical era (c. 600 B.C.E.–c. 600 C.E.).

DOCUMENT	PAGE	DOCUMENT NAME
1	120	Image and description of Queen Boudica
2	124	Image and description of the Trung sisters
3	153	Excerpt from *Lessons for Women*, Ban Zhao
4	177	Quote from the North African Carthagian writer Tertullian
5	251	Description of the Moche Lady of Cao

Long-Essay Question

When answering the following question, refer to the "Advice for Responding to an LEQ" on the inside of the back cover.

5. Evaluate the extent to which belief systems in ONE of the following regions experienced continuities and changes from 3500 B.C.E. to 500 C.E., and analyze the reasons for these continuities and changes.
- East Asia
- Middle East
- South Asia

PART THREE

AN AGE OF ACCELERATING CONNECTIONS

600 C.E.–1450

Contents

DEFINING A MILLENNIUM

History seldom turns sharp corners, and historians often have difficulty deciding just when one phase of the human story ends and another begins. Between roughly 200 and 850 C.E., many of the second-wave states and civilizations (Han dynasty China, the western Roman Empire, Gupta India, Meroë, Axum, Maya, Teotihuacán, Moche) experienced severe disruption, decline, or collapse. For many historians, this has marked the end of an era and the start of a new period of world history. Furthermore, almost everyone agrees that the transatlantic voyages of Columbus beginning in 1492 represent yet another new departure in world history. This coupling of the Eastern and Western hemispheres set in motion historical processes that transformed most of the world and signaled the beginning of the modern era.

But how are we to understand the thousand years (roughly 600 to 1450) between the end of the second-wave era and the beginning of modern world history? Frankly, historians have had some difficulty defining a distinct identity for this millennium, a problem reflected in the vague terms used to describe it: a postclassical era, a medieval or "middle" period between the ancient and modern, or, as in this book, an age of third-wave civilizations. At best, these terms indicate where this period falls in the larger time frame of world history, but none of them are very descriptive.

AP® EXAM TIP

The historical processes and events in Part Three make up 20 percent of the AP® World History exam.

Third-Wave Civilizations: Something New, Something Old, Something Blended

A large part of the problem lies in the rather different trajectories of various regions of the world during this millennium. It is not easy to identify clearly defined features that encompass all major civilizations or human communities during this period and to distinguish them from what went before. We can, however, point to several distinct patterns during this third-wave era.

In some areas, for example, wholly new but smaller civilizations arose where none had existed before. Along the East African coast, Swahili civilization emerged in a string of thirty or more city-states, very much engaged in the commercial life of the Indian Ocean basin. The kingdoms of Ghana, Mali, Songhay, and others, stimulated and sustained by long-distance trade across the Sahara, represented a new West African civilization. In the area now encompassed by

Ukraine and western Russia, another new civilization, known as Kievan Rus, likewise took shape with a good deal of cultural borrowing from Mediterranean civilization. East and Southeast Asia also witnessed new centers of civilization. Those in Japan, Korea, and Vietnam were strongly influenced by China, while Srivijaya on the Indonesian island of Sumatra, and later the Angkor kingdom centered in present-day Cambodia, drew on the Hindu and Buddhist traditions of India.

All of these represent a continuation of a well-established pattern in world history—the globalization of civilization. Each of the new third-wave civilizations was, of course, culturally unique, but like their predecessors of the first and second waves, they too featured states, cities, specialized economic roles, sharp class and gender inequalities, and other elements of "civilized" life. As newcomers to the growing number of civilizations, all of them borrowed heavily from larger or more established centers.

The largest, most expansive, and most widely influential of the new third-wave civilizations was surely that of Islam. It began in Arabia in the seventh century c.e., projecting the Arab peoples into a prominent role as builders of an enormous empire while offering a new, vigorous, and attractive religion. Viewed as a new civilization defined by its religion, the world of Islam came to encompass many other centers of civilization—Egypt, Mesopotamia, Persia, India, the interior of West Africa and the coast of East Africa, Spain, southeastern Europe, and more. Here was a uniquely cosmopolitan or "umbrella" civilization that "came closer than any had ever come to uniting all mankind under its ideals."[1]

Yet another, and quite different, historical pattern during the third-wave millennium involved those older civilizations that persisted or were reconstructed. The Byzantine Empire, embracing the eastern half of the old Roman Empire, continued the patterns of Mediterranean Christian civilization and persisted until 1453, when it was overrun by the Ottoman Turks. In China, following almost four centuries of fragmentation, the Sui, Tang, and Song dynasties (589–1279) restored China's imperial unity and reasserted its Confucian tradition. Indian civilization retained its ancient patterns of caste and Hinduism amid vast cultural diversity, even as parts of India fell under the control of Muslim rulers.

Variations on this theme of continuing or renewing older traditions took shape in the Western Hemisphere, where two centers of civilization—in Mesoamerica and in the Andes—had been long established. In Mesoamerica, the collapse of classical Maya civilization and of the great city-state of Teotihuacán by about 900 c.e. opened the way for other peoples to give new shape to this ancient civilization. The most well-known of these efforts was associated with the Mexica or Aztec people, who created a powerful and impressive state in the fifteenth century. About the same time, on the western rim of South America, a Quechua-speaking people, now known as the Incas, incorporated various centers of Andean civilization into a huge bureaucratic empire. Both the Aztecs and the Incas gave a new political expression to much older patterns of civilized life.

Yet another pattern took shape in Western Europe following the collapse of the Roman Empire. There, would-be kings and church leaders alike sought to maintain links with the older Greco-Roman-Christian traditions of classical Mediterranean civilization. In the absence of empire, however, new and far more decentralized societies emerged, led now by Germanic peoples and centered in Northern and Western Europe, considerably removed from the older centers of Rome and Athens. It was a hybrid civilization, combining old and new, Greco-Roman and Germanic elements, in a distinctive blending. For five centuries or more, this region was a relative backwater, compared to the more vibrant, prosperous, and powerful civilizations of Byzantium, the Islamic world, and China. During the centuries after 1000 c.e., however, Western European civilization emerged as a rapidly growing and expansive set of competitive states, willing, like other new civilizations, to borrow extensively from their more developed neighbors.

The Ties That Bind: Transregional Interaction in the Third-Wave Era

These quite-different patterns of development within particular civilizations have made it difficult to devise a single, all-encompassing definition of the third-wave era. In one way, however, a common theme emerges, for during this time, the world's various regions, cultures, and peoples interacted with one another far more extensively. More than before, change in human societies was the product of contact with strangers, or at least with their ideas, armies, goods, or diseases. In a variety of places—Island Southeast Asia, coastal East Africa, Central Asian cities, parts of Western Europe, the Islamic Middle East, and the Inca Empire—local cosmopolitan regions emerged in which trade, migration, or empire had brought peoples of different cultures together in a restricted space. These "mini-globalizations," both larger and more common than before, became a distinctive feature of third-wave civilizations.

None of these civilizations were wholly isolated or separate from their neighbors, although the range and intensity of cross-cultural interaction certainly varied over time. In limited ways, this had been true for earlier civilizations as well. But the scale and pace of such interaction accelerated considerably between 600 and 1450. Much of Part Three highlights these intersections and spells out their many and varied consequences.

One pattern of interaction lay in long-distance trade, which grew considerably during the third-wave millennium—along the Silk Roads of Eurasia, within the Indian Ocean basin, across the Sahara, and along the Mississippi and other rivers. Everywhere it acted as an agent of change for all its participants. In places where such commerce was practiced extensively, it required that more people devote their energies to producing for a distant market rather than for the consumption of their own communities. Those who controlled this kind of trade often became extremely wealthy, exciting envy or outrage among those less fortunate. Many societies learned about new products via these trade routes. Europe's knowledge of pepper and other spices, for example, derived from Roman seaborne trade with India beginning in the first century c.e. Such exchange among distant lands also had political consequences, as many new states or empires were constructed on the basis of resources derived from long-distance commerce. Furthermore, religious ideas, technologies, and diseases also made their ways along these paths of commerce, disrupting older ways of living and offering new opportunities as well.

Yet another mechanism of cross-cultural interaction lay in large empires. Not only did they incorporate many distinct cultures within a single political system, but their size and stability also provided the security that encouraged travelers and traders to journey long distances from their homelands. Empires, of course, were nothing new in world history, but many of those associated with third-wave civilizations were distinctive. In the first place, they were larger. The Arab Empire, which accompanied the initial spread of Islam, stretched from Spain to India. Even more extensive was the Mongol Empire of the thirteenth and fourteenth centuries. In the Western Hemisphere, the Inca Empire encompassed dozens of distinct peoples in a huge state that ran some 2,500 miles along the spine of the Andes Mountains.

Furthermore, the largest of these empires were the creation of nomadic or pastoral peoples. Earlier empires in the Mediterranean basin, China, India, and Persia had been the work of settled farming societies. But now, in the thousand years between 600 and 1450, peoples with a recent history of a nomadic or herding way of life entered the stage of world history as empire builders — Arabs, Berbers, Turks, Mongols, Aztecs — ruling over agricultural peoples and established civilizations.

Together, large-scale empires and long-distance trade facilitated the spread of ideas, technologies, food crops, and germs far beyond their points of origin. Buddhism spread from India to much of Asia; Christianity encompassed Europe and took root in distant Russia, even as it contracted in the Middle East and North Africa. Hinduism attracted followers in Southeast Asia; and more than any other religion, Islam became an Afro-Eurasian phenomenon with an enormous reach. Beyond the connections born of commerce and conquest, those of culture and religion generated lasting ties among many peoples of the Eastern Hemisphere.

Technologies, too, were diffused widely. Until the sixth century c.e., China maintained a monopoly on the manufacture of raw silk. Then this technology spread beyond East Asia, allowing the development of a silk industry in the eastern Mediterranean and later in Italy. India too contributed much to the larger world — many food crops, crystallized sugar, a system of numerals and the concept of zero, and techniques for making cotton textiles. In the Americas, corn gradually diffused from Mesoamerica, where it was initially domesticated, to North America, where it stimulated population growth and the development of more complex societies. Disease also linked distant communities. The plague, or Black Death, decimated many parts of Eurasia and North Africa as it made its deadly way from east to west in the fourteenth century.

A focus on these accelerating connections across cultural boundaries puts the historical spotlight on merchants, travelers, missionaries, migrants, soldiers, and administrators—people who traveled abroad rather than those who stayed at home. This cross-cultural emphasis in world history raises provocative questions about what happens when cultures interact or when strangers meet. How did external stimuli operate to produce change within particular societies? How did individuals or societies decide what to accept and what to reject when confronted with new ideas or practices? In what ways did they alter foreign customs or traditions to better meet their own needs and correspond to their own values?

Much of the readily visible "action" in third-wave civilizations, as in all earlier civilizations, featured male actors. The vast majority of rulers, traders, soldiers, religious officials, and long-distance travelers were men, as were most heads of households and families. The building of states and empires, so prominent in the third-wave era, meant war and conquest, fostering distinctly masculine warrior values and reinforcing the dominant position of men. Much of what follows in Part Three is, frankly, men's history.

But it is useful to remember that behind all of this lay a vast realm of women's activity, long invisible to historians or simply assumed. Women sustained the family life that was the foundation of all human community; they were the repositories of language, religious ritual, group knowledge, and local history; their labor generated many of the products that entered long-distance trade routes as well as those that fed and clothed their communities. The changing roles and relationships of men and women and their understandings of gender also figure in the chapters that follow.

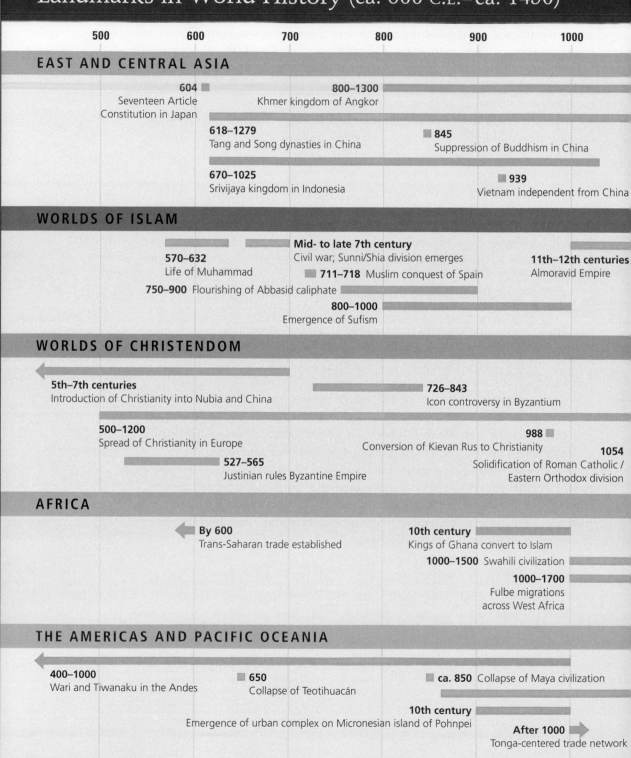

Landmarks in World History (ca. 600 C.E.–ca. 1450)

500 · 600 · 700 · 800 · 900 · 1000

EAST AND CENTRAL ASIA

604
Seventeen Article
Constitution in Japan

800–1300
Khmer kingdom of Angkor

618–1279
Tang and Song dynasties in China

845
Suppression of Buddhism in China

670–1025
Srivijaya kingdom in Indonesia

939
Vietnam independent from China

WORLDS OF ISLAM

570–632
Life of Muhammad

Mid- to late 7th century
Civil war; Sunni/Shia division emerges

11th–12th centuries
Almoravid Empire

711–718 Muslim conquest of Spain

750–900 Flourishing of Abbasid caliphate

800–1000
Emergence of Sufism

WORLDS OF CHRISTENDOM

5th–7th centuries
Introduction of Christianity into Nubia and China

726–843
Icon controversy in Byzantium

500–1200
Spread of Christianity in Europe

988
Conversion of Kievan Rus to Christianity

1054
Solidification of Roman Catholic /
Eastern Orthodox division

527–565
Justinian rules Byzantine Empire

AFRICA

By 600
Trans-Saharan trade established

10th century
Kings of Ghana convert to Islam

1000–1500 Swahili civilization

1000–1700
Fulbe migrations
across West Africa

THE AMERICAS AND PACIFIC OCEANIA

400–1000
Wari and Tiwanaku in the Andes

650
Collapse of Teotihuacán

ca. 850 Collapse of Maya civilization

10th century
Emergence of urban complex on Micronesian island of Pohnpei

After 1000
Tonga-centered trade network

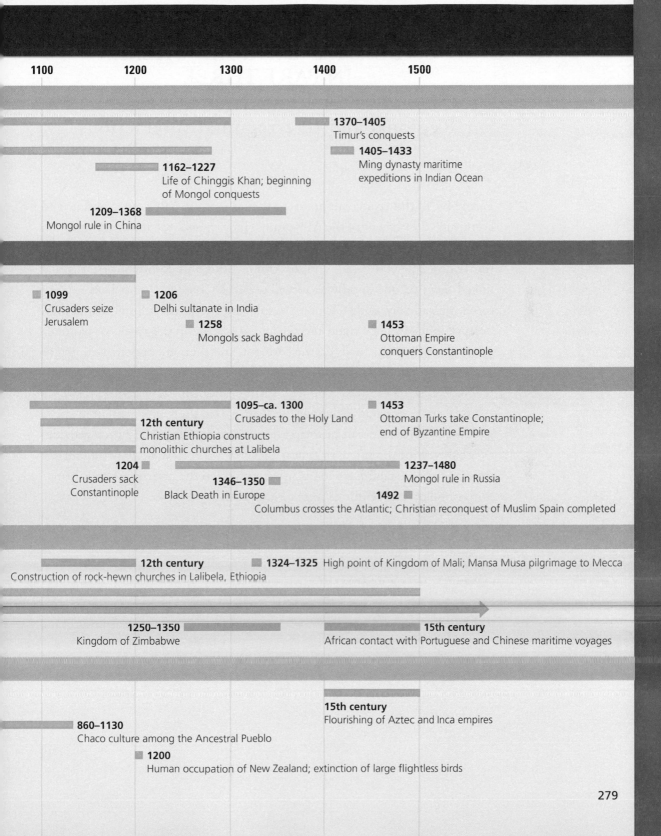

1100   1200   1300   1400   1500

1370–1405
Timur's conquests

1405–1433
Ming dynasty maritime
expeditions in Indian Ocean

1162–1227
Life of Chinggis Khan; beginning
of Mongol conquests

1209–1368
Mongol rule in China

1099
Crusaders seize
Jerusalem

1206
Delhi sultanate in India

1258
Mongols sack Baghdad

1453
Ottoman Empire
conquers Constantinople

1095–ca. 1300
Crusades to the Holy Land

1453
Ottoman Turks take Constantinople;
end of Byzantine Empire

12th century
Christian Ethiopia constructs
monolithic churches at Lalibela

1204
Crusaders sack
Constantinople

1346–1350
Black Death in Europe

1237–1480
Mongol rule in Russia

1492
Columbus crosses the Atlantic; Christian reconquest of Muslim Spain completed

12th century
Construction of rock-hewn churches in Lalibela, Ethiopia

1324–1325 High point of Kingdom of Mali; Mansa Musa pilgrimage to Mecca

1250–1350
Kingdom of Zimbabwe

15th century
African contact with Portuguese and Chinese maritime voyages

15th century
Flourishing of Aztec and Inca empires

860–1130
Chaco culture among the Ancestral Pueblo

1200
Human occupation of New Zealand; extinction of large flightless birds

279

UNDERSTANDING AP® THEMES
IN PART THREE

Regional and Interregional Interactions

Part Three of this text corresponds to Period 3 of the AP® course outline and constitutes 20 percent of the AP® exam. Here we will focus our attention on both the disparate histories of various civilizations and societies during the third-wave era (600–1450) and the connections and common patterns that linked them to one another. You will see that Chapters 7 and 11 are structured thematically, with Chapter 7 exploring the cross-cultural interactions born of long-distance trade and Chapter 11 probing the world of pastoralism with a particular focus on the Mongols and their encounters with major Eurasian civilizations. Sandwiched between the thematic landscapes, Chapters 8, 9, and 10 examine Chinese, Islamic, and Christian civilizations in a regional and comparative manner, with an eye on their engagement in larger patterns of Afro-Eurasian historical development. Chapter 12 then provides a global view of the fifteenth century. It serves to review the human journey thus far and to establish a benchmark from which the enormous transformations of following centuries might be assessed.

Environment	Cultures	State Building	Economies	Social Structures
Long-distance commerce and environmental variations	Spread of Buddhism in Asia	The development of Southeast Asian states	Silk Road trading networks	Slavery in West African civilizations
China and northern barbarians: interaction across an ecological frontier	Indian cultural influence in Southeast Asia	The development of Swahili city-states	Indian Ocean trading networks	Women in Song dynasty China
Ecological patterns in Arabia	Cross-cultural encounters and perceptions of "others"	The development of West African empires	Trans-Saharan trading networks	Comparing women's lives in Korea, Vietnam, and Japan
Islam's "Green Revolution"	Assimilation and resistance: Buddhism in China	State structure in Song and Tang China	Commercial networks in the Americas	Chinese elites at leisure
Ecology, agriculture, and technology in Europe	The rise of Islam	In the shadow of China: state building in Korea, Vietnam, and Japan	China's economic revolution	Women in Mongol-ruled China
Environmental effects of European economic growth in the Middle Ages	Cultural encounters: Islam in India, Anatolia, West Africa, and Spain	Rise and fragmentation of an Arab Empire	Chinese technological innovations	Men and women in early Islam
Pastoralism as an environmental adaptation	Christianity ■ Contraction in Asia and Africa ■ Expansion in Europe and Russia ■ Conflicts between Roman Catholic and Eastern Orthodox	The Byzantine state	Islam and the making of a hemispheric exchange network	Women and work in the emerging European civilization
Environmental effects of Mongol conquests		A new Russian state	European technological borrowing and innovation	European feudalism as a social system
Disease as a historical actor: the Black Death	Faith and reason in European Christianity	Rise of a state system in Europe	Comparing European and Chinese economic patterns	Urban societies in medieval Europe
Australian environmental adaptations	Cultural exchange in the Mongol Empire	The Crusades	Mongol Empire as a Eurasian economic network	Commonality and variation in pastoral societies
	Varying perceptions of the Mongols	Pastoral empires	Networks of connection in the 15th century	Women in pastoral societies
	Islam and the European Renaissance	The Mongol conquests: comparing China, Persia, and Russia		Social variations and gender roles in 15th-century societies
		Comparing 15th-century states: Chinese, European, Islamic world		Gender parallelism in the Aztec and Inca empires
		Comparing European and Chinese maritime voyages		Gender roles among the Iroquois
		Aztec and Inca empires		

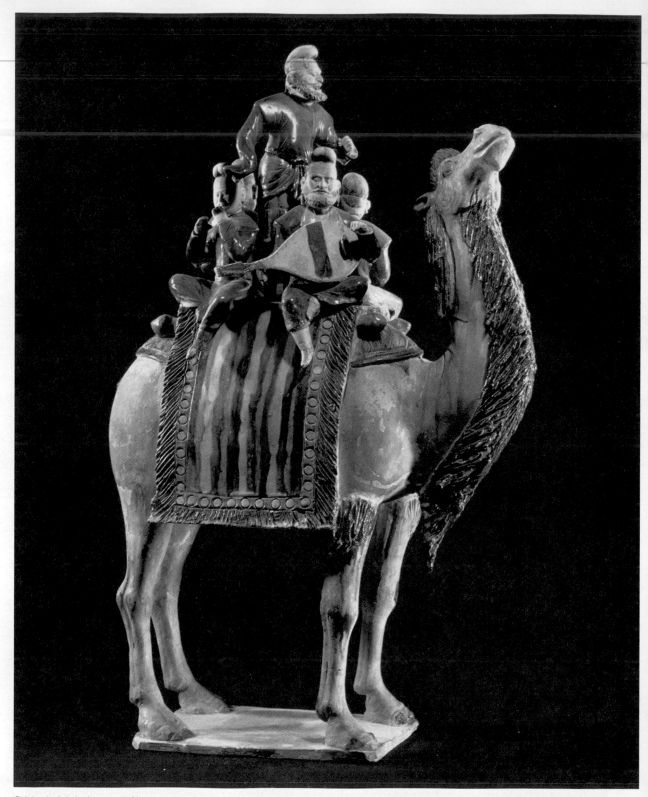

Commerce and Culture

600–1450

"In the spring of 2004, I was looking for an appropriate college graduation present for my son Ateesh and decided on an Apple iPod music player. . . . I placed my order online. . . . I was astonished by what followed. I received a confirmation e-mail within minutes . . . [and learned that] the product was being shipped not from California but from Shanghai, China. . . . Ateesh's personalized iPod landed on our New Haven [Connecticut] doorstep barely 40 hours after I had clicked 'Buy.'"[1] To Nayan Chanda, a fifty-eight-year-old journalist, born and educated in India and at the time working at Yale University, this was an astonishing transaction. Probably it was less surprising to his son. But both of them, no doubt, understood this kind of commercial exchange as something quite recent in human history.

And in the speed of the transaction, it surely was. But from the perspective of world history, exchange among distant peoples is not altogether new, and the roots of economic globalization lie deep in the past. In fact, just three years after purchasing his son's iPod, Nayan Chanda wrote a well-received book titled *Bound Together*, describing how traders, preachers, adventurers, and warriors had long created links among peoples living in widely separated cultures and civilizations. Those early transregional interactions and their capacity for transforming human societies, for better and for worse, played an increasingly significant role in this era of third-wave civilizations, a millennium of accelerating connections.

The exchange of goods among communities occupying different ecological zones has long been a prominent feature of human history. Coastlands and highlands, steppes and farmlands,

---

Travels on the Silk Road This Chinese ceramic figurine from the Tang dynasty (618–907 C.E.) shows a group of musicians riding on a camel along the famous Silk Road commercial network that long linked the civilizations of western and eastern Eurasia. The bearded figures represent Central Asian merchants, while the others depict Chinese.

islands and mainlands, valleys and mountains, deserts and forests—each generates different products. Furthermore, some societies have been able to monopolize, at least temporarily, the production of particular products—such as silk in China, certain spices in Southeast Asia, and incense in southern Arabia—that others have found valuable. This uneven distribution of goods and resources, whether natural or resulting from human activity, has long motivated exchange, not only within particular civilizations or regions but among them as well. In the world of 500 to 1500, long-distance trade became more important than ever before in linking and shaping distant societies and peoples. For the most part, it was indirect, a chain of separate transactions in which goods traveled farther than individual merchants. Nonetheless, a network of exchange and communication extending all across the Afro-Eurasian world, and separately in parts of the Americas as well, slowly came into being.

Why was trade important? How did it generate change within the societies that it connected? Economically speaking, commerce often altered consumption and shaped daily life. West Africans, for example, imported scarce salt, necessary for human diets and useful for seasoning and preserving food, from distant mines in the Sahara in exchange for the gold of their region. Over several millennia, incense such as frankincense and myrrh, grown in southern Arabia and the adjacent region of northern Somalia, found eager consumers in ancient Egypt and Babylon, India and China, Greece and Rome. Used for medicinal purposes, religious ceremonies, and as an antidote to the odors of unsanitary cities, incense also bore the "aroma of eros." "I have perfumed my bed with myrrh, aloes, and cinnamon," declared a harlot featured in the Old Testament book of Proverbs. "Come, let us take our fill of love till morning."[2] Trade also affected the working lives of many people, encouraging them to specialize in producing particular products for sale in distant markets rather than for use in their own communities.

Trade, in short, diminished the economic self-sufficiency of local societies, even as it altered the structure of those societies as well. Merchants often became a distinct social group, viewed with suspicion by others because of their impulse to accumulate wealth without actually producing anything themselves. In some societies, trade became a means of social mobility, as Chinese merchants, for example, were able to purchase landed estates and establish themselves within the gentry class. Long-distance trade also enabled elite groups in society to distinguish themselves from commoners by acquiring prestigious goods from a distance—silk, tortoiseshell, jade, rhinoceros horn, or particular feathers. The association with faraway or powerful societies, signaled by the possession of their luxury goods, often conveyed status in communities more remote from major civilizations.

Trade also had the capacity to transform political life. The wealth available from controlling and taxing trade motivated the creation of states in various parts of the world and sustained those states once they had been constructed. Furthermore, commerce posed a set of problems to governments everywhere. Should trade be left in private hands, as in the Aztec Empire, or should it be controlled by the state,

A MAP OF TIME

430 B.C.E.	Trade-borne disease enters Greece from Egypt
200 B.C.E.–200 C.E.	Initial flourishing of Silk Road commerce
By 1st century B.C.E.	Spread of Buddhism to Central Asian cities and northern China
Early centuries C.E.	Knowledge of monsoons enables expansion of Indian Ocean commerce
300–400 C.E.	Beginning of trans-Saharan trade
350	All-water route opened between India and China
6th century	Chinese monopoly on silk production broken
7th century	Rise of Islam
670–1025	Srivijaya kingdom
800–1300	Khmer kingdom of Angkor
1000–1500	Swahili civilization along East African coast
13th and 14th centuries	Mongol Empire revitalizes Silk Road commerce
1250–1350	Kingdom of Zimbabwe in southeastern Africa
1275–1292	Marco Polo in China
1346–1350	Black Death enters Europe via transcontinental trade routes
1354	Ibn Battuta visits West Africa
15th century	Aztec and Inca empires facilitate commercial exchange in the Americas

as in the Inca Empire? How should state authorities deal with men of commerce, who were both economically useful and potentially disruptive?

Moreover, the saddlebags of camel caravans or the cargo holds of merchant vessels carried more than goods. Trade became a vehicle for the spread of religious ideas, technological innovations, disease-bearing germs, and plants and animals to regions far from their places of origin. In just this fashion, Buddhism made its way from India to Central and East Asia, and Islam crossed the Sahara into West Africa. So did the pathogens that devastated much of Eurasia during the Black Death. These immense cultural and biological transformations were among the most significant outcomes of the increasingly dense network of long-distance commerce during the era of third-wave civilizations.

SEEKING THE MAIN POINT

In what ways did long-distance commerce act as a motor of change in premodern world history?

Silk Roads: Exchange across Eurasia

AP® EXAM TIP

The goods, ideas, technology, and peoples that traveled the Silks Roads, and their effects on Eurasian cultures, are "must know" information for success on the AP® exam.

The Eurasian landmass has long been home to the majority of humankind as well as to the world's most productive agriculture, largest civilizations, and greatest concentration of pastoral peoples. Beyond its many separate societies and cultures, Eurasia also gave rise to one of the world's most extensive and sustained networks of exchange among its diverse peoples. Known as the Silk Roads, a reference to their most famous product, these land-based trade routes linked pastoral and agricultural peoples as well as the large civilizations on the continent's outer rim (see Map 7.1). None of its numerous participants knew the full extent of this network's reach, for it was largely a "relay trade" in which goods were passed down the line, changing hands many times before reaching their final destination. Nonetheless, the Silk Roads provide a certain unity and coherence to Eurasian history alongside the distinct stories of its separate civilizations and peoples.

The Growth of the Silk Roads

The beginnings of the Silk Roads lay in both geography and history. As a geographic unit, Eurasia is often divided into inner and outer zones that represent quite different environments. Outer Eurasia consists of relatively warm, well-watered areas, suitable for agriculture, which provided the setting for the great civilizations of China, India, the Middle East, and the Mediterranean. Inner Eurasia—the lands of eastern Russia and Central Asia—lies farther north and has a harsher and drier climate, much of it not conducive to agriculture. Herding their animals from horseback, the pastoral people of this region had for centuries traded with and raided their agricultural neighbors to the south. Products of the forest and of semi-arid northern grasslands known as the steppes—such as hides, furs, livestock, wool, and amber—were exchanged for the agricultural products and manufactured goods of adjacent civilizations. The movement of pastoral peoples for thousands of years also served to diffuse Indo-European languages, bronze metallurgy, horse-based technologies, and more all across Eurasia.

Guided Reading Question

■ CHANGE
What lay behind the emergence of Silk Road commerce, and what kept it going for so many centuries?

    The construction of the second-wave civilizations and their imperial states during the last five centuries B.C.E. added another element to these earlier Eurasian connections. From the south, the Persian Empire invaded the territory of pastoral peoples in present-day Turkmenistan and Uzbekistan. From the west, Alexander the Great's empire stretched well into Central Asia. From the east, China's Han dynasty extended its authority westward, seeking to control the nomadic Xiongnu and to gain access to the powerful "heavenly horses" that were so important to Chinese military forces. By the early centuries of the Common Era, indirect trading connections, often brokered by pastoral peoples, linked these Eurasian civilizations in a network of transcontinental exchange.

    Silk Road trading networks prospered most when large and powerful states provided security for merchants and travelers. Such conditions prevailed during the second-wave era when the Roman and Chinese empires anchored long-distance commerce at the western and eastern ends of Eurasia. Silk Road trade flourished again during the seventh and eighth centuries C.E. as the Byzantine Empire, the Muslim Abbasid (ah-BAH-sihd) dynasty, and Tang dynasty China created an almost continuous belt of strong states across Eurasia. In the thirteenth and fourteenth centuries, the Mongol Empire briefly encompassed almost the entire route of the Silk Roads in a single state, giving a renewed vitality to long-distance trade. Over many centuries, various technological innovations, such as yokes, saddles, and stirrups, made the use of camels, horses, and oxen more effective means of transportation across the vast distances of the Silk Roads.

Goods in Transit

During prosperous times especially, a vast array of goods (detailed in the Snapshot on page 286) made its way across the Silk Roads, often carried in large camel caravans that traversed the harsh and dangerous steppes, deserts, and oases of Central Asia. In high demand and hard to find, most of these goods were luxury products, destined for an elite and wealthy market, rather than staple goods, for only readily moved commodities of great value could compensate for the high costs of transportation across such long and forbidding distances.

Of all these luxury goods, it was silk that came to symbolize this Eurasian network of exchange. From the time of silk's origin in China, by 3000 B.C.E. or earlier,

Map 7.1
The Silk Roads

For 2,000 years, goods, ideas, technologies, and diseases made their way across Eurasia on the several routes of the Silk Roads.

AP® EXAM TIP

Know the relationships between governments and trade routes across time and place.

SNAPSHOT   Economic Exchange along the Silk Roads

Region	Products Contributed to Silk Road Commerce
China	silk, bamboo, mirrors, gunpowder, paper, rhubarb, ginger, lacquerware, chrysanthemums
Forest lands of Siberia and grasslands of Central Asia	furs, walrus tusks, amber, livestock, horses, falcons, hides, copper vessels, tents, saddles, slaves
India	cotton textiles, herbal medicine, precious stones, spices, pepper, pearls, ebony
Middle East	dates, nuts, dried fruit, dyes, lapis lazuli, swords
Mediterranean basin	gold coins, glassware, glazes, grapevines, jewelry, artworks, perfume, wool and linen textiles, olive oil

that civilization long held a monopoly on its production. After 300 B.C.E. or so, that precious fabric increasingly found a growing market all across the linked commercial network of the Afro-Eurasian world. Although the silk trade itself was largely in the hands of men, women figured hugely in the process in terms of both supply and demand. For many centuries, Chinese women, mostly in rural areas, were responsible for every step of the ingenious and laborious enterprise of silk production. They tended the mulberry trees on whose leaves silkworms fed; they unwound the cocoons in very hot water to extract the long silk fibers; they turned these fibers into thread and wove them into textiles. Thus Chinese homes became the primary site of textile production with rural women as its main labor force. By the time of the Tang dynasty (618–907 C.E.), women were making a large contribution to the household economy, to technological innovation in the silk industry, and to the state, which depended heavily on peasant taxes, often paid in cloth. Despite these contributions, many rural families persisted in poverty, as the thirteenth-century writer Wen-hsiang indicated:

> The silkworms have finished their third sleep and are famished. The family is poor, without cash to buy the mulberry leaves to feed them. What can they do? Hungry silkworms do not produce silk. . . . The daughter is twenty but does not have wedding clothes. Those the government sends to collect taxes are like tigers. If they have no clothes to dress their daughter, they can put the [wedding] off. If they have no silk to turn over to the government, they will go bankrupt.[3]

Elite Chinese women, and their men as well, also furnished part of the demand for these luxurious fabrics, which marked their high status. So too did Chinese officials, who required huge quantities of silk to exchange for much-needed horses and to buy off "barbarian" invaders from the north. Beyond China, women in many cultures ardently sought Chinese silk for its comfort and its value as a fashion

Guided Reading Question

■ SIGNIFICANCE
What made silk such a highly desired commodity across Eurasia?

statement. The demand for silk, as well as for cotton textiles from India, was so great in the Roman Empire that various Roman writers were appalled at the drain of resources that it represented. They also were outraged at the moral impact of wearing revealing silk garments. "I can see clothes of silk," lamented Seneca the Younger in the first century C.E., "if materials that do not hide the body, nor even one's decency, can be called clothes. . . . Wretched flocks of maids labour so that the adulteress may be visible through her thin dress, so that her husband has no more acquaintance than any outsider or foreigner with his wife's body."[4]

By the sixth century C.E., the knowledge and technology for producing raw silk had spread beyond China. An old Chinese story attributes it to a Chinese princess who smuggled out silkworms in her turban when she was married off to a Central Asian ruler. In a European version of the tale, Christian monks living in China did the deed by hiding some silkworms in a bamboo cane, an act of industrial espionage that allowed an independent silk-producing and silk-weaving industry to take hold in the Byzantine Empire. However it happened, Koreans, Japanese, Indians, and Persians likewise learned how to produce this precious fabric.

As the supply of silk increased, its many varieties circulated even more extensively across Afro-Eurasian trade routes. In Central Asia, silk was used as currency and as a means of accumulating wealth. In both China and the Byzantine Empire, silk became a symbol of high status, and governments passed laws that restricted silk clothing to members of the elite. Furthermore, silk became associated with the sacred in the expanding world religions of Buddhism and Christianity. Chinese Buddhist pilgrims who made their way to India seeking religious texts and relics took with them large quantities of silk as gifts to the monasteries they visited. Buddhist monks in China received purple silk robes from Tang dynasty emperors as a sign of high honor. In the world of Christendom, silk wall hangings, altar covers, and vestments became highly prestigious signs of devotion and piety. Because no independent silk industry developed in Western Europe until the twelfth century C.E., a considerable market developed for silks imported from the Islamic world. Ironically, the splendor of Christian churches depended in part on Islamic trading networks and on silks manufactured in the Muslim world. Some of those silks were even inscribed with passages in Arabic from the Quran, unbeknownst to their European buyers.[5] By the twelfth century, the West African king of Ghana was wearing silk, and that fabric circulated in Egypt, Ethiopia, and along the East African coast as well.

Compared to contemporary global commerce, the volume of trade on the Silk Roads was modest, and its focus on luxury goods limited its direct impact on most people. Nonetheless, it had important economic and social consequences. Peasants in the Yangzi River delta of southern China sometimes gave up the cultivation of food crops, choosing to focus instead on producing silk, paper, porcelain, lacquerware, or iron tools, many of which were destined for the markets of the Silk Roads. In this way, the impact of long-distance trade trickled down to affect the lives of ordinary farmers. Furthermore, favorably placed individuals could benefit immensely

AP® EXAM TIP

The AP® exam often includes questions that ask you to compare features of Han China to those of Imperial Rome.

AP® EXAM TIP

You should know that the goods transported along the Silk Roads focused on luxury items.

Guided Reading Question

■ **CONNECTION**
What were the major economic, social, and cultural consequences of Silk Road commerce?

from long-distance trade. The twelfth-century Persian merchant Ramisht made a personal fortune from his long-distance trading business and with his profits purchased an enormously expensive silk covering for the Kaaba, the central shrine of Islam in Mecca.

Cultures in Transit

AP® EXAM TIP

Understanding that Buddhism, like other major religions, spread along trade routes is fundamental to success on the AP® exam.

More important even than the economic impact of the Silk Roads was their role as a conduit of culture. Buddhism in particular, a cultural product of Indian civilization, spread widely throughout Central and East Asia, owing much to the activities of merchants along the Silk Roads. From its beginnings in India during the sixth century B.C.E., Buddhism had appealed to merchants, who preferred its universal message to that of a Brahmin-dominated Hinduism that privileged the higher castes. Indian traders and Buddhist monks, sometimes supported by rulers such as Ashoka, brought the new religion to the trans-Eurasian trade routes. To the west, Persian Zoroastrianism largely blocked the spread of Buddhism, but in the oasis cities of Central Asia, such as Merv, Samarkand, Khotan, and Dunhuang, Buddhism quickly took hold. By the first century B.C.E., many of the inhabitants of these towns had converted to Buddhism, and foreign merchant communities soon introduced it to northern China as well.

Guided Reading Question

■ CHANGE
What accounted for the spread of Buddhism along the Silk Roads?

Particularly important in this process were the Sogdians, a Central Asian people, whose merchants established an enduring network of exchange with China. Two such Sogdians, living in China during the second century C.E., were instrumental in translating Sanskrit Buddhist texts into Chinese. Sogdians dominated Silk Road trade for much of the first millennium C.E., and their language became a medium of communication all along that commercial network. In their Central Asian homeland, however, Sogdians practiced Zoroastrianism, Manichaeism, and local traditions as well as Buddhism.

AP® EXAM TIP

Know examples of merchant groups who traveled far from their homes along trade routes, like the Sogdians.

Conversion to Buddhism in the oasis cities was a voluntary process, without the pressure of conquest or foreign rule. Dependent on long-distance trade, the inhabitants and rulers of those sophisticated and prosperous cities found in Buddhism a link to the larger, wealthy, and prestigious civilization of India. Well-to-do Buddhist merchants could earn religious merit by building monasteries and supporting monks. The monasteries in turn provided convenient and culturally familiar places of rest and resupply for merchants making the long and arduous trek across Central Asia. Many of these cities became cosmopolitan centers of learning and commerce. Scholars have found thousands of Buddhist texts in the city of Dunhuang, where several branches of the Silk Roads joined to enter western China, together with hundreds of cave temples, lavishly decorated with murals and statues.

Outside of the oasis communities, Buddhism progressed only slowly among pastoral peoples of Central Asia. The absence of a written language was an obstacle to the penetration of a highly literate religion, and their nomadic ways made the founding of monasteries, so important to Buddhism, quite difficult. But as pastoralists became involved in long-distance trade or came to rule settled agricultural

Dunhuang
Located in western China at a critical junction of the Silk Road trading network, Dunhuang was also a center of Buddhist learning, painting, and sculpture as that religion made its way from India to China and beyond. In some 492 caves, carved out of the rock between about 400 and 1400 C.E., a remarkable gallery of Buddhist art has been preserved, of which this painting is but one example. (Steve Vidler/© Prisma Bildagentur AG/Alamy)

peoples, Buddhism seemed more attractive. The nomadic Jie people, who controlled much of northern China after the collapse of the Han dynasty, are a case in point. Their ruler in the early fourth century C.E., Shi Le, became acquainted with a Central Asian Buddhist monk called Fotudeng, who had traveled widely on the Silk Roads. The monk's reputation as a miracle worker, a rainmaker, and a fortune-teller and his skills as a military strategist cemented a personal relationship with Shi Le and led to the conversions of thousands and the construction of hundreds of Buddhist temples. In China itself, Buddhism remained for many centuries a religion of foreign merchants or foreign rulers. Only slowly did it become popular among the Chinese themselves, a process examined more closely in Chapter 8.

As Buddhism spread across the Silk Roads from India to Central Asia, China, and beyond, it also changed. The original faith had shunned the material world, but Buddhist monasteries in the rich oasis towns of the Silk Roads found themselves very much involved in secular affairs. Some of them became quite wealthy, receiving gifts from well-to-do merchants, artisans, and local rulers. The begging bowls of the monks became a symbol rather than a daily activity. Sculptures and murals in the monasteries depicted musicians and acrobats, women applying makeup, and even drinking parties.

Doctrines changed as well. It was the more devotional Mahayana form of Buddhism (see Chapter 4) — featuring the Buddha as a deity, numerous bodhisattvas, an emphasis on compassion, and the possibility of earning merit—that flourished on the Silk Roads, rather than the more austere psychological teachings of the original Buddha. Moreover, Buddhism picked up elements of other cultures while in transit on the Silk Roads. In the Sogdian city of Samarkand, the use of Zoroastrian fire rituals apparently became a part of Buddhist practice. And in the area northwest of India that had been influenced by the invasions of Alexander the Great, statues of the Buddha reveal distinctly Greek influences. The Greco-Roman mythological figure of Heracles, the son of Zeus and a figure associated with great strength, courage, masculinity, and sexual prowess, was used to represent Vajrapani, one of the divine protectors of the Buddha. In a similar way, the gods of many peoples along the Silk Roads were incorporated into Buddhist practice as bodhisattvas.

Disease in Transit

AP® EXAM TIP

The spread of diseases across trade routes in different places and eras is an important concept in AP® World History.

Guided Reading Question

■ **CONNECTION**
What was the impact of disease along the Silk Roads?

Beyond goods and cultures, diseases too traveled the trade routes of Eurasia, and with devastating consequences. Each of the major population centers of the Afro-Eurasian world had developed characteristic disease patterns, mechanisms for dealing with them, and in some cases immunity to them. But when contact among previously isolated human communities occurred, people were exposed to unfamiliar diseases for which they had little immunity or few effective methods of coping. The epidemics that followed often brought suffering and death on an enormous scale to rich and poor alike. An early example involved the Greek city-state of Athens, which in 430–429 B.C.E. was suddenly afflicted by a new and still-unidentified infectious disease that had entered Greece via seaborne trade from Egypt, killing perhaps 25 percent of its army and permanently weakening the city-state.

Even more widespread diseases affected the Roman Empire and Han dynasty China as the Silk Roads promoted contact all across Eurasia. Smallpox and measles devastated the populations of both empires, contributing to their political collapse. Paradoxically, these disasters may well have strengthened the appeal of Christianity in Europe and Buddhism in China, for both of them offered compassion in the face of immense suffering.

Again in the period between 534 and 750 C.E., intermittent outbreaks of bubonic plague ravaged the coastal areas of the Mediterranean Sea as the black rats that carried the disease arrived via the seaborne trade with India, where they originally lived. What followed was catastrophic. Constantinople, the capital city of the Byzantine Empire, lost thousands of people per day during a forty-day period in 534 C.E., according to a contemporary historian. Disease played an important role in preventing Byzantium from reintegrating Italy into its version of a renewed Roman Empire encompassing the Mediterranean basin. The repeated recurrence of the disease over the next several centuries also weakened the ability of Christendom to resist Muslim armies from Arabia in the seventh century C.E.

The most well-known dissemination of disease was associated with the Mongol Empire, which briefly unified much of the Eurasian landmass during the thirteenth and fourteenth centuries C.E. (see Chapter 11). That era of intensified interaction facilitated the spread of the Black Death—identified variously with the bubonic plague, anthrax, or a package of epidemic diseases—from China to Europe. Its consequences were enormous. Between 1346 and 1348, up to half of the population of Europe perished from the plague. "A dead man," wrote the Italian writer Boccaccio, "was then of no more account than a dead goat."⁶ Despite the terrible human toll, some among the living benefited. Tenant farmers and urban workers, now in short supply, could demand higher wages or better terms. Some landowning nobles, on the other hand, were badly hurt as the price of their grains dropped and the demands of their dependents grew.

A similar death toll afflicted China and parts of the Islamic world. The Central Asian steppes, home to many nomadic peoples, including the Mongols, also suffered terribly, undermining Mongol rule and permanently altering the balance between pastoral and agricultural peoples to the advantage of settled farmers. In these and many other ways, disease carried by long-distance trade shaped the lives of millions and altered their historical development. (See Chapter 11 for more on the Black Death.)

In the long run of world history, the exchange of diseases gave Europeans a certain advantage when they confronted the peoples of the Western Hemisphere after 1500. Exposure over time had provided them with some degree of immunity to Eurasian diseases. In the Americas, however, the absence of domesticated animals, the less intense interaction among major centers of population, and isolation from the Eastern Hemisphere ensured that native peoples had little defense against the diseases of Europe and Africa. Thus, when their societies were suddenly confronted by Europeans and Africans from across the Atlantic, they perished in appalling numbers. Such was the long-term outcome of the very different histories of the two hemispheres.

Sea Roads: Exchange across the Indian Ocean

If the Silk Roads linked Eurasian societies by land, sea-based trade routes likewise connected distant peoples all across the Eastern Hemisphere. For example, since the days of the Phoenicians, Greeks, and Romans, the Mediterranean Sea had been an avenue of maritime commerce throughout the region, a pattern that continued during the third-wave era. The Italian city of Venice emerged by 1000 C.E. as a major center of that commercial network, with its ships and merchants active in the Mediterranean and Black seas as well as on the Atlantic coast. Much of its wealth derived from control of expensive and profitable imported goods from Asia, many of which came up the Red Sea through the Egyptian port of Alexandria. There Venetian merchants picked up those goods and resold them throughout the Mediterranean basin. This type of transregional exchange linked the maritime commerce of the Mediterranean Sea to the much larger and more extensive network of seaborne trade in the Indian Ocean basin.

Until the creation of a genuinely global oceanic system of trade after 1500, the Indian Ocean represented the world's largest sea-based system of communication

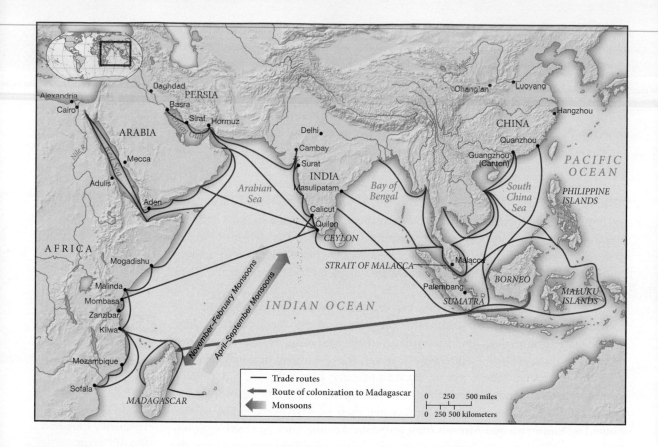

Map 7.2
The Sea Roads

Paralleling the Silk Road trading network, a sea-based commerce in the Indian Ocean basin connected the many peoples between China and East Africa.

and exchange, stretching from southern China to eastern Africa (see Map 7.2). Like the Silk Roads, these transoceanic trade routes—the Sea Roads—also grew out of the vast environmental and cultural diversities of the region. The desire for various goods not available at home—such as porcelain from China, spices from the islands of Southeast Asia, cotton goods and pepper from India, ivory and gold from the East African coast, incense from southern Arabia—provided incentives for Indian Ocean commerce. Transportation costs were lower on the Sea Roads than on the Silk Roads because ships could accommodate larger and heavier cargoes than camels. This meant that the Sea Roads could eventually carry more bulk goods and products destined for a mass market—textiles, pepper, timber, rice, sugar, wheat—whereas the Silk Roads were limited largely to luxury goods for the few.

What made Indian Ocean commerce possible were the monsoons, alternating wind currents that blew predictably northeast during the summer months and southwest during the winter (see Map 7.2). An understanding of monsoons and a gradually accumulating technology of shipbuilding and oceanic navigation drew on the ingenuity of many peoples—Chinese, Malays, Indians, Arabs, Swahilis, and others. Collectively they made "an interlocked human world joined by the common highway of the Indian Ocean."[7]

But this world of Indian Ocean commerce did not occur between entire regions and certainly not between "countries," even though historians sometimes write about India, Indonesia, Southeast Asia, or East Africa as a matter of shorthand or convenience. It operated rather across an "archipelago of towns" whose merchants often had more in common with one another than with the people of their own hinterlands.[8] These urban centers, strung out around the entire Indian Ocean basin, provided the nodes of this widespread commercial network.

Weaving the Web of an Indian Ocean World

The world of Indian Ocean commerce was long in the making, dating back to the time of the First Civilizations. Seaborne trade via the Persian Gulf between ancient Mesopotamia and the Indus Valley civilization is reflected in archeological finds in both places. Perhaps the still-undeciphered Indian writing system was stimulated by Sumerian cuneiform. The ancient Egyptians, and later the Phoenicians, likewise traded down the Red Sea, exchanging their manufactured goods for gold, ivory, frankincense, and slaves from the coasts of Ethiopia, Somalia, and southern Arabia. These ventures mostly hugged the coast and took place over short distances. Malay sailors, however, were an exception to this rule. Speaking Austronesian languages, they jumped off from the islands of present-day Indonesia during the first millennium B.C.E. and made their way in double-outrigger canoes across thousands of miles of open ocean to the East African island of Madagascar. There they introduced their language and their crops—bananas, coconuts, and taro—which soon spread to the mainland, where they greatly enriched the diets of African peoples. Also finding its way to the continent was a Malayo-Polynesian xylophone, which is still played in parts of Africa today. A casualty of this migration, coupled with the later arrival of Bantu-speaking Africans, was the extinction of the "elephant bird," a huge flightless bird weighing up to 600 pounds and found only in Madagascar.

The tempo of Indian Ocean commerce picked up in the era of second-wave civilizations during the early centuries of the Common Era, as mariners learned how to ride the monsoons. Various technological innovations also facilitated Indian Ocean trade—improvements in sails, new kinds of ships called junks with sternpost rudders and keels for greater stability, new means of calculating latitude such as the astrolabe, and evolving versions of the magnetic needle or compass. Around the time of Christ, the Greek geographer Strabo reported that "great fleets [from the Roman Empire] are sent as far as India, whence the most valuable cargoes are brought back to Egypt and thence exported again to other places."[9] Merchants from the Roman world, mostly Greeks, Syrians, and Jews, established settlements in southern India and along the East African coast. The introduction of Christianity into both Axum and Kerala (in southern India) testifies to the long-term cultural impact of that trade. In the eastern Indian Ocean and the South China Sea, Chinese and Southeast Asian merchants likewise generated a growing commerce, and by 100 C.E. Chinese traders had reached India.

AP® EXAM TIP

Study the map on the opposite page closely. You must know the effects of the monsoon winds on trade in the Indian Ocean. You should also know that, like on the Silk Roads, people from many different societies participated in exchanges in the Indian Ocean network.

AP® EXAM TIP

Take note of the technological developments that aided Indian Ocean trade.

SNAPSHOT   Economic Exchange In the Indian Ocean Basin

Region	Products Contributed to Indian Ocean Commerce
Mediterranean basin	ceramics, glassware, wine, gold, olive oil
East Africa	ivory, gold, iron goods, slaves, tortoiseshells, quartz, leopard skins
Arabia	frankincense, myrrh, perfumes
India	grain, ivory, precious stones, cotton textiles, spices, timber, tortoiseshells
Southeast Asia	tin, sandalwood, cloves, nutmeg, mace
China	silks, porcelain, tea

Guided Reading Question

■ CHANGE
What lay behind the flourishing of Indian Ocean commerce in the postclassical millennium?

The fulcrum of this growing commercial network lay in India itself. Its ports bulged with goods from both west and east, as illustrated in the Snapshot above. Its merchants were in touch with Southeast Asia by the first century C.E., and settled communities of Indian traders appeared throughout the Indian Ocean basin and as far away as Alexandria in Egypt. Indian cultural practices, such as Hinduism and Buddhism, as well as South Asian political ideas began to take root in Southeast Asia.

In the era of third-wave civilizations between 500 and 1500, two major processes changed the landscape of the Afro-Eurasian world and wove the web of Indian Ocean exchange even more densely than before. One was the economic and political revival of China, some four centuries after the collapse of the Han dynasty (see Chapter 8). Especially during the Tang and Song dynasties (618–1279), China reestablished an effective and unified state, which actively encouraged maritime trade. Furthermore, the impressive growth of the Chinese economy sent Chinese products pouring into the circuits of Indian Ocean commerce, while providing a vast and attractive market for Indian and Southeast Asian goods. Chinese technological innovations, such as larger ships and the magnetic compass, likewise added to the momentum of commercial growth.

A second transformation in the world of Indian Ocean commerce involved the sudden rise of Islam in the seventh century C.E. and its subsequent spread across much of the Afro-Eurasian world (see Chapter 9). Unlike Confucian culture, which was quite suspicious of merchants, Islam was friendly to commercial life; the Prophet Muhammad himself had been a trader. The creation of an Arab Empire, stretching from the Atlantic Ocean through the Mediterranean basin and all the way to India, brought together in a single political system an immense range of economies and cultural traditions and provided a vast arena for the energies of Muslim traders.

Those energies greatly intensified commercial activity in the Indian Ocean basin. Middle Eastern gold and silver flowed into southern India to purchase pepper, pearls, textiles, and gemstones. Muslim merchants and sailors, as well as Jews and Christians living within the Islamic world, established communities of traders from East Africa to the south China coast. Efforts to reclaim wasteland in Mesopotamia to produce sugar and dates for export stimulated a slave trade from East Africa, which landed thousands of Africans in southern Iraq to work on plantations and in salt mines under horrendous conditions. A massive fifteen-year revolt (868–883) among these slaves badly disrupted the Islamic Abbasid Empire before that rebellion was brutally crushed.

Beyond these specific outcomes, the expansion of Islam gave rise to an international maritime culture by 1000, shared by individuals living in the widely separated port cities around the Indian Ocean. The immense prestige, power, and prosperity of the Islamic world stimulated widespread conversion, which in turn facilitated commercial transactions. Even those who did not convert to Islam, such as Buddhist rulers in Burma, nonetheless regarded it as commercially useful to assume Muslim names. Thus was created "a maritime Silk Road . . . a commercial and informational network of unparalleled proportions."[10] After 1000, the culture of this network was increasingly Islamic.

Sea Roads as a Catalyst for Change: Southeast Asia

Oceanic commerce transformed all of its participants in one way or another, but nowhere more so than in Southeast Asia and East Africa, at opposite ends of the Indian Ocean network. In both regions, trade stimulated political change as ambitious or aspiring rulers used the wealth derived from commerce to construct larger and more centrally governed states or cities. Both areas likewise experienced cultural change as local people were attracted to foreign religious ideas from Confucian, Hindu, Buddhist, or Islamic sources. As on the Silk Roads, trade was a conduit for culture.

Located between the major civilizations of China and India, Southeast Asia was situated by geography to play an important role in the evolving world of Indian Ocean commerce. During the third-wave era, a series of cities and states or kingdoms emerged on both the islands and mainland of Southeast Asia, representing new civilizations in this vast region (see Map 7.3). That process paralleled a similar development of new civilizations in East and West Africa, Japan, Russia, and Western Europe in what was an Afro-Eurasian phenomenon. In Southeast Asia, many of those new societies were stimulated and decisively shaped by their interaction with the sea-based trade of the Indian Ocean.[11]

The case of Srivijaya (SREE-vih-juh-yuh) illustrates the connection between commerce and state building. When Malay sailors, long active in the waters around Southeast Asia, opened an all-sea route between India and China through the Straits of Malacca around 350 C.E., the many small ports along the Malay Peninsula and the coast of Sumatra began to compete intensely to attract the growing number of traders and travelers making their way through the straits. From this competition emerged the Malay kingdom of Srivijaya, which dominated this critical choke

Guided Reading Question

■ CONNECTION
In what ways did Indian influence register in Southeast Asia?

Map 7.3   Southeast Asia, ca. 1200 C.E.

Both mainland and island Southeast Asia were centrally involved in the commerce of the Indian Ocean basin, and both were transformed by that experience.

point of Indian Ocean trade from 670 to 1025. A number of factors—Srivijaya's plentiful supply of gold; its access to the source of highly sought-after spices, such as cloves, nutmeg, and mace; and the taxes levied on passing ships—provided resources to attract supporters, to fund an embryonic bureaucracy, and to create the military and naval forces that brought some security to the area.

The inland states on the mainland of Southeast Asia, whose economies were based more on domestically produced rice than on international trade, nonetheless participated in the commerce of the region. The state of Funan, which flourished during the first six centuries of the Common Era in what is now southern Vietnam and eastern Cambodia, hosted merchants from both India and China. Archeologists have found Roman coins as well as trade goods from Persia, Central Asia, and Arabia in the ruins of its ancient cities. The Khmer kingdom of Angkor (flourished 800–1300) exported exotic forest products, receiving in return Chinese and Indian handicrafts, while welcoming a considerable community of Chinese merchants. Traders from Champa in what is now central and southern Vietnam operated in China, Java, and elsewhere, practicing piracy when trade dried up. Champa's effort to control the trade between China and Southeast Asia provoked warfare with its commercial rivals.

Beyond the exchange of goods, commercial connections served to spread elements of Indian culture across much of Southeast Asia, even as Vietnam was incorporated into the Chinese sphere of influence. (See Chapter 8 for more on Chinese influence in Vietnam.) Indian alphabets such as Sanskrit and Pallava were used to write a number of Southeast Asian languages. Indian artistic forms provided models for Southeast Asian sculpture and architecture, while the Indian epic *Ramayana* became widely popular across the region.

Politically, Southeast Asian rulers and elites found attractive the Indian belief that leaders were god-kings, perhaps reincarnations of a Buddha or the Hindu deity Shiva, while the idea of karma conveyed legitimacy to the rich and powerful based on their moral behavior in earlier lives. Srivijayan monarchs, for example, employed Indians as advisers, clerks, or officials and assigned Sanskrit titles to their subordinates. The capital city of Palembang was a cosmopolitan place, where even the parrots were said to speak four languages. While these rulers drew on indigenous beliefs that chiefs possessed magical powers and were responsible for the prosperity of their people, they also made use of imported Indian political ideas and Buddhist religious concepts, which provided a "higher level of magic" for rulers as well as the prestige of association with Indian civilization.[12] They also sponsored the creation of images of the Buddha and various bodhisattvas whose faces resembled those of deceased kings and were inscribed with traditional curses against anyone who would destroy them. Srivijaya grew into a major center of Buddhist observance and teaching, attracting thousands of monks and students from throughout the Buddhist world. The seventh-century Chinese monk Yi Jing was so impressed that he advised Buddhist monks headed for India to study first in Srivijaya for several years.

Elsewhere as well, elements of Indian culture took hold in Southeast Asia. The Sailendra kingdom in central Java, an agriculturally rich region closely allied with Srivijaya, mounted a massive building program between the eighth and tenth centuries featuring Hindu temples and Buddhist monuments. The most famous, known as Borobudur, is an enormous mountain-shaped structure of ten levels, with a three-mile walkway and elaborate carvings illustrating the spiritual journey from ignorance and illusion to full enlightenment. The largest Buddhist monument anywhere in the world, it is nonetheless a distinctly Javanese creation, whose carved figures have Javanese features and whose scenes are clearly set in Java, not India. Its shape resonated with an ancient Southeast Asian veneration of mountains as sacred places and the abode of ancestral spirits. Borobudur represents the process of Buddhism becoming culturally grounded in a new place.

Hinduism too, though not an explicitly missionary religion, found a place in Southeast Asia. It was well rooted in the Champa kingdom, for example, where Shiva was worshipped, cows were honored, and phallic imagery was prominent. But it was in the prosperous and powerful Angkor kingdom of the twelfth century C.E. that Hinduism found its most stunning architectural expression in the temple complex known as Angkor Wat. The largest religious structure in the premodern

Borobudur

This huge Buddhist monument, constructed probably in the ninth century C.E., was subsequently abandoned and covered with layers of volcanic ash and vegetation as Java came under Islamic influence. It was rediscovered by British colonial authorities in the early nineteenth century and has undergone several restorations over the past two centuries. Although Indonesia is a largely Muslim country, its small Buddhist minority still celebrates the Buddha's birthday at Borobudur. (© Luca Tettoni/ Robert Harding World Imagery/ Alamy)

AP® EXAM TIP

Angkor Wat and the temple of Borobudur are examples of architecture influenced by religion.

Angkor Wat
Constructed in the early twelfth century, the Angkor Wat complex was designed as a state temple, dedicated to the Hindu god Vishnu and lavishly decorated with carved bas-reliefs depicting scenes from Hindu mythology. By the late thirteenth century, it was in use by Buddhists, as it is to this day. This photo shows a small section of the temple and three Buddhist monks in their saffron robes. (© Jose Fuste Raga/Corbis)

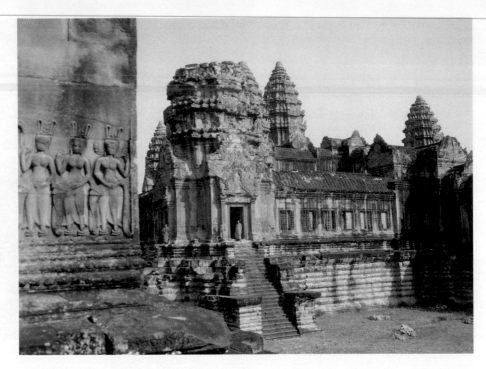

world, it sought to express a Hindu understanding of the cosmos, centered on a mythical Mount Meru, the home of the gods in Hindu tradition. Later, it was used by Buddhists as well, with little sense of contradiction. To the west of Angkor, the state of Pagan likewise devoted enormous resources to shrines, temples, and libraries inspired by both Hindu and Buddhist faiths.

This extensive Indian influence in Southeast Asia has led some scholars to speak of the "Indianization" of the region, similar perhaps to the earlier spread of Greek culture within the empires of Alexander the Great and Rome. In the case of Southeast Asia, however, no imperial control accompanied Indian cultural influence. It was a matter of voluntary borrowing by independent societies that found Indian traditions and practices useful and were free to adapt those ideas to their own needs and cultures. Traditional religious practices mixed with the imported faiths or existed alongside them with little conflict. And much that was distinctively Southeast Asian persisted despite influences from afar. In family life, for example, most Southeast Asian societies traced an individual's ancestry from both the mother's and father's line in contrast to India and China, where patrilineal descent was practiced. Furthermore, women had fewer restrictions and a greater role in public life than in the more patriarchal civilizations of both East and South Asia. They were generally able to own property together with their husbands and to initiate divorce. A Chinese visitor to Angkor observed, "It is the women who are concerned with commerce." Women in Angkor also served as gladiators, warriors, and members of the palace staff, and as poets, artists, and religious teachers. Almost 1,800 realistically carved images of women decorate the temple complex of Angkor Wat. In neighboring Pagan, a thirteenth-century queen, Pwa Saw, exercised extensive political and religious influence for some forty years amid internal intrigue and external threats, while donating some of her lands and property to a Buddhist temple. Somewhat later, but also via Indian Ocean commerce, Islam too began to penetrate Southeast Asia as the world of seaborne trade brought yet another cultural tradition to the region.

Sea Roads as a Catalyst for Change: East Africa

On the other side of the Indian Ocean, the transformative processes of long-distance trade were likewise at work, giving rise to an East African civilization known as Swahili. Emerging in the eighth century C.E., this civilization took shape as a set of commercial city-states stretching all along the East African coast, from present-day Somalia to Mozambique.

The earlier ancestors of the Swahili lived in small farming and fishing communities, spoke Bantu languages, and traded with the Arabian, Greek, and Roman merchants who occasionally visited the coast during the second-wave era. But what stimulated the growth of Swahili cities was the far more extensive commercial life of the western Indian Ocean following the rise of Islam. As in Southeast Asia, local people and aspiring rulers found opportunity for wealth and power in the growing demand for East African products associated with an expanding Indian Ocean commerce. Gold, ivory, quartz, leopard skins, and sometimes slaves acquired from interior societies, as well as iron and processed timber manufactured along the coast, found a ready market in Arabia, Persia, India, and beyond. At least one East African giraffe found its way to Bengal in northeastern India, and from there was sent on to China. In response to such commercial opportunities, an African merchant class developed, villages turned into sizable towns, and clan chiefs became kings. A new civilization was in the making.

Between 1000 and 1500, that civilization flourished along the coast, and it was a very different kind of society from the farming and pastoral cultures of the East African interior. It was thoroughly urban, centered in cities of 15,000 to 18,000 people, such as Lamu, Mombasa, Kilwa, Sofala, and many others. Like the city-states of ancient Greece, each Swahili city was politically independent, was generally governed by its own king, and was in sharp competition with other cities. No imperial system or larger territorial states unified the world of Swahili civilization. Nor did any of these city-states control a critical choke point of trade, as Srivijaya did for the Straits of Malacca. Swahili cities were commercial centers that accumulated goods from the interior and exchanged them for the products of distant civilizations, such as Chinese porcelain and silk, Persian rugs, and Indian cottons. While the transoceanic journeys occurred largely in Arab vessels, Swahili craft navigated the coastal waterways, concentrating goods for shipment abroad. This long-distance trade generated class-stratified urban societies with sharp distinctions between a mercantile elite and commoners.

AP® EXAM TIP

Take good notes on East Africa's contributions to the Indian Ocean network.

Guided Reading Question

■ CONNECTION
What was the role of Swahili civilization in the world of Indian Ocean commerce?

The Swahili Coast of East Africa

Culturally as well as economically, Swahili civilization participated in the larger Indian Ocean world. Arab, Indian, and Persian merchants were welcome visitors, and some settled permanently. Many ruling families of Swahili cities claimed Arab or Persian origins as a way of bolstering their prestige, even while they dined from Chinese porcelain and dressed in Indian cottons. The Swahili language, widely spoken in East Africa today, was grammatically an African tongue within the larger Bantu family of languages, but it was written in Arabic script and contained a number of Arabic loan words. A small bronze lion found in the Swahili city of Shanga and dating to about 1100 illustrates the distinctly cosmopolitan character of Swahili culture. It depicted a clearly African lion, but it was created in a distinctly Indian artistic style and was made from melted-down Chinese copper coins.[13]

Furthermore, Swahili civilization rapidly became Islamic. Introduced by Arab traders, Islam was voluntarily and widely adopted within the Swahili world. Like Buddhism in Southeast Asia, Islam linked Swahili cities to the larger Indian Ocean world, and these East African cities were soon dotted with substantial mosques. When Ibn Battuta (IH-buhn ba-TOO-tuh), a widely traveled Arab scholar, merchant, and public official, visited the Swahili coast in the early fourteenth century, he found altogether Muslim societies in which religious leaders often spoke Arabic, and all were eager to welcome a learned Islamic visitor. But these were African Muslims, not colonies of transplanted Arabs. A prominent historian of Ibn Battuta's travels commented on Swahili society: "The rulers, scholars, officials, and big merchants as well as the port workers, farmers, craftsmen, and slaves, were dark-skinned people speaking African tongues in everyday life."[14]

Islam sharply divided the Swahili cities from their African neighbors to the west, for neither the new religion nor Swahili culture penetrated much beyond the coast until the nineteenth century. Economically, however, the coastal cities acted as intermediaries between the interior producers of valued goods and the Arab merchants who carried them to distant markets. Particularly in the southern reaches of the Swahili world, this relationship extended the impact of Indian Ocean trade well into the African interior. Hundreds of miles inland, between the Zambezi and Limpopo rivers, lay rich sources of gold, much in demand on the Swahili coast. The emergence of a powerful state, known as Great Zimbabwe, seems clearly connected to the growing trade in gold to the coast as well as to the wealth embodied in its large herds of cattle. At its peak between 1250 and 1350, Great Zimbabwe had the resources and the labor power to construct huge stone enclosures entirely without mortar, with walls sixteen feet thick and thirty-two feet tall. "[It] must have been an astonishing sight," writes a recent historian, "for the subordinate chiefs and kings who would have come there to seek favors at court."[15] Here in the interior of southeastern Africa lay yet another example of the reach and transforming power of Indian Ocean commerce.

AP® EXAM TIP

Features of the Swahili and Great Zimbabwe civilizations in East Africa are a frequent topic on the AP® exam.

PRACTICING AP® HISTORICAL THINKING

To what extent did the Silk Roads and the Sea Roads operate in a similar fashion? How did they differ?

Sand Roads: Exchange across the Sahara

In addition to the Silk Roads and the Sea Roads, another important pattern of long-distance trade—this one across the vast reaches of the Sahara—linked North Africa and the Mediterranean world with the land and peoples of interior West Africa. Like the others, these Sand Road commercial networks had a transforming impact, stimulating and enriching West African civilization and connecting it to larger patterns of world history during the third-wave era.

Commercial Beginnings in West Africa

Trans-African trade, like the commerce of the Silk Roads and the Sea Roads, was rooted in environmental variation. The North African coastal regions, long part of Roman or later Arab empires, generated cloth, glassware, weapons, books, and other manufactured goods. The great Sahara held deposits of copper and especially salt, while its oases produced sweet and nutritious dates. While the sparse populations of the desert were largely pastoral and nomadic, farther south lived agricultural peoples who grew a variety of crops, produced their own textiles and metal products, and mined a considerable amount of gold. These agricultural regions of sub-Saharan Africa are normally divided into two ecological zones: the savanna grasslands immediately south of the Sahara, which produced grain crops such as millet and sorghum, and the forest areas farther south, where root and tree crops such as yams and kola nuts predominated. These quite varied environments provided the economic incentive for the exchange of goods.

The earliest long-distance trade within this huge region was not across the Sahara at all, but largely among the agricultural peoples themselves in the area later known to Arabs as the Sudan, or "the land of black people." During the first millennium B.C.E., the peoples of Sudanic West Africa began to exchange metal goods, cotton textiles, gold, and various food products across considerable distances using boats along the Niger River and donkeys overland. On the basis of this trade, a number of independent urban clusters emerged by the early centuries of the Common Era. The most well known was Jenne-jeno, which was located at a crucial point on the Niger River where goods were transshipped from boat to donkey or vice versa. This was the Niger Valley civilization, described in Chapter 6.

AP® EXAM TIP

Note the key raw materials carried within and out of Africa along the Sand Roads.

Gold, Salt, and Slaves: Trade and Empire in West Africa

A major turning point in African commercial life occurred with the introduction of the camel to North Africa and the Sahara in the early centuries of the Common Era. (See Zooming In: The Arabian Camel, page 302.) This remarkable animal, which could go for ten days without water, finally made possible the long trek across the Sahara. It was camel-owning dwellers of desert oases who initiated regular trans-Saharan commerce by 300 to 400 C.E. Several centuries later, North African Arabs, now bearing the new religion of Islam, also organized caravans across the desert.

AP® EXAM TIP

Understand the significance of the introduction of the camel into Africa from Southwest Asia.

The Arabian Camel

Animals have their own histories, and they have long played a large role in human history as well. Consider the single-humped Arabian camel, for thousands of years an important means of transport and a beast of burden on the Silk and Sand Roads. Even today, the Arabian camel is a common sight across northern Africa and the Middle East. But it took millennia for this breed of camel to spread beyond its native Arabian Peninsula, where it had been domesticated by 3000 B.C.E. Camels were initially valued by Arab tribesmen for their milk; however, over time their endurance and ability to carry heavy loads resulted in their adoption as pack animals along the caravan routes between the frankincense- and myrrh-producing regions of southern Arabia and cities on the northern edges of the peninsula.

This trade slowly introduced Arabian camels to the rest of the Middle East, where they were well established

Part of a camel caravan.

by 500 B.C.E. But it was the invention of a new saddle, which allowed each animal to carry a heavier load, that transformed the camel into the most versatile and efficient form of transport in the region by 100 B.C.E. Ultimately the camel displaced the ox and cart, which for millennia had been a mainstay for moving goods. The advantages of the camel were significant. Camels ate desert plants that thrived on lands unsuitable to agriculture, while oxen required fodder grown on arable land. Moreover, camels carried loads on their backs rather than pulling carts made of wood, a scarce resource in the Middle East. In many parts of the region, the camel's triumph was complete. By 500 C.E., wheeled vehicles had disappeared entirely from most of the Middle East, and the camel maintained its dominance for fifteen

photo: From the "Maqamat" of Abu Mohammed al Qasim ibn Ali Hariri (1054–1122), 1237. © Scala/White Images/Art Resource, NY

Guided Reading Question

■ CONNECTION
What changes did trans-Saharan trade bring to West Africa?

What they sought, above all else, was gold, which was found in some abundance in the border areas straddling the grasslands and the forests of West Africa. From its source, it was transported by donkey to transshipment points on the southern edge of the Sahara and then transferred to camels for the long journey north across the desert. African ivory, kola nuts, and slaves were likewise in considerable demand in the desert, the Mediterranean basin, and beyond. In return, the peoples of the Sudan received horses, cloth, dates, various manufactured goods, and especially salt from the rich deposits in the Sahara.

Thus the Sahara was no longer simply a barrier to commerce and cross-cultural interaction; it quickly became a major international trade route that fostered new relationships among distant peoples. The caravans that made the desert crossing could be huge, with as many as 5,000 camels and hundreds of people. Traveling mostly at night to avoid the daytime heat, the journey might take up to seventy days, covering fifteen to twenty-five miles per day. For well over 1,000 years, such caravans traversed the desert, linking the interior of West Africa with lands and people far to the north.

hundred years. In the 1780s, a French traveler in Syria commented, "It is noteworthy that in all of Syria no wagon or cart is seen."[16] Only with the emergence of the automobile in the twentieth century did the camel decisively lose its advantage over wheeled vehicles. From the Middle East, Arabian camels and related hybrid species moved along the Silk Roads, becoming a major means of transport as far away as modern Afghanistan. Only the cold climatic conditions of Central Asia halted their spread. In the frigid Gobi Desert, it was the Arabian camel's cousin—the two-humped Bactrian camel—that traders relied upon to carry their loads.

The Arabian camel had perhaps an even more profound impact on long-distance trade across the Sahara. Before the arrival of the camel, the western Sahara proved an imposing barrier to trade. Just a trickle of goods flowed across the vast arid region, often through indirect exchange. The first camels most likely filtered into western Africa from the Middle East along the southern borders of the Sahara around 200 B.C.E., and they probably arrived after 100 C.E. in Roman North Africa, where they were used for a variety of purposes, including the plowing of fields. From the time of their arrival, camels stimulated trade and contact across the Sahara, but these exchanges really took off when the Arab conquerors of North Africa brought their expertise in camel caravan trading to the region in the sixth century C.E. At their height, caravans of up to 5,000 camels regularly crossed the Sahara on several established routes. It could take seventy days to traverse the desert, but profits from trade in gold, ivory, salt, and slaves made the journey worthwhile. These trade routes facilitated the emergence of empires in West Africa and the spread of Islam into the region. The Arabian camel remained the chief source of transport between sub-Saharan West Africa and the Mediterranean for over a thousand years, until European ships sailing along the Atlantic coast challenged their dominance in the fifteenth century.

Questions: Was the disappearance of the wheel an advance in terms of transport in the Middle East? What impact did the Arabian camel have on long-distance trade in Eurasia and Africa? How might reliance on the camel rather than the wheel affect human settlements?

As in Southeast Asia and East Africa, this long-distance trade across the Sahara provided both incentives and resources for the construction of new and larger political structures. It was the peoples of the western and central Sudan, living between the forests and the desert, who were in the best position to take advantage of these new opportunities. Between roughly 500 and 1600, they constructed a series of states, empires, and city-states that reached from the Atlantic coast to Lake Chad, including Ghana, Mali, Songhay, Kanem, and the city-states of the Hausa people (see Map 7.4). All of them were monarchies with elaborate court life and varying degrees of administrative complexity and military forces at their disposal. All drew on the wealth of trans-Saharan trade, taxing the merchants who conducted it. In the wider world, these states soon acquired a reputation for great riches. An Arab traveler in the tenth century C.E. described the ruler of Ghana as "the wealthiest king on the face of the earth because of his treasures and stocks of gold."[17] At its high point in the fourteenth century, Mali's rulers monopolized the import of strategic goods such as horses and metals; levied duties on salt, copper, and other merchandise; and reserved large nuggets of gold for themselves while

> **AP® EXAM TIP**
>
> Features of the West African Islamic kingdoms of Ghana, Mali, and Songhay are "must know" information for the AP® exam.

Map 7.4   The Sand Roads

For a thousand years or more, the Sahara was an ocean of sand that linked the interior of West Africa with the world of North Africa and the Mediterranean but separated them as well.

permitting the free export of gold dust. (See Working with Evidence, Source 7.3, page 318, for an early sixteenth-century account of this West African civilization.)

This growing integration with the world of international commerce generated the social complexity and hierarchy characteristic of all civilizations. Royal families and elite classes, mercantile and artisan groups, military and religious officials, free peasants and slaves—all of these were represented in this emerging West African civilization. So too were gender hierarchies, although without the rigidity of more established Eurasian civilizations. Rulers, merchants, and public officials were almost always male, and by 1200 earlier matrilineal descent patterns had been largely replaced by those tracing descent through the male line. Male bards, the repositories for their communities' history, often viewed powerful women as dangerous, not to be trusted, and a seductive distraction for men. But ordinary women were central to agricultural production and weaving; royal women played important political roles in many places; and oral traditions and mythologies frequently portrayed a complementary rather than hierarchal relationship between the sexes. According to a recent scholar:

> Men [in West African civilization] derive their power and authority by releasing and accumulating *nyama* [a pervasive vital power] through acts of transforming one thing into another—making a living animal dead in hunting, making a lump of metal into a fine bracelet at the smithy. Women derive their power from similar acts of transformation—turning clay into pots or turning the bodily fluids of sex into a baby.[18]

Certainly, the famous Muslim traveler Ibn Battuta, visiting Mali in the fourteenth century, was surprised, and appalled, at the casual intimacy of unmarried men and women, despite their evident commitment to Islam.

As in all civilizations, slavery found a place in West Africa. Early on, most slaves had been women, working as domestic servants and concubines. As West African civilization crystallized, however, male slaves were put to work as state officials, porters, craftsmen, miners harvesting salt from desert deposits, and especially agricultural laborers producing for the royal granaries on large estates or plantations. Most came from non-Islamic and stateless societies farther south, which were raided during the dry season by cavalry-based forces of West African states, though some white slave women from the eastern Mediterranean also made an appearance in Mali. A song in honor of one eleventh-century ruler of Kanem boasted of his slave-raiding achievements:

> The best you took (and sent home) as the first fruits of battle.
> The children crying on their mothers you snatched away from their mothers. You took the slave wife from a slave, and set them in lands far removed from one another.[19]

Most of these slaves were used within this emerging West African civilization, but a trade in slaves also developed across the Sahara. Between 1100 and 1400, perhaps 5,500 slaves per year made the perilous trek across the desert, where most were put to work in the homes of the wealthy in Islamic North Africa.

These states of Sudanic Africa developed substantial urban and commercial centers—such as Koumbi-Saleh, Jenne, Timbuktu, Gao, Gobir, and Kano—where traders congregated and goods were exchanged. Some of these cities also became centers of manufacturing, creating finely wrought beads, iron tools, or cotton textiles, some of which entered the circuits of commerce. Visitors described them as cosmopolitan places where court officials, artisans, scholars, students, and local and foreign merchants all rubbed elbows. As in East Africa, Islam accompanied trade and became an important element in the urban culture of West Africa. The growth of long-distance trade had stimulated the development of a West African civilization, which was linked to the wider networks of exchange in the Eastern Hemisphere.

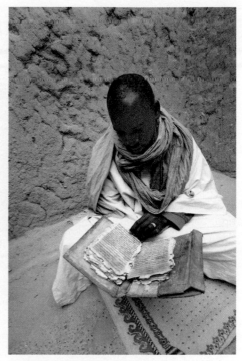

Manuscripts of Timbuktu
The West African city of Timbuktu, a terminus of the Sand Road commercial network, became an intellectual center of Islamic learning—both scientific and religious. Its libraries were stocked with books and manuscripts, often transported across the Sahara from the heartland of Islam. Many of these have been preserved and are now being studied once again. (Alex Dissanayake/Lonely Planet Images/Getty Images)

An American Network: Commerce and Connection in the Western Hemisphere

Before the voyages of Columbus, the world of the Americas developed quite separately from that of Afro-Eurasia. Intriguing hints of occasional contacts with Polynesia and other distant lands have been proposed, but the only clearly demonstrated connection was that occasioned by the brief Viking voyages to North America around the year 1000. (See Zooming In: Thorfinn Karlsefni, page 306.) Certainly, no sustained interaction between the peoples of the two hemispheres took place. But if the Silk, Sea, and Sand Roads linked the diverse peoples of the Eastern Hemisphere, did a similar network of interaction join and transform the various societies of the Western Hemisphere?

Thorfinn Karlsefni, Viking Voyager

While the peoples of the Eastern and Western hemispheres remained almost completely isolated from one another before Columbus, the Viking journeys to North America, part of a larger age of Viking expansion, represent an exception to that generalization. Between 800 and 1050, Scandinavian Vikings had raided, traded, and sometimes settled across much of Europe, generating a fearful reputation. They also colonized Iceland and Greenland, and from that base sought yet more land in North America. Yet their transatlantic voyages, although impressive feats of oceanic exploration, represented a historical dead end, for they bore no long-term consequences. Their significance lies in their role as a prelude to Columbus rather than in any immediate outcomes.

Among those voyagers was Thorfinn Karlsefni, who set off from southern Greenland in the spring of 1007 bound for what he called Vinland, and what we know as North America. A well-born, wealthy merchant and seaman of Norwegian Viking background, he had come the previous summer from his home in Iceland to the small Viking community in Greenland on a trading mission.

A Viking ship similar to that used by Thorfinn Karlsefni and other Viking explorers.

There he found winter accommodations with Eric the Red, a pioneer of Nordic settlement in Greenland. He also found a wife, Gudrid, the widow of one of Eric's sons. Two of Eric's sons, including Leif Ericsson, had previously made the journey to Vinland. And so, during that long winter, talk turned to another voyage, for that land was reputed to be rich in furs, timber, and other valuable resources. Thus Thorfinn came to lead 160 people, including his new wife and other women, on three ships heading to a virtually unknown land. The story of that voyage comes to us from two Icelandic sagas, based on oral traditions and committed to writing several hundred years after the events they describe.[20]

Arriving along the coast of what is now Newfoundland, Thorfinn and his people first looked for pastureland for the cattle that had accompanied them. With food in short supply, the first winter was very difficult and provoked a religious controversy. The Christians among the group "made prayers to God for food," but Thorhall, a

photo: © Yvette Cardozo/Alamy

Guided Reading Question

....

■ COMPARISON

In what ways did networks of interaction in the Western Hemisphere differ from those in the Eastern Hemisphere?

Clearly, direct connections among the various civilizations and cultures of the Americas were less densely woven than in the Afro-Eurasian region. The llama and the potato, both domesticated in the Andes, never reached Mesoamerica; nor did the writing system of the Maya diffuse to Andean civilizations. The Aztecs and the Incas, contemporary civilizations in the fifteenth century, had little if any direct contact with each other. The limits of these interactions owed something to the absence of horses, donkeys, camels, wheeled vehicles, and large oceangoing vessels, all of which facilitated long-distance trade and travel in Afro-Eurasia.

Geographic or environmental differences added further obstacles. The narrow bottleneck of Panama, largely covered by dense rain forests, surely inhibited contact between South and North America. Furthermore, the north/south orientation large, solitary, and "foul-mouthed" hunter, declared: "Has it not been that the Redbeard [Thor, the Norse god of thunder] has proved a better friend than your Christ?"

The following spring, the small Viking community had its first encounter with native peoples when dozens of canoes described in the sagas as "black, and ill favoured" appeared offshore. What followed was a kind of mutual inspection, as the natives "stayed a while in astonishment" and then rowed away. They returned the following year, this time to barter. The Vikings offered red cloth and milk porridge in exchange for furs and skins. But what began as a peaceful encounter ended badly when a bull from the Norsemen's herd erupted out of the forest, bellowing loudly. The surprised and frightened locals quickly departed, and when they returned three weeks later, violence erupted. Considerably outnumbered and attacked with catapults and a "great shower of missiles," Thorfinn and his company reacted with "great terror."

This encounter and the "fear of hostilities" that it provoked persuaded the Vikings "to depart and return to their own country." As they made their way north along the coast, they came upon a group of five natives sleeping near the sea. Perhaps in revenge, the Vikings simply killed them. In another incident before departing for home, they captured two boys, baptized them as Christians, and taught them the Viking language. After

three difficult years in this remote land, Thorfinn and Gudrid returned home, with a son named Snorri, the first European born in the Western Hemisphere.

Although intermittent Viking voyages to North America probably occurred over the next several centuries, the Vikings established no permanent presence. Their numbers were small, and they lacked the support of a strong state, such as Columbus and the Spanish conquistadores later enjoyed. For some time, many doubted that those voyages had occurred at all. But in the 1960s, archeological work on the northern tip of the island of Newfoundland uncovered the remains of a Norse settlement dating to the time of Thorfinn's visit. Eight sod dwellings, evidence of ironworking and boat repair, and household items such as needles and spindles confirmed the existence of a Viking settlement, consisting of both men and women. The interaction of Thorfinn and the other Vikings with native peoples of North America raised, but did not answer, the question of how the epic encounter of these two continents would turn out. The later voyages of Columbus and other West Europeans provided that answer.

Question: How might these interactions have appeared if the descriptions of these encounters had been derived from the sagas of the native peoples of North America?

of the Americas—which required agricultural practices to move through, and adapt to, quite distinct climatic and vegetation zones—slowed the spread of agricultural products. By contrast, the east/west axis of Eurasia meant that agricultural innovations could diffuse more rapidly because they were entering roughly similar environments. Thus nothing equivalent to the long-distance trade of the Silk, Sea, or Sand Roads of the Eastern Hemisphere arose in the Americas, even though local and regional commerce flourished in many places. Nor did distinct cultural traditions spread widely to integrate distant peoples, as Buddhism, Christianity, and Islam did in the Afro-Eurasian world.

Nonetheless, scholars have discerned "a loosely interactive web stretching from the North American Great Lakes and upper Mississippi south to the Andes."[21]

AP® EXAM TIP

Be prepared to compare and contrast characteristics of exchange zones in the Americas with those of Afro-Eurasia.

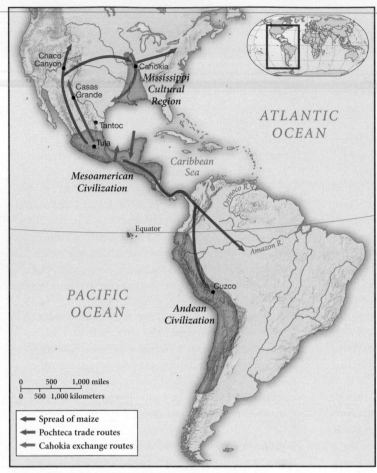

Map 7.5   The American Web

Transcontinental interactions within the American web were more modest than those of the Afro-Eurasian hemisphere. The most intense areas of exchange and communication occurred within the Mississippi valley, Mesoamerican, and Andean regions.

(See Map 7.5.) Partly, it was a matter of slowly spreading cultural elements, such as the gradual diffusion of maize from its Mesoamerican place of origin to the southwestern United States and then on to eastern North America as well as to much of South America in the other direction. A game played with rubber balls on an outdoor court has left traces in the Caribbean, Mexico, and northern South America. Construction in the Tantoc region of northeastern Mexico resembled the earlier building styles of Cahokia, indicating the possibility of some interaction between the two regions. The spread of particular pottery styles and architectural conventions likewise suggests at least indirect contact over wide distances. This kind of diffusion likely extended from the Americas to the Pacific islands as well. Scholars believe that the sweet potato, indigenous to South America, passed into Pacific Oceania around 1000 to 1100 C.E., introduced by Polynesian voyagers who had landed on the west coast of that continent and then returned home with sweet potatoes, which spread widely within Oceania.[22]

Commerce too played an important role in the making of this "American web." A major North American chiefdom at Cahokia, near present-day St. Louis, flourished from about 900 to 1250 at the confluence of the Mississippi, Illinois, and Missouri rivers (see Chapter 6, pages 257–58). Cahokia lay at the center of a widespread trading network that brought it shells from the Atlantic coast, copper from the Lake Superior region, buffalo hides from the Great Plains, obsidian from the Rocky Mountains, and mica from the southern Appalachian Mountains. Sturdy dugout canoes plied the rivers of the eastern woodlands, loosely connecting their diverse societies. Early European explorers and travelers along the Amazon and Orinoco rivers of South America reported active networks of exchange that may well have operated for many centuries among densely populated settlements of agricultural peoples. Caribbean peoples using large oceangoing canoes had long conducted an inter-island trade, and the Chincha people of southern coastal Peru undertook a privately organized ocean-based exchange in copper, beads, and shells along the Pacific coasts of Peru and Ecuador in large seagoing rafts. Another regional commercial network, centered in Mesoamerica, extended north to what is now the southwestern United States and south to Ecuador and Colombia. Many items from Mesoamerica—copper bells, macaw feathers, tons of shells—have been found in the Chaco region of New Mexico. Residents of Chaco also drank liquid chocolate, using jars of Maya origin and cacao beans imported from Mesoamerica, where the practice began. Turquoise, mined and worked by the Ancestral Pueblo (see Chapter 6, pages 255–56), flowed in the other direction.

But the most active and dense networks of communication and exchange in the Americas lay within, rather than between, the regions that housed the two great civilizations of the Western Hemisphere—Mesoamerica and the Andes. During the flourishing of Mesoamerican civilization (200–900 C.E.), both the Maya cities in the Yucatán area of Mexico and Guatemala and the huge city-state of Teotihuacán in central Mexico maintained commercial relationships with one another and throughout the region. In addition to this land-based trade, the Maya conducted a seaborne commerce, using large dugout canoes holding forty to fifty people, along both the Atlantic and Pacific coasts.

Although most of this trade was in luxury goods rather than basic necessities, it was critical to upholding the position and privileges of royal and noble families. Items such as cotton clothing, precious jewels, and feathers from particular birds marked the status of elite groups and served to attract followers. Controlling access to such high-prestige goods was an important motive for war among Mesoamerican states. Among the Aztecs of the fifteenth century, professional merchants known as *pochteca* (pohch-TEH-cah) undertook large-scale trading expeditions both within and well beyond the borders of their empire, sometimes as agents for the state or for members of the nobility, but more often acting on their own as private businessmen.

Unlike in the Aztec Empire, in which private traders largely handled the distribution of goods, economic exchange in the Andean Inca Empire during the fifteenth century was a state-run operation, and no merchant group similar to the Aztec pochteca emerged there. Instead, great state storehouses bulged with immense quantities of food, clothing, military supplies, blankets, construction materials, and more, all carefully recorded on *quipus* (knotted cords used to record numerical data) by a highly trained class of accountants. From these state centers, goods were transported as needed by caravans of human porters and llamas across the numerous roads and bridges of the empire. Totaling some 20,000 miles, Inca roads traversed the coastal plain and the high Andes in a north/south direction, while lateral roads linked these diverse environments and extended into the eastern rain forests and

Inca Roads
Used for transporting goods by pack animal or sending messages by foot, the Inca road network included some 2,000 inns where travelers might find food and shelter. Messengers, operating in relay, could cover as many as 150 miles a day. Here contemporary hikers still make use of an old Inca trail road. (William H. Mullins/Science Source)

AP® EXAM TIP

Take notes on the ways that the American trade network was similar to and different from the Sand, Sea, and Silk Roads.

plains as well. Despite the general absence of private trade, local exchange took place at highland fairs and along the borders of the empire with groups outside the Inca state.

REFLECTIONS

Economic Globalization— Ancient and Modern

The densely connected world of the modern era, linked by ties of commerce and culture around the planet, certainly has roots in much earlier patterns. Particularly in the era of third-wave civilizations from 500 to 1500, the Silk, Sea, and Sand Roads of the Afro-Eurasian world and the looser networks of the American web linked distant peoples both economically and culturally, prompted the emergence of new states, and sustained elite privileges in many ancient civilizations. In those ways, they resembled the globalized world of modern times.

In other respects, though, the networks and webs of the premodern millennium differed sharply from those of more recent centuries. Most people still produced primarily for their own consumption rather than for the market, and a much smaller range of goods was exchanged in the marketplaces of the world. Far fewer people then were required to sell their own labor for wages, an almost universal practice in modern economies. Because of transportation costs and technological limitations, most trade was in luxury goods rather than in necessities. In addition, the circuits of commerce were rather more limited than the truly global patterns of exchange that emerged after 1500.

Furthermore, the world economy of the modern era increasingly had a single center—industrialized Western European countries—which came to dominate much of the world both economically and politically during the nineteenth century. Though never completely equal, the economic relationships of earlier times occurred among much more equivalent units. For example, no one region dominated the complex pattern of Indian Ocean exchange, although India and China generally offered manufactured goods, while Southeast Asia and East Africa mostly contributed agricultural products or raw materials. And with the exception of the brief Mongol control of the Silk Roads and the Inca domination of the Andes for a century, no single power exercised political control over the major networks of world commerce.

Economic relationships among third-wave civilizations, in short, were more balanced and multicentered than those of the modern era. Although massive inequalities occurred within particular regions or societies, interaction among the major civilizations operated on a rather more equal basis than in the globalized world of the past several centuries. With the rise of China, India, Turkey, and Brazil as major players in the world economy of the twenty-first century, are we perhaps witnessing a return to that earlier pattern?

Chapter Review

What's the Significance?

Big Picture Questions

1. What motivated and sustained the long-distance commerce of the Silk Roads, Sea Roads, and Sand Roads?
2. Why did the peoples of the Eastern Hemisphere develop long-distance trade more extensively than did those of the Western Hemisphere?
3. "Cultural change often derived from commercial exchange in the third-wave era." What evidence from this chapter supports this observation?
4. In what ways was Afro-Eurasia a single interacting zone, and in what respects was it a vast region of separate cultures and civilizations?
5. **Looking Back:** Compared to the cross-cultural interactions of earlier times, what was different about those of the third-wave era?

Next Steps: For Further Study

Jerry Bentley, *Old World Encounters* (1993). A wonderfully succinct and engaging history of cross-cultural interaction all across Afro-Eurasia before 1500.

William J. Bernstein, *A Splendid Exchange* (2008). A global account of "how trade shaped the world."

E. W. Bovill, *The Golden Trade of the Moors* (1970). A classic account of the trans-Saharan trade.

Nayan Chanda, *Bound Together* (2007). Places contemporary globalization in a rich world historical context.

K. N. Chaudhuri, *Trade and Civilization in the Indian Ocean* (1985). A well-regarded study that treats the Indian Ocean basin as a single region linked by both commerce and culture during the third wave era.

Philip Curtin, *Cross-Cultural Trade in World History* (1984). Explores long-distance trade as a generator of social change on a global level.

Xinru Liu, *The Silk Road in World History* (2010). A brief, accessible, and up-to-date account by a leading scholar.

"The Last Salt Caravan," http://www.youtube.com/watch?v=yNwQeLFk74o. A ten-minute trailer for a documentary showing an early twenty-first-century camel caravan crossing the Sahara, reminiscent of much earlier caravans of the Sand Roads network.

Silk Road Seattle, http://depts.washington.edu/silkroad/. A wonderful Web site about the Silk Road with many artistic images and maps as well as extensive narrative description of that vast network of exchange.

WORKING WITH EVIDENCE

Travelers' Tales and Observations

During the third-wave millennium, as long-distance trade flourished and large transregional empires grew, opportunities increased for individuals to travel far beyond their homelands. Their accounts have provided historians with invaluable information about particular regions and cultures, as well as about interactions among disparate peoples. The authors of these accounts, perhaps inadvertently, also reveal much about themselves and about the perceptions and misperceptions generated by cross-cultural encounters. The selections that follow provide three examples of intrepid long-distance travelers and their impressions of the societies they encountered on their arduous journeys.

Source 7.1

A Chinese Buddhist in India

In 629, Xuanzang (SCHWEN-ZAHNG) (600–664 C.E.), a highly educated Buddhist monk from China, made a long and difficult journey to India through some of the world's most daunting deserts and mountain ranges, returning home in 645 C.E. after sixteen years abroad. His motives, like those of many other Buddhist travelers to India, were essentially religious. "I regretted that the teachings of [Buddhism] were not complete and the scriptures deficient in my own country," he wrote. "I have doubts and have puzzled in my mind, but I could find no one to solve them. That was why I decided to travel to the West."[23] In India, the homeland of Buddhism, he hoped to find the teachers and the sacred texts that would answer his questions, enrich Buddhist practice in China, and resolve the many disputes that had created serious divisions within the Buddhist community of his own country.

During a ten-year stay in India, Xuanzang visited many of the holy sites associated with the Buddha's life and studied with leading Buddhist teachers, particularly those at Nalanda University, a huge monastic complex dedicated to Buddhist scholarship (see Map 7.1, page 285, and the Zooming In feature on Nalanda in Chapter 4, page 162). He traveled widely within India and established a personal relationship with Harsha, the ruler of the state that then encompassed much of northern India. On his return journey to China, he carried hundreds of manuscripts, at least seven statues of the Buddha, and even some relics. Warmly greeted by the Chinese emperor, Xuanzang spent the last two decades of his life translating the texts he had collected into Chinese. He also wrote an account of his travels, known as the *Record of the Western Regions*, and shared his recollections with a fellow monk and translator named Huili, who subsequently wrote a biography of Xuanzang. The selections that follow derive from these two accounts and convey something of Xuanzang's impressions of Indian civilization in the seventh century C.E.

■ What surprised or impressed Xuanzang on his visit to India? What features of Indian life might seem most strange to a Chinese visitor?

■ How might these selections serve to illustrate or to contradict the descriptions of Indian civilization found in Chapters 3–5?

■ What can this document contribute to our understanding of Buddhist practice in India?

HUILI

A Biography of the Tripitaka Master

Seventh Century C.E.

[*Certainly the emotional highlight of Xuanzang's travels in India was his visit to the site of the Buddha's enlightenment under the famous Bodhi tree. The great traveler's biographer, Huili, recorded his Master's response.*]

Upon his arrival there, the Master worshipped the Bodhi tree and the image of the Buddha attaining enlightenment made by Maitreya Bodhisattva. After having looked at the image with deep sincerity, he prostrated himself before it and deplored sadly, saying with self-reproach, "I do not know where I was born in the course of transmigration at the time when the Buddha attained enlightenment. I could only come here at this time. . . . It makes me think that my karmic hindrances must have been very heavy!" While he was saying so, his eyes brimmed with sorrowful tears. As that was the time when the monks dismissed the summer retreat, several thousand people forgathered from far and near. Those who saw the Master were choked by sobs in sympathy with him.

Source: Li Rongxi, trans., *A Biography of the Tripitaka Master of the Great Ci'en Monastery of the Great Tang Dynasty* (Berkeley, CA: Numata Center for Buddhist Translation, 1995), 89–90.

XUANZANG

Record of the Western Region

Seventh Century C.E.

[*Selections from Xuanzang's more general description of Indian civilization follow here, drawn from his own account.*]

On Towns and Villages

The towns and villages have inner gates; the walls are wide and high; the streets and lanes are tortuous, and the roads winding. The thoroughfares are dirty and the stalls arranged on both sides of the road with appropriate signs. Butchers, fishers, dancers, executioners, and scavengers, and so on [untouchables], have their abodes without [outside] the city. In coming and going these persons are bound to keep on the left side of the road till they arrive at their homes. Their houses are surrounded by low walls and form the suburbs. The earth being soft and muddy, the walls of the towns are mostly built of brick or tiles. . . .

On Buddhist Studies

The different schools are constantly at variance, and their contending utterances rise like the angry waves of the sea. The different sects have their separate masters. . . . There are eighteen schools, each claiming pre-eminence. The partisans of the Great and Little Vehicle are content to dwell apart. There are some who give themselves up to quiet contemplation, and devote themselves, whether walking or standing still or sitting down, to the acquirement of wisdom and insight; others, on the contrary, differ from these in raising noisy contentions about their faith. According to their fraternity, they are governed by distinctive rules and regulations. . . .

The *Vinaya* discourses [rules governing monastic life] are equally Buddhist books. He who can entirely explain one class of these books is exempted from the control of the *karmadâna* [a high monastic official]. If he can explain two classes, he receives in addition the equipments of an upper seat (*room*); he who can explain three classes has allotted to him different servants to attend to and obey him; he who can explain four classes has "pure men" allotted to him as attendants; he who can explain five classes of books is then allowed an elephant carriage; he who can explain six classes of books is allowed a surrounding escort. When a man's renown has reached to a high distinction, then at different times he convokes an assembly for discussion. He judges of the superior or inferior talent of those who take part in it; he distinguishes their good or bad points; he praises the clever and reproves the faulty; if one of the assembly distinguishes himself by refined language, subtle investigation, deep pen-

etration, and severe logic, then he is mounted on an elephant covered with precious ornaments, and conducted by a numerous suite to the gates of the convent.

If, on the contrary, one of the members breaks down in his argument, or uses poor and inelegant phrases, or if he violates a rule in logic and adapts his words accordingly, they proceed to disfigure his face with red and white, and cover his body with dirt and dust, and then carry him off to some deserted spot or leave him in a ditch. Thus they distinguish between the meritorious and the worthless, between the wise and the foolish.

On Caste and Marriage

With respect to the division of families, there are four classifications. The first is called the Brâhman, men of pure conduct. They guard themselves in religion, live purely, and observe the most correct principles. The second is called Kshattriya, the royal caste. For ages they have been the governing class: they apply themselves to virtue and kindness. The third is called Vaiśyas, the merchant class: they engage in commercial exchange, and they follow profit at home and abroad. The fourth is called Sûdra, the agricultural class: they labor in plowing and tillage. In these four classes purity or impurity of caste assigns to every one his place. When they marry they rise or fall in position according to their new relationship. They do not allow promiscuous marriages between relations. A woman once married can never take another husband. Besides these there are other classes of many kinds that intermarry according to their several callings.

On Manners and Justice

With respect to the ordinary people, although they are naturally light-minded, yet they are upright and honorable. In money matters they are without craft, and in administering justice they are considerate. They dread the retribution of another state of existence, and make light of the things of the present world. They are not deceitful or treacherous in their conduct, and are faithful to their oaths and promises. In their rules of government there is remarkable rectitude, whilst in their behavior there is much gentleness and sweetness. With respect to criminals or rebels, these are few in number, and only occasionally troublesome. When the laws are broken or the power of the ruler violated, then the matter is clearly sifted and the offenders imprisoned. There is no infliction of corporal punishment; they are simply left to live or die, and are not counted among men. When the rules of propriety or justice are violated, or when a man fails in fidelity or filial piety, then they cut his nose or his ears

off, or his hands and feet, or expel him from the country or drive him out into the desert wilds. For other faults, except these, a small payment of money will redeem the punishment. In the investigation of criminal cases there is no use of rod or staff to obtain proofs (*of guilt*).

Source: Samuel Beal, trans., *Su-Yu-Ki: Buddhist Records of the Western World* (London: K. Paul, Trench, Trubner, 1906), vol. 1, bk. 2, 73–74, 77, 79–84.

Source 7.2
A European Christian in China

Of all the travelers along the Silk Road network, the best known and most celebrated, at least in the West, was Marco Polo (1254–1324). Born and raised in the prosperous commercial city-state of Venice in northern Italy, Marco Polo was a member of a family prominent in the long-distance trade of the Mediterranean and Black sea regions. At the age of seventeen, Marco accompanied his father and an uncle on an immense journey across Eurasia that, by 1275, brought the Polos to China, recently conquered by the Mongols. It was, in fact, the relative peace that the Mongols had created in their huge transcontinental empire that facilitated the Polos' journey (see Map 11.1, page 466). For the next seventeen years, they lived in China, where they were employed in minor administrative positions by Khubilai Khan, the country's Mongol ruler. During these years, Marco Polo apparently traveled widely within China, where he gathered material for the book about his travels, which he dictated to a friend after returning home in 1295.

Marco Polo's journey and the book that described it, generally known as *The Travels of Marco Polo*, were important elements of the larger process by which an emerging West European civilization reached out to and became aware of the older civilizations of the East. Christopher Columbus carried a marked-up copy of the book on his transatlantic journeys, believing that he was seeking by sea the places Marco Polo had visited by land. Some modern scholars are skeptical about parts of Marco Polo's report, and a few even question whether he ever got to China at all, largely because he omitted any mention of certain prominent features of Chinese life, for example, foot binding, the Great Wall, and tea drinking. Most historians, however, accept the basic outlines of Marco Polo's account, even as they notice exaggerations as well as an inflated perception of his own role within China. The selection that follows conveys Marco Polo's description of the city of Hangzhou, which he referred to as Kinsay. At the time of Marco Polo's visit, it was among the largest cities in the world.

- How would you describe Marco Polo's impressions of the city? What did he notice? What surprised him?

- Why did Marco Polo describe the city as "the finest and the noblest in the world"?

- What marks his account of the city as that of a foreigner and a Christian?

- What evidence of China's engagement with a wider world does this account offer?

MARCO POLO

The Travels of Marco Polo
1299

The city is beyond dispute the finest and the noblest in the world. In this we shall speak according to the written statement which the Queen of this Realm sent to Bayan, the [Mongol] conqueror of the country for transmission to the Great Kaan, in order that he might be aware of the surpassing grandeur of the city and might be moved to save it from destruction or injury. I will tell you all the truth as it was set down in that document. For truth it was, as the said Messer Marco Polo at a later date was able to witness with his own eyes. . . .

First and foremost, then, the document stated the city of Kinsay to be so great that it hath an hundred miles of compass. And there are in it 12,000 bridges of stone. . . . [Most scholars consider these figures a considerable exaggeration.] And though the bridges be so high, the approaches are so well contrived that carts and horses do cross them.

The document aforesaid also went on to state that there were in this city twelve guilds of the different crafts, and that each guild had 12,000 houses in the occupation of its workmen. Each of these houses contains at least twelve men, whilst some contain twenty and some forty. . . . And yet all these craftsmen had full occupation, for many other cities of the kingdom are supplied from this city with what they require.

The document aforesaid also stated that the number and wealth of the merchants, and the amount of goods that passed through their hands, were so enormous that no man could form a just estimate thereof. And I should have told you with regard to those masters of the different crafts who are at the head of such houses as I have mentioned, that neither they nor their wives ever touch a piece of work with their own hands, but live as nicely and delicately as if they were kings and queens. The wives indeed are most dainty and angelical creatures! Moreover it was an ordinance laid down by the King that every man should follow his father's business and no other, no matter if he possessed 100,000 bezants [a Byzantine gold coin].

Inside the city there is a Lake . . . and all round it are erected beautiful palaces and mansions, of the richest and most exquisite structure that you can imagine, belonging to the nobles of the city. There are also on its shores many abbeys and churches of the Idolaters [Buddhists]. In the middle of the Lake are two Islands, on each of which stands a rich, beautiful, and spacious edifice, furnished in such style as to seem fit for the palace of an Emperor. And when any one of the citizens desired to hold a marriage feast, or to give any other entertainment, it used to be done at one of these palaces.

And everything would be found there ready to order, such as silver plate, trenchers, and dishes, napkins and table-cloths, and whatever else was needful. . . . Sometimes there would be at these palaces an hundred different parties; some holding a banquet, others celebrating a wedding . . . in so well-ordered a manner that one party was never in the way of another. . . .

Both men and women are fair and comely, and for the most part clothe themselves in silk, so vast is the supply of that material, both from the whole district of Kinsay, and from the imports by traders from other provinces. And you must know they eat every kind of flesh, even that of dogs and other unclean beasts, which nothing would induce a Christian to eat. . . .

You must know also that the city of Kinsay has some 3,000 baths, the water of which is supplied by springs. They are hot baths, and the people take great delight in them, frequenting them several times a month, for they are very cleanly in their persons. They are the finest and largest baths in the world. . . .

And the Ocean Sea comes within twenty-five miles of the city at a place called Ganfu, where there is a town and an excellent haven, with a vast amount of shipping which is engaged in the traffic to and from India and other foreign parts, exporting and importing many kinds of wares, by which the city benefits. . . .

I repeat that everything appertaining to this city is on so vast a scale, and the Great Kaan's yearly revenues therefrom are so immense, that it is not easy even to put it in writing. . . .

In this part are the ten principal markets, though besides these there are a vast number of others in the different parts of the town. . . . [T]oward the [market] squares are built great houses of stone, in which the merchants from India and other foreign parts store their wares, to be handy for the markets. In each of the squares is held a market three days in the week, frequented by 40,000 or 50,000 persons, who bring thither for sale every possible necessary of life, so that there is always an ample supply of every kind of meat and game. . . .

Those markets make a daily display of every kind of vegetables and fruits. . . . [V]ery good raisins are brought from abroad, and wine likewise. . . . From the Ocean Sea also come daily supplies of fish in great quantity, brought twenty-five miles up the river. . . . All the ten market places are encompassed by lofty houses, and below these are shops where all sorts of crafts are carried on, and all sorts of wares are on sale, including spices and jewels and pearls. Some of these shops are entirely devoted to the sale of wine made from rice and spices, which is constantly made fresh, and is sold very cheap. Certain of the streets are occupied by the women of the town, who are in such a number that I dare not say what it is. They are found not only in the vicinity of the market places, where usually a quarter is assigned to them, but all over the city. They exhibit themselves splendidly attired and abundantly perfumed, in finely garnished houses, with trains of waiting-women. These women are extremely accomplished in all the arts of allurement, and readily adapt their conversation to all sorts of persons, insomuch that strangers who have once tasted their attractions seem to get bewitched, and are so taken with their blandishments and their fascinating ways that they never can get these out of their heads. . . .

Other streets are occupied by the Physicians, and by the Astrologers, who are also teachers of reading and writing; and an infinity of other professions have their places round about those squares. In each of the squares there are two great palaces facing one another, in which are established the officers appointed by the King to decide differences arising between merchants, or other inhabitants of the quarter. . . .

The crowd of people that you meet here at all hours . . . is so vast that no one would believe it possible that victuals enough could be provided for their consumption, unless they should see how, on every market-day, all those squares are thronged and crammed with purchasers, and with the traders who have brought in stores of provisions by land or water; and everything they bring in is disposed of. . . .

The natives of the city are men of peaceful character, both from education and from the example of their kings, whose disposition was the same. They know nothing of handling arms, and keep none in their houses. You hear of no feuds or noisy quarrels or dissensions of any kind among them. Both in their commercial dealings and in their manufactures they are thoroughly honest and truthful, and there is such a degree of good will and neighborly attachment among both men and women that you would take the people who live in the same street to be all one family.

And this familiar intimacy is free from all jealousy or suspicion of the conduct of their women. These they treat with the greatest respect, and a man who should presume to make loose proposals to a married woman would be regarded as an infamous rascal. They also treat the foreigners who visit them for the sake of trade with great cordiality and entertain them in the most winning manner, affording them every help and advice on their business. But on the other hand they hate to see soldiers, and not least those of the Great Kaan's garrisons, regarding them as the cause of their having lost their native kings and lords.

Source: *The Book of Sir Marco Polo the Venetian Concerning the Kingdoms and Marvels of the East*, 3rd ed., translated and edited by Henry Yule, revised by Henri Cordier (London: John Murray, 1903), 2:185–206.

Source 7.3
A Moroccan Diplomat in West Africa

Known to the world by his European-derived nickname of Leo Africanus, this widely traveled Arabic-speaking Muslim of Berber background was actually born as al-Hassan Ibn Muhammad al Wazzan in Granada, Spain, during the late fifteenth century, just as Islam was being pushed out of that country. His family moved to Fez in Morocco, where he was educated in Islamic law. Later, he served the sultan of Morocco as a diplomat and commercial agent, traveling widely in North Africa, the Middle East, Italy, and West Africa. On one of these journeys, he was captured by pirates, winding up in Rome, where he came to the attention of Pope Leo X. There he was apparently converted to Christianity, at least for a time, though he later chose to live in Muslim North Africa and likely returned to his original Muslim faith. It was during his stay in Italy that he completed in 1526 the book for which he is most clearly remembered, *The History and Description of Africa*, based on observations and knowledge picked up during his travels. Later published in many languages, it became a major source of European knowledge of the African Islamic world, much as Marco Polo's writings introduced Europeans to China. In the following excerpts from that book, Leo Africanus describes several of the major kingdoms and cities of West African civilization.

■ Based on these accounts, how does Leo Africanus characterize West African civilization? What can you infer about his own attitude toward this civilization?

■ What connections between West Africa and a wider world are evident in these passages?

■ What can you learn about the role of slavery in West Africa at a time before the Atlantic slave trade had become big business?

■ Why do you think these passages say so little about the practice of Islam, focusing instead on political and economic matters? (Keep in mind that the book was first published in Italy and in Italian.) Despite this omission, what can you infer about variations in Islamic observance in West African civilization at this time?

LEO AFRICANUS

The History and Description of Africa
1526

The Kingdom of Mali

In this kingdom there is a large and ample village containing more than six thousand families, and named Mali, which is also the name of the whole kingdom. Here the king has his residence. The region itself yields great abundance of wheat, meat, and cotton. Here are many craftsmen and merchants in all places: and yet the king honorably entertains all strangers. The inhabitants are rich and have plenty of merchandise. Here is a great number of temples [mosques], clergymen, and teachers, who read their lectures in the mosques because they have no colleges at all. The people of the region excel all other Negroes in wit, civility, and industry, and were the first that embraced the law of Muhammad. . . .

The City of Timbuktu

All its houses are . . . cottages, built of mud and covered with thatch. However, there is a most stately mosque to be seen, whose walls are made of stone and lime, and a princely palace also constructed by the highly skilled craftsmen of Granada. Here there are many shops of artisans and merchants, especially of those who weave linen and cotton, and here Barbary [Muslim North African] merchants bring European cloth. The inhabitants, and especially resident aliens, are exceedingly rich, since the present king married both of his daughters to rich merchants. Here are many wells, containing sweet water. Whenever the Niger River overflows, they carry the water into town by means of sluices. This region yields great quantities of grain, cattle, milk, and butter, but salt is very scarce here, for it is brought here by land from Tegaza, which is five hundred miles away. When I was there, I saw one camel-load of salt sold for eighty ducats.

The rich king of Timbuktu has many plates and scepters of gold, some of which weigh 1,300 pounds, and he keeps a magnificent and well-furnished court. When he travels anywhere, he rides upon a camel, which is led by some of his noblemen. He does so likewise when going to war, and all his soldiers ride upon horses. Whoever wishes to speak to this king must first of all fall down before his feet and then taking up earth must sprinkle it on his own head and shoulders. . . . [The king] always has under arms 3,000 horsemen and a great number of foot soldiers who shoot poisoned arrows. They often skirmish with those who refuse to pay tribute and whomever they capture they sell to the merchants of Timbuktu. Here very few horses are bred. . . . Their best horses are brought out of North Africa. As soon as the king learns that any merchants have come to the town with horses, he commands that a certain number be brought before him. Choosing the best horse for himself, he pays a most liberal price for it. . . .

Here are great numbers of [Islamic] religious teachers, judges, scholars and other learned persons, who are bountifully maintained at the king's expense. Here too are brought various [Arabic] manuscripts or written books from Barbary, which are sold for more money than any other merchandise.

The coin of Timbuktu is gold, without any stamp or inscription, but in matters of small value they use certain shells from the kingdom of Persia. Four hundred of these are worth a ducat, and six pieces of Timbuktu's golden coin weigh two-thirds of an ounce.

The inhabitants are gentle and cheerful and spend a great part of the night in singing and dancing throughout the city streets. They keep large numbers of male and female slaves, and their town is greatly vulnerable to fire. At the time of my second visit, almost half the town burned down in the space of five hours.

The Town and Kingdom of Gao

Here are very rich merchants and to here journey continually large numbers of Negroes who purchase here cloth from Barbary and Europe. The town abounds in grain and meat but lacks wine, trees, and fruits. However, there are plenty of melons, lemons and rice. Here there are many wells, which also contain very sweet and wholesome water. Here also is a certain place where slaves are sold, especially upon those days when merchants assemble. A young slave of fifteen years of age is sold for six ducats, and children are also sold.

The king of this region has a certain private palace in which he keeps a large number of concubines and slaves, who are watched by eunuchs. To guard his person he maintains a sufficient troop of horsemen and foot soldiers. Between the first gate of the palace and the inner part, there is a walled enclosure wherein the king personally decides all of his subjects' controversies. Although the king is most diligent in this regard and conducts all business in these matters, he has in his company counsellors and such other officers as his secretaries, treasurers, stewards, and auditors.

It is a wonder to see the quality of merchandise that is daily brought here and how costly and sumptuous everything is. Horses purchased in Europe for ten ducats are sold here for forty and sometimes fifty ducats apiece. There is not European cloth so coarse as to sell for less than four ducats an ell [unit of measure]. If it is anywhere near fine quality, they will give fifteen ducats for an ell, and an ell of the scarlet of Venice or of Turkish cloth is here worth thirty ducats. A sword is here valued at three or four crowns, and likewise are spears, bridles, and similar commodities, and spices are all sold at a high rate. However, of all other items, salt is the most expensive.

The rest of this kingdom contains nothing but villages and hamlets inhabited by herdsmen and shepherds, who in winter cover their bodies with the skins of animals, but in summer they go naked, save for their private parts. . . . They are an ignorant and rude people, and you will scarcely find one learned person in the square of a hundred miles. They are continually burdened by heavy taxes; to the point that they scarcely have anything left on which to live.

The Kingdom of Borno

They embrace no religion at all, being neither Christian, Muhametans [Muslims], nor Jews, nor any other profession, but living after a brutish manner, having wives and children in common. . . . They have a most powerful prince. . . . He has in readiness as many as three thousand horsemen and a huge number of foot soldiers; for all his subjects are so serviceable and obedient to him, that whenever he commands them, they will arm themselves and will follow him wherever he leads them. They pay him no tribute except tithes on their grain; neither does the king have any revenues to support his state except the spoils he gets from his enemies by frequent invasions and assaults. He is in a state of perpetual hostility with a certain people who live beyond the desert of Seu, who in times past marching with a huge army of footsoldiers over the said desert, devastated a great part of the Kingdom of Borno. Whereupon the king sent for the merchants of Barbary and ordered them to bring him a great store of horses: for in this country they exchange horses for slaves, and sometimes give fifteen or twenty slaves for a horse. And by this means there were a great many horses bought although the merchants were forced to stay for their slaves until the king returned home as a conqueror with a great number of captives, and satisfied his creditors for his horses. Frequently it happens that the merchants must stay three months before the king returned from the wars. . . . Sometimes he does not bring home enough slaves to satisfy the merchants and sometimes they are forced to wait a whole year. . . . And yet the king seems marvelously rich, because his spurs, bridles, platters, dishes, pots, and other vessels are made of gold. The king is extremely covetous and would rather pay his debts in slaves rather than gold.

Source: Leo Africanus, *The History and Description of Africa*, edited by Robert Brown (London: The Hakluyt Society, 1896), 3:823–27, 832–34.

DOING HISTORY

Travelers' Tales and Observations

1. **Describing a foreign culture:** Each of these documents was written by an outsider to the people or society he is describing. What different postures toward these foreign cultures are evident in the sources? How did the travelers' various religions shape their perception of places they visited? How did they view the women of their host societies? Were these travelers more impressed by the similarities or by the differences between their home cultures and the ones they visited?

2. **Defining the self-perception of authors:** What can we learn from these documents about the men who wrote them? What motivated them to travel so far from home? How did they define themselves in relationship to the societies they observed?

3. **Assessing the credibility of sources:** What information in these sources would be most valuable for historians seeking to understand India, China, and West Africa in the third-wave era? What statements in these sources might be viewed with the most skepticism? You will want to consider the authors' purposes and their intended audiences in evaluating their writings.

4. **Considering outsiders' accounts:** What are the advantages and limitations for historians in drawing on the writings of foreign observers?

China and the World

East Asian Connections
600–1300

"China will be the next superpower."[1] That was the frank assertion of an article in the British newspaper the *Guardian* in June 2006. Nor was it alone in that assessment. As the new millennium dawned, headlines with this message appeared with increasing frequency in public lectures, in newspaper and magazine articles, and in book titles all across the world. China's huge population, its booming economy, its massive trade surplus with the United States, its entry into world oil markets, its military potential, and its growing presence in global political affairs—all of this suggested that China was headed for a major role, perhaps even a dominant role, in the world of the twenty-first century. Few of these authors, however, paused to recall that China's prominence on the world stage was hardly something new or that its nineteenth- and twentieth-century position as a "backward," weak, or dependent country was distinctly at odds with its long history. Is China perhaps poised to resume in the twenty-first century a much older and more powerful role in world affairs?

In the world of third-wave civilizations, even more than in earlier times, China cast a long shadow. Its massive and powerful civilization, widely imitated by adjacent peoples, gave rise to a China-centered set of relationships encompassing most of eastern Asia. China extended its borders deep into Central Asia, while its wealthy and cosmopolitan culture attracted visitors from all over Eurasia. None of its many neighbors—whether nomadic peoples to the north and west or smaller peripheral states such as Tibet, Korea, Japan, and Vietnam—could escape its gravitational pull. All of them

Chinese Astronomy The impressive achievements of Chinese astronomy included the observation of sunspots, supernovae, and solar and lunar eclipses as well as the construction of elaborate star maps and astronomical devices such as those shown here. The print itself is of Japanese origin and depicts a figure wearing the dragon robes of a Chinese official. It illustrates the immense cultural influence of China on its smaller Japanese neighbor.

had to deal with China. Far beyond these near neighbors, China's booming economy and many technological innovations had ripple effects all across the Afro-Eurasia world.

Even as China so often influenced the world, it too was changed by its many interactions with non-Chinese peoples. Northern nomads—"barbarians" to the Chinese—frequently posed a military threat and on occasion even conquered and ruled parts of China. The country's growing involvement in international trade stimulated important social, cultural, and economic changes within China itself. Buddhism, a religion of Indian origin, took root in China, and, to a much lesser extent, so did Christianity and Islam. In short, China's engagement with the wider world became a very significant element in a global era of accelerating connections.

SEEKING THE MAIN POINT

Chinese history has often been viewed in the West as impressive perhaps, but largely static or changeless and self-contained or isolated. In what ways might the material in this chapter counteract such impressions?

Together Again: The Reemergence of a Unified China

The collapse of the Han dynasty around 220 C.E. ushered in more than three centuries of political fragmentation in China and signaled the rise of powerful and locally entrenched aristocratic families. It also meant the incursion of northern nomads, many of whom learned Chinese, dressed like Chinese, married into Chinese families, and governed northern regions of the country in a Chinese fashion. Such conditions of disunity, unnatural in the eyes of many thoughtful Chinese, discredited Confucianism and opened the door to a greater acceptance of Buddhism and Daoism among the elite. (See Zooming In: Ge Hong in Chapter 5, page 196.)

Those centuries also witnessed substantial Chinese migration southward toward the Yangzi River valley, a movement of people that gave southern China some 60 percent of the country's population by 1000. That movement of Chinese people, accompanied by their intensive agriculture, set in motion a vast environmental transformation, marked by the destruction of the old-growth forests that once covered much of the country and the retreat of the elephants that had inhabited those lands. Around 800 C.E., the Chinese official and writer Liu Zongyuan lamented what was happening:

AP® EXAM TIP

Be prepared to contrast the aftermath of Rome's fall near the end of the classical era with that of the fall of the Han dynasty in China.

A tumbled confusion of lumber as flames on the hillside crackle
Not even the last remaining shrubs are safeguarded from destruction
Where once mountain torrents leapt—nothing but rutted gullies.[2]

A "Golden Age" of Chinese Achievement

Unlike the fall of the western Roman Empire, where political fragmentation proved to be a permanent condition, China regained its unity under the Sui dynasty (589–618). Its emperors solidified that unity by a vast extension of the country's canal system, stretching some 1,200 miles in length and described by one scholar as

A MAP OF TIME

39 C.E.	Trung sisters' rebellion against China in Vietnam
4th–7th centuries	Early state building in Korea
300–800	Buddhism takes root in China
589–618	Sui dynasty and the reunification of China
604	Seventeen Article Constitution in Japan
618–907	Tang dynasty in China
688	Withdrawal of Chinese military forces from Korea
794–1192	Heian period in Japanese history
845	Suppression of Buddhism in China
868	First printed book in China
939	Vietnam establishes independence from China
960–1279	Song dynasty in China
ca. 1000	Invention of gunpowder in China; beginning of foot binding
1000	*The Tale of Genji* (Japan)
1279–1369	Mongol rule in China

"an engineering feat without parallel in the world of its time."[3] Those canals linked northern and southern China economically and contributed much to the prosperity that followed. But the ruthlessness of Sui emperors and a futile military campaign to conquer Korea exhausted the state's resources, alienated many people, and prompted the overthrow of the dynasty.

This dynastic collapse, however, witnessed no prolonged disintegration of the Chinese state. The two dynasties that followed—the Tang (618–907) and the Song (960–1279)—built on the Sui foundations of renewed unity (see Map 8.1). Together they established patterns of Chinese life that endured into the twentieth century, despite a fifty-year period of disunity between the two dynasties. Culturally, this era has long been regarded as a "golden age" of arts and literature, setting standards of excellence in poetry, landscape painting, and ceramics. (See Working with Evidence: The Leisure Life of China's Elites, page 356.) Particularly during the Song dynasty, an explosion of scholarship gave rise to Neo-Confucianism, an effort to revive Confucian thinking while incorporating into it some of the insights of Buddhism and Daoism.

Politically, the Tang and Song dynasties built a state structure that endured for a thousand years. Six major ministries—personnel, finance, rites, army, justice, and public works—were accompanied by the Censorate, an agency that exercised

Guided Reading Question

■ CHANGE

Why are the centuries of the Tang and Song dynasties in China sometimes referred to as a "golden age"?

Map 8.1   Tang and Song Dynasty China
During the third-wave millennium, China interacted extensively with its neighbors. The Tang
dynasty extended Chinese control deep into Central Asia, while the Song dynasty witnessed
incursions by the nomadic Jurchen people, who created the Jin Empire, which ruled parts of
northern China.

surveillance over the rest of the government, checking on the character and competence of public officials. To staff this bureaucracy, the examination system was
revived and made more elaborate, facilitated by the ability to print books for the
first time in world history. Efforts to prevent cheating on the exams included
searching candidates entering the examination hall and placing numbers rather than

names on their papers. Schools and colleges proliferated to prepare candidates for the rigorous exams, which became a central feature of upper-class life. A leading world historian has described Tang dynasty China as "the best ordered state in the world."[4]

Selecting officials on the basis of merit represented a challenge to established aristocratic families' hold on public office. Still, a substantial percentage of official positions went to the sons of the privileged, even if they had not passed the exams. Moreover, because education and the examination system grew far more rapidly than the number of official positions, many who passed lower-level exams could not be accommodated with a bureaucratic appointment. Often, however, they were able to combine landowning and success in the examination system to maintain an immense cultural prestige and prominence in their local areas. Despite the state's periodic efforts to redistribute land in favor of the peasantry, the great families of large landowners continued to encroach on peasant plots, a recurring pattern in rural China from ancient times to the present.

Underlying these cultural and political achievements was an "economic revolution" that made Song dynasty China "by far the richest, most skilled, and most populous country on earth."[5] The most obvious sign of China's prosperity was its rapid growth in population, which jumped from about 50 million or 60 million during the Tang dynasty to 120 million by 1200. Behind this doubling of the population were remarkable achievements in agricultural production, particularly the adoption of a fast-ripening and drought-resistant strain of rice from Vietnam.

Many people found their way to the cities, making China the most urbanized country in the world. Dozens of Chinese cities numbered over 100,000, while the Song dynasty capital of Hangzhou was home to more than a million people. A Chinese observer in 1235 provided a vivid description of that city.[6] Specialized markets abounded for meat, herbs, vegetables, books, rice, and much more, with troupes of actors performing for the crowds. Restaurants advertised their unique offerings—sweet bean soup, pickled dates, juicy lungs, meat pies, pigs' feet—and some offered vegetarian fare for religious banquets. Inns of various kinds appealed to different groups. Those that served only wine, a practice known as "hitting the cup," were regarded as "unfit for polite company." "Luxuriant inns," marked by red lanterns, featured prostitutes and "wine chambers equipped with beds." Specialized agencies managed elaborate dinner parties for the wealthy, complete with a Perfume and Medicine Office to "help sober up the guests." Schools for musicians offered thirteen different courses. Numerous clubs provided companionship for poets, fishermen, Buddhists, physical fitness enthusiasts, antiques collectors, horse lovers, and many other groups. No wonder the Italian visitor Marco Polo described Hangzhou later in the thirteenth century as "beyond dispute the finest and noblest [city] in the world."[7] (See Working with Evidence, Source 7.2, page 315, for a fuller description of Marco Polo's impressions of Hangzhou.)

AP® EXAM TIP

Know that throughout history, China has had the world's highest population and the greatest number of urban areas with high population.

Gunpowder

The Chinese Tang and Song dynasties (618–1279) witnessed a golden age of technological innovation in China. Both woodblock and movable type generated the world's first printed books, while Chinese innovations in navigational and shipbuilding technologies led the world. Among these many developments, the invention of gunpowder stands out because it spawned a permanent revolution in military affairs that had global dimensions. But gunpowder, a mixture of saltpeter, sulfur, and charcoal, was not originally developed for use in war. Instead, it was an accidental byproduct of the search by Daoist alchemists for an elixir of immortality. Indeed, the first reference to gunpowder appeared in a mid–ninth-century Daoist text that warns alchemists not to mix together its component parts because "smoke and flames result, so that [the alchemists'] hands and faces have been burnt, and even the whole house where they were working burned down."[8] This association with alchemy may explain why the Chinese referred to gunpowder as *huo yao*, or "fire drug." The same properties that made gunpowder so dangerous in an alchemist's lab attracted the interest of those

A twelfth-century Chinese Buddhist carving showing an early handheld gun.

seeking to entertain and amaze audiences through fireworks and pyrotechnic displays, especially at the Chinese imperial court.

Military authorities also noticed its potential as a weapon, and its uses in war developed rapidly during the Song dynasty. At first, military engineers drew on the incendiary rather than the explosive possibilities of gunpowder. In 1044, an imperial official wrote a tract for the emperor on military technologies that included two recipes for gunpowder, both for weapons designed to set fire to their targets. Decades later, Song engineers borrowed techniques from fireworks makers to produce "Thunderclap Bombs" designed to scare and disorient opposing troops through noise and light. While these bombs were not yet powerful enough to kill large numbers of the enemy, a chronicler of a siege of the Song capital in 1127 described them as "hitting the lines of the enemy well and throwing them into great confusion."

Through the twelfth and early thirteenth centuries, both the Song dynasty, which controlled southern

photo: Cave number 149, Pei Shan complex, Temples at Ta-tsu, Szechuan, China/Ancient Art & Architecture Collection, Ltd.

AP® EXAM TIP

Understand China's extensive network of canals and their contributions to its economy.

Supplying these cities with food was made possible by an immense network of internal waterways—canals, rivers, and lakes—stretching perhaps 30,000 miles. They provided a cheap transportation system that bound the country together economically and created the "world's most populous trading area."[9]

Industrial production likewise soared. In both large-scale enterprises employing hundreds of workers and in smaller backyard furnaces, China's iron industry increased its output dramatically. By the eleventh century, it was providing the government with 32,000 suits of armor and 16 million iron arrowheads annually, in addition to supplying metal for coins, tools, construction, and bells in Buddhist

China, and the Jin, which controlled much of the north, continued to develop ever more powerful gunpowder weapons. Engineers experimented with gunpowder blends that included larger quantities of saltpeter, the nitrate-rich substance that gives gunpowder its explosiveness. When the Mongols invaded northern China in 1231, the defenders of the capital, Kaifeng, were able to deploy what they called the "Heaven-Shaking Thunder Crash Bomb" against Mongol forces. An eyewitness recorded that "the attacking soldiers were blown to bits, not even a trace being left behind."

The Mongols recognized the effectiveness of gunpowder and, following their conquest of China, encouraged engineers to continue to develop new weapons. During the thirteenth and fourteenth centuries, powerful bombs were produced with such names as "Match for Ten Thousand Enemies Bomb" and the "Bone-Burning and Bruising Fire Oil Magic Bomb." At the same time, Chinese technicians developed the first rockets, which were employed in battle from the middle of the thirteenth century. These experiments with more powerful forms of gunpowder culminated in the emergence of weapons designed to fire projectiles. The first of these evolved from earlier fire lances, bamboo or metal tubes filled with gunpowder that spewed flames and sparks. However, unlike the fire lance, which used the incendiary properties of gunpowder to attack the enemy, these new guns used its explosive power as a propellant to fire projectiles. Cannons were in common

use in China by the 1350s. But the first evidence of a handheld gun comes from a carving, dating from the 1120s and located, strangely enough, in a Buddhist cave featuring Kuan-yin, "the one who answers every prayer." A prayer inscribed in that cave asks "that weapons of war be forever stilled."

Gunpowder and gunpowder-based weapons spread rapidly across Eurasia from the thirteenth century, changing the nature of warfare wherever they were adopted. While there is some debate as to exactly when gunpowder arrived in India, the Middle East, and Europe, it is clear that the Mongols' use of gunpowder weapons in their conquests spurred its spread and use. Its rapid adoption ensured that by the sixteenth century the "fire drug" developed by Daoist alchemists in search of immortality had sparked what scholars have labeled the gunpowder revolution in warfare, transforming military conflict across the globe. Gunpowder remained the dominant explosive used in war until the advent of nitroglycerin in the mid-nineteenth century.

It is more than a little ironic that a substance originally derived from a search for happiness and immortality would result in unimaginable human suffering and an untold number of deaths. Such are the unintended outcomes of human effort.

Question: What can the development of gunpowder-based weapons tell us about technological innovation in China?

---

monasteries. This industrial growth was fueled almost entirely by coal, which also came to provide most of the energy for heating homes and cooking. This no doubt generated considerable air pollution. Technological innovation in other fields also flourished. Inventions in printing, both woodblock and movable type, generated the world's first printed books, and by 1000 relatively cheap books on religious, agricultural, mathematical, and medical topics became widely available in China. Its navigational and shipbuilding technologies led the world. The Chinese invention of gunpowder created within a few centuries a revolution in military affairs that had global dimensions. (See Zooming In: Gunpowder, above.) But China's remarkable

AP EXAM TIP
Know the origins, uses, and spread of gunpowder technology during the postclassical era.

Kaifeng
This detail comes from a huge watercolor scroll, titled *Upper River during Qing Ming Festival*, originally painted during the Song dynasty. It illustrates the urban sophistication of Kaifeng and other Chinese cities at that time and has been frequently imitated and copied since then. (View Stock RF/age fotostock)

industrial revolution stalled as the country was repeatedly invaded and devastated by nomadic peoples from the north, culminating in the Mongol conquests of the thirteenth century.

Most remarkably, perhaps, all of this occurred within the world's most highly commercialized society, in which producing for the market, rather than for local consumption, became a very widespread phenomenon. Cheap transportation allowed peasants to grow specialized crops for sale, while they purchased rice or other staples on the market. In addition, government demands for taxes paid in cash rather than in kind required peasants to sell something—their products or their labor—in order to meet their obligations. The growing use of paper money as well as financial instruments such as letters of credit and promissory notes further contributed to the commercialization of Chinese society. Two prominent scholars have described the outcome: "Output increased, population grew, skills multiplied, and a burst of inventiveness made Song China far wealthier than ever before—or than any of its contemporaries."[10] (See Snapshot, page 347.)

AP® EXAM TIP

China had the world's leading economy in the postclassical era, and you should know its features, like paper money.

Women in the Song Dynasty

The "golden age" of Song dynasty China was perhaps less than "golden" for many of its women, for that era marked yet another turning point in the history of Chinese patriarchy. Under the influence of steppe nomads, whose women led less restricted lives, elite Chinese women of the Tang dynasty era, at least in the north, had participated in social life with greater freedom than in earlier times. Paintings and statues show aristocratic women riding horses, while the Queen Mother of the West, a Daoist deity, was widely worshipped by female Daoist priests and practitioners. (See Working with Evidence, Sources 8.2 and 8.4, pages 358 and 360.) By the Song dynasty, however, a reviving Confucianism and rapid economic growth seemed to tighten patriarchal restrictions on women and to restore some of the earlier Han dynasty notions of female submission and passivity.

Once again, Confucian writers highlighted the subordination of women to men and the need to keep males and females separate in every domain of life. The Song dynasty historian and scholar Sima Guang (1019–1086) summed up the prevailing view: "The boy leads the girl, the girl follows the boy; the duty of husbands to be resolute and wives to be docile begins with this."[11] For men, masculinity came to be defined less in terms of horseback riding, athleticism, and the warrior values of northern nomads and more in terms of the refined pursuits of calligraphy, scholarship, painting, and poetry. Corresponding views of feminine qualities emphasized women's weakness, reticence, and delicacy. Women were also frequently viewed as a distraction to men's pursuit of a contemplative and introspective life. The remarriage of widows, though legally permissible, was increasingly condemned, for "to walk through two courtyards is a source of shame for a woman."[12]

The most compelling expression of a tightening patriarchy lay in foot binding. Apparently beginning among dancers and courtesans in the tenth or eleventh century C.E., this practice involved the tight wrapping of young girls' feet, usually breaking the bones of the foot and causing intense pain. During and after the Song dynasty, foot binding found general acceptance among elite families and later became even more widespread in Chinese society. It was associated with new images of female beauty and eroticism that emphasized small size, frailty, and deference and served to keep women restricted to the "inner quarters," where Confucian tradition asserted that they belonged. Many mothers imposed this painful procedure on their daughters, perhaps to enhance their marriage prospects and to assist them in competing with concubines for the attention of their husbands.[13] For many women, it became a rite of passage, and their tiny feet and the beautiful slippers that encased them became a source of some pride, even a topic of poetry for some literate women. Foot binding also served to distinguish Chinese women from their "barbarian" counterparts and elite women from commoners and peasants.

Furthermore, a rapidly commercializing economy undermined the position of women in the textile industry. Urban workshops and state factories, run by men,

AP® EXAM TIP

It is essential to understand the status of women and their roles in society during the Tang and Song dynasties, and you must know the factors that led to continuities and changes in women's status throughout China's, and all of humanity's, history.

Guided Reading Question

■ CHANGE
In what ways did women's lives change during the Tang and Song dynasties?

Foot Binding
While the practice of foot binding painfully deformed the feet of young girls and women, it was also associated aesthetically with feminine beauty, particularly in the delicate and elaborately decorated shoes that encased their bound feet. (foot: Jodi Cobb/National Geographic Creative; shoe: ClassicStock/Masterfile)

increasingly took over the skilled tasks of weaving textiles, especially silk, which had previously been the work of rural women in their homes. Although these women continued to tend silkworms and spin silk thread, they had lost the more lucrative income-generating work of weaving silk fabrics. But as their economic role in textile production declined, other opportunities beckoned in an increasingly prosperous Song China. In the cities, women operated restaurants, sold fish and vegetables, and worked as maids, cooks, and dressmakers. The growing prosperity of elite families funneled increasing numbers of women into roles as concubines, entertainers, courtesans, and prostitutes. Their ready availability surely reduced the ability of wives to negotiate as equals with their husbands, setting women against one another and creating endless household jealousies.

In other ways, the Song dynasty witnessed more positive trends in the lives of women. Their property rights expanded, allowing women to control their own dowries and to inherit property from their families. "Neither in earlier nor in later periods," writes one scholar, "did as much property pass through women's hands" as during the Song dynasty.[14] Furthermore, lower-ranking but ambitious officials strongly urged the education of women, so that they might more effectively raise their sons and increase the family's fortune. Song dynasty China, in short, offered a mixture of tightening restrictions and new opportunities to its women.

China and the Northern Nomads: A Chinese World Order in the Making

From early times to the nineteenth century, China's many interactions with a larger Eurasian world shaped both China's own development and that of world history more generally. The country's most enduring and intense interaction with foreigners lay to the north, involving the many nomadic pastoral or semi-agricultural peoples of the steppes. Living in areas unable to sustain Chinese-style farming, the northern nomads had long focused their economies around the raising of livestock (sheep, cattle, goats) and the mastery of horse riding. Organized locally in small, mobile, kinship-based groups, sometimes called tribes, these peoples also periodically created much larger and powerful states or confederations that could draw on the impressive horsemanship and military skills of virtually the entire male population of their societies. Such specialized pastoral societies needed grain and other agricultural products from China, and their leaders developed a taste for Chinese manufactured and luxury goods—wine and silk, for example—with which they could attract and reward followers. Thus the nomads were drawn like a magnet toward China, trading, raiding, and extorting to obtain the resources so vital to their way of life. For 2,000 years or more, pressure from the steppes and the intrusion of nomadic peoples were constant factors in China's historical development.

From the nomads' point of view, the threat often came from the Chinese, who periodically directed their own military forces deep into the steppes, built the Great Wall to keep the nomads out, and often proved unwilling to allow pastoral peoples easy access to trading opportunities within China. And yet the Chinese needed the nomads. Their lands were the source of horses, which were essential for the Chinese military. Other products of the steppes and the forests beyond, such as skins, furs, hides, and amber, were also of value in China. Furthermore, pastoral nomads controlled much of the Silk Road trading network, which funneled goods from the West into China. The continuing interaction between China and the northern nomads brought together peoples occupying different environments, practicing different economies, governing themselves with different institutions, and thinking about the world in quite different ways.

> ### AP® EXAM TIP
> An important topic across world history is how civilizations responded to outside groups, as illustrated here with the response of China's governments to northern nomads.

Guided Reading Question

■ CONNECTION
How did the Chinese and their nomadic neighbors to the north view each other?

The Tribute System in Theory

An enduring outcome of this cross-cultural encounter was a particular view the Chinese held of themselves and of their neighbors, fully articulated by the time of the Han dynasty (ca. 200 B.C.E.–200 C.E.) and lasting for more than two millennia. That understanding cast China as the "middle kingdom," the center of the world, infinitely superior to the "barbarian" peoples beyond its borders. With its long history, great cities, refined tastes, sophisticated intellectual and artistic achievements, bureaucratic state, literate elite, and prosperous economy, China represented "civilization." All of this, in Chinese thinking, was in sharp contrast to the rude cultures and primitive life of the northern nomads, who continually moved about "like beasts and birds," lived in tents, ate mostly meat and milk, and practically lived on their horses, while making war on everyone within reach. Educated Chinese saw their own society as self-sufficient, requiring little from the outside world, while barbarians, quite understandably, sought access to China's wealth and wisdom. Furthermore, China was willing to permit that access under controlled conditions, for its sense of superiority did not preclude the possibility that barbarians could become civilized Chinese. China was a "radiating civilization," graciously shedding its light most fully to nearby barbarians and with diminished intensity to those farther away.

Guided Reading Question

■ CONNECTION
What assumptions underlay the tribute system?

Such was the general understanding of literate Chinese about their own civilization in relation to northern nomads and other non-Chinese peoples. That worldview also took shape as a practical system for managing China's relationship with these people. Known as the tribute system, it was a set of practices that required non-Chinese authorities to acknowledge Chinese superiority and their own subordinate place in a Chinese-centered world order. Foreigners seeking access to China had to send a delegation to the Chinese court, where they would perform the kowtow, a series of ritual bowings and prostrations, and present their tribute—products of value from their countries—to the Chinese emperor. In return for these expressions of submission, he would grant permission for foreigners to trade in China's rich markets and would provide them with gifts or "bestowals," often worth far more than the tribute they had offered. This was the mechanism by which successive Chinese dynasties attempted to regulate their relationships with northern nomads; with neighboring states such as Korea, Vietnam, Tibet, and Japan; and, after 1500, with those European barbarians from across the sea.

Often, this system seemed to work. Over the centuries, countless foreign delegations proved willing to present their tribute, say the required words, and perform the rituals necessary for gaining access to the material goods of China. Aspiring non-Chinese rulers also gained prestige as they basked in the reflected glory of even this subordinate association with the great Chinese civilization. The official titles, seals of office, and ceremonial robes they received from China proved useful in their local struggles for power.

The Tribute System in Practice

AP® EXAM TIP

Know the features of China's tribute system of exchange with nomadic groups, such as the Xiongnu.

But the tribute system also disguised some realities that contradicted its assumptions. On occasion, China was confronting not separate and small-scale barbarian societies, but large and powerful nomadic empires able to deal with China on at least equal terms. An early nomadic confederacy was that of the Xiongnu, established about the same time as the Han dynasty and eventually reaching from Manchuria to Central Asia (see Map 3.5, page 123). Devastating Xiongnu raids into northern China persuaded the Chinese emperor to negotiate an arrangement that recognized the nomadic state as a political equal, promised its leader a princess in marriage, and, most important, agreed to supply him annually with large quantities

The Tribute System
This Qing dynasty painting shows an idealized Chinese version of the tribute system. The Chinese emperor receives barbarian envoys, who perform rituals of subordination and present tribute in the form of a horse. (Musée des Arts Asiatiques–Guimet, Paris, France/© RMN–Grand Palais/Art Resource, NY)

of grain, wine, and silk. Although these goods were officially termed "gifts," granted in accord with the tribute system, they were in fact tribute in reverse or even protection money. In return for these goods, so critical for the functioning of the nomadic state, the Xiongnu agreed to refrain from military incursions into China. The basic realities of the situation were summed up in this warning to the Han dynasty in the first century B.C.E.:

> Just make sure that the silks and grain stuffs you bring the Xiongnu are the right measure and quality, that's all. What's the need for talking? If the goods you deliver are up to measure and good quality, all right. But if there is any deficiency or the quality is no good, then when the autumn harvest comes, we will take our horses and trample all over your crops.[15]

Something similar occurred during the Tang dynasty as a series of Turkic empires arose in Mongolia. Like the Xiongnu, they too extorted large "gifts" from the Chinese. One of these peoples, the Uighurs, actually rescued the Tang dynasty from a serious internal revolt in the 750s. In return, the Uighur leader gained one of the Chinese emperor's daughters as a wife and arranged a highly favorable exchange of poor-quality horses for high-quality silk, which brought half a million rolls of the precious fabric annually into the Uighur lands. Despite the rhetoric of the tribute system, the Chinese were not always able to dictate the terms of their relationship with the northern nomads.

Steppe nomads were generally not much interested in actually conquering and ruling China. It was easier and more profitable to extort goods from a functioning Chinese state. On occasion, however, that state broke down, and various nomadic groups moved in to "pick up the pieces," conquering and governing parts of China. Such a process took place following the fall of the Han dynasty and again after the collapse of the Tang dynasty, when the Khitan (kee-THAN) (907–1125) and then the Jin, or Jurchen (JER-chihn) (1115–1234), peoples established states that encompassed parts of northern China as well as major areas of the steppes to the north.

Both of them required the Chinese Song dynasty, located farther south, to deliver annually huge quantities of silk, silver, and tea, some of which found its way into the Silk Road trading network. The practice of "bestowing gifts on barbarians," long a part of the tribute system, allowed the proud Chinese to imagine that they were still in control of the situation even as they were paying heavily for protection from nomadic incursion. Those gifts, in turn, provided vital economic resources to nomadic states.

Cultural Influence across an Ecological Frontier

AP® EXAM TIP

Know the purpose of the Great Wall.

When nomadic peoples actually ruled parts of China, some of them adopted Chinese ways, employing Chinese advisers, governing according to Chinese practice, and, at least for the elite, immersing themselves in Chinese culture and learning. This process of "becoming Chinese" went furthest among the Jurchen, many of whom lived in northern China and learned to speak Chinese, wore Chinese clothing, married Chinese husbands and wives, and practiced Buddhism or Daoism. On the whole, however, Chinese culture had only a modest impact on the nomadic people of the northern steppes. Unlike the native peoples of southern China, who were gradually absorbed into Chinese culture, the pastoral societies north of the Great Wall generally retained their own cultural patterns. Few of them were incorporated, at least not for long, within a Chinese state, and most lived in areas where Chinese-style agriculture was simply impossible. Under these conditions, there were few incentives for adopting Chinese culture wholesale. But various modes of interaction—peaceful trade, military conflict, political negotiations, economic extortion, some cultural influence—continued across the ecological frontier that divided two quite distinct and separate ways of life. Each was necessary for the other.

Guided Reading Question

■ **CONNECTION**
In what ways did China and the nomads influence each other?

On the Chinese side, elements of steppe culture had some influence in those parts of northern China that were periodically conquered and ruled by nomadic peoples. The founders of the Sui and Tang dynasties were in fact of mixed nomad and Chinese ancestry and came from the borderland region where a blended Chinese/Turkic culture had evolved. High-ranking members of the imperial family personally led their troops in battle in the style of Turkic warriors. Furthermore, Tang dynasty China was awash with foreign visitors from all over Asia—delegations bearing tribute, merchants carrying exotic goods, bands of clerics or religious pilgrims bringing new religions such as Christianity, Islam, Buddhism, and Manichaeism. For a time in the Tang dynasty, almost anything associated with "Western barbarians"—Central Asians, Persians, Indians, Arabs—had great appeal among northern Chinese elites. Their music, dancing, clothing, foods, games, and artistic styles found favor among the upper classes. The more traditional southern Chinese, feeling themselves heir to the legacy of the Han dynasty, were sharply critical of their northern counterparts for allowing women too much freedom, for drinking yogurt rather than tea, and for listening to "Western" music, all of which they attrib uted to barbarian influence. Around 800 C.E., the poet Yuan Chen gave voice to a growing backlash against this too-easy acceptance of things "Western":

> Ever since the Western horsemen began raising smut and dust,
> Fur and fleece, rank and rancid, have filled Hsien and Lo [two Chinese cities].
> Women make themselves Western matrons by the study of Western makeup.
> Entertainers present Western tunes, in their devotion to Western music.[16]

Coping with China: Comparing Korea, Vietnam, and Japan

Also involved in tributary relationships with China were the newly emerging states and civilizations of Korea, Vietnam, and Japan. Unlike the northern nomads, these societies were thoroughly agricultural and sedentary. During the first millennium C.E., they were part of a larger process — the globalization of civilization — which produced new city- and state-based societies in various parts of the world. Proximity to their giant Chinese neighbor decisively shaped the histories of these new East Asian civilizations, for all of them borrowed major elements of Chinese culture. But unlike the native peoples of southern China, who largely became Chinese, the peoples of Korea, Vietnam, and Japan did not. They retained distinctive identities, which have lasted into modern times. While resisting Chinese political domination, they also appreciated Chinese culture and sought the source of Chinese wealth and power. In such ways, these smaller East Asian civilizations resembled the "developing" Afro-Asian societies of the twentieth century, which embraced "modernity" and elements of Western culture, while trying to maintain their political and cultural independence from the European and American centers of that modern way of life. Korea, Vietnam, and Japan, however, encountered China and responded to it in quite different ways.

AP® EXAM TIP

Know the interactions between major empires and the states near them, like China with Korea, and Vietnam with China.

Korea and China

Immediately adjacent to northeastern China, the Korean peninsula and its people have long lived in the shadow of their imposing neighbor (see Map 8.2). Temporary Chinese conquest of northern Korea during the Han dynasty and some colonization by Chinese settlers provided an initial channel for Chinese cultural influence, particularly in the form of Buddhism. Early Korean states, which emerged in the fourth through seventh centuries C.E., all referred to their rulers with the Chinese term *wang* (king). Bitter rivals with one another, these states strenuously resisted Chinese political control, except when they found it advantageous to join with China against a local enemy. In the seventh century, one of these states — the Silla (SHEE-lah) kingdom — allied with Tang dynasty China to bring some political

Guided Reading Question

■ CONNECTION

In what ways did China have an influence in Korea, Vietnam, and Japan? In what ways was that influence resisted?

Map 8.2 Korean Kingdoms, ca. 500 C.E.

The three early kingdoms of Korea were brought together by the seventh century in a unified state, which was subsequently governed by a series of dynastic regimes.

unity to the peninsula for the first time. But Chinese efforts to set up puppet regimes and to assimilate Koreans to Chinese culture provoked sharp military resistance, persuading the Chinese to withdraw their military forces in 688 and to establish a tributary relationship with a largely independent Korea.

Under a succession of dynasties—the Silla (688–900), Koryo (918–1392), and Joseon (1392–1910)—Korea generally maintained its political independence while participating in China's tribute system. Its leaders actively embraced the connection with China and, especially during the Silla dynasty, sought to turn their small state into a miniature version of Tang China.

Tribute missions to China provided legitimacy for Korean rulers and knowledge of Chinese court life and administrative techniques, which they sought to replicate back home. A new capital city of Kumsong was modeled directly on the Chinese capital of Chang'an (chahng-ahn). Tribute missions also enabled both official and private trade, mostly in luxury goods such as ceremonial clothing, silks, fancy teas, Confucian and Buddhist texts, and artwork—all of which enriched the lives of a Korean aristocracy that was becoming increasingly Chinese in culture. Thousands of Korean students were sent to China, where they studied primarily Confucianism but also natural sciences and the arts. Buddhist monks visited centers of learning and pilgrimage in China and brought back popular forms of Chinese Buddhism, which quickly took root in Korea. Schools for the study of Confucianism, using texts in the Chinese language, were established in Korea. In these ways, Korea became a part of the expanding world of Chinese culture, and refugees from the peninsula's many wars carried Chinese culture to Japan as well.

These efforts to plant Confucian values and Chinese culture in Korea had what one scholar has called an "overwhelmingly negative" impact on Korean women, particularly after 1300.[17] Early Chinese observers noticed, and strongly disapproved of, "free choice" marriages in Korea as well as the practice of women singing and dancing together late at night. With the support of the Korean court, Chinese models of family life and female behavior, especially among the elite, gradually replaced the more flexible Korean patterns. Earlier, a Korean woman had generally given birth and raised her young children in her parents' home, where she was often joined by her husband. This was now strongly discouraged, for it was deeply offensive to those who espoused Confucian orthodoxy, which held that a married woman belonged to her husband's family. Some Korean customs—funeral rites in which a husband was buried in the sacred plot of his wife's family, the remarriage of widowed or divorced women, and female inheritance of property—eroded under the pressure of Confucian orthodoxy. So too did the practice of plural marriages for men. In 1413, a legal distinction between primary and secondary wives required men to identify one of their wives as primary. Because she and her children now had special privileges and status, sharp new tensions emerged within families. Korean restrictions on elite women, especially widows, came to exceed even those in China itself.

Still, Korea remained Korean. After 688, the country's political independence, though periodically threatened, was largely intact. Chinese cultural influence, except for Buddhism, had little impact beyond the aristocracy and certainly did not penetrate the lives of Korea's serf-like peasants. Nor did it register among Korea's many slaves, amounting to about one-third of the country's population by 1100. In fact, Korean Buddhist monasteries used slaves to cultivate their lands. A Chinese-style examination system to recruit government officials, though encouraged by some Korean rulers, never assumed the prominence that it gained in Tang and Song dynasty China. Korea's aristocratic class was able to maintain an even stronger monopoly on bureaucratic office than its Chinese counterpart did. And in the 1400s, Korea moved toward greater cultural independence by developing a phonetic alphabet, known as *hangul* (HAHN-gool), for writing the Korean language. Although resisted by conservative male elites, who were long accustomed to using the more prestigious Chinese characters to write Korean, this new form of writing gradually took hold, especially in private correspondence, in popular fiction, and among women. Clearly part of the Chinese world order, Korea nonetheless retained a distinctive culture as well as a separate political existence.

Vietnam and China

At the southern fringe of the Chinese cultural world, the people who eventually came to be called Vietnamese had a broadly similar historical encounter with China (see Map 8.3). As in Korea, the elite culture of Vietnam borrowed heavily from China—adopting Confucianism, Daoism, Buddhism, administrative techniques, the examination system, artistic and literary styles—even as its popular culture remained distinctive. And, like Korea, Vietnam achieved political independence, while participating fully in the tribute system as a vassal state.

But there were differences as well. The cultural heartland of Vietnam in the Red River valley was fully incorporated into the Chinese state for more than a thousand years (111 B.C.E.–939 C.E.), far longer than corresponding parts of Korea.

AP® EXAM TIP

You should know about the effects of the spread of Confucianism and Buddhism on areas outside their places of origin.

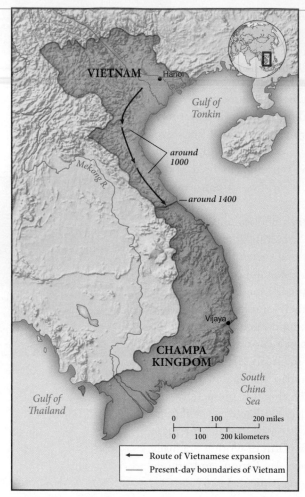

Map 8.3   Vietnam

As Vietnam threw off Chinese control, it also expanded to the south, while remaining wary of its larger Chinese neighbor to the north.

Regarded by the Chinese as "southern barbarians," the Vietnamese were ruled by Chinese officials who expected to fully assimilate this rich rice-growing region into China culturally as well as politically. To these officials, it was simply a further extension of the southward movement of Chinese civilization. Thus Chinese-style irrigated agriculture was introduced; Vietnamese elites were brought into the local bureaucracy and educated in Confucian-based schools; Chinese replaced the local language in official business; Chinese clothing and hairstyles became mandatory; and large numbers of Chinese, some fleeing internal conflicts at home, flooded into the relative security of what they referred to as "the pacified south," while often despising the local people. The heavy pressure of the Chinese presence generated not only a Vietnamese elite thoroughly schooled in Chinese culture but also periodic rebellions, on several occasions led by women. (See Zooming In: Trung Trac, Chapter 3, page 124.)

The weakening of the Tang dynasty in the early tenth century C.E. finally enabled a particularly large rebellion to establish Vietnam as a separate state, though one that carefully maintained its tributary role, sending repeated missions to do homage at the Chinese court. Nonetheless, successive Vietnamese dynasties found the Chinese approach to government useful, styling their rulers as emperors, claiming the Mandate of Heaven, and making use of Chinese court rituals, while expanding their state steadily southward. More so than in Korea, a Chinese-based examination system in Vietnam functioned to undermine an established aristocracy, to provide some measure of social mobility for commoners, and to create a merit-based scholar-gentry class to staff the bureaucracy. Furthermore, members of the Vietnamese elite class remained deeply committed to Chinese culture, viewing their own country less as a separate nation than as a southern extension of a universal civilization, the only one they knew.

Beyond the elite, however, there remained much that was uniquely Vietnamese, such as a distinctive language, a fondness for cockfighting, and the habit of chewing betel nuts. More importantly, Vietnam long retained a greater role for women in social and economic life, despite heavy Chinese influence. In the third century C.E., a woman leader of an anti-Chinese resistance movement declared: "I want to drive away the enemy to save our people. I will not resign myself to the usual lot of women who bow their heads and become concubines." Female nature deities and a "female Buddha" continued to be part of Vietnamese popular religion, even as Confucian-based ideas took root among the elite. In the centuries following independence from China, as Vietnam expanded to the south, northern officials tried in vain to impose more orthodox Confucian gender practices in place of local customs that allowed women to choose their own husbands and married men to live in the households of their wives. So persistent were these practices that a seventeenth-century Chinese visitor opined, with disgust, that Vietnamese preferred the birth of a girl to that of a boy. These features of Vietnamese life

Independence for Vietnam
In 938, Vietnamese forces under the leadership of General Ngo Quyen defeated the Chinese in the Battle of Bach Dang River, thus ending a thousand years of direct Chinese rule. This image is one of many that celebrate that victory. (Pictures from History/CPA Media)

reflected larger patterns of Southeast Asian culture that distinguished it from China. And like Koreans, the Vietnamese developed a variation of Chinese writing called *chu nom* ("southern script"), which provided the basis for an independent national literature and a vehicle for the writing of most educated women.

Japan and China

Unlike Korea and Vietnam, the Japanese islands were physically separated from China by 100 miles or more of ocean and were never successfully invaded or conquered by their giant mainland neighbor (see Map 8.4). Thus Japan's very extensive borrowing from Chinese civilization was wholly voluntary, rather than occurring under conditions of direct military threat or outright occupation. The high point of that borrowing took place during the seventh to the ninth centuries C.E., as the first more or less unified Japanese state began to emerge from dozens of small clan-based aristocratic chiefdoms. That state found much that was useful in Tang dynasty China and set out, deliberately and systematically, to transform Japan into a centralized bureaucratic state on the Chinese model.

The initial leader of this effort was Shotoku Taishi (572–622), a prominent aristocrat from one of the major clans. He launched a series of large-scale missions to China, which took hundreds of Japanese monks, scholars, artists, and students to the mainland, and when they returned, they put into practice what they had learned. In 604 C.E. Shotoku issued the Seventeen Article Constitution, proclaiming the Japanese ruler as a Chinese-style emperor and encouraging both Buddhism and Confucianism. In good Confucian fashion, that document emphasized the

AP® EXAM TIP

Note the differences in the ways Chinese culture was introduced into Japan, compared to its introduction into Korea and Vietnam.

Map 8.4   Japan

Japan's distance from China enabled it to maintain its political independence and to draw selectively from Chinese culture.

AP® EXAM TIP

It will be helpful to remember that Japan has a long history of voluntarily borrowing from other cultures.

moral quality of rulers as a foundation for social harmony. In the decades that followed, Japanese authorities adopted Chinese-style court rituals and a system of court rankings for officials as well as the Chinese calendar. Subsequently, they likewise established Chinese-based taxation systems, law codes, government ministries, and provincial administration, at least on paper. Two capital cities, first Nara and then Heian-kyo (Kyoto), arose, both modeled on the Chinese capital of Chang'an.

Chinese culture, no less than its political practices, also found favor in Japan. Various schools of Chinese Buddhism took root, first among the educated and literate classes and later more broadly in Japanese society, deeply affecting much of Japanese life. Art, architecture, education, medicine, views of the afterlife, attitudes toward suffering and the impermanence of life—all of this and more reflected the influence of Buddhist culture in Japan. The Chinese writing system—and with it an interest in historical writing, calligraphy, and poetry—likewise proved attractive among the elite.

The absence of any compelling threat from China made it possible for the Japanese to be selective in their borrowing. By the tenth century, deliberate efforts to absorb additional elements of Chinese culture diminished, and formal tribute missions to China stopped, although private traders and Buddhist monks continued to make the difficult journey to the mainland. Over many centuries, the Japanese combined what they had assimilated from China with elements of their own tradition into a distinctive Japanese civilization, which differed from Chinese culture in many ways.

In the political realm, for example, the Japanese never succeeded in creating an effective centralized and bureaucratic state to match that of China. Although the court and the emperor retained an important ceremonial and cultural role, their real political authority over the country gradually diminished in favor of competing aristocratic families, both at court and in the provinces. A Chinese-style university trained officials, but rather than serving as a mechanism for recruiting talented commoners into the political elite, it enrolled students who were largely the sons of court aristocrats.

As political power became increasingly decentralized, local authorities developed their own military forces, the famous *samurai* warrior class of Japanese society. Bearing their exquisite curved swords, the samurai developed a distinctive set of values featuring bravery, loyalty, endurance, honor, great skill in martial arts, and a preference for death over surrender. This was *bushido* (boo-shee-doh), the way of the warrior. Japan's celebration of the samurai and of military virtues contrasted sharply with China's emphasis on intellectual achievements and political office holding, which were accorded higher prestige than bearing arms. "The educated men of the land," wrote a Chinese minister in the eleventh century, "regard the carrying of arms as a disgrace."[18] The Japanese, clearly, did not agree.

Religiously as well, Japan remained distinctive. Although Buddhism in many forms took hold in the country, it never completely replaced the native beliefs and practices, which focused attention on numerous *kami*, sacred spirits associated with human ancestors and various natural phenomena. Much later referred to as Shinto, this tradition provided legitimacy to the imperial family, based on claims of descent from the sun goddess. Because veneration of the kami lacked an elaborate philosophy or ritual, it conflicted very little with Buddhism. In fact, numerous kami were assimilated into Japanese Buddhism as local expressions of Buddhist deities or principles.

Japanese literary and artistic culture likewise evolved in distinctive ways, despite much borrowing from China. As in Korea and Vietnam, there emerged a unique writing system that combined Chinese characters with a series of phonetic symbols. A highly stylized Japanese poetic form, known as tanka, developed early and has remained a favored means of expression ever since. (See Zooming In: Izumi Shikibu, page 344, for the life of Japan's best-known female tanka poet.) Particularly during the Heian period of Japanese history (794–1192), a highly refined aesthetic culture found expression at the imperial court, even as the court's real political authority melted away. Court aristocrats and their ladies lived in splendor, composed poems, arranged flowers, and conducted their love affairs. "What counted," wrote one scholar, "was the proper costume, the right ceremonial act, the successful turn of phrase in a poem, and the appropriate expression of refined taste."[19] Much of our knowledge of this courtly culture comes from the work of women writers, who composed their diaries and novels in the vernacular Japanese script, rather than in the

Guided Reading Question

■ COMPARISON

In what different ways did Japanese and Korean women experience the pressures of Confucian orthodoxy?

The Samurai of Japan

This late nineteenth-century image shows a samurai warrior on horseback clad in armor and a horned helmet while carrying a sword as well as a bow and arrows. The prominence of martial values in Japanese culture was one of the ways in which Japan differed from its Chinese neighbor, despite much borrowing. (Library of Congress, ID #pd 01046)

Izumi Shikibu,
Japanese Poet and Lover

Nowhere in world history has poetry played a more central role than in the imperial court of Japan, located in the capital city of Heian-kyo (now Kyoto) between the ninth and twelfth centuries. There, amid the political posturing and the love affairs of aristocratic women and men, almost every event, public or private, called for a poem—the first sighting of spring blossoms or a new moon; births, deaths, and marriages; various official rituals; the morning after a romantic encounter. "It is poetry," wrote one famous Japanese author in the early tenth century, "which . . . awakens the world of invisible spirits . . . , softens the relationship between men and women, and consoles the hearts of fierce warriors."[20] Izumi Shikibu, Japan's most illustrious female poet, was a master of this art, particularly in the lyric five-line, thirty-one-syllable form known as tanka. In her exquisite poetry, we can catch a glimpse of her erotic intensity, expressed in many scandalous love affairs, as well as her engagement in more spiritual pursuits.

Born around 975 as the daughter of a mid-level official, Izumi grew up in the imperial court, where a literary

Izumi Shikibu.

education was essential for girls of her status, for at least in matters of poetry and the arts, women and men operated on an equal basis. At about the age of twenty, Izumi married a provincial governor, but she soon began an affair with Prince Tam-etaka, son of the emperor, shocking court society partly because of the sharp difference in their social positions. Tametaka's death in 1002, widely credited to his sexual excess with Izumi, only deepened the scandal and led to Izumi's divorce from her husband and estrangement from her family. Addressing her parents and sisters in a poem, she declared: "One of you / I was, but am no more."[21]

Less than a year later, she ignited another scandal by taking up with Tametaka's brother, Prince Atsumichi. The first year of this affair became the subject of Izumi's famous *Diary*. When the prince sent her a sprig of orange blossoms, she responded with a poem: "Rather than recall / in these flowers / the fragrance of the past, /

photo: Pictures from History/CPA Media

classical Chinese used by elite men. *The Tale of Genji*, a Japanese novel written by the woman author Murasaki Shikibu around 1000, provides an intimate picture of the intrigues and romances of court life.

At this level of society, Japan's women, unlike those in Korea, largely escaped the more oppressive features of Chinese Confucian culture, such as the prohibition of remarriage for widows, seclusion within the home, and foot binding. Perhaps this is because the most powerful Chinese influence on Japan occurred during the Tang dynasty, when Chinese elite women enjoyed considerable freedom. Japanese women continued to inherit property; Japanese married couples often lived apart or with the wife's family; and marriages were made and broken easily. None of this corresponded to Confucian values. When Japanese women did begin to lose status

I would like to hear this nightingale's voice, / to know if his song is as sweet." What followed was a year of nocturnal visits, frequent absences, rumors and gossip, doubts and longings, and the endless exchange of poems. Finally, Izumi took up residence in the prince's compound, much to the distress of his principal wife. Atsumichi's death in 1007 prompted an outpouring of poetry mourning the loss of her great love. "I long for the sound / of your voice. / The face / I see so clearly / doesn't say a word."[22]

Despite Izumi's behavior, she was subsequently appointed as a lady-in-waiting for the Empress Akiko, for her literary reputation added splendor to the court. But the scandal of her personal life continued to shadow her. A rival literary figure at the court, the renowned Lady Murasaki, author of *The Tale of Genji*, commented, "How interestingly Izumi Shikibu writes. Yet what a disgraceful person she is."[23] A subsequent marriage to a much older provincial governor took Izumi away from the court for the rest of her life. But her affairs continued. "I do not feel in the least disposed to sleep alone," she wrote.[24]

Her poetry gave frequent expression to erotic love and to the anguished yearning that accompanied it. "Lying alone, / my black hair tangled, / uncombed / I long for the one / who touched it first." To a monk who left his fan behind after a visit, she wrote, "I think / you may have briefly forgotten / this fan, / but everyone must know / how it came to be dropped."

Izumi's experiences of love within her social circle gave her an acute sense of the ephemerality of all things. "Come quickly—as soon as / these blossoms open, / they fall. / This world exists / as a sheen of dew on flowers." Her understanding of impermanence was reinforced by her Buddhist faith with its emphasis on the transience of human life. From time to time, she felt the desire to withdraw into a monastery, and she did take periodic retreats in mountain temples. Even there, however, Izumi experienced the pull of the world. "Although I try / to hold the single thought / of Buddha's teaching in my heart, / I cannot help but hear / the many crickets' voices calling as well."[25]

Perhaps Izumi's best-known poem was composed when she was still in her teens, though it has sometimes been viewed as a prayer on her deathbed. Written to a Buddhist cleric, it reveals her early and continuing desire for spiritual enlightenment, symbolized here as the light of the moon. "From utter darkness / I must embark upon an / even darker road / O distant moon, cast your light / from the rim of the mountains."[26]

Question: How do you understand Izumi's involvement in multiple love relationships and her religious sensibilities?

in the twelfth century and later, it had less to do with Confucian pressures than with the rise of a warrior culture. As the personal relationships of samurai warriors to their lords replaced marriage alliances as a political strategy, the influence of women in political life was reduced, but this was an internal Japanese phenomenon, not a reflection of Chinese influence.

Japan's ability to borrow extensively from China while developing its own distinctive civilization perhaps provided a model for its encounter with the West in the nineteenth century. Then, as before, Japan borrowed selectively from a foreign culture without losing either its political independence or its cultural uniqueness.

PRACTICING AP® HISTORICAL THINKING

In what different ways did Korea, Vietnam, Japan, and northern nomads experience and respond to Chinese influence?

China and the Eurasian World Economy

Beyond China's central role in East Asia was its economic interaction with the wider world of Eurasia generally. On the one hand, China's remarkable economic growth, taking place during the Tang and Song dynasties, could hardly be contained within China's borders and clearly had a major impact throughout Eurasia. On the other hand, China was recipient as well as donor in the economic interactions of the third-wave era, and its own economic achievements owed something to the stimulus of contact with the larger world.

Spillovers: China's Impact on Eurasia

AP® EXAM TIP

Know examples of technological contributions from China to the rest of Asia and to Europe.

One of the outcomes of China's economic revolution lay in the diffusion of its many technological innovations to peoples and places far from East Asia as the movements of traders, soldiers, slaves, and pilgrims conveyed Chinese achievements abroad. (See Snapshot, opposite, for a wider view of Chinese technological achievements.) Chinese techniques for producing salt by solar evaporation spread to the Islamic world and later to Christian Europe. Papermaking, known in China since the Han dynasty, spread to Korea and Vietnam by the fourth century C.E., to Japan and India by the seventh, to the Islamic world by the eighth, to Muslim Spain by 1150, to France and Germany in the 1300s, and to England in the 1490s. Printing, likewise a Chinese invention, rapidly reached Korea, where movable type became a highly developed technique, and Japan as well. Both technologies were heavily influenced by Buddhism, which accorded religious merit to the reproduction of sacred texts. The Islamic world, however, highly valued handwritten calligraphy and generally resisted printing as impious until the nineteenth century. The adoption of printing in Europe was likewise delayed because of the absence of paper until the twelfth century. Then movable type was reinvented by Johannes Gutenberg in the fifteenth century, although it is unclear whether he was aware of Chinese and Korean precedents. With implications for mass literacy, bureaucracy, scholarship, the spread of religion, and the exchange of information, papermaking and printing were Chinese innovations of revolutionary and global dimensions.

Guided Reading Question

■ CONNECTION

In what ways did China participate in the world of Eurasian commerce and exchange, and with what outcomes?

Chinese technologies were seldom simply transferred from one place to another. More often, a particular Chinese technique or product stimulated innovations in more distant lands in accordance with local needs.[27] For example, as the Chinese formula for gunpowder, invented around 1000, became available in Europe, together with some early and simple firearms, these innovations triggered the development of cannons in the early fourteenth century. Soon cannons appeared in the Islamic world and, by 1356, in China itself, which first used cast iron rather than bronze in their construction. But the highly competitive European state system drove the "gunpowder revolution" much further and more rapidly than in China's imperial state. Chinese textile, metallurgical, and naval technologies likewise stimulated

SNAPSHOT Chinese Technological Achievements

Before the technological explosion of the European Industrial Revolution during the eighteenth and nineteenth centuries, China had long been the major center of global technological innovation.[28] Many of those inventions spread to other civilizations, where they stimulated imitation or modification. Since Europe was located at the opposite end of the Eurasian continent from China, it often took considerable time for those innovations to give rise to something similar in the West. That lag is also a measure of the relative technological development of the two civilizations in premodern times.

Innovation	First Used in China (approximate)	Adoption/Recognition in the West: Time Lag in Years (approximate)
Iron plow	6th–4th century B.C.E.	2,000+
Cast iron	4th century B.C.E.	1,000–1,200
Efficient horse collar	3rd–1st century B.C.E.	1,000
Paper	2nd century B.C.E.	1,000
Wheelbarrow	1st century B.C.E.	900–1,000
Rudder for steering ships	1st century C.E.	1,100
Iron chain suspension bridge	1st century C.E.	1,000–1,300
Porcelain	3rd century C.E.	1,500
Magnetic compass for navigation	9th–11th century C.E.	400
Gunpowder	9th century C.E.	400
Chain drive for transmission of power	976 C.E.	800
Movable type printing	1045 C.E.	400

imitation and innovation all across Eurasia. An example is the magnetic compass, a Chinese invention eagerly embraced by mariners of many cultural backgrounds as they traversed the Indian Ocean.

In addition to its technological influence, China's prosperity during the Song dynasty greatly stimulated commercial life and market-based behavior all across the Afro-Eurasian trading world. China's products — silk, porcelain, lacquerware — found eager buyers from Japan to East Africa, and everywhere in between. The immense size and wealth of China's domestic economy also provided a ready market for hundreds of commodities from afar. For example, the lives of many thousands of people in the spice-producing islands of what is now Indonesia were transformed as they came to depend on Chinese consumers' demand for their products. "[O]ne hundred million [Chinese] people," wrote historian William McNeill,

AP® EXAM TIP

Be able to list mass-produced Chinese products that were made for export.

"increasingly caught up within a commercial network, buying and selling to supplement every day's livelihood, made a significant difference to the way other human beings made their livings throughout a large part of the civilized world."[29] Such was the ripple effect of China's economic revolution.

On the Receiving End: China as Economic Beneficiary

If Chinese economic growth and technological achievements significantly shaped the Eurasian world of the third-wave era, that pattern of interaction was surely not a one-way street, for China too was changed by its engagement with a wider world. During this period, for example, China had learned about the cultivation and processing of both cotton and sugar from India. From Vietnam, around 1000, China gained access to the new, fast-ripening, and drought-resistant strains of rice that made a highly productive rice-based agriculture possible in the drier and more rugged regions of southern China. This marked a major turning point in Chinese history as the frontier region south of the Yangzi River grew rapidly in population, overtaking the traditional centers of Chinese civilization in the north. In the process, the many non-Chinese peoples of the area were painfully overwhelmed by Chinese military forces and by the migration of at least a million Han Chinese farmers by 1400. Some of them were attracted by new economic opportunities, while others were forcibly relocated by the Chinese state, intent on thoroughly integrating the south into Chinese civilization.

Technologically as well, China's extraordinary burst of creativity owed something to the stimulus of cross-cultural contact. Awareness of Persian windmills, for example, spurred the development of a distinct but related device in China. Printing arose from China's growing involvement with the world of Buddhism, which put a spiritual premium on the reproduction of the Buddha's image and of short religious texts that were carried as charms. It was in Buddhist monasteries during the Tang dynasty that the long-established practice of printing with seals was elaborated by Chinese monks into woodblock printing. The first printed book, in 868 C.E., was a famous Buddhist text, the *Diamond Sutra*.

A further transforming impact of China's involvement with a wider world derived from its growing participation in Indian Ocean trade. By the Tang dynasty, thousands of ships annually visited the ports of southern China, and settled communities of foreign merchants—Arabs, Persians, Indians, Southeast Asians—turned some of these cities into cosmopolitan centers. Buddhist temples, Muslim mosques and cemeteries, and Hindu phallic sculptures graced the skyline of Quanzhou, a coastal city in southern China. Occasionally the tensions of cultural diversity erupted in violence, such as the massacre of tens of thousands of foreigners in Canton during the 870s when Chinese rebel forces sacked the city. Indian Ocean commerce also contributed much to the transformation of southern China from a subsistence economy to one more heavily based on producing for export.

In the process, merchants achieved a degree of social acceptance not known before, including their frequent appointment to high-ranking bureaucratic positions. Finally, much-beloved stories of the monkey god, widely popular even in contemporary China, derived from Indian sources transmitted by Indian Ocean commerce.

China and Buddhism

By far the most important gift that China received from India was neither cotton nor sugar, but a religion, Buddhism. The gradual assimilation of this South Asian religious tradition into Chinese culture illustrates the process of cultural encounter and adaptation and invites comparison with the spread of Christianity into Europe. Until the adoption of Marxism in the twentieth century, Buddhism was the only large-scale cultural borrowing in Chinese history. It also made China into a launching pad for Buddhism's dispersion to Korea and from there to Japan as well. Thus, as Buddhism faded in the land of its birth, it became solidly rooted in much of East Asia, providing an element of cultural commonality for a vast region (see Map 8.5).

> **AP® EXAM TIP**
>
> Be sure you know the causes and effects of the spread of Buddhism into South, East, and Southeast Asia.

Making Buddhism Chinese

Buddhism initially entered China via the Silk Road trading network during the first and second centuries C.E. The stability and prosperity of the Han dynasty, then at its height, ensured that the new "barbarian" religion held little appeal for native Chinese. Furthermore, the Indian culture from which Buddhism sprang was at odds with Chinese understandings of the world in many ways. Buddhism's commitment to a secluded and monastic life for monks and nuns seemed to dishonor Chinese family values, and its concern for individual salvation or enlightenment appeared selfish, contradicting the social orientation of Confucian thinking. Its abstract philosophy ran counter to the more concrete, "this-worldly" concerns of Chinese thinkers, and the Buddhist concept of infinite eons of time, endlessly repeating themselves, was quite a stretch for the Chinese, who normally thought in terms of finite family generations or dynastic cycles. No wonder that for the first several centuries C.E., Buddhism was largely the preserve of foreign merchants and monks living in China.

In the half millennium between roughly 300 and 800 C.E., however, Buddhism took solid root in China within both elite and popular culture, becoming a permanent, though fluctuating, presence in Chinese life. How did this remarkable transformation unfold? It began, arguably, with the collapse of the Han dynasty around 200 C.E. The chaotic, violent, and politically fragmented centuries that followed seriously discredited Confucianism and opened the door to alternative understandings of the world. Nomadic rulers, now governing much of northern China, found Buddhism useful in part because it was foreign. "We were born out of the marches," declared one of them, "and though we are unworthy, we have complied with our

Guided Reading Question

....

■ CHANGE
What facilitated the rooting of Buddhism within China?

Map 8.5   The World of Asian Buddhism

Originating in India, Buddhism later spread widely throughout much of Asia to provide a measure of cultural or religious commonality across this vast region.

AP® EXAM TIP

Study the routes and the broad time-table of the spread of Buddhism.

appointed destiny and govern the Chinese as their prince. . . . Buddha being a bar-barian god is the very one we should worship."[30] Rulers and elite families provided patronage for Buddhist monasteries, temples, and works of art. In southern China, where many northern aristocrats had fled following the disastrous decline of the Han dynasty, Buddhism provided some comfort in the face of a collapsing society.

Its emphasis on ritual, morality, and contemplation represented an intellectually and aesthetically satisfying response to times that were so clearly out of joint.

Meanwhile, Buddhist monasteries increasingly provided an array of social services for ordinary people. In them, travelers found accommodation; those fleeing from China's many upheavals discovered a place of refuge; desperate people received charity; farmers borrowed seed for the next planting; the sick were treated; and children learned to read. And for many, Buddhism was associated with access to magical powers as reports of miracles abounded. Battles were won, rain descended on drought-ridden areas, diseases were cured, and guilt was relieved—all through the magical ministrations of charismatic monks.

Accompanying all of this was a serious effort by monks, scholars, and translators to present this Indian religion in terms that Chinese could more readily grasp. Thus the Buddhist term *dharma*, referring to the Buddha's teaching, was translated as *dao*, or "the way," a notion long familiar in both Daoist and Confucian thinking (see Chapter 4). The Buddhist notion of "morality" was translated with the Confucian term that referred to "filial submission and obedience." Some Indian concepts were modified in the process of translation. For example, the idea that "husband supports wife," which reflected a considerable respect for women and mothers in early Indian Buddhism, became in translation "husband controls wife."[31]

As Buddhism took hold in China, it was primarily in its broader Mahayana form—complete with numerous deities, the veneration of relics, many heavens and hells, and bodhisattvas to aid the believer—rather than its more psychological and individualistic Theravada form (see Chapter 4). One of the most popular expressions of Buddhism in China was the Pure Land School, in which faithfully repeating the name of an earlier Buddha, the Amitabha, was sufficient to ensure rebirth in a beautifully described heavenly realm, the Pure Land. In its emphasis on salvation by faith, without arduous study or intensive meditation, Pure Land Buddhism became a highly popular and authentically Chinese version of the Indian faith.

China's reunification under the Sui and early Tang dynasties witnessed growing state support for Buddhism. The Sui emperor Wendi (r. 581–604 C.E.) had monasteries constructed at the base of China's five sacred mountains, further identifying the imported religion with traditional Chinese culture. He even used Buddhism to justify his military campaigns. "With a hundred victories in a hundred battles," he declared, "we promote the practice of the ten Buddhist virtues."[32] By 600 C.E., some 4,000 monasteries had been established. With state support and growing popular acceptance, they became centers of great wealth. They were largely exempt from taxation and owned large estates; ran businesses such as oil presses, water mills, and pawn shops; collected gems, gold, and lavish works of art; and employed millions of slaves, serfs, and other unfree and dependent workers. But Buddhism, while solidly entrenched in Chinese life by the early Tang dynasty, never achieved the independence from state authorities that the Christian Church acquired in

Europe. The examinations for becoming a monk were supervised by the state, and education in the monasteries included the required study of the Confucian classics. In the mid-ninth century, the state showed quite dramatically just how much control it could exercise over the Buddhist establishment.

Losing State Support: The Crisis of Chinese Buddhism

The impressive growth of Chinese Buddhism was accompanied by a persistent undercurrent of resistance and criticism. Some saw the Buddhist establishment, at least potentially, as a "state within a state" and a challenge to imperial authority. More important was a deepening resentment of its enormous wealth. One fifth-century critic, referring to monks, put the issue squarely: "Why is it that their ideals are noble and far-reaching and their activities still are base and common? [They] become merchants and engage in barter, wrangling with the masses for profit."[33] Nor did the environmental impact of Buddhist monasteries escape the notice of state officials. In 707 C.E., one such official wrote: "Extensive construction of monasteries are undertaken and large mansions are built. Even though for such works trees are felled to the point of stripping the mountains, it does not suffice. . . . Though earth is moved to the point of obstructing roads, it does not suffice."[34] When state treasuries were short of funds, government officials cast a covetous eye on these wealthy and tax-exempt monasteries. Furthermore, Buddhism was clearly of foreign origin and offensive for that reason to some Confucian and Daoist thinkers. The celibacy of the monks and their withdrawal from society, the critics argued, undermined the Confucian-based family system of Chinese tradition.

Guided Reading Question

■ **CHANGE**
What were the major sources of opposition to Buddhism within China?

Such criticisms took on new meaning in the changed environment of China after about 800 C.E. Following centuries of considerable foreign influence in China, a growing resentment against foreign culture, particularly among the literate classes, increasingly took hold. The turning point may well have been the An Lushan rebellion (755–763), in which a general of foreign origin led a major revolt against the Tang dynasty. Whatever its origin, an increasingly xenophobic reaction set in among the upper classes, reflected in a desire to return to an imagined "purity" of earlier times. In this setting, the old criticisms of Buddhism became more sharply focused. In 819, Han Yu, a leading figure in the Confucian counterattack on Buddhism, wrote a scathing memorial to the emperor, criticizing his willingness to honor a relic of the Buddha's finger.

> Now the Buddha was of barbarian origin. His language differed from Chinese speech; his clothes were of a different cut; his mouth did not pronounce the prescribed words of the Former Kings. . . . He did not recognize the relationship between prince and subject, nor the sentiments of father and son. . . . I pray that Your Majesty will turn this bone over to the officials that it may be cast into water or fire.[35]

Several decades later, the Chinese state took direct action against the Buddhist establishment as well as against other foreign religions. A series of imperial decrees between 841 and 845 ordered some 260,000 monks and nuns to return to normal life as tax-paying citizens. Thousands of monasteries, temples, and shrines were either destroyed or turned to public use, while the state confiscated the lands, money, metals, and serfs belonging to monasteries. Buddhists were now forbidden to use gold, silver, copper, iron, and gems in constructing their images. These actions dealt a serious blow to Chinese Buddhism. Its scholars and monks were scattered, its creativity diminished, and its institutions came even more firmly under state control.

Despite this persecution, Buddhism did not vanish from China. At the level of elite culture, its philosophical ideas played a role in the reformulation of Confucian thinking that took place during the Song dynasty. At the village level, Buddhism became one element of Chinese popular religion, which also included the veneration of ancestors, the honoring of Confucius, and Daoist shrines and rituals. Temples frequently included statues of Confucius, Laozi, and the Buddha, with little sense of any incompatibility among them. "Every black-haired son of Han," the Chinese have long said, "wears a Confucian thinking cap, a Daoist robe, and Buddhist sandals." (See photo, page 146.) Unlike in Europe, where an immigrant religion triumphed over and excluded all other faiths, Buddhism in China became assimilated into Chinese culture alongside its other traditions.

REFLECTIONS

Why Do Things Change?

The rapidity of change in modern societies is among the most distinctive features of recent history, but change and transformation, though at various rates, have been constants in the human story since the very beginning. Explaining how and why human societies change is perhaps the central issue that historians confront, no matter which societies or periods of time they study. Those who specialize in the history of some particular culture or civilization often emphasize sources of change operating within those societies, although there is intense disagreement as to which are most significant. The ideas of great thinkers, the policies of leaders, struggles for power, the conflict of classes, the invention of new technologies, the growth or decline in population, variations in climate or weather—all of these and more have their advocates as the primary motor of historical transformation.

Of course, it is not necessary to choose among them. The history of China illustrates the range of internal factors that have driven change in that civilization. The political conflicts of the "era of warring states" provided the setting and the motivation for the emergence of Confucianism and Daoism, which in turn have certainly shaped the character and texture of Chinese civilization over many centuries. The personal qualities and brutal policies of Shihuangdi surely played a role in China's unification and in the brief duration of the Qin dynasty. The subsequent creation of a widespread network of canals and waterways as well as the country's technological achievements served to maintain that unity over very long periods of time. But the massive inequalities of Chinese society generated the peasant upheavals, which periodically shattered that unity and led to new ruling dynasties. Sometimes natural events, such as droughts and floods, triggered those rebellions.

World historians, more than those who study particular civilizations or nations, have been inclined to find the primary source of change in contact with strangers, in external connections and interactions, whether direct or indirect. The history of China and East Asia provides plenty of examples for this point of view as well. Conceptions of China as the "middle kingdom," infinitely superior to all surrounding societies, grew out of centuries of involvement with its neighbors. Some of those neighbors became Chinese as China's imperial reach grew, especially to the south. Even those that did not, such as Korea, Vietnam, and Japan, were decisively transformed by proximity to the "radiating civilization" of China. China's own cuisine, so distinctive in recent centuries, may well be a quite recent invention, drawing heavily on Indian and Southeast Asian cooking. Buddhism, of course, is an obvious borrowing from abroad, although its incorporation into Chinese civilization and its ups and downs within China owed much to internal cultural and political realities.

In the end, clear distinctions between internal and external sources of change in China's history — or that of any other society — are perhaps misleading. The boundary between "inside" and "outside" is itself a constantly changing line. Should the borderlands of northern China, where Chinese and Turkic peoples met and mingled, be regarded as internal or external to China itself? And, as the histories of Chinese Buddhism and of Japanese culture so clearly indicate, what comes from beyond is always transformed by what it encounters within.

Chapter Review

What's the Significance?

Sui dynasty, 324–25
Tang dynasty, 325–27
Song dynasty, 325–32
Hangzhou, 327
gunpowder, 328–29
economic revolution, 328–30
foot binding, 331–32
tribute system, 333–36
Xiongnu, 334–36

Khitan and Jurchen people, 335–36
Silla dynasty (Korea), 337–38
hangul, 339
chu nom, 341
Shotoku Taishi, 341
bushido, 343
Izumi Shikibu, 344–45
Chinese Buddhism, 349–53
Emperor Wendi, 351

Big Picture Questions

1. How can you explain the changing fortunes of Buddhism in China?
2. How did China influence the world of the third-wave era? How was China itself transformed by its encounters with a wider world?
3. How might China's posture in the world during the Tang and Song dynasty era compare to its emerging role in global affairs in the twenty-first century?
4. **Looking Back:** In what ways did Tang and Song dynasty China resemble the earlier Han dynasty period, and in what ways had China changed?

Next Steps: For Further Study

Samuel Adshead, *Tang China: The Rise of the East in World History* (2004). Explores the role of China within the larger world.

Patricia Buckley Ebrey, *The Inner Quarters* (1993). A balanced account of the gains and losses experienced by Chinese women during the changes of the Song dynasty.

Mark Elvin, *The Pattern of the Chinese Past* (1973). A classic account of the Chinese economic revolution.

James L. Huffman, *Japan in World History* (2010). The first three chapters of this recent work place Japan's early history in the framework of world history.

Paul S. Ropp, *China in World History* (2010). An up-to-date telling of China's historical development, cast in a global context.

Arthur F. Wright, *Buddhism in Chinese History* (1959). An older account filled with wonderful stories and anecdotes.

"Lost Treasurers of the Ancient World—Japan," http://www.youtube.com/watch?v=i9ObeuCWhiE. A Discovery Channel video presentation of Japanese history.

Upper River during the Qing Ming Festival, http://www.ibiblio.org/ulysses/gec/painting/qingming/full.htm. A scrolling reproduction of a huge Chinese painting, showing in detail the Song dynasty city of Kaifeng.

WORKING WITH EVIDENCE

The Leisure Life of China's Elites

From the earliest centuries of Chinese civilization, that country's artists have painted—on pottery, paper, wood, and silk; in tombs, on coffins, and on walls; in albums and on scrolls. Relying largely on ink rather than oils, their brushes depicted human figures, landscapes, religious themes, and images of ordinary life. While Chinese painting evolved over many centuries, in terms of both subject matter and technique, by most accounts it reached a high point of artistic brilliance during the Tang and Song dynasties.

Here, however, we are less interested in the aesthetic achievements of Chinese painting than in what those works can show us about the life of China's elite class—those men who had passed the highest-level examinations and held high office in the state bureaucracy and those women who lived within the circles of the imperial court. While they represented only a tiny fraction of China's huge population, such elite groups established the tone and set the standards of behavior for Chinese civilization. For such people, leisure was a positive value, a time for nurturing relationships and cultivating one's character in good Confucian or Daoist fashion. According to the Tang dynasty writer and scholar Duan Chengshi,

> Leisure is good.
> Dusty affairs don't entangle the mind.
> I sit facing the tree outside the window
> And watch its shadow change direction three times.[36]

Action and work, in the Chinese view of things, need to be balanced by self-reflection and leisure. In the images that follow, we can catch a glimpse of how the Chinese elite lived and interacted with one another, particularly in their leisure time.

Leading court officials and scholar-bureaucrats must have been greatly honored to be invited to an elegant banquet, hosted by the emperor himself, such as that shown in Source 8.1. Usually attributed to the emperor Huizong (1082–1135)—who was himself a noted painter, poet, calligrapher, and collector—the painting shows a refined dinner gathering of high officials drinking tea and wine with the emperor presiding at the left. This emperor's great attention to the arts rather than to affairs of state gained him a reputation as a negligent and dissolute ruler. His reign ended in disgrace as China suffered a humiliating defeat at the hands of northern nomadic Jin people, who took the emperor captive.

Ink and color on silk, 15th century/Private Collection/Photo © Christie's Images/Bridgeman Images

Source 8.1 A Banquet with the Emperor

- What features of this painting contribute to the impression of imperial elegance?

- What mood does this painting evoke?

- What social distinction among the figures in the painting can you discern?

- How is the emperor depicted in this painting in comparison to that on page 335? How would you explain the difference?

- How might you imagine the conversation around this table?

Elite women of the court likewise gathered to eat, drink, and talk, as illustrated in Source 8.2, an anonymous Tang dynasty painting on silk. Hosting the event is the empress, shown seated upright in the middle of the left side of the table, holding a fan and wearing a distinctive headdress. Her guests and paid professional musicians sit around the table.

- How does this gathering of elite women differ from that of the men in Source 8.1? How might their conversation differ from that of the men?

- To what extent are the emperor and empress in Sources 8.1 and 8.2 distinguished from their guests? How do you think the emperor and

National Palace Museum, Taipei, Taiwan/Werner Forman/Art Resource, NY

Source 8.2 At Table with the Empress

empress viewed their roles at these functions? Were they acting as private persons among friends or in an official capacity?

■ What differences in status among these women can you identify?

■ What view of these women does the artist seek to convey?

■ What does the posture of the women suggest about the event?

Confucian cultural ideals gave great prominence to literature, poetry, and scholarly pursuits as leisure activities appropriate for "gentlemen." Confucius himself had declared that "gentlemen make friends through literature, and through friendship increase their benevolence." For some, a more reclusive life devoted to study, painting, poetry, and conversation with friends represented an honorable alternative to government service. Thus literary gatherings of scholars and officials, often in garden settings, were common themes in Tang and Song dynasty paintings. Source 8.3, by the tenth-century painter Zhou Wenju, provides an illustration of such a gathering.

Source 8.3 A Literary Gathering

(Formerly attributed to) Scholars of the Liuli Hall, late 13th century, China. Song Dynasty (9601279). Handscroll: ink and color on silk. Image: 12⅜ × 50¹⁵⁄₁₆ in. (31.4 × 128.4 cm.). Overall with mounting: 15⅛ x 329½ in. (38.4 x 836.9 cm.). Gift of Mrs. Sheila Riddell, in memory of Sir Percival David, 1977 (1977.49). The Metropolitan Museum of Art, New York, NY, USA/Image copyright © The Metropolitan Museum of Art/Image Source: Art Resource, NY

- What marks these figures as cultivated men of literary or scholarly inclination?

- What meaning might you attribute to the outdoor garden setting of this image and that of Source 8.1?

- Notice the various gazes of the four figures. What do they suggest about the character of this gathering and the interpersonal relationships among its participants? Are they interacting or engaged in solitary pursuits?

- Do you think the artist was seeking to convey an idealized image of what a gathering of "gentlemen" ought to be or a realistic portrayal of an actual event? What elements of the painting support your answer?

Not all was poetry and contemplation of nature in the leisure-time activities of China's elite. Nor were men and women always so strictly segregated as the preceding sources may suggest. Source 8.4 illustrates another side of Chinese elite life. These images are part of a long tenth-century scroll painting

© Beijing Eastphoto Stockimages, Co., Ltd./Alamy

Source 8.4 An Elite Night Party

titled *The Night Revels of Han Xizai*. Apparently, the Tang dynasty emperor Li Yu became concerned that one of his ministers, Han Xizai, was overindulging in suspicious nightlong parties in his own home. He therefore commissioned the artist Gu Hongzhong to attend these parties secretly and to record the events in a painting, which he hoped would shame his wayward but talented official into more appropriate and dignified behavior. The entire scroll shows men and women together, sometimes in flirtatious situations, while open sleeping areas suggest sexual activity.

- What kinds of entertainment were featured at this gathering?

- What aspects of these parties shown in the scroll paintings might have caused the emperor some concern? Refer back to the female musicians shown on page 211, which derives from the same painting. In what respects might these kinds of gatherings run counter to Confucian values?

- How are women portrayed in these images? In what ways are they relating to the men in the paintings?

DOING HISTORY

The Leisure Life of China's Elites

1. **Describing elite society:** Based on these paintings, write a brief description of the social life of Chinese elites during the Tang and Song dynasties.

2. **Defining the self-image of an elite:** What do these sources suggest about how members of the elite ideally viewed themselves? In what ways do those self-portraits draw upon Confucian, Daoist, or Buddhist teachings?

3. **Noticing differences in the depiction of women:** In what different ways are women represented in these paintings? Keep in mind that all the artists were men. How might this affect the way women were depicted? How might female artists have portrayed them differently?

4. **Using images to illustrate change:** Reread the sections on Chinese women (pages 211–13 and 331–32). How might these images be used to illustrate the changes in women's lives that are described in those pages?

5. **Seeking additional sources:** What other kinds of visual sources might provide further insight into the lives of Chinese elites?

From the *"Maqamat" of Abu Mohammed el Qasim ibn Ali Hariri* (1054–1122), 1237/© BnF, Dist. RMN–Grand Palais/Art Resource, NY

CHAPTER 9

The Worlds of Islam

Afro-Eurasian Connections
600–1450

Hassan Kargbo, a citizen of the small West African country of Sierra Leone, is a "ChrisMus," which in local parlance is a person who identifies with both Christianity and Islam. "I see it as the same religion," he stated. Interviewed in early 2014, he acknowledged going to church every Sunday, wearing a Jesus bracelet, and praying at a mosque every day. Kelfala Conteh, the caretaker of an ancient mosque in Sierra Leone's capital of Freetown, reported, "Of course [Christians] come here. We have both Christians and Muslims praying side by side." Wurie Bah, another Muslim from Freetown, said, "We all believe in God. If my friends invite me to church, of course I will go." On one of the colorfully decorated minibuses that carry passengers around the city is the declaration that "God loves Allah."[1]

In the world of the early twenty-first century, where headlines often highlight violence among Muslims and violent conflict with Christians or Jews, it is perhaps useful to recall places such as Sierra Leone where religious tolerance is both practiced and celebrated. Nor is it alone. Indonesia, the most heavily populated Muslim country in the world, has inscribed freedom of religion in its constitution; has officially recognized Christian, Hindu, and Buddhist holidays as well as those of Islam; and has generally maintained peace among its various religious communities. Tunisia, the cradle of the Arab Spring, adopted a new constitution in early 2014 that represented a compromise between advocates of a secular state and those committed to a more Islamic regime. It commits the country to democracy, freedom of conscience, and gender equality.

The many faces of contemporary Islam echo the earlier history of this newest of humankind's major religions. During the first Muslim

The Hajj   The pilgrimage to Mecca, known as the hajj, has long been a central religious ritual in Islamic practice. It also embodies the cosmopolitan character of Islam as pilgrims from all over the vast Islamic realm assemble in the city where the faith was born. This painting shows a group of joyful pilgrims, led by a band, on their way to Mecca.

millennium (600–1600), the Islamic world found expression in various forms, some displaying a broad acceptance for diversity and others engaged in serious and at times violent conflict with those of a different religious outlook. Furthermore, both then and now, the world of Islam occupied a central position in the larger international arena, interacting with most of the other civilizations.

As in China, Muslim societies over much of the past century have been seeking to overcome several hundred years of humiliating European intrusion and to find their place in the modern world. In doing so, many Muslims have found inspiration and encouragement in the early history of their civilization and their faith. For a thousand years (roughly 600–1600), peoples claiming allegiance to Islam represented a highly successful, prosperous, and expansive civilization, encompassing parts of Africa, Europe, the Middle East, and Asia. While Chinese culture and Buddhism provided the cultural anchor for East Asia during the third-wave millennium and Christianity did the same for Europe, the realm of Islam touched on both of them and decisively shaped the history of the entire Afro-Eurasian world.

The significance of a burgeoning Islamic world during the third-wave era was enormous. It thrust the previously marginal and largely nomadic Arabs into a central role in world history, for it was among them and in their language that the newest of the world's major religions was born. The sudden emergence and rapid spread of that religion in the seventh century C.E. was accompanied by the creation of a huge empire that stretched from Spain to India. Both within that empire and beyond it, a new and innovative civilization took shape, drawing on Arab, Persian, Turkish, Greco-Roman, South Asian, and African cultures. It was clearly the largest and most influential of the new third-wave civilizations. Finally, the broad reach of Islam generated many of the great cultural encounters of this age of accelerating connections, as Islamic civilization challenged and provoked Christendom, penetrated and was transformed by African cultures, and also took root in India, Central Asia, and Southeast Asia. The spread of Islam continued in the modern era so that by 2013 some 1.6 billion people, or 23 percent of the world's population, identified as Muslims. It was second only to Christianity as the world's most widely practiced religion, and it extended far beyond the Arab lands where it had originated.

SEEKING THE MAIN POINT

In what ways did the civilization of Islam draw on other civilizations in the Afro-Eurasian world? And in what respects did it shape or transform those civilizations?

The Birth of a New Religion

AP® EXAM TIP

Pay close attention to these similarities and differences in major religions.

Most of the major religious or cultural traditions of the second-wave era had emerged from the core of established civilizations—Confucianism and Daoism from China, Hinduism and Buddhism from India, Greek philosophy from the Mediterranean world, and Zoroastrianism from Persia. Christianity and Islam, by contrast, emerged more from the margins of Mediterranean and Middle Eastern civilizations. Christianity, of course, appeared among a small Middle Eastern people, the Jews, in a

A MAP OF TIME

570–632	Life of Muhammad
632–661	Era of Rightly Guided Caliphs
633–644	Muslim conquest of Persia
650s	Quran compiled
656–661; 680–692	Civil war; emergence of Sunni/Shia split
661–750	Umayyad caliphate
711–718	Conquest of Spain
750–900	High point of Abbasid caliphate
751	Battle of Talas River
756	Baghdad established as capital of Abbasid caliphate
800–1000	Emergence of Sufism
1099	Crusaders seize Jerusalem
1206	Delhi sultanate established in India
1258	Mongols sack Baghdad; formal end of Abbasid caliphate
1324	Mansa Musa's pilgrimage to Mecca
1453	Ottoman Empire conquers Constantinople; end of Byzantine Empire
1492	Christian reconquest of Spain complete; end of Muslim Spain
1526	Mughal Empire established in India

remote province of the Roman Empire, while Islam took hold in the cities and deserts of the Arabian Peninsula.

The Homeland of Islam

The central region of the Arabian Peninsula had long been inhabited by nomadic Arabs, known as Bedouins, who herded their sheep and camels in seasonal migrations. These peoples lived in fiercely independent clans and tribes, which often engaged in bitter blood feuds with one another. They recognized a variety of gods, ancestors, and nature spirits; valued personal bravery, group loyalty, and hospitality; and greatly treasured their highly expressive oral poetry. But there was more to Arabia than camel-herding nomads. In scattered oases, the highlands of Yemen, and interior mountain communities, sedentary village-based agriculture was practiced,

AP® EXAM TIP

Know the major features of Islam's roots.

Map 9.1   Arabia at the Time of Muhammad

Located adjacent to the Byzantine and Persian empires, the eastern coast of Arabia was the site of a major trade route between the Indian Ocean and the Mediterranean Sea.

Guided Reading Question

■ DESCRIPTION

In what ways did the early history of Islam reflect its Arabian origins?

AP® EXAM TIP

Cross-cultural connections of major belief systems are important concepts on the AP® exam.

and in the northern and southern regions of Arabia, small kingdoms had flourished in earlier times. Arabia also sat astride increasingly important trade routes that connected the Indian Ocean world with that of the Mediterranean Sea, a location that gave rise to cosmopolitan commercial cities, whose values and practices were often in conflict with those of traditional Arab tribes (see Map 9.1).

One of those cities, Mecca, came to occupy a distinctive role in Arabia. Though somewhat off the major long-distance trade routes, Mecca was the site of the Kaaba, the most prominent religious shrine in Arabia, which housed representations of some 360 deities and was the destination for many pilgrims. Mecca's dominant tribe, the Quraysh (koor-EYE'SH), had come to control access to the Kaaba and had grown wealthy by taxing the local trade that accompanied the annual pilgrimage season. By the sixth century, Mecca was home to people from various tribes and clans as well as an assortment of individual outlaws, exiles, refugees, and foreign merchants, but much of its growing wealth was concentrated in the hands of a few ruling Quraysh families.

Furthermore, Arabia was located on the periphery of two established and rival civilizations of that time—the Byzantine Empire, heir to the Roman world, and the Sassanid Empire, heir to the imperial traditions of Persia. This location, coupled with long-distance trade, ensured some familiarity with the larger world, particularly in the cities and settled farming regions of the peninsula. Many Jews and Christians as well as some Zoroastrians lived among the Arabs, and their monotheistic ideas became widely known. By the time of Muhammad, most of the settled Arabs had acknowledged the preeminent position of Allah, the supreme god of the Arab pantheon, although they usually found the lesser gods, including the three daughters of Allah, far more accessible. Moreover, they increasingly identified Allah with Yahweh, the Jewish High God, and regarded themselves too as "children of Abraham." A few Arabs were beginning to explore the possibility that Allah/Yahweh was the only God and that the many others, residing in the Kaaba and in shrines across the peninsula, were nothing more than "helpless and harmless idols."[2]

To an outside observer around 600, it might well have seemed that Arabs were moving toward Judaism religiously or that Christianity, the most rapidly growing religion in western Asia, would encompass Arabia as well. Any such expectations, however, were thoroughly confounded by the dramatic events of the seventh century.

The Messenger and the Message

The catalyst for those events and for the birth of this new religion was a single individual, Muhammad Ibn Abdullah (570–632 C.E.), who was born in Mecca to a Quraysh family. As a young boy, Muhammad lost his parents, came under the care of an uncle, and worked as a shepherd to pay his keep. Later he became a trader and traveled as far north as Syria. At the age of twenty-five, he married a wealthy widow, Khadija, herself a prosperous merchant, with whom he fathered six children. A highly reflective man deeply troubled by the religious corruption and social inequalities of Mecca, he often undertook periods of withdrawal and meditation in the arid mountains outside the city. There, like the Buddha and Jesus, Muhammad had a powerful, overwhelming religious experience that left him convinced, albeit reluctantly, that he was Allah's messenger to the Arabs, commissioned to bring to them a scripture in their own language. (See Working with Evidence: The Life of the Prophet, page 399, for images from the life of Muhammad.)

According to Muslim tradition, the revelations began in 610 and continued periodically over the next twenty-two years. Those revelations, recorded in the Quran, became the sacred scriptures of Islam, which to this day most Muslims regard as the very words of God and the core of their faith. Intended to be recited rather than simply read for information, the Quran, Muslims claim, when heard in its original Arabic, conveys nothing less than the very presence of the Divine. Its unmatched poetic beauty, miraculous to Muslims, convinced many that it was indeed a revelation from God. One of the earliest converts testified to its power: "When I heard the Quran, my heart was softened and I wept and Islam entered into me."[3]

In its Arabian setting, the Quran's message, delivered through Muhammad, was revolutionary. Religiously, it was radically monotheistic, presenting Allah as the only God, the all-powerful Creator, good, just, and ever merciful. Allah was the "Lord sustainer of the worlds, the Compassionate, the Caring, master of the day of reckoning" and known to human beings "on the farthest horizon and within their own selves."[4] Here was an exalted conception of Deity that drew heavily on traditions of Jewish and Christian monotheism. As "the Messenger of God," Muhammad presented himself in the line of earlier prophets — Abraham, Moses, Jesus, and many others. He was the last, "the seal of the prophets," bearing God's

Guided Reading Question

■ DESCRIPTION

What did the Quran expect from those who followed its teachings?

Muslims, Jews, and Christians
The close relationship of three Middle Eastern monotheistic traditions is illustrated in this fifteenth-century Persian painting, which portrays Muhammad leading Moses, Abraham, and Jesus in prayer. The fire surrounding the Prophet's head represents his religious fervor. The painting reflects the Islamic belief that the revelations granted to Muhammad built on and completed those given earlier to Jews and Christians. (From *Miradj*, by Mir Haydar, Royal workshop of the Timurid Dynasty in Herat, Afghanistan, 1436. © BnF, Dist. RMN–Grand Palais/Art Resource, NY)

final revelation to humankind. It was not so much a call to a new faith as an invitation to return to the old and pure religion of Abraham from which Jews, Christians, and Arabs alike had deviated. Jews had wrongly conceived of themselves as a uniquely "chosen people"; Christians had made their prophet into a god; and Arabs had become wildly polytheistic. To all of this, the message of the Quran was a corrective.

Submission to Allah ("Muslim" means "one who submits") was the primary obligation of believers and the means of achieving a God-conscious life in this world and a place in Paradise after death. According to the Quran, however, submission was not merely an individual or a spiritual act, for it involved the creation of a whole new society. Over and again, the Quran denounced the prevailing social practices of an increasingly prosperous Mecca: the hoarding of wealth, the exploitation of the poor, the charging of high rates of interest on loans, corrupt business deals, the abuse of women, and the neglect of widows and orphans. Like the Jewish prophets of the Old Testament, the Quran demanded social justice and laid out a prescription for its implementation. It sought a return to the older values of Arab tribal life—solidarity, equality, concern for the poor—which had been undermined, particularly in Mecca, by growing wealth and commercialism.

The message of the Quran challenged not only the ancient polytheism of Arab religion and the social injustices of Mecca but also the entire tribal and clan structure of Arab society, which was so prone to war, feuding, and violence. The just and moral society of Islam was the *umma* (OOM-mah), the community of all believers, replacing tribal, ethnic, or racial identities. Such a society would be a "witness over the nations," for according to the Quran, "You are the best community evolved for mankind, enjoining what is right and forbidding what is wrong."[5] In this community, women too had an honored and spiritually equal place. "The believers, men and women, are protectors of one another," declared the Quran.[6] The umma, then, was to be a new and just community, bound by common belief rather than by territory, language, or tribe.

The core message of the Quran—the remembrance of God—was effectively summarized as a set of five requirements for believers, known as the Pillars of Islam. The first pillar expressed the heart of the Islamic message: "There is no god but God, and Muhammad is the messenger of God." The second pillar was ritual prayer, performed five times a day. Accompanying practices, including cleansing, bowing, kneeling, and prostration, expressed believers' submission to Allah and provided a frequent reminder, amid the busyness of daily life, that they were living in the presence of God. The third pillar, almsgiving, reflected the Quran's repeated demands for social justice by requiring believers to give generously to support the poor and needy of the community. The fourth pillar established a month of fasting during Ramadan, which meant abstaining from food, drink, and sexual relations from the first light of dawn to sundown. It provided an occasion for self-purification and a reminder of the needs of the hungry. The fifth pillar encouraged a pilgrimage to Mecca, known as the hajj (HAHJ), during which believers from all over the Islamic

AP® EXAM TIP

You must know that the major religions had core rules of behavior, like the Pillars of Islam, and that they developed more expansive rules that developed over time.

world assembled once a year and put on identical simple white clothing as they reenacted key events in Islamic history. For at least the few days of the hajj, the many worlds of Islam must surely have seemed a single realm.

A further requirement for believers, sometimes called the sixth pillar, was "struggle," or *jihad* in Arabic. Its more general meaning, which Muhammad referred to as the "greater jihad," was an interior personal effort of each believer against greed and selfishness, a spiritual striving toward living a God-conscious life. In its "lesser" form, the "jihad of the sword," the Quran authorized armed struggle against the forces of unbelief and evil as a means of establishing Muslim rule and of defending the umma from the threats of infidel aggressors. The understanding and use of the jihad concept have varied widely over the many centuries of Islamic history and remain a matter of much controversy among Muslims in the twenty-first century.

The Transformation of Arabia

As the revelations granted to Muhammad became known in Mecca, they attracted a small following of some close relatives, a few prominent Meccan leaders, and an assortment of lower-class dependents, freed slaves, and members of poorer clans. Those teachings also soon attracted the vociferous opposition of Mecca's elite families, particularly those of Muhammad's own tribe, the Quraysh. Muhammad's claim to be a "messenger of Allah," his unyielding monotheism, his call for social reform, his condemnation of Mecca's business practices, and his apparent disloyalty to his own tribe enraged the wealthy and ruling families of Mecca. So great had this opposition become that in 622 Muhammad and his small band of followers emigrated to the more welcoming town of Yathrib, soon to be called Medina, the city of the Prophet. This agricultural settlement of mixed Arab and Jewish population had invited Muhammad to serve as an arbitrator of their intractable conflicts. The emigration to Yathrib, known in Arabic as the *hijra* (HIJJ-ruh) ("the journey"), was a momentous turning point in the early history of Islam and thereafter marked the beginning of a new Islamic calendar.

The new community, or umma, that took shape in Medina was a kind of "supertribe," but very different from the traditional tribes of Arab society. Membership was a matter of belief rather than birth, allowing the community to expand rapidly. Furthermore, all authority, both political and religious, was concentrated in the hands of Muhammad, who proceeded to introduce radical changes. Usury was outlawed, tax-free marketplaces were established, and a mandatory payment to support the poor was imposed.

In Medina, Muhammad not only began to create a new society but also declared his movement's independence from its earlier affiliation with Judaism. In the early years, he had anticipated a warm response from Jews and Christians, based on a common monotheism and prophetic tradition, and had directed his followers to pray facing Jerusalem. But when some Jewish groups allied with his enemies, Muhammad acted harshly to suppress them, exiling some and enslaving or killing

AP® EXAM TIP

It is important for you to know the names of founders of major religions, like Muhammad.

Guided Reading Question

■ CHANGE
How was Arabia transformed by the rise of Islam?

others. This was not, however, a general suppression of Jews since others among them remained loyal to Muhammad's new state. But the Prophet now redirected his followers' prayer toward Mecca, essentially declaring Islam an Arab religion, though one with a universal message.

From its base in Medina, the Islamic community rapidly extended its reach throughout Arabia. Early military successes against Muhammad's Meccan opponents convinced other Arab tribes that the Muslims and their God were on the rise, and they sought to negotiate alliances with the new power. Growing numbers converted. The religious appeal of the new faith, its promise of material gain, the end of incessant warfare among feuding tribes, periodic military actions skillfully led by Muhammad, and the Prophet's willingness to enter into marriage alliances with leading tribes—all of this contributed to the consolidation of Islamic control throughout Arabia. In 630, Muhammad triumphantly and peacefully entered Mecca itself, purging the Kaaba of its idols and declaring it a shrine to the one God, Allah. By the time Muhammad died in 632, most of Arabia had come under the control of this new Islamic state, and many had embraced the new faith.

Thus the birth of Islam differed sharply from that of Christianity. Jesus' teaching about "giving to Caesar what is Caesar's and to God what is God's" reflected the minority and subordinate status of the Jews within the Roman Empire. Early Christians found themselves periodically persecuted by Roman authorities for more than three centuries, requiring them to work out some means of dealing with an often-hostile state. The answer lay in the development of a separate church hierarchy and the concept of two coexisting authorities, one religious and one political, an arrangement that persisted even after the state became Christian.

The young Islamic community, by contrast, constituted a state, and soon a huge empire, at the very beginning of its history. Muhammad was not only a religious figure but also, unlike Jesus or the Buddha, a political and military leader able to implement his vision of an ideal Islamic society. Nor did Islam give rise to a separate religious organization, although tension between religious and political goals frequently generated conflict. No professional clergy mediating between God and humankind emerged within Islam. Teachers, religious scholars, prayer leaders, and judges within an Islamic legal system did not have the religious role that priests held within Christianity. No distinction between religious law and civil law, so important in the Christian world, existed within the realm of Islam. One law, known as the *sharia* (shah-REE-ah), regulated every aspect of life. The sharia (literally, "a path to water," which is the source of life) evolved over the several centuries following the birth of this new religion and found expression in a number of separate schools of Islamic legal practice.

In little more than twenty years (610–632), a profound transformation had occurred in the Arabian Peninsula. What would subsequently become a new religion had been born, though it was one with roots in earlier Jewish, Christian, and Zoroastrian traditions. A new and vigorous state had emerged, bringing peace to the warring tribes of Arabia. Within that state, a distinctive society had

AP® EXAM TIP

Be prepared to explain similarities and differences between major religions.

begun to take shape, one that served ever after as a model for Islamic communities everywhere. In his farewell sermon, Muhammad described the outlines of this community:

> All mankind is from Adam and Eve, an Arab has no superiority over a non-Arab nor a non-Arab has any superiority over an Arab; also a white has no superiority over a black nor a black has any superiority over a white—except by piety and good action. Learn that every Muslim is a brother to every Muslim and that the Muslims constitute one brotherhood.[7]

The Making of an Arab Empire

It did not take long for the immense transformations occurring in Arabia to have an impact beyond the peninsula. In the centuries that followed, the energies born of those vast changes profoundly transformed much of the Afro-Eurasian world. The new Arab state became a huge empire, encompassing all or part of Egyptian, Roman/Byzantine, Persian, Mesopotamian, and Indian civilizations. The Islamic faith spread widely within and outside that empire. So too did the culture and language of Arabia, as many Arabs migrated far beyond their original homeland and many others found it advantageous to learn Arabic. From the mixing and blending of these many peoples emerged the new and distinctive third-wave civilization of Islam, bound by the ties of a common faith but divided by differences of culture, class, politics, gender, and religious understanding. These enormously consequential processes—the making of a new religion, a new empire, and a new civilization—were central to world history during the third-wave millennium.

War, Conquest, and Tolerance

Within a few years of Muhammad's death in 632, Arab armies engaged the Byzantine and Persian Sassanid empires, the great powers of the region. It was the beginning of a process that rapidly gave rise to an Arab empire that stretched from Spain to India, penetrating both Europe and China and governing most of the lands between them (see Map 9.2). In creating that empire, Arabs were continuing a long pattern of tribal raids into surrounding civilizations, but now these Arabs were newly organized in a state of their own with a central command able to mobilize the military potential of the entire population. The Byzantine and Persian empires had for a century or more suffered periodic epidemics of the plague that decimated their urban populations, while the more remote and scattered Arabs of the Arabian Desert were more protected from this pestilence. Furthermore, these great empires, weakened by decades of war with each other and by internal revolts, continued to view the Arabs as a mere nuisance rather than a serious threat. But by 644, the Sassanid Empire had been defeated by Arab forces, while Byzantium, the remaining eastern regions of the old Roman Empire, soon lost the southern half of its

AP® EXAM TIP

Be knowledgeable as to the extent of the spread of Islam in the era ca. 600–ca. 1450.

Map 9.2   The Arab Empire and the Initial Expansion of Islam, 622–900 C.E.

Far more so than with Buddhism or Christianity, the initial spread of Islam was both rapid and extensive. And unlike the other two world religions, Islam quickly gave rise to a huge empire, ruled by Muslim Arabs, which encompassed many of the older civilizations of the region.

territories. Beyond these victories, Muslim forces, operating on both land and sea, swept westward across North Africa, conquered Spain in the early 700s, and attacked southern France. To the east, Arab armies reached the Indus River and seized some of the major oases towns of Central Asia. In 751, they inflicted a crushing defeat on Chinese forces in the Battle of Talas River, which had lasting consequences for the cultural evolution of Asia, for it checked the further expansion of China to the west and made possible the conversion to Islam of Central Asia's Turkic-speaking people. Most of the violence of conquest involved imperial armies, though on occasion civilians too were caught up in the fighting and suffered terribly. In 634, for example, a battle between Byzantine and Arab forces in Palestine resulted in the death of some 4,000 villagers.

The motives driving the creation of the Arab Empire were broadly similar to those of other empires. The merchant leaders of the new Islamic community wanted to capture profitable trade routes and wealthy agricultural regions. Individual Arabs found in military expansion a route to wealth and social promotion. The need to harness the immense energies of the Arabian transformation was also

Guided Reading Question

■ CHANGE

Why were Arabs able to construct such a huge empire so quickly?

important. The fragile unity of the umma threatened to come apart after Muhammad's death, and external expansion provided a common task for the community.

While many among the new conquerors viewed the mission of empire in terms of jihad, bringing righteous government to the peoples they conquered, this did not mean imposing a new religion. In fact, for the better part of a century after Muhammad's death, his followers usually referred to themselves as "believers," a term that appears in the Quran far more often than "Muslims" and one that included pious Jews and Christians as well as newly monotheistic Arabs. Such a posture eased the acceptance of the new political order, for many people recently incorporated in the emerging Arab Empire were already monotheists and familiar with the core ideas and practices of the Believers' Movement—prayer, fasting, pilgrimage, revelation, and prophets. Furthermore, the new rulers were remarkably tolerant of established Jewish and Christian faiths. The first governor of Arab-ruled Jerusalem was a Jew. Many old Christian churches continued to operate and new ones were constructed. A Nestorian Christian patriarch in Iraq wrote to one of his bishops around 647 C.E. observing that the new rulers "not only do not fight Christianity, they even commend our religion, show honor to the priests and monasteries and saints of the Lord, and make gifts to the monasteries and churches."[8] Formal agreements or treaties recognized Jews, Christians, and Zoroastrians as "people of the book," giving them the status of *dhimmis* (dihm-mees), protected but second-class subjects. Such people were permitted to freely practice their own religion, so long as they paid a special tax known as the *jizya*. Theoretically the tax was a substitute for military service, supposedly forbidden to non-Muslims. In practice, many dhimmis served in the highest offices within Muslim kingdoms and in their armies as well.

In other ways too, the Arab rulers of an expanding empire sought to limit the disruptive impact of conquest. To prevent indiscriminate destruction and exploitation of conquered peoples, occupying Arab armies were restricted to garrison towns, segregated from the native population. Local elites and bureaucratic structures were incorporated into the new Arab Empire. Nonetheless, the empire worked many changes on its subjects, the most enduring of which was the mass conversion of Middle Eastern peoples to what became by the eighth century the new and separate religion of Islam.

AP® EXAM TIP

Know the ways Islam applied the concept of "people of the book" to different peoples over place and time.

Conversion

For some people, no doubt, converting to Islam was or subsequently became a matter of profound spiritual or psychological transformation, but far more often, at least initially, it was "social conversion," motivated more by convenience than conviction.[9] It happened at various rates and in different ways, but in the four centuries or so after the death of Muhammad, millions of individuals and many whole societies within the Arab Empire found their cultural identity bound up with a belief in Allah and the message of his prophet. They had become Muslims. How had this immense cultural change occurred?

Guided Reading
Question

····················

■ EXPLANATION
What accounts for the
widespread conversion to
Islam?

AP® EXAM TIP

Add this to your
examples of simi-
larities among
major religions.

AP® EXAM TIP

Knowledge of the
ways religions adapt
to local cultures is
also important.

In some ways, perhaps, the change was not so dramatic, as major elements of Islam—monotheism; ritual prayer and cleansing ceremonies; fasting; divine revelation; the ideas of Heaven, Hell, and final judgment—were quite familiar to Jews, Christians, and Zoroastrians. Furthermore, Islam was from the beginning associated with the sponsorship of a powerful state, quite unlike the experience of early Buddhism or Christianity. Conquest called into question the power of old gods, while the growing prestige of the Arab Empire attracted many to Allah. Although deliberately forced conversion was rare and forbidden, living in an Islamic-governed state provided a variety of incentives for claiming Muslim identity. Slaves and prisoners of war were among the early converts, particularly in Persia. Converts could also avoid the jizya, the tax imposed on non-Muslims. People aspiring to official positions found conversion to Islam an aid to social mobility. In Islam, merchants found a religion friendly to commerce. The Prophet himself had been a trader, acting as a commercial agent for his wife Khadija. As Islamic law developed over several centuries, it defined what merchants might expect from one another and so reduced the uncertainty of long-distance commerce. And in the expansive Arab Empire, merchants enjoyed a huge and secure arena for trade.

Conversion was not an automatic or easy process. Vigorous resistance delayed conversion for centuries among the Berbers of North Africa; a small group of zealous Spanish Christians in the ninth century provoked their own martyrdom by publicly insulting the Prophet; and some Persian Zoroastrians fled to avoid Muslim rule. More generally, though, a remarkable and lasting religious transformation occurred throughout the Arab Empire.

In Persia, for example, between 750 and 900, about 80 percent of the population made the transition to a Muslim religious identity. But they did so in a manner quite distinct from the people of Iraq, Syria, Egypt, and North Africa. In these regions, converts to Islam gradually abandoned their native languages, adopted Arabic, and came to see themselves as Arabs. In Iran or Persia, by contrast, Arab conquest did not involve cultural Arabization, despite some initial efforts to impose the Arabic language. By the tenth century, the vast majority of Persians had become Muslims, but the Persian language (called Farsi in Iran) flourished, enriched now by a number of Arabic loan words and written in an Arabic script. In 1010, that language received its classic literary expression when the Persian poet Ferdowsi completed his epic work, the *Shahnama* (*The Book of Kings*). A huge text of some 60,000 rhyming couplets, it recorded the mythical and pre-Islamic history of Iran and gave an enduring expression to a distinctly Persian cultural identity. Thus, in places where large-scale Arab migration had occurred, such as Egypt, North Africa, and Iraq, Arabic culture and language, as well as the religion of Islam, took hold. Such areas are today both Muslim and Arab, while the peoples of Iran, Turkey, Pakistan, Indonesia, and West Africa, for example, have "Islamized" without "Arabizing."

The preservation of Persian language and culture had enormous implications for the world of Islam. Many religious ideas of Persian Zoroastrianism—an evil satanic power, final judgment, Heaven and Hell, Paradise—found their way into

Islam, often indirectly via Jewish or Christian precedents. In Iran, Central Asia, India, and later in the Ottoman Empire, Islam was accompanied by pervasive Persian influences. Persian administrative and bureaucratic techniques; Persian court practices with their palaces, gardens, and splendid garments; Persian architecture, poetry, music, and painting—all of this decisively shaped the high culture of these eastern Islamic lands. One of the Abbasid caliphs, himself an Arab, observed: "The Persians ruled for a thousand years and did not need us Arabs even for a day. We have been ruling them for one or two centuries and cannot do without them for an hour."[10]

Divisions and Controversies

The ideal of a unified Muslim community, so important to Muhammad, proved difficult to realize as conquest and conversion vastly enlarged the Islamic umma. A central problem involved leadership and authority in the absence of Muhammad's towering presence. Who should hold the role of caliph (KAY-lihf), the successor to Muhammad as the political leader of the umma, the protector and defender of the faith? That issue crystallized a variety of emerging conflicts within the Islamic world—between early and later converts, among various Arab tribes and factions, between Arabs and non-Arabs, between privileged and wealthy rulers and their far less fortunate subjects. Many of these political and social conflicts found expression in religious terms as various understandings of the Quran and of Muhammad's life and teachings took shape within the growing Islamic community.

The first four caliphs, known among most Muslims as the Rightly Guided Caliphs (632–661), were close "companions of the Prophet," selected by the Muslim elders of Medina. Division surfaced almost immediately as a series of Arab tribal rebellions and new "prophets" persuaded the first caliph, Abu Bakr, to suppress them forcibly. The third and fourth caliphs, Uthman and Ali, were both assassinated, and by 656, less than twenty-five years after Muhammad's death, civil war pitted Muslim against Muslim.

Out of that conflict emerged one of the deepest and most enduring rifts within the Islamic world. On one side were the Sunni (SOON-nee) Muslims, who held that the caliphs were rightful political and military leaders, selected by the Islamic community. On the other side of this sharp divide was the Shia (SHEE-ah) (an Arabic word meaning "party" or "faction") branch of Islam. Its adherents felt strongly that leadership in the Islamic world should derive from the line of Ali and his son Husayn, blood relatives of Muhammad, both of whom died at the hands of their political or religious enemies. If the caliph was the idealized communal leader for Sunnis, imams (leaders) served this purpose for most of the Shia Muslims. They were widely thought to have some special charisma based on descent from the Prophet, giving them a religious authority that the caliphs lacked and allowing them to infallibly interpret divine revelation and law.

Thus what began as a purely political conflict acquired over time a deeper significance. For much of early Islamic history, Shia Muslims saw themselves as the

Guided Reading Question

■ COMPARISON
What is the difference between Sunni and Shia Islam?

AP® EXAM TIP

You must know that major belief systems tend to fragment over time as they spread.

The Kaaba
Located in Mecca, this stone structure, covered with a black cloth and known as the Kaaba, was originally home to the numerous deities of pre-Islamic Arabia. Cleansed by Muhammad, it became the sacred shrine of Islam and the destination of countless pilgrims undertaking the hajj. Part of that ritual involves circling the Kaaba seven times, as shown here in a photograph from 2013. (Ibraheem Abu Mustafa/Reuters/Landov)

minority opposition within Islam. They felt that history had taken a wrong turn and that they were "the defenders of the oppressed, the critics and opponents of privilege and power," while the Sunnis were the advocates of the established order.[11] Various armed revolts by Shias over the centuries, most of which failed, led to a distinctive conception of martyrdom and to the expectation that their defeated leaders were merely in hiding and not really dead and that they would return in the fullness of time. Thus a messianic element entered Shia Islam. The Sunni/Shia schism became a lasting division in the Islamic world, reflected in conflicts among various Islamic states, and was exacerbated by further splits among the Shia. Those divisions echo still in the twenty-first century.

As the Arab Empire grew, its caliphs were transformed from modest Arab chiefs into absolute monarchs, "the shadow of God on earth," of the Byzantine or Persian variety, complete with elaborate court rituals, a complex bureaucracy, a standing army, and centralized systems of taxation and coinage. They were also subject to the dynastic rivalries and succession disputes common to other empires. The first dynasty, following the era of the Rightly Guided Caliphs, came from the Umayyad (oo-MEYE-ahd) family (r. 661–750). Under its leadership, the Arab Empire expanded greatly, caliphs became hereditary rulers, and the capital moved from Medina to the cosmopolitan Roman/Byzantine city of Damascus in Syria. Its ruling class was an

Arab military aristocracy, drawn from various tribes. But Umayyad rule provoked growing criticism and unrest. The Shia viewed the Umayyad caliphs as illegitimate usurpers, and non–Arab Muslims resented their second-class citizenship in the empire. Many Arabs protested the luxurious living and impiety of their rulers. The Umayyads, they charged, "made God's servants slaves, God's property something to be taken by turns among the rich, and God's religion a cause of corruption."[12]

Such grievances lay behind the overthrow of the Umayyads in 750 and their replacement by a new Arab dynasty, the Abbasids. With a splendid new capital in Baghdad, the Abbasid caliphs presided over a flourishing and prosperous Islamic civilization in which non-Arabs, especially Persians, now played a prominent role. But the political unity of the Abbasid Empire did not last long. Beginning in the mid-ninth century, many local governors or military commanders effectively asserted the autonomy of their regions, while still giving formal allegiance to the caliph in Baghdad. Long before Mongol conquest put an official end to the Abbasid Empire in 1258, the Islamic world had fractured politically into a series of "sultanates," many ruled by Persian or Turkish military dynasties.

A further tension within the world of Islam, though one that seldom produced violent conflict, lay in different answers to one central question: what does it mean to be a Muslim, to submit wholly to Allah? That question took on added urgency as the expanding Arab Empire incorporated various peoples and cultures that had been unknown during Muhammad's lifetime. One answer lay in the development of the sharia, the body of Islamic law developed primarily in the eighth and ninth centuries by religious scholars, Sunni and Shia alike, known as the *ulama*.

Based on the Quran, the life and teachings of Muhammad, deductive reasoning, and the consensus of scholars, the emerging sharia addressed in great detail practically every aspect of life. It was a blueprint for an authentic Islamic society, providing meticulous guidance for prayer and ritual cleansing; marriage, divorce, and inheritance; business and commercial relationships; the treatment of slaves; political life; personal hygiene; dietary requirements; and much more. Debates among the ulama led to the creation of four schools of law among Sunni Muslims and still others in the lands of Shia Islam. To the ulama and their followers, living as a Muslim meant following the sharia and thus participating in the creation of an Islamic society.

A second and quite different understanding of the faith emerged among those who saw the worldly success of Islamic civilization as a distraction and deviation from the purer

Guided Reading Question

■ COMPARISON
In what ways were Sufi Muslims critical of mainstream Islam?

Sufis and Worldly Power
This early seventeenth-century painting from India illustrates the tension between Sufis and worldly authorities. Here the Muslim Mughal emperor Jahangir, seated on an hourglass throne, gives his attention to the white-bearded Sufi holy man rather than to the prominent men, including a European figure, shown in the bottom left. (bpk, Berlin/Museum für Islamische Kunst, Staatliche Museum, Berlin, Germany/Photo: Georg Niedermeiser/Art Resource, NY)

Mullah Nasruddin, the Wise Fool of Islam

In the Islamic world, a mullah was a man of some learning, often a local cleric or leader of a village mosque. Far and away the most famous and beloved of mullahs is Nasruddin, considered both a wise man and a fool, both a sage and a simpleton. Stories about him have circulated for centuries and were well known long before the earliest written references to him appeared in the thirteenth century. Many peoples have claimed him, some have sought to find a historical figure on which he is based, and in the Turkish city of Aksehir there is even a tomb and an annual Nasruddin festival, where people dress in costumes to reenact his jokes and stories.

In fact, Mullah Nasruddin has long been an imaginary folk character within the world of Islam and especially among Sufis, gently expressing a skeptical attitude toward the rational mind, sanctimonious posturing, human vanity, and the many faces of the ego. His tales usually take place in a village setting and highlight the limitations of the intellect; the role of humor and intuition in spiritual life; the

Mullah Nasruddin.

importance of generosity, tolerance, and humility; and the many mysteries of existence. The only way to get acquainted with Mullah Nasruddin is to reflect on some of his tales. Here are just a few of the thousands:[13]

- The Mullah was in Mecca for the pilgrimage and had fallen asleep with his feet pointing toward the Kaaba, the large black cube that is the central shrine of Islam. He was awakened and rebuked by some pious Muslims, who told him it was offensive to have his dirty feet pointing at the Kaaba, where God himself resided. The Mullah apologized profusely and then added, "Perhaps you could move my feet to some place where God is *not* present."

- Mullah Nasruddin was invited to a formal reception and upon entering took the seat of greatest honor. Approached by the chief of the guard, he was asked if he was a diplomat, a minister of the king, or perhaps the king himself in disguise. To each of these queries,

photo: Turkish miniature, ca. 1500/© akg-images/The Image Works

spirituality of Muhammad's time. Known as Sufis (SOO-fees), they represented Islam's mystical dimension, in that they sought a direct and personal experience of the Divine. Through renunciation of the material world, meditation on the words of the Quran, the chanting of the names of God, the use of music and dance, and the veneration of Muhammad and various "saints," Sufis pursued an interior life, seeking to tame the ego and achieve spiritual union with Allah. To describe that inexpressible experience, they often resorted to metaphors of drunkenness or the embrace of lovers. "Stain your prayer rug with wine," urged the famous Sufi poet Hafiz, referring to the intoxication of the believer with the Divine Presence. (See the Zooming In feature on Mullah Nasruddin, above, for an expression of popular or folk Sufism.)

he replied, "No, I am more than that." "Then who are you?" demanded the guard. His answer: "I am nobody."

- A villager rushed to tell the Mullah about visions of God he had been having. He asked if this meant he had become enlightened. The Mullah replied by asking him about his goats and servants. The man was enraged at this apparent dismissal of his visions. Then the Mullah explained, "If you are becoming more tender and kind toward your goats and servants, then you are on the way to enlightenment. If not, your visions are an illusion of your ego."

- Mullah Nasruddin was asked to present a lecture on "the nature of Allah" in the local mosque together with many highly learned scholars. When the scholars had finished their eloquent and wise expositions, the humble Mullah arose and hesitantly began his talk by declaring "Allah is an eggplant," while holding one of the vegetables aloft. An uproar followed at this blasphemy. When he was finally given a chance to explain himself, the Mullah declared, "Everyone before me has spoken of what they do not know or have never seen. But we can all see this eggplant. Can anyone deny that Allah is manifest in all things?" When no one was willing to dispute the point, the Mullah concluded, "Well, then Allah is an eggplant."

- One evening, after spending many hours in the local tavern, a thoroughly intoxicated Mullah was stumbling along the streets. A local police official approached him and asked, "Who are you? Where did you come from? Where are you going? Why are you out so late?" The Mullah replied, "If I had answers to all those questions, I'd be home already." [Note: To Sufis, taverns and drunkenness often symbolized spiritual insight or mystical "intoxication" with the Divine.]

- When some neighbors told Nasruddin that his donkey was lost, the Mullah exclaimed, "Thank goodness I was not on the donkey or I'd be lost as well." [Note: In Sufi circles, the donkey has long symbolized the unruly human ego.]

The Mullah's tales have been understood on several levels. Most obviously, they are jokes. But they also convey moral teachings about individual behavior as well as social commentary. And especially for Sufis, they have become a spiritual resource, gradually dissolving limited and culturally conditioned thinking, while opening the way to more fully realizing humanity's divine potential.

Questions: Pick several of these tales and explain in your own words the lessons they might convey for Muslims. In what ways might these tales be considered subversive of established authorities? Might they strike a chord with contemporary sensibilities of our own time?

This mystical tendency in Islamic practice, which had won widely popular by the ninth and tenth centuries, was at times sharply critical of the more scholarly and legalistic practitioners of the sharia. To Sufis, establishment teachings about the law and correct behavior, while useful for daily living, did little to bring the believer into the presence of God. For some, even the Quran had its limits. Why spend time reading a love letter (the Quran), asked one Sufi master, when one might be in the very presence of the Beloved who wrote it?[14] Furthermore, Sufis felt that many of the ulama had been compromised by their association with worldly and corrupt governments. Sufis therefore often charted their own course to God, implicitly challenging the religious authority of the ulama. For these orthodox religious scholars, Sufi ideas and practice sometimes verged on heresy, as Sufis on occasion claimed unity with God, received new revelations, or incorporated novel religious practices from outside the Islamic world.

Despite their differences, adherents of the legalistic emphasis of the sharia and practitioners of Sufi spirituality coexisted, mostly peacefully, mixing and mingling, collaborating and disagreeing, in various combinations. For many centuries, roughly 1100 to 1800, Sufism was central to mainstream Islam, and many, perhaps most, Muslims affiliated with one or another Sufi organization, making use of its spiritual practices. A major Islamic thinker, al-Ghazali (1058–1111), himself both a legal scholar and a Sufi practitioner, in fact worked out an intellectual accommodation among these different strands of Islamic thought. Rational philosophy alone could never enable believers to know Allah, he argued. Nor were revelation and the law sufficient, for Muslims must know God in their hearts, through direct personal encounter with Allah. Nonetheless, differences in emphasis remained an element of tension and sometimes discord within the world of Islam.

Women and Men in Early Islam

What did the rise of Islam and the making of the Arab Empire mean for the daily lives of women and their relationship with men? Virtually every aspect of this question has been and remains highly controversial. The debates begin with the Quran itself. Did its teachings release women from earlier restrictions, or did they impose new limitations? At the level of spiritual life, the Quran was quite clear and explicit: men and women were equal. Numerous passages in the Quran use gender-inclusive language, referring to "believers, both men and women."

> Those who surrender themselves to Allah and accept the true faith; who are devout, sincere, patient, humble, charitable, and chaste; who fast and are ever mindful of Allah—on these, both men and women, Allah will bestow forgiveness and rich reward.[15]

But in social terms, and especially within marriage, the Quran, like the written texts of almost all civilizations, viewed women as inferior and subordinate: "Men have authority over women because Allah has made the one superior to the other, and because they spend their wealth to maintain them. Good women are obedient."[16] More specifically, the Quran provided a mix of rights, restrictions, and protections for women. Female infanticide, for example, widely practiced in many cultures as a means of gender selection, was now forbidden for Muslims. Women were given control over their own property, particularly their dowries, and were granted rights of inheritance, but at half the rate of their male counterparts. Marriage was considered a contract between consenting parties, thus making marriage by capture illegitimate. Divorce was possible for both parties, although it was far more readily available for men. The practice of taking multiple husbands, which operated in some pre-Islamic Arab tribes, was prohibited, while polygyny (the practice of having multiple wives) was permitted, though more clearly regulated than before. Men were limited to four

AP® EXAM TIP

The expectations for gender roles over time as practiced by the major belief systems are "must know" information.

Guided Reading Question

■ CHANGE
How did the rise of Islam change the lives of women?

wives and required to treat each of them equally. (The difficulty of doing so has been interpreted by some as virtually requiring monogamy.) Men were, however, permitted to have sexual relations with female slaves, but any children born of those unions were free, as was the mother once her owner died. Furthermore, men were strongly encouraged to marry orphans, widows, and slaves.

Such Quranic prescriptions were but one factor shaping the lives of women and men. At least as important were the long-established practices of the societies into which Islam spread and the growing sophistication, prosperity, and urbanization of Islamic civilization. As had been the case in Athens and China during their "golden ages," Muslim women, particularly in the upper classes, experienced growing restrictions as Islamic civilization flourished culturally and economically in the Abbasid era. In early Islamic times, a number of women played visible public roles, particularly Muhammad's youngest wife, Aisha. Women prayed in the mosques, although separately, standing beside the men. Nor were women generally veiled or secluded. As the Arab Empire grew in size and splendor, however, the position of women became more limited. The second caliph, Umar, asked women to offer prayers at home. Now veiling and the seclusion of women became standard practice among the upper and ruling classes, removing them from public life. Separate quarters within the homes of the wealthy were the domain of women, from which they could emerge only completely veiled. The caliph Mansur (r. 754–775) carried this separation of the sexes even further when he ordered a separate bridge for women to be built over the Euphrates River in the new capital of Baghdad. Such seclusion was less possible for lower-class women, who lacked the servants of the rich and had to leave the home for shopping or work.

AP® EXAM TIP
You should be able to compare expectations of gender roles among major religions over time.

Such practices derived far more from established traditions of Middle Eastern cultures than from the Quran itself, but they soon gained an Islamic rationale in the writings of Muslim thinkers. The famous philosopher and religious scholar al-Ghazali clearly saw a relationship between Muslim piety and the separation of the sexes:

> It is not permissible for a stranger to hear the sound of a pestle being pounded by a woman he does not know. If he knocks at the door, it is not proper for the woman to answer him softly and easily because men's hearts can be drawn to [women] for the most trifling [reason]. . . . However, if the woman has to answer the knock, she should stick her finger in her mouth so that her voice sounds like that of an old woman.[17]

Other signs of a tightening patriarchy—such as "honor killing" of women by their male relatives for violating sexual taboos and, in some places, clitoridectomy (female genital cutting)—likewise derived from local cultures, with no sanction in the Quran or Islamic law. Where they were practiced, such customs often came to be seen as Islamic, but they were certainly not limited to the Islamic world. In many cultures, concern with family honor linked to women's sexuality dictated harsh punishments for women who violated sexual taboos.

Negative views of women, presenting them variously as weak, deficient, and a sexually charged threat to men and social stability, emerged in the *hadiths* (hah-DEETHS), traditions about the sayings or actions of Muhammad, which became an important source of Islamic law. A changing interpretation of the Adam and Eve story illustrates the point. The Quran attaches equal blame to both Adam and Eve for yielding to the temptation of Satan, and both alike ask for and receive God's forgiveness. Nothing suggests that Eve tempted or seduced Adam into sin. In later centuries, however, several hadiths and other writings took up Judeo-Christian versions of the story that blamed Eve, and thus women in general, for Adam's sin and for the punishment that followed, including expulsion from the garden and pain in childbirth.[18]

Even as women faced growing restrictions in society generally, Islam, like Buddhism and Christianity, also offered new outlets for them in religious life. The Sufi practice of mystical union with Allah allowed a greater role for women than did mainstream Islam. Some Sufi orders had parallel groups for women, and a few welcomed women as equal members. Among the earliest of well-known Sufi practitioners was Rabia, an eighth-century woman from Basra in southern Iraq, who renounced numerous proposals of marriage and engaged, apparently successfully, in repeated religious debates with men. The greatest of the Sufi scholars, Ibn al-Arabi (1165–1240), sang the praises of divine beauty in an explicitly feminine form. The spiritual equality that the Quran accorded to male and female alike allowed women also to aspire to union with God. But for some male Sufi scholars, such as the twelfth-century mystical poet Attar, doing so meant that "she is a man and one cannot any more call her a woman."[19]

Beyond Sufi practice, within the world of Shia Islam, women teachers of the faith were called mullahs, the same as their male counterparts. Islamic education, either in the home or in Quranic schools, allowed some to become literate and a few to achieve higher levels of learning. Visits to the tombs of major Islamic figures as well as the ritual of the public bath likewise provided some opportunity for women to interact with other women beyond their own family circle.

Islam and Cultural Encounter: A Four-Way Comparison

AP® EXAM TIP

Be sure you understand the relationships between politics and religion.

In its earliest centuries, the rapid spread of Islam had been accompanied by the creation of an immense Arab Empire, very much in the tradition of earlier Mediterranean and Middle Eastern empires. By the tenth century, however, little political unity remained, and in 1258 even the powerless symbol of that earlier unity vanished as Mongol forces sacked Baghdad and killed the last Abbasid caliph. But even as the empire disintegrated, the civilization that was born within it grew and flourished. Perhaps the most significant sign of a flourishing Islamic civilization was the continued spread of the religion both within and beyond the boundaries of a vanishing Arab Empire (see Map 9.3), although that process differed considerably

Map 9.3   The Growing World of Islam, 900–1500
Islam as a religion, a civilization, and an arena of commerce continued to grow even as the Arab
Empire fragmented.

from place to place. The examples of India, Anatolia, West Africa, and Spain illustrate the various ways that Islam penetrated these societies as well as the rather different outcomes of these epic cultural encounters.

The Case of India

In South Asia, Islam found a permanent place in a long-established civilization as invasions by Turkic speaking warrior groups from Central Asia, recently converted to Islam, brought the faith to northern India. Thus the Turks became the third major carrier of Islam, after the Arabs and Persians, as their conquests initiated an enduring encounter between Islam and a Hindu-based Indian civilization. Beginning around 1000, those conquests gave rise to a series of Turkic and Muslim regimes that governed much of India until the British takeover in the eighteenth and nineteenth centuries. The early centuries of this encounter were violent indeed, as the invaders smashed Hindu and Buddhist temples and carried off vast quantities of Indian treasure. With the establishment of the Sultanate of Delhi in 1206 (see Map 9.4), Turkic rule became more systematic, although the Turks' small numbers and internal conflicts allowed only a very modest penetration of Indian society.

In the centuries that followed, substantial Muslim communities emerged in India, particularly in regions less tightly integrated into the dominant Hindu culture. Disillusioned Buddhists as well as low-caste Hindus and untouchables found the more egalitarian Islam attractive. So did peoples just beginning to make the transition to settled agriculture. Others benefited from converting to Islam by avoiding the tax imposed on non-Muslims. Sufis were particularly important in facilitating conversion, for India had always valued "god-filled men" who were detached from worldly affairs. Sufi holy men, willing to accommodate local gods and religious festivals, helped to develop a "popular Islam" that was not always so sharply distinguished from the more devotional (*bhakti*) forms of Hinduism.

Unlike the earlier experience of Islam in the Middle East, North Africa, and Persia, where Islam rapidly became the dominant faith, in India it was never able to claim more than 20 to 25 percent of the total population. Furthermore, Muslim communities were especially concentrated in the Punjab and Sind regions of northwestern India and in Bengal to the east. The core regions of Hindu culture in the northern Indian plain were not seriously challenged by the new faith, despite centuries of Muslim rule. One reason perhaps lay in the sharpness of the cultural divide between Islam and Hinduism. Islam was the most radically monotheistic of the world's religions, forbidding any representation of Allah, while Hinduism was surely among the most prolifically polytheistic, generating endless statues and images of the Divine in many forms. The Muslim notion of the equality of all believers contrasted sharply with the hierarchical assumptions of the caste system. Believing in sexual modesty, Muslims were deeply offended by the open eroticism of some Hindu religious art.

Although such differences may have limited the appeal of Islam in India, they also may have prevented it from being absorbed into the tolerant and inclusive embrace of Hinduism, as so many other religious ideas, practices, and communities had been. The religious exclusivity of Islam, born of its firm monotheistic belief and the idea of a unique revelation, set a boundary that the great sponge of Hinduism could not completely absorb.

Guided Reading Question

■ COMPARISON

What similarities and differences can you identify in the spread of Islam to India, Anatolia, West Africa, and Spain?

AP® EXAM TIP

Take good notes on the political and cultural features of the Delhi sultanate.

Sultanate of Delhi, ca. 1300

Vijayanagar, ca. 1500

Map 9.4   The Sultanate of Delhi

Between 1206 and 1526 a number of Muslim dynasties ruled northern India as the Delhi sultanate, while an explicitly Hindu kingdom of Vijayanagar arose in the south after 1340. It drew on north Indian Muslim architectural features and made use of Muslim mercenaries for its military forces.

Certainly, not all was conflict across that boundary. Many prominent Hindus willingly served in the political and military structures of a Muslim-ruled India. Mystical seekers after the Divine blurred the distinction between Hindu and Muslim, suggesting that God was to be found "neither in temple nor in mosque." "Look within your heart," wrote the great fifteenth-century mystic poet Kabir, "for there you will find both [Allah] and Ram [a famous Hindu deity]."[20] During the early sixteenth century, a new and distinct religious tradition emerged in India, known as Sikhism (SIHK-iz'm), which blended elements of Islam, such as devotion to one universal God, with Hindu concepts, such as karma and rebirth. "There is no Hindu and no Muslim. All are children of God," declared Guru Nanak (1469–1539), the founder of Sikhism.

Nonetheless, Muslims usually lived quite separately, remaining a distinctive minority within an ancient Indian civilization, which they now largely governed but which they proved unable to completely transform.

Map 9.5 **The Ottoman Empire by the Mid-Fifteenth Century**

As Turkic-speaking migrants bearing the religion of Islam penetrated Anatolia, the Ottoman Empire took shape, reaching into southeastern Europe and finally displacing the Christian Byzantine Empire. Subsequently, it came to control much of the Middle East and North Africa as well.

The Case of Anatolia

At the same time as India was being subjected to Turkic invasion, so too was Anatolia (now modern Turkey), where the largely Christian and Greek-speaking population was then governed by the Byzantine Empire (see Map 9.2 and Map 9.5). Here, as in India, the invaders initially wreaked havoc as Byzantine authority melted away in the eleventh century. Sufi practitioners likewise played a major role in the process of conversion. The outcome, however, was a far more profound cultural transformation than in India. By 1500, the population was 90 percent Muslim and largely Turkic-speaking, and Anatolia was the heartland of the powerful Turkish Ottoman Empire that had overrun Christian Byzantium. Why did the Turkic intrusion into Anatolia generate a much more thorough Islamization than in India?

One factor clearly lies in a very different demographic balance. The population of Anatolia—perhaps 8 million—was far smaller than India's roughly 48 million people, but far more Turkic-speaking peoples settled in Anatolia, giving them a much greater cultural weight than the smaller colonizing force in India. Furthermore, the disruption of Anatolian society was much more extensive. Massacres,

Guided Reading Question

■ CHANGE

In what ways was Anatolia changed by its incorporation into the Islamic world?

enslavement, famine, and flight led to a sharp drop in the native population. The Byzantine state had been fatally weakened. Church properties were confiscated, and monasteries were destroyed or deserted. Priests and bishops were sometimes unable to serve their congregations. Christians, though seldom forced to convert, suffered many discriminations. They had to wear special clothing and pay special taxes, and they were forbidden to ride saddled horses or carry swords. Not a few Christians came to believe that these disasters represented proof that Islam was the true religion. Thus Byzantine civilization in Anatolia, previously focused on the centralized institutions of church and state, was rendered leaderless and dispirited, whereas India's decentralized civilization, lacking a unified political or religious establishment, was better able to absorb the shock of external invasion while retaining its core values and identity.

The Turkish rulers of Anatolia built a new society that welcomed converts and granted them material rewards and opportunity for high office. Moreover, the cultural barriers to conversion were arguably less severe than in India. The common monotheism of Islam and Christianity, and Muslim respect for Jesus and the Christian scriptures, made conversion easier than crossing the great gulf between Islam and Hinduism. Such similarities lent support to the suggestion of some Sufi teachers that the two religions were but different versions of the same faith. Sufis also established schools, mills, orchards, hospices, and rest places for travelers and thus replaced the destroyed or decaying institutions of Christian Anatolia. All of this contributed to the thorough religious transformation of Anatolia and laid a foundation for the Ottoman Empire, which by 1500 had become the most impressive and powerful state within the Islamic world.

But the Islamization of Anatolia occurred within a distinctly Turkish context. A Turkish language, not Arabic, predominated. Some Sufi religious practices, such as ecstatic turning dances, actually derived from Central Asian Turkic shamanism. And Turkic tradition, common among pastoral peoples, offered a freer, more gender-equal life for women. This practice caught the attention of the Arab Moroccan visitor Ibn Battuta during his travels among the Turks in the fourteenth century. He commented, "A remarkable thing that I saw . . . was the respect shown to women by the Turks, for they hold a more dignified position than the men. . . . The windows of the tent are open and her face is visible, for the Turkish women do not veil themselves."[21] He was not pleased.

The Case of West Africa

AP® EXAM TIP

Take note of the features of Islam in West Africa that made it unique in the Muslim world.

Still another pattern of Islamic expansion prevailed in West Africa. Here Islam accompanied Muslim traders across the Sahara rather than being brought by invading Arab or Turkic armies. Its gradual acceptance in the emerging civilization of West African states in the centuries after 1000 was largely peaceful and voluntary, lacking the incentives associated elsewhere with foreign conquest. Introduced by Muslim merchants from an already-Islamized North Africa, the new faith was accepted primarily in the urban centers of the West African empires—Ghana, Mali,

Map 9.6   West Africa and the World of Islam

Both trans-Saharan commerce and Islam linked the civilization of West Africa to the larger Muslim world.

Songhay, Kanem-Bornu, and others (see Map 9.6 and Zooming In: Mansa Musa, page 390). For African merchant communities, Islam provided an important link to Muslim trading partners, much as Buddhism had done in Southeast Asia. For the monarchs and their courts, it offered a source of literate officials to assist in state administration as well as religious legitimacy, particularly for those who gained the prestige conferred by a pilgrimage to Mecca. Islam was a world religion with a single Creator-God, able to comfort and protect people whose political and economic horizons had expanded well beyond the local realm where ancestral spirits and traditional deities might be effective. It had a religious appeal for societies that were now participating in a wider world.

By the sixteenth century, a number of West African cities had become major centers of Islamic religious and intellectual life, attracting scholars from throughout the Muslim world. Timbuktu boasted more than 150 lower-level Quranic schools and several major centers of higher education with thousands of students from all over West Africa and beyond. Libraries held tens of thousands of books and scholarly manuscripts (see the image on page 305). Monarchs subsidized the construction of mosques as West Africa became an integral part of a larger Islamic world. Arabic became an important language of religion, education, administration, and trade, but it did not become the dominant language of daily life. Nor did West

The Great Mosque at Jenne
This mosque in the city of Jenne, initially constructed in the thirteenth century, illustrates the assimilation of Islam into West African civilization. (Antonello Lanzellotto/TIPS Images/age fotostock)

Africa experience the massive migration of Arab peoples that had promoted the Arabization of North Africa and the Middle East. Moreover, in contrast to India and Anatolia, Sufi holy men played a far more modest role until at least the eighteenth century. Scholars, merchants, and rulers, rather than mystic preachers, initially established Islam in West Africa.

Islam remained the culture of urban elites and spread little into the rural areas of West Africa until the nineteenth century. No thorough religious transformation occurred in West Africa as it had in Anatolia. Although many rulers adopted Islam, they governed people who steadfastly practiced African religions and whose sensibilities they had to respect if social peace were to prevail. Thus they made few efforts to impose the new religion on their rural subjects or to govern in strict accordance with Islamic law. The fourteenth-century Arab visitor Ibn Battuta was appalled that practicing Muslims in Mali permitted their women to appear in public almost naked and to mingle freely with unrelated men. "The association of women with men is agreeable to us," he was told, "and a part of good conduct to which no suspicion attaches. They are not like the women of your country."[22] Ibn Battuta also noted with disapproval a "dance of the masks" on the occasion of an Islamic festival and the traditional practice of sprinkling dust on one's head as a sign of respect for the king. Sonni Ali, a fifteenth-century ruler of Songhay, observed Ramadan and built mosques, but he also consulted traditional diviners and performed customary sacrifices. In such ways, Islam became Africanized even as parts of West Africa became Islamized.

The Case of Spain

The chief site of Islamic encounter with Christian Europe occurred in Spain, called al-Andalus by Muslims, which was conquered by Arab and Berber forces in the early eighth century during the first wave of Islamic expansion. By the tenth century, Muslim Spain was a vibrant civilization, often portrayed as a place of harmony and tolerance between its Muslim rulers and its Christian and Jewish subjects.

Certainly, Spain's agricultural economy was the most prosperous in Europe during this time, and its capital of Córdoba was among the largest and most splendid cities in the world. Muslims, Christians, and Jews alike contributed to a brilliant high culture in which astronomy, medicine, the arts, architecture, and literature flourished. Furthermore, social relationships among upper-class members of different faiths were easy and frequent. By 1000, perhaps 75 percent of the population had converted to Islam. Many of the remaining Christians learned Arabic, veiled their women, stopped eating pork, appreciated Arabic music and poetry, and sometimes married Muslims. One Christian bishop complained that Spanish Christians knew the rules of Arabic grammar better than those of Latin. During the reign of Abd al-Rahman III (r. 912–961), freedom of worship was declared as well as the opportunity for all to rise in the bureaucracy of the state.

But this so-called golden age of Muslim Spain was both limited and brief. Even assimilated or Arabized Christians remained religious infidels and second-class citizens in the eyes of their Muslim counterparts, and by the late tenth century toleration began to erode. The Córdoba-based regime fragmented into numerous rival states. Warfare with the remaining Christian kingdoms in northern Spain picked up in the tenth and eleventh centuries, and more puritanical and rigid forms of Islam entered Spain from North Africa. Under the rule of al-Mansur (r. 981–1002), an official policy of tolerance turned to one of overt persecution against Christians, which now included the plundering of churches and the seizure of their wealth, although he employed many Christian mercenaries in his armies. Social life also changed. Devout Muslims avoided contact with Christians; Christian homes had to be built lower than those of Muslims; priests were forbidden to carry a cross or a Bible, lest they offend Muslim sensibilities; and Arabized Christians were permitted to live only in particular places. Thus, writes one scholar, "the era of harmonious interaction between Muslim and Christian in Spain came to an end, replaced by intolerance, prejudice, and mutual suspicion."[23]

That intolerance intensified as the Christian reconquest of Spain gained ground after 1200. The end came in 1492, when Ferdinand and Isabella, the Catholic monarchs of a unified Spain, took Granada, the last Muslim stronghold on the Iberian Peninsula. To Christopher Columbus, who witnessed the event before leaving on his first transatlantic voyage, it was a grand Christian triumph. "I saw the royal banners of your Highnesses planted by force of arms upon the towers of the Alhambra," he wrote. To Muslims, it was a catastrophe. Tradition has it that Abu Abdullah, the final ruler of Muslim Granada, wept as he left his beloved city for the last time. Observing his grief, Abu Abdullah's mother famously said to him: "Thou dost weep like a woman for what thou couldst not defend as a man."

After the conquest, many Muslims were forced to emigrate, replaced by Christian settlers. While those who remained under Christian rule were legally guaranteed freedom of worship, they were forbidden to make converts, to give the call to prayer, or to go on pilgrimage. And all Jews, some 200,000 of them, were expelled from the country. In the early seventeenth century, even Muslim converts to Christianity were likewise banished from Spain. And yet cultural interchange persisted for a time. The translation of Arab texts into Latin continued under Christian rule, while Christian churches and palaces were constructed on the sites of older mosques and incorporated Islamic artistic and architectural features.

Mansa Musa, West African Monarch and Muslim Pilgrim

In 1324, Mansa Musa, the ruler, or *mansa*, of the Kingdom of Mali, set out on an arduous journey from his West African homeland to the holy city of Mecca. His kingdom stretched from the Atlantic coast a thousand miles or more to the fabled inland city of Timbuktu and beyond, even as his pilgrimage to Mecca reflected the growing penetration of Islam in this emerging West African civilization. A pious Muslim, Mansa Musa was fluent in Arabic, was an avid builder of mosques, and was inclined on occasion to free a few slaves.

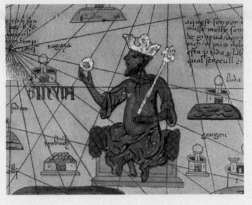

Mansa Musa.

In the fourteenth century, Mali was an expanding empire. According to Musa, one of his immediate predecessors had launched a substantial maritime expedition "to discover the furthest limits of the Atlantic Ocean."[24] The voyagers never returned, and no other record of this trip exists, but it is intriguing to consider that Africans and Europeans alike may have been exploring the Atlantic at roughly the same time. Mansa Musa, however, was more inclined to expand on land as he sought access to the goldfields to the south and the trans-Saharan

trade network to the north. Control of this lucrative commercial complex enriched Mansa Musa's empire, enabled a major building program of mosques and palaces, and turned the city of Timbuktu into a thriving center of trade, religion, and intellectual life. Merchants and scholars from across West and North Africa flocked to the city.

Mansa Musa's journey to Mecca fascinated observers at the time and continues to intrigue historians today. Such a pilgrimage has long been one of the duties—and privileges—of all Muslims. It also added the prestigious title of *hajji* to their names. For rulers in particular, it conveyed a spiritual power known as *baraka*, which helped legitimate their rule.

When Mansa Musa began his journey in 1324, he was accompanied by an enormous entourage, with thousands of fellow pilgrims, some 500 slaves, his wife and other women, hundreds of camels, and a huge quantity of gold. It was the gold that attracted the most attention, as he dis-

photo: Detail from the *Catalan Atlas*, 1375, by Abraham Cresques (1375–1387)/ Bibliothèque National de France, Paris, France/Bridgeman Images

---

Thus Spain, unlike most other regions incorporated into the Islamic world, experienced a religious reversal as Christian rule was reestablished and Islam painfully eradicated from the Iberian Peninsula. In world historical terms, perhaps the chief significance of Muslim Spain was its role in making the rich heritage of Islamic learning available to Christian Europe. As a cross-cultural encounter, it was largely a one-way street. European scholars wanted the secular knowledge—Greek as well as Arab—that had accumulated in the Islamic world, and they flocked to Spain to acquire it. That knowledge of philosophy, mathematics, medicine, optics, astronomy, botany, and more played a major role in the making of a new European civilization in the thirteenth century and beyond. Muslim Spain remained only as a memory.

PRACTICING AP® HISTORICAL THINKING

"Islam had a revolutionary impact on every society that it touched." What evidence might support this statement, and what might challenge it?

tributed it lavishly along his journey. Egyptian sources reported that the value of gold in their country was depressed for years after his visit. On his return trip, Mansa Musa apparently had exhausted his supply and had to borrow money from Egyptian merchants at high interest rates. Those merchants also made a killing on Musa's pilgrims, who, unsophisticated in big-city shopping, were made to pay far more than their purchases were worth. Europeans too now became aware of Mansa Musa, featuring him holding a large nugget of gold in a famous map from 1375 with a caption reading: "This Negro lord is called Musa Mali. . . . So abundant is the gold found in his country that he is the richest and most noble king in all the land."[25]

In Cairo, Mansa Musa displayed both his pride and his ignorance of Islamic law. Invited to see the sultan of Egypt, he was initially reluctant because of a protocol requirement to kiss the ground and the sultan's hand. He consented only when he was persuaded that he was really prostrating before God, not the sultan. And in conversation with learned clerics, Mansa Musa was surprised to learn that Muslim rulers were not allowed to take the beautiful unmarried women of their realm as concubines. "By God, I did not know that," he replied. "I hereby leave it and abandon it utterly."[26]

In Mecca, Mansa Musa completed the requirements of the hajj, dressing in the common garb of all pilgrims, repeatedly circling the Kaaba, performing ritual prayers, and visiting various sites associated with Muhammad's life, including a side trip to the Prophet's tomb in Medina. He also sought to recruit a number of sharifs, prestigious descendants of Muhammad's family, to add Islamic luster to his kingdom. After considerable difficulty and expense, he found four men who were willing to return with him to what Arabs understood to be the remote frontier of the Islamic world. Some reports suggested that they were simply freed slaves, hoping for better lives.

In the end, perhaps Mansa Musa's goals for the pilgrimage were achieved. On a personal level, one source reported that he was so moved by the pilgrimage that he actually considered abandoning his throne altogether and returning to Mecca, where he might live as "a dweller near the sanctuary [the Kaaba]."[27] His visit certainly elevated Mali's status in the Islamic world. Some 200 years after that visit, one account of his pilgrimage placed the sultan of Mali as one of four major rulers in the Islamic world, equal to those of Baghdad and Egypt. Mansa Musa would have been pleased.

Question: What significance did Mansa Musa likely attach to his pilgrimage? How might Egyptians, Arabians, and Europeans have viewed it?

The World of Islam as a New Civilization

As the religion spread and the Abbasid dynasty declined, the civilization of Islam, unlike that of China but similar to Western Christendom, operated without a dominant political center, bound more by a shared religious culture than by a shared state. Twice that civilization was threatened from outside. The most serious intrusion came during the thirteenth century from the Mongols, whose conquest of Central Asia and Persia proved devastating while incorporating many Muslims within the huge Mongol domains (see Chapter 11). Less serious but more well known, at least in the West, were the Christian Crusaders who established in the twelfth and thirteenth centuries several small and temporary outposts along the eastern Mediterranean (see Chapter 10).

AP® EXAM TIP

You should know features of the travels of Mansa Musa, the Muslim monarch of Mali, as described in the Zooming In box above.

Despite these external threats and its various internal conflicts, Islamic civilization flourished and often prospered, embracing at least parts of virtually every other civilization in the Afro-Eurasian hemisphere. It was in that sense "history's first truly global civilization," although the Americas, of course, were not involved.[28] What held this Islamic world together? What enabled many people to feel themselves part of a single civilization despite its political fragmentation, religious controversies, and cultural and regional diversity?

Networks of Faith

At the core of that vast civilization was a common commitment to Islam. No group was more important in the transmission of those beliefs and practices than the ulama. These learned scholars were not "priests" in the Christian sense, for in Islam, at least theoretically, no person could stand between the believer and Allah. Rather, they served as judges, interpreters, administrators, prayer leaders, and reciters of the Quran, but especially as preservers and teachers of the sharia. Supported mostly by their local communities, some also received the patronage of sultans, or rulers, and were therefore subject to criticism for corruption and undue submission to state authority. In their homes, mosques, shrines, and Quranic schools, the ulama passed on the core teachings of the faith. Beginning in the eleventh century, formal colleges called *madrassas* offered more advanced instruction in the Quran and the sayings of Muhammad; grammar and rhetoric; sometimes philosophy, theology, mathematics, and medicine; and, above all else, law. Teaching was informal, mostly oral, and involved much memorization of texts. It was also largely conservative, seeking to preserve an established body of Islamic learning.

Guided Reading Question

∙∙∙∙∙∙∙∙∙∙∙∙∙∙∙∙∙∙∙∙∙∙∙∙∙∙∙∙∙∙∙∙∙

■ DESCRIPTION
What makes it possible to speak of the Islamic world as a distinct and coherent civilization?

The ulama were an "international elite," and the system of education they created served to bind together an immense and diverse civilization. Common texts were shared widely across the world of Islam. Students and teachers alike traveled great distances in search of the most learned scholars. From Indonesia to West Africa, educated Muslims inhabited a "shared world of debate and reference."[29]

Paralleling the educational network of the ulama were the emerging religious orders of the Sufis. By the tenth century, particular Sufi *shaykhs* (shakes), or teachers, began to attract groups of disciples who were eager to learn their unique devotional practices and techniques of personal transformation. The disciples usually swore allegiance to their teacher and valued highly the chain of transmission by which those teachings and practices had come down from earlier masters. In the twelfth and thirteenth centuries, Sufis began to organize in a variety of larger associations, some limited to particular regions and others with chapters throughout the Islamic world. The Qadiriya order, for example, began in Baghdad but spread widely throughout the Arab world and into sub-Saharan Africa.

Sufi orders were especially significant in the frontier regions of Islam because they followed conquering armies or traders into Central and Southeast Asia, India, Anatolia, parts of Africa, and elsewhere. Their devotional teachings, modest ways of living, and reputation for supernatural powers gained a hearing for the new faith. Their emphasis on personal experience of the Divine, rather than on the law, allowed the Sufis to accommodate elements of local belief and practice and encouraged the growth of a popular or blended Islam. The veneration of deceased Sufi "saints," or "friends of God," particularly at their tombs, created sacred spaces that enabled Islam to take root in many places despite its foreign origins. But that flexibility also often earned Sufi practitioners the enmity of the ulama, who were sharply critical of any deviations from the sharia.

Like the madrassas and the sharia, Sufi religious ideas and institutions spanned the Islamic world and were yet another thread in the cosmopolitan web of Islamic civilization. Particular devotional teachings and practices spread widely, as did the writings of such famous Sufi poets as Hafiz and Rumi. Devotees made pilgrimages to the distant tombs of famous teachers, who, they often believed, might intercede with God on their behalf. Wandering Sufis, in search of the wisdom of renowned shaykhs, found fellow seekers and welcome shelter in the compounds of these religious orders.

In addition to the networks of the Sufis and the ulama, many thousands of people, from kings to peasants, made the grand pilgrimage to Mecca—the hajj—no doubt gaining some sense of the umma. There men and women together, hailing from all over the Islamic world, joined as one people to rehearse the central elements of their faith. The claims of local identities based on family, clan, tribe, ethnicity, or state never disappeared, but now overarching them all was the inclusive unity of the Muslim community.

Networks of Exchange

The world of Islamic civilization cohered not only as a network of faith but also as an immense arena of exchange in which goods, technologies, food products, and ideas circulated widely. Now large areas of the Afro-Eurasian world operated within a single political system, practiced Islam, and spoke Arabic. This huge region rapidly became a vast trading zone of hemispheric dimensions. In part, this was due to its central location in the Afro-Eurasian world and the breaking down of earlier political barriers between the Byzantine and Persian empires. Furthermore, commerce was valued positively within Islamic teaching, and laws regulating it figured prominently in the sharia, creating a predictable framework for exchange across many cultures. The pilgrimage to Mecca, as well as the urbanization that accompanied the growth of Islamic civilization, likewise fostered commerce. Baghdad, established in 756 as the capital of the Abbasid Empire, soon grew into a magnificent city of half a million people. The appetite of urban elites for luxury goods stimulated both craft production and the desire for foreign products.

Thus Muslim merchants, Arabs and Persians in particular, quickly became prominent and sometimes dominant players in all the major Afro-Eurasian trade routes of the third-wave era—in the Mediterranean Sea, along the revived Silk Roads, across the Sahara, and throughout the Indian Ocean basin (see Chapter 7).

AP® EXAM TIP

You are expected to know the features, participants, and extent of the Muslim trade networks.

Guided Reading Question

■ CONNECTION

In what ways was the world of Islam a "cosmopolitan civilization"?

AP® EXAM TIP

These examinations of the "Islamic Green (agricultural) Revolution" and the accompanying spread of technology and science across the Muslim world are very important.

By the eighth century, Arab and Persian traders had established a commercial colony in Canton in southern China, thus linking the Islamic heartland with Asia's other giant and flourishing economy. Various forms of banking, partnerships, business contracts, and instruments for granting credit facilitated these long-distance economic relationships and generated a prosperous, sophisticated, and highly commercialized economy that spanned the Old World.

The vast expanse of Islamic civilization also contributed to ecological change as agricultural products and practices spread from one region to another, a process already under way in the earlier Roman and Persian empires. Among the food crops that circulated within and beyond the Islamic world were different varieties of sugarcane, rice, apricots, artichokes, eggplants, lemons, oranges, almonds, figs, and bananas. Equally significant were water-management practices, so important to the arid or semi-arid environments of many parts of the Islamic world. Persian-style reservoirs and irrigation technologies spread as far as Tunisia and Morocco, the northern fringes of the Sahara, Spain, and Yemen. By connecting different environmental zones, particularly those where water availability was the major obstacle to agricultural growth, particular regions could draw upon a wide range of crops and practices. All of this contributed to an "Islamic Green Revolution" of increased food production as well as to population growth, urbanization, and industrial development across the Islamic world.

Technology too diffused widely within the realm of Islam. Muslim technicians made improvements on rockets, first developed in China, by developing one that carried a small warhead and another used to attack ships. Paper-making techniques entered the Abbasid Empire from China in the eighth century or earlier, with paper mills soon operating in Persia, Iraq, and Egypt. This revolutionary technology, which everywhere served to strengthen bureaucratic governments, passed from the Middle East into India and Europe over the following centuries. Everywhere it spurred the emergence of books and written culture at the expense of earlier orally based cultural expressions.

A Muslim Astronomical Observatory
Drawing initially on Greek, Indian, and Persian astronomy, the Islamic world after 1000 developed its own distinctive tradition of astronomical observation and prediction, reflected in this Turkish observatory constructed in 1557. Muslim astronomy subsequently exercised considerable influence in both China and Europe. (University Library, Istanbul, Turkey/Bridgeman Images)

Ideas likewise circulated across the Islamic world. The religion itself drew heavily and quite openly on Jewish and Christian precedents. Persia also contributed much in the way of bureaucratic practice, court ritual, and poetry, with Persian becoming a major literary language in elite circles. Scientific, medical, and philosophical texts, especially from ancient Greece, the Hellenistic world, and India, were systematically translated into Arabic, providing an enormous boost to Islamic scholarship and science for several centu-

SNAPSHOT Key Achievements in Islamic Science and Scholarship

Person/Dates	Achievement
al-Khwarazim (790–840)	Mathematician; spread use of Arabic numerals in Islamic world; wrote first book on algebra
al-Razi (865–925)	Discovered sulfuric acid; wrote a vast encyclopedia of medicine drawing on Greek, Syrian, Indian, and Persian work and his own clinical observation
al-Biruni (973–1048)	Mathematician, astronomer, cartographer; calculated the radius of the earth with great accuracy; worked out numerous mathematical innovations; developed a technique for displaying a hemisphere on a plane
Ibn Sina (Avicenna) (980–1037)	Prolific writer in almost all fields of science and philosophy; especially known for *Canon of Medicine*, a fourteen-volume work that set standards for medical practice in Islamic and Christian worlds for centuries
Omar Khayyam (1048–1131)	Mathematician; critic of Euclid's geometry; measured the solar year with great accuracy; Sufi poet; author of *The Rubaiyat*
Ibn Rushd (Averroës) (1126–1198)	Translated and commented widely on Aristotle; rationalist philosopher; made major contributions in law, mathematics, and medicine
Nasir al-Din Tusi (1201–1274)	Founder of the famous Maragha observatory in Persia (data from Maragha probably influenced Copernicus); mapped the motion of stars and planets
Ibn Khaldun (1332–1406)	Greatest Arab historian; identified trends and structures in world history over long periods of time

ries. In 830, the Abbasid caliph al-Mamun, himself a poet and scholar with a passion for foreign learning, established the House of Wisdom in Baghdad as an academic center for this research and translation. Stimulated by Greek texts, a school of Islamic thinkers known as Mutazalites ("those who stand apart") argued that reason, rather than revelation, was the "surest way to truth."[30] In the long run, however, the philosophers' emphasis on logic, rationality, and the laws of nature was subject to increasing criticism by those who held that only the Quran, the sayings of the Prophet, or mystical experience represented a genuine path to God.

But the realm of Islam was much more than a museum of ancient achievements from the civilizations that it encompassed. Those traditions mixed and blended to generate a distinctive Islamic civilization with many new contributions to the world of learning. (See Snapshot, above.) Using Indian numerical notation, for example, Arab scholars developed algebra as a novel mathematical discipline. They also undertook much original work in astronomy and optics. They built on earlier Greek and Indian practice to create a remarkable tradition in medicine and pharmacology. Arab physicians such as al-Razi and Ibn Sina accurately diagnosed many diseases, such as hay fever, measles, smallpox, diphtheria, rabies, and diabetes. In addition, treatments such as using a mercury ointment for scabies, cataract and hernia operations, and filling teeth with gold emerged from Arab doctors. The first hospitals, traveling clinics, and examinations for physicians and pharmacologists were also developed within the Islamic world. In the eleventh and twelfth centuries, this enormous body of Arab medical scholarship entered Europe via Spain, and it remained at the core of European medical practice for many centuries.

REFLECTIONS

Past and Present: Choosing Our History

Prominent among the many uses of history is the perspective it provides on the present. Although historians sometimes worry that an excessive "present-mindedness" may distort our perception of the past, all of us look to history, almost instinctively, to comprehend the world we now inhabit. Given the obvious importance of the Islamic world in the international arena of the twenty-first century, how might some grasp of the early development of Islamic civilization assist us in understanding our present circumstances?

Certainly, that history reminds us of the central role that Islam played in the Afro-Eurasian world for a thousand years or more. From 600 to 1600 or later, it was a proud, cosmopolitan, often prosperous, and frequently powerful civilization that spanned Africa, Europe, the Middle East, and Asia. What followed were several centuries of European or Western imperialism that many Muslims found humiliating, even if some were attracted by elements of modern Western culture. In their recent efforts to overcome those centuries of subordination and exploitation, Muslims have found encouragement and inspiration in reflecting on the more distant and perhaps more glorious past. But they have not all chosen to emphasize the same past. Those labeled as "fundamentalists" have often viewed the early Islamic community associated with Medina, Mecca, and Muhammad as a model for Islamic renewal in the present. Others, often known as Islamic modernizers, have looked to the somewhat later achievements of Islamic science and scholarship as a foundation for a more open engagement with the West and the modern world.

The history of Islam also reveals to us a world of great diversity and debate. Sharp religious differences between Sunni and Shia understandings of the faith; differences in emphasis between advocates of the sharia and of Sufi spirituality; political conflicts among various groups and regions within the larger Islamic world; different postures toward women in Arab lands and in West Africa—all of this and more divided the umma and divide it still. Recalling that diversity is a useful reminder for any who would tag all Muslims with a single label.

A further dimension of that diversity lies in the many cultural encounters that the spread of Islam has spawned. Sometimes great conflict and violence have accompanied those encounters, as in the Crusades and in Turkic invasions of India and Anatolia. At other times and places, Muslims and non-Muslims have lived together in relative tranquillity and tolerance—in Spain, in West Africa, in India, and in the Ottoman Empire. Some commentaries on the current interaction of Islam and the West seem to assume an eternal hostility or an inevitable clash of civilizations. The record of the past, however, shows considerable variation in the interaction of Muslims and others. While the past certainly shapes and conditions what happens next, the future, as always, remains open. Within limits, we can choose the history on which we seek to build.

Chapter Review

What's the Significance?

Quran, 367–69

umma, 368

Pillars of Islam, 368

hijra, 369

sharia, 370

jizya, 373

Umayyad caliphate, 376–77

Abbasid caliphate, 377

ulama, 377, 392

Sufism, 377–80

Mullah Nasruddin, 378–79

al-Ghazali, 380

Sikhism, 385

Ibn Battuta, 386–88

Timbuktu, 387

al-Andalus, 388–90

Mansa Musa, 390–91

madrassas, 392

House of Wisdom, 395

Ibn Sina, 395–96

Big Picture Questions

1. How might you account for the immense religious and political/military success of Islam in its early centuries?

2. In what ways might Islamic civilization be described as cosmopolitan, international, or global?

3. "Islam was simultaneously a single world of shared meaning and interaction and a series of separate, distinct, and conflicting communities." What evidence could you provide to support both sides of this argument?

4. What changes did Islamic expansion generate in those societies that encountered it, and how was Islam itself transformed by those encounters?

5. **Looking Back:** What distinguished the early centuries of Islamic history from a similar phase in the history of Christianity and Buddhism?

Next Steps: For Further Study

Reza Aslan, *No God but God* (2005). A well-written and popular history of Islam by an Iranian immigrant to the United States.

Fred M. Donner, *Muhammad and the Believers* (2010). An innovative account of the first century of Islam by a leading scholar of that era.

Richard Eaton, *Islamic History as Global History* (1990). A short account by a major scholar that examines Islam in a global framework.

John Esposito, ed., *The Oxford History of Islam* (1999). Up-to-date essays on various periods and themes in Islamic history. Beautifully illustrated.

Francis Robinson, ed., *Cambridge Illustrated History of the Islamic World* (1996). A series of essays by major scholars, with lovely pictures and maps.

Judith Tucker, *Gender and Islamic History* (1994). A brief overview of the changing lives of Islamic women.

The Man Who Walked across the World, http://topdocumentaryfilms.com/man-who-walked-across-world/. A documentary travelogue tracing the many journeys of Ibn Battuta.

"Religions: Islam," http://www.bbc.co.uk/religion/religions/islam/. A BBC Web site providing information about all aspects of Islamic life and culture.

WORKING WITH EVIDENCE

The Life of the Prophet

In addition to the teachings of the Quran, Muslims have long revered their Prophet as the most complete expression of God-conscious humanity and an example for all who would follow the path of Islam. In the several centuries after his death, Muslim scholars collected every detail of his life and sought to draw lessons about behavior based on his moral qualities and actions: his utter devotion to Allah; his bravery and decisiveness in battle; his honesty in business affairs; his flexibility, compassion, and willingness to forgive in dealing with enemies; his habit of consulting with companions before making a decision; his generosity and kindness to the poor and enslaved. Early biographies of Muhammad also made much of his sexual virility and attraction to women, which combined with his tenderness toward them to create a new model of Islamic masculinity.[31] The images that follow illustrate four major events in the life of Muhammad, long familiar to Muslims everywhere.

These images derive from the tradition of Persian or Turkish miniature painting—small, colorful, and exquisitely detailed works often used to illustrate books or manuscripts. One art historian described them as "little festivals of color in images separated from each other by pages of text."[32] Scenes from the life of the Prophet Muhammad appeared occasionally in this art form, which flourished especially from the thirteenth through the sixteenth centuries. They provide a window into the ways Muslims have understood their prophet and sought to learn from his example.

Representation of the Prophet Muhammad has long been controversial within Islamic societies. While not prohibited in the Quran, visual depictions of the Prophet have often been discouraged or even forbidden to prevent idolatry. Nonetheless, Muhammad was on occasion portrayed in Persian and Turkish miniature painting, sometimes in full face, but often with his face obscured. Such depictions, however, were limited to illustrations of particular events in books of history or poetry. They were never used to decorate mosques or the Quran. Nor were they employed as a teaching tool or for devotional purposes, as was frequently the case in Christian religious art.

According to all Muslims, the central and defining experience in Muhammad's life occurred in the year 610 C.E. in his initial encounter with an angel, usually identified as Gabriel, an event that marked the beginning of his revelations.[33] For some time before this dramatic event, Muhammad had been in the habit of withdrawing to a cave outside Mecca for prayer and meditation. On this occasion, however, a towering and overpowering presence of the angel appeared to him, filling the entire horizon, squeezing the very breath from his body, and commanding him to "recite" or to "read." After repeated protests that "I am not a reciter/reader," Muhammad found himself speaking what became the first revelation of the Quran.

When the vision passed, Muhammad fled in terror to his wife Khadija, fearing that he might be mad or possessed of some demonic spirit. Seeking to comfort him, Khadija took her husband to her learned cousin Waraqa, a Christian, who assured Muhammad that "he is the prophet of his people" and the recipient of revelation from the same God who had earlier granted similar messages to Abraham, Moses, and Jesus, among others. Further revelations followed over the next twenty-two years until Muhammad's death in 632, after which they were compiled into the Quran.

Source 9.1, an early fourteenth-century Persian miniature painting, depicts this encounter between Muhammad and Gabriel.

- What impression of this encounter does the artist seek to convey by the posture of the two figures?

- What religious meaning might Muslims derive from the idea that the revelation to Muhammad came through an angelic messenger rather than directly from Allah?

- Traditional accounts of Muhammad's encounter with the angel stress the mysterious and overpowering "otherness" of the Divine Presence, which accounts for Muhammad's initial fear and terror. What is the religious significance of such a depiction of the Divine? To what extent does this image convey that impression?

- Muslims have traditionally stressed that their prophet was illiterate, based in part on his response to the angel: "I am not a reader." Why might it be important to Muslims to believe that Muhammad was illiterate?

By far the most frequently portrayed event in the life of Muhammad was the *miraj*, the Prophet's Night Journey, said to have taken place in 619 or 620. The Quran refers briefly to God's taking the Prophet "from the sacred place of worship to the far distant place of worship." This passage became the basis for a story, much embellished over the centuries, of rich and deep meaning for Muslims. In this religious narrative, Muhammad was led one night by the angel Gabriel from Mecca to Jerusalem. For the journey he was given a *buraq*, a mythical winged creature with the body of a mule or donkey and the face of a woman. Upon arriving in Jerusalem, Muhammad led prayers for an assembly of earlier prophets including Abraham, Moses, and Jesus. (See page 367 for

Source 9.1 Muhammad and the Archangel Gabriel

Miniature from the "Jami' al-Tawarikh" of Rashid al-Din, ca. 1307/Edinburgh University Library, Scotland/With kind permission of the University of Edinburgh/ Bridgeman Images

a fifteenth-century Persian painting illustrating this event.) Then, accompanied by many angels, Muhammad made his way through seven heavens almost into the presence of God, where, according to the Quran, "he did see some of the most profound of his Sustainer's symbols." There too Allah spoke to Muhammad about the importance of regular prayer, commanding fifty prayers a day, a figure later reduced to five on the advice of Moses.

From the beginning, Muslims have been divided on how to interpret this journey of the Prophet. For most, perhaps, it was taken quite literally as a miraculous event. Some, however, viewed it as a dream or a vision, while others understood it as the journey of Muhammad's soul but not his body.

Source 9.2 The Night Journey of Muhammad

The Prophet's youngest wife, Aisha, for example, reported that "his body did not leave its place." Source 9.2, dating from the early sixteenth century, is one of many representations of the Night Journey that emerged within Persian miniature painting.

- What significance might attach to the female head of the buraq?

- What are the accompanying angels offering to the Prophet during his journey?

- What meaning might the artist seek to convey by the image of the world below and slightly to the right of the buraq?

- What is the significance of Muhammad's encounter with earlier prophets such as Abraham, Moses, and Jesus?

- Review the discussion of the Sufi tradition of Islam on pages 377–80. How might Sufis have understood the Night Journey?

The circumstances of Muhammad's life required that he act as a political leader at the same time as he was seeking to convey a new religious message. By 622, intense hostility to that revolutionary message had forced him out of Mecca to a new base in Medina, where he became a lawgiver, creating a social and political framework for his small band of followers. Violent opposition from various quarters and the absence of any overall political authority in the Arabian Peninsula made it necessary for Muhammad to also become a military strategist to protect his fledgling community. In these ways, his task was very different from that of the Buddha or Jesus.

Among the leading adversaries of the embryonic community of "believers" in Medina were the forces of Muhammad's own Quraysh clan in Mecca. An important turning point in that struggle occurred in 624 at the Battle of Badr in western Arabia. Despite being outnumbered more than three to one (about 1,000 Meccans but only around 300 "believers" from Medina), Muhammad's forces emerged victorious. While the Meccans fought in traditional Arab style with much individual bravado and no unified command, Muhammad's men were carefully drilled, well organized, and effectively led. To Muslims, however, it was not human ingenuity but divine intervention that occasioned this unlikely triumph. The Quran reported that Allah had sent some 3,000 angels to assist Muhammad's forces and reminded the believers that "it was not you that slew the enemy, but it was God that slew them."

This battle established the new Muslim community as a force to be reckoned with in Arabia and was enormously encouraging to the "believers." It was also the occasion for a series of revelations to Muhammad about the treatment of prisoners. They should not be abused in any way, but released, offered for ransom, or allowed to earn enough money to purchase their freedom. According to a traditional saying (hadith) of the Prophet, Muhammad asked his followers to treat captives as members of their own families. "You must feed them as you feed yourselves and clothe them as you clothe yourselves."

Visual Source 9.3, a sixteenth-century Turkish miniature painting, shows the preparation for the battle at Badr. Muhammad, shown in green dress with his face obscured, is sending waves of horsemen into the struggle. While other followers watch from behind, two of his close associates appear at the bottom right, and an angel hovers over the scene.

From the *Siyar-i-Nabi* (Volume IV) of Murad III (1546–1595), 1595 /Musée du Louvre, Paris, France/© Christian Larrieu/Bridgeman Images

Source 9.3 The Battle at Badr

- What elements of this image might suggest a natural or human understanding of the Muslim victory at Badr? And what might indicate divine intervention as an explanation?

- Documentary sources report only two horses and seventy camels on the side of the "believers" at this battle and suggest a more ragtag group of fighters than the image portrays. Why do you think the artist presented a rather more impressive picture?

- What religious meanings did Muhammad and Muslims in general extract from the battle at Badr?

In 630, just six years after the battle at Badr, Muhammad and some 10,000 soldiers triumphantly entered Mecca, almost completely without violence, and in a posture of reconciliation rather than revenge. In sharp contrast to traditional Arab practice, Muhammad issued a general amnesty for those who had opposed him. Then he turned his attention to the religious rationale of his entire movement. Riding his favorite camel, Muhammad circled the Kaaba seven times, shouting "Allahu Akbar" (God is greater), thus declaring the triumph of the Believer's Movement. Refusing to enter the Kaaba until it had been purified from its idolatry, Muhammad ordered its 360 idols and paintings removed. He then smashed each one, reciting a Quranic verse: "The truth has come and falsehood has vanished away." Muslim sources record that the Prophet invited his cousin and son-in-law Ali, the first male convert to the new faith, to stand on his shoulders to strike down the highest idols. Thus the Kaaba was cleansed and, in Muslim thinking, restored to its original purpose as a focal point for the worship of Allah alone.

Source 9.4, a fifteenth-century Persian image, portrays this dramatic event, showing Muhammad with Ali on his shoulders, both enveloped in holy fire, smashing the offensive idols while their followers look on.

- What view of pre-Islamic Arab religion do the images of the idols suggest?

- What fundamental religious teachings or spiritual truths does this painting seek to convey? How might you understand the Muslim concern with idolatry?

- Some traditions suggest that Muhammad ordered pictures of Mary and Jesus within the Kaaba to be left intact. What purpose might this tradition serve?

Source 9.4 The Destruction of the Idols

Miniature from "Raudat as-Safa" ("Garden of Purity"), by Mir Havand (d. 1489), Iran: Shiraz, ca. 1590/bpk, Berlin/
Museum für Islamische Kunst, Staatliche Museen, Berlin, Germany/Photo: Wolfgang Selbach/Art Resource, NY

DOING HISTORY

The Life of the Prophet

1. **Noticing point of view:** Consider these four visual sources together with the other images within the chapter. What general impression of the Islamic world emerges? What point of view, if any, is reflected in this selection of visual sources? Do they convey a positive, negative, or neutral impression of Islamic civilization? Explain your answer with specific references to the various images.

2. **Considering Muhammad:** How might you describe the understanding of Muhammad that these images present? In what ways is Muhammad an exemplar for Muslims of a fully realized human being? Do such images have any usefulness for knowing "what really happened" as opposed to grasping Muslim views of their prophet?

3. **Reflecting on religious history:** What do these images reveal about Muslims' understandings of their relationship to earlier religious practices? What did they accept from the past, and what did they reject? How does that understanding compare with Buddhists' and Christians' views of their place in religious history?

4. **Comparing narrative textbook and visual sources:** What do these images add to the understanding of Islam you derived from the narrative text of this chapter?

From the Psalter of Charles the Bold, 15th century/Victoria & Albert Museum, London, UK/Bridgeman Images

CHAPTER 10

The Worlds of Christendom

Contraction, Expansion, and Division
600–1300

Yao Hong, a Chinese woman, was about twenty years of age around 1990, when, distraught at discovering that her husband was having an affair, she became a Christian. As a migrant from a rural village to the huge city of Shanghai, Yao Hong found support and a sense of family in a Christian community. Interviewed in 2010, she observed, "Whether they know you or not, they treat you as a brother or sister. If you have troubles, they help out with money or material assistance or spiritual aid." Nor did she find the Christian faith alien to her Chinese culture. To the contrary, she felt conversion to Christianity as a patriotic act, even a way of becoming more fully modern. "God is rising here in China," she declared. "If you look at the United States or England, their gospel is very advanced. Their churches are rich, because God blesses them. So I pray for China."[1]

Yao Hong is but one of many millions who have made Christianity a very rapidly growing faith in China over the past thirty years or so. Other Asian countries—South Korea, Taiwan, Singapore, the Philippines, Vietnam, and parts of India—also host substantial Christian communities. Even more impressively, the non-Muslim regions of Africa witnessed an explosive advance of Christianity during the twentieth century, while Latin America, long a primarily Catholic region, has experienced a spectacular growth of Pentecostal Protestant Christianity since the 1970s. In the early twenty-first century, over 60 percent of the world's Christians lived in Asia, Africa, or Latin America. Thus Europe and North America, long regarded as the centers of the Christian world, have been increasingly outnumbered in the census of global Christianity.

Charlemagne This fifteenth-century manuscript painting depicts Charlemagne, king of the Franks, who was crowned emperor by the pope in 800 C.E. His reign illustrates the close and sometimes-conflicted relationship of political and religious authorities in an emerging European civilization. It also represents the futile desire of many in Western Europe to revive the old Roman Empire, even as a substantially new civilization was taking shape in the aftermath of the Roman collapse several centuries earlier.

AP® EXAM TIP

Knowledge of the spread and extent of Christianity over time is essential for success on the AP® exam.

Interestingly enough, the sixth- and seventh-century world of Christendom revealed a broadly similar pattern. Christianity then enjoyed an Afro-Eurasian reach with flourishing communities in Anatolia, Arabia, Egypt, North Africa, Ethiopia, Nubia, Syria, Armenia, Persia, India, and China, as well as Europe (see Chapter 4, pages 172–80). But during the next thousand years, radical changes reshaped that Christian world. Its African and Asian outposts largely vanished, declined, or were marginalized as Christianity became primarily a European phenomenon for the next thousand years or more.

During this millennium, Christianity came to provide a measure of cultural commonality for the diverse peoples of western Eurasia, much as Chinese civilization and Buddhism did for those of East Asia and Islam did for the Middle East and beyond. By 1300, almost all of these societies—from Ireland and England in the west to Russia in the east—had embraced in some form the teachings of the Jewish artisan called Jesus. At the same time, that part of the Christian world became deeply divided. Its eastern half, known as the Byzantine Empire or Byzantium (bihz-ANN-tee-uhm), encompassed much of the eastern Mediterranean basin while continuing the traditions of the Greco-Roman world, though on a smaller scale, until its conquest by the Muslim Ottoman Empire in 1453. Centered on the magnificent city of Constantinople, Byzantium gradually evolved a particular form of Christianity known as Eastern Orthodoxy within a distinctive third-wave civilization.

In Western, or Latin, Christendom, encompassing what we now know as Western Europe, the setting was far different. There the Roman imperial order had largely vanished by 500 C.E., accompanied by the weakening of many features of Roman civilization. Roads fell into disrepair, cities decayed, and long-distance trade shriveled. What replaced the old Roman order was a highly localized society—fragmented, decentralized, and competitive—in sharp contrast to the unified state of Byzantium. Like Byzantium, the Latin West ultimately became thoroughly Christian, but it was a gradual process lasting centuries, and its Roman Catholic version of the faith, increasingly centered on the pope, had an independence from political authorities that the Eastern Orthodox Church did not. Moreover, the Western Church in particular and its society in general were far more rural than Byzantium and certainly had nothing to compare to the splendor of Constantinople. However, slowly at first and then with increasing speed after 1000, Western Europe emerged as an especially dynamic, expansive, and innovative third-wave civilization, combining elements of its Greco-Roman past with the culture of Germanic and Celtic peoples to produce a distinctive hybrid, or blended, civilization.

SEEKING THE MAIN POINT

In what different ways did the history of Christianity unfold in various parts of the Afro-Eurasian world during the third-wave era?

Thus the story of global Christendom in the era of third-wave civilizations is one of contractions and expansions. As a religion, Christianity contracted sharply in Asia and Africa even as it expanded in Western Europe and Russia. As a civilization, Christian Byzantium flourished for a time, then gradually con-

A MAP OF TIME

4th century	Christianity becomes state religion of Armenia, Axum, and Roman Empire
5th–6th centuries	Introduction of Christianity into Nubia
476	Collapse of western Roman Empire
527–565	Justinian rules Byzantine Empire
7th century	Introduction of Christianity into China; initial spread of Islam
726–843	Icon controversy in Byzantium
800	Charlemagne crowned as new "Roman emperor"
988	Conversion of Kievan Rus to Christianity
1054	Mutual excommunication of pope and patriarch
1095–1291	Crusaders in the Islamic world
12th–13th centuries	Translations of Greek and Arab works available in Europe
1346–1350	Black Death in Europe
1453	Turks capture Constantinople; end of Byzantine Empire
1492	Christian reconquest of Spain completed; Columbus's first voyage

tracted and finally disappeared. The trajectory of civilization in the West traced an opposite path, at first contracting as the Roman Empire collapsed and later expanding as a new and blended civilization took hold in Western Europe.

Christian Contraction in Asia and Africa

How had Christianity become by 1500 a largely European faith, with its earlier and promising Asian and African communities diminished, defeated, or dissolved? The answer, in large measure, was Islam. The wholly unforeseen birth of yet another monotheistic faith in the Middle East, its rapid spread across much of the Afro-Eurasian world, the simultaneous creation of a large and powerful Arab Empire, the emergence of a cosmopolitan and transcontinental Islamic civilization—these were the conditions, described more fully in Chapter 9, that led to the contraction of Christendom in Asia and Africa, leaving Europe as the principal center of the Christian faith.[2]

Asian Christianity

**Guided Reading
Question**

■ COMPARISON

What variations in the
experience of African and
Asian Christian communi-
ties can you identify?

It was in Arabia, the homeland of Islam, that the decimation of earlier Christian communities occurred most completely and most quickly, for within a century or so of Muhammad's death in 632, only a few Christian groups remained. During the eighth century, triumphant Muslims marked the replacement of the old religion by using pillars of a demolished Christian cathedral to construct the Grand Mosque of Sana'a in southern Arabia.

Elsewhere in the Middle East, other Jewish and Christian communities soon felt the impact of Islam. When expanding Muslim forces took control of Jerusalem in 638 and subsequently constructed the Muslim shrine known as the Dome of the Rock (687–691), that precise location had long been regarded as sacred. To Jews, it contained the stone on which Abraham prepared to offer his son Isaac as a sacrifice to God, and it was the site of the first two Jewish temples. To Christians, it was a place that Jesus had visited as a youngster to converse with learned teachers and later to drive out the money changers. Thus, when the Umayyad caliph (successor to the Prophet) Abd al-Malik ordered a new construction on that site, he was appropriating for Islam both Jewish and Christian legacies. But he was also demonstrating the victorious arrival of a new faith and announcing to Christians and Jews that "the Islamic state was here to stay."[3]

AP® EXAM TIP

You should know
examples of accom-
modation and resis-
tance among major
belief systems.

In Syria and Persia, with more concentrated populations of Christians, accommodating policies generally prevailed. Certainly, Arab conquest of these adjacent areas involved warfare, largely against the military forces of existing Byzantine and Persian authorities, but not to enforce conversion. In both areas, however, the majority of people turned to Islam voluntarily, attracted perhaps by its aura of success. A number of Christian leaders in Syria, Jerusalem, Armenia, and elsewhere negotiated agreements with Muslim authorities whereby remaining Christian communities were guaranteed the right to practice their religion, largely in private, in return for payment of a special tax.

The Dome of the Rock, Jerusalem
To Muslims, the Dome of the Rock was constructed on the site from which Muhammad ascended into the presence of Allah during his Night Journey. It was the first large-scale building in the Islamic world and drew heavily on Roman, Byzantine, and Persian precedents. Its location in Jerusalem marked the arrival of a competing faith to Jews and Christians who had long considered the city sacred. (© Aaron Horowitz/Corbis)

Much depended on the attitudes of local Muslim rulers. On occasion, churches were destroyed, villages plundered, fields burned, and Christians forced to wear distinctive clothing. By contrast, a wave of church building took place in Syria under Muslim rule, and Christians were recruited into the administration, schools, translation services, and even the armed forces of the Arab Empire. In 649, only fifteen years after Damascus had been conquered by Arab forces, a Nestorian bishop wrote: "These Arabs fight not against our Christian religion; nay rather they defend our faith, they revere our priests and Saints, and they make gifts to our churches and monasteries."[4]

Thus the Nestorian Christian communities of Syria, Iraq, and Persia, sometimes called the Church of the East, survived the assault of Islam, but they did so as shrinking communities of second-class subjects, regulated minorities forbidden from propagating their message to Muslims. They also abandoned their religious paintings and sculptures, fearing to offend Muslims, who generally objected to any artistic representation of the Divine.

But further east, a small and highly creative Nestorian Church, initiated in

Nestorian Stele
The Nestorian Stele, erected in 781 C.E., is a large limestone block inscribed with a text detailing the early history of Christianity in China. (Nestorian Stele of the Tang Dynasty erected in 781, Xian, China/photo: Ancient Art & Architecture Collection Ltd./Kadokawa Shoten/Bridgeman Images)

635 by a Persian missionary monk, had taken root in China with the approval of the country's Tang dynasty rulers. Both its art and literature articulated the Christian message using Buddhist and Daoist concepts. The written texts themselves, known as the Jesus Sutras, refer to Christianity as the "Religion of Light from the West" or the "Luminous Religion." They describe God as the "Cool Wind," sin as "bad karma," and a good life as one of "no desire" and "no action." "People can live only by dwelling in the living breath of God," the Jesus Sutras declare. "All the Buddhas are moved by this wind, which blows everywhere in the world."[5] The contraction of this remarkable experiment owed little to Islam, but derived rather from the vagaries of Chinese politics. In the mid-ninth century, the Chinese state turned against all religions of foreign origin, Islam and Buddhism as well as Christianity (see Chapter 8, pages 352–53). Wholly dependent on the goodwill of Chinese authorities, this small outpost of Christianity withered.

Later the Mongol conquest of China in the thirteenth century offered a brief opportunity for Christianity's renewal, as the religiously tolerant Mongols welcomed Nestorian Christians as well as people of various other faiths. A number of prominent Mongols became Christians, including one of the wives of Chinggis Khan. Considering Jesus a powerful shaman, Mongols also appreciated that Christians, unlike Buddhists, could eat meat and, unlike Muslims, could drink alcohol, even including it in their worship. But Mongol rule was short, ending in 1368, and the

AP® EXAM TIP

Remember this example of syncretism (blending) of belief systems when you read about similar processes in the Americas after the arrival of Europeans (see Chapter 15).

small number of Chinese Christians ensured that the faith almost completely vanished with the advent of the vigorously Confucian Ming dynasty.

African Christianity

The churches of Africa, like those of the Middle East and Asia, also found themselves on the defensive and declining in the face of an expanding Islam. Across coastal North Africa, widespread conversion to Islam over several centuries reduced to virtual extinction Christian communities that had earlier provided many of the martyrs and intellectuals of the early Church.

In Egypt, however, Christianity had become the religion of the majority by the time of the Muslim conquest around 640, and for the next 500 years or so, large numbers continued to speak Coptic and practice their religion as *dhimmis*, legally inferior but protected people paying a special tax, under relatively tolerant Muslim rulers. Many found Arab government less oppressive than that of their former Byzantine overlords, who considered Egyptian Christians heretics. By the thirteenth century, things changed dramatically as Christian Crusaders from Europe and Mongol invaders from the east threatened Egypt. In these circumstances, the country's Muslim rulers came to suspect the political loyalty of their Christian subjects. The mid-fourteenth century witnessed violent anti-Christian pogroms, destruction of churches, and the forced removal of Christians from the best land. Many felt like "exiles in their own country." As a result, most rural Egyptians converted to Islam and moved toward the use of Arabic rather than Coptic, which largely died out. Although Egypt was becoming an Arab and Muslim country, a substantial Christian minority persisted among the literate in urban areas and in monasteries located in remote regions. In the early twenty-first century, Egyptian Christians still numbered about 10 percent of the population.

Even as Egyptian Christianity was contracting, a new center of African Christianity was taking shape during the fifth and sixth centuries in the several kingdoms of Nubia to the south of Egypt, where the faith had been introduced by Egyptian traders and missionaries. Parts of the Bible were translated into the Nubian language, while other writings appeared in Greek, Arabic, and the Ethiopian language of Ge'ez. A great cathedral in the Nubian city of Faras was decorated with magnificent murals, and the earlier practice of burying servants to provide for rulers in the afterlife stopped abruptly. At times, kings served as priests, and Christian bishops held state offices. By the mid-seventh century, both the ruling class and many commoners had become Christian. At the same time, Nubian armies twice defeated Arab incursions, and following these defeats an agreement with Muslim Egypt protected this outpost of Christianity for some 600 years. But pressures mounted in the thirteenth and fourteenth centuries as Egypt adopted a more hostile stance toward Christians, while Islamized tribes from the desert and Arab migrants pushed against Nubia. By 1500, Nubian Christianity, like its counterparts in coastal North Africa, had largely disappeared.

An important exception to these various contractions of Asian and African Christianity lay in Ethiopia. There the rulers of Axum had adopted Christianity in the fourth century, and it subsequently took root among the general population as well. (See Chapter 4, page 178, and Chapter 6, pages 237–39.) Over the centuries of Islamic expansion, Ethiopia became a Christian island in a Muslim sea, protected by its mountainous geography and its distance from major centers of Islamic power. Many Muslims also remembered gratefully that Christian Ethiopia had sheltered some of the beleaguered and persecuted followers of Muhammad in Islam's early years. Nonetheless, the spread of Islam largely cut Ethiopia off from other parts of Christendom and rendered its position in northeast Africa precarious.

The Church of St. George, Lalibela, Ethiopia
Excavated from solid rock in the twelfth century, the churches of Lalibela were distinctive Christian structures, invisible from a distance and apparent only when looking down on them from ground level. Local legend has it that their construction was aided by angels. This one in the shape of a cross is named for Saint George, the patron saint of Ethiopia. (© Gavin Hellier/Robert Harding World Imagery/Corbis)

In its isolated location, Ethiopian Christianity developed some of its most distinctive features. One of these was a fascination with Judaism and Jerusalem, reflected in a much-told story about the visit of an Ethiopian Queen of Sheba to King Solomon. The story includes an episode in which Solomon seduces the queen, producing a child who becomes the founding monarch of the Ethiopian state. Since Solomon figures in the line of descent to Jesus, it meant that Ethiopia's Christian rulers could legitimate their position by tracing their ancestry to Jesus himself. Furthermore, Ethiopian monks long maintained a presence in Jerusalem's Church of the Holy Sepulcher, said to mark the site where Jesus was crucified and buried. Then, in the twelfth century, the rulers of a new Ethiopian dynasty constructed a remarkable series of twelve linked underground churches, apparently attempting to create a New Jerusalem on Christian Ethiopian soil, as the original city lay under Muslim control. Those churches are in use to this day in modern Ethiopia, where over 60 percent of the country's population retains an affiliation with this ancient Christian church.

> **AP® EXAM TIP**
>
> Know the political and social effects of the Christian presence in Ethiopia over time.

Byzantine Christendom: Building on the Roman Past

The contraction of the Christian faith and Christian societies in Asia and Africa left Europe and Anatolia, largely by default, as the centers of Christendom. The initial expansion of Islam and the Arab Empire had quickly stripped away what had been

AP® EXAM TIP

You must know the political, social, and economic features and legacies of the Byzantine Empire. Also, be sure to take good notes on the continuities that carried over from the Roman Empire to the Byzantine Empire.

Guided Reading Question

■ CONTINUITY AND CHANGE

In what respects did Byzantium continue the patterns of the classical Roman Empire? In what ways did it diverge from those patterns?

the Middle Eastern and North African provinces of the Roman Empire and had brought Spain under Muslim control. But after the Mediterranean frontier between the Islamic and Christian worlds stabilized somewhat in the early eighth century, the immediate threat of Muslim incursions into the heartland of Christendom lifted, although border conflicts persisted. It was within this space of relative security, unavailable to most African and Asian Christian communities, that the diverging histories of the Byzantine Empire and Western Europe took shape.

Unlike most empires, Byzantium has no clear starting point. Its own leaders, as well as its neighbors and enemies, viewed it as simply a continuation of the Roman Empire. Some historians date its beginning to 330 C.E., when the Roman emperor Constantine, who began to favor Christianity during his reign, established a new capital, Constantinople, on the site of an ancient Greek city called Byzantium. At the end of that century, the Roman Empire was formally divided into eastern and western halves, thus launching a division of Christendom that has lasted into the twenty-first century.

Although the western Roman Empire collapsed during the fifth century, the eastern half persisted for another thousand years. Housing the ancient civilizations of Egypt, Greece, Syria, and Anatolia, the eastern Roman Empire (Byzantium) was far wealthier, more urbanized, and more cosmopolitan than its western counterpart; it possessed a much more defensible capital in the heavily walled city of Constantinople; and it had a shorter frontier to guard. Byzantium also enjoyed access to the Black Sea and command of the eastern Mediterranean. With a stronger army, navy, and merchant marine as well as clever diplomacy, its leaders were able to deflect the Germanic and Hun invaders who had overwhelmed the western Roman Empire.

Much that was late Roman—its roads, taxation system, military structures, centralized administration, imperial court, laws, Christian Church—persisted in the east for many centuries. Like Tang dynasty China seeking to restore the glory of the Han era, Byzantium consciously sought to preserve the legacy of classical Greco-Roman civilization. Constantinople was to be a "New Rome," and people referred to themselves as "Romans." Fearing contamination by "barbarian" customs, emperors forbade the residents of Constantinople from wearing boots, trousers, clothing made from animal skins, and long hairstyles, all of which were associated with Germanic peoples, and insisted instead on Roman-style robes and sandals. But much changed as well over the centuries, marking the Byzantine Empire as the home of a distinctive civilization.

The Byzantine State

Perhaps the most obvious change was one of scale, as the Byzantine Empire never approximated the size of its Roman predecessor (see Map 10.1). The western Roman Empire was permanently lost to Byzantium, despite Emperor Justinian's (r. 527–565) impressive but short-lived attempt to reconquer the Mediterranean basin. The rapid Arab/Islamic expansion in the seventh century resulted in the loss

Map 10.1   The Byzantine Empire

The Byzantine Empire reached its greatest extent under Emperor Justinian in the mid-sixth century
C.E. It subsequently lost considerable territory to various Christian European powers as well as to
Muslim Arab and Turkic invaders.

of Syria/Palestine, Egypt, and North Africa. Nonetheless, until roughly 1200, a
more compact Byzantine Empire remained a major force in the eastern Mediterranean, controlling Greece, much of the Balkans (southeastern Europe), and Anatolia. A reformed administrative system gave appointed generals civil authority in
the empire's provinces and allowed them to raise armies from the landowning
peasants of the region. From that territorial base, the empire's naval and merchant
vessels were active in both the Mediterranean and Black seas.

In its heyday, the Byzantine state was an impressive creation. Political authority
remained tightly centralized in Constantinople, where the emperor claimed to
govern all creation as God's worldly representative, styling himself the "peer of the
Apostles" and the "sole ruler of the world." The imperial court tried to imitate the
awesome grandeur of what it thought was God's heavenly court, but in fact it
resembled ancient Persian imperial splendor. Aristocrats trained in Greek rhetoric
and literature occupied high positions in the administration, participating in court
ceremonies that maintained their elite status. Parades of these silk-clad officials

AP® EXAM TIP

You must know ex-
amples of the struc-
tures of postclassical
empires, such as the
Byzantine.

added splendor to the imperial court, which also included mechanical lions that roared, birds that sang, and an immense throne that quickly elevated the emperor high above his presumably awestruck visitors. Nonetheless, this centralized state touched only lightly on the lives of most people, as it focused primarily on collecting taxes, maintaining order, and suppressing revolts. "Personal freedom in the provinces was constrained more by neighbors and rival households," concluded one historian, "than by the imperial government."[6]

After 1085, Byzantine territory shrank, owing to incursions by aggressive Western European powers, by Catholic Crusaders, and by Turkic Muslim invaders. The end came in 1453 when the Turkic Ottoman Empire, then known as the "sword of Islam," finally took Constantinople. One eyewitness to the event wrote a moving lament to his fallen city:

> And the entire city was to be seen in the tents of the [Turkish] camp, the city deserted, lying lifeless, naked, soundless, without either form or beauty. O city, head of all cities, center of the four corners of the world, pride of the Romans, civilizer of the barbarians. . . . Where is your beauty, O paradise . . . ? Where are the bodies of the Apostle of my Lord . . . ? Where are the relics of the saints, those of the martyrs? Where are the remains of Constantine the Great and the other emperors? . . . Oh, what a loss![7]

AP® EXAM TIP

Be able to list the causes of the decline of the Byzantine Empire.

The Byzantine Church and Christian Divergence

AP® EXAM TIP

You should know examples of connections between governments and religions throughout history, such as those described here.

Intimately tied to the state was the Church, a relationship that became known as caesaropapism. Unlike in Western Europe, where the Roman Catholic Church maintained some degree of independence from political authorities, in Byzantium the emperor assumed something of the role of both "Caesar," as head of state, and the pope, as head of the Church. Thus he appointed the patriarch, or leader, of the Orthodox Church; sometimes made decisions about doctrine; called church councils into session; and generally treated the Church as a government department. "The [Empire] and the church have a great unity and community," declared a twelfth-century patriarch. "Indeed they cannot be separated."[8] A dense network of bishops and priests brought the message of the Church to every corner of the empire, while numerous monasteries accommodated holy men, whose piety, self-denial, and good works made them highly influential among both elite and ordinary people.

Guided Reading Question

■ COMPARISON
How did Eastern Orthodox Christianity differ from Roman Catholicism?

Eastern Orthodox Christianity had a pervasive influence on every aspect of Byzantine life. It legitimated the supreme and absolute authority of the emperor, for he was a God-anointed ruler, a reflection of the glory of God on earth. It also provided a cultural identity for the empire's subjects. Even more than being "Roman," they were orthodox, or "right-thinking," Christians for whom the empire and the Church were equally essential to achieving eternal salvation. Constantinople was filled with churches and the relics of numerous saints. And the churches were filled with icons—religious paintings, some of them artistic masterpieces, of Jesus, Mary, and numerous saints—that many believed conveyed Divine Presence to the faithful. Complex theological issues about the Trinity and especially about the relationship of God and Jesus engaged the attention of ordinary people. One fourth-century bishop complained: "I wish to know the price of bread; one answers 'The Father is greater than the Son.' I inquire whether my bath is ready; one answers 'The Son has been made out of nothing.'"[9] Partisans of competing chariot-racing teams, known as the Greens and the Blues, vigorously debated theological issues as well as the merits of their favorite drivers.

In its early centuries and beyond, the Christian movement was rent by theological controversy and political division. Followers of Arius, an Egyptian priest, held that Jesus had been created by God the Father rather than living eternally with him. Nestorius, the fifth-century bishop of Constantinople, argued that Mary had given birth only to the human Jesus, who then became the "temple" of God. This view, defined as heretical in the Western Christian world, predominated in a separate Persian Church, which spread its views to India, China, and Arabia.

But the most lasting and deepest division within the Christian world occurred as Eastern Orthodoxy came to define itself against an emerging Latin Christianity centered on papal Rome. Both had derived, of course, from the growth of Christianity in the Roman Empire and therefore had much in common—the teachings of Jesus; the Bible; the sacraments; a church hierarchy of patriarchs, bishops, and priests; a missionary impulse; and intolerance toward other religions. Despite these shared features, any sense of a single widespread Christian community was increasingly replaced by an awareness of difference, competition, and outright hostility that even a common fear of Islam could not overcome. In part, this growing religious divergence reflected the political separation and rivalry between the Byzantine Empire and the emerging kingdoms of Western Europe. As the growth of Islam in the seventh century submerged earlier centers of Christianity in the Middle East and North Africa, Constantinople and Rome alone remained as alternative hubs of the Church. But they were now in different states that competed with each other for territory and for the right to claim the legacy of imperial Rome.

Beyond such political differences were those of language and culture. Although Latin remained the language of the Church and of elite communication in the West, it was abandoned in the Byzantine Empire in favor of Greek, which remained the basis for Byzantine education. More than in the West, Byzantine thinkers sought to formulate Christian doctrine in terms of Greek philosophical concepts.

Differences in theology and church practice likewise widened the gulf between Orthodoxy and Catholicism, despite agreement on fundamental doctrines. Disagreements about the nature of the Trinity, the source of the Holy Spirit, original sin, and the relative importance of faith and reason gave rise to much controversy. So too, for a time, did the Byzantine efforts to prohibit the use of icons, popular paintings of saints and biblical scenes, usually painted on small wooden panels. Other more modest differences also occasioned mutual misunderstanding and disdain.

St. Mark's Basilica
Consecrated in 1094, this ornate cathedral, although located in Venice, Italy, is a classic example of Byzantine architecture. Such churches represented perhaps the greatest achievement of Byzantine art and were certainly the most monumental expressions of Byzantine culture. (Erich Lessing/Art Resource, NY)

Priests in the West shaved and, after 1050 or so, were supposed to remain celibate, while those in Byzantium allowed their beards to grow long and were permitted to marry. Orthodox ritual called for using bread leavened with yeast in the Communion, but Catholics used unleavened bread. Far more significant was the question of authority. Eastern Orthodox leaders sharply rejected the growing claims of Roman popes to be the sole and final authority for all Christians everywhere.

This rift in the world of Christendom grew gradually from the seventh century on, punctuated by various efforts to bridge the mounting divide between the Western and Eastern branches of the Church. A sign of this continuing deterioration occurred in 1054 when representatives of both churches mutually excommunicated each other, declaring in effect that those in the opposing tradition were not true Christians. The Crusades, launched in 1095 by the Catholic pope against the forces of Islam, made things worse. Western Crusaders, passing through the Byzantine Empire on their way to the Middle East, engaged in frequent conflict with local people and thus deepened the distrust between them. From the Western viewpoint, Orthodox practices were "blasphemous, even heretical." One Western observer of the Second Crusade noted that the Greeks "were judged not to be Christians and the Franks [French] considered killing them a matter of no importance."[10] During the Fourth Crusade in 1204, Western forces seized and looted Constantinople and ruled Byzantium for the next half century. Their brutality only confirmed Byzantine views of their Roman Catholic despoilers as nothing more than barbarians. According to one Byzantine account, "They sacked the sacred places and trampled on divine things . . . they tore children from their mothers . . . and they defiled virgins in the holy chapels, fearing neither God's anger nor man's vengeance."[11] After this, the rupture in the world of Christendom proved irreparable.

Byzantium and the World

Beyond its tense relationship with Western Europe, the Byzantine Empire, located astride Europe and Asia, also interacted intensively with its other neighbors. On a political and military level, Byzantium continued the long-term Roman struggle with the Persian Empire. That persisting conflict weakened both of them and was one factor in the remarkable success of Arab armies as they marched out of Arabia in the seventh century. Although Persia quickly became part of the Islamic world, Byzantium held out, even as it lost considerable territory to the Arabs. A Byzantine military innovation known as "Greek fire"—a potent and flammable combination of oil, sulfur, and lime that was launched from bronze tubes—helped hold off the Arabs. It operated something like a flamethrower and subsequently passed into Arab and Chinese arsenals as well. Byzantium's ability to defend its core regions delayed for many centuries the Islamic advance into southeastern Europe, which finally occurred at the hands of the Turkish Ottoman Empire in the fifteenth and sixteenth centuries.

AP® EXAM TIP

Features of the political, social, and economic connections between the Byzantine Empire and its neighbors are "must know" facts for the AP® exam.

Economically, the Byzantine Empire was a central player in the long-distance trade of Eurasia, with commercial links to Western Europe, Russia, Central Asia, the Islamic world, and China. Its gold coin, the bezant, was a widely used currency in the Mediterranean basin for more than 500 years, and wearing such coins as pendants was a high-status symbol in the less developed kingdoms of Western Europe. The luxurious products of Byzantine craftspeople—jewelry, gemstones, silver and gold work, linen and woolen textiles, purple dyes—were much in demand. Its silk industry, based on Chinese technology, supplied much of the Mediterranean basin with this precious fabric.

Guided Reading Question

....

■ **CONNECTION**
In what ways was the Byzantine Empire linked to a wider world?

The cultural influence of Byzantium was likewise significant. Preserving much of ancient Greek learning, the Byzantine Empire transmitted this classical heritage to the Islamic world as well as to the Christian West. In both places, it had an immensely stimulating impact among scientists, philosophers, theologians, and other intellectuals. Some saw it as an aid to faith and to an understanding of the world, while others feared it as impious and distracting. (See "Reason and Faith," page 442.)

Byzantine religious culture also spread widely among Slavic-speaking peoples in the Balkans and Russia. As lands to the south and the east were overtaken by Islam, Byzantium looked to the north. By the early eleventh century, steady military pressure had brought many of the Balkan Slavic peoples and the Bulgars under Byzantine control. Christianity and literacy accompanied this Byzantine offensive. Already in the ninth century, two Byzantine missionaries, Cyril and Methodius, had developed an alphabet, based on Greek letters, with which Slavic languages could be written. This Cyrillic script made it possible to translate the Bible and other religious literature into these languages and greatly aided the process of conversion.

ZOOMING IN

988 and the Conversion of Rus

The baptism of Prince Vladimir.

In 988, Prince Vladimir of Rus underwent his celebrated religious conversion, a decision that initiated the Christianization of what later became Russia and Ukraine. About 125 years later, a charming account of that event appeared in the *Russian Primary Chronicle*, a major source of information about early Russian history. In that account, the prince essentially went shopping for a religion, sending emissaries to investigate the faiths of Judaism, Islam, Roman Catholicism, and Eastern Orthodoxy. Based on these reports, Vladimir rejected Islam, for it prohibited eating pork and drinking alcohol, and "drinking is the joy of the Russes." Circumcision and the dispersal of the Jews from their homeland counted against Judaism, while the emissaries reported that they "beheld no glory" among the Catholics. It was a different story when they described Eastern Orthodox Christianity and the great church of Hagia Sophia in Constantinople. There, they declared, "we knew not whether we were in heaven or on earth." And so Vladimir was baptized; married a sister of the Byzantine emperor; threw an idol of Perun, the god of thunder, into the river; and ordered the inhabitants of Kiev to

take part in a mass baptism. "There was joy in heaven and on earth," the *Chronicle* concludes, "to behold so many souls saved."[12]

Most historians are highly skeptical that any such systematic search for a new religion actually occurred. But the story reflects several historical realities of the time. Through trade and warfare, the emerging kingdom of Kievan Rus was becoming aware of its neighbors, especially the towering Byzantine Empire but also nearby Jewish, Catholic, and Muslim peoples. Nor is it hard to imagine that ruling elites sought ways to integrate the diverse peoples and cultures of their state. But the coming of Christianity to Rus was not nearly so abrupt as the *Chronicle* suggests. And the motives for this process were not quite so spiritual or religious as portrayed in this account.

In fact, the story began in 860, when the Byzantine Empire, subjected to fearsome raids by wild and ferocious warriors from Rus, sought to tame these "barbarians" by converting them to Christianity, a common practice

photo: Detail from the *Radziwill Chronicle*, Library of the Academy of Sciences of Russia, St. Petersburg, Russia/Photo by Fine Art Images/Heritage Images/Getty Images

The Conversion of Russia

AP® EXAM TIP

You should know the factors that gave rise to the Russian state.

The most significant expansion of Orthodox Christianity occurred among the Slavic peoples of what is now Ukraine and western Russia. In this culturally diverse region, which also included Finnic and Baltic peoples as well as Viking traders, a modest state known as Kievan Rus (KEE-yehv-ihn ROOS)—named after the most prominent city, Kiev—emerged in the ninth century. As in many of the new third-wave civilizations, the development of Rus was stimulated by trade, in this case along the Dnieper River, linking Scandinavia and Byzantium. Loosely led by various princes, especially the prince of Kiev, Rus was a society of slaves and freemen, privileged people and commoners, dominant men and subordinate women. This stratification marked it as a third-wave civilization in the making (see Map 10.3, page 429).

among threatened Christian rulers all across Europe. A Byzantine mission to the lands of Rus resulted in a church or two and a small number of individual converts, but no wholesale religious change. Then, in 911, a treaty between Rus and Byzantium was signed in Constantinople, where the delegates from Rus were shown "the beauties of the churches, the golden palace, and the riches contained therein." Furthermore, Byzantine clerics "instructed the Russes in their faith and expounded to them the true belief." By 957, some among the royal court in Rus had become interested in the new faith. A princess named Olga visited Constantinople and was baptized a Christian. But she was unable to persuade others in ruling circles to follow her example. Even her son spurned Christianity, fearing that his warrior followers would mock him if he converted. During this time, however, a brisk trade had developed between Rus and Byzantium; some warriors from Rus had served as mercenaries in Byzantine armies; and the notables of Rus had become aware of the cultural splendor and material riches of the Byzantine Empire.

And so it is perhaps not surprising that when Vladimir had consolidated his own power by 980, he moved decisively toward the Byzantine Empire and Orthodox Christianity. The occasion was a request in 987 for military assistance from a Byzantine emperor threatened by an internal rebellion. In the negotiations that followed, Vladimir agreed to supply 6,000 soldiers and to convert to Christianity. In return, he gained a new wife, Anna, the sister of the emperor, together with numerous priests and advisers. Perhaps most importantly, Vladimir gained recognition as an equal Christian ruler from the dominant civilization in the region. Here was a turning point in the century-long interaction of Rus and Byzantium and the beginning of an extended process, born of political need on both sides, by which Rus—and later Russia and Ukraine—became thoroughly Christian lands.

A thousand years after Vladimir's conversion, in 1988, the millennial anniversary of that event was celebrated in a Soviet Union still ruled by a Communist Party that had spared little effort to destroy the Russian Orthodox Church. As the Soviet Union disintegrated in the several years that followed, many closed churches, seminaries, and monasteries reopened, returning to the control of the faithful, who flooded into them. The Church has again become an important bulwark of the new Russian and Ukrainian states. And in the memory of many Russians, 988 still remains a major turning point in their country's history.

Questions: How did the *Russian Primary Chronicle* simplify the conversion story? What aspects of the conversion process are emphasized in the *Chronicle*?

Religion reflected the region's cultural diversity, with the gods and practices of many peoples much in evidence. Ancestral spirits, household deities, and various gods related to the forces of nature were in evidence, with Perun, the god of thunder, perhaps the most prominent. Small numbers of Christians, Muslims, and Jews were likewise part of the mix. Then, in the late tenth century, 988 to be precise, a decisive turning point occurred. The growing interaction of Rus with the larger world prompted Prince Vladimir of Kiev to affiliate with the Eastern Orthodox faith of the Byzantine Empire. He was searching for a religion that would unify the diverse peoples of his region, while linking Rus into wider networks of communication and exchange. (See Zooming In: 988 and the Conversion of Rus, above, for a closer look at this momentous decision.)

Guided Reading Question

■ CONNECTION

How did links to Byzantium transform the new civilization of Kievan Rus?

As elsewhere in Europe, the coming of Christianity to Rus was a top-down process in which ordinary people followed their rulers into the Church. It was also a slow process, and elements of traditional religious sensibility long lingered among those who defined themselves as Christian. Perun continued to speak to some, and "magicians" sometimes led people astray in the eyes of church authorities. But building churches on the site where idols to Perun and other gods once stood helped to anchor the new faith in its new land.

It was a fateful choice with long-term implications for Russian history, for it brought this fledgling civilization firmly into the world of Orthodox Christianity, separating it from both the realm of Islam and the Roman Catholic West. Like many new civilizations, Rus borrowed extensively from its older and more sophisticated neighbor. Among these borrowings were Byzantine architectural styles, the Cyrillic alphabet, the extensive use of icons, a monastic tradition stressing prayer and service, and political ideals of imperial control of the Church, all of which became part of a transformed Rus. Orthodoxy also provided a more unified identity for this emerging civilization and religious legitimacy for its rulers. Centuries later, when Byzantium had fallen to the Turks, a few Russian church leaders proclaimed the doctrine of a "third Rome." The original Rome had abandoned the true Orthodox faith for Roman Catholicism, and the second Rome, Constantinople, had succumbed to Muslim infidels. Moscow was now the third Rome, the final protector and defender of Orthodox Christianity. Though not widely proclaimed in Russia itself, such a notion reflected the "Russification" of Eastern Orthodoxy and its growing role as an element of Russian national identity. It was also a reminder of the enduring legacy of a thousand years of Byzantine history, long after the empire itself had vanished.

AP® EXAM TIP

Be knowledgeable about cities that arose during the postclassical period, like Kiev and Moscow.

Western Christendom: Rebuilding in the Wake of Roman Collapse

The western half of the European Christian world followed a rather different path than that of the Byzantine Empire. For much of the third-wave millennium, it was distinctly on the margins of world history, partly because of its geographic location at the far western end of the Eurasian landmass. Thus it was at a distance from the growing routes of world trade—by sea in the Indian Ocean and by land across the Silk Roads to China and the Sand Roads to West Africa. Not until the Eastern and Western hemispheres were joined after 1500 did Western Europe occupy a geographically central position in the global network. Internally, Europe's geography made political unity difficult. It was a region in which population centers were divided by mountain ranges and dense forests as well as by five major peninsulas and two large islands (Britain and Ireland). However, its extensive coastlines and interior river systems facilitated exchange within Europe, while a moderate climate, plentiful rainfall, and fertile soils enabled a productive agriculture that could support a growing population.

Political Life in Western Europe

In the early centuries of this era, history must have seemed more significant than geography, for the Roman Empire, long a fixture of the western Mediterranean region, was gone. The traditional date marking the collapse of the empire is 476, when the German general Odoacer overthrew the last Roman emperor in the West. In itself not very important, this event has come to symbolize a major turning point in the West, for much that had characterized Roman civilization also weakened, declined, or disappeared in the several centuries before and after 476. Any semblance of large-scale centralized rule vanished. Disease and warfare reduced Western Europe's population by more than 25 percent. Land under cultivation contracted, while forests, marshland, and wasteland expanded. Urban life too diminished sharply, as Europe reverted to a largely rural existence. Rome at its height was a city of 1 million people, but by the tenth century it numbered perhaps 10,000. Public buildings crumbled from lack of care. Outside Italy, long-distance trade dried up as Roman roads deteriorated, and money exchange gave way to barter in many places. Literacy lost ground as well. Germanic peoples, whom the Romans had viewed as barbarians—Goths, Visigoths, Franks, Lombards, Angles, Saxons—now emerged as the dominant peoples of Western Europe. In the process, Europe's center of gravity moved away from the Mediterranean toward the north and west.

Yet much that was classical or Roman persisted, even as a new order emerged in Europe. On the political front, a series of regional kingdoms—led by Visigoths in Spain, Franks in France, Lombards in Italy, and Angles and Saxons in England—arose to replace Roman authority. But many of these Germanic peoples, originally organized in small kinship-based tribes with strong warrior values, had already been substantially Romanized. Contact with the Roman Empire in the first several centuries C.E. had generated more distinct ethnic identities among them, militarized their societies, and given greater prominence to Woden, their god of war. As Germanic peoples migrated into or invaded Roman lands, many were deeply influenced by Roman culture, especially if they served in the Roman army. On the funeral monument of one such person was a telling inscription: "I am a Frank by nationality, but a Roman soldier under arms."[13]

The prestige of things Roman remained high, even after the empire itself had collapsed. Now as leaders of their own kingdoms, the Germanic rulers actively embraced written Roman law, using fines and penalties to provide order and justice in their new states in place of feuds and vendettas. One Visigoth ruler named Athaulf (r. 410–415), who had married a Roman noblewoman, gave voice to the continuing attraction of Roman culture and its empire:

AP® EXAM TIP

You must know the effects of the fall of the Roman Empire on the Mediterranean region.

AP® EXAM TIP

As you develop your skills in writing comparison essays, study similarities in political fragmentation between South Asia and Western Europe. Look back at Chapter 3.

Guided Reading Question

■ CHANGE

What replaced the Roman order in Western Europe?

At first I wanted to erase the Roman name and convert all Roman territory into a Gothic empire. . . . But long experience has taught me that . . . without law a state is not a state. Therefore I have more prudently chosen the different glory of reviving the Roman name with Gothic vigour, and I hope to be acknowledged by posterity as the initiator of a Roman restoration.[14]

Several of the larger, though relatively short-lived, Germanic kingdoms also had aspirations to re-create something of the unity of the Roman Empire. Charlemagne (SHAHR-leh-mane) (r. 768–814), ruler of the Carolingian Empire, occupying what is now France, Belgium, the Netherlands, and parts of Germany and Italy, erected an embryonic imperial bureaucracy, standardized weights and measures, and began to act like an imperial ruler. On Christmas Day of the year 800, he was crowned as a new Roman emperor by the pope, although his realm splintered shortly after his death (see Map 10.2). Later Otto I of Saxony (r. 936–973) gathered much of Germany under his control, saw himself as renewing Roman rule, and was likewise invested with the title of emperor by the pope. Otto's realm, subsequently known as the Holy Roman Empire, was largely limited to Germany and soon proved little more than a collection of quarreling principalities. Though unsuccessful in reviving anything approaching Roman imperial authority, these efforts testify to the continuing appeal of the classical world, even as a new political system of rival kingdoms blended Roman and Germanic elements.

AP® EXAM TIP

Be able to cite several examples of political division and unity throughout European history.

The Carolingian Empire in the Ninth Century C.E.

- Kingdom of Charles the Bald
- Kingdom of Louis the German
- Kingdom of Lothar
- Charlemagne's territory

Map 10.2 Western Europe in the Ninth Century

Charlemagne's Carolingian Empire brought a temporary political unity to parts of Western Europe, but it was subsequently divided among his three sons, who waged war on one another.

Society and the Church

Within these new kingdoms, a highly fragmented and decentralized society widely known as feudalism emerged with great local variation. In thousands of independent, self-sufficient, and largely isolated landed estates or manors, power—political, economic, and social—was exercised by a warrior elite of landowning lords. In the constant competition of these centuries, lesser lords and knights swore allegiance to greater lords or kings and thus became their vassals, frequently receiving lands and plunder in return for military service.

Such reciprocal ties between superior and subordinate were also apparent at the bottom of the social hierarchy, as Roman-style slavery gradually gave way to serfdom. Unlike slaves, serfs were not the personal property of their masters, could not be arbitrarily thrown off their land, and were allowed to live in families. However, they were bound to their masters' estates as peasant laborers and owed various payments and services to the lord of the manor. One family on a manor near Paris in the ninth century owed four silver coins, wine, wood, three hens, and fifteen eggs per year. Women generally were required to weave cloth and make clothing for the lord, while men labored in the lord's fields. In return, the serf family received a small farm and such protection as the lord could provide. In a violent and insecure world adjusting to the absence of Roman authority, the only security available to many individuals or families lay in these communities, where the ties to kin, manor, and lord constituted the primary human loyalties. It was a world apart from the stability of life in imperial Rome or its continuation in Byzantium.

Also filling the vacuum left by the collapse of empire was the Church, later known as Roman Catholic, yet another link to the now-defunct Roman world. Its hierarchical organization of popes, bishops, priests, and monasteries was modeled on that of the Roman Empire and took over some of its political, administrative, educational, and welfare functions. Latin continued as the language of the Church even as it gave way to various vernacular languages in common speech. In fact, literacy in the classical languages of Greek and Latin remained the hallmark of educated people in the West well into the twentieth century.

Like the Buddhist establishment in China, the Church subsequently became quite wealthy, with reformers often accusing it of forgetting its central spiritual mission. It also provided a springboard for the conversion of Europe's many "pagan" peoples. Numerous missionaries, commissioned by the pope, monasteries, or already-converted rulers, fanned out across Europe, generally pursuing a "top-down" strategy. Frequently it worked, as local kings and warlords found status and legitimacy in association with a literate and "civilized" religion that still bore something of the grandeur that was Rome. With "the wealth and protection of the powerful," ordinary people followed their rulers into the fold of the Church.[15]

This process was similar to Buddhism's appeal for the nomadic rulers of northern and western China following the collapse of the Han dynasty. Christianity, like Buddhism, also bore the promise of superior supernatural powers, and its spread was frequently associated with reported miracles of healing, rainfall, fertility, and victory in battle.

But it was not an easy sell. Outright coercion was sometimes part of the process. More often, however, softer methods prevailed. The Church proved willing to accommodate a considerable range of earlier cultural practices, absorbing them into an emerging Christian tradition. For example, amulets and charms to ward off evil became medals with the image of Jesus or the Virgin Mary; traditionally sacred wells and springs became the sites of churches; and festivals honoring ancient gods became Christian holy days. December 25 was selected as the birthday of Jesus, for it was associated with the winter solstice, the coming of more light, and the birth or rebirth of various deities in pre-Christian European traditions. By 1100, most of Europe had embraced Christianity. Even so, for centuries priests and bishops had to warn their congregations against the worship of rivers, trees, and mountains, and for many people, ancient gods, monsters, trolls, and spirits still inhabited the land. The spreading Christian faith, like the new political framework of European civilization, was a blend of many elements. (For more on the rooting of Christianity in Western Europe, see Working with Evidence: The Making of Christian Europe, page 448.)

Church authorities and the nobles/warriors who exercised political influence reinforced each other. Rulers provided protection for the papacy and strong encouragement for the faith. In return, the Church offered religious legitimacy for the powerful and the prosperous. "It is the will of the Creator," declared the teaching of the Church, "that the higher shall always rule over the lower. Each individual and class should stay in its place [and] perform its tasks."[16] But Church and political authorities competed as well as cooperated, for they were rival centers of power in post-Roman Europe. Particularly controversial was the right to appoint bishops and the pope himself; this issue, known as the investiture conflict, was especially prominent in the eleventh and twelfth centuries. Was the right to make such appointments the responsibility of the Church alone, or did kings and emperors also have a role? In the compromise that ended the conflict, the Church won the right to appoint its own officials, while secular rulers retained an informal and symbolic role in the process.

Accelerating Change in the West

The pace of change in this emerging civilization picked up considerably in the several centuries after 1000. For many centuries before this, the world of European Christendom had been subject to repeated invasions. The incursion of Germanic peoples had accompanied the decline and fall of the western Roman Empire. In the fifth century C.E., the Central Asian Huns had penetrated as far as France and briefly, under the leadership of Attila, established a large state across much of Central and Eastern Europe. Muslim armies had conquered Christian North Africa and Spain and threatened the rest of Europe. In the ninth and tenth centuries, Magyar (Hungarian) invasions from the east and Viking incursions from the north likewise disrupted and threatened post-Roman Europe (see Map 10.3). But by the year 1000, these invasions had been checked; the invaders had been absorbed into settled society and in some cases had converted to Christianity. The greater security and stability that came with relative peace arguably opened the way to an accelerating tempo of change. The climate also seemed to cooperate. A generally warming trend after 750 reached its peak in the eleventh and twelfth centuries, enhancing agricultural production, especially in northern and highland regions.

AP® EXAM TIP

A key theme in AP® World History is how the environment has affected human activity, as discussed here and again on page 430.

Map 10.3   Europe in the Middle Ages

By the eleventh century, the national monarchies that would organize European political life—France, Spain, England, Poland, and Germany—had begun to take shape. The earlier external attacks on Europe from Vikings, Magyars, and Muslims had largely ceased, although it was clear that European civilization was developing in the shadow of the Islamic world.

Whatever may have launched this new phase of European civilization, commonly called the High Middle Ages (1000–1300), the signs of expansion and growth were widely evident. The population of Europe grew from perhaps 35 million in 1000 to about 80 million in 1340. With more people, many new lands were opened for cultivation in a process paralleling China's expansion to the south at the same time. Great lords, bishops, and religious orders organized new villages on what had recently

Guided Reading Question

■ CHANGE

In what ways was European civilization changing after 1000?

been forest or wasteland. Marshes were drained in many regions, and land was reclaimed from the sea, especially along the North Sea coast.

Warmer weather during the summer months allowed farmers and pastoralists to herd their flocks into previously wild highland regions. Everywhere trees were felled at tremendous rates to clear agricultural land and to use as fuel or building material. By 1300, the forest cover of Europe had been reduced to about 20 percent of the land area. "I believe that the forest . . . covers the land to no purpose," declared a German abbot, "and hold this to be an unbearable harm."[17] These developments took a heavy toll on both the terrestrial and aquatic environments. Deforestation, overfishing, human waste, and the proliferation of new watermills and their associated ponds damaged freshwater ecosystems in many places. Lamenting the declining availability of fish, the French king Philip IV declared in 1289: "Today each and every river and waterside of our realm, large and small, yields nothing."[18]

The increased production associated with this agricultural expansion stimulated a considerable growth in long-distance trade, much of which had dried up in the aftermath of the Roman collapse. One center of commercial activity lay in Northern Europe from England to the Baltic coast and involved the exchange of wood, beeswax, furs, rye, wheat, salt, cloth, and wine. The other major trading network centered on northern Italian towns such as Florence, Genoa, and Venice. Their trading partners were the more established civilizations of Islam and Byzantium, and the primary objects of trade included silks, drugs, precious stones, and spices from Asia. At great trading fairs, particularly those in the Champagne area of France near Paris, merchants from Northern and Southern Europe met to exchange the products of their respective areas, such as northern woolens for Mediterranean spices. Thus the self-sufficient communities of earlier centuries increasingly forged commercial bonds among themselves and with more distant peoples.

The population of towns and cities likewise grew on the sites of older Roman towns, at trading crossroads and fortifications, and around cathedrals all over Europe. Some towns had only a few hundred people, but others became much larger. In the early 1300s, London had about 40,000 people, Paris had approximately 80,000, and Venice by the end of the fourteenth century could boast perhaps 150,000. To keep these figures in perspective, Constantinople housed some 400,000 people in 1000, Córdoba in Muslim Spain about 500,000, the Song dynasty capital of Hangzhou more than 1 million in the thirteenth century, and the Aztec capital of Tenochtitlán perhaps 200,000 by 1500. Nonetheless, urbanization was proceeding apace in Europe, though never hosting more than 10 percent of Europe's population. These towns gave rise to and attracted new groups of people, particularly merchants, bankers, artisans, and university-trained professionals such as lawyers, doctors, and scholars. Many of these groups, including university professors and students, organized themselves into guilds (associations of people pursuing the same line of work) to regulate their respective professions. Thus, from the rural social order of lord and peasant, a new more productive and complex division of labor took shape in European society.

AP® EXAM TIP

Be able to list factors that led to the revival of cities during Europe's Middle Ages.

A further sign of accelerating change in the West lay in the growth of territorial states with more effective institutions of government commanding the loyalty, or at least the obedience, of their subjects. Since the disintegration of the Roman Empire, Europeans' loyalties had focused on the family, the manor, or the religious community, but seldom on the state. Great lords may have been recognized as kings, but their authority was extremely limited and was exercised through a complex and decentralized network of feudal relationships with earls, counts, barons, and knights, who often felt little obligation to do the king's bidding. But in the eleventh through the thirteenth centuries, the nominal monarchs of Europe gradually and painfully began to consolidate their authority, and the outlines of French, English, Spanish, Scandinavian, and other states began to appear, each with its own distinct language and culture (see Map 10.3, page 429). Royal courts and fledgling bureaucracies were established, and groups of professional administrators appeared. Such territorial kingdoms were not universal, however. In Italy, city-states flourished as urban areas grew wealthy and powerful, whereas the Germans remained divided among a large number of small principalities within the Holy Roman Empire.

AP® EXAM TIP

Know the features of Europe's feudal system.

These changes, which together represented the making of a new civilization, had implications for the lives of countless women and men. (See Zooming In: Cecilia Penifader, page 432, for an account of a rural unmarried woman's life in England during this time.) Economic growth and urbanization initially offered European women substantial new opportunities. Women were active in a number of urban professions, such as weaving, brewing, milling grain, midwifery, small-scale retailing, laundering, spinning, and prostitution. In twelfth-century Paris, for example, a list of 100 occupations identified 86 as involving women workers, of which 6 were exclusively female. In England, women worked as silk weavers, hat-makers, tailors, brewers, and leather processors and were entitled to train female apprentices in some of these trades. In Frankfurt, about one-third of the crafts and trades were entirely female, another 40 percent were dominated by men, and the rest were open to both. Widows of great merchants sometimes continued their husbands' businesses, and one of them, Rose Burford, lent a large sum of money to the king of England to finance a war against Scotland in 1318.

Much as economic and technological change in China had eroded female silk production, by the fifteenth century artisan opportunities were declining for European women as well. Most women's guilds were gone, and women were restricted or banned from many others. Even brothels were run by men. In England, guild regulations now outlawed women's participation in manufacturing particular fabrics and forbade their being trained on new and larger weaving machines. Women might still spin thread, but the more lucrative and skilled task of weaving fell increasingly to men. Technological progress may have been one reason for this change. Water- and animal-powered grain mills replaced the hand-grinding previously undertaken by women, and larger looms making heavier cloth replaced the lighter looms that women had worked. Men increasingly took over these professions and trained their sons as apprentices, making it more difficult for women to remain active in these fields.

Cecilia Penifader, an English Peasant and Unmarried Woman

Born in 1297 in a small English village, Cecilia Penifader was an illiterate peasant woman, who seldom if ever traveled more than twenty miles beyond her birthplace. She was of no particular historical importance outside of her family and community. Nonetheless, her life, reconstructed from court records by historian Judith Bennett, provides a window into the conditions of ordinary rural people as a new European civilization was taking shape.[19]

From birth to death, Cecilia lived in Brigstock, a royal manor owned by the king of England or a member of the royal family. Free tenants such as Cecilia owed rents and various dues to the lord of the manor. Thus Cecilia occupied a social position above the serfs, unfree people who owed labor service to the lord, but infinitely below the clergy and nobility to whom the lower orders of society owed constant deference. But within the class of "those who work"—the peasantry—Cecilia was fortunate. She was born the seventh of eight children, six of whom survived to adulthood, an unusual occurrence at a time when roughly half of village children died. Her family had

A European peasant woman such as Cecilia Penifader.

substantially larger landholdings than most of their neighbors and no doubt lived in a somewhat larger house. Still, it was probably a single-room dwelling measuring about thirty by fifteen feet, with a dirt floor, and surely it was smoky, for chimneys were not a part of peasant homes.

Between 1315 and 1322, as Cecilia entered early adulthood, England and much of the rest of Europe experienced an immense famine, caused by several years of especially cold and wet weather that marked the end of centuries of favorable climatic conditions. During those years, Cecilia first entered the court records of Brigstock. In 1316, another peasant lodged a complaint against Cecilia and her father for ignoring his boundary stones and taking hay from his fields. Such petty quarrels and minor crimes proliferated as neighborliness broke down in the face of bad harvests and desperate circumstances. Furthermore, both of Cecilia's parents died during the famine years.

photo: *August*, from a series of labors of the month, ca. 1450. English stained glass roundel/Victoria & Albert Museum, London, UK/V&A Images/Art Resource, NY

AP® EXAM TIP

Compare leadership roles for women in the Roman Catholic and Buddhist faiths (see Chapter 5).

The Church had long offered some women an alternative to home, marriage, family, and rural life. As in Buddhist lands, substantial numbers of women, particularly from aristocratic families, were attracted to the secluded monastic life of poverty, chastity, and obedience within a convent, in part for the relative freedom from male control that it offered. Here was one of the few places where women might exercise authority as abbesses of their orders and obtain a measure of education. The twelfth-century abbess Hildegard of Bingen, for example, won wide acclaim for her writings on theology, medicine, botany, and music.

But by 1300, much of the independence that such abbesses and their nuns had enjoyed was curtailed and male control tightened, even as veneration of the Virgin Mary swept across Western Christendom. Restrictions on women hearing confes-

Thus Cecilia was left a single woman in her early twenties, but the relative prosperity of her family allowed her to lead a rather independent life. In 1317, she acquired her first piece of land, probably with financial assistance from her father and her own earnings as a day laborer. In fact, Cecilia benefited from the famine because it forced desperate peasants to sell their land at reduced prices. As a result, Cecilia was able to accumulate additional land. By the time of her death in 1344, she was a fairly prosperous woman with a house and farmyard, seventy acres of pasture, and two acres of good farming land. She hired servants or day laborers to work her lands and depended considerably on her brothers, who lived nearby.

If class and family shaped Cecilia's life, so did gender. As a woman, she was unable to hold office in the manor; she was paid about one-third less than men when she worked as an unskilled day laborer; and she could not serve as an official ale-taster, responsible for the quality of the beverage, although women brewed the ale. Like all women, she suffered under a sexual double standard. Two of her brothers, one of whom was a priest, produced children out of wedlock, with no apparent damage to their reputations. But should Cecilia have done so, scandal would surely have ensued.

Unlike most women of her time, Cecilia never married. Did her intended perhaps die during the famine? Did she have a socially inappropriate lover? Did she have an intimate relationship with Robert Malin, a man to whom she left one-third of her estate? Or did she consider marriage a disadvantage? Married women and their property were legally under the control of their husbands, but as a free tenant and head of household, Cecilia bought and sold land on her own and participated as a full member in the deliberations of the local court, which regulated the legal affairs of the manor.

For a woman, the pros and cons of marriage depended very much on whom she married. As a medieval poem put it: "The good and bad happenstances that some women have had / Stands in the choice of a good husband or bad." So while Cecilia missed out on the social approval and support that marriage offered as well as the pleasures of intimacy and children, she also avoided the potential abuse and certain dependency that married life carried for women.

Cecilia's death in 1344 provoked sharp controversy within her family network over the familiar issues of inheritance, kinship, and land. She left her considerable property to the illegitimate son of her brother, to the daughter of her sister Agnes, and to the mysterious Robert Malin. Aggrieved parties, particularly her sister Christina and a nephew Martin, succeeded in having her will overturned.

Question: In what ways did class, family, gender, and natural catastrophe shape Cecilia's life?

sions, preaching, and chanting the Gospel were now more strictly enforced. The educational activities of monastic centers, where men and women could both participate, now gave way to the new universities, where only ordained men could study and teach. Furthermore, older ideas of women's intellectual inferiority, the impurity of menstruation, and their role as sexual temptresses were mobilized to explain why women could never be priests and must operate under male control.

Another religious opportunity for women, operating outside of monastic life and the institutional church, was that of the Beguines. These were groups of laywomen, often from poorer families in Northern Europe, who lived together, practiced celibacy, and devoted themselves to weaving and to working with the sick, the old, and the poor. Though widely respected for their piety and service, their independence from the church hierarchy prompted considerable opposition from both religious and secular authorities suspicious of women operating outside of male control, and the movement gradually faded away. More acceptable to male authorities was the role of anchoress, a woman who withdrew to a locked cell, usually attached to a church, where she devoted herself to prayer and fasting. Some anchoresses gained reputations for great holiness and were much sought after for spiritual guidance. The English mystic and anchoress Julian of Norwich (1342–1416), for example, acquired considerable public prominence and spiritual influence, even as she emphasized the feminine dimension of the Divine and portrayed Jesus as a mother, who "feeds us with Himself."[20]

Thus tightening male control of women took place in Europe as it did in Song dynasty China at about the same time. Accompanying this change was a new understanding of masculinity, at least in the growing towns and cities. No longer able to function as warriors protecting their women, men increasingly defined themselves as "providers"; a man's role was to brave the new marketplaces "to win wealth for himself and his children." In one popular tale, a woman praised her husband: "He was a good provider; he knew how to rake in the money and how to save it." By 1450, the English word "husband" had become a verb meaning "to keep" or "to save."[21]

Europe Outward Bound: The Crusading Tradition

Accompanying the growth of a new European civilization after 1000 were efforts to engage more actively with both near and more distant neighbors. This "medieval expansion" of Western Christendom took place as the Byzantine world was contracting under pressure from the West, from Arab invasion, and later from Turkish conquest (see Map 10.1, page 417). The western half of Christendom was on the rise, while the eastern part was in decline. It was a sharp reversal of their earlier trajectories.

Guided Reading Question

■ CHANGE
What was the impact of the Crusades in world history?

Expansion, of course, has been characteristic of virtually every civilization and has taken a variety of forms—territorial conquest, empire building, settlement of new lands, vigorous trading initiatives, and missionary activity. European civilization was no exception. As population mounted, settlers cleared new land, much of it on the eastern fringes of Europe. The Vikings of Scandinavia, having raided much of Europe, set off on a maritime transatlantic venture around 1000 that briefly established a colony in Newfoundland in North America, and more durably in Greenland and Iceland. (See Zooming In: Thorfinn Karlsefni, Chapter 7, page 306.) As Western economies grew, merchants, travelers, diplomats, and missionaries brought European society into more intensive contact with more distant peoples and with Eurasian commercial networks. By the thirteenth and fourteenth centuries, Europeans had direct, though limited, contact with India, China, and Mongolia. Europe clearly was outward bound.

Nothing more dramatically revealed European expansiveness and the religious passions that informed it than the Crusades, a series of "holy wars" that captured the imagination of Western Christendom for several centuries, beginning in 1095. In European thinking and practice, the Crusades were wars undertaken at God's command and authorized by the pope as the Vicar of Christ on earth. They required participants to swear a vow and in return offered an indulgence, which removed the penalties for any confessed sins, as well as various material benefits, such as immunity from lawsuits and a moratorium on the repayment of debts. Any number of political, economic, and social motives underlay the Crusades, but at their core they were religious wars. Within Europe, the amazing support for the Crusades reflected an understanding of them "as providing security against mortal enemies threatening the spiritual health of all Christendom and all Christians."[22] Crusading drew on both Christian piety and the warrior values of the elite, with little sense of contradiction between these impulses.

The most famous Crusades were those aimed at wresting Jerusalem and the holy places associated with the life of Jesus from Islamic control and returning them to Christendom (see Map 10.4). Beginning in 1095, wave after wave of Crusaders

> **AP® EXAM TIP**
>
> You do not need to know details of the individual Crusades, but a firm understanding of the political, social, and economic causes and effects of the Crusades as a whole is very important.

Map 10.4   The Crusades

Western Europe's crusading tradition reflected the expansive energy and religious impulses of an emerging civilization. It was directed against Muslims in the Middle East, Sicily, and Spain as well as the Eastern Orthodox Christians of the Byzantine Empire. The Crusades also involved attacks on Jewish communities, probably the first organized mass pogroms against Jews in Europe's history.

The Crusades
This fourteenth-century painting illustrates the Christian seizure of Jerusalem during the First Crusade in 1099. The crowned figure in the center is Godefroi de Bouillon, a French knight and nobleman who played a prominent role in the attack and was briefly known as the king of Jerusalem. (Bibliothèque Nationale de France, Paris, France/Bridgeman Images)

from all walks of life and many countries flocked to the eastern Mediterranean, where they temporarily carved out four small Christian states, the last of which was recaptured by Muslim forces in 1291. Led or supported by an assortment of kings, popes, bishops, monks, lords, nobles, and merchants, the Crusades demonstrated a growing European capacity for organization, finance, transportation, and recruitment, made all the more impressive by the absence of any centralized direction for the project. They also demonstrated considerable cruelty. The seizure of Jerusalem in 1099 was accompanied by the slaughter of many Muslims and Jews as the Crusaders made their way to the tomb of Christ, according to no doubt exaggerated reports, through streets littered with corpses and ankle deep in blood.

Crusading was not limited to targets in the Islamic Middle East, however. Those Christians who waged war for centuries to reclaim the Iberian Peninsula from Muslim hands were likewise declared "crusaders," with a similar set of spiritual and material benefits. So too were Scandinavian and German warriors who took part in wars to conquer, settle, and convert lands along the Baltic Sea. The Byzantine Empire and Russia, both of which followed Eastern Orthodox Christianity, were also on the receiving end of Western crusading, as were Christian heretics, Jews, and various enemies of the pope in Europe itself. Crusading, in short, was a pervasive feature of European expansion, which persisted as Europeans began their oceanic voyages in the fifteenth century and beyond.

Surprisingly perhaps, the Crusades had little lasting impact, either politically or religiously, in the Middle East. European power was not sufficiently strong or long-lasting to induce much conversion, and the small European footholds there had come under Muslim control by 1300. The penetration of Turkic-speaking peoples from Central Asia and the devastating Mongol invasions of the thirteenth century were far more significant in Islamic history than were the temporary incursions of European Christians. In fact, Muslims largely forgot about the Crusades until the late nineteenth and early twentieth centuries, when their memory was revived in the context of a growing struggle against European imperialism.

In Europe, however, crusading in general and interaction with the Islamic world in particular had very significant long-term consequences. Spain, Sicily, and the Baltic region were brought permanently into the world of Western Christendom, while a declining Byzantium was further weakened by the Crusader sacking of Constantinople in 1204 and left even more vulnerable to Muslim Turkish conquest. In Europe itself, popes strengthened their position, at least for a time, in their continuing struggles with secular authorities. Tens of thousands of Europeans came into personal contact with the Islamic world, from which they picked up a taste for the many luxury goods available there, stimulating a demand for Asian goods. They also learned techniques for producing sugar on large plantations using slave labor, a process that had incalculable consequences in later centuries as Europeans transferred the plantation system to the Americas. Muslim scholarship, together with the Greek learning that it incorporated, also flowed into Europe, largely through Spain and Sicily.

If the cross-cultural contacts born of crusading opened channels of trade, technology transfer, and intellectual exchange, they also hardened cultural barriers between peoples. The rift between Eastern Orthodoxy and Roman Catholicism deepened further and remains to this day a fundamental divide in the Christian world. Christian anti-Semitism was both expressed and exacerbated as Crusaders on their way to Jerusalem found time to massacre Jews, regarded as "Christ-killers," in a number of European cities, particularly in Germany. Such pogroms, however, were not sanctioned by the Church. A leading figure in the Second Crusade, Bernard of Clairvaux, declared, "It is good that you march against the Muslims, but anyone who touches a Jew to take his life, is as touching Jesus himself."[23] European empire building, especially in the Americas, continued the crusading notion that "God wills it." And more recently, over the past two centuries, as the world of the Christian West and that of Islam collided, both sides found many occasions for which images of the Crusades, however distorted, proved politically popular or ideologically useful.

AP® EXAM TIP

The results of cross-cultural connections throughout history are "must know" information.

PRACTICING AP® HISTORICAL THINKING

How did the historical development of the European West differ from that of Byzantium in the third-wave era?

The West in Comparative Perspective

At one level, the making of Western civilization was unremarkable. Civilizations had risen, fallen, renewed themselves, and evolved at many times and in many places. The European case has received extraordinary scrutiny, not so much because of its special significance at the time, but because of its later role as a globally dominant region. However we might explain Europe's subsequent rise to prominence on the world stage, its development in the several centuries after 1000 made only modest ripples beyond its own region. In some respects, Europe was surely distinctive, but it was not yet a major player in the global arena. Comparisons, particularly with China and the Islamic world, help to place these European developments in a world history context.

Catching Up

As the civilization of the West evolved, it was clearly less developed in comparison to Byzantium, China, India, and the Islamic world. Europe's cities were smaller, its political authorities weaker, its economy less commercialized, and its technology inferior. Muslim observers who encountered Europeans saw them as barbarians. An Arab geographer of the tenth century commented on Europeans: "Their bodies are large, their manners harsh, their understanding dull, and their tongues heavy. . . . Those of them who are farthest to the north are the most subject to stupidity, grossness and brutishness."[24] Muslim travelers over the next several centuries saw more to be praised in West African kingdoms, where Islam was practiced and gold was plentiful.

Furthermore, thoughtful Europeans who directly encountered other peoples often acknowledged their own comparative backwardness. "In our time," wrote a twelfth-century European scholar, "it is in Toledo [a Spanish city long under Muslim rule] that the teaching of the Arabs . . . is offered to the crowds. I hastened there to listen to the teaching of the wisest philosophers of this world."[25] The Italian traveler Marco Polo in the thirteenth century proclaimed Hangzhou in China "the finest and noblest [city] in the world." In the early sixteenth century, Spanish invaders of Mexico were stunned at the size and wealth of the Aztec capital, especially its huge market, claiming that they "had never seen such a thing before."[26]

Curious about the rest of the world, Europeans proved quite willing to engage with and borrow from the more advanced civilizations to the east. Growing European economies, especially in the northwest, reconnected with the Eurasian trading system, with which they had lost contact after the fall of Rome. Now European elites eagerly sought spices, silks, porcelain, and sugar from afar even as they assimilated various technological, intellectual, and cultural innovations, as the Snapshot opposite demonstrates. When the road to China opened in the thirteenth and fourteenth centuries, many Europeans, including the merchant-traveler Marco Polo, were more than willing to make the long and difficult journey, returning with amazing tales of splendor and abundance far beyond what was available in Europe. When Europeans took to the oceans in the fifteenth and sixteenth centuries, they were seeking out the sources of African and Asian wealth. Thus the accelerating growth of European civilization was accompanied by its reintegration into the larger Afro-Eurasian networks of exchange and communication.

In this willingness to borrow, Europe resembled several other third-wave civilizations of the time. Japan, for example, took much from China; West Africa drew heavily on Islamic civilization; and Russia actively imitated Byzantium. All of them were then developing civilizations, in a position analogous perhaps to the developing countries of the twentieth century.

Technological borrowing required adaptation to the unique conditions of Europe and was accompanied by considerable independent invention as well. Together these processes generated a significant tradition of technological innovation that

AP® EXAM TIP

You need to know factors that led to the revival of Western Europe in politics, economics, and culture.

Guided Reading Question

■ CHANGE

In what ways did borrowing from abroad shape European civilization after 1000?

AP® EXAM TIP

Be prepared to supply examples of cultural borrowing in world history.

SNAPSHOT   European Borrowing

Like people in other emerging civilizations of the third-wave era, Europeans borrowed extensively from their near and more distant counterparts. They adapted these imports, both technological and cultural, to their own circumstances and generated distinctive innovations as well.

Borrowing	Source	Significance
Horse collar	China / Central Asia via Tunisia	Enabled heavy plowing and contributed to European agricultural development
Stirrup	India/Afghanistan	Revolutionized warfare by enhancing cavalry forces
Gunpowder	China	Enhanced the destructiveness of warfare
Paper	China	Enabled bureaucracy; fostered literacy; prerequisite for printing
Spinning wheel	India	Sped up production of yarn, usually by women at home
Wheelbarrow	China	Laborsaving device for farm and construction work
Aristotle	Byzantium / Islamic Spain	Recovery of classical Greek thought
Medical knowledge/treatments	Islamic world	Sedatives, antiseptics, surgical techniques, optics, and knowledge of contagious diseases enriched European medicine
Christian mysticism	Muslim Spain	Mutual influence of Sufi, Jewish, and Christian mysticism
Music/poetry	Muslim Spain	Contributed to tradition of troubadour poetry about chivalry and courtly love
Mathematics	India / Islamic world	Foundation for European algebra
Chess	India/Persia	A game of prestige associated with European nobility

allowed Europe by 1500 to catch up with, and in some areas perhaps to surpass, China and the Islamic world. That achievement bears comparison with the economic revolution of Tang and Song dynasty China, although Europe began at a lower level and depended more on borrowing than did its Chinese counterpart (see Chapter 8). But in the several centuries surrounding 1000, at both ends of Eurasia, major processes of technological innovation were under way.

In Europe, technological breakthroughs first became apparent in agriculture as Europeans adapted to the very different environmental conditions north of the Alps in the several centuries following 500 C.E. They developed a heavy wheeled plow that could handle the dense soils of Northern Europe far better than the light, or "scratch," plow used in Mediterranean agriculture. To pull the plow, Europeans began to rely increasingly on horses rather than oxen and to use iron horseshoes and a more efficient collar, which probably originated in China or Central Asia and could support much heavier loads. In addition, Europeans developed a

European Technology
Europeans' fascination with technology and their religious motivation for investigating the world are apparent in this thirteenth-century portrayal of God as a divine engineer, laying out the world with a huge compass. (From the *Bible Moralisée*, mid-13th century/Oesterreichische Nationalbibliothek, Vienna, Austria/Erich Lessing/Art Resource, NY)

AP® EXAM TIP

You must know examples of Chinese technology that influenced Europe in the postclassical period.

new three-field system of crop rotation, which allowed considerably more land to be planted at any one time. These were the technological foundations for a more productive agriculture that could support the growing population of European civilization, especially in its urban centers, far more securely than before.

Beyond agriculture, Europeans began to tap non-animal sources of energy in a major way, particularly after 1000. A new type of windmill, very different from an earlier Persian version, was widely used in Europe by the twelfth and thirteenth centuries. The water-driven mill was even more important. The Romans had used such mills largely to grind grain, but their development was limited, since few streams flowed all year and many slaves were available to do the work. By the ninth century, however, watermills were rapidly becoming more evident in Europe. In the early fourteenth century, a concentration of sixty-eight mills dotted a one-mile stretch of the Seine River near Paris. In addition to grinding grain, these mills provided power for sieving flour, tanning hides, making beer, sawing wood, manufacturing iron, and making paper. Devices such as cranks, flywheels, camshafts, and complex gearing mechanisms, when combined with water or wind power, enabled Europeans of the High Middle Ages to revolutionize production in a number of industries and to break with the ancient tradition of depending almost wholly on animal or human muscle as sources of energy. So intense was the interest of European artisans and engineers in tapping mechanical sources of energy that a number of them experimented with perpetual-motion machines, an idea borrowed from Indian philosophers.

Technological borrowing was also evident in the arts of war. Gunpowder was invented in China, but Europeans were probably the first to use it in cannons, in the early fourteenth century, and by 1500 they had the most advanced arsenals in the world. In 1517, one Chinese official, on first encountering European ships and weapons, remarked with surprise, "The westerns are extremely dangerous because of their artillery. No weapon ever made since memorable antiquity is superior to their cannon."[27] Advances in shipbuilding and navigational techniques—including the magnetic compass and sternpost rudder from China and adaptations of the Mediterranean or Arab lateen sail, which enabled vessels to sail against the wind—provided the foundation for European mastery of the seas.

Europe's passion for technology was reflected in its culture and ideas as well as in its machines. About 1260, the English scholar and Franciscan friar Roger Bacon wrote of the possibilities he foresaw, and in doing so, he expressed the confident spirit of the age:

> Machines of navigation can be constructed, without rowers . . . which are borne under the guidance of one man at a greater speed than if they were full of men. Also a chariot can be constructed, that will move with incalculable speed without any draught animal. . . . Also flying machines may be constructed so that a man may sit in the midst of the machine turning a certain instrument by means of which wings artificially constructed would beat the air after the manner of a bird flying . . . and there are countless other things that can be constructed.[28]

Pluralism in Politics

Unlike the large centralized states of Byzantium, the Islamic world, and China, this third-wave European civilization never regained the earlier unity it had under Roman rule. Rather, political life gradually crystallized into a system of competing states (France, Spain, England, Sweden, Prussia, the Netherlands, and Poland, among others) that has persisted into the twenty-first century and that the European Union still confronts. Geographic barriers, ethnic and linguistic diversity, and the shifting balances of power among its many states prevented the emergence of a single European empire, despite periodic efforts to re-create something resembling the still-remembered unity of the Roman Empire.

This multicentered political system shaped the emerging civilization of the West in many ways. It gave rise to frequent wars, enhanced the role and status of military men, and drove the "gunpowder revolution." Thus European society and values were militarized far more than in China, which gave greater prominence to scholars and bureaucrats. Intense interstate rivalry, combined with a willingness to borrow, also stimulated European technological development. By 1500, Europeans had gone a long way toward catching up with their more advanced Asian counterparts in agriculture, industry, war, and sailing.

Thus endemic warfare did not halt European economic growth. Capital, labor, and goods found their way around political barriers, while the common assumptions of Christian culture and the use of Latin and later French by the literate elite fostered communication across political borders. Europe's multistate system thus provided enough competition to stimulate innovation, but it also preserved enough order and unity to allow the economy to grow.

The states within this emerging European civilization also differed from those to the east. Their rulers generally were weaker and had to contend with competing sources of power. Unlike the Orthodox Church in Byzantium, with its practice of caesaropapism, the Roman Catholic Church in the West maintained a degree of independence from state authority that served to check the power of kings and lords. European vassals had certain rights in return for loyalty to their lords and

AP® EXAM TIP

Be ready to compare the features of European political systems with those of other major political systems in the postclassical period.

Guided Reading Question

■ **COMPARISON**

Why was Europe unable to achieve the kind of political unity that China experienced? What impact did this have on the subsequent history of Europe?

kings. By the thirteenth century, this meant that high-ranking nobles, acting through formal councils, had the right to advise their rulers and to approve new taxes.

This three-way struggle for power among kings, warrior aristocrats, and church leaders, all of them from the nobility, enabled urban-based merchants in Europe to achieve an unusual independence from political authority. Many cities, where wealthy merchants exercised local power, won the right to make and enforce their own laws and appoint their own officials. Some of them — Venice, Genoa, Pisa, and Milan, for example — became almost completely independent city-states. Elsewhere, kings granted charters that allowed cities to have their own courts, laws, and governments, while paying their own kind of taxes to the king instead of feudal dues. Powerful, independent cities were a distinctive feature of European life after 1100 or so. By contrast, Chinese cities, which were far larger than those of Europe, were simply part of the empire and enjoyed few special privileges. Although commerce was far more extensive in China than in the emerging European civilization, the powerful Chinese state favored the landowners over merchants, monopolized the salt and iron industries, and actively controlled and limited merchant activity far more than the new and weaker royal authorities of Europe were able to do.

The relative weakness of Europe's rulers allowed urban merchants more leeway and, according to some historians, opened the way to a more thorough development of capitalism in later centuries. It also led to the development of representative institutions or parliaments through which the views and interests of these contending forces could be expressed and accommodated. Intended to strengthen royal authority by consulting with major social groups, these embryonic parliaments did not represent the "people" or the "nation" but instead embodied the three great "estates of the realm" — the clergy (the first estate), the landowning nobility (the second estate), and urban merchants (the third estate).

Reason and Faith

A further feature of this emerging European civilization was a distinctive intellectual tension between the claims of human reason and those of faith. Christianity had developed in a world suffused with Greek rationalism. Some early Christian thinkers sought to maintain a clear separation between the new religion and the ideas of Plato and Aristotle. "What indeed has Athens to do with Jerusalem?" asked Tertullian (150–225 C.E.), an early church leader from North Africa. More common, however, was the notion that Greek philosophy could serve as a "handmaiden" to faith, more fully disclosing the truths of Christianity. In the reduced circumstances of Western Europe after the collapse of the Roman Empire, the Church had little direct access to the writings of the Greeks, although some Latin translations and commentaries provided a continuing link to the world of classical thought.

But intellectual life in Europe changed dramatically in the several centuries after 1000, amid a rising population, a quickening commercial life, emerging towns and cities, and the Church's growing independence from royal or noble authorities. Moreover, the West was developing a legal system that provided a measure of independence for a variety of institutions—towns and cities, guilds, professional associations, and especially universities. An outgrowth of earlier cathedral schools, these European universities—in Paris, Bologna, Oxford, Cambridge, Salamanca—became "zones of intellectual autonomy" in which scholars could pursue their studies with some freedom from the dictates of religious or political authorities, although that freedom was never complete and was frequently contested.[29]

This was the setting in which European Christian thinkers, a small group of literate churchmen, began to emphasize, quite self-consciously, the ability of human reason to penetrate divine mysteries and to grasp the operation of the natural order. An early indication of this new emphasis occurred in the late eleventh century when students in a monastic school in France asked their teacher, Anselm, to provide them a proof for the existence of God based solely on reason, without using the Bible or other sources of divine revelation.

The new interest in rational thought was applied first and foremost to theology, the "queen of the sciences" to European thinkers. Here was an effort to provide an intellectual foundation for faith, not to replace faith or to rebel against it. Logic, philosophy, and rationality would operate in service to Christ. Of course, some opposed this new emphasis on human reason. Bernard of Clairvaux, a twelfth-century French abbot, declared, "Faith believes. It does not dispute."[30] His contemporary and intellectual opponent, the French scholar William of Conches, lashed out: "You poor fools. God can make a cow out of a tree, but has he ever done so? Therefore show some reason why a thing is so or cease to hold that it is so."[31]

European intellectuals also applied their newly discovered confidence in human reason to law, medicine, and the world of nature, exploring optics, magnetism, astronomy, and alchemy. Slowly and never completely, the scientific study of nature, known as "natural philosophy," began to separate itself from theology. In European universities, natural philosophy was studied in the faculty of arts, which was separate from the faculty of theology, although many scholars contributed to both fields.

This mounting enthusiasm for rational inquiry stimulated European scholars to seek out original Greek texts, particularly those of Aristotle. They found them in the Greek-speaking world of Byzantium and in the Islamic world, where they had long ago been translated into Arabic. In the twelfth and thirteenth centuries, an explosion of translations from Greek and Arabic into Latin, many of them undertaken in Spain, gave European scholars direct access to the works of ancient Greeks and to the remarkable results of Arab scholarship in astronomy, optics, medicine, pharmacology, and more. Much of this Arab science was now translated into Latin and provided a boost to Europe's changing intellectual life, centered in the new universities. One of these translators, Adelard of Bath (1080–1142), remarked that

Guided Reading Question

■ COMPARISON

In what different ways did classical Greek philosophy and science have an impact in the West, in Byzantium, and in the Islamic world?

AP® EXAM TIP

You should know the influences of classical Greek thought on Europeans in the post-classical period.

European University Life in the Middle Ages
This fourteenth-century manuscript painting shows a classroom scene from the University of Bologna in Italy. Note the sleeping and disruptive students. Some things apparently never change. (From the *Liber ethicorum*, by Fra Henricus de Allemania, illuminated manuscript page by Laurentius de Voltolina, ca. 1360–1390/bpk, Berlin/Kupferstichkabinett, Staatliche Museen, Berlin, Germany/Photo: Joerg P. Anders/Art Resource, NY)

he had learned, "under the guidance of reason from Arabic teachers," not to trust established authority.[32]

It was the works of the prolific Aristotle, with his logical approach and "scientific temperament," that made the deepest impression. His writings became the basis for university education and largely dominated the thought of Western Europe in the five centuries after 1200. In the work of the thirteenth-century theologian Thomas Aquinas, Aristotle's ideas were thoroughly integrated into a logical and systematic presentation of Christian doctrine. In this growing emphasis on human rationality, which some considered to be at least partially separate from divine revelation, lay one of the foundations of the later Scientific Revolution and the secularization of European intellectual life.

Surprisingly, nothing comparable occurred in the Byzantine Empire, where knowledge of the Greek language was widespread and access to Greek texts was easy. Although Byzantine scholars kept the classical tradition alive, their primary interest lay in the humanities (literature, philosophy, history) and theology rather than in the natural sciences or medicine. Furthermore, both state and church had serious reservations about Greek learning. In 529, the emperor Justinian closed

Plato's Academy in Athens, claiming that it was an outpost of paganism. Its scholars dispersed into lands that soon became Islamic, carrying Greek learning into the Islamic world. Church authorities as well were suspicious of Greek thought, sometimes persecuting scholars who were too enamored with the ancients. Even those who did study the Greek writers did so in a conservative spirit, concerned with preserving and transmitting the classical heritage rather than with using it as a springboard for creating new knowledge. "The great men of the past," declared the fourteenth-century Byzantine scholar and statesman Theodore Metochites, "have said everything so perfectly that they have left nothing for us to say."[33]

In the Islamic world, Greek thought was embraced "with far more enthusiasm and creativity" than in Byzantium.[34] A massive translation project in the ninth and tenth centuries made Aristotle and many other Greek writers available in Arabic. That work contributed to a flowering of Arab scholarship, especially in the sciences and natural philosophy, between roughly 800 and 1200 (see Chapter 9), but it also stimulated a debate about faith and reason among Muslim thinkers, many of whom greatly admired Greek philosophical, scientific, and medical texts. As in the Christian world, the issue was whether secular Greek thought was an aid or a threat to the faith. Western European church authorities after the thirteenth century had come to regard natural philosophy as a wholly legitimate enterprise and had thoroughly incorporated Aristotle into university education, but learned opinion in the Islamic world swung the other way. Though never completely disappearing from Islamic scholarship, the ideas of Plato and Aristotle receded after the thirteenth century in favor of teachings that drew more directly from the Quran or from mystical experience. Nor was natural philosophy a central concern of Islamic higher education, as it was in the West. The integration of political and religious life in the Islamic world, as in Byzantium, contrasted with their separation in the West, where there was more space for the independent pursuit of scientific subjects.

AP® EXAM TIP

Note the influences of classical Greek thought on the Muslim world in the postclassical era.

REFLECTIONS

Remembering and Forgetting: Continuity and Surprise in the Worlds of Christendom

Many of the characteristic features of Christendom, which emerged during the era of third-wave civilizations, have had a long life, extending well into the modern era. The crusading element of European expansion was prominent among the motives of Spanish and Portuguese explorers. Europe's grudging freedom for merchant activity and its eagerness to borrow foreign technology arguably contributed to the growth of capitalism and industrialization in later centuries. The endemic military conflicts of European states, unable to recover the unity of the Roman Empire, found terrible expression in the world wars of the twentieth century. The controversy about reason and faith resonates still, at least in the United States, in debates about the authority of the Bible in secular and scientific matters. The rift between Eastern Orthodoxy and Roman Catholicism remains one of the major divides in the Christian world. Modern universities and the separation of religious and political authority likewise have their origins in the European Middle Ages. Such a perspective, linking the past with what came later, represents one of the great contributions that the study of history makes to human understanding. We are limited and shaped by our histories.

Yet that very strength of historical study can be misleading, particularly if it suggests a kind of inevitability, in which the past determines the future. Knowing the outcome of the stories we tell can be a serious disadvantage, for it may rob the people we study of the freedom and uncertainty that they surely experienced. In 500, few people would have predicted that Europe would become the primary center of Christianity, while the African and Asian expressions of that faith withered away. As late as 1000, the startling reversal of roles between the Eastern and Western wings of Christendom, which the next several centuries witnessed, was hardly on the horizon. At that time, the many small, rural, unsophisticated, and endlessly quarreling warrior-based societies of Western Europe would hardly have borne comparison with the powerful Byzantine Empire and its magnificent capital of Constantinople. Even in 1500, when Europe had begun to catch up with China and the Islamic world in various ways, there was little to predict its remarkable transformation over the next several centuries and the dramatic change in the global balance of power that this transformation produced.

Usually students of history are asked to remember. But forgetting can also be an aid to historical understanding. To recapture the unexpectedness of the historical process and to allow ourselves to be surprised, it may be useful on occasion to forget—or at least set aside—what we know about what happened next and to see the world as contemporaries viewed it.

Chapter Review

What's the Significance?

Big Picture Questions

1. What accounts for the different historical trajectories of the Byzantine and West European expressions of Christendom?
2. How did Byzantium and Western Europe interact with each other and with the larger world of the third-wave era?
3. In what respects was the civilization of the Latin West distinctive and unique, and in what ways was it broadly comparable to other third-wave civilizations?
4. **Looking Back:** How does the evolution of the Christian world in the third-wave era compare with that of Tang and Song dynasty China and of the Islamic world?

Next Steps: For Further Study

Bonnie S. Anderson and Judith P. Zinsser, *A History of Their Own* (2000). An overview of European women's history by two prominent scholars.

Edward Grant, *Science and Religion from Aristotle to Copernicus* (2004). Demonstrates the impact of Greek philosophy and science in Europe, with comparisons to Byzantium and the Islamic world.

Barbara A. Hanawalt, *The Middle Ages: An Illustrated History* (1999). A brief and beautifully illustrated introduction to the Middle Ages in European history.

Rowena Loverance, *Byzantium* (2004). A lavishly illustrated history of the Byzantine Empire, drawing on the rich collection of artifacts in the British Museum.

Diarmaid MacCulloch, *Christianity: The First Three Thousand Years* (2010). A recent and much-praised overview of the history of Christendom.

Christopher Tyerman, *Fighting for Christendom: Holy Wars and the Crusades* (2005). A very well-written, up-to-date history of the Crusades designed for nonspecialists.

"Byzantine Empire," http://www.history.com/topics/ancient-history/byzantine-empire. A History channel Web site that features a number of short, thoughtful videos about Byzantium.

"Middle Ages," http://www.learner.org/interactives/middleages/. An interactive Web site with text and images relating to life in Europe after the collapse of the Roman Empire.

WORKING WITH EVIDENCE

The Making of Christian Europe

Like Buddhism and Islam, Christianity became a universal religion, taking root well beyond its place of origin. In its early centuries, this new faith, born in a Jewish context in Roman Palestine, spread throughout the Roman Empire, where it received state support during the fourth century C.E. In the centuries that followed the collapse of the western Roman Empire, Christianity also took hold among the peoples of Western Europe in what are now England, France, Germany, and Scandinavia. While we often think about this region as solidly Christian, Western Europe in the period between 500 and 1000 C.E. was very much on the frontier of the Christian world. During those centuries, a number of emerging monarchs of post-Roman Europe found the Christian faith and the Church useful in consolidating their new and fragile states by linking them to the legacy of the Roman Empire. But the making of Christian Europe was a prolonged and tentative process, filled with setbacks, resistance, and struggles among variant versions of the faith as well as growing acceptance and cultural compromise. The documents that follow illustrate that process.

Source 10.1
The Conversion of Clovis

Among the Germanic peoples of post-Roman Western Europe, none were of greater significance than the Franks, occupying the region of present-day France (see Map 10.1, page 417). By the early sixth century, a loosely unified Frankish kingdom had emerged under the leadership of Clovis (r. 485–511), whose Merovingian dynasty ruled the area until 751. Clovis's conversion to Christianity was described about a century later by a well-known bishop and writer, Gregory of Tours (538–594). It was an important step in the triumph of Christianity over Frankish "paganism." It also marked the victory of what would later become Roman Catholicism, based on the idea of the Trinity, over a rival form of the Christian faith, known as Arianism, which held that Jesus was a created divine being subordinate to God the Father.

■ According to Gregory, what led to the conversion of Clovis?

■ What issues are evident in the religious discussions of Clovis and his wife, Clotilda?

- Notice how Gregory modeled his picture of Clovis on that of Constantine, the famous Roman emperor whose conversion to Christianity in the fourth century gave official legitimacy and state support to the faith (see Chapter 4). What message did Gregory seek to convey in making this implied comparison?

- How might a modern secular historian use this document to help explain the spread of Christianity among the Franks?

GREGORY OF TOURS

History of the Franks

Late Sixth Century

[Clovis] had a first-born son by queen Clotilda, and as his wife wished to consecrate him in baptism, she tried unceasingly to persuade her husband, saying: "The gods you worship are nothing, and they will be unable to help themselves or any one else. For they are graven out of stone or wood or some metal. . . . They are endowed rather with the magic arts than with the power of the divine name. But he [God] ought rather to be worshipped who created by his word heaven and earth, the sea and all that in them is out of a state of nothingness . . . [and] by whose hand mankind was created. . . ."

But though the queen said this, the spirit of the king was by no means moved to belief, and he said: "It was at the command of our gods that all things were created and came forth, and it is plain that your God has no power and, what is more, he is proven not to belong to the family of the gods." Meantime the faithful queen made her son ready for baptism; she gave command to adorn the church with hangings and curtains, in order that he who could not be moved by persuasion might be urged to belief by this mystery. The boy, whom they named Ingomer, died after being baptized, still wearing the white garments in which he became regenerate. At this the king was violently angry, and reproached the queen harshly, saying: "If the boy had been dedicated in the name of my gods he would certainly have lived; but as it is, since he was baptized in the name of your God, he could not

live at all." To this the queen said: "I give thanks to the omnipotent God, creator of all, who has judged me not wholly unworthy, that he should deign to take to his kingdom one born from my womb. My soul is not stricken with grief for his sake, because I know that, summoned from this world as he was in his baptismal garments, he will be fed by the vision of God. . . ."

The queen did not cease to urge him to recognize the true God and cease worshipping idols. But he could not be influenced in any way to this belief, until at last a war arose with the Alamanni [a Germanic people], in which he was driven by necessity to confess what before he had of his free will denied. It came about that as the two armies were fighting fiercely, there was much slaughter, and Clovis's army began to be in danger of destruction. He saw it and raised his eyes to heaven, and with remorse in his heart he burst into tears and cried: "Jesus Christ, whom Clotilda asserts to be the son of the living God . . . , I beseech the glory of thy aid, with the vow that if thou wilt grant me victory over these enemies . . . , I will believe in thee and be baptized in thy name. For I have invoked my own gods but, as I find, they have withdrawn from aiding me; and therefore I believe that they possess no power, since they do not help those who obey them. . . ." And when he said thus, the Alamanni turned their backs, and began to disperse in flight. And when they saw that their king was killed, they submitted to the dominion of

Clovis, saying: "Let not the people perish further, we pray; we are yours now." And he stopped the fighting, and after encouraging his men, retired in peace and told the queen how he had had merit to win the victory by calling on the name of Christ. This happened in the fifteenth year of his reign. . . .

And so the king confessed all-powerful God in the Trinity, and was baptized in the name of the Father, Son and Holy Spirit, and was anointed with the holy ointment with the sign of the cross of Christ. And of his army more than 3,000 were baptized.

Source: Gregory Bishop of Tours, *History of the Franks*, translated by Ernest Brehaut (New York: Columbia University Press, 1916; copyright renewed 1944), bk. 2, selections from secs. 27, 29, 30, 31, 36–41.

Source 10.2
Advice on Dealing with "Pagans"

In their dealings with the "pagan," or non-Christian, peoples and kings of Western Europe, church authorities such as missionaries, bishops, and the pope himself sometimes advocated compromise with existing cultural traditions rather than overt hostility to them. Here Pope Gregory (r. 590–604) urges the bishop of England to adopt a strategy of accommodation with the prevailing religious practices of the Anglo-Saxon peoples of the island. Gregory's advice was included in a famous work about the early Christian history of England, composed by a Benedictine monk known as the Venerable Bede and completed about 731.

- What can we learn about the religious practices of the Anglo-Saxons from Bede's account?

- In what specific ways did the pope urge toleration? And why did he advocate accommodation or compromise with existing religious practices? Keep in mind that the political authorities in England at the time had not yet become thoroughly Christian.

- What implication might Gregory's policies have for the beliefs and practices of English converts?

POPE GREGORY
Advice to the English Church
601

The temples of the idols in that nation [England] ought not to be destroyed; but let the idols that are in them be destroyed; let holy water be made and sprinkled in the said temples, let altars be erected, and relics placed. For if those temples are well built, it is requisite that they be converted from the worship of devils to the service of the true God; that the nation, seeing that their temples are not destroyed, may remove error from their hearts, and knowing and adoring the true God, may the more familiarly resort to the places to which they have been accustomed.

And because they have been used to slaughter many oxen in the sacrifices to devils, some solemnity must be exchanged for them on this account, as that on the day of the dedication, or the nativities of the holy martyrs, whose relics are there deposited, they may build themselves huts of the boughs of trees, about those churches which have been turned to that use from temples, and celebrate the solemnity with religious feasting, and no more offer beasts to the Devil, but kill cattle to the praise of God in their eating, and return thanks to the Giver of all things for their sustenance; to the end that, while some gratifications are outwardly permitted them, they may the more easily consent to the inward consolations of the grace of God. For there is no doubt that it is impossible to efface everything at once from their obdurate minds; because he who endeavors to ascend to the highest place, rises by degrees or steps, and not by leaps.

Thus the Lord made Himself known to the people of Israel in Egypt; and yet He allowed them the use of the sacrifices which they were wont to offer to the Devil, in his own worship; so as to command them in his sacrifice to kill beasts, to the end that, changing their hearts, they might lay aside one part of the sacrifice, while they retained another; that while they offered the same beasts which they were wont to offer, they should offer them to God, and not to idols; and thus they would no longer be the same sacrifices.

Source: The Venerable Bede, *The Ecclesiastical History of the English Nation*, edited by Ernest Rhys (London: J. M. Dent and Sons; New York: E. P. Dutton, 1910), 52–53.

Source 10.3
Charlemagne and the Saxons

The policies of peaceful conversion and accommodation described in Source 10.2 did not prevail everywhere, as Charlemagne's dealings with the Saxons reveals. During the late eighth and early ninth centuries C.E., Charlemagne (r. 768–814) was the powerful king of the Franks. He turned his Frankish kingdom into a Christian empire that briefly incorporated much of continental Europe, and he was crowned as a renewed Roman emperor by the pope. In the course of almost-constant wars of expansion, Charlemagne struggled for over thirty years (772–804) to subdue the Saxons, a "pagan" Germanic people who inhabited a region on the northeastern frontier of Charlemagne's growing empire (see Map 10.2, page 426). The document known as the *Capitulary on Saxony* outlines a series of laws, regulations, and punishments (known collectively as a capitulary) regarding religious practice of the Saxons. This source reveals both the coercive policies of Charlemagne and the vigorous resistance of the Saxons to their forcible incorporation into his Christian domain.

- What does this document reveal about the kind of resistance that the Saxons mounted against their enforced conversion?

- How did Charlemagne seek to counteract that resistance?

- What does this document suggest about Charlemagne's views of his duties as ruler?

CHARLEMAGNE

Capitulary on Saxony

785

1. It was pleasing to all that the churches of Christ, which are now being built in Saxony and consecrated to God, should not have less, but greater and more illustrious honor, than the fanes [temples] of the idols had had. . . .

3. If any one shall have entered a church by violence and shall have carried off anything in it by force or theft, or shall have burned the church itself, let him be punished by death.

4. If any one, out of contempt for Christianity, shall have despised the holy Lenten fast and shall have eaten flesh, let him be punished by death. But, nevertheless, let it be taken into consideration by a priest, lest perchance any one from necessity has been led to eat flesh.

5. If any one shall have killed a bishop or priest or deacon, let him likewise be punished capitally.

6. If any one deceived by the devil shall have believed, after the manner of the pagans, that any man or woman is a witch and eats men, and on this account shall have burned the person, or shall have given the person's flesh to others to eat, or shall have eaten it himself, let him be punished by a capital sentence.

7. If any one, in accordance with pagan rites, shall have caused the body of a dead man to be burned and shall have reduced his bones to ashes, let him be punished capitally. . . .

9. If any one shall have sacrificed a man to the devil, and after the manner of the pagans shall have presented him as a victim to the demons, let him be punished by death.

10. If any one shall have formed a conspiracy with the pagans against the Christians, or shall have wished to join with them in opposition to the Christians, let him be punished by death; and whoever shall have consented to this same fraudulently against the king and the Christian people, let him be punished by death. . . .

17. Likewise, in accordance with the mandate of God, we command that all shall give a tithe of their property and labor to the churches and priests;

18. That on the Lord's day no meetings and public judicial assemblages shall be held, unless perchance in a case of great necessity or when war compels it, but all shall go to the church to hear the word of God, and shall be free for prayers or good works. Likewise, also, on the especial festivals they shall devote themselves to God and to the services of the church, and shall refrain from secular assemblies.

19. Likewise, . . . all infants shall be baptized within a year. . . .

21. If any one shall have made a vow at springs or trees or groves, or shall have made any offerings after the manner of the heathen and shall have partaken of a repast in honor of the demons, if he shall be a noble, [he must pay a fine of] 60 solidi [gold coins], if a freeman 30, if a litus [neither a slave nor a free person] 15.

Source: D. C. Munro, trans., *Translations and Reprints from the Original Sources of European History*, vol. 6, no. 5, *Selections from the Laws of Charles the Great* (Philadelphia: University of Pennsylvania Press, 1900), 2–4.

Sources 10.4 and 10.5
The Persistence of Tradition

Conversion to Christianity in Western Europe was neither easy nor simple. Peoples thought to have been solidly converted to the new faith continued to engage in earlier practices. Others blended older traditions with Christian rituals. The two documents that follow illustrate both patterns. Source 10.4 describes the encounter between Saint Boniface (672–754), a leading missionary to the Hessians, a Germanic people, during the eighth century. It was written by one of Boniface's devoted followers, Willibald, who subsequently composed a biography of the missionary. Source 10.5 comes from a tenth-century Anglo-Saxon manuscript known as the *Leechbook*, a medical text that describes cures for various problems caused by "elfkind and nightgoers."

- What practices of the Hessians conflicted with Boniface's understanding of Christianity? How did he confront the persistence of these practices?

- What do these documents reveal about the process of conversion to Christianity?

- How might Pope Gregory (Source 10.2), Charlemagne (Source 10.3), and Boniface (Source 10.4) have responded to the cures and preventions described in the *Leechbook*?

WILLIBALD
Life of Boniface
ca. 760

Now many of the Hessians who at that time had acknowledged the Catholic faith were confirmed by the grace of the Holy Spirit and received the laying-on of hands. But others, not yet strong in the spirit, refused to accept the pure teachings of the church in their entirety. Moreover, some continued secretly, others openly, to offer sacrifices to trees and springs, to inspect the entrails of victims; some practiced divination, legerdemain, and incantations; some turned their attention to auguries, auspices, and other sacrificial rites; while others, of a more reasonable character, forsook all the profane practices of the [heathens] and committed none of these crimes.

With the counsel and advice of the latter persons, Boniface in their presence attempted to cut down . . .

a certain oak of extraordinary size, called in the old tongue of the pagans the Oak of Jupiter. Taking his courage in his hands (for a great crowd of pagans stood by watching and bitterly cursing in their hearts the enemy of the gods), he cut the first notch. But when he had made a superficial cut, suddenly, the oak's vast bulk, shaken by a mighty blast of wind from above crashed to the ground shivering its topmost branches into fragments in its fall. As if by the express will of God (for the brethren present had done nothing to cause it) the oak burst asunder into four parts, each part having a trunk of equal length.

At the sight of this extraordinary spectacle the heathens who had been cursing ceased to revile and began, on the contrary, to believe and bless the Lord. Thereupon the holy bishop took counsel with the brethren, built an oratory [a place of prayer] from the timber of the oak and dedicated it to Saint Peter the Apostle. He then set out on a journey to Thuringia. . . . Arrived there, he addressed the elders and the chiefs of the people, calling on them to put aside their blind ignorance and to return to the Christian religion that they had formerly embraced.

Source: Willibald, "Life of Boniface," in *The Anglo-Saxon Missionaries in Germany*, translated by C. H. Talbot (London: Sheed and Ward, 1954), 45–46.

Leechbook
Tenth Century

Work a salve against elfkind and night-goers, . . . and the people with whom the Devil has intercourse. Take eowohumelan, wormwood, bishopwort, lupin, ashthroat, henbane, harewort, haransprecel, heathberry plants, cropleek, garlic, hedgerife grains, githrife, fennel. Put these herbs into one cup, set under the altar, sing over them nine masses; boil in butter and in sheep's grease, add much holy salt, strain through a cloth; throw the herbs in running water. If any evil temptation, or an elf or nightgoers, happen to a man, smear his forehead with this salve, and put on his eyes, and where his body is sore, and cense him [with incense], and sign [the cross] often. His condition will soon be better.

. . . Against elf disease . . . Take bishopwort, fennel, lupin, the lower part of *ælfthone*, and lichen from the holy sign of Christ [cross], and incense; a handful of each. Bind all the herbs in a cloth, dip in hallowed font water thrice. Let three masses be sung over it, one "Omnibus sanctis [For all the saints]," a second "Contra tribulationem [Against tribulation]," a third "Pro infirmis [For the sick]." Put then coals in a coal pan, and lay the herbs on it.

Smoke the man with the herbs before . . . [9 A.M.] and at night; and sing a litany, the Creed [Nicene], and the Pater noster [Our Father]; and write on him Christ's mark on each limb. And take a little handful of the same kind of herbs, similarly sanctified, and boil in milk; drip holy water in it thrice. And let him sip it before his meal. It will soon be well with him.

Against the Devil and against madness, . . . a strong drink. Put in ale hassock, lupin roots, fennel, ontre, betony, hind heolothe, marche, rue, wormwood, nepeta (catmint), helenium, *ælfthone*, wolfs comb. Sing twelve masses over the drink; and let him drink. It will soon be well with him.

A drink against the Devil's temptations: thefanthorn, cropleek, lupin, ontre, bishopwort, fennel, hassock, betony. Sanctify these herbs; put into ale holy water. And let the drink be there in where the sick man is. And continually before he drinks sing thrice over the drink, . . . "God, in your name make me whole (save me)."

Source: Karen Louise Jolly, *Popular Religion in Late Saxon England: Elf Charms in Context* (Chapel Hill: University of North Carolina Press, 1996), 159–67.

DOING HISTORY

The Making of Christian Europe

1. **Describing cultural encounters:** Consider the spread of Christianity in Europe from the viewpoint of those seeking to introduce the new religion. What obstacles did they encounter? What strategies did they employ? What successes and failures did they experience?

2. **Describing cultural encounters . . . from another point of view:**
    Consider the same process from the viewpoint of new adherents to
    Christianity. What were the motives for or the advantages of conversion
    for both political elites and ordinary people? To what extent was it
    possible to combine prevailing practices and beliefs with the teachings
    of the new religion?

3. **Defining a concept:** The notion of "conversion" often suggests a
    quite rapid and complete transformation of religious commitments based
    on sincere inner conviction. In what ways do these documents support
    or challenge this understanding of religious change?

4. **Noticing point of view and assessing credibility:** From what point
    of view is each of the documents written? Which statements in each
    document might historians find unreliable, and which would they find
    most useful?

From *History of the Mongols*, India (Lahore), Moghul, Court of Akbar the Great, ca. 1590/Library, Golestan Palace, Teheran, Iran/Werner Forman/Art Resource, NY

CHAPTER 11

Pastoral Peoples on the Global Stage

The Mongol Moment

1200–1450

In late 2012, the Central Asian nation of Mongolia celebrated a "Day of Mongolian Pride," marking the birth of the country's epic hero Chinggis Khan 850 years earlier. Officials laid wreaths at a giant monument to the warrior leader; wrestlers and archers tested their skills in competition; dancers performed; over 100 scholars made presentations; traditional costumes abounded. In central London, no less, a large bronze statue of Mongolia's founder was unveiled for the occasion. For this small and somewhat remote country, seeking to navigate between its two giant neighbors, China and Russia, it was an occasion to express its own distinctive identity. And Chinggis Khan is central to that identity. With his bloody conquests played down, Chinggis Khan is celebrated as a unifier of the Mongolian peoples, the creator of an empire tolerant of various faiths, and a promoter of economic and cultural ties among distant peoples.

The 2012 celebrations marked a shift in Mongolian thinking about Chinggis Khan that has been under way since the 1990s. Under the country's earlier Soviet-backed communist government, the great Mongol leader had been regarded in very negative terms. After all, his forces had decimated Russia in the thirteenth century, and resentment lingered. But as communism faded in both Russia and Mongolia at the end of the twentieth century, the memory of Chinggis Khan made a remarkable comeback in the land of his birth. Vodka, cigarettes, a chocolate bar, two brands of beer, the country's best rock band, and the central square of the capital city all bore his name, while his picture appeared on Mongolia's stamps and money. Rural young people on horseback sang songs in his honor, and their counterparts in urban Internet cafés constructed Web sites to celebrate

---

Chinggis Khan at Prayer This sixteenth-century Indian painting shows Chinggis Khan at prayer in the midst of battle. He is perhaps praying to Tengri, the great sky god, on whom the Mongol conqueror based his power.

his achievements. The elaborate celebrations in 2012 for his 850th birthday represent just the latest expression of his continuing centrality to modern Mongolia.

All of this is a reminder of the enormous and surprising role that the Mongols played in the Eurasian world of the thirteenth and fourteenth centuries and of the continuing echoes of that long-vanished empire. More generally, the story of the Mongols serves as a useful corrective to the almost-exclusive focus that historians often devote to agricultural peoples and their civilizations, for the Mongols, and many other such peoples, were pastoralists who disdained farming while centering their economic lives around their herds of animals. Normally they did not construct elaborate cities, enduring empires, or monumental works of art, architecture, and written literature. Nonetheless, they left an indelible mark on the historical development of the entire Afro-Eurasian hemisphere, and particularly on the agricultural civilizations with which they so often interacted.

SEEKING THE MAIN POINT

What has been the role in world history of pastoral peoples in general and the Mongols in particular?

Looking Back and Looking Around: The Long History of Pastoral Peoples

AP® EXAM TIP

You must know the features and contributions of pastoral peoples.

The "revolution of domestication," beginning around 11,500 years ago, involved both plants and animals. People living in more favored environments were able to combine farming with animal husbandry and on this economic foundation generated powerful and impressive civilizations with substantial populations. But on the arid margins of agricultural lands, where productive farming was difficult or impossible, an alternative kind of food-producing economy emerged around 4000 B.C.E., focused on the raising of livestock. Peoples practicing such an economy learned to use the milk, blood, wool, hides, and meat of their animals, allowing them to occupy lands that could not support agricultural societies. Some of those animals also provided new baggage and transportation possibilities. Horses, camels, goats, sheep, cattle, yaks, and reindeer were the primary animals that separately, or in some combination, enabled the construction of pastoral or herding societies. Such societies took shape in the vast grasslands of inner Eurasia and sub-Saharan Africa, in the Arabian and Saharan deserts, in the subarctic regions of the Northern Hemisphere, and in the high plateau of Tibet. (See Snapshot, page 460.) Pastoralists had their greatest impact in the Afro-Eurasian world, because in most parts of the Americas the absence of large animals that could be domesticated precluded a herding economy. Only in the Andes did llamas and alpacas allow for some pastoralism.

The World of Pastoral Societies

Despite their many differences, pastoral societies shared several important features that distinguished them from settled agricultural communities and civilizations. Pastoral societies' generally less productive economies and their need for large graz-

A MAP OF TIME

ca. 4000 B.C.E.	Beginning of pastoral economies
ca. 1000 B.C.E.	Beginning of horseback riding
ca. 200 B.C.E.–200 C.E.	Xiongnu Empire
6th–10th centuries	Various Turkic empires
7th–10th centuries	Arab Empire
10th–14th centuries	Conversion of Turkic peoples to Islam
11th–12th centuries	Almoravid Empire
1162–1227	Life of Temujin (Chinggis Khan)
1209–1368	Mongol rule in China
1237–1480	Mongol rule in Russia
1241–1242	Mongol attacks on Eastern Europe
1258	Mongol seizure of Baghdad
1274, 1281	Failed Mongol attacks on Japan
1295	Mongol ruler of Persia converts to Islam
1348–1350	High point of Black Death in Europe

ing areas meant that they supported far smaller populations than did agricultural societies. People generally lived in small and widely scattered encampments or seasonal settlements made up of related kinfolk rather than in the villages, towns, and cities characteristic of agrarian civilizations. Beyond the family unit, pastoral peoples organized themselves in kinship-based groups or clans that claimed a common ancestry, usually through the male line. Related clans might on occasion come together as a tribe, which could also absorb unrelated people into the community. Although their values stressed equality and individual achievement, in some pastoral societies clans were ranked as noble or commoner, and considerable differences emerged between wealthy aristocrats owning large flocks of animals and poor herders. Many pastoral societies held slaves as well.

Furthermore, pastoral peoples generally offered women a higher status, fewer restrictions, and a greater role in public life than their counterparts in agricultural civilizations. Everywhere women were involved in productive labor as well as having domestic responsibility for food and children. The care of smaller animals such as sheep and goats usually fell to women, although only rarely did women own or control their own livestock. Among the Mongols, the remarriage of widows carried none of the negative connotations that it did among the Chinese, and women could initiate divorce. Mongol women frequently served as political advisers and

Guided Reading Question

■ COMPARISON
In what ways did pastoral societies differ from their agricultural counterparts?

SNAPSHOT   Varieties of Pastoral Societies

Region and Peoples	Primary Animals	Features
Inner Eurasian steppes (Xiongnu, Yuezhi, Turks, Uighurs, Mongols, Huns, Kipchaks)[1]	Horses; also sheep, goats, cattle, Bactrian (two-humped) camel	Domestication of horse by 4000 B.C.E.; horseback riding by 1000 B.C.E.; site of largest pastoral empires
Southwestern and Central Asia (Seljuks, Ghaznavids, Mongol il-khans, Uzbeks, Ottomans)	Sheep and goats; used horses, camels, and donkeys for transport	Close economic relationship with neighboring towns; pastoralists provided meat, wool, milk products, and hides in exchange for grain and manufactured goods
Arabian and Saharan deserts (Bedouin Arabs, Berbers, Tuareg)	Dromedary (one-humped) camel; sometimes sheep	Camel caravans made possible long-distance trade; camel-mounted warriors central to early Arab/Islamic expansion
Grasslands of sub-Saharan Africa (Fulbe, Nuer, Turkana, Masai)	Cattle; also sheep and goats	Cattle were a chief form of wealth and central to ritual life; little interaction with wider world until nineteenth century
Subarctic Scandinavia, Russia (Sami, Nenets)	Reindeer	Reindeer domesticated only since 1500 C.E.; many also fished
Tibetan plateau (Tibetans)	Yaks; also sheep, cashmere goats, some cattle	Tibetans supplied yaks as baggage animals for overland caravan trade; exchanged wool, skins, and milk with valley villagers and received barley in return
Andean Mountains	Llamas and alpacas	Andean pastoralists in a few places relied on their herds for a majority of their subsistence, supplemented with horticulture and hunting

were active in military affairs as well. (See Zooming In: Khutulun, page 477.) A thirteenth-century European visitor, the Franciscan friar Giovanni DiPlano Carpini, recorded his impressions of Mongol women:

> Girls and women ride and gallop as skillfully as men. We even saw them carrying quivers and bows, and the women can ride horses for as long as the men; they have shorter stirrups, handle horses very well, and mind all the property. [Mongol] women make everything: skin clothes, shoes, leggings, and everything made of leather. They drive carts and repair them, they load camels, and are quick and vigorous in all their tasks. They all wear trousers, and some of them shoot just like men.[2]

Certainly, literate observers from adjacent civilizations noticed and clearly disapproved of the freedom granted to pastoral women. Ancient Greek writers thought that the pastoralists with whom they were familiar were "women governed." To Han Kuan, a Chinese Confucian scholar in the first century B.C.E., China's northern pastoral neighbors "[made] no distinction between men and women."[3]

The most characteristic feature of pastoral societies was their mobility, as local environmental conditions largely dictated their patterns of movement. In some favorable regions, pastoralists maintained seasonal settlements, migrating, for instance, between highland pastures in the summer and less harsh lowland environments in the winter. Others lived more nomadic lives, moving their herds frequently in regular patterns to systematically follow the seasonal changes in vegetation and water supply. But even the most nomadic pastoralists were not homeless; they took their homes, often elaborate felt tents, with them. Whatever their patterns of movement, pastoralists shared a life based on turning grass, which people cannot eat, into usable food and energy through their animals.

Although pastoralists represented an alternative to the agricultural way of life that they disdained, they were almost always deeply connected to, and often dependent on, their agricultural neighbors. Few of these peoples could live solely from the products of their animals, and most of them actively sought access to the foodstuffs, manufactured goods, and luxury items available from the urban workshops and farming communities of nearby civilizations. Particularly among the pastoral peoples of inner Eurasia, this desire for the fruits of civilization periodically stimulated the creation of tribal confederations or states that could more effectively deal with the powerful agricultural societies on their borders. The Mongol Empire of

Guided Reading Question

■ **CONNECTION**

In what ways did pastoral societies interact with their agricultural neighbors?

The Scythians
An ancient horse-riding pastoral people during the second-wave era, the Scythians occupied a region in present-day Kazakhstan and southern Russia. Their pastoral way of life is apparent in this detail from an exquisite gold necklace from the fourth century B.C.E. (Historical Museum, Kiev, Ukraine/Photo © Boltin Picture Library/Bridgeman Images)

the thirteenth century was but the most recent and largest in a long line of such efforts, dating back to the first millennium B.C.E.

Constructing a large state among pastoralists was no easy task. Such societies generally lacked the surplus wealth needed to pay for the professional armies and bureaucracies that everywhere sustained the states and empires of agricultural civilizations. And the fierce independence of widely dispersed pastoral clans and tribes as well as their internal rivalries made any enduring political unity difficult to achieve. Nonetheless, charismatic leaders, such as Chinggis Khan, were periodically able to weld together a series of tribal alliances that for a time became powerful states. In doing so, they often employed the device of "fictive kinship," designating allies as blood relatives and treating them with a corresponding respect.

Despite their limited populations, such states had certain military advantages in confronting larger and more densely populated civilizations. They could draw on the horseback-riding and hunting skills of virtually the entire male population and some women as well. Easily transferred to the role of warrior, these skills, which were practiced from early childhood, were an integral part of inner Eurasian pastoral life. But what sustained these states was their ability to extract wealth, through raiding, trading, or extortion, from agricultural civilizations such as China, Persia, and Byzantium. As long as that wealth flowed into pastoral states, rulers could maintain the fragile alliances among fractious clans and tribes. When it was interrupted, however, those states often fragmented.

Pastoralists interacted with their agricultural neighbors not only economically and militarily but also culturally as they "became acquainted with and tried on for size all the world and universal religions."[4] At one time or another, Judaism, Buddhism, Islam, and several forms of Christianity all found a home somewhere among the pastoral peoples of inner Eurasia. So did Manichaeism, a religious tradition born in third-century Persia and combining elements of Zoroastrian, Christian, and Buddhist practice. Usually conversion was a top-down process as pastoral elites and rulers adopted a foreign religion for political purposes, sometimes changing religious allegiance as circumstances altered. Pastoral peoples, in short, did not inhabit a world totally apart from their agricultural and civilized neighbors.

Surely the most fundamental contribution of pastoralists to the larger human story was their mastery of environments unsuitable for agriculture. Through the creative use of their animals, they brought a version of the food-producing revolution and a substantial human presence to the arid grasslands and desert regions of Afro-Eurasia. As the pastoral peoples of the Inner Asian steppes learned the art of horseback riding, by roughly 1000 B.C.E., their societies changed dramatically. Now they could accumulate and tend larger herds of horses, sheep, and goats and move more rapidly over a much wider territory. New technologies, invented or adapted by pastoral societies, added to the mastery of their environment and spread widely across the Eurasian steppes, creating something of a common culture in this vast region. These innovations included complex horse harnesses, saddles with iron stirrups, a small compound bow that could be fired from horseback, various forms of armor, and new kinds of swords. Agricultural peoples were amazed at the centrality of the horse in pastoral life. As a Roman historian noted about the Huns, "From their horses, by day and night every one of that nation buys and sells, eats and drinks, and bowed over the narrow neck of the animal relaxes in a sleep so deep as to be accompanied by many dreams."[5]

Before the Mongols: Pastoralists in History

What enabled pastoral peoples to make their most visible entry onto the stage of world history was the military potential of horseback riding, and of camel riding somewhat later. Their mastery of mounted warfare made possible a long but intermittent series of pastoral empires across the steppes of inner Eurasia and parts of Africa. For 2,000 years, those states played a major role in Afro-Eurasian history and represented a standing challenge to and influence upon the agrarian civilizations on their borders.

One early large-scale pastoral empire was associated with the people known as the Xiongnu, who lived in the Mongolian steppes north of China (see Chapter 8). Provoked by Chinese penetration of their territory, the Xiongnu in the third and second centuries B.C.E. created a huge military confederacy that stretched from Manchuria deep into Central Asia. Under the charismatic leadership of Modun (r. 210–174 B.C.E.), the Xiongnu Empire effected a revolution in pastoral life. Earlier fragmented and egalitarian societies were now transformed into a far more centralized and hierarchical political system in which

The Xiongnu Confederacy

power was concentrated in a divinely sanctioned ruler and differences between "junior" and "senior" clans became more prominent. "All the people who draw the bow have now become one family," declared Modun. Tribute, exacted from other pastoral peoples and from China itself, sustained the Xiongnu Empire and forced the Han dynasty emperor Wen to acknowledge, unhappily, the equality of people he regarded as barbarians. "Our two great nations," he declared, no doubt reluctantly, "the Han and the Xiongnu, stand side by side."[6]

Although it subsequently disintegrated under sustained Chinese counterattacks, the Xiongnu Empire created a model that later Turkic and Mongol empires emulated. Even without a powerful state, various nomadic or semi-nomadic peoples played a role in the collapse of the already-weakened Chinese and Roman empires and in the subsequent rebuilding of those civilizations (see Chapter 3).

It was during the era of third-wave civilizations (500–1500) that pastoral peoples made their most significant mark on the larger canvas of world history. Arabs, Berbers, Turks, and Mongols—all of them of pastoral origin—created the largest and most influential empires of that millennium. The most expansive religious tradition of the era, Islam, derived from a largely pastoral people, the Arabs, and was carried to new regions by another pastoral people, the Turks. In that millennium, most of the great civilizations of outer Eurasia—Byzantium, Persia, India, and China— had come under the control of previously pastoral people, at least for a time. But as

AP® EXAM TIP
Know the characteristics and general locations of pastoral societies before the Mongols.

Guided Reading Question

■ SIGNIFICANCE
In what ways did the Xiongnu, Arabs, Turks, and Berbers make an impact on world history?

Seljuk Tiles
Among the artistic achievements of Turkic Muslims were lovely ceramic tiles used to decorate mosques, minarets, palaces, and other public spaces. They contained intricate geometric designs, images of trees and birds, and inscriptions from the Quran. This one, dating from the thirteenth century, was used in a Seljuk palace, built as a summer residence for the sultan in the city of Konya in what is now central Turkey. (© Images & Stories/Alamy)

AP® EXAM TIP

Take note of the characteristics and regions of Arab and Turkic pastoralists before the rise of Islam.

pastoralists entered and shaped the arena of world history, they too were transformed by the experience.

The first and most dramatic of these incursions came from Arabs. In the Arabian Peninsula, the development of a reliable camel saddle somewhere between 500 and 100 B.C.E. enabled pastoral Bedouin (desert-dwelling) Arabs to fight effectively from atop their enormous beasts. With this new military advantage, they came to control the rich trade routes in incense running through Arabia. Even more important, these camel pastoralists served as the shock troops of Islamic expansion, providing many of the new religion's earliest followers and much of the military force that carved out the Arab Empire. Although intellectual and political leadership came from urban merchants and settled farming communities, the Arab Empire was in some respects a pastoralist creation that subsequently became the foundation of a new and distinctive civilization.

Even as the pastoral Arabs encroached on the world of Eurasian civilizations from the south, Turkic-speaking pastoralists were making inroads from the north. Never a single people, various Turkic-speaking clans and tribes migrated from their homeland in Mongolia and southern Siberia generally westward and entered the historical record as creators of a series of empires between 552 and 965 C.E., most of them lasting little more than a century. Like the Xiongnu Empire, they were fragile alliances of various tribes headed by a supreme ruler known as a *kaghan*, who was supported by a faithful corps of soldiers called "wolves," for the wolf was the mythical ancestor of Turkic peoples. From their base in the steppes, these Turkic states confronted the great civilizations to their south—China, Persia, Byzantium—alternately raiding them, allying with them against common enemies, trading with them, and extorting tribute payments from them. Turkic language and culture spread widely over much of Inner Asia, and elements of that culture entered the agrarian civilizations. In the courts of northern China, for example, yogurt thinned with water, a drink derived from the Turks, replaced for a time the traditional beverage of tea, and at least one Chinese poet wrote joyfully about the delights of snowy evenings in a felt tent.[7]

A major turning point in the history of the Turks occurred with their conversion to Islam between the tenth and fourteenth centuries. This extended process represented a major expansion of the faith and launched the Turks into a new role as the third major carrier of Islam, following the Arabs and the Persians. It also brought the Turks into an increasingly important position within the heartland of an established Islamic civilization as they migrated southward into the Middle East. There they served first as slave soldiers within the Abbasid caliphate, and then, as the caliphate declined, they increasingly took political and military power themselves. In the Seljuk Turkic Empire of the eleventh and twelfth centuries, centered in Persia and present-day Iraq, Turkic rulers began to claim the Muslim title of *sultan* (ruler) rather than the Turkic *kaghan*. Although the Abbasid caliph remained the formal ruler, real power was exercised by Turkic sultans.

AP® EXAM TIP

Be prepared to list the roles that Islam played in the lives of pastoral peoples of Southwest Asia and North Africa.

Not only did Turkic peoples become Muslims themselves, but they carried Islam to new areas as well. Their invasions of northern India solidly planted Islam in that ancient civilization. In Anatolia, formerly ruled by Christian Byzantium, they brought both Islam and a massive infusion of Turkic culture, language, and people, even as they created the Ottoman Empire, which by 1500 became one of the great powers of Eurasia (see Chapter 12, page 516). In both places, Turkic dynasties governed and would continue to do so well into the modern era. Thus Turkic people, many of them at least, had transformed themselves from pastoralists to sedentary farmers, from creators of steppe empires to rulers of agrarian civilizations, and from polytheistic worshippers of their ancestors and various gods to followers and carriers of a monotheistic Islam.

The Almoravid Empire

Broadly similar patterns prevailed in Africa as well. All across northern Africa and the Sahara, the introduction of the camel, probably during the first millennium B.C.E., gave rise to pastoral societies. Much like the Turkic-speaking pastoralists of Central Asia, many of these peoples later adopted Islam, but at least initially had little formal instruction in the religion. In the eleventh century C.E., a reform movement arose among the Sanhaja Berber pastoralists living in the western Sahara; they had only recently converted to Islam and were practicing it rather superficially. The movement was sparked by a scholar, Ibn Yasin, who returned from a pilgrimage to Mecca around 1039 seeking to purify the practice of the faith among his own people in line with orthodox principles. That religious movement soon became an expansive state, the Almoravid Empire, which incorporated a large part of northwestern Africa and in 1086 crossed into southern Spain, where it offered vigorous opposition to Christian efforts to conquer the region.

For a time, the Almoravid state enjoyed considerable prosperity, based on its control of much of the West African gold trade and the grain-producing Atlantic plains of Morocco. The Almoravids also brought to Morocco the sophisticated Islamic culture of southern Spain, still visible in the splendid architecture of the city of Marrakesh, for a time the capital of the Almoravid Empire. By the mid-twelfth century, that empire had been overrun by its longtime enemies, Berber farming people from the Atlas Mountains. But for roughly a century, the Almoravid movement represented an African pastoral people, who had converted to Islam, came into conflict with their agricultural neighbors, built a short-lived empire, and had a considerable impact on neighboring civilizations in both North Africa and Europe.

Breakout: The Mongol Empire

Of all the pastoral peoples who took a turn on the stage of world history, the Mongols made the most stunning entry. Their thirteenth-century breakout from Mongolia gave rise to the largest land-based empire in all of human history, stretching from the Pacific coast of Asia to Eastern Europe (see Map 11.1). This empire joined the pastoral peoples of the inner Eurasian steppes with the settled agricultural civilizations of outer Eurasia more extensively and more intimately than ever before. It also brought the major civilizations of Eurasia—Europe, China, and the Islamic world—into far more direct contact than in earlier times. Both the enormous destructiveness of the process and the networks of exchange and communication

Map 11.1   The Mongol Empire

Encompassing much of Eurasia, the Mongol Empire was divided into four khanates after the death of Chinggis Khan.

that it spawned were the work of the Mongols, numbering only about 700,000 people. It was another of history's unlikely twists.

For all of its size and fearsome reputation, the Mongol Empire left a surprisingly modest cultural imprint on the world it had briefly governed. Unlike the Arabs, the Mongols bequeathed to the world no new language, religion, or civilization. Whereas Islam offered a common religious home for all converts—conquerors and conquered alike—the Mongols never tried to spread their own faith among subject peoples. Their religion centered on rituals invoking the ancestors, which were performed around the family hearth. Rulers sometimes consulted religious specialists, known as shamans, who might predict the future, offer sacrifices, and communicate with the spirit world, particularly with Tengri, the supreme sky god of the Mongols. There was little in this tradition to attract outsiders, and in any event the Mongols proved uninterested in religious imperialism.

The Mongols offered the majority of those they conquered little more than the status of defeated, subordinate, and exploited people, although people with skills were put to work in ways useful to Mongol authorities. Unlike the Turks, whose languages and culture flourish today in many places far from the Turkic homeland, Mongol culture remains confined largely to Mongolia. Furthermore, the Mongol Empire, following in the tradition of Xiongnu and Turkic state building, proved to be "the last, spectacular bloom of pastoral power in Inner Eurasia."[8] Some Mongols themselves became absorbed into the settled societies they conquered. After the decline and disintegration of the Mongol Empire, the tide turned against the pastoralists of inner Eurasia, who were increasingly swallowed up in the expanding Russian or Chinese empires. Nonetheless, while it lasted and for a few centuries thereafter, the Mongol Empire made an enormous impact throughout the entire Eurasian world.

From Temujin to Chinggis Khan: The Rise of the Mongol Empire

World historians are prone to focus attention on large-scale and long-term processes of change in explaining "what happened in history," but in understanding the rise of the Mongol Empire, most scholars have found themselves forced to look closely at the role of a single individual—Temujin (TEM-oo-chin) (1162–1227), later known as Chinggis Khan (universal ruler). The twelfth-century world into which he was born found the Mongols an unstable and fractious collection of tribes and clans, much reduced from a somewhat earlier and more powerful position in the shifting alliances in what is now Mongolia. "Everyone was feuding," declared a leading Mongol shaman. "Rather than sleep, they robbed each other of their possessions. . . . There was no respite, only battle. There was no affection, only mutual slaughter."[9]

The early life of Temujin showed few signs of a prominent future. The boy's father had been a minor chieftain of a noble clan, but he was murdered by tribal rivals before Temujin turned ten, and the family was soon deserted by other members of the clan. As social outcasts without livestock, Temujin's small family, headed

AP® EXAM TIP

Knowledge of the methods of rule of the Mongol Empire is vital to success on the AP® exam.

Guided Reading Question

■ DESCRIPTION
Identify the major steps in the rise of the Mongol Empire.

by his resourceful mother, was forced to abandon pastoralism, living instead by hunting, fishing, and gathering wild foods. It was an enormous and humiliating drop in their social status. In these desperate circumstances, Temujin's remarkable character came into play. His personal magnetism and courage and his inclination to rely on trusted friends rather than ties of kinship allowed him to build up a small following and to ally with a more powerful tribal leader. This alliance received a boost from Chinese patrons, who were always eager to keep the pastoralists divided. Military victory over a rival tribe resulted in Temujin's recognition as a chief in his own right with a growing band of followers.

Temujin's rise to power within the complex tribal politics of Mongolia was a surprise to everyone. It took place amid shifting alliances and betrayals, a mounting string of military victories, the indecisiveness of his enemies, a reputation as a leader generous to friends and ruthless to enemies, and the incorporation of warriors from defeated tribes into his own forces. In 1206, a Mongol tribal assembly recognized Temujin as Chinggis Khan, supreme leader of a now unified Great Mongol Nation. (See Working with Evidence, Source 11.1, page 488.) It was a remarkable achievement, but one little noticed beyond the highland steppes of Mongolia. That would soon change.

The unification of the Mongol tribes raised an obvious question: what was Chinggis Khan to do with the powerful army he had assembled? Without a common task, the new and fragile unity of the Mongols would surely dissolve into quarrels and chaos; and without external resources to reward his followers, Chinggis Khan would be hard-pressed to maintain his supreme position. Both considerations pointed in a single direction—expansion, particularly toward China, long a source of great wealth for pastoral peoples.

In 1209, the first major attack on the settled agricultural societies south of Mongolia set in motion half a century of a Mongol world war, a series of military campaigns, massive killing, and empire building without precedent in world history. In the process, Chinggis Khan, followed by his sons and grandsons (Ogodei, Mongke, and Khubilai), constructed an empire that contained China, Korea, Central Asia, Russia, much of the Islamic Middle East, and parts of Eastern Europe (see Map 11.1, page 466). "In a flash," wrote a recent scholar, "the Mongol warriors would defeat every army, capture every fort, and bring down the walls of every city they encountered. Christians, Muslims, Buddhists, and Hindus would soon kneel before the dusty boots of illiterate young Mongol horsemen."[10]

Various setbacks marked the outer limits of the Mongol Empire—the Mongols' withdrawal from Eastern Europe (1242), their defeat at Ain Jalut in Palestine at the hands of Egyptian forces (1260), the failure of their invasion of Japan owing to typhoons, and the difficulty of penetrating the tropical jungles of Southeast Asia. But what an empire it was! How could a Mongol confederation, with a total population of less than 1 million people and few resources beyond their livestock, assemble an imperial structure of such staggering transcontinental dimensions? (See Zooming In: A Mongol Failure, page 470.)

Explaining the Mongol Moment

Like the Roman Empire but far more rapidly, the Mongol realm grew of its own momentum without any grand scheme or blueprint for world conquest. Each fresh victory brought new resources for making war and new threats or insecurities that seemed to require further expansion. As the empire took shape and certainly by the end of his life, Chinggis Khan had come to see his career in terms of a universal mission. "I have accomplished a great work," he declared, "uniting the whole world in one empire."[11] Thus the Mongol Empire acquired an ideology in the course of its construction.

What made this "great work" possible? The odds seemed overwhelming, for China alone outnumbered the Mongols 100 to 1 and possessed incomparably greater resources. Furthermore, the Mongols did not enjoy any technological superiority over their many adversaries. They did, however, enjoy the luck of good timing, for China was divided, having already lost control of its northern territory to the pastoral Jurchen people, while the decrepit Abbasid caliphate, once the center of the Islamic world, had shrunk to a fraction of its earlier size. But clearly, the key to the Mongols' success lay in their army. According to one scholar, "Mongol armies were simply better led, organized, and disciplined than those of their opponents."[12] In an effort to diminish a divisive tribalism, Chinggis Khan reorganized the entire social structure of the Mongols into military units of 10, 100, 1,000, and 10,000 warriors, an arrangement that allowed for effective command and control. Conquered tribes, especially, were broken up, and their members were scattered among these new units, which enrolled virtually all men and supplied the cavalry forces of Mongol armies. A highly prestigious imperial guard, also recruited across tribal lines, marked the further decline of the old tribalism as a social revolution, imposed from above, reshaped Mongol society.

An impressive discipline and loyalty to their leaders characterized Mongol military forces, and discipline was reinforced by the provision that should any members of a unit desert in battle, all were subject to the death penalty. More positively, loyalty was cemented by the leaders' willingness to share the hardships of their men. "I eat the same food and am dressed in the same rags as my humble herdsmen," wrote Chinggis Khan. "I am always in the forefront, and in battle I am never at the rear."[13] (See Working with Evidence,

AP® EXAM TIP

Note this comparison between the Roman and Mongol empires as you develop your essay-writing skills.

A Mongol Warrior
Horseback-riding skills, honed in herding animals and adapted to military purposes, were central to Mongol conquests, as illustrated in this Ming dynasty Chinese painting of a mounted Mongol archer. (Victoria & Albert Museum, London, UK/Bridgeman Images)

A Mongol Failure: The Invasion of Japan

The Mongols are best known for their remarkable military victories, which gave them one of the largest empires in history, but they experienced stunning defeats as well.[14] None was more dramatic than the failed invasion of Japan in 1281. The armada assembled by the Mongols for this campaign was one of the largest in history, comprising thousands of ships and as many as 140,000 sailors and soldiers. With little experience in naval warfare, the Mongols built their armada by drawing on the resources of their vassal state in Korea and their recently conquered subjects in China. But even with the aid of these seafaring peoples, this huge invasion fleet stretched the resources of the Mongols, who resorted to commuting the death sentences of criminals willing to serve in the fleet.

The invasion was the culmination of a deteriorating relationship between Japanese authorities and the Mongol ruler Khubilai Khan, grandson of Chinggis Khan and founder of the Chinese Yuan dynasty. In the 1260s,

Japanese samurai attacking a Mongol warship.

Japan's government ignored the khan's demands that it become a vassal state of the Mongol Empire. In 1274, the khan dispatched a raiding force against Japan that briefly landed on the main Japanese island of Kyushu. This force both scouted a suitable invasion route and put pressure on the Japanese to accept Mongol demands. In the years that followed, tensions increased, especially when the Japanese summarily beheaded Mongol envoys sent to demand their submission.

Following the final conquest of China in 1279, the khan shifted his attention to subjugating Japan. The massive invasion fleet sailed from ports in Korea and southern China with plans to combine off the shores of Japan. The fleet from Korea arrived first and attacked the mainland without waiting for the Chinese fleet. The Mongols sought to establish a beachhead at the site where Mongol forces had briefly come ashore in 1274, but the

photo: Detail from a Japanese scroll painting on paper, ca. 1293, attributed to Tosa Nagataka and Tosa Nagaaki/The Granger Collection, NYC—All rights reserved.

Source 11.2, page 490.) Such discipline and loyalty made possible the elaborate tactics of encirclement, retreat, and deception that proved decisive in many a battle. Furthermore, the enormous flow of wealth from conquered civilizations benefited all Mongols, though not equally. Even ordinary Mongols could now dress in linens and silks rather than hides and felt, could own slaves derived from the many prisoners of war, and had far greater opportunities to improve their social position in a constantly expanding empire.

To compensate for their own small population, the Mongols incorporated huge numbers of conquered peoples into their military forces. "People who lived in felt tents"—mostly Mongol and Turkic pastoralists—were conscripted en masse into the cavalry units of the Mongol army, while settled agricultural peoples supplied the infantry and artillery forces. As the Mongols penetrated major civilizations, with their walled cities and elaborate fortifications, they quickly acquired Chinese techniques and technology of siege warfare. Some 1,000 Chinese artillery crews, for heavily outnumbered Japanese forces were waiting for them behind recently constructed defensive walls. Unable to establish a beachhead, the Mongol fleet anchored in the harbor, where it was attacked by groups of Japanese warriors, known as samurai, in small open boats, like the one depicted in a contemporary scroll recounting the battle (see photo opposite). In daring raids, often at night, the samurai boarded the much larger Mongol ships and engaged their crews in deadly close-quarters combat.

Under pressure, the Korean fleet withdrew and made its rendezvous with the Chinese fleet that had arrived in the waters off Japan. The combined forces then moved against another Japanese island, where they engaged in a fierce all-night sea battle that once again pitted the large seagoing ships of the Mongol armada against heavily outnumbered groups of samurai in small raiding boats. It was at this moment that a typhoon, named the *kamikaze*, or "divine wind," by the Japanese defenders, struck, destroying perhaps 30 percent of the Korean fleet and between 60 and 90 percent of the Chinese flotilla. In the aftermath, the Mongol commanders abandoned the invasion, leaving behind thousands of shipwrecked soldiers and sailors on the beaches. Such was the role of natural events in confounding human plans.

The defeat had little impact on Khubilai Khan, whose empire recovered quickly from the setback. But the khan never again turned his attentions to Japan, instead seeking to expand his empire elsewhere, including the islands of Southeast Asia, the target of another ambitious but unsuccessful naval expedition in the 1290s. In Japan, the Mongol invasion had a much greater long-term impact. The destruction of the Mongol fleet through what was perceived as divine intervention strengthened Japanese conceptions of their island nation as the *shinkoku*, or "land of the gods." Memories of triumph over the Mongols continued to resonate into the twentieth century. At the end of World War II, when Japan was again faced with foreign invasion, Japanese suicide pilots who sought to stop the Allied advance took the name *kamikazes*, evoking the memory of the typhoon that had turned back the Mongol invasion centuries earlier.

Question: How does the Mongols' military defeat at the hands of the Japanese shape your understanding of the Mongols and their empire?

example, took part in the Mongol invasion of distant Persia. Beyond military recruitment, Mongols demanded that their conquered people serve as laborers, building roads and bridges and ferrying supplies over long distances. Artisans, craftsmen, and skilled people generally were carefully identified, spared from massacre, and often sent to distant regions of the empire where their services were required. A French goldsmith, captured by Mongol forces in Hungary, wound up as a slave in the Mongol capital of Karakorum (kah-rah-KOR-um), where he constructed an elaborate silver fountain that dispensed wine and other intoxicating drinks.

A further element in the military effectiveness of Mongol forces lay in a growing reputation for a ruthless brutality and utter destructiveness. Chinggis Khan's policy was clear: "Whoever submits shall be spared, but those who resist, they shall be destroyed with their wives, children and dependents . . . so that the others who hear and see should fear and not act the same."[15] City after city was utterly destroyed, and enemy soldiers were passed out in lots to Mongol troops for execution, while

AP® EXAM TIP

Know the legendary thoroughness of Mongol conquest.

women and skilled craftsmen were enslaved. Unskilled civilians served as human shields for attacks on the next city or were used as human fill in the moats surrounding those cities. (See Working with Evidence, Sources 11.3 and 11.4, pages 492 and 494.)

One scholar explained such policies in this way: "Extremely conscious of their small numbers and fearful of rebellion, Chinggis often chose to annihilate a region's entire population, if it appeared too troublesome to govern."[16] These policies also served as a form of psychological warfare, a practical inducement to surrender for those who knew of the Mongol terror. Historians continue to debate the extent and uniqueness of the Mongols' brutality, but their reputation for unwavering harshness proved a military asset.

Underlying the purely military dimensions of the Mongols' success was an impressive ability to mobilize both the human and material resources of their growing empire. Elaborate census taking allowed Mongol leaders to know what was available to them and made possible the systematic taxation of conquered people. An effective system of relay stations, about a day's ride apart, provided rapid communication across the empire and fostered trade as well. Marco Polo, the Venetian trader who traveled through Mongol domains in the thirteenth century, claimed that the Mongols maintained some 10,000 such stations, together with 200,000 horses available to authorized users. The beginnings of a centralized bureaucracy with various specialized offices took shape in the new capital of Karakorum. There scribes translated official decrees into the various languages of the empire, such as Persian, Uighur, Chinese, and Tibetan.

AP® EXAM TIP

Take note of the kinds of administrative techniques that the Mongols used.

Other policies appealed to various groups among the conquered peoples of the empire. Interested in fostering commerce, Mongol rulers often offered merchants 10 percent or more above their asking price and allowed them the free use of the relay stations for transporting their goods. In administering the conquered regions, Mongols held the highest decision-making posts, but Chinese and Muslim officials held many advisory and lower-level positions in China and Persia respectively. In religious matters, the Mongols welcomed and supported many religious traditions—Buddhist, Christian, Muslim, Daoist—as long as they did not become the focus of political opposition. This policy of religious toleration allowed Muslims to seek converts among Mongol troops and afforded Christians much greater freedom than they had enjoyed under Muslim rule. Toward the end of his life, apparently feeling his approaching death, Chinggis Khan himself summoned a famous Daoist master from China and begged him to "communicate to me the means of preserving life." (See Working with Evidence, Source 11.2, page 490.) One of his successors, Mongke, arranged a debate among representatives of several religious faiths, after which he concluded: "Just as God gave different fingers to the hand, so has He given different ways to men."[17] Such economic, administrative, and religious policies provided some benefits and a place within the empire—albeit subordinate—for many of its conquered peoples.

PRACTICING AP® HISTORICAL THINKING

What accounts for the political and military success of the Mongols?

Encountering the Mongols: Comparing Three Cases

The Mongol moment in world history represented an enormous cultural encounter between pastoralists and the settled civilizations of Eurasia. Differences among those civilizations—Confucian China, Muslim Persia, Christian Russia—ensured considerable diversity as this encounter unfolded across a vast realm. The process of conquest, the length and nature of Mongol rule, the impact on local people, and the extent of Mongol assimilation into the cultures of the conquered—all this and more varied considerably across the Eurasian domains of the empire. The experiences of China, Persia, and Russia provide brief glimpses into several expressions of this massive clash of cultures.

AP® EXAM TIP

Study this discussion of comparisons of Mongol rule as a guide for good essay construction.

China and the Mongols

Long the primary target for pastoral steppe dwellers in search of agrarian wealth, China proved the most difficult and extended of the Mongols' many conquests, lasting some seventy years, from 1209 to 1279. The invasion began in northern China, which had been ruled for several centuries by various dynasties of pastoral origin and was characterized by destruction and plunder on a massive scale. Southern China, under the control of the native Song dynasty, was a different story, for there the Mongols were far less violent and more concerned with accommodating the local population. Landowners, for example, were guaranteed their estates in exchange for their support or at least their neutrality. By whatever methods, the outcome was the unification of a divided China, a treasured ideal among educated Chinese. This achievement persuaded some of them that the Mongols had indeed been granted the Mandate of Heaven and, despite their foreign origins, were legitimate rulers. One highly educated Chinese scholar wrote a short biography of a recently deceased Mongol official, praising him for curtailing the violence of Mongol soldiers, offering leniency to rebels, and providing tax relief and food during a famine. In short, he was behaving like a good Chinese official.

Having acquired China, what were the Mongols to do with it? One possibility, apparently considered by the Great Khan Ogodei (ERG-uh-day) in the 1230s, was to exterminate everyone in northern China and turn the country into pastureland for Mongol herds. That suggestion, fortunately, was rejected in favor of extracting as much wealth as possible from the country's advanced civilization. Doing so meant some accommodation to Chinese culture and ways of governing, for the Mongols had no experience with the operation of a complex agrarian society.

That accommodation took many forms. The Mongols made use of Chinese administrative practices and techniques of taxation as well as their postal system. They gave themselves a Chinese dynastic title, the Yuan, suggesting a new beginning in Chinese history. They transferred their capital from Karakorum in Mongolia to what is now Beijing, building a wholly new capital city there known as Khanbalik, the "city of the khan." Thus the Mongols were now rooting themselves

Guided Reading Question

■ CHANGE
How did Mongol rule change China? In what ways were the Mongols changed by China?

Marco Polo and Khubilai Khan

In ruling China, the Mongols employed in high positions a number of Muslims and a few Europeans, such as Marco Polo, shown here kneeling before Khubilai Khan in a painting from the fifteenth century. (From *Livre des Merveilles du Monde*, ca. 1410–1412, Boucicaut Master [fl. 1390–1430], and workshop/Bibliothèque Nationale de France, Paris, France/Bridgeman Images)

AP® EXAM TIP

Be able to list examples of travelers in the postclassical era, such as Marco Polo and Ibn Battuta (see Chapter 9), and the places they traveled.

solidly on the soil of a highly sophisticated civilization, well removed from their homeland on the steppes. Khubilai Khan (koo-buh-l'eye kahn), the grandson of Chinggis Khan and China's Mongol ruler from 1271 to 1294, ordered a set of Chinese-style ancestral tablets to honor his ancestors and posthumously awarded them Chinese names. Many of his policies evoked the values of a benevolent Chinese emperor as he improved roads, built canals, lowered some taxes, patronized scholars and artists, limited the death penalty and torture, supported peasant agriculture, and prohibited Mongols from grazing their animals on peasants' farmland. Mongol khans also made use of traditional Confucian rituals, supported the building of some Daoist temples, and were particularly attracted to a Tibetan form of Buddhism, which returned the favor with strong political support for the invaders.

Despite these accommodations, Mongol rule was still harsh, exploitative, foreign, and resented. Marco Polo, who was in China at the time, reported that some Mongol officials or their Muslim intermediaries treated Chinese "just like slaves," demanding bribes for services, ordering arbitrary executions, and seizing women at will—all of which generated outrage and hostility. The Mongols did not become Chinese, nor did they accommodate every aspect of Chinese culture. Deep inside the new capital, the royal family and court could continue to experience something of steppe life as their animals roamed freely in large open areas, planted with steppe grass. Many of the Mongol elite much preferred to live, eat, sleep, and give birth in the traditional tents that sprouted everywhere. In administering the country, the Mongols largely ignored the traditional Chinese examination system and relied heavily on foreigners, particularly Muslims from Central Asia and the Middle East, to serve as officials, while keeping the top decision-making posts for themselves. Few Mongols learned Chinese, and Mongol law discriminated against the Chinese, reserving for them the most severe punishments. Furthermore, the Mongols honored and supported merchants and artisans far more than Confucian bureaucrats had been inclined to do.

In social life, the Mongols forbade intermarriage and prohibited Chinese scholars from learning the Mongol script. Mongol women never adopted foot binding and scandalized the Chinese by mixing freely with men at official gatherings and riding to the hunt with their husbands. The Mongol ruler Khubilai Khan retained the Mongol tradition of relying heavily on female advisers, the chief of which was his favorite wife, Chabi. Ironically, she urged him to accommodate his Chinese subjects, forcefully and successfully opposing an early plan to turn Chinese farmland into pastureland. Unlike many Mongols, biased as they were against farming, Chabi recognized the advantages of agriculture and its ability to generate tax revenue. With a vision of turning Mongol rule into a lasting dynasty that might rank with the splendor of the Tang, she urged her husband to emulate the best practices of that earlier era of Chinese history.

However one assesses Mongol rule in China, it was relatively brief, lasting little more than a century. By the mid-fourteenth century, intense factionalism among the Mongols, rapidly rising prices, furious epidemics of the plague, and growing peasant rebellions combined to force the Mongols out of China. By 1368, rebel forces had triumphed, and thousands of Mongols returned to their homeland in the steppes. For several centuries, they remained a periodic threat to China, but during the Ming dynasty that followed, the memory of their often-brutal and alien rule stimulated a renewed commitment to Confucian values and restrictive gender practices and an effort to wipe out all traces of the Mongols' impact.

Persia and the Mongols

A second great civilization conquered by the Mongols was Islamic Persia. There the Mongol takeover was far more abrupt than the extended process of conquest in China. A first invasion (1219–1221), led by Chinggis Khan himself, was followed thirty years later by a second assault (1251–1258) under his grandson Hulegu (HE-luh-gee), who became the first il-khan (subordinate khan) of Persia. Although Persia had been repeatedly attacked, from the invasion of Alexander the Great to that of the Arabs, nothing prepared them for the Mongols. Before the Mongols, the most recent incursion had featured Turkic peoples, but they had been Muslims, recently converted, small in number, and seeking only acceptance within the Islamic world. The Mongols, however, were infidels in Muslim eyes, and their stunning victory was a profound shock to people accustomed to viewing history as the progressive expansion of Islamic rule. Furthermore, Mongol military victory brought in its wake a degree of ferocity and slaughter that had no parallel in Persian experience. (See Working with Evidence, Source 11.3, page 492, for a description of the Mongol

AP® EXAM TIP

Look for patterns in reasons for the fall of empires in world history, such as peasant rebellions, diseases, and a poor economy.

seizure of the city of Bukhara.) The Persian historian Juvaini described it in fearful terms:

> Every town and every village has been several times subjected to pillage and massacre and has suffered this confusion for years so that even though there be generation and increase until the Resurrection the population will not attain to a tenth part of what it was before.[18]

The sacking of Baghdad in 1258, which put an end to the Abbasid caliphate, was accompanied by the massacre of more than 200,000 people, according to Hulegu himself.

Beyond this human catastrophe lay the damage to Persian and Iraqi agriculture and to those who tilled the soil. Heavy taxes, sometimes collected twenty or thirty times a year and often under torture or whipping, pushed large numbers of peasants off their land. Furthermore, the in-migration of pastoral Mongols, together with their immense herds of sheep and goats, turned much agricultural land into pasture and sometimes into desert. As a result, a fragile system of underground water channels that provided irrigation to the fields was neglected, and much good agricultural land was reduced to waste. Some sectors of the Persian economy gained, however. Wine production increased because the Mongols were fond of alcohol, and the Persian silk industry benefited from close contact with a Mongol-ruled China. In general, though, even more so than in China, Mongol rule in Persia represented "disaster on a grand and unparalleled scale."[19]

Nonetheless, the Mongols in Persia were themselves transformed far more than their counterparts in China. They made extensive use of the sophisticated Persian bureaucracy, leaving the greater part of government operations in Persian hands. During the reign of Ghazan (haz-ZAHN) (1295–1304), they made some efforts to repair the damage caused by earlier policies of ruthless exploitation by rebuilding damaged cities and repairing neglected irrigation works. Most important, the Mongols who conquered Persia became Muslims, following the lead of Ghazan, who converted to Islam in 1295. No such widespread conversion to the culture of the conquered occurred in China or in Christian Russia. Members of the court and Mongol elites learned at least some Persian, unlike most of their counterparts in China. A number of Mongols also turned to farming, abandoning their pastoral ways, while some married local people.

When the Mongol dynasty of Hulegu's descendants collapsed in the 1330s for lack of a suitable heir, the Mongols were not driven out of Persia as they had been from China. Rather, they and their Turkic allies simply disappeared, assimilated into Persian society. From a Persian point of view, the barbarians had been civilized, and Persians had successfully resisted cultural influence from their uncivilized conquerors. When the great Persian historian Rashid al-Din wrote his famous history of the Mongols, he apologized for providing information about women, generally unmentioned in Islamic writing, explaining that Mongols treated their women equally and included them in decisions of the court.[20] Now Persian rulers could return to their more patriarchal ways.

Khutulun, a Mongol Wrestler Princess

A Mongol woman riding with Chinggis Khan, as Khutulun rode with her father.

Born around 1260 into the extended family network of Chinggis Khan, Khutulun was the only girl among fourteen brothers.[21] Even among elite Mongol women, many of whom played important roles in public life, Khutulun was unique. Her father, Qaidu Khan, was the Mongol ruler of Central Asia and a bitter opponent of Khubilai Khan, the Mongol ruler of China who was trying to extend his control over Central Asia. A large and well-built young woman, Khutulun excelled in horse riding, archery, and wrestling, outperforming her brothers. Winning fame as a wrestler in public competitions, she soon joined her father on the battlefield, was awarded a medallion of office normally reserved for men alone, and gained a reputation for being blessed of the gods. According to Marco Polo, during battle Khutulun would often seize one of the enemy, "as deftly as a hawk pounces on a bird," and carry him off to her father.

It was when she became of marriageable age that trouble began. She turned down the possibility of marrying a cousin who governed Mongol Persia, for this woman of the steppes had no desire to live as a secluded urban wife. In fact, she declared that she would only marry someone who could defeat her in wrestling. Many suitors tried, wagering 10, 100, or in one case 1,000 horses that they could defeat her. All of them failed, and, in the process, Khutulun accumulated a very substantial herd of horses.

Khutulun's extraordinary public life and her unwillingness to marry provided an opening for her enemies. Rumors circulated that she refused to marry because she was engaged in an incestuous relationship with her father. To put an end to such stories, Khutulun finally agreed to wed one of her father's followers without any wrestling contest. Still, the decision was hers. As the Mongol chronicles put it, "She chose him herself for her husband."

Even after her marriage, Khutulun continued to campaign with Qaidu Khan, and together they protected the steppe lands of Central Asia from incorporation into Mongol-ruled China. In 1301, her father was wounded in battle and, shortly thereafter, died. Some accounts suggest that he tried to name Khutulun as khan in his place, but the resistance of her brothers nixed that plan. "You should mind your scissors and needles," declared her rivals. "What have you to do with kingship?" Khutulun herself supported one of her brothers as khan, while she remained at the head of the army. She died in 1306, though whether in battle or as the result of an assassination remains unclear.

In her public and military life and in her fierce independence about marriage, Khutulun reflected the relative freedom and influence of Mongol women, particularly of the elite class. In her preference for the open life of the steppes and in her resistance to the intrusion of Mongol-ruled China, she aligned with those who saw themselves as "true Mongols," in opposition to those who had come under the softening influence of neighboring Chinese or Persian civilizations. To this day, when Mongolian men wrestle, they wear a vest with an open chest in honor of Khutulun, ensuring that they are wrestling with other men rather than with a woman who might throw them to the ground.

Question: What does the life of Khutulun reveal about Mongol gender relationships?

Mongol Rulers and Their Women

The wives of Mongol rulers exercised considerable influence at court. This fourteenth-century painting shows Chinggis Khan's fourth son, Tului, the ruler of the Mongol heartland after his father's death, with his Christian wife Sorgaqtani. After her husband's early death from alcoholism, she maneuvered her children, including Khubilai Khan, into powerful positions and strongly encouraged them in the direction of religious toleration. (By Rashid al-Din, *Djamil el Tawarak*, 15th century Persian illumination/ Bibliothèque Nationale de France, Paris, France/akg-images)

Russia and the Mongols

When the Mongol military machine rolled over Russia between 1237 and 1240, it encountered a relatively new third-wave civilization, located on the far eastern fringe of Christendom (see Chapter 10). Whatever political unity this new civilization of Kievan Rus had earlier enjoyed was now gone, and various independent princes proved unable to unite even in the face of the Mongol onslaught. Although they had interacted extensively with pastoral people of the steppes north of the Black Sea, Mongol ferocity was stunning. City after city fell to Mongol forces, which were now armed with the catapults and battering rams adopted from Chinese or Muslim sources. The slaughter that sometimes followed was described in horrific terms by Russian chroniclers, although twentieth-century historians often regard such accounts as exaggerated. (See Working with Evidence, Source 11.4, page 494, for one such account.) From the survivors and the cities that surrendered early, laborers and skilled craftsmen were deported to other Mongol lands or sold into slavery. A number of Russian crafts were so depleted of their workers that they did not recover for a century or more.

If the violence of initial conquest bore similarities to the experiences of Persia, Russia's incorporation into the Mongol Empire was very different. To the Mongols, it was the Kipchak (KIP-chahk) Khanate, named after the Kipchak Turkic-speaking peoples north of the Caspian and Black seas, among whom the Mongols had settled. To the Russians, it was the "Khanate of the Golden Horde." By whatever name, the Mongols had conquered Russia, but they did not occupy it as they had China and Persia. Because there were no garrisoned cities, permanently sta-

AP® EXAM TIP

You might see questions on the AP® exam regarding interactions between Russians and Mongols.

Guided Reading Question

■ COMPARISON

What was distinctive about the Russian experience of Mongol rule?

tioned administrators, or Mongol settlers, the Russian experience of Mongol rule was quite different from that of conquered peoples elsewhere. From the Mongol point of view, Russia had little to offer. Its economy was not nearly so sophisticated or productive as that of more established civilizations; nor was it located on major international trade routes. It was simply not worth the expense of occupying. Furthermore, the availability of extensive steppe lands for pasturing their flocks north of the Black and Caspian seas meant that the Mongols could maintain their preferred pastoral way of life, while remaining in easy reach of Russian cities when the need arose to send further military expeditions. They could dominate and exploit Russia from the steppes.

And exploit they certainly did. Russian princes received appointment from the khan and were required to send substantial tribute to the Mongol capital at Sarai, located on the lower Volga River. A variety of additional taxes created a heavy burden, especially on the peasantry, while continuing border raids sent tens of thousands of Russians into slavery. The Mongol impact was highly uneven, however. Some Russian princes benefited considerably because they were able to manipulate their role as tribute collectors to grow wealthy. The Russian Orthodox Church likewise flourished under the Mongol policy of religious toleration, for it received exemption from many taxes. Nobles who participated in Mongol raids earned a share of the loot. Some cities, such as Kiev, resisted the Mongols and were devastated, while others collaborated and were left undamaged. Moscow in particular emerged as the primary collector of tribute for the Mongols, and its princes parlayed this position into a leading role as the nucleus of a renewed Russian state when Mongol domination receded in the fifteenth century.

The absence of direct Mongol rule had implications for the Mongols themselves, for they were far less influenced by or assimilated within Russian cultures than their counterparts in China and Persia had been. The Mongols in China had turned themselves into a Chinese dynasty, with the khan as a Chinese emperor. Some learned calligraphy, and a few came to appreciate Chinese poetry. In Persia, the Mongols had converted to Islam, with some becoming farmers. Not so in Russia. There "the Mongols of the Golden Horde were still spending their days in the saddle and their nights in tents."[22] They could dominate Russia from the adjacent steppes without in any way adopting Russian culture. Even though they remained culturally separate from Christian Russians, eventually the Mongols

Mongol Russia
This sixteenth-century painting depicts the Mongol burning of the Russian city of Ryazan in 1237. Similar destruction awaited many Russian towns that resisted the invaders. (Sovfoto/Universal Images Group/akg-images)

assimilated to the culture and the Islamic faith of the Kipchak people of the steppes, and in the process they lost their distinct identity and became Kipchaks.

Despite this domination from a distance, "the impact of the Mongols on Russia was, if anything, greater than on China and Iran [Persia]," according to a leading scholar.[23] Russian princes, who were more or less left alone if they paid the required tribute and taxes, found it useful to adopt the Mongols' weapons, diplomatic rituals, court practices, taxation system, and military draft. Mongol policies facilitated, although not intentionally, the rise of Moscow as the core of a new Russian state, and that state made good use of the famous Mongol mounted courier service, which Marco Polo had praised so highly. Mongol policies also strengthened the hold of the Russian Orthodox Church and enabled it to penetrate the rural areas more fully than before. Some Russians, seeking to explain their country's economic backwardness and political autocracy in modern times, have held the Mongols responsible for both conditions, though most historians consider such views vastly exaggerated.

Divisions among the Mongols, the disruptive influence of plague, and the growing strength of the Russian state, centered now on the city of Moscow, enabled the Russians to break the Mongols' hold by the end of the fifteenth century. With the earlier demise of Mongol rule in China and Persia, and now in Russia, the Mongols had retreated from their brief but spectacular incursion into the civilizations of outer Eurasia. Nonetheless, they continued to periodically threaten these civilizations for several centuries, until their homelands were absorbed into the expanding Russian and Chinese empires. But the Mongol moment in world history was over.

AP® EXAM TIP

Compare the decline of Mongol rule in Russia with the decline in China and Persia.

The Mongol Empire as a Eurasian Network

During the third-wave millennium, Chinese culture and Buddhism provided a measure of integration among the peoples of East Asia; Christianity did the same for Europe, while the realm of Islam connected most of the lands in between. But it was the Mongol Empire, during the thirteenth and fourteenth centuries, that brought all of these regions into a single interacting network. It was a unique moment in world history and an important step toward the global integration of the modern era.

Toward a World Economy

The Mongols themselves did not produce much of value for distant markets, nor were they active traders. Nonetheless, they consistently promoted international commerce, largely so that they could tax it and thus extract wealth from more developed civilizations. The Great Khan Ogodei, for example, often paid well over the asking price to attract merchants to his capital of Karakorum. The Mongols also provided financial backing for caravans, introduced standardized weights and measures, and gave tax breaks to merchants.

In providing a relatively secure environment for merchants making the long and arduous journey across Central Asia between Europe and China, the Mongol Empire brought the two ends of the Eurasian world into closer contact than ever before and launched a new phase in the history of the Silk Roads. Marco Polo was only the most famous of many European merchants, mostly from Italian cities, who made their way to China through the Mongol Empire. So many traders attempted the journey that guidebooks circulated with much useful advice about the trip. Merchants returned with tales of rich lands and prosperous commercial opportunities, but what they described were long-established trading networks of which Europeans had been largely ignorant.

The Mongol trading circuit was a central element in an even larger commercial network that linked much of the Afro-Eurasian world in the thirteenth century (see Map 11.2). Mongol-ruled China was the fulcrum of this vast system, connecting the overland route through the Mongol Empire with the oceanic routes through the South China Sea and Indian Ocean.

Guided Reading Question

■ CONNECTION

What kinds of cross-cultural interactions did the Mongol Empire generate?

AP® EXAM TIP

The features and extent of the political, economic, and cultural conditions established by the Mongols are "must know" material for the AP® exam.

Diplomacy on a Eurasian Scale

Not only did the Mongol Empire facilitate long-distance commerce, but it also prompted diplomatic relationships from one end of Eurasia to the other. As their invasion of Russia spilled over into Eastern Europe, Mongol armies destroyed Polish, German, and Hungarian forces in 1241–1242 and seemed poised to march on Central and Western Europe. But the death of the Great Khan Ogodei required Mongol leaders to return to Mongolia, and Western Europe lacked adequate pasture for Mongol herds. Thus Western Europe was spared the trauma of conquest, but fearing the possible return of the Mongols, both the pope and European rulers dispatched delegations to the Mongol capital, mostly led by Franciscan friars. They hoped to learn something about Mongol intentions, to secure Mongol aid in the Christian crusade against Islam, and, if possible, to convert Mongols to Christianity.

These efforts were largely in vain, for no alliance or widespread conversion occurred. In fact, one of these missions came back with a letter for the pope from the Great Khan Guyuk, demanding that Europeans submit to him. "But if you should not believe our letters and the command of God nor hearken to our counsel," he warned, "then we shall know for certain that you wish to have war. After that we do not know what will happen."[24] Perhaps the most important outcome of these diplomatic probings was the useful information about lands to the east that European missions brought back. Those reports contributed to a dawning European awareness of a wider world, and they have certainly provided later historians with much useful information about the Mongols. Somewhat later, in 1287, the il-khanate of Persia sought an alliance with European powers to take Jerusalem and crush the forces of Islam, but the Persian Mongols' conversion to Islam soon put an end to any such anti-Muslim coalition.

Map 11.2   Trade and Disease in the Fourteenth Century

The Mongol Empire played a major role in the commercial integration of the Eurasian world as well as in the spread of the plague across this vast area.

Within the Mongol Empire itself, close relationships developed between the courts of Persia and China. They regularly exchanged ambassadors, shared intelligence information, fostered trade between their regions, and sent skilled workers back and forth. Thus political authorities all across Eurasia engaged in diplomatic relationships with one another to an unprecedented degree.

Cultural Exchange in the Mongol Realm

Accompanying these transcontinental economic and political relationships was a substantial exchange of peoples and cultures. Mongol policy forcibly transferred many thousands of skilled craftsmen and educated people from their homelands to distant parts of the empire, while the Mongols' religious tolerance and support of merchants drew missionaries and traders from afar. The Mongol capital at Karakorum was a cosmopolitan city with places of worship for Buddhists, Daoists, Muslims, and Christians. Chinggis Khan and several other Mongol rulers married Christian women. Actors and musicians from China, wrestlers from Persia, and a jester from Byzantium provided entertainment for the Mongol court. Persian and Arab doctors and administrators were sent to China, while Chinese physicians and engineers found their skills in demand in the Islamic world.

> **AP® EXAM TIP**
>
> Remember that the Mongols practiced religious toleration among their conquered subjects.

This movement of people facilitated the exchange of ideas and techniques, a process actively encouraged by Mongol authorities. A great deal of Chinese technology and artistic conventions—such as painting, printing, gunpowder weapons, compass navigation, high-temperature furnaces, and medical techniques—flowed westward. Acupuncture, for example, was poorly received in the Middle East because it required too much bodily contact for Muslim taste, but Chinese techniques for diagnosing illness by taking the pulse of patients proved quite popular, as they involved minimal body contact. Muslim astronomers brought their skills and knowledge to China because Mongol authorities wanted "second opinions on the reading of heavenly signs and portents" and assistance in constructing the accurate calendars needed for ritual purposes.[25] Plants and crops likewise circulated within the Mongol domain. Lemons and carrots from the Middle East found a welcome reception in China, while the Persian il-khan Ghazan sent envoys to India, China, and elsewhere to seek "seeds of things which are unique in that land."[26]

Europeans arguably gained more than most from these exchanges, for they had long been cut off from the fruitful interchange with Asia, and in comparison to the Islamic and Chinese worlds, they were less technologically developed. Now they could reap the benefits of new technology, new crops, and new knowledge of a wider world. And almost alone among the peoples of Eurasia, they could do so without having suffered the devastating consequences of Mongol conquest. In these circumstances, some historians have argued, lay the roots of Europe's remarkable rise to global prominence in the centuries that followed.

> **AP® EXAM TIP**
>
> Pay attention to this discussion of the many important effects of exchanges between the Mongols and their subjects.

The Plague: An Afro-Eurasian Pandemic

Any benefits derived from participation in Mongol networks of communication and exchange must be measured alongside the hemispheric catastrophe known as the "plague" or the "pestilence" and later called the Black Death. Originating most likely in China, the bacteria responsible for the disease, known as *Yersinia pestis*, spread across the trade routes of the vast Mongol Empire in the early fourteenth century (see Map 11.2, page 482). Carried by rodents and transmitted by fleas to humans, the plague erupted initially in 1331 in northeastern China and had reached the Middle East and Western Europe by 1347. One lurid but quite uncertain story has the Mongols using catapults to hurl corpses infected with the plague into the Genoese city of Caffa in the Crimea. In 1409, the plague reached East Africa, probably by way of the famous Chinese maritime expeditions that encompassed the Indian Ocean basin.

Guided Reading Question

■ CHANGE

Disease changes societies. How might this argument apply to the plague?

AP® EXAM TIP

Most Westerners think of the bubonic plague and its effects on Europe, but here you see that it spread much farther.

The disease itself was associated with swelling of the lymph nodes, most often in the groin; terrible headaches; high fever; and internal bleeding just below the skin. Infected people generally died within a few days. In the densely populated civilizations of China, the Islamic world, and Europe as well as in the steppe lands of the pastoralists, the plague claimed enormous numbers of human victims, causing a sharp contraction in Eurasian population for a century or more. Chroniclers reported rates of death that ranged from 50 to 90 percent of the affected population, depending on the time and place. A recent study suggests that about half of Europe's people perished during the initial outbreak of 1348–1350.[27] A fifteenth-century Egyptian historian wrote that within a month of the plague's arrival in 1349, "Cairo had become an abandoned desert. . . . Everywhere one heard lamentations and one could not pass by any house without being overwhelmed by the howling."[28] The Middle East generally had lost perhaps one-third of its population by the early fifteenth century.[29] The intense first wave of the plague was followed by periodic visitations over the next several centuries. However, other regions of the Eastern Hemisphere, especially India and sub-Saharan Africa, were much less affected, so the plague's impact varied significantly.

In those places where it struck hardest, the plague left thoughtful people grasping for language with which to describe a horror of such unprecedented dimensions. One Italian man, who had buried all five of his children with his own hands, wrote in 1348 that "so many have died that everyone believes it is the end of the world."[30] Another Italian, the Renaissance scholar Francesco Petrarch, was equally stunned by the impact of the Black Death; he wrote to a friend in 1349:

> When at any time has such a thing been seen or spoken of? Has what happened in these years ever been read about: empty houses, derelict cities, ruined estates, fields strewn with cadavers, a horrible and vast solitude encompassing the whole world? Consult historians, they are silent; ask physicians, they are stupefied; seek the answers from philosophers, they shrug their shoulders, furrow their brows, and with fingers pressed against their lips, bid you be silent. Will posterity believe these things, when we who have seen it can scarcely believe it?[31]

In the Islamic world, the famous historian Ibn Khaldun, who had lost both of his parents to the plague, also wrote about it in apocalyptic terms:

AP® EXAM TIP

You need to know the long-term demographic (population), economic, and political effects of the bubonic plague on Afro-Eurasia.

> Civilization in both the East and the West was visited by a destructive plague which devastated nations and caused populations to vanish. It swallowed up many of the good things of civilization and wiped them out. . . . It was as if the voice of existence had called out for oblivion and restriction, and the world responded to its call.[32]

Beyond its immediate devastation, the Black Death worked longer-term social changes in Europe, the region where the plague's impact has been most thoroughly studied. Labor shortages following the initial outburst provoked sharp conflict between scarce workers, who sought higher wages or better conditions, and the rich, who resisted those demands. A series of peasant revolts in the fourteenth century reflected this tension, which also undermined the practice of serfdom. That labor shortage also may have fostered a greater interest in technological innovation and created, at least for a time, more employment opportunities for women. Thus a resilient European civilization survived a cataclysm that had the power to destroy it. In a strange way, that catastrophe may have actually fostered its future growth.

Whatever its impact in particular places, the plague also had larger consequences. Ironically, that human disaster, born of the Mongol network, was a primary reason for the demise of that network in the fourteenth and fifteenth centuries. Population contracted, cities declined, and the volume of trade diminished all across the Mongol world. By 1350, the Mongol Empire itself was in disarray, and within a century the Mongols had lost control of Chinese, Persian, and Russian civilizations. The Central Asian trade route, so critical to the entire Afro-Eurasian world economy, largely closed.

This disruption of the Mongol-based land routes to the east, coupled with a desire to avoid Muslim intermediaries, provided incentives for Europeans to take to the sea in their continuing efforts to reach the riches of Asia. Their naval technology gave them military advantages on the seas, much as the Mongols' skill with the bow and their mobility on horseback gave these pastoralists a decisive edge in land battles. As Europeans penetrated Asian and Atlantic waters in the sixteenth century, they took on, in some ways, the role of the Mongols in organizing and fostering world trade and in creating a network of communication and exchange over an even larger area. Like the Mongols, Europeans were people on the periphery of the major established civilizations; they too were economically less developed in comparison to Chinese and Islamic civilizations. Both Mongols and Europeans were apt to forcibly plunder the wealthier civilizations they encountered, and European empire building in the Americas, like that of the Mongols in Eurasia, brought devastating disease and catastrophic population decline in its wake.[33] Europeans, of course, brought far more of their own culture and many more of their own people to the societies they conquered, as Christianity, European languages, settler societies, and Western science and technology took root within their empires. Although their imperial presence lasted far longer and operated on a much larger scale, European actions at the beginning of their global expansion bore some resemblance to those of their Mongol predecessors. They were, as one historian put it, "the Mongols of the seas."[34]

The Plague
This illustration depicts a European doctor visiting a patient with the plague. Notice that the doctor and others around the bedside cover their noses to prevent infection. During the Black Death, doctors were often criticized for refusing to treat dying patients, as they feared for their own lives.
(The Granger Collection, NYC—All rights reserved.)

AP® EXAM TIP

Take good notes on these causes of European exploration and review them when you reach Chapter 12.

Changing Images of Pastoral Peoples

Historians frequently change their minds, and long-term consensus on most important matters has been difficult to achieve. For example, until recently, pastoralists generally received bad press in history books. Normally they entered the story only when they were threatening or destroying established civilizations. In presenting a largely negative image of pastoral peoples, historians were reflecting the long-held attitudes of literate elites in the civilizations of Eurasia. Fearing and usually despising such peoples, educated observers in China, the Middle East, and Europe often described them as bloodthirsty savages or barbarians, bringing only chaos and destruction in their wake. Han Kuan, a Chinese scholar of the first century B.C.E., described the Xiongnu people as "abandoned by Heaven . . . in foodless desert wastes, without proper houses, clothed in animal hides, eating their meat uncooked and drinking blood."[35] To the Christian Saint Jerome (340–420 C.E.), the Huns "filled the whole earth with slaughter and panic alike as they flitted hither and thither on their swift horses."[36] Almost a thousand years later, the famous Arab historian Ibn Khaldun described pastoralists in a very similar fashion: "It is their nature to plunder whatever other people possess."[37]

Because pastoral peoples generally did not have written languages, the sources available to historians came from less-than-unbiased observers in adjacent agricultural civilizations. Furthermore, in the long-running conflict across the farming/pastoral frontier, agricultural civilizations ultimately triumphed. Over the centuries, some pastoralist or semi-agricultural peoples, such as the Germanic tribes of Europe and the Arabs, created new civilizations. Others, such as the Turkic and Mongol peoples, took over existing civilizations or were encompassed within established agrarian empires. By the early twentieth century, and in most places much earlier, pastoral peoples everywhere had lost their former independence and had often shed their pastoral life as well. Since "winners" usually write history, the negative views of pastoralists held by agrarian civilizations normally prevailed.

Reflecting more inclusive contemporary values, historians in recent decades have sought to present a more balanced picture of pastoralists' role in world history, emphasizing what they created as well as what they destroyed. These historians have highlighted the achievements of herding peoples, such as their adaptation to inhospitable environments; their technological innovations; their development of horse-, camel-, or cattle-based cultures; their role in fostering cross-cultural exchange; and their state-building efforts.

A less critical or judgmental posture toward the Mongols may also owe something to the "total wars" and genocides of the twentieth century, in which the mass slaughter of civilians became a strategy to induce enemy surrender. During the cold war, the United States and the Soviet Union were prepared, apparently, to obliterate each other's entire population with nuclear weapons in response to an attack. In light of this recent history, Mongol massacres may appear a little less unique. Historians living in the glass houses of contemporary societies are perhaps more reluctant to cast stones at the Mongols. In understanding the Mongols, as in so much else, historians are shaped by the times and circumstances of their own lives as much as by "what really happened" in the past.

Chapter Review

What's the Significance?

pastoralism, 458–65

Modun, 463

Xiongnu, 463

Turks, 463–65

Almoravid Empire, 465

Temujin/Chinggis Khan, 467–69

the Mongol world war, 469–72

Yuan dynasty China, 473–75

Khubilai Khan, 474–75

Hulegu, 475

Khutulun, 477

Kipchak Khanate/Golden Horde, 478–80

Black Death/plague, 483–85

Big Picture Questions

1. What accounts for the often-negative attitudes of settled societies toward the pastoral peoples living on their borders?

2. Why have historians often neglected pastoral peoples' role in world history? How would you assess the perspective of this chapter toward the Mongols? Does the chapter strike you as negative and critical of the Mongols, as bending over backward to portray them in a positive light, or as a balanced presentation?

3. In what different ways did Mongol rule affect the Islamic world, Russia, China, and Europe? In what respects did it foster Eurasian integration?

4. Why did the Mongol Empire last only a relatively short time?

5. **Looking Back:** In what ways did the Mongol Empire resemble previous empires (Arab, Roman, Chinese, or the Greek empire of Alexander, for example), and in what ways did it differ from them?

Next Steps: For Further Study

John Aberth, *The First Horseman: Disease in Human History* (2007). A global study of the history of disease, with a fine chapter on the Black Death.

Thomas Allsen, *Culture and Conquest in Mongol Eurasia* (2001). A history of cultural exchange within the Mongol realm, particularly between China and the Islamic world.

Thomas J. Barfield, *The Nomadic Alternative* (1993). An anthropological and historical survey of pastoral peoples on a global basis.

Carter Finley, *The Turks in World History* (2005). The evolution of Turkic-speaking people, from their nomadic origins to the twentieth century.

Jack Weatherford, *Genghis Khan and the Making of the Modern World* (2004). A lively, well-written, and balanced account of the world the Mongols made and the legacy they left for the future.

"Horseback Riding and Bronze Age Pastoralism in the Eurasian Steppes," http://www.youtube.com/watch?v=QapUGZ0ObjA. An illustrated lecture on the origins of pastoralism by David W. Anthony, a prominent scholar.

"The Mongols in World History," http://afe.easia.columbia.edu/mongols. A wonderful resource on the Mongols generally, with a particular focus on their impact in China.

WORKING WITH EVIDENCE

Perspectives on the Mongols

How did the Mongols understand themselves and the enormous empire they had created? How did the peoples who were forcibly incorporated within that empire or threatened by it view the Mongols? What did outsiders who encountered the Mongols notice about their ways of living? In studying the Mongol phenomenon, historians use documents that reflect both the Mongols' perception of themselves and the perspectives of others. The first two documents derive from Mongol sources, while the final three represent views from Persian, Russian, and European observers.

Sorting through these various perceptions of the Mongols raises questions about the kinds of understandings—or misunderstandings—that arise as culturally different peoples meet, especially under conditions of conquest. These documents also require reflection on the relative usefulness of sources that come from the Mongols themselves as well as those that derive from the victims of Mongol aggression.

Source 11.1
Mongol History from a Mongol Source

The major literary work to emerge from the Mongols themselves, widely known as *The Secret History of the Mongols*, was written a decade or two after the death in 1227 of Chinggis Khan. The unknown author of this work was clearly a contemporary of the Great Khan and likely a member of the royal household. The first selection discusses the Mongol practice of *anda*, a very close relationship between two unrelated men. The anda relationship of Temujin, the future Chinggis Khan, and his friend Jamugha was important in Temujin's rise to power, although they later broke with one another. The second selection from the *Secret History* describes the process by which Temujin was elevated to the rank of Chinggis Khan, the ruler of a united Mongol nation, while the third recounts the reflections of Ogodei, Chinggis Khan's son and successor, probably toward the end of his reign, which lasted from 1229 to 1241.

■ How would you describe the anda relationship?

■ What does the *Secret History* suggest about the nature of political authority and political relationships among the Mongols?

■ What did Ogodei regard as his greatest achievements and his most notable mistakes?

■ What evidence do these selections from the *Secret History* provide that the author was an insider?

The Secret History of the Mongols
ca. 1240

Anda: Temujin and Jamugha

Temujin and Jamugha pitched their tents in the Khorkonagh Valley. With their people united in one great camp, the two leaders decided they should renew their friendship, their pledge of anda. They remembered when they'd first made that pledge, and said, "We should love one another again."

That first time they'd met Temujin was eleven years old. . . . So Temujin and Jamugha said to each other: "We've heard the elders say, 'When two men become anda their lives become one, one will never desert the other and will always defend him.' This is the way we'll act from now on. We'll renew our old pledge and love each other forever."

Temujin took the golden belt he'd received in the spoils from Toghtoga's defeat and placed it around Anda Jamugha's waist. Then he led out the Merkid chief's warhorse, a light yellow mare with black mane and tail, and gave it to Anda Jamugha to ride. Jamugha took the golden belt he'd received in the spoils from Dayir Usun's defeat and placed it around the waist of Anda Temujin. Then he led out the whitish tan warhorse of Dayir Usun and had Anda Temujin ride on it.

Before the cliffs of Khuldaghar in the Khorkonagh Valley, beneath the Great Branching Tree of the Mongol, they pledged their friendship and promised to love one another. They held a feast on the spot and there was great celebration. Temujin and Jamugha spent that night alone, sharing one blanket to cover them both. Temujin and Jamugha loved each other for one year, and when half of the second year had passed they agreed it was time to move camp. . . .

Temujin Becomes Chinggis Khan

Then they moved the whole camp to the shores of Blue Lake in the Gurelgu Mountains. Altan, Khuchar, and Sacha Beki conferred with each other there, and then said to Temujin: "We want you to be khan. Temujin, if you'll be our khan we'll search through the spoils for the beautiful women and virgins, for the great palace tents, . . . for the finest geldings and mares. We'll gather all these and bring them to you. When we go off to hunt for wild game, we'll go out first to drive them together for you to kill. We'll drive the wild animals of the steppe together so that their bellies are touching. We'll drive the wild game of the mountains together so that they stand leg to leg. If we disobey your command during battle, take away our possessions, our children, and wives. Leave us behind in the dust, cutting off our heads where we stand and letting them fall to the ground. If we disobey your counsel in peacetime, take away our tents and our goods, our wives, and our children. Leave us behind when you move, abandoned in the desert without a protector." Having given their word, having taken this oath, they proclaimed Temujin khan of the Mongol and gave him the name Chingis Khan. . . .

Reflections of Ogodei

Then Ogodei Khan spoke these words: "Since my father the Khan passed away and I came to sit on his great throne, what have I done? I went to war against the people of Cathay [China] and I destroyed them. For my second accomplishment I established a network of post stations so that my words are carried across the land with great speed. Another of my accomplishments has been to have my commanders dig wells in the desert so that there would be pasture and water for the people there. Lastly I placed spies and agents among all the people of the cities. In all directions I've brought peace to the Nation and the people. . . .

"Since the time of my father the Khan, I added these four accomplishments to all that he did. But also since my father passed away and I came to sit on his great throne with the burden of all the numerous people on my shoulders, I allowed myself to be conquered by wine. This was one of my mistakes. Another of my mistakes was to listen to a woman with no principles and because of her take away the daughters who belonged to my Uncle Odchigin. Even though I'm the Khan, the Lord of the Nation, I have no right to go against established principle, so this was my mistake.

"Another mistake was to secretly harm Dok-holkhu. If you ask, 'Why was this wrong?' I would say that to secretly harm Dokholkhu, a man who had served his proper lord, my father the Khan, performing heroic deeds in his service, was a mistake. Now that I've done this, who'll perform heroic deeds in my service? Then my last mistake was to desire too much, to say to myself, 'I'm afraid that all the wild game born under Heaven will run off toward the land of my brothers.' So I ordered earthen walls to be built to keep the wild game from running away, but even as these walls were being built I heard my brothers speaking badly of me. I admit that I was wrong to do this. Since the time of my father the Khan I've added four accomplishments to all that he'd done and I've done four things which I admit were wrong."

Source: Paul Kahn, *The Secret History of the Mongols: The Origin of Chingis Khan* (San Francisco: North Point Press, 1984), 44–45, 48–49, 192–93.

Source 11.2
Chinggis Khan and Changchun

Source 11.2 begins with a remarkable letter that Chinggis Khan sent to the seventy-two-year-old Chinese Daoist master Changchun in 1219, requesting a personal meeting with the teacher.

- Why did Chinggis Khan seek a meeting with Changchun? Do you think he was satisfied with the outcome of that meeting?

- How does Chinggis Khan define his life's work? What is his image of himself?

- How would you describe the tone of Chinggis Khan's letter to Changchun? What does the letter suggest about Mongol attitudes toward the belief systems of conquered peoples?

- How do Sources 11.1 and 11.2 help explain the success of the Mongols' empire-building efforts?

- What core Mongol values do these documents suggest?

Chinggis Khan

Letter to Changchun

1219

Heaven has abandoned China owing to its haughtiness and extravagant luxury. But I, living in the northern wilderness, have not inordinate passions. I hate luxury and exercise moderation. I have only one coat and one food. I eat the same food and am dressed in the same tatters as my humble herdsmen. I consider the people my children, and take an interest in talented men as if they were my brothers. . . . At military exercises I am always in the front, and in time of battle am never behind. In the space of seven years I have succeeded in accomplishing a great work, and uniting the whole world into one empire. I have not myself distinguished qualities. But the government of the [Chinese] is inconstant, and therefore Heaven assists me to obtain the throne. . . . All together have acknowledged my supremacy. It seems to me that since the remote time . . . such an empire has not been seen. . . . Since the time I came to the throne I have always taken to heart the ruling of my people; but I could not find worthy men to occupy [high offices]. . . . With respect to these circumstances I inquired, and heard that thou, master, hast penetrated the truth. . . . For a long time thou hast lived in the caverns of the rocks, and hast retired from the world; but to thee the people who have acquired sanctity repair, like clouds on the paths of the immortals, in innumerable multitudes. . . . But what shall I do? We are separated by mountains and plains of great extent, and I cannot meet thee. I can only descend from the throne and stand by the side. I have fasted and washed. I have ordered my adjutant . . . to prepare an escort and a cart for thee. Do not be afraid of the thousand *li* [a great distance]. I implore thee to move thy sainted steps. Do not think of the extent of the sandy desert. Commiserate the people in the present situation of affairs, or have pity upon me, and communicate to me the means of preserving life. I shall serve thee myself. I hope that at least thou wilt leave me a trifle of thy wisdom. Say only one word to me and I shall be happy.

[*After a long journey, Changchun arrived at the camp of Chinggis Khan, located in what is now Afghanistan. One of Changchun's disciples recorded what happened in their initial meeting.*]

[T]he master presented himself to the Emperor, who greeted him, and said: "You were invited by the other courts (the Kin and the Sung), but you refused. Now you have come to see me, having traversed a road of ten thousand li. I am much gratified." The master answered: "The wild man of the mountains came to see the emperor by order of your majesty; it was the will of Heaven." Chinghiz invited him to sit down, and ordered a meal to be set before him. After this he asked: "Sainted man, you have come from a great distance. Have you a medicine of immortality?" The master replied: "There are means for preserving life, but no medicines for immortality." Chinghiz lauded him for his sincerity and candour. By imperial order two tents were pitched for the master east of the emperor's tents. The emperor gave him the title of *shen sien* (the immortal).

Source: E. Bretschneider, *Mediaeval Researches from Eastern Asiatic Sources,* vol. 1 (London, 1875), 37–39, 86.

Source 11.3
The Conquest of Bukhara:
A Persian View

While Chinggis Khan was hosting Changchun, he was also personally leading Mongol forces into the lands of the Persian Empire, then ruled by the Turkic Khwarazmian dynasty. The thirteenth-century Persian historian Juvaini, himself a high official in the Mongol government of his homeland, wrote an account of the creation of the Mongol Empire titled *The History of the World Conqueror*. This excerpt from that work describes the conquest of the city of Bukhara, a major commercial and intellectual center of the Persian Islamic world.

■ What can we learn about the policies and strategies of the Mongols from Juvaini's account? What parts of this account seem most reliable?

■ How might you describe Juvaini's posture toward the Mongols? Keep in mind that he was working for them.

■ What aspects of Mongol behavior would be most offensive to Muslims?

■ How did Chinggis Khan justify his conquest of Bukhara?

JUVAINI
The History of the World Conqueror
1219

[Chinggis Khan's] troops were more numerous than ants or locusts, being in their multitude beyond estimation or computation. Detachment after detachment arrived, each like a billowing sea, and encamped round about the town. At sunrise twenty thousand men from the Sultan's [Muslim ruler of Bukhara] auxiliary army issued forth from the citadel together with most of the inhabitants. . . . When these forces reached the banks of the Oxus, the patrols and advance parties of the Mongol army fell upon them and left no trace of them.

On the following day when from the reflection of the sun that plain seemed to be a tray filled with blood, the people of Bukhara opened their gates and closed the door of strife and battle. The imams and notables came on a deputation to Chingis-

Khan, who entered to inspect the town and citadel. He rode into the Juma Mosque. . . . Chingis-Khan asked those present whether this was the palace of the Sultan; they replied it was the house of God. Then he too got down from his horse, and mounting two or three steps of the pulpit he exclaimed: "The countryside is empty of fodder, fill our horses' bellies." Whereupon they opened all the magazines in the town and began carrying off the grain. And they brought the cases in which the Qurans were kept out in the courtyard of the mosque, where they cast the Qurans right and left and turned the cases into mangers for their horses. After which they circulated cups and sent for the singing-girls of the town to sing and dance for them, while the Mongols raised their voices to the tunes of their own songs. Meanwhile, the imams, shaikhs, sayyids, doctors and scholars of the age kept watch over their horses in the stables. . . . After an hour or two Chingis-Khan arose to return to his camp. . . . [T]he leaves of the Quran were trampled beneath the dirt beneath their own feet and their horses' hooves.

When Chingis-Khan left the town he went to the festival muhalla and mounted the pulpit; and, the people having assembled, he asked which were wealthy amongst them. Two hundred and eighty persons were designated (a hundred and ninety of them being natives of the town and the rest strangers, i.e., ninety merchants from various places) and were led before him. He then began a speech, in which, after describing the resistance and treachery of the Sultan, he addressed them as follows: "O People! know that you have committed great sins, and that the great ones among you have committed these sins. If you ask me what proof I have for these words, I say it is because I am the punishment of God. If you had not committed these great sins, God would not have sent a punishment like me upon you." When he had finished speaking in this strain, he continued his discourse with words of admonition, saying, "There is no need to declare your property that is on the face of the earth; tell me of that which is in the belly of the earth." . . . [A]lthough not subjecting them to disgrace or humiliation, they began to exact money from these men; and when they delivered it up they did not torment them by excessive punishment or demanding what was beyond their power to pay.

Chingis-Khan had given orders for the Sultan's troops to be driven out of the interior of the town and the citadel. . . . [H]e now gave orders for all quarters of the town to be set on fire; and since the houses were built entirely out of wood, within several days the greater part of the town had been consumed, with the exception of the Juma mosque and some of the palaces, which were built with baked bricks. Then the people of Bukhara were driven against the citadel. And on either side the furnace of battle was heated. On the outside, mangonels [catapults] were erected, bows bent, and stones and arrows discharged, and, on the inside, . . . pots of naphtha [a flammable liquid] were set in motion. It was like a red hot furnace. . . . For days they fought in this manner; the garrison made sallies against the besiegers. . . . But finally they were reduced to the last extremity; resistance was no longer in their power; and they stood excused before God and man. The moat had been filled with animate and inanimate and raised up with levies and Bukharans; . . . their khans, leaders and notables, who were the chief men of the age and the favorites of the Sultan who in their glory would set their feet on the head of Heaven, now became captives of abasement and were drowned in the sea of annihilation. . . . Of the Qanqli [Turkic defenders of the city] no male was spared who stood higher than the butt of a whip and more than thirty thousand were counted amongst the slain; whilst their small children, the children of their nobles and their womenfolk, slender as the cypress, were sold to slavery.

When the town and the citadel had been purged of rebels and the walls and outworks levelled with the dust, the inhabitants of the town, men and women, ugly and beautiful, were driven out onto the field of the *musalla* [an open space outside of a mosque]. Chingis-Khan spared their lives, but the youths and full-grown men that were fit for such service were pressed into a levy for the attack on Samarqand and Dabusiya.

Source: Juvaini, *The History of the World Conqueror*, translated by John Boyle (Manchester: Manchester University Press, 1958), 103–6.

Source 11.4

A Russian View of the Mongols

In 1238, some nineteen years after their initial assault on Persia, Mongol forces began their conquest of Russia. Source 11.4 offers a Russian commentary on those events, drawn from *The Chronicle of Novgorod*, one of the major sources for the history of early Russia.

■ How did the Russian writer of the *Chronicle* account for what he saw as the disaster of the Mongol invasion?

■ Can you infer from the document any additional reasons for the Mongol success?

■ Beyond the conquest itself, what other aspects of Mongol rule offended the Russians?

■ To what extent was the Mongol conquest of Russia also a clash of cultures?

■ What similarities and differences do you notice between this account of Mongol conquest and that of Juvaini in Source 11.3?

The Chronicle of Novgorod
1238

That same year [1238] foreigners called Tartars [Mongols] came in countless numbers, like locusts, into the land of Ryazan, and on first coming they halted at the river Nukhla, and took it, and halted in camp there. And thence they sent their emissaries to the *Knyazes* [princes] of Ryazan, a sorceress and two men with her, demanding from them one-tenth of everything: of men and *Knyazes* and horses—of everything one-tenth. And the *Knyazes* of Ryazan . . . without letting them into their towns, went out to meet them to Voronazh. And the *Knyazes* said to them: "Only when none of us remain then all will be yours." . . . And the *Knyazes* of Ryazan sent to Yuri of Volodimir asking for help, or himself to come. But Yuri neither went himself nor listened to the request of the *Knyazes* of Ryazan, but he himself wished to make war separately. But it was too late to oppose the wrath of God. . . . Thus also did God before these men take from us our strength and put into us perplexity and thunder and dread and trembling for our sins. And then the pagan foreigners surrounded Ryazan and fenced it in with a stockade. . . . And the Tartars took the town on December 21, and they had advanced against it on the 16th of the same month. They likewise killed the *Knyaz* and *Knyaginya*, and men, women, and children, monks, nuns and priests, some by fire, some by the sword, and violated nuns, priests' wives, good women and girls in the presence of their mothers and sisters. But God saved the Bishop, for he had departed the same moment when the troops invested the town. And who, brethren, would not lament over this, among those of us left alive when they suffered this bitter and violent death? And we, indeed, having seen it, were terrified and wept with sighing day and night over our sins, while we sigh every day and night, taking thought for our possessions and for the hatred of brothers.

The pagan and godless Tartars, then, having taken Ryazan, went to Volodimir. . . . And when the lawless ones had already come near and set up battering rams, and took the town and fired it on Friday . . . , the *Knyaz* and *Knyaginya* and *Vladyka*, seeing that the town was on fire and that the people were already perishing, some by fire and others by the sword, took refuge in the Church of the Holy Mother of God and shut themselves in the Sacristy. The pagans breaking down the doors, piled up wood and set fire to the sacred church; and slew all, thus they perished, giving up their souls to God. . . . And Rostov and Suzhdal went each its own way. And the accursed ones having come thence took Moscow, Pereyaslavi, Yurev, Dmitrov, *Volok*, and Tver; there also they killed the son of Yaroslav. And thence the lawless ones came and invested Torzhok on the festival of the first Sunday in Lent. They fenced it all round with a fence as they had taken other towns, and here the accursed ones fought with battering rams for two weeks. And the people in the town were exhausted and from Novgorod there was no help for them; but already every man began to be in perplexity and terror. And so the pagans took the town, and slew all from the male sex even to the female, all the priests and the monks, and all stripped and reviled gave up their souls to the Lord in a bitter and a wretched death, on March 5 . . . Wednesday in Easter week.

Source: Robert Mitchell and Nevill Forbes, trans., *The Chronicle of Novgorod, 1016–1471* (New York: AMS Press, 1970; repr. from the edition of 1914, London), 81–83, 88.

Source 11.5
Mongol Women through European Eyes

Source 11.5 provides some insight into the roles of Mongol women and men through the eyes of a European observer, William of Rubruck (1220–1293). A Flemish Franciscan friar, William was one of several emissaries sent to the Mongol court by the pope and the king of France. The Mongols' invasion of Russia and their incursions into Central Europe looked ominous to many European leaders. They hoped that these diplomatic missions might lead to the conversion of the Mongols to Christianity, or perhaps to an alliance with the Mongols against Islam, or at least to some useful intelligence about Mongol intentions. While no agreements with the Mongols came from these missions, William of Rubruck left a detailed account of Mongol life in the mid-thirteenth century, which included observations about the domestic roles of men and women.

■ How does William of Rubruck portray the lives of Mongol women? What was the class background of the Mongol women he describes?

■ What do you think he would have found most upsetting about the position of women in Mongol society?

■ Based on this account, how might you compare the life of Mongol women to that of women in more established civilizations, such as China, Europe, or the Islamic world?

WILLIAM OF RUBRUCK
Journey to the Land of the Mongols
ca. 1255

The matrons (married women) make for themselves most beautiful (luggage) carts. . . . A single rich Mo'al or Tartar (Mongol) has quite one hundred or two hundred such carts with coffers. Baatu [grandson of Chinggis Khan] has twenty-six wives, each of whom has a large dwelling, exclusive of the other little ones which they set up after the big one, and which are like closets, in which the sewing girls live, and to each of these (large) dwellings are attached quite two hundred carts. And when they set up their houses, the first wife places her dwelling on the extreme west side, and after her the others according to their rank, so that the last wife will be in the extreme east; and there will be the distance of a stone's throw between the yurt of one wife and that of another. The *ordu* [residence] of a rich Mo'al seems like a large town, though there will be very few men in it.

When they have fixed their dwelling, the door turned to the south, they set up the couch of the master on the north side. The side for the women is always the east side . . . on the left of the house of the master, he sitting on his couch his face turned to the south. The side for the men is the west side . . . on the right. Men coming into the house would never hang up their bows on the side of the woman.

It is the duty of the women to drive the carts, get the dwellings on and off them, milk the cows, make butter and *gruit* [sour curd], and to dress and sew skins, which they do with a thread made of tendons. They divide the tendons into fine shreds, and then twist them into one long thread. They also sew the boots, the socks, and the clothing. They never wash clothes, for they say that God would be angered, and that it would thunder if they hung them up to dry. They will even beat those they find washing [their clothes]. Thunder they fear extraordinarily; and when it thunders they will turn out of their dwellings all strangers, wrap themselves in black felt, and thus hide themselves till it has passed away. Furthermore, they never wash their bowls, but when the meat is cooked they rinse out the dish in which they are about to put it with some of the boiling broth from the kettle, which they pour back into it. They [the women] also make the felt and cover the houses.

The men make bows and arrows, manufacture stirrups and bits, make saddles, do the carpentering on their dwellings and the carts; they take care of the horses, milk the mares, churn the *cosmos* or mare's milk, make the skins in which it is put; they also look after the camels and load them. Both sexes look after the sheep and goats, sometimes the men, other times the women, milking them.

They dress skins with a thick mixture of sour ewe's milk and salt. When they want to wash their hands or head, they fill their mouths with water, which they let trickle onto their hands, and in this way they also wet their hair and wash their heads.

As to their marriages, you must know that no one among them has a wife unless he buys her; so it sometimes happens that girls are well past marriageable age before they marry, for their parents always keep them until they sell them. . . . Among them no widow marries, for the following reason: they believe that all who serve them in this life shall serve them in the next, so as regards a widow they believe that she will always return to her first husband after death. Hence this shameful custom prevails among them, that sometimes a son takes to wife all his father's wives, except his own mother; for the *ordu* of the father and mother always belongs to the youngest son, so it is he who must provide for all his father's wives . . . and if he wishes it, he uses them as wives, for he esteems not himself injured if they return to his father after death. When then anyone has made a bargain with another to take his daughter, the father of the girl gives a feast, and the girl flees to her relatives and hides there. Then the father says: "Here, my daughter is yours: take her wheresoever you find her." Then he searches for her with his friends till he finds her, and he must take her by force and carry her off with a semblance of violence to his house.

Source: *The Journey of William of Rubruck* . . . , translated from the Latin and edited, with an introductory notice, by William Woodville Rockhill (London: Hakluyt Society, 1900), chaps. 2, 7.

DOING HISTORY

Perspectives on the Mongols

1. **Assessing sources:** What are the strengths and limitations of these documents for understanding the Mongols? Taking the positions of their authors into account, what exaggerations, biases, or misunderstandings can you identify in these sources? What information seems credible, and what should be viewed more skeptically?

2. **Characterizing the Mongols:** Based on these documents and on the text of Chapter 11, write an essay assessing the Mongol moment in world history. How might you counteract the view of many that the Mongols were simply destructive barbarians? How do your own values affect your understanding of the Mongol moment?

3. **Considering values and practice:** How would you describe the core values of Mongol culture? (Consider the leaders' goals, their attitudes toward conquered peoples, the duties of rulers, the views of political authority, and the role of women.) To what extent were these values put into practice in acquiring and ruling the Mongols' huge empire? And in what ways were these values undermined or eroded as that empire took shape?

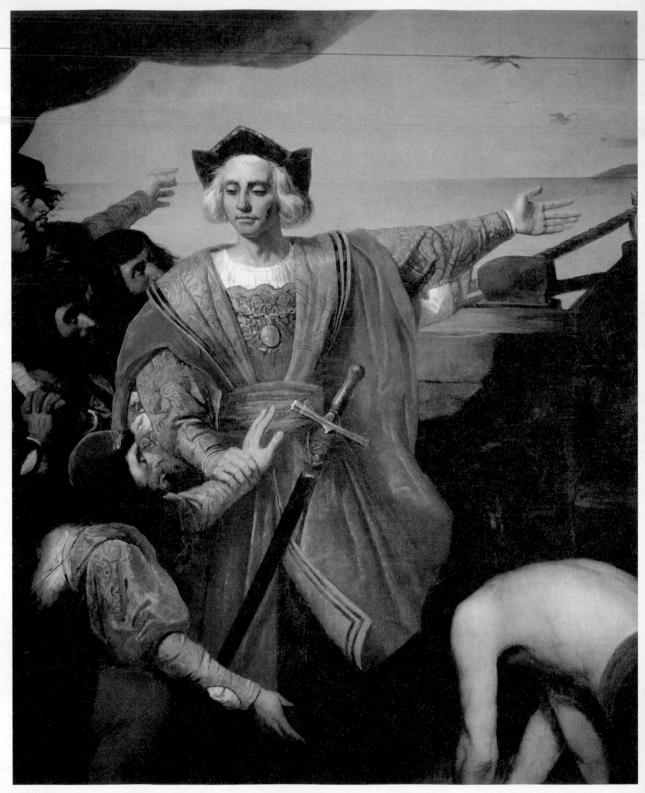

French painting, 19th century/Monastery of La Rabida, Huelva, Andalusia, Spain/Bridgeman Images

CHAPTER 12

The Worlds of the Fifteenth Century

"Columbus was a perpetrator of genocide . . . , a slave trader, a thief, a pirate, and most certainly not a hero. To celebrate Columbus is to congratulate the process and history of the invasion."[1] This was the view of Winona LaDuke, president of the Indigenous Women's Network, on the occasion in 1992 of the 500th anniversary of Columbus's arrival in the Americas. Much of the commentary surrounding the event echoed the same themes, citing the history of death, slavery, racism, and exploitation that followed in the wake of Columbus's first voyage to what was for him an altogether New World. A century earlier, in 1892, the tone of celebration had been very different. A presidential proclamation cited Columbus as a brave "pioneer of progress and enlightenment" and instructed Americans to "express honor to the discoverer and their appreciation of the great achievements of four completed centuries of American life." The century that followed witnessed the erosion of Western dominance in the world and the discrediting of racism and imperialism and, with it, the reputation of Columbus.

This sharp reversal of opinion about Columbus provides a reminder that the past is as unpredictable as the future. Few Americans in 1892 could have guessed that their daring hero could emerge so tarnished only a century later. And few people living in 1492 could have imagined the enormous global processes set in motion by the voyage of Columbus's three small ships — the Atlantic slave trade, the decimation of the native peoples of the Americas, the massive growth of world population, the Industrial Revolution, and the growing prominence of Europeans on the world stage. None of these developments were even remotely foreseeable in 1492.

The Meeting of Two Worlds This nineteenth-century painting shows Columbus on his first voyage to the New World. He is reassuring his anxious sailors by pointing to the first sight of land. In light of its long-range consequences, this voyage represents a major turning point in world history.

Thus, in historical hindsight, that voyage of Columbus was arguably the single most important event of the fifteenth century. But it was not the only significant marker of that century. A Central Asian Turkic warrior named Timur launched the last major pastoral invasion of adjacent civilizations. Russia emerged from two centuries of Mongol rule to begin a huge empire-building project across northern Asia. A new European civilization was taking shape in the Renaissance. In 1405, an enormous Chinese fleet, dwarfing that of Columbus, set out across the entire Indian Ocean basin, only to voluntarily withdraw twenty-eight years later. The Islamic Ottoman Empire put a final end to Christian Byzantium with the conquest of Constantinople in 1453, even as Spanish Christians completed the "reconquest" of the Iberian Peninsula from the Muslims in 1492. And in the Americas, the Aztec and Inca empires gave a final and spectacular expression to Mesoamerican and Andean civilizations before they were both swallowed up in the burst of European imperialism that followed the arrival of Columbus.

Because the fifteenth century was a hinge of major historical change on many fronts, it provides an occasion for a bird's-eye view of the world through a kind of global tour. This excursion around the world will serve to briefly review the human saga thus far and to establish a baseline from which the enormous transformations of the centuries that followed might be measured. How, then, might we describe the world, and the worlds, of the fifteenth century?

SEEKING THE MAIN POINT

What predictions about the future might a global traveler in the fifteenth century have reasonably made?

The Shapes of Human Communities

One way to describe the world of the fifteenth century is to identify the various types of societies that it contained. Bands of hunters and gatherers, villages of agricultural peoples, newly emerging chiefdoms or small states, pastoral communities, established civilizations and empires—all of these social or political forms would have been apparent to a widely traveled visitor in the fifteenth century. Representing alternative ways of organizing human life, all of them were long established by the fifteenth century, but the balance among these distinctive kinds of societies in 1500 was quite different than it had been a thousand years earlier.

AP® EXAM TIP

Recall the Paleolithic (gathering and hunting) societies from Chapter 1 and note that they continued to exist into the era ca. 600– ca. 1450.

Paleolithic Persistence: Australia and North America

Despite millennia of agricultural advance, substantial areas of the world still hosted gathering and hunting societies, known to historians as Paleolithic (Old Stone Age) peoples. All of Australia, much of Siberia, the arctic coastlands, and parts of Africa and the Americas fell into this category. These peoples were not simply relics of a bygone age. They too had changed over time, though more slowly than their agricultural counterparts, and they too interacted with their neighbors. In short, they had a history, although most history books largely ignore them after the age of agri-

A MAP OF TIME

1345–1521	Aztec Empire in Mesoamerica
1368–1644	Ming dynasty in China
1370–1405	Conquests of Timur
15th century	Spread of Islam in Southeast Asia Civil war among Japanese warlords Rise of Hindu state of Vijayanagara in southern India European Renaissance Flourishing of African states of Ethiopia, Kongo, Benin, Zimbabwe
1405–1433	Chinese maritime voyages
1415	Beginning of Portuguese exploration of West African coast
1438–1533	Inca Empire along the Andes
1453	Ottoman seizure of Constantinople
1464–1591	Songhay Empire in West Africa
1492	Christian reconquest of Spain from Muslims completed; Columbus's first transatlantic voyage
1497–1520s	Portuguese entry into the Indian Ocean world
1501	Founding of Safavid Empire in Persia
1526	Founding of Mughal Empire in India

culture arrived. Nonetheless, this most ancient way of life still had a sizable and variable presence in the world of the fifteenth century.

Consider, for example, Australia. That continent's many separate groups, some 250 of them, still practiced a gathering and hunting way of life in the fifteenth century, a pattern that continued well after Europeans arrived in the late eighteenth century. Over many thousands of years, these people had assimilated various material items or cultural practices from outsiders—outrigger canoes, fishhooks, complex netting techniques, artistic styles, rituals, and mythological ideas—but despite the presence of farmers in nearby New Guinea, no agricultural practices penetrated the Australian mainland. Was it because large areas of Australia were unsuited for the kind of agriculture practiced in New Guinea? Or did the peoples of Australia, enjoying an environment of sufficient resources, simply see no need to change their way of life?

Despite the absence of agriculture, Australia's peoples had mastered and manipulated their environment, in part through the practice of "firestick farming," a pattern of deliberately set fires, which they described as "cleaning up the country."

Guided Reading Question

■ COMPARISON

In what ways did the gathering and hunting people of Australia differ from those of the northwest coast of North America?

AP® EXAM TIP

Make sure you are aware of common features of Paleolithic societies.

These controlled burns served to clear the underbrush, thus making hunting easier and encouraging the growth of certain plant and animal species. In addition, native Australians exchanged goods among themselves over distances of hundreds of miles, created elaborate mythologies and ritual practices, and developed sophisticated traditions of sculpture and rock painting. They accomplished all of this on the basis of an economy and technology rooted in the distant Paleolithic past.

A very different kind of gathering and hunting society flourished in the fifteenth century along the northwest coast of North America among the Chinookan, Tulalip, Skagit, and other peoples. With some 300 edible animal species and an abundance of salmon and other fish, this extraordinarily bounteous environment provided the foundation for what scholars sometimes call "complex" or "affluent" gathering and hunting cultures. What distinguished the northwest coast peoples from those of Australia were permanent village settlements with large and sturdy houses, considerable economic specialization, ranked societies that sometimes included slavery, chiefdoms dominated by powerful clan leaders or "big men," and extensive storage of food.

Although these and other gathering and hunting peoples persisted still in the fifteenth century, both their numbers and the area they inhabited had contracted greatly as the Agricultural Revolution unfolded across the planet. That relentless advance of the farming frontier continued in the centuries ahead as the Russian, Chinese, and European empires encompassed the lands of the remaining Paleolithic peoples. By the early twenty-first century, what was once the only human way of life had been reduced to minuscule pockets of people whose cultures seemed doomed to a final extinction.

Agricultural Village Societies: The Igbo and the Iroquois

Far more numerous than gatherers and hunters were those many peoples who, though fully agricultural, had avoided incorporation into larger empires or civilizations and had not developed their own city- or state-based societies. Living usually in small village-based communities and organized in terms of kinship relations, such people predominated during the fifteenth century in much of North America; in most of the tropical lowlands of South America and the Caribbean; in parts of the Amazon River basin, Southeast Asia, and Africa south of the equator; and throughout Pacific Oceania. Historians have largely relegated such societies to the periphery of world history, viewing them as marginal to the cities, states, and large-scale civilizations that predominate in most accounts of the global past. Viewed from within their own circles, though, these societies were at the center of things, each with its own history of migration, cultural transformation, social conflict, incorporation of new people, political rise and fall, and interaction with strangers. In short, they too changed as their histories took shape.

East of the Niger River in the heavily forested region of West Africa lay the lands of the Igbo (EE-boh) peoples. By the fifteenth century, their neighbors, the

Yoruba and Bini, had begun to develop small states and urban centers. But the Igbo, whose dense population and extensive trading networks might well have given rise to states, declined to follow suit. The deliberate Igbo preference was to reject the kingship and state-building efforts of their neighbors. They boasted on occasion that "the Igbo have no kings." Instead, they relied on other institutions to maintain social cohesion beyond the level of the village: title societies in which wealthy men received a series of prestigious ranks, women's associations, hereditary ritual experts serving as mediators, and a balance of power among kinship groups. It was a "stateless society," famously described in Chinua Achebe's *Things Fall Apart*, the most widely read novel to emerge from twentieth-century Africa.

But the Igbo peoples and their neighbors did not live in isolated, self-contained societies. They traded actively among themselves and with more distant peoples, such as the large African kingdom of Songhay (sahn-GEYE) far to the north. Cotton cloth, fish, copper and iron goods, decorative objects, and more drew neighboring peoples into networks of exchange. Common artistic traditions reflected a measure of cultural unity in a politically fragmented region, and all of these peoples seem to have changed from a matrilineal to a patrilineal system of tracing their descent. Little of this registered in the larger civilizations of the Afro-Eurasian world, but to the peoples of the West African forest during the fifteenth century, these processes were central to their history and their daily lives. Soon, however, all of them would be caught up in the transatlantic slave trade and would be changed substantially in the process.

Across the Atlantic in what is now central New York State, other agricultural village societies were also in the process of substantial change during the several centuries preceding their incorporation into European trading networks and empires. The Iroquois-speaking peoples of that region had only recently become fully agricultural, adopting maize- and bean-farming techniques that had originated centuries earlier in Mesoamerica. As this productive agriculture took hold by 1300 or so, the population grew, the size of settlements increased, and distinct peoples emerged. Frequent warfare also erupted among them. Some scholars have speculated that as agriculture, largely seen as women's work, became the primary economic activity, "warfare replaced successful food getting as the avenue to male prestige."[2]

Whatever caused it, this increased level of conflict among Iroquois peoples triggered a remarkable political innovation around the fifteenth century: a loose alliance or confederation among five Iroquois-speaking peoples—the Mohawk, Oneida, Onondaga, Cayuga, and Seneca. Based on an agreement known as the Great Law of Peace (see Map 12.5, page 523), the Five Nations, as they called themselves, agreed to settle their differences peacefully through a confederation council of clan leaders, some fifty of them altogether, who had the authority to adjudicate disputes and set reparation payments. Operating by consensus, the Iroquois League of Five

Igbo Art
Widely known for their masks, used in a variety of ritual and ceremonial occasions, the Igbo were also among the first to produce bronze castings using the "lost wax" method. This exquisite bronze pendant in the form of a human head derives from the Igbo Ukwu archeological site in eastern Nigeria and dates to the ninth century C.E. (The British Museum, London, UK/ Werner Forman/Art Resource, NY)

Nations effectively suppressed the blood feuds and tribal conflicts that had only recently been so widespread. It also coordinated their peoples' relationship with outsiders, including the Europeans, who arrived in growing numbers in the centuries after 1500.

The Iroquois League gave expression to values of limited government, social equality, and personal freedom, concepts that some European colonists found highly attractive. One British colonial administrator declared in 1749 that the Iroquois had "such absolute Notions of Liberty that they allow no Kind of Superiority of one over another, and banish all Servitude from their Territories."[3] Such equality extended to gender relationships, for among the Iroquois, descent was matrilineal (reckoned through the woman's line), married couples lived with the wife's family, and women controlled agriculture and property. While men were hunters, warriors, and the primary political officeholders, women selected and could depose those leaders.

Wherever they lived in 1500, over the next several centuries independent agricultural peoples such as the Iroquois and Igbo were increasingly encompassed in expanding economic networks and conquest empires based in Western Europe, Russia, China, or India. In this respect, they replicated the experience of many other village-based farming communities that had much earlier found themselves forcibly included in the powerful embrace of Egyptian, Mesopotamian, Roman, Indian, Chinese, and other civilizations.

Pastoral Peoples: Central Asia and West Africa

AP® EXAM TIP

Timur's empire encompassed a key portion of the Silk Roads.

Guided Reading Question

■ SIGNIFICANCE
What role did Central Asian and West African pastoralists play in their respective regions?

Pastoral peoples had long impinged more directly and dramatically on civilizations than did hunting and gathering or agricultural village societies. The Mongol incursion, along with the enormous empire to which it gave rise, was one in a long series of challenges from the steppes, but it was not quite the last. As the Mongol Empire disintegrated, a brief attempt to restore it occurred in the late fourteenth and early fifteenth centuries under the leadership of a Turkic warrior named Timur, born in what is now Uzbekistan and known in the West as Tamerlane (see Map 12.1, page 506).

With a ferocity that matched or exceeded that of his model, Chinggis Khan, Timur's army of pastoralists brought immense devastation yet again to Russia, Persia, and India. Timur himself died in 1405, while preparing for an invasion of China. Conflicts among his successors prevented any lasting empire, although his descendants retained control of the area between Persia and Afghanistan for the rest of the fifteenth century. That state hosted a sophisticated elite culture, combining Turkic and Persian elements, particularly at its splendid capital of Samarkand, as its rulers patronized artists, poets, traders, and craftsmen. Timur's conquest proved to be the last great military success of pastoral peoples from Central Asia. In the centuries that followed, their homelands were swallowed up in the expanding Russian and Chinese empires, as the balance of power between steppe pastoralists of inner Eurasia and the civilizations of outer Eurasia turned decisively in favor of the latter.

In Africa, pastoral peoples stayed independent of established empires several centuries longer than those of Inner Asia, for not until the late nineteenth century were they incorporated into European colonial states. The experience of the Fulbe, West Africa's largest pastoral society, provides an example of an African herding people with a highly significant role in the fifteenth century and beyond. From their homeland in the western fringe of the Sahara along the upper Senegal River, the Fulbe had migrated gradually eastward in the centuries after 1000 C.E. (see Map 12.3, page 514). Unlike the pastoral peoples of Inner Asia, they generally lived in small communities among agricultural peoples and paid various grazing fees and taxes for the privilege of pasturing their cattle. Relations with their farming hosts often were tense because the Fulbe resented their subordination to agricultural peoples, whose way of life they despised. That sense of cultural superiority became even more pronounced as the Fulbe, in the course of their eastward movement, slowly adopted Islam. Some of them in fact dropped out of a pastoral life and settled in towns, where they became highly respected religious leaders. In the eighteenth and nineteenth centuries, the Fulbe were at the center of a wave of religiously based uprisings, or jihads, which greatly expanded the practice of Islam and gave rise to a series of new states, ruled by the Fulbe themselves.

Civilizations of the Fifteenth Century: Comparing China and Europe

Beyond the foraging, farming, and pastoral societies of the fifteenth-century world were its civilizations, those city-centered and state-based societies that were far larger and more densely populated, more powerful and innovative, and much more unequal in terms of class and gender than other forms of human community. Since the First Civilizations had emerged between 3500 and 1000 B.C.E., both the geographic space they encompassed and the number of people they embraced had grown substantially. By the fifteenth century, a considerable majority of the world's population lived within one or another of these civilizations, although most of these people no doubt identified more with local communities than with a larger civilization. What might an imaginary global traveler notice about the world's major civilizations in the fifteenth century?

Ming Dynasty China

Such a traveler might well begin his or her journey in China, heir to a long tradition of effective governance, Confucian and Daoist philosophy, a major Buddhist presence, sophisticated artistic achievements, and a highly productive economy. That civilization, however, had been greatly disrupted by a century of Mongol rule, and its population had been sharply reduced by the plague. During the Ming dynasty (1368–1644), however, China recovered (see Map 12.1). The early decades of that dynasty witnessed an effort to eliminate all signs of foreign rule, discouraging the use of Mongol names and dress, while promoting Confucian learning and orthodox

AP® EXAM TIP

You should know the time frames of each of the major Chinese dynasties, such as the Ming (fourteenth to seventeenth centuries).

Map 12.1   Asia in the Fifteenth Century

The fifteenth century in Asia witnessed the massive Ming dynasty voyages into the Indian Ocean, the last major eruption of pastoral power in Timur's empire, and the flourishing of the maritime city of Malacca.

AP® EXAM TIP

Always pay attention to examples of governments' methods of political control.

Guided Reading Question

■ DESCRIPTION

How would you define the major achievements of Ming dynasty China?

gender roles, based on earlier models from the Han, Tang, and Song dynasties. Emperor Yongle (YAHNG-leh) (r. 1402–1422) sponsored an enormous *Encyclopedia* of some 11,000 volumes. With contributions from more than 2,000 scholars, this work sought to summarize or compile all previous writing on history, geography, philosophy, ethics, government, and more. Yongle also relocated the capital to Beijing, ordered the building of a magnificent imperial residence known as the Forbidden City, and constructed the Temple of Heaven, where subsequent rulers performed Confucian-based rituals to ensure the well-being of Chinese society. Two empresses wrote instructions for female behavior, emphasizing traditional expectations after the disruptions of the previous century. Culturally speaking, China was looking to its past.

Politically, the Ming dynasty reestablished the civil service examination system that had been neglected under Mongol rule and went on to create a highly centralized government. Power was concentrated in the hands of the emperor himself, while a cadre of eunuchs (castrated men) personally loyal to the emperor exercised great authority, much to the dismay of the official bureaucrats. The state acted vigorously to repair the damage of the Mongol years by restoring millions of acres to cultivation; rebuilding canals, reservoirs, and irrigation works; and planting, according to some estimates, a billion trees in an effort to reforest China. As a result, the economy rebounded, both international and domestic trade flourished, and the population grew. During the fifteenth century, China had recovered and was perhaps the best governed and most prosperous of the world's major civilizations.

China also undertook the largest and most impressive maritime expeditions the world had ever seen. Since the eleventh century, Chinese sailors and traders had been a major presence in the South China Sea and in Southeast Asian port cities, with much of this activity in private hands. But now, after decades of preparation, an enormous fleet, commissioned by Emperor Yongle himself, was launched in 1405, followed over the next twenty-eight years by six more such expeditions. On board more than 300 ships of the first voyage was a crew of some 27,000, including 180 physicians, hundreds of government officials, 5 astrologers, 7 high-ranking or grand eunuchs, carpenters, tailors, accountants, merchants, translators, cooks, and thousands of soldiers and sailors. Visiting many ports in Southeast Asia, Indonesia, India, Arabia, and East Africa, these fleets, captained by the Muslim eunuch Zheng He (JUHNG-huh), sought to enroll distant peoples and states in the Chinese tribute system (see Map 12.1). Dozens of rulers accompanied the fleets back to China, where they presented tribute, performed the required rituals of submission, and received in return abundant gifts, titles, and trading opportunities. Chinese officials were amused by some of the exotic products to be found abroad — ostriches, zebras, and giraffes, for example. Officially described as "bringing order to the world," Zheng He's expeditions served to establish Chinese power and prestige in the Indian Ocean and to exert Chinese control over foreign trade in the region. The Chinese, however, did not seek to conquer new territories, establish Chinese settlements, or spread their culture, though they did intervene in a number of local disputes. (See Zooming In: Zheng He, page 508.)

AP® EXAM TIP

Compare the purposes, sizes, discoveries, and effects of Zheng He's expedition with those from Europe in the fifteenth century.

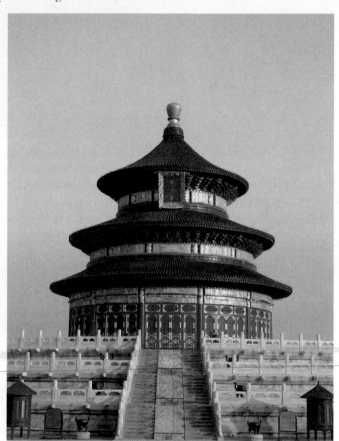

Temple of Heaven
Set in a forest of more than 650 acres, the Temple of Heaven was constructed in the early fifteenth century. In Chinese thinking, it was the primary place where Heaven and Earth met. From his residence in the Forbidden City, the Chinese emperor led a procession of thousands twice a year to this sacred site, where he offered sacrifices, implored the gods for a good harvest, and performed the rituals that maintained the cosmic balance. (Imaginechina for AP Images)

Zheng He,
China's Non-Chinese Admiral

At the helm of China's massive maritime expeditions in the early fifteenth century was a most unusual person named Zheng He.[4] Born in 1371 in the frontier region of Yunnan in southwestern China, his family roots were in Central Asia in what is now Uzbekistan. Both his father and grandfather were devout Muslims who had made the pilgrimage to Mecca. The family had also achieved local prominence as high officials serving the Mongol rulers of China for a century. Zheng He would surely have continued in this tradition had not a major turning point in China's history decisively altered the trajectory of his life.

Zheng He's birth, as it happened, coincided with the end of Mongol rule. His own father was killed resisting the forces of the new Ming dynasty that ousted the Mongols from Yunnan in 1382. Eleven-year-old Zheng He was taken prisoner along with hundreds of Mongols and their Muslim supporters. But young Zheng He lost more than his freedom; he also lost his male sex organs as he underwent castration, becoming a eunuch. The practice had a long history in China as well as in Chris-

Among the acquisitions of Zheng He's expeditions, none excited more interest in the Chinese court than an African giraffe.

tian and Islamic civilizations. During the 276 years of the Ming dynasty (1368–1644), some 1 million eunuchs served the Chinese emperor and members of the elite. A small number became powerful officials, especially at the central imperial court, where their utter dependence upon and loyalty to the emperor gained them the enduring hostility of the scholar-bureaucrats of China's civil service. Strangely enough, substantial numbers of Chinese men voluntarily became eunuchs, trading their manhood for the possibility of achieving power, prestige, and wealth.

After his castration, pure chance shaped Zheng He's life as he was assigned to Zhu Di, the fourth son of the reigning emperor, who was then establishing himself in the northern Chinese region around Beijing. Zheng He soon won the confidence of his master, and eventually the almost seven-foot-tall eunuch proved himself an effective military leader in various skirmishes against the Mongols

photo: *Tribute Giraffe with Attendant*, 1414, China, Ming Dynasty (1368–1644), Yongle Period (1403–1424), ink and color on silk/Gift of John T. Dorrance, 1977 (1977-42-1)/The Philadelphia Museum of Art/Art Resource, NY

The most surprising feature of these voyages was how abruptly and deliberately they were ended. After 1433, Chinese authorities simply stopped such expeditions and allowed this enormous and expensive fleet to deteriorate in port. "In less than a hundred years," wrote a recent historian of these voyages, "the greatest navy the world had ever known had ordered itself into extinction."[5] Part of the reason involved the death of the emperor Yongle, who had been the chief patron of the enterprise. Many high-ranking officials had long seen the expeditions as a waste of resources because China, they believed, was the self-sufficient "middle kingdom," and in the civil war that brought Zhu Di to power as the emperor Yongle in 1402. With his master as emperor, Zheng He served first as Grand Director of Palace Servants. Now he could don the prestigious red robe, rather than the blue one assigned to lower-ranking eunuchs. But soon Zheng He found himself with a far more ambitious assignment—commander of China's huge oceangoing fleet.

The seven voyages that Zheng He led between 1405 and 1433 have defined his role in Chinese and world history. But they also revealed something of the man himself. Clearly, he was not an explorer in the mold of Columbus, for he sailed in well-traveled waters and usually knew where he was going. While his journeys were largely peaceful, with no effort to establish colonies or control trade, on several occasions Zheng He used force to suppress piracy or to punish those who resisted Chinese overtures. Once he personally led 2,000 Chinese soldiers against a hostile ruler in the interior of Ceylon. He also had a keen eye for the kind of exotica that the imperial court found fascinating, returning to China with ostriches, zebras, lions, elephants, and a giraffe.

The voyages also disclose Zheng He's changing religious commitments. Born and raised a Muslim, he had not lived in a primarily Islamic setting since his capture at the age of eleven. Thus it is hardly surprising that he adopted the more eclectic posture toward religion common in China. During his third voyage in Ceylon, he erected a trilingual tablet recording lavish gifts and praise to the Buddha, to Allah, and to a local form of the Hindu deity Vishnu. He also apparently expressed some interest in a famous relic said to be a tooth of the Buddha. And Zheng He credited the success of his journeys to the Daoist goddess Tianfei, protector of sailors and seafarers.

To Zheng He, the voyages surely represented the essential meaning of his own life. In an inscription erected just prior to his last voyage, Zheng He summarized his achievements: "When we arrived at the foreign countries, barbarian kings who resisted transformation [by Chinese civilization] and were not respectful we captured alive, and bandit soldiers who looted and plundered recklessly we exterminated. Because of this, the sea routes became pure and peaceful and the foreign peoples could rely upon them and pursue their occupations in safety." But after his death, Zheng He vanished from the historical record, even as his country largely withdrew from the sea, and most Chinese forgot about the unusual man who had led those remarkable voyages. In the early twenty-first century, however, Zheng He has been resurrected as a potent symbol of China's growing global position and of its peaceful intentions. In such ways, the past is appropriated, and sometimes distorted, as it proves useful in the present.

Questions: How might you describe the arc of Zheng He's life? What were its major turning points? How did Zheng He's castration shape his life?

requiring little from the outside world. In their eyes, the real danger to China came from the north, where barbarians constantly threatened. Finally, they viewed the voyages as the project of the court eunuchs, whom these officials despised. Even as these voices of Chinese officialdom prevailed, private Chinese merchants and craftsmen continued to settle and trade in Japan, the Philippines, Taiwan, and Southeast Asia, but they did so without the support of their government. The Chinese state quite deliberately turned its back on what was surely within its reach—a large-scale maritime empire in the Indian Ocean basin.

European Comparisons: State Building and Cultural Renewal

At the other end of the Eurasian continent, similar processes of demographic recovery, political consolidation, cultural flowering, and overseas expansion were under way. Western Europe, having escaped Mongol conquest but devastated by the plague, began to regrow its population during the second half of the fifteenth century. As in China, the infrastructure of civilization proved a durable foundation for demographic and economic revival.

Guided Reading Question

■ COMPARISON

What political and cultural differences stand out in the histories of fifteenth-century China and Western Europe? What similarities are apparent?

Politically too Europe joined China in continuing earlier patterns of state building. In China, however, this meant a unitary and centralized government that encompassed almost the whole of its civilization, while in Europe a decidedly fragmented system of many separate, independent, and highly competitive states made for a sharply divided Western civilization (see Map 12.2). Many of these states—Spain, Portugal, France, England, the city-states of Italy (Milan, Venice, and Florence), various German principalities—learned to tax their citizens more efficiently, to create more effective administrative structures, and to raise standing armies. A small Russian state centered on the city of Moscow also emerged in the fifteenth century as Mongol rule faded away. Much of this state building was driven by the needs of war, a frequent occurrence in such a fragmented and competitive political environment. England and France, for example, fought intermittently for more than a century in the Hundred Years' War (1337–1453) over rival claims to territory in France. Nothing remotely similar disturbed the internal life of Ming dynasty China.

A renewed cultural blossoming, known in European history as the Renaissance, likewise paralleled the revival of all things Confucian in Ming dynasty China. In Europe, however, that blossoming celebrated and reclaimed a classical Greco-Roman tradition that earlier had been lost or obscured. Beginning in the vibrant commercial cities of Italy between roughly 1350 and 1500, the Renaissance reflected the belief of the wealthy male elite that they were living in a wholly new era, far removed from the confined religious world of feudal Europe. Educated citizens of these cities sought inspiration in the art and literature of ancient Greece and Rome; they were "returning to the sources," as they put it. Their purpose was not so much to reconcile these works with the ideas of Christianity, as the twelfth- and thirteenth-century university scholars had done, but to use them as a cultural standard to imitate and then to surpass. The elite patronized great Renaissance artists such as Leonardo da Vinci, Michelangelo, and Raphael, whose paintings and sculptures were far more naturalistic, particularly in portraying the human body, than those of their medieval counterparts. Some of these artists looked to the Islamic world for standards of excellence, sophistication, and abundance. (See Working with Evidence: Islam and Renaissance Europe, page 536.)

Although religious themes remained prominent, Renaissance artists now included portraits and busts of well-known contemporary figures, scenes from ancient

AP® EXAM TIP

One important feature of the Renaissance was that artists were funded by wealthy elites—part of a pattern since the beginning of civilizations.

Map 12.2   Europe in 1500

By the end of the fifteenth century, Christian Europe had assumed its early modern political shape as a system of competing states threatened by an expanding Muslim Ottoman Empire.

mythology, and depictions of Islamic splendor. In the work of scholars, known as humanists, reflections on secular topics such as grammar, history, politics, poetry, rhetoric, and ethics complemented more religious matters. For example, Niccolò Machiavelli's (1469–1527) famous work *The Prince* was a prescription for political success based on the way politics actually operated in a highly competitive Italy of rival city-states rather than on idealistic and religiously based principles. To the question of whether a prince should be feared or loved, Machiavelli replied:

> One ought to be both feared and loved, but as it is difficult for the two to go together, it is much safer to be feared than loved. . . . For it may be said of men in general that they are ungrateful, voluble, dissemblers, anxious to avoid danger,

AP® EXAM TIP

Machiavelli's political theories influenced totalitarian leaders of the early twentieth century (see Chapter 21).

The Waldseemüller Map of 1507
Just fifteen years after Columbus landed in the Western Hemisphere, this map, which was created by the German cartographer Martin Waldseemüller, reflected a dawning European awareness of the planet's global dimensions and the location of the world's major landmasses. (bpk, Berlin/Staatsbibliothek zu Berlin, Stiftung Preussischer Kulturbesitz/Photo: Ruth Schacht/Art Resource, NY)

and covetous of gain. . . . Fear is maintained by dread of punishment which never fails. . . . In the actions of men, and especially of princes, from which there is no appeal, the end justifies the means.[6]

While the great majority of Renaissance writers and artists were men, among the remarkable exceptions to that rule was Christine de Pizan (1363–1430), the daughter of a Venetian official, who lived mostly in Paris. Her writings pushed against the misogyny of so many European thinkers of the time. In her *City of Ladies*, she mobilized numerous women from history, Christian and pagan alike, to demonstrate that women too could be active members of society and deserved an education equal to that of men. Aiding in the construction of this allegorical city is Lady Reason, who offers to assist Christine in dispelling her poor opinion of her own sex. "No matter which way I looked at it," she wrote, "I could find no evidence from my own experience to bear out such a negative view of female nature and habits. Even so . . . I could scarcely find a moral work by any author which didn't devote some chapter or paragraph to attacking the female sex."[7]

Heavily influenced by classical models, Renaissance figures were more interested in capturing the unique qualities of particular individuals and in describing the world as it was than in portraying or exploring eternal religious truths. In its focus on the affairs of this world, Renaissance culture reflected the urban bustle and commercial preoccupations of Italian cities. Its secular elements challenged the other-worldliness of Christian culture, and its individualism signaled the dawning of a more capitalist economy of private entrepreneurs. A new Europe was in the making, one more different from its own recent past than Ming dynasty China was from its pre-Mongol glory.

European Comparisons: Maritime Voyaging

A global traveler during the fifteenth century might be surprised to find that Europeans, like the Chinese, were also launching outward-bound maritime expeditions. Initiated in 1415 by the small country of Portugal, those voyages sailed ever farther down the west coast of Africa, supported by the state and blessed by the pope (see Map 12.3). As the century ended, two expeditions marked major breakthroughs, although few suspected it at the time. In 1492, Christopher Columbus, funded by Spain, Portugal's neighbor and rival, made his way west across the Atlantic hoping to arrive in the East and, in one of history's most consequential mistakes, ran into the Americas. Five years later, in 1497, Vasco da Gama launched a voyage that took him around the tip of South Africa, along the East African coast, and, with the help of a Muslim pilot, across the Indian Ocean to Calicut in southern India.

The differences between the Chinese and European oceangoing ventures were striking, most notably perhaps in terms of size. Columbus captained three ships and a crew of about 90, while da Gama had four ships, manned by perhaps 170 sailors. These were minuscule fleets compared to Zheng He's hundreds of ships and a crew in the many thousands. "All the ships of Columbus and da Gama combined," according to a recent account, "could have been stored on a single deck of a single vessel in the fleet that set sail under Zheng He."[8]

Motivation as well as size differentiated the two ventures. Europeans were seeking the wealth of Africa and Asia — gold, spices, silk, and more. They also were in search of Christian converts and of possible Christian allies with whom to continue their long crusading struggle against threatening Muslim powers. China, by contrast, faced no equivalent power, needed no military allies in the Indian Ocean basin, and required little that these regions produced. Nor did China possess an impulse to convert foreigners to its culture or religion, as the Europeans surely did. Furthermore, the confident and overwhelmingly powerful Chinese fleet sought neither conquests nor colonies, while the Europeans soon tried to monopolize by force the commerce of the Indian Ocean and violently carved out huge empires in the Americas.

The most striking difference in these two cases lay in the sharp contrast between China's decisive ending of its voyages and the continuing, indeed escalating, European effort, which soon brought the world's oceans and growing numbers of the world's people under its control. This is why Zheng He's voyages were so long neglected in China's historical memory. They led nowhere, whereas the initial

Guided Reading Question

■ COMPARISON
In what ways did European maritime voyaging in the fifteenth century differ from that of China? What accounts for these differences?

Map 12.3   Africa in the Fifteenth Century

By the fifteenth century, Africa was a virtual museum of political and cultural diversity, encompassing large empires, such as Songhay; smaller kingdoms, such as Kongo; city-states among the Yoruba, Hausa, and Swahili peoples; village-based societies without states at all, as among the Igbo; and pastoral peoples, such as the Fulbe. Both European and Chinese maritime expeditions touched on Africa during that century, even as Islam continued to find acceptance in the northern half of the continent.

European expeditions, so much smaller and less promising, were but the first steps on a journey to world power. But why did the Europeans continue a process that the Chinese had deliberately abandoned?

In the first place, Europe had no unified political authority with the power to order an end to its maritime outreach. Its system of competing states, so unlike

China's single unified empire, ensured that once begun, rivalry alone would drive the Europeans to the ends of the earth. Beyond this, much of Europe's elite had an interest in overseas expansion. Its budding merchant communities saw opportunity for profit; its competing monarchs eyed the revenue from taxing overseas trade or from seizing overseas resources; the Church foresaw the possibility of widespread conversion; impoverished nobles might imagine fame and fortune abroad. In China, by contrast, support for Zheng He's voyages was very shallow in official circles, and when the emperor Yongle passed from the scene, those opposed to the voyages prevailed within the politics of the court.

AP® EXAM TIP

Take note of factors that led to China's withdrawal from exploration.

Finally, the Chinese were very much aware of their own antiquity, believed strongly in the absolute superiority of their culture, and felt with good reason that, should they desire something from abroad, others would bring it to them. Europeans too believed themselves unique, particularly in religious terms as the possessors of Christianity, the "one true religion." In material terms, though, they were seeking out the greater riches of the East, and they were highly conscious that Muslim power blocked easy access to these treasures and posed a military and religious threat to Europe itself. All of this propelled continuing European expansion in the centuries that followed.

The Chinese withdrawal from the Indian Ocean actually facilitated the European entry. It cleared the way for the Portuguese to penetrate the region, where they faced only the eventual naval power of the Ottomans. Had Vasco da Gama encountered Zheng He's massive fleet as his four small ships sailed into Asian waters in 1498, world history may well have taken quite a different turn. As it was, however, China's abandonment of oceanic voyaging and Europe's embrace of the seas marked different responses to a common problem that both civilizations shared—growing populations and land shortage. In the centuries that followed, China's rice-based agriculture was able to expand production internally by more intensive use of the land, while the country's territorial expansion was inland toward Central Asia. By contrast, Europe's agriculture, based on wheat and livestock, expanded primarily by acquiring new lands in overseas possessions, which were gained as a consequence of a commitment to oceanic expansion.

Civilizations of the Fifteenth Century: The Islamic World

Beyond the domains of Chinese and European civilization, our fifteenth-century global traveler would surely have been impressed with the transformations of the Islamic world. Stretching across much of Afro-Eurasia, the enormous realm of Islam experienced a set of remarkable changes during the fifteenth and early sixteenth centuries, as well as the continuation of earlier patterns. The most notable change lay in the political realm, for an Islamic civilization that had been severely fragmented since at least 900 now crystallized into four major states or empires (see Map 12.4). At the same time, a long-term process of conversion to Islam continued the cultural transformation of Afro-Eurasian societies both within and beyond these new states.

In the Islamic Heartland: The Ottoman and Safavid Empires

Guided Reading Question

....

■ COMPARISON

What differences can you identify among the four major empires in the Islamic world of the fifteenth and sixteenth centuries?

AP® EXAM TIP

You must know examples of the Ottoman Empire's economic, cultural, and political significance.

The most impressive and enduring of the new Islamic states was the Ottoman Empire, which lasted in one form or another from the fourteenth to the early twentieth century. It was the creation of one of the many Turkic warrior groups that had migrated into Anatolia, slowly and sporadically, in the several centuries following 1000 C.E. By the mid-fifteenth century, these Ottoman Turks had already carved out a state that encompassed much of the Anatolian peninsula and had pushed deep into southeastern Europe (the Balkans), acquiring in the process a substantial Christian population. During the sixteenth century, the Ottoman Empire extended its control to much of the Middle East, coastal North Africa, the lands surrounding the Black Sea, and even farther into Eastern Europe.

The Ottoman Empire was a state of enormous significance in the world of the fifteenth century and beyond. In its huge territory, long duration, incorporation of many diverse peoples, and economic and cultural sophistication, it was one of the great empires of world history. In the fifteenth century, only Ming dynasty China and the Incas matched it in terms of wealth, power, and splendor. The empire represented the emergence of the Turks as the dominant people of the Islamic world, ruling now over many Arabs, who had initiated this new faith more than 800 years before. In adding "caliph" (successor to the Prophet) to their other titles, Ottoman sultans claimed the legacy of the earlier Abbasid Empire. They sought to bring a renewed unity to the Islamic world, while also serving as protector of the faith, the "strong sword of Islam."

The Ottoman Empire also represented a new phase in the long encounter between Christendom and the world of Islam. In the Crusades, Europeans had taken the aggressive initiative in that encounter, but the rise of the Ottoman Empire reversed their roles. The seizure of Constantinople in 1453 marked the final demise of Christian Byzantium and allowed Ottoman rulers to see themselves as successors to the Roman Empire. (See Zooming In: 1453 in Constantinople, page 518.) It also opened the way to further expansion in heartland Europe, and in 1529 a rapidly expanding Ottoman Empire laid siege to Vienna in the heart of Central Europe. The political and military expansion of Islam, at the expense of Christendom, seemed clearly under way. Many Europeans spoke fearfully of the "terror of the Turk."

In the neighboring Persian lands to the east of the Ottoman Empire, another Islamic state was also taking shape in the late fifteenth and early sixteenth centuries—the Safavid (SAH-fah-vihd) Empire. Its leadership was also Turkic, but in this case it had emerged from a Sufi religious order founded several centuries earlier by Safi al-Din (1252–1334). The long-term significance of the Safavid Empire, which was established in the decade following 1500, was its decision to forcibly

Map 12.4   Empires of the Islamic World

The most prominent political features of the vast Islamic world in the fifteenth and sixteenth centuries were four large states: the Songhay, Ottoman, Safavid, and Mughal empires.

impose a Shia version of Islam as the official religion of the state. Over time, this form of Islam gained popular support and came to define the unique identity of Persian (Iranian) culture.

This Shia empire also introduced a sharp divide into the political and religious life of heartland Islam, for almost all of Persia's neighbors practiced a Sunni form of the faith. For a century (1534–1639), periodic military conflict erupted between the Ottoman and Safavid empires, reflecting both territorial rivalry and sharp religious differences. In 1514, the Ottoman sultan wrote to the Safavid ruler in the most bitter of terms:

> You have denied the sanctity of divine law . . . you have deserted the path of salvation and the sacred commandments . . . you have opened to Muslims the gates of tyranny and oppression . . . you have raised the standard of irreligion

1453 in Constantinople

On May 29, 1453, forces of the Muslim Ottoman sultan Mehmed II seized control of the great Christian city of Constantinople, an event that marked the final end of the Roman/Byzantine Empire and the ascendency of the Ottoman Empire. In retrospect, this event acquired a certain air of inevitability about it, for the Byzantine Empire had been retreating for almost two centuries before the steady advance of the Ottomans. By 1453, that once-great empire, heir to all things Roman, had shrunk to little more than the city itself, with only some 50,000 inhabitants and 8,000 active defenders compared to a vast Ottoman army of 60,000 soldiers. And little was left of the fabled wealth of the city. But what later observers see as inevitable generally occurs only with great human effort and amid vast uncertainty about the outcome. So it was in Constantinople in 1453.

Constantine XI, the last Byzantine emperor, was well aware of the odds he faced. Yet his great city, protected by water on two sides and a great wall on a third, had repeatedly withstood many attacks and sieges. Furthermore, until the very end, he had hoped for assistance

Ottoman Turks storm the walls of Constantinople in 1453.

from Western Christians, even promising union with the Roman Church to obtain it. But no such help arrived, at least not in sufficient quantities to make a difference, though rumors of a fleet from Venice persisted. The internal problems of the Western powers as well as the long-standing hostility between Eastern Orthodoxy and Roman Catholicism ensured that Constantinople would meet its end alone.

On the Ottoman side, enormous effort was expended with no assurance of success. In 1451, a new sultan came to the throne of the Ottoman Empire, Mehmed II, only nineteen years old and widely regarded as not very promising. Furthermore, some among the court officials had reservations about an attack on Constantinople. But the young sultan seemed determined to gain the honor promised in Islamic prophesies going back to Muhammad himself to the one who conquered the city. Doing so could also rid him of a potential rival to the Ottoman throne, who had taken refuge in Constantinople.

and heresy. . . . [Therefore] the *ulama* and our doctors have pronounced a sentence of death against you, perjurer and blasphemer.[9]

This Sunni/Shia hostility has continued to divide the Islamic world into the twenty-first century.

On the Frontiers of Islam: The Songhay and Mughal Empires

While the Ottoman and Safavid empires brought both a new political unity and a sharp division to the heartland of Islam, two other states performed a similar role on the expanding African and Asian frontiers of the faith. In the West African savan-

And so preparations began for an assault on the once-great city. The Ottomans assembled a huge fleet, gathered men and materials, and constructed a fortress to control access to Constantinople by water. In late 1452, Mehmed secured the services of a Hungarian master cannon builder named Orban, who constructed a number of huge cannons, one of which could hurl a 600-pound stone ball over a mile. These weapons subsequently had a devastating effect on the walls surrounding Constantinople. Interestingly enough, Orban had first offered his services to the Byzantine emperor, who simply could not afford to pay for this very expensive project.

In early April of 1453, the siege began, and it lasted for fifty-seven days. As required by Islamic law, Mehmed offered three times to spare the emperor and his people if they surrendered. Constantine apparently considered the offer seriously, but he finally refused, declaring, "We have all decided to die with our own free will." After weeks of furious bombardment, an ominous silence descended on May 28. Mehmed had declared a day of rest and prayer before the final assault the next day. That evening, the Byzantine emperor ordered a procession of icons and relics about the city and then entered the ancient Christian church of Hagia Sophia, seeking forgiveness for his sins and receiving Holy Communion.

And then, early the next day, the final assault began as Ottoman forces breached the walls of Constantinople and took the city. The Christians bravely defended their city, and Constantine discarded his royal regalia and died fighting like a common soldier. A later legend suggested that angels turned Constantine into marble and buried him in a nearby cave from which he would eventually reappear to retake the city for Christendom.

Islamic law required that soldiers be permitted three days of plundering the spoils, but Mehmed was reluctant, eager to spare the city he longed for as his capital. So he limited plundering to one day. Even so, the aftermath was terrible. According to a Christian eyewitness, "The enraged Turkish soldiers . . . gave no quarter. When they had massacred and there was no longer any resistance, they were intent on pillage and roamed through the town stealing, disrobing, pillaging, killing, raping, taking captive men, women, children, monks, priests."[10] When Mehmed himself entered the city, praying at the Christian altar of Hagia Sophia, he reportedly wept at seeing the destruction that had occurred.

Constantinople was now a Muslim city, capital of the Ottoman Empire, and Hagia Sophia became a mosque. A momentous change had occurred in the relationship between the world of Islam and that of Christendom.

Questions: What factors contributed to Mehmed's victory? Under what circumstances might a different outcome have been possible?

nas, the Songhay Empire rose in the second half of the fifteenth century. It was the most recent and the largest in a series of impressive states that operated at a crucial intersection of the trans-Saharan trade routes and that derived much of their revenue from taxing that commerce. Islam was a growing faith in Songhay but was limited largely to urban elites. This cultural divide within Songhay largely accounts for the religious behavior of its fifteenth-century monarch Sonni Ali (r. 1465–1492), who gave alms and fasted during Ramadan in proper Islamic style but also enjoyed a reputation as a magician and possessed a charm thought to render his soldiers invisible to their enemies. Nonetheless, Songhay had become a major center of Islamic learning and commerce by the early sixteenth century. A North African traveler known as Leo Africanus remarked on the city of Timbuktu:

AP® EXAM TIP

The AP® exam often asks questions about features of the Songhay Empire.

Ottoman Janissaries
Originating in the fourteenth century, the Janissaries became the elite infantry force of the Ottoman Empire. Complete with uniforms, cash salaries, and marching music, they were the first standing army in the region since the days of the Roman Empire. When gunpowder technology became available, Janissary forces soon were armed with muskets, grenades, and handheld cannons. This Turkish miniature painting dates from the sixteenth century. (Turkish miniature, Topkapi Palace Library, Istanbul, Turkey/Album/Art Resource, NY)

> Here are great numbers of [Muslim] religious teachers, judges, scholars, and other learned persons who are bountifully maintained at the king's expense. Here too are brought various manuscripts or written books from Barbary [North Africa] which are sold for more money than any other merchandise. . . . Here are very rich merchants and to here journey continually large numbers of negroes who purchase here cloth from Barbary and Europe. . . . It is a wonder to see the quality of merchandise that is daily brought here and how costly and sumptuous everything is.[11]

See Working with Evidence, Source 7.3, page 318, for more from Leo Africanus about West Africa in the early sixteenth century. Sonni Ali's successor made the pilgrimage to Mecca and asked to be given the title "Caliph of the Land of the Blacks." Songhay then represented a substantial Islamic state on the African frontier of a still-expanding Muslim world. (See the photo on page 305 for manuscripts long preserved in Timbuktu.)

The Mughal (MOO-guhl) Empire in India bore similarities to Songhay, for both governed largely non-Muslim populations. Much as the Ottoman Empire initiated a new phase in the interaction of Islam and Christendom, so too did the Mughal Empire continue an ongoing encounter between Islamic and Hindu civilizations. Established in the early sixteenth century, the Mughal Empire was the creation of yet another Islamized Turkic group, which invaded India in 1526. Over the next century, the Mughals (a Persian term for Mongols) established unified control over most of the Indian peninsula, giving it a rare period of political unity and laying the foundation for subsequent British colonial rule. During its first 150 years, the Mughal Empire, a land of great wealth and imperial splendor, undertook a remarkable effort to blend many Hindu groups and a variety of Muslims into an effective partnership. The inclusive policies of the early Mughal emperors showed that Muslim rulers could accommodate their overwhelmingly Hindu subjects in somewhat the same fashion as Ottoman authorities provided religious autonomy for their Christian minority. In southernmost India, however, the distinctly Hindu kingdom of Vijayanagara flourished in the fifteenth century, even as it borrowed architectural styles from the Muslim states of northern India and sometimes employed Muslim mercenaries in its military forces.

AP® EXAM TIP

Know the Mughal Empire's significance in South Asian history.

Together these four Muslim empires—Ottoman, Safavid, Songhay, and Mughal—brought to the Islamic world a greater measure of political coherence, military power, economic prosperity, and cultural brilliance than it had known since the early centuries of Islam. This new energy, sometimes called a "second flowering of Islam," impelled the continuing spread of the faith to yet new regions. The most prominent of these was oceanic Southeast Asia, which for centuries had been intimately bound up in the world of Indian Ocean commerce, while borrowing elements of both Hindu and Buddhist traditions. By the fifteenth century, that trading network was largely in Muslim hands, and the demand for Southeast Asian spices was mounting as the Eurasian world recovered from the devastation of Mongol conquest and the plague. Growing numbers of Muslim traders, many of them from India, settled in Java and Sumatra, bringing their faith with them. Eager to attract those traders to their port cities, a number of Hindu or Buddhist rulers along the Malay Peninsula and in Indonesia converted to Islam, while transforming themselves into Muslim sultans and imposing Islamic law. Thus, unlike in the Middle East and India, where Islam was established in the wake of Arab or Turkic conquest, in Southeast Asia, as in West Africa, it was introduced by traveling merchants and solidified through the activities of Sufi holy men.

The rise of Malacca, strategically located on the waterway between Sumatra and Malaya, was a sign of the times (see Map 12.1, page 506). During the fifteenth century, it was transformed from a small fishing village to a major Muslim port city. A Portuguese visitor in 1512 observed that Malacca had "no equal in the world. . . . Commerce between different nations for a thousand leagues on every hand must come to Malacca."[12] That city also became a springboard for the spread of Islam

AP® EXAM TIP

Malacca was an important city for trade and culture during the post-classical era (ca. 600–ca. 1450).

throughout the region. In the eclectic style of Southeast Asian religious history, the Islam of Malacca demonstrated much blending with local and Hindu/Buddhist traditions, while the city itself, like many port towns, had a reputation for "rough behavior." An Arab Muslim pilot in the 1480s commented critically: "They have no culture at all. . . . You do not know whether they are Muslim or not."[13] Nonetheless, Malacca, like Timbuktu on the West African frontier of an expanding Islamic world, became a center for Islamic learning, and students from elsewhere in Southeast Asia were studying there in the fifteenth century. As the more central regions of Islam were consolidating politically, the frontier of the faith continued to move steadily outward.

PRACTICING AP® HISTORICAL THINKING

In what ways did the civilizations of China, Europe, and the Islamic world in the fifteenth century seem to be moving in the same direction, and in what respects were they diverging from one another?

Civilizations of the Fifteenth Century: The Americas

Across the Atlantic, centers of civilization had long flourished in Mesoamerica and in the Andes. The fifteenth century witnessed new, larger, and more politically unified expressions of those civilizations, embodied in the Aztec and Inca empires. Both were the work of previously marginal peoples who had forcibly taken over and absorbed older cultures, giving them new energy, and both were decimated in the sixteenth century at the hands of Spanish conquistadores and their diseases. To conclude this global tour of world civilizations, we will send our intrepid traveler to the Western Hemisphere for a brief look at these American civilizations (see Map 12.5).

AP® EXAM TIP

The Aztec and Inca civilizations are significant parts of the AP® curriculum. Study them closely.

The Aztec Empire

Guided Reading Question

■ COMPARISON
What distinguished the Aztec and Inca empires from each other?

The empire known to history as the Aztec state was largely the work of the Mexica (meh-SHEEH-kah) people, a semi-nomadic group from northern Mexico who had migrated southward and by 1325 had established themselves on a small island in Lake Texcoco. Over the next century, the Mexica developed their military capacity, served as mercenaries for more powerful people, negotiated elite marriage alliances with them, and built up their own capital city of Tenochtitlán. In 1428, a Triple Alliance between the Mexica and two other nearby city-states launched a highly aggressive program of military conquest, which in less than 100 years brought more of Mesoamerica within a single political framework than ever before. Aztec authorities, eager to shed their rather undistinguished past, now claimed descent from earlier Mesoamerican peoples such as the Toltecs and Teotihuacán.

With a core population recently estimated at 5 to 6 million people, the Aztec Empire was a loosely structured and unstable conquest state that witnessed frequent rebellions by its subject peoples. Conquered peoples and cities were required to provide labor for Aztec projects and to regularly deliver to their Aztec rulers

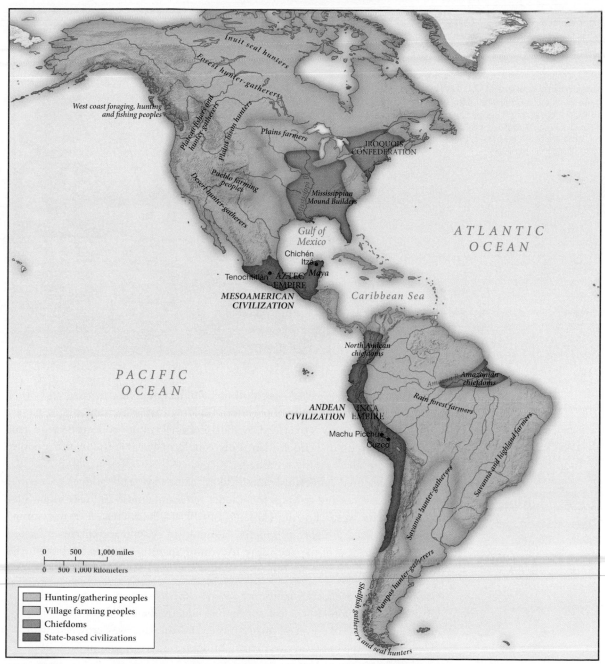

Map 12.5 key:
- Hunting/gathering peoples
- Village farming peoples
- Chiefdoms
- State-based civilizations

Map 12.5   The Americas in the Fifteenth Century

The Americas before Columbus represented a world almost completely separate from Afro-Eurasia. It featured similar kinds of societies, though with a different balance among them, but it largely lacked the pastoral economies that were so important in the Eastern Hemisphere.

Aztec Women

Within the home, Aztec women cooked, cleaned, spun and wove cloth, raised their children, and undertook ritual activities. Outside the home, they served as officials in palaces, priestesses in temples, traders in markets, teachers in schools, and members of craft workers' organizations. This domestic image comes from the sixteenth-century Florentine Codex, which was compiled by the Spanish but illustrated by Aztec artists. (Facsimile from Book IV of Florentine Codex, *General History of Things in New Spain*, 16th century, Mexico/Museo del Templo Mayor, Mexico City, Mexico/De Agostino Picture Library/Bridgeman Images)

impressive quantities of textiles and clothing, military supplies, jewelry and other luxuries, various foodstuffs, animal products, building materials, rubber balls, paper, and more. The process was overseen by local imperial tribute collectors, who sent the required goods on to Tenochtitlán, a metropolis of 150,000 to 200,000 people, where they were meticulously recorded.

That city featured numerous canals, dikes, causeways, and bridges. A central walled area of palaces and temples included a pyramid almost 200 feet high. Surrounding the city were "floating gardens," artificial islands created from swamplands that supported a highly productive agriculture. Vast marketplaces reflected the commercialization of the economy. A young Spanish soldier who beheld the city in 1519 described his reaction:

> Gazing on such wonderful sights, we did not know what to say, or whether what appeared before us was real, for on one side, on the land there were great cities, and in the lake ever so many more, and the lake was crowded with canoes, and in the causeway were many bridges at intervals, and in front of us stood the great city of Mexico.[14]

Beyond tribute from conquered peoples, ordinary trade, both local and long-distance, permeated Aztec domains. The extent of empire and rapid population growth stimulated the development of markets and the production of craft goods, particularly in the fifteenth century. Virtually every settlement, from the capital city to the smallest village, had a marketplace that hummed with activity during weekly market days. The largest was that of Tlatelolco, near the capital city, which stunned the Spanish with its huge size, its good order, and the immense range of goods available. Hernán Cortés, the Spanish conquistador who defeated the Aztecs, wrote that "every kind of merchandise such as can be met with in every land is for sale there, whether of food and victuals, or ornaments of gold and silver, or lead, brass, copper, tin, precious stones, bones, shells, snails and feathers."[15] Professional merchants, known as *pochteca*, were legally commoners, but their wealth, often exceeding that of the nobility, allowed them to rise in society and become "magnates of the land."

Among the "goods" that the pochteca obtained were slaves, many of whom were destined for sacrifice in the bloody rituals so central to Aztec religious life. Long a part of Mesoamerican and many other world cultures, human sacrifice assumed an unusually prominent role in Aztec public life and thought during the fifteenth century. Tlacaelel (1398–1480), who was for more than half a century a prominent official of the Aztec Empire, is often credited with crystallizing the ideology of state that gave human sacrifice such great importance.

In that cyclical understanding of the world, the sun, central to all life and identified with the Aztec patron deity Huitzilopochtli (wee-tsee-loh-pockt-lee), tended to lose its energy in a constant battle against encroaching darkness. Thus the Aztec world hovered always on the edge of catastrophe. To replenish its energy and thus postpone the descent into endless darkness, the sun required the life-giving force found in human blood. Because the gods had shed their blood ages ago in creating humankind, it was wholly proper for people to offer their own blood to nourish the gods in the present. The high calling of the Aztec state was to supply this blood, largely through its wars of expansion and from prisoners of war, who were destined for sacrifice. The victims were "those who have died for the god." The growth of the Aztec Empire therefore became the means for maintaining cosmic order and avoiding utter catastrophe. This ideology also shaped the techniques of Aztec warfare, which put a premium on capturing prisoners rather than on killing the enemy. As the empire grew, priests and rulers became mutually dependent, and "human sacrifices were carried out in the service of politics."[16] Massive sacrificial rituals, together with a display of great wealth, served to impress enemies, allies, and subjects alike with the immense power of the Aztecs and their gods.

Alongside these sacrificial rituals was a philosophical and poetic tradition of great beauty, much of which mused on the fragility and brevity of human life. Such an outlook characterized the work of Nezahualcoyotl (1402–1472), a poet and king of the city-state of Texcoco, which was part of the Aztec Empire:

> Truly do we live on Earth?
> Not forever on earth; only a little while here.
> Although it be jade, it will be broken.
> Although it be gold, it is crushed.
> Although it be a quetzal feather, it is torn asunder.
> Not forever on earth; only a little while here.[17]

AP® EXAM TIP
The *pochteca* are an important feature of the Aztec economy.

Guided Reading Question
■ DESCRIPTION
How did Aztec religious thinking support the empire?

AP® EXAM TIP
You will need to know much more about the Aztecs than just ritual beheadings. Study their form of government, interactions with neighboring groups, trade systems, and gender roles.

The Inca Empire

AP® EXAM TIP

Remember the location of the Aztecs (Mesoamerica) and the Incas (Andes Mountains in South America). Also, note these similarities and differences between the Aztecs and Incas.

Guided Reading Question

....

■ **DESCRIPTION**
In what ways did Inca authorities seek to integrate their vast domains?

While the Mexica were constructing an empire in Mesoamerica, a relatively small community of Quechua-speaking people, known to us as the Incas, was building the Western Hemisphere's largest imperial state along the entire spine of the Andes Mountains. Much as the Aztecs drew on the traditions of the Toltecs and Teotihuacán, the Incas incorporated the lands and cultures of earlier Andean civilizations: the Chavín, Moche, Wari, and Tiwanaku. The Inca Empire, however, was much larger than the Aztec state; it stretched some 2,500 miles along the Andes and contained perhaps 10 million subjects. Although the Aztec Empire controlled only part of the Mesoamerican cultural region, the Inca state encompassed practically the whole of Andean civilization during its short life in the fifteenth and early sixteenth centuries. In the speed of its creation and the extent of its territory, the Inca Empire bears some similarity to that of the Mongols.

Both the Aztec and Inca empires represent rags-to-riches stories in which quite modest and remotely located people very quickly created by military conquest the largest states ever witnessed in their respective regions, but the empires themselves were quite different. In the Aztec realm, the Mexica rulers largely left their conquered people alone, if the required tribute was forthcoming. No elaborate administrative system arose to integrate the conquered territories or to assimilate their people to Aztec culture.

The Incas, on the other hand, erected a rather more bureaucratic empire. At the top reigned the emperor, an absolute ruler regarded as divine, a descendant of the creator god Viracocha and the son of the sun god Inti. Each of the some eighty provinces in the empire had an Inca governor. In theory, the state owned all land and resources, though in practice state lands, known as "lands of the sun," existed alongside properties owned by temples, elites, and traditional communities. At least in the central regions of the empire, subjects were grouped into hierarchical units of 10, 50, 100, 500, 1,000, 5,000, and 10,000 people, each headed by local officials, who were appointed and supervised by an Inca governor or the emperor. A separate set of "inspectors" provided the imperial center with an independent check on provincial officials. Births, deaths, marriages, and other population data were carefully recorded on *quipus*, the knotted cords that served as an accounting device. A resettlement program moved one-quarter or more of the population to new locations, in part to disperse conquered and no doubt resentful people and sometimes to reward loyal followers with promising opportunities. Efforts at cultural integration required the leaders of conquered peoples to learn Quechua. Their sons were removed to the capital of Cuzco for instruction in Inca culture and language. Even now, millions of people from Ecuador to Chile still speak Quechua, and it is the official second language of Peru after Spanish.

But the sheer human variety of the Incas' enormous empire required great flexibility. In some places Inca rulers encountered bitter resistance; in others local elites were willing to accommodate Incas and thus benefit from their inclusion in the

Machu Picchu
Machu Picchu, high in the Andes Mountains, was constructed by the Incas in the fifteenth century on a spot long held sacred by local people. Its 200 buildings stand at some 8,000 feet above sea level, making it a "city in the sky." It was probably a royal retreat or religious center, rather than serving administrative, commercial, or military purposes. The outside world became aware of Machu Picchu only in 1911, when it was discovered by a Yale University archeologist. (fStop/Superstock)

empire. Where centralized political systems already existed, Inca overlords could delegate control to native authorities. Elsewhere they had to construct an administrative system from scratch. Everywhere they sought to incorporate local people into the lower levels of the administrative hierarchy. While the Incas required their subject peoples to acknowledge major Inca deities, these peoples were then largely free to carry on their own religious traditions. The Inca Empire was a fluid system that varied greatly from place to place and over time. It depended as much on the posture of conquered peoples as on the demands and desires of Inca authorities.

Like the Aztec Empire, the Inca state represented an especially dense and extended network of economic relationships within the "American web," but these relationships took shape in quite a different fashion. Inca demands on their conquered people were expressed, not so much in terms of tribute, but as labor service, known as *mita*, which was required periodically of every household. What people produced at home usually stayed at home, but almost everyone also had to work for the state. Some labored on large state farms or on "sun farms," which supported temples and religious institutions; others herded, mined, served in the military, or toiled on state-directed construction projects.

AP® EXAM TIP

Know the meaning and significance of the *mita* system.

AP® EXAM TIP

The AP® exam frequently includes questions about the Inca economic system.

Those with particular skills were put to work manufacturing textiles, metal goods, ceramics, and stonework. The most well-known of these specialists were the "chosen women," who were removed from their homes as young girls, trained in Inca ideology, and set to producing corn beer and cloth at state centers. Later they were given as wives to men of distinction or sent to serve as priestesses in various temples, where they were known as "wives of the Sun." In return for such labor services, Inca ideology, expressed in terms of family relationships, required the state to arrange elaborate feasts at which large quantities of food and drink were consumed and to provide food and other necessities when disaster struck. Thus the authority of the state penetrated and directed Inca society and economy far more than did that of the Aztecs. (See Working with Evidence, Source 13.4, page 596, for an early Spanish account of Inca governing practices.)

If the Inca and Aztec civilizations differed sharply in their political and economic arrangements, they resembled each other more closely in their gender systems. Both societies practiced what scholars call "gender parallelism," in which "women and men operate in two separate but equivalent spheres, each gender enjoying autonomy in its own sphere."[18]

AP® EXAM TIP

Note these continued comparisons between the Aztecs and Incas. Pay attention to their social structures.

In both Mesoamerican and Andean societies, such systems had emerged long before their incorporation into the Aztec and Inca empires. In the Andes, men reckoned their descent from their fathers and women from their mothers, while Mesoamericans had long viewed children as belonging equally to their mothers and fathers. Parallel religious cults for women and men likewise flourished in both societies. Inca men venerated the sun, while women worshipped the moon, with matching religious officials. In Aztec temples, both male and female priests presided over rituals dedicated to deities of both sexes. Particularly among the Incas, parallel hierarchies of male and female political officials governed the empire, while in Aztec society, women officials exercised local authority under a title that meant "female person in charge of people." Social roles were clearly defined and different for men and women, but the domestic concerns of women—childbirth, cooking, weaving, cleaning—were not regarded as inferior to the activities of men. Among the Aztecs, for example, sweeping was a powerful and sacred act with symbolic significance as "an act of purification and a preventative against evil elements penetrating the center of the Aztec universe, the home."[19] In the Andes, men broke the ground, women sowed, and both took part in the harvest.

This was gender complementarity, not gender equality. Men occupied the top positions in both political and religious life, and male infidelity was treated more lightly than was women's unfaithfulness. As the Inca and Aztec empires expanded, military life, limited to men, grew in prestige, perhaps skewing an earlier gender parallelism. The Incas in particular imposed a more rigidly patriarchal order on their subject peoples. In other ways, the new Aztec and Inca rulers adapted to the gender systems of the people they had conquered. Among the Aztecs, the tools of women's work, the broom and the weaving spindle, were ritualized as weapons; sweeping the home was believed to assist men at war; and childbirth was regarded by women as "our kind of war."[20] Inca rulers replicated the gender parallelism of their subjects at a higher level, as the *sapay Inca* (the Inca ruler) and the *coya* (his female consort) governed jointly, claiming descent respectively from the sun and the moon.

Webs of Connection

Few people in the fifteenth century lived in entirely separate and self-contained communities. Almost all were caught up, to one degree or another, in various and overlapping webs of influence, communication, and exchange.[21] Perhaps most obvious were the webs of empire, large-scale political systems that brought together a variety of culturally different people. Christians and Muslims encountered each other directly in the Ottoman Empire, as did Hindus and Muslims in the Mughal Empire. And no empire tried more diligently to integrate its diverse peoples than the fifteenth-century Incas.

Religion too linked far-flung peoples, and divided them as well. Christianity provided a common religious culture for peoples from England to Russia, although the great divide between Roman Catholicism and Eastern Orthodoxy endured, and in the sixteenth century the Protestant Reformation would shatter permanently the Christian unity of the Latin West. Although Buddhism had largely vanished from its South Asian homeland, it remained a link among China, Korea, Tibet, Japan, and parts of Southeast Asia, even as it splintered into a variety of sects and practices. More than either of these, Islam actively brought together its many peoples. In the hajj, the pilgrimage to Mecca, Africans, Arabs, Persians, Turks, Indians, and many others joined as one people as they rehearsed together the events that gave birth to their common faith. And yet divisions and conflicts persisted within the vast realm of Islam, as the violent hostility between the Sunni Ottoman Empire and the Shia Safavid Empire so vividly illustrates.

Long-established patterns of trade among peoples occupying different environments and producing different goods were certainly much in evidence during the fifteenth century, as they had been for millennia. Hunting societies of Siberia funneled furs and other products of the forest into the Silk Road trading network traversing the civilizations of Eurasia. In the fifteenth century, some of the agricultural peoples in southern Nigeria were receiving horses brought overland from the drier regions of Africa to the north, where those animals flourished better. The Mississippi River in North America and the Orinoco and Amazon rivers in South America facilitated a canoe-borne commerce along those waterways. Coastal shipping in large seagoing canoes operated in the Caribbean and along the Pacific coast between Mexico and Peru. In Pacific Polynesia, the great voyaging networks across vast oceanic distances that had flourished especially since 1000 were in decline by 1500 or earlier, leading to the abandonment of a number of islands. Ecological devastation perhaps played a role, and some scholars believe that a cooling and fluctuating climate change known as the Little Ice Age created less favorable conditions

AP® EXAM TIP

Pay close attention to this section about political, cultural, and economic links in the fifteenth-century world.

Guided Reading Question

■ CONNECTION
In what different ways did the peoples of the fifteenth century interact with one another?

Map 12.6   Religion and Commerce in the Afro-Eurasian World

By the fifteenth century, the many distinct peoples and societies of the Eastern Hemisphere were linked to one another by ties of religion and commerce. Of course, most people were not directly involved in long-distance trade, and many people in areas shown as Buddhist or Islamic on the map practiced other religions. While much of India, for example, was ruled by Muslims, the majority of its people followed some form of Hinduism. And although Islam had spread to West Africa, that religion had not penetrated much beyond the urban centers of the region.

for inter-island exchange. The great long-distance trading patterns of the Afro-Eurasian world, in operation for a thousand years or more, continued in the fifteenth century, although the balance among them was changing (see Map 12.6). The Silk Road overland network, which had flourished under Mongol control in the thirteenth and fourteenth centuries, contracted in the fifteenth century as the Mongol Empire broke up and the devastation of the plague reduced demand for its products. The rise of the Ottoman Empire also blocked direct commercial contact between Europe and China, but oceanic trade from Japan, Korea, and China through the islands of Southeast Asia and across the Indian Ocean picked up considerably. Larger ships made it possible to trade in bulk goods such as grain as well as luxury products, while more sophisticated partnerships and credit mechanisms greased the wheels of commerce. A common Islamic culture over much of this vast region likewise smoothed the passage of goods among very different peoples, as it also did for the trans-Saharan trade.

A Preview of Coming Attractions: Looking Ahead to the Modern Era, 1450–2015

While ties of empire, culture, commerce, and disease surely linked many of the peoples in the world of the fifteenth century, none of those connections operated on a genuinely global scale. Although the densest webs of connection had been woven within the Afro-Eurasian zone of interaction, this huge region had no sustained ties with the Americas, and neither of them had sustained contact with the peoples of Pacific Oceania. That situation was about to change as Europeans in the sixteenth century and beyond forged a set of genuinely global relationships that generated sustained interaction among all of these regions. That huge process and the many outcomes that flowed from it marked the beginning of what world historians commonly call the modern age—the more than five centuries that followed the voyages of Columbus starting in 1492.

> **AP® EXAM TIP**
>
> Hold on to this summary of the next 500 years to guide you through Chapters 13–23.

Over those five centuries, the previously separate worlds of Afro-Eurasia, the Americas, and Pacific Oceania became inextricably linked, with enormous consequences for everyone involved. Global empires, a global economy, global cultural exchanges, global migrations, global disease, global wars, and global environmental changes have made the past 500 years a unique phase in the human journey. Those webs of communication and exchange—the first defining feature of the modern era—have progressively deepened, so much so that by the end of the twentieth century few if any people lived beyond the cultural influences, economic ties, or political relationships of a globalized world.

Several centuries after the Columbian voyages, and clearly connected to them, a second distinctive feature of the modern era took shape: the emergence of a radically new kind of human society, first in Europe during the nineteenth century and then in various forms elsewhere in the world. The core feature of such societies was industrialization, with its sustained growth of technological innovation and its massive consumption of energy and raw materials. The human ability to create wealth made an enormous leap forward in a very short period of time, at least by world history standards. Accompanying this economic or industrial revolution was an equally distinctive and unprecedented jump in human numbers, a phenomenon that has affected not only human beings but also many other living species and the earth itself. (See Snapshot, page 532.)

Moreover, these modern societies were far more urbanized and much more commercialized than ever before, as more and more people began to work for wages, to produce for the market, and to buy the requirements of daily life rather

SNAPSHOT   World Population Growth, 1000–2000[22]

than growing or making those products for their own use. These societies gave prominence and power to holders of urban wealth—merchants, bankers, industrialists, educated professionals—at the expense of rural landowning elites, while simultaneously generating a substantial factory working class and diminishing the role of peasants and handicraft artisans.

Modern societies were generally governed by states that were more powerful and intrusive than earlier states and empires had been, and they offered more of their people an opportunity to play an active role in public and political life. Literacy in modern societies was far more widespread than ever before, while new national identities became increasingly prominent, competing with more local loyalties and with those of empire. To the mix of established religious ideas and folk traditions were now added the challenging outlook and values of modern science, with its secular emphasis on the ability of human rationality to know and manipulate the world. Modernity has usually meant a self-conscious awareness of living and thinking in new ways that deliberately departed from tradition.

This revolution of modernity, comparable in its pervasive consequences only to the Agricultural Revolution of some 10,000 years ago, introduced new divisions and new conflicts into the experience of humankind. The ancient tensions between rich and poor within particular societies were now paralleled by new economic inequalities among entire regions and civilizations and a much-altered global balance of power. The first societies to experience the modern transformation—those in Western Europe and North America—became both a threat and a source of envy to much of the rest of the world. As modern societies emerged and spread, they were enormously destructive of older patterns of human life, even as they gave rise to many new ways of living. Sorting out what was gained and what was lost during the modern transformation has been a persistent and highly controversial thread of human thought over the past several centuries.

A third defining feature of the last 500 years was the growing prominence of European peoples on the global stage. In ancient times, the European world, focused in the Mediterranean basin of Greek culture and the Roman Empire, was but one of several second-wave civilizations in the Eastern Hemisphere. After 500 C.E., Western Europe was something of a backwater, compared to the more prosperous and powerful civilizations of China and the Islamic world.

In the centuries following 1500, however, this western peninsula of the Eurasian continent became the most innovative, most prosperous, most powerful, most expansive, and most imitated part of the world. European empires spanned the globe. European peoples created new societies all across the Americas and as far away as South Africa, Australia, and New Zealand. Their languages were spoken and their Christian religion was widely practiced throughout the Americas and in parts of Asia and Africa. Their businessmen bought, sold, and produced goods around the world. It was among Europeans that the Scientific and Industrial Revolutions first took shape, with enormously powerful intellectual and economic consequences for the entire planet. The quintessentially modern ideas of liberalism, nationalism, feminism, and socialism all bore the imprint of their European origin. By the beginning of the twentieth century, Europeans or peoples of European descent exercised unprecedented influence and control over the earth's many other peoples, a wholly novel experience in human history.

For the rest of the world, growing European dominance posed a common challenge. Despite their many differences, the peoples of Asia, Africa, the Middle East, the Americas, and Pacific Oceania all found themselves confronted by powerful and intrusive Europeans. The impact of this intrusion and how various peoples responded to it—resistance, submission, acceptance, imitation, adaptation—represent critically important threads in the world history of the past five centuries.

REFLECTIONS

What If? Chance and Contingency in World History

Seeking meaning in the stories they tell, historians are inclined to look for deeply rooted or underlying causes for the events they recount. And yet, is it possible that, at least on occasion, historical change derives less from profound and long-term sources than from coincidence, chance, or the decisions of a few that might well have gone another way?

Consider, for example, the problem of explaining the rise of Europe to a position of global power in the modern era. What if the Great Khan Ogodei had not died in 1241, requiring the Mongol forces then poised for an assault on Germany to return to Mongolia? It is surely possible that Central and Western Europe might have been overrun by Mongol armies as so many other civilizations had been, a prospect that could have drastically altered the trajectory of European history. Or what if the Chinese had decided in 1433 to continue their huge maritime expeditions, creating an empire in the Indian Ocean basin and perhaps moving on to "discover" the Americas and Europe? Such a scenario suggests a wholly different future for world history than the one that in fact occurred. Or what if the forces of the Ottoman Empire had taken the besieged city of Vienna in 1529? Might they then have incorporated even larger parts of Europe into their expanding domain, requiring a halt to Europe's overseas empire-building enterprise?

None of this necessarily means that the rise of Europe was merely a fluke or an accident of history, but it does raise the issue of "contingency," the role of unforeseen or small events in the unfolding of the human story. An occasional "what if" approach to history reminds us that alternative possibilities existed in the past and that the only certainty about the future is that we will be surprised.

Chapter Review

What's the Significance?

Paleolithic persistence, 500–2

Igbo, 502–3

Iroquois, 503–4

Timur, 504

Fulbe, 505

Ming dynasty China, 505–9

Zheng He, 507–9

European Renaissance, 510–13

Ottoman Empire, 516

seizure of Constantinople in 1453, 516, 518–19

Safavid Empire, 516–18

Songhay Empire, 518–20

Timbuktu, 519–20

Mughal Empire, 521

Malacca, 521–22

Aztec Empire, 522–25

Inca Empire, 526–29

Big Picture Questions

1. Assume for the moment that the Chinese had not ended their maritime voyages in 1433. How might the subsequent development of world history have been different? What value is there in asking this kind of "what if" or counterfactual question?

2. How does this chapter distinguish among the various kinds of societies contained in the world of the fifteenth century? What other ways of categorizing the world's peoples might work as well or better?

3. What common patterns might you notice across the world of the fifteenth century? And what variations in the historical trajectories of various regions can you identify?

4. **Looking Back:** What would surprise a knowledgeable observer from 500 or 1000 C.E., were he or she to make a global tour in the fifteenth century? What features of that earlier world might still be recognizable?

Next Steps: For Further Study

Terence N. D'Altroy, *The Incas* (2002). A history of the Inca Empire that draws on recent archeological and historical research.

Edward L. Dreyer, *Zheng He: China and the Oceans in the Early Ming Dynasty* (2006). The most recent scholarly account of the Ming dynasty voyages.

Halil Inalcik and Donald Quataert, *An Economic and Social History of the Ottoman Empire, 1300–1914* (1994). A classic study of the Ottoman Empire.

Robin Kirkpatrick, *The European Renaissance, 1400–1600* (2002). A beautifully illustrated history of Renaissance culture as well as the social and economic life of the period.

Charles C. Mann, *1491: New Revelations of the Americas before Columbus* (2005). A review of Western Hemisphere societies and academic debates about their pre-Columbian history.

J. R. McNeill and William H. McNeill, *The Human Web* (2003). A succinct account of the evolving webs or relationships among human societies in world history.

Michael Smith, *The Aztecs* (2003). A history of the Aztec Empire, with an emphasis on the lives of ordinary people.

"Italian Renaissance," http://www.history.com/topics/italian-renaissance. A History channel presentation of the European Renaissance, with a number of brief videos.

"Ming Dynasty," http://www.metmuseum.org/toah/hd/ming/hd_ming.htm. A sample of Chinese art from the Ming dynasty from the collection of the Metropolitan Museum of Art.

WORKING WITH EVIDENCE

Islam and Renaissance Europe

The Renaissance era in Europe, roughly 1400 to 1600, represented the crystallization of a new civilization at the western end of Eurasia. In cultural terms, its writers and artists sought to link themselves to the legacy of the pre-Christian Greeks and Romans. But if Europeans were reaching back to their classical past, they were also reaching out—westward to the wholly new world of the Americas, southward to Africa, and eastward to Asia generally and the Islamic world in particular. The European Renaissance, in short, was shaped not only from within but also by its encounters with a wider world.

Interaction with the world of Islam was, of course, nothing new. Centuries of Muslim rule in Spain, the Crusades, and the expansion of the Ottoman Empire were markers in the long relationship of conflict, cooperation, and mutual influence between Christendom and the realm of Islam. Politically, that relationship was changing in the fifteenth century. The Christian reconquest of Spain from Muslim rule was completed by 1492. At the other end of the Mediterranean Sea, the Turkish Ottoman Empire was expanding into the previously Christian regions of the Balkans (southeastern Europe), seizing the ancient capital of the Byzantine Empire, Constantinople, in 1453, while becoming a major player in European international politics. Despite such conflicts, commerce flourished across political and religious divides. European bulk goods such as wool, timber, and glassware, along with silver and gold, were exchanged for high-value luxury goods from the Islamic world or funneled through it from farther east. These included spices, silks, carpets, tapestries, brocades, art objects, precious stones, gold, dyes, and pigments. In 1384, a Christian pilgrim from the Italian city of Florence wrote: "Really all of Christendom could be supplied for a year with the merchandise of Damascus."[23] And a fifteenth-century Italian nobleman said of Venice: "It seems as if all the world flocks here, and that human beings have concentrated there all their force for trading."[24]

The acquisition of such Eastern goods was important for elite Europeans as they sought to delineate and measure their emerging civilization. As that civilization began to take shape in the centuries after 1100 or so, it had drawn extensively on Arab or Muslim learning—in medicine, astronomy, philosophy, architecture, mathematics, business practices, and more. As early as the twelfth century, a Spanish priest and Latin translator of Arab texts wrote, "It befits us to imitate the Arabs, for they are as it were our teachers and the pioneers." During the Renaissance centuries as well, according to a recent account, "Europe began to define itself by purchasing and emulating the opulence and cultured sophistication of the cities, merchants, scholars, and empires of the Ottomans, Persians, and the Egyptian Mamluks." That engagement with the Islamic world found various expressions in Renaissance art, as the images that follow illustrate.

The year 1453 marked a watershed in the long relationship between Christendom and the Islamic world, for it was in that year that the Ottoman sultan Mehmed II decisively conquered the great Christian city of Constantinople, bringing the thousand-year history of Byzantium to an inglorious end. To many Europeans, that event was a catastrophe and Mehmed was the "terror of the world." On hearing the news, one Italian bishop, later to become the pope, foresaw a dismal future for both the Church and Western civilization: "Who can doubt that the Turks will vent their wrath upon the churches of God? . . . This will be a second death to Homer and a second destruction of Plato." Others, however, saw opportunity. Less than a year after that event, the northern Italian city of Venice signed a peace treaty with the Ottoman sultan, declaring, "It is our intention to live in peace and friendship with the Turkish emperor." Some even expressed admiration for the conquering Muslim ruler. George of Trebizond, a Greek-speaking Renaissance scholar, described Mehmed as "a wise king and one who philosophizes about the greatest matters."

For his part, Mehmed admired both classical and contemporary European culture, even as his armies threatened European powers. This cosmopolitan emperor employed Italian scholars to read to him from ancient Greek and Roman literature, stocked his library with Western texts, and decorated the walls of his palace with Renaissance-style frescoes. Seeing himself as heir to Roman imperial authority, he now added "Caesar" to his other titles. Although Islam generally prohibited the depiction of human figures, Mehmed's long interest in caricatures and busts and his desire to celebrate his many conquests led him to commission numerous medals by European artists, bearing his image. In 1480, he also had his portrait painted by the leading artist of Venice, Gentile Bellini, who had been sent to the Ottoman court as a cultural ambassador of his city.

Source 12.1 shows Bellini's portrait of the emperor sitting under a marble arch, a symbol of triumph that evokes his dramatic conquest of Constantinople. The three golden crowns on the upper left and right likely represent the lands recently acquired for the Ottoman Empire, and the inscription at the bottom describes Mehmed as "Conqueror of the World." Not long after the painting was made, Mehmed died, and shortly thereafter his son and successor sold it to Venetian merchants to help finance a large mosque complex. Thus the portrait returned to Venice.

National Gallery, London, UK/Bridgeman Images

Source 12.1 Gentile Bellini, Portrait of Mehmed II

- What overall impression of the sultan does this portrait convey?

- Why might this Muslim ruler want his portrait painted by a Christian artist from Venice?

- Why might Bellini and the city government of Venice be willing— even eager—to undertake the assignment, less than thirty years after the Muslim conquest of Constantinople?

■ The candelabra decorating the arch were a common feature in Venetian church architecture. Why might the sultan have agreed to this element of Christian symbolism in his portrait?

■ What does the episode surrounding this portrait indicate about the relationship of Venice and the Ottoman Empire in the wake of the conquest of Constantinople?

Venice had long been the primary point of commercial contact between Europe and the East and the source of the much-desired luxury goods that its merchants obtained from Alexandria in Egypt. At that time, Muslim Egypt was ruled by the Mamluks, a warrior caste of slave origins, who had checked the westward advance of the Mongols in 1260 and had driven the last of the European Crusaders out of the Middle East in 1291. Venetian traders, however, were more interested in commerce than in religion and by the fifteenth century enjoyed a highly profitable relationship with the Mamluk rulers of Egypt and Syria, despite the periodic opposition of the pope and threats of excommunication. Thus it is not surprising that the Renaissance artists of Venice were prominent among those who reflected the influence of the Islamic world in their work. By the late fifteenth century, something of a fad for oriental themes surfaced in Venetian pictorial art.

Source 12.2, painted by an anonymous Venetian artist in 1511, expresses this intense interest in the Islamic world. The setting is Damascus in Syria, then ruled by the Egyptian Mamluk regime. The local Mamluk governor of the city, seated on a low platform with an elaborate headdress, is receiving an ambassador from Venice, shown in a red robe and standing in front of the governor. Behind him in black robes are other members of the Venetian delegation, while in the foreground various members of Damascus society—both officials and merchants—are distinguished from one another by variations in their turbans. Behind the wall lies the city of Damascus with its famous Umayyad mosque, formerly a Roman temple to Jupiter and later a Christian church, together with its three minarets. The city's lush gardens and its homes with wooden balconies and rooftop terraces complete the picture of urban Islam.

■ What impressions of the city and its relationship with Venice does the artist seek to convey?

■ How are the various social groups of Damascus distinguished from one another in this painting? What does the very precise visual description of these differences suggest about Venetian understanding of urban Mamluk society?

■ What does the total absence of women suggest about their role in the public life of Damascus?

Louvre, Paris, France/Bridgeman Images

Source 12.2 The Venetian Ambassador Visits Damascus

> ■ How would you know that this is a Muslim city? What role, if any, does
> religion play in this depiction of the relationship between Christian
> Venice and Islamic Damascus?

Beyond political and commercial relationships, Europeans had long engaged
with the Islamic world intellectually as well. Source 12.3 illustrates that engagement in a work by Girolamo da Cremona, a fifteenth-century Italian painter
known for his "illuminations" of early printed books. Created in 1483 (only
some forty years after the invention of the printing press in Europe), it served
as the frontispiece for one of the first printed versions of Aristotle's writings,
translated into Latin, along with commentaries by the twelfth-century Muslim scholar Ibn Rushd, better known in the West as Averroes.

Aristotle, of course, was the great Greek philosopher of the fourth century
B.C.E. whose writings presented a systematic and rational view of the world,
while commenting on practically every branch of knowledge. The legacy of
Greek thought in general and Aristotle in particular passed into both the
Christian and Islamic worlds. Ibn Rushd (1126–1198), who wrote volumi-
nous commentaries on Aristotle's works and much else as well, lived in Muslim Spain, where he argued for the compatibility of Aristotelian philosophy
and the religious perspectives of Islam. While that outlook faced growing

Source 12.3 Aristotle and Averroes

opposition in the Islamic world, Aristotle's writings found more fertile ground among European scholars in the new universities of the twelfth and thirteenth centuries, where they became the foundation of university curricula and nourished the growth of "natural philosophy." In large measure it was through translations of Ibn Rushd's Arabic commentaries on Aristotle that Europeans regained access to the thinking of that ancient philosopher. A long line of European scholars defined themselves as "Averroists."

The painting in Source 12.3 is presented as a parchment leaf, torn to disclose two worlds behind Aristotle's text. At the top in a rural setting, Aristotle, dressed in a blue robe, is speaking to Ibn Rushd, clad in a yellow robe with a round white turban. The bottom of the painting depicts the world of classical Greek mythology. The painted jewels, gems, and pearls testify to the great value placed on such illuminated and printed texts.

- What might the possession of such a book say about the social status, tastes, and outlook of its owner?

- What overall impression of Renaissance thinking about the classical world and the world of Islam does this painting convey?

- Notice the gestures of the two men at the top as well as the pen in Ibn Rushd's hand and the book at his feet. How might you describe the relationship between them?

- What made it possible for at least some European Christians of the Renaissance era to embrace both the pagan Aristotle and the Islamic Ibn Rushd?

Despite the fluid relationship of Renaissance Europe with the world of Islam, the Ottoman Empire, apparently expanding inexorably, was a growing threat to Christian Europe, and Islam was a false religion to many Christians. Those themes too found expression in the art of the Renaissance. Source 12.4 provides an example. Painted during the first decade of the sixteenth century by the Venetian artist Vittore Carpaccio, it reflects the popular "orientalist" style with its elaborate and exotic depiction of Eastern settings, buildings, and costumes. This particular painting was part of a series illustrating the life of Saint George, a legendary soldier-saint who rescued a Libyan princess, slew the dragon about to devour her, and by his courageous example converted a large number of pagans to Christianity. Earlier paintings in this series portrayed the killing of the dragon, while this one shows the conversion of the infidels to the "true faith."

The setting for Source 12.4 is Muslim-ruled Jerusalem, where the action focuses on Saint George, on the right, baptizing a bareheaded Muslim ruler and a woman (perhaps his wife). Several others await their turns below the steps, while a group of Mamluk musicians play in honor of the occasion.

By Vittore Carpaccio (ca. 1460–1523), 1501–1507/Scuola di San Giorgio degli Schiavoni, Venice, Italy/Giraudon/Bridgeman Images

Source 12.4 Saint George Baptizes the Pagans of Jerusalem

■ What posture toward the Islamic world does this painting represent? Does it convey resistance to Ottoman expansion, or does it hold out the hope for the peaceful conversion of that powerful empire?

■ What is the significance of the large Ottoman turban at the foot of the steps?

■ Why might the legend of Saint George provide a potent symbol for European interaction with the Islamic world in the circumstances of the early sixteenth century?

■ Compare this urban scene with that of Source 12.2. What common features do you notice? Apart from any religious meanings, what do these paintings suggest about Venetian interests in the Islamic world?

An even more vitriolic anti-Muslim sensibility had long circulated in Europe, based on the fear of Islamic power, the distortions growing out of the Crusades, and the perception of religious heresy. In the early fourteenth century, the Italian poet Dante, author of *The Divine Comedy*, placed Muhammad in the eighth circle of Hell, where the "sowers of discord" were punished and mutilated. To many Christians, Muhammad was a "false prophet," sometimes portrayed as drunk. Protestants such as Martin Luther on occasion equated their great enemy, the pope, with the Muslim "Turk," both of them leading people away from authentic religion.

The most infamous Renaissance example of hostility to Islam as a religion is displayed in Source 12.5, a fresco by the Italian artist Giovanni da Modena, painted on a church wall in the northern Italian city of Bologna in 1415. It was a small part of a much larger depiction of Hell, featuring a gigantic image of Satan devouring and excreting the damned, while many others endured horrific punishments. Among them was Muhammad—naked, bound to a rock, and tortured by a winged demon with long horns. It reflected common understandings of Muhammad as a religious heretic, a false prophet, and even the anti-Christ and therefore "hell-bound."

Detail, from the Bolognini Chapel, San Pietro, Bologna, Italy/Scala/Art Resource, NY

Source 12.5 Giovanni da Modena, Muhammad in Hell

■ How does this fresco depict Hell? What does the larger context of the fresco as a whole suggest about Modena's view of Muhammad?

■ How does this image differ from that of Source 12.4, particularly in its posture toward Islam?

■ Italian Muslims have long objected to this image, noting that Islam portrays Jesus in a very positive light. In 2002 a radical group linked to al-Qaeda plotted unsuccessfully to blow up the church that housed this image in order to destroy the offending portrayal of their prophet. What particular objections do you imagine motivated Muslim opposition to this element of the fresco?

DOING HISTORY

Islam and Renaissance Europe

1. **Making comparisons:** What range of postures toward the Islamic world do these images convey? How might you account for the differences among them?

2. **Imagining reactions:** How might the artists who created the first four images respond to Source 12.5?

3. **Examining the content of visual sources:** While all of these images deal with the Islamic world, with what different aspects of that world are they concerned?

4. **Considering art and society:** In what ways were these images shaped by the concrete political, economic, and cultural conditions of Renaissance Europe? What role did the Islamic world play in the emerging identity of European civilization?

Multiple-Choice Questions

For questions 1–3, use the map on page 350 of this text to answer the following questions.

1. According to the map, where did Buddhism originate?
   a. In southern India
   b. Near the Ganges River in northeastern India
   c. In China
   d. Along the Silk Roads

2. According to the map, what may have delayed the spread of Buddhism into Tibet centuries after it spread to other regions?
   a. The people of Tibet were resistant to Buddhist teachings.
   b. The Himalayas and Taklamakan Desert were natural barriers to exchanges into Tibet.
   c. Buddhist monks were not interested in spreading Buddhism into Tibet.
   d. Political strife between Tibet and India made cultural exchanges impossible.

3. According to the map, why did Buddhism spread in the directions and time frame indicated?
   a. Buddhism spread in random patterns.
   b. Buddhism spread along established land and sea exchange routes.
   c. Buddhism spread as millions of Indians migrated throughout Asia.
   d. Buddhism spread farther west than it did to the east or south.

Short-Answer Question

4. Answer parts A, B, and C.
   A. Identify ONE political, social, or economic factor that fostered changes in East Africa in the period 600–1450.
   B. Briefly explain ONE change in East Africa that resulted from the factor that you indicated in part A.
   C. Briefly explain ANOTHER change in East Africa that resulted from the factor that you indicated in part A.

Document-Based Question

Directions: *Question 5 refers to the following documents. You will likely need to flip back and forth between these documents to answer the question adequately. Use scrap pieces of paper or sticky notes to tab these documents. When answering the question, refer to the "Advice for Responding to a DBQ" on the inside of the back cover.*

5. Using the following documents from this textbook and your knowledge of world history, analyze relationships between religion and politics in Afro-Eurasia in the postclassical era (c. 600–c. 1450 C.E.).

DOCUMENT	PAGE	DOCUMENT NAME
1	314	Xuanzang, "On Buddhist Studies"
2	320	Leo Africanus, "The Kingdom of Borno"
3	404	The Battle at Badr
4	408	Charlemagne
5	449–50	Gregory of Tours, *History of the Franks*
6	452	Charlemagne, *Capitulary on Saxony*
7	494–95	*The Chronicle of Novgorod*

Long-Essay Question

When answering the following question, refer to the "Advice for Responding to an LEQ" on the inside of the back cover.

6. In ONE of the following regions, analyze the effects of pastoral groups in the period 600 to 1450.
- Central Asia
- East Asia
- Southwest Asia

PART FOUR

THE EARLY MODERN WORLD

1450–1750

Contents

DEBATING THE CHARACTER OF AN ERA

For the sake of clarity and coherence, historians often characterize a particular period of time in a brief phrase—the age of First Civilizations, the age of empires, the era of revolutions, and so on. Though useful and even necessary, such capsule descriptions leave a lot out and vastly oversimplify what actually happened. Historical reality is always more messy, more complicated, and more uncertain than any shorthand label can convey. Such is surely the case when we examine the three centuries spanning the years from roughly 1450 to 1750.

AP® EXAM TIP

The historical processes and events in Part Four make up 20 percent of the AP® exam.

An Early Modern Era?

Those three centuries, which are addressed in Chapters 13 through 15, are conventionally labeled as "the early modern era." In using this term, historians are suggesting that during these three centuries we can find some initial signs or markers of the modern world, such as those described at the end of Chapter 12: the beginnings of genuine globalization, elements of distinctly modern societies, and a growing European presence in world affairs.

The most obvious expression of globalization, of course, lay in the oceanic journeys of European explorers and the European conquest and colonial settlement of the Americas. The Atlantic slave trade linked Africa permanently to the Western Hemisphere, while the global silver trade allowed Europeans to use New World precious metals to buy their way into ancient Asian trade routes. The massive transfer of plants, animals, diseases, and people, known to historians as the Columbian exchange, created wholly new networks of interaction across both the Atlantic and Pacific oceans, with enormous global implications. Missionaries carried Christianity far beyond Europe, allowing it to become a genuinely world religion, with a presence in the Americas, China, Japan, the Philippines, and south-central Africa. Other threads in the emerging global web were also woven as Russians marched across Siberia to the Pacific, as China expanded deep into Inner Asia, and as the Ottoman Empire encompassed much of the Middle East, North Africa, and southeastern Europe (see Chapter 13).

Scattered signs of what later generations thought of as "modernity" appeared in various places around the world. The most obviously modern cultural development took place in Europe, where the Scientific Revolution transformed, at least for a few people, their view of the world, their approach to knowledge, and their understanding of traditional Christianity. Demographically, China,

Japan, India, and Europe experienced the beginnings of modern population growth as Eurasia recovered from the Black Death and Mongol wars and as the foods of the Americas—corn and potatoes, for example—provided nutrition to support larger numbers. World population more than doubled between 1400 and 1800 (from about 374 million to 968 million), even as the globalization of disease produced a demographic catastrophe in the Americas and the slave trade limited African population growth. More highly commercialized economies centered in large cities developed in various parts of Eurasia and the Americas. By the early eighteenth century, for example, Japan was one of the most urbanized societies in the world, with Edo (Tokyo) housing more than a million inhabitants and ranking as the world's largest city. In China, Southeast Asia, India, and across the Atlantic basin, more and more people found themselves, sometimes willingly and at other times involuntarily, producing for distant markets rather than for the use of their local communities.

Stronger and more cohesive states represented yet another global pattern as they incorporated various local societies into larger units while actively promoting trade, manufacturing, and a common culture within their borders. France, the Dutch Republic, Russia, Morocco, the Mughal Empire, Vietnam, Burma, Siam, and Japan all represent this kind of state.[1] Their military power likewise soared as the "gunpowder revolution" kicked in around the world. Thus large-scale empires proliferated across Asia and the Middle East, while various European powers carved out new domains in the Americas. Within these empires, human pressures on the land intensified as forests were felled, marshes drained, and the hunting grounds of foragers and the grazing lands of pastoralists were confiscated for farming or ranching.

A Late Agrarian Era?

All of these developments give some validity to the notion of an early modern era. But this is far from the whole story, and it may be misleading if it suggests that European world domination and more fully modern societies were a sure thing, an inevitable outgrowth of early modern developments. In fact, that future was far from clear in 1750.

Although Europeans ruled the Americas and controlled the world's sea routes, their political and military power in mainland Asia and Africa was very limited. Eighteenth-century China and Japan strictly controlled the European missionaries and merchants who operated in their societies, and African authorities frequently set the terms under which the slave trade was conducted. Islam, not Christianity, was the most rapidly spreading faith in much of Asia and Africa, and in 1750 Europe, India, and China were roughly comparable in their manufacturing output. In short, it was not obvious that Europeans would soon dominate the planet. Moreover, populations and economies had surged at various points in the past, only to fall back again in a cyclical pattern. Nothing guaranteed that the early modern surge would be any more lasting than the others.

Nor was there much to suggest that anything approaching modern industrial society was on the horizon. Animal and human muscles, wind, and water still provided almost all of the energy that powered human economies. Handicraft techniques of manufacturing had nowhere been displaced by factory-based production or steam power. Long-established elites, not middle-class upstarts, everywhere provided leadership and enjoyed the greatest privileges, while rural peasants, not urban workers, represented the primary social group in the lower classes. Kings and nobles, not parliaments and parties, governed. Female subordination was assumed to be natural almost everywhere. While the texture of patriarchy varied among cultures and fluctuated over time, nowhere had ideas of gender equality taken root. Modern society, with its promise of liberation from ancient inequalities and from mass poverty, hardly seemed around the corner.

Most of the world's peoples, in fact, continued to live in long-established ways, and their societies operated according to traditional principles. Kings ruled most of Europe, and male landowning aristocrats remained at the top of the social hierarchy. Another change in ruling dynasties occurred in China, while that huge country affirmed Confucian values and a social structure that privileged landowning and office-holding elites, all of them men. Most Indians practiced some form of Hinduism and owed their most fundamental loyalty to local castes, even as South Asia continued its centuries-long incorporation into the Islamic world. The realm of Islam maintained its central role in the Eastern Hemisphere as the Ottoman Empire revived the political fortunes of Islam, and the religion sustained its long-term expansion into Africa and Southeast Asia.

In short, for the majority of humankind, the three centuries between 1450 and 1750 marked less an entry into the modern era than the continuing development of older agrarian societies. It was as much a late agrarian era as an early modern age. Persistent patterns rooted in the past characterized that period, along with new departures and sprouts of modernity. And change was not always in the direction of what we now regard as "modern." In European, Islamic, and Chinese societies alike, some people urged a return to earlier ways of living and thinking rather than embracing what was new and untried. Although Europeans were increasingly prominent on the world stage, they certainly did not hold all the leading roles in the global drama of these three centuries.

From this mixture of what was new and what was old during the early modern era, the three chapters that follow highlight the changes. Chapter 13 turns the spotlight on the new empires of those three centuries—European, Middle Eastern, and Asian. New global patterns of long-distance trade in spices, sugar, silver, fur, and slaves represent the themes of Chapter 14. New cultural trends—both within the major religious traditions of the world and in the emergence of modern science—come together in Chapter 15. With the benefit of hindsight, we may see many of these developments as harbingers of a modern world to come, but from the viewpoint of 1700 or so, the future was open and uncertain, as it almost always is.

Landmarks in World History (ca. 1450–ca. 1750)

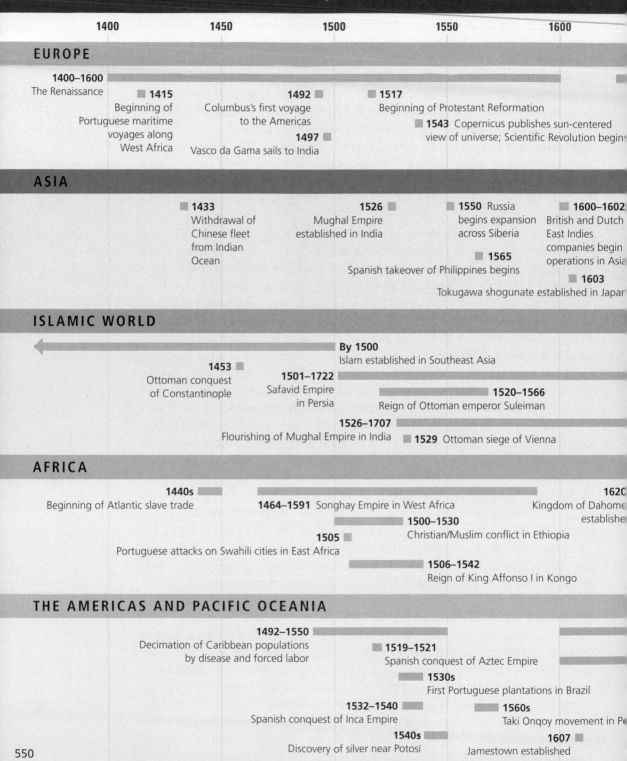

	1400	1450	1500	1550	1600

EUROPE

1400–1600
The Renaissance

■ 1415
Beginning of
Portuguese maritime
voyages along
West Africa

1492 ■
Columbus's first voyage
to the Americas

1497 ■
Vasco da Gama sails to India

■ 1517
Beginning of Protestant Reformation

■ 1543 Copernicus publishes sun-centered
view of universe; Scientific Revolution begin

ASIA

■ 1433
Withdrawal of
Chinese fleet
from Indian
Ocean

1526 ■
Mughal Empire
established in India

■ 1550 Russia
begins expansion
across Siberia

■ 1565
Spanish takeover of Philippines begins

■ 1600–1602
British and Dutch
East Indies
companies begin
operations in Asia

■ 1603
Tokugawa shogunate established in Japan

ISLAMIC WORLD

◀——

By 1500
Islam established in Southeast Asia

1453 ■
Ottoman conquest
of Constantinople

1501–1722
Safavid Empire
in Persia

1520–1566
Reign of Ottoman emperor Suleiman

1526–1707
Flourishing of Mughal Empire in India

■ 1529 Ottoman siege of Vienna

AFRICA

1440s
Beginning of Atlantic slave trade

1464–1591 Songhay Empire in West Africa

1500–1530
Christian/Muslim conflict in Ethiopia

1505 ■
Portuguese attacks on Swahili cities in East Africa

1506–1542
Reign of King Affonso I in Kongo

1620
Kingdom of Dahome
establishe

THE AMERICAS AND PACIFIC OCEANIA

1492–1550
Decimation of Caribbean populations
by disease and forced labor

■ 1519–1521
Spanish conquest of Aztec Empire

1530s
First Portuguese plantations in Brazil

1532–1540
Spanish conquest of Inca Empire

1560s
Taki Onqoy movement in Pe

1540s
Discovery of silver near Potosí

1607 ■
Jamestown established

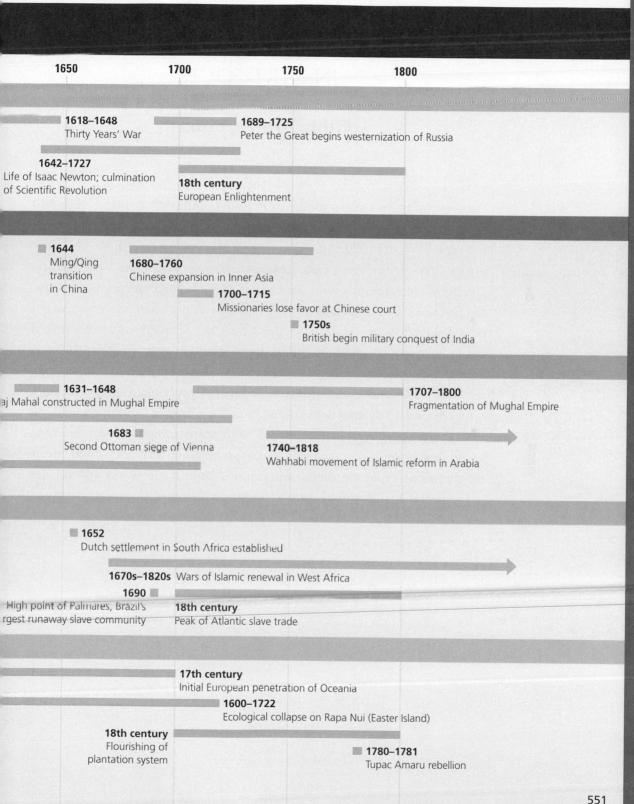

1650   1700   1750   1800

1618–1648
Thirty Years' War

1689–1725
Peter the Great begins westernization of Russia

1642–1727
Life of Isaac Newton; culmination
of Scientific Revolution

18th century
European Enlightenment

1644
Ming/Qing
transition
in China

1680–1760
Chinese expansion in Inner Asia

1700–1715
Missionaries lose favor at Chinese court

1750s
British begin military conquest of India

1631–1648
aj Mahal constructed in Mughal Empire

1707–1800
Fragmentation of Mughal Empire

1683
Second Ottoman siege of Vienna

1740–1818
Wahhabi movement of Islamic reform in Arabia

1652
Dutch settlement in South Africa established

1670s–1820s Wars of Islamic renewal in West Africa

1690
High point of Palmares, Brazil's
rgest runaway slave community

18th century
Peak of Atlantic slave trade

17th century
Initial European penetration of Oceania

1600–1722
Ecological collapse on Rapa Nui (Easter Island)

18th century
Flourishing of
plantation system

1780–1781
Tupac Amaru rebellion

UNDERSTANDING AP® THEMES
IN PART FOUR

Global Interactions

Part Four of this text corresponds to Period 4 of the AP® course outline and constitutes 20 percent of the AP® exam. Encompassing the three centuries between 1450 and 1750, this part is commonly referred to as the "early modern era." While this designation remains controversial among some historians, these centuries represent a new phase in the human journey because for the first time the interactions among distinct cultures and societies occurred on a genuinely global scale. Now the Americas became permanently linked into a network of communication and exchange with the Afro-Eurasian world, and sub-Saharan Africa was more thoroughly connected to an emerging world system. The three chapters of Part Four are organized thematically, with Chapter 13 dealing with empire building, Chapter 14 with the making of a global economy, and Chapter 15 with transregional cultural developments, both religious and secular. These processes in turn had major effects on the social evolution of human cultures around the world and on the demographic and environmental settings in which they operated.

Environment	Cultures	State Building	Economies	Social Structures
Global population growth and environmental change	Muslim/Hindu encounters in India	European conquest and empire building in the Americas	The spice trade: empires of European commerce in Asia	Class and gender in the early modern era
Disease and demographic collapse: the Americas and Siberia	Muslim/Christian encounters in Ottoman realm	A Spanish colonial state in the Philippines	Asian commercial networks in Asia	Comparing colonial social structures in North and South America
The Columbian exchange: global biological transformations	Protestant Reformation	The making of a Russian Empire	Global silver trade: effects on • Spanish America • Japan • China • Europe	Women in American colonial societies
The Little Ice Age: global cooling and its consequences	Christianity in • The Philippines • Siberia • Spanish America • Russia • China • Japan • Mughal India	Peter the Great and Russia's "catching up" efforts		Emergence of mestizo/mulatto classes in the Americas
Environmental effects of silver mining in Bolivia		A Central Asian Chinese empire	The fur trade: North America and Russia compared	The fur trade and gender roles in North America
Reforestation in Japan	African religious cultures in the Americas	The Mughals: a Muslim empire in India	The Atlantic slave trade • Origins • Operations • Outcomes	Erosion of women's roles in the colonial Philippines
Deforestation in China	Islamic expansion in Southeast Asia	The Ottomans: a Muslim empire in the Middle East and Southeast Europe		Female merchants in Southeast Asia
Species depletion and the fur trade (in Russia and North America)	Islamic renewal: the Wahhabi example	The Tokugawa state in Japan	Plantation economies in the Americas	Erosion of pastoralism in Russian and Chinese empires
Demographic history of slave trade	Neo-Confucianism, *kaozheng*, and popular culture in China	Japan and China: limiting European incursions	Forced labor and the hacienda system	Multiculturalism in China
	Bhakti tradition in India	African state building and state disintegration in the slave-trade era	Silver-mining economy: Potosí	Women in Mughal and Ottoman empires
	Emergence of Sikhism in India		Settler economies in the Americas	Slavery in Africa
	Emergence of modern science in Europe	Early modern state building: primary sources from Asia, the Middle East, Europe, and the Americas	Erosion of hunting and herding economies in Russian Empire	Gender and social change in Africa as a result of the slave trade
	The European Enlightenment			Expressing social status via trade goods
	Responses to European science: China, Japan, and the Islamic world			Women in the Scientific Revolution and the Enlightenment

Illustration from the *Padshahnama*, ca. 1630–1640 (bodycolour with gold on paper)/Royal Collection Trust © Her Majesty Queen Elizabeth II, 2014/Bridgeman Images

CHAPTER 13

Political Transformations

Empires and Encounters

1450–1750

"What he [Vladimir Putin] wants to do, you can just see the lust in his eyes, he wants to re-create the Russian empire, and this move on Crimea is his first step." So said U.S. senator Bill Nelson in March of 2014, referring to the Russian president's actions in seizing Crimea and in pressuring Ukraine to remain within a Russian sphere of influence. In reflecting on this very current political situation, the senator, and many others as well, invoked the Russian Empire, which had taken shape during the early modern era. In the same vein, commentators on the economic and political resurgence of twenty-first-century Turkey often refer to it as an effort "to rebuild the Ottoman Empire," likewise a creation of the early modern era.[1] In such ways, the memories of these earlier empires continue to shape understanding of current events and perhaps to inspire actions in the present as well.

As these comments imply, empire building has been largely discredited during the twentieth and twenty-first centuries, and "imperialist" has become a term of insult rather than a source of pride. How very different were the three centuries (1450–1750) of the early modern era, when empire building was a global process! In the Americas, the Aztec and Inca empires flourished before they were incorporated into the rival empires of the Spanish, Portuguese, British, French, and Dutch, constructed all across the Western Hemisphere. Within those imperial systems, vast transformations took place: old societies were destroyed, and new societies arose as Native Americans, Europeans, and Africans came into sustained contact with one another for the first time in world history.

The Mughal Empire   Among the most magnificent of the early modern empires was that of the Mughals in India. In this painting by an unknown Mughal artist, the seventeenth-century emperor Shah Jahan is holding a *durbar*, or ceremonial assembly, in the audience hall of his palace. The material splendor of the setting shows the immense wealth of the court, while the halo around Shah Jahan's head indicates the special spiritual grace or enlightenment associated with emperors.

It was a revolutionary encounter with implications that extended far beyond the Americas themselves.

But European empires in the Americas were not alone on the imperial stage of the early modern era. Across the immense expanse of Siberia, the Russians constructed what was then the world's largest territorial empire, making Russia an Asian as well as a European power. Qing (chihng) dynasty China penetrated deep into Inner Asia, doubling the size of the country while incorporating millions of non-Chinese people who practiced Islam, Buddhism, or animistic religions. On the South Asian peninsula, the Islamic Mughal Empire brought Hindus and Muslims into a closer relationship than ever before, sometimes quite peacefully and at other times with great conflict. In the Middle East, the Turkish Ottoman Empire reestablished something of the earlier political unity of heartland Islam and posed a serious military and religious threat to European Christendom.

Thus the early modern era was an age of empire. Within their borders, those empires mixed and mingled diverse peoples in a wide variety of ways. Those relationships represented a new stage in the globalization process and new arenas of cross-cultural encounter. The transformations they set in motion echo still in the twenty-first century.

SEEKING THE MAIN POINT

In what ways did European empires in the Americas resemble their Russian, Chinese, Mughal, and Ottoman counterparts, and in what respects were they different? Do you find the similarities or the differences more striking?

European Empires in the Americas

AP® EXAM TIP

Take good notes on the progression of European conquest of the Americas.

Among the early modern empires, those of Western Europe were distinctive because the conquered territories lay an ocean away from the imperial heartland, rather than adjacent to it. Following the breakthrough voyages of Columbus, the Spanish focused their empire-building efforts in the Caribbean and then, in the early sixteenth century, turned to the mainland, with stunning conquests of the powerful but fragile Aztec and Inca empires. Meanwhile, the Portuguese established themselves along the coast of present-day Brazil. In the early seventeenth century, the British, French, and Dutch launched colonial settlements along the eastern coast of North America. From these beginnings, Europeans extended their empires to encompass most of the Americas, at least nominally, by the mid-eighteenth century (see Map 13.1). It was a remarkable achievement. What had made it possible?

The European Advantage

Guided Reading Question

....

■ CONNECTION
What enabled Europeans to carve out huge empires an ocean away from their homelands?

Geography provides a starting point for explaining Europe's American empires. Countries on the Atlantic rim of Europe (Portugal, Spain, Britain, and France) were simply closer to the Americas than were any potential Asian competitors. Furthermore, the fixed winds of the Atlantic blew steadily in the same direction. Once these air currents were understood and mastered, they provided a far different maritime environment than the alternating monsoon winds of the Indian Ocean, in

A MAP OF TIME

1453	Ottoman conquest of Constantinople
1464–1591	Songhay Empire in West Africa
1480	Russia emerges from Mongol rule
1494	Treaty of Tordesillas divides the Americas between Spain and Portugal
1501	Safavid Empire established in Persia/Iran
1519–1521	Spanish conquest of Aztec Empire
1526	Mughal Empire established in India
1529	Ottoman siege of Vienna
1530s	First Portuguese plantations in Brazil
1532–1540	Spanish conquest of Inca Empire
1550	Russian expansion across Siberia begins
1565	Spanish takeover of Philippines begins
1607	Jamestown, Virginia: first permanent English settlement in Americas
1608	French colony established in Quebec
1680–1760	Chinese expansion into Inner Asia
1683	Second Ottoman siege of Vienna
After 1707	Fragmentation of Mughal Empire

which Asian powers had long operated. European innovations in mapmaking, navigation, sailing techniques, and ship design—building on earlier models from the Mediterranean, Indian Ocean, and Chinese regions—likewise enabled Europeans to penetrate the Atlantic Ocean. The enormously rich markets of the Indian Ocean world provided little incentive for its Chinese, Indian, or Muslim participants to venture much beyond their own waters.

Europeans, however, were powerfully motivated to do so. After 1200 or so, European elites were increasingly aware of their region's marginal position in the rich world of Eurasian commerce and were determined to gain access to that world. Once the Americas were discovered, windfalls of natural resources, including highly productive agricultural lands, drove further expansion, ultimately underpinning the long-term growth of the European economy into the nineteenth and twentieth centuries. Beyond these economic or ecological stimuli, rulers were driven by the enduring rivalries of competing states. The growing and relatively independent merchant class in a rapidly commercializing Europe sought direct access to Asian wealth

AP® EXAM TIP

Make a list of the powerful motivations for European exploration.

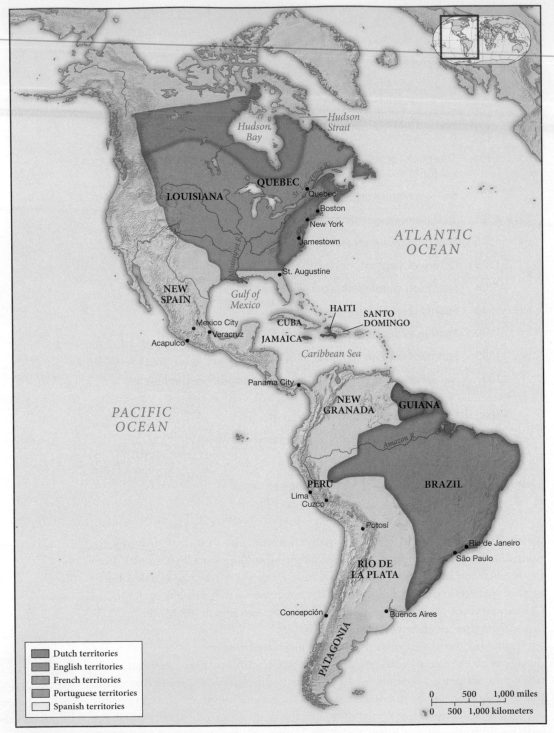

Hudson
Strait

Hudson
Bay

QUEBEC

LOUISIANA

Quebec

St. Lawrence R.

Boston

New York

ATLANTIC
OCEAN

Jamestown

Mississippi R.

NEW
SPAIN

St. Augustine

Gulf of
Mexico

HAITI

Mexico City
Veracruz

CUBA

SANTO
DOMINGO

Acapulco

JAMAICA

Caribbean Sea

Panama City

NEW
GRANADA

GUIANA

PACIFIC
OCEAN

Amazon R.

BRAZIL

PERU

Lima
Cuzco

Potosí

Rio de Janeiro

São Paulo

RÍO DE
LA PLATA

Concepción

Buenos Aires

PATAGONIA

Dutch territories
English territories
French territories
Portuguese territories
Spanish territories

0   500   1,000 miles
0   500   1,000 kilometers

Map 13.1   European Colonial Empires in the Americas

By the beginning of the eighteenth century, European powers had laid claim to most of the Western Hemisphere. Their wars and rivalries during that century led to an expansion of Spanish and
English claims, at the expense of the French.

to avoid the reliance on Muslim intermediaries that they found so distasteful. Impoverished nobles and commoners alike found opportunity for gaining wealth and status in the colonies. Missionaries and others were inspired by crusading zeal to enlarge the realm of Christendom. Persecuted minorities were in search of a new start in life. All of these compelling motives drove the relentlessly expanding imperial frontier in the Americas. Summarizing their intentions, one Spanish conquistador declared: "We came here to serve God and the King, and also to get rich."[2]

In carving out these empires, often against great odds and with great difficulty, Europeans nonetheless bore certain advantages, despite their distance from home. Their states and trading companies enabled the effective mobilization of both human and material resources. Their seafaring technology, built on Chinese and Islamic precedents, allowed them to cross the Atlantic with growing ease, transporting people and supplies across great distances. Their ironworking technology, gunpowder weapons, and horses initially had no parallel in the Americas, although many peoples subsequently acquired them.

Divisions within and between local societies provided allies for the determined European invaders. Various subject peoples of the Aztec Empire, for example, resented Mexica domination and willingly joined Hernán Cortés in the Spanish assault on that empire. In the final attack on the Aztec capital of Tenochtitlán, Cortés's forces contained fewer than 1,000 Spaniards and many times that number of Tlaxcalans, former subjects of the Aztecs. After their defeat, tens of thousands of Aztecs themselves joined Cortés as he carved out a Spanish Mesoamerican empire far larger than that of the Aztecs. (See Zooming In: Doña Marina, page 558.) Much of the Inca elite, according to a recent study, "actually welcomed the Spanish invaders as liberators and willingly settled down with them to share rule of Andean farmers and miners."[3] A violent dispute between two rival contenders for the Inca throne, the brothers Atahualpa and Huáscar, certainly helped the European invaders recruit allies to augment their own minimal forces. In short, Spanish military victories were not solely of their own making, but the product of alliances with local peoples, who supplied the bulk of the Europeans' conquering armies.

Perhaps the most significant of European advantages lay in their germs and diseases, with which Native Americans had no familiarity. Those diseases decimated society after society, sometimes in advance of the Europeans' actual arrival. In particular regions such as the Caribbean, Virginia, and New England, the rapid buildup of immigrant populations, coupled with the sharply diminished native numbers, allowed Europeans to actually outnumber local peoples within a few decades.

The Great Dying and the Little Ice Age

Whatever combination of factors explains the European acquisition of empires in the Americas, there is no doubting their global significance. Chief among the consequences was the demographic collapse of Native American societies. Although precise figures remain the subject of much debate, scholars generally agree that the

Doña Marina:
Between Two Worlds

In her brief life, she was known variously as Malinal, Doña Marina, and La Malinche.[4] By whatever name, she was a woman who experienced the encounter of the Old World and the New in particularly intimate ways, even as she became a bridge between them. Born around 1505, Malinal was the daughter of an elite and cultured family in the borderlands between the Maya and Aztec cultures in what is now southern Mexico. Two dramatic events decisively shaped her life. The first occurred when her father died and her mother remarried, bearing a son to her new husband. To protect this boy's inheritance, Malinal's family sold her into slavery. Eventually, she came into the possession of a Maya chieftain in Tabasco on the Gulf of Mexico.

Here her second life-changing event took place in March 1519, when the Spanish conquistador Hernán Cortés landed his troops and inflicted a sharp military defeat on Tabasco. In the negotiations that followed, Tabasco authorities gave lavish gifts to the Spanish, including twenty women, one of whom was Malinal.

Doña Marina (center left) translating for Cortés.

Described by Bernal Díaz, one of Cortés's associates, as "good-looking, intelligent, and self-assured," the teenage Malinal soon found herself in service to Cortés himself. Since Spanish men were not supposed to touch non-Christian women, these newcomers were distributed among his officers, quickly baptized, and given Christian names. Thus Malinal became Doña Marina.

With a ready ear for languages and already fluent in Mayan and Nahuatl, the language of the Aztecs, Doña Marina soon picked up Spanish and quickly became indispensable to Cortés as an interpreter, cross-cultural broker, and strategist. She accompanied him on his march inland to the Aztec capital, Tenochtitlán, and on several occasions her language skills and cultural awareness allowed her to uncover spies and plots that might well have seriously impeded Cortés's defeat of the Aztec Empire. Díaz reported that "Doña Marina, who understood full well what was happening, told [Cortés] what

pre-Columbian population of the Western Hemisphere was substantial, perhaps 60 to 80 million. The greatest concentrations of people lived in the Mesoamerican and Andean zones, which were dominated by the Aztec and Inca empires. Long isolation from the Afro-Eurasian world and the lack of most domesticated animals meant the absence of acquired immunities to Old World diseases such as smallpox, measles, typhus, influenza, malaria, and, later, yellow fever.

Therefore, when Native American peoples came into contact with these European and African diseases, they died in appalling numbers, in many cases losing up to 90 percent of the population. As one recent historian has noted, "It was as if the suffering these diseases had caused in Eurasia over the past millennia were concentrated into the span of decades."[5] The densely settled peoples of Caribbean islands was going on." In the Aztec capital, where Cortés took the emperor Moctezuma captive, it fell to Doña Marina to persuade him to accept this humiliating position and surrender his wealth to the Spanish. Even Cortés, who was never very gracious with his praise for her, acknowledged that "after God, we owe this conquest of New Spain to Doña Marina." Aztecs soon came to see this young woman as the voice of Cortés, referring to her as La Malinche, a Spanish approximation of her original name. So paired did Cortés and La Malinche become in Aztec thinking that Cortés himself was often called "Malinche."

More than an interpreter for Cortés, Doña Marina also became his mistress and bore him a son. But after the initial conquest of Mexico was complete and he no longer needed her skills, Cortés married Doña Marina off to another Spanish conquistador, Juan Jaramillo, with whom she lived until her death, probably around 1530. Cortés did provide her with several pieces of land, one of which, ironically, had belonged to Moctezuma. Her son, however, was taken from her and raised in Spain.

In 1523, Doña Marina performed one final service for Cortés, accompanying him on a mission to Honduras to suppress a rebellion. There her personal life seemed to come full circle, for near her hometown she encountered her mother, who had sold her into slavery, and her half brother. Díaz reported that they "were very much afraid

of Doña Marina," thinking that they would surely be put to death by their now-powerful and well-connected relative. But in a replay of the biblical story of Joseph and his brothers, Doña Marina quickly reassured and forgave them, while granting them "many golden jewels and some clothes."

In the centuries since her death, Doña Marina has been highly controversial. For much of the colonial era, she was viewed positively as an ally of the Spanish. But after independence, some came to see her as a traitor to her own people, shunning her heritage and siding with the invaders. Still others have considered her as the mother of Mexico's mixed-race, or mestizo, culture. Should she be understood primarily as a victim or as a skillful survivor negotiating hard choices under difficult circumstances?

Whatever the judgments of later generations, Doña Marina herself seems to have made a clear choice to cast her lot with the Europeans. Even when Cortés had given her to another man, Doña Marina expressed no regret. According to Díaz, she declared, "Even if they were to make me mistress of all the provinces of New Spain, I would refuse the honor, for I would rather serve my husband and Cortés than anything else in the world."

Questions: How might you define the significance of Doña Marina's life? In what larger contexts might that life find a place?

virtually vanished within fifty years of Columbus's arrival. Central Mexico, with a population estimated at some 10 to 20 million before the Spanish conquest, declined to about 1 million by 1650. A native Nahuatl (nah-watl) account depicted the social breakdown that accompanied the smallpox pandemic: "A great many died from this plague, and many others died of hunger. They could not get up to search for food, and everyone else was too sick to care for them, so they starved to death in their beds."[6]

The situation was similar in Dutch and British territories of North America. A Dutch observer in New Netherland (later New York) reported in 1656 that "the Indians . . . affirm that before the arrival of the Christians, and before the small pox broke out amongst them, they were ten times as numerous as they are now, and that their population had been melted down by this disease, whereof nine-tenths of them have died."[7] To Governor Bradford of Plymouth colony (in present-day Massachusetts), such conditions represented the "good hand of God" at work, "sweeping away great multitudes of the natives . . . that he might make room for us."[8] Not until the late seventeenth century did native numbers begin to recuperate somewhat from this catastrophe, and even then, they did not recover everywhere.

As the Great Dying took hold in the Americas, it interacted with another natural phenomenon, this time one of genuinely global proportions. Known as the Little Ice Age, it was a period of unusually cool temperatures that spanned much of the early modern period, most prominently in the Northern Hemisphere. Scholars continue to debate its causes. Some have suggested a low point in sunspot activity, leading to less intense solar irradiation of the earth, while others have argued that the chief cause was volcanic eruptions, whose ash and gases blocked the sun's warming energy in the upper atmosphere. More recently, some scientists have linked the Little Ice Age to the demographic collapse in the Americas. The Great Dying, they argue, resulted in the desertion of large areas of Native American farmland and ended the traditional practices of forest management through burning in many regions. These changes sparked a resurgence of plant life, which in turn took large amounts of carbon dioxide, a greenhouse gas, out of the atmosphere, contributing to global cooling. Whatever the causes, shorter growing seasons and less hospitable weather conditions adversely affected food production in regions across the globe.

While the onset, duration, and effects of the Little Ice Age varied from region to region, the impact of a cooler climate reached its peak in many regions in the mid-seventeenth century, helping to spark what scholars term the General Crisis. Much of China, Europe, and North America experienced record or near-record cold winters during this period. Regions near the equator in the tropics and Southern Hemisphere also experienced extreme conditions and irregular rainfall, resulting, for instance, in the growth of the Sahara Desert. Wet, cold summers reduced harvests dramatically in Europe, while severe droughts ruined crops in many other regions, especially China, which suffered its worst years of drought in the previous five centuries between 1637 and 1641. Difficult weather conditions accentuated other stresses in societies, leading to widespread famines, epidemics, uprisings, and wars in which millions perished. Eurasia did not escape lightly from these stresses: the collapse of the Ming dynasty in China, nearly constant warfare in Europe, and civil war in Mughal India all occurred in the context of the General Crisis, which only fully subsided when more favorable weather patterns returned in the eighteenth century.

Nor were the Americas, already devastated by the Great Dying, spared the suffering that accompanied the Little Ice Age and the General Crisis of the seventeenth century. In central Mexico, heartland of the Aztec Empire and the center of Spanish colonial rule in the area, severe drought in the five years after 1639 sent the price of maize skyrocketing, left granaries empty and many people without water, and prompted an unsuccessful plot to declare Mexico's independence from Spain.

AP® EXAM TIP

You need to know examples of the effects of environmental events on human history.

Continuing drought years in the decades that followed witnessed repeated public processions of the statue of Our Lady of Guadalupe, who had gained a reputation for producing rain. The Caribbean region during the 1640s experienced the opposite condition—torrential rains that accompanied more frequent El Niño weather patterns—which provided ideal conditions for the breeding of mosquitoes that carried both yellow fever and malaria. A Maya chronicle for 1648 noted, "There was bloody vomit and we began to die."[9]

Like the Great Dying, the General Crisis reminds us that climate often plays an important role in shaping human history. But it also reminds us that human activity—the importation of deadly diseases to the Americas, in this case—may also help shape the climate, and that this has been true long before the twenty-first century.

The Columbian Exchange

In sharply diminishing the population of the Americas, the Great Dying and the impact of the Little Ice Age created an acute labor shortage and certainly did make room for immigrant newcomers, both colonizing Europeans and enslaved Africans. Over the several centuries of the colonial era and beyond, various combinations of indigenous, European, and African peoples created entirely new societies in the Americas, largely replacing the many and varied cultures that had flourished before 1492. To those colonial societies, Europeans and Africans brought not only their

germs and their people but also their plants and animals. Wheat, rice, sugarcane, grapes, and many garden vegetables and fruits, as well as numerous weeds, took hold in the Americas, where they transformed the landscape and made possible a recognizably European diet and way of life. Even more revolutionary were their animals—horses, pigs, cattle, goats, sheep—all of which were new to the Americas and multiplied spectacularly in an environment largely free of natural predators. These domesticated animals made possible the ranching economies and cowboy cultures of both North and South America. Horses also transformed many Native American societies, particularly in the North American West as settled farming peoples such

Disease and Death among the Aztecs
Smallpox, which accompanied the Spanish to the Americas, devastated native populations. This image, drawn by an Aztec artist and contained in the sixteenth-century *Florentine Codex*, illustrates the impact of the disease in Mesoamerica. (Private Collection/Peter Newark American Pictures/Bridgeman Images)

as the Pawnee abandoned their fields to hunt bison from horseback. In the process, women lost much of their earlier role as food producers as a male-dominated hunting and warrior culture emerged. Both environmentally and socially, these changes were nothing less than revolutionary.

Guided Reading Question

▬ CHANGE
What large-scale transformations did European empires generate?

AP® EXAM TIP

Make a chart of places in Africa, Asia, and Europe, and list the American plants that had a major impact.

In the other direction, American food crops such as corn, potatoes, and cassava spread widely in the Eastern Hemisphere, where they provided the nutritional foundation for the immense population growth that became everywhere a hallmark of the modern era. In Europe, calories derived from corn and potatoes helped push human numbers from some 60 million in 1400 to 390 million in 1900. Those Amerindian crops later provided cheap and reasonably nutritious food for millions of industrial workers. Potatoes, especially, allowed Ireland's population to grow enormously and then condemned many of the Irish to starvation or emigration when an airborne fungus, also from the Americas, destroyed the crop in the mid-nineteenth century. In China, corn, peanuts, and especially sweet potatoes supplemented the traditional rice and wheat to sustain China's modern population explosion. By the early twentieth century, food plants of American origin represented about 20 percent of total Chinese food production. In Africa, corn took hold quickly and was used as a cheap food for the human cargoes of the transatlantic trade. Scholars have speculated that corn, together with peanuts and cassava, underwrote some of Africa's population growth and partially offset the population drain of the slave trade.

Beyond food crops, American stimulants such as tobacco and chocolate were soon used around the world. By the seventeenth century, how-to manuals instructed Chinese users on smoking techniques, and tobacco had become, in the words of one enamored Chinese poet, "the gentleman's companion, it warms my heart and leaves my mouth feeling like a divine furnace."[10] Tea from China and coffee from the Islamic world also spread globally, contributing to this worldwide biological exchange. Never before in human history had such a large-scale and consequential diffusion of plants and animals operated to remake the biological environment of the planet.

Furthermore, the societies that developed within the American colonies drove the processes of globalization and reshaped the world economy of the early modern era (see Chapter 14 for a more extended treatment). The silver mines of Mexico and Peru fueled both transatlantic and transpacific commerce, encouraged Spain's unsuccessful effort to dominate Europe, and enabled Europeans to buy the Chinese tea, silk, and porcelain that they valued so highly. The plantation owners of the tropical lowland regions needed workers and found them by the millions in Africa. The Atlantic slave trade, which brought these workers to the colonies, and the sugar and cotton trade, which distributed the fruits of their labor abroad, created a lasting link among Africa, Europe, and the Americas, while scattering peoples of African origin throughout the Western Hemisphere.

This enormous network of communication, migration, trade, disease, and the transfer of plants and animals, all generated by European colonial empires in the

Americas, has been dubbed the "Columbian exchange." It gave rise to something wholly new in world history: an interacting Atlantic world connecting four continents. Millions of years ago, the Eastern and Western hemispheres had physically drifted apart, and, ecologically speaking, they had remained largely apart. Now these two "old worlds" were joined, increasingly creating a single biological regime, a "new world" of global dimensions.

The long-term benefits of this Atlantic network were very unequally distributed. Western Europeans were clearly the dominant players in the Atlantic world, and their societies reaped the greatest rewards. Mountains of new information flooded into Europe, shaking up conventional understandings of the world and contributing to a revolutionary new way of thinking known as the Scientific Revolution. The wealth of the colonies—precious metals, natural resources, new food crops, slave labor, financial profits, colonial markets—provided one of the foundations on which Europe's Industrial Revolution was built. The colonies also provided an outlet for the rapidly growing population of European societies and represented an enormous extension of European civilization. In short, the colonial empires of the Americas greatly facilitated a changing global balance of power, which now thrust the previously marginal Western Europeans into an increasingly central and commanding role on the world stage. "Without a New World to deliver economic balance in the Old," concluded a prominent world historian, "Europe would have remained inferior, as ever, in wealth and power, to the great civilizations of Asia."[11]

> **AP® EXAM TIP**
>
> Take notes on this very important explanation of some long-term effects of the Columbian exchange.

Comparing Colonial Societies in the Americas

What the Europeans had encountered across the Atlantic was another "old world," but their actions surely gave rise to a "new world" in the Americas. Their colonial empires—Spanish, Portuguese, British, and French alike—did not simply conquer and govern established societies, but rather generated wholly new societies, born of the decimation of Native American populations and the introduction of European and African peoples, cultures, plants, and animals.

Furthermore, all the European rulers of these empires viewed their realms through the lens of the prevailing economic theory known as mercantilism. This view held that European governments served their countries' economic interests best by encouraging exports and accumulating bullion (precious metals such as silver and gold), believed to be the source of national prosperity. In this scheme of things, colonies provided closed markets for the manufactured goods of the "mother country" and, if they were lucky, supplied great quantities of bullion as well. Mercantilist thinking thus fueled European wars and colonial rivalries around the world in the early modern era. Particularly in Spanish America, however, it was a theory largely ignored or evaded in practice. Spain had few manufactured goods to sell, and piracy and smuggling allowed Spanish colonists to exchange goods with Spain's rivals.

> **AP® EXAM TIP**
>
> Make a chart of similarities and differences between European colonial rule in the Caribbean and North America and European colonial rule in South America.

But variations across the immense colonial world of the Western Hemisphere were at least as noticeable as these similarities. Some differences grew out of the societies of the colonizing power, such as the contrast between a semi-feudal and Catholic Spain and a more rapidly changing Protestant England. The kind of economy established in particular regions—settler-dominated agriculture, slave-based plantations, ranching, or mining—likewise influenced their development. So too did the character of the Native American cultures—the more densely populated and urbanized Mesoamerican and Andean civilizations differed greatly from the more sparsely populated rural villages of North America, for example.

Furthermore, women and men often experienced colonial intrusion in quite distinct ways. Beyond the common burdens of violent conquest, epidemic disease, and coerced labor, both Native American and enslaved African women had to cope with the additional demands made on them as females. Conquest was often accompanied by the transfer of women to the new colonial rulers. Cortés, for example, marked his alliance with the city of Tlaxcala (tlah-SKAH-lah) against the Aztecs by an exchange of gifts in which he received hundreds of female slaves and eight daughters of elite Tlaxcalan families, whom he distributed to his soldiers. And he commanded the Aztec ruler: "You are to deliver women with light skins, corn, chicken, eggs, and tortillas."[12]

Soon after conquest, many Spanish men married elite native women. It was a long-standing practice in Amerindian societies and was encouraged by both Spanish and indigenous male authorities as a means of cementing their new relationship. It was also advantageous for some of the women involved. One of Aztec emperor Moctezuma's daughters, who was mistress to Cortés and eventually married several other Spaniards, wound up with the largest landed estate in the valley of Mexico. Below this elite level of interaction, however, far more women experienced sexual violence and abuse. Rape accompanied conquest in many places, and dependent or enslaved women working under the control of European men frequently found themselves required to perform sexual services. This was tragedy and humiliation for native and enslaved men as well, for they were unable to protect their women from such abuse. Such variations in culture, policy, economy, and gender generated quite different colonial societies in several major regions of the Americas.

In the Lands of the Aztecs and the Incas

The Spanish conquest of the Aztec and Inca empires in the early sixteenth century gave Spain access to the most wealthy, urbanized, and densely populated regions of the Western Hemisphere. Within a century and well before the British had even begun their colonizing efforts in North America, the Spanish in Mexico and Peru had established nearly a dozen major cities; several impressive universities; hundreds of cathedrals, churches, and missions; an elaborate administrative bureaucracy; and a network of regulated international commerce.

The economic foundation for this emerging colonial society lay in commercial agriculture, much of it on large rural estates, and in silver and gold mining. In both cases, native peoples, rather than African slaves or European workers, provided most of the labor, despite their much-diminished numbers. Almost everywhere it was forced labor, often directly required by colonial authorities. In a legal system known as *encomienda*, the Spanish Crown granted to particular Spanish settlers a number of local native people from whom they could require labor, gold, or agricultural produce and to whom they owed "protection" and instruction in the Christian faith. It turned into an exploitative regime not far removed from slavery and was replaced by a similar system, *repartimiento*, with slightly more control by the Crown and Spanish officials. By the seventeenth century, the *hacienda* system had taken shape by which the owners of large estates directly employed native workers. With low wages, high taxes, and large debts to the landowners, the *peons* who worked these estates enjoyed little control over their lives or their livelihood.

On this economic base, a distinctive social order grew up, replicating something of the Spanish class and gender hierarchy while accommodating the racially and culturally different Indians and Africans as well as growing numbers of racially mixed people. At the top of this colonial society were the male Spanish settlers, who were politically and economically dominant and seeking to become a landed aristocracy. One Spanish official commented in 1619: "The Spaniards, from the able and rich to the humble and poor, all hold themselves to be lords and will not serve [do manual labor]."[13] Politically, they increasingly saw themselves not as colonials, but as residents of a Spanish kingdom, subject to the Spanish monarch, yet separate and distinct from Spain itself and deserving of a large measure of self-government. Therefore, they chafed under the heavy bureaucratic restrictions imposed by the Crown. "I obey but I do not enforce" was a slogan that reflected local authorities' resistance to orders from Spain.

But the Spanish minority, never more than 20 percent of the population, was itself a divided community. Descendants of the original conquistadores sought to protect their privileges against immigrant newcomers; Spaniards born in the Americas (*creoles*) resented the pretensions to superiority of those born in Spain (*peninsulares*); landowning Spaniards felt threatened by the growing wealth of commercial and mercantile groups practicing less prestigious occupations. Spanish missionaries and church authorities

Racial Mixing in Colonial Mexico
This eighteenth-century painting by the famous Zapotec artist Miguel Cabrera shows a Spanish man, a *mestiza* woman, and their child, who was labeled as *castiza*. By the twentieth century, such mixed-race people represented the majority of the population of Mexico, and cultural blending had become a central feature of the country's identity. (Museo de América, Madrid, Spain/Bridgeman Images)

AP® EXAM TIP

It is important to remember that "politics" is more than just government—it's about who is in power in societies and relationships.

were often sharply critical of how these settlers treated native peoples. While Spanish women shared the racial privileges of their husbands, they were clearly subordinate in gender terms, unable to hold public office and viewed as weak and in need of male protection. But they were also regarded as the "bearers of civilization," and through their capacity to produce legitimate children, they were the essential link for transmitting male wealth, honor, and status to future generations. This required strict control of their sexuality and a continuation of the Iberian obsession with "purity of blood." In Spain, that concern had focused on potential liaisons with Jews and Muslims; in the colonies, the alleged threat to female virtue derived from Native American and African men.

From a male viewpoint, the problem with Spanish women was that there were very few of them. This demographic fact led to the most distinctive feature of these new colonial societies in Mexico and Peru—the emergence of a *mestizo* (mehs-TEE-zoh), or mixed-race, population, initially the product of unions between Spanish men and Indian women. Rooted in the sexual imbalance among Spanish immigrants (seven men to one woman in early colonial Peru, for example), the emergence of a mestizo population was facilitated by the desire of many surviving Indian women for the relative security of life in a Spanish household, where they and their children would not be subject to the abuse and harsh demands made on native peoples. Over the 300 years of the colonial era, mestizo numbers grew substantially, becoming the majority of the population in Mexico sometime during the nineteenth century. Such mixed-race people were divided into dozens of separate groups known as *castas* (castes), based on their racial heritage and skin color.

AP® EXAM TIP

Look back at other empires in history. How were non-elites treated? Compare these examples from Latin America with others you've read about.

Mestizos were largely Hispanic in culture, but Spaniards looked down on them during much of the colonial era, regarding them as illegitimate, for many were not born of "proper" marriages. Despite this attitude, their growing numbers and the economic usefulness of their men as artisans, clerks, supervisors of labor gangs, and lower-level officials in both church and state bureaucracies led to their recognition as a distinct social group. *Mestizas*, women of mixed racial background, worked as domestic servants or in their husbands' shops, wove cloth, and manufactured candles and cigars, in addition to performing domestic duties. A few became quite wealthy. An illiterate mestiza named Mencia Perez married successively two reasonably well-to-do Spanish men and upon their deaths took over their businesses, becoming in her own right a very rich woman by the 1590s. At that point, no one would have referred to her as a mestiza.[14] Particularly in Mexico, mestizo identity blurred the sense of sharp racial difference between Spanish and Indian peoples and became a major element in the identity of modern Mexico.

At the bottom of Mexican and Peruvian colonial societies were the indigenous peoples, known to Europeans as "Indians." Traumatized by the Great Dying, they were subject to gross abuse and exploitation as the primary labor force for the mines and estates of the Spanish Empire and were required to render tribute payments to their Spanish overlords. Their empires dismantled by Spanish conquest, their religions attacked by Spanish missionaries, and their diminished numbers forcibly relocated into larger settlements, many Indians gravitated toward the world of their conquerors. Many learned Spanish, converted to Christianity; moved to cities to work for wages; ate the meat of cows, chickens, and pigs; used plows and draft animals rather than traditional digging sticks; and took their many grievances to Spanish courts. Indian women endured some distinctive conditions as Spanish legal codes generally defined them as minors rather than responsible adults. As those codes took hold, Indian women were increasingly excluded from the courts or represented by their menfolk. This made it more difficult to maintain female property rights. In 1804, for example, a Maya legal petition identified eight men and ten women from a particular family as owners of a piece of land, but the Spanish translation omitted the women's names altogether.[15]

But much that was indigenous persisted. At the local level, Indian male authorities retained a measure of autonomy, and traditional markets operated regularly. Both Andean and Maya women continued to leave personal property to their female descendants. Maize, beans, and squash persisted as the major elements of Indian diets in Mexico. Christian saints in many places blended easily with specialized indigenous gods, while belief in magic, folk medicine, and communion with the dead remained strong. Memories of the past also endured. The Tupac Amaru revolt in Peru during 1780–1781 was made in the name of the last independent Inca emperor. In that revolt, the wife of the leader, Micaela Bastidas, was referred to as La Coya, the female Inca, evoking the parallel hierarchies of male and female officials who had earlier governed the Inca Empire (see Chapter 12, pages 528–29).

Thus Spaniards, mestizos, and Indians represented the major social categories in the colonial lands of what had been the Inca and Aztec empires, while African slaves and freemen were less numerous than elsewhere in the Americas. Despite the sharp divisions among these groups, some movement was possible. Indians who acquired an education, wealth, and some European culture might "pass" as mestizo. Likewise, more fortunate mestizo families might be accepted as Spaniards over time. Colonial Spanish America was a vast laboratory of ethnic mixing and cultural change. It was dominated by Europeans, to be sure, but with a rather more fluid and culturally blended society than in the racially rigid colonies of British North America.

Colonies of Sugar

Another and quite different kind of colonial society emerged in the lowland areas of Brazil, ruled by Portugal, and in the Spanish, British, French, and Dutch colonies in the Caribbean. These regions lacked the great civilizations of Mexico and Peru. Nor did they provide much mineral wealth until the Brazilian gold rush of the 1690s and the discovery of diamonds a little later. Still, Europeans found a very profitable substitute in sugar, which was much in demand in Europe, where it was used as a medicine, a spice, a sweetener, a preservative, and in sculptured forms as a decoration that indicated high status. Although commercial agriculture in the

AP® EXAM TIP

It is essential that you read and understand this section on Latin American sugar colonies.

Spanish Empire served a domestic market in its towns and mining camps, these sugar-based colonies produced almost exclusively for export, while importing their food and other necessities.

Large-scale sugar production had been pioneered by Arabs, who had introduced it in the Mediterranean. Europeans learned the technique and transferred it to their Atlantic island possessions and then to the Americas. For a century (1570–1670), Portuguese planters along the northeast coast of Brazil dominated the world market for sugar. Then the British, French, and Dutch turned their Caribbean territories into highly productive sugar-producing colonies, breaking the Portuguese and Brazilian monopoly.

Sugar decisively transformed Brazil and the Caribbean. Its production, which involved both growing the sugarcane and processing it into usable sugar, was very labor-intensive and could most profitably occur in a large-scale, almost industrial setting. It was perhaps the first modern industry in that it produced for an international and mass market, using capital and expertise from Europe, with production facilities located in the Americas. However, its most characteristic feature—the massive use of slave labor—was an ancient practice. In the absence of a Native American population, which had been almost totally wiped out in the Caribbean or had fled inland in Brazil, European sugarcane planters turned to Africa and the Atlantic slave trade for an alternative workforce. The vast majority of the African captives transported across the Atlantic, some 80 percent or more, ended up in Brazil and the Caribbean. (See Chapter 14 for a more extensive description of the Atlantic slave trade.)

Slaves worked on sugar-producing estates in horrendous conditions. The heat and fire from the cauldrons, which turned raw sugarcane into crystallized sugar, reminded many visitors of scenes from Hell. These conditions, combined with disease, generated a high death rate, perhaps 5 to 10 percent per year, which required plantation owners to constantly import fresh slaves. A Jesuit observer in 1580 aptly summarized the situation: "The work is great and many die."[16]

More male slaves than female slaves were imported from Africa into the sugar economies of the Americas, leading to major and persistent gender imbalances. Nonetheless, female slaves did play distinctive roles in these societies. Women made up about half of the field gangs that did the heavy work of planting and harvesting sugarcane. They were subject to the same brutal punishments and received the same rations as their male counterparts, though they were seldom permitted to undertake the more skilled labor inside the sugar mills. Women who worked in urban areas, mostly for white female owners, did domestic chores and were often hired out as laborers in various homes, shops, laundries, inns, and brothels. Discouraged from establishing stable families, women had to endure, often alone, the wrenching separation from their children that occurred when they were sold. Mary Prince, a Caribbean slave who wrote a brief account of her life, recalled the pain of families torn apart: "The great God above alone knows the thoughts of the poor slave's heart, and the bitter pains which follow such separations as these. All that we love taken away from us—oh, it is sad, sad! and sore to be borne!"[17]

Guided Reading Question

■ COMPARISON

How did the plantation societies of Brazil and the Caribbean differ from those of southern colonies in British North America?

AP® EXAM TIP

After reading these paragraphs, return to Chapter 5 (page 204) and compare Latin American slavery to that of earlier eras.

AP® EXAM TIP

You must know demographic features and effects of African slavery in the Americas and in Africa.

The extensive use of African slave labor gave these plantation colonies a very different ethnic and racial makeup than that of highland Spanish America, as the Snapshot on page 570 indicates. Thus, after three centuries of colonial rule, a substantial majority of Brazil's population was either partially or wholly of African descent. In the French Caribbean colony of Haiti in 1790, the corresponding figure was 93 percent.

As in Spanish America, a considerable amount of racial mixing took place in Brazil. Cross-racial unions accounted for only about 10 percent of all marriages in Brazil, but the use of concubines and informal liaisons among Indians, Africans, and Portuguese produced a substantial mixed-race population. From their ranks derived much of the urban skilled workforce and many of the supervisors in the sugar industry. *Mulattoes*, the product of Portuguese-African unions, predominated, but as many as forty separate and named groups, each indicating a different racial mixture, emerged in colonial Brazil.

The plantation complex of the Americas, based on African slavery, extended beyond the Caribbean and Brazil to encompass the southern colonies of British North America, where tobacco, cotton, rice, and indigo were major crops, but the social outcomes of these plantation colonies were quite different from those farther south. Because European women had joined the colonial migration to North

Plantation Life in the Caribbean
This painting from 1823 shows the use of slave labor on a plantation in Antigua, a British-ruled island in the Caribbean. Notice the overseer with a whip supervising the tilling and planting of the field. (Breaking Up the Land, from *Ten Views in the Island of Antigua*, 1823, color engraving by William Clark [fl. 1823]/British Library, London, UK/© British Library Board. All Rights Reserved/Bridgeman Images)

AP® EXAM TIP

Compare slavery in Latin America and the Caribbean with slavery in British North America.

SNAPSHOT   Ethnic Composition of Colonial Societies in Latin America (1825)[18]

	Highland Spanish America	Portuguese America (Brazil)
Europeans	18.2 percent	23.4 percent
Mixed-race	28.3 percent	17.8 percent
Africans	11.9 percent	49.8 percent
Native Americans	41.7 percent	9.1 percent

America at an early date, these colonies experienced less racial mixing and certainly demonstrated less willingness to recognize the offspring of such unions and accord them a place in society. A sharply defined racial system (with black Africans, "red" Native Americans, and white Europeans) evolved in North America, whereas both Portuguese and Spanish colonies acknowledged a wide variety of mixed-race groups.

Slavery too was different in North America than in the sugar colonies. By 1750 or so, slaves in what became the United States proved able to reproduce themselves, and by the time of the Civil War almost all North American slaves had been born in the New World. That was never the case in Latin America, where large-scale importation of new slaves continued well into the nineteenth century. Nonetheless, many more slaves were voluntarily set free by their owners in Brazil than in North America, and free blacks and mulattoes in Brazil had more economic opportunities than did their counterparts in the United States. At least a few among them found positions as political leaders, scholars, musicians, writers, and artists. Some were even hired as slave catchers.

Does this mean, then, that racism was absent in colonial Brazil? Certainly not, but it was different from racism in North America. For one thing, in North America, any African ancestry, no matter how small or distant, made a person "black"; in Brazil, a person of African and non-African ancestry was considered not black, but some other mixed-race category. Racial prejudice surely persisted, for white characteristics were prized more highly than black features, and people regarded as white had enormously greater privileges and opportunities than others. Nevertheless, skin color in Brazil, and in Latin America generally, was only one criterion of class status, and the perception of color changed with the educational or economic standing of individuals. A light-skinned mulatto who had acquired some wealth or education might well pass as a white. One curious visitor to Brazil was surprised to find a darker-skinned man serving as a local official. "Isn't the governor a mulatto?" inquired the visitor. "He was, but he isn't any more," was the reply. "How can a governor be a mulatto?"[19]

Settler Colonies in North America

Yet another distinctive type of colonial society emerged in the northern British colonies of New England, New York, and Pennsylvania. Because the British were the last of the European powers to establish a colonial presence in the Americas, a full century after Spain, they found that "only the dregs were left."[20] The lands they acquired were widely regarded in Europe as the unpromising leftovers of the New World, lacking the obvious wealth and sophisticated cultures of the Spanish possessions. Until at least the eighteenth century, these British colonies remained far less prominent on the world stage than those of Spain or Portugal.

The British settlers came from a more rapidly changing society than did those from an ardently Catholic, semi-feudal, authoritarian Spain. When Britain launched its colonial ventures in the seventeenth century, it had already experienced considerable conflict between Catholics and Protestants, the rise of a merchant capitalist class distinct from the nobility, and the emergence of Parliament as a check on the authority of kings. Although they brought much of their English culture with them, many of the British settlers—Puritans in Massachusetts and Quakers in Pennsylvania, for example—sought to escape aspects of an old European society rather than to re-create it, as was the case for most Spanish and Portuguese colonists. The easy availability of land and the outsider status of many British settlers made it even more difficult to follow the Spanish or Portuguese colonial pattern of sharp class hierarchies, large rural estates, and dependent laborers.

Thus men in Puritan New England became independent heads of family farms, a world away from Old England, where most land was owned by nobles and gentry and worked by servants, tenants, and paid laborers. But if men escaped the class restrictions of the old country, women were less able to avoid its gender limitations. While Puritan Christianity extolled the family and a woman's role as wife and mother, it reinforced largely unlimited male authority. "Since he is thy Husband," declared Boston minister Benjamin Wadsworth in 1712 to the colony's women, "God has made him the Head and set him above thee."[21] Women were prosecuted for the crime of "fornication" far more often than their male companions; the inheritance of daughters was substantially less than that of sons; few girls attended school; and while women were the majority of church members, they could never become ministers.

Furthermore, British settlers were far more numerous than their Spanish counterparts, outnumbering them five to one by 1750. This disparity was the most obvious distinguishing feature of the New England and middle Atlantic colonies. By the time of the American Revolution, some 90 percent or more of these colonies' populations were Europeans. Devastating diseases and a highly aggressive military policy had largely cleared the colonies of Native Americans, and their numbers, which were far smaller to start with than those of their Mesoamerican and Andean counterparts, did not rebound in subsequent centuries as they did in the lands of the Aztecs and the Incas. Moreover, slaves were not needed in an agricultural economy

AP® EXAM TIP

Previous AP® exams have asked questions about differences between the British American and Spanish/Portuguese colonies.

Guided Reading Question

■ COMPARISON

What distinguished the British settler colonies of North America from their counterparts in Latin America?

AP® EXAM TIP

Notice features of this paragraph that can help you improve your essays, such as the many specific examples, the comparisons, and the ranking of evidence.

dominated by numerous small-scale independent farmers working their own land, although elite families, especially in urban areas, sometimes employed household slaves. These were almost pure settler colonies, without the racial mixing that was so prominent in Spanish and Portuguese territories.

Other differences likewise emerged. A largely Protestant England was far less interested in spreading Christianity among the remaining native peoples than were the large and well-funded missionary societies of Catholic Spain. Although religion loomed large in the North American colonies, the church and colonial state were not so intimately connected as they were in Latin America. The Protestant emphasis on reading the Bible for oneself led to a much greater mass literacy than in Latin America, where three centuries of church education still left some 95 percent of the population illiterate at independence. By contrast, well over 75 percent of white males in British North America were literate by the 1770s, although women's literacy rates were somewhat lower. Furthermore, British settler colonies evolved traditions of local self-government more extensively than in Latin America. Preferring to rely on joint stock companies or wealthy individuals operating under a royal charter, Britain had nothing resembling the elaborate imperial bureaucracy that governed Spanish colonies. For much of the seventeenth century, a prolonged power struggle between the English king and Parliament meant that the British government paid little attention to the internal affairs of the colonies. Therefore, elected colonial assemblies, seeing themselves as little parliaments defending "the rights of Englishmen," vigorously contested the prerogatives of royal governors sent to administer their affairs.

AP® EXAM TIP

Take notes on this discussion of the reversal of relationships between the northern and southern continents.

PRACTICING AP® HISTORICAL THINKING

In what ways might European empire building in the Americas be understood as a single phenomenon? And in what respects should it be viewed as a set of distinct and separate processes?

The grand irony of the modern history of the Americas lay in the reversal of long-established relationships between the northern and southern continents. For thousands of years, the major centers of wealth, power, commerce, and innovation lay in Mesoamerica and the Andes. That pattern continued for much of the colonial era, as the Spanish and Portuguese colonies seemed far more prosperous and successful than their British or French counterparts in North America. In the nineteenth and twentieth centuries, however, the balance shifted. What had once been the "dregs" of the colonial world became the United States, more politically stable, more democratic, more economically successful, and more internationally powerful than a divided, unstable, and much less prosperous Latin America.

The Steppes and Siberia: The Making of a Russian Empire

At the same time as Western Europeans were building their empires in the Americas, the Russian Empire, which subsequently became the world's largest state, was beginning to take shape. When Columbus crossed the Atlantic, a small Russian state centered on the city of Moscow was emerging from two centuries of Mongol rule. That state soon conquered a number of neighboring Russian-speaking cities and incorporated them into its expanding territory. Located on the remote, cold, and heavily forested eastern fringe of Christendom, it was perhaps an unlikely candidate for constructing one of the great empires of the modern era. And yet, over the next three centuries, it did precisely that, extending Russian domination over the vast tundra, forests, and grasslands of northern Asia that lay to the south and east of Moscow, all the way to the Pacific Ocean. Furthermore, Russians also expanded westward, bringing numerous Poles, Germans, Ukrainians, Belorussians, and Baltic peoples into the Russian Empire.

Russian attention was drawn first to the grasslands south and east of the Russian heartland, an area long inhabited by various nomadic pastoral peoples, who were organized into feuding tribes and clans and adjusting to the recent disappearance of the Mongol Empire. From the viewpoint of the emerging Russian state, the problem was security because these pastoral peoples, like the Mongols before them, frequently raided their agricultural Russian neighbors and sold many into slavery. To the east, across the vast expanse of Siberia, Russian motives were quite different, for the scattered peoples of its endless forests and tundra posed no threat to Russia. Numbering only some 220,000 in the seventeenth century and speaking more than 100 languages, they were mostly hunting, gathering, and herding people, living in small-scale societies and largely without access to gunpowder weapons. What drew the Russians across Siberia was opportunity—primarily the "soft gold" of fur-bearing animals, whose pelts were in great demand on the world market.

Whatever motives drove it, this enormous Russian Empire took shape in the three centuries between 1500 and 1800 (see Map 13.2). A growing line of wooden forts offered protection to frontier towns and trading centers as well as to mounting numbers of Russian farmers. Empire building was an extended process, involving the Russian state and its officials as well as a variety of private interests—merchants, hunters, peasants, churchmen, exiles, criminals, and adventurers. For the Russian migrants to these new eastern lands, the empire offered "economic and social improvements over what they had known at home—from more and better land to fewer lords and officials."[22] Political leaders and educated Russians generally defined the empire in grander terms: defending Russian frontiers; enhancing the power of the Russian state; and bringing Christianity, civilization, and enlightenment to savages. But what did that empire mean to those on its receiving end?

Experiencing the Russian Empire

First, of course, empire meant conquest. Although resistance was frequent, especially from nomadic peoples, in the long run Russian military might, based in modern weaponry and the organizational capacity of a state, brought both the steppes and Siberia under Russian control. Everywhere Russian authorities demanded an oath of allegiance by which native peoples swore "eternal submission to the grand tsar,"

Guided Reading Question

■ **DESCRIPTION**
What motivated Russian empire building?

AP® EXAM TIP

The AP® exam frequently includes questions about empire building throughout world history. Note this example of how the Russian Empire developed.

Map 13.2   The Russian Empire

From its beginnings as a small principality under Mongol control, Moscow became the center of a vast Russian Empire during the early modern era.

the monarch of the Russian Empire. They also demanded *yasak*, or "tribute," paid in cash or in kind. In Siberia, this meant enormous quantities of furs, especially the extremely valuable sable, which Siberian peoples were compelled to produce. As in the Americas, devastating epidemics accompanied conquest, particularly in the more remote regions of Siberia, where local people had little immunity to smallpox or measles. Also accompanying conquest was an intermittent pressure to convert to Christianity. Tax breaks, exemptions from paying tribute, and the promise of land or cash provided incentives for conversion, while the destruction of many mosques and the forced resettlement of Muslims added to the pressures. Yet the Russian state did not pursue conversion with the single-minded intensity that Spanish authorities exercised in Latin America, particularly if missionary activity threatened political and social stability. The empress Catherine the Great, for example, established religious tolerance for Muslims in the late eighteenth century and created a state agency to oversee Muslim affairs.

The most profoundly transforming feature of the Russian Empire was the influx of Russian settlers, whose numbers by the end of the eighteenth century had overwhelmed native peoples, giving their lands a distinctively Russian character. By 1720, some 700,000 Russians lived in Siberia, thus reducing the native Siberians to 30 percent of the total population, a proportion that dropped to 14 percent in the nineteenth century. The loss of hunting grounds and pasturelands to Russian agricultural settlers undermined long-standing economies and rendered local people dependent on Russian markets for grain, sugar, tea, tobacco, and alcohol. Pressures to encourage pastoralists to abandon their nomadic ways included the requirement to pay fees and to obtain permission to cross agricultural lands. Kazakh herders responded with outrage: "The grass and the water belong to Heaven, and why should we pay any fees?"[23] Intermarriage, prostitution, and sexual abuse resulted in some mixed-race offspring, but these were generally absorbed as Russians rather than identified as distinctive communities, as in Latin America.

Over the course of three centuries, both Siberia and the steppes were incorporated into the Russian state. Their native peoples were not driven into reservations or eradicated as in the Americas. Many of them, though, were Russified, adopting the Russian language and converting to Christianity, even as their traditional ways of life—hunting and herding—were much disrupted. The Russian Empire represented the final triumph of an agrarian civilization over the hunting societies of Siberia and over the pastoral peoples of the grasslands.

Guided Reading Question

■ CHANGE
How did the Russian Empire transform the life of its conquered people and of the Russian homeland itself?

The Cossacks
In the vanguard of Russian expansion across Siberia were the Cossacks, bands of fiercely independent warriors consisting of peasants who had escaped serfdom as well as criminals and other adventurers. Here the sixteenth-century Cossack warrior Yermak is shown leading his troops. (De Agostini Picture Library/akg-images)

Russians and Empire

If the empire transformed the conquered peoples, it also fundamentally changed Russia itself. Within an increasingly multiethnic empire, Russians diminished as a proportion of the overall population, although they remained politically dominant. Among the growing number of non-Russians in the empire, Slavic-speaking Ukrainians and Belorussians predominated, while the vast territories of Siberia and the steppes housed numerous separate peoples, but with quite small populations.[24] The wealth of empire—rich agricultural lands, valuable furs, mineral deposits—played a major role in making Russia one of the great powers of Europe by the eighteenth century, and it has enjoyed that position ever since.

Unlike its expansion to the east, Russia's westward movement occurred in the context of military rivalries with the major powers of the region—the Ottoman Empire, Poland, Sweden, Lithuania, Prussia, and Austria. During the late seventeenth and eighteenth centuries, Russia acquired substantial territories in the Baltic region, Poland, and Ukraine. This contact with Europe also fostered an awareness of Russia's backwardness relative to Europe and prompted an extensive program of westernization, particularly under the leadership of Peter the Great (r. 1689–1725). His massive efforts included vast administrative changes, the enlargement and modernization of Russian military forces, a new educational system for the sons of noblemen, and dozens of manufacturing enterprises. Russian nobles were instructed to dress in European styles and to shave their sacred and much-revered beards. The newly created capital city of St. Petersburg was to be Russia's "window on the West." One of Peter's successors, Catherine the Great (r. 1762–1796), followed up with further efforts to Europeanize Russian cultural and intellectual life, viewing herself as part of the European Enlightenment. Thus Russians were the first of many peoples to measure themselves against the West and to mount major "catch-up" efforts.

But this European-oriented and Christian state had also become an Asian power, bumping up against China, India, Persia, and the Ottoman Empire. It was on the front lines of the encounter between Christendom and the world of Islam. This straddling of Asia and Europe was the source of a long-standing identity problem that has troubled educated Russians for 300 years. Was Russia a backward European country, destined to follow the lead of more highly developed Western European societies? Or was it different, uniquely Slavic or even Asian, shaped by its Mongol legacy and its status as an Asian power? It is a question that Russians have not completely answered even in the twenty-first century. Either way, the very size of that empire, bordering on virtually all of the great agrarian civilizations of outer Eurasia, turned Russia, like many empires before it, into a highly militarized state, "a society organized for continuous war," according to one scholar.[25] It also reinforced the highly autocratic character of the Russian Empire because such a huge state arguably required a powerful monarchy to hold its vast domains and highly diverse peoples together.

AP® EXAM TIP

Russia's "westernization" process in this—and the next—era is a common topic on the AP® exam.

Clearly, the Russians had created an empire, similar to those of Western Europe in terms of conquest, settlement, exploitation, religious conversion, and feelings of superiority. Nonetheless, the Russians had acquired their empire under different circumstances than did the Western Europeans. The Spanish and the British had conquered and colonized the New World, an ocean away and wholly unknown to them before 1492. They acquired those empires only after establishing themselves as distinct European states. The Russians, on the other hand, absorbed adjacent territories, and they did so at the same time that a modern Russian state was taking shape. "The British had an empire," wrote historian Geoffrey Hosking. "Russia *was* an empire."[26] Perhaps this helps explain the unique longevity of the Russian Empire. Whereas the Spanish, Portuguese, and British colonies in the Americas long ago achieved independence, the Russian Empire remained intact until the collapse of the Soviet Union in 1991. So thorough was Russian colonization that Siberia and much of the steppes remain still an integral part of the Russian state.

Asian Empires

Even as West Europeans were building their empires in the Americas and the Russians were expanding across Siberia, other imperial projects were likewise under way. The Chinese pushed deep into central Eurasia; Turko-Mongol invaders from Central Asia created the Mughal Empire, bringing much of Hindu South Asia within a single Muslim-ruled political system; and the Ottoman Empire brought Muslim rule to a largely Christian population in southeastern Europe and Turkish rule to largely Arab populations in North Africa and the Middle East. None of these empires had the global reach or worldwide impact of Europe's American colonies; they were regional rather than global in scope. Nor did they have the same devastating and transforming impact on their conquered peoples, for those peoples were not being exposed to new diseases. Nothing remotely approaching the catastrophic population collapse of Native American peoples occurred in these Asian empires. Moreover, the process of building these empires did not transform the imperial homeland as fundamentally as did the wealth of the Americas and to a lesser extent Siberia for European imperial powers. Nonetheless, these expanding Asian empires reflected the energies and vitality of their respective civilizations in the early modern era, and they gave rise to profoundly important cross-cultural encounters, with legacies that echoed for many centuries.

Making China an Empire

In the fifteenth century, China had declined an opportunity to construct a maritime empire in the Indian Ocean, as Zheng He's massive fleet was withdrawn and left to wither away (see Chapter 12, pages 507–9). In the seventeenth and eighteenth centuries, however, China built another kind of empire on its northern and western frontiers that vastly enlarged the territorial size of the country and incorporated

AP® EXAM TIP
As you read this section, compare the features of the expansion of land-based empires such as Russia and China to those of the expansion of sea-based empires such as Spain in the Americas.

a number of non-Chinese peoples. Undertaking this enormous project of imperial expansion was China's Qing, or Manchu, dynasty (1644–1912). Strangely enough, the Qing dynasty was itself of foreign and nomadic origin, hailing from Manchuria, north of the Great Wall. Having conquered China, the Qing rulers sought to maintain their ethnic distinctiveness by forbidding intermarriage between themselves and the Chinese. Nonetheless, their ruling elites also mastered the Chinese language and Confucian teachings and used Chinese bureaucratic techniques to govern the empire. Perhaps because they were foreigners, Qing rulers went to great lengths to reinforce traditional Confucian gender roles, honoring men who were loyal sons, officials, and philanthropists and women who demonstrated loyalty to their spouses by resisting rape or remaining chaste as widows.

For many centuries, the Chinese had interacted with the nomadic peoples, who inhabited the dry and lightly populated regions now known as Mongolia, Xinjiang, and Tibet. Trade, tribute, and warfare ensured that these ecologically and culturally different worlds were well known to each other, quite unlike the New World "discoveries" of the Europeans. Chinese authority in the area had been intermittent and actively resisted. Then, in the early modern era, Qing dynasty China undertook an eighty-year military effort (1680–1760) that brought these huge regions solidly under Chinese control. It was largely security concerns, rather than economic need, that motivated this aggressive posture. During the late seventeenth century, the creation of a substantial state among the western Mongols, known as the Zunghars, revived Chinese memories of an earlier Mongol conquest. As in so many other cases, Chinese expansion was viewed as a defensive necessity. The eastward movement of the Russian Empire likewise appeared potentially threatening, but this

Guided Reading Question

■ DESCRIPTION

What were the distinctive features of Chinese empire building in the early modern era?

Chinese Conquests in Central Asia
Painted by the Chinese artist Jin Tingbiao in the mid-eighteenth century, this image portrays Machang, a leading warrior involved in the westward extension of the Chinese empire. The painting was commissioned by the emperor himself and served to honor the bravery of Machang. (Pictures from History/ CPA Media)

danger was resolved diplomatically, rather than militarily, in the Treaty of Nerchinsk (1689), which marked the boundary between Russia and China.

Although undertaken by the non-Chinese Manchus, the Qing dynasty campaigns against the Mongols marked the evolution of China into a Central Asian empire. The Chinese, however, have seldom thought of themselves as an imperial power. Rather, they spoke of the "unification" of the peoples of central Eurasia within a Chinese state. Nonetheless, historians have seen many similarities between Chinese expansion and other cases of early modern empire building, while noting some clear differences as well.

Clearly the Qing dynasty takeover of central Eurasia was a conquest, making use of China's more powerful military technology and greater resources. Furthermore, the area was ruled separately from the rest of China through a new office called the Court of Colonial Affairs. Like other colonial powers, the Chinese made active use of local notables—Mongol aristocrats, Muslim officials, Buddhist leaders—as they attempted to govern the region as inexpensively as possible. Sometimes these native officials abused their authority, demanding extra taxes or labor service from local people and thus earning their hostility. In places, those officials imitated Chinese ways by wearing peacock feathers, decorating their hats with gold buttons, or adopting a Manchu hairstyle that was much resented by many Chinese who were forced to wear it.

More generally, however, Chinese or Qing officials did not seek to assimilate local people into Chinese culture and showed considerable respect for the Mongolian, Tibetan, and Muslim cultures of the region. People of noble rank, Buddhist monks, and those associated with monasteries were excused from the taxes and labor service required of ordinary people. Nor was the area flooded with Chinese settlers. In parts of Mongolia, for example, Qing authorities sharply restricted the entry of Chinese merchants and other immigrants in an effort to preserve the area as a source of recruitment for the Chinese military. They feared that the "soft" and civilized Chinese ways might erode the fighting spirit of the Mongols.

The long-term significance of this new Chinese imperial state was tremendous. It greatly expanded the territory of China and added a small but important minority of non-Chinese people to the empire's vast population (see Map 13.3). The borders of contemporary China are essentially those created during the Qing dynasty. Some of those peoples, particularly those in Tibet and Xinjiang, have retained their older identities and in recent decades have actively sought greater autonomy or even independence from China.

Map 13.3   China's Qing Dynasty Empire
After many centuries of intermittent expansion into Central Asia, the Qing dynasty brought this vast region firmly within the Chinese empire.

Even more important, Chinese conquests, together with the expansion of the Russian Empire, utterly transformed Central Asia. For centuries, that region had been the cosmopolitan crossroads of Eurasia, hosting the Silk Road trading network, welcoming all the major world religions, and generating an enduring encounter between the nomads of the steppes and the farmers of settled agricultural regions. Now under Russian or Chinese rule, it became the backward and impoverished region known to nineteenth- and twentieth-century observers. Land-based commerce across Eurasia increasingly took a backseat to oceanic trade. Indebted Mongolian nobles lost their land to Chinese merchants, while nomads, no longer able to herd their animals freely, fled to urban areas, where many were reduced to begging. The incorporation of inner Eurasia into the Russian and Chinese empires "eliminated permanently as a major actor on the historical stage the nomadic pastoralists, who had been the strongest alternative to settled agricultural society since the second millennium B.C.E."[27] It was the end of a long era.

Muslims and Hindus in the Mughal Empire

If the creation of a Chinese imperial state in the early modern era provoked a final clash of nomadic pastoralists and settled farmers, India's Mughal Empire hosted a different kind of encounter—a further phase in the long interaction of Islamic and Hindu cultures in South Asia. That empire was the product of Central Asian warriors, who were Muslims in religion and Turkic in culture and who claimed descent from Chinggis Khan and Timur (see Chapters 11 and 12). Their brutal conquests in the sixteenth century provided India with a rare period of relative political unity (1526–1707), as Mughal emperors exercised a fragile control over a diverse and fragmented subcontinent, which had long been divided into a bewildering variety of small states, principalities, tribes, castes, sects, and ethno-linguistic groups.

The central division within Mughal India was religious. The ruling dynasty and perhaps 20 percent of the population were Muslims; most of the rest practiced some form of Hinduism. Mughal India's most famous emperor, Akbar (r. 1556–1605), clearly recognized this fundamental reality and acted deliberately to accommodate the Hindu majority. After conquering the warrior-based and Hindu Rajputs of northwestern India, Akbar married several of their princesses but did not require them to convert to Islam. He incorporated a substantial number of Hindus into the political-military elite of the empire and supported the building of Hindu temples as well as mosques, palaces, and forts. (See Working with Evidence, Source 13.1, page 590.) But Akbar acted to soften some Hindu restrictions on women, encouraging the remarriage of widows, discouraging child marriages and *sati* (the practice in which a widow followed her husband to death by throwing herself on his funeral pyre), and persuading merchants to set aside special market days for women so as to moderate their seclusion in the home. Nur Jahan, the twentieth and favorite wife of Emperor Jahangir (r. 1605–1627), was widely regarded as the power behind the throne of her alcohol- and opium-addicted husband, giving audiences to visiting dignitaries, consulting with ministers, and even having a coin issued in her name.

In directly religious matters, Akbar imposed a policy of toleration, deliberately restraining the more militantly Islamic *ulama* (religious scholars) and removing the special tax (*jizya*) on non-Muslims. He constructed a special House of Worship where he presided over intellectual discussion with representatives of many religions—Muslim, Hindu, Christian, Buddhist, Jewish, Jain, and Zoroastrian. His son Jahangir wrote proudly of his father: "He associated with the good of every race and creed and persuasion. . . . The professors of various faiths had room in the broad expanse of his incomparable sway."[28] Akbar went so far as to create his own state cult, a religious faith aimed at the Mughal elite, drawing on Islam, Hinduism, and Zoroastrianism and emphasizing loyalty to the emperor himself. The overall style of the Mughal Empire was that of a blended elite culture in which both Hindus and various Muslim groups could feel comfortable. Thus Persian artists and writers were welcomed into the empire, and the Hindu epic *Ramayana* was translated into Persian, while various Persian classics appeared in Hindi and Sanskrit. In short, Akbar and his immediate successors downplayed a distinctly Islamic identity for the Mughal Empire in favor of a cosmopolitan and hybrid Indian-Persian-Turkic culture.

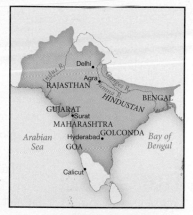

The Mughal Empire

Such policies fostered sharp opposition among some Muslims. The philosopher Shaykh Ahmad Sirhindi (1564–1624), claiming to be a "renewer" of authentic Islam in his time, strongly objected to this cultural synthesis. The worship of saints, the sacrifice of animals, and support for Hindu religious festivals all represented impure intrusions of Sufi Islam or Hinduism that needed to be rooted out. In Sirhindi's view, it was primarily women who had introduced these deviations: "Because of their utter stupidity women pray to stones and idols and ask for their help. This practice is common, especially when small pox strikes, and there is hardly a woman who is not involved in this polytheistic practice. Women participate in the holidays of Hindus and Jews. They celebrate Diwali [a major Hindu festival] and send their sisters and daughters presents similar to those exchanged by the infidels."[29] It was therefore the duty of Muslim rulers to impose the sharia (Islamic law), to enforce the jizya, and to remove non-Muslims from high office.

This strain of Muslim thinking found a champion in the emperor Aurangzeb (ow-rang-ZEHB) (r. 1658–1707), who reversed Akbar's policy of accommodation and sought to impose Islamic supremacy. While Akbar had discouraged the Hindu practice of sati, Aurangzeb forbade it outright. Music and dance were now banned at court, and previously tolerated vices such as gambling, drinking, prostitution, and narcotics were actively suppressed. Dancing girls were ordered to get married or leave the empire altogether. Some Hindu temples were destroyed, and the jizya was reimposed. "Censors of public morals," posted to large cities, enforced Islamic law.

AP® EXAM TIP

Features of Akbar's rule over the Mughal Empire sometimes appear on the AP® exam.

Aurangzeb's religious policies, combined with intolerable demands for taxes to support his many wars of expansion, antagonized Hindus and prompted various movements of opposition to the Mughals. "Your subjects are trampled underfoot," wrote one anonymous protester. "Every province of your empire is impoverished. . . . God is the God of all mankind, not the God of Mussalmans [Muslims] alone."[30] These opposition movements, some of them self-consciously Hindu, fatally fractured the Mughal Empire, especially after Aurangzeb's death in 1707, and opened the way for a British takeover in the second half of the eighteenth century.

Thus the Mughal Empire was the site of a highly significant encounter between two of the world's great religious traditions. It began with an experiment in multicultural empire building and ended in growing antagonism between Hindus and Muslims. In the centuries that followed, both elements of the Mughal experience would be repeated.

Muslims and Christians in the Ottoman Empire

Like the Mughal state, the Ottoman Empire was also the creation of Turkic warrior groups, whose aggressive raiding of agricultural civilization was now legitimized in Islamic terms. Beginning around 1300 from a base area in northwestern Anatolia, these Ottoman Turks over the next three centuries swept over much of the Middle East, North Africa, and southeastern Europe to create the Islamic world's most significant empire (see Map 13.4). During those centuries, the Ottoman state was transformed from a small frontier principality to a prosperous, powerful, cosmopolitan empire, heir both to the Byzantine Empire and to leadership within the Islamic world. Its sultan combined the roles of a Turkic warrior prince, a Muslim caliph, and a conquering emperor, bearing the "strong sword of Islam" and serving as chief defender of the faith.

Gaining such an empire transformed Turkish social life as well. The relative independence of Central Asian pastoral women, their open association with men, and their political influence in society all diminished as the Turks adopted Islam, beginning in the tenth century, and later acquired an empire in the heartland of ancient and patriarchal Mediterranean civilizations. Now elite Turkish women found themselves secluded and often veiled; slave women from the Caucasus Mountains and the Sudan grew more numerous; official imperial censuses did not count women; and orthodox Muslim reformers sought to restrict women's religious gatherings.

And yet within the new constraints of a settled Islamic empire, Turkish women retained something of the social power they had enjoyed in pastoral societies. From around 1550 to 1650, women of the royal court had such an influence in political matters that their critics referred to the "sultanate of women." Islamic law permitted women important property rights, which enabled some to become quite

AP® EXAM TIP

Remember that an empire that unites South Asia is the exception to the norm.

AP® EXAM TIP

Return to Chapter 9 and compare features of those Islamic caliphates with features of this Islamic empire.

Map 13.4   The Ottoman Empire

At its high point in the mid-sixteenth century, the Ottoman Empire encompassed a vast diversity of peoples; straddled Europe, Africa, and Asia; and battled both the Austrian and Safavid empires.

wealthy, endowing religious and charitable institutions. Many women actively used the Ottoman courts to protect their legal rights in matters of marriage, divorce, and inheritance, sometimes representing themselves or acting as agents for female relatives. In 1717, the wife of an English ambassador to the Ottoman Empire compared the lives of Turkish and European women, declaring, "'Tis very easy to see that they have more liberty than we have."[31]

Within the Islamic world, the Ottoman Empire represented the growing prominence of Turkic people, for their empire now incorporated a large number of

Guided Reading Question

■ SIGNIFICANCE
In what ways was the Ottoman Empire important for Europe in the early modern era?

Arabs, among whom the religion had been born. The responsibility and the prestige of protecting Mecca, Medina, and Jerusalem—the holy cities of Islam—now fell to the Ottoman Empire. A century-long conflict (1534–1639) between the Ottoman Empire, espousing the Sunni version of Islam, and the Persian Safavid Empire, holding fast to the Shia form of the faith, expressed a deep and enduring division within the Islamic world. Nonetheless, Persian culture, especially its poetry, painting, and traditions of imperial splendor, occupied a prominent position among the Ottoman elite.

The Ottoman Empire, like its Mughal counterpart, was the site of a highly significant cross-cultural encounter in the early modern era, adding yet another chapter to the long-running story of interaction between the Islamic world and Christendom. As the Ottoman Empire expanded across Anatolia, its mostly Christian population converted in large numbers to Islam as the Byzantine state visibly weakened and large numbers of Turks settled in the region. By 1500, some 90 percent of Anatolia's inhabitants were Muslims and Turkic speakers. The climax of this Turkic assault on the Christian world of Byzantium occurred in 1453, when Constantinople fell to the invaders. Renamed Istanbul, that splendid Christian city became the capital of the Ottoman Empire. Byzantium, heir to the glory of Rome and the guardian of Orthodox Christianity, was no more.

In the empire's southeastern European domains, known as the Balkans, the Ottoman encounter with Christian peoples unfolded quite differently than it had in Anatolia. In the Balkans, Muslims ruled over a large Christian population, but the scarcity of Turkish settlers and the willingness of the Ottoman authorities to accommodate the region's Christian churches led to far fewer conversions. By the early sixteenth century, only about 19 percent of the area's people were Muslims, and 81 percent were Christians.

Many of these Christians had welcomed Ottoman conquest because taxes were lighter and oppression less pronounced than under their former Christian rulers. Christian communities such as the Eastern Orthodox and Armenian Churches were granted considerable autonomy in regulating their internal social, religious, educational, and charitable affairs. Nonetheless, many Christian and Jewish women appealed legal cases dealing with marriage and inheritance to Muslim courts, where their property rights were greater. A substantial number of Christian men—Balkan landlords, Greek merchants, government officials, and high-ranking clergy—became part of the Ottoman elite, sometimes without converting to Islam. Jewish refugees, fleeing Christian persecution in a Spain recently "liberated" from Islamic rule, likewise found greater opportunity in the Ottoman Empire, where they became prominent in trade and banking circles. In these ways, Ottoman dealings with the Christian and Jewish populations of their empire broadly resembled Akbar's policies toward the Hindu majority of Mughal India. In another way, however, Turkish rule bore heavily on Christians. Through a process known as the *devshirme* (devv-shirr-MEH) (the collecting or gathering), Ottoman authorities siphoned off

The Ottoman Siege of Vienna, 1683
In this late seventeenth-century painting by the Flemish artist Frans Geffels, the last Ottoman incursion into the Austrian Empire is pushed back with French and Polish help, marking the end of a serious Muslim threat to Christian Europe. (Wien Museum Karlsplatz, Vienna, Austria/Erich Lessing/Art Resource, NY)

many thousands of young boys from Christian families into the service of the state. (See Zooming In: Devshirme, page 586.)

Even though Ottoman authorities were relatively tolerant toward Christians within their borders, the empire itself represented an enormous threat to Christendom generally. The seizure of Constantinople, the conquest of the Balkans, Ottoman naval power in the Mediterranean, and the siege of Vienna in 1529 and again in 1683 raised anew "the specter of a Muslim takeover of all of Europe."[32] (See Working with Evidence, Source 13.2, page 593.) One European ambassador reported fearfully in 1555 from the court of the Turkish ruler Suleiman:

> He tramples the soil of Hungary with 200,000 horses, he is at the very gates of Austria, threatens the rest of Germany, and brings in his train all the nations that extend from our borders to those of Persia.[33]

Indeed, the "terror of the Turk" inspired fear across much of Europe and placed Christendom on the defensive, even as Europeans were expanding aggressively across the Atlantic and into the Indian Ocean.

AP® EXAM TIP

The Muslim conquest of Constantinople was a major turning point in the political and cultural history of Europe, North Africa, and Southwest Asia.

Devshirme: The "Gathering" of Christian Boys in the Ottoman Empire

Every few years, Ottoman official recruiters descended on rural Christian villages in the Balkan provinces of the empire, mostly among Serbs, Greeks, and Albanians. There they required the village priest to present the birth records of the village and to assemble boys of about ten to eighteen years of age. Then they selected a certain number of these boys, dressed them in red uniforms, and marched them off to Constantinople. Once the boys arrived, they were circumcised, converted to Islam, given a Muslim name, and enrolled in a long training program to prepare them for administrative or military positions within the Ottoman government.

Ottoman officials selecting Christian boys, in red, for the devshirme.

This was the *devshirme*, or "gathering," of Christian boys, a distinctive practice that began in the mid- to late fourteenth century when the rapid expansion of the Ottoman Empire required more soldiers and officials. It extended a much older Islamic tradition of using prisoners captured in war as slave soldiers. The devshirme enabled the sultan to create a cadre of civil and military officials personally loyal to and dependent upon him, thus avoiding reliance on the Turkish nobility. Boys with the greatest potential received a prestigious education, lasting some fourteen years, in Arabic, Turkish, and Persian languages; mathematics; Islamic studies; horsemanship; weaponry; and more. They were tracked into civil administrative careers, often in the palace itself. Others entered a rigorous training for military service and generally ended up in the Janissary corps, an elite military unit responsible directly to the sultan.

Technically, the devshirme recruits were slaves, but they were quite different from ordinary purchased slaves. They were absorbed into Ottoman society in distinctive and privileged roles, and some of them were able to rise to very prominent positions, including that of grand vizier, the chief adviser to the sultan himself. One such official recalled that he was taken "weeping and in distress," but also reported with some pride that "a shepherd may be [transported] to a sultan's domain."[34]

photo: From the "Suleymanname" (Mss Hazine, 1517 f. 31v.), 1558 (ink and gold leaf on vellum)/Topkapi Palace Museum, Istanbul, Turkey/Bridgeman Images

AP® EXAM TIP

Pay close attention to examples of diplomatic relationships in the era ca.1450–ca.1750.

But the Ottoman encounter with Christian Europe spawned admiration and cooperation as well as fear and trembling. Italian Renaissance artists portrayed the splendor of the Islamic world. (See Working with Evidence, Chapter 12, page 536.) The sixteenth-century French philosopher Jean Bodin praised the religious tolerance of the Ottoman sultan in contrast to Christian intolerance: "The King of the Turks who rules over a great part of Europe safeguards the rites of religion as well as any prince in this world. Yet he constrains no-one, but on the contrary permits everyone to live as his conscience dictates."[35] The French government on occasion found it useful to ally with the Ottoman Empire against their common enemy of Habsburg Austria, while European merchants willingly violated a papal ban on selling firearms to the Turks. Cultural encounter involved more than conflict.

So prestigious were such positions—or so desperate were impoverished Christians—that some Christian families voluntarily offered their sons to the recruiters, and some free Muslim families schemed to get their children into the exalted ranks of the devshirme.

Yet there is little doubt that the devshirme system brought great suffering to the empire's Christian subjects and was widely hated and resisted. In 1395, an Eastern Orthodox metropolitan, or archbishop, named Isidore Glabas from Thessaloniki in Greece delivered a scathing public sermon denouncing the practice, no doubt reflecting the views of his parishioners. "My eyes are filled with tears and can no longer bear to see my beloved ones," he began. Then he outlined the various ways that the devshirme brought grief to his people: their children were "forced to change over to alien customs and to become a vessel of barbaric garb, speech, impiety, and other contaminations, all in a moment." His words reflected the Greeks' view of Turks as "barbarians" and their fear that their children might be subjected to castration as eunuchs or exposed to the homosexuality widely regarded as a part of Janissary life. Furthermore, according to the archbishop, the devshirme threatened the continuity of family life, for a father "will not have his son to send him to his grave in fitting manner." And who, he asked, would not "lament his son because a free child becomes a slave?" Worst of all, in the archbishop's view, was the danger to the immortal soul of a Christian boy who was circumcised and converted to Islam, for "he is shamefully separated from God and has become miserably entangled with the devil, and in the end will be sent to darkness and hell with the demons."[36]

It was no wonder then that Ottoman Christians deployed many strategies to avoid the devshirme. Some communities required their boys to formally marry at a very young age; parish priests might conveniently lose names from the parish registries; families sometimes fled to avoid the recruiters; Eastern Orthodox Christians on occasion appealed to the pope or to Catholic military orders for help, "lest we lose our children." On several occasions, villagers murdered the recruiters and many times sought to bribe them.

By the mid-seventeenth century, the devshirme system had been largely abandoned, as recruitment to these positions was opened to free Muslim Turks. But the memory lingered well into the twentieth century as an irritant in the conflicted relations of Greeks and Turks. A song recently sung in northern Greece recalled the memory: "Be Dammed, Emperor, thrice be dammed. . . . You catch and shackle the old and the archpriests, in order to take the children as janissaries. Their parents weep, their sisters and brothers, too."[37]

Questions: How might you summarize the origins and outcomes of the devshirme system? How does this practice alter your understanding of slavery?

The Centrality of Context in World History

World history is, to put it mildly, a big subject. To teachers and students alike, it can easily seem overwhelming in its detail. And yet the central task of world history is *not* the inclusion of endless facts or particular cases. It is rather to establish contexts or frameworks within which carefully selected facts and cases take on new meaning. In world history, every event, every process, every historical figure, and every culture, society, or civilization gain significance from their incorporation into some larger context or framework. Contextual thinking is central to world history.

AP® EXAM TIP

In this section the author says it is essential to understand historical context if you wish to understand world history, and that understanding is precisely what the AP® exam will test. Now that you are about halfway through this text, consider the political (e.g., empire building), social (e.g., relations between governments and religions), and economic (e.g., the empires' policies on trade) connections and comparisons that you have made thus far.

The broad outlines of European colonization in the Americas are familiar to most American and European students. And yet, when that story is set in the context of other empire-building projects of the early modern era, it takes on new and different meanings. Such a context helps to counter any remaining Eurocentrism in our thinking about the past by reminding us that Western Europe was not the only center of vitality and expansion and that the interaction of culturally different peoples, so characteristic of the modern age, derived from multiple sources. How often do we notice that a European Christendom creating empires across the Atlantic was also the victim of Ottoman imperial expansion in the Balkans?

This kind of contextualizing also allows us to see more clearly the distinctive features of European empires as we view them in the mirror of other imperial creations. The Chinese, Mughal, and Ottoman empires continued older patterns of historical development, while those of Europe represented something wholly new in human history—an interacting Atlantic world of Europe, Africa, and the Americas. Furthermore, the European empires had a far greater impact on the peoples they incorporated than did other empires. Nowhere else did empire building generate such a catastrophic population collapse as in the Americas. Nor did Asian empires foster the kind of slave-based societies and transcontinental trade in slaves that were among the chief outcomes of Europe's American colonies. Finally, Europe was enriched and transformed by its American possessions far more than China and the Ottomans were by their territorial acquisitions. Europeans gained enormous new biological resources from their empires—corn, potatoes, tomatoes, chocolate, tobacco, timber, and much more—as well as enormous wealth in the form of gold, silver, and land.

Should we need a motto for world history, consider this one: in world history, nothing stands alone; context is everything.

Chapter Review

What's the Significance?

Big Picture Questions

1. The experience of empire for conquered peoples was broadly similar whoever their rulers were. Does the material in this chapter support or challenge this idea?
2. In thinking about the similarities and differences among the empires of the early modern era, what categories of comparison might be most useful to consider?
3. Have a look at the maps in this chapter with an eye to the areas of the world that were not incorporated into a major empire. Pick one or more of them and do a little research as to what was happening there in the early modern era.
4. **Looking Back:** Compared to the world of the fifteenth century, what new patterns of development are visible in the empire-building projects of the centuries that followed?

Next Steps: For Further Study

Jane Burbank and Frederick Cooper, *Empires in World History* (2010). Chapters 5–7 of this recent work describe and compare the empires of the early modern world.

Jorge Canizares-Esguerra and Erik R. Seeman, eds., *The Atlantic in Global History* (2007). A collection of essays that treats the Atlantic basin as a single interacting region.

Alfred W. Crosby, *The Columbian Voyages, the Columbian Exchange, and Their Historians* (1987). A brief and classic account of changing understandings of Columbus and his global impact.

John Kicza, *Resilient Cultures: America's Native Peoples Confront European Colonization, 1500–1800* (2003). An account of European colonization in the Americas that casts the native peoples as active agents rather than passive victims.

Charles C. Mann, *1493: Uncovering the New World Columbus Created* (2011). A global account of the Columbian exchange that presents contemporary scholarship in a very accessible fashion.

Peter Perdue, *China Marches West: The Qing Conquest of Central Eurasia* (2005). Describes how China became an empire as it incorporated the non-Chinese people of Central Asia.

Willard Sutherland, *Taming the Wild Fields: Colonization and Empire on the Russian Steppe* (2004). An up-to-date account of Russian expansion in the steppes.

"Discover the Ottomans," http://www.theottomans.org/english/index.asp. A series of essays and images that traces the history of the Ottoman Empire over six centuries.

"1492: An Ongoing Voyage," http://www.ibiblio.org/expo/1492.exhibit/Intro.html. An interactive Web site based on an exhibit from the Library of Congress that provides a rich context for exploring the meaning of Columbus and his voyages.

State Building in the Early Modern Era

The empires of the early modern era were the projects of states, though these states often made use of various private groups—missionaries, settlers, merchants, mercenaries—to achieve the goals of empire. Such imperial states—Mughal India, the Ottoman Empire, France, and the Inca Empire, for example—were invariably headed by kings or emperors who were the source of ultimate political authority in their lands. Each of those rulers sought to govern societies divided by religion, region, ethnicity, or class.

During the three centuries between 1450 and 1750, all of these states, and a number of non-imperial states as well, moved toward greater political integration and centralization. In all of them, more effective central bureaucracies curtailed, though never eliminated, entrenched local interests; royal courts became more elaborate; and the role of monarchs grew more prominent. The growth of empire accompanied this process of political integration, and perhaps helped cause it. However, efforts at state building differed considerably across the early modern world, depending on variations in historical backgrounds, the particular problems and circumstances that each state faced, the cultural basis of political authority, and the policies that individual leaders followed.

The documents that follow allow us to examine this state-building effort in several distinct settings. Two of them were written by monarchs themselves and two by outside observers. What similarities and variations in this process of state building can you notice as you study the documents? How did these early modern states differ from the states of later centuries or those of today? To what extent was government personal rather than institutional? In what ways was power exercised—through coercion and violence, through accommodation with established elites, through the operation of new bureaucratic structures, or by persuading people that the central authority was in fact legitimate?

Source 13.1
The Memoirs of Emperor Jahangir

The peoples of India had only rarely experienced a political system that encompassed most of the subcontinent. Its vast ethnic and cultural diversity and the division between its Hindu and Muslim peoples usually generated a fragmented political order of many competing states and principalities. But in the early modern era, the Mughal Empire gave to South Asia a rare period of substantial political unity. Source 13.1 offer excerpts from the memoirs of Jahangir, who ruled the Mughal state from 1605 to 1627, following the reign of his more famous father Akbar (see pages 580–81). Written in Persian, the literary language of the eastern Islamic world, Jahangir's account of his reign followed the tradition of earlier Mughal emperors in noting major events of his lifetime, but it departed from that tradition in reflecting personally on art, politics, family life, and more.

- Why do you think Jahangir mounted such an elaborate coronation celebration for himself?

- In what ways did Jahangir seek to ensure the effective authority of the state he led?

- In what ways was Jahangir a distinctly Muslim ruler? In what respects did he and his father depart from Islamic principles?

- Based on these selections, what concrete problems of governance can you infer were facing Jahangir?

JAHANGIR
Memoirs
1605–1627

At the age of thirty-eight, I became Emperor. . . . As at the very instant that I seated myself on the throne, the sun rose from the horizon; I accepted this as the omen of victory, and as indicating a reign of unvarying prosperity. Hence I assumed the titles of . . . the world-subduing emperor, the world-subduing king.

On this occasion I made use of the throne prepared by my father, and enriched at an expense without parallel for the celebration of the festival of the new year. . . . Having thus seated myself on the throne of my expectations and wishes, I caused also the imperial crown, which my father had caused to be made after the manner of that which was worn by the great kings of Persia, to be brought before me, and then, in the presence of the whole assembled Emirs, having placed it on my brows, as an omen auspicious to the stability and happiness of my reign, kept it there for the space of a full astronomical hour. . . .

For forty days and forty nights I caused the . . . great imperial state drum, to strike up, without ceasing, the strains of joy and triumph; and . . . around my throne, the ground was spread by my directions with the most costly brocades and gold embroidered carpets. Censers [containers for burning incense] of gold and silver were disposed in different directions for the purpose of burning odoriferous drugs, and nearly three thousand camphorated wax lights . . . illuminated the scene from night till morning. Numbers of blooming youths, beautiful as young Joseph in the pavilions of Egypt, clad in dresses of the most costly materials . . . awaited my commands, rank after rank, and in attitude most respectful. And finally, the Emirs of the empire . . . covered from head to foot in gold and jewels, and shoulder to shoulder, stood round in brilliant array, also waiting for the commands of their sovereign. For forty days and forty nights did I keep open to the world these scenes of festivity and splendor, furnishing altogether an example of imperial magnificence seldom paralleled in this stage of earthly existence. . . .

I instituted . . . special regulations . . . as rules of conduct, never to be deviated from in their respective stations.

1. I remitted [canceled] altogether to my subjects three sources of revenue taxes or duties. . . .

2. I directed, when the district lay waste or destitute of inhabitants, that towns should be built. . . . I charged the Jaguir-daurs [local rulers granted a certain territory by the emperor], or feudatories of the empire, in such deserted places to erect mosques and substantial . . . stations for the accommodation of travelers, in order to render the district once more an inhabited country, and that wayfaring men might again be able to pass and repass in safety.

3. Merchants traveling through the country were not to have their bales or packages of any kind opened without their consent. But when they were perfectly willing to dispose of any article of merchandise, purchasers were permitted to deal with them, without, however, offering any species of molestation. . . .

5. No person was permitted either to make or sell either wine or any other kind of intoxicating liquor. I undertook to institute this regulation, although it is sufficiently notorious that I have myself the strongest inclination for wine, in which from the age of sixteen I have liberally indulged. . . .

6. No person [official] was permitted to take up his abode obtrusively in the dwelling of any subject of my realm. . . .

7. No person was to suffer, for any offense, the loss of a nose or ear. If the crime were theft, the offender was to be scourged with thorns, or deterred from further transgression by an attestation on the Koran.

8. [High officials] were prohibited from possessing themselves by violence of the lands of the subject, or from cultivating them on their own account. . . .

10. The governors in all the principal cities were directed to establish infirmaries or hospitals, with competent medical aid for the relief of the sick. . . .

11. During the month of my birth . . . the use of all animal food was prohibited both in town and country; and at equidistant periods throughout the year a day was set apart, on which all slaughtering of animals was strictly forbidden.

[H]aving on one occasion asked my father [Akbar] the reason why he had forbidden any one to prevent or interfere with the building of these haunts of idolatry [Hindu temples], his reply was in the following terms: "My dear child," said he, "I find myself a powerful monarch, the shadow of God upon earth. I have seen that he bestows the blessings of his gracious providence upon all his creatures without distinction. Ill should I discharge the duties of my exalted station, were I to withhold my compassion and indulgence from any of those entrusted to my charge. With all of the human race, with all of God's creatures, I am at peace: why then should I permit myself, under any consideration, to be the cause of molestation or aggression to any one? Besides, are not five parts in six of mankind either Hindus or aliens to the faith; and were I to be governed by motives of the kind suggested in your inquiry, what alternative can I have but to put them all to death! I have thought it therefore my wisest plan to let these men alone. Neither is it to be forgotten, that the class of whom we are speaking . . . are usefully engaged, either in the pursuits of science or the arts, or of improvements for the benefit of mankind, and have in numerous instances arrived at the highest distinctions in the state, there being, indeed, to be found in this city men of every description, and of every religion on the face of the earth."

Source: *The Memoirs of the Emperor Jahangir*, translated from the Persian by Major David Price (London: Oriental Translation Committee, 1829), 1–3, 5–8, 15.

Source 13.2
An Outsider's View of the Ottoman Empire

Under Suleiman I (r. 1520–1566), the Ottoman Empire reached its greatest territorial extent and perhaps its golden age in terms of culture and economy (see Map 13.4, page 583). A helpful window into the life of this most powerful of Muslim states comes from the writings of Ogier Ghiselin de Busbecq, a Flemish nobleman who served as a diplomat for the Austrian Empire, which then felt under great threat from Ottoman expansion into Central Europe. Busbecq's letters to a friend, excerpted in Source 13.2, present his view of the Ottoman court and his reflections on Ottoman military power.

- How do you think Busbecq's outsider status shaped his perceptions of Ottoman political and military life? To what extent does his role as a foreigner enhance or undermine the usefulness of his account for historians?

- How did he define the differences between the Ottoman Empire and Austria? What do you think he hoped to accomplish by highlighting these differences?

- What sources of Ottoman political authority are apparent in Busbecq's account?

- What potential problems of the Ottoman Empire does this document imply or state?

Ogier Ghiselin de Busbecq
The Turkish Letters
1555–1562

On his [Suleiman's] arrival we were admitted to an audience. . . . His air [attitude], was by no means gracious, and his face wore a stern, though dignified, expression. On entering we were separately conducted into the royal presence by the chamberlains, who grasped our arms. This has been the Turkish fashion of admitting people to the Sovereign ever since a Croat, in order to avenge the death of his master . . . asked Amurath [an earlier Sultan] for an audience, and took advantage of it to slay him. After having gone through a pretense of kissing his hand, we were conducted backward to the wall opposite his seat, care being taken that we should never turn our backs on him. . . .

The Sultan's hall was crowded with people, among whom were several officers of high rank. Besides these there were all the troopers of the Imperial guard and a large force of Janissaries; but there was not in all that great assembly a single man who owed his position to aught save his valor and his merit. No distinction is attached to birth among the Turks. . . . In making his appointments the Sultan pays no regard to any pretensions on the score of wealth or rank, nor does he take into consideration recommendations or popularity. . . . It is by merit that men rise in the service, a system which ensures that posts should only be assigned to the competent. . . . Those who receive the highest offices from the Sultan are for the most part the sons of shepherds or herdsmen, and so far from being ashamed of their parentage, they actually glory in it, and consider it a matter of boasting that they owe nothing to the accident of birth. . . .

Among the Turks, therefore, honors, high posts, and judgeships are the rewards of great ability and good service. If a man be dishonest, or lazy, or careless, he remains at the bottom of the ladder, an object of contempt; for such qualities there are no honors in Turkey! This is the reason that they are successful in their undertakings, that they lord it over others, and are daily extending the bounds of their empire. These are not our ideas, with us [Europeans] there is no opening left for merit; birth is the standard for everything; the prestige of birth is the sole key to advancement in the public service. . . .

[T]ake your stand by my side, and look at the sea of turbaned heads, each wrapped in twisted folds of the whitest silk; look at those marvelously handsome dresses of every kind and every color; time would fail me to tell how all around is glittering with gold, with silver, with purple, with silk, and with velvet; words cannot convey an adequate idea of that strange and wondrous sight: it was the most beautiful spectacle I ever saw.

With all this luxury, great simplicity and economy are combined; every man's dress, whatever his position may be, is of the same pattern; no fringes or useless points are sewn on, as is the case with us, appendages which cost a great deal of money, and are worn out in three days. . . . I was greatly struck with the silence and order that prevailed in this great crowd. There were no cries, no hum of voices, the usual accompaniments of a motley gathering, neither was there any jostling; without the slightest disturbance each man took his proper place according to his rank. . . .

On leaving the assembly we had a fresh treat in the sight of the household cavalry returning to their quarters; the men were mounted on splendid horses, excellently groomed, and gorgeously accoutred. And so we left the royal presence, taking with us but little hope of a successful issue to our embassy.

The Turkish monarch going to war takes with him over 40,000 camels and nearly as many baggage mules, of which a great part, when he is invad-ing Persia, are loaded with rice and other kinds of grain. . . . The invading army carefully abstains from encroaching on its magazines [supplies] at the outset. . . . The Sultan's magazines are opened, and a ration just sufficient to sustain life is daily weighed out to the Janissaries and other troops of the royal household.

From this you will see that it is the patience, self-denial, and thrift of the Turkish soldier that enable him to face the most trying circumstances. . . . What a contrast to our men! Christian soldiers on a campaign refuse to put up with their ordinary food, and call for thrushes, beccaficos [small birds], and such like dainty dishes! If these are not supplied they grow mutinous and work their own ruin; and, if they are supplied, they are ruined all the same. For each man is his own worst enemy, and has no foe more deadly than his own intemperance, which is sure to kill him, if the enemy be not quick.

It makes me shudder to think of what the result of a struggle between such different systems must be; one of us must prevail and the other be destroyed. . . . On their side is the vast wealth of their empire, unimpaired resources, experience and practice in arms, a veteran soldiery, an uninterrupted series of victories, readiness to endure hardships, union, order, discipline, thrift, and watchfulness. On ours are found an empty exchequer, luxurious habits, exhausted resources, broken spirits, a raw and insubordinate soldiery, and greedy generals; there is no regard for discipline, license runs riot, the men indulge in drunkenness and debauchery, and, worst of all, the enemy are accustomed to victory, we, to defeat. Can we doubt what the result must be? The only obstacle is Persia, whose position on his rear forces the invader to take precautions. The fear of Persia gives us a respite, but it is only for a time. When he has secured himself in that quarter, he will fall upon us with all the resources of the East. How ill prepared we are to meet such an attack it is not for me to say.

[In the following passage, Busbecq reflects on a major problem of the Ottoman state, succession to the throne.]

The sons of Turkish Sultans are in the most wretched position in the world, for, as soon as one of them succeeds his father, the rest are doomed to certain death. The Turk can endure no rival to the throne, and, indeed, the conduct of the Janissaries renders it impossible for the new Sultan to spare his brothers; for if one of them survives, the Janissaries are forever asking largesses. If these are refused, forthwith the cry is heard, "Long live the brother!" "God preserve the brother!"—a tolerably broad

hint that they intend to place him on the throne. So that the Turkish Sultans are compelled to celebrate their succession by imbruing their hands in the blood of their nearest relatives.

Source: Charles Thornton Forester and F. H. Blackburne Daniell, *The Life and Letters of Ogier Ghiselin de Busbecq* (London: C. Kegan Paul, 1881), 114–15, 152–56, 219–22.

Source 13.3
French State Building and Louis XIV

Like their counterparts in the Middle East and Asia, a number of European states in the early modern era also pursued the twin projects of imperial expansion abroad and political integration at home. But consolidating central authority was a long and difficult task. Obstacles to the ambitions of kings in Europe were many—the absence of an effective transportation and communication infrastructure; the difficulty of acquiring information about the population and resources; the entrenched interests of privileged groups such as the nobility, church, town councils, and guilds; and the division between Catholics and Protestants.

Perhaps the most well-known example of such European state-building efforts is that of France under the rule of Louis XIV (r. 1643–1715). Louis and other European monarchs, such as those in Spain and Russia, operated under a set of assumptions known as absolutism, which held that kings ruled by "divine right" and could legitimately claim sole and uncontested authority in their realms. Louis's famous dictum *"L'état, c'est moi"* ("I am the state") summed up the absolutist ideal. Source 13.3 illustrates at least one way in which Louis attempted to realize this ideal.

Written by Louis himself, this document focuses on the importance of "spectacle" and public display in solidifying the exalted role of the monarch. The "carousel" described here was an extravagant pageant, held in Paris in June 1662. It featured various exotic animals, slaves, princes, and nobles arrayed in fantastic costumes representing distant lands, as well as many equestrian competitions. Unifying this disparate assembly was King Louis himself, dressed as a Roman emperor, while on the shields of the nobles was that grand symbol of the monarchy, the sun.

■ What posture does Louis take toward his subjects in this document?

■ How does he understand the role of spectacle in general and the carousel in particular?

■ What does the choice of the sun as a royal symbol suggest about Louis's conception of his role in the French state and empire?

LOUIS XIV

Memoirs

1670

It was necessary to conserve and cultivate with care all that which, without diminishing the authority and the respect due to me, linked me by bonds of affection to my peoples and above all to the people of rank, so as to make them see by this very means that it was neither aversion for them nor affected severity, nor harshness of spirit, but simply reason and duty, that made me more reserved and more exact toward them in other matters. That sharing of pleasures, which gives people at court a respectable familiarity with us, touches them and charms them more than can be expressed. The common people, on the other hand, are delighted by shows in which, at bottom, we always have the aim of pleasing them; and all our subjects, in general, are delighted to see that we like what they like, or what they excel in. By this means we hold on to their hearts and their minds, sometimes more strongly perhaps than by recompenses and gifts; and with regard to foreigners, in a state they see flourishing and well ordered, that which is spent on expenses and which could be called superfluous, makes a very favorable impression on them, of magnificence, of power, of grandeur. . . .

The carousel, which has furnished me the subject of these reflections, had only been conceived at first as a light amusement; but little by little, we were carried away, and it became a spectacle that was fairly grand and magnificent, both in the number of exercises, and by the novelty of the costumes and the variety of the [heraldic] devices. It was

then that I began to employ the one that I have always kept since and which you see in so many places . . . it ought to represent in some way the duties of a prince, and constantly encourage me to fulfill them. For the device they chose the sun, which . . . is the most noble of all, and which, by its quality of being unique, by the brilliance that surrounds it, by the light that it communicates to the other stars which form for it a kind of court, by the just and equal share that the different climates of the world receive of this light, by the good it does in all places, ceaselessly producing as it does, in every sphere of life, joy and activity, by its unhindered movement, in which it nevertheless always appears calm, by its constant and invariable course, from which it never departs nor wavers, is the most striking and beautiful image of a great monarch.

Those who saw me governing with a good deal of ease and without being confused by anything, in all the numerous attentions that royalty demands, persuaded me to add the earth's globe, and for motto, *nec pluribus impar* (not unequal to many things): by which they meant something that flattered the aspirations of a young king, namely that, being sufficient to so many things, I would doubtless be capable of governing other empires, just as the sun was capable of lighting up other worlds if they were exposed to its rays.

Source: Robert Campbell, *Louis XIV* (London: Longmans, 1993), 117–18.

Source 13.4

An Outsider's View of the Inca Empire

Pedro de Cieza de León (1520–1554), a Spanish chronicler of the Inca Empire of the early sixteenth century, came to the Americas as a boy at the age of thirteen. For the next seventeen years, Cieza took part as a soldier in a number of expeditions that established Spanish rule in various parts of South America. Along the way, he collected a great deal of information, especially about the Inca Empire, which he began to publish on his return to Spain in 1550. Despite a very limited education, Cieza wrote a series of works that have become a major source for historians about the workings of the Inca Empire and about the Spanish conquest of that land. The selection that follows focuses on the techniques that the Incas used to govern their huge empire.

- How would you describe Cieza's posture toward the Inca Empire? What in particular did he seem to appreciate about it?

- Based on this account, what difficulties did the Inca rulers face in governing their large and diverse realm?

- What policies or practices did the Inca authorities follow in seeking to integrate their empire?

- Some modern observers have described the Inca Empire as "totalitarian" or "socialist." Do such terms seem appropriate? How else might you describe the Inca state?

- How does Cieza's relationship to the Inca Empire compare to that of Busbecq to the Ottoman Empire?

PEDRO DE CIEZA DE LEÓN
Chronicles of the Incas
ca. 1550

The Incas had the seat of their empire in the city of Cuzco, where the laws were given and the captains set out to make war. . . . As soon as one of these large provinces was conquered, ten or twelve thousand of the men and their wives, or six thousand, or the number decided upon were ordered to leave and remove themselves from it. These were transferred to another town or province of the same climate and nature as that which they left. . . . And they had another device to keep the natives from hating them, and this was that they never divested the natural chieftains of their power. If it so happened that one of them committed a crime or in some way deserved to be stripped of his power, it was vested in his sons or brothers, and all were ordered to obey them. . . .

One of the things most to be envied in these rulers is how well they knew to conquer such vast lands. . . .

[T]hey entered many lands without war, and the soldiers who accompanied the Inca were ordered to do no damage or harm, robbery or violence. If there was a shortage of food in the province, he ordered supplies brought in from other regions so that those newly won to his service would not find his rule and acquaintance irksome. . . .

In many others, where they entered by war and force of arms, they ordered that the crops and houses of the enemy be spared. . . . But in the end the Incas always came out victorious, and when they had vanquished the others, they did not do them further harm, but released those they had taken prisoner, if there were any, and restored the booty, and put them back in possession of their property and rule, exhorting them not to be foolish and try to compete with his royal majesty nor abandon his friendship, but to be his friends as their neighbors were. And saying this, he gave them a number of beautiful women and fine pieces of wool or gold. . . .

They never deprived the native chieftains of their rule. They were all ordered to worship the sun as God, but they were not prohibited from observing their own religions and customs. . . .

It is told for a fact of the rulers of this kingdom that in the days of their rule they [the Incas] had their representatives in the capitals of all the provinces. . . . They served as head of the provinces or regions, and from every so many leagues around the tributes were brought to one of these capitals. . . . This was so well organized that there was not a village that did not know where it was to send its tribute. In all these capitals the Incas had temples of the sun, mints, and many silversmiths who did nothing but work rich pieces of gold or fair vessels of silver. . . . The tribute paid by each of these districts where the capital was situated, and that turned over by the natives, whether gold, silver, clothing, arms, and all else they gave, was entered in the accounts of the [quipu-] camayocs, who kept the quipus and did everything ordered by the governor in the matter of finding the soldiers or supplying whomever the Inca ordered, or making delivery to Cuzco; but when they came from the city of Cuzco to go over the accounts, or they were ordered to go to Cuzco to give an accounting, the accountants themselves gave it by the quipus, or went to give it where there could be no fraud, but everything had to come out right. Few years went by in which an accounting of all these things was not made. . . .

When the Incas set out to visit their kingdom, it is told that they traveled with great pomp, riding in rich litters set upon smooth, long poles of the finest wood and adorned with gold and silver. . . .

So many people came to see his passing that all the hills and slopes seemed covered with them, and all called down blessings upon him. . . .

He [the Inca] traveled four leagues each day, or as much as he wished; he stopped wherever he liked to inquire into the state of his kingdom; he willingly listened to those who came to him with complaints, righting wrongs and punishing those who had committed an injustice. . . .

[T]hese rulers, as the best measure, ordered and decreed, with severe punishment for failure to obey, that all the natives of their empire should know

and understand the language of Cuzco, both they and their women. . . . This was carried out so faithfully that in the space of a very few years a single tongue was known and used in an extension of more than 1,200 leagues; yet, even though this language was employed, they all spoke their own [languages], which were so numerous that if I were to list them it would not be credited. . . .

[The Inca] appointed those whose duty it was to punish wrongdoers, and to this end they were always traveling about the country. The Incas took such care to see that justice was meted out that nobody ventured to commit a felony or theft. This was to deal with thieves, ravishers of women, or conspirators against the Inca; however, there were many provinces that warred on one another, and the Incas were not wholly able to prevent this. By the river [Huatanay] that runs through Cuzco justice was executed on those who were caught or brought in as prisoners from some other place. There they had their heads cut off, or were put to death in some other manner which they chose. Mutiny and conspiracy were severely punished, and, above all, those who were thieves and known as such; even their wives and children were despised and considered to be tarred with the same brush. . . .

[I]n each of the many provinces there were many storehouses filled with supplies and other needful things; thus, in times of war, wherever the armies went they draw upon the contents of these storehouses, without ever touching the supplies of their confederates or laying a finger on what they had in their settlements. And when there was no war, all this stock of supplies and food was divided up among the poor and the widows. These poor were the aged, or the lame, crippled, or paralyzed, or those afflicted with some other diseases. . . . If there came a lean year, the storehouses were opened and the provinces were lent what they needed in the way of supplies; then, in a year of abundance, they paid back all they had received.

Source: *The Incas of Pedro de Cieza de León*, translated by Harriet de Onis (Norman: University of Oklahoma Press, 1959), 56–57, 158–60, 165–73, 177–78.

DOING HISTORY

State Building in the Early Modern Era

1. **Making comparisons:** To what extent did these four early modern states face similar problems and devise similar solutions? How did they differ? In particular, how did the rulers of these states deal with subordinates? How did they use violence? What challenges to imperial authority did they face?

2. **Assessing spectacle:** In what different ways was spectacle, royal splendor, or public display evident in the documents? How would you define the purpose of such display? How effective do you think spectacle has been in consolidating state authority?

3. **Distinguishing power and authority:** Some scholars have made a distinction between "power," the ability of a state to coerce its subjects into some required behavior, and "authority," the ability of a state to persuade its subjects to do its bidding voluntarily by convincing them that it is proper, right, or natural to do so. What examples of power and authority can you find in these documents? How were power and authority related? What are the advantages and disadvantages of each, from the viewpoint of ambitious rulers?

4. **Comparing past and present:** It is important to recognize that early modern states differed in many ways from twentieth- or twenty-first-century states. How would you define those differences? Consider, among other things, the personal role of the ruler, the use of violence, the means of establishing authority, and the extent to which the state could shape the lives of its citizens.

5. **Comparing insiders' and outsiders' accounts:** What differences do you notice between the two passages written by monarchs themselves and the two composed by foreign observers? What advantages and limitations do these two types of sources offer to historians seeking to use them as evidence?

Slave Merchant in Gorée Island, Senegal, from *Encyclopédie des Voyages*, engraved by L. F. Labrousse, 1796/Bibliothèque des Arts Décoratifs, Paris, France/Archives Charmet/Bridgeman Images

CHAPTER 14

Economic Transformations

Commerce and Consequence

1450–1750

"I have come full circle back to my destiny: from Africa to America and back to Africa. I could hear the cries and wails of my ancestors. I weep with them and for them."[1] This is what an African American woman from Atlanta wrote in 2002 in the guest book of the Cape Coast Castle, one of the many ports of embarkation for slaves located along the coast of Ghana in West Africa. There she no doubt saw the whips and leg irons used to discipline the captured Africans as well as the windowless dungeons in which hundreds were crammed while waiting for the ships that would carry them across the Atlantic to the Americas. Almost certainly she also caught sight of the infamous "gate of no return," through which the captives departed to their new life as slaves.

This visitor's emotional encounter with the legacy of the Atlantic slave trade reminds us of the enormous significance of this commerce in human beings for the early modern world and of its continuing echoes even in the twenty-first century. The slave trade, however, was only one component of those international networks of exchange that shaped human interactions during the centuries between 1450 and 1750. Europeans now smashed their way into the ancient spice trade of the Indian Ocean, developing new relationships with Asian societies as a result. Silver, obtained from mines in Spanish America, enriched Western Europe, even as much of it made its way to China, where it allowed Europeans to participate more fully in the rich commerce of East Asia. Furs from North America and Siberia found a ready market in Europe and China, while the hunting and trapping of those fur-bearing animals transformed

---

The Atlantic Slave Trade This eighteenth-century French engraving shows the sale of slaves at Gorée, a major slave-trading port in what is now Dakar in Senegal. A European merchant and an African authority figure negotiate the arrangement, while the shackled victims themselves wait for their fate to be decided.

both natural environments and human societies. Despite their growing prominence in long-distance exchange, Europeans were far from the only actors in early modern commerce. Southeast Asians, Chinese, Indians, Armenians, Arabs, Africans, and Native Americans likewise played major roles in the making of the world economy during the early modern era.

Thus commerce joined empire as the twin creators of a global network during these centuries. Together they gave rise to new relationships, disrupted old patterns, brought distant peoples into contact with one another, enriched some, and impoverished or enslaved others. They also generated new ways of expressing status, as the Working with Evidence feature on pages 634–41 illustrates. From the various "old worlds" of the premodern era, a single "new world" emerged—slowly, amid much suffering, and accompanied by growing inequalities. What was gained and what was lost in the transformations born of global commerce have been the subject of great controversy ever since.

SEEKING THE MAIN POINT

In what different ways did global commerce transform human societies and the lives of individuals during the early modern era?

Europeans and Asian Commerce

AP® EXAM TIP

You should know the factors leading to Europe's involvement in the Indian Ocean trade.

Schoolchildren everywhere know that European empires in the Western Hemisphere grew out of an accident—Columbus's unknowing encounter with the Americas—and that new colonial societies and new commercial connections across the Atlantic were the result. In Asia, it was a very different story. The voyage (1497–1499) of the Portuguese mariner Vasco da Gama, in which Europeans sailed to India for the first time, was certainly no accident. It was the outcome of a deliberate, systematic, century-long Portuguese effort to explore a sea route to the East, by creeping slowly down the West African coast, around the tip of South Africa, up the East African coast, and finally across the Indian Ocean to Calicut in southern India in 1498. There Europeans encountered an ancient and rich network of commerce that stretched from East Africa to China. They were certainly aware of the wealth of that commercial network, but largely ignorant of its workings.

Guided Reading Question

■ CAUSATION
What drove European involvement in the world of Asian commerce?

The most immediate motivation for this massive effort was the desire for tropical spices—cinnamon, nutmeg, mace, cloves, and, above all, pepper—which were widely used as condiments and preservatives and were sometimes regarded as aphrodisiacs. A fifteenth-century English book declared: "Pepper [from Java] is black and has a good smack, And every man doth buy it."[2] Other products of the East, such as Chinese silk, Indian cottons, rhubarb for medicinal purposes, emeralds, rubies, and sapphires, were also in great demand.

Underlying this growing interest in Asia was the more general recovery of European civilization following the disaster of the Black Death in the early fourteenth century. During the fifteenth century, Europe's population was growing again, and its national monarchies—in Spain, Portugal, England, and France—were learning how to tax their subjects more effectively and to build substantial military forces equipped with gunpowder weapons. Its cities were growing too. Some of them—

A MAP OF TIME

Early 15th century	Beginning of Portuguese voyages along the coast of West Africa
1440s	First European export of slaves from West Africa
1492	Columbus reaches the Americas
1497	Vasco da Gama reaches India
1545	Founding of Potosí as silver mining town in Bolivia
1565	Beginning of Spanish takeover of the Philippines
1570s	Beginning of silver shipments from Mexico to Manila
17th century	Russian conquest of Siberia
1601–1602	British and Dutch East India companies established in Asia
18th century	Peak of the transatlantic slave trade
1750s	British begin military conquest of India

AP® EXAM TIP

This timeline will help you connect the important sequence of events of Chapters 13 and 14.

in England, the Netherlands, and northern Italy, for example—were becoming centers of international commerce, giving birth to economies based on market exchange, private ownership, and the accumulation of capital for further investment.

For many centuries, Eastern goods had trickled into the Mediterranean through the Middle East from the Indian Ocean commercial network. From the viewpoint of an increasingly dynamic Europe, several major problems accompanied this pattern of trade. First, of course, the source of supply for these much-desired goods lay solidly in Muslim hands. Most immediately, Muslim Egypt was the primary point of transfer into the Mediterranean basin and its European Christian customers. The Italian commercial city of Venice largely monopolized the European trade in Eastern goods, annually sending convoys of ships to Alexandria in Egypt. Venetians resented the Muslim monopoly on Indian Ocean trade, and other European powers disliked relying on Venice as well as on Muslims. Circumventing these monopolies was yet another impetus—both religious and political—for the Portuguese to attempt a sea route to India that bypassed both Venetian and Muslim intermediaries. In addition, many Europeans of the time were persuaded that a mysterious Christian monarch, known as Prester John, ruled somewhere in Asia or Africa. Joining with his mythical kingdom to continue the Crusades and combat a common Islamic enemy was likewise a goal of the Portuguese voyages.

A further problem for Europeans lay in paying for Eastern goods. Few products of an economically less developed Europe were attractive in Eastern markets. Thus Europeans were required to pay cash—gold or silver—for Asian spices or textiles.

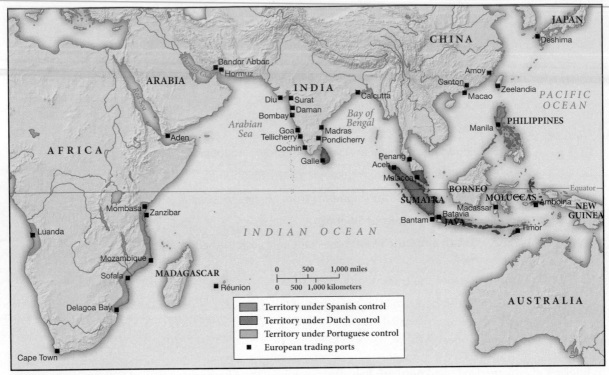

Map 14.1   Europeans in Asia in the Early Modern Era

The early modern era witnessed only very limited territorial control by Europeans in Asia. Trade, rather than empire, was the chief concern of the Western newcomers, who were not, in any event, a serious military threat to major Asian states.

This persistent trade deficit contributed much to the intense desire for precious metals that attracted early modern European explorers, traders, and conquerors. Portuguese voyages along the West African coast, for example, were seeking direct access to African goldfields. The enormously rich silver deposits of Mexico and Bolivia provided at least a temporary solution to this persistent European problem.

First the Portuguese and then the Spanish, French, Dutch, and British found their way into the ancient Asian world of Indian Ocean commerce (see Map 14.1). How they behaved in that world and what they created there differed considerably among the various European countries, but collectively they contributed much to the new regime of globalized trade.

A Portuguese Empire of Commerce

The arena of Indian Ocean commerce into which Vasco da Gama and his Portuguese successors sailed was a world away from anything they had known. It was vast, both in geographic extent and in the diversity of those who participated in it. East Africans, Arabs, Persians, Indians, Malays, Chinese, and others traded freely.

Most of them were Muslims, though hailing from many separate communities, but Hindus, Buddhists, Christians, Jews, and Chinese likewise had a role in this commercial network. Had the Portuguese sought simply to participate in peaceful trading, they certainly could have done so, but it was quickly apparent that European trade goods were crude and unattractive in Asian markets and that Europeans would be unable to compete effectively. Moreover, the Portuguese soon learned that most Indian Ocean merchant ships were not heavily armed and certainly lacked the onboard cannons that Portuguese ships carried. Since the withdrawal of the Chinese fleet from the Indian Ocean early in the fifteenth century, no major power was in a position to dominate the sea lanes, and the many smaller-scale merchants generally traded openly, although piracy was sometimes a problem.

Given these conditions, the Portuguese saw an opening, for their ships could outgun and outmaneuver competing naval forces, while their onboard cannons could devastate coastal fortifications. Although their overall economy lagged behind that of Asian producers, Europeans had more than caught up in the critical area of naval technology and naval warfare. This military advantage enabled the Portuguese to quickly establish fortified bases at several key locations within the Indian Ocean world—Mombasa in East Africa, Hormuz at the entrance to the Persian Gulf, Goa on the west coast of India, Malacca in Southeast Asia, and Macao on the south coast of China. With the exception of Macao, which had been obtained through bribery and negotiations with Chinese authorities, these Portuguese bases were obtained forcibly against small and weak states. In Mombasa, for example, the commander of a Portuguese fleet responded to local resistance in 1505 by burning and sacking the city, killing some 1,500 people, and seizing large quantities of cotton and silk textiles and carpets. The king of Mombasa wrote a warning to a neighboring city:

> This is to inform you that a great lord has passed through the town, burning it and laying it waste. He came to the town in such strength and was of such a cruelty that he spared neither man nor woman, or old nor young   nay, not even the smallest child. . . . Nor can I ascertain nor estimate what wealth they have taken from the town.[3]

What the Portuguese created in the Indian Ocean is commonly known as a "trading post empire," for they aimed to control commerce, not large territories or populations, and to do so by force of arms rather than by economic competition. Seeking to monopolize the spice trade, the Portuguese king grandly titled himself "Lord of the Conquest, Navigation, and Commerce of Ethiopia, Arabia, Persia, and India." Portuguese authorities in the East tried to require all merchant vessels to purchase a *cartaz*, or pass, and to pay duties of 6 to 10 percent on their cargoes. They partially blocked the traditional Red Sea route to the Mediterranean and for a century or so monopolized the highly profitable route around Africa to Europe. Even so, they never succeeded in controlling much more than half of the spice trade to Europe.

Guided Reading Question

■ CONNECTION

To what extent did the Portuguese realize their own goals in the Indian Ocean?

AP® EXAM TIP

The AP® exam might ask you to compare Europeans' interactions in the Indian Ocean trade network with their interactions in the trade network of the Americas.

The Spice Trade

For thousands of years, spices were a major trade item in the Indian Ocean commercial network, as this fifteenth-century French depiction of the gathering of pepper in southern India illustrates. In the early modern era, Europeans gained direct access to this ancient network for the first time. (From the *Livres des Merveilles du Monde*, ca. 1410–1412, by Master Boucicaut [fl. 1390–1430] and workshop/Bibliothèque Nationale, Paris, France /Archives Charmet/Bridgeman Images)

Failing to dominate Indian Ocean commerce as they had hoped, the Portuguese gradually assimilated themselves to its ancient patterns. They became heavily involved in carrying Asian goods to Asian ports, selling their shipping services because they were largely unable to sell their goods. Even in their major settlements, the Portuguese were outnumbered by Asian traders, and many married Asian women. Hundreds of Portuguese escaped the control of their government altogether and settled in Asian or African ports, where they learned local languages, sometimes converted to Islam, and became simply one more group in the diverse trading culture of the East.

By 1600, the Portuguese trading post empire was in steep decline. This small European country was overextended, and rising Asian states such as Japan, Burma, Mughal India, Persia, and the sultanate of Oman actively resisted Portuguese commercial control. Unwilling to accept a dominant Portuguese role in the Indian Ocean, other European countries also gradually contested Portugal's efforts to monopolize the rich spice trade to Europe.

AP® EXAM TIP

Note the factors that led to Portugal's decline as a power in the Indian Ocean trade network.

Spain and the Philippines

Spain was the first to challenge Portugal's position. As precious and profitable spices began to arrive in Europe on Portuguese ships in the early sixteenth century, the Spanish soon realized that they were behind in the race to gain access to the riches of the East. In an effort to catch up, they established themselves on what became the Philippine Islands, named after the Spanish king Philip II. The Spanish first encountered the region during the famous round-the-world voyage (1519–1521) of Ferdinand Magellan, a Portuguese mariner sailing on behalf of the Spanish Crown. There they found an archipelago of islands, thousands of them, occupied by culturally diverse peoples and organized in small and highly competitive chiefdoms. One of the local chiefs later told the Spanish: "There is no king and no sole authority in this land; but everyone holds his own view and opinion, and does as he prefers."[4] Some were involved in tribute trade with China, and a small number of Chinese settlers lived in the port towns. Nonetheless, the region was of little interest to the governments of China and Japan, the major powers in the area.

These conditions—proximity to China and the spice islands, small and militarily weak societies, the absence of competing claims—encouraged the Spanish to establish outright colonial rule on the islands, rather than to imitate a Portuguese-style trading post empire. Accomplished largely from Spanish Mexico, conquest and colonization involved small-scale military operations, gunpowder weapons, local alliances, gifts and favors to chiefs, and the pageantry of Catholic ritual, all of which contributed to a relatively easy and often-bloodless Spanish takeover of the islands in the century or so after 1565. They remained a Spanish colonial territory until the end of the nineteenth century, when the United States assumed control following the Spanish-American War of 1898.

Accompanying Spanish rule was a major missionary effort, which turned Filipino society into the only major outpost of Christianity in Asia. That effort also opened up a new front in the long encounter of Christendom and Islam, for on the southern island of Mindanao, Islam was gaining strength and provided an ideology of resistance to Spanish encroachment for 300 years. Indeed, Mindanao remains a contested part of the Philippines into the twenty-first century.

Beyond the missionary enterprise, other features of Spanish colonial practice in the Americas found expression in the Philippines. People living in scattered settlements were persuaded or forced to relocate into more concentrated Christian communities. Tribute, taxes, and unpaid labor became part of ordinary life. Large landed estates emerged, owned by Spanish settlers, Catholic religious orders, or prominent Filipinos. Women who had played major roles as ritual specialists, healers, and midwives were now displaced by male Spanish priests, and the ceremonial instruments of these women were deliberately defiled and disgraced. Short-lived revolts and flight to interior mountains were among the Filipino responses to colonial oppression.

Yet others fled to Manila, the new capital of the colonial Philippines. By 1600, it had become a flourishing and culturally diverse city of more than 40,000 inhabitants and was home to many Spanish settlers and officials and growing numbers of Filipino migrants. Its rising prosperity also attracted some 3,000 Japanese and more than 20,000 Chinese. Serving as traders, artisans, and sailors, the Chinese in particular became an essential element in the Spanish colony's growing economic

Guided Reading Question

■ **COMPARISON**

How did the Portuguese, Spanish, Dutch, and British initiatives in Asia differ from one another?

AP® EXAM TIP

Take notes on Spain's reasons for taking over the Philippines.

relationship with China; however, their economic prominence and their resistance to conversion earned them Spanish hostility and clearly discriminatory treatment. Periodic Chinese revolts, followed by expulsions and massacres, were the result. On one occasion in 1603, the Spanish killed about 20,000 people, nearly the entire Chinese population of the island.

The East India Companies

Far more important than the Spanish as European competitors for the spice trade were the Dutch and English, both of whom entered Indian Ocean commerce in the early seventeenth century. Together they quickly overtook and displaced the Portuguese, often by force, even as they competed vigorously with each other as well. These rising Northern European powers were both militarily and economically stronger than the Portuguese. During the sixteenth century, the Dutch had become a highly commercialized and urbanized society, and their business skills and maritime shipping operations were the envy of Europe. Around 1600, both the British and the Dutch, unlike the Portuguese, organized their Indian Ocean ventures through private trading companies, which were able to raise money and share risks among a substantial number of merchant investors. The British East India Company and the Dutch East India Company received charters from their respective governments granting them trading monopolies and the power to make war and to govern conquered peoples. Thus they established their own parallel and competing trading post empires, with the Dutch focused on the islands of Indonesia and the English on India. Somewhat later, a French company also established settlements in the Indian Ocean basin.

Guided Reading Question

∙∙∙∙∙∙∙∙∙∙∙∙∙∙∙∙∙∙∙∙∙∙∙∙∙∙∙∙∙∙∙

■ **CHANGE**

To what extent did the British and Dutch trading companies change the societies they encountered in Asia?

Operating in a region of fragmented and weak political authority, the Dutch acted to control not only the shipping of cloves, cinnamon, nutmeg, and mace but also their production. With much bloodshed, the Dutch seized control of a number of small spice-producing islands, forcing their people to sell only to the Dutch and destroying the crops of those who refused. On the Banda Islands, famous for their nutmeg, the Dutch killed, enslaved, or left to starve virtually the entire population of some 15,000 people and then replaced them with Dutch planters, using a slave labor force to produce the nutmeg crop. One Indonesian sultan asked a Dutch commander, "Do you believe that God has preserved for your trade alone islands which lie so far from your homeland?"[5] Apparently the Dutch did. And for a time in the seventeenth century, they were able to monopolize the trade in nutmeg, mace, and cloves and to sell these spices in Europe and India at fourteen to seventeen times the price they paid in Indonesia.[6] While Dutch profits soared, the local economy of the Spice Islands was shattered, and their people were impoverished.

The Dutch East India Company also established itself briefly on the large island of Taiwan, off the coast of southern China, between 1624 and 1662, hoping to produce deerskins, rice, and sugar for export. Finding the local people unwilling to take part in commercial agriculture, the Dutch opened the island to large-scale

Chinese immigration. Thus, under a regime of Dutch and Chinese "co-colonization," Taiwan became ethnically Chinese. Later in the century, Chinese forces expelled the Dutch, bringing Taiwan into China politically as well. And so Taiwan emerged as a site of intersection between European and Chinese expansion in the early modern era.[7]

The British East India Company operated differently from its Dutch counterpart. Less well financed and less commercially sophisticated, the British were largely excluded from the rich Spice Islands by the Dutch monopoly. Thus they fell back on India, where they established three major trading settlements during the seventeenth century: Bombay (now Mumbai), on India's west coast, and Calcutta and Madras, on the east coast. Although British naval forces soon gained control of the Arabian Sea and the Persian Gulf, largely replacing the Portuguese, on land they were no match for the powerful Mughal Empire, which ruled most of the Indian subcontinent. Therefore, the British were unable to practice "trade by warfare," as the Dutch did in Indonesia.[8] Rather, they secured their trading bases with the permission of Mughal authorities or local rulers, with substantial payments and bribes as the price of admission to the Indian market. When some independent English traders plundered a Mughal ship in 1636, local authorities detained British East India Company officials for two months and forced them to pay a whopping fine. Although pepper and other spices remained important in British trade, British merchants came to focus much more heavily on Indian cotton textiles, which were becoming widely popular in England and its American colonies. Hundreds of villages in the interior of southern India became specialized producers for this British market.

Like the Portuguese before them, both the Dutch and English became heavily involved in trade within Asia. The profits from this "carrying trade" enabled them to purchase Asian goods without paying for them in gold or silver from Europe. Dutch and English traders also began to deal in bulk goods for a mass market — pepper, textiles, and later, tea and coffee — rather than just luxury goods for an elite market. In the second half of the eighteenth century, both the Dutch and British trading post empires slowly evolved into a more conventional form of colonial domination, in which the British came to rule India and the Dutch controlled Indonesia.

A European View of Asian Commerce
The various East India companies (British, French, and Dutch) represented the major vehicle for European commerce in Asia during the early modern era. This wall painting, dating from 1778 and titled *The East Offering Its Riches to Britannia*, hung in the main offices of the British East India Company. (*The East Offering Its Riches to Britannia*, by Roma Spiridione [d. 1787]/British Library, London, UK/© British Library Board. All Rights Reserved/Bridgeman Images)

AP® EXAM TIP

Know ways that European trade in the Indian Ocean evolved over time in the era ca. 1450– ca. 1750.

Asians and Asian Commerce

The attention of historians often falls disproportionately on what is new. Although European commerce in the Indian Ocean and the South China Sea certainly qualifies as "something new," the European presence was far less significant in Asia than it was in the Americas or Africa during these centuries. European political control was limited to the Philippines, parts of Java, and a few of the Spice Islands. The small Southeast Asian state of Siam was able to expel the French in 1688, outraged by their aggressive religious efforts at conversion and their plotting to extend French influence. To the great powers of Asia—Mughal India, China, and Japan—Europeans represented no real military threat and played minor roles in their large and prosperous economies. Japan provides a fascinating case study in the ability of major Asian powers to control the European intruders.

When Portuguese traders and missionaries first arrived in that island nation in the mid-sixteenth century, soon followed by Spanish, Dutch, and English merchants, Japan was plagued by endemic conflict among numerous feudal lords, known as *daimyo*, each with his own cadre of *samurai* warriors. In these circumstances, the European newcomers found a hospitable welcome, for their military technology, shipbuilding skills, geographic knowledge, commercial opportunities, and even religious ideas proved useful or attractive to various elements in Japan's fractious and competitive society. The second half of the sixteenth century, for example, witnessed the growth of a substantial Christian movement, with some 300,000 converts and a Japanese-led church organization.

By the early seventeenth century, however, a series of remarkable military figures had unified Japan politically, under the leadership of a supreme military commander known as the *shogun*, who hailed from the Tokugawa clan. With the end of Japan's civil wars, successive shoguns came to view Europeans as a threat to the country's newly established unity rather than an opportunity. They therefore expelled Christian missionaries and violently suppressed the practice of Christianity. This policy included the execution, often under torture, of some sixty-two missionaries and thousands of Japanese converts. Shogunate authorities also forbade Japanese from traveling abroad and banned most European traders altogether, permitting only the Dutch, who appeared less interested in spreading Christianity, to trade at a single site. Thus, for two centuries (1650–1850), Japanese authorities of the Tokugawa shogunate largely closed their country off from the emerging world of European commerce, although they maintained their trading ties to China, Korea, and Southeast Asia.

In the early seventeenth century, a large number of Japanese traders began to operate in Southeast Asia, where they behaved much like the newly arriving Europeans, frequently using force in support of their commercial interests. But unlike European states, the Japanese government of the Tokugawa shogunate explicitly disavowed any responsibility for or connection with these Japanese merchants. In one of many letters to rulers of Southeast Asian states, the Tokugawa shogun wrote

AP® EXAM TIP

You need to know the roles of the *samurai* and the *daimyo* during the Tokugawa shogunate.

AP® EXAM TIP

Take notes on the interactions between Japan and European traders in this era.

to officials in Cambodia in 1610: "Merchants from my country [Japan] go to several places in your country [Cambodia] as well as Cochinchina and Champa [Vietnam]. There they become cruel and ferocious. . . . These men cause terrible damage. . . . They commit crimes and cause suffering. . . . Their offenses are extremely serious. Please punish them immediately according to the laws of your country. It is not necessary to have any reservations in this regard."[9] Thus Japanese merchants lacked the kind of support from their government that European merchants consistently received, but they did not refrain from trading in Southeast Asia.

Nor did other Asian merchants disappear from the Indian Ocean, despite European naval dominance. Arab, Indian, Chinese, Javanese, Malay, Vietnamese, and other traders benefited from the upsurge in seaborne commerce. Resident communities of Chinese merchants inhabited many Southeast Asian port cities and dominated the growing spice trade between that region and China. Southeast Asian merchants, many of them women, continued a long tradition of involvement in international trade. Malay proverbs from the sixteenth century, for example, encouraged "teaching daughters how to calculate and make a profit."[10] Overland trade within Asia remained wholly in Asian hands and grew considerably. Christian merchants from Armenia were particularly active in the commerce linking Europe, the Middle East, and Central Asia. Tens of thousands of Indian merchants and moneylenders, mostly Hindus representing sophisticated family firms, lived throughout Central Asia, Persia, and Russia, thus connecting this vast region to markets in India. These international Asian commercial networks, equivalent in their commercial sophistication to those of Europe, continued to operate successfully even as Europeans militarized the seaborne commerce of the Indian Ocean.

Within India, large and wealthy family firms, such as the one headed by Virji Vora during the seventeenth century, were able to monopolize the buying and selling of particular products, such as pepper or coral, and thus dictate terms and prices to the European trading companies. "He knoweth that wee must sell," complained one English trader about Vora, "and so beats us downe till we come to his owne rates." Furthermore, Vora was often the only source of loans for the cash-strapped Europeans, forcing them to pay interest rates as high as 12 to 18 percent annually. Despite their resentments, Europeans had little choice, because "none but Virji Vora hath moneye to lend or will lend."[11]

AP® EXAM TIP

Pay attention to features of Asia's land-based trade networks that are continuities from the postclassical era, as seen in Chapter 7.

Silver and Global Commerce

Even more than the spice trade of Eurasia, it was the silver trade that gave birth to a genuinely global network of exchange (see Map 14.2). As one historian put it, silver "went round the world and made the world go round."[12] The mid–sixteenth-century discovery of enormously rich silver deposits in Bolivia, and simultaneously in Japan, suddenly provided a vastly increased supply of that precious metal. Spanish America alone produced perhaps 85 percent of the world's silver during the early modern era. Spain's sole Asian colony, the Philippines, provided a critical link in

AP® EXAM TIP

You must know features and effects of the global trade of silver in this era.

Map 14.2   The Global Silver Trade

Silver was one of the first major commodities to be exchanged on a genuinely global scale.

this emerging network of global commerce. Manila, the colonial capital of the Philippines, was the destination of annual Spanish shipments of silver, which were drawn from the rich mines of Bolivia, transported initially to Acapulco in Mexico, and from there shipped across the Pacific to the Philippines. This trade was the first direct and sustained link between the Americas and Asia, and it initiated a web of Pacific commerce that grew steadily over the centuries.

At the heart of that Pacific web, and of early modern global commerce generally, was China's huge economy, especially its growing demand for silver. In the 1570s, Chinese authorities consolidated a variety of tax levies into a single tax, which its huge population was now required to pay in silver. This sudden new demand for the white metal caused its value to skyrocket. It meant that foreigners with silver could now purchase far more of China's silks and porcelains than before.

This demand set silver in motion around the world, with the bulk of the world's silver supply winding up in China and much of the rest elsewhere in Asia. The routes by which this "silver drain" operated were numerous. Chinese, Portuguese, and Dutch traders flocked to Manila to sell Chinese goods in exchange for silver. European ships carried Japanese silver to China. Much of the silver shipped across the Atlantic to Spain was spent in Europe generally and then used to pay for the Asian goods that the French, British, and Dutch so greatly desired. Silver paid for some African slaves and for spices in Southeast Asia. The standard Spanish silver

Guided Reading Question

■ CONNECTION

What was the significance of the silver trade in the early modern era of world history?

coin, known as a "piece of eight," was used by merchants in North America, Europe, India, Russia, and West Africa as a medium of exchange. By 1600, it circulated widely in southern China. A Portuguese merchant in 1621 noted that silver "wanders throughout all the world . . . before flocking to China, where it remains as if at its natural center."[13]

In its global journeys, silver transformed much that it touched, and nowhere more profoundly than at Potosí, the site of a huge silver-mining operation in what is now Bolivia. (See Zooming In: Potosí, page 614.) In Spain itself, which was the initial destination for much of Latin America's silver, the precious metal vastly enriched the Crown, making Spain the envy of its European rivals during the sixteenth century. Spanish rulers could now pursue military and political ambitions in both Europe and the Americas far beyond the country's own resource base. "New World mines," concluded several prominent historians, "supported the Spanish empire."[14] Nonetheless, this vast infusion of wealth did not fundamentally transform the Spanish economy, because it generated more inflation of prices than real economic growth. A rigid economy laced with monopolies and regulations, an aristocratic class that preferred leisure to enterprise, and a crusading insistence on religious uniformity all prevented the Spanish from using their silver windfall in a productive fashion. When the value of silver dropped in the early seventeenth century, Spain lost its earlier position as the dominant Western European power. More generally, the flood of American silver that circulated in Europe drove prices higher, further impoverished many, stimulated uprisings across the continent, and, together with the Little Ice Age of global cooling, contributed to what historians sometimes call a "General Crisis" of upheaval and instability in the seventeenth century. (For a broader discussion of the General Crisis, see Chapter 13, page 560.)

Japan, another major source of silver production in the sixteenth century, did better. Its military rulers, the Tokugawa shoguns, used silver-generated profits to defeat hundreds of rival feudal lords and unify the country. Unlike their Spanish counterparts, the shoguns allied with the country's vigorous domestic merchant class to develop a market-based economy and to invest heavily in agricultural and industrial enterprises. Japanese state and local authorities alike acted vigorously to protect and renew Japan's dwindling forests, while millions of families in the eighteenth century took steps to have fewer children by practicing late marriages, contraception, abortion, and infanticide. The outcome was the dramatic slowing of Japan's population growth, the easing of an impending ecological crisis, and a flourishing, highly commercialized economy. These were the foundations for Japan's remarkable nineteenth-century Industrial Revolution.

In China, silver deepened the already-substantial commercialization of the country's economy. To obtain the silver needed to pay their taxes, more and more people had to sell something—either their labor or their products. Communities that devoted themselves to growing mulberry trees, on which silkworms fed, had to buy their rice from other regions. Thus the Chinese economy became more

> **AP® EXAM TIP**
>
> Questions about the Potosí silver mines have appeared on past AP® exams.

Potosí, a Mountain of Silver

China's insatiable demand for silver during the early modern period drove global commerce, transforming the economies and societies of far distant lands. Perhaps nowhere did the silver trade have a greater impact than at Cerro de Potosí, a mountain located in a barren and remote stretch of Andean highlands, ten weeks' travel by mule from Lima, Peru. In 1545, Spanish prospectors discovered the richest deposit of silver in history at Potosí, and within a few decades this single mountain was producing over half of the silver mined in the world each year. At its foot, the city of Potosí grew rapidly. "New people arrive by the hour, attracted by the smell of silver," commented a Spanish observer in the 1570s. Within just a few decades, Potosí's population had reached 160,000 people, making it the largest city in the Americas and equivalent in size to London, Amsterdam, or Seville.

The mines of Potosí.

The silver was mined and processed at great human and environmental cost. The Spanish authorities forced Native American villages across a wide region of the Andes to supply workers for the mines, with as many as 14,000 to 16,000 at a time laboring in horrendous conditions. A Spanish priest observed, "Once inside, they spend the whole week in there without emerging, working with tallow candles. They are in great danger inside there, for one very small stone that falls injures or kills anyone it strikes. If 20 healthy Indians enter on Monday, half may emerge crippled on Saturday."[15] Work aboveground, often undertaken by slaves of African descent, was also dangerous because extracting silver from the mined ore required mixing it with the toxic metal mercury. Many thousands died. Mortality rates were so high that some families held funeral

regionally specialized. Particularly in southern China, this surging economic growth resulted in the loss of about half the area's forest cover as more and more land was devoted to cash crops. No Japanese-style conservation program emerged to address this growing problem. An eighteenth-century Chinese poet, Wang Dayue, gave voice to the fears that this ecological transformation generated:

> Rarer, too, their timber grew, and rarer still and rarer
> As the hills resembled heads now shaven clean of hair.
> For the first time, too, moreover, they felt an anxious mood
> That all their daily logging might not furnish them with fuel.[16]

China's role in the silver trade is a useful reminder of Asian centrality in the world economy of the early modern era. Its large and prosperous population, services for men drafted to work in the mines before they embarked for Potosí. Beyond the human cost, the environment suffered as well when highly intensive mining techniques deforested the region and poisoned and eroded the soil.

Although some indigenous merchants, muleteers, and chiefs were enriched by mining, much of the wealth generated flowed to the Europeans who owned the mines and to the Spanish government, which impounded one-fifth of the silver as well as collecting other taxes and duties. European elites in Potosí lived in luxury, with all the goods of Europe and Asia at their disposal. Merchants brought to Potosí French hats, Venetian glass, German swords, Persian carpets, Southeast Asian spices, and Chinese porcelain and silks. Potosí also imported almost all of its basic needs because the dry, cold region was unable to support the city. Pack trains of llamas brought large quantities of foodstuffs, cloth, and other necessities from Ecuador, Peru, Chile, and Argentina. By the early seventeenth century, the economies of many regions in Spanish South America were structured to supply this huge mining operation.

While the mines caused much suffering, the silver-fueled economy of Potosí also offered opportunity to groups beyond the mine-owning European elite, not least to women. To earn a few pesos for the household, Spanish women might rent out buildings they owned for commercial purposes or send their slaves into the streets as small-scale traders. Less well-to-do Spanish women often ran stores, pawnshops, bakeries, and taverns. Indian and *mestiza* women likewise opened businesses that provided the city with beverages, food, clothing, and credit. The wealth created a hive of commercial activity in this otherwise-barren backwater.

But the silver that created Potosí also caused its decline. After a century of intensive mining, all that remained were lower-quality ores that were difficult to extract from the ground. This led the mines to shut down. By 1800, Potosí, which had once rivaled the largest cities in Europe, was just a shadow of its former self. The history of this remote region of the Andes reminds us of the profound and often-conflicting results of world trade during the early modern period. While many suffered in the hellish conditions of the mines, others grew wealthy off the demand for silver.

Question: What can Potosí tell us about the consequences of global trade in the early modern period?

increasingly operating within a silver-based economy, fueled global commerce, vastly increasing the quantity of goods exchanged and the geographic range of world trade. Despite their obvious physical presence in the Americas, Africa, and Asia, economically speaking Europeans were essentially middlemen, funneling American silver to Asia and competing with one another for a place in the rich markets of the East. The productivity of the Chinese economy was evident in Spanish America, where cheap and well-made Chinese goods easily outsold those of Spain. In 1594, the Spanish viceroy of Peru observed that "a man can clothe his wife in Chinese silks for [25 pesos], whereas he could not provide her with clothing of Spanish silks with 200 pesos."[17] Indian cotton textiles likewise outsold European woolen or linen textiles in the seventeenth century to such an extent that French laws in 1717 prohibited the wearing of Indian cotton or Chinese silk clothing as a means of protecting French industry.

"The World Hunt": Fur in Global Commerce

In the early modern era, furs joined silver, textiles, and spices as major items of global commerce.[18] Their production had an important environmental impact as well as serious implications for the human societies that generated and consumed them. Furs, of course, had long provided warmth and conveyed status in colder regions of the world, but the integration of North America and of northern Asia (Siberia) into a larger world economy vastly increased their significance in global trade.

By 1500, European population growth and agricultural expansion had sharply diminished the supply of fur-bearing animals, such as beaver, rabbits, sable, marten, and deer. Furthermore, much of the early modern era witnessed a period of cooling temperatures and harsh winters, known as the Little Ice Age, which may well have increased the demand for furs. "The weather is bitterly cold and everyone is in furs although we are almost in July," observed a surprised visitor from Venice while in London in 1604.[19] These conditions pushed prices higher. The cost of a good-quality beaver pelt, for example, quadrupled in France between 1558 and 1611. This price increase translated into strong economic incentives for European traders to tap the immense wealth of fur-bearing animals found in North America. At the same time, the collapse of Native American populations in North America caused by the Great Dying led to the regrowth of forest habitats for fur-bearing animals and deer herds.

Like other aspects of imperial expansion, the fur trade was a highly competitive enterprise. The French were most prominent in the St. Lawrence valley, around the Great Lakes, and later along the Mississippi River; British traders pushed into the Hudson Bay region; and the Dutch focused their attention along the Hudson River in what is now New York. They were frequently rivals for the great prize of North American furs. In the southern colonies of British North America, deerskins by the hundreds of thousands found a ready market in England's leather industry (see Map 14.3).

Only a few Europeans directly engaged in commercial trapping or hunting. They usually waited for Indians to bring the furs or skins initially to their coastal settlements and later to their fortified trading posts in the interior of North America. European merchants paid for the furs with a variety of trade goods, including guns, blankets, metal tools, rum, and brandy, amid much ceremony, haggling over prices, and ritualized gift giving. Native Americans represented a cheap labor force in this international commercial effort, but they were not a directly coerced labor force.

Over the three centuries of the early modern era, enormous quantities of furs and deerskins found their way to Europe, where they considerably enhanced the standard of living in those cold climates. The environmental price was paid in the Americas, and it was high. A consistent demand for beaver hats led to the near extinction of that industrious animal in much of North America by the early nineteenth century and with it the degradation or loss of many wetland habitats. Other

Guided Reading Question

■ CHANGE
Describe the impact of the fur trade on North American native societies.

Map 14.3   The North American Fur Trade

North America, as well as Russian Siberia, funneled an apparently endless supply of furs into the circuits of global trade during the early modern era.

fur-bearing species were also seriously depleted as the trade moved inexorably westward. By the 1760s, hunters in southeastern British colonies took about 500,000 deer every year, seriously diminishing the deer population of the region. As early as 1642, Miantonomo, a chief of the New England Narragansett people, spoke of the environmental consequences of English colonialism:

You know our fathers had plenty of deer and skins and our plains were full of game and turkeys, and our coves and rivers were full of fish. But, brothers, since these Englishmen have seized our country, they have cut down the grass with scythes, and the trees with axes. Their cows and horses eat up the grass, and their hogs spoil our bed of clams; and finally we shall all starve to death.[20]

For the Native American peoples who hunted, trapped, processed, and transported these products, the fur trade bore various benefits, particularly at the beginning. The Hurons, for example, who lived on the northern shores of Lakes Erie and Ontario in the early seventeenth century, annually exchanged some 20,000 to 30,000 pelts, mostly beaver, and in return received copper pots, metal axes, knives, cloth, firearms, and alcohol. Many of these items were of real value, which strengthened the Hurons in their relationships with neighboring peoples. These goods also enhanced the authority of Huron chiefs by providing them with gifts to distribute among their followers. At least initially, competition among Europeans ensured that Native American leaders could negotiate reasonable prices for their goods. Furthermore, their important role in the lucrative fur trade protected them for a time from the kind of extermination, enslavement, or displacement that was the fate of native peoples in Portuguese Brazil.

Nothing, however, protected them against the diseases carried by Europeans. In the 1630s and 1640s, to cite only one example of many, about half of the Hurons perished from influenza, smallpox, and other European-borne diseases. Furthermore, the fur trade generated warfare beyond anything previously known. Competition among Native American societies became more intense as the economic stakes grew higher. Catastrophic population declines owing to disease stimulated "mourning wars," designed to capture people who could be assimilated into much-diminished societies. A century of French-British rivalry for North America (1664–1763) forced Native American societies to take sides, to fight, and to die in these European imperial conflicts. Firearms, of course, made warfare far more deadly than before.

Beyond the fur trade, many Native American peoples sought actively to take advantage of the new commercial economy now impinging upon them. The Iroquois, for example, began to sell new products such as ginseng root, much in demand in China as a medicine. They also rented land to Europeans, worked for wages in various European enterprises, and started to use currency, when barter was ineffective. But as they became enmeshed in these commercial relationships, Native Americans grew dependent on European trade goods. Among the Algonquians, for example, iron tools and cooking pots replaced those of stone, wood, or bone; gunpowder weapons took the place of bows and arrows; European textiles proved more attractive than traditional beaver and deerskin clothing; and flint and steel were found to be more effective for starting fires than wooden drills. A wide range of traditional crafts were thus lost, while the native peoples did not gain a corresponding ability to manufacture the new items for themselves. Enthusiasm for these imported goods and continued European demands for furs and skins frequently eroded the customary restraint that characterized traditional hunting practices, resulting in the depletion of many species. One European observer wrote of the Creek Indians: "[They] wage eternal war against deer and bear . . . which is indeed carried to an unreasonable and perhaps criminal excess, since the white people have dazzled their senses with foreign superfluities."[21]

Alongside germs and guns, yet another highly destructive European import was alcohol—rum and brandy, in particular. Whiskey, a locally produced grain-based alcohol, only added to the problem. With no prior experience of alcohol and little time to adjust to its easy availability, these drinks "hit Indian societies with explosive force."[22] Binge drinking, violence among young men, promiscuity, and addiction followed in many places. In 1753, Iroquois leaders complained bitterly to European authorities in Pennsylvania: "These wicked Whiskey Sellers, when they have once got the Indians in liquor, make them sell their very clothes from their backs. . . . If this practice be continued, we must be inevitably ruined."[23] In short, it was not so much the fur trade itself that decimated Native American societies, but all that accompanied it—disease, dependence, guns, alcohol, and the growing encroachment of European colonial empires.

All of this had particular implications for women. A substantial number of native women married European traders according to the "custom of the country"—with no sanction from civil or church authorities. Such marriages eased the difficulties of this cross-cultural exchange, providing traders with guides, interpreters, and negotiators. But sometimes these women were left abandoned when their husbands returned to Europe. More generally, the fur trade enhanced the position of men in their societies since hunting or trapping animals was normally a male occupation. Among the Ojibwa, a gathering and hunting people in the northern Great Lakes region, women had traditionally acquired economic power by creating

Fur and the Russians
This colored engraving shows a sixteenth-century Russian ambassador and his contingent arriving at the court of the Holy Roman Emperor and bearing gifts of animal pelts, the richest fruit of the expanding Russian Empire. (Contemporary color line engraving, 1576/The Granger Collection, NYC—All rights reserved)

food, utensils, clothing, and decorations from the hides and flesh of the animals that their husbands caught. With the fur trade in full operation, women spent more time processing those furs for sale than in producing household items, some of which were now available for purchase from Europeans. And so, as one scholar put it, "women lost authority and prestige." At the same time, however, women generated and controlled the trade in wild rice and maple syrup, both essential to the livelihood of European traders.[24] Thus the fur trade offered women a mix of opportunities and liabilities.

Paralleling the North American fur trade was the one simultaneously taking shape within a rapidly expanding Russian Empire, which became a major source of furs for Western Europe, China, and the Ottoman Empire. The profitability of that trade in furs was the chief incentive for Russia's rapid expansion during the sixteenth and seventeenth centuries across Siberia, where the "soft gold" of fur-bearing animals was abundant. The international sale of furs greatly enriched the Russian state as well as many private merchants, trappers, and hunters. Here the silver trade and the fur trade intersected, as Europeans paid for Russian furs largely with American gold and silver.

The consequences for native Siberians were similar to those in North America as disease took its toll, as indigenous people became dependent on Russian goods, as the settler frontier encroached on native lands, and as many species of fur-bearing mammals were seriously depleted. In several ways, however, the Russian fur trade was unique. Whereas several European nations competed in North America and generally obtained their furs through commercial negotiations with Indian societies, no such competition accompanied Russian expansion across Siberia. Russian authorities imposed a tax or tribute, payable in furs, on every able-bodied Siberian male between eighteen and fifty years of age. To enforce the payment, they took hostages from Siberian societies, with death as a possible outcome if the required furs were not forthcoming. A further difference lay in the large-scale presence of private Russian hunters and trappers, who competed directly with their Siberian counterparts.

Guided Reading Question

■ COMPARISON
How did the North American and Siberian fur trades differ from each other? What did they have in common?

PRACTICING AP® HISTORICAL THINKING

What differences can you identify in the operation and impact of the spice, silver, and fur trades?

Commerce in People: The Atlantic Slave Trade

Of all the commercial ties that linked the early modern world into a global network of exchange, none had more profound or enduring human consequences than the Atlantic slave trade. Between 1500 and 1866, this trade in human beings took an estimated 12.5 million people from African societies, shipped them across the Atlantic in the infamous Middle Passage, and deposited some 10.7 million of them in the Americas, where they lived out their often-brief lives as slaves. About 1.8 million (14.4 percent) died during the transatlantic crossing, while countless others perished in the process of capture and transport to the African coast.[25] (See Map 14.4.)

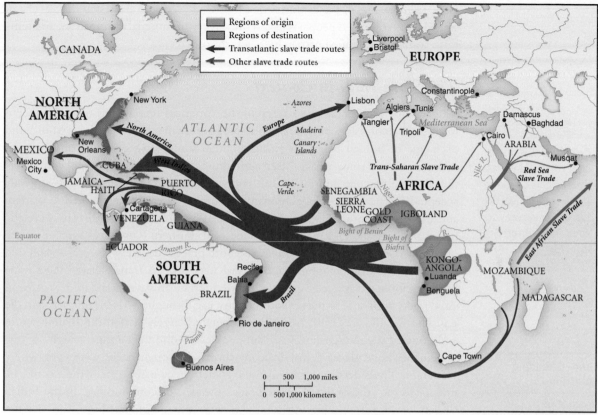

Map 14.4   The Atlantic Slave Trade

Stimulated by the plantation complex of the Americas, the Atlantic slave trade represented an enormous extension of the ancient practice of people owning and selling other people.

Beyond the multitude of individual tragedies that it spawned—capture and sale, displacement from home cultures, forced labor, beatings and brandings, broken families—the Atlantic slave trade transformed all of its participants. Within Africa itself, that commerce thoroughly disrupted some societies, strengthened others, and corrupted many. Elites often enriched themselves, while the slaves, of course, were victimized almost beyond imagination.

In the Americas, the slave trade added a substantial African presence to the mix of European and Native American peoples. This African diaspora (the global spread of African peoples) injected into these new societies issues of race that endure still in the twenty-first century. It also introduced elements of African culture, such as religious ideas, musical and artistic traditions, and cuisine, into the making of American cultures. The profits from the slave trade and the forced labor of African slaves certainly enriched European and Euro-American societies, even as the practice of slavery contributed much to the racial stereotypes of European peoples. Finally, slavery became a metaphor for many kinds of social oppression, quite different from plantation slavery, in the centuries that followed. Workers protested the slavery of wage labor, colonized people rejected the slavery of imperial domination, and feminists sometimes defined patriarchy as a form of slavery.

The Slave Trade in Context

The Atlantic slave trade and slavery in the Americas represented the most recent large-scale expression of a very widespread human practice—the owning and exchange of human beings. It was present in some early gathering and hunting societies, among some village-based agricultural peoples, and in pastoral communities. But the practice flourished most widely in civilizations where it was generally accepted as a perfectly normal human enterprise and was closely linked to warfare and capture. Before 1500, the Mediterranean and Indian Ocean basins were the major arenas of the Old World slave trade, and southern Russia was a major source of slaves. Many African societies likewise both practiced slavery themselves and sold slaves into these international commercial networks. A trans-Saharan slave trade had long funneled African captives into Mediterranean slavery, and an East African slave trade from at least the seventh century C.E. brought Africans into the Middle East and the Indian Ocean basin. Both operated largely within the Islamic world and initiated the movement of African peoples beyond the continent itself.

Guided Reading Question

■ COMPARISON

What was distinctive about the Atlantic slave trade? What did it share with other patterns of slave owning and slave trading?

Furthermore, slavery came in many forms. Although slaves were everywhere vulnerable "outsiders" to their masters' societies, in many places they could be integrated into their owners' households, lineages, or communities. In the Indian Ocean world, for example, African slaves were often assimilated into the societies of their owners and lost the sense of a distinctive identity that was so prominent in North America. In some places, children inherited the slave status of their parents; elsewhere those children were free persons. Within the Islamic world, where most slaves worked in domestic settings, the preference was for female slaves by a two-to-one margin, while the later Atlantic slave trade, which funneled captives into plantation labor, favored males by a similar margin. Not all slaves, however, occupied degraded positions. Some in the Islamic world acquired prominent military or political status. Most slaves in the premodern world worked in their owners' households, farms, or shops, with smaller numbers laboring in large-scale agricultural or industrial enterprises.

The slavery that emerged in the Americas was distinctive in several ways. One was simply the immense size of the traffic in slaves and its centrality to the economies of colonial America. Furthermore, this New World slavery was largely based on plantation agriculture and treated slaves as a form of dehumanized property, lacking any rights in the society of their owners. Slave status throughout the Americas was inherited across generations, and there was little hope of eventual freedom for the vast majority. Nowhere else, with the possible exception of ancient Greece, was widespread slavery associated with societies that affirmed values of human freedom and equality. Perhaps most distinctive was the racial dimension: Atlantic slavery came to be identified wholly with Africa and with "blackness." How did this exceptional form of slavery emerge?

The origins of Atlantic slavery clearly lie in the Mediterranean world and with that now-common sweetener known as sugar. Until the Crusades, Europeans knew nothing of sugar and relied on honey and fruits to sweeten their bland diets. However, as they learned from the Arabs about sugarcane and the laborious techniques for producing usable sugar, Europeans established sugar-producing plantations within the Mediterranean and later on various islands off the coast of West Africa. It was a "modern" industry, perhaps the first one, in that it required huge capital investment, substantial technology, an almost factory-like discipline among workers, and a mass market of consumers. The immense difficulty and danger of the work, the limitations attached to serf labor, and the general absence of wageworkers all pointed to slavery as a source of labor for sugar plantations.

Initially, Slavic-speaking peoples from the Black Sea region furnished the bulk of the slaves for Mediterranean plantations, so much so that "Slav" became the basis for the word "slave" in many European languages. In 1453, however, when the Ottoman Turks seized Constantinople, the supply of Slavic slaves was effectively cut off. At the same time, Portuguese mariners were exploring the coast of West Africa; they were looking primarily for gold, but they also found there an alternative source of slaves available for sale. Thus, when sugar, and later tobacco and cotton, plantations took hold in the Americas, Europeans had already established links to a West African source of supply. They also now had religious justification for their actions, for in 1452 the pope formally granted to the kings of Spain and Portugal "full and free permission to invade, search out, capture, and subjugate the Saracens [Muslims] and pagans and any other unbelievers . . . and to reduce their persons into perpetual slavery."[26] Largely through a process of elimination, Africa became the primary source of slave labor for the plantation economies of the Americas. Slavic peoples were no longer available; Native Americans quickly perished from European diseases; marginal Europeans were Christians and therefore supposedly exempt from slavery; and European indentured servants, who agreed to work for a fixed period in return for transportation, food, and shelter, were expensive and temporary. Africans, on the other hand, were skilled farmers; they had some immunity to both tropical and European diseases; they were not Christians; they were, relatively speaking, close at hand; and they were readily available in substantial numbers through African-operated commercial networks.

Moreover, Africans were black. The precise relationship between slavery and European racism has long been a much-debated subject. Historian David Brion Davis has suggested the controversial view that "racial stereotypes were transmitted, along with black slavery itself, from Muslims to Christians."[27] For many centuries, Muslims had drawn on sub-Saharan Africa as one source of slaves and in the process had developed a form of racism. The fourteenth-century Tunisian scholar

Guided Reading Question

■ CAUSATION
What explains the rise of the Atlantic slave trade?

AP® EXAM TIP

Note the characteristics of slavery in the Mediterranean before the Atlantic slave trade began.

Ibn Khaldun wrote that black people were "submissive to slavery, because Negroes have little that is essentially human and have attributes that are quite similar to those of dumb animals."[28]

Other scholars find the origins of racism within European culture itself. For the English, argues historian Audrey Smedley, the process of conquering Ireland had generated by the sixteenth century a view of the Irish as "rude, beastly, ignorant, cruel, and unruly infidels," perceptions that were then transferred to Africans enslaved on English sugar plantations of the West Indies.[29] Whether Europeans borrowed such images of Africans from their Muslim neighbors or developed them independently, slavery and racism soon went hand in hand. "Europeans were better able to tolerate their brutal exploitation of Africans," writes a prominent world historian, "by imagining that these Africans were an inferior race, or better still, not even human."[30]

The Slave Trade in Practice

The European demand for slaves was clearly the chief cause of this tragic commerce, and from the point of sale on the African coast to the massive use of slave labor on American plantations, the entire enterprise was in European hands. Within Africa itself, however, a different picture emerges, for over the four centuries of the Atlantic slave trade, European demand elicited an African supply. A few early efforts by the Portuguese at slave raiding along the West African coast convinced Europeans that such efforts were unwise and unnecessary, for African societies were quite capable of defending themselves against European intrusion, and many were willing to sell their slaves peacefully. Furthermore, Europeans died like flies when they entered the interior because they lacked immunities to common tropical diseases. Thus the slave trade quickly came to operate largely with Europeans waiting on the coast, either on their ships or in fortified settlements, to purchase slaves from African merchants and political elites. Certainly, Europeans tried to exploit African rivalries to obtain slaves at the lowest possible cost, and the firearms they funneled into West Africa may well have increased the warfare from which so many slaves were derived. But from the point of initial capture to sale on the coast, the entire enterprise was normally in African hands. Almost nowhere did Europeans attempt outright military conquest; instead they generally dealt as equals with local African authorities.

An arrogant agent of the British Royal Africa Company in the 1680s learned the hard way who was in control when he spoke improperly to the king of Niumi, a small state in what is now Gambia. The company's records describe what happened next:

> [O]ne of the grandees [of the king], by name Sambalama, taught him better manners by reaching him a box on the ears, which beat off his hat, and a few thumps on the back, and seizing him . . . and several others, who together with the agent were taken and put into the king's pound and stayed there three or four days till their ransom was brought, value five hundred bars.[31]

AP® EXAM TIP

Pay attention to this discussion of important factors in the development of the Atlantic slave trade.

Guided Reading Question

■ CONNECTION

What roles did Europeans and Africans play in the unfolding of the Atlantic slave trade?

In exchange for slaves, African sellers sought both European and Indian textiles, cowrie shells (widely used as money in West Africa), European metal goods, firearms and gunpowder, tobacco and alcohol, and various decorative items such as beads. Europeans purchased some of these items—cowrie shells and Indian textiles, for example—with silver mined in the Americas. Thus the slave trade connected with commerce in silver and textiles as it became part of an emerging worldwide network of exchange. Issues about the precise mix of goods African authorities desired, about the number and quality of slaves to be purchased, and always about the price of everything were settled in endless negotiation. Most of the time, a leading historian concluded, the slave trade took place "not unlike international trade anywhere in the world of the period."[32]

For the slaves themselves—seized in the interior, often sold several times on the harrowing journey to the coast, sometimes branded, and held in squalid slave dungeons while awaiting transportation to the New World—it was anything but a normal commercial transaction. One European engaged in the trade noted that "the negroes are so willful and loath to leave their own country, that they have often leap'd out of the canoes, boat, and ship, into the sea, and kept under water till they were drowned, to avoid being taken up and saved by our boats."[33]

Over the four centuries of the slave trade, millions of Africans underwent such experiences, but their numbers varied considerably over time. During the sixteenth century, slave exports from Africa averaged fewer than 3,000 annually. In those years, the Portuguese were at least as much interested in African gold, spices, and textiles. Furthermore, as in Asia, they became involved in transporting African goods, including slaves, from one African port to another, thus becoming the "truck drivers" of coastal West African commerce.[34] In the seventeenth century, the pace picked up as the slave trade became highly competitive, with the

The Middle Passage
This mid-nineteenth-century painting of slaves held belowdecks on a Spanish slave ship illustrates the horrendous conditions of the transatlantic voyage, a journey experienced by many millions of captured Africans. (Watercolor by Lt. Francis Meinelli, British Royal Navy/The Granger Collection, NYC—All rights reserved)

British, Dutch, and French contesting the earlier Portuguese monopoly. The century and a half between 1700 and 1850 marked the high point of the slave trade as the plantation economies of the Americas boomed. (See Snapshot, opposite.)

Where did these Africans come from, and where did they go? Geographically, the slave trade drew mainly on the societies of West and South-Central Africa, from present-day Mauritania in the north to Angola in the south. Initially focused on the coastal regions, the slave trade progressively penetrated into the interior as the demand for slaves picked up. Socially, slaves were mostly drawn from various marginal groups in African societies—prisoners of war, criminals, debtors, people who had been "pawned" during times of difficulty. Thus Africans did not generally sell "their own people" into slavery. Divided into hundreds of separate, usually small-scale, and often rival communities—cities, kingdoms, microstates, clans, and villages—the various peoples of West Africa had no concept of an "African" identity. Those whom they captured and sold were normally outsiders, vulnerable people who lacked the protection of membership in an established community. When short-term economic or political advantage could be gained, such people were sold. In this respect, the Atlantic slave trade was little different from the experience of enslavement elsewhere in the world.

The destination of enslaved Africans, half a world away in the Americas, was very different. The vast majority wound up in Brazil or the Caribbean, where the labor demands of the plantation economy were most intense. Smaller numbers found themselves in North America, mainland Spanish America, or in Europe itself. Their journey across the Atlantic was horrendous, with the Middle Passage having an overall mortality rate of more than 14 percent.

Enslaved Africans frequently resisted their fates in a variety of ways. About 10 percent of the transatlantic voyages experienced a major rebellion by desperate captives, and resistance continued in the Americas, taking a range of forms from surreptitious slowdowns of work to outright rebellion. One common act was to flee. Many who escaped joined free communities of former slaves known as maroon societies, which were founded in remote regions, especially in South America and the Caribbean. The largest such settlement was Palmares in Brazil, which endured for most of the seventeenth century, housing 10,000 or more people, mostly of African descent but also including Native Americans, mestizos, and renegade whites. While slave owners feared wide-scale slave rebellions, these were rare, and even small-scale rebellions were usually crushed with great brutality. It was only with the Haitian Revolution of the 1790s that a full-scale slave revolt brought lasting freedom for its participants.

Consequences: The Impact of the Slave Trade in Africa

From the viewpoint of world history, the chief outcome of the slave trade lay in the new transregional linkages that it generated as Africa became a permanent part of an interacting Atlantic world. Millions of its people were now compelled to make

SNAPSHOT   The Slave Trade in Numbers (1501–1866)[35]

The Rise and Decline of the Slave Trade

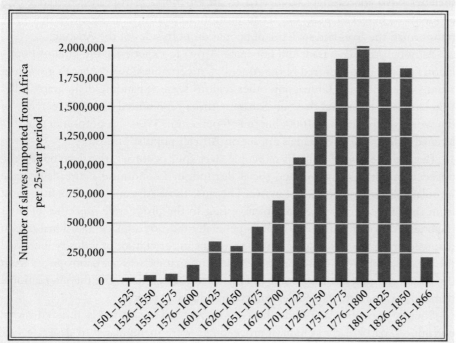

The Destinations of Slaves

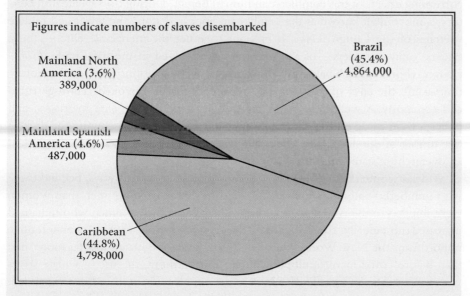

Figures indicate numbers of slaves disembarked

Mainland North America (3.6%) 389,000

Mainland Spanish America (4.6%) 487,000

Caribbean (44.8%) 4,798,000

Brazil (45.4%) 4,864,000

AP® EXAM TIP

Charts and graphs frequently show up on the AP® exam, so develop your skills in "reading" all parts of these documents for information like trends over time.

their lives in the Americas, where they made an enormous impact both demographically and economically. Until the nineteenth century, they outnumbered European immigrants to the Americas by three or four to one, and West African societies were increasingly connected to an emerging European-centered world economy. These vast processes set in motion a chain of consequences that have transformed the lives and societies of people on both sides of the Atlantic.

Although the slave trade did not cause Africa to experience the kind of population collapse that occurred in the Americas, it certainly slowed Africa's growth at a time when Europe, China, and other regions were expanding demographically. Scholars have estimated that sub-Saharan Africa represented about 18 percent of the world's population in 1600, but only 6 percent in 1900.[36] A portion of that difference reflects the slave trade's impact on Africa's population history.

Beyond the loss of millions of people over four centuries, the slave trade produced economic stagnation and social disruption. Economically, the slave trade stimulated little positive change in Africa because those Africans who benefited most from the traffic in people were not investing in the productive capacities of their societies. Although European imports generally did not displace traditional artisan manufacturing, no technological breakthroughs in agriculture or industry increased the wealth available to these societies. Maize and manioc (cassava), introduced from the Americas, added a new source of calories to African diets, but the international demand was for Africa's people, not its agricultural products.

Socially too, the slave trade shaped African societies. It surely fostered moral corruption, particularly as judicial proceedings were manipulated to generate victims for the slave trade. A West African legend that cowrie shells, a major currency of the slave trade, grew on corpses of the slaves was a symbolic recognition of the corrupting effects of this commerce in human beings. During the seventeenth century, a movement known as the Lemba cult appeared along the lower and middle stretches of the Congo River. It brought together the mercantile elite—chiefs, traders, caravan leaders—of a region heavily involved in the slave trade. Complaining about stomach pains, breathing problems, and sterility, they sought protection against the envy of the poor and the sorcery that it provoked. Through ritual and ceremony as well as efforts to control markets, arrange elite marriages, and police a widespread trading network, Lemba officials sought to counter the disruptive impact of the slave trade and to maintain elite privileges in an area that lacked an overarching state authority.

African women felt the impact of the slave trade in various ways, beyond those who numbered among its transatlantic victims. Since far more men than women were shipped to the Americas, the labor demands on those women who remained increased substantially, compounded by the growing use of cassava, a labor-intensive import from the New World. Unbalanced sex ratios also meant that far more men than before could marry multiple women. Furthermore, the use of female slaves within West African societies also grew as the export trade in male slaves expanded. Retaining female slaves for their own use allowed warriors and nobles in the Senegambia region to distinguish themselves more clearly from ordinary peasants. In the Kongo, female slaves provided a source of dependent laborers for the plantations that sustained the lifestyle of urban elites. A European merchant on the Gold Coast in the late eighteenth century observed that every free man had at least one or two slaves.

For much smaller numbers of women, the slave trade provided an opportunity to exercise power and accumulate wealth. In the Senegambia region, where women had long been involved in politics and commerce, marriage to European traders offered advantage to both partners. For European male merchants, as for fur traders in North America, such marriages afforded access to African-operated commercial networks as well as the comforts of domestic life. Some of the women involved in these cross-cultural marriages, known as *signares*, became quite wealthy, operating their own trading empires, employing large numbers of female slaves, and acquiring elaborate houses, jewelry, and fashionable clothing.

Furthermore, the state-building enterprises that often accompanied the slave trade in West Africa offered yet other opportunities to a few women. As the Kingdom of Dahomey (deh-HOH-mee) expanded during the eighteenth century, the royal palace, housing thousands of women and presided over by a powerful Queen Mother, served to integrate the diverse regions of the state. Each lineage was required to send a daughter to the palace even as well-to-do families sent additional girls to increase their influence at court. In the Kingdom of Kongo, women held lower-level administrative positions, the head wife of a nobleman exercised authority over hundreds of junior wives and slaves, and women served on the council that advised the monarch. The neighboring region of Matamba was known for its female rulers, most notably the powerful Queen Nzinga (1626–1663), who guided the state amid the complexities and intrigues of various European and African rivalries and gained a reputation for her resistance to Portuguese imperialism.

Within particular African societies, the impact of the slave trade differed considerably from place to place and over time. Many small-scale kinship-based societies, lacking the protection of a strong state, were thoroughly disrupted by raids from more powerful neighbors, and insecurity was pervasive. Oral traditions in southern Ghana, for example, reported that "there was no rest in the land," that people went about in groups rather than alone, and that mothers kept their children inside when European ships appeared.[37] Some larger kingdoms such as Kongo and Oyo slowly disintegrated as access to trading opportunities and firearms enabled outlying regions to establish their independence. (For an account of one young man's journey to slavery and back, see Zooming In: Ayuba Suleiman Diallo, page 630.)

However, African authorities also sought to take advantage of the new commercial opportunities and to manage the slave trade in their own interests. The Kingdom of Benin, in the forest area of present-day Nigeria, successfully avoided a deep involvement in the trade while diversifying the exports with which it purchased European firearms and other goods. As early as 1516, its ruler began to

AP® EXAM TIP

Remember that merchants in the Atlantic slave trade consisted of three groups: Europeans, European colonists in the Americas, and Africans.

Ayuba Suleiman Diallo:
To Slavery and Back

February 1730 found Ayuba Suleiman Diallo, less than thirty years of age, living between the Gambia and Senegal rivers in West Africa among the Fulbe-speaking people.[38] Like his father, a prominent Islamic scholar and teacher, Ayuba was a Muslim who was literate in Arabic, a prayer leader in the local mosque, and a *hafiz*, someone who had memorized the entire Quran. He was also husband to two wives and father to four children. Now his father sent the young man on an errand. He was to take several of their many slaves to a location some 200 miles away, where an English trading ship had anchored, and exchange them for paper and other goods. The paper was especially important, for his father's income depended on inscribing passages from the Quran on small slips of paper and selling them as protective charms.

To put it mildly, things did not go as planned. Unable to reach an agreement with the English merchant Captain

Ayuba Suleiman Diallo.

Stephen Pike, Ayuba traveled farther south and traded his slaves for a number of cows in the land of the Mandinka people. Well beyond the safety of his own country, he was in dangerous territory. As he and his companions stopped to rest on the journey home, they were seized, their heads were shaved, and they were sold as slaves to the very same Captain Pike. Although Ayuba was able to send a message to his father asking to be ransomed in exchange for some of their slaves, the ship sailed before a reply was received. And so Ayuba, along with 168 other slaves, both men and women, headed for the British American colony of Maryland, where 150 of them arrived alive.

Sold to a local planter, Ayuba was immediately sent to the tobacco fields, but when he became ill from this heavy and unaccustomed work, his owner assigned him

photo: By William Hoare of Bath (1707–1792), 1733, oil on canvas/photo © Christie's Images/Bridgeman Images

restrict the slave trade and soon forbade the export of male slaves altogether, a ban that lasted until the early eighteenth century. By then, the ruler's authority over outlying areas had declined, and the country's major exports of pepper and cotton cloth had lost out to Asian and then European competition. In these circumstances, Benin felt compelled to resume limited participation in the slave trade. The neighboring kingdom of Dahomey, on the other hand, turned to a vigorous involvement in the slave trade in the early eighteenth century under strict royal control. The army conducted annual slave raids, and the government soon came to depend on the trade for its essential revenues. The slave trade in Dahomey became the chief business of the state and remained so until well into the nineteenth century.

the less arduous and more familiar task of tending cattle Alone with the cattle, Ayuba was able to withdraw into a nearby forest to pray, but he was spotted by a young white boy who mocked him and threw dirt in his face. Sometime later, no doubt in despair, Ayuba ran away, but he was soon captured and housed in the county jail, located in the back room of a tavern. There he became something of a local curiosity and attracted the attention of a lawyer named Thomas Bluett. When Ayuba refused wine, wrote a few lines in Arabic, and mentioned "Allah" and "Muhammad," Bluett realized that he was "no common slave." After locating an old slave who could translate for him, Bluett became fascinated by Ayuba's story, and he initiated a process that took both of them to England in 1733, where philanthropists purchased Ayuba's freedom.

Ayuba's reception in England was amazing. Now fluent in English, Ayuba was received by the English royal family and various members of the nobility, hosted by leading scholars, and entertained by wealthy merchants, eager to tap his knowledge of economic conditions in West Africa. The prominent artist William Hoare painted his portrait, complete with a small Quran hanging from his neck.

In 1734, he finally set off for home, loaded with gifts from his English friends. There he encountered, quite by chance, the same Mandinka men who had sold him only a few years before. Francis Moore, a European trader accompanying Ayuba, wrote that he "fell into a most terrible passion and was for killing them" and was restrained from doing so only with difficulty. He arrived in his hometown to find that his father had recently died. His wives and children, however, were all alive and welcomed him warmly. One of his wives had remarried, believing him gone forever, but her new husband readily gave way, and Ayuba resumed his place of prominence in his own community until his death in 1773.

He also resumed his life as a slave owner. Selling some of the gifts he had acquired in England, he purchased a woman slave and two horses soon after his arrival back in West Africa. According to Moore, he "spoke always very handsomely of the English," and he continued his association with the Royal African Company, the primary English trading firm in West Africa, in their rivalry with French traders.[39] The last mention of Ayuba in the records of that company noted that he was seeking compensation for the loss of two slaves and a watch, probably the one given him in England by Queen Caroline.

Questions: What might you infer about Ayuba's own view of slavery and the slave trade? What insights or questions about the slave trade does his remarkable story suggest?

REFLECTIONS

Economic Globalization—Then and Now

AP® EXAM TIP

Make a brief list of continuities and changes in global commerce from this era to the early twenty-first century.

The study of history reminds us of two quite contradictory truths. One is that our lives in the present bear remarkable similarities to those of people long ago. We are perhaps not so unique as we might think. The other is that our lives are very different from theirs and that things have changed substantially. This chapter about global commerce—long-distance trade in spices and textiles, silver and gold, beaver pelts and deerskins, slaves and sugar—provides both perspectives.

If we are accustomed to thinking about globalization as a product of the late twentieth century, early modern world history provides a corrective. Those three centuries reveal much that is familiar to people of the twenty-first century—the global circulation of goods; an international currency; production for a world market; the growing economic role of the West on the global stage; private enterprise, such as the British and Dutch East India companies, operating on a world scale; national governments eager to support their merchants in a highly competitive environment. By the eighteenth century, many Europeans dined from Chinese porcelain dishes called "china," wore Indian-made cotton textiles, and drank chocolate from Mexico, tea from China, and coffee from Yemen while sweetening these beverages with sugar from the Caribbean or Brazil. The millions who worked to produce these goods, whether slave or free, were operating in a world economy. Some industries were thoroughly international. New England rum producers, for example, depended on molasses imported from the Caribbean, while the West Indian sugar industry used African labor and European equipment to produce for a global market.

Nonetheless, early modern economic globalization was a far cry from that of the twentieth century. The most obvious differences, perhaps, were scale and speed. By 2000, immensely more goods circulated internationally, and far more people produced for and depended on the world market than was the case even in 1750. Back-and-forth communications between England and India that took eighteen months in the eighteenth century could be accomplished in an hour by telegraph in the late nineteenth century and almost instantaneously via the Internet in the late twentieth century. Moreover, by 1900 globalization was firmly centered in the economies of Europe and North America. In the early modern era, by contrast, Asia in general and China in particular remained major engines of the world economy, despite the emerging presence of Europeans around the world. By the end of the twentieth century, the booming economies of Turkey, Brazil, India, and China suggested at least a partial return to that earlier pattern.

Early modern globalization differed in still other ways from that of the contemporary world. Economic life then was primarily preindustrial: it was still powered by human and animal muscles, wind, and water and lacked the enormous productive capacity that accompanied the later technological breakthrough of the steam engine and the Industrial Revolution. Finally, the dawning of a genuinely global economy in the early modern era was tied unapologetically to empire building and to slavery, both of which had been discredited by the late twentieth century. Slavery lost its legitimacy during the nineteenth century, and formal territorial empires largely disappeared in the twentieth. Most people during the early modern era would have been surprised to learn that a global economy, as it turned out, could function effectively without either of these long-standing practices.

Chapter Review

What's the Significance?

Big Picture Questions

1. To what extent did Europeans transform earlier patterns of commerce, and in what ways did they assimilate into those older patterns?
2. How should we distribute the moral responsibility for the Atlantic slave trade? Is this an appropriate task for historians?
3. What lasting legacies of early modern globalization are evident in the twenty-first century? Pay particular attention to the legacies of the slave trade.
4. **Looking Back:** Asians, Africans, and Native Americans experienced early modern European expansion in quite different ways. Based on Chapters 13 and 14, how might you describe and explain those differences? In what respects were they active agents in the historical process rather than simply victims of European actions?

Next Steps: For Further Study

Glenn J. Ames, *The Globe Encompassed: The Age of European Discovery, 1500–1700* (2007). An up-to-date survey of European expansion in the early modern era.

Andre Gunder Frank, *ReOrient: Global Economy in the Asian Age* (1998). An account of the early modern world economy that highlights the centrality of Asia.

Erik Gilbert and Jonathan Reynolds, *Trading Tastes: Commodity and Cultural Exchange to 1750* (2006). A world historical perspective on transcontinental and transoceanic commerce.

David Northrup, ed., *The Atlantic Slave Trade* (2002). A fine collection of essays about the origins, practice, impact, and abolition of Atlantic slavery.

John Richards, *The Endless Frontier* (2003). Explores the ecological consequences of early modern commerce.

John K. Thornton, *A Cultural History of the Atlantic World, 1250–1820* (2012). A recent account of the intersection of European, African, and Native American people by a highly respected historian.

"Atlantic Slave Trade and Slave Life in the Americas: A Visual Record," http://hitchcock.itc.virginia.edu/Slavery/index.php. An immense collection of maps and images, illustrating the slave trade and the life of slaves in the Americas.

"The Spice of Life: Pepper, the Master Spice," https://www.youtube.com/watch?v=NuZujx-LMfg. A BBC film that presents the history of pepper, so central to the spice trade of the early modern era.

WORKING WITH EVIDENCE

Exchange and Status in the Early Modern World

In many cultures across many centuries, the possession of scarce foreign goods has served not only to meet practical needs and desires but also to convey status. For centuries, Chinese silk signified rank, position, or prestige across much of Eurasia. Pepper and other spices from South and Southeast Asia likewise appealed to elite Romans and Chinese, eager to demonstrate their elevated position in society. In the late twentieth century, American blue jeans were much in demand among Russian young people who sought to display their independence from an oppressive communist regime, while Americans who could afford a German Porsche or an Italian Ferrari acquired an image of sophistication or glamour, setting them apart from others.

As global commerce expanded in the early modern era, so too did the exchange of foods, fashions, finery, and more. Already in 1500, according to a recent study, "it would be possible for a person in the Persian Gulf to wear cotton cloth from India while eating a bowl of rice also from India while sitting under a roof made of timber imported from East Africa. As he finished the rice he would see a Chinese character—the bowl itself came from China."[40] In the centuries that followed, growing numbers of people all across the world, particularly in elite social circles, had access to luxury goods from far away with which they could display, and perhaps enhance, their status. Some of these goods—sugar, pepper, tobacco, tea, and Indian cotton textiles, for example—gradually dropped in price, becoming more widely available. The images that follow illustrate this relationship between global trade and the display of status during the several centuries after 1500.

More than the peoples of other major civilizations, Europeans in the early modern era embraced the goods of the world. They had long been fascinated by and impressed with the wealth and splendor of Asia, which Marco Polo had described in the early fourteenth century after returning from his famous sojourn in China. Now in the early modern era, Western Europe was increasingly at the hub of a growing network of global commerce with access to products from around the world. Tea, porcelain, and silk from China; cotton textiles and spices from India and Southeast Asia; sugar, chocolate, and tobacco from the Americas; coffee from the Middle East—all of this and much more flooded into Europe. By the eighteenth century, a fascination for things Chinese had seized the elite classes of Europe—Chinese textiles, porcelains, tea, wallpaper, furniture, gardens, and artistic styles. The son of King George II of England built a "Mandarin yacht" resembling a Chinese pleasure boat to sail on a large artificial lake near London.

Source 14.1, which shows a German painting from the early eighteenth century, illustrates the growing popularity of tea as a beverage of choice in Europe as well as Chinese teacups. Long popular in China and Japan, tea made its entry into Europe in the sixteenth century aboard Portuguese ships. Initially, it was extremely expensive and limited to the very wealthy, but the price dropped as the supply increased, and by the eighteenth century it was widely consumed in Europe. Chinese teacups without handles also became popular and arrived packed in tea or rice via European merchant vessels. Like many other porcelains, these teacups had been created by Chinese artisans

Staatliche Schloesser und Gaerton, Karlsruhe. Germany/Eric Lessing/Art Resource, NY

Source 14.1 Tea and Porcelain in Europe

specifically for a European market. Those sitting on the table in the foreground of the image were manufactured in China between 1662 and 1722. Notice the practice of pouring the tea into the saucer to cool it.

■ What foreign trade items can you identify in this painting?

■ Note the European house on the teacup at the bottom left. What does this indicate about the willingness of the Chinese to cater to the tastes of European customers?

■ From what social class do you think the woman in the image comes?

■ How might you explain the great European interest in Chinese products and styles during the eighteenth century? Why might their possession have suggested status?

Like tea from China and coffee from Ethiopia, chocolate from Mesoamerica also became an elite beverage and an indicator of high status in Europe during the early modern era. It was the Olmecs, the Maya, and the Aztecs who first discovered how to process the seeds of the cacao tree into a chocolate drink. After the Spanish conquest of the Aztec Empire, that drink was introduced into Spain, where it became highly fashionable in court and aristocratic circles. And from Spain it spread to much of the rest of Europe, also limited to the elite social classes, who could afford to purchase this expensive import. Not until the Industrial Revolution made it possible to produce solid chocolate candy for mass consumption did this Mesoamerican acquisition become more widely available. Unlike tobacco and coffee, however, chocolate did not take hold in the Islamic world or China until more recent times.

A part of the larger Columbian exchange, chocolate in Europe lost the religious or ritual associations with which the Aztecs had invested it, becoming a medicine, sometimes an aphrodisiac, and in general a recreational beverage. Hernán Cortés, the Spanish conqueror of the Aztecs, described chocolate as "the divine drink which builds up resistance and fights fatigue" and reported, "A cup of this precious drink permits a man to walk for a whole day without food."[41] After some debate, the Church approved it as a nutritional substitute during times of fasting, when taking solid food was forbidden. Europeans also innovated with the beverage, adding sugar, cinnamon, and other spices, and later milk. With ingredients from the Americas and Asia, some of them produced by African slave labor, chocolate illustrated the process by which Europe was becoming the center of an emerging world economy.

Source 14.2, a painted tile panel from the early eighteenth century, shows a *chocolatada*, or "chocolate party," in Valencia, Spain. Notice the saucer, or *mancerina*, also a European innovation, for drinking chocolate without spilling it.

Museu de Ceramica, Barcelona, Spain/Album/Art Resource, NY

Source 14.2 A Chocolate Party in Spain

- What marks this event as an upper-class occasion?

- What steps in the preparation of the chocolate drink can you observe in the image?

- Why do you think Europeans embraced a practice of people they regarded as uncivilized, bloodthirsty, and savage? What does this suggest about the process of cultural borrowing?

Europeans, of course, were not the only people to embrace foreign tastes newly available in the early modern era. Tobacco and coffee, like tea, soon found a growing range of consumers all across Eurasia. Originating in the Americas, tobacco smoking spread quickly to Europe and Asia. Well before 1700, it had become perhaps the first global recreation. In the Ottoman Empire, as elsewhere, it provoked strenuous opposition on the grounds that it was an intoxicant, like wine, and was associated with unwholesome and promiscuous behavior. It was also associated with coffee, which had entered the Ottoman Empire in the sixteenth century from its place of origin in Ethiopia and Yemen. Coffee too encountered considerable opposition, partly because it was consumed in the new social arena of the coffeehouse. To moralists and other critics, the coffeehouse was a "refuge of Satan," which drew people away from the mosques even as it drew together all different classes. Authorities suspected that coffeehouses were places of political intrigue. None of this stopped the spread of either tobacco or coffee, and the coffeehouse, in the Ottoman Empire and in Europe, came to embody a new "public culture of fun" as it wore away at earlier religious restrictions on the enjoyment of life.[42]

Source 14.3 is a sixteenth-century miniature painting depicting a Turkish coffeehouse in the Ottoman Empire.

- What activities can you identify in the painting?

- Would you read this painting as critical of the coffeehouse, as celebrating it, or as a neutral description? Notice that the musicians and those playing board games at the bottom were engaged in activities considered rather disreputable. How would you describe the general demeanor of the men in the coffeehouse?

- Notice the cups that the patrons are using and those stacked in the upper right. Do they look similar to those shown in Source 14.1? Certainly Ottoman elites by the sixteenth century preferred Chinese porcelain to that manufactured within their own empire.

The emerging colonial societies of Spanish and Portuguese America gave rise to a wide variety of recognized mixed-race groups known as *castas*, or "castes," defined in terms of the precise mixture of Native American, European, and African ancestry that an individual possessed. While this system slotted people into a hierarchical social order defined by race and heritage, it did allow for some social mobility. If individuals managed to acquire some education, land, or money, they might gain in social prestige and even pass as members of a more highly favored category (see Chapter 13, pages 565–67). Adopting the dress and lifestyle of higher-ranking groups could facilitate this process.

Source 14.4 shows a woman of Indian ancestry and a man of African/ Indian descent as well as their child, who is categorized as a *loba*, or "wolf." It comes from a series of "casta paintings" created in eighteenth-century Mexico by the well-known Zapotec artist Miguel Cabrera to depict some eighteen or more mixed-race couples and their children, each with a distinct designation. The woman in this image is wearing a lovely *huipil*, a traditional Maya tunic or blouse, while the man is dressed in a European-style waistcoat, vest, and lace shirt, while holding a black tricorne hat, widely popular in Europe during the seventeenth and eighteenth centuries. Interest in such

Source 14.3 An Ottoman Coffeehouse

De Chino cambujoy dIndia ; Loba

Source 14.4 Clothing and Status in Colonial Mexico

paintings reflected both a Spanish fascination with race and a more general European concern with classification, which was characteristic of eighteenth-century scientific thinking.

■ What indications of status ambition or upward mobility can you identify in this image? Keep in mind that status here is associated with race and gender as well as the possession of foreign products.

■ Why do you think the woman is shown in more traditional costume, while the man is portrayed in European dress?

■ Notice the porcelain items at the bottom right. Where might they have come from?

■ In what cultural tradition do you think this couple raised their daughter? What problems might they have experienced in the process?

DOING HISTORY

Exchange and Status in the Early Modern World

1. **Analyzing the display of status:** In what different ways did the possession of foreign objects convey status in the early modern world? Toward whom were these various claims of status directed? Notice the difference between the display of status in public and private settings.

2. **Noticing gender differences:** In what ways are men and women portrayed in these visual sources? Why might women be absent in Sources 14.2 and 14.3?

3. **Exploring the functions of trade:** How might you use these images to support the idea that trade served more than economic needs?

4. **Raising questions about cultural borrowing:** What issues about cross-cultural borrowing do these visual sources suggest?

5. **Evaluating images as evidence:** What are the strengths and limitations of visual sources as a means of understanding the relationship of trade and status in the early modern era? What other kinds of sources would be useful for pursuing this theme?

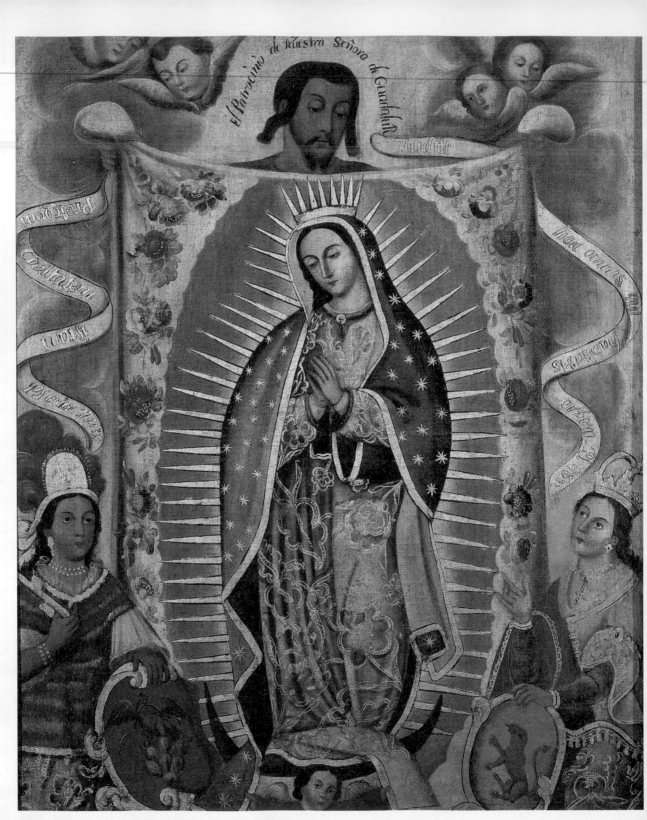

El Patrocinio de Nuestra Señora de Guadalupe

CHAPTER 15

Cultural Transformations

Religion and Science
1450–1750

Nigerian pastor Daniel Ajayi-Adeniran is a missionary to the United States, with his mission field in the Bronx. The church he represents, the Redeemed Christian Church of God, began in Nigeria in 1952. It has acquired millions of members in Nigeria and boasts a missionary network with a presence in 100 countries. According to its leader, the church was "made in heaven, assembled in Nigeria, exported to the world." And the Redeemed Church of God is not alone. As secularism and materialism born of the Scientific Revolution and modern life have eroded religious faith in the West, many believers in Asia, Africa, and Latin America have felt called to reinvigorate a declining Christianity in Europe and North America. In a remarkable reversal of an earlier pattern, they now seek to "re-evangelize" the West, from which they originally received the faith. After all, more than 60 percent of the world's professing Christians now live outside Europe and North America, and, within the United States, one in six Catholic diocesan priests and one in three seminary students are foreign-born. For example, hundreds of Filipino priests, nuns, and lay workers now serve churches in the West. "We couldn't just throw up our hands and see these churches turned into nightclubs or mosques," declared Tokunboh Adeyemo, another Nigerian church leader seeking to minister to an "increasingly godless West."[1]

The early modern era of world history gave birth to two intersecting cultural trends that continue to play out in the twenty-first century. The first was the spread of Christianity to Asians, Africans, and Native Americans, some of whom now seem to be returning the favor. The second was the emergence of a modern scientific outlook, which sharply challenged Western Christianity even as it too acquired a global presence.

The Virgin of Guadalupe   According to Mexican tradition, a dark-skinned Virgin Mary appeared to an indigenous peasant named Juan Diego in 1531, an apparition reflected in this Mexican painting from 1720. Belief in the Virgin of Guadalupe represented the incorporation of Catholicism into the emerging culture and identity of Mexico.

And so, alongside new empires and new patterns of commerce, the early modern centuries also witnessed novel cultural transformations that likewise connected distant peoples. Riding the currents of European empire building and commercial expansion, Christianity was established solidly in the Americas and the Philippines; far more modestly in Siberia, China, Japan, and India; and hardly at all within the vast and still-growing domains of Islam. A cultural tradition largely limited to Europe in 1500 now became a genuine world religion, spawning a multitude of cultural encounters. While this ancient faith was spreading, a new understanding of the universe and a new approach to knowledge were taking shape among European thinkers of the Scientific Revolution, giving rise to another kind of cultural encounter — that between science and religion. Science was a new and competing worldview, and for some it became almost a new religion. In time, it grew into a defining feature of global modernity, achieving a worldwide acceptance that exceeded that of Christianity or any other religious tradition.

Although Europeans were central players in the globalization of Christianity and the emergence of modern science, they did not act alone in the cultural transformations of the early modern era. Asian, African, and Native American peoples largely determined how Christianity would be accepted, rejected, or transformed as it entered new cultural environments. Science emerged within an international and not simply a European context, and it met varying receptions in different parts of the world. Islam continued a long pattern of religious expansion and renewal, even as Christianity began to compete with it as a world religion. Buddhism maintained its hold in much of East Asia, as did Hinduism in South Asia and numerous smaller-scale religious traditions in Africa. And Europeans themselves were certainly affected by the many "new worlds" that they now encountered. The cultural interactions of the early modern era, in short, did not take place on a one-way street.

SEEKING THE MAIN POINT

To what extent did the cultural changes of the early modern world derive from cross-cultural interaction? And to what extent did they grow from within particular societies or civilizations?

The Globalization of Christianity

AP® EXAM TIP

You need to know the expansion patterns of all major religions to do well on the AP® exam.

Despite its Middle Eastern origins and its earlier presence in many parts of the Afro-Asian world, Christianity was largely limited to Europe at the beginning of the early modern era. In 1500, the world of Christendom stretched from Spain and England in the west to Russia in the east, with small and beleaguered communities of various kinds in Egypt, Ethiopia, southern India, and Central Asia. Internally, the Christian world was seriously divided between the Roman Catholics of Western and Central Europe and the Eastern Orthodox of Eastern Europe and Russia. Externally, it was very much on the defensive against an expansive Islam. Muslims had ousted Christian Crusaders from their toeholds in the Holy Land by 1300, and with the Ottoman seizure of Constantinople in 1453, they had captured the prestigious capital of Eastern Orthodoxy. The Ottoman siege of Vienna in 1529 marked a Muslim advance into the heart of Central Europe. Except in Spain and Sicily,

A MAP OF TIME

1453	Ottoman conquest of Constantinople
1469–1539	Life of Guru Nanak; beginning of Sikh tradition
1472–1529	Life of Wang Yangming in China
1498–1547	Life of Mirabai, bhakti poet of India
1517	Luther's Ninety-Five Theses; beginning of Protestant Reformation
1543	Publication of Copernicus's masterwork about a sun-centered universe
1545–1563	Council of Trent
1560s	Taki Onqoy movement in Peru
1582–1610	Matteo Ricci in China
1598	Edict of Nantes proclaiming religious toleration in France
Early 17th century	European missionaries expelled from Japan
1618–1648	Thirty Years' War in Europe
1642–1727	Life of Isaac Newton; culmination of European Scientific Revolution
18th century	European Enlightenment
Early 18th century	Missionaries lost favor in the Chinese court
1740–1818	Wahhabi movement of Islamic reform in Arabia

which had recently been reclaimed for Christendom after centuries of Muslim rule, the future, it must have seemed, lay with Islam rather than Christianity.

Western Christendom Fragmented: The Protestant Reformation

As if these were not troubles enough, in the early sixteenth century the Protestant Reformation shattered the unity of Roman Catholic Christianity, which for the previous 1,000 years had provided the cultural and organizational foundation of an emerging Western European civilization. The Reformation began in 1517 when a German priest, Martin Luther (1483–1546), publicly invited debate about various abuses within the Roman Catholic Church by issuing a document, known as the Ninety-Five Theses, allegedly nailing it to the door of a church in Wittenberg. In itself, this was nothing new, for many people were critical of the luxurious life of the popes, the corruption and immorality of some clergy, the Church's selling of

AP® EXAM TIP

Refer back to the sections in Chapter 4 on variations within Buddhism and in Chapter 9 on variations within Islam and compare them to variations in Christianity in this chapter.

The Protestant Reformation
An engraving of Martin Luther nailing his Ninety-Five Theses to the door of the Wittenberg castle church in 1517, thus launching the Protestant Reformation. (Photo © Tarker/Bridgeman Images)

Guided Reading Question

■ CHANGE

In what ways did the Protestant Reformation transform European society, culture, and politics?

indulgences (said to remove the penalties for sin), and other aspects of church life and practice.

What made Luther's protest potentially revolutionary, however, was its theological basis. A troubled and brooding man anxious about his relationship with God, Luther had recently come to a new understanding of salvation: he believed that it came through faith alone. Neither the good works of the sinner nor the sacraments of the Church had any bearing on the eternal destiny of the soul, for faith was a free gift of God, graciously granted to his needy and undeserving people. To Luther, the source of these beliefs, and of religious authority in general, was not the teaching of the Church, but the Bible alone, interpreted according to the individual's conscience. All of this challenged the authority of the Church and called into question the special position of the clerical hierarchy and of the pope in particular. In sixteenth-century Europe, this was the stuff of revolution. (See the Snapshot, opposite, for a brief summary of Catholic and Protestant differences.)

Contrary to Luther's original intentions, his ideas provoked a massive schism within the world of Catholic Christendom, for they came to express a variety of political, economic, and social tensions as well as religious differences. Some kings and princes, many of whom had long disputed the political authority of the pope, found in these ideas a justification for their own independence and an opportunity to gain the lands and taxes previously held by the Church. In the Protestant idea

SNAPSHOT   Catholic/Protestant Differences in the Sixteenth Century

	Catholic	Protestant
Religious authority	Pope and church hierarchy	The Bible, as interpreted by individual Christians
Role of the pope	Ultimate authority in faith and doctrine	Authority of the pope denied
Ordination of clergy	Apostolic succession: direct line between original apostles and all subsequently ordained clergy	Apostolic succession denied; ordination by individual congregations or denominations
Salvation	Importance of church sacraments as channels of God's grace	Importance of faith alone; God's grace is freely and directly granted to believers
Status of Mary	Highly prominent, ranking just below Jesus; provides constant intercession for believers	Less prominent; Mary's intercession on behalf of the faithful denied
Prayer	To God, but often through or with Mary and saints	To God alone; no role for Mary and saints
Holy Communion	Transubstantiation: bread and wine become the actual body and blood of Christ	Transubstantiation denied; bread and wine have a spiritual or symbolic significance
Role of clergy	Priests are generally celibate, sharp distinction between priests and laypeople; priests are mediators between God and humankind	Ministers may marry; priesthood of all believers; clergy have different functions (to preach, administer sacraments) but no distinct spiritual status
Role of saints	Prominent spiritual exemplars and intermediaries between God and humankind	Generally disdained as a source of idolatry; saints refer to all Christians

that all vocations were of equal merit, middle-class urban dwellers found a new religious legitimacy for their growing role in society, since the Roman Catholic Church was associated in their eyes with the rural and feudal world of aristocratic privilege. For common people, who were offended by the corruption and luxurious living of some bishops, abbots, and popes, the new religious ideas served to express their opposition to the entire social order, particularly in a series of German peasant revolts in the 1520s. Although large numbers of women were attracted to Protestantism, Reformation teachings and practices did not offer them a substantially greater role in the church or society. In Protestant-dominated areas, the veneration of Mary and female saints ended, leaving the male Christ figure as the sole

AP® EXAM TIP

Take notes on the causes of the Protestant Reformation within Christianity.

Map 15.1
Reformation Europe in the Sixteenth Century

The rise of Protestantism added yet another set of religious divisions, both within and between states, to the world of Christendom, which was already sharply divided between the Roman Catholic Church and the Eastern Orthodox Church.

Protestant dominant
Some Protestant influence
Catholic
Eastern Orthodox Christian
Boundary of the Holy Roman Empire

object of worship. Protestant opposition to celibacy and monastic life closed the convents, which had offered some women an alternative to marriage. Nor were Protestants (except the Quakers) any more willing than Catholics to offer women an official role within their churches. The importance that Protestants gave to reading the Bible for oneself stimulated education and literacy for women, but given the emphasis on women as wives and mothers subject to male supervision, they had little opportunity to use that education outside of the family.

Reformation thinking spread quickly both within and beyond Germany, thanks in large measure to the recent invention of the printing press. Luther's many pamphlets and his translation of the New Testament into German were soon widely available. "God has appointed the [printing] Press to preach, whose voice the pope is never able to stop," declared one Reformation leader.[2] As the movement spread to France, Switzerland, England, and elsewhere, it also splintered, amoeba-like, into a variety of competing Protestant churches—Lutheran, Calvinist, Anglican, Quaker, Anabaptist—many of which subsequently subdivided, producing a bewildering array of Protestant denominations. Each was distinctive, but none gave allegiance to Rome or the pope.

Thus to the sharp class divisions and the fractured political system of Europe was now added the potent brew of religious difference, operating both within and between states (see Map 15.1). For more than thirty years (1562–1598), French society was torn by violence between Catholics and the Protestant minority known as Huguenots (HYOO-guh-naht). On a single day, August 24, 1572, Catholic mobs in Paris massacred some 3,000 Huguenots, and thousands more perished in provincial towns in the weeks that followed. Finally, a war-weary monarch, Henry IV, issued the Edict of Nantes (nahnt) in 1598, granting a substantial measure of religious toleration to French Protestants, though with the intention that they would soon return to the Catholic Church. The culmination of European religious conflict took shape in the Thirty Years' War (1618–1648), a Catholic–Protestant struggle that began in the Holy Roman Empire but eventually engulfed most of Europe. It was a horrendously destructive war, during which, scholars estimate, between 15 and 30 percent of the German population perished from violence, famine, or disease. Finally, the Peace of Westphalia (1648) brought the conflict to an end, with some reshuffling of boundaries and an agreement that each state was sovereign, authorized to control religious affairs within its own territory. Whatever religious unity Catholic Europe had once enjoyed was now permanently splintered.

The Protestant breakaway, combined with reformist tendencies within the Catholic Church itself, provoked a Catholic Reformation, or Counter-Reformation. In the Council of Trent (1545–1563), Catholics clarified and reaffirmed their unique doctrines and practices, such as the authority of the pope, priestly celibacy, the veneration of saints and relics, and the importance of church tradition and good works, all of which Protestants had rejected. Moreover, they set about correcting the abuses and corruption that had stimulated the Protestant movement by placing a new emphasis on the education of priests and their supervision by bishops. A crackdown on dissidents included the censorship of books, fines, exile, penitence, and occasionally the burning of heretics. Renewed attention was given to individual spirituality and personal piety. New religious orders, such as the Society of Jesus (Jesuits), provided a dedicated brotherhood of priests committed to the renewal of the Catholic Church and its extension abroad.

Although the Reformation was profoundly religious, it encouraged a skeptical attitude toward authority and tradition, for it had, after all, successfully challenged the immense prestige and power of the pope and the established Church. Protestant

Map 15.2
**The Globalization
of Christianity**

The growing Christian
presence in Asia, Africa,
and especially the Ameri-
cas, combined with older
centers of that faith, gave
the religion derived from
Jesus a global dimension
during the early modern
era.

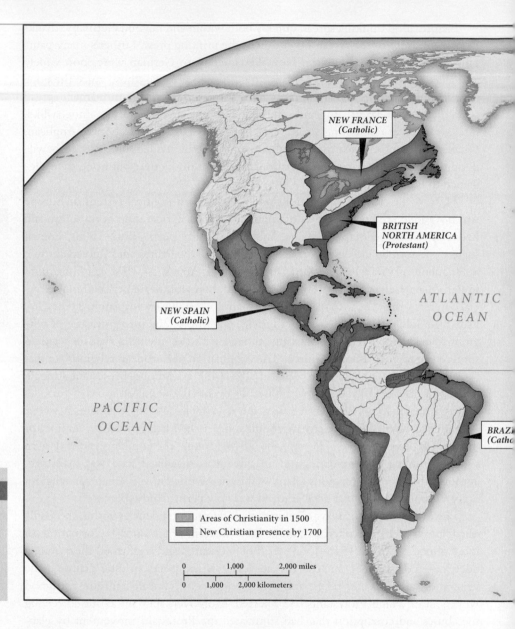

NEW FRANCE
(Catholic)

BRITISH
NORTH AMERICA
(Protestant)

NEW SPAIN
(Catholic)

ATLANTIC
OCEAN

PACIFIC
OCEAN

BRAZI
(Catho

Areas of Christianity in 1500
New Christian presence by 1700

0   1,000   2,000 miles

0   1,000   2,000 kilometers

AP® EXAM TIP

Keep track of the
global changes
over time in the
size of Christianity's
influence.

reformers fostered religious individualism, as people were now encouraged to read
and interpret the scriptures for themselves and to seek salvation without the media-
tion of the Church. In the centuries that followed, some people turned that skepticism and the habit of thinking independently against all conventional religion.
Thus the Protestant Reformation opened some space for new directions in European intellectual life.

In short, it was a more highly fragmented but also a renewed and revitalized Christianity that established itself around the world in the several centuries after 1500
(see Map 15.2).

WESTERN EUROPE
(Catholic/Protestant divide)

RUSSIAN EMPIRE
(Russian Orthodox)

SIBERIA
(Russian
Orthodox)

QING EMPIRE
(Minor Catholic
presence)

PACIFIC
OCEAN

ARMENIA
(Armenian
Orthodox)

MUGHAL EMPIRE
(Minor Catholic
presence)

JAPAN
(Christian Century,
Catholic, 1549–1650)

EGYPT
(Minority
Coptic)

ETHIOPIA
(Ethiopian
Orthodox)

SOUTH INDIA
(St. Thomas
Christians)

PHILIPPINES
(Spanish Catholic)

Equator

KONGO
(Court-adopted
Catholic)

INDIAN
OCEAN

DUTCH
SOUTH AFRICA
(Protestant)

Christianity Outward Bound

Christianity motivated European political and economic expansion and also benefited from it. The resolutely Catholic Spanish and Portuguese both viewed their movement overseas as a continuation of a long crusading tradition, which only recently had completed the liberation of their countries from Muslim control. When Vasco da Gama's small fleet landed in India in 1498, local authorities understandably asked, "What brought you hither?" The reply: they had come "in search of Christians and of spices."[3] Likewise, Columbus, upon arriving in the Americas, expressed the no doubt sincere hope that the people "might become Christians," even as he promised his Spanish patrons an abundant harvest of gold, spice, cotton, aloe wood, and slaves.[4] Neither man sensed any contradiction or hypocrisy in this blending of religious and material concerns.

If religion drove and justified European ventures abroad, it is difficult to imagine the globalization of Christianity (see Map 15.2) without the support of empire. Colonial settlers and traders, of course, brought their faith with them and sought to replicate it in their newly conquered homelands. New England Puritans, for example, planted a distinctive Protestant version of Christianity in North America, with an emphasis on education, moral purity, personal conversion, civic responsibility, and little tolerance for competing expressions of the faith. They did not show much interest in converting native peoples but sought rather to push them out of their ancestral territories. It was missionaries, mostly Catholic, who actively spread the Christian message beyond European communities. Organized in missionary orders such as the Dominicans, Franciscans, and Jesuits, Portuguese missionaries took the lead in Africa and Asia, while Spanish and French missionaries were most prominent in the Americas. Missionaries of the Russian Orthodox Church likewise accompanied the expansion of the Russian Empire across Siberia, where priests and monks ministered to Russian settlers and trappers, who often donated their first sable furs to a church or monastery.

Missionaries had their greatest success in Spanish America and in the Philippines, areas that shared two critical elements beyond their colonization by Spain. Most important, perhaps, was an overwhelming European presence, experienced variously as military conquest, colonial settlement, missionary activity, forced labor, social disruption, and disease. Surely it must have seemed as if the old gods had been bested and that any possible future lay with the powerful religion of the European invaders. A second common factor was the absence of a literate world religion in these two regions. Throughout the modern era, peoples solidly rooted in Confucian, Buddhist, Hindu, or Islamic traditions proved far more resistant to the Christian message than those who practiced more localized, small-scale, orally based religions. (See Working with Evidence, page 679, for images illustrating the global spread of Christianity.)

Conversion and Adaptation in Spanish America

Spanish America and China illustrate the difference between those societies in which Christianity became widely practiced and those that largely rejected it. Both cases, however, represent major cultural encounters of a kind that was becoming more frequent as European expansion brought the Christian faith to distant peoples with very different cultural traditions.

The decisive conquest of the Aztec and Inca empires and all that followed from it—disease, population collapse, loss of land to Europeans, forced labor, resettlement into more compact villages—created a setting in which the religion of the victors took hold in Spanish American colonies. Europeans saw their political and military success as a demonstration of the power of the Christian God. Native American

Guided Reading Question

■ CONNECTION

How was European imperial expansion related to the spread of Christianity?

AP® EXAM TIP

Past AP® exams have asked questions about methods of conversion to Christianity in Latin America, so pay attention here!

Guided Reading Question

■ CONNECTION

In what ways was European Christianity assimilated into the Native American cultures of Spanish America?

peoples generally agreed, and by 1700 or earlier the vast majority had been baptized and saw themselves in some respects as Christians. After all, other conquerors
such as the Aztecs and the Incas had always imposed their gods in some fashion on
defeated peoples. So it made sense, both practically and spiritually, to affiliate with
the Europeans' God, saints, rites, and rituals. Many millions accepted baptism, contributed to the construction of village churches, attended services, and embraced
images of saints. Despite the prominence of the Virgin Mary as a religious figure
across Latin America, the cost of conversion was high, especially for women. Many
women, who had long served as priests, shamans, or ritual specialists, had no corresponding role in a Catholic church, led by an all-male clergy. And, with a few
exceptions, convent life, which had provided some outlet for female authority and
education in Catholic Europe, was reserved largely for Spanish women in the
Americas. (See Zooming In: Úrsula de Jesús, page 654, for an exception.)

Earlier conquerors had made no attempt to eradicate local deities and religious
practices. The flexibility and inclusiveness of Mesoamerican and Andean religions
had made it possible for subject people to accommodate the gods of their new rulers
while maintaining their own traditions. But Europeans were different. They claimed
an exclusive religious truth and sought the utter destruction of local gods and everything associated with them. Operating within a Spanish colonial regime that actively
encouraged conversion, missionaries often proceeded by persuasion and patient teaching. At times, though, their frustration with the persistence of "idolatry, superstition,

Andean Christianity
In 1753, Marcos Zapata, a native Peruvian artist trained in European techniques, painted this rendering of Jesus' Last
Supper with his disciples, which included a number of Andean elements. The central dish on the table was a roasted
guinea pig, a traditional sacrificial animal, while a local fermented corn drink called *chicha* was also part of the meal.
Side dishes featured pomegranates, a Eurasian fruit brought to Peru by the Columbian exchange symbolizing the
passion of Christ. At the bottom right, looking away from Jesus while grasping a money bag, is the figure of Judas,
painted, some say, to resemble Francisco Pizarro, the Spanish conqueror of the Inca Empire. (© Yadid Levy/age fotostock)

Úrsula de Jesús, an Afro-Peruvian Slave and Christian Visionary

Úrsula de Jesús was born in the prosperous Spanish colonial city of Lima, Peru, in 1606, the daughter of a slave mother. Thus she entered life at the lowest rung of Spanish colonial society. But among enslaved people, Úrsula was fortunate. Her mother's owner was a wealthy aristocratic woman, and at age eight Úrsula was sent to live in the home of another elite woman with a reputation for piety and religious visions. Five years later, Úrsula accompanied a third woman into the Convent of Santa Clara, where she spent the rest of her life. There Úrsula found a place for herself in the world of colonial Peru and Latin American Christianity—but not easily or immediately.[5]

For the next quarter of a century, Úrsula was one of more than a hundred slaves in the convent, where she attended to the personal needs of her mistress and participated in communal labor—cooking, cleaning, and attending the sick. In the convent, as in the larger society, Úrsula was at the bottom of the social ladder as nuns, novices, and *doñadas* (religious laywomen) all

A wealthy white Peruvian woman and her African slave.

enjoyed a higher status. But the wealth of her mistress or perhaps her own day labor allowed her to dress well and to elevate herself above common slaves. She later noted that she went about "beautifully adorned from head to toe." She recalled, "I used to wear fancy clothes and parade about the choir."

The year 1642 marked a dramatic turning point in Úrsula's life, when she almost fell into a deep well. Crediting her deliverance from certain death to the Virgin of Carmen, Úrsula turned decisively away from her earlier vain and self-centered ways and embraced an ever-deepening spirituality. She sold her lovely clothes, devoted every spare moment to prayer, and sought out the most onerous tasks such as caring for contagious patients and washing soiled garments. She took to whipping herself twice daily, wearing a coarse and painful hair shirt, and placing a crown of thorns beneath her hair. In Catholic

AP® EXAM TIP

You should know examples of resistance to forced cultural conversions in history.

and error" boiled over into violent campaigns designed to uproot old religions once and for all. In 1535, the bishop of Mexico proudly claimed that he had destroyed 500 pagan shrines and 20,000 idols. During the seventeenth and early eighteenth centuries, church authorities in the Andean region periodically launched movements of "extirpation," designed to fatally undermine native religion. They destroyed religious images and ritual objects, publicly urinated on native "idols," desecrated the remains of ancestors, flogged "idolaters," and held religious trials and "processions of shame" aimed at humiliating offenders.

It is hardly surprising that such aggressive action generated resistance. Writing around 1600, the native Peruvian nobleman Guaman Poma de Ayala commented on the posture of native women toward Christianity: "They do not confess; they religious thinking of the time, such "mortification" of the body served to enhance identification with Jesus' suffering.

Úrsula's new religious fervor incurred the displeasure of her mistress, who felt neglected by her slave. By 1645, a deeply unhappy Úrsula determined to leave the convent and find a new owner. Then one of the nuns, hoping to retain her pious services, purchased Úrsula's freedom. Nonetheless, Úrsula chose to stay in the convent as a *doñada*. Doing so represented a modest elevation in her social status, an opportunity to pursue her spiritual life with fewer restrictions, and a measure of social and economic security.

Still, she continued to perform the same exhausting tasks she had as a slave and complained frequently about them. "I was up to my ears with cooking and other things," she confided to her diary, "desiring only to be in the mountains where there are no people." Even as she struggled with the restrictions of her position in the convent, Úrsula enhanced her reputation as a "servant of God," a woman of extraordinary devotion and humility, and as a visionary and a mystic.

In her diary, Úrsula recounted numerous direct encounters with God, Jesus, Mary, and with dead souls seeking her intervention to shorten their time in the purifying fires of purgatory. These visions frequently reflected the tensions of class, race, and position within the convent and in the larger society. Several priests, suffering in purgatory for their sexual sins, luxurious living, and mistreatment of slaves, appealed to Úrsula. So too did nuns who had been lax in their spiritual practices or placed their business interests above their religious duties. Úrsula had a special concern for the female slaves and servants who asked for her intercession. One feared becoming an "orphan" in purgatory with no one to remember her. Another confessed to a lesbian love affair with a nun. Although Úrsula once questioned "whether black women went to heaven," it was later revealed to her as an abode of "great harmony," but not of social equality, for "everyone had their place . . . in accordance with their standing and the obligations of their class." By the end of her life, however, Úrsula was able to affirm the spiritual equality of all. "In memory, understanding, and will," she declared, "they [blacks and whites] are all one."

When Úrsula died in 1666, a prominent nun confirmed that she had entered Heaven directly, with no intervening time in purgatory. Her funeral was attended by many high officials of both state and church, and she was buried beneath the chapel of the convent she had served.

Question: To what extent did Úrsula shape her own life, and in what way was it shaped by larger historical forces?

do not attend catechism classes . . . nor do they go to mass. . . . And resuming their ancient customs and idolatry, they do not want to serve God or the crown."[6] Occasionally, overt resistance erupted. One such example was the religious revivalist movement in central Peru in the 1560s, known as Taki Onqoy (dancing sickness). Possessed by the spirits of local gods, or *huacas*, traveling dancers and teachers predicted that an alliance of Andean deities would soon overcome the Christian God, inflict the intruding Europeans with the same diseases that they had brought to the Americas, and restore the world of the Andes to an imagined earlier harmony. They called on native peoples to cut off all contact with the Spanish, to reject Christian worship, and to return to traditional practices. "The world has turned about," one member declared, "and this time God and the Spaniards [will be] defeated and all the Spaniards killed and their cities drowned; and the sea will rise and overwhelm them, so that there will remain no memory of them."[7]

More common than such frontal attacks on Christianity, which colonial authorities quickly smashed, were efforts at blending two religious traditions, reinterpreting Christian practices within an Andean framework, and incorporating local elements into an emerging Andean Christianity. Even female dancers in the Taki Onqoy movement sometimes took the names of Christian saints, seeking to appropriate for themselves the religious power of Christian figures. Within Andean Christian communities, women might offer the blood of a llama to strengthen a village church or make a cloth covering for the Virgin Mary and a shirt for an image of a huaca with the same material. Although the state cults of the Incas faded away, missionary attacks did not succeed in eliminating the influence of local huacas. Images and holy sites might be destroyed, but the souls of the huacas remained, and their representatives gained prestige. One resilient Andean resident inquired of a Jesuit missionary: "Father, are you tired of taking our idols from us? Take away that mountain if you can, since that is the God I worship."[8]

In Mexico as well, an immigrant Christianity was assimilated into patterns of local culture. Parishes were organized largely around precolonial towns or regions. Churches built on or near the sites of old temples became the focus of community identity. *Cofradias*, church-based associations of laypeople, organized community processions and festivals and made provisions for proper funerals and burials for their members. Central to an emerging Mexican Christianity were the saints who closely paralleled the functions of precolonial gods. Saints were imagined as parents of the local community and the true owners of its land, and their images were paraded through the streets on the occasion of great feasts and were collected by individual households. Mexico's Virgin of Guadalupe neatly combined both Mesoamerican and Spanish notions of Divine Motherhood (see the chapter-opening photo on page 642). Although parish priests were almost always Spanish, the *fiscal*, or leader of the church staff, was a native Christian of great local prestige, who carried on the traditions and role of earlier religious specialists.

Throughout the colonial period and beyond, many Mexican Christians also took part in rituals derived from the past, with little sense of incompatibility with Christian practice. Incantations to various gods for good fortune in hunting, farming, or healing; sacrifices of self-bleeding; offerings to the sun; divination; the use of hallucinogenic drugs—all of these practices provided spiritual assistance in those areas of everyday life not directly addressed by Christian rites. Conversely, these practices also showed signs of Christian influence. Wax candles, normally used in Christian services, might now appear in front of a stone image of a precolonial god. The anger of a neglected saint, rather than that of a traditional god, might explain someone's illness and require offerings, celebration, or a new covering to regain his or her favor. In such ways did Christianity take root in the new cultural environments of Spanish America, but it was a distinctly Andean or Mexican Christianity, not merely a copy of the Spanish version.

An Asian Comparison: China and the Jesuits

The Chinese encounter with Christianity was very different from that of Native Americans in Spain's New World empire. The most obvious difference was the political context. The peoples of Spanish America had been defeated, their societies thoroughly disrupted, and their cultural confidence sorely shaken. China, on the other hand, encountered European Christianity between the sixteenth and eighteenth centuries during the powerful and prosperous Ming (1368–1644) and Qing (1644–1912) dynasties. Although the transition between these two dynasties occasioned several decades of internal conflict, at no point was China's political independence or cultural integrity threatened by the handful of European missionaries and traders working there.

The reality of a strong, independent, confident China required a different missionary strategy, for Europeans needed the permission of Chinese authorities to operate in the country. Whereas Spanish missionaries working in a colonial setting sought primarily to convert the masses, the leading missionary order in China, the Jesuits, took deliberate aim at the official Chinese elite. Following the example of their most famous missionary, Matteo Ricci (in China 1582–1610), many Jesuits learned Chinese, became thoroughly acquainted with classical Confucian texts, and dressed like Chinese scholars. Initially, they downplayed their mission to convert and instead emphasized their interest in exchanging ideas and learning from China's ancient culture. As highly educated men, the Jesuits carried the recent secular knowledge of Europe—science, technology, geography, mapmaking—to an audience of curious Chinese scholars. In presenting Christian teachings, Jesuits were at pains to be respectful of Chinese culture, pointing out parallels between Confucianism and Christianity rather than portraying it as something new and foreign. They chose to define Chinese rituals honoring the emperor or venerating ancestors as secular or civil observances rather than as religious practices that had to be abandoned. Such efforts to accommodate Chinese culture contrast sharply with the frontal attacks on Native American religions in the Spanish Empire undertaken by many missionaries.

The religious and cultural outcomes of the missionary enterprise likewise differed greatly in the two regions. Nothing approaching mass conversion to Christianity took place in China, as it had in Latin America. During the sixteenth and seventeenth centuries, a modest number of Chinese scholars and officials did become Christians, attracted by the personal lives of the missionaries, by their interest in Western science, and by the moral certainty that Christianity offered. Jesuit missionaries found favor for a time at the Chinese imperial court, where their mathematical, astronomical, technological, and mapmaking skills rendered them useful. For more than a century, they were appointed to head the Chinese Bureau of Astronomy. Among ordinary people, Christianity spread very modestly amid tales of miracles attributed to the Christian God, while missionary teachings about "eternal life" sounded to some like Daoist prescriptions for immortality. At most, though,

Guided Reading Question

■ COMPARISON
Why were missionary efforts to spread Christianity so much less successful in China than in Spanish America?

AP® EXAM TIP

You should know about some of the scientific and religious contributions of Jesuit missionaries in China.

missionary efforts over the course of some 250 years (1550–1800) resulted in 200,000 to 300,000 converts, a minuscule number in a Chinese population approaching 300 million by 1800. What explains the very limited acceptance of Christianity in early modern China?

Fundamentally, the missionaries offered little that the Chinese really wanted. Confucianism for the elites and Buddhism, Daoism, and a multitude of Chinese gods and spirits at the local level adequately supplied the spiritual needs of most Chinese. Furthermore, it became increasingly clear that Christianity was an all-or-nothing faith that required converts to abandon much of traditional Chinese culture. Christian monogamy, for example, seemed to require Chinese men to put away their concubines. What would happen to these deserted women?

By the early eighteenth century, the papacy and competing missionary orders came to oppose the Jesuit policy of accommodation. The pope claimed authority over Chinese Christians and declared that sacrifices to Confucius and the veneration of ancestors were "idolatry" and thus forbidden to Christians. The pope's pronouncements represented an unacceptable challenge to the authority of the emperor and an affront to Chinese culture. In 1715, an outraged Emperor Kangxi wrote:

> I ask myself how these uncultivated Westerners dare to speak of the great precepts of China. . . . [T]heir doctrine is of the same kind as the little heresies of the Buddhist and Taoist monks. . . . These are the greatest absurdities that have ever been seen. As from now I forbid the Westerners to spread their doctrine in China; that will spare us a lot of trouble.[9]

This represented a major turning point in the relationship of Christian missionaries and Chinese society. Many were subsequently expelled, and missionaries lost favor at court.

In other ways as well, missionaries played into the hands of their Chinese opponents. Their willingness to work under the Manchurian Qing dynasty, which came to power in 1644, discredited them with those Chinese scholars who viewed the Qing as uncivilized foreigners and their rule in China as disgraceful and illegitimate. Missionaries' reputation as miracle workers further damaged their standing as men of science and rationality, for elite Chinese often regarded miracles and supernatural religion as superstitions, fit only for the uneducated masses. Some viewed the Christian ritual of Holy Communion as a kind of cannibalism. Others came to see missionaries as potentially subversive, for various Christian groups met in secret, and such religious sects had often provided the basis for peasant rebellion. Nor did it escape Chinese notice that European Christians had taken over the Philippines and that their warships were active in the Indian Ocean. Perhaps the missionaries, with their great interest in maps, were spies for these aggressive foreigners. All of this contributed to the general failure of Christianity to secure a prominent presence in China.

Persistence and Change in Afro-Asian Cultural Traditions

Although Europeans were central players in the globalization of Christianity, theirs was not the only expanding or transformed culture of the early modern era. African religious ideas and practices, for example, accompanied slaves to the Americas. Common African forms of religious revelation—divination, dream interpretation, visions, spirit possession—found a place in the Africanized versions of Christianity that emerged in the New World. Europeans frequently perceived these practices as evidence of sorcery, witchcraft, or even devil worship and tried to suppress them. Nonetheless, syncretic (blended) religions such as Vodou in Haiti, Santería in Cuba, and Candomblé and Macumba in Brazil persisted. They derived from various West African traditions and featured drumming, ritual dancing, animal sacrifice, and spirit possession. Over time, they incorporated Christian beliefs and practices such as church attendance, the search for salvation, and the use of candles and crucifixes and often identified their various spirits or deities with Catholic saints.

> **AP® EXAM TIP**
>
> Compare these "blended" forms of Afro-Asian Christianity with those developed by native believers in Latin America.

Expansion and Renewal in the Islamic World

The early modern era likewise witnessed the continuation of the "long march of Islam" across the Afro-Asian world. In sub-Saharan Africa, in the eastern and western wings of India, and in Central and Southeast Asia, the expansion of the Islamic frontier, a process already a thousand years in the making, extended farther still. Conversion to Islam generally did not mean a sudden abandonment of old religious practices in favor of the new. Rather, it was more often a matter of "assimilating Islamic rituals, cosmologies, and literatures into . . . local religious systems."[10]

Continued Islamization was not usually the product of conquering armies and expanding empires. It depended instead on wandering Muslim holy men or Sufis, Islamic scholars, and itinerant traders, none of whom posed a threat to local rulers. In fact, such people often were useful to those rulers and their village communities.

> **Guided Reading Question**
>
> ■ EXPLANATION
> What accounts for the continued spread of Islam in the early modern era and for the emergence of reform or renewal movements within the Islamic world?

They offered literacy in Arabic, established informal schools, provided protective charms containing passages from the Quran, served as advisers to local authorities and healers to the sick, often intermarried with local people, and generally did not insist that new converts give up their older practices. What they offered, in short, was connection to the wider, prestigious, prosperous world of Islam. Islamization extended modestly even to the Americas, where enslaved African Muslims practiced their faith in North America, particularly in Brazil, where Muslims led a number of slave revolts in the early nineteenth century. (See Zooming In: Ayuba Suleiman Diallo in Chapter 14, page 630.)

The islands of Southeast Asia illustrate the diversity of belief and practice that accompanied the spread of Islam in the early modern era. During the seventeenth century in Aceh, a Muslim sultanate on the northern tip of Sumatra, authorities sought to enforce the dietary codes and almsgiving practices of Islamic law. After four successive women ruled the area in the late seventeenth century, women were forbidden from exercising political power. On Muslim Java, however, numerous women served in royal courts, and women throughout Indonesia continued their longtime role as buyers and sellers in local markets. Among ordinary Javanese, traditional animistic practices of spirit worship coexisted easily with a tolerant and accommodating Islam, while merchants often embraced a more orthodox version of the religion in line with Middle Eastern traditions.

To such orthodox Muslims, religious syncretism, which accompanied Islamization almost everywhere, became increasingly offensive, even heretical. Such sentiments played an important role in movements of religious renewal and reform that emerged throughout the vast Islamic world of the eighteenth century. The leaders of such movements sharply criticized those practices that departed from earlier patterns established by Muhammad and from the authority of the Quran. For example, in India, which was governed by the Muslim Mughal Empire, religious resistance to official policies that accommodated Hindus found concrete expression during the reign of the emperor Aurangzeb (r. 1658–1707) (see Chapter 13, page 581). A series of religious wars in West Africa during the eighteenth and early nineteenth centuries took aim at corrupt Islamic practices and the rulers, Muslim and non-Muslim alike, who permitted them. In Southeast and Central Asia, tension grew between practitioners of localized and blended versions of Islam and those who sought to purify such practices in the name of a more authentic and universal faith.

The most well-known and widely visible of these Islamic renewal movements took place during the mid-eighteenth century in Arabia itself, where the religion had been born more than 1,000 years earlier. This movement originated in the teachings of the Islamic scholar Muhammad Ibn Abd al-Wahhab (1703–1792). The growing difficulties of the Islamic world, such as the weakening of the Ottoman Empire, were directly related, he argued, to deviations from the pure faith of early Islam. Al-Wahhab was particularly upset by common religious practices in central Arabia that seemed to him idolatry—the widespread veneration of Sufi saints and their tombs, the adoration of natural sites, and even the respect paid to Muhammad's

AP® EXAM TIP
You need to know ways that Islam changed as it spread into Southeast Asia and also ways that it stayed the same.

tomb at Medina. All of this was a dilution of the absolute monotheism of authentic Islam.

The Wahhabi movement took a new turn in the 1740s when it received the political backing of Muhammad Ibn Saud, a local ruler who found al-Wahhab's ideas compelling. With Ibn Saud's support, the religious movement became an expansive state in central Arabia. Within that state, offending tombs were razed; "idols" were eliminated; books on logic were destroyed; the use of tobacco, hashish, and musical instruments was forbidden; and certain taxes not authorized by religious teaching were abolished.

Al-Wahhab's ideas about the role of women have attracted considerable attention in light of the highly restrictive practices of Wahhabi Islam in contemporary Saudi Arabia. He did on one occasion reluctantly authorize the stoning of a woman who persisted in an adulterous sexual relationship after numerous warnings, but more generally he emphasized the rights of women within a patriarchal Islamic framework. These included the right to consent to and stipulate conditions for a marriage, to control her dowry, to divorce, and to engage in commerce. Such rights, long embedded in Islamic law, had apparently been forgotten or ignored in eighteenth-century Arabia. Furthermore, he did not insist on head-to-toe covering of women in public and allowed for the mixing of unrelated men and women for business or medical purposes.

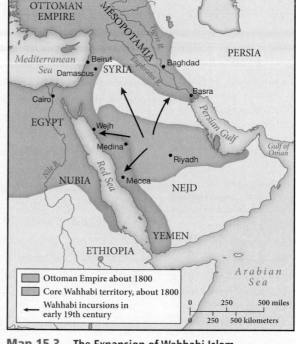

Map 15.3 The Expansion of Wahhabi Islam

From its base in central Arabia, the Wahhabi movement represented a challenge to the Ottoman Empire, while its ideas subsequently spread widely within the Islamic world.

By the early nineteenth century, this new reformist state encompassed much of central Arabia, with Mecca itself coming under Wahhabi control in 1803 (see Map 15.3). Although an Egyptian army broke the power of the Wahhabis in 1818, the movement's influence continued to spread across the Islamic world. Together with the ongoing expansion of the religion, these movements of reform and renewal signaled the continuing cultural vitality of the "abode of Islam," even as the European presence on the world stage assumed larger dimensions. In the nineteenth and twentieth centuries, such movements persisted and became associated with resistance to the political, military, and cultural intrusion of the European West into the affairs of the Islamic world.

AP® EXAM TIP

Take notes on elements of the Wahhabi movement within Islam.

China: New Directions in an Old Tradition

Neither China nor India experienced cultural or religious change as dramatic as that of the Reformation in Europe, nor did Confucian or Hindu cultures during the early modern era spread widely, as did Christianity and Islam. Nonetheless, neither of these traditions remained static. As in Christian Europe, challenges to established orthodoxies in China and India emerged as commercial and urban life, as well as political change, fostered new thinking.

China during the Ming and Qing dynasties continued to operate broadly within a Confucian framework, enriched now by the insights of Buddhism and Daoism to generate a system of thought called Neo-Confucianism. Chinese Ming dynasty rulers, in their aversion to the despised Mongols, embraced and actively supported this native Confucian tradition, whereas the foreign Manchu or Qing rulers did so to woo Chinese intellectuals to support the new dynasty. Within this context, a considerable amount of controversy, debate, and new thinking emerged during the early modern era.

During late Ming times, for example, the influential thinker Wang Yangming (1472–1529) argued that "intuitive moral knowledge exists in people . . . even robbers know that they should not rob."[11] Thus anyone could achieve a virtuous life by introspection and contemplation, without the extended education, study of classical texts, and constant striving for improvement that traditional Confucianism prescribed for an elite class of "gentlemen." Such ideas figured prominently among Confucian scholars of the sixteenth century, although critics later contended that such thinking promoted an excessive individualism. They also argued that Wang Yangming's ideas had undermined the Ming dynasty and contributed to China's conquest by the foreign Manchus. Some Chinese Buddhists as well sought to make their religion more accessible to ordinary people, by suggesting that laypeople at home could undertake practices similar to those performed by monks in monasteries. Withdrawal from the world was not necessary for enlightenment. This kind of moral or religious individualism bore some similarity to the thinking of Martin Luther, who argued that individuals could seek salvation by "faith alone," without the assistance of a priestly hierarchy.

Another new direction in Chinese elite culture took shape in a movement known as *kaozheng*, or "research based on evidence." Intended to "seek truth from facts," kaozheng was critical of the unfounded speculation of conventional Confucian philosophy and instead emphasized the importance of verification, precision, accuracy, and rigorous analysis in all fields of inquiry. During the late Ming years, this emphasis generated works dealing with agriculture, medicine, pharmacology, botany, craft techniques, and more. In the Qing era, kaozheng was associated with the recovery and critical analysis of ancient historical documents, which sometimes led to sharp criticism of Neo-Confucian orthodoxy. It was a genuinely scientific approach to knowledge, but it was applied more to the study of the past than to the natural world of astronomy, physics, or anatomy, which was the focus in the West.

While such matters occupied the intellectual elite of China, in the cities a lively popular culture emerged among the less educated. For city-dwellers, plays, paintings, short stories, and especially novels provided diversion and entertainment that were a step up from what could be found in teahouses and wineshops. Numerous "how-to" painting manuals allowed a larger public to participate in this favorite

Guided Reading Question

■ CHANGE
What kinds of cultural changes occurred in China and India during the early modern era?

AP® EXAM TIP

Pay attention to factors that led to the rise of Neo-Confucianism. List the ways in which it differed from traditional Confucianism.

Chinese art form. Even though Confucian scholars disdained popular fiction, a vigorous printing industry responded to the growing demand for exciting novels. The most famous was Cao Xueqin's mid-eighteenth-century novel *The Dream of the Red Chamber*, a huge book that contained 120 chapters and some 400 characters, most of them women. It explored the social life of an eighteenth-century elite family with connections to the Chinese court.

India: Bridging the Hindu/Muslim Divide

In a largely Hindu India, ruled by the Muslim Mughal Empire, several significant cultural departures took shape in the early modern era that brought Hindus and Muslims together in new forms of religious expression. At the level of elite culture, the Mughal ruler Akbar formulated a state cult that combined elements of Islam, Hinduism, and Zoroastrianism (see Chapter 13, page 581). The Mughal court also embraced Renaissance Christian art, and soon murals featuring Jesus, Mary, and Christian saints appeared on the walls of palaces, garden pavilions, and harems. The court also commissioned a prominent Sufi spiritual master to compose an illustrated book describing various Hindu yoga postures. Intended to bring this Hindu tradition into Islamic Sufi practice, the book, known as the *Ocean of Life*, portrayed some of the yogis in a Christ-like fashion.

Within popular culture, the flourishing of a devotional form of Hinduism known as *bhakti* also bridged the gulf separating Hindu and Muslim. Through songs, prayers, dances, poetry, and rituals, devotees sought to achieve union with one or another of India's many deities. Appealing especially to women, the bhakti movement provided an avenue for social criticism. Its practitioners often set aside caste distinctions and disregarded the detailed rituals of the Brahmin priests in favor of direct contact with the Divine. This emphasis had much in common with mystical Sufi forms of Islam and helped blur the distinction between these two traditions in India.

Among the most beloved of bhakti poets was Mirabai (1498–1547), a high-caste woman from northern India who abandoned her upper-class family and conventional Hindu practice. Upon her husband's death, tradition asserts, she declined to burn herself on his funeral pyre (a practice known as *sati*). She further offended caste restrictions by

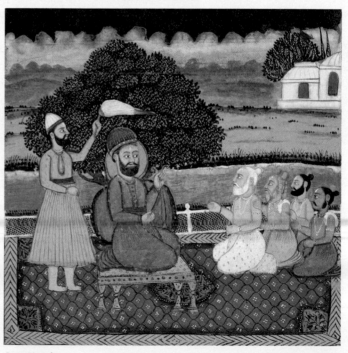

Guru Nanak
This painting shows a seated Guru Nanak, the founder of Sikhism, disputing with four kneeling Hindu holy men. (British Library, London, UK/© British Library Board. All Rights Reserved/Robena/Art Resource, NY)

taking as her guru (religious teacher) an old untouchable shoemaker. To visit him, she apparently tied her saris together and climbed down the castle walls at night. Then she would wash his aged feet and drink the water from these ablutions. Much of her poetry deals with her yearning for union with Krishna, a Hindu deity she regarded as her husband, lover, and lord. She wrote:

> What I paid was my social body, my town body, my family body, and all my inherited jewels. Mirabai says: The Dark One [Krishna] is my husband now.[12]

Yet another major cultural change that blended Islam and Hinduism emerged with the growth of Sikhism as a new and distinctive religious tradition in the Punjab region of northern India. Its founder, Guru Nanak (1469–1539), had been involved in the bhakti movement but came to believe that "there is no Hindu; there is no Muslim; only God." His teachings and those of subsequent gurus also generally ignored caste distinctions and untouchability and ended the seclusion of women, while proclaiming the "brotherhood of all mankind" as well as the essential equality of men and women. Drawing converts from Punjabi peasants and merchants, both Muslim and Hindu, the Sikhs gradually became a separate religious community. They developed their own sacred book, known as the Guru Granth (teacher book); created a central place of worship and pilgrimage in the Golden Temple of Amritsar; and prescribed certain dress requirements for men, including keeping hair and beards uncut, wearing a turban, and carrying a short sword. During the seventeenth century, Sikhs encountered hostility from both the Mughal Empire and some of their Hindu neighbors. In response, Sikhism evolved from a peaceful religious movement, blending Hindu and Muslim elements, into a militant community whose military skills were highly valued by the British when they took over India in the late eighteenth century.

PRACTICING AP® HISTORICAL THINKING

In what ways did religious changes in Asia and the Middle East parallel those in Europe, and in what ways were they different?

A New Way of Thinking: The Birth of Modern Science

AP® EXAM TIP

You must know about the causes, as well as the consequences, of the Scientific Revolution to have success on the AP® exam.

While some Europeans were actively attempting to spread the Christian faith to distant corners of the world, others were nurturing an understanding of the cosmos at least partially at odds with traditional Christian teaching. These were the makers of Europe's Scientific Revolution, a vast intellectual and cultural transformation that took place between the mid-sixteenth and early eighteenth centuries. These men of science would no longer rely on the external authority of the Bible, the Church, the speculations of ancient philosophers, or the received wisdom of cultural tradition. For them, knowledge would be acquired through rational inquiry based on evidence, the product of human minds alone. Those who created this revolution—Copernicus from Poland, Galileo from Italy, Descartes from France,

Newton from England, and many others—saw themselves as departing radically from older ways of thinking. "The old rubbish must be thrown away," wrote a seventeenth-century English scientist. "These are the days that must lay a new Foundation of a more magnificent Philosophy."[13]

The long-term significance of the Scientific Revolution can hardly be overestimated. Within early modern Europe, it fundamentally altered ideas about the place of humankind within the cosmos and sharply challenged both the teachings and the authority of the Church. Over the past several centuries, it has substantially eroded religious belief and practice in the West, particularly among the well educated. When applied to the affairs of human society, scientific ways of thinking challenged ancient social hierarchies and political systems and played a role in the revolutionary upheavals of the modern era. But science was also used to legitimize racial and gender inequalities, giving new support to old ideas about the natural inferiority of women and enslaved people. When married to the technological innovations of the Industrial Revolution, science fostered both the marvels of modern production and the horrors of modern means of destruction. By the twentieth century, science had become so widespread that it largely lost its association with European culture and became the chief marker of global modernity. Like Buddhism, Christianity, and Islam, modern science became a universal worldview, open to all who could accept its premises and its techniques.

The Question of Origins: Why Europe?

Why did the breakthrough of the Scientific Revolution occur first in Europe and during the early modern era? The realm of Islam, after all, had generated the most advanced science in the world during the centuries between 800 and 1400. Arab scholars could boast of remarkable achievements in mathematics, astronomy, optics, and medicine, and their libraries far exceeded those of Europe.[14] And what of China? Its elite culture of Confucianism was both sophisticated and secular, less burdened by religious dogma than that of the Christian or Islamic worlds; its technological accomplishments and economic growth were unmatched anywhere in the several centuries after 1000. In neither civilization, however, did these achievements lead to the kind of intellectual innovation that occurred in Europe.

Europe's historical development as a reinvigorated and fragmented civilization arguably gave rise to conditions particularly favorable to the scientific enterprise. By the twelfth and thirteenth centuries, Europeans had evolved a legal system that guaranteed a measure of independence for a variety of institutions—the Church, towns and cities, guilds, professional associations, and universities. This legal revolution was based on the idea of a "corporation," a collective group of people that was treated as a unit, a legal person, with certain rights to regulate and control its own members.

Most important for the development of science in the West was the autonomy of its emerging universities. By 1215, the University of Paris was recognized as a

Guided Reading Question

■ COMPARISON
Why did the Scientific Revolution occur in Europe rather than in China or the Islamic world?

AP® EXAM TIP

Here's another example of the roles played by cities in world history: the rise of universities in major European towns.

"corporation of masters and scholars," which could admit and expel students, establish courses of instruction, and grant a "license to teach" to its faculty. Such universities — for example, in Paris, Bologna, Oxford, Cambridge, and Salamanca — became "neutral zones of intellectual autonomy" in which scholars could pursue their studies in relative freedom from the dictates of church or state authorities. Within them, the study of the natural order began to slowly separate itself from philosophy and theology and to gain a distinct identity. Their curricula featured "a basically scientific core of readings and lectures" that drew heavily on the writings of the Greek thinker Aristotle, which had only recently become available to Western Europeans. Most of the major figures in the Scientific Revolution had been trained in and were affiliated with these universities.

In the Islamic world, by contrast, science was patronized by a variety of local authorities, but it occurred largely outside the formal system of higher education. Within colleges known as madrassas, Quranic studies and religious law held the central place, whereas philosophy and natural science were viewed with great suspicion. To religious scholars, the Quran held all wisdom, and scientific thinking might well challenge it. An earlier openness to free inquiry and religious toleration was increasingly replaced by a disdain for scientific and philosophical inquiry, for it seemed to lead only to uncertainty and confusion. "May God protect us from useless knowledge" was a saying that reflected this outlook. Nor did Chinese authorities permit independent institutions of higher learning in which scholars could conduct their studies in relative freedom. Instead, Chinese education focused on preparing for a rigidly defined set of civil service examinations and emphasized the humanistic and moral texts of classical Confucianism. "The pursuit of scientific subjects," one recent historian concluded, "was thereby relegated to the margins of Chinese society."[15]

Beyond its distinctive institutional development, Western Europe was in a position to draw extensively on the knowledge of other cultures, especially that of the Islamic world. Arab medical texts, astronomical research, and translations of Greek classics played a major role in the birth of European natural philosophy (as science was then called) between 1000 and 1500. Then, in the sixteenth through the eighteenth centuries, Europeans found themselves at the center of a massive new exchange of information as they became aware of lands, peoples, plants, animals, societies, and religions from around the world. This tidal wave of new knowledge, uniquely available to Europeans, shook up older ways of thinking and opened the way to new conceptions of the world. The sixteenth-century Italian doctor, mathematician, and writer Girolamo Cardano (1501–1576) clearly expressed this sense of wonderment: "The most unusual [circumstance of my life] is that I was born in this century in which the whole world became known; whereas the ancients were familiar with but a little more than a third part of it." He worried, however, that amid this explosion of knowledge, "certainties will be exchanged for uncertainties."[16] It was precisely those uncertainties — skepticism about established views — that provided such a fertile cultural ground for the emergence of modern science.

AP® EXAM TIP

Read this paragraph twice and take notes; it's a good example of how cross-cultural interactions create change.

The Reformation too contributed to that cultural climate in its challenge to authority, its encouragement of mass literacy, and its affirmation of secular professions.

Science as Cultural Revolution

Before the Scientific Revolution, educated Europeans held a view of the world
that derived from Aristotle, perhaps the greatest of the ancient Greek philosophers,
and from Ptolemy, a Greco-Egyptian mathematician and astronomer who lived
in Alexandria during the second century C.E. To medieval European thinkers, the
earth was stationary and at the center of the universe, and around it revolved the
sun, moon, and stars embedded in ten spheres of transparent crystal. This understanding coincided well with the religious outlook of the Catholic Church because
the attention of the entire universe was centered on the earth and its human inhabitants, among whom God's plan for salvation unfolded. It was a universe of divine
purpose, with angels guiding the hierarchically arranged heavenly bodies along
their way while God watched over the whole from his realm beyond the spheres.
The Scientific Revolution was revolutionary because it fundamentally challenged
this understanding of the universe.

The initial breakthrough in the Scientific Revolution came from the Polish
mathematician and astronomer Nicolaus Copernicus, whose famous book *On the
Revolutions of the Heavenly Spheres* was published in the year of his death, 1543. Its
essential argument was that "at the middle of all things lies the sun" and that the
earth, like the other planets, revolved around it. Thus the earth was no longer
unique or at the obvious center of God's attention.

Other European scientists built on Copernicus's central insight, and some even
argued that other inhabited worlds and other kinds of humans existed. Less specula-
tively, in the early seventeenth century Johannes Kepler, a German mathematician,
showed that the planets followed elliptical orbits, undermining the ancient belief that
they moved in perfect circles. The Italian Galileo (gal-uh-LAY-oh) developed an
improved telescope, with which he made many observations that undermined established understandings of the cosmos. (See Zooming In: Galileo and the Telescope,
page 668.) Some thinkers began to discuss the notion of an unlimited universe in
which humankind occupied a mere speck of dust in an unimaginable vastness. The
French mathematician and philosopher Blaise Pascal (1623–1662) perhaps spoke for
many when he wrote, "The eternal silence of infinite space frightens me."[17]

The culmination of the Scientific Revolution came in the work of Sir Isaac
Newton (1642–1727), the Englishman who formulated the modern laws of motion
and mechanics, which remained unchallenged until the twentieth century. At the
core of Newton's thinking was the concept of universal gravitation. "All bodies
whatsoever," Newton declared, "are endowed with a principle of mutual gravitation."[18] Here was the grand unifying idea of early modern science. The radical
implication of this view was that the heavens and the earth, long regarded as separate
and distinct spheres, were not so different after all, for the motion of a cannonball

AP® EXAM TIP

The Scientific Revo-
lution marked a
major turning point
in the way Western-
ers saw the world
around them. Pay
close attention to
this section.

**Guided Reading
Question**

■ CHANGE
What was revolutionary
about the Scientific
Revolution?

ZOOMING IN

Galileo and the Telescope: Reflecting on Science and Religion

The Scientific Revolution was predicated on the idea that knowledge of how the universe worked was acquired through a combination of careful observations, controlled experiments, and the formulation of general laws, expressed in mathematical terms. New scientific instruments capable of making precise empirical observations underpinned some of the most important break-

Galileo on trial.

throughs of the period. Perhaps no single invention produced more dramatic discoveries than the telescope, the first of which were produced in the early seventeenth century by Dutch eyeglass makers.

The impact of new instruments depended on how scientists employed them. In the case of the telescope, it was the brilliant Italian mathematician and astronomer Galileo Galilei (1564–1642) who unlocked its potential when he used it to observe the night sky. Within months of creating his own telescope, which improved on earlier designs, Galileo made a series of discoveries that put into question well-established understandings of the cosmos. He observed craters on the moon and sunspots, or blemishes, moving across the face of the sun, which challenged the traditional notion that no imperfection or change

marred the heavenly bodies. Moreover, his discovery of the moons of Jupiter and many new stars suggested a cosmos far larger than the finite universe of traditional astronomy. In 1610, Galileo published his remarkable findings in a book titled *The Starry Messenger*, where he emphasized time and again that his precise observations provided irrefutable evidence of a cosmos unlike that described by traditional authorities. "With the aid of the telescope," he argued, "this has been scrutinized so directly and with such ocular certainty that all the disputes which have vexed the philosophers through so many ages have been resolved, and we are at last freed from wordy debates about it."[19]

Galileo's empirical evidence transformed the debate over the nature of the cosmos. His dramatic and unexpected discoveries were readily grasped, and with the aid of a telescope anyone could confirm their veracity. His initial findings were heralded by many in the scientific community, including Christoph Clavius, the Church's leading astronomer in Rome. Galileo's findings led him

photo: *Trial of Galileo*, 1633, oil on canvas, Italian/Private Collection/Bridgeman Images

or the falling of an apple obeyed the same natural laws that governed the orbiting planets.

By the time Newton died, a revolutionary new understanding of the physical universe had emerged among educated Europeans: the universe was no longer propelled by supernatural forces but functioned on its own according to scientific principles that could be described mathematically. Articulating this view, Kepler wrote, "The machine of the universe is not similar to a divine animated being but similar to a clock."[20] Furthermore, it was a machine that regulated itself, requiring neither God nor angels to account for its normal operation. Knowledge of that universe could be obtained through human reason alone — by observation, deduction, and experimentation — without the aid of ancient authorities or divine reveto conclude that Copernicus (1473–1543), an earlier astronomer and mathematician, had been correct when he had advanced the theory that the sun rather than the earth was at the center of the solar system. But Galileo's evidence could not definitively prove Copernicus's theory to the satisfaction of critics, leading Galileo to study other phenomena, such as the tides, that could provide further evidence that the earth was in motion.

When the Church condemned Copernicus's theory in 1616, it remained silent on Galileo's astronomical observations, instead warning him to refrain from teaching or promoting Copernicus's ideas. Ultimately, though, Galileo came into conflict with church authorities when in 1629 he published, with what he thought was the consent of the Church, the *Dialogue Concerning the Two Chief World Systems*, a work sympathetic to Copernicus's sun-centric system. In 1632, Galileo was tried by the Roman Inquisition, an ecclesiastical court charged with maintaining orthodoxy, and convicted of teaching doctrines against the express orders of the Church. He recanted his beliefs and at the age of sixty-nine was sentenced to house arrest.

Although Galileo was formally convicted of disobeying the Church's order to remain silent on the issue of Copernicus's theory, the question most fundamentally at stake in the trial was "What does it mean, 'to know something'?"[21] This question of the relationship between scientific knowledge, primarily concerned with how the universe works, and other forms of "knowledge," derived from divine revelation or mystical experience, has persisted in the West. Over 350 years after the trial, Pope John Paul II spoke of Galileo's conviction in a public speech in 1992, declaring it a "sad misunderstanding" that belongs to the past, but one with ongoing resonance because "the underlying problems of this case concern both the nature of science and the message of faith." Addressing the central question of what it means to know something, the pope declared scientific and religious knowledge to be compatible: "There exist two realms of knowledge, one which has its source in Revelation and one which reason can discover by its own power. . . . The distinction between the two realms of knowledge ought not to be understood as opposition. . . . The methodologies proper to each make it possible to bring out different aspects of reality."[22]

Strangely enough, Galileo himself had expressed something similar centuries earlier. "Nor is God," he wrote, "any less excellently revealed in Nature's actions than in the sacred statements of the Bible."[23] Finding the place of new scientific knowledge in a constellation of older wisdom traditions proved a fraught but highly significant development in the emergence of the modern world.

Question: What can Galileo's discoveries with his telescope and his conviction by the Inquisition tell us about the Scientific Revolution?

lation. The French philosopher René Descartes (day-KAHRT) resolved "to seek no other knowledge than that which I might find within myself, or perhaps in the book of nature."[24]

Like the physical universe, the human body also lost some of its mystery. The careful dissections of cadavers and animals enabled doctors and scientists to describe the human body with much greater accuracy and to understand the circulation of the blood throughout the body. The heart was no longer the mysterious center of the body's heat and the seat of its passions; instead it was just another machine, a complex muscle that functioned as a pump.

The movers and shakers of this enormous cultural transformation were almost entirely male. European women, after all, had been largely excluded from the

The Telescope
Johannes Hevelius, an astronomer of German Lutheran background living in what is now Poland, constructed extraordinarily long telescopes in the mid-seventeenth century with which he observed sunspots, charted the surface of the moon, and discovered several comets. Such telescopes played a central role in transforming understandings of the universe during the Scientific Revolution. (© World History Archive/Alamy)

AP® EXAM TIP

Compare examples of cooperation and conflict between science and religion in Europe to examples of these in the Islamic world in this era.

universities where much of the new science was discussed. A few aristocratic women, however, had the leisure and connections to participate informally in the scientific networks of their male relatives. Through her marriage to the Duke of Newcastle, Margaret Cavendish (1623–1673) joined in conversations with a circle of "natural philosophers," wrote six scientific texts, and was the only seventeenth-century English woman to attend a session of the Royal Society of London, created to foster scientific learning. In Germany, a number of women took part in astronomical work as assistants to their husbands or brothers. Maria Winkelman, for example, discovered a previously unknown comet, though her husband took credit for it. After his death, she sought to continue his work in the Berlin Academy of Sciences but was refused on the grounds that "mouths would gape" if a woman held such a position.

Much of this scientific thinking developed in the face of strenuous opposition from the Catholic Church, for both its teachings and its authority were under attack. The Italian philosopher Giordano Bruno, proclaiming an infinite universe and many worlds, was burned at the stake in 1600, and Galileo was compelled by the Church to publicly renounce his belief that the earth moved around an orbit and rotated on its axis.

But scholars have sometimes exaggerated the conflict of science and religion, casting it in military terms as an almost unbroken war. None of the early scientists rejected Christianity. Copernicus in fact published his famous book with the support of several leading Catholic churchmen and dedicated it to the pope. After all, several earlier Catholic writers had proposed the idea of the earth in motion. He more likely feared the criticism of fellow scientists than that of the church hierarchy. Galileo himself proclaimed the compatibility of science and faith, and his lack of diplomacy in dealing with church leaders was at least in part responsible for his quarrel with the Church.[25] Newton was a serious biblical scholar and saw no inherent contradiction between his ideas and belief in God. "This most beautiful system of the sun, planets, and comets," he declared, "could only proceed from the counsel and dominion of an intelligent Being."[26] Thus the Church gradually accommodated as well as resisted the new ideas, largely by compartmentalizing them. Science might prevail in its limited sphere of describing the physical universe, but religion was still the arbiter of truth about those ultimate questions concerning human salvation, righteous behavior, and the larger purposes of life.

Science and Enlightenment

Initially limited to a small handful of scholars, the ideas of the Scientific Revolution spread to a wider European public during the eighteenth century. That process was aided by novel techniques of printing and bookmaking, by a popular press, by growing literacy, and by a host of scientific societies. Moreover, the new approach to knowledge—rooted in human reason, skeptical of authority, expressed in natural laws—was now applied to human affairs, not just to the physical universe. The Scottish professor Adam Smith (1723–1790), for example, formulated laws that accounted for the operation of the economy and that, if followed, he believed, would generate inevitably favorable results for society. Growing numbers of people believed that the long-term outcome of scientific development would be "enlightenment," a term that has come to define the eighteenth century in European history. If human reason could discover the laws that governed the universe, surely it could uncover ways in which humankind might govern itself more effectively.

"What is Enlightenment?" asked the prominent German intellectual Immanuel Kant (1724–1804). "It is man's emergence from his self-imposed . . . inability to use one's own understanding without another's guidance. . . . Dare to know! 'Have the courage to use your own understanding' is therefore the motto of the enlightenment."[27] Although they often disagreed sharply with one another, European Enlightenment thinkers shared this belief in the power of knowledge to transform human society. They also shared a satirical, critical style, a commitment to open-mindedness and inquiry, and in various degrees a hostility to established political and religious authority. Many took aim at arbitrary governments, the "divine right of kings," and the aristocratic privileges of European society. The English philosopher John Locke (1632–1704) offered principles for constructing a constitutional government, a contract between rulers and ruled that was created by human ingenuity rather than divinely prescribed. Much of Enlightenment thinking was directed against the superstition, ignorance, and corruption of established religion. In his *Treatise on Toleration*, the French writer Voltaire (1694–1778) reflected the outlook of the Scientific Revolution as he commented sarcastically on religious intolerance:

> This little globe, nothing more than a point, rolls in space like so many other globes; we are lost in its immensity. Man, some five feet tall, is surely a very small part of the universe. One of these imperceptible beings says to some of his neighbors in Arabia or Africa: "Listen to me, for the God of all these worlds has enlightened me; there are nine hundred million little ants like us on the earth, but only my anthill is beloved of God; He will hold all others in horror through all eternity; only mine will be blessed, the others will be eternally wretched."[28]

Voltaire's own faith, like that of many others among the "enlightened," was deism. Deists believed in a rather abstract and remote Deity, sometimes compared to a clockmaker, who had created the world, but not in a personal God who intervened

AP® EXAM TIP

The AP® exam might ask you to explain how Europe's new views of science led to new ideas about human government and philosophies.

Guided Reading Question

■ CHANGE

In what ways did the Enlightenment challenge older patterns of European thinking?

The Philosophers of the Enlightenment
This painting shows the French philosopher Voltaire with a group of intellectual luminaries at the summer palace of the Prussian king Frederick II. Such literary gatherings, sometimes called salons, were places of lively conversation among mostly male participants and came to be seen as emblematic of the European Enlightenment. (Painting by Adolph Menzel [1815–1905], 1850/© akg-images/The Image Works)

in history or tampered with natural law. Others became *pantheists*, who believed that God and nature were identical. Here was a conception of religion shaped by the outlook of science. Sometimes called "natural religion," it was devoid of mystery, revelation, ritual, and spiritual practice, while proclaiming a God that could be "proven" by human rationality, logic, and the techniques of scientific inquiry. In this view, all else was superstition. Among the most radical of such thinkers were the several Dutchmen who wrote the *Treatise of Three Imposters*, which claimed that Moses, Jesus, and Muhammad were fraudulent impostors who based their teachings on "the ignorance of Peoples [and] resolved to keep them in it."[29]

Prominent among the debates spawned by the Enlightenment was the question of women's nature, their role in society, and the education most appropriate for them. Although well-to-do Parisian women hosted in their elegant salons many gatherings of the largely male Enlightenment figures, most of those men were anything but ardent feminists. The male editors of the famous *Encyclopédie*, a vast compendium of Enlightenment thought, included very few essays by women. One of the male authors expressed a common view: "[Women] constitute the

AP® EXAM TIP

Pay attention to how the Enlightenment led to new ideas about women's roles in Western society.

principal ornament of the world. . . . May they, through submissive discretion and . . . artless cleverness, spur us [men] on to virtue." In his treatise *Emile*, Jean-Jacques Rousseau described women as fundamentally different from and inferior to men and urged that "the whole education of women ought to be relative to men."

Such views were sharply contested by any number of other Enlightenment figures—men and women alike. The *Journal des Dames* (Ladies Journal), founded in Paris in 1759, aggressively defended women. "If we have not been raised up in the sciences as you have," declared Madame Beaulmer, the *Journal*'s first editor, "it is you [men] who are the guilty ones; for have you not always abused . . . the bodily strength that nature has given you?"[30] The philosopher Condorcet looked forward to the "complete destruction of those prejudices that have established an inequality of rights between the sexes." And in 1792, the British writer Mary Wollstonecraft directly confronted Rousseau's view of women and their education: "What nonsense! . . . Til women are more rationally educated, the progress of human virtue and improvement in knowledge must receive continual checks." Thus was initiated a debate that echoed throughout the centuries that followed.

Though solidly rooted in Europe, Enlightenment thought was influenced by the growing global awareness of its major thinkers. Voltaire, for example, idealized China as an empire governed by an elite of secular scholars selected for their talent, which stood in sharp contrast to continental Europe, where aristocratic birth and military prowess were far more important. The example of Confucianism—supposedly secular, moral, rational, and tolerant—encouraged Enlightenment thinkers to imagine a future for European civilization without the kind of supernatural religion that they found so offensive in the Christian West.

The central theme of the Enlightenment—and what made it potentially revolutionary—was the idea of progress. Human society was not fixed by tradition or divine command but could be changed, and improved, by human action guided by reason. No one expressed this soaring confidence in human possibility more clearly than the French thinker the Marquis de Condorcet (1743–1794), who boldly declared that "the perfectibility of humanity is indefinite." Belief in progress was a sharp departure from much of premodern social thinking, and it inspired those who later made the great revolutions of the modern era in the Americas, France, Russia, China, and elsewhere. Born of the Scientific Revolution, that was the faith of the Enlightenment. For some, it was virtually a new religion.

The age of the Enlightenment, however, also witnessed a reaction against too much reliance on human reason. Jean-Jacques Rousseau (1712–1778) minimized the importance of book learning for the education of children and prescribed instead an immersion in nature, which taught self-reliance and generosity rather than the greed and envy fostered by "civilization." The Romantic movement in art and literature appealed to emotion, intuition, passion, and imagination rather than cold reason and scientific learning. Religious awakenings—complete with fiery sermons, public repentance, and intense personal experience of sin and redemption—shook Protestant Europe and North America in the eighteenth and early

AP® EXAM TIP

It's important to note that the Scientific Revolution led to the Enlightenment ("Age of Reason"), which led to major political and social reforms during the eighteenth and nineteenth centuries.

nineteenth centuries. The Methodist movement — with its emphasis on Bible study, confession of sins, fasting, enthusiastic preaching, and resistance to worldly pleasures — was a case in point.

Various forms of "enlightened religion" also arose in the early modern centuries, reflecting the influence of Enlightenment thinking. Quakers, for example, emphasized tolerance, an absence of hierarchy and ostentation, a benevolent God, and an "inner light" available to all people. Unitarians denied the Trinity, original sin, predestination, and the divinity of Jesus, but honored him as a great teacher and a moral prophet. Later, in the nineteenth century, proponents of the "social gospel" saw the essence of Christianity not in personal salvation but in ethical behavior. Science and the Enlightenment surely challenged religion, and for some they eroded religious belief and practice. Just as surely, though, religion persisted, adapted, and revived for many others.

Looking Ahead: Science in the Nineteenth Century and Beyond

The perspectives of the Enlightenment were challenged not only by romanticism and religious "enthusiasm" but also by the continued development of European science itself. This remarkable phenomenon justifies a brief look ahead at several scientific developments in the nineteenth and twentieth centuries.

Guided Reading Question

■ CHANGE
How did nineteenth-century developments in the sciences challenge the faith of the Enlightenment?

Modern science was a cumulative and self-critical enterprise, which in the nineteenth century and later was applied to new domains of human inquiry in ways that undermined some of the assumptions of the Enlightenment. In the realm of biology, for example, Charles Darwin (1809–1882) laid out a complex argument that all life was in constant change, that an endless and competitive struggle for survival over millions of years constantly generated new species of plants and animals, while casting others into extinction. Human beings were not excluded from this vast process, for they too were the work of evolution operating through natural selection. Darwin's famous books *The Origin of Species* (1859) and *The Descent of Man* (1871) were threatening to many traditional Christian believers, perhaps more so than Copernicus's ideas about a sun-centered universe had been several centuries earlier.

At the same time, Karl Marx (1818–1883) articulated a view of human history that likewise emphasized change and struggle. Conflicting social classes — slave owners and slaves, nobles and peasants, capitalists and workers — successively drove the process of historical transformation. Although he was describing the evolution of human civilization, Marx saw himself as a scientist. He based his theories on extensive historical research; like Newton and Darwin, he sought to formulate general laws that would explain events in a rational way. Nor did he believe in heavenly intervention, chance, or the divinely endowed powers of kings. The coming of socialism, in this view, was not simply a good idea; it was inscribed in the laws of historical development. (See Working with Evidence, Source 17.1, page 776.)

Like the intellectuals of the Enlightenment, Darwin and Marx believed strongly in progress, but in their thinking, conflict and struggle rather than reason and education were the motors of progress. The Enlightenment image of the thoughtful, rational, and independent individual was fading. Individuals—plant, animal, and human alike—were now viewed as enmeshed in vast systems of biological, economic, and social conflict.

The work of the Viennese doctor Sigmund Freud (1856–1939) applied scientific techniques to the operation of the human mind and emotions and in doing so cast further doubt on Enlightenment conceptions of human rationality. At the core of each person, Freud argued, lay primal impulses toward sexuality and aggression, which were only barely held in check by the thin veneer of social conscience derived from civilization. Our neuroses arose from the ceaseless struggle between our irrational drives and the claims of conscience. This too was a far cry from the Enlightenment conception of the human condition.

And in the twentieth century, developments in physics, such as relativity and quantum theory, called into question some of the established verities of the Newtonian view of the world, particularly at the subatomic level and at speeds approaching that of light. In this new physics, time is relative to the position of the observer; space can warp and light can bend; matter and energy are equivalent; black holes and dark matter abound; and probability, not certain prediction, is the best that scientists can hope for. None of this was even on the horizon of those who made the original Scientific Revolution in the early modern era.

European Science beyond the West

In the long run, the achievements of the Scientific Revolution spread globally, becoming the most widely sought-after product of European culture and far more desired than Christianity, democracy, socialism, or Western literature. In the early modern era, however, interest in European scientific thinking within major Asian societies was both modest and selective. The telescope provides an example. Invented in early seventeenth-century Europe and endlessly improved in the centuries that followed, the telescope provoked enormous excitement in European scientific circles. It made possible any number of astronomical discoveries, including the rugged surface of the moon, the moons of Jupiter, the rings of Saturn, and the phases of Venus. "We are here . . . on fire with these things," wrote an English astronomer in 1610.[31] Soon the telescope was available in China, Mughal India, and the Ottoman Empire. But in none of these places did it evoke much interest or evolve into the kind of "discovery machine" that it was rapidly becoming in Europe.

In China, Qing dynasty emperors and scholars were most interested in European techniques, derived largely from Jesuit missionaries, for predicting eclipses, reforming the calendar, and making accurate maps of the empire. European medicine, however, was of little importance for Chinese physicians before the nineteenth century. But the reputation of the Jesuits suffered when it became apparent in the 1760s that for two centuries the missionaries had withheld information about Copernican views of a sun-centered solar system because those ideas had been condemned by the Church. Nonetheless, European science had a substantial impact on

Guided Reading Question

■ CONNECTION

In what ways was European science received in the major civilizations of Asia in the early modern era?

a number of Chinese scholars as it seemed compatible with the data-based kaozheng movement, described by one participant as "an ant-like accumulation of facts."[32] European mathematics was of particular interest to kaozheng researchers who were exploring the history of Chinese mathematics. To convince their skeptical colleagues that the barbarian Europeans had something to offer in this field, some Chinese scholars argued that European mathematics had in fact grown out of much earlier Chinese ideas and could therefore be adopted with comfort.[33] In such ways, early modern Chinese thinkers selectively assimilated Western science very much on their own terms.[34]

AP® EXAM TIP

Know that Japan has a greater tradition of cultural borrowing than China. This will become more evident in the nineteenth century.

Although Japanese authorities largely closed their country off from the West in the early seventeenth century (see Chapter 14), one window remained open. Alone among Europeans, the Dutch were permitted to trade in Japan at a single location near Nagasaki, but not until 1720 did the Japanese lift the ban on importing Western books. Then a number of European texts in medicine, astronomy, geography, mathematics, and other disciplines were translated and studied by a small group of Japanese scholars. They were especially impressed with Western anatomical studies, for in Japan dissection was work fit only for outcasts. Returning from an autopsy conducted by Dutch physicians in the mid-eighteenth century, several Japanese observers reflected on their experience: "We remarked to each other how amazing the autopsy had been, and how inexcusable it had been for us to be ignorant of the anatomical structure of the human body."[35] Nonetheless, this small center of "Dutch learning," as it was called, remained isolated amid a pervasive Confucian-based culture. Not until the mid-nineteenth century, when Japan was forcibly opened to Western penetration, would European-style science assume a prominent place in Japanese culture.

AP® EXAM TIP

Pay attention to the similar reactions of China, Japan, and the Ottoman Empire to the Scientific Revolution.

Like China and Japan, the Ottoman Empire in the sixteenth and seventeenth centuries was an independent, powerful, successful society whose intellectual elites saw no need for a wholesale embrace of things European. Ottoman scholars were conscious of the rich tradition of Muslim astronomy and chose not to translate the works of major European scientists such as Copernicus, Kepler, or Newton, although they were broadly aware of European scientific achievements by 1650. Insofar as they were interested in these developments, it was for their practical usefulness in making maps and calendars rather than for their larger philosophical implications. In any event, the notion of a sun-centered solar system did not cause the kind of upset that it did in Europe.

More broadly, theoretical science of any kind—Muslim or European—faced an uphill struggle in the face of a conservative Islamic educational system. In 1580, for example, a highly sophisticated astronomical observatory was dismantled under pressure from conservative religious scholars and teachers, who interpreted an outbreak of the plague as God's disapproval with those who sought to understand his secrets. As in Japan, the systematic embrace of Western science would have to await the nineteenth century, when the Ottoman Empire was under far more intense European pressure and reform seemed more necessary.

Cultural Borrowing and Its Hazards

Ideas are important in human history. They shape the mental or cultural worlds that people everywhere inhabit, and they often influence behavior as well. Many of the ideas developed or introduced during the early modern era have had enormous and continuing significance in the centuries that followed. The Western Hemisphere was solidly incorporated into Christendom. A Wahhabi version of Islam remains the official faith of Saudi Arabia into the twenty-first century and has influenced many contemporary Islamic revival movements, including al-Qaeda. Modern science and the associated notions of progress have become for many people something approaching a new religion.

Accompanying the development of these ideas has been a great deal of cultural borrowing. Filipinos, Siberians, and many Native American peoples borrowed elements of Christianity from Europeans. Numerous Asian and African peoples borrowed Islam from the Arabs. North Indian Sikhs drew on both Hindu and Muslim teachings. Europeans borrowed scientific and medical ideas from the Islamic world and subsequently contributed their own rich scientific thinking to the entire planet.

In virtually every case, though, borrowing was selective rather than wholesale, even when it took place under conditions of foreign domination or colonial rule. Many peoples who appropriated Christianity or Islam certainly did not accept the rigid exclusivity and ardent monotheism of more orthodox versions of those faiths. Elite Chinese were far more interested in European mapmaking and mathematics than in Western medicine, while Japanese scholars became fascinated with the anatomical work of the Dutch. Neither, however, adopted Christianity in a widespread manner.

Borrowing was frequently the occasion for serious conflict. Some objected to much borrowing at all, particularly when it occurred under conditions of foreign domination or foreign threat. Thus members of the Taki Onqoy movement in Peru sought to wipe out Spanish influence and control, while Chinese and Japanese authorities clamped down firmly on European missionaries, even as they maintained some interest in European technological and scientific skills. Another kind of conflict derived from the efforts to control the terms of cultural borrowing. For example, European missionaries and Muslim reformers alike sought to root out "idolatry" among native converts.

To ease the tensions of cultural borrowing, efforts to "domesticate" foreign ideas and practices proliferated. Thus the Jesuits in China tried to point out similarities between Christianity and Confucianism, and Native American converts identified Christian saints with their own gods and spirits. By the late seventeenth century, some local churches in central Mexico had come to associate Catholicism less with the Spanish than with ancient pre-Aztec communities and beliefs that were now, supposedly, restored to their rightful position.

The pace of global cultural borrowing and its associated tensions stepped up even more as Europe's modern transformation unfolded in the nineteenth century and as its imperial reach extended and deepened around the world.

Chapter Review

What's the Significance?

Big Picture Questions

1. Why did Christianity take hold in some places more than in others?
2. In what ways was the missionary message of Christianity shaped by the cultures of Asian and American peoples?
3. In what ways did the spread of Christianity, Islam, and modern science give rise to culturally based conflicts?
4. **Looking Back:** Based on Chapters 13 through 15, how might you challenge a Eurocentric understanding of the early modern era while acknowledging the growing role of Europeans on the global stage?

Next Steps: For Further Study

Natana J. Delong-Bas, *Wahhabi Islam: From Revival and Reform to Global Jihad* (2004). A careful study of the origins of Wahhabi Islam and its subsequent development.

Patricia Buckley Ebrey et al., *East Asia: A Cultural, Social, and Political History* (2005). A broad survey by major scholars in the field.

Geoffrey C. Gunn, *First Globalization: The Eurasian Exchange, 1500–1800* (2003). Explores the two-way exchange of ideas between Europe and Asia in the early modern era.

Toby E. Huff, *The Rise of Early Modern Science* (2003). A fascinating and controversial explanation as to why modern science arose in the West rather than in China or the Islamic world.

Úrsula de Jesús, *The Souls of Purgatory: The Spiritual Diary of a Seventeenth-Century Afro-Peruvian Mystic* (2004). A scholarly introduction by Nancy E. van Deusen places Úrsula in a broader context.

Diarmaid MacCulloch, *Christianity: The First Three Thousand Years* (2009). A masterful exploration of global Christianity with extensive coverage of the early modern era.

Deva Sobel, *A More Perfect Heaven: How Copernicus Revolutionized the Cosmos* (2011). A fascinating account of a major breakthrough in the Scientific Revolution.

"Christianity: A History of 'Dark Continents,' " http://vimeo.com/15944175.

Internet Modern History Sourcebook, "The Scientific Revolution," http://www.fordham.edu/halsall/mod/modsbook09.html. A collection of primary-source documents dealing with the breakthrough to modern science in Europe.

WORKING WITH EVIDENCE

Global Christianity in the Early Modern Era

During the early modern centuries, the world of European Christendom, long divided between its Roman Catholic and Eastern Orthodox branches, underwent two major transformations. First, the Reformation sharply divided Western Christendom into bitterly hostile Protestant and Catholic halves. And while that process was unfolding in Europe, missionaries—mostly Roman Catholic—rode the tide of European expansion to establish the faith in the Americas and parts of Africa and Asia. In those places, native converts sometimes imitated European patterns and at other times adapted the new religion to their own cultural traditions. Furthermore, smaller but ancient Christian communities persisted in Ethiopia, Armenia, Egypt, southern India, and elsewhere. Thus the Christian world of the early modern era was far more globalized and much more varied than before 1500. That variety found expression in both art and architecture, as the sources that follow illustrate.

Some of the differences between Protestant and Catholic Christianity become apparent in the interiors of their churches. To Martin Luther, the founder of Protestant Christianity, elaborate church interiors, with their many sculptures and paintings, represented a spiritual danger, for he feared that the wealthy few who endowed such images would come to believe that they were buying their way into Heaven rather than relying on God's grace. "It would be better," he wrote, "if we gave less to the churches and altars, . . . and more to the needy."[36] John Calvin, the prominent French-born Protestant theologian, went even further, declaring that "God forbade . . . the making of any images representing him."[37]

Behind such statements lay different understandings of the church building. While Roman Catholics generally saw a church as a temple or "house of God," sacred because it is where God dwells on earth, Protestants viewed churches more as meetinghouses, gathering places for a congregation. They were not sacred in themselves as places, but only on account of the worship that occurred within them.[38] Furthermore, to Protestants, images of the saints were an invitation to idolatry. Acting on such ideas, Protestants in various places stripped older churches of the offending images, decapitated statues, and sometimes ritually burned statues and paintings at the stake. The new

Interior of the Choir of St. Bavo's Church at Haarlem, 1660 (oil on panel), by Pieter Jansz Saenredam (1597–1665)/Worcester Art Museum, Massachusetts, USA/Bridgeman Images

Source 15.1 Interior of a Dutch Reformed Church

churches they created were often quite different from their Catholic counterparts. Source 15.1, a painting by the seventeenth-century Dutch artist Pieter Saenredam, portrays the interior of a Dutch Reformed (Protestant) church in the city of Haarlem.

Roman Catholic response to the Reformation took shape in the Catholic Reformation, or Counter-Reformation (see page 649). That vigorous movement found expression in a style of church architecture known as Baroque, which emerged powerfully in Catholic Europe as well as in the Spanish and Portuguese colonies of Latin America during the seventeenth and eighteenth centuries. The interiors of such churches were ornately adorned with paintings, ceiling frescoes, and statues, depicting Jesus on the cross, the Virgin and child, numerous saints, and biblical stories. The exuberant art of these church interiors appealed to the senses, seeking to provoke an emotional response of mystery, awe, and grandeur while kindling the faith of the worshippers and binding them firmly to the Catholic Church in the face of Protestant competition. Source 15.2 is a photograph of the interior of the Pilgrimage Church of Mariazell, located in present-day Austria. A church site since the twelfth century, the building was enlarged and refurbished in Baroque style in the seventeenth century.

Erich Lessing/Art Resource, NY

Source 15.2 Catholic Baroque, Interior of Pilgrimage Church, Mariazell, Austria

- What obvious differences do you notice between these two church interiors? What kind of emotional responses would each of them have evoked?

- In what ways do these church interiors reflect differences between Protestant and Catholic theology? (See Snapshot, page 647.)

- How might Protestants and Catholics have reacted upon entering each other's churches?

- Keep in mind that Source 15.1 is a painting. Why do you think the artist showed the people disproportionately small?

Throughout Latin America, Christianity was established in the context of European conquest and colonial rule (see pages 652–56). As the new faith took hold across the region, it incorporated much that was of European origin, as the construction of many large and ornate Baroque churches illustrates. But local communities also sought to blend this European Catholic Christianity with religious symbols and concepts drawn from their own traditions in a process that historians call syncretism. In the Andes, for example, Inca religion featured a supreme creator god (Viracocha); a sun god (Inti), regarded as the creator of the Inca people; a moon goddess (Killa), who was the wife of Inti and was attended by an order of priestesses; and an earth mother goddess (Pachamama), associated with mountain peaks and fertility. Those religious figures found their way into Andean understanding of Christianity, as Source 15.3 illustrates.

Painted around 1740 by an unknown artist, this striking image shows the Virgin Mary placed within the "rich mountain" of Potosí in Bolivia, from which the Spanish had extracted so much silver (see Chapter 14, page 614). Thus Christianity was visually expressed in an Andean tradition that viewed mountains as the embodiment of the gods. A number of smaller figures within the mountain represent the native miners whose labor had enriched their colonial rulers. A somewhat larger figure at the bottom of the mountain is an Inca ruler dressed in royal garb receiving tribute from his people. At the bottom left are the pope and a cardinal, while on the right stand the Habsburg emperor Charles V and perhaps his wife.

- What is Mary's relationship to the heavenly beings standing above her (God the Father on the right; the dove, symbolizing the Holy Spirit, in the center; and Jesus on the left) as well as to the miners at work in the mountain? What is the significance of the crown above her head and her outstretched arms?

- The European figures at the bottom are shown in a posture of prayer or thanksgiving. What might the artist have been trying to convey? How would you interpret the relative size of the European and Andean figures?

- Why do you think the artist placed Mary actually inside the mountain rather than on it, while depicting her dress in a mountain-like form?

Museo de la Casa de la Moneda, Potosi, Bolivia/Gilles Mermet/akg-images

15.3 Cultural Blending in Andean Christianity

- What marks this painting and the one on page 653 as examples of syncretism?

- Do you read these two images from the Andes as subversive of the colonial order or as supportive of it? Do you think the artist who painted Source 15.3 was a European or a Native American Christian?

In China, unlike in Latin America, Christian missionaries operated in a setting wholly outside of European political control, bringing their faith to a powerful and proud civilization, long dominant in eastern Asia, where Confucianism, Daoism, and Buddhism had for many centuries mixed and mingled. The outcome of those missionary efforts was far more modest and much less successful than in the Americas. Nonetheless, in China too the tendency toward syncretism was evident. Jesuit missionaries themselves sought to present the Christian message within a Chinese cultural context to the intellectual and political elites who were their primary target audience. And Chinese Christians often transposed the new religion into more familiar cultural concepts. European critics of the Jesuit approach, however, feared that syncretism watered down the Christian message and risked losing its distinctive character.

Source 15.4 provides an example of Christianity becoming Chinese.[39] In the early seventeenth century, the Jesuits published several books in the Chinese language describing the life of Christ and illustrated them with a series of woodblock prints created by Chinese artists affiliated with the Jesuits. Although they were clearly modeled on European images, those prints cast Christian

Roma, ARSI, Jap. Sin I 43

Source 15.4 Making Christianity Chinese

figures into an altogether Chinese setting. The print in Source 15.4 portrays the familiar biblical story of the Annunciation, when an angel informs Mary that she will be the mother of Jesus. The house and furniture shown in the print suggest the dwelling of a wealthy Chinese scholar. The reading table in front of Mary was a common item in the homes of the literary elite of the time. The view from the window shows a seascape, mountains in the distance, a lone tree, and a "scholar's rock"—all of which were common features in Chinese landscape painting. The clouds that appear at the angel's feet and around the shaft of light shining on Mary are identical to those associated with sacred Buddhist and Daoist figures. To Chinese eyes, the angel might well appear as a Buddhist bodhisattva, while Mary may resemble a Ming dynasty noblewoman or perhaps Kuanyin, the Chinese Buddhist goddess of mercy and compassion.

- What specifically Chinese elements can you identify in this image?

- To whom might this image have been directed?

- How might educated Chinese have responded to this image?

- The European engraving on which this Chinese print was modeled included in the background the scene of Jesus' crucifixion. Why might the Chinese artist have chosen to omit that scene from his image?

- How would European critics of the Jesuits' approach to missionary work have reacted to this image? To what extent has the basic message of Catholic Christianity been retained or altered in this Chinese cultural setting?

As Chinese emperors welcomed Jesuit missionaries at court, so too did the rulers of Mughal India during the time of Akbar (r. 1556–1605) and Jahangir (r. 1605–1627). But while Chinese elite circles received the Jesuits for their scientific skills, especially in astronomy, the Mughal court seemed more interested in the religious and artistic achievements of European civilization. Akbar invited the Jesuits to take part in cross-religious discussions that included Muslim, Hindu, Jain, and Zoroastrian scholars. Furthermore, the Mughal emperors eagerly embraced the art of late Renaissance Europe, which the Jesuits provided to them, much of it devotional and distinctly Christian. Mughal artists quickly learned to paint in the European style, and soon murals featuring Jesus, Mary, and Christian saints appeared on the walls of palaces, garden pavilions, and harems of the Mughal court, while miniature paintings adorned books, albums, and jewelry.

In religious terms, however, the Jesuit efforts were "a fantastic and extravagant failure,"[40] for these Muslim rulers of India were not in the least interested in abandoning Islam for the Christian faith, and few conversions of any kind occurred. Akbar and Jahangir, however, were cosmopolitan connoisseurs of art, which they collected, reproduced, and displayed. European religious art also had propaganda value in enhancing their status. Jesus and Mary, after all, had a prominent place within Islam. Jesus was seen both as an earlier prophet and as a mystical figure, similar to the Sufi masters who were so important in Indian Islam. Mughal paintings, pairing the adult Jesus and Mary side by side, were placed above the imperial throne as well as on the emperor's jewelry and his official seal, suggesting an identification of Jesus and a semi-divine emperor. That the mothers of both Akbar and Jahangir were named Mary only added to the appeal. Thus Akbar and Jahangir sought to incorporate European-style Christian art into their efforts to create a blended and tolerant religious culture for the elites of their vast and diverse realm. It was a culture that drew on Islam, Hinduism, Zoroastrianism, and Christianity.

But as Catholic devotional art was reworked by Mughal artists, it was also subtly changed. Source 15.5 shows an early seventeenth-century depiction of the Holy Family painted by an Indian artist.

The Free Library of Philadelphia/Bridgeman Images

Source 15.5 Christian Art at the Mughal Court

■ Why do you think that this Mughal painter portrayed Mary and Joseph as rather distinguished and educated persons rather than as the humble carpenter and his peasant wife, as in so many European images? Why might he have placed the family in rather palatial surroundings instead of a stable?

■ How do you imagine European missionaries responded to this representation of the Holy Family?

■ How might more orthodox Muslims have reacted to the larger project of creating a blended religion making use of elements from many traditions?

■ What similarities can you identify between this Indian image and the Chinese print in Source 15.4? Pay attention to the setting, the clothing, the class status of the human figures, and the scenes outside the windows.

DOING HISTORY

Global Christianity in the Early Modern Era

1. **Making comparisons:** What common Christian elements can you identify in these visual sources? What differences in the expression of Christianity can you define?

2. **Considering Mary:** The Catholic Christian tradition as it developed in Latin America, China, and India as well as Europe assigned a very important role to representations of the Virgin Mary. Why might such images of Mary have been so widely appealing? But in what ways does the image of the Holy Mother differ in Sources 15.3, 15.4, and 15.5? In what ways were those images adapted to the distinctive cultures in which they were created?

3. **Pondering syncretism:** From a missionary viewpoint, develop arguments for and against religious syncretism using these visual sources as points of reference.

4. **Considering visual sources as evidence:** What are the strengths and limitations of these visual sources, as opposed to texts, as historians seek to understand the globalization of Christianity in the early modern era? What other visual sources might be useful?

Multiple-Choice Questions

Refer to the painting on page 565 and its caption to answer the following questions.

1. What was the most likely purpose of this painting?

a. To show the superiority of men over women in colonial Latin America

b. To warn against the mixing of ethnic groups in colonial Latin America

c. To show cultural blending that occurred throughout colonial Latin America

d. To train religious officials in classifying people into social classes

2. What level of society do the people in the painting seem to represent?

a. They are members of the lower class since they represent an interracial marriage.

b. They are members of the upper class, perhaps a Spanish man married to a descendant of native royalty.

c. They are members of the working class, indicated by the many shoes in the background.

d. They are members of the *peninsulares* class, born in Europe and living in the Americas.

3. Which of these is the best definition of the term *castas*?

a. The religious beliefs of people in Latin America

b. The laws set up in the Americas by Spain and Portugal

c. The system of acquiring slaves in Latin America

d. The socioeconomic hierarchy in Latin America

Short-Answer Question

4. Answer parts A, B, and C.

A. Briefly explain why ONE of the following developments best represents the beginning of global trade.

- European transatlantic voyages in the late fifteenth century
- Spanish transpacific voyages in the early sixteenth century
- The chartering of joint stock corporations such as the Dutch East India Company in the early seventeenth century

B. Provide at least ONE example of a specific historical event or development to support your explanation in part A.

C. Briefly explain why ONE of the other options is not as persuasive as the one you chose in part A.

Document-Based Question

Directions: *Question 5 refers to the following documents. You will likely need to flip back and forth between these documents to answer the question adequately. Use scrap pieces of paper or sticky notes to tab these documents. When answering the question, refer to the "Advice for Responding to a DBQ" on the inside of the back cover.*

5. Using the following documents from this textbook and your knowledge of world history, discuss ways in which political leaders in the era c. 1450–c. 1750 used spectacle (i.e., ceremony, art, proclamations, lifestyle) to maintain their positions of power.

DOCUMENT	PAGE	DOCUMENT NAME
1	552	Illustration from the *Padshahnama*
2	591–92	Jahangir, "Memoirs"
3	593–95	Ogier Ghiselin de Busbecq, "The Turkish Letters"
4	596	Louis XIV, "Memoirs"
5	597–98	Pedro de Cieza de León, "Chronicles of the Incas"
6	619	Fur and the Russians

Long-Essay Question

When answering the following question, refer to the "Advice for Responding to an LEQ" on the inside of the back cover.

6. In ONE of the following regions, analyze causes for the development of syncretic beliefs and practices between 1450 and 1750.
   - Caribbean and Latin America
   - South Asia
   - Southeast Asia

PART FIVE

THE EUROPEAN MOMENT IN WORLD HISTORY

1750–1900

Contents

THE BIG PICTURE

EUROPEAN CENTRALITY AND THE PROBLEM OF EUROCENTRISM

During the century and a half between 1750 and 1900, sometimes referred to as the "long nineteenth century," two new and related phenomena held center stage in the global history of humankind and represent the major themes of the four chapters that follow. The first of these, explored in Chapters 16 and 17, was the creation of a new kind of human society, commonly called "modern." It emerged from the intersection of the Scientific, French, and Industrial Revolutions, all of which took shape initially in Western Europe. Those societies generated many of the transformative ideas that have guided human behavior over the past several centuries: that movement toward social equality and the end of poverty was possible; that ordinary people might participate in political life; that nations might trump empires; that women could be equal to men; that slavery was no longer necessary.

The second theme of this long nineteenth century, which is addressed in Chapters 18 and 19, was the growing ability of these modern societies to exercise enormous power and influence over the rest of humankind. In some places, this occurred within expanding European empires, such as those that governed India, Southeast Asia, Africa, and Pacific Oceania. Elsewhere, it took place through less formal means — economic penetration, military intervention, diplomatic pressure, missionary activity — in states that remained officially independent, such as China, Japan, the Ottoman Empire, and various countries in Latin America.

Together, these two phenomena thrust Western Europe, and to a lesser extent North America, into a new and far more prominent role in world history than ever before. While various regions had experienced sprouts of modernity during the "early modern" centuries, it was in Western European societies that these novel ways of living emerged most fully. Those societies, and their North American offspring, also came to exercise a wholly unprecedented role in world affairs, as they achieved, collectively, something approaching global dominance by the early twentieth century.

But if Europeans were moving toward dominance over other peoples, they were also leading a human intervention in the natural order of unprecedented dimensions, largely the product of industrialization. The demand for raw materials to supply new factories and to feed their workers drove developments

689

across the globe, leaving a mark on such remote regions as the high peaks of the Andes, the guano islands of the Pacific, and the plains of Kansas and Argentina as well as on the industrial cities of Western Europe and North America. Growing numbers of scientists and other scholars now argue that humankind was then entering a new era, not only in human history but also in the history of the planet—its biological regime, its atmosphere, its climate, even its geology. They have called it the Anthropocene, or the "age of man."

Historically, scientists have viewed human activity as incidental to the larger processes that have shaped the physical and biological evolution of the earth. But now they are suggesting that over the past several centuries, humankind itself has become an active agent of change in this domain, rapidly reshaping the planet. While these changes became more pronounced and obvious in the second half of the twentieth century, the European moment of the long nineteenth century takes on an added significance as the starting point of an epic transformation in the relationship of humanity to the earth, equivalent perhaps to the early stages of the Agricultural Revolution. While human beings have long felt themselves vulnerable to nature, in recent centuries unprecedented numbers of humans, possessing unprecedented powers and material desires, have left nature increasingly vulnerable to humans.

Eurocentric Geography and History

The unprecedented power that Europeans accumulated during the long nineteenth century included the ability to rewrite geography and history in ways that centered the human story on Europe and to convey those views powerfully to other people. Thus flat maps placed Europe at the center of the world, while dividing Asia in half. Europe was granted continental status, even though it was more accurately only the western peninsula of Asia, much as India was its southern peninsula. Other regions of the world, such as the Far East or the Near (Middle) East, were defined in terms of their distance from Europe. The entire world came to measure longitude from a line, known as the prime meridian, which passes through the Royal Astronomical Observatory in Greenwich, England.

History textbooks as well often reflected a Europe-centered outlook, sometimes blatantly. In 1874, the American author William O. Swinton wrote *An Outline of the World's History*, a book intended for use in high school and college classes, in which he flatly declared that "the race to which we belong, the Aryan, has always played the leading part in the great drama of the world's progress."[1] Other peoples and civilizations, by contrast, were long believed to be static or stagnant, thus largely lacking any real history. Most Europeans assumed that these "backward" peoples and regions must either imitate the Western model or face further decline and possible extinction. Until the mid-twentieth century, such ideas went largely unchallenged in the Western world.

They implied that history was a race toward the finish line of modernity. The fact that Europeans arrived there first seemed to suggest something unique, special, or superior about them or their culture, while everyone else struggled to overcome their inadequacy and catch up.

As the discipline of world history took shape in the decades after World War II, scholars and teachers actively sought to counteract such Eurocentric understandings of the past, but they faced a special problem in dealing with recent centuries. How can we avoid Eurocentrism when dealing with a phase of world history in which Europeans were in fact central? The long nineteenth century, after all, was "the European moment," a time when Europeans were clearly the most powerful, most innovative, most prosperous, most expansive, and most widely imitated people on the planet.

Countering Eurocentrism

At least five answers to this dilemma are reflected in the chapters that follow. The first is simply to remind ourselves how recent and perhaps how brief the European moment in world history has been. Other peoples too had times of "cultural flowering" that granted them a period of primacy or influence—for example, the Greeks (500 B.C.E.–200 C.E.), Indians of South Asia (200–600 C.E.), Arabs (600–1000), Chinese (1000–1500), Mongols (1200–1350), and Incas and Aztecs (fifteenth century)—but all of these were limited to particular regions of Afro-Eurasia or the Americas.[2] Even though the European moment operated on a genuinely global scale, Western peoples have enjoyed their worldwide primacy for at most two centuries. Some scholars have suggested that the events of the late twentieth and early twenty-first centuries—the end of colonial empires, the rise of India and especially China, and the assertion of Islam—mark the end, or at least the erosion, of the age of European predominance.

Second, we need to remember that the rise of Europe occurred within an international context. It was the withdrawal of the Chinese naval fleet that allowed Europeans to enter the Indian Ocean in the sixteenth century, while Native Americans' lack of immunity to European diseases and their own divisions and conflicts greatly assisted the European takeover of the Western Hemisphere. The Industrial Revolution, explored in Chapter 17, likewise benefited from New World resources and markets and from the stimulus of superior Asian textile and pottery production. Chapters 18 and 19 make clear that European control of other regions everywhere depended on the cooperation of local elites. Such observations remind us that the remarkable—indeed revolutionary—transformations of the European moment in world history did not derive wholly from some special European genius or long-term advantage. Rather, they emerged from a unique intersection of European historical development with that of other peoples, regions, and cultures. Europeans, like everyone else, were embedded in a web of relationships that shaped their own histories.

A third reminder is that the rise of Europe to a position of global dominance was not an easy or automatic process. Frequently it occurred in the face of ferocious resistance and rebellion, which often required Europeans to modify their policies and practices. The so-called Indian mutiny in mid-nineteenth-century South Asia, a massive uprising against British colonial rule, did not end British control, but it substantially transformed the character of the colonial experience. In Africa, fear of offending Muslim sensibilities persuaded the British to keep European missionaries and mission schools out of northern Nigeria during the colonial era. Even when Europeans exercised political power, they could not do so precisely as they pleased. Empire, formal and informal alike, was always in some ways a negotiated arrangement.

Fourth, peoples the world over made active use of Europeans and European ideas for their own purposes, seeking to gain advantage over local rivals or to benefit themselves in light of new conditions. In Southeast Asia, for example, a number of highland minority groups, long oppressed by the dominant lowland Vietnamese, viewed the French invaders as liberators and assisted in their takeover of Vietnam. Hindus in India used the railroads, introduced by the British, to go on pilgrimages to holy sites more easily, while the printing press made possible the more widespread distribution of their sacred texts. During the Haitian Revolution, examined in Chapter 16, enslaved Africans made use of radical French ideas about "the rights of man" in ways that most Europeans never intended. The leaders of a massive Chinese peasant upheaval in the mid-nineteenth century adopted a unique form of Christianity to legitimate their revolutionary assault on an ancient social order. Recognizing that Asian and African peoples remained active agents, pursuing their own interests even in oppressive conditions, is another way of countering residual Eurocentrism.

Moreover, what was borrowed from Europe was always adapted to local circumstances. Thus Japanese or Russian industrial development did not wholly follow the pattern of England's Industrial Revolution. The Christianity that took root in the Americas or later in Africa evolved in culturally distinctive ways. Ideas of nationalism, born in Europe, were used to oppose European imperialism throughout Asia and Africa. Russian and Chinese socialism in the twentieth century departed in many ways from the vision of Karl Marx. The most interesting stories of modern world history are not simply those of European triumph or the imposition of Western ideas and practices but those of encounters, though highly unequal, among culturally different peoples. It was from these encounters, not just from the intentions and actions of Europeans, that the dramatic global changes of the modern era arose.

A fifth and final antidote to Eurocentrism in an age of European centrality lies in the recognition that although Europeans gained an unprecedented prominence on the world stage, they were not the only game in town, nor were they the sole preoccupation of Asian, African, and Middle Eastern peoples. While China confronted Western aggression in the nineteenth century, it was also absorbing a huge population increase and experiencing massive peasant rebellions that grew out of distinctly Chinese conditions. The long relationship of Muslim and Hindu cultures in India continued to evolve under British colonial rule, as it had for centuries under other political systems. West African societies in the nineteenth century experienced a wave of religious wars that created new states and extended and transformed the practice of Islam, and that faith continued its centuries-long spread on the continent even under European colonial rule. A further wave of wars and state formation in southern Africa transformed the political and ethnic landscape, even as European penetration picked up speed.

None of this diminishes the significance of the European moment in world history, but it sets that moment in a larger context of continuing patterns of historical development and of interaction and exchange with other peoples.

Landmarks in World History (ca. 1750–ca. 1900)

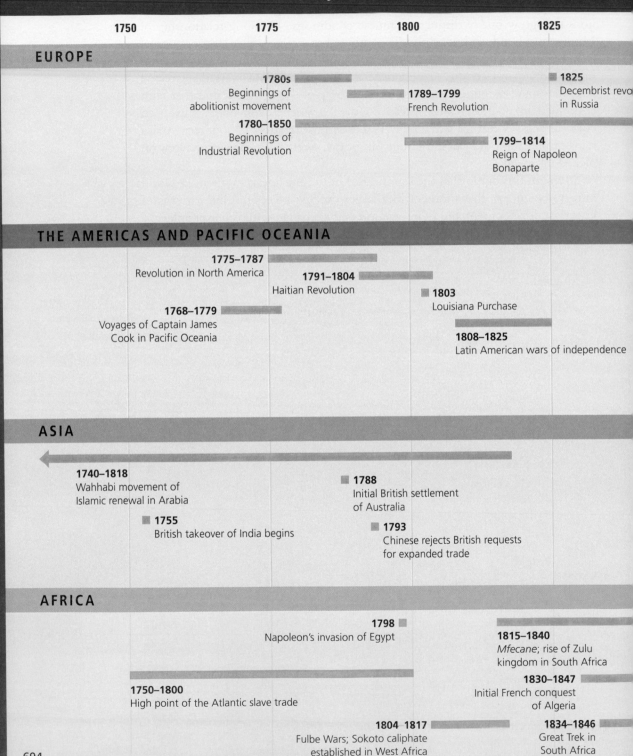

1750   1775   1800   1825

EUROPE

1780s
Beginnings of
abolitionist movement

1789–1799
French Revolution

1825
Decembrist revo
in Russia

1780–1850
Beginnings of
Industrial Revolution

1799–1814
Reign of Napoleon
Bonaparte

THE AMERICAS AND PACIFIC OCEANIA

1775–1787
Revolution in North America

1791–1804
Haitian Revolution

1803
Louisiana Purchase

1768–1779
Voyages of Captain James
Cook in Pacific Oceania

1808–1825
Latin American wars of independence

ASIA

1740–1818
Wahhabi movement of
Islamic renewal in Arabia

1788
Initial British settlement
of Australia

1755
British takeover of India begins

1793
Chinese rejects British requests
for expanded trade

AFRICA

1798
Napoleon's invasion of Egypt

1815–1840
Mfecane; rise of Zulu
kingdom in South Africa

1750–1800
High point of the Atlantic slave trade

1830–1847
Initial French conquest
of Algeria

1804–1817
Fulbe Wars; Sokoto caliphate
established in West Africa

1834–1846
Great Trek in
South Africa

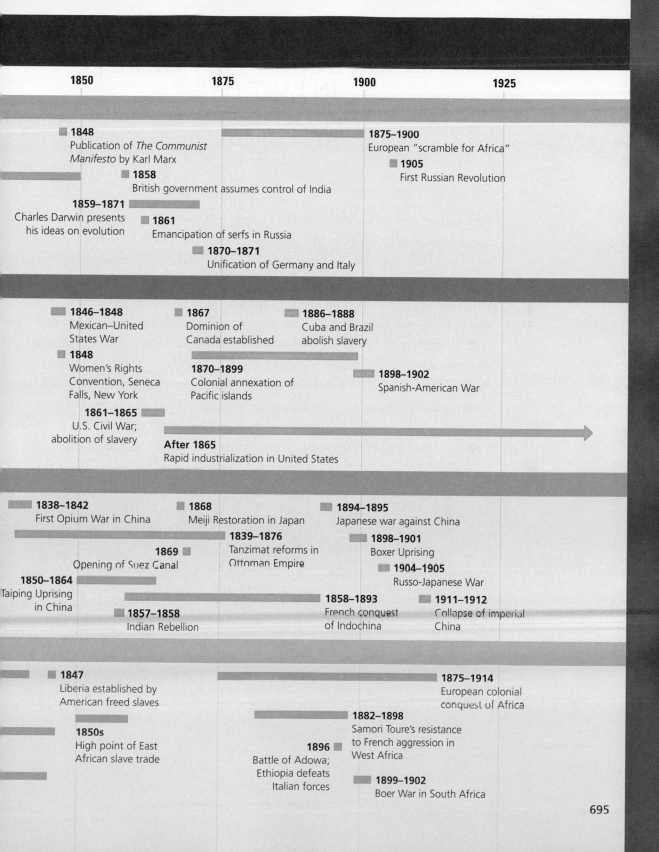

1850   1875   1900   1925

1848
Publication of *The Communist Manifesto* by Karl Marx

1875–1900
European "scramble for Africa"

1905
First Russian Revolution

1858
British government assumes control of India

1859–1871
Charles Darwin presents his ideas on evolution

1861
Emancipation of serfs in Russia

1870–1871
Unification of Germany and Italy

1846–1848
Mexican–United States War

1867
Dominion of Canada established

1886–1888
Cuba and Brazil abolish slavery

1848
Women's Rights Convention, Seneca Falls, New York

1870–1899
Colonial annexation of Pacific islands

1898–1902
Spanish-American War

1861–1865
U.S. Civil War; abolition of slavery

After 1865
Rapid industrialization in United States

1838–1842
First Opium War in China

1868
Meiji Restoration in Japan

1894–1895
Japanese war against China

1839–1876
Tanzimat reforms in Ottoman Empire

1898–1901
Boxer Uprising

1869
Opening of Suez Canal

1904–1905
Russo-Japanese War

1850–1864
Taiping Uprising in China

1857–1858
Indian Rebellion

1858–1893
French conquest of Indochina

1911–1912
Collapse of imperial China

1847
Liberia established by American freed slaves

1875–1914
European colonial conquest of Africa

1850s
High point of East African slave trade

1882–1898
Samori Toure's resistance to French aggression in West Africa

1896
Battle of Adowa; Ethiopia defeats Italian forces

1899–1902
Boer War in South Africa

UNDERSTANDING AP® THEMES
IN PART FIVE

Industrial and Global Integration

Part Five of this text corresponds to Period 5 of the AP® course outline and constitutes 20 percent of the AP® exam. The 150 years addressed in these chapters have great historical significance in many ways. Environmentally, they mark the advent of the Anthropocene era, when human activity began to affect the planet in ways that will be apparent for centuries to come. Much of this activity was occasioned by the Industrial Revolution (IR), a thorough transformation of economic life that began in Europe but grew to global dimensions. That economic transformation, in turn, lay at the heart of what we have come to call "modernity," as new kinds of social life and new cultural outlooks began to take shape. In political terms, all of this led to a mounting influence of European peoples and countries, amounting to an unprecedented, albeit temporary, dominance of one part of the world over the entire globe.

Environment	Cultures	State Building	Economies	Social Structures
Industrial Revolution (IR) and • Population growth • Energy shortage • Ecological windfall from the Americas	Enlightenment ideas and revolution in the Atlantic world	Revolutions compared and connected: North American, French, Haitian, Latin American, Decembrist	Industrial Revolutions compared: British, French, U.S., Russian, Japanese, Latin American	Women in Atlantic revolutions
	Cultural expressions of nationalism			Early feminism
Environmental effects of IR		Post-independence state building in U.S., Haiti, Latin America	Destruction of plantation economy in Haiti	Abolition of slavery
	Marxist socialism as an idea and a movement			End of serfdom in Russia
Romantic poets and early environmentalism	Ideologies of imperialism	U.S. "informal empire" in Latin America	Post-slavery labor regimes in the Americas	Class in colonial North America
IR as beginning of the Anthropocene era	Colonial racism and racial identity	European empires and the IR	"Dependent development": Latin America in the world economy	Class and gender outcomes of French Revolution
Changing roles of agriculture in industrial economies	Colonial education and westernization	Conquest and colonial states in Asia and Africa	Colonial economies compared • Forced labor systems • Cash-crop production • Mining economies • Settler economies	Class, race, and social upheaval in Haiti
	Missionaries and "female circumcision"			Absence of social change in Latin American revolutions
Disease in the colonial world	Africanization of Christianity	Taiping Uprising in China		Class and IR: aristocracy, middle classes, artisans, workers
	"Tribalism" and pan-Africanism	Opium Wars	Scarcity of colonial industrialization	
Environmental effects of cash-crop agriculture: ex.: Burma and Vietnam	Hinduism: emergence of a distinct tradition in India and spread to the West	The end of imperial China	Taiping Uprising and the devastation of China's economy	Gender and IR: domesticity and return to the workforce
		Contraction and reform in Ottoman Empire		Patterns of migration: European, Asian, African
Ecological damage of Bantustan policy in South Africa	Ottoman ideologies: Islamic modernism, secularism, nationalism	Meiji Restoration in Japan	Opium trade and its outcomes	
American food crops and Chinese population growth		Meiji Japan and women's rights	Failure of Chinese industrialization	African women and colonial economies
	Japanese westernization	Japan as an imperial power	Japan's industrial revolution	New and old elites in colonial regimes
				Gender policies of Taiping rebels
				Tokugawa society and social change
				Women and reform in Meiji Japan

Vive le Roi, Vive la Nation.

Jsavois ben Qu'jaurions not tour.

Atlantic Revolutions, Global Echoes

1750–1900

The Haitian earthquake of January 2010 not only devastated an already-impoverished country but also reawakened issues deriving from that country's revolution against slavery and French colonial rule, which finally succeeded in 1804. Twenty-one years later, the French government demanded from Haiti a payment of 150 million gold francs in compensation for the loss of its richest colony and its "property" in slaves. With French warships hovering offshore, Haitian authorities agreed. To make the heavy payments, even after they were somewhat reduced, Haiti took out major loans from French, German, and North American banks. Repaying those loans, finally accomplished only in 1947, represented a huge drain on the country's budget, costing 80 percent of the government's revenue in 1915. In 2010, with the country in ruins, an international petition signed by over 100 prominent people called on the French government to repay some $17 billion, effectively returning the "independence debt" extorted from Haiti 185 years earlier. While the French government dismissed those claims, the issue provided a reminder of the continuing echoes of events from an earlier age of revolution.

The Haitian Revolution was part of and linked to a much larger set of upheavals that shook both sides of the Atlantic world between 1775 and 1825. Haitians had drawn inspiration from the earlier North American and French revolutions, even as their successful overthrow of French rule helped shape the Latin American independence struggles that followed. These four closely related upheavals reflect the new connections among Europe, Africa,

Revolution and the Reversal of Class Roles   Three French female figures, representing from right to left the clergy, nobility, and commoners (Third Estate), show the reversal of class roles that the revolution generated. Now the commoner rides on the back of the noblewoman and is shown in a dominant position over the nun.

697

SEEKING THE MAIN POINT

What were the most important outcomes of the Atlantic revolutions,
both immediately and in the century
that followed?

North America, and South America, which took
shape in the wake of Columbus's voyages and the
European conquests that followed. Together, they
launched a new chapter in the history of the Atlantic
world, while the echoes of those revolutions reverberated in the larger world.

Atlantic Revolutions in a Global Context

Writing to a friend in 1772, before any of the Atlantic revolutions had occurred,
the French intellectual Voltaire asked, "My dear philosopher, doesn't this appear
to you to be the century of revolutions?"[1] He was certainly on target, and not only
for the European/Atlantic world. From the early eighteenth century to the mid-
nineteenth, many parts of the world witnessed political and social upheaval, leading
some historians to think in terms of a "world crisis" or "converging revolutions."
By the 1730s, the Safavid dynasty that had ruled Persia (now Iran) for several centuries had completely collapsed, even as the powerful Mughal Empire governing
India also fragmented. About the same time, the Wahhabi movement in Arabia
seriously threatened the Ottoman Empire, and its religious ideals informed major
political upheavals in Central Asia and elsewhere (see Chapter 15, pages 659–61).
The Russian Empire under Catherine the Great experienced a series of peasant
uprisings, most notably one led by the Cossack commander Pugachev in 1773–
1774, which briefly proclaimed the end of serfdom before that rebellion was crushed.
China too in the late eighteenth and early nineteenth centuries hosted a number
of popular though unsuccessful rebellions, a prelude perhaps to the huge Taiping
revolution of 1850–1864. Beginning in the early nineteenth century, a wave of
Islamic revolutions shook West Africa, while in southern Africa a series of wars and
migrations known as the *mfecane* (the breaking or crushing) involved widespread and
violent disruptions as well as the creation of new states and societies.

AP® EXAM TIP

Note that the era
ca. 1750–ca. 1900
is full of political,
social, and techno-
logical revolutions.

Thus the Atlantic revolutions in North America, France, Haiti, and Latin America took place within a larger global framework. Like many of the other upheavals,
they too occurred in the context of expensive wars, weakening states, and destabi-
lizing processes of commercialization. But compared to upheavals elsewhere, the
Atlantic revolutions were distinctive in various ways. The costly wars that strained
European imperial states—Britain, France, and Spain in particular—were global
rather than regional. In the so-called Seven Years' War (1754–1763), Britain and
France joined battle in North America, the Caribbean, West Africa, and South
Asia. The expenses of those conflicts prompted the British to levy additional taxes
on their North American colonies and the French monarchy to seek new revenue
from its landowners. These actions contributed to the launching of the North
American and French revolutions, respectively.

Furthermore, the Atlantic revolutions were distinctive in that they were closely
connected to one another. The American revolutionary leader Thomas Jefferson

A MAP OF TIME

1775–1787	North American Revolution
1780s	Beginnings of antislavery movement
1789–1799	French Revolution
1791–1804	Haitian Revolution
1793–1794	Execution of Louis XVI; the Terror in France
1799–1814	Reign of Napoleon
1807	End of slave trade in British Empire
1808–1825	Latin American wars of independence
1810–1811	Hidalgo-Morelos rebellion in Mexico
1822	Brazil gains independence from Portugal
1848	Women's Rights Convention, Seneca Falls, New York
1861	Emancipation of serfs in Russia
1861–1865	Civil War and abolition of slavery in United States
1870–1871	Unification of Germany and Italy
1886–1888	Cuba and Brazil abolish slavery
1920	Women gain the vote in United States

was the U.S. ambassador to France on the eve of the French Revolution. While there, he provided advice and encouragement to French reformers and revolutionaries. Simón Bolívar, a leading figure in Spanish American struggles for independence, twice visited Haiti, where he received military aid from the first black government in the Americas.

Beyond such direct connections, the various Atlantic revolutionaries shared a set of common ideas. The Atlantic basin had become a world of intellectual and cultural exchange as well as one of commercial and biological interaction. The ideas that animated the Atlantic revolutions derived from the European Enlightenment and were shared across the ocean in newspapers, books, and pamphlets. At the heart of these ideas was the radical notion that human political and social arrangements could be engineered, and improved, by human action. Thus conventional and long-established ways of living and thinking—the divine right of kings, state control of trade, aristocratic privilege, the authority of a single church—were no longer sacrosanct and came under repeated attack. New ideas of liberty, equality, free trade, religious tolerance, republicanism, and human rationality were in the air. Politically, the core notion was "popular sovereignty," which meant that the authority to govern derived from the people rather than from God or from

AP® EXAM TIP

Be prepared for AP® exam questions about political revolutions in the Atlantic world.

established tradition. As the Englishman John Locke (1632–1704) had argued, the "social contract" between ruler and ruled should last only as long as it served the people well. In short, it was both possible and desirable to start over in the construction of human communities. In the late eighteenth and early nineteenth centuries, these ideas were largely limited to the Atlantic world. While all of the Atlantic revolutions involved the elimination of monarchs, at least temporarily, across Asia and the Middle East such republican political systems were virtually inconceivable until much later. There the only solution to a bad monarch was a new and better one.

In the world of the Atlantic revolutions, ideas born of the Enlightenment generated endless controversy. Were liberty and equality compatible? What kind of government—unitary and centralized or federal and decentralized—best ensured freedom? And how far should liberty be extended? Except in Haiti, the chief beneficiaries of these revolutions were propertied white men of the "middling classes." Although women, slaves, Native Americans, and men without property did not gain much from these revolutions, the ideas that accompanied those upheavals gave them ammunition for the future. Because their overall thrust was to extend political rights further than ever before, these Atlantic movements have often been referred to as "democratic revolutions."

A final distinctive feature of the Atlantic revolutions lies in their immense global impact, extending well beyond the Atlantic world. The armies of revolutionary France, for example, invaded Egypt, Germany, Poland, and Russia, carrying seeds of change. The ideals that animated these Atlantic revolutions inspired efforts in many countries to abolish slavery, to extend the right to vote, to develop constitutions, and to secure greater equality for women. Nationalism, perhaps the most potent ideology of the modern era, was nurtured in the Atlantic revolutions and shaped much of nineteenth- and twentieth-century world history. The ideas of human equality articulated in these revolutions later found expression in feminist, socialist, and communist movements. The Universal Declaration of Human Rights, adopted by the United Nations in 1948, echoed and amplified those principles while providing the basis for any number of subsequent protests against oppression, tyranny, and deprivation. In 1989, a number of Chinese students, fleeing the suppression of a democracy movement in their own country, marched at the head of a huge parade in Paris, celebrating the bicentennial of the French Revolution. And in 2011, the Middle Eastern uprisings known as the Arab Spring initially prompted numerous comparisons with the French Revolution. The Atlantic revolutions had a long reach.

Comparing Atlantic Revolutions

Despite their common political vocabulary and a broadly democratic character, the Atlantic revolutions differed substantially from one another. They were triggered by different circumstances, expressed quite different social and political tensions,

Guided Reading Question

■ CAUSATION

In what ways did the ideas of the Enlightenment contribute to the Atlantic revolutions?

AP® EXAM TIP

You can expect to see questions on the AP® exam about effects of the revolutions found in this chapter.

and varied considerably in their outcomes. Liberty, noted Simón Bolívar, "is a suc-culent morsel, but one difficult to digest."[2] "Digesting liberty" occurred in quite distinct ways in the various sites of the Atlantic revolutions.

The North American Revolution, 1775–1787

Every schoolchild in the United States learns early that the American Revolution was a struggle for independence from oppressive British rule. That struggle was launched with the Declaration of Independence in 1776, resulted in an unlikely military victory by 1781, and generated a federal constitution in 1787, joining thir-teen formerly separate colonies into a new nation (see Map 16.1). It was the first in a series of upheavals that rocked the Atlantic world and beyond in the century that followed. But was it a genuine revolution? What, precisely, did it change?

By effecting a break with Britain, the American Revolution marked a decisive political change, but in other ways it was, strangely enough, a conservative move-ment, because it originated in an effort to preserve the existing liberties of the colo-nies rather than to create new ones. For much of the seventeenth and eighteenth centuries, the British colonies in North America enjoyed a considerable degree of local autonomy, as the British government was embroiled in its own internal con-flicts and various European wars. Furthermore, Britain's West Indian colonies seemed more profitable and of greater significance than those of North America. In these circumstances, local elected assemblies in North America, dominated by the wealth-ier property-owning settlers, achieved something close to self-government. Colo-nists came to regard such autonomy as a birthright and part of their English heritage. Thus, until the mid-eighteenth century, almost no one in the colonies thought of breaking away from England because participation in the British Empire provided many advantages — protection in war, access to British markets, and confirmation of the settlers' continuing identity as "Englishmen" — and few drawbacks.

There were, however, real differences between Englishmen in England and those in the North American colonies. Within the colonies, English settlers had developed societies described by a leading historian as "the most radical in the con-temporary Western world." Certainly class distinctions were real and visible, and a small class of wealthy "gentlemen" — the Adamses, Washingtons, Jeffersons, and Hancocks — wore powdered wigs, imitated the latest European styles, were promi-nent in political life, and were generally accorded deference by ordinary people. But the ready availability of land following the dispossession of Native Americans, the scarcity of people, and the absence of both a titled nobility and a single estab-lished church meant that social life was far more open than in Europe. No legal distinctions differentiated clergy, aristocracy, and commoners, as they did in France. All free men enjoyed the same status before the law, a situation that excluded black slaves and, in some ways, white women as well. These conditions made for less poverty, more economic opportunity, fewer social differences, and easier relation-ships among the classes than in Europe. The famous economist Adam Smith observed

Guided Reading Question

■ CHANGE
What was revolutionary about the American Revo-lution, and what was not?

Map 16.1   The United States after the American Revolution

The union of the thirteen British colonies in North America created the embryonic United States, shown here in 1788. Over the past two centuries and more of anticolonial struggles, it was the only example of separate colonies joining together after independence to form a larger and enduring nation.

that British colonists were "republican in their manners . . . and their government" well before their independence from England.[3]

Thus the American Revolution grew not from social tensions within the colonies, but from a rather sudden and unexpected effort by the British government to tighten its control over the colonies and to extract more revenue from them. As

Britain's global struggle with France drained its treasury and ran up its national debt, British authorities, beginning in the 1760s, looked to America to make good these losses. Abandoning its neglectful oversight of the colonies, Britain began to act like a genuine imperial power, imposing a variety of new taxes and tariffs on the colonies without their consent, for they were not represented in the British Parliament. Many of the colonists were infuriated, because such measures challenged their economic interests, their established traditions of local autonomy, and their identity as true Englishmen. Armed with the ideas of the Enlightenment—popular sovereignty, natural rights, the consent of the governed—they went to war, and by 1781 they had prevailed, with considerable aid from the French, who were only too pleased to harm the interests of their British rivals.

What was revolutionary about the American experience was not so much the revolution itself but the kind of society that had already emerged within the colonies. Independence from Britain was not accompanied by any wholesale social transformation. Rather, the revolution accelerated the established democratic tendencies of the colonial societies. Political authority remained largely in the hands of existing elites who had led the revolution, although property requirements for voting were lowered and more white men of modest means, such as small farmers and urban artisans, were elected to state legislatures.

This widening of political participation gradually eroded the power of traditional gentlemen, but no women or people of color shared in these gains. Land was not seized from its owners, except in the case of pro-British loyalists who had fled the country. Although slavery was gradually abolished in the northern states, where it counted for little, it remained firmly entrenched in the southern states, where it counted for much. Chief Justice John Marshall later gave voice to this conservative understanding of the American Revolution: "All contracts and rights, respecting property, remained unchanged by the Revolution."[4] In the century that followed independence, the United States did become the world's most democratic country, but this development was less the direct product of the revolution and more the gradual working out in a reformist fashion of earlier practices and the principles of equality announced in the Declaration of Independence.

Nonetheless, many American patriots felt passionately that they were creating "a new order for the ages." James Madison in the *Federalist Papers* made the point clearly: "We pursued a new and more noble course . . . and accomplished a revolution that has no parallel in the annals of human society." Supporters abroad agreed. On the eve of the French Revolution, a Paris newspaper proclaimed that the United States was "the hope and model of the human race."[5] In both cases, they were referring primarily to the political ideas and practices of the new country. The American Revolution, after all, initiated the political dismantling of Europe's New World empires. The "right to revolution," proclaimed in the Declaration of Independence and made effective only in a great struggle, inspired revolutionaries and nationalists from Simón Bolívar in nineteenth-century Latin America to Ho Chi Minh in twentieth-century Vietnam. Moreover, the new U.S. Constitution—with

AP® EXAM TIP

Make sure you can connect the American Revolution to global politics.

AP® EXAM TIP

Take notes here so you can compare outcomes of the American Revolution with those of later Latin American revolutions.

its Bill of Rights, checks and balances, separation of church and state, and federalism—was one of the first sustained efforts to put the political ideas of the Enlightenment into practice. That document, and the ideas that it embraced, echoed repeatedly in the political upheavals of the century that followed.

The French Revolution, 1789–1815

Act Two in the drama of the Atlantic revolutions took place in France, beginning in 1789, although it was closely connected to Act One in North America. Thousands of French soldiers had provided assistance to the American colonists and now returned home full of republican enthusiasm. Thomas Jefferson, the U.S. ambassador in Paris, reported that France "has been awakened by our revolution."[6] More immediately, the French government, which had generously aided the Americans in an effort to undermine its British rivals, was teetering on the brink of bankruptcy and had long sought reforms that would modernize the tax system and make it more equitable. In a desperate effort to raise taxes against the opposition of the privileged classes, the French king, Louis XVI, had called into session an ancient representative body, the Estates General. It consisted of male representatives of the three "estates," or legal orders, of prerevolutionary France: the clergy, the nobility, and the commoners. The first two estates comprised about 2 percent of the population, and the Third Estate included everyone else. When that body convened in 1789, representatives of the Third Estate soon organized themselves as the National Assembly, claiming the sole authority to make laws for the country. A few weeks later, they drew up the Declaration of the Rights of Man and Citizen, which forthrightly declared that "men are born and remain free and equal in rights." These actions, unprecedented and illegal in the *ancien régime* (the old regime), launched the French Revolution and radicalized many of the participants in the National Assembly.

Guided Reading Question

■ COMPARISON
How did the French Revolution differ from the American Revolution?

The French Revolution was quite different from its North American predecessor. Whereas the American Revolution expressed the tensions of a colonial relationship with a distant imperial power, the French insurrection was driven by sharp conflicts within French society. Members of the titled nobility—privileged, prestigious, and wealthy—resented and resisted the monarchy's efforts to subject them to new taxes. Educated middle-class men such as doctors, lawyers, lower-level officials, and merchants were growing in numbers and sometimes in wealth and were offended by the remaining privileges of the aristocracy, from which they were excluded. Ordinary urban men and women, many of whose incomes had declined for a generation, were hit particularly hard in the late 1780s by the rapidly rising price of bread and widespread unemployment. Peasants in the countryside, though largely free of serfdom, were subject to hated dues imposed by their landlords, taxes from the state, obligations to the Church, and the requirement to work without pay on public roads. As Enlightenment ideas penetrated French society, more and more people, mostly in the Third Estate but also including some priests and nobles, found a language with which to articulate these grievances. The famous French writer Jean-Jacques Rousseau had told them that it was "manifestly contrary to the law of nature . . . that a handful of people should gorge themselves with superfluities while the hungry multitude goes in want of necessities."[7]

These social conflicts gave the French Revolution, especially during its first five years, a much more violent, far-reaching, and radical character than its American counterpart. It was a profound social upheaval, more comparable to the revolutions of Russia and China in the twentieth century than to the earlier American Revolution. Initial efforts to establish a constitutional monarchy and promote harmony among the classes (see Working with Evidence, Source 16.1, page 731) gave way to more radical measures, as internal resistance and foreign opposition produced a fear that the revolution might be overturned. In the process, urban crowds organized insurrections. Some peasants attacked the residences of their lords, burning the documents that recorded their dues and payments. The National Assembly decreed the end of all legal privileges and eliminated what remained of feudalism in France. Even slavery was abolished, albeit briefly. Church lands were sold to raise revenue, and priests were put under government authority. (See Sources 16.2 and 16.3, pages 732 and 733, for images reflecting this more radical phase of the revolution.)

AP® EXAM TIP

Take notes on this violent phase of the French Revolution to compare it with the later Russian and Chinese revolutions of the twentieth century.

In 1793, King Louis XVI and his queen, Marie Antoinette, were executed, an act of regicide that shocked traditionalists all across Europe and marked a new stage in revolutionary violence. (See Source 16.4, page 734.) What followed was the Terror of 1793–1794. Under the leadership of Maximilien Robespierre (ROHBS-pee-air) and his Committee of Public Safety, tens of thousands deemed enemies of the revolution lost their lives on the guillotine. Shortly thereafter, Robespierre himself was arrested and guillotined, accused of leading France into tyranny and dictatorship. "The revolution," remarked one of its victims, "was devouring its own children."

Accompanying attacks on the old order were efforts to create a wholly new society, symbolized by a new calendar with the Year 1 in 1792, marking a fresh start for France. Unlike the Americans, who sought to restore or build on earlier freedoms, French revolutionaries perceived themselves to be starting from scratch and looked to the future. For the first time in its history, the country became a republic and briefly passed universal male suffrage, although it was never implemented. The old administrative system was rationalized into eighty-three territorial departments, each with a new name. As revolutionary France

The Execution of Robespierre
The beheading of the radical leader Robespierre, who had himself brought thousands of others to the guillotine, marked a decisive turning point in the unfolding of the French Revolution and the end of its most violent phase. (Musée de la Ville de Paris, Musée Carnavalet, Paris, France/Bridgeman Images)

prepared for war against its threatened and threatening neighbors, it created the world's largest army, with some 800,000 men, and all adult males were required to serve. Led by officers from the middle and even lower classes, this was an army of citizens representing the nation.

In terms of gender roles, the French Revolution did not create a new society, but it did raise the question of female political equality far more explicitly than the American Revolution had done. Partly this was because French women were active in the major events of the revolution. In July 1789, they took part in the famous storming of the Bastille, a large fortress, prison, and armory that had come to symbolize the oppressive old regime. In October of that year, some 7,000 Parisian women, desperate about the shortage of bread, marched on the palace at Versailles, stormed through the royal apartments searching for the despised Queen Marie Antoinette, and forced the royal family to return with them to Paris.

Backed by a few male supporters, women also made serious political demands. They signed petitions detailing their complaints: lack of education, male competition in female trades, the prevalence of prostitution, the rapidly rising price of bread and soap. One petition, reflecting the intersection of class and gender, referred to women as the "Third Estate of the Third Estate." Another demanded the right to bear arms in defense of the revolution. Over sixty women's clubs were established throughout the country. A small group called the Cercle Social (Social Circle) campaigned for women's rights, noting that "the laws favor men at the expense of women, because everywhere power is in your hands."[8] The French playwright and journalist Olympe de Gouges appropriated the language of the Declaration of Rights to insist that "woman is born free and lives equal to man in her rights."

But the assertion of French women in the early years of the revolution seemed wildly inappropriate and threatening to most men, uniting conservatives and revolutionaries alike in defense of male privileges. And so in late 1793, the country's all-male legislative body voted to ban all women's clubs. "Women are ill-suited for elevated thoughts and serious meditation," declared one of the male representatives. "A woman should not leave her family to meddle in affairs of government." Here was a conception of gender that defined masculinity in terms of exercising political power. Women who aspired to do so were, in the words of one revolutionary orator, "denatured *viragos*" (domineering women), in short, not really women at all.[9] Thus French revolutionaries were distinctly unwilling to offer any political rights to women, even though they had eliminated class restrictions, at least in theory; granted religious freedom to Jews and Protestants; and abolished slavery. Nonetheless, according to a leading historian, "the French Revolution, more than any other event of its time, opened up the question of women's rights for consideration" and thus laid the foundations for modern feminism.[10]

If not in terms of gender, the immediate impact of the revolution was felt in many other ways. Streets got new names; monuments to the royal family were destroyed; titles vanished; people referred to one another as "citizen so-and-so." Real politics in the public sphere emerged for the first time as many people joined political clubs, took part in marches and demonstrations, served on local committees, and ran for public office. Ordinary men and women, who had identified primarily with their local communities, now began to think of themselves as belonging to a nation. The state replaced the Catholic Church as the place for registering births, marriages, and deaths, and revolutionary festivals substituted for church holidays.

More radical revolutionary leaders deliberately sought to convey a sense of new beginnings and endless possibilities. At a Festival of Unity held in 1793 to mark the first anniversary of the end of monarchy, participants burned the crowns and scepters of the royal family in a huge bonfire while releasing a cloud of 3,000 white doves. The Cathedral of Notre Dame was temporarily turned into the Temple of Reason, while the "Hymn to Liberty" combined traditional church music with the explicit message of the Enlightenment:

> Oh Liberty, sacred Liberty
> Goddess of an enlightened people
> Rule today within these walls.
> Through you this temple is purified.
> Liberty! Before you reason chases out deception,
> Error flees, fanaticism is beaten down.
> Our gospel is nature
> And our cult is virtue.
> To love one's country and one's brothers, To serve the Sovereign People—
> These are the sacred tenets
> And pledge of a Republican.[11]

Elsewhere too the French Revolution evoked images of starting over. Witnessing that revolution in 1790, the young William Wordsworth, later a famous British Romantic poet, imagined "human nature seeming born again." "Bliss it was in that dawn to be alive," he wrote. "But to be young was very heaven."

The French Revolution also differed from the American Revolution in the way its influence spread. At least until the United States became a world power at the end of the nineteenth century, what inspired others was primarily the example of its revolution and its constitution. French influence, by contrast, spread through conquest, largely under the leadership of Napoleon Bonaparte (r. 1799–1814). A highly successful general who seized power in 1799, Napoleon is often credited with taming the revolution in the face of growing disenchantment with its more radical features and with the social conflicts it generated. He preserved many of its more moderate elements, such as civil equality, a secular law code, religious freedom, and promotion by merit, while reconciling with the Catholic Church and suppressing the revolution's more democratic elements in a military dictatorship. In short, Napoleon kept the revolution's emphasis on social equality for men but dispensed with liberty.

Like many of the revolution's ardent supporters, Napoleon was intent on spreading its benefits far and wide. In a series of brilliant military campaigns, his forces

AP® EXAM TIP

If you haven't already done so, now is a good time to make a chart of political and social similarities and differences between the French and American revolutions.

Map 16.2   Napoleon's European Empire

The French Revolution spawned a French empire, under Napoleon's leadership, that encompassed most of Europe and served to spread the principles of the revolution.

subdued most of Europe, thus creating the continent's largest empire since the days of the Romans (see Map 16.2). Within that empire, Napoleon imposed such revolutionary practices as ending feudalism, proclaiming equality of rights, insisting on religious toleration, codifying the laws, and rationalizing government administration. In many places, these reforms were welcomed, and seeds of further change were planted. But French domination was also resented and resisted, stimulating national consciousness throughout Europe. That too was a seed that bore fruit in the century that followed. More immediately, national resistance, particularly from Russia and Britain, brought down Napoleon and his amazing empire by 1815 and marked an end to the era of the French Revolution, though not to the potency of its ideas.

The Haitian Revolution, 1791–1804

Nowhere did the example of the French Revolution echo more loudly than in the French Caribbean colony of Saint Domingue, later renamed Haiti (see Map 16.3, page 712). Widely regarded as the richest colony in the world, Saint Domingue boasted 8,000 plantations, which in the late eighteenth century produced some 40 percent of the world's sugar and perhaps half of its coffee. A slave labor force of about 500,000 people made up the vast majority of the colony's population. Whites numbered about 40,000, sharply divided between very well-to-do plantation owners, merchants, and lawyers and those known as *petits blancs* (peh-TEE blahnk), or poor whites. A third social group consisted of some 30,000 *gens de couleur libres* (free people of color), many of them of mixed-race background. Saint Domingue was a colonial society very different from the New England colonies or even the southern colonies of British North America. Given its enormous inequalities and its rampant exploitation, this Caribbean colony was primed for explosion.

In such a volatile setting, the ideas and example of the French Revolution lit several fuses and set in motion a spiral of violence that engulfed the colony for more than a decade. The principles of the revolution, however, meant different things to different people. To the *grands blancs*—the rich white landowners—it suggested greater autonomy for the colony and fewer economic restrictions on trade, but they resented the demands of the *petits blancs*, who sought equality of citizenship for all whites. Both white groups were adamantly opposed to the insistence of free people of color that the "rights of man" meant equal treatment for all free people regardless of race. To the slaves, the promise of the French Revolution was a personal freedom that challenged the entire slave labor system. In a massive revolt beginning in 1791, triggered by rumors that the French king had already declared an end to slavery, slaves burned 1,000 plantations and killed hundreds of whites as well as mixed-race people.

Soon warring factions of slaves, whites, and free people of color battled one another. Spanish and British forces, seeking to enlarge their own empires at the expense of the French, only added to the turmoil. Amid the confusion, brutality, and massacres of the 1790s, power gravitated toward the slaves, now led by the astute Toussaint Louverture, himself a former slave. He and his successor overcame internal resistance, outmaneuvered the foreign powers, and even defeated an attempt by Napoleon to reestablish French control.

When the dust settled in the early years of the nineteenth century, it was clear that something remarkable and unprecedented had taken place, a revolution unique in the Atlantic world and in world history. Socially, the last had become first. In the only completely successful slave revolt in world history, "the lowest order of the society—slaves—became equal, free, and independent citizens."[12] Politically, they had thrown off French colonial rule, creating the second independent republic in the Americas and the first non-European state to emerge from Western colonialism. They renamed their country "Haiti," a term meaning "mountainous" or "rugged" in the language of the original Taino people. It was a symbolic break with

AP® EXAM TIP

The AP® exam often asks questions about the Haitian Revolution partly because it was inspired by revolutions on both sides of the Atlantic: the American and the French.

Guided Reading Question

■ COMPARISON
What was distinctive about the Haitian Revolution, both in world history generally and in the history of Atlantic revolutions?

The Haitian Revolution
This early nineteenth-century engraving, titled *Revenge Taken by the Black Army*, shows black Haitian soldiers hanging a large number of French soldiers, thus illustrating both the violence and the racial dimension of the upheaval in Haiti. (From *An Historic Account of the Black Empire of Haiti*, engraving by Marcus Rainsford [ca. 1750–1805]/Private Collection/Bridgeman Images)

Europe and represented an effort to connect with the long-deceased native inhabitants of the land. Some, in fact, referred to themselves as "Incas." At the formal declaration of Haiti's independence on January 1, 1804, Jean-Jacques Dessalines, the new country's first head of state, declared: "I have given the French cannibals blood for blood; I have avenged America."[13] In defining all Haitian citizens as "black" and legally equal regardless of color or class, Haiti directly confronted elite preferences for lighter skin even as it disallowed citizenship for most whites. Economically, the country's plantation system, oriented wholly toward the export of sugar and coffee, had been largely destroyed. As whites fled or were killed, both private and state lands were redistributed among former slaves and free blacks, and Haiti became a nation of small-scale farmers producing mostly for their own needs, with a much smaller export sector.

The destructiveness of the Haitian Revolution, its bitter internal divisions of race and class, and continuing external opposition contributed much to Haiti's abiding poverty as well as to its authoritarian and unstable politics. So too did the enormous "independence debt" that the French forced on the fledgling republic in 1825, a financial burden that endured for well over a century (see page 697). "Freedom" in Haiti came to mean primarily the end of slavery rather than the establishment of political rights for all. In the early nineteenth century, however, Haiti was a source of enormous hope and of great fear. Within weeks of the Haitian slave uprising in 1791, Jamaican slaves had composed songs in its honor, and it was not long before slave owners in the Caribbean and North America observed a new "insolence" in their slaves. Certainly, its example inspired other slave rebellions, gave a boost to the dawning abolitionist movement, and has been a source of pride for people of African descent ever since.

To whites throughout the hemisphere, the cautionary saying "Remember Haiti" reflected a sense of horror at what had occurred there and a determination not to allow political change to reproduce that fearful outcome again. Particularly in Latin America, the events in Haiti injected a deep caution and social conservatism in the elites who led their countries to independence in the early nineteenth century. Ironically, though, the Haitian Revolution also led to a temporary expansion of slavery elsewhere. Cuban plantations and their slave workers considerably

AP® EXAM TIP

The AP® exam always features questions about how people see themselves and others, known as questions of identity.

increased their production of sugar as that of Haiti declined. Moreover, Napoleon's defeat in Haiti persuaded him to sell to the United States the French territories known as the Louisiana Purchase, from which a number of "slave states" were carved out. Nor did the example of Haiti lead to successful independence struggles in the rest of the thirty or so Caribbean colonies. Unlike mainland North and South America, Caribbean decolonization had to await the twentieth century. In such contradictory ways did the echoes of the Haitian Revolution reverberate in the Atlantic world.

Spanish American Revolutions, 1808–1825

The final act in a half century of Atlantic revolutionary upheaval took place in the Spanish and Portuguese colonies of mainland Latin America (see Map 16.3). Their revolutions were shaped by preceding events in North America, France, and Haiti as well as by their own distinctive societies and historical experiences. As in British North America, native-born elites (known as *creoles*) in the Spanish colonies were offended and insulted by the Spanish monarchy's efforts during the eighteenth century to exercise greater power over its colonies and to subject them to heavier taxes and tariffs. Creole intellectuals had also become familiar with ideas of popular sovereignty, republican government, and personal liberty derived from the European Enlightenment. But these conditions, similar to those in North America, led initially only to scattered and uncoordinated protests rather than to outrage, declarations of independence, war, and unity, as had occurred in the British colonies. Why did Spanish colonies win their independence almost fifty years later than those of British North America?

Spanish colonies had long been governed in a rather more authoritarian fashion than their British counterparts and were more sharply divided by class. In addition, whites throughout Latin America were vastly outnumbered by Native Americans, people of African ancestry, and those of mixed race. All of this inhibited the growth of a movement for independence, notwithstanding the example of North America and similar provocations.

Despite their growing disenchantment with Spanish rule, creole elites did not so much generate a revolution as have one thrust upon them by events in Europe. In 1808, Napoleon invaded Spain and Portugal, deposing the Spanish king Ferdinand VII and forcing the Portuguese royal family into exile in Brazil. With legitimate royal authority now in disarray, Latin Americans were forced to take action. The outcome, ultimately, was independence for the various states of Latin America, established almost everywhere by 1826. But the way in which independence occurred and the kind of societies it generated differed greatly from the experience of both North America and Haiti.

The process lasted more than twice as long as it did in North America, partly because Latin American societies were so divided by class, race, and region. In North America, violence was directed almost entirely against the British and seldom

Guided Reading Question

■ CONNECTION
How were the Spanish American revolutions shaped by the American, French, and Haitian revolutions that happened earlier?

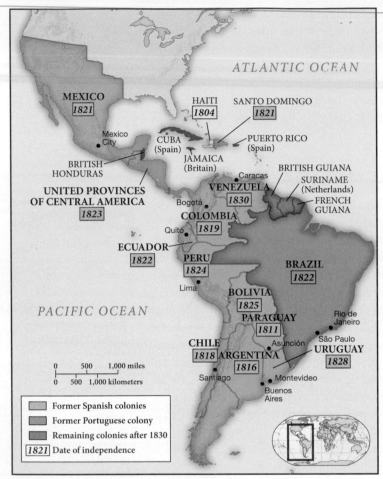

ATLANTIC OCEAN

MEXICO
1821

Mexico City

HAITI
1804

SANTO DOMINGO
1821

CUBA
(Spain)

PUERTO RICO
(Spain)

JAMAICA
(Britain)

BRITISH HONDURAS

Caracas

BRITISH GUIANA

SURINAME
(Netherlands)

UNITED PROVINCES
OF CENTRAL AMERICA
1823

Bogotá

VENEZUELA
1830

FRENCH GUIANA

COLOMBIA
1819

Quito

ECUADOR
1822

PERU
1824

Lima

BRAZIL
1822

PACIFIC OCEAN

BOLIVIA
1825

PARAGUAY
1811

Rio de Janeiro

São Paulo

CHILE
1818

Asunción

URUGUAY
1828

ARGENTINA
1816

Santiago

Montevideo

Buenos Aires

0   500   1,000 miles
0   500   1,000 kilometers

Former Spanish colonies
Former Portuguese colony
Remaining colonies after 1830
1821 Date of independence

Map 16.3   Latin American Independence

With the exception of Haiti, Latin American revolutions brought independence to new states but offered little social change or political opportunity for the vast majority of people.

spilled over into domestic disputes, except for some bloody skirmishes with loyalists. Even then, little lasting hostility occurred, and some loyalists were able to reenter U.S. society after independence was achieved. In Mexico, by contrast, the move toward independence began in 1810 in a peasant insurrection, driven by hunger for land and by high food prices and led successively by two priests, Miguel Hidalgo and José Morelos. Alarmed by the social radicalism of the Hidalgo-Morelos rebellion, creole landowners, with the support of the Church, raised an army and crushed the insurgency. Later that alliance of clergy and creole elites brought Mexico to a more socially controlled independence in 1821. Such violent conflict among Latin Americans, along lines of race, class, and ideology, accompanied the struggle against Spain in many places.

The entire independence movement in Latin America took place under the shadow of a great fear—the dread of social rebellion from below—that had little counterpart in North America. The extensive violence of the French and Haitian revolutions was a lesson to Latin American elites that political change could easily get out of hand and was fraught with danger to themselves. An abortive rebellion of Native Americans in Peru in the early 1780s, led by a man who claimed direct descent from the last Inca emperor, Tupac Amaru, reminded whites that they sat atop a potentially explosive society, most of whose members were exploited and oppressed people of color. So too did the Hidalgo-Morelos rebellion in Mexico.

And yet the creole sponsors of independence movements, both regional military leaders such as Simón Bolívar and José de San Martín and their civilian counterparts, required the support of "the people," or at least some of them, if they were to prevail against Spanish forces. The answer to this dilemma was found in nativism, which cast all of those born in the Americas—creoles, Indians, mixed-race people, free blacks—as Americanos, while the enemy was defined as those born in

Spain or Portugal.[14] This was no easy task, because many creole whites and mestizos saw themselves as Spanish and because great differences of race, culture, and wealth divided the Americanos. Nonetheless, nationalist leaders made efforts to mobilize people of color into the struggle with promises of freedom, the end of legal restrictions, and social advancement. Many of these leaders were genuine liberals, who had been influenced by the ideals of the Enlightenment, the French Revolution, and Spanish liberalism. In the long run, however, few of those promises were kept. Certainly, the lower classes, Native Americans, and slaves benefited little from independence. "The imperial state was destroyed in Spanish America," concluded one historian, "but colonial society was preserved."[15]

AP® EXAM TIP

A trend throughout these Latin American revolutions is that women did not gain many political or social rights until the early twentieth century.

Nor did women as a group gain much from the independence struggle, though they had participated in it in various ways. Upper-class or wealthy women gave and raised money for the cause and provided safe havens for revolutionary meetings. In Mexico, some women disguised themselves as men to join the struggle, while numerous working-class and peasant women served as cooks and carriers of supplies in a "women's brigade." A considerable number of women were severely punished for their disloyalty to the Crown, with some forty-eight executed in Colombia. Yet, after independence, few social gains attended these efforts. General San Martín of Argentina accorded national recognition to a number of women, and modest improvement in educational opportunities for women appeared. But Latin American women continued to be wholly excluded from political life and remained under firm legal control of the men in their families.

A further difference in the Latin American situation lay in the apparent impossibility of uniting the various Spanish colonies, so much larger than the small British territories of North America, despite several failed efforts to do so. Thus no United States of Latin America emerged. Distances among the colonies and geographic obstacles to effective communication were certainly greater than in the Eastern Seaboard colonies of North America, and their longer colonial experience had given rise to distinct and deeply rooted regional identities. Shortly before his death in 1830, the "great liberator" Bolívar, who so admired George Washington and had so ardently hoped for greater unity, wrote in despair to a friend: "[Latin] America is ungovernable. Those who serve the revolution plough the sea."[16]

Simón Bolívar
Among the heroic figures of Spanish American independence movements, none was more significant than Simón Bolívar, shown here in a moment of triumph entering his hometown of Caracas in present-day Venezuela. But Bolívar was immensely disappointed in the outcomes of independence as his dream of a unified South America perished amid the rivalries of separate countries. (By R. Weibezahl, 1829/Sammlung Archiv für Kunst und Geschichte/akg-images)

The aftermath of independence in Latin America marked a reversal in the earlier relationship of the two American continents. The United States, which began its history as the leftover "dregs" of the New World, grew increasingly wealthy, industrialized, democratic, internationally influential, and generally stable, with the major exception of the Civil War. The Spanish colonies, which took shape in the wealthiest areas and among the most sophisticated cultures of the Americas, were widely regarded as the more promising region compared to England's North American territories, which had a backwater reputation. But in the nineteenth century, as newly independent countries in both regions launched a new phase of their histories, those in Latin America became relatively underdeveloped, impoverished, undemocratic, politically unstable, and dependent on foreign technology and investment (see Chapter 17, pages 766–72). Begun in broadly similar circumstances, the Latin American and North American revolutions occurred in very different societies and gave rise to very different historical trajectories.

PRACTICING AP® HISTORICAL THINKING

Compare the North American, French, Haitian, and Spanish American revolutions. What are the most significant categories of comparisons?

Echoes of Revolution

AP® EXAM TIP

You need to know that Europe experienced three decades of political revolutions in the first half of the nineteenth century.

The repercussions of the Atlantic revolutions reverberated far beyond their places of origin and persisted long after those upheavals had been concluded. Britain's loss of its North American colonies, for example, fueled its growing interest and interventions in Asia, contributing to British colonial rule in India and the Opium Wars in China. Napoleon's brief conquest of Egypt opened the way for a modernizing regime to emerge in that ancient land and stimulated westernizing reforms in the Ottoman Empire (see Chapter 19, pages 844–49). During the nineteenth century, the idea of a "constitution" found advocates in Poland, Latin America, the Spanish-ruled Philippines, China, the Ottoman Empire, and British-governed India.

Within Europe, which was generally dominated by conservative governments following Napoleon's final defeat, smaller revolutionary eruptions occurred in 1830, more widely in 1848, and in Paris in 1870. They reflected ideas of republicanism, greater social equality, and national liberation from foreign rule. Such ideas and social pressures pushed the major states of Western Europe, the United States, and Argentina to enlarge their voting publics, generally granting universal male suffrage by 1914. An abortive attempt to establish a constitutional regime even broke out in autocratic Russia in 1825. (See Zooming In: The Russian Decembrist Revolt, page 716.) More generally, the American and French revolutions led sympathetic elites in Central Europe and elsewhere to feel that they had fallen behind, that their countries were "sleeping." As early as 1791, a Hungarian poet gave voice to such sentiments: "O you still in the slave's collar . . . And you too! Holy consecrated kings . . . turn your eyes to Paris! Let France set out the fate of both king and shackled slave."[17]

Beyond these echoes of the Atlantic revolutions, three major movements arose to challenge continuing patterns of oppression or exclusion. Abolitionists sought the end of slavery; nationalists hoped to foster unity and independence from foreign rule; and feminists challenged male dominance. Each of these movements bore the marks of the Atlantic revolutions, and although they took root first in Europe and the Americas, each came to have a global significance in the centuries that followed.

The Abolition of Slavery

In little more than a century, from roughly 1780 to 1890, a remarkable transformation occurred in human affairs as slavery, widely practiced and little condemned since at least the beginning of civilization, lost its legitimacy and was largely ended. In this amazing process, the ideas and practices of the Atlantic revolutions played an important role.

Enlightenment thinkers in eighteenth-century Europe had become increasingly critical of slavery as a violation of the natural rights of every person, and the public pronouncements of the American and French revolutions about liberty and equality likewise focused attention on this obvious breach of those principles. To this secular antislavery thinking was added an increasingly vociferous religious voice, expressed first by Quakers and then by Protestant evangelicals in Britain and the United States. To them, slavery was "repugnant to our religion" and a "crime in the sight of God."[18] What made these moral arguments more widely acceptable was the growing belief that, contrary to much earlier thinking, slavery was not essential for economic progress. After all, England and New England were among the most prosperous regions of the Western world in the early nineteenth century, and both were based on free labor. Slavery in this view was out of date, unnecessary in the new era of industrial technology and capitalism. Thus moral virtue and economic success were joined. It was an attractive argument. The actions of slaves themselves likewise hastened the end of slavery. The dramatically successful Haitian Revolution was followed by three major rebellions in the British West Indies, all of which were harshly crushed, in the early nineteenth century. The Great Jamaica Revolt of 1831–1832 was particularly important in prompting Britain to abolish slavery throughout its empire in 1833. These revolts demonstrated clearly that slaves were hardly "contented," and the brutality with which they were suppressed appalled British public opinion. Growing numbers of the British public came to believe that slavery was "not only morally wrong and economically inefficient, but also politically unwise."[19]

These various strands of thinking—secular, religious, economic, and political—came together in abolitionist movements, most powerfully in Britain, which brought growing pressure on governments

AP® EXAM TIP

The abolition of slavery in the Atlantic world was the greatest political and social achievement of the nineteenth century.

Guided Reading Question

■ **CHANGE**
What accounts for the end of Atlantic slavery during the nineteenth century?

Abolitionism
This antislavery medallion was commissioned in the late eighteenth century by English Quakers, who were among the earliest participants in the abolitionist movement. Its famous motto, "Am I not a man and a brother," reflected both Enlightenment and Christian values of human equality. (The Art Archive at Art Resource, NY)

The Russian Decembrist Revolt

The Decembrists in Siberian exile.

It must surely rank among the world's shortest and least impressive revolts. On December 26, 1825, a group of radicalized military officers persuaded around 3,000 Russian soldiers stationed in the capital of St. Petersburg to stage an uprising, refusing to swear an oath of allegiance to the new tsar, Nicholas I. But expected reinforcements never arrived, and several of their leaders deserted the cause. Soon some 9,000 soldiers loyal to the tsar had reached the square where the rebels were assembled, together with the tsar himself. After some hesitation and failed negotiations, Nicholas ordered artillery fire, and soon about seventy of the rebels lay dead. The rest scattered and the uprising was over, in less than a day. This was the Decembrist revolt, named for the month in which it occurred.

Many of those who planned and executed this uprising were well-educated, often French-speaking, army officers from aristocratic families. They had accompanied the Russian forces that had chased Napoleon out of their country, serving in France itself or elsewhere in Europe. There they had been exposed to the ideas of the European Enlightenment and the French Revolution, and some had become intoxicated with these ideas. The contrast between the backwardness of Russia and what they witnessed in Europe was striking indeed. Russia was still ruled by an absolute monarch, backed by the Church; it had no constitution and no representative assemblies to provide an outlet for grievances; and the ancient institution of serfdom still persisted.

When these officers returned to Russia, some of them formed a secret society known as the Union of Salvation, whose goals were to bring Enlightenment sensibilities to life in their homeland. But they differed on precisely how to do so. Some favored gradual change toward a constitutional monarchy along British lines. Others were more radical, seeking to overthrow the tsarist regime altogether: they wanted to kill the royal family, establish a republic, abolish class distinctions, and end serfdom immediately. Growing frustration with the reactionary and repressive policies of Tsar Alexander I inclined this small cadre of revolutionaries to action. Alexander's death in November 1825, followed by a confusing succession struggle,

photo: © Mary Evans Picture Library/John Massey Stewart Russian Collection/ The Image Works

AP® EXAM TIP

When you read the Zooming In box above, note that the Decembrist revolt failed but inspired Russian revolutionaries in the early twentieth century.

to close down the trade in slaves and then to ban slavery itself. In the late eighteenth century, such a movement gained wide support among middle- and working-class people in Britain. Its techniques included pamphlets with heartrending descriptions of slavery, numerous petitions to Parliament, lawsuits, and boycotts of slave-produced sugar. Frequent public meetings dramatically featured the testimony of Africans who had experienced the horrors of slavery firsthand. In 1807, Britain forbade the sale of slaves within its empire and in 1834 emancipated those who remained enslaved. Over the next half century, other nations followed suit, responding to growing international pressure, particularly from Britain, then the world's leading economic and military power. British naval vessels patrolled the Atlantic, provided the occasion for that action. And so they struck in the abortive uprising of December 1825. The revolt itself marked the first open breach between a section of the educated Russian nobility and the tsarist regime, a gulf that grew much wider over the next century. But its quick failure demonstrated how little social support the rebels enjoyed.

Russian authorities arrested hundreds of participants in the revolt, and the tsar himself interrogated their leaders. Five were executed, others were imprisoned, and over 100 were sent to live in exile in Siberia, including a number of high-ranking nobles. Some months later, after a ceremonial ritual to remove the stain of bloodshed and treason, the tsar declared: "The fatherland is cleansed of the marks of infection." Nicholas now forbade all mention of the Decembrists and sought to erase the memory of the uprising, while defining himself as "conqueror," a defender of Russia and the monarchy from the insidious forces of revolution.

But erasing memory is more easily declared than accomplished. The Decembrists in fact gained a nearly mythic status among a segment of the Russian intelligentsia, many of whom felt increasingly alienated from their autocratic regime. Through veiled references in literary publications, in letters among members of the elite, and by word of mouth, the Decembrists came to symbolize an untarnished heroic morality in sharp contrast to a corrupt and repressive society.[20] They provided inspiration when the revolutionary impulse resurfaced in the 1860s to 1870s.

This shining image of the rebels also gained strength from their behavior in Siberian exile. While sentenced to hard labor and living under close supervision, they were able to establish schools, clinics, theaters, and libraries; organize symposia and concerts; and introduce modern agricultural innovations. To identify with the poor, some dressed like peasants and refused to trim their beards in proper aristocratic fashion.

The wives of these upper-class Siberian exiles likewise gained notoriety for voluntarily joining their husbands in exile. A special law after the revolt permitted the wives of the revolutionaries to be considered widows and to remarry. But a number refused the privilege, leaving their children, titles, and wealth behind. "Whatever your fate, I will share it," declared Maria Volkonskaya in a letter to her exiled husband. And she did. These women came to personify the self-sacrificial loyalty of the ideal Russian feminine. All of this generated a legendary image of the Decembrists in various parts of Siberia.

Although an obvious failure at the time, the Decembrist uprising looked both backward and forward. It represented a distant echo of the earlier French Revolution, and it marked the beginning of a Russian revolutionary movement that came to fruition only in 1917.

Question: Are failures or dead ends in history worthy of the same consideration as more successful ventures? Why or why not?

intercepted illegal slave ships, and freed their human cargoes in a small West African settlement called Freetown, in present-day Sierra Leone. Following their independence, most Latin American countries abolished slavery by the 1850s. Brazil, in 1888, was the last to do so, bringing more than four centuries of Atlantic slavery to an end. A roughly similar set of conditions—fear of rebellion, economic inefficiency, and moral concerns—persuaded the Russian tsar (zahr) to free the many serfs of that huge country in 1861, although there it occurred by fiat from above rather than from growing public pressure.

None of this happened easily. Slave economies continued to flourish well into the nineteenth century, and plantation owners vigorously resisted the onslaught of abolitionists. So did slave traders, both European and African, who together shipped millions of additional captives, mostly to Cuba and Brazil, long after the trade had been declared illegal. Osei Bonsu, the powerful king of the West African state of Asante, was puzzled as to why the British would no longer buy his slaves. "If they think it bad now," he asked a local British representative in 1820, "why did they think it good before?"[21] Nowhere was the persistence of slavery more evident and resistance to abolition more intense than in the southern states of the United States. It was the only slaveholding society in which the end of slavery occurred through such a bitter, prolonged, and highly destructive civil war (1861–1865).

The end of Atlantic slavery during the nineteenth century surely marked a major and quite rapid turn in the world's social history and in the moral thinking of humankind. Nonetheless, the outcomes of that process were often surprising and far from the expectations of abolitionists or the newly freed slaves. In most cases, the economic lives of the former slaves did not improve dramatically. Nowhere in the Atlantic world, except Haiti, did a redistribution of land follow the end of slavery. But freedmen everywhere desperately sought economic autonomy on their own land, and in parts of the Caribbean such as Jamaica, where unoccupied land was available, independent peasant agriculture proved possible for some. Elsewhere, as in the southern United States, various forms of legally free but highly dependent labor, such as sharecropping, emerged to replace slavery and to provide low-paid and often-indebted workers for planters. The understandable reluctance of former slaves to continue working in plantation agriculture created labor shortages and set in motion a huge new wave of global migration. Large numbers of indentured servants from India and China were imported into the Caribbean, Peru, South Africa, Hawaii, Malaya, and elsewhere to work in mines, on plantations, and in construction projects. There they often toiled in conditions not far removed from slavery itself.

Newly freed people did not achieve anything close to political equality, except in Haiti. White planters, farmers, and mine owners retained local authority in the Caribbean, where colonial rule persisted until well into the twentieth century. In the southern United States, a brief period of "radical reconstruction," during which newly freed blacks did enjoy full political rights and some power, was followed by harsh segregation laws, denial of voting rights, a wave of lynching, and a virulent racism that lasted well into the twentieth century. For most former slaves, emancipation usually meant "nothing but freedom."[22] Unlike the situation in the Americas, the end of serfdom in Russia transferred to the peasants a considerable portion of the nobles' land, but the need to pay for this land with "redemption dues" and the rapid growth of Russia's rural population ensured that most peasants remained impoverished and politically volatile.

In both West and East Africa, the closing of the external slave trade decreased the price of slaves and increased their use within African societies to produce the export crops that the world economy now sought. Thus, as Europeans imposed colonial rule on Africa in the late nineteenth century, one of their justifications for

---

Guided Reading Question

■ CHANGE

How did the end of slavery affect the lives of the former slaves?

AP® EXAM TIP

It's important to know that the end of slavery led to a reemergence of indentured servitude in the Caribbean sugar plantations.

doing so was the need to emancipate enslaved Africans. The fact that Europeans proclaimed the need to end slavery in a continent from which they had extracted slaves for more than four centuries was surely among the more ironic outcomes of the abolitionist process.

In the Islamic world, where slavery had long been practiced and elaborately regulated, the freeing of slaves, though not required, was strongly recommended as a mark of piety. Some nineteenth-century Muslim authorities opposed slavery altogether on the grounds that it violated the Quran's ideals of freedom and equality. But unlike Europe and North America, the Islamic world generated no popular grassroots antislavery movements. There slavery was outlawed gradually only in the twentieth century under the pressure of international opinion.

Nations and Nationalism

In addition to contributing to the end of slavery, the Atlantic revolutions also gave new prominence to a relatively recent kind of human community—the nation. By the end of the twentieth century, the idea that humankind was divided into separate nations, each with a distinct culture and territory and deserving an independent political life, was so widespread as to seem natural and timeless. And yet for most of human experience, states did not usually coincide with the culture of a particular people, for all the great empires and many smaller states governed culturally diverse societies. Few people considered rule by foreigners itself a terrible offense because the most important identities and loyalties were local, limited to clan, village, or region, with only modest connection to the larger state or empire that governed them. People might on occasion consider themselves part of larger religious communities (such as Christians or Muslims) or ethno-linguistic groupings such as Greek, Arab, or Maya, but such identities rarely provided the basis for enduring states.

All of that began to change during the era of Atlantic revolutions. Independence movements in both North and South America were made in the name of new nations. The French Revolution declared that sovereignty lay with "the people," and its leaders mobilized this people to defend the "French nation" against its external enemies. In 1793, the revolutionary government of France declared a mass conscription (*levée en masse*) with a stirring call to service:

Guided Reading Question

■ EXPLANATION
What accounts for the growth of nationalism as a powerful political and personal identity in the nineteenth century?

> Henceforth, until the enemies have been driven from the territory of the Republic, all the French are in permanent requisition for army service. The young men shall go to battle; the married men shall forge arms and transport provisions; the women shall make tents and clothes, and shall serve in the hospitals; the children shall turn old linen into lint; the old men shall repair to the public places, to stimulate the courage of the warriors and preach the unity of the Republic and the hatred of kings.[23]

Napoleon's conquests likewise stimulated national resistance in many parts of Europe. European states had long competed and fought with one another, but increasingly in the nineteenth century, those states were inhabited by people who felt themselves to be citizens of a nation, deeply bound to their fellows by ties of blood, culture, or common experience, not simply common subjects of a ruling dynasty. It was a novel form of political loyalty.

Europe's modern transformation also facilitated nationalism, as older identities and loyalties eroded. Science weakened the hold of religion on some. Migration to industrial cities or abroad diminished allegiance to local communities. At the same time, printing and the publishing industry standardized a variety of dialects into a smaller number of European languages, a process that allowed a growing reading public to think of themselves as members of a common linguistic group or nation. All of this encouraged political and cultural leaders to articulate an appealing idea of their particular nations and ensured a growing circle of people receptive to such ideas. Thus the idea of the "nation" was constructed or even invented, but it was often imagined and presented as a reawakening of older linguistic or cultural identities, and it certainly drew on the songs, dances, folktales, historical experiences, and collective memories of earlier cultures (see Map 16.4).

Whatever its precise origins, nationalism proved to be an infinitely flexible and enormously powerful idea in nineteenth-century Europe and beyond. It inspired the political unification of both Germany and Italy, gathering their previously fragmented peoples into new states by 1871. It encouraged Greeks and Serbs to assert their independence from the Ottoman Empire; Czechs and Hungarians to demand more autonomy within the Austrian Empire; Poles and Ukrainians to become more aware of their oppression within the Russian Empire; and the Irish to seek "home rule" and separation from Great Britain. By the end of the nineteenth century, a small Zionist movement, seeking a homeland in Palestine, had emerged among Europe's frequently persecuted Jews. Popular nationalism made the normal rivalry among European states even more acute and fueled a highly competitive drive for colonies in Asia and Africa. The immensity of the suffering and sacrifice that nationalism generated in Europe was vividly disclosed during the horrors of World War I. Furthermore, nationalism fueled rivalries among the various European-derived states in the Americas, reflected, for example, in the Mexican–United States War of 1846–1848 and the devastating conflict between Paraguay and the Triple Alliance of Argentina, Brazil, and Uruguay between 1864 and 1870.

Governments throughout the Western world now claimed to act on behalf of their nations and deliberately sought to instill national loyalties in their citizens through schools, public rituals, the mass media, and military service. Russian authorities, for example, imposed the use of the Russian language, even in parts of the country where it was not widely spoken. They succeeded, however, only in producing a greater awareness of Ukrainian, Polish, and Finnish nationalism.

As it became more prominent in the nineteenth century, nationalism took on a variety of political ideologies. Some supporters of liberal democracy and representative government, as in France or the United States, saw nationalism, with its emphasis on "the people," as an aid to their aspirations toward wider involvement

AP® EXAM TIP

Take notes on all the ways nationalism was promoted by political and cultural leaders and the media.

AP® EXAM TIP

Study this paragraph as an example of writing that is full of specific evidence.

Map 16.4   The Nations and Empires of Europe, ca. 1880

By the end of the nineteenth century, the national principle had substantially reshaped the map of Europe, especially in the unification of Germany and Italy. However, several major empires (Russian, Austro-Hungarian, and Ottoman) remained, each with numerous subject peoples who likewise sought national independence.

AP® EXAM TIP

Knowledge of the map of Europe in the late nineteenth century is essential because you may see it on the AP® exam.

Nationalism in Poland

In the eighteenth century, Poland had been divided among Prussia, Austria, and Russia and disappeared as a separate and independent state. Polish nationalism found expression in the nineteenth century in a series of revolts against Poland's Russian occupiers. This painting shows Russian officers surrendering their standards to Polish insurgents during the November Uprising of 1830. The revolt was subsequently crushed.

in political life. Often called civic nationalism, such a view identified the nation with a particular territory and maintained that people of various cultural backgrounds could assimilate into the dominant culture, as in the process of "becoming American." Other versions of nationalism, in Germany for example, sometimes defined the nation in racial terms, which excluded those who did not share a common ancestry, such as Jews. In the hands of conservatives, nationalism could be used to combat socialism and feminism, for those movements allegedly divided the nation along class or gender lines. Thus nationalism generated endless controversy because it provided no clear answer to the questions of who belonged to the nation or who should speak for it.

Nor was nationalism limited to the Euro-American world in the nineteenth century. An "Egypt for the Egyptians" movement arose in the 1870s as British and French intervention in Egyptian affairs deepened. When Japan likewise confronted European aggression in the second half of the nineteenth century, its long sense of itself as a distinct culture was readily transformed into an assertive modern nationalism. Small groups of Western-educated men in British-ruled India began to think of their enormously diverse country as a single nation. The Indian National Congress, established in 1885, gave expression to this idea. The notion of the Ottoman Empire as a Turkish national state rather than a Muslim or dynastic empire took hold among a few people. By the end of the nineteenth century, some Chinese intellectuals began to think in terms of a Chinese nation beset both by a foreign ruling dynasty and by predatory Europeans. Along the West African coast, the idea of an "African nation" stirred among a handful of freed slaves and missionary-educated men. Although Egyptian and Japanese nationalism gained broad support, elsewhere in Asia and Africa such movements would have to wait until the twentieth century, when they exploded with enormous power on the stage of world history.

Feminist Beginnings

A third echo of the Atlantic revolutions lay in the emergence of a feminist movement. Although scattered voices had earlier challenged patriarchy, never before had an organized and substantial group of women called into question this most fundamental and accepted feature of all preindustrial civilizations—the subordination of women to men. But in the century following the French Revolution, such a challenge took shape, especially in Europe and North America. Then, in the twentieth century, feminist thinking transformed "the way in which women and men work, play, think, dress, worship, vote, reproduce, make love and make war."[24] How did this extraordinary process get launched in the nineteenth century?

Thinkers of the European Enlightenment had challenged many ancient traditions, including on occasion that of women's intrinsic inferiority (see Chapter 15, pages 672–73). The French writer Condorcet, for example, called for "the complete destruction of those prejudices that have established an inequality of rights between the sexes." The French Revolution then raised the possibility of re-creating human societies on new foundations. Many women participated in these events, and a few insisted, unsuccessfully, that the revolutionary ideals of liberty and equality must include women. In neighboring England, the French Revolution stimulated the writer Mary Wollstonecraft to pen her famous *Vindication of the Rights of Woman*, one of the earliest expressions of a feminist consciousness. "Who made man the exclusive judge," she asked, "if woman partake with him of the gift of reason?"

Within the growing middle classes of industrializing societies, more women found both educational opportunities and some freedom from household drudgery. Such women increasingly took part in temperance movements, charities, abolitionism, and missionary work, as well as socialist and pacifist organizations. Some of their working-class sisters became active trade unionists. On both sides of the Atlantic, small numbers of these women began to develop a feminist consciousness that viewed women as individuals with rights equal to those of men. The first organized expression of this new feminism took place at the Women's Rights Convention in Seneca

Guided Reading Question

■ SIGNIFICANCE

What were the achievements and limitations of nineteenth-century feminism?

Falls, New York, in 1848. At that meeting, Elizabeth Cady Stanton drafted a statement that began by paraphrasing the Declaration of Independence: "We hold these truths to be self-evident, that all men and women are created equal."

From the beginning, feminism became a transatlantic movement in which European and American women attended the same conferences, corresponded regularly, and read one another's work. Access to schools, universities, and the professions were among their major concerns as growing numbers of women sought these previously unavailable opportunities. The more radical among them refused to take their husbands' surname or wore trousers under their skirts. Elizabeth Cady Stanton published a Women's Bible, excising the parts she found offensive. As heirs to the French Revolution, feminists ardently believed in progress and insisted that it must now include a radical transformation of the position of women.

AP® EXAM TIP

Take notes on examples of nineteenth-century feminism as a transatlantic movement. It is important to note that nineteenth-century feminism was largely an upper- and middle-class movement.

By the 1870s, feminist movements in the West were focusing primarily on the issue of suffrage and were gaining a growing constituency. Now many ordinary middle-class housewives and working-class mothers joined their better-educated sisters in the movement. By 1914, some 100,000 women took part in French feminist organizations, while the National American Woman Suffrage Association claimed 2 million members. Most operated through peaceful protest and persuasion, but the British Women's Social and Political Union organized a campaign of violence that included blowing up railroad stations, slashing works of art, and smashing department store windows. One British activist, Emily Davison, threw herself in front of the king's horse during a race in Britain in 1913 and was trampled to death. By the beginning of the twentieth century in the most highly industrialized countries of the West, the women's movement had become a mass movement.

That movement had some effect. By 1900, upper- and middle-class women had gained entrance to universities, though in small numbers, and women's literacy rates were growing steadily. In the United States, a number of states passed legislation allowing women to manage and control their own property and wages, separate from their husbands. Divorce laws were liberalized in some places. Professions such as medicine opened to a few, and teaching beckoned to many more. In Britain, Florence Nightingale professionalized nursing and attracted thousands of women into it, while Jane Addams in the United States virtually invented "social work," which also became a female-dominated profession. Progress was slower in the political domain. In 1893, New Zealand became the first country to give the vote to all adult women; Finland followed in 1906. Elsewhere widespread voting rights for women in national elections were not achieved until after World War I, and in France not until 1945.

Beyond these concrete accomplishments, the movement prompted an unprecedented discussion about the role of women in modern society. In Henrik Ibsen's play *A Doll's House* (1879), the heroine, Nora, finding herself in a loveless and oppressive marriage, leaves both her husband and her children. European audiences were riveted, and many were outraged. Writers, doctors, and journalists addressed previously taboo sexual topics, including homosexuality and birth control. Social-

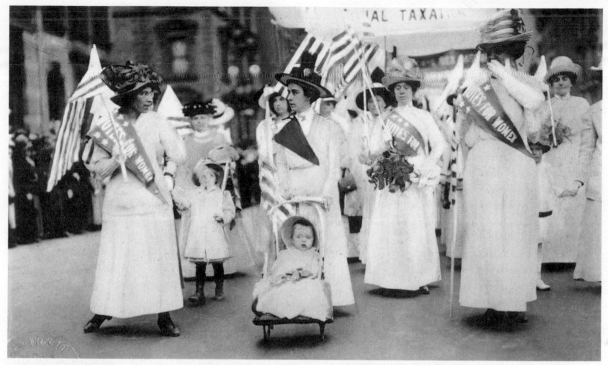

Women's Suffrage
What began as a few isolated voices of feminist protest in the early nineteenth century had become by the end of the century a mass movement in the United States and Western Europe. Here, in a photograph of an American suffrage parade in 1912, is an illustration of that movement in action. (The Granger Collection, NYC—All rights reserved)

ists too found themselves divided about women's issues. Did the women's movement distract from the class solidarity that Marxism proclaimed, or did it provide added energy to the workers' cause? Feminists themselves disagreed about the proper basis for women's rights. Some took their stand on the modern idea of human equality: "Whatever is right for a man is right for a woman." Others, particularly in France, based their claims more on the distinctive role of women as mothers. "It is above all this holy function of motherhood," wrote one advocate of "maternal feminism," "which requires that women watch over the futures of their children and gives women the right to intervene not only in all acts of civil life, but also in all acts of political life."[25]

Not surprisingly, feminism provoked bitter opposition. Some academic and medical experts argued that the strains of education and life outside the home would cause serious reproductive damage and as a consequence depopulate the nation. Thus feminists were viewed as selfish, willing to sacrifice the family or even the nation while pursuing their individual goals. Some saw suffragists, like Jews and socialists, as "a foreign body in our national life." Never before in any society had such a passionate and public debate about the position of women erupted. It was a novel feature of Western historical experience in the aftermath of the Atlantic revolutions.

AP® EXAM TIP

It's important to recognize that as with all major movements promoting social change, feminism had opposition.

Kartini:
Feminism and Nationalism in Java

The ideas of the European Enlightenment and the Atlantic revolutions resonated deeply in the life of a remarkable young Javanese woman named Kartini during the late nineteenth century, when her country was part of the Dutch East Indies (now Indonesia).[26] Born in 1879 into a large aristocratic Javanese family, young Kartini attended a Dutch elementary school where she learned the Dutch language and observed the relative freedom of her European classmates, in sharp contrast to the constraints and ritualized interactions of her own family. At the age of twelve, in keeping with Javanese Muslim custom, Kartini was abruptly removed from her school. For the next four years, she never left her home.

Through her father, a high official in the Dutch colonial administration who much admired Western education, Kartini still had access to Dutch books, and later she was tutored by several Europeans, including one woman with strong socialist and feminist leanings. She also read widely on her own and began an extensive correspondence, largely with Dutch friends in the Netherlands, which lasted until her death. By the time she

Kartini.

photo: Royal Tropical Institute

was twenty, Kartini had acquired an impressive Western education and a network of relationships with prominent Europeans both in the Netherlands and in Java.

From her letters, we learn something of Kartini's thinking. In light of her exposure to Europeans and European thought, she found the absolute subordination of Javanese women completely unacceptable. The seclusion of girls, the total separation of the sexes, the absence of educational opportunities—all of this drove her almost to despair. "Are fine women of no use to civilization?" she asked. But it was the prospect of a traditional high-class Javanese marriage that she found most appalling. Her husband would be "a stranger, an unknown man, whom my parents would choose for me . . . without my knowledge." During the wedding ceremony, she would be expected to prostrate herself before the bridegroom and kiss his feet as a sign of her future submission. Even then, she would be only one of several wives. "Do you understand now," she

AP® EXAM TIP

Pay attention to these examples of nineteenth-century feminism beyond the West.

Like nationalism, a concern with women's rights spread beyond Western Europe and the United States, though less widely. An overtly feminist newspaper was established in Brazil in 1852, and an independent school for girls was founded in Mexico in 1869. A handful of Japanese women and men, including the empress Haruko, raised issues about marriage, family planning, and especially education as the country began its modernizing process after 1868, but the state soon cracked down firmly, forbidding women from joining political parties or even attending political meetings. In Russia, the most radical feminist activists operated within socialist or anarchist circles, targeting the oppressive tsarist regime. Within the Islamic world and in China, some modernists came to believe that education and a wrote to a Dutch confidante, "the deep aversion I have for marriage?"

Kartini was equally outraged by particular features of Dutch colonial rule, especially its racism. Conscious of her membership in a "despised brown race," she deplored the need for "creeping in the dust" before Europeans. Javanese generally were not supposed to speak Dutch with their colonial masters, as if "Dutch is too beautiful to be spoken by a brown mouth." And yet, for Kartini, it was Dutch education and its universal Enlightenment values—"freedom, equality, fraternity," as she put it, echoing the slogan of the French Revolution—that would lead to Javanese emancipation from both Dutch and Javanese oppression. "Europe will teach us to be truly free," she wrote.

Nonetheless, Kartini openly embraced much of her own culture—its art, music, and poetry; its regard for the dead; its hospitality to the poor; its spiritual depth—and she certainly did not seek to transform Javanese into "half-Europeans." But she did believe that "contact with another civilization" and modern European education in particular would enable Javanese "to develop the fine qualities that are peculiar to their race." "Emancipation is in the air," she declared in early 1901.

Kartini's fondest hope was to contribute to that emancipation by studying in the Netherlands and then opening a school for girls in Java. But these grand dreams were thwarted by opposition from her own family, from

Javanese officials, and from much of the Dutch colonial bureaucracy. Java's leading newspaper denounced her intentions as "outrageous," and local gossip had it that she simply wanted to marry a European and become a Europeanized woman. A backup plan to study in the colonial capital of Batavia likewise came to naught with a sudden announcement in mid-1903 that her father had arranged for her to be married to a much older and polygamous man of her social class. Kartini was devastated. "My crown has fallen from my head. My golden illusions of purity and chastity lie shattered in the dust. . . . Now I am nothing more than all the rest."[27]

Although Kartini felt that she was "done with all personal happiness," she determined to make her marriage a model for the future, actually meeting her husband before the wedding and extracting from him a written promise that she could continue with her plans to create a school for girls. But she soon became pregnant, and four days after the birth of her son in 1904, she died at the age of twenty-five. As her writings subsequently became known in Indonesia, Kartini came to be regarded as a pioneer of both feminist and nationalist thinking, and a number of "Kartini schools" were established in her memory.

Question: In what ways was Kartini's life shaped by living at the intersection of Javanese and European worlds?

higher status for women strengthened the nation in its struggles for development and independence and therefore deserved support. (See Zooming In: Kartini, above, for an example from the Dutch East Indies.) Huda Sharawi, founder of the first feminist organization in Egypt, returned to Cairo in 1923 from an international conference in Italy and threw her veil into the sea. Many upper-class Egyptian women soon followed her example.

Nowhere did nineteenth-century feminism have thoroughly revolutionary consequences. But as an outgrowth of the French and Industrial Revolutions, it raised issues that echoed repeatedly and more loudly in the century that followed.

REFLECTIONS

Revolutions: Pro and Con

Long after the dust had settled from the Atlantic upheavals, their legacies have continued to provoke controversy. Were these revolutions necessary? Did they really promote the freedoms that they advertised? Did their benefits outweigh their costs in blood and treasure?

To the people who made these revolutions, benefited from them, or subsequently supported them, they represented an opening to new worlds of human possibility, while sweeping away old worlds of oppression, exploitation, and privilege. Modern revolutionaries acted on the basis of Enlightenment ideas, believing that the structure of human societies was not forever ordained by God or tradition and that it was both possible and necessary to reconstruct those societies. They saw themselves as correcting ancient and enduring injustices. To those who complained about the violence of revolutions, supporters pointed to the violence that maintained the status quo and the unwillingness of favored classes to accommodate changes that threatened those unjust privileges. It was persistent injustice that made revolution necessary and perhaps inevitable.

To their victims, critics, and opponents, revolutions appeared in a quite different light. Conservatives generally viewed human societies not as machines whose parts could be easily rearranged but as organisms that evolved slowly. Efforts at radical and sudden change only invited disaster, as the unrestrained violence of the French Revolution at its height demonstrated. The brutality and bitterness of the Haitian Revolution arguably contributed to the unhappy future of that country. Furthermore, critics charged that revolutions were largely unnecessary since societies were in fact changing. France was becoming a modern society, and feudalism was largely gone well before the revolution exploded. Slavery was ended peacefully in many places, and democratic reform proceeded gradually throughout the nineteenth century. Was this not a preferable alternative to revolutionary upheaval?

Historians too struggle with the passions of revolution—both pro and con—as they seek to understand the origins and consequences of these momentous events. Were revolutions the product of misery, injustice, and oppression? Or did they reflect the growing weakness of established authorities, the arrival of new ideas, or the presence of small groups of radical activists able to fan the little fires of ordinary discontent into revolutionary conflagrations? The outcomes of revolutions have been as contentious as their beginnings. Did the American Revolution enable the growth of the United States as an economic and political "great power"? Did the Haitian Revolution stimulate the later end of slavery elsewhere in the Atlantic world? Did the French Revolution and the threat of subsequent revolutions encourage the democratic reforms that followed in the nineteenth century? Such questions have been central to an understanding of the Atlantic revolutions as well as to those that followed in Russia, China, and elsewhere in the twentieth century.

Chapter Review

What's the Significance?

North American Revolution, 701–4

Declaration of the Rights of Man and
   Citizen, 704

French Revolution, 704–8

Napoleon Bonaparte, 707–8

Haitian Revolution, 709–11

Spanish American revolutions, 711–14

abolitionist movement, 715–19

Decembrists, 716–17

nationalism, 719–23

Vindication of the Rights of Woman, 723

Elizabeth Cady Stanton, 724

maternal feminism, 725

Kartini, 726–27

Big Picture Questions

1. Do revolutions originate in oppression and injustice, in the weakening of political authorities, in new ideas, or in the activities of small groups of determined activists?
2. "The influence of revolutions endured long after they ended and far beyond where they started." To what extent does this chapter support or undermine this idea?
3. Did the Atlantic revolutions fulfill or betray the goals of those who made them? Consider this question in both short- and long-term perspectives.
4. **Looking Back:** To what extent did the Atlantic revolutions reflect the influence of early modern historical developments (1450–1750)?

Next Steps: For Further Study

Benedict Anderson, *Imagined Communities: Reflections on the Origins and Spread of Nationalism* (1991). A now-classic though controversial examination of the process by which national identities were created.

Bonnie S. Anderson, *Joyous Greetings: The First International Women's Movement, 1830–1860* (2000). Describes the beginnings of transatlantic feminism.

David Armitage and Sanjay Subrahmanyam, eds., *The Age of Revolutions in Global Context, c. 1760–1840* (2010). A recent collection of scholarly essays that seeks to explore revolutions within a global framework.

Laurent Dubois and John Garrigus, *Slave Revolution in the Caribbean, 1789–1804* (2006). A brief and up-to-date summary of the Haitian Revolution, combined with a number of documents.

Eric Hobsbawm, *The Age of Revolution, 1789–1848* (1999). A highly respected survey by a well-known British historian.

Lynn Hunt, ed., *The French Revolution and Human Rights* (1996). A collection of documents, with a fine introduction by a prominent scholar.

Égalité for All: Toussaint Louverture and the Haitian Revolution, http://www.youtube.com/watch?v=IQGVqOYX6SU. A thoughtful PBS documentary on the Haitian Revolution, focusing on its principal leader.

"Liberty, Equality, Fraternity: Exploring the French Revolution," http://chnm.gmu.edu/revolution/. A collection of cartoons, paintings, and artifacts illustrating the French Revolution.

WORKING WITH EVIDENCE

Representing the French Revolution

The era of the French Revolution, generally reckoned to have lasted from 1789 to 1815, unfolded as a complex and varied process. Its first several years were relatively moderate, but by 1792 it had become far more radical and violent. After 1795, a reaction set in against the chaos and upheaval that it had generated, culminating in the seizure of power in 1799 by the successful general Napoleon Bonaparte. Nor was the revolution a purely French affair. Conservative opposition in the rest of Europe prompted prolonged warfare, and French efforts under Napoleon to spread the revolution led to a huge French empire in Europe and much resistance to it (see pages 704–8).

All of this provoked enormous controversy, which found visual expression in paintings, cartoons, drawings, and portraits. The four visual sources that follow suggest something of the changing nature of the revolution and the varied reactions it elicited.

Like all major social upheavals, the French Revolution unleashed both enormous hopes and great fears, largely depending on an individual's position in French society. Nonetheless, in the early stages of the revolution (1789–1791), many people believed that France could become a constitutional monarchy with a far more limited role for the king and that the three estates— clergy, nobility, and commoners—could live together in harmony. Source 16.1 represents this phase of the revolution as it depicts the peaceful interaction of members of the three estates. The text that originally accompanied this image read: "Then Messieur we drink to the health of our good King and the Fatherland, that we may be in agreement, at least for this life. And that virtue may be our guide and we will taste together the true pleasures of life."

■ What changes during the first year of the French Revolution does this image reveal? Consider the activity portrayed in the painting and the posture of the three figures. What continuities with the past does it also suggest?

■ How does the image portray the ideal of national unity?

■ How are the representatives of the three estates distinguished from one another?

Source 16.1 The Patriotic Snack, Reunion of the Three Estates, August 4, 1789

■ Notice the peasants hunting in the background. Keep in mind that before the revolution peasants who hunted on the estates of the nobility were subject to harsh punishment or even death. Why do you suppose the artist chose to include them in the painting?

Despite the hope for harmony, many soon came to see the revolution as a sharp reversal of class roles. Source 16.2, titled *The Awakening of the Third Estate*, illustrates this stage of the revolution. In the foreground are male figures representing the three estates of old France. While a member of the Third Estate breaks his chains and takes up arms, members of the clergy and nobility recoil in horror. In the background is the Bastille, the fortress/prison and symbol of the old regime, which was seized by a crowd in July 1789 and subsequently demolished. Also displaying this reversal of class roles is the painting on page 696. Here three female figures symbolize the three estates, with the

Source 16.2 A Reversal of Roles: The Three Estates of Revolutionary France

Third Estate, holding a child, now riding on the back of the nobility and in a superior position to that of the clergy. The caption reads: "I really knew we would have our turn."

- What different impressions of the revolution are conveyed by these images as compared to that of Source 16.1?

- What particular fears might animate the horror with which the clergy and nobility greet the awakening of the Third Estate?

- Notice that the woman representing the Third Estate in the chapter-opening image holds a distaff, a tool used for spinning, as well as a child. What does this suggest about the roles of women in the new order?

© Musée Carnavalet/Roger-Viollet/The Image Works

Source 16.3 Revolution and Religion: "Patience, Monsignor, your turn will come."

In its more radical phase, the French Revolution witnessed not only serious class conflict but also a vigorous attack on the Catholic Church and on Christianity itself. The Church was brought under state control, and members of the clergy were required to swear an oath of allegiance to the revolution. The revolutionary government closed many church buildings or sold them to the highest bidder. The government also seized church property to finance France's wars. For a time, revolutionaries tried to establish a Cult of Reason to replace the Christian faith. This attack on the Church also involved the closure of monasteries and efforts to force priests to abandon their vocation and even to marry. Source 16.3 suggests some of the reasons that ardent revolutionaries were so opposed to supernatural religion in general and the Catholic Church in particular.

- How does this visual source reflect the outlook of the Enlightenment? (See Chapter 15, pages 671–74.)

- What criticisms of the Church are suggested by this image? Why is the bishop on the left portrayed as a fat, even bloated, figure? What is the significance of efforts to "squeeze" the priests? Based on their dress, what class do you think the pressmen represent?

- The caption reads: "Patience, Monsignor, your turn will come." What do you imagine was the reaction of devout Catholics to such images and to the policies of de-Christianization?

Library of Congress, Prints and Photographs Division, LC–DIG–ppmsca–10742

Source 16.4 An English Response to Revolution: "Hell Broke Loose, or, The Murder of Louis"

Attacks on the Church and religion in general were among the actions of the revolution that prompted fear, outrage, and revulsion, both within France and in the more conservative societies of Europe. So too was the execution of Louis XVI and Marie Antoinette, as well as the widespread violence of the Terror. Source 16.4, a British political cartoon, conveys this highly critical, indeed horrified, outlook on the French Revolution. Captioned "Hell Broke Loose," it depicts the execution of Louis XVI and was printed shortly after his death in January 1793. The flying demonic figures in the image are repeating popular slogans of the revolution: "*Vive la nation*" ("Long live the nation") and "*Ca ira*" ("That will go well," or more loosely, "We will win").

■ What is the significance of the demons and dragons in the cartoon? Notice how the soldiers at the bottom of the image are portrayed.

■ What meaning would you attribute to the caption, "Hell Broke Loose"? What disasters might critics of the revolution have imagined coming in its wake?

■ How do you understand the beam of light from Heaven that falls on Louis XVI?

■ Why was regicide regarded with such horror in England in the 1790s?

DOING HISTORY

Representing the French Revolution

1. **Considering political art as evidence:** Based on these four visual sources, together with those in the text itself, what are the advantages and limitations of political or satirical art in understanding a complex phenomenon such as the French Revolution?

2. **Making comparisons:** In what different ways was the French Revolution portrayed in these visual sources? How might you account for those differences? Consider issues of class, nationality, religious commitment, time period, and gender.

3. **Defining the French Revolution:** Based on these visual sources, what was revolutionary about the French Revolution? And what earlier patterns of French life persisted?

4. **Identifying opponents of the revolution:** Based on these visual sources and the text narrative, which groups of people likely opposed the revolution? Why?

Vivian's copper foundry, Swansea, Wales, engraving by Durand-Brager/Bibliothèque des Arts décoratifs, Paris, France/Gianni Dagli Orti/The Art Archive at Art Resource, NY

Revolutions of Industrialization

1750–1900

"Industrialization is, I am afraid, going to be a curse for mankind. . . . God forbid that India should ever take to industrialism after the manner of the West. The economic imperialism of a single tiny island kingdom (England) is today [1928] keeping the world in chains. If an entire nation of 300 millions took to similar economic exploitation, it would strip the world bare like locusts. . . . Industrialization on a mass scale will necessarily lead to passive or active exploitation of the villagers. . . . The machine produces much too fast."[1]

Such were the views of the famous Indian nationalist and spiritual leader Mahatma Gandhi, who subsequently led his country to independence from British colonial rule by 1947, only to be assassinated a few months later. However, few people anywhere have agreed with the heroic Indian figure's views on industrialization. Since its beginning in Great Britain in the late eighteenth century, the idea of industrialization, if not always its reality, has been embraced in every kind of society, both for the wealth it generates and for the power it conveys. Even Gandhi's own country, once it achieved its independence, largely abandoned its founding father's vision of small-scale, village-based handicraft manufacturing in favor of modern industry. As the twenty-first century dawned, India was moving rapidly to develop a major high-technology industrial sector. At that time, across the river from the site in New Delhi where Gandhi was cremated in 1948, a large power plant belched black smoke.

No element of Europe's modern transformation held a greater significance for the history of humankind than the Industrial Revolution, which took place initially in the century and a half

---

Industrial Britain The dirt, smoke, and pollution of early industrial societies are vividly conveyed in this nineteenth-century engraving of a copper foundry in Wales.

between 1750 and 1900. It drew on the Scientific Revolution and accompanied the unfolding legacy of the French Revolution to utterly transform European society and to propel Europe into a temporary position of global dominance. Not since the breakthrough of the Agricultural Revolution some 12,000 years ago had human ways of life been so fundamentally altered. Also transformed was the human relationship to the natural world as our species learned to access energy resources derived from outside of the biosphere—coal, oil, gas, and the nucleus of atoms. But the Industrial Revolution, unlike its agricultural predecessor, began independently in only one place, Western Europe, and more specifically Great Britain. From there, it spread much more rapidly than agriculture, though very unevenly, to achieve a worldwide presence in less than 250 years. Far more than Christianity, democracy, or capitalism, Europe's Industrial Revolution has been enthusiastically welcomed virtually everywhere.

In any long-term reckoning, the history of industrialization is very much an unfinished story. It is hard to know whether we are at the beginning of a movement leading to worldwide industrialization, stuck in the middle of a world permanently divided into rich and poor countries, or approaching the end of an environmentally unsustainable industrial era. Whatever the future holds, this chapter focuses on the early stages of an immense transformation in the global condition of humankind.

Explaining the Industrial Revolution

The global context for this epochal economic transformation lies in a very substantial increase in human numbers from about 375 million people in 1400 to about 1 billion in the early nineteenth century. Accompanying this growth in population was an emerging energy crisis, most pronounced in Western Europe, China, and Japan, as wood and charcoal, the major industrial fuels, became scarcer and their prices rose. In short, "global energy demands began to push against the existing local and regional ecological limits."[2] In broad terms, the Industrial Revolution marks a human response to that dilemma as nonrenewable fossil fuels such as coal, oil, and natural gas replaced the endlessly renewable energy sources of wind, water, wood, and the muscle power of people and animals. It was a breakthrough of unprecedented proportions that made available for human use, at least temporarily, immensely greater quantities of energy. Sustaining the Industrial Revolution was another breakthrough, which lay in the exploitation of guano, or seabird excrement, from the islands off the coast of Peru as well as various mineral sources of nitrates and phosphates in South America and Pacific Oceania. This was an agricultural breakthrough, as these substances made excellent fertilizers, enriching the soils and enabling highly productive input-intensive farming. In much of Western Europe, North America, Australia, and New Zealand, they sustained the produc-

A MAP OF TIME

1712	Early steam engine in Britain
1780s	Beginning of British Industrial Revolution
1812	Locomotives first used to haul coal in England
1832	Reform Bill gives vote to middle-class men in England
1848	Karl Marx, *The Communist Manifesto*
1850s	Beginning of railroad building in Argentina, Cuba, Chile, Brazil
1861	Freeing of serfs in Russia
1864–1876	First International socialist organization in Europe
After 1865	Rapid growth of U.S. industrialization
After 1868	Takeoff of Japanese industrialization
1869	Opening of transcontinental railroad across United States
1871	Unification of Germany
1889–1916	Second International socialist organization in Europe
1890s	Rapid growth of Russian industrialization
1891–1916	Building of trans-Siberian railroad
1905	Failed revolution in Russia
1910 1920	Mexican Revolution
1917	Russian Revolution

AP® EXAM TIP

Look closely at this Map of Time and notice connections between the Industrial Revolution and political revolutions of this era.

tion of food to feed both the draft animals and the growing human populations of the industrializing world.[3]

All of this wrought, of course, a mounting impact on the environment. The massive extraction of nonrenewable raw materials to feed and to fuel industrial machinery—coal, iron ore, petroleum, guano, and much more—altered the landscape in many places. Sewers and industrial waste emptied into rivers, turning them into poisonous cesspools. In 1858, the Thames River running through London smelled so bad that the British House of Commons had to suspend its session. Smoke from coal-fired industries and domestic use polluted the air in urban areas and sharply increased the incidence of respiratory illness. (See the chapter-opening image on page 736.) Against these conditions a number of individuals and small groups raised their voices. Romantic poets such as William Blake and William Wordsworth inveighed against the "dark satanic mills" of industrial England and nostalgically urged a return to the "green and pleasant land" of an earlier time. Here

AP® EXAM TIP

Remember that human interactions with the environment are always important subjects in this course and are fair game for AP® exam questions.

were early and local signs of what became by the late twentieth century an issue of unprecedented and global proportions. For many historians, the Industrial Revolution marked a new era in both human history and the history of the planet that scientists increasingly call the Anthropocene, or the "age of man." More and more, human industrial activity left a mark not only on human society but also on the ecological, atmospheric, and geological history of the earth.

More immediately and more obviously, however, access to huge new sources of energy gave rise to an enormously increased output of goods and services. In Britain, where the Industrial Revolution began, industrial output increased some fiftyfold between 1750 and 1900. It was a wholly unprecedented and previously unimaginable jump in the capacity of human societies to produce wealth. Lying behind it was a great acceleration in the rate of technological innovation, not simply this or that invention — the spinning jenny, power loom, steam engine, or cotton gin — but a "culture of innovation," a widespread and almost obsessive belief that things could be endlessly improved.

Early signs of the technological creativity that spawned the Industrial Revolution appeared in eighteenth-century Britain, where a variety of innovations transformed cotton textile production. It was only in the nineteenth century, though, that Europeans in general and the British in particular more clearly forged ahead of the rest of the world. The great breakthrough was the coal-fired steam engine, which provided an inanimate and almost limitless source of power beyond that of wind, water, or muscle and could be used to drive any number of machines as well as locomotives and oceangoing ships. Soon the Industrial Revolution spread beyond the textile industry to iron and steel production, railroads and steamships, food processing, and construction. Later in the nineteenth century, a so-called second Industrial Revolution focused on chemicals, electricity, precision machinery, the telegraph and telephone, rubber, printing, and much more. Agriculture too was affected as mechanical reapers, chemical fertilizers, pesticides, and refrigeration transformed this most ancient of industries. Technical innovation occurred in more modest ways as well. Patents for horseshoes in the United States, for example, grew from fewer than five per year before 1840 to thirty to forty per year by the end of the century. Furthermore, industrialization soon spread beyond Britain to continental Western Europe and then, in the second half of the century, to the United States, Russia, and Japan.

In the twentieth century, the Industrial Revolution became global as a number of Asian, African, and Latin American countries developed substantial industrial sectors. Oil, natural gas, and nuclear reactions joined coal as widely available sources of energy, and new industries emerged in automobiles, airplanes, consumer durable goods, electronics, computers, and on and on. It was a cumulative process that, despite periodic ups and downs, accelerated over time. More than anything else, this continuous emergence of new techniques of production, together with the massive economic growth they made possible and the environmental impact they generated, marks the past 250 years as a distinct phase of human history.

AP® EXAM TIP

Take notes on this excellent summary of the first and second Industrial Revolutions.

AP® EXAM TIP

As always in world history, when a process "goes global" like the Industrial Revolution, pay attention to the social, economic, and political consequences.

Why Europe?

The Industrial Revolution has long been a source of great controversy among scholars. Why did it occur first in Europe? Within Europe, why did it occur earliest in Great Britain? And why did it take place in the late eighteenth and nineteenth centuries? Some explanations have sought the answer in unique and deeply rooted features of European society, history, or culture. One recent account, for example, argued that Europeans have been distinguished for several thousand years by a rest-less, creative, and freedom-loving culture with its roots in the aristocratic warlike societies of early Indo-European invaders.[4] While not denying certain distinctive qualities of the West, many world historians have challenged views that seem to suggest that Europe alone was destined to lead the way to modern economic life. Such an approach, they argue, not only is Eurocentric and deterministic but also flies in the face of much recent research.

Historians now know that other areas of the world had experienced times of great technological and scientific flourishing. Between 750 and 1100 C.E., the Islamic world generated major advances in shipbuilding, the use of tides and falling water to generate power, papermaking, textile production, chemical technologies, water mills, clocks, and much more.[5] India had long been the world center of cot-ton textile production, the first place to turn sugarcane juice into crystallized sugar, and the source of many agricultural innovations and mathematical inventions. To the Arabs of the ninth century C.E., India was a "place of marvels."[6] More than either of these, China was clearly the world leader in technological innovation between 700 and 1400 C.E., prompting various scholars to suggest that China was on the edge of an industrial revolution by 1200 or so. For reasons much debated among historians, all of these flowerings of technological creativity had slowed down considerably or stagnated by the early modern era, when the pace of techno-logical change in Europe began to pick up. But these earlier achievements certainly suggest that Europe was not alone in its capacity for technological innovation.

Nor did Europe enjoy any overall economic advantage as late as 1750. Over the past several decades, historians have carefully examined the economic conditions of various Eurasian societies in the eighteenth century and found "a world of surpris-ing resemblances." Economic indicators such as life expectancies, patterns of con-sumption and nutrition, wage levels, general living standards, widespread free mar-kets, and prosperous merchant communities suggest broadly similar conditions across the major civilizations of Europe and Asia.[7] Thus Europe had no obvious economic lead, even on the eve of the Industrial Revolution. Rather, according to one leading scholar, "there existed something of a global economic parity between the most advanced regions in the world economy."[8]

A final reason for doubting a unique European capacity for industrial develop-ment lies in the relatively rapid spread of industrial techniques to many parts of the world over the past 250 years, a fairly short time by world history standards. Although the process has been highly uneven, industrialization has taken root, to one degree

Guided Reading Question

■ **CHANGE**

In what respects did the roots of the Industrial Revo-lution lie within Europe? In what ways did that transformation have global roots?

or another, in Japan, China, India, Brazil, Mexico, Turkey, Indonesia, South Africa, Saudi Arabia, Thailand, South Korea, and elsewhere. Such a pattern weakens any suggestion that European culture or society was exceptionally compatible with industrial development.

Thus, while sharp debate continues, many contemporary historians are inclined to see the Industrial Revolution erupting rather quickly and quite unexpectedly between 1750 and 1850 (see Map 17.1). Two intersecting factors help explain why this process occurred in Europe rather than elsewhere. One lies in certain patterns of Europe's internal development that favored innovation. Its many small and highly competitive states, taking shape in the twelfth or thirteenth centuries, arguably provided an "insurance against economic and technological stagnation," which the larger Chinese, Ottoman, or Mughal empires perhaps lacked.[9] If so, then Western Europe's failure to re-create the earlier unity of the Roman Empire may have acted as a stimulus to innovation.

Furthermore, the relative newness of these European states and their monarchs' desperate need for revenue in the absence of an effective tax-collecting bureaucracy pushed European royals into an unusual alliance with their merchant classes. Small groups of merchant capitalists might be granted special privileges, monopolies, or even tax-collecting responsibilities in exchange for much-needed loans or payments to the state. It was therefore in the interest of governments to actively encourage commerce and innovation. Thus states granted charters and monopolies to private trading companies, and governments founded scientific societies and offered prizes to promote innovation. In this way, European merchants and other innovators from the fifteenth century onward gained an unusual degree of freedom from state control and in some places a higher social status than their counterparts in more established civilizations. In Venice and Holland, merchants actually controlled the state. By the eighteenth century, major Western European societies were highly commercialized and governed by states generally supportive of private commerce. In short, they were well on their way toward capitalist economies—where buying and selling on the market was a widely established practice—before they experienced industrialization. Such internally competitive economies, coupled with a highly competitive system of rival states, arguably fostered innovation in the new civilization taking shape in Western Europe.

Europe's societies, of course, were not alone in developing market-based economies by the eighteenth century. Japan, India, and especially China were likewise highly commercialized or market driven. However, in the several centuries after 1500, Western Europe was unique in a second way. That region alone "found itself at the hub of the largest and most varied network of exchange in history."[10] Widespread contact with culturally different peoples was yet another factor that historically has generated extensive change and innovation. This new global network, largely the creation of Europeans themselves, greatly energized commerce and brought Europeans into direct contact with peoples around the world.

AP® EXAM TIP

Government tax policies are an important continuity since the earliest days of civilization.

Map 17.1   The Early Phase of Europe's Industrial Revolution

From its beginning in Great Britain, industrialization had spread by 1850 across Western Europe to include parts of France, Germany, Belgium, Bohemia, and Italy.

AP® EXAM TIP

Notice that most industrial areas developed near sources of coal and iron.

For example, Asia, home to the world's richest and most sophisticated societies, was the initial destination of European voyages of exploration. The German philosopher Gottfried Wilhelm Leibniz (1646–1716) encouraged Jesuit missionaries in China "not to worry so much about getting things European to the Chinese but rather about getting remarkable Chinese inventions to us."[11] Inexpensive and well-made Indian textiles began to flood into Europe, causing one English observer to note: "Almost everything that used to be made of wool or silk, relating either to dress of the women or the furniture of our houses, was supplied by the Indian trade."[12] The competitive stimulus of these Indian cotton textiles was certainly one factor driving innovation in the British textile industry. Likewise, the popularity of Chinese porcelain and Japanese lacquerware prompted imitation and innovation in England, France, and Holland.[13] Thus competition from desirable, high-quality, and newly available Asian goods played a role in stimulating Europe's Industrial Revolution.

In the Americas, Europeans found a windfall of silver that allowed them to operate in Asian markets. They also found timber, fish, maize, potatoes, and much else to sustain a growing population. Later, slave-produced cotton supplied an emerging textile industry with its key raw material at low prices, while sugar, similarly produced with slave labor, furnished cheap calories to European workers. "Europe's Industrial Revolution," concluded historian Peter Stearns, "stemmed in great part from Europe's ability to draw disproportionately on world resources."[14] The new societies of the Americas further offered a growing market for European machine-produced goods and generated substantial profits for European merchants and entrepreneurs. None of the other empires of the early modern era enriched their imperial heartlands so greatly or provided such a spur to technological and economic growth.

Thus the intersection of new, highly commercialized, competitive European societies with the novel global network of their own making provides a context for understanding Europe's Industrial Revolution. Commerce and cross-cultural exchange, acting in tandem, sustained the impressive technological changes of the first industrial societies.

Why Britain?

If the Industrial Revolution was initially a Western European phenomenon generally, it clearly began in Britain in particular. The world's first Industrial Revolution unfolded spontaneously in a country that concentrated some of the more general features of European society. It was both unplanned and unexpected.

With substantial imperial possessions in the Caribbean, in North America, and, by the late eighteenth century, in India as well, Britain was the most highly commercialized of Europe's larger countries. Its landlords had long ago "enclosed" much agricultural land, pushing out the small farmers and producing for the market. A series of agricultural innovations—crop rotation, selective breeding of animals, lighter plows, higher-yielding seeds—increased agricultural output, kept food prices low, and freed up labor from the countryside. The guilds, which earlier had protected Britain's urban artisans, had largely disappeared by the eighteenth century, allowing employers to run their manufacturing enterprises as they saw fit. Coupled with a rapidly growing population, these processes ensured a ready supply of industrial workers who had few alternatives available to them. Furthermore, British aris-

---

Guided Reading Question

■ COMPARISON

What was distinctive about Britain that may help explain its status as the breakthrough point of the Industrial Revolution?

tocrats, unlike their counterparts in Europe, had long been interested in the world of business, and some took part in new mining and manufacturing enterprises. British commerce, moreover, extended around the world, its large merchant fleet protected by the Royal Navy. The wealth of empire and global commerce, however, were not themselves sufficient for spawning the Industrial Revolution, for Spain, the earliest beneficiary of American wealth, was one of the slowest-industrializing European countries into the twentieth century.

British political life encouraged commercialization and economic innovation. Its policy of religious toleration, formally established in 1688, welcomed people with technical skills regardless of their faith, whereas France's persecution of its Protestant minority had chased out some of its most skilled workers. The British government favored men of business with tariffs that kept out cheap Indian textiles, with laws that made it easy to form companies and to forbid workers' unions, with roads and canals that helped create a unified internal market, and with patent laws that served to protect the interests of inventors. Checks on royal prerogative—trial by jury and the growing authority of Parliament, for example—provided a freer arena for private enterprise than elsewhere in Europe.

Europe's Scientific Revolution also took a distinctive form in Great Britain in ways that fostered technological innovation.[15] Whereas science in continental Europe was largely based on logic, deduction, and mathematical reasoning, in Britain it was much more concerned with observation, experiment, precise measurements, mechanical devices, and practical commercial applications. This kind of science played a role in the invention and improvement of the steam engine. Even though most inventors were artisans or craftsmen rather than scientists, in eighteenth-century Britain, they were in close contact with scientists, makers of scientific instruments, and entrepreneurs, whereas in continental Europe these groups were largely separate. The British Royal Society, an association of "natural philosophers" (scientists) established in 1660, saw its role as promoting "useful knowledge." To this end, it established "mechanics' libraries," published broadsheets and pamphlets on recent scientific advances, and held frequent public lectures and demonstrations. The integration of science and technology became widespread and permanent after 1850, but for a century before, it was largely a British phenomenon.

Finally, several accidents of geography and history contributed something to Britain's Industrial Revolution. The country had a ready supply of coal and iron ore, often located close to each other and within easy reach of major industrial centers. Although Britain took part in the wars against Napoleon, the country's island location protected it from the kind of invasions that so many continental European states experienced during the era of the French Revolution. Moreover, Britain's relatively fluid society allowed for adjustments in the face of social changes without widespread revolution. By the time the dust settled from the immense disturbance of the French Revolution, Britain was well on its way to becoming the world's first industrial society.

The First Industrial Society

Wherever it took hold, the Industrial Revolution generated, within a century or less, an economic miracle, at least in comparison with earlier technologies. The British textile industry, which used 52 million pounds of cotton in 1800, consumed 588 million pounds in 1850. Britain's output of coal soared from 5.23 million tons in 1750 to 68.4 million tons a century later.[16] Railroads crisscrossed Britain and much of Europe like a giant spider web (see Map 17.1, page 743). Most of this dramatic increase in production occurred in mining, manufacturing, and services. Thus agriculture, for millennia the overwhelmingly dominant economic sector in every civilization, shrank in relative importance. In Britain, for example, agriculture generated only 8 percent of national income in 1891 and employed fewer than 8 percent of working Britons in 1914. Accompanying this vast economic change was an epic transformation of social life. "In two centuries," wrote one prominent historian, "daily life changed more than it had in the 7,000 years before."[17] Nowhere were the revolutionary dimensions of industrialization more apparent than in Great Britain, the world's first industrial society.

The social transformation of the Industrial Revolution both destroyed and created. Referring to the impact of the Industrial Revolution on British society, historian Eric Hobsbawm wrote: "In its initial stages it destroyed their old ways of living and left them free to discover or make for themselves new ones, if they could and knew how. But it rarely told them how to set about it."[18] For many people, it was an enormously painful, even traumatic process, full of social conflict, insecurity, and false starts as well as new opportunities, an eventually higher standard of living, and greater participation in public life. Scholars, politicians, journalists, and ordinary people have endlessly debated the gains and losses associated with the Industrial Revolution. Amid the controversy, however, one thing is clear: not everyone was affected in the same way.

Railroads

The popularity of railroads, long a symbol of the Industrial Revolution, is illustrated in this early nineteenth-century watercolor, which shows a miniature train offered as a paid amusement for enthusiasts in London's Euston Square. (*Richard Trevithick's Railroad, Euston Square in 1809*, by Thomas Rowlandson [1756–1827]/Science Museum, London, UK/Bridgeman Images)

The British Aristocracy

Individual landowning aristocrats, long the dominant class in Britain, suffered little in material terms from the Industrial Revolution. In the mid-nineteenth century, a few thousand families still owned more than half of the cultivated land in Britain, most of it leased to tenant farmers, who in turn employed agricultural wage laborers to work it. Rapidly growing population and urbanization sustained a demand for food products grown on that land. For most of the nineteenth century, landowners continued to dominate the British Parliament.

As a class, however, the British aristocracy declined as a result of the Industrial Revolution, as have large landowners in every industrial society. As urban wealth became more important, landed aristocrats had to make way for the up-and-coming businessmen, manufacturers, and bankers, newly enriched by the Industrial Revolution. The aristocracy's declining political clout was demonstrated in the 1840s when high tariffs on foreign agricultural imports, designed to protect the interests of British landlords, were finally abolished. By the end of the century, landownership had largely ceased to be the basis of great wealth, and businessmen, rather than aristocrats, led the major political parties. Even so, the titled nobility of dukes, earls, viscounts, and barons retained great social prestige and considerable personal wealth. Many among them found an outlet for their energies and opportunities for status and enrichment in the vast domains of the British Empire, where they went as colonial administrators or settlers. Famously described as a "system of outdoor relief for the aristocracy," the empire provided a cushion for a declining class.

The Middle Classes

Those who benefited most conspicuously from industrialization were members of that amorphous group known as the middle class. At its upper levels, this middle class contained extremely wealthy factory and mine owners, bankers, and merchants. Such rising businessmen readily assimilated into aristocratic life, buying country houses, obtaining seats in Parliament, sending their sons to Oxford or Cambridge University, and gratefully accepting titles of nobility from Queen Victoria.

Far more numerous were the smaller businessmen, doctors, lawyers, engineers, teachers, journalists, scientists, and other professionals required in any industrial society. Such people set the tone for a distinctly middle-class society with its own values and outlooks. Politically they were liberals, favoring constitutional government, private property, free trade, and social reform within limits. Their agitation resulted in the Reform Bill of 1832, which broadened the right to vote to many men of the middle class, but not to middle-class women. Ideas of thrift and hard work, a rigid morality, and cleanliness characterized middle-class culture. The central value of that culture was "respectability," a term that combined notions of social status and virtuous behavior. Nowhere were these values more effectively displayed than in the Scotsman Samuel Smiles's famous book *Self-Help*, published in 1859. Individuals are responsible for their own destiny, Smiles argued. An hour a day devoted to self-improvement "would make an ignorant man wise in a few years." According to Smiles, this enterprising spirit was what distinguished the prosperous middle class from Britain's poor. The misery of the poorer classes was

Guided Reading Question

■ CHANGE

How did the Industrial Revolution transform British society?

AP® EXAM TIP

Pay attention to changes in British society due to the Industrial Revolution because they will repeat throughout the industrialized world.

Guided Reading Question

■ CHANGE

How did Britain's middle classes change during the nineteenth century?

The Industrial Middle Class
This late nineteenth-century painting shows a prosperous French middle-class family, attended by a servant. (*Family Reunion at the Home of Madame Adolphe Brisson*, 1893, by Marcel André Baschet [1862–1941]/Château de Versailles, France/ Giraudon/Bridgeman Images)

"voluntary and self-imposed—the results of idleness, thriftlessness, intemperance, and misconduct."[19] Women in such middle-class families were increasingly cast as homemakers, wives, and mothers, charged with creating an emotional haven for their men and a refuge from a heartless and cutthroat capitalist world. They were also expected to be the moral centers of family life, the educators of "respectability," and the managers of household consumption as "shopping"—a new concept in eighteenth-century Britain—became a central activity for the middle classes. An "ideology of domesticity" defined homemaking, child rearing, charitable endeavors, and "refined" activities such as embroidery, music, and drawing as the proper sphere for women, while paid employment and the public sphere of life outside the home beckoned to men.

Male elites in many civilizations had long established their status by detaching women from productive labor. The new wealth of the Industrial Revolution now allowed larger numbers of families to aspire to that kind of status. With her husband as "provider," such a woman was now a "lady." "She must not work for profit," wrote the Englishwoman Margaretta Greg in 1853, "or engage in any occupation that money can command."[20] Employing even one servant became a proud marker of such middle-class status. But the withdrawal of middle-class women from the labor force turned out to be only a temporary phenomenon. By the late nineteenth century, some middle-class women began to enter the teaching, clerical, and nursing professions, and in the second half of the twentieth century, educated middle-class women flooded into the labor force. By contrast, the withdrawal of children from productive labor into schools has proved a more enduring phenomenon as industrial economies increasingly required a more educated workforce.

As Britain's industrial economy matured, it also gave rise to a sizable lower middle class, which included people employed in the growing service sector as clerks, salespeople, bank tellers, hotel staff, secretaries, telephone operators, police officers, and the like. By the end of the nineteenth century, this growing segment of the middle class represented about 20 percent of Britain's population and provided new employment opportunities for women as well as men. In just twenty years (1881–1901), the number of female secretaries in Britain rose from 7,000 to 90,000. Almost all were single and expected to return to the home after marriage. Telephone operators had initially been boys or men, but by the end of the nineteenth century in both Britain and the United States that work had become a wholly female occupation. For both men and women, such employment represented a claim on membership in the larger middle class and a means of distinguishing themselves clearly from a working class tainted by manual labor. The mounting ability of these middle classes to consume all manner of material goods—and their appetite for doing so—was among the factors that sustained the continuing growth of the industrializing process.

AP® EXAM TIP

You must know how the Industrial Revolution changed gender roles beginning in the early nineteenth century.

The Laboring Classes

The overwhelming majority of Britain's nineteenth-century population—some 70 percent or more—were neither aristocrats nor members of the middle classes. They were manual workers in the mines, ports, factories, construction sites, workshops, and farms of an industrializing Britain. Although their conditions varied considerably and changed over time, it was the laboring classes who suffered most and benefited least from the epic transformations of the Industrial Revolution. Their efforts to accommodate, resist, protest, and change those conditions contributed much to the texture of the first industrial society.

The lives of the laboring classes were shaped primarily by the new working conditions of the industrial era. Chief among those conditions was rapid urbanization. Liverpool's population alone grew from 77,000 to 400,000 in the first half of the nineteenth century. By 1851, a majority of Britain's population lived in towns and cities, an enormous change from the overwhelmingly rural life of almost all

AP® EXAM TIP

How the Industrial Revolution affected the lower classes— for better and worse—is a very important topic in AP® World History.

DEATH'S DISPENSARY.

OPEN TO THE POOR, GRATIS, BY PERMISSION OF THE PARISH.

The Urban Poor of Industrial Britain

This 1866 political cartoon shows an impoverished urban family forced to draw its drinking water from a polluted public well, while a figure of Death operates the pump.

previous civilizations. By the end of the century, London was the world's largest city, with more than 6 million inhabitants.

These cities were vastly overcrowded and smoky, with wholly insufficient sanitation, periodic epidemics, endless row houses and warehouses, few public services or open spaces, and inadequate and often-polluted water supplies. This was the environment in which most urban workers lived in the first half of the nineteenth century. By 1850, the average life expectancy in England was only 39.5 years, less than it had been some three centuries earlier. Nor was there much personal contact between the rich and the poor of industrial cities. Benjamin Disraeli's novel *Sybil*, published in 1845, described these two ends of the social spectrum as "two nations between whom there is no intercourse and no sympathy; who are ignorant of each other's habits, thoughts and feelings, as if they were dwellers in different zones or inhabitants of different planets."

The industrial factories to which growing numbers of desperate people looked for employment offered a work environment far different from the artisan's shop or the tenant's farm. Long hours, low wages, and child labor were nothing new for the poor, but the routine and monotony of work, dictated by the factory whistle and the needs of machines, imposed novel and highly unwelcome conditions of labor. Also objectionable were the direct and constant supervision and the rules and fines aimed at enforcing work discipline. The ups and downs of a capitalist economy made industrial work insecure as well as onerous.

In the early decades of the nineteenth century, Britain's industrialists favored girls and young unmarried women as employees in the textile mills, for they were often willing to accept lower wages, while male owners believed them to be both docile and more suitable for repetitive tasks such as tending machines. (See Zooming In: Ellen Johnston, page 752.) A gendered hierarchy of labor emerged in these factories, with men in supervisory and more skilled positions while women occupied the less skilled and "lighter" jobs that offered little opportunity for advancement. Nor were women welcome in the unions that eventually offered men some ability to shape the conditions under which they labored.

Thus, unlike their middle-class counterparts, many girls and young women of the laboring classes engaged in industrial work or found jobs as domestic servants for upper- and middle-class families to supplement meager family incomes. But after marriage, they too usually left outside paid employment because a man who could not support his wife was widely considered a failure. Within the home, however, many working-class women continued to earn money by taking in boarders, doing laundry, or sewing clothes in addition to the domestic and child-rearing responsibilities long assigned to women.

Social Protest

For workers of the laboring classes, industrial life "was a stony desert, which they had to make habitable by their own efforts."[21] Such efforts took many forms. By 1815, about 1 million workers, mostly artisans, had created a variety of "friendly societies." With dues contributed by members, these working-class self-help groups provided insurance against sickness, a decent funeral, and an opportunity for social life in an otherwise-bleak environment. Other skilled artisans, who had been displaced by machine-produced goods and forbidden to organize in legal unions, sometimes wrecked the offending machinery and burned the mills that had taken their jobs. (See Zooming In: The English Luddites and Machine Breaking, page 758.) The class consciousness of working people was such that one police informer reported that "most every creature of the lower order both in town and country are on their side."[22] Others acted within the political arena by joining movements aimed at obtaining the vote for working-class men, a goal that was gradually achieved in the second half of the nineteenth century. When trade unions were legalized in 1824, growing numbers of factory workers joined these associations in their efforts to achieve better wages and working conditions. Initially their strikes, attempts at nationwide organization, and threat of violence made them fearful indeed to the upper classes. One British newspaper in 1834 described unions as "the most dangerous institutions that were ever permitted to take root, under shelter of law, in any country,"[23] although they later became rather more "respectable" organizations.

Socialist ideas of various kinds gradually spread within the working class, challenging the assumptions of a capitalist society. Robert Owen (1771–1858), a wealthy British cotton textile manufacturer, urged the creation of small industrial communities where workers and their families would be well treated. He established one such community, with a ten-hour workday, spacious housing, decent wages, and education for children, at his mill in New Lanark in Scotland.

Of more lasting significance was the socialism of Karl Marx (1818–1883). German by birth, Marx spent much of his life in England, where he witnessed the brutal conditions of Britain's Industrial Revolution and wrote voluminously about history and economics. His probing analysis led him to the conclusion that industrial capitalism was an inherently unstable system, doomed to collapse in a revolutionary

AP® EXAM TIP

Social, political, and economic reactions to the Industrial Revolution are "must know" information for this course.

Ellen Johnston, Factory Worker and Poet

Born around 1835 to a working-class family in an industrializing Scotland, Ellen Johnston worked in a variety of textile mills throughout her life, lived as a single mother, and, most unusually, became a published poet with a modest local reputation. Through her brief autobiography and her poetry, we can catch a glimpse of one working-class woman's experience during Britain's Industrial Revolution.[24]

Shortly after her birth, Ellen's father, a stonemason, decided to emigrate to America. Her mother, however, refused to join him and returned with her young daughter to her father's house, where she supported her small family as a dressmaker. Ellen remembered with pleasure those early years, in which she wandered the area with her doll and her dog. When she was eight, her mother remarried, to an abusive man who forced young Ellen into factory work a few years later. "No language can paint the suffering," she wrote about her stepfather, "which I afterwards endured from my tormentor." She repeatedly ran away from his home and entered into

A young British woolen factory worker in a setting similar to that in which Ellen Johnston labored.

photo: Science and Society/SuperStock

a love affair that left her a single mother at age seventeen. Nonetheless, in a time of expanding literacy, Ellen read widely, calling herself a "self-taught scholar." She especially liked to read "love adventures" and developed a romantic image of herself as a "heroine of the modern style." She also began to write poetry for the "penny press," inexpensive newspapers of the region.

Ellen's troubled home life made her resistant to the emerging ideology of domesticity, which defined women's roles as tranquil homemakers, wives, and mothers, a view that was taking hold even within the working classes by the mid-nineteenth century. "Fallen women"—those who gave birth outside of marriage—were considered beyond the confines of "true womanhood" and were generally expected to withdraw from public life in disgrace. Ellen Johnston, however, was unrepentant. "I did not . . . feel inclined to die," she wrote, "when I could no longer conceal what

(See Working with Evidence, page 775, for the various voices of a socialist tradition inspired by Marx.)

Guided Reading Question

■ **CHANGE**

How did Karl Marx understand the Industrial Revolution? In what ways did his ideas have an impact in the industrializing world of the nineteenth century?

upheaval that would give birth to a classless socialist society, thus ending forever the ancient conflict between rich and poor. (See Working with Evidence, page 775, for the various voices of a socialist tradition inspired by Marx.)

In his writings, the combined impact of Europe's industrial, political, and scientific revolutions found expression. Industrialization created both the social conditions against which Marx protested so bitterly and the enormous wealth he felt would make socialism possible. The French Revolution, still a living memory in Marx's youth, provided evidence that grand upheavals, giving rise to new societies, had in fact taken place and could do so again. Moreover, Marx regarded himself as a scientist, discovering the laws of social development in much the same fashion as the world falsely calls a woman's shame." Descriptions of home life in her writing are almost always negative. Referring to her aunt's marriage to an alcoholic, she wrote: "Now the dark cup of sorrow embitters thy life / To a hard hearted drunkard, ah! thou art a wife."

Johnston supported herself and her daughter by working intermittently in the textile mills of industrial Scotland, occasionally withdrawing for health reasons or to write poetry that she signed as "the factory girl." Through her poetry, Johnston made clear her awareness of the inequalities and exploitation of industrial life, writing in one poem: "It is the puir [poor] man's hard-won toil that fills the rich man's purse . . . / What care the gentry if they're well, though all the poor would die." Another poem urged unionization for boatbuilders and boilermakers.

In response to industrial misery, however, Johnston did not advocate for socialism or revolutionary upheaval. Rather, she implicitly called on the "master" of the mill to behave in a benevolent fashion toward his employees and to create within the factory a sense of community. At times she recited her poetry at factory-organized gatherings, sometimes toasting the owner: "May he still have wealth; may we still have health / To remain his servants of toil."

On a personal level, this "factory girl" stood up for herself, at one point taking her foreman to court to recover a week's wages when she was fired without notice. But it was within the factory, not the family, that Johnston found emotional and personal satisfaction. In the mills, she discovered camaraderie, an emotional and spiritual home, and a status higher than that of domestic labor, which was the lot of so many young working-class women. Celebrating one of the factories where she worked, Johnston proclaimed: "I would not leave thee, dear beloved place / A crown, a sceptre, or a throne to grace, / To be a queen—the nation's flag unfurl—/ A thousand times I'd be a Factory Girl!"

Johnston had hoped to make her living as a poet and thus escape the poverty to which factory wages condemned her. She did receive occasional financial support from upper-class benefactors, including a small gift from Queen Victoria, and a published collection of her work appeared in 1867. She was, however, aware that both class and gender made it difficult for her to win acceptance among middle- and upper-class members of the literary establishment, a recognition expressed in her writing. "I am so small I cannot shine / Amidst the great that read my rhyme." In 1870, only a year after the publication of the second edition of her book of poetry, she had to apply for "poor relief," and in 1874, Ellen Johnston died in a Scottish poorhouse, not yet forty years of age.

Question: How would you describe Ellen Johnston's outlook on industrial Britain?

Newton discovered the laws of motion. His was therefore a "scientific socialism," embedded in these laws of historical change; revolution was a certainty and the socialist future was inevitable.

It was a grand, compelling, prophetic, utopian vision of human freedom and community—and it inspired socialist movements of workers and intellectuals amid the grim harshness of Europe's industrialization in the second half of the nineteenth century. Socialists established political parties in most European states and linked them together in international organizations as well. These parties recruited members, contested elections as they gained the right to vote, agitated for reforms, and in some cases plotted revolution.

AP® EXAM TIP

You will see AP® exam questions on Marx's economic theories and their effects.

The Socialist Outlook

This 1911 poster was first published in the newspaper of the Industrial Workers of the World, a radical American trade union organization. It illustrates a socialist perspective on capitalist societies. At the bottom of the pyramid, supporting the entire social edifice, are the workers, while above them are arrayed the various oppressive layers of the social hierarchy: the bourgeoisie, the police and militias, religious figures, and state officials. (From *Pyramid of Capitalist System*, issued by Nedelkovich, Brashick and Kuharich, Cleveland [International Publishing Company, 1911]/photo: IAM/akg-images)

AP® EXAM TIP

Take notes on how governments in Western Europe responded to Marx's ideas.

In the later decades of the nineteenth century, such ideas echoed among more radical trade unionists and some middle-class intellectuals in Britain, and even more so in a rapidly industrializing Germany and elsewhere. By then, however, the British working-class movement was not overtly revolutionary. When a working-class political party, the Labour Party, was established in the 1890s, it advocated a reformist program and a peaceful democratic transition to socialism, largely rejecting the class struggle and revolutionary emphasis of classical Marxism. Generally known as "social democracy," this approach to socialism was especially prominent in Germany during the late nineteenth century and spread more widely in the twentieth century when it came into conflict with the more violent and revolutionary movements calling themselves "communist."

Improving material conditions during the second half of the nineteenth century helped move the working-class movement in Britain, Germany, and elsewhere away from a revolutionary posture. Marx had expected industrial capitalist societies to polarize into a small wealthy class and a huge and increasingly impoverished proletariat. However, standing between "the captains of industry" and the workers was a sizable middle and lower middle class, constituting perhaps 30 percent of the population, most of whom were not really wealthy but were immensely proud that they were not manual laborers. Marx had not foreseen the development of this intermediate social group, nor had he imagined that workers could better their standard of living within a capitalist framework. But they did. Wages rose under pressure from unions; cheap imported food improved working-class diets; infant mortality rates fell; and shops and chain stores catering to working-class families multiplied. As English male workers gradually obtained the right to vote, politicians had an incentive to legislate in their favor, by abolishing child labor, regulating factory conditions, and even, in 1911, inaugurating a system of relief for the unemployed. Sanitary reform considerably cleaned up the "filth and stink" of early nineteenth-century cities, and urban parks made a modest appearance. Contrary to Marx's expectations, capitalist societies demonstrated some capacity for reform.

Further eroding working-class radicalism was a growing sense of nationalism, which bound workers in particular countries to their middle-class employers and compatriots, offsetting to some extent the economic and social antagonism between them. When World War I broke out, the "workers of the world," far from uniting against their bourgeois enemies as Marx had urged them, instead set off to slaughter one another in enormous numbers on the battlefields of Europe. National loyalty had trumped class loyalty.

Nonetheless, as the twentieth century dawned, industrial Britain was hardly a stable or contented society. Immense inequalities still separated the classes. Some 40 percent of the working class continued to live in conditions then described as "poverty." A mounting wave of strikes from 1910 to 1913 testified to the intensity of class conflict. The Labour Party was becoming a major force in Parliament. Some socialists and some feminists were becoming radicalized. "Wisps of violence hung in the English air," wrote Eric Hobsbawm, "symptoms of a crisis in economy and society, which the [country's] self-confident opulence . . . could not quite conceal."[25] The world's first industrial society remained dissatisfied and conflicted.

It was also a society in economic decline relative to industrial newcomers such as Germany and the United States. Britain paid a price for its early lead, for its businessmen became committed to machinery that became obsolete as the century progressed. Latecomers invested in more modern equipment and in various ways had surpassed the British by the early twentieth century.

Europeans in Motion

Europe's Industrial Revolution prompted a massive migratory process that uprooted many millions, setting them in motion both internally and around the globe. Within Europe itself, the movement of men, women, and families from the countryside to the cities involved half or more of the region's people by the mid-nineteenth century. More significant for world history was the exodus between 1815 and 1939 of fully 20 percent of Europe's population, some 50 to 55 million people, who left home for the Americas, Australia, New Zealand, South Africa, and elsewhere (see Map 17.2). They were pushed by poverty, a rapidly growing population, and the displacement of peasant farming and artisan manufacturing. And they were pulled abroad by the enormous demand for labor overseas, the ready availability of land in some places, and the relatively cheap transportation of railroads and steamships. But not all found a satisfactory life in their new homes, and perhaps 7 million returned to Europe.[26]

This huge process had a transformative global impact, temporarily increasing Europe's share of the world's population and scattering Europeans around the world. In 1800, less than 1 percent of the total world population consisted of overseas Europeans and their descendants; by 1930, they represented 11 percent.[27] In particular regions, the impact was profound. Australia and New Zealand became settler colonies, outposts of European civilization in the South Pacific that overwhelmed their native populations through conquest, acquisition of their lands, and disease. In Australia, the initial settlers derived from the unwanted of British

AP® EXAM TIP

Causes and effects of global migrations, triggered by the Industrial Revolution, are key elements of the AP® World History curriculum.

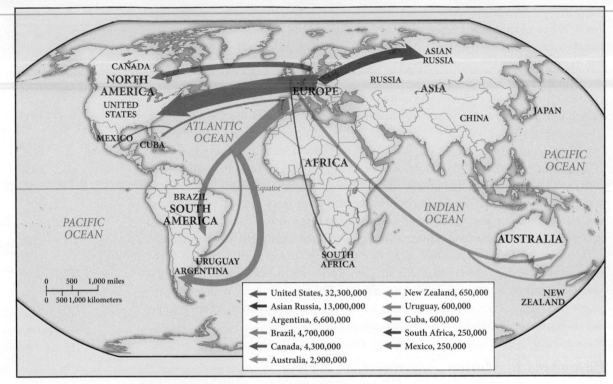

Map 17.2   European Migration in the Industrial Age

The Industrial Revolution not only transformed European society but also scattered millions of Europeans to the far corners of the world.

society: convicts were sentenced to penal colonies on the island continent, and by 1867 over 165,000 of them had arrived. By the end of the nineteenth century, New Zealand's European population, based on immigration of free people, out-numbered the native Maori by 700,000 to 40,000. Smaller numbers of Europeans found their way to South Africa, Kenya, Rhodesia, Algeria, and elsewhere, where they injected a sharp racial divide into those colonized territories.

But it was the Americas that felt the brunt of this huge movement of people. Latin America received about 20 percent of the European migratory stream, mostly from Italy, Spain, and Portugal, with Argentina and Brazil accounting for some 80 percent of those immigrants. Considered "white," they enhanced the social weight of the European element in those countries and thus enjoyed economic advantages over the mixed-race, Indian, and African populations.

In several ways the immigrant experience in the United States was distinctive. It was far larger and more diverse than elsewhere, with some 32 million newcomers arriving from all over Europe between 1820 and 1930. Furthermore, the United

States offered affordable land to many and industrial jobs to many more, neither of which was widely available in Latin America. And the United States was unique in turning the immigrant experience into a national myth—that of the melting pot. Despite this ideology of assimilation, the earlier immigrants, mostly Protestants from Britain and Germany, were anything but welcoming to Catholics and Jews from Southern and Eastern Europe who arrived later. The newcomers were seen as distinctly inferior, even "un-American," and blamed for crime, labor unrest, and socialist ideas. Nonetheless, this surge of immigration contributed much to the westward expansion of the United States, to the establishment of a European-derived culture in a vast area of North America, and to the displacement of the Native American peoples of the region.

In the vast domains of the Russian Empire, a parallel process of European migration likewise unfolded. After the freeing of the serfs in 1861, some 13 million Russians and Ukrainians migrated to Siberia, where they overwhelmed the native population of the region, while millions more settled in Central Asia. By the end of the century, native Siberians totaled only 10 percent of that region's population. The availability of land, the prospect of greater freedom from tsarist restrictions and from the exploitation of aristocratic landowners, and the construction of the trans-Siberian railroad—all of this facilitated the continued Europeanization of Siberia. As in the United States, the Russian government encouraged and aided this process, hoping to forestall Chinese pressures in the region and relieve growing population pressures in the more densely settled western lands of the empire.

Variations on a Theme: Industrialization in the United States and Russia

Not for long was the Industrial Revolution confined to Britain. It soon spread to continental Western Europe, and by the end of the nineteenth century it was well under way in the United States, Russia, and Japan. The globalization of industrialization had begun. Everywhere it took hold, industrialization bore a range of broadly similar outcomes. New technologies and sources of energy generated vast increases in production and spawned an unprecedented urbanization as well. Class structures changed as aristocrats, artisans, and peasants declined as classes, while the middle classes and a factory working class grew in numbers and social prominence. Middle-class women generally withdrew from paid labor altogether, and their working-class counterparts sought to do so after marriage. Working women usually received lower wages than their male counterparts, had difficulty joining unions, and were accused of taking jobs from men. Working-class frustration and anger gave rise to trade unions and socialist movements, injecting a new element of social conflict into industrial societies.

Nevertheless, different histories, cultures, and societies ensured that the Industrial Revolution unfolded variously in the diverse countries in which it became

AP® EXAM TIP

Always pay special attention to discussions of comparisons in world history.

The English Luddites and Machine Breaking

If you do Not Cause those Dressing Machines to be Remov'd Within the Bounds of Seven Days . . . your factory and all that it Contains Will and Shall Surely Be Set on fire . . . it is Not our Desire to Do you the Least Injury, But We are fully Determin'd to Destroy Both Dressing Machines and Steam Looms.[28]

B etween 1811 and 1813, this kind of warning was sent to hundreds of English workshops in the woolen and cotton industry, where more efficient machines, some of them steam powered, threatened the jobs and livelihood of workers. Over and over, that threat was carried out as well-organized bands of skilled artisans destroyed the offending machines, burned buildings, and on occasion attacked employers. These were the Luddites, taking their name from a mythical Robin Hood–like figure, Ned Ludd. A song called "General Ludd's Triumph" expressed their sentiments: "These Engines of mischief were sentenced to die / By unanimous vote of the Trade / And Ludd who can all opposition defy / Was the Grand executioner made."

So widespread and serious was this Luddite uprising that the British government sent 12,000 troops to sup-

Luddites smashing a loom.

press it, more than it was then devoting to the struggle against Napoleon in continental Europe. And a new law, rushed through Parliament as an "emergency measure" in 1812, made those who destroyed mechanized looms subject to the death penalty. Some sixty to seventy alleged Luddites were in fact hanged, and sometimes beheaded as well, for machine breaking.

In the governing circles of England, Luddism was widely regarded as blind protest, an outrageous, unthinking, and futile resistance to progress. It has remained in more recent times a term of insult applied to those who resist or reject technological innovation. And yet, a closer look suggests that we might view that movement with some sympathy as an understandable response to a painful transformation of social life when few alternatives for expressing grievances were available.

At the time of the Luddite uprising, England was involved in an increasingly unpopular war with Napoleon's France, and mutual blockades substantially reduced trade and hurt the textile industry. The country was also

established. Differences in the pace and timing of industrialization, the size and shape of major industries, the role of the state, the political expression of social conflict, and many other factors have made this process rich in comparative possibilities. French industrialization, for example, occurred more slowly and perhaps less disruptively than did that of Britain. Germany focused initially on heavy industry — iron, steel, and coal — rather than on the textile industry with which Britain had begun. Moreover, German industrialization was far more highly concentrated in huge companies called cartels, and it generated a rather more militant and Marxist-oriented labor movement than in Britain.

in the early phase of an Industrial Revolution in which mechanized production was replacing skilled artisan labor. All of this, plus some bad weather and poor harvests, combined to generate real economic hardship, unemployment, and hunger. Bread riots and various protests against high prices proliferated.

Furthermore, English elites were embracing new laissez-faire, or free market, economic principles, which eroded customary protections for the poor and working classes. Over the previous several decades, many laws that had regulated wages and apprenticeships and prohibited certain laborsaving machines had been repealed, despite repeated workers' appeals to Parliament to maintain some minimal protections for their older way of life. A further act of Parliament in 1799 had forbidden trade unions and collective bargaining. In these circumstances, some form of direct action is hardly surprising.

At one level, the Luddite machine-breaking movement represented "collective bargaining by riot," a way of pressuring employers when legal negotiations with them had been outlawed. And the issues involved more than laborsaving machines. Luddites also argued for price reductions, minimum wages, and prohibitions on the flooding of their industry by unapprenticed workers. They wanted to return to a time when "full fashioned work at the old fashioned price is established by custom and law," according to one of their songs. More generally, Luddites sought to preserve elements of an older way of life in which industry existed to provide a livelihood for workers, in which men could take pride in their craft, in which government and employers felt some paternalistic responsibility to the lower classes, and in which journeymen workers felt some bonds of attachment to a larger social and moral order. All of this was rapidly eroding in the new era of capitalist industrialization. In these ways, the Luddite movement looked backward to idealized memories of an earlier time.

And yet in other ways, the rebels anticipated the future with their demands for minimum wage and an end to child labor, their concern about inferior-quality products produced by machines, and their desire to organize trade unions. At the height of the Luddite movement, some among them began to move beyond local industrial action toward a "general insurrection" that might bring real political change to the entire country. In one letter from a Luddite in 1812, the writer expressed "hope for assistance from the French emperor [Napoleon] in shaking off the yoke of the rottenest, wickedest, and most tyranious government that ever existed." He continued, "Then we will be governed by a just republic."

After 1813, the organized Luddite movement faded away. But it serves as a cautionary reminder that what is hailed as progress claims victims as well as beneficiaries.

Questions: To what extent did the concerns of the Luddites come to pass as the Industrial Revolution unfolded? How does your understanding of the Luddites affect your posture toward technological change in our time?

Nowhere were the variations in the industrializing process more apparent than in those two vast countries that lay on the periphery of Europe. To the west across the Atlantic Ocean was the United States, a young, vigorous, democratic, expanding country, populated largely by people of European descent, along with a substantial number of slaves of African origin. To the east was Russia, with its Eastern Orthodox Christianity, an autocratic tsar, a huge population of serfs, and an empire stretching across all of northern Asia. In the 1830s, the French observer Alexis de Tocqueville famously commented on these two emerging giants in his book *Democracy in America*:

The Anglo-American relies upon personal interest to accomplish his ends and gives free scope to the unguided strength and common sense of the people; the Russian centers all the authority of society in a single arm. . . . Their starting-point is different and their courses are not the same; yet each of them seems marked out by the will of Heaven to sway the destinies of half the globe.

By the early twentieth century, his prediction seemed to be coming true. Industrialization had turned the United States into a major global power and had spawned in Russia an enormous revolutionary upheaval that made that country the first outpost of global communism.

The United States: Industrialization without Socialism

American industrialization began in the textile factories of New England during the 1820s but grew explosively in the half century following the Civil War (1861–1865) (see Map 17.3). The country's huge size, the ready availability of natural resources, its expanding domestic market, and its relative political stability combined to make the United States the world's leading industrial power by 1914. At that time, it produced 36 percent of the world's manufactured goods, compared to 16 percent for Germany, 14 percent for Great Britain, and 6 percent for France. Furthermore, U.S. industrialization was closely linked to that of Europe. About one-third of the capital investment that financed its remarkable growth came from British, French, and German capitalists. But unlike Latin America, which also received much foreign investment, the United States was able to use those funds to generate an independent Industrial Revolution of its own.

Guided Reading Question

■ COMPARISON
What were the differences between industrialization in the United States and that in Russia?

As in other second-wave industrializing countries, the U.S. government played an important role, though less directly than in Germany or Japan. Tax breaks, huge grants of public land to the railroad companies, laws enabling the easy formation of corporations, and the absence of much overt regulation of industry all fostered the rise of very large business enterprises. The U.S. Steel Corporation, for example, by 1901 had an annual budget three times the size of that of the federal government. In this respect, the United States followed the pattern of Germany but differed from that of France and Britain, where family businesses still predominated.

The United States also pioneered techniques of mass production, using interchangeable parts, the assembly line, and "scientific management" to produce for a mass market. The nation's advertising agencies, Sears Roebuck's and Montgomery Ward's mail-order catalogs, and urban department stores generated a middle-class "culture of consumption." When the industrialist Henry Ford in the early twentieth century began producing the Model T at a price that many ordinary people could afford, he famously declared: "I am going to democratize the automobile." More so than in Europe, with its aristocratic traditions, self-made American industrialists of fabulous wealth such as Henry Ford, Andrew Carnegie, and John D.

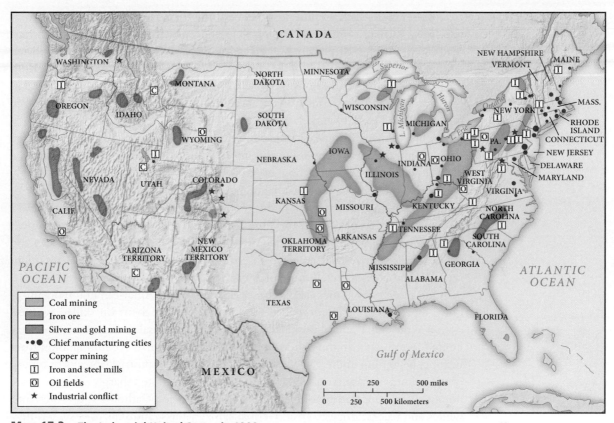

Map 17.3   The Industrial United States in 1900

By the early twentieth century, manufacturing industries were largely in the Northeast and Midwest, whereas mining operations were more widely scattered across the country.

Rockefeller became cultural heroes, widely admired as models of what anyone could achieve with daring and hard work in a land of endless opportunity.

Nevertheless, well before the first Model T rolled off the assembly line, serious social divisions of a kind common to European industrial societies mounted. Preindustrial America had boasted of a relative social equality, quite unlike that of Europe, but by the end of the nineteenth century a widening gap separated the classes. In Carnegie's Homestead steel plant near Pittsburgh, employees worked every day except Christmas and the Fourth of July, often for twelve hours a day. In Manhattan, where millions of European immigrants disembarked, many lived in five- or six-story buildings with four families and two toilets on each floor. In every large city, such conditions prevailed close by the mansions of elite neighborhoods. To some, the contrast was a betrayal of American ideals, while others saw it as a natural outcome of competition and "the survival of the fittest."

Guided Reading Question

■ EXPLANATION

Why did Marxist socialism not take root in the United States?

As elsewhere, such conditions generated much labor protest, the formation of unions, and strikes, sometimes leading to violence. In 1877, when the eastern railroads announced a 10 percent wage cut for their workers, strikers disrupted rail service across the eastern half of the country, smashed equipment, and rioted. Both state militias and federal troops were called out to put down the movement. Class consciousness and class conflict were intense in the industrial America of the late nineteenth and early twentieth centuries.

Unlike in many European countries, however, no major political party emerged in the United States to represent the interests of the working class. Nor did the ideas of socialism, especially those of Marxism, appeal to American workers nearly as much as they did to European laborers. At its high point, the Socialist Party of America garnered just 6 percent of the vote for its presidential candidate in the 1912 election, whereas socialists at the time held more seats in Germany's Parliament than any other party. Even in the depths of the Great Depression of the 1930s, no major socialist movement emerged to champion American workers. How might we explain this distinctive feature of American industrial development?

One answer lies in the relative conservatism of major American union organizations, especially the American Federation of Labor. Its focus on skilled workers excluded the more radical unskilled laborers, and its refusal to align with any party limited its influence in the political arena. Furthermore, massive immigration from Europe, beginning in the 1840s, created a very diverse industrial labor force on top of the country's sharp racial divide. This diversity contrasted sharply with the more homogeneous populations of many European countries. Catholics and Protestants; whites and blacks; English, Irish, Germans, Slavs, Jews, and Italians—such differences undermined the class solidarity of American workers, making it far more difficult to sustain class-oriented political parties and a socialist labor movement. Moreover, the country's remarkable economic growth generated on average a higher standard of living for American workers than their European counterparts experienced. Land was cheaper, and home ownership was more available. Workers with property generally found socialism less attractive than those without. By 1910, a particularly large group of white-collar workers in sales, services, and offices outnumbered factory laborers. Their middle-class aspirations further diluted impulses toward radicalism.

But political challenges to the abuses of capitalist industrialization did arise. In the 1890s, among small farmers in the U.S. South, West, and Midwest, "populists" railed against banks, industrialists, monopolies, the existing money system, and both major political parties, all of which they thought were dominated by the corporate interests of the eastern elites. More successful, especially in the early twentieth century, were the Progressives, who pushed for specific reforms, such as wages-and-hours legislation, better sanitation standards, antitrust laws, and greater governmental intervention in the economy. Socialism, however, came to be defined as fundamentally "un-American" in a country that so valued individualism and so feared "big government." It was a distinctive feature of the American response to industrialization.

Russia: Industrialization and Revolution

As a setting for the Industrial Revolution, it would be hard to imagine two more different environments than the United States and Russia. If the United States was the Western world's most exuberant democracy during the nineteenth century, Russia remained the sole outpost of absolute monarchy, in which the state exercised far greater control over individuals and society than anywhere in the Western world.

At the beginning of the twentieth century, Russia still had no national parliament, no legal political parties, and no nationwide elections. The tsar, answerable to God alone, ruled unchecked. Furthermore, Russian society was dominated by a titled nobility of various ranks. Its upper levels included great landowners, who furnished the state with military officers and leading government officials. Until 1861, most Russians were peasant serfs, bound to the estates of their masters, subject to sale, greatly exploited, and largely at the mercy of their owners. A vast cultural gulf separated these two classes. Many nobles were highly westernized, some speaking French better than Russian, whereas their serfs were steeped in a backwoods Orthodox Christianity that incorporated pre-Christian spirits, spells, curses, and magic.

A further difference between Russia and the United States lay in the source of social and economic change. In the United States, such change bubbled up from society as free farmers, workers, and businessmen sought new opportunities and operated in a political system that gave them varying degrees of expression. In autocratic Russia, change was far more often initiated by the state itself, in its continuing

Russian Serfdom
This nineteenth-century cartoon by the French artist Gustave Doré shows Russian noblemen gambling with tied bundles of stiff serfs. Serfdom was not finally abolished in Russia until 1861.

efforts to catch up with the more powerful and innovative states of Europe. This kind of "transformation from above" found an early expression in the reign of Peter the Great (r. 1689–1725). (See Chapter 13, page 576.) Such state-directed change continued in the nineteenth century with the freeing of the serfs in 1861, an action stimulated by military defeat at the hands of British and French forces in the Crimean War (1854–1856). To many thoughtful Russians, serfdom seemed incompatible with modern civilization and held back the country's overall development, as did its economic and industrial backwardness. Thus, beginning in the 1860s, Russia began a program of industrial development, which was more heavily directed by the state than was the case in Western Europe or the United States.

By the 1890s, Russia's Industrial Revolution was launched and growing rapidly. It focused particularly on railroads and heavy industry and was fueled by a substantial amount of foreign investment. By 1900, Russia ranked fourth in the world in steel production and had major industries in coal, textiles, and oil. Its industrial enterprises, still modest in comparison to those of Europe, were concentrated in a few major cities—Moscow, St. Petersburg, and Kiev, for example—and took place in factories far larger than in most of Western Europe.

All of this contributed to the explosive social outcomes of Russian industrialization. A growing middle class of businessmen and professionals increasingly took shape. As modern and educated people, many in the middle class objected strongly to the deep conservatism of tsarist Russia and sought a greater role in political life, but they were also dependent on the state for contracts and jobs and for suppressing the growing radicalism of the workers, which they greatly feared. Although factory workers constituted only about 5 percent of Russia's total population, they quickly developed a radical class consciousness, based on harsh conditions and the absence of any legal outlet for their grievances. As in Western Europe, millions flocked to the new centers of industrial development. By 1897, over 70 percent of the population in Moscow and St. Petersburg were recent migrants from the rural areas. Their conditions of life resembled those of industrial migrants in New York or Berlin. One observer wrote: "People live in impossible conditions: filth, stench, suffocating heat. They lie down together barely a few feet apart; there is no division between the sexes and adults sleep with children."[29] Until 1897, a thirteen-hour working day was common, while ruthless discipline and overt disrespect from supervisors created resentment. In the absence of legal unions or political parties, these grievances often erupted in the form of large-scale strikes.

In these conditions, a small but growing number of educated Russians found in Marxist socialism a way of understanding the changes they witnessed daily as well as hope for the future in a revolutionary upheaval of workers. In 1898, they created an illegal Russian Social-Democratic Labor Party and quickly became involved in workers' education, union organizing, and, eventually, revolutionary action. By the early twentieth century, the strains of rapid change and the state's continued intransigence had reached the bursting point, and in 1905, following its defeat in a

Guided Reading Question

■ CHANGE

What factors contributed to the making of a revolutionary situation in Russia by the beginning of the twentieth century?

AP® EXAM TIP

Comparative responses to the Industrial Revolution are a popular topic on the AP® exam.

naval war with Japan, Russia erupted in spontaneous insurrection (see Map 17.4). Workers in Moscow and St. Petersburg went on strike and created their own representative councils, called soviets. Peasant uprisings, student demonstrations, revolts of non-Russian nationalities, and mutinies in the military all contributed to the upheaval. Recently formed political parties, representing intellectuals of various persuasions, came out into the open.

The 1905 revolution, though brutally suppressed, forced the tsar's regime to make more substantial reforms than it had ever contemplated. It granted a constitution, legalized both trade unions and political parties, and permitted the election of a national assembly, called the Duma. Censorship was eased, and plans were under way for universal primary education. Industrial development likewise continued at a rapid rate, so that by 1914 Russia stood fifth in the world in terms of overall output. But in the first half of that year, some 1,250,000 workers, representing about 40 percent of the entire industrial workforce, went out on strike.

Thus the tsar's limited political reforms, which had been granted with great reluctance and were often reversed in practice, failed to tame working-class radicalism or to bring social stability to Russia. In Russian political life, the people generally, and even the middle class, had only a very limited voice. Rep-

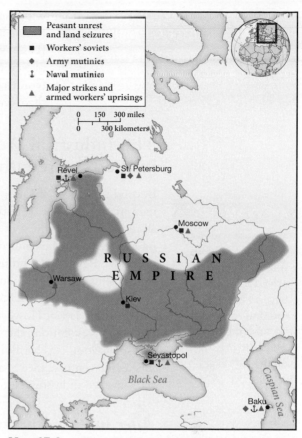

Map 17.4 Industrialization and Revolution in Russia, 1905
Only in Russia did industrialization lead to violent revolutionary upheavals, both in 1905 and more successfully in 1917.

resentatives of even the privileged classes had become so alienated by the government's intransigence that many felt revolution was inevitable. Various revolutionary groups, many of them socialist, published pamphlets and newspapers, organized trade unions, and spread their messages among workers and peasants. Particularly in the cities, these revolutionary parties had an impact. They provided a language through which workers could express their grievances; they created links among workers from different factories; and they furnished leaders who were able to act when the revolutionary moment arrived.

World War I provided that moment. The enormous hardships of that war, coupled with the immense social tensions of industrialization within a still-autocratic political system, sparked the Russian Revolution of 1917 (see Chapter 21). That massive upheaval quickly brought to power the most radical of the socialist groups operating in the country—the Bolsheviks, led by the charismatic Vladimir Ilyich Ulyanov, better known as Lenin. Only in Russia was industrialization associated

AP® EXAM TIP

Pay attention to this latest example of causes of the fall of a major empire, as this is an example of continuity over time.

PRACTICING AP® HISTORICAL THINKING

What was common to industrialization everywhere, and in what ways did it vary from place to place?

with violent social revolution. This was the most distinctive feature of Russia's modern historical development. And only in Russia was a socialist political party, inspired by the teachings of Karl Marx, able to seize power, thus launching the modern world's first socialist society, with enormous implications for the twentieth century.

The Industrial Revolution and Latin America in the Nineteenth Century

AP® EXAM TIP

Make sure you study the ways the Industrial Revolution affected regions beyond Europe and the United States because they are frequently found on the AP® exam.

Beyond the world of Europe and North America, only Japan underwent a major industrial transformation during the nineteenth century, part of that country's overall response to the threat of European aggression. (See Chapter 19, pages 852–60, for a more detailed examination of Japan's industrialization.) Elsewhere—in colonial India, Egypt, the Ottoman Empire, China, and Latin America—very modest experiments in modern industry were undertaken, but nowhere did they drive the kind of major social transformation that had taken place in Britain, Europe, North America, and Japan. However, even in societies that did not experience their own Industrial Revolution, the profound impact of European and North American industrialization was hard to avoid. Such was the case in Latin America during the nineteenth century. (See Snapshot, opposite, for the global economic divisions that accompanied industrialization.)

After Independence in Latin America

The struggle for independence in Latin America had lasted far longer and proved far more destructive than in North America. Decimated populations, diminished herds of livestock, flooded or closed silver mines, abandoned farms, shrinking international trade and investment capital, and empty national treasuries—these were the conditions that greeted Latin Americans upon independence. Furthermore, the four major administrative units (viceroyalties) of Spanish America ultimately dissolved into eighteen separate countries, and regional revolts wracked Brazil in the early decades of its independent life. A number of international wars in the post-independence century likewise shook these new nations. Peru and Bolivia briefly united and then broke apart in a bitter conflict (1836–1839); Mexico lost huge territories to the United States (1846–1848); and an alliance of Argentina, Brazil, and Uruguay went to war with Paraguay (1864–1870) in a conflict that devastated Paraguay's small population.

Within these new countries, political life was turbulent and unstable. Conservatives favored centralized authority and sought to maintain the social status quo of the colonial era in alliance with the Catholic Church, which at independence owned perhaps half of all productive land. Their often-bitter opponents were liberals, who attacked the Church in the name of Enlightenment values, sought at least

SNAPSHOT   The Industrial Revolution and the Global Divide

During the nineteenth century, the Industrial Revolution generated an enormous and unprecedented economic division in the world, as measured by the share of manufacturing output. What patterns can you see in this table?[30]

SHARE OF TOTAL WORLD MANUFACTURING OUTPUT (percentage)

	1750	1800	1860	1880	1900
EUROPE AS A WHOLE	23.2	28.1	53.2	61.3	62.0
United Kingdom	1.9	4.3	19.9	22.9	18.5
France	4.0	4.2	7.9	7.8	6.8
Germany	2.9	3.5	4.9	8.5	13.2
Russia	5.0	5.6	7.0	7.6	8.8
UNITED STATES	0.1	0.8	7.2	14.7	23.6
JAPAN	3.8	3.5	2.6	2.4	2.4
THE REST OF THE WORLD	73.0	67.7	36.6	20.9	11.0
China	32.8	33.3	19.7	12.5	6.2
South Asia (India/Pakistan)	24.5	19.7	8.6	2.8	1.7

modest social reforms, and preferred federalism. In many countries, conflicts between these factions, often violent, enabled military strongmen known as *caudillos* (kaw-DEE-yos) to achieve power as defenders of order and property, although they too succeeded one another with great frequency. One of them, Antonio López de Santa Anna of Mexico, was president of his country at least nine separate times between 1833 and 1855. Constitutions too replaced one another with bewildering speed. Bolivia had ten constitutions during the nineteenth century, while Ecuador and Peru each had eight.

Social life did not change fundamentally in the aftermath of independence. As in Europe and North America, women remained disenfranchised and wholly outside of formal political life. Slavery, it is true, was abolished in most of Latin America by midcentury, although it persisted in both Brazil and Cuba until the late 1880s. Most of the legal distinctions among various racial categories also disappeared, and all free people were considered, at least officially, equal citizens. Nevertheless, productive economic resources such as businesses, ranches, and plantations remained overwhelmingly in the hands of creole white men, who were culturally oriented toward Europe. The military provided an avenue of mobility for a few skilled and ambitious mestizo men, some of whom subsequently became caudillos. Other mixed-race men and women found a place in a small middle class as teachers,

AP® EXAM TIP

Take notes on this paragraph about social continuities in nineteenth-century Latin America.

shopkeepers, or artisans. The vast majority—blacks, Indians, and many mixed-race people of both sexes—remained impoverished, working small subsistence farms or laboring in the mines or on the *haciendas* (ah-see-EHN-duhz) (plantations) of the well-to-do. Only rarely did the poor and dispossessed actively rebel against their social betters. One such case was the Caste War of Yucatán (1847–1901), a prolonged struggle of the Maya people of Mexico, aimed at cleansing their land of European and mestizo intruders.

Facing the World Economy

During the second half of the nineteenth century, a measure of political consolidation took hold in Latin America, and countries such as Mexico, Peru, and Argentina entered periods of greater stability. At the same time, Latin America as a whole became more closely integrated into a world economy driven by the industrialization of Western Europe and North America. The new technology of the steamship cut the sailing time between Britain and Argentina almost in half, while the underwater telegraph instantly brought the latest news and fashions of Europe to Latin America.

The most significant economic outcome of this growing integration was a rapid growth of Latin American exports to the industrializing countries, which now needed the food products, raw materials, and markets of these new nations. Latin American landowners, businessmen, and governments proved eager to supply those needs, and in the sixty years or so after 1850, an export boom increased the value of Latin American goods sold abroad by a factor of ten.

Mexico continued to produce large amounts of silver, providing more than half the world's new supply until 1860. Now added to the list of raw materials flowing out of Latin America were copper from Chile, a metal that the growing electrical industry required; tin from Bolivia, which met the mounting demand for tin cans; and nitrates from Chile and guano (bird droppings) from Peru, both of which were used for fertilizer. Wild rubber from the Amazon rain forest was in great demand for bicycle and automobile tires, as was sisal from Mexico, used to make binder twine for the proliferating mechanical harvesters of North America. Bananas from Central America, beef from Argentina, cacao from Ecuador, coffee from Brazil and Guatemala, and sugar from Cuba also found eager markets in the rapidly growing and increasingly prosperous world of industrializing countries. In return for these primary products, Latin Americans imported the textiles, machinery, tools, weapons, and luxury goods of Europe and the United States (see Map 17.5).

Accompanying this burgeoning commerce was large-scale investment of European capital in Latin America, $10 billion alone between 1870 and 1919. Most of this capital came from Great Britain, which invested more in Argentina in the late nineteenth century than in its colony of India, although France, Germany, Italy, and the United States also contributed to this substantial financial transfer. By 1910, U.S. business interests controlled 40 percent of Mexican property and produced

Guided Reading Question

■ CONNECTION

In what ways was Latin America linked to the global economy of the nineteenth century, and what was the impact of these links?

AP® EXAM TIP

Pay attention to the economic and social connections between several world regions on Map 17.5.

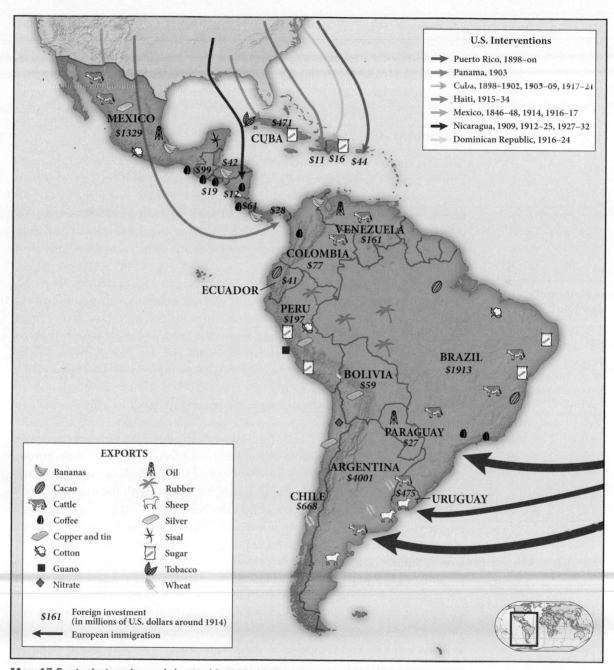

U.S. Interventions

→ Puerto Rico, 1898–on
→ Panama, 1903
→ Cuba, 1898–1902, 1903–09, 1917–21
→ Haiti, 1915–34
→ Mexico, 1846–48, 1914, 1916–17
→ Nicaragua, 1909, 1912–25, 1927–32
→ Dominican Republic, 1916–24

MEXICO
$1329

CUBA
$471
$11 $16 $44

$42
$99
$19 $12
$61 $28

VENEZUELA
$161

COLOMBIA
$77

ECUADOR
$41

PERU
$197

BOLIVIA
$59

BRAZIL
$1913

PARAGUAY
$27

ARGENTINA
$4001

CHILE
$668

URUGUAY
$475

EXPORTS

🍌 Bananas   Oil
   Cacao   Rubber
   Cattle   Sheep
   Coffee   Silver
   Copper and tin Sisal
   Cotton   Sugar
   Guano   Tobacco
   Nitrate   Wheat

$161   Foreign investment
       (in millions of U.S. dollars around 1914)

←   European immigration

Map 17.5   Latin America and the World, 1825–1935

During the nineteenth and early twentieth centuries, Latin American countries interacted with the industrializing world via investment, trade, immigration, and military intervention from the United States.

half of its oil. Much of this capital was used to build railroads, largely to funnel Latin American exports to the coast, where they were shipped to overseas markets. Mexico had only 390 miles of railroad in 1876; it had 15,000 miles in 1910. By 1915, Argentina, with 22,000 miles of railroad, had more track per person than the United States had.

Becoming like Europe?

To the economic elites of Latin America, intent on making their countries resemble Europe or the United States, all of this was progress. In some respects, they were surely right. Economies were growing, producing more than ever before. The population was also burgeoning; it increased from about 30 million in 1850 to more than 77 million in 1912 as public health measures (such as safe drinking water, inoculations, sewers, and campaigns to eliminate mosquitoes that carried yellow fever) brought down death rates.

Guided Reading Question

■ COMPARISON
Did Latin America follow or diverge from the historical path of Europe during the nineteenth century?

Urbanization also proceeded rapidly. By the early twentieth century, wrote one scholar, "Latin American cities lost their colonial cobblestones, white-plastered walls, and red-tiled roofs. They became modern metropolises, comparable to urban giants anywhere. Streetcars swayed, telephones jangled, and silent movies flickered from Montevideo and Santiago to Mexico City and Havana."[31] Buenos Aires, Argentina's metropolitan center, boasted 750,000 people in 1900 and billed itself as the "Paris of South America." There the educated elite, just like the English, drank tea in the afternoon, while discussing European literature, philosophy, and fashion, usually in French.

To become more like Europe, Latin America sought to attract more Europeans. Because civilization, progress, and modernity apparently derived from Europe, many Latin American countries actively sought to increase their "white" populations by deliberately recruiting impoverished Europeans with the promise, mostly unfulfilled, of a new and prosperous life in the New World. Argentina received the largest wave of European immigrants (some 2.5 million between 1870 and 1915), mostly from Spain and Italy. Brazil and Uruguay likewise attracted substantial numbers of European newcomers.

Only a quite modest segment of Latin American society saw any great benefits from the export boom and all that followed from it. Upper-class landowners certainly gained as exports flourished and their property values soared. Middle-class urban dwellers—merchants, office workers, lawyers, and other professionals—also grew in numbers and prosperity as their skills proved valuable in a modernizing society. As a percentage of the total population, however, these were narrow elites. In Mexico in the mid-1890s, for example, the landowning upper class made up no more than 1 percent and the middle classes perhaps 8 percent of the population. Everyone else was lower class, and most of them were impoverished.[32]

A new but quite small segment of this vast lower class emerged among urban workers who labored in the railroads, ports, mines, and a few factories. They initially organized themselves in a variety of mutual aid societies, but by the end of the nineteenth century they were creating unions and engaging in strikes. To authoritarian governments interested in stability and progress, such activity was highly provocative and threatening, and they acted harshly to crush or repress unions and strikes. In 1906, the Mexican dictator Porfirio Díaz invited the Arizona Rangers to suppress a strike at Cananea, near the U.S. border, an action that resulted in dozens of deaths. The following year in the Chilean city of Iquique, more than 1,000 men, women, and children were slaughtered by police when nitrate miners protested their wages and working conditions.

The vast majority of the lower class lived in rural areas, where they suffered the most and benefited the least from the export boom. Government attacks on communal landholding and peasant indebtedness to wealthy landowners combined to push many farmers off their land or into remote and poor areas where they could barely make a living. Many wound up as dependent laborers or peons on the haciendas of the wealthy, where their wages were often too meager to support a family. Thus women and children, who had earlier remained at home to tend the family plot, were required to join their menfolk as field laborers. Many immigrant Italian farmworkers in Argentina and Brazil were unable to acquire their own farms, as they had expected, and so drifted into the growing cities or returned to Italy.

Although local protests and violence were frequent, only in Mexico did these vast inequalities erupt into a nationwide revolution. There, in the early twentieth century, middle-class reformers joined with workers and peasants to overthrow the long dictatorship of Porfirio Díaz (r. 1876–1911). What followed was a decade of bloody conflict (1910–1920) that cost Mexico some 1 million lives, or roughly 10 percent of the population. Huge peasant armies under charismatic leaders such as Pancho Villa and Emiliano Zapata helped oust Díaz. Intent on seizing land and redistributing it to the peasants, they then went on to attack many of Mexico's large haciendas. But unlike the leaders of the later Russian and Chinese revolutions, whose most radical elements seized state power, Villa and Zapata proved unable to do so on a long-term basis, in part because they were hobbled by factionalism and focused on local or regional issues. Despite this

The Mexican Revolution Women were active participants in the Mexican Revolution. They prepared food, nursed the wounded, washed clothes, and at times served as soldiers on the battlefield, as illustrated in this cover image from a French magazine in 1913. (© Archivio Iconografico, S.A./Corbis)

limitation and its own internal conflicts, the Mexican Revolution transformed the country. When the dust settled, Mexico had a new constitution (1917) that proclaimed universal male suffrage; provided for the redistribution of land; stripped the Catholic Church of any role in public education and forbade it to own land; announced unheard-of rights for workers, such as a minimum wage and an eight-hour workday; and placed restrictions on foreign ownership of property. Much of Mexico's history in the twentieth century involved working out the implications of these nationalist and reformist changes. The revolution's direct influence, however, was largely limited to Mexico itself and a few places in Central America and the Andes; the upheaval did not have the wider international impact of the Russian and Chinese revolutions.

Perhaps the most significant outcome of the export boom lay in what did *not* happen, for nowhere in Latin America did it jump-start a thorough Industrial Revolution, despite a few factories that processed foods or manufactured textiles, clothing, and building materials. The reasons are many. A social structure that relegated some 90 percent of its population to an impoverished lower class generated only a very small market for manufactured goods. Moreover, economically powerful groups such as landowners and cattlemen benefited greatly from exporting agricultural products and had little incentive to invest in manufacturing. Domestic manufacturing enterprises could only have competed with cheaper and higher-quality foreign goods if they had been protected for a time by high tariffs. But Latin American political leaders had thoroughly embraced the popular European doctrine of prosperity through free trade, and many governments depended on taxing imports to fill their treasuries.

Instead of its own Industrial Revolution, Latin Americans developed a form of economic growth that was largely financed by capital from abroad and dependent on European and North American prosperity and decisions. Brazil experienced this kind of dependence when its booming rubber industry suddenly collapsed in 1910–1911, after seeds from the wild rubber tree had been illegally exported to Britain and were used to start competing and cheaper rubber plantations in Malaysia.

Later critics saw this "dependent development" as a new form of colonialism, expressed in the power exercised by foreign investors. The influence of the U.S.-owned United Fruit Company in Central America was a case in point. Allied with large landowners and compliant politicians, the company pressured the governments of these "banana republics" to maintain conditions favorable to U.S. business. This indirect or behind-the-scenes imperialism was supplemented by repeated U.S. military intervention in support of American corporate interests in Cuba, Haiti, the Dominican Republic, Nicaragua, and Mexico. The United States also controlled the Panama Canal and acquired Puerto Rico as a territory in the aftermath of the Spanish-American War (see Map 17.5, page 769).

Thus, despite Latin America's domination by people of European descent and its close ties to the industrializing countries of the Atlantic world, that region's historical trajectory in the nineteenth century diverged considerably from that of Europe and North America.

AP® EXAM TIP

Make sure you understand the concept of "dependent development" because it is sometimes seen on the AP® exam.

History and Horse Races

Historians and students of history seem endlessly fascinated by "firsts"—the first breakthrough to agriculture, the first domestication of horses, the first civilization, the first use of gunpowder, the first printing press, and so on. Each of these firsts presents a problem of explanation: why did it occur in some particular time and place rather than somewhere else or at some other time? Such questions have assumed historical significance because "first achievements" represent something new in the human journey and because many of them conveyed unusual power, wealth, status, or influence on their creators.

Nonetheless, the focus on firsts can be misleading as well. Those who accomplished something first may see themselves as generally superior to those who embraced that innovation later. Historians too can sometimes adopt a winners-and-losers mentality, inviting a view of history as a horse race toward some finish line of accomplishment. Most first achievements in history, however, were not the result of intentional efforts but rather the unexpected outcome of converging circumstances.

The Industrial Revolution is a case in point. Understanding the European beginnings of this immense breakthrough is certainly justified by its pervasive global consequences and its global spread over the past several centuries. In terms of human ability to dominate the natural environment and to extract wealth from it, the Industrial Revolution marks a decisive turning point in the history of our species. But Europeans' attempts to explain their Industrial Revolution have at times stated or implied their own unique genius. In the nineteenth century, many Europeans saw their technological mastery as a sure sign of their cultural and racial superiority as they came to use "machines as the measure of men."[33] In pondering the "why Europe?" question, historians too have sometimes sought an answer in some distinct or even superior feature of European civilization.

In emphasizing the unexpectedness of the first Industrial Revolution, and the global context within which it occurred, world historians have attempted to avoid a "history as horse race" outlook. Clearly, the first industrial breakthrough in Britain was not a self-conscious effort to win a race; it was the surprising outcome of countless decisions by many people to further their own interests. Subsequently, however, other societies and their governments quite deliberately tried to catch up, seeking the wealth and power that the Industrial Revolution promised.

The rapid spread of industrialization across the planet, though highly uneven, may diminish the importance of the "why Europe?" issue. Just as no one views agriculture as a Middle Eastern phenomenon even though it occurred first in that region, it seems likely that industrialization will be seen increasingly as a global process rather than one uniquely associated with Europe. If industrial society proves to be a sustainable future for humankind—and this is presently an open question—historians of the future may well be more interested in the pattern of its global spread and in efforts to cope with its social and environmental consequences than in its origins in Western Europe.

Chapter Review

What's the Significance?

steam engine, 740

Indian cotton textiles, 743–44

middle-class values, 747–49

lower middle class, 749

Karl Marx, 751–53

Ellen Johnston, 752–53

Labour Party, 754–55

Luddites, 758–59

socialism in the United States, 762

Progressives, 762

Russian Revolution of 1905, 764–65

caudillos, 767

Latin American export boom, 768

Mexican Revolution, 771–72

dependent development, 772

Big Picture Questions

1. What did humankind gain from the Industrial Revolution, and what did it lose?

2. In what ways might the Industrial Revolution be understood as a global rather than simply a European phenomenon?

3. How might you situate the Industrial Revolution in the long history of humankind? How do you think the material covered in this chapter will be viewed 50, 100, or 200 years into the future?

4. **Looking Back:** How did the Industrial Revolution interact with the Scientific Revolution and the French Revolution to generate Europe's modern transformation?

Next Steps: For Further Study

John Charles Chasteen, *Born in Blood and Fire* (2006). A lively and well-written account of Latin America's turbulent history since the sixteenth century.

Jack Goldstone, *Why Europe? The Rise of the West in World History, 1500–1850* (2009). An original synthesis of recent research provided by a leading world historian.

David S. Landes, *The Wealth and Poverty of Nations* (1998). An argument that culture largely shapes the possibilities for industrialization and economic growth.

Robert B. Marks, *The Origins of the Modern World* (2007). An effective summary of new thinking about the origins of European industrialization.

Peter Stearns, *The Industrial Revolution in World History* (1998). A global and comparative perspective on the Industrial Revolution.

Peter Waldron, *The End of Imperial Russia, 1855–1917* (1997). A brief account of Russian history during its early industrialization.

Bridging World History, Units 18 and 19, http://www.learner.org/channel/courses/worldhistory. An innovative world history Web site that provides pictures, video, and text dealing with "Rethinking the Rise of the West" and "Global Industrialization."

"A History of Women in Industry," http://www.nwhm.org/online-exhibits/industry/womenindustry_intro .html. An exhibit of the National Women's History Museum that provides commentary, images, and primary sources about the lives of American women during the Industrial Revolution.

WORKING WITH EVIDENCE

Voices of European Socialism

Among the ideologies and social movements that grew out of Europe's Industrial Revolution, none was more important than socialism. The socialist dream of equality, justice, and community has an ancient pedigree, but the early currents of modern socialism took shape during the first quarter of the nineteenth century in the minds of various thinkers—the Englishman Robert Owen and the Frenchman Charles Fourier, for example—both of whom were appalled by the social divisions that industrial society generated. As an alternative, they proposed small-scale, voluntary, and cooperative communities, and their followers actually established a number of such experimental groups in Europe and the United States. But they seldom lasted long and never spread widely.

Far more important were the socialist ideas and movements inspired by the writings of Karl Marx, who disdained the voluntary communities as merely "utopian." The historical significance of Marxist socialism was immense. It offered an exuberant and thoroughly modern praise of the Industrial Revolution, embracing the new science and technology that generated such amazing wealth. But Marx also provided a devastating critique of the social inequalities, the economic instability, and the blatant exploitation that accompanied this process. In short, Marx distinguished sharply between the technological achievements of industrialization and the capitalist socioeconomic system in which it occurred. Marxist thinking sharpened the social conflicts that characterized industrializing Europe by dramatically highlighting, and simplifying, those conflicts. On one side of this great divide was the wealthy industrial business class, the bourgeoisie, those who owned and managed the mines, factories, and docks of an industrializing Europe. On the other stood the proletariat, the workers in those enterprises—often impoverished, exploited, and living in squalid conditions.

In the political realm, Marx's ideas inspired a variety of movements and parties that aimed to create the socialist society that he predicted. By the end of the nineteenth century, socialism had become a major element of European political and intellectual life, and it enjoyed a modest presence in the United States and Japan and among a handful of intellectuals elsewhere. For many people, those ideas also served as a way of understanding the world, perhaps akin to a religion, or as a substitute for religion. Marxism offered an alternative model for industrializing societies, imagining a future that would more fully realize the promise of modern industry and more equally distribute its benefits. Thus nineteenth-century Marxism provided the foundation for twentieth-century world communism as it took shape in Russia, China, Vietnam, Cuba, and elsewhere.

The documents that follow illustrate some of the ways that Marxist socialism was expressed and debated within a nineteenth-century European context.

Source 17.1

Socialism According to Marx

The life of Karl Marx (1818–1883) coincided with perhaps the harshest phase of capitalist industrialization in Europe. At that time, an encompassing market economy was rudely shattering older institutions and traditions, but the benefits of this new and highly productive system were not yet widely shared (see pages 746–66). But in this brutal process, Marx discerned the inevitable approach of a new world. Source 17.1 presents excerpts from the most famous of Marx's writings, *The Communist Manifesto*, first published in 1848. In this effort and throughout much of his life, Marx was assisted by another German thinker, Friedrich Engels (1820–1895), the son of a successful textile manufacturer. Engels became radicalized as he witnessed the devastating social results of capitalist industrialization. Marx and Engels's *Manifesto* begins with a summary description of the historical process. Much of the document then analyzes what the authors call the "bourgeoisie" or the "bourgeois epoch," terms that refer to the age of industrial capitalism.

- How do Marx and Engels understand the motor of change in human history? How do they view the role of class?

- What are their criticisms of the existing social system? What do they see as its major achievements?

- Why do they believe that the capitalist system is doomed?

- What kind of society do Marx and Engels envisage after the collapse of capitalism? Why do they believe that only a revolution, "the forcible overthrow of all existing social conditions," will enable the creation of a socialist society?

- Which of Marx and Engels's descriptions and predictions ring true even now? In what respects was their analysis disproved by later developments?

KARL MARX AND FRIEDRICH ENGELS
The Communist Manifesto
1848

The history of all hitherto existing society is the history of class struggles. Freeman and slave, patrician and plebeian, lord and serf, guild-master and journeyman, in a word, oppressor and oppressed, stood in constant opposition to one another, carried on an uninterrupted, now hidden, now open fight, a fight that each time ended, either in a revolutionary reconstitution of society at large, or in the common ruin of the contending classes. . . .

Our epoch, the epoch of the bourgeoisie, possesses, however, this distinct feature: it has simplified class antagonisms. Society as a whole is more and more splitting up into two great hostile camps, into two great classes directly facing each other—bourgeoisie and proletariat.

Modern industry has established the world market, for which the discovery of America paved the way. This market has given an immense development to commerce, to navigation, to communication by land. . . .

[T]he bourgeoisie has at last, since the establishment of Modern Industry and of the world market, conquered for itself, in the modern representative state, exclusive political sway. The executive of the modern state is but a committee for managing the common affairs of the whole bourgeoisie. . . .

The bourgeoisie, wherever it has got the upper hand, has put an end to all feudal, patriarchal, idyllic relations. It has pitilessly torn asunder the motley feudal ties that bound man to his "natural superiors," and has left no other nexus between people than naked self-interest, than callous "cash payment." It has drowned out the most heavenly ecstasies of religious fervor, of chivalrous enthusiasm, of philistine sentimentalism, in the icy water of egotistical calculation. It has resolved personal worth into exchange value, and in place of the numberless indefeasible chartered freedoms, has set up that single, unconscionable freedom—Free Trade. In one word, for exploitation, veiled by religious and political illusions, it has substituted naked, shameless, direct, brutal exploitation.

The bourgeoisie has stripped of its halo every occupation hitherto honored and looked up to with reverent awe. It has converted the physician, the lawyer, the priest, the poet, the man of science, into its paid wage laborers.

The bourgeoisie has torn away from the family its sentimental veil, and has reduced the family relation into a mere money relation. . . .

It has been the first to show what man's activity can bring about. It has accomplished wonders far surpassing Egyptian pyramids, Roman aqueducts, and Gothic cathedrals. . . .

The need of a constantly expanding market for its products chases the bourgeoisie over the entire surface of the globe. It must nestle everywhere, settle everywhere, establish connections everywhere. . . .

All old-established national industries have been destroyed or are daily being destroyed. They are dislodged by new industries, whose introduction becomes a life and death question for all civilized nations, by industries that no longer work up indigenous raw material, but raw material drawn from the remotest zones; industries whose products are consumed, not only at home, but in every quarter of the globe. In place of the old wants, satisfied by the production of the country, we find new wants, requiring for their satisfaction the products of distant lands and climes. In place of the old local and national seclusion and self-sufficiency, we have intercourse in every direction, universal interdependence of nations. . . .

The bourgeoisie, by the rapid improvement of all instruments of production, by the immensely facilitated means of communication, draws all, even the most barbarian, nations into civilization.

The cheap prices of commodities are the heavy artillery with which it forces the barbarians' intensely obstinate hatred of foreigners to capitulate. It compels all nations, on pain of extinction, to adopt the bourgeois mode of production; it compels them to introduce what it calls civilization into their midst, i.e., to become bourgeois themselves. In one word, it creates a world after its own image.

The bourgeoisie has subjected the country to the rule of the towns. It has created enormous cities, has greatly increased the urban population as compared with the rural, and has thus rescued a considerable part of the population from the idiocy of rural life. Just as it has made the country dependent on the towns, so it has made barbarian and semibarbarian countries dependent on the civilized ones, nations of peasants on nations of bourgeois, the East on the West. . . . The bourgeoisie, during its rule of scarce one hundred years, has created more massive and more colossal productive forces than have all preceding generations together. Subjection of nature's forces to man, machinery, application of chemistry to industry and agriculture, steam navigation, railways, electric telegraphs, clearing of whole continents for cultivation, canalization of rivers, whole populations conjured out of the ground—what earlier century had even a presentiment that such productive forces slumbered in the lap of social labor? . . .

It is enough to mention the commercial crises that, by their periodical return, put the existence of the entire bourgeois society on its trial, each time more threateningly. . . . In these crises, there breaks out an epidemic that, in all earlier epochs, would have seemed an absurdity—the epidemic of overproduction. . . .

But not only has the bourgeoisie forged the weapons that bring death to itself; it has also called into existence the men who are to wield those weapons—the modern working class—the proletarians. . . .

These laborers, who must sell themselves piecemeal, are a commodity, like every other article of commerce, and are consequently exposed to all the vicissitudes of competition, to all the fluctuations of the market.

Owing to the extensive use of machinery, and to the division of labor, the work of the proletarians has lost all individual character, and, consequently, all charm for the workman. He becomes an appendage of the machine, and it is only the most simple, most monotonous, and most easily acquired knack, that is required of him. . . .

Masses of laborers, crowded into the factory, are organized like soldiers. As privates of the industrial army, they are placed under the command of a perfect hierarchy of officers and sergeants. Not only are they slaves of the bourgeois class, and of the bourgeois state; they are daily and hourly enslaved by the machine, by the overlooker, and, above all, by the individual bourgeois manufacturer himself. . . .

The lower strata of the middle class—the small tradespeople, shopkeepers, and retired tradesmen generally, the handicraftsmen and peasants—all these sink gradually into the proletariat. . . . Thus, the proletariat is recruited from all classes of the population. . . .

This organization of the proletarians into a class, and, consequently, into a political party, is continually being upset again by the competition between the workers themselves. But it ever rises up again, stronger, firmer, mightier. . . .

Finally, in times when the class struggle nears the decisive hour, . . . a small section of the ruling class cuts itself adrift, and joins the revolutionary class, the class that holds the future in its hands. . . . What the bourgeoisie therefore produces, above all, are its own grave-diggers. Its fall and the victory of the proletariat are equally inevitable. . . .

We have seen above that the first step in the revolution by the working class is to raise the proletariat to the position of ruling class, to win the battle of democracy.

The proletariat will use its political supremacy to wrest, by degree, all capital from the bourgeoisie, to centralize all instruments of production in the hands of the state, i.e., of the proletariat organized as the ruling class; and to increase the total productive forces as rapidly as possible.

Of course, in the beginning, this cannot be effected except by means of despotic inroads on the rights of property. . . .

These measures will, of course, be different in different countries. Nevertheless, in most advanced countries, the following will be pretty generally applicable.

1. Abolition of property in land and application of all rents of land to public purposes.
2. A heavy progressive or graduated income tax.
3. Abolition of all rights of inheritance.
4. Confiscation of the property of all emigrants and rebels.
5. Centralization of credit in the banks of the state, by means of a national bank with state capital and an exclusive monopoly.
6. Centralization of the means of communication and transport in the hands of the state.
7. Extension of factories and instruments of production owned by the state; the bringing into cultivation of waste lands, and the improvement of the soil generally in accordance with a common plan.
8. Equal obligation of all to work. Establishment of industrial armies, especially for agriculture.
9. Combination of agriculture with manufacturing industries; gradual abolition of all the distinction between town and country by a more equable distribution of the populace over the country.
10. Free education for all children in public schools. Abolition of children's factory labor in its present form. Combination of education with industrial production, etc.

When, in the course of development, class distinctions have disappeared, and all production has been concentrated in the hands of a vast association of the whole nation, the public power will lose its political character. Political power, properly so called, is merely the organized power of one class for oppressing another. If the proletariat during its contest with the bourgeoisie is compelled, by the force of circumstances, to organize itself as a class; if, by means of a revolution, it makes itself the ruling class, and, as such, sweeps away by force the old conditions of production, then it will, along with these conditions, have swept away the conditions for the existence of class antagonisms and of classes generally, and will thereby have abolished its own supremacy as a class.

In place of the old bourgeois society, with its classes and class antagonisms, we shall have an association in which the free development of each is the condition for the free development of all. . . .

The Communists disdain to conceal their views and aims. They openly declare that their ends can be attained only by the forcible overthrow of all existing social conditions. Let the ruling classes tremble at a communist revolution. The proletarians have nothing to lose but their chains. They have a world to win.

Source: John E. Toews, ed., *The Communist Manifesto by Karl Marx and Frederick Engels with Related Documents* (Boston: Bedford/St. Martin's, 1999), 63–96.

Source 17.2
Socialism without Revolution

Karl Marx and Friedrich Engels provided the set of ideas that informed much of the European socialist movement during the second half of the nineteenth century. Organized in various national parties and joined together in international organizations as well, socialists usually referred to themselves as social democrats, for they were seeking to extend the principles of democracy from the political arena (voting rights, for example) into the realm of the economy and society. By the 1890s, however, some of them had begun to question at least part of Marx's teachings, especially the need for violent revolution. The chief spokesperson for this group of socialists, known as "revisionists," was Eduard Bernstein (1850–1932), a prominent member of the German Social Democratic Party. His ideas provoked a storm of controversy within European socialist circles. Source 17.2 is drawn from the preface of Bernstein's 1899 book, *Evolutionary Socialism*.

- In what ways and for what reasons was Bernstein critical of Marx and Engels's analysis of capitalism?

- Why do you think Bernstein refers so often to Engels?

- What strategy does Bernstein recommend for the German Social Democratic Party?

- What does he mean by saying that "the movement means everything for me and . . . 'the final aim of socialism' is nothing"?

- Why would some of Marx's followers have considered Bernstein a virtual traitor to the socialist cause?

Eduard Bernstein
Evolutionary Socialism
1899

It has been maintained in a certain quarter that the practical deductions from my treatises would be the abandonment of the conquest of political power by the proletariat organized politically and economically. That [idea] . . . I altogether deny.

I set myself against the notion that we have to expect shortly a collapse of the bourgeois economy. . . .

The adherents of this theory of a catastrophe base it especially on the conclusions of the *Communist Manifesto*. This is a mistake. . . .

Social conditions have not developed to such an acute opposition of things and classes as is depicted in the *Manifesto*. It is not only useless, it is the greatest folly to attempt to conceal this from ourselves. The number of members of the possessing classes is today not smaller but larger. The enormous increase of social wealth is not accompanied by a decreasing number of large capitalists but by an increasing number of capitalists of all degrees. The middle classes change their character but they do not disappear from the social scale.

The concentration in productive industry is not being accomplished even today in all its departments with equal thoroughness and at an equal rate. . . . Trade statistics show an extraordinarily elaborated graduation of enterprises in regard to size. . . .

In all advanced countries we see the privileges of the capitalist bourgeoisie yielding step by step to democratic organizations. Under the influence of this, and driven by the movement of the working classes which is daily becoming stronger, a social reaction has set in against the exploiting tendencies of capital. . . . Factory legislation, the democratizing of local government, and the extension of its area of work, the freeing of trade unions and systems of cooperative trading from legal restrictions, the consideration of standard conditions of labor in the work undertaken by public authorities—all these characterize this phase of the evolution.

But the more the political organizations of modern nations are democratized, the more the needs and opportunities of great political catastrophes are diminished. . . .

[Engels] points out in conformity with this opinion that the next task of the party should be "to work for an uninterrupted increase of its votes" or to carry on a slow *propaganda of parliamentary activity*. . . .

Shall we be told that he [Engels] abandoned the conquest of political power by the working classes . . . ?

[F]or a long time yet the task of social democracy is, instead of speculating on a great economic crash, "to organize the working classes politically and develop them as a democracy and to fight for all reforms in the State which are adapted to raise the working classes and transform the State in the direction of democracy." . . .

[T]he movement means everything for me and that what is *usually* called "the final aim of socialism" is nothing. . . .

The conquest of political power by the working classes, the expropriation of capitalists, are not ends themselves but only means for the accomplishment of certain aims and endeavors. . . . But the conquest of political power necessitates the possession of political *rights*; German social democracy [must] devise the best ways for the extension of the political and economic rights of the German working classes.

Source: Eduard Bernstein, *Evolutionary Socialism*, translated by Edith C. Harvey (New York: Schocken Books, 1961), xxiv–xxx.

Source 17.3
Socialism and Women

Marxist socialism focused largely on issues of class, but that movement coincided with the emergence of feminism, giving rise to what many socialists called "the woman question." The main theoretical issue was the source of female subjugation. Did it derive from private property and the class structure of capitalist society, or was it the product of deeply rooted cultural attitudes independent of class? While middle-class feminists generally assumed the second view, orthodox Marxist thinking aligned with the first one, believing that the lack of economic independence was the root cause of women's subordination. Their liberation would follow, more or less automatically, after the creation of socialist societies. On a more practical level, the question was whether socialist parties should seek to enroll women by actively supporting their unique concerns—suffrage, equal pay, education, maternity insurance. Or did such efforts divide the working class and weaken the socialist movement? Should socialists treat women as members of an oppressed class or as members of an oppressed sex? Among the leading figures addressing such issues was Clara Zetkin (1857–1933), a prominent German socialist and feminist. In Source 17.3, Zetkin outlines the efforts of the German Social Democratic Party to reach out to women and describes the party's posture toward middle-class feminism.

■ How would you describe Zetkin's view of the relationship between socialism and feminism? Which one has priority, in her thinking?

- Why is she so insistent that the Social Democratic Party of Germany address the concerns of women? How precisely did it do so?

- Why does she believe that women's issues will be better served within a socialist framework than in a bourgeois women's rights movement?

- How might critics—both feminist and socialist—argue with Zetkin?

CLARA ZETKIN

The German Socialist Women's Movement

1909

In 1907 the Social-Democratic Party of Germany [SDP] embraced 29,458 women members, in 1908 they numbered 62,257. . . . One hundred and fifty lecture and study circles for women have been established. . . . Socialist propaganda amongst the workers' wives and women wage-earners has been carried on by many hundred public meetings, in which women comrades addressed more particularly working-class women. . . .

The women's office works now in conjunction with the Party's Executive. . . . They are to make a vigorous propaganda that the wage-earning women shall in large numbers exercise the franchise to the administrative bodies of the State Sick-Insurance, the only kind of franchise women possess in Germany. The women comrades were further engaged to form local committees for the protection of children. . . . Besides this, Socialist women were reminded to found and improve protective committees for women workers, and collect their grievances on illegal and pernicious conditions of labor, forwarding them to the factory inspector.

Besides their activity in that line, the Socialist women have continued their propaganda in favor of the full political emancipation of their sex. The struggle for universal suffrage . . . was a struggle for adult suffrage for both sexes, vindicated in meetings and leaflets. . . . The work of our trade unions to enlighten, train, and organize wage-earning women is not smaller nor less important than what

the S.D.P. has done to induce women to join in political struggles of the working class. . . .

The most prominent feature of the Socialist women's movement in Germany is its clearness and revolutionary spirit as to Socialist theories and principles. The women who head it are fully conscious that the social fate of their sex is indissolubly connected with the general evolution of society. . . . The integral human emancipation of all women depends in consequence on the social emancipation of labor; that can only be realized by the class-war of the exploited majority. Therefore, our Socialist women oppose strongly the bourgeois women righters' credo that the women of all classes must gather into an unpolitical, neutral movement striving exclusively for women's rights. In theory and practice they maintain the conviction that the class antagonisms are much more powerful, effective, and decisive than the social antagonisms between the sexes. . . . [T]hus the working-class women will [only] win their full emancipation . . . in the class war of all the exploited, without difference of sex, against all who exploit, without difference of sex. That does not mean at all that they undervalue the importance of the political emancipation of the female sex. On the contrary, they employ much more energy than the German women-righters to conquer the suffrage. But the vote is, according to their views, not the last word and term of their aspirations, but only a weapon—a means in struggle for a revolutionary aim—the Socialistic order.

The Socialist women's movement in Germany . . . strives to help change the world by awakening the consciousness and the will of working-class women to join in performing the most Titanic deed that history will know: the emancipation of labor by the laboring class themselves.

Source: Clara Zetkin, *The German Socialist Women's Movement* (1909; Marxists Internet Archive, 2007), http://www.marxists.org /archive/zetkin/1909/10/09.htm.

Source 17.4
Lenin and Russian Socialism

By the late nineteenth century, most West European socialist parties were operating in a more or less democratic environment in which they could organize legally, contest elections, and serve in parliament. Some of them, following Eduard Bernstein, had largely abandoned any thoughts of revolution in favor of a peaceful and democratic path to socialism. For others, this amounted to a betrayal of the Marxist vision. This was particularly the case for Vladimir Ilyich Ulyanov, better known as Lenin, then a prominent figure in the small Russian Social Democratic Labor Party, established in 1898. Lenin was particularly hostile to what he called "economism" or "trade-unionism," which focused on immediate reforms such as higher wages, shorter hours, and better working conditions. He was operating in a still-autocratic Russian state, where neither political parties nor trade unions were legal and where no national parliament or elections allowed for the expression of popular grievances.

In a famous pamphlet titled *What Is to Be Done?* (1902), Lenin addressed many of these issues, well before he became the leader of the world's first successful socialist revolution in 1917.

- What were Lenin's objections to economism?

- What kind of party organization did he favor?

- Why did Lenin believe that workers were unlikely to come to a revolutionary consciousness on their own? What was necessary to move them in that direction?

- Was Lenin more faithful to the views of Marx himself than the revisionists and economists were?

- In what ways did Lenin's views reflect the specific conditions of Russia?

LENIN

What Is to Be Done?

1902

The history of all countries shows that the working class, exclusively by its own effort, is able to develop only trade union consciousness, i.e., it may itself realize the necessity for combining in unions, for fighting against the employers, and for striving to compel the government to pass necessary labor legislation, etc. The theory of socialism, however, grew out of the philosophic, historical, and economic theories that were elaborated by the educated representatives of the propertied classes, the intellectuals. . . . [I]n Russia . . . it arose as a natural and inevitable outcome of the development of ideas among the revolutionary socialist intelligentsia.

It is only natural that a Social Democrat, who conceives the political struggle as being identical with the "economic struggle against the employers and the government," should conceive of an "organization of revolutionaries" as being more or less identical with an "organization of workers." . . .

[O]n questions of organization and politics, the Economists are forever lapsing from Social Democracy into trade unionism. The political struggle carried on by the Social Democrats is far more extensive and complex than the economic struggle the workers carry on against the employers and the government. Similarly . . . the organization of a revolutionary Social Democratic Party must inevitably *differ* from the organizations of the workers designed for the latter struggle. A workers' organization . . . must be as wide as possible; and . . . it must be as public as conditions will allow. . . . On the other hand, the organizations of revolutionaries must consist first and foremost of people whose profession is that of a revolutionary. . . . Such an organization must of necessity be not too extensive and as secret as possible. . . .

I assert:

1. that no movement can be durable without a stable organization of leaders to maintain continuity;

2. that the more widely the masses are spontaneously drawn into the struggle and form the basis of the movement and participate in it, the more necessary is it to have such an organization. . . .

3. that the organization must consist chiefly of persons engaged in revolutionary activities as a profession;

4. that in a country with an autocratic government, the more we restrict the membership of this organization to persons who are engaged in revolutionary activities as a profession and who have been professionally trained in the art of combating the political police, the more difficult will it be to catch the organization. . . .

The centralization of the more secret functions in an organization of revolutionaries will not diminish, but rather increase the extent and the quality of the activity of a large number of other organizations intended for wide membership. . . . [I]n order to "serve" the mass movement we must have people who will devote themselves exclusively to Social Democratic activities, and that such people must *train* themselves patiently and steadfastly to be professional revolutionaries. . . .

Let no active worker take offense at these frank remarks, for as far as insufficient training is concerned, I apply them first and foremost to myself. I used to work in a circle that set itself great and all-embracing tasks; and every member of that circle suffered to the point of torture from the realization that we were proving ourselves to be amateurs at a moment in history when we might have been able to say, paraphrasing a well-known epigram: "Give us an organization of revolutionaries, and we shall overturn the whole of Russia!"

Source: V. I. Lenin, *What Is to Be Done?* (Pamphlet, 1902; Marxists Internet Archive, 1999), https://www.marxists.org/archive/lenin/works/1901/witbd/index.htm.

Voices of European Socialism

1. **Comparing socialisms:** While the various strands of Marxist socialism in nineteenth-century Europe shared some common views and values, it was also a sharply divided movement. How would you describe those commonalities as well as the divisions and controversies?

2. **Connecting socialist thinking with the Atlantic revolutions:** To what extent did socialist thinking reflect the concerns of the Atlantic revolutions explored in Chapter 16? In what ways did it diverge from those earlier revolutionary movements?

3. **Considering the appeal of Marxism:** These documents were written by intellectuals within the socialist movement. In what ways might their ideas have appealed to ordinary workers?

4. **Considering responses to socialism:** With which of the variant forms of socialism might Marx himself have been most and least sympathetic? Which of them do you think would have had the most appeal in the United States? How might a manager or owner of an industrial enterprise respond to these ideas?

CHAPTER 18

Colonial Encounters in Asia, Africa, and Oceania

1750–1950

In mid-1967, I (Robert Strayer) was on summer break from a teaching assignment with the Peace Corps in Ethiopia and was traveling with some friends in neighboring Kenya, just four years after that country had gained its independence from British colonial rule. The bus we were riding on broke down, and I found myself hitchhiking across Kenya, heading for Uganda. Soon I was picked up by a friendly Englishman, one of Kenya's many European settlers who had stayed on after independence. At one point, he pulled off the road to show me a lovely view of Kenya's famous Rift Valley, and we were approached by a group of boys selling baskets and other tourist items. They spoke to us in good English, but my British companion replied to them in Swahili. He later explained that Europeans generally did not speak English with the "natives." I was puzzled, but reluctant to inquire further.

Several years later, while conducting research about British missionaries in Kenya in the early twentieth century, I found a clue about the origins of this man's reluctance to speak his own language with Kenyans. It came in a letter from a missionary in which the writer argued against the teaching of English to Africans. Among his reasons were "the danger in which such a course would place our white women and girls" and "the danger of organizing against the government and Europeans."[1] Here, clearly displayed, was the European colonial insistence on maintaining distance and distinction between whites and blacks, for both sexual and political reasons. Such monitoring of racial boundaries was a central feature of many nineteenth- and

The Imperial Durbar of 1903 To mark the coronation of British monarch Edward VII and his installation as the Emperor of India, colonial authorities in India mounted an elaborate assembly, or durbar. The durbar was intended to showcase the splendor of the British Empire, and its pageantry included sporting events; a state ball; a huge display of Indian arts, crafts, and jewels; and an enormous parade in which a long line of British officials and Indian princes passed by on bejeweled elephants.

early twentieth-century colonial societies and, in the case of my new British acquaintance, a practice that persisted even after the colonial era had ended.

For many millions of Africans, Asians, and Pacific Islanders, colonial rule—by the British, French, Germans, Italians, Belgians, Portuguese, Russians, or Americans—was the major new element in their historical experience during the long nineteenth century (1750–1914). Of course, no single colonial experience characterized this vast region. Much depended on the cultures and prior history of various colonized people. Policies of the colonial powers sometimes differed sharply and changed over time. Men and women experienced the colonial era differently, as did traditional elites, Western-educated groups, artisans, peasant farmers, and migrant laborers. Furthermore, the varied actions and reactions of such people, despite their oppression and exploitation, shaped the colonial experience, perhaps as much as the policies, practices, and intentions of their temporary European rulers. All of them—colonizers and colonized alike—were caught up in the flood of change that accompanied this new burst of European imperialism.

SEEKING THE MAIN POINT

In what ways did colonial rule transform the societies that it encompassed?

Industry and Empire

Behind much of Europe's nineteenth-century expansion lay the massive fact of its Industrial Revolution, a process that gave rise to new economic needs, many of which found solutions abroad. The enormous productivity of industrial technology and Europe's growing affluence now created the need for extensive raw materials and agricultural products: wheat from the American Midwest and southern Russia; meat from Argentina; bananas from Central America; rubber from Brazil; cocoa and palm oil from West Africa; tea, copra, and coconut oil from Ceylon; gold and diamonds from South Africa; gutta-percha, a natural latex used to insulate underwater telegraph lines, from Southeast Asia. This demand radically changed patterns of economic and social life in the countries of their origin.

Furthermore, Europe needed to sell its own products. One of the peculiarities of industrial capitalism was that it periodically produced more manufactured goods than its own people could afford to buy. By 1840, for example, Britain was exporting 60 percent of its cotton-cloth production, annually sending 200 million yards to Europe, 300 million yards to Latin America, and 145 million yards to India. This last figure is particularly significant because for centuries Europe had offered little that Asian societies were willing to buy. Part of European and American fascination with China during the nineteenth and twentieth centuries lay in the enormous market potential represented by its huge population.

Much the same could be said for capital, for European investors often found it more profitable to invest their money abroad than at home. Between 1910 and

Guided Reading Question

■ CHANGE

In what ways did the Industrial Revolution shape the character of nineteenth-century European imperialism?

A MAP OF TIME

1750s	Beginnings of British takeover of India
1788	Initial British settlement of Australia
1798	Napoleon's invasion of Egypt
1830	French invasion of Algeria
1840s	Beginning of major British settlement in New Zealand
1857–1858	Indian Rebellion
1858–1893	French conquest of Indochina
1869	Opening of Suez Canal
1875–1900	Scramble for Africa
1898	United States acquires the Philippines from Spain and annexes Hawaii
1899–1902	Boer War in South Africa
1901–1910	Completion of Dutch conquest of Indonesia
1904–1905	Maji Maji rebellion in East Africa
1910	Japan annexes Korea
Twentieth century	Spread of Christianity in non-Muslim Africa
1920s–1947	Gandhi's leadership of Indian National Congress

1913, Britain was sending about half of its savings overseas as foreign investment. In 1914, it had some 3.7 billion pounds sterling invested abroad, about equally divided between Europe, North America, and Australia on the one hand and Asia, Africa, and Latin America on the other.

Wealthy Europeans also saw social benefits to foreign markets, which served to keep Europe's factories humming and its workers employed. The English imperialist Cecil Rhodes confided his fears to a friend in the late nineteenth century:

Yesterday I attended a meeting of the unemployed in London and having listened to the wild speeches which were nothing more than a scream for bread, I returned home convinced more than ever of the importance of imperialism. . . . In order to save the 40 million inhabitants of the United Kingdom from a murderous civil war, the colonial politicians must open up new areas to absorb the excess population and create new markets for the products of the mines and factories. . . . The British Empire is a matter of bread and butter. If you wish to avoid civil war, then you must become an imperialist.[2]

THE DEVILFISH IN EGYPTIAN WATERS.

An American View of British Imperialism
In this American cartoon dating to 1882, the British Empire is portrayed as an octopus whose tentacles are already attached to many countries, while one tentacle is about to grasp yet another colony, Egypt. (The Granger Collection, NYC — All rights reserved)

Thus imperialism promised to solve the class conflicts of an industrializing society while avoiding revolution or the serious redistribution of wealth.

But what made imperialism so broadly popular in Europe, especially in the last quarter of the nineteenth century, was the growth of mass nationalism. By 1871, the unification of Italy and Germany made Europe's already-competitive international relations even more so, and much of this rivalry spilled over into the struggle for colonies or economic concessions in Asia, Africa, and Pacific Oceania. Colonies and spheres of influence abroad became symbols of "Great Power" status for a nation, and their acquisition was a matter of urgency, even if they possessed little immediate economic value. After 1875, it seemed to matter, even to ordinary people, whether some remote corner of Africa or some obscure Pacific island was in British, French, or German hands. Imperialism, in short, appealed on economic and social grounds to the wealthy or ambitious, seemed politically and strategically necessary in the game of international power politics, and was emotionally satisfying to almost everyone. This was a potent mix!

If the industrial era made overseas expansion more desirable or even urgent, it also provided new means for achieving those goals. Steam-driven ships, moving through the new Suez Canal, completed in 1869, allowed Europeans to reach distant Asian, African, and Pacific ports more quickly and predictably and to penetrate interior rivers as well. The underwater telegraph made possible almost instant communication with far-flung outposts of empire. The discovery of quinine to prevent malaria greatly reduced European death rates in the tropics. Breech-loading rifles and machine guns vastly widened the military gap between Europeans and everyone else.

Industrialization also occasioned a marked change in the way Europeans perceived themselves and others. In earlier centuries, Europeans had defined others largely in religious terms. "They" were heathen; "we" were Christian. Even as they held on to this sense of religious superiority, Europeans nonetheless adopted many of the ideas and techniques of more advanced societies. They held many aspects of Chinese and Indian civilization in high regard; they freely mixed and mingled with

Asian and African elites and often married their women; some even saw more technologically simple peoples as "noble savages."

With the advent of the industrial age, however, Europeans developed a secular arrogance that fused with or in some cases replaced their notions of religious superiority. They had, after all, unlocked the secrets of nature, created a society of unprecedented wealth, and used both to produce unsurpassed military power. These became the criteria by which Europeans judged both themselves and the rest of the world.

By such standards, it is not surprising that their opinions of other cultures dropped sharply. The Chinese, who had been highly praised in the eighteenth century, were reduced in the nineteenth century to the image of "John Chinaman"—weak, cunning, obstinately conservative, and, in large numbers, a distinct threat, represented by the "yellow peril" in late nineteenth-century European thinking. African societies, which had been regarded even in the slave-trade era as nations, and their leaders, who had been regarded as kings, were demoted in nineteenth-century European eyes to the status of tribes led by chiefs as a means of emphasizing their "primitive" qualities.

Peoples of Pacific Oceania and elsewhere could be regarded as "big children," who lived "closer to nature" than their civilized counterparts and correspondingly distant from the high culture with which Europeans congratulated themselves. Upon visiting Tahiti in 1768, the French explorer Bougainville concluded: "I thought I was walking in the Garden of Eden."[3] Such views could be mobilized to criticize the artificiality and materialism of modern European life, but they could also serve to justify the conquest of people who were, apparently, doing little to improve what nature had granted them. Writing in 1854, a European settler in Australia declared: "The question comes to this; which has the better right—the savage, born in a country, which he runs over but can scarcely be said to occupy . . . or the civilized man, who comes to introduce into this . . . unproductive country, the industry which supports life?"[4]

Increasingly, Europeans viewed the culture and achievements of Asian and African peoples through the prism of a new kind of racism, expressed now in terms of modern science. Although physical differences had often been a basis of fear or dislike, in the nineteenth century Europeans increasingly used the prestige and apparatus of science to support their

Guided Reading Question

■ CHANGE

What contributed to changing European views of Asians and Africans in the nineteenth century?

AP® EXAM TIP

You must know about ideas regarding race in history, especially since ca. 1450.

PROGRESSIVE DEVELOPMENT OF MAN.—(2) EVOLUTION ILLUSTRATED WITH THE SIX CORRESPONDING LIVING FORMS.

European Racial Images

This nineteenth-century chart, depicting the "Progressive Development of Man" from apes to modern Europeans, reflected the racial categories that were so prominent at the time. It also highlights the influence of Darwin's evolutionary ideas as they were applied to varieties of human beings. (The Granger Collection, NYC—All rights reserved) racial preferences and prejudices. Phrenologists, craniologists, and sometimes physicians used allegedly scientific methods and numerous instruments to classify the size and shape of human skulls and concluded, not surprisingly, that those of whites were larger and therefore more advanced. Nineteenth-century biologists, who classified the varieties of plants and animals, applied these notions of rank to varieties of human beings as well. The result was a hierarchy of races, with the whites on top and the less developed "child races" beneath them. Race, in this view, determined human intelligence, moral development, and destiny. "Race is everything," declared the British anatomist Robert Knox in 1850. "Civilization depends on it."[5] Furthermore, as the germ theory of disease took hold in nineteenth-century Europe, it was accompanied by fears that contact with "inferiors" threatened the health and even the biological future of more advanced or "superior" peoples.

These ideas influenced how Europeans viewed their own global expansion. Almost everyone saw it as inevitable, a natural outgrowth of a superior civilization. For many, though, this viewpoint was tempered with a genuine, if condescending, sense of responsibility to the "weaker races" that Europe was fated to dominate. "Superior races have a right, because they have a duty," declared the French politician Jules Ferry in 1883. "They have the duty to civilize the inferior races."[6] That "civilizing mission" included bringing Christianity to the heathen, good government to disordered lands, work discipline and production for the market to "lazy natives," a measure of education to the ignorant and illiterate, clothing to the naked, and health care to the sick, all while suppressing "native customs" that ran counter to Western ways of living. In European thinking, this was "progress" and "civilization."

A harsher side to the ideology of imperialism derived from an effort to apply, or perhaps misapply, the evolutionary thinking of Charles Darwin to an understanding of human societies. The key concept of this "social Darwinism," though not necessarily shared by Darwin himself, was "the survival of the fittest," suggesting that European dominance inevitably involved the displacement or destruction of backward peoples or "unfit" races. Referring to native peoples of Australia, a European bishop declared:

> Everyone who knows a little about aboriginal races is aware that those races which are of a low type mentally and who are at the same time weak in constitution rapidly die out when their country comes to be occupied by a different race much more rigorous, robust, and pushing than themselves.[7]

Such views made imperialism, war, and aggression seem both natural and progressive, for they were predicated on the notion that weeding out "weaker" peoples of the world would allow the "stronger" to flourish. These were some of the ideas with which industrializing and increasingly powerful Europeans confronted the peoples of Asia and Africa in the nineteenth century.

AP® EXAM TIP

The concept of social Darwinism is important and will likely appear on the AP® exam.

A Second Wave of European Conquests

If the sixteenth- and seventeenth-century takeover of the Americas represented the first phase of European colonial conquests, the century and a half between 1750 and 1914 was a second and quite distinct round of that larger process. Now it was focused in Asia, Africa, and Oceania rather than in the Western Hemisphere. And it featured a number of new players—Germany, Italy, Belgium, the United States, and Japan—who were not at all involved in the earlier phase, while the Spanish and Portuguese now had only minor roles. In general, Europeans preferred informal control, which operated through economic penetration and occasional military intervention but without a wholesale colonial takeover. Such a course was cheaper and less likely to provoke wars. But where rivalry with other European states made it impossible or where local governments were unable or unwilling to cooperate, Europeans proved more than willing to undertake the expense and risk of conquest and outright colonial rule.

The construction of these new European empires in the Afro-Asian world, like empires everywhere, involved military force or the threat of it. Initially, the European military advantage lay in organization, drill and practice, and command structure. Increasingly in the nineteenth century, the Europeans also possessed overwhelming advantages in firepower, deriving from the recently invented repeating rifles and machine guns. A much-quoted jingle by the English writer Hilaire Belloc summed up the situation:

> Whatever happens we have got
> The Maxim gun [an automatic machine gun] and they have not.

Nonetheless, Europeans had to fight, often long and hard, to create their new empires, as countless wars of conquest attest. In the end, though, they prevailed almost everywhere, largely against adversaries who did not have Maxim guns or in some cases any guns at all. Thus were African, Asian, and Oceanic peoples of all kinds incorporated within one or another of the European empires. Gathering and hunting bands in Australia, agricultural village societies or chiefdoms on Pacific islands and in parts of Africa, pastoralists of the Sahara and Central Asia, residents of states large and small, and virtually everyone in the large and complex civilizations of India and Southeast Asia—all of them alike lost the political sovereignty and freedom of action they had previously exercised. For some, such as Hindus governed by the Muslim Mughal Empire, it was an exchange of one set of foreign rulers for another. But now all were subjects of a European colonial state.

The passage to colonial status occurred in various ways. For the peoples of India and Indonesia, colonial conquest grew out of earlier interaction with European trading firms. Particularly in India, the British East India Company, rather than the British government directly, played the leading role in the colonial takeover of South Asia. The fragmentation of the Mughal Empire and the absence of any overall

Guided Reading Question

■ COMPARISON

In what different ways was colonial rule established in various parts of Africa and Asia?

AP® EXAM TIP

Know examples of acceptance and rejection of European imperialism by Africans and Asians.

sense of cultural or political unity both invited and facilitated European penetration. A similar situation of many small and rival states assisted the Dutch acquisition of Indonesia. However, neither the British nor the Dutch had a clear-cut plan for conquest. Rather, it evolved slowly as local authorities and European traders made and unmade a variety of alliances over roughly a century in India (1750–1850). In Indonesia, a few areas held out until the early twentieth century (see Map 18.1).

For most of Africa, mainland Southeast Asia, and the Pacific islands, colonial conquest came later, in the second half of the nineteenth century, and rather more abruptly and deliberately than in India or Indonesia. The "scramble for Africa," for example, pitted half a dozen European powers against one another as they partitioned the entire continent among themselves in only about twenty-five years (1875–1900). (See Working with Evidence: The Scramble for Africa, page 825, for various perspectives on the "scramble.") European leaders themselves were surprised by the intensity of their rivalries and the speed with which they acquired huge territories, about which they knew very little (see Map 18.2).

That process involved endless but peaceful negotiations among the competing Great Powers about "who got what" and extensive and bloody military action, sometimes lasting decades, to make their control effective on the ground. It took the French sixteen years (1882–1898) to finally conquer the recently created West African empire led by Samori Toure. Among the most difficult to subdue were those decentralized societies without any formal state structure. In such cases, Europeans confronted no central authority with which they could negotiate or that they might decisively defeat. It was a matter of village-by-village conquest against extended resistance. As late as 1925, one British official commented on the process as it operated in central Nigeria: "I shall of course go on walloping them until they surrender. It's a rather piteous sight watching a village being knocked to pieces and I wish there was some other way, but unfortunately there isn't."[8] Another very difficult situation for the British lay in South Africa, where they were initially defeated by a Zulu army in 1879 at the Battle of Isandlwana. And twenty years later, in what became known as the Boer War (1899–1902), the Boers, white descendants of the earlier Dutch settlers in South Africa, fought bitterly for three years before succumbing to British forces. Perhaps the great disparity in military forces made the final outcome of European victory inevitable, but the conquest of Africa was intensely contested.

Europeans and Americans had been drawn into the world of Pacific Oceania during the eighteenth century through exploration and scientific curiosity, by the missionary impulse for conversion, and by their economic interests in sperm whale oil, coconut oil, guano, mineral nitrates and phosphates, sandalwood, and other products. Primarily in the second half of the nineteenth century, these entanglements morphed into competitive annexations as Britain, France, the Netherlands, Germany, and the United States, now joined by Australia, claimed control of all the islands of Oceania. Chile too, in search of valuable guano and nitrates, entered the fray and gained a number of coastal islands as well as Rapa Nui (Easter Island), the easternmost island of Polynesia.

Map 18.1 Colonial Asia in the Early Twentieth Century
By the early twentieth century, several of the great population centers of Asia had come under the colonial control of Britain, the Netherlands, France, the United States, or Japan.

The colonization of the South Pacific territories of Australia and New Zealand, both of which were taken over by the British during the nineteenth century, was more similar to the earlier colonization of North America than to contemporary patterns of Asian and African conquest. In both places, conquest was accompanied by large-scale European settlement and diseases that reduced native numbers by 75 percent or more by 1900. Like Canada and the United States, these became settler colonies, "neo-European" societies in the Pacific. Aboriginal Australians constituted only about 2.4 percent of their country's population in the early twenty-first century, and the indigenous Maori were a minority of about 15 percent in New Zealand. In other previously isolated regions as well—Polynesia, Amazonia, Siberia— disease took a terrible toll on peoples who lacked immunities to European pathogens. For example, in Polynesia the population of Hawaii declined from around 142,000 in 1823 to only 39,000 in 1896, while in Rapa Nui the number of residents dropped

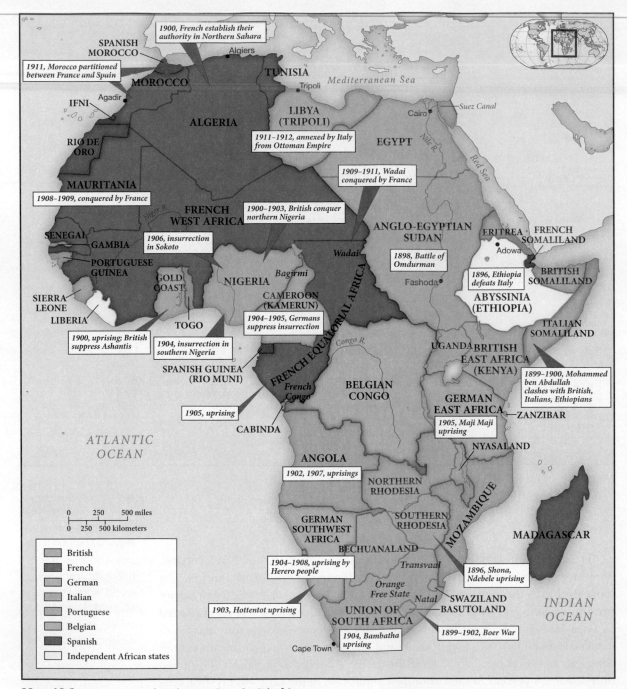

Map 18.2   Conquest and Resistance in Colonial Africa

By the early twentieth century, the map of Africa reflected the outcome of the "scramble for Africa," a conquest that was heavily resisted in many places. The boundaries established during that process still provide the political framework for Africa's independent states.

from around 3,000 in 1863 to 111 in 1877. Unlike these remote areas, most of Africa and Asia shared with Europe a broadly similar disease environment and so were less susceptible to the pathogens of the conquerors.

Elsewhere other variations on the theme of imperial conquest unfolded. The westward expansion of the United States, for example, overwhelmed Native American populations and involved the country in an imperialist war with Mexico. Seeking territory for white settlement, the United States practiced a policy of removing, sometimes almost exterminating, Indian peoples. On the "reservations" to which Indians were confined and in boarding schools to which many of their children were removed, reformers sought to "civilize" the remaining Native Americans, eradicating tribal life and culture, under the slogan "Kill the Indian and Save the Man."

Japan's takeover of Taiwan and Korea bore marked similarities to European actions, as that East Asian nation joined the imperialist club. Russian penetration of Central Asia brought additional millions under European control as the Russian Empire continued its earlier territorial expansion. Filipinos acquired new colonial rulers when the United States took over from Spain following the Spanish-American War of 1898. Some 13,000 freed U.S. slaves, seeking greater freedom than was possible at home, migrated to West Africa, where they became, ironically, a colonizing elite in the land they named Liberia. Ethiopia and Siam (Thailand) were notable for avoiding the colonization to which their neighbors succumbed. Those countries' military and diplomatic skills, their willingness to make modest concessions to the Europeans, and the rivalries of the imperialists all contributed to these exceptions to the rule of colonial takeover in East Africa and Southeast Asia. Ethiopia, in fact, considerably expanded its own empire, even as it defeated Italy at the famous Battle of Adowa in 1896. (See Zooming In: The Battle of Adowa in Chapter 19, page 850, for an account of Ethiopia's defeat of Italian forces.)

These broad patterns of colonial conquest dissolved into thousands of separate encounters as the target societies of Western empire builders were confronted with decisions about how to respond to encroaching European power in the context of their local circumstances. Many initially sought to enlist Europeans in their own internal struggles for power or in their external rivalries with neighboring states or peoples. As pressures mounted and European demands escalated, some tried to play off imperial powers against one another, while others resorted to military action. Many societies were sharply divided between those who wanted to fight and those who believed that resistance was futile. After extended resistance against French aggression, the nineteenth-century Vietnamese emperor Tu Duc argued with those who wanted the struggle to go on:

> Do you really wish to confront such a power with a pack of [our] cowardly soldiers? It would be like mounting an elephant's head or caressing a tiger's tail. . . . With what you presently have, do you really expect to dissolve the enemy's rifles into air or chase his battleships into hell?[9]

AP® EXAM TIP

Be able to compare motivations and outcomes of nineteenth- and early twentieth-century imperialism.

Still others negotiated, attempting to preserve as much independence and power as possible. The rulers of the East African kingdom of Buganda, for example, saw opportunity in the British presence and negotiated an arrangement that substantially enlarged their state and personally benefited the kingdom's elite class.

Under European Rule

In many places and for many people, incorporation into European colonial empires was a traumatic experience. Especially for small-scale societies, the loss of life, homes, cattle, crops, and land was devastating. In 1902, a British soldier in East Africa described what happened in a single village: "Every soul was either shot or bayoneted. . . . We burned all the huts and razed the banana plantations to the ground."[10]

For the Vietnamese elite, schooled for centuries in Chinese-style Confucian thinking, conquest meant that the natural harmonies of life had been badly disrupted; it was a time when "water flowed uphill." Nguyen Khuyen (1835–1909), a senior Vietnamese official, retired to his ancestral village to farm and write poetry after the French conquest. In his poems he expressed his anguish at the passing of the world he had known:

> Fine wine but no good friends,
> So I buy none though I have the money.
> A poem comes to mind, but I choose not to write it down.
> If it were written, to whom would I give it?
> The spare bed hangs upon the wall in cold indifference.
> I pluck the lute, but it just doesn't sound right.[11]

Many others also withdrew into private life, feigning illness when asked to serve in public office under the French.

Cooperation and Rebellion

Although violence was a prominent feature of colonial life both during conquest and after, various groups and many individuals willingly cooperated with colonial authorities to their own advantage. Many men found employment, status, and security in European-led armed forces. The shortage and expense of European administrators and the difficulties of communicating across cultural boundaries made it necessary for colonial rulers to rely heavily on a range of local intermediaries. Thus Indian princes, Muslim emirs, and African rulers, often from elite or governing families, found it possible to retain much of their earlier status and many of their privileges while gaining considerable wealth by exercising authority, legally and otherwise, at the local level. For example, in French West Africa, an area eight times the size of France and with a population of about 15 million in the late 1930s, the colonial state consisted of just 385 French administrators and more than 50,000

African "chiefs." Thus colonial rule rested on and reinforced the most conservative segments of colonized societies.

Both colonial governments and private missionary organizations had an interest in promoting a measure of European education. From this process arose a small Western-educated class, whose members served the colonial state, European businesses, and Christian missions as teachers, clerks, translators, and lower-level administrators. A few received higher education abroad and returned home as lawyers, doctors, engineers, or journalists. As colonial governments and business enterprises became more sophisticated, Europeans increasingly depended on the Western-educated class at the expense of the more traditional elites.

If colonial rule enlisted the willing cooperation of some, it provoked the bitter opposition of many others. Thus periodic rebellions, both large and small, erupted in colonial regimes everywhere. The most famous among them was the Indian Rebellion of 1857–1858, which was triggered by the introduction into the colony's military forces of a new cartridge smeared with animal fat from cows and pigs. Because Hindus venerated cows and Muslims regarded pigs as unclean, both groups viewed the innovation as a plot to render them defiled and to convert them to Christianity. Behind this incident were many groups of people with a whole series of grievances generated by the British colonial presence: local rulers who had lost power; landlords deprived of their estates or their rent; peasants overtaxed and exploited by urban moneylenders and landlords alike; unemployed weavers displaced by machine-manufactured textiles; and religious leaders outraged by missionary preaching. A mutiny among Indian troops in Bengal triggered the rebellion, which soon spread to other regions of the colony and other social groups. Soon much of India was aflame. Some rebel leaders presented their cause as an effort to revive an almost-vanished Mughal Empire and thereby attracted support from those with strong resentments against the British. Although it was crushed in 1858, the rebellion greatly widened the racial divide in colonial India and eroded British tolerance for those they viewed as "nigger natives" who had betrayed their trust. Fear of provoking another rebellion made the British more conservative and cautious about deliberately trying to change Indian society. Moreover, the rebellion convinced the British government to assume direct control over India, ending the era of British East India Company rule in the subcontinent.

Colonial Empires with a Difference

At one level, European colonial empires were but the latest in a very long line of imperial creations, all of which had enlisted cooperation and experienced resistance from their subject peoples, but the nineteenth-century European version of empire was distinctive in several remarkable ways. One was the prominence of race in distinguishing rulers and ruled, as the high tide of "scientific racism" in Europe coincided with the acquisition of Asian and African colonies. In East Africa, for

Guided Reading Question

■ EXPLANATION
Why might subject people choose to cooperate with the colonial regime? What might prompt them to violent rebellion or resistance?

example, white men expected to be addressed as *bwana* (Swahili for "master"), whereas Europeans regularly called African men "boy." Education for colonial subjects was both limited and skewed toward practical subjects rather than scientific and literary studies, which were widely regarded as inappropriate for the "primitive mind" of "natives." Particularly affected by European racism were those whose Western education and aspirations most clearly threatened the racial divide. Europeans were exceedingly reluctant to allow even the most highly educated Asians and Africans to enter the higher ranks of the colonial civil service. A proposal in 1883 to allow Indian judges to hear cases involving whites provoked outrage and massive demonstrations among European inhabitants of India.

Guided Reading Question

....

■ COMPARISON
What was distinctive about European colonial empires of the nineteenth century?

In those colonies that had a large European settler population, the pattern of racial separation was much more pronounced than in places such as Nigeria, which had few permanently settled whites. The most extreme case was South Africa, where a large European population and the widespread use of African labor in mines and industries brought blacks and whites into closer and more prolonged contact than elsewhere. The racial fears that were aroused resulted in extraordinary efforts to establish race as a legal, not just a customary, feature of South African society. This racial system provided for separate "homelands," educational systems, residential areas, public facilities, and much more. In what was eventually known as apartheid, South African whites attempted the impossible task of creating an industrializing economy based on cheap African labor, while limiting African social and political integration in every conceivable fashion.

A further distinctive feature of nineteenth-century European empires lay in the extent to which colonial states were able to penetrate the societies they governed. Centralized tax-collecting bureaucracies, new means of communication and transportation, imposed changes in landholding patterns, integration of colonial economies into a global network of exchange, public health and sanitation measures, and the activities of missionaries—all of this touched the daily lives of many people far more deeply than in earlier empires. Not only were Europeans foreign rulers, but they also bore the seeds of a very different way of life, which grew out of their own modern transformation.

Nineteenth-century European colonizers were extraordinary as well in their penchant for counting and classifying their subject people. With the assistance of anthropologists and missionaries, colonial governments collected a vast amount of information, sought to organize it "scientifically," and used it to manage the unfamiliar, complex, varied, and fluctuating societies that they governed. In India, the British found in classical texts and Brahmin ideology an idealized description of the caste system, based on the notion of four ranked and unchanging varnas, which made it possible to bring order out of the immense complexity and variety of caste as it actually operated. Thus the British invented or appropriated a Brahmin version of "traditional India" that they favored and sought to preserve, while scorning as "non-Indian" the new elite who had been educated in European schools and were enthusiastic about Western ways of life. This view of India reflected the great influence of Brahmins on British thinking and clearly served the interests of this Indian upper class.

Likewise, within African colonies Europeans identified, and sometimes invented, distinct tribes, each with its own clearly defined territory, language, customs, and chief. The notion of a "tribal Africa" expressed the Western view that African societies were primitive or backward, representing an earlier stage of human development. It was also a convenient idea, for it reduced the enormous complexity and fluidity of African societies to a more manageable state and thus made colonial administration easier.

Gender too entered into the efforts of Europeans to define both themselves and their newly acquired subject peoples. European colonizers—mostly male—took pride in their "active masculinity" while defining the "conquered races" as soft, passive, and feminine. Indian Bengali men, wrote a British official in 1892, "are disqualified for political enfranchisement by the possession of essentially feminine characteristics."[12] By linking the inferiority of women with that of people of color, gender ideology and race prejudice were joined in support of colonial rule. But the intersection of race, gender, and empire was complex and varied. European men in the colonies often viewed their own women as the bearers and emblems of civilization, "upholding the moral dignity of the white community" amid the darkness of inferior peoples.[13] As such, European women had to be above reproach in sexual matters, protected against the alleged lust of native men by their separation from local African or Asian societies. Furthermore, certain colonized people, such as the Sikhs and Gurkhas in India, the Kamba in Kenya, and the Hausa in Nigeria, were gendered as masculine or "martial races" and targeted for recruitment into British military or police forces.

Finally, the colonial policies of Europeans contradicted their own core values and their practices at home to an unusual degree. While nineteenth-century Britain and France were becoming more democratic, their colonies were essentially dictatorships, offering perhaps order and stability, but certainly not democratic government, because few colonial subjects were participating citizens. Empire, of course, was wholly at odds with European notions of national independence, and ranked racial classifications went against the grain of both Christian and Enlightenment ideas of human equality. Furthermore, many Europeans were distinctly reluctant to encourage within their colonies the kind of modernization—urban growth, industrialization, individual values, religious skepticism—that was sweeping their own societies. They feared that this kind of social change, often vilified as "detribalization," would encourage unrest and challenge colonial rule. As a model for social development, they much preferred "traditional" rural society, with its established authorities and social hierarchies, though shorn of abuses such as slavery and *sati* (widow burning). Such contradictions between what Europeans embraced at home and what they practiced in the colonies became increasingly apparent to many Asians and Africans and played a major role in undermining the foundations of colonial rule in the twentieth century.

Ways of Working: Comparing Colonial Economies

Colonial rule affected the lives of its subject people in many ways, but the most pronounced change was in their ways of working. The colonial state—with its power to tax, to seize land for European enterprises, to compel labor, and to build railroads, ports, and roads—played an important role in these transformations. Even more powerful was the growing integration of colonized societies into a world economy that increasingly demanded their gold, diamonds, copper, tin, rubber, coffee, cotton, sugar, cocoa, and many other products. But the economic transformations born of these twin pressures were far from uniform. Various groups— migrant workers and cash-crop farmers, plantation laborers and domestic servants, urban elites and day laborers, men and women—experienced the colonial era differently as their daily working lives underwent profound changes.

To various degrees, old ways of working were eroded almost everywhere in the colonial world. Subsistence farming, in which peasant families produced largely for their own needs, diminished as growing numbers directed at least some of their energies to working for wages or selling what they produced for a cash income. That money was both necessary to pay taxes and school fees and useful for buying the various products—such as machine-produced textiles, bicycles, and kerosene— that the industrial economies of Europe sent their way. As in Europe, artisans suffered greatly when cheaper machine-manufactured merchandise displaced their own handmade goods. A flood of inexpensive textiles from Britain's new factories ruined the livelihood of tens of thousands of India's handloom weavers. Iron smelting largely disappeared in Africa, and occupations such as blacksmithing and tanning lost ground. Furthermore, Asian and African merchants, who had earlier handled the trade between their countries and the wider world, were squeezed out by well-financed European commercial firms.

Economies of Coercion: Forced Labor and the Power of the State

Many of the new ways of working that emerged during the colonial era derived directly from the demands of the colonial state. The most obvious was required and unpaid labor on public projects, such as building railroads, constructing government buildings, and transporting goods. In French Africa, all "natives" were legally obligated for "statute labor" of ten to twelve days a year, a practice that lasted through 1946. It was much resented. A resident of British West Africa, interviewed in 1996, bitterly recalled this feature of colonial life: "They [British officials] were rude, and they made us work for them a lot. They came to the village and just rounded us up and made us go off and clear the road or carry loads on our heads."[14]

The most infamous cruelties of forced labor occurred during the early twentieth century in the Congo Free State, then governed personally by King Leopold II of Belgium. Private companies in the Congo, operating under the authority of the state, forced villagers to collect rubber, which was much in demand for bicycle and automobile tires, with a reign of terror and abuse that cost millions of lives. One refugee from these horrors described the process:

> We were always in the forest to find the rubber vines, to go without food, and our women had to give up cultivating the fields and gardens. Then we starved. . . . We begged the white man to leave us alone, saying we could get no more rubber, but the white men and their soldiers said "Go. You are only beasts yourselves. . . ." When we failed and our rubber was short, the soldiers came to our towns and killed us. Many were shot, some had their ears cut off; others were tied up with ropes round their necks and taken away.[15]

Eventually such outrages were widely publicized in Europe, where they created a scandal, forcing the Belgian government to take control of the Congo in 1908 and ending Leopold's reign of terror.

Meanwhile, however, this late nineteenth- and early twentieth-century commerce in rubber and ivory, made possible by the massive use of forced labor in both the Congo and the neighboring German colony of Cameroon, laid the foundations for

Colonial Violence in the Congo
These young boys with severed hands were among the victims of a brutal regime of forced labor undertaken in the Congo during the late nineteenth and early twentieth centuries. Such mutilation was punishment for their villages' inability to supply the required amount of wild rubber. (Universal History Archive/Universal Images Group/UIG via Getty Images)

the modern AIDS epidemic. It was in southeastern Cameroon that the virus causing AIDS made the jump from chimpanzees to humans, and it was in the crowded and hectic Congolese city of Kinshasa, with its new networks of sexual interaction, where that disease found its initial breakout point, becoming an epidemic. "Without the scramble [for Africa]," concludes a recent account, "it's hard to see how HIV could have made it out of southeastern Cameroon to eventually kill tens of millions of people."[16]

A variation on the theme of forced labor took shape in the so-called cultivation system of the Netherlands East Indies (Indonesia) during the nineteenth century. Peasants were required to cultivate 20 percent or more of their land in cash crops such as sugar or coffee to meet their tax obligation to the state. Sold to government contractors at fixed and low prices, those crops, when resold on the world market, proved highly profitable for Dutch traders and shippers as well as for the Dutch state and its citizens. According to one scholar, the cultivation system "performed a miracle for the Dutch economy," enabling it to avoid taxing its own people and providing capital for its Industrial Revolution.[17] It also enriched and strengthened the position of those "traditional authorities" who enforced the system, often by using lashings and various tortures, on behalf of the Dutch. For the peasants of Java, however, it meant a double burden of obligations to the colonial state as well as to local lords. Many became indebted to moneylenders when they could not meet those obligations. Those demands, coupled with the loss of land and labor now excluded from food production, contributed to a wave of famines during the mid-nineteenth century in which hundreds of thousands perished.

On occasion, the forced cultivation of cash crops was successfully resisted. In German East Africa, for example, colonial authorities in the late nineteenth century imposed the cultivation of cotton, which seriously interfered with production of local food crops. Here is how one man remembered the experience:

> The cultivation of cotton was done by turns. Every village was allotted days on which to cultivate. . . . After arriving you all suffered very greatly. Your back and your buttocks were whipped and there was no rising up once you stooped to dig. . . . And yet he [the German] wanted us to pay him tax. Were we not human beings?[18]

Such conditions prompted a massive rebellion in 1904–1905, known as Maji Maji, and persuaded the Germans to end the forced growing of cotton. In Mozambique, where the Portuguese likewise brutally enforced cotton cultivation, a combination of peasant sabotage, the planting of unauthorized crops, and the smuggling of cotton across the border to more profitable markets ensured that Portugal never achieved its goal of becoming self-sufficient in cotton production. Thus the actions of colonized peoples could alter or frustrate the plans of the colonizers.

Economies of Cash-Crop Agriculture: The Pull of the Market

AP® EXAM TIP

Return to Chapter 14 and compare the plantation systems in the Americas to those discussed here.

Many Asian and African peoples had produced quite willingly for an international market long before they were enclosed within colonial societies. They offered for trade items such as peanuts and palm oil in West Africa, cotton in Egypt, spices in Indonesia, and pepper and textiles in India. In some places, colonial rule created conditions that facilitated and increased cash-crop production to the advantage of local farmers. British authorities in Burma, for example, acted to encourage rice production among small farmers by ending an earlier prohibition on rice exports, providing irrigation and transportation facilities, and enacting land tenure laws that facilitated private ownership of small farms. Under these conditions, the population of the Irrawaddy Delta boomed, migrants from Upper Burma and India poured into the region, and rice exports soared. Local small farmers benefited considerably because they were now able to own their own land, build substantial houses, and buy imported goods. For several decades in the late nineteenth century, standards of living improved sharply, and huge increases in rice production fed millions of people in other parts of Asia and elsewhere. It was a very different situation from that of peasants forced to grow crops that seriously interfered with their food production.

But that kind of colonial development, practiced also in the Mekong River delta of French-ruled Vietnam, had important environmental consequences. It involved the destruction of mangrove forests and swamplands along with the fish and shellfish that supplemented local diets. New dikes and irrigation channels inhibited the depositing of silt from upstream and thus depleted soils in the deltas of these major river systems. And, unknown to anyone at the time, this kind of agriculture generates large amounts of methane gas, a major contributor to global warming.

Profitable cash-crop farming also developed in the southern Gold Coast (present-day Ghana), a British territory in West Africa. Unlike in Burma, it was African farmers themselves who took the initiative to develop export agriculture. Planting cacao trees in huge quantities, they became the world's leading supplier of cocoa, used to make chocolate, by 1911. Cacao was an attractive crop because, unlike cotton, it was compatible with the continued production of foods and did not require so much labor time. In the early twentieth century, it brought a new prosperity to many local farmers. "A hybrid society was taking shape," wrote one scholar, "partly peasant, in that most members farmed their own land with family labor . . . and partly capitalist, in that a minority employed wage laborers, produced chiefly for the market, and reinvested profits."[19]

That success brought new problems in its wake. A shortage of labor fostered the employment of former slaves as dependent and exploited workers and also generated tensions between the sexes when some men married women for their labor power but refused to support them adequately. Moreover, the labor shortage brought a huge influx of migrants from the drier interior parts of West Africa, generating ethnic and class tensions. Furthermore, many colonies came to specialize in one or two cash crops, creating an unhealthy dependence when world market prices dropped. Thus African and Asian farmers were increasingly subject to the uncertain rhythms of the international marketplace as well as to those of weather and climate.

Guided Reading Question

■ CHANGE
How did cash-crop agriculture transform the lives of colonized peoples?

Economies of Wage Labor: Migration for Work

Yet another new way of working in colonial societies involved wage labor in some European enterprise. Driven by the need for money, by the loss of land adequate to support their families, or sometimes by the orders of colonial authorities, millions of colonial subjects across Asia, Africa, and Oceania sought employment in European-owned plantations, mines, construction projects, and homes. Often this required migration to distant work sites, many of them overseas. In this process, colonized migrants were joined by millions of Chinese, Japanese, and others, who lived in more independent states. Together they generated vast streams of migration

Economic Change in the Colonial World
These workers on a Ceylon tea plantation in the early twentieth century are moving sacks of tea into a drying house in preparation for export. The Lipton label on the bags is a reminder of the role of large-scale foreign investment in the economic transformations of the colonial era. (© Hulton-Deutsch Collection/Corbis)

that paralleled and at least equaled in numbers the huge movement of Europeans during the nineteenth and early twentieth centuries (see Chapter 17, pages 755–57). For Europeans, Asians, and Africans alike, the globalizing world of the colonial era was one of people in motion. (See the Snapshot on long-distance migration, opposite.)

The African segment of this migratory stream moved in several directions. For much of the nineteenth century, the Atlantic slave trade continued, funneling well over 3 million additional people to the Americas, mostly to Brazil. As the slave trade diminished and colonial rule took shape in Africa, internal migration mounted within or among particular colonies. More than in Asia, Africans migrated to European farms or plantations because they had lost their own land. In the settler colonies of Africa—Algeria, Kenya, Southern Rhodesia (Zimbabwe), and South Africa, for example—permanent European communities, with the help of colonial governments, obtained huge tracts of land, much of which had previously been home to African societies. A 1913 law in South Africa legally defined 88 percent of the land as belonging to whites, who were then about 20 percent of the population. Much of highland Kenya, an enormously rich agricultural region that was home to the Gikuyu and Kamba peoples, was taken over by some 4,000 white farmers. In

SNAPSHOT   Long-Distance Migration in an Age of Empire, 1846–1940

AP® EXAM TIP

Massive migrations in the late nineteenth and early twentieth centuries are a major concept in the AP® course.

The age of empire was also an age of global migration. Beyond the three major patterns of long-distance migration shown here, shorter migrations within particular regions or colonies set millions more into motion.[20]

Origins	Destination	Numbers
Europe	Americas	55–58 million
India, southern China	Southeast Asia, Indian Ocean rim, South Pacific	48–52 million
Northeast Asia, Russia	Manchuria, Siberia, Central Asia, Japan	46–51 million

such places, some Africans stayed on as "squatters," working for the new landowners as the price of remaining on what had been their own land. Others were displaced to "native reserves," limited areas that could not support their growing populations, and many were thus forced to work for wages on European farms. Most notably in South Africa, such reserved areas, known as Bantustans, became greatly overcrowded: soil fertility declined, hillsides were cleared, forests shrank, and erosion scarred the land. This kind of ecological degradation was among the environmental consequences of African wage labor on European farms and estates.

The gold and diamond mines of South Africa likewise set in motion a huge pattern of labor migration that encompassed all of Africa south of the Belgian Congo. With skilled and highly paid work reserved for white miners, Africans worked largely as unskilled laborers at a fraction of the wages paid to whites. Furthermore, they were recruited on short-term contracts, lived in all-male prison-like barracks that were often surrounded by barbed wire, and were forced to return home periodically to prevent them from establishing a permanent family life near the mines.

Asians too were in motion and in large numbers. Some 29 million Indians and 19 million Chinese migrated variously to Southeast Asia, the South Pacific, East and South Africa, the Caribbean islands, or the lands around the Indian Ocean basin. All across Southeast Asia in the later nineteenth and early twentieth centuries, huge plantations sprouted, which were financed from Europe and which grew sugarcane, rubber, tea, tobacco, sisal (used for making rope), and more. Impoverished workers by the hundreds of thousands came from great distances (India, China, Java) to these plantations, where they were subject to strict control, often housed in barracks, and paid poorly, with women receiving 50 to 75 percent of a man's wage. Disease was common, and death rates were at least double that of the colony as a whole. In 1927 in southern Vietnam alone, one in twenty plantation workers died. British colonial authorities in India facilitated the migration of millions of Indians to work sites elsewhere in the British Empire — Trinidad, Jamaica, Fiji, Malaysia, Ceylon, South Africa, Kenya, and Uganda, for example — with some working as indentured laborers, receiving free passage and enough money to survive in return for five to seven years of heavy labor. Others operated as independent merchants. Particularly in the Caribbean region, Indian migration rose as the end of slavery created a need for additional labor. Since the vast majority of these Asian migrants were male, it altered gender ratios in the islands and in their countries of origin, where women faced increased workloads.

Mines were another source of wage labor for many Asians. In the British-ruled Malay States (Malaysia), tin mining accelerated greatly in the late nineteenth century, and by 1895 that colony produced some 55 percent of the world's tin. Operated initially by Chinese and later by European entrepreneurs, Malaysian tin mines drew many millions of impoverished Chinese workers on strictly controlled three-year contracts. Appalling living conditions, disease, and accidents generated extraordinarily high death rates.

Beyond Southeast Asia, Chinese migrants moved north to Manchuria in substantial numbers, encouraged by a Chinese government eager to prevent Russian encroachment in the area. The gold rushes of Australia and California also attracted hundreds of thousands of Chinese, who often found themselves subject to sharp discrimination from local people, including recently arrived European migrants. For example, Dennis Kearney, who led a California anti-immigrant labor organization with the slogan "The Chinese must go," was himself an Irish-born immigrant. Canada, Australia, New Zealand, and the United States all enacted measures to restrict or end Chinese immigration in the late nineteenth century.

A further destination of African and Asian migrants lay in the rapidly swelling cities of the colonial world—Lagos, Nairobi, Cairo, Calcutta, Rangoon, Batavia, Singapore, Saigon. Racially segregated, often unsanitary, and greatly overcrowded, these cities nonetheless were seen as meccas of opportunity for people all across the social spectrum. Traditional elites, absentee landlords, and wealthy Chinese businessmen occupied the top rungs of Southeast Asian cities. Western-educated people everywhere found opportunities as teachers, doctors, and professional specialists, but more often as clerks in European business offices and government bureaucracies. Skilled workers on the railways or in the ports represented a working-class elite, while a few labored in the factories that processed agricultural goods or manufactured basic products such as beer, cigarettes, cement, and furniture. Far more numerous were the construction workers, rickshaw drivers, food sellers, domestic servants, prostitutes, and others who made up the urban poor of colonial cities. In 1955, a British investigating commission described life in Nairobi, the capital of Kenya, one of Britain's richest colonies:

> The wages of the majority of African workers are too low to enable them to obtain accommodation which is adequate to any standard. The high cost of housing relative to wages is in itself a cause of overcrowding, because housing is shared to lighten the cost. This, with the high cost of food in towns, makes family life impossible for the majority.[21]

Guided Reading Question

■ CHANGE

What kinds of wage labor were available in the colonies? Why might people take part in it? How did doing so change their lives?

AP® EXAM TIP

You should know about factors that led to the growth of colonial cities in this era.

Thus, after more than half a century of colonial rule, British authorities themselves acknowledged that normal family life in the colony's major urban center proved out of reach for the vast majority. It was quite an admission.

Women and the Colonial Economy: Examples from Africa

If economic life in European empires varied greatly from place to place, even within the same colony, it also offered a different combination of opportunities and hardships to women than it did to men, as the experience of colonial Africa shows.[22] In precolonial Africa, women were almost everywhere active farmers, with responsibility for planting, weeding, and harvesting in addition to food preparation and child care. Men cleared the land, built houses, herded the cattle, and in some cases assisted with field work. Within this division of labor, women were expected to feed their own families and were usually allocated their own fields for that purpose. Many were also involved in local trading activity. Though clearly subordinate to men, African women nevertheless had a measure of economic autonomy.

As the demands of the colonial economy grew, women's lives increasingly diverged from those of men. In colonies where cash-crop agriculture was dominant, men often withdrew from subsistence production in favor of more lucrative export crops. Among the Ewe people of southern Ghana, men almost completely dominated the highly profitable cacao farming, whereas women assumed near total responsibility for domestic food production. In neighboring Ivory Coast, women had traditionally grown cotton for their families' clothing, but when that crop acquired a cash value, men insisted that cotton grown for export be produced on their own personal fields. Thus men acted to control the most profitable aspects of cash-crop agriculture and in doing so greatly increased the subsistence workload of women. One study from Cameroon estimated that women's working hours increased from forty-six per week in precolonial times to more than seventy by 1934.

Further increasing women's workload and differentiating their lives from those of men was labor migration. As growing numbers of men sought employment in the cities, on settler farms, or in the mines, their wives were left to manage the domestic economy almost alone. In many cases, women also had to supply food to men in the cities to compensate for very low urban wages. They often took over such traditionally male tasks as breaking the ground for planting, milking the cows, and supervising the herds, in addition to their normal responsibilities. In South Africa, where the demands of the European economy were particularly heavy, some 40 to 50 percent of able-bodied adult men were absent from the rural areas, and women headed 60 percent of households. In Botswana, which supplied much male labor to South Africa, married couples by the 1930s rarely lived together for more than two months at a time. Increasingly, men and women lived in different worlds, with one focused on the cities and working for wages and the other on village life and subsistence agriculture. (See Zooming In: Wanjiku of Kenya, page 810).

Guided Reading Question

■ CHANGE

How were the lives of African women altered by colonial economies?

Wanjiku of Kenya

Born in 1910 among the Gikuyu people of East Africa, Wanjiku witnessed almost the entire twentieth century.[23] Her life encompassed the dramatic intrusion of British colonialism, the coming of Christianity, the Mau Mau rebellion against European rule, the achievement of independence for Kenya in 1963, and the challenges of modernization in the decades that followed.

Women of Kenya forming a Home Guard.

eligible for marriage. Described as "buying maturity with pain," the operation was, as Wanjiku later recalled, "like being slaughtered." Circumcision also marked Wanjiku's entry into an age-set, a group of girls who had undergone this initiation into womanhood together. As adults, they worked together in the fields, provided help and gifts at the birth of children, and protected one another from sexual abuse by men.

And yet, the first thirty years or more of Wanjiku's life were shaped far more by the customary patterns of rural Gikuyu culture than by the transformations of colonial rule. She grew up in her father's compound, where her mother, three other wives, and more than a dozen children also lived. As a child, she began contributing to the household — fetching water, firewood, and vegetables — even as she learned the stories, riddles, and proverbs of Gikuyu folklore. At age fourteen, she had her ears pierced, thus achieving a "new stage of maturity."

Far more important, however, was her "circumcision," a procedure that involved the cutting of her genitals and the excision of the clitoris. For Wanjiku, as for virtually all Gikuyu girls, this procedure was a prerequisite for becoming "a grown-up person" and

Now Wanjiku was also able to attend the evening dances where young men and women mingled. There she met her first husband, Wamai, who initiated the long process of negotiation between families and the payment of numerous goats and cows to the bride's father. She said of her marriage, "[It] was a big change — learning about sex and my husband's habits." Tragedy struck, however, when both her husband and her first child died. A few years later, Wanjiku married Kamau, the younger brother of her first husband, with whom she had three sons. Her second marriage, unlike the first, was accompanied by a church service and a wedding ring,

photo: © Bettmann/Corbis

Women coped with these difficult circumstances in a number of ways. Many sought closer relations with their families of birth rather than with their absent husbands' families, as would otherwise have been expected. Among the Luo of Kenya, women introduced laborsaving crops, adopted new farm implements, and earned some money as traders. In the cities, they established a variety of self-help associations, including those for prostitutes and for brewers of beer.

The colonial economy sometimes provided a measure of opportunity for enterprising women, particularly in small-scale trade and marketing. In some parts of West Africa, women came to dominate this sector of the economy by selling food-signs of encroaching Western culture. Both marriages were apparently relatively satisfying, and she reported with pride that neither man mistreated or beat her.

During the 1940s and 1950s, the new realities of colonial life began to touch Wanjiku more personally than before. She and Kamau became Christians around 1940, and in 1948 Wanjiku "became saved." "The saved ones," she declared, "do not take tobacco nor drink. And they don't abuse anybody." She then joined a church-based "Mother's Union," vowing "never again to carry out old Gikuyu customs." For Wanjiku, this group became a major source of social support that operated outside of traditional Gikuyu culture.

In 1952, Wanjiku found herself caught up in the Gikuyu-based Mau Mau rebellion against colonial rule. To separate the general population from the Mau Mau "freedom fighters" in the surrounding forests, the colonial government forced most Gikuyu to relocate into compact villages where they were closely and brutally supervised by the Home Guard, local African police appointed by European authorities. Wanjiku and many others were required to dig a large trench around the village to keep the rebels out. "We were like prisoners," Wanjiku reported. "If we started to drag behind working, we were beaten." Caught between the opposing forces of the Home Guard and the Mau Mau fighters, Wanjiku lived in fear. "If you made a mistake with the Home Guard, you would die. If you made a mistake with the Mau Mau, you would die too."

The British crushed the Mau Mau rebellion by 1956, but by 1963 Kenya, like dozens of other African countries, had achieved its independence. Wanjiku remembered the day with exhilaration. "We spent the whole night singing and dancing. We were so happy because we would never be ruled by foreigners again. It also meant the end of the beatings." It was perhaps the high point of Wanjiku's consciousness as a public person and a participant in a new nation.

In the decades following independence, Wanjiku experienced still further changes. She and her husband began to grow tea as a cash crop, an undertaking that had been limited to European farmers for much of the colonial era. Kenya's new government tried to forbid female circumcision, and, as young people were increasingly drawn to the larger cities, older rural social patterns broke down. Boys and girls of different age-sets mingled far more freely than before. Educated young people felt superior and sometimes behaved disrespectfully to illiterate elders such as Wanjiku.

By the 1990s, Wanjiku was an old woman afflicted with arthritis and much-diminished vision. She saw herself less as a Kenyan than as a Gikuyu. No longer able to farm, she counseled her children, looked after her grandchildren, and enjoyed recounting her life story to a visiting anthropologist.

Question: How does Wanjiku's life reflect both the continuities and changes of the twentieth century in African history?

---

stuffs, cloth, and inexpensive imported goods, while men or foreign firms controlled the more profitable wholesale and import-export trade. Such opportunities sometimes gave women considerable economic autonomy. By the 1930s, for example, Nupe women in northern Nigeria had gained sufficient wealth as itinerant traders that they were contributing more to the family income than their husbands and frequently lent money to them. Among some Igbo groups in southern Nigeria, men were responsible for growing the prestigious yams, but women's crops—especially cassava—came to have a cash value during the colonial era, and women were entitled to keep the profits from selling them. "What is man? I have my own money" was a popular saying that expressed the growing economic independence of such women.[24]

At the other end of the social scale, women of impoverished rural families, by necessity, often became virtually independent heads of household in the absence of their husbands. Others took advantage of new opportunities in mission schools, towns, and mines to flee the restrictions of rural patriarchy. Such challenges to patriarchal values elicited various responses from men, including increased accusations of witchcraft against women and fears of impotence. Among the Shona in Southern Rhodesia, and no doubt elsewhere, senior African men repeatedly petitioned the colonial authorities for laws and regulations that would criminalize adultery and restrict women's ability to leave their rural villages. The control of women's sexuality and mobility was a common interest of European and African men.

Assessing Colonial Development

AP® EXAM TIP

Take notes on this important discussion of the legacies of nineteenth-century imperialism.

Beyond the many and varied changes that transformed the working lives of millions in the colonial world lies the difficult and highly controversial question of the overall economic impact of colonial rule on Asian and African societies. Defenders, both then and now, praise it for jump-starting modern economic growth, but numerous critics cite a record of exploitation and highlight the limitations and unevenness of that growth.

Amid the continuing debates, three things seem reasonably clear. First, colonial rule served, for better or worse, to further the integration of Asian and African economies into a global network of exchange, now centered in Europe. In many places, that process was well under way before conquest imposed foreign rule, and elsewhere it occurred without formal colonial control. Nonetheless, it is apparent that within the colonial world far more land and labor were devoted to production for the global market at the end of the colonial era than at its beginning. Many colonized groups and individuals benefited from their new access to global markets—Burmese rice farmers and West African cocoa farmers, for example. Others were devastated. In India, large-scale wheat exports to Britain continued unchecked—or even increased—despite a major drought and famine that claimed between 6 and 10 million lives in the late 1870s. A colonial government committed to free market principles declined to interfere with those exports or to provide much by way of relief. One senior official declared it "a mistake to spend so much money to save a lot of black fellows."[25]

Guided Reading Question

············

■ CHANGE
Did colonial rule bring "economic progress" in its wake?

Second, Europeans could hardly avoid conveying to the colonies some elements of their own modernizing process. It was in their interests to do so, and many felt duty bound to "improve" the societies they briefly governed. Modern administrative and bureaucratic structures facilitated colonial control; communication and transportation infrastructure (railroads, motorways, ports, telegraphs, postal services) moved products to the world market; schools trained the army of intermediaries on which colonial rule depended; and modest health care provisions fulfilled some of the "civilizing mission" to which many Europeans felt committed. These elements of modernization made an appearance, however inadequately, during the colonial era.

Third, nowhere in the colonial world did a major breakthrough to modern industrial society occur. When India became independent after two centuries of colonial rule by the world's first industrial society, it was still one of the poorest of the world's developing countries. The British may not have created Indian poverty, but neither did they overcome it to any substantial degree. Scholars continue to debate the reasons for that failure: was it the result of deliberate British policies, or was it due to the conditions of Indian society? The nationalist movements that surged across Asia and Africa in the twentieth century had their own answer. To their many millions of participants, colonial rule, whatever its earlier promise, had become an economic dead end, whereas independence represented a grand opening to new and more hopeful possibilities. Paraphrasing a famous teaching of Jesus, Kwame Nkrumah, the first prime minister of an independent Ghana, declared, "Seek ye first the political kingdom, and all these other things [schools, factories, hospitals, for example] will be added unto you."

> **PRACTICING AP® HISTORICAL THINKING**
>
> In what different ways did the colonial experience reshape the economic lives of Asian and African societies?

Believing and Belonging: Identity and Cultural Change in the Colonial Era

The experience of colonial rule—its racism, its exposure to European culture, its social and economic upheavals—contributed much to cultural change within Asian, African, and Oceanic societies. Coping with these enormous disruptions induced many colonized peoples to alter the ways they thought about themselves and their communities. Cultural identities, of course, are never static, but the transformations of the colonial era catalyzed substantial and quite rapid changes in what people believed and in how they defined the societies to which they belonged. Those transformed identities continued to echo long after European rule had ended.

Education

For an important minority, it was the acquisition of Western education, obtained through missionary or government schools, that generated a new identity. To many European colonizers, education was a means of "uplifting native races," a paternalistic obligation of the superior to the inferior. To previously illiterate people, the knowledge of reading and writing of any kind often suggested an almost magical power. Within the colonial setting, it could mean an escape from some of the most onerous obligations of living under European control, such as forced labor. More positively, it meant access to better-paying positions in government bureaucracies, mission organizations, or business firms and to the exciting imported goods that

> **AP® EXAM TIP**
>
> It is important to know examples of colonial elites who received education from their colonizers, because they became leaders of independence movements in the twentieth century.

their salaries could buy. Moreover, education often provided social mobility and elite status within their own communities and an opportunity to achieve, or at least approach, equality with whites in racially defined societies. An African man from colonial Kenya described an encounter he had as a boy in 1938 with a relative who was a teacher in a mission school:

> Aged about 25, he seems to me like a young god with his smart clothes and shoes, his watch, and a beautiful bicycle. I worshipped in particular his bicycle that day and decided that I must somehow get myself one. As he talked with us, it seemed to me that the secret of his riches came from his education, his knowledge of reading and writing, and that it was essential for me to obtain this power.[26]

Guided Reading Question

■ CHANGE
What impact did Western education have on colonial societies?

Many such people ardently embraced European culture, dressing in European clothes, speaking French or English, building European-style houses, getting married in long white dresses, and otherwise emulating European ways. Some of the early Western-educated Bengalis from northeastern India boasted about dreaming in English and deliberately ate beef, to the consternation of their elders. In a well-known poem titled "A Prayer for Peace," Léopold Senghor, a highly educated West African writer and political leader, enumerated the many crimes of colonialism and yet confessed, "I have a great weakness for France." Asian and African colonial societies now had a new cultural divide: between the small numbers who had mastered to varying degrees the ways of their rulers and the vast majority who had not. Literate Christians in the East African kingdom of Buganda referred with contempt to their "pagan" neighbors as "those who do not read."

Many among the Western-educated elite saw themselves as a modernizing vanguard, leading the regeneration of their societies in association with colonial authorities. For them, at least initially, the colonial enterprise was full of promise for a better future. The Vietnamese teacher and nationalist Nguyen Thai Hoc, while awaiting execution in 1930 by the French for his revolutionary activities, wrote about his earlier hopes: "At the beginning, I had thought to cooperate with the French in Indochina in order to serve my compatriots, my country, and my people, particularly in the areas of cultural and economic development."[27] Senghor too wrote wistfully about an earlier time when "we could have lived in harmony [with Europeans]."

AP® EXAM TIP

The rise of national pride within African and Asian colonies is an important concept in AP® World History.

In nineteenth-century India, Western-educated men organized a variety of reform societies, which drew inspiration from the classic texts of Hinduism while seeking a renewed Indian culture that was free of idolatry, caste restrictions, and other "errors" that had entered Indian life over the centuries. Much of this reform effort centered on improving the status of women. Thus reformers campaigned against *sati*, the ban on remarriage of widows, female infanticide, and child marriages, while advocating women's education and property rights. For a time, some of these Indian reformers saw themselves working in tandem with British colonial authorities. One of them, Keshub Chunder Sen (1838–1884), spoke to his fellow Indians in 1877: "You are bound to be loyal to the British government that came

The Educated Elite
Throughout the Afro-Asian world of the nineteenth century, the European presence generated a small group of people who enthusiastically embraced the culture and lifestyle of Europe. Here King Chulalongkorn of Siam poses with the crown prince and other young students, all of them impeccably garbed in European clothing. (© Hulton-Deutsch Collection/Corbis)

to your rescue, as God's ambassador, when your country was sunk in ignorance and superstition. . . . India in her present fallen condition seems destined to sit at the feet of England for many long years, to learn western art and science."[28] Such fond hopes for the modernization or renewal of Asian and African societies within a colonial framework would be bitterly disappointed. Europeans generally declined to treat their Asian and African subjects—even those with a Western education— as equal partners in the enterprise of renewal. The frequent denigration of their cultures as primitive, backward, uncivilized, or savage certainly rankled, particularly among the well educated. "My people of Africa," wrote the West African intellectual James Aggrey in the 1920s, "we were created in the image of God, but men have made us think that we are chickens, and we still think we are; but we are eagles. Stretch forth your wings and fly."[29] In the long run, the educated classes in colonial societies everywhere found European rule far more of an obstacle to their countries' development than a means of achieving it. Turning decisively against a now-despised foreign imperialism, they led the many struggles for independence that came to fruition in the second half of the twentieth century.

Religion

Religion too provided the basis for new or transformed identities during the colonial era. Most dramatic were those places where widespread conversion to Christianity took place, such as Pacific Oceania and especially non-Muslim Africa. Some 10,000 missionaries had descended on Africa by 1910; by the 1960s, about 50 million Africans, roughly half of the non-Muslim population, claimed a Christian identity. The attractions of the new faith were many. As in the Americas centuries earlier, military defeat shook confidence in the old gods and local practices, fostering openness to new sources of supernatural power that could operate in the wider world now impinging on Oceanic and African societies. Furthermore, Christianity was widely associated with modern education, and, especially in Africa, mission schools were the primary providers of Western education. The young, the poor, and many women—all of them oppressed groups in many African societies—found new opportunities and greater freedom in some association with missions. Moreover, the spread of the Christian message was less the work of European missionaries than of those many thousands of African teachers, catechists, and pastors who brought the new faith to remote villages as well as the local communities that begged for a teacher and supplied the labor and materials to build a small church or school. In Oceania, local authorities, such as those in Fiji, Tonga, and Hawaii, sought to strengthen their position by associating with Christian missionaries, widely regarded as linked to the growing influence of European or American power in the region. In many of these small island societies, mission Christianity with its schools, clinics, political counsel, and new social conventions provided a measure of social cohesion for peoples devastated by disease and other disruptions that accompanied Western incursions.

But missionary teaching and practice also generated conflict and opposition, particularly when they touched on gender roles. A wide range of issues focusing on the lives of women proved challenging for missionaries and spawned opposition from converts or potential converts. Female nudity offended Western notions of modesty. Polygyny contradicted Christian monogamy, though such prescriptions sat uneasily beside Old Testament practices, and the question of what male converts should do with their additional wives was always difficult. Bride wealth made marriage seem "a mere mercantile transaction." Marriages between Christians and non-Christians remained problematic. Sexual activity outside of monogamous marriage often resulted in disciplinary action or expulsion from the church. Missionaries' efforts to enforce Western gender norms were in part responsible for considerable turnover in the ranks of African church members.

Among the more explosive issues that agitated nascent Christian communities in colonial Kenya was that of "female circumcision," the excision of a pubescent

Guided Reading Question

■ CHANGE

What were the attractions of Christianity within some colonial societies?

The Missionary Factor
Among the major change agents of the colonial era were the thousands of Christian missionaries who brought not only a new religion but also elements of European medicine, education, gender roles, and culture. Here is an assembly at a mission school for girls in New Guinea in the early twentieth century. (The Granger Collection, NYC — All rights reserved)

girl's clitoris and adjacent genital tissue as a part of initiation rites marking her coming-of-age.[30] To the Gikuyu people, among whom it was widely practiced, it was a prerequisite for adult status and marriage. To missionaries, it was physically damaging to girls and brought "unnecessary attention . . . to the non-spiritual aspects of sex." When missionaries in 1929 sought to enforce a ban on the practice among their African converts, outrage ensued. Thousands abandoned mission schools and churches, but they did not abandon Christianity or modern education. Rather, they created a series of independent schools and churches in which they could practice their new faith and pursue their educational goals without missionary intrusion. Some recalled that the New Testament itself had declared that "circumcision is nothing and uncircumcision is nothing." Accordingly, wrote one angry convert to a local missionary, "Has God spoken to you this time and informed you that those who circumcise will not enter in to God's place? It is better for a European like you to leave off speaking about such things because you can make the Gospel to be evil spoken of." (See Zooming In: Wanjiku, page 810, for the experience of a Gikuyu woman.)

As elsewhere, Christianity in Africa soon became Africanized. Within mission-based churches, many converts continued using protective charms and medicines and consulting local medicine men, all of which caused their missionary mentors to

Vivekananda, a Hindu Monk in America

The modern colonial era is associated with the "westernization" of the peoples of Asia, Africa, and the Middle East. Less frequently noticed has been traffic in the other direction, as Eastern, and especially Indian, religious culture penetrated Europe and the Americas. The Transcendentalist writers of early nineteenth-century New England warmly welcomed the translations of Hindu texts that derived from British scholars in colonial India. At his cabin on Walden Pond, Henry David Thoreau remarked, "In the morning I bathe my intellect in the stupendous . . . philosophy of the Bhagavad Gita . . . in comparison with which our modern world and its literature seem puny and trivial."[31] Since then, many Americans and Europeans have embraced elements of the universal and inclusive Hindu philosophical system known as Vedanta, and far more have practiced the physical and mental disciplines of yoga, both of which derive from ancient India.

A seminal moment in the coming of Indian spirituality to the United States occurred in Chicago during September 1893. The occasion was the World's Parlia-

Swami Vivekananda.

ment of Religions, an interfaith gathering that drew representatives from many of the world's religious traditions. The man who made the most vivid impression at the conference was a handsome thirty-year-old Hindu monk known as Swami Vivekananda. Appearing in an orange robe and a yellow turban and speaking fluent and eloquent English, he had only recently arrived from India, where he had received an excellent European education as well as a deep immersion in Hindu philosophy and practice.

In his initial speech to the parliament on its opening day, Vivekananda began by addressing his audience as "sisters and brothers of America." The intimacy of his greeting alone prompted prolonged applause. "I am proud," he continued, "to belong to a religion which has taught the world both tolerance and universal acceptance. . . . We accept all religions as true." He concluded with a plea that the parliament might mark the end of sectarianism, fanaticism, and persecution "between persons wending their way to the same goal."

photo: Roland and Sabrina Michaud/akg-images

speak frequently of "backsliding." Other converts continued to believe in their old gods and spirits but now deemed them evil and sought their destruction. Furthermore, thousands of separatist movements established a wide array of independent churches, which were thoroughly Christian but under African rather than missionary control and which in many cases incorporated African cultural practices and modes of worship. It was a twentieth-century "African Reformation."

In India, where Christianity made only very modest inroads, leading intellectuals and reformers began to define their region's endlessly varied beliefs, practices, sects, rituals, and philosophies as a more distinct, unified, and separate religion now

In further speeches at the parliament and in subsequent travels around the country, Vivekananda expressed the major themes of his modernized Vedanta outlook: that all human beings possess a divine nature; that awakening to that nature can be pursued through a variety of paths; and that spiritual practice and realization are far more important than dogma or doctrine. He argued that the disciplines of the mind and body that derived from Hindu tradition represented a psychological, experimental, and almost scientific approach to spiritual development and certainly did not require "conversion" to an alien faith. On occasion, he was sharply critical of Christian missionaries for their emphasis on conversion. "The people of India have more than religion enough," he declared. "What they want is bread." He described England as "the most prosperous Christian nation in the world with her foot on the neck of 250 million Asiatics."

Vivekananda emerged from the parliament a sensation and a celebrity, widely acclaimed but also widely criticized. His critique of Christian missionaries offended many. More conservative Christians objected to his assertion of the equality of all religious traditions. "We believe that Christianity is to supplant all other religions," declared the leading organizer of the parliament.

Vivekananda's time in the United States represented India speaking back to the West. After a century of European missionary activity and colonial rule in his country, he was declaring that India could offer spiritual support to a Western world mired in materialism and militarism. He proclaimed, "The whole of the Western world is a volcano which may burst tomorrow. . . . Now is the time to work so that India's spiritual ideas may penetrate deep into the West."[32]

And so he established a number of Vedanta Societies, some of which have persisted to the present day. In exposing Americans to Indian spirituality, Vivekananda's followers did not seek converts, but invited participants to apply Vedanta principles and practices within their own religious traditions. They also spoke about Jesus with great respect and displayed his image along with that of the Buddha and various Hindu sacred figures. In the early twentieth century, these Vedanta centers attracted a modest following among Americans who were disillusioned with the superficiality of modern life as well as with the rigidity of Christian doctrine and the many divisions and conflicts among Christian churches. In the 1960s and later, interest in Eastern religion exploded in the West as hundreds of Indian teachers arrived, many of them bearing the same universal message that Vivekananda had presented in Chicago. The growing numbers of Americans who claim to be "spiritual but not religious" are following in the path of that orange-robed monk.

Question: What accounts for the appeal of Vivekananda's message, and what accounts for opposition to it?

known as Hinduism. It was in part an effort to provide for India a religion wholly equivalent to Christianity, "an accessible tradition and a feeling of historical worth when faced with the humiliation of colonial rule."[33] To Swami Vivekananda (1863–1902), one of nineteenth-century India's most influential religious figures, as well as others active in reform movements, a revived Hinduism, shorn of its distortions, offered a means of uplifting the country's village communities, which were the heart of Indian civilization. In his famous travels to America, Vivekananda focused his attention on the cultivation of an inner life rather than on service and social reform as he did in India. (See Zooming In: Vivekananda, above.)

Guided Reading Question

■ CHANGE

How and why did Hinduism emerge as a distinct religious tradition during the colonial era in India?

This new notion of Hinduism provided a cultural foundation for emerging ideas of India as a nation, but it also contributed to a clearer sense of Muslims as a distinct community in India. Before the British takeover, little sense of commonality united the many diverse communities who practiced Islam—urban and rural dwellers; nomads and farmers; artisans, merchants, and state officials. But the British had created separate inheritance laws for all Muslims and others for all Hindus; in their census taking, they counted the numbers of people within these now sharply distinguished groups; and they allotted seats in local councils according to these artificial categories. As some anti-British patriots began to cast India in Hindu terms, the idea of Muslims as a separate community, which was perhaps threatened by the much larger number of Hindus, began to make sense to some who practiced Islam. In the early twentieth century, a young Hindu Bengali schoolboy noticed that "our Muslim school-fellows were beginning to air the fact of their being Muslims rather more consciously than before and with a touch of assertiveness."[34] Here were the beginnings of what became in the twentieth century a profound religious and political division within the South Asian peninsula.

"Race" and "Tribe"

AP® EXAM TIP

Racial identity, the way that groups are viewed by others and how they view themselves, is a crucial theme in the AP® course.

In Africa as well, intellectuals and ordinary people alike forged new ways of belonging as they confronted the upheavals of colonial life. Central to these new identities were notions of race and ethnicity. By the end of the nineteenth century, a number of African thinkers, familiar with Western culture, began to define the idea of an "African identity." Previously, few if any people on the continent had regarded themselves as Africans. Rather, they were members of particular local communities, usually defined by language; some were also Muslims; and still others inhabited some state or empire. Now, however, influenced by the common experience of colonial oppression and by a highly derogatory European racism, well-educated Africans began to think in broader terms, similar to those of Indian reformers who were developing the notion of Hinduism. It was an effort to revive the cultural self-confidence of their people by articulating a larger, common, and respected "African tradition," equivalent to that of Western culture.

Guided Reading Question

■ CHANGE

In what ways were "race" and "tribe" new identities in colonial Africa?

This effort took various shapes. One line of argument held that African culture and history in fact possessed the very characteristics that Europeans exalted. Knowing that Europeans valued large empires and complex political systems, African intellectuals pointed with pride to the ancient kingdoms of Ethiopia, Mali, Songhay, and others. C. A. Diop, a French-educated scholar from Senegal, insisted that Egyptian civilization was in fact the work of black Africans. Reversing European assumptions, Diop argued that Western civilization owed much to Egyptian influence and was therefore derived from Africa. Black people, in short, had a history of achievement fully comparable to that of Europe and therefore deserved just as much respect and admiration.

An alternative approach to defining an African identity lay in praising the differences between African and European cultures. The most influential proponent of such views was Edward Blyden (1832–1912), a West African born in the West Indies and educated in the United States who later became a prominent scholar and political official in Liberia. Blyden accepted the assumption that the world's various races were different but argued that each had its own distinctive contribution to make to world civilization. The uniqueness of African culture, Blyden wrote, lay in its communal, cooperative, and egalitarian societies, which contrasted sharply with Europe's highly individualistic, competitive, and class-ridden societies; in its harmonious relationship with nature as opposed to Europe's efforts to dominate and exploit the natural order; and particularly in its profound religious sensibility, which Europeans had lost in centuries of attention to material gain. Like Vivekananda in India, Blyden argued that Africa had a global mission "to be the spiritual conservatory of the world."[35]

In the twentieth century, such ideas resonated with a broader public. Hundreds of thousands of Africans took part in World War I, during which they encountered other Africans as well as Europeans. Some were able to travel widely. Contact with American black leaders, such as Booker T. Washington, W. E. B. DuBois, and Marcus Garvey, as well as various West Indian intellectuals further stimulated among a few a sense of belonging to an even larger pan-African world. Such notions underlay the growing nationalist movements that contested colonial rule as the twentieth century unfolded.

For the vast majority, however, the most important new sense of belonging that evolved from the colonial experience was not the notion of "Africa"; rather, it was the idea of "tribe" or, in the language of contemporary scholars, that of ethnic identity. African peoples, of course, had long recognized differences among themselves based on language, kinship, clan, village, or state, but these were seldom clearly defined. Boundaries fluctuated and were hazy; local communities often incorporated a variety of culturally different peoples. The idea of an Africa sharply divided into separate and distinct "tribes" was in fact a European notion that facilitated colonial administration and reflected Europeans' belief in African primitiveness. For example, when the British began to rule the peoples living along the northern side of Lake Tanganyika, in present-day Tanzania, they found a series of communities that were similar to one another in language and customs but that governed themselves separately and certainly had not regarded themselves as a distinct "tribe." It was British attempts to rule them as a single people, first through a "paramount chief" and later through a council of chiefs and elders, that resulted in their being called, collectively, the Nyakyusa. A tribe had been born. By requiring people to identify their tribe on applications for jobs, schools, and identity cards, colonial governments spread the idea of tribe widely within their colonies.

New ethnic identities were not simply imposed by Europeans, for Africans themselves increasingly found ethnic or tribal labels useful. This was especially true in rapidly growing urban areas. Surrounded by a bewildering variety of people and in a setting where competition for jobs, housing, and education was very intense, migrants to the city found it helpful to categorize themselves and others in larger ethnic terms. Thus, in many colonial cities, people who spoke similar languages, shared a common culture, or came from the same general part of the country began to think of themselves as a single people—a new tribe. They organized a rich variety of ethnic or tribal associations to provide mutual assistance while in the cities and to send money back home to build schools or clinics. Migrant workers, far from home and concerned about protecting their rights to land and to their wives and families, found a sense of security in being part of a recognized tribe, with its chiefs, courts, and established authority.

The Igbo people of southeastern Nigeria represent a case in point. Prior to the twentieth century, they were organized in a series of independently governed village groups. Although they spoke related languages, they had no unifying political system and no myth of common ancestry. Occupying a region of unusually dense population, many of these people eagerly seized on Western education and moved in large numbers to the cities and towns of colonial Nigeria. There they gradually discovered what they had in common and how they differed from the other peoples of Nigeria. By the 1940s, they were organizing on a national level and calling on Igbos everywhere to "sink all differences" to achieve "tribal unity, cooperation, and progress of all the Igbos." Fifty years earlier, however, no one had regarded himself or herself as an Igbo. One historian summed up the process of creating African ethnic identities in this way: "Europeans believed Africans belonged to tribes; Africans built tribes to belong to."[36]

REFLECTIONS

Who Makes History?

Winners may write history, but they do not make history, at least not alone. Dominant groups everywhere—slave owners, upper classes, men generally, and certainly colonial rulers—have found their actions constrained and their choices limited by the sheer presence of subordinated people and the ability of those people to act. Europeans who sought to make their countries self-sufficient in cotton by requiring colonized Africans to grow it generally found themselves unable to achieve that goal. Missionaries who tried to impose their own understanding of Christianity in the colonies found their converts often unwilling to accept missionary authority or the cultural framework in which the new religion was presented. In the twentieth century, colonial rulers all across Asia and Africa found that their most highly educated subjects became the leaders of those movements seeking to end colonial rule. Clearly, this was not what they had intended.

In recent decades, historians have been at pains to uncover the ways in which subordinated people—slaves, workers, peasants, women, the colonized—have been able to act in their own interests, even within the most oppressive conditions. This kind of "history from below" found expression in a famous book about American slavery that was subtitled *The World the Slaves Made*. Historians of women's lives have sought to show women not only as victims of patriarchy but also as historical actors in their own right.

Likewise, colonized people in any number of ways actively shaped the history of the colonial era. On occasion, they resisted and rebelled; in various times and places, they embraced, rejected, and transformed a transplanted Christianity; many eagerly sought Western education but later turned it against the colonizers; women both suffered from and creatively coped with the difficulties of colonial life; and everywhere people created new ways of belonging. None of this diminishes the hardships, the enormous inequalities of power, or the exploitation and oppression of the colonial experience. Rather, it suggests that history is often made through the struggle of unequal groups and that the outcome corresponds to no one's intentions.

Perhaps we might let Karl Marx have the last word on this endlessly fascinating topic: "Men make their own history," he wrote, "but they do not make it as they please nor under conditions of their own choosing." In the colonial experience of the nineteenth and early twentieth centuries, both the colonizers and the colonized "made history," but neither was able to do so as they pleased.

Chapter Review

What's the Significance?

European racism, 790–92
scramble for Africa, 794
Indian Rebellion, 1857–1858, 799
Congo Free State / Leopold II, 802–3
cultivation system, 803–4
cash-crop agriculture, 804–5

Wanjiku, 810–11
Western-educated elite, 813–16
Africanization of Christianity, 816–18
Swami Vivekananda, 818–19
Edward Blyden, 821

Big Picture Questions

1. In what ways did colonial rule rest on violence and coercion, and in what ways did it elicit voluntary cooperation or generate benefits for some people?
2. In what respects were colonized people more than victims of colonial conquest and rule? To what extent could they act in their own interests within the colonial situation?
3. Was colonial rule a transforming, even a revolutionary, experience, or did it serve to freeze or preserve existing social and economic patterns? What evidence can you find to support both sides of this argument?
4. **Looking Back:** How would you compare the colonial experience of Asian and African peoples during the long nineteenth century to the earlier colonial experience in the Americas?

Next Steps: For Further Study

A. Adu Boahen, *African Perspectives on Colonialism* (1987). An examination of the colonial experience by a prominent African scholar.

Alice Conklin and Ian Fletcher, *European Imperialism, 1830–1930* (1999). A collection of both classical reflections on empire and examples of modern scholarship.

Scott B. Cook, *Colonial Encounters in the Age of High Imperialism* (1996). Seven case studies of the late nineteenth-century colonial experience.

Adam Hochschild, *King Leopold's Ghost* (1999). A journalist's evocative account of the horrors of early colonial rule in the Congo.

Douglas Peers, *India under Colonial Rule* (2006). A concise and up-to-date exploration of colonial India.

Bonnie Smith, ed., *Imperialism* (2000). A fine collection of documents, pictures, and commentary on nineteenth- and twentieth-century empires.

Margaret Strobel, *Gender, Sex, and Empire* (1994). A brief account of late twentieth-century historical thinking about colonial life and gender.

Bridging World History, Unit 21: "Colonial Identities," http://www.learner.org/courses/worldhistory/unit _main_21.html. Provides text, primary and secondary sources, images, and video to explore the question of identity during the colonial era via clothing.

"The Magnificent African Cake," http://www.youtube.com/watch?v=irDWdqOvjVA. A thoughtful documentary on the colonial experience in Africa, from the series *Africa: A Voyage of Discovery* by the well-known historian Basil Davidson.

WORKING WITH EVIDENCE

The Scramble for Africa

The centerpiece of Europe's global expansion during the nineteenth century occurred in the so-called scramble for Africa, during which a half dozen or so European countries divided up almost the entire continent into colonial territories (see Map 18.2, page 796). The "scramble" took place very quickly (between roughly 1875 and 1900), surprising even the European leaders who initiated it, as well as the many African societies that suddenly found themselves confronting highly aggressive and well-armed foreign forces. Each of the rival powers—Britain, France, Germany, Belgium, Portugal, Spain, and Italy—sought to get a piece of a continent that many believed held the promise of great wealth. Given Europe's wars over colonial possessions in the early modern era, it is remarkable that the entire partition of Africa took place without any direct military conflict between the competing imperial countries. But in establishing their control on the ground, Europeans faced widespread African resistance, making the scramble an extremely bloody process of military conquest. The images that follow illustrate some of the distinctive features of the scramble for Africa as well as the differing ways in which it was perceived and represented.

As the Atlantic slave trade diminished over the course of the nineteenth century, Europeans began to look at Africa in new ways—as a source of raw materials, as an opportunity for investment, as a market for industrial products, as a field for exploration, and as an opportunity to spread Christianity. But it was not until the last quarter of the nineteenth century that Europeans showed much interest in actually acquiring territory and ruling large populations in Africa. Source 18.1, from a late nineteenth-century French board game, illustrates the widespread interest in the growing missionary enterprise in Africa as well as in the celebrated adventures of the intrepid explorers who penetrated the dangerous interior of the continent. This game, featuring the travels of David Livingstone and Henry Stanley, enabled ordinary Europeans to participate in exciting events in distant lands. Livingstone (1813–1873) was a British missionary and explorer of Central Africa whose work in exposing the horrors of the Arab slave trade gave him an almost mythic status among Europeans. Stanley (1841–1904), a British journalist and explorer, gained lasting fame by finding Livingstone, long out of touch with his homeland, deep in the African interior.

Private Collection/Archives Charmet/Bridgeman Images

Source 18.1 Prelude to the Scramble

- What images of Africa are suggested by this board game? Notice carefully the landscape, the animals, and the activities in which people are engaged.

- How does the game depict European activities in Africa?

- What might be the meaning of the large sun arising at the top of the image?

- What nineteenth-century realities are missing from this portrayal of Africa?

As the scramble for Africa got under way in earnest in the 1880s and 1890s, it became a highly competitive process. French designs on Africa, for example, focused on obtaining an uninterrupted east-west link from the Red Sea to the Atlantic Ocean. But the British, entrenched in Egypt and in control of the

Suez Canal, were determined that no major European power should be allowed to control the headwaters of the Nile on which Egypt depended. Those conflicting goals came to a head in 1898, when British forces moving south from Egypt met a French expedition moving northeast from the Atlantic coast of what is now Gabon. That encounter took place along the Nile River at Fashoda in present-day Sudan, threatening war between France and Great Britain. In the end, negotiations persuaded the French to withdraw.

Source 18.2, the cover of a French publication, shows the commander of the French expedition, Jean-Baptiste Marchand, who gained heroic stature in leading his troops on an epic journey across much of Africa for more than eighteen months.

- How did the artist portray Marchand? How might a British artist have portrayed him?

- What does this source suggest about the role of violence in the scramble for Africa?

- Notice the large number of African troops among Marchand's forces. What does that suggest about the process of colonial conquest? Why might Africans have agreed to fight on behalf of a European colonial power?

- How do you understand the fallen soldier lying between Marchand's legs?

Nowhere did the vaulting ambition of European colonial powers in Africa emerge more clearly than in the British vision of a north-south corridor of British territories along the eastern side of the continent stretching from South Africa to Egypt, or in the popular phrase of the time, "from the Cape to Cairo." A part of this vision was an unbroken railroad line running the entire length of the African continent. That grand idea was popularized by Cecil Rhodes, a British-born businessman and politician who made a fortune in South African diamonds and became an enthusiastic advocate of British imperialism. Source 18.3, an 1892 cartoon published in the popular British magazine of satire and humor named *Punch*, shows Rhodes bestriding the continent with one foot in Egypt and the other in South Africa.

- Is this famous image criticizing or celebrating Rhodes's Cape-to-Cairo dream? Explain your reasoning.

- What does this source suggest about the purpose of the Cape-to-Cairo scheme and the means to achieve it? Notice the telegraph wire in Rhodes's hands and the rifle on his shoulder.

- How did the artist portray the African continent? What does the absence of African people suggest? How does this image compare to Source 18.1?

© Musée de l'Armée/Dist. RMN-Grand Palais/Art Resource, NY

Source 18.2 Conquest and Competition

THE RHODES COLOSSUS
STRIDING FROM CAPE TOWN TO CAIRO.

Source 18.3 From the Cape to Cairo

■ Scholars have sometimes argued that the scramble for Africa was driven less by concrete economic interests than by emotional, even romantic, notions of national grandeur and personal adventure. In what ways do Sources 18.2 and 18.3 support or challenge this interpretation?

In North Africa, the primary European rivalries for territory involved Great Britain, which occupied Egypt in 1881; France, which came to control Tunisia, Algeria, and Morocco; and Italy, which seized Libya in 1912. Source 18.4 portrays two of these rivals—Britain, on the right, and France, on the left—toasting one another while standing on piles of skeletons. This image appeared in the Cairo *Punch*, a British-owned magazine in Egypt published in Arabic, probably around 1910.

A. H. Zaki/© Corbis

Source 18.4 British and French in North Africa

This image refers specifically to two incidents. On the British side, the cartoon evokes a 1906 quarrel between British soldiers hunting pigeons and local villagers of Denshway that resulted in the death of one of the soldiers. In response, outraged British authorities hanged several people and flogged dozens of others. The following year in Morocco, French civilians building a small railway near the harbor of Casablanca dug up parts of a Muslim cemetery, "churning up piles of bones." When attacks against European laborers followed, killing eight, the French bombarded the Arab quarter of the city, with many casualties—European and Arab alike—in the fighting that ensued. Both incidents stimulated nationalist feelings in these two North African countries.

- What references to the incidents described here can you find in Source 18.4?

- The British and French generally saw themselves as rivals in the scramble for Africa. How are they portrayed here?

- What criticisms of colonial rule does this image contain? While the artist remains unknown, do you think it more likely to have been an Egyptian or a European?

The Scramble for Africa

1. **Distinguishing viewpoints:** From what different perspectives do these sources represent the scramble for Africa? What criticisms of the scramble can you read in them?

2. **Portraying Africans and Europeans:** Both Africans and Europeans are portrayed variously in these images. What differences can you identify?

3. **Using images selectively:** In what ways might sources such as these be most useful to historians seeking to understand the scramble for Africa? For what kinds of questions about the scramble might they have little to offer?

4. **Considering moral visions:** How do these visual sources deal with issues of morality or visions of right and wrong?

The Chinese Cake, from *Le Petit Journal*, 1898, lithograph by Henri Meyer (1844–1899)/Private Collection/Roger-Viollet, Paris, France/Bridgeman Images

CHAPTER 19

Empires in Collision

Europe, the Middle East, and East Asia
1800–1900

"In the 170-plus years since the Opium War of 1840, our great country has weathered untold hardships. . . . Following the Opium War, China gradually became a semi-colonial . . . society, and foreign powers stepped up their aggression against China."[1] Speaking in 2011, Chinese president Hu Jintao thus reminded his listeners of Britain's violent intrusion into China's history in order to sell highly addictive opium to China's people. This conflict marked the beginning of what the Chinese still describe as a "century of humiliation." In Hu Jintao's view, it was only the victory of the Chinese Communist Party that enabled his country to finally escape from that shameful past. Memories of the Opium War remain a central element of China's "patriotic education" for the young, serve as a warning against uncritical admiration of the West, and provide a rejoinder to any Western criticism of China. Some 170 years after that clash between the Chinese and British empires, the Opium War retains an emotional resonance for many Chinese and offers a politically useful tool for the country's government.

China was among the countries that confronted an aggressive and industrializing West while maintaining its formal independence, unlike the colonized areas discussed in Chapter 18. So too did Japan, the Ottoman Empire, Persia (now Iran), Ethiopia, and Siam (now Thailand). Latin America also falls in this category (see Chapter 17, pages 766–72). These states avoided outright incorporation into European colonial empires, retaining some ability to resist European aggression and to reform or transform their

---

Carving Up the Pie of China   In this French cartoon from the late 1890s, the Great Powers of the day (from left to right: Great Britain's Queen Victoria, Germany's Kaiser Wilhelm, Russia's Tsar Nicholas II, a female figure representing France, and the Meiji emperor of Japan) participate in dividing China, while a Chinese figure behind them tries helplessly to stop the partition of his country.

own societies. But they shared with their colonized counterparts the need to deal with four dimensions of the European moment in world history. First, they faced the immense military might and political ambitions of rival European states. Second, they became enmeshed in networks of trade, investment, and sometimes migration that arose from an industrializing and capitalist Europe to generate a new world economy. Third, they were touched by various aspects of traditional European culture, as some among them learned the French, English, or German language; converted to Christianity; or studied European literature and philosophy. Fourth, and finally, they too engaged with the culture of modernity—its scientific rationalism; its technological achievements; its belief in a better future; and its ideas of nationalism, socialism, feminism, and individualism. In those epic encounters, they sometimes resisted, at other times accommodated, and almost always adapted what came from the West. They were active participants in the global drama of nineteenth-century world history, not simply its passive victims or beneficiaries.

Dealing with Europe, however, was not the only item on their agendas. Population growth and peasant rebellion wracked China; internal social and economic changes eroded the stability of Japanese public life; the great empires of the Islamic world shrank or disappeared; rivalry among competing elites troubled Latin American societies; Ethiopia launched its own empire-building process even as it resisted European intrusions. (See Zooming In: 1896: The Battle of Adowa, page 850.)

SEEKING THE MAIN POINT

What differences can you identify in how China, the Ottoman Empire, and Japan experienced Western imperialism and responded to it? How might you account for those differences?

Encounters with an expansive Europe were conditioned everywhere by particular local circumstances. Among those societies that remained independent, albeit sometimes precariously, while coping simultaneously with their internal crises and the threat from the West, this chapter focuses primarily on China, the Ottoman Empire, and Japan. Together with Latin America, they provide a range of experiences, responses, and outcomes and many opportunities for comparison.

Reversal of Fortune: China's Century of Crisis

In 1793, just a decade after King George III of Britain lost his North American colonies, he received yet another rebuff, this time from China. In a famous letter to the British monarch, the Chinese emperor Qianlong (chyan-loong) sharply rejected British requests for a less restricted trading relationship with his country. "Our Celestial Empire possesses all things in prolific abundance," he declared. "There was therefore no need to import the manufactures of outside barbarians." Qianlong's snub simply continued the pattern of the previous several centuries, during which Chinese authorities had strictly controlled and limited the activities of European missionaries and merchants. But by 1912, little more than a century later, China's long-established imperial state had collapsed, and the country had been transformed from a central presence in the global economy to a weak and dependent

A MAP OF TIME

1793	Chinese reject British requests for open trade
1798	Napoleon invades Egypt
1830s	Famine and rebellions in Japan
1838–1842	First Opium War in China
1839–1876	Tanzimat reforms in the Ottoman Empire
1850–1864	Taiping Uprising in China
1853	Admiral Perry arrives in Japan
1856–1858	Second Opium War in China
1868	Meiji Restoration in Japan
1894–1895	Japanese war against China
1896	Ethiopian defeat of Italy preserves Ethiopia's independence
1898–1901	Boxer Uprising in China
1904–1905	Russo-Japanese War
1908	Young Turk takeover in Ottoman Empire
1910	Japan annexes Korea
1911–1912	Chinese revolution; end of Qing dynasty

participant in a European-dominated world system in which Great Britain was the major economic and political player. It was a stunning reversal of fortune for a country that in Chinese eyes was the civilized center of the entire world—in their terms, the Celestial Empire or the Middle Kingdom.

The Crisis Within

In many ways, China was the victim of its own earlier success. Its robust economy and American food crops had enabled substantial population growth, from about 100 million people in 1685 to some 430 million in 1853. Unlike in Europe, though, where a similar population spurt took place, no Industrial Revolution accompanied this vast increase in the number of people, nor was agricultural production able to keep up. Neither did China's internal expansion to the west and south generate anything like the wealth and resources that derived from Europe's overseas empires. The result was growing pressure on the land, smaller farms for China's huge peasant population, and, in all too many cases, unemployment, impoverishment, misery, and starvation.

AP® EXAM TIP

Here is another example of a continuity in history: an empire falling due to internal and external factors.

Guided Reading Question

▪ CAUSATION

What accounts for the massive peasant rebellions of nineteenth-century China?

Furthermore, China's famed centralized and bureaucratic state did not enlarge itself to keep pace with the growing population. Thus the state was increasingly unable to effectively perform its many functions, such as tax collection, flood control, social welfare, and public security. Gradually the central state lost power to provincial officials and local gentry. Among such officials, corruption was endemic, and harsh treatment of peasants was common. According to an official report issued in 1852, "Day and night soldiers are sent out to harass taxpayers. Sometimes corporal punishments are imposed upon tax delinquents; some of them are so badly beaten to exact the last penny that blood and flesh fly in all directions."[2] Finally, European military pressure and economic penetration during the first half of the nineteenth century (see pages 838–41) disrupted internal trade routes, created substantial unemployment, and raised peasant taxes.

This combination of circumstances, traditionally associated with a declining dynasty, gave rise to growing numbers of bandit gangs roaming the countryside and, even more dangerous, to outright peasant rebellion. Beginning in the late eighteenth century, such rebellions drew on a variety of peasant grievances and found leadership in charismatic figures proclaiming a millenarian religious message. Increasingly they also expressed opposition to the Qing dynasty because of its foreign Manchu origins. "We wait only for the northern region to be returned to a Han emperor," declared one rebel group in the early nineteenth century.[3]

The culmination of China's internal crisis lay in the Taiping Uprising, which set much of the country aflame between 1850 and 1864. This was a different kind of peasant upheaval. Its leaders largely rejected Confucianism, Daoism, and Buddhism alike, finding their primary ideology in a unique form of Christianity. Its leading figure, Hong Xiuquan (1814–1864), proclaimed himself the younger brother of Jesus, sent to cleanse the world of demons and to establish a "heavenly kingdom of great peace." Nor were these leaders content to restore an idealized Chinese society; instead they insisted on genuinely revolutionary change. They called for the abolition of private property, a radical redistribution of land, the end of prostitution and opium smoking, and the organization of society into sexually segregated military camps of men and women. Hong fiercely denounced the Qing dynasty as foreigners who had "poisoned China" and "defiled the emperor's throne." His cousin, Hong

Taiping Uprising
The Taiping rebels captured the city of Nanjing in 1853, making it their capital. Eleven years later, in 1864, imperial forces retook the city as illustrated in this Chinese print, effectively ending the Taiping Uprising. (School of Oriental and African Studies/Eileen Tweedy/The Art Archive at Art Resource, NY)

Rengan, developed plans for transforming China into an industrial nation, complete with railroads, health insurance for all, newspapers, and widespread public education.

Among the most revolutionary dimensions of the Taiping Uprising was its posture toward women and gender roles. This outlook reflected its origins among the minority Hakka people of southern China, where women were notably less restricted than Confucian orthodoxy prescribed. During the uprising, Hakka women, whose feet had never been bound, fought as soldiers in their own regiments; in liberated regions, Taiping officials ordered that the feet of other women be unbound. The Taiping land reform program promised women and men equal shares of land. Women were now permitted to sit for civil service examinations and were appointed to supervisory positions, though usually ones in which they exercised authority over other women rather than men. Mutual attraction rather than family interests was promoted as a basis for marriage.

AP® EXAM TIP

Compare the causes and results of the Taiping Uprising to those of the rebellions you learned about in Chapter 16.

None of these reforms were consistently implemented during the short period of Taiping power, and the movement's leadership demonstrated considerable ambivalence about equality for women. Hong himself reflected a much more traditional understanding of elite women's role when he assembled a large personal harem and declared: "The duty of the palace women is to attend to the needs of their husbands; and it is arranged by Heaven that they are not to learn of the affairs outside."[4] Nonetheless, the Taiping posture toward women represented a sharp challenge to long-established gender roles and contributed to the hostility that the movement generated among many other Chinese, including women.

With a rapidly swelling number of followers, Taiping forces swept out of southern China and established their capital in Nanjing in 1853. For a time, the days of the Qing dynasty appeared to be over. But divisions and indecisiveness within the Taiping leadership, along with their inability to link up with several other rebel groups also operating separately in China, provided an opening for Qing dynasty loyalists to rally and by 1864 to crush this most unusual of peasant rebellions. Western military support for pro-Qing forces likewise contributed to their victory. It was not, however, the imperial military forces of the central government that defeated the rebels. Instead provincial military leaders, fearing the radicalism of the Taiping program, mobilized their own armies, which in the end crushed the rebel forces.

Thus the Qing dynasty was saved, but it was also weakened as the provincial gentry consolidated their power at the expense of the central state. The intense conservatism of both imperial authorities and their gentry supporters postponed any resolution of China's peasant problem, delayed any real change for China's women, and deferred vigorous efforts at modernization until the communists came to power in the mid-twentieth century. More immediately, the devastation and destruction occasioned by this massive civil war seriously disrupted and weakened China's economy. Estimates of the number of lives lost range from 20 to 30 million. In human terms, it was the most costly conflict in the world during the nineteenth century, and it took China more than a decade to recover from its devastation. China's internal crisis in general and the Taiping Uprising in particular also provided a highly unfavorable setting for the country's encounter with a Europe newly invigorated by the Industrial Revolution.

Western Pressures

Nowhere was the shifting balance of global power in the nineteenth century more evident than in China's changing relationship with Europe, a transformation that registered most dramatically in the famous Opium Wars. Derived from Arab traders in the eighth century or earlier, opium had long been used on a small scale as a drinkable medicine; it was regarded as a magical cure for dysentery and described by one poet as "fit for Buddha."[5] It did not become a serious problem until the late eighteenth century, when the British began to use opium, grown and processed in India, to cover their persistent trade imbalance with China. By the 1830s, British, American, and other Western merchants had found an enormous, growing, and very profitable market for this highly addictive drug. From 1,000 chests (each weighing roughly 150 pounds) in 1773, China's opium imports exploded to more than 23,000 chests in 1832. (See Snapshot, below.)

SNAPSHOT   Chinese/British Trade at Canton, 1835–1836

What do these figures suggest about the role of opium in British trade with China? Calculate opium exports as a percentage of British exports to China, Britain's trade deficit without opium, and its trade surplus with opium. What did this pattern mean for China?[6]

	Item	Value (in Spanish dollars)
British Exports to Canton	Opium	17,904,248
	Cotton	8,357,394
	All other items (sandalwood, lead, iron, tin, cotton yarn and piece goods, tin plates, watches, clocks)	6,164,981
	Total	32,426,623
British Imports from Canton	Tea (black and green)	13,412,243
	Raw silk	3,764,115
	Vermilion	705,000
	All other goods (sugar products, camphor, silver, gold, copper, musk)	5,971,541
	Total	23,852,899

By then, Chinese authorities recognized a mounting problem on many levels. Because opium importation was illegal, it had to be smuggled into China, thus flouting Chinese law. Bribed to turn a blind eye to the illegal trade, many officials were corrupted. Furthermore, a massive outflow of silver to pay for the opium reversed China's centuries-long ability to attract much of the world's silver supply, and this imbalance caused serious economic problems. Finally, China found itself with many millions of addicts—men and women, court officials, students preparing for exams, soldiers going into combat, and common laborers seeking to overcome the pain and drudgery of their work. Following an extended debate at court in 1836 on whether to legalize the drug or crack down on its use, the emperor decided on suppression. An upright official, Commissioner Lin Zexu (lin zuh-SHOO), led the campaign against opium use as a kind of "drug czar." (See Zooming In: Lin Zexu, page 840.) The British, offended by the seizure of their property in opium and emboldened by their new military power, sent a large naval expedition to China, determined to end the restrictive conditions under which they had long traded with that country. In the process, they would teach the Chinese a lesson about the virtues of free trade and the "proper" way to conduct relations among countries. Thus began the first Opium War, in which Britain's industrialized military might proved decisive. The Treaty of Nanjing, which ended the war in 1842, largely on British terms, imposed numerous restrictions on Chinese sovereignty and opened five ports to European traders. Its provisions reflected the changed balance of global power that had emerged with Britain's Industrial Revolution. To the Chinese, that agreement represented the first of the "unequal treaties" that seriously eroded China's independence by the end of the century.

But it was not the last of those treaties. Britain's victory in a second Opium War (1856–1858) was accompanied by the brutal vandalizing of the emperor's exquisite Summer Palace outside Beijing and resulted in further humiliations. Still more ports were opened to foreign traders. Now those foreigners were allowed to travel freely and buy land in China, to preach Christianity under the protection of Chinese authorities, and to patrol some of China's rivers. Furthermore, the Chinese were forbidden to use the character for "barbarians" to refer to the

Guided Reading Question

■ CONNECTION

How did Western pressures stimulate change in China during the nineteenth century?

Addiction to Opium
Throughout the nineteenth century, opium imports created a massive addiction problem in China, as this photograph of an opium den from around 1900 suggests. Not until the early twentieth century did the British prove willing to curtail the opium trade from their Indian colony. (© Hulton-Deutsch Collection/Corbis)

Lin Zexu:
Confronting the Opium Trade

When the Chinese emperor decided in 1838 on firm measures to suppress the opium trade, he selected Lin Zexu to enforce that policy.[7] Born in 1785, Lin was the son of a rather poor but scholarly father, who had never achieved an official position. Lin, however, excelled academically, passing the highest-level examinations in 1811 after two failed attempts and then rising rapidly in the ranks of China's bureaucracy. In the process, he gained a reputation as a strict and honest official; he was immune to bribery, genuinely concerned with the welfare of the peasantry, and unafraid to confront the corruption and decadence of rich and poor alike.

And so in December of 1838, after some nineteen personal audiences with the emperor, Lin found himself in Canton, the center of the opium trade and the only Chinese city legally open to foreign merchants. He was facing the greatest challenge of his professional life. Undertaken with the best of intentions, his actions propelled the country into a cen-

Commissioner Lin Zexu.

tury of humiliating subservience to an industrializing Europe and forced growing numbers of Chinese to question their vaunted civilization.

In established Confucian fashion, Lin undertook his enormous task with a combination of moral appeals, reasoned argument, political pressure, and coercion, while hoping to avoid outright armed conflict. It was an approach that focused on both the demand and supply sides of the problem. In dealing with Chinese opium users, Lin emphasized the health hazards of the drug and demanded that people turn in their supplies of opium and the pipes used to smoke it. By mid-1839, he had confiscated some 50,000 pounds of the drug together with over 70,000 pipes and arrested some 1,700 dealers. Hundreds of local students were summoned to an assembly where they were invited to identify opium

photo: Commissioner Lin Zexu. From Alexander Murray, *Doings in China: Being the personal narrative of an officer engaged in the late Chinese Expedition, from the Recapture of Chusan in 1841, to the Peace of Nankin in 1842* (London: Richard Bentley, New Burlington Street, Publisher in Ordinary to Her Majesty, 1843), pl. ii/Visual Connection Archive

British in official documents. Following military defeats at the hands of the French (1885) and Japanese (1895), China lost control of Vietnam, Korea, and Taiwan. By the end of the century, the Western nations plus Japan and Russia had all carved out spheres of influence within China, granting themselves special privileges to establish military bases, extract raw materials, and build railroads. Many Chinese believed that their country was being "carved up like a melon" (see Map 19.1 and the chapter-opening photo on page 832).

Coupled with its internal crisis, China's encounter with European imperialism had reduced the proud Middle Kingdom to dependency on the Western pow-distributors and to suggest ways of dealing with the problem. Opium-using officials became the target of investigations, and five-person teams were established to enforce the ban on opium smoking on one another.

Lin applied a similar mix of methods to the foreign suppliers of opium. A moralistic appeal to Queen Victoria argued that the articles the English imported from China—silk, tea, and rhubarb—were all beneficial. "By what right," he asked, "do [the barbarians] use this poisonous drug to injure Chinese people?" He pointedly reminded Europeans that new regulations, applying to Chinese and foreigners alike, fixed the penalty for dealing in opium at "decapitation or strangling." Then he demanded that foreign traders hand over their opium, and without compensation. When the merchants hesitated, Lin tightened the screws, ordering all Chinese employed by foreigners to leave their jobs and blockading the Europeans in their factories. After six weeks of negotiations, the Europeans capitulated, turning over some 3 million pounds of raw opium to Lin Zexu.

Disposing of the drug was an enormous task. Workers, stripped and searched daily to prevent looting, dug three huge trenches into which they placed the opium mixed with water, salt, and lime and then flushed the concoction into the sea. Lin offered a sacrifice to the Sea Spirit, apologizing for introducing this poison into its domain and "advising the Spirit to tell the creatures of the water to move away for a time." He informed the emperor that throngs of local people flocked to witness the destruction of the opium. And foreigners too came to observe the spectacle. Lin reported, "[The foreigners] do not dare to show any disrespect, and indeed I should judge from their attitudes that they have the decency to feel heartily ashamed."

Had Lin been correct in his appraisal, history would have taken a very different turn. But neither Lin nor his superiors anticipated the response that these actions provoked from the British government. They were also largely unaware of European industrial and military advances, which had decisively shifted the balance of power between China and the West. Arriving in 1840, a British military expedition quickly demonstrated its superiority and initiated the devastating Opium War that marked Lin's policies in Canton as a failure.

As a punishment for his unsatisfactory performance, the emperor sent Lin to a remote post in western China. Although his career rebounded somewhat after 1845, he died in 1850 while on the way to an appointment aimed at suppressing the Taiping rebellion. While his reputation suffered in the nineteenth century, it recovered in the twentieth as an intensely nationalist China recalled his principled stand against Western imperialism.

Questions: How might Lin Zexu have handled his task differently or more successfully? Or had he been given an impossible mission?

ers as it became part of a European-based "informal empire." China was no longer the center of civilization to which barbarians paid homage and tribute, but just one weak and dependent nation among many others. The Qing dynasty remained in power, but in a weakened condition, which served European interests well and Chinese interests poorly. Restrictions imposed by the unequal treaties clearly inhibited China's industrialization, as foreign goods and foreign investment flooded the country largely unrestricted. Chinese businessmen mostly served foreign firms, rather than developing as an independent capitalist class capable of leading China's own Industrial Revolution.

Map 19.1   China and the World in the Nineteenth Century

As China was reeling from massive internal upheavals during the nineteenth century, it also faced external assaults from Russia, Japan, and various European powers. By the end of the century, large parts of China were divided into spheres of influence, each affiliated with one of the major industrial powers of the day.

AP® EXAM TIP

Make comparisons between this map showing a divided China and Map 13.3 on page 579 showing a unified China.

The Failure of Conservative Modernization

Chinese authorities were not passive in the face of their country's mounting crises, both internal and external. Known as "self-strengthening," their policies during the 1860s and 1870s sought to reinvigorate a traditional China while borrowing cautiously from the West. An overhauled examination system, designed to recruit qualified candidates for official positions, sought the "good men" who could cope with the massive reconstruction that China faced in the wake of the Taiping rebellion. Support for landlords and the repair of dikes and irrigation helped restore rural social and economic order. A few industrial factories producing textiles and steel were established, coal mines were expanded, and a telegraph system was initiated. One Chinese general in 1863 confessed his humiliation that "Chinese weapons are far inferior to those of foreign countries."[8] A number of modern arsenals, shipyards, and foreign-language schools sought to remedy this deficiency.

Self-strengthening as an overall program for China's modernization was inhibited by the fears of conservative leaders that urban, industrial, or commercial development would erode the power and privileges of the landlord class. Furthermore, the new industries remained largely dependent on foreigners for machinery, materials, and expertise. And they served to strengthen local authorities, who largely controlled those industries, rather than the central Chinese state.

The general failure of "self-strengthening" became apparent at the end of the century, when an antiforeign movement known as the Boxer Uprising (1898–1901) erupted in northern China. Led by militia organizations calling themselves the Society of Righteous and Harmonious Fists, the "Boxers" killed numerous Europeans and Chinese Christians and laid siege to the foreign embassies in Beijing. When Western powers and Japan occupied Beijing to crush the rebellion and imposed a huge payment on China as a punishment, it was clear that China remained a dependent country, substantially under foreign control.

No wonder, then, that growing numbers of educated Chinese, including many in official elite positions, became highly disillusioned with the Qing dynasty, which was both foreign and ineffective in protecting China. By the late 1890s, such people were organizing a variety of clubs, study groups, and newspapers to examine China's desperate situation and to explore alternative paths. The names of these organizations reflect their outlook—the National Rejuvenation Study Society, Society to Protect the Nation, and Understand the National Shame Society. They admired not only Western science and technology but also Western political practices that limited the authority of the ruler and permitted wider circles of people to take part in public life. They believed that only a truly unified nation in which rulers and ruled were closely related could save China from dismemberment at the hands of foreign imperialists. Despite the small number of women who took part in these discussions, traditional gender roles became yet another focus of opposition. No one expressed that issue more forcefully than Qiu Jin (1875–1907), the rebellious daughter of a gentry family who left a husband and two children to study in Japan. Upon her return to China, she started a women's journal, arguing that liberated women were essential for a strong Chinese nation, and became involved in revolutionary politics. (For more on Qiu Jin, see Working with Evidence, Source 19.3, page 867.) Thus was born the immensely powerful force of Chinese nationalism, directed alike against Western imperialists, the foreign Qing dynasty, and aspects of China's traditional culture.

The Qing dynasty response to these new pressures proved inadequate. A flurry of progressive imperial edicts in 1898, known as the Hundred Days of Reform, was

Guided Reading Question

....

■ CONNECTION

What strategies did China adopt to confront its various problems? In what ways did these strategies reflect China's own history and culture as well as the new global order?

soon squelched by conservative forces. More extensive reform in the early twentieth century, including the end of the old examination system and the promise of a national parliament, was a classic case of too little too late. (See Working with Evidence: Changing China, page 863.) In 1912 the last Chinese emperor abdicated as the ancient imperial order that had governed China for two millennia collapsed, with only a modest nudge from organized revolutionaries. It was the end of a long era in China and the beginning of an immense struggle over the country's future.

The Ottoman Empire and the West in the Nineteenth Century

AP® EXAM TIP

As you read about the Ottoman Empire in the nineteenth century, make comparisons with China in the same era.

Like China, the Islamic world represented a highly successful civilization that felt little need to learn from the "infidels" or "barbarians" of the West until it collided with an expanding and aggressive Europe in the nineteenth century. Unlike China, though, Islamic civilization had been a near neighbor to Europe for 1,000 years. Its most prominent state, the Ottoman Empire, had long governed substantial parts of the Balkans and had posed a clear military and religious threat to Europe in the sixteenth and seventeenth centuries. But if its encounter with the West was less abrupt than that of China, it was no less consequential. Neither the Ottoman Empire nor China fell under direct colonial rule, but both were much diminished as the changing balance of global power took hold; both launched efforts at "defensive modernization" aimed at strengthening their states and preserving their independence; and in both societies, some people held tightly to old identities and values, even as others embraced new loyalties associated with nationalism and modernity.

"The Sick Man of Europe"

In 1750, the Ottoman Empire was still the central political fixture of a widespread Islamic world. From its Turkish heartland in Anatolia, it ruled over much of the Arab world, from which Islam had come. It protected pilgrims on their way to Mecca, governed Egypt and coastal North Africa, and incorporated millions of Christians in the Balkans. Its ruler, the sultan, claimed the role of caliph, successor to the Prophet Muhammad, and was widely viewed as the leader, defender, and primary representative of the Islamic world. But by the middle, and certainly by the end, of the nineteenth century, the Ottoman Empire was no longer able to deal with Europe from a position of equality, let alone superiority. Among the Great Powers of the West, it was now known as "the sick man of Europe." Within the Muslim world, the Ottoman Empire, once viewed as "the strong sword of Islam," was unable to prevent region after region—India, Indonesia, West Africa, Central Asia—from falling under the control of Christian powers.

The Ottoman Empire's own domains shrank considerably at the hands of Russian, British, Austrian, and French aggression (see Map 19.2). In 1798, Napoleon's invasion of Egypt, which had long been a province of the Ottoman Empire, was a

Map 19.2   The Contraction of the Ottoman Empire

Foreign aggression and nationalist movements substantially diminished the Ottoman Empire during the nineteenth century, but they also stimulated a variety of efforts to revive and reform Ottoman society.

particularly stunning blow. A contemporary observer, Abd al-Rahman al-Jabarti, described the French entry into Cairo:

> The French entered the city like a torrent rushing through the alleys and streets without anything to stop them, like demons of the Devil's army. . . . And the French trod in the Mosque of al-Azhar with their shoes, carrying swords and rifles. . . . They plundered whatever they found in the mosque. . . . They treated the books and Quranic volumes as trash. . . . Furthermore, they soiled the mosque, blowing their spit in it, pissing and defecating in it. They guzzled wine and smashed bottles in the central court.[9]

When the French left, a virtually independent Egypt pursued a modernizing and empire-building program of its own during the early and mid-nineteenth century and on one occasion came close to toppling the Ottoman Empire itself.

Beyond territorial losses to stronger European powers, other parts of the empire, such as Greece, Serbia, Bulgaria, and Romania, achieved independence based on their own surging nationalism and support from the British or the Russians. The continued independence of the core region of the Ottoman Empire owed much

Guided Reading Question

■ CHANGE

What lay behind the decline of the Ottoman Empire in the nineteenth century?

to the inability of Europe's Great Powers to agree on how to divide it up among themselves.

Behind the contraction of the Ottoman Empire lay other problems. As in China, the central Ottoman state had weakened, particularly in its ability to raise necessary revenue, as provincial authorities and local warlords gained greater power. Moreover, the Janissaries, once the effective and innovative elite infantry units of Ottoman military forces, lost their military edge, becoming a highly conservative force within the empire. The technological and military gap with the West was clearly growing.

Economically, the earlier centrality of the Ottoman and Arab lands in Afro-Eurasian commerce diminished as Europeans achieved direct oceanic access to the treasures of Asia. Competition from cheap European manufactured goods hit Otto-man artisans hard and led to urban riots protesting foreign imports. Furthermore, a series of agreements, known as capitulations, between European countries and the Ottoman Empire granted Westerners various exemptions from Ottoman law and taxation. Like the unequal treaties with China, these agreements facilitated European penetration of the Ottoman economy and became widely resented. Such measures eroded Ottoman sovereignty and reflected the changing position of that empire relative to Europe. So too did the growing indebtedness of the Ottoman Empire, which came to rely on foreign loans to finance its efforts at economic development. By 1881, its inability to pay the interest on those debts led to foreign control of much of its revenue-generating system, while a similar situation in Egypt led to its outright occupation by the British. Like China, the Ottoman Empire had fallen into a position of considerable dependency on Europe.

Reform and Its Opponents

AP® EXAM TIP

Take notes on political and social continuities in the Ottoman Empire in this era.

The leadership of the Ottoman Empire recognized many of its problems and dur-ing the nineteenth century mounted increasingly ambitious programs of "defensive modernization" that were earlier, more sustained, and far more vigorous than the timid and halfhearted measures of self-strengthening in China. One reason perhaps lay in the absence of any internal upheaval, such as the Taiping Uprising in China, which threatened the very existence of the ruling dynasty. Nationalist revolts on the empire's periphery, rather than Chinese-style peasant rebellion at the center, represented the primary internal crisis of nineteenth-century Ottoman history. Nor did the Middle East in general experience the explosive population growth that contributed so much to China's nineteenth-century crisis. Furthermore, the long-established Ottoman leadership was Turkic and Muslim, culturally similar to its core population, whereas China's Qing dynasty rulers were widely regarded as foreign-ers from Manchuria.

Guided Reading Question

■ CHANGE
In what different ways did the Ottoman state respond to its various problems?

Ottoman reforms began in the late eighteenth century when Sultan Selim III sought to reorganize and update the army, drawing on European advisers and tech-niques. Even these modest innovations stirred the hostility of powerful factions among both the *ulama* (religious scholars) and the elite military corps of Janissaries, who saw them in conflict with both Islam and their own institutional interests. Opposition to his measures was so strong that Selim was overthrown in 1807 and then murdered. Subsequent sultans, however, crushed the Janissaries and brought the ulama more thoroughly under state control than elsewhere in the Islamic world.

Then, in the several decades after 1839, more far-reaching reformist measures, known as Tanzimat (tahn-zee-MAHT) (reorganization), took shape as the Ottoman leadership sought to provide the economic, social, and legal underpinnings for a strong and newly recentralized state. Factories producing cloth, paper, and armaments; modern mining operations; reclamation and resettlement of agricultural land; telegraphs, steamships, railroads, and a modern postal service; Western-style law codes and courts; new elementary and secondary schools—all of these new departures began a long process of modernization and westernization in the Ottoman Empire.

AP® EXAM TIP

You need to know about the goals and outcomes of the Tanzimat reforms.

Even more revolutionary, at least in principle, were changes in the legal status of the empire's diverse communities, which now gave non-Muslims equal rights under the law. An imperial proclamation of 1856 declared:

> Every distinction or designation tending to make any class whatever of the subjects of my Empire inferior to another class, on account of their religion, language or race shall be forever effaced. . . . No subject of my Empire shall be hindered in the exercise of the religion that he professes. . . . All the subjects of my Empire, without distinction of nationality, shall be admissible to public employment.

This declaration represented a dramatic change that challenged the fundamentally Islamic character of the state. Mixed tribunals with representatives from various religious groups were established to hear cases involving non-Muslims. More Christians were appointed to high office. A mounting tide of secular legislation and secular schools, drawing heavily on European models, now competed with traditional Islamic institutions.

Although Tanzimat-era reforms did not directly address gender issues, they did stimulate modest educational openings for women, mostly in Istanbul, with a training program for midwives in 1842, a girls' secondary school in 1858, and a teacher training college for women in 1870. Furthermore, the reform-minded class that emerged from the Tanzimat era generally favored greater opportunities for women as a means of strengthening the state, and a number of upper- and middle-class women were involved in these discussions. During the 1870s and 1880s, the prominent female poet Sair Nigar Hanim held weekly "salons" in which reformist intellectuals of both sexes participated.

The reform process raised profound and highly contested questions. What was the Ottoman Empire, and who were its people? Were they Ottoman subjects of a dynastic state, Turkish citizens of a national state, or Muslim believers in a religiously defined state? For decades, the answers oscillated as few people wanted to choose decisively among these alternative identities.

Guided Reading
Question
....
■ COMPARISON
In what different ways did
various groups define the
Ottoman Empire during the
nineteenth century?

To those who supported the reforms, the Ottoman Empire was an inclusive state, all of whose people were loyal to the dynasty that ruled it. This was the outlook of a new class spawned by the reform process itself—lower-level officials, military officers, writers, poets, and journalists, many of whom had a modern Western-style education. Dubbed the Young Ottomans, they were active during the middle decades of the nineteenth century, as they sought major changes in the Ottoman political system itself. They favored a more European-style parliamentary and constitutional regime that could curtail the absolute power of the sultan. Only such a political system, they felt, could mobilize the energies of the country to overcome backwardness and preserve the state against European aggression. Known as Islamic modernism, such ideas found expression in many parts of the Muslim world in the second half of the century. Muslim societies, the Young Ottomans argued, needed to embrace Western technical and scientific knowledge, while rejecting its materialism. Islam in their view could accommodate a full modernity without sacrificing its essential religious character. After all, the Islamic world had earlier hosted impressive scientific achievements and had incorporated elements of Greek philosophical thinking.

In 1876, the Young Ottomans experienced a short-lived victory when Sultan Abd al-Hamid II (r. 1876–1909) accepted a constitution and an elected parliament, but not for long. Under the pressure of war with Russia, the sultan soon suspended the reforms and reverted to an older style of despotic rule for the next thirty years,

The First Ottoman Constitution
This Ottoman-era postcard celebrates the short-lived constitutional period of 1876–1878 and the brief political victory of the Young Ottoman reformers. The country is represented by an unveiled woman being released from her chains, while an angel carries a banner inscribed with the slogan of the French Revolution: liberty, equality, fraternity. ("The Ottoman Constitution, December 1895," color postcard. Artist unknown/Visual Connection Archive)

even renewing the claim that he was the caliph, the successor to the Prophet and the protector of Muslims everywhere.

Opposition to this revived despotism soon surfaced among both military and civilian elites known as the Young Turks. Largely abandoning any reference to Islam, they advocated a militantly secular public life, were committed to thorough modernization along European lines, and increasingly thought about the Ottoman Empire as a Turkish national state. "There is only one civilization, and that is European civilization," declared Abdullah Cevdet, a prominent figure in the Young Turk movement. "Therefore we must borrow western civilization with both its rose and its thorn."[10]

A military coup in 1908 finally allowed the Young Turks to exercise real power. They pushed for a radical secularization of schools, courts, and law codes; permitted elections and competing parties; established a single Law of Family Rights for all regardless of religion; and encouraged Turkish as the official language of the empire. They also opened modern schools for women, including access to Istanbul University; allowed women to wear Western clothing; restricted polygamy; and permitted women to obtain divorces in some situations. Women established a number of publications and organizations, some of them linked to British suffrage groups. In the western cities of the empire, some women abandoned their veils.

But the nationalist Turkish conception of Ottoman identity antagonized non-Turkic peoples and helped stimulate Arab and other nationalisms in response. For some, a secular nationality was becoming the most important public loyalty, with Islam relegated to private life. Nationalist sentiments contributed to the complete disintegration of the Ottoman Empire following World War I, but the secularizing and westernizing principles of the Young Turks informed the policies of the Turkish republic that replaced it.

Outcomes: Comparing China and the Ottoman Empire

By the beginning of the twentieth century, both China and the Ottoman Empire, recently centers of proud and vibrant civilizations, had experienced the consequences of a rapidly shifting balance of global power. Now they were "semi-colonies" within the "informal empires" of Europe, although they retained sufficient independence for their governments to launch catch-up efforts of defensive modernization, the Ottomans earlier and the Chinese later. But neither was able to create the industrial economies or strong states required to fend off European intrusion and restore their former status in the world. Despite their diminished power, however, both China and the Ottoman Empire gave rise to new nationalist conceptions of society, which were initially small and limited in appeal but of great significance for the future.

In the early twentieth century, that future witnessed the end of both the Chinese and Ottoman empires. In China, the collapse of the imperial system in 1912 was followed by a vast revolutionary upheaval that by 1949 led to a communist regime within largely the same territorial space as the old empire. By contrast, the

1896: The Battle of Adowa

On March 1, 1896, two armies faced one another near the small town of Adowa in northern Ethiopia. On one side lay the Italian forces, who had intruded into Ethiopia from their adjacent colony of Eritrea, supplemented by a large number of African troops. On the other side stood the much larger Ethiopian army, personally led by Emperor Menelik II, accompanied by his forceful wife, Empress Taytu. The battle that followed proved a decisive victory for the Ethiopians and a rout for the Italians. That victory placed Ethiopia, like China, Persia, the Ottoman Empire, Japan, and Thailand, in the category of countries that retained their independence in an era of rampant European empire building. It was, in fact, the only part of Africa to enjoy that status. How had it happened?

One answer lies in circumstances. Ethiopia's location in the mountainous highlands of eastern Africa made external invasion difficult. Its long tradition of independent statehood and a common Christian culture provided a strong sense of identity alongside the ethnic diversity of its population and the political rivalries of its governing elites. Ethiopia's Italian adversary had become a unified

Emperor Menelik II of Ethiopia at the Battle of Adowa.

country only in 1871 and possessed a less robust military than Britain, France, or Germany did. Nonetheless, as the scramble for Africa unfolded, the Italians had established colonial rule in both Somalia and Eritrea. Now they were seeking to enlarge their African holdings at the expense of Ethiopia.

Building on these circumstances, Menelik's diplomacy and military strategy proved highly effective. After becoming emperor in 1889, Menelik actively took advantage of European rivalries for territory in northeastern Africa to pursue agreements with and to buy arms from Russia, France, Germany, Britain, and Italy. To obtain an agreement with Italy, he was willing to cede some territory in northern Ethiopia and to acknowledge Italian control of Eritrea in return for financial assistance and military supplies. But a dispute arose when the Italians interpreted the treaty as implying an Italian protectorate over Ethiopia. This, of course, Menelik decisively rejected. When Italian forces moved into Ethiopian territory in early 1895, he prepared for war.

photo: Color lithographic illustration by Louis Fortune Meaulle (1844–1901) from *Le Petit Journal*, 1898/Private Collection/Bridgeman Images

collapse of the Ottoman Empire following World War I led to the creation of the new but much smaller nation-state of Turkey in the Anatolian heartland of the old empire, which lost its vast Arab and European provinces.

China's twentieth-century revolutionaries rejected traditional Confucian culture far more thoroughly than the secularizing leaders of modern Turkey rejected Islam. Almost everywhere in the Islamic world, including Turkey, traditional religion retained its hold on the private loyalties of most people and later in the twentieth century became a basis for social renewal in many places. Islamic civilization, unlike its Chinese counterpart, had many independent centers and was never so

Imposing a special tax to pay for more guns and ammunition, Menelik ordered the expulsion of all Italians from Ethiopia and called for national mobilization. Troops under the command of various regional rulers began to assemble, and in October 1895 a huge force began a five-month, 580-mile march from the capital of Addis Ababa to Adowa, where the decisive battle took place.

The echoes of Adowa resonated far and wide. For Italy, it was a national humiliation, "a shameful scar" according to a leading poet. That wound failed to heal and played a large role in motivating Mussolini's invasion of Ethiopia in 1935, a step on the road to World War II. As the avenger of Adowa, he had a large bust of himself placed on that battlefield.

For Ethiopia itself, Adowa had an immense significance that bears comparison with the experience of Japan. Like Japan, Ethiopia was a long-established independent state, threatened by European expansion, which actually defeated a major European power, and it did so a decade before Japan's victory over Russia in 1905. Both Japan and Ethiopia became beacons of hope and inspiration to societies that had fallen under colonial rule. Furthermore, both nations went on to construct empires of their own. In Ethiopia's case, Menelik practically doubled the territorial size of his country as he expanded Ethiopian control to the south and east. Successfully resisting the European scramble for Africa, he also proceeded to take part in it. These successes enabled Menelik to solidify his hold on the throne, to unify the country in its modern form, and to emerge with an almost mythic reputation. Within Africa and among African Americans, Ethiopia came to symbolize African bravery and resistance to white oppression. It is no accident that Addis Ababa, the capital of Ethiopia, was chosen as the headquarters of the Organization of African Unity in 1963. A huge stained-glass wall in the main building depicts Ethiopians leading the rest of Africa to independence.

But in another way, Ethiopian and Japanese history sharply diverged. Japan was able to join its political and military success with a thorough economic transformation of the country. Ethiopia was not able to do this and remains one of the least developed countries of the Global South. Menelik did initiate a number of modernizing projects—banks, railroads, schools, hospitals, and a few factories—but nothing approached the scale of Japan's transformation. His success, in fact, strengthened the more conservative forces within Ethiopian society.

When I (Robert Strayer) taught high school history in Ethiopia in the mid-1960s, I was told that Italians were perhaps the most well-liked Europeans in the country, but that they were careful to stay at home on the anniversary of the Battle of Adowa.

Question: How might you describe the significance of the Battle of Adowa in Ethiopian, African, and world history?

---

closely associated with a single state. Furthermore, it was embedded in a deeply religious tradition that was personally meaningful to millions of adherents, in contrast to the more elitist and secular outlook of Confucianism. Many rural Chinese, however, retained traditional Confucian values such as filial piety, and Confucianism has made something of a comeback in China over the past several decades. Nonetheless, Islam retained a hold on its civilization in the twentieth century rather more firmly than Confucianism did in China.

PRACTICING AP® HISTORICAL THINKING

In what ways were the histories of China and the Ottoman Empire similar during the nineteenth century? And how did they differ?

The Japanese Difference:
The Rise of a New East Asian Power

AP® EXAM TIP

Questions comparing China and Japan in this era have appeared on the AP® exam.

Like China and the Ottoman Empire, the island country of Japan confronted the aggressive power of the West during the nineteenth century, most notably in the form of U.S. commodore Matthew Perry's "black ships," which steamed into Tokyo Bay in 1853 and forcefully demanded that this reclusive nation open up to more "normal" relations with the world. However, the outcome of that encounter differed sharply from the others. In the second half of the nineteenth century, Japan undertook a radical transformation of its society—a "revolution from above," according to some historians—turning it into a powerful, modern, united, industrialized nation. It was an achievement that neither China nor the Ottoman Empire was able to duplicate. Far from succumbing to Western domination, Japan joined the club of imperialist countries by creating its own East Asian empire, at the expense of China and Korea. In building a society that was both modern and distinctly Japanese, Japan demonstrated that modernity was not a uniquely European phenomenon. This "Japanese miracle," as some have called it, was both promising and ominous for the rest of Asia. How had it occurred?

The Tokugawa Background

For 250 years prior to Perry's arrival, Japan had been governed by a shogun (a military ruler) from the Tokugawa family who acted in the name of a revered but powerless emperor, who lived in Kyoto, 300 miles away from the seat of power in Edo (Tokyo). The chief task of this Tokugawa shogunate was to prevent the return of civil war among some 260 rival feudal lords, known as daimyo, each of whom had a cadre of armed retainers, the famed samurai warriors of Japanese tradition.

Based on their own military power and political skills, successive shoguns gave Japan more than two centuries of internal peace (1600–1850). To control the restive daimyo, they required these local authorities to create second homes in Edo, the country's capital, where they had to live during alternate years. When they left for their rural residences, families stayed behind, almost as hostages. Nonetheless, the daimyo, especially the more powerful ones, retained substantial autonomy in their own domains and behaved in some ways like independent states with separate military forces, law codes, tax systems, and currencies. With no national army, no uniform currency, and little central authority at the local level, Tokugawa Japan was "pacified . . . but not really unified."[11] To further stabilize the country, the Tokugawa regime issued highly detailed rules governing the occupation, residence, dress, hairstyles, and behavior of the four hierarchically ranked status groups into which Japanese society was divided—samurai at the top, then peasants, artisans, and, at the bottom, merchants.

Much was changing within Japan during these 250 years of peace in ways that belied the control and orderliness of Tokugawa regulations. For one thing, the samurai, in the absence of wars to fight, evolved into a salaried bureaucratic or administrative class amounting to 5 to 6 percent of the total population, but they were still fiercely devoted to their daimyo lords and to their warrior code of loyalty, honor, and self-sacrifice.

More generally, centuries of peace contributed to a remarkable burst of economic growth, commercialization, and urban development. Entrepreneurial peasants, using fertilizers and other agricultural innovations, grew more rice than ever before and engaged in a variety of rural manufacturing enterprises as well. By 1750, Japan had become perhaps the world's most urbanized country, with about 10 percent of its population living in sizable towns or cities. Edo, with perhaps a million residents, was among the world's largest cities. Well-functioning networks of exchange linked urban and rural areas, marking Japan as an emerging market economy. The influence of Confucianism encouraged education and generated a remarkably literate population, with about 40 percent of men and 15 percent of women able to read and write. Although no one was aware of it at the time, these changes during the Tokugawa era provided a solid foundation for Japan's remarkable industrial growth in the late nineteenth century.

Such changes also undermined the shogunate's efforts to freeze Japanese society in the interests of stability. Some samurai found the lowly but profitable path of commerce too much to resist. "No more shall we have to live by the sword," declared one of them in 1616 while renouncing his samurai status. "I have seen that great profit can be made honorably. I shall brew *sake* and soy sauce, and we shall prosper."[12] Many merchants, though hailing from the lowest-ranking status group, prospered in the new commercial environment and supported a vibrant urban culture, while not a few daimyo found it necessary, if humiliating, to seek loans from these social inferiors. Thus merchants had money, but little status, whereas samurai enjoyed high status but were often indebted to inferior merchants. Both resented their positions.

Despite prohibitions to the contrary, many peasants moved to the cities, becoming artisans or merchants and imitating the ways of their social betters. A decree of 1788 noted that peasants "have become accustomed to luxury and forgetful of their status." They wore inappropriate clothing, used umbrellas rather than straw hats in the rain, and even left the villages for the city. "Henceforth," declared the shogun, "all luxuries should be avoided by the peasants. They are to live simply and devote themselves to farming."[13] This decree, like many others before it, was widely ignored.

More than social change undermined the Tokugawa regime. Corruption was widespread, to the disgust of many. The shogunate's failure to deal successfully with a severe famine in the 1830s eroded confidence in its effectiveness. At the same time, a mounting wave of local peasant uprisings and urban riots expressed the many grievances of the poor. The most striking of these outbursts left the city of Osaka in flames in 1837. Its leader, Oshio Heihachiro, no doubt spoke for many ordinary people when he wrote:

Guided Reading Question

■ CHANGE

In what ways was Japan changing during the Tokugawa era?

We must first punish the officials who torment the people so cruelly; then we must execute the haughty and rich Osaka merchants. Then we must distribute the gold, silver, and copper stored in their cellars, and bands of rice hidden in their storehouses.[14]

From the 1830s on, one historian concluded, "there was a growing feeling that the *shogunate* was losing control."[15]

American Intrusion and the Meiji Restoration

It was foreign intervention that brought matters to a head. Since the expulsion of European missionaries and the harsh suppression of Christianity in the early seventeenth century (see Chapter 14, page 610), Japan had deliberately limited its contact with the West to a single port, where only the Dutch were allowed to trade. By the early nineteenth century, however, various European countries and the United States were knocking at the door. All were turned away, and even shipwrecked sailors or whalers were expelled, jailed, or executed. As it happened, it was the United States that forced the issue, sending Commodore Perry in 1853 to demand

The Black Ships of the United States
The initial occasion for serious Japanese reflection on the West occurred in 1853–1854, in the context of American commodore Matthew Perry's efforts to "open" Japan to regular commercial relationships with the United States. His nine coal-fired steamships, belching black smoke and carrying a crew of some 1,800 men and more than 100 mounted cannons, became known in Japan as the "black ships." Created around 1854, this image represents perhaps the best known of many such Japanese depictions of the American warships. (The Granger Collection, NYC — All rights reserved)

humane treatment for castaways, the right of American vessels to refuel and buy provisions, and the opening of ports for trade. Authorized to use force if necessary, Perry presented his reluctant hosts with, among other gifts, a white flag for surrender should hostilities follow.

In the end, the Japanese avoided war. Aware of what had happened to China as a result of resisting European demands, Japan agreed to a series of unequal treaties with various Western powers. That humiliating capitulation to the demands of the "foreign devils" further eroded support for the shogunate, triggered a brief civil war, and by 1868 led to a political takeover by a group of young samurai from southern Japan. This decisive turning point in Japan's history was known as the Meiji (MAY-jee) Restoration, for the country's new rulers claimed that they were restoring to power the young emperor, then a fifteen-year-old boy whose throne name was Meiji, or Enlightened Rule. Despite his youth, he was regarded as the most recent link in a chain of descent that traced the origins of the imperial family back to the sun goddess Amaterasu. Having eliminated the shogunate, the patriotic young men who led the takeover soon made their goals clear—to save Japan from foreign domination not by futile resistance, but by a thorough transformation of Japanese society drawing on all that the modern West had to offer. "Knowledge shall be sought throughout the world," they declared, "so as to strengthen the foundations of imperial rule."

Japan now had a government committed to a decisive break with the past, and it had acquired that government without massive violence or destruction. By contrast, the defeat of the Taiping Uprising had deprived China of any such opportunity for a fresh start, while saddling it with enormous devastation and massive loss of life. Furthermore, Japan was of less interest to Western powers than either China, with its huge potential market and reputation for riches, or the Ottoman Empire, with its strategic location at the crossroads of Asia, Africa, and Europe. The American Civil War and its aftermath likewise deflected U.S. ambitions in the Pacific for a time, further reducing the Western pressure on Japan.

> **AP® EXAM TIP**
>
> You should know the features of the Meiji Restoration.

Modernization Japanese-Style

These circumstances gave Japan some breathing space, and its new rulers moved quickly to take advantage of that unique window of opportunity. Thus they launched a cascading wave of dramatic changes that rolled over the country in the last three decades of the nineteenth century. Like the more modest reforms of China and the Ottoman Empire, Japanese modernizing efforts were defensive, based on fears that Japanese independence was in grave danger. Those reforms, however, were revolutionary in their cumulative effect, transforming Japan far more thoroughly than even the most radical of the Ottoman efforts, let alone the limited "self-strengthening" policies of the Chinese.

The first task was genuine national unity, which required an attack on the power and privileges of both the daimyo and the samurai. In a major break with the past,

> **Guided Reading Question**
>
> ■ CHANGE
>
> In what respects was Japan's nineteenth-century transformation revolutionary?

the new regime soon ended the semi-independent domains of the daimyo, replacing them with governors appointed by and responsible to the national government. The central state, not the local authorities, now collected the nation's taxes and raised a national army based on conscription from all social classes.

Thus the samurai relinquished their ancient role as the country's warrior class and with it their cherished right to carry swords. The old Confucian-based social order with its special privileges for various classes was largely dismantled, and almost all Japanese became legally equal as commoners and as subjects of the emperor. Limitations on travel and trade likewise fell as a nationwide economy came to parallel the centralized state. Although there was some opposition to these measures, including a brief rebellion of resentful samurai in 1877, it was on the whole a remarkably peaceful process in which a segment of the old ruling class abolished its own privileges. Many, but not all, of these displaced elites found a soft landing in the army, bureaucracy, or business enterprises of the new regime, thus easing a painful transition.

Accompanying these social and political changes was a widespread and eager fascination with almost everything Western. Knowledge about the West—its science and technology; its various political and constitutional arrangements; its legal and educational systems; its dances, clothing, and hairstyles—was enthusiastically sought out by official missions to Europe and the United States, by hundreds of students sent to study abroad, and by many ordinary Japanese at home. Western writers were translated into Japanese; for example, Samuel Smiles's *Self-Help*, which focused on "achieving success and rising in the world," sold a million copies. "Civilization and Enlightenment" was the slogan of the time, and both were to be found in the West. The most prominent popularizer of Western knowledge, Fukuzawa Yukichi, summed up the chief lesson of his studies in the mid-1870s—Japan was backward and needed to learn from the West: "If we compare the knowledge of the Japanese and Westerners, in letters, in technique, in commerce, or in industry, from the largest to the smallest matter, there is not one thing in which we excel. . . . In Japan's present condition there is nothing in which we may take pride vis-à-vis the West."[16]

After this initial wave of uncritical enthusiasm for everything Western receded, Japan proceeded to borrow more selectively and to combine foreign and Japanese elements in distinctive ways. For example, the Constitution of 1889, drawing heavily on German experience, introduced an elected parliament, political parties, and democratic ideals, but that constitution was presented as a gift from a sacred emperor descended from the sun goddess. The parliament could advise, but ultimate power, and particularly control of the military, lay theoretically with the emperor and in practice with an oligarchy of prominent reformers acting in his name. Likewise, a modern educational system, which achieved universal primary schooling by the early twentieth century, was laced with Confucian-based moral instruction and exhortations of loyalty to the emperor. Christianity made little headway in Meiji Japan, but Shinto, an ancient religious tradition featuring ancestors and nature spirits, was elevated to the status of an official state cult. Japan's earlier experience in borrowing massively but selectively from Chinese culture perhaps served it better in these new circumstances than either the Chinese disdain for foreign cultures or the reluctance of many Muslims to see much of value in the infidel West.

Like their counterparts in China and the Ottoman Empire, some reformers in Japan—male and female alike—argued that the oppression of women was an obstacle to the country's modernization and that family reform was essential to gaining the respect of the West. The widely read commentator Fukuzawa Yukichi urged an end to concubinage and prostitution, advocated more education for girls, and called for gender equality in matters of marriage, divorce, and property rights. But most male reformers understood women largely in the context of family life, seeing them as "good wife, wise mother." By the 1880s, however, a small feminist movement arose, demanding—and modeling—a more public role for women. Some even sought the right to vote at a time when only a small fraction of men could do so. A leading feminist, Kishida Toshiko, not yet twenty years old, astonished the country in 1882 when she undertook a two-month speaking tour, where she addressed huge audiences. Only "equality and equal rights," she argued, would allow Japan "to build a new society." Japan must rid itself of the ancient habit of "respecting men and despising women."

While the new Japanese government included girls in their plans for universal education, it was with a gender-specific curriculum and in schools segregated by sex. Any thought of women playing a role in public life was harshly suppressed. A Peace Preservation Law of 1887, in effect until 1922, forbade women from joining political parties and even from attending meetings where political matters were discussed. The Constitution of 1889 made no mention of any political rights for women. The Civil Code of 1898 accorded absolute authority to the male head of the family, while grouping all wives with "cripples and disabled persons" as those who "cannot undertake any legal action." To the authorities of Meiji Japan, a serious transformation of gender roles was more of a threat than an opportunity.

At the core of Japan's effort at defensive modernization lay its state-guided industrialization program. More than in Europe or the United States, the government itself established a number of enterprises, later selling many of them to private investors. It also acted to create a modern infrastructure by building railroads, creating a postal system, and establishing a national currency and banking system. By the early twentieth century, Japan's industrialization, organized around a number of large firms called *zaibatsu*, was well under way. The country became a major exporter of textiles, in part as a way to pay for needed imports of raw materials, such as cotton, owing to its limited natural resources. Soon the country was able to produce its own munitions and industrial goods as well. Its major cities enjoyed mass-circulation newspapers, movie theaters, and electric lights. All of this was accomplished through its own resources and without the massive foreign debt that so afflicted Egypt and the Ottoman Empire. No other country outside of Europe

AP® EXAM TIP

Take notes on changing gender roles in Japan in this era.

Japan's Modernization

In Japan, as in Europe, railroads quickly became a popular symbol of the country's modernization, as this woodblock print from the 1870s illustrates. (*Commodore Perry's Gift of a Railway to the Japanese in 1853*, by Ando or Utagawa Hiroshige [1797–1858]/Private Collection/Bridgeman Images)

and North America had been able to launch its own Industrial Revolution in the nineteenth century. It was a distinctive feature of Japan's modern transformation.

Less distinctive, however, were the social results of that process. Taxed heavily to pay for Japan's ambitious modernization program, many peasant families slid into poverty. Their sometimes-violent protests peaked in 1883–1884 as the Japanese countryside witnessed infanticide, the sale of daughters, and starvation.

While state authorities rigidly excluded women from political life and denied them adult legal status, they badly needed female labor in the country's textile industry, which was central to Japan's economic growth. Accordingly, the majority of Japan's textile workers were young women from poor families in the countryside. Recruiters toured rural villages, contracting with parents for their daughters' labor in return for a payment that the girls had to repay from their wages. That pay was low and their working conditions were terrible. Most lived in factory-provided dormitories and worked twelve or more hours per day. While some committed suicide or ran away and many left after earning enough to pay off their contracts, others organized strikes and joined the anarchist or socialist movements that were emerging among a few intellectuals. One such woman, Kanno Sugako, was hanged in 1911 for participating in a plot to assassinate the emperor. Efforts to create unions and organize strikes, both illegal in Japan at the time, were met with harsh repression even as corporate and state authorities sought to depict the company as a family unit to which workers should give their loyalty, all under the beneficent gaze of the divine emperor.

Japan and the World

Japan's modern transformation soon registered internationally. By the early twentieth century, its economic growth, openness to trade, and embrace of "civilization and enlightenment" from the West persuaded the Western powers to revise the unequal treaties in Japan's favor. This had long been a primary goal of the Meiji regime, and the Anglo-Japanese Treaty of 1902 now acknowledged Japan as an equal player among the Great Powers of the world.

Not only did Japan escape from its semi-colonial entanglements with the West, but it also launched its own empire-building enterprise, even as European powers and the United States were carving up much of Asia, Africa, and Pacific Oceania into colonies or spheres of influence. It was what industrializing Great Powers did in the late nineteenth century, and Japan followed suit, in part to compensate for the relative poverty of its natural resource base. Successful wars against China (1894–1895) and Russia (1904–1905) established Japan as a formidable military competitor in East Asia and the first Asian state to defeat a major European power. Through those victories, Japan also gained colonial control of Taiwan and Korea and a territorial foothold in Manchuria. And in the aftermath of World War I, Japan acquired a growing influence in China's Shandong Peninsula and control over a number of Micronesian islands under the auspices of the League of Nations. Japan's entry onto the broader global stage was felt in many places (see Map 19.3). It added yet one more imperialist power to those already burdening a beleaguered China. Defeat at the hands of Japanese upstarts shocked Russia and triggered the 1905 revolution in that country. To Europeans and Americans, Japan was now an economic, political, and military competitor in Asia.

In the world of subject peoples, the rise of Japan and its defeat of Russia generated widespread admiration among those who saw Japan as a model for their own modern development and perhaps as an ally in the struggle against imperialism. Some Poles, Finns, and Jews viewed the Russian defeat in 1905 as an opening for their own liberation from the Russian Empire and were grateful to Japan for the opportunity. Despite Japan's aggression against their country, many Chinese reformers and nationalists found in the Japanese experience valuable lessons for themselves. Thousands flocked to Japan to study its achievements. Newspapers throughout the Islamic world celebrated Japan's victory over Russia as an "awakening of the East," which might herald Muslims' own liberation. Some Turkish women gave their children Japanese names. Indonesian Muslims from Aceh wrote to the Meiji emperor asking for help in their struggle against the Dutch, and Muslim poets wrote odes in his honor. The Egyptian nationalist Mustafa Kamil spoke for many when he declared: "We are amazed by Japan because it is the first Eastern government to utilize Western civilization to resist the shield of European imperialism in Asia."[17]

Those who directly experienced Japanese imperialism in Taiwan or Korea no doubt had a less positive view, for its colonial policies matched or exceeded the

Guided Reading Question

■ **CONNECTION**

How did Japan's relationship to the larger world change during its modernization process?

Map 19.3   The Rise of Japan

As Japan modernized after the Meiji Restoration, it launched an empire-building program that provided a foundation for further expansion in the 1930s and during World War II.

brutality of European practices. In the twentieth century, China and much of Southeast Asia suffered bitterly under Japanese imperial aggression. Nonetheless, both the idea of Japan as a liberator of Asia from the European yoke and the reality of Japan as an oppressive imperial power in its own right derived from the country's remarkable modern transformation and its distinctive response to the provocation of Western intrusion.

Success and Failure in History

Beyond describing what happened in the past and explaining why, historians often find themselves evaluating the events they study. When they make judgments about the past, notions of success and failure frequently come into play. Should Europe's Industrial Revolution and its rise to global power be regarded as a success? If so, does that imply that other civilizations were failures? Should we consider Japan more successful than China or the Ottoman Empire during the nineteenth century? Three considerations suggest that we should be very careful in applying these ideas to the complexities of the historical record.

First, and most obviously, is the question of criteria. If the measure of success is national wealth and power, then the Industrial Revolution surely counts as a great accomplishment. But if preservation of the environment, spiritual growth, and the face-to-face relationships of village life are more highly valued, then industrialization, as Gandhi argued, might be more reasonably considered a disaster.

Second, there is the issue of "success for whom?" British artisans who lost their livelihood to industrial machines as well as Japanese women textile workers who suffered through the early stages of industrialization might be forgiven for not appreciating the "success" of their countries' transformation, even if their middle-class counterparts and subsequent generations benefited. In such cases, issues of both social and generational justice complicate any easy assessment of the past.

Third, and finally, success is frequently associated with good judgment and wise choices, yet actors in the historical drama are never completely free in making their decisions, and none, of course, have the benefit of hindsight, which historians enjoy. Did the leaders of China and the Ottoman Empire fail to push industrial development more strongly, or were they not in a position to do so? Were Japanese leaders wiser and more astute than their counterparts elsewhere, or did their knowledge of China's earlier experience and their unique national history simply provide them with circumstances more conducive to modern development? Such questions regarding the possibilities and limitations of human action have no clear-cut answers, but they might caution us about any easy assessment of success and failure.

Chapter Review

What's the Significance?

Big Picture Questions

1. "The response of each society to European imperialism grew out of its larger historical development and its internal problems." What evidence might support this statement?
2. "Deliberate government policies were more important than historical circumstances in shaping the history of China, the Ottoman Empire, and Japan during the nineteenth century." How might you argue for and against this statement?
3. What kinds of debates, controversies, and conflicts were generated by European intrusion within each of the societies examined in this chapter?
4. **Looking Back:** How did the experiences of China, the Ottoman Empire, Japan, and Latin America, all of which retained their independence despite much European pressure, differ from those of Africa, India, Southeast Asia, and Pacific Oceania, which fell under formal colonial rule?

Next Steps: For Further Study

William Bowman et al., *Imperialism in the Modern World* (2007). A collection of short readings illustrating the various forms and faces of European expansion over the past several centuries.

Carter V. Finley, *The Turks in World History* (2004). A study placing the role of Turkish-speaking peoples in general and the Ottoman Empire in particular in a global context.

Marius B. Jansen, *The Making of Modern Japan* (2002). A well-regarded account of Japan since 1600 by a leading scholar.

Jonathan D. Spence, *The Search for Modern China* (1999). Probably the best single-volume account of Chinese history from about 1600 through the twentieth century.

E. Patricia Tsurumi, *Factory Girls: Women in the Thread Mills of Meiji Japan* (1990). An examination of the lives of women in Japan's nineteenth-century textile factories.

Arthur Waley, *The Opium War through Chinese Eyes* (1968). An older classic that views the Opium War from various Chinese points of view.

"The Decline of the Ottoman Empire," http://www.youtube.com/watch?v=T-SUlb4rwls. A ten-minute video that offers an interpretation of the declining fortunes of the Ottoman Empire.

"Visualizing Cultures: Image-Driven Scholarship," http://ocw.mit.edu/ans7870/21f/21f.027/home/index.html. A collection, provided by MIT, of thoughtful essays and stunning images dealing with China and Japan during the nineteenth century.

WORKING WITH EVIDENCE

Changing China

By the end of the nineteenth century, growing numbers of thoughtful Chinese recognized that their country was in crisis. Repeated European military interventions since the first Opium War in 1839 had humiliated the once-proud Middle Kingdom, reducing it to a semi-colonial dependent of various European powers. A decisive military defeat in a war with Japan in 1894–1895 represented a further humiliation at the hands of a small country long under the cultural influence of China. China also continued to face the enormous problem of widespread poverty among its peasant population, a dilemma reflected in repeated upheavals in the countryside. Both of these issues—foreign imperialism and peasant rebellion—found expression in the Boxer Uprising of 1898–1901 (see page 843). This upheaval demonstrated—once again—the ability of China's vast peasant population to make its presence felt in the political life of the country, as it had in the Taiping Uprising of the 1850s and 1860s (see pages 836–38). The Boxer rebellion's virulent antiforeign and anti-Christian outlook disclosed the depth of feeling against imperialism even among rural people. The outcome of that rebellion—foreign occupation of Beijing and large reparation payments from China's government—revealed China's continuing weakness relative to European and Japanese powers.

In this context, many educated Chinese began to consider alternatives to the status quo and to make plans for changing China. Some of their proposals were reformist and aimed at preserving the Qing dynasty regime; others were more revolutionary and sought to replace dynastic China with a new society and political system altogether. During a brief three-month period in 1898, known as the Hundred Days of Reform, and then again in the decade following the Boxer Uprising, some of the more reformist proposals began to be implemented, including the end of the traditional civil service examination system and the creation of elected provincial assemblies. But more substantial change in China had to await the collapse of the Qing dynasty and the end of the monarchy in 1912, and the most dramatic changes occurred after the communists came to power in 1949. Nonetheless, the proposals of the late nineteenth and early twentieth centuries were significant, for they reveal both the mounting pressures for a new path and the obstacles that confronted those who advocated such changes.

Source 19.1

Toward a Constitutional Monarchy

Among the leading advocates of reform in the aftermath of China's defeat by Japan was Kang Youwei (1858–1927), a brilliant Confucian scholar, whose views informed the Hundred Days of Reform in 1898. Understanding Confucius as a reformer, Kang Youwei argued that the Chinese emperor could be an active agent for China's transformation while operating in a parliamentary and constitutional setting. With its emphasis on human goodness, self-improvement, and the moral example of superiors, Confucianism could provide a framework for real change even as it protected China from "moral degeneration" and an indiscriminate embrace of Western culture. In an appeal to the emperor in early 1898, Kang Youwei spelled out his understanding of what China needed.

■ In what ways does Kang Youwei express a Confucian outlook, and in what respects does he show an awareness of a larger world?

■ What obstacles to reform does Kang Youwei identify?

■ Why does he advocate the Russia of Peter the Great and the Japan of the Meiji reforms as models for China?

KANG YOUWEI

An Appeal to Emperor Guangxu
1898

A survey of all states in the world will show that those states that undertook reforms became stronger while those states which clung to the past perished. . . . If Your Majesty, with your discerning brilliance, observes the trends in other countries, you will see that if we can change, we can preserve ourselves; but if we cannot change, we shall perish.

It is a principle of things that the new is strong but the old is weak. . . . [T]here are no institutions that should remain unchanged for a hundred years. Moreover our present institutions are but unworthy vestiges of the Han, Tang, Yuan, and Ming dynasties. . . . [T]hey are the products of fancy writing and corrupt dealing of the petty officials rather than the original ideas of the ancestors. To say that they are ancestral institutions is an insult to the ancestors. Furthermore institutions are for the purpose of preserving one's territories. Now that the ancestral territory cannot be preserved, what good is it to maintain the ancestral institutions? . . .

Nowadays the court has been undertaking some reforms, but the action of the emperor is obstructed by the ministers, and the recommendations of the able scholars are attacked by old-fashioned bureaucrats. If the charge is not "using barbarian ways to change China," then it is "upsetting ancestral institutions." Rumors and scandal are rampant, and people fight each other like fire and water. A reform in this way is as effective as attempting a forward march by walking backward. . . . I beg Your Majesty to make up your mind and to decide on the national policy.

After studying ancient and modern institutions, Chinese and foreign, I have found that the institutions of the sage-kings and the Three Dynasties [Xia, Shang, and Zhou dynasties of very ancient times] were excellent, but ancient times were different from today. I hope that Your Majesty will daily read Mencius [a famous Confucian writer] and follow his example of loving the people. The development of the Han, Tang, Song and Ming dynasties may be learned, but it should be remembered that the [present] age of universal unification is different from that of sovereign nations. . . .

As to the republican governments of the United States and France and the constitutional governments of Britain and Germany, these countries are far away and their customs are different from ours. . . . Consequently I beg Your Majesty to adopt the purpose of Peter the Great of Russia as our purpose and to take the Meiji Reform of Japan as the model of our reform. The time and place of Japan's reforms are not remote and her religion and customs are somewhat similar to ours. Her success is manifest; her example can be followed.

Source: Wm. Theodore de Bary and Richard Lufrano, eds., *Sources of Chinese Tradition: From 1600 through the Twentieth Century* (New York: Columbia University Press, 2000), 269–70.

Source 19.2
Education and Examination

At the heart of Chinese elite culture and government lay the country's fabled examination system and the Confucian-based education on which it rested. Those examinations had long been used to select the officials who governed China. The classical texts and rhetorical style that the examinations tested were widely regarded as essential to preserving the essence of Chinese culture while creating common values among the elite. But for those seeking fundamental change in China, the examination system represented everything that was conservative, backward, and out of date, preventing the country from effectively modernizing. In 1905, that ancient examination system was formally and permanently abolished. The two brief selections that follow make the case for educational reform. The first comes from an anonymous editorial in a Chinese newspaper in 1898, while the second was part of an edict from the reforming Emperor Guangxu during the Hundred Days of Reform, also in 1898.

■ What criticisms of the old examination system do these excerpts make?

■ What kind of education do they advocate?

■ How might conservatives respond to these documents?

ANONYMOUS

Editorial on China's Examination System

1898

The dynasty's examination system is extremely annoying and cumbersome. . . . Students go through innumerable hardships before they can obtain the right to wear the robes designating them as officially authorized students. Hence year after year they persist in their studies until their hair turns white. One half of each year is taken up with examinations, and the other half is burdened with wife, children, home, and family. Any spare time is spent trying to master the eight-legged essay. And yet it is very difficult to attain satisfactory competence in the eight-legged style, even though it is considered so vital. What then, if in addition, one wants to read useful books and study useful subjects? . . .

For the court to use poetry, rhyme-prose, and fine script as the criteria for passing or failing the examinations for men of ability is truly vulgar and ridiculous. . . . [T]he multitude of problems on the coast [a reference to European penetration] has steadily weakened the nation. Poetry and rhyme-prose are not adequate to cope with this changing situation, and fine script is not adequate to withstand the enemy. How are we to devise a policy to bring peace and to emulate the wealth and power [of the Western nations]? Every meaningless and extravagant custom should be reformed. . . . Only then will officials of the court . . . be able to devote themselves to useful studies. Their ambitions will no longer be diverted by eight-legged essays, poetry, rhyme-prose and fine script, nor will their minds be disturbed by all the various examinations.

EMPEROR GUANGXU

Edict on Education

1898

Our scholars are now without solid and practical education; our artisans are without scientific instructors; when compared with other countries, we soon see how weak we are. Does anyone think that our troops are as well drilled or as well led as those of the foreign armies? Or that we can successfully stand against them? Changes must be made to accord with the necessities of the times. . . . Keeping in mind the morals of the sages and wise men, we must make them the basis on which to build newer and better structures. We must substitute modern arms and western organization for our old regime; we must select our military officers according to western methods of military education; we must establish elementary and high schools, colleges and universities, in accordance with those of foreign countries; we must abolish the Wen-chang (literary essay) and obtain a knowledge of ancient and modern world-history, a right conception of the present-day state of affairs, with special reference to the governments and institutions of the countries of the five great continents; and we must understand their arts and sciences.

Sources: J. Mason Gentzler, *Changing China* (New York: Praeger, 1977), 88–89; Isaac Taylor Headland, *Court Life in China* (New York: F. H. Revell, 1909).

Source 19.3

Gender, Reform, and Revolution

Among those seeking to change China, the question of women's roles in society frequently arose. Kang Youwei (see Source 19.1), for example, looked forward to the end of traditional marriage, hoping it would be replaced by a series of one-year contracts between a man and woman, which he thought would ensure gender equality. But the most well-known advocate for women was Qiu Jin (1875–1907). Born into a well-to-do family with liberal inclinations, she received a fine literary education, developing a passion for reading as well as for swordplay, horseback riding, and martial arts.

Married to a much older man at age eighteen, she was distinctly unsatisfied in such a conventional life and developed a growing feminist awareness, sometimes dressing in men's clothes and Western styles. "My aim is to dress like a man!" she told a friend. "[I]n China men are strong, and women are oppressed because they're supposed to be weak. . . . If I first take on the form of a man, then I think my mind too will eventually become that of a man. My hair is cut in a foreigner's style, something Chinese aren't supposed to do, and I'm wearing Western clothes."[18]

In 1903, Qiu Jin did something even more unthinkable for a Chinese woman when she left her husband and children to pursue an education in Japan, selling her jewelry to finance the trip. "Cut off from my family I leave my native land," she wrote. "Unbinding my feet I clean out a thousand years of poison."[19]

Returning to China in 1906, she started a women's magazine, the *Chinese Women's Journal*, which was a strong advocate for women's independence and education. "Of the enlightened countries today," declared an article in the *Journal*, "there is not one which does not stress education for women, and thus their countries are strong."[20] Soon Qiu Jin became active in revolutionary circles. For her role in an abortive plot to overthrow the Qing dynasty, she was arrested, tortured, and beheaded in 1907 at the age of thirty-two. Asked to write a confession moments before her execution, she instead penned a short verse of seven characters that included her surname, Qiu, which literally means "autumn" in Chinese: "Autumn rain, autumn wind, they make one die of sorrow."[21]

The selection that follows comes from her most famous appeal for the rights of women.

■ How did Qiu Jin describe the difficulties that faced Chinese women?

■ How did she account for these sad conditions?

■ What did she advocate as a remedy for the problems she identified? Did she seem to have a political agenda?

■ To what extent do you think she was writing from personal experience?

QIU JIN

Address to Two Hundred Million Fellow Countrywomen

1904

Alas, the most unfairly treated things on this earth are the two hundred million who are born as Chinese women. We consider ourselves lucky to be born to a kind father. If we are unlucky, our father will be an ill-tempered and unreasonable person who repeatedly says, "How unlucky I am, yet another useless one," as if at any instant he could pick us up and throw us to our death. He will resent us and say things like "she's eventually going to someone else's family" and give us cold and contemptuous looks. When we grow a few years older, without bothering to ask us our thoughts, they will bind our tender, white and natural feet with a strip of cloth, never loosening them even while we sleep. In the end, the flesh is mangled and the bones broken, all so that relatives, friends and neighbors can say, "the girl from so and so's family has tiny feet."

When the time comes (for the parents) to select a husband, everything is based on the promises of two shameless matchmakers. The daughter's parents will go along with any proposal as long as his family is rich and powerful. Her parents do not bother to ask if the man's family is respectable, or inquire about the groom's temperament and level of education. On the wedding day, one will sit in the brightly decorated bridal sedan chair barely able to breathe. When we arrive at the new home, if the husband is found to be unambitious but even-tempered, her family will say we are blessed with good fortune from a previous life. If he is no good, her family will blame it "on our wrong conduct in a previous life," or simply "bad luck." If we dare complain, or otherwise try to counsel our husbands, then a scolding and beating will befall us. Others who hear of the abuse will say: "She is a woman of no virtue. She does not act as a wife should!" Can you believe such words? These aspersions are cast

without the chance for an appeal! Further inequities will follow if the husband dies. The wife will have to wear a mourning dress for three years and will not be allowed to remarry. Yet, if the wife dies, the husband only needs to wear a blue (mourning) braid. Some men find even that unbecoming and do not bother to wear it at all. Even when the wife has only been dead for three days, he can go out and cavort and indulge himself. A new wife is allowed to enter the household even before the official seven weeks of mourning is over. In the beginning, Heaven created all people with no differences between men and women. Ask yourselves this, how could these people have been born without women? Why are things so unjust? Everyday these men say, "We ought to be equal and treat people kindly." Then why do they treat women so unfairly and unequally as if they were African slaves?

A woman has to learn not to depend on others, but to rely on herself instead. . . . Why can't we reject footbinding? Are they afraid of women being educated, knowledgeable, and perhaps surpassing them? Men do not allow us to study. We must not simply go along with their decision without even challenging them. . . .

However, from now on I hope we can leave the past behind us and focus on our future. Assuming we have died in the past and are reincarnated into our next life, the elders should not say "too old to be of any use." If you have a decent husband who wants to establish a school, do not stop him. If you have a fine son who wishes to study abroad, do not stop him. The middle-aged wife should not hinder her husband by causing him to have no ambition and achieve nothing. If you have a son, send him to school. Do the same for your daughter and never bind her feet. If you have a young girl, the best choice would be for her to attend school, but even if she is unable to attend schools, you should teach her to read and write at home. If you come from a family of officials that has money, you should persuade your husband to establish schools and factories and do good deeds that will help common people. If your family is poor, you should work hard to help your husband. Do not be lazy and do nothing. These are my hopes. All of you are aware that we are about to lose our country. Men can scarcely protect themselves. How can we rely on them? We must revitalize ourselves. Otherwise all will be too late when the country is lost. Everybody! Everybody! Please keep my hopes alive!

Source: David G. Atwill and Lurong Y. Atwill, *Sources in Chinese History* (Upper Saddle River, NJ: Prentice Hall, 2010), 140–41.

Source 19.4
Prescriptions for a Revolutionary China

While some advocates for change pressed for various reforms within the framework of Qing dynasty China, others felt that the millennia-old monarchy itself had to be overthrown if China was to modernize and prosper as a nation. The leading figure among China's late nineteenth-century revolutionaries was Sun Yat-sen (1866–1925), a convert to Christianity, a trained medical doctor, and by the 1890s an ardent revolutionary. From exile in Europe, the United States, and Japan, Sun plotted various uprisings against the Qing dynasty and in 1905 created the Revolutionary Alliance in an effort to bring together the various groups seeking to end the ancient imperial system. But what kind of society and political structure did Sun envisage for his country? In 1906, Sun spelled out an early formulation of his "three people's principles"—nationalism, democracy, and people's livelihood—that articulated his vision for China's future.

- Why does Sun Yat-sen believe that China requires a revolution rather than reform?

- In his view, who are the enemies of the Chinese nation?

- What elements of Sun's prescriptions for China's future derive from traditional Chinese practice and which reflect Western influence?

- Is Sun Yat-sen advocating a socialist future for China?

- How might Kang Youwei in Source 19.1 respond to Sun Yat-sen's prescriptions for the future?

SUN YAT-SEN

The Three People's Principles and the Future of the Chinese People

1906

Nationalism . . . has to do with human nature and applies to everyone. Today, more than 260 years have passed since the Manchus entered China proper, yet even as children we Han [ethnic Chinese] would certainly not mistake them for fellow Han. This is the root of nationalism. . . . It simply means not allowing such people [the Manchu rulers of the Qing dynasty] to seize our political power, for only when we Han are in control politically do we have a nation. . . .

Actually we are already a people without a nation. . . . Our nation is the most populous, most ancient, and most civilized in the world, yet today we are a lost nation. . . . We Han are now swiftly being caught up in a tidal wave of nationalist revolution, yet the Manchus continue to discriminate against the Han. They boast that their forefathers conquered the Han because of their superior unity and that they intend . . . to dominate the Han forever. . . . Certainly once we Han unite, our power will be thousands of times greater than theirs and the success of our nationalist revolution will be assured.

As for the Principle of Democracy, it is the foundation of the political revolution. . . . For several thousand years China has been a monarchial autocracy, a type of political system intolerable to those living in freedom and equality. A nationalist revolution is not itself sufficient to get rid of such a system . . . a political revolution is an absolute necessity. The aim of the political revolution is to create a constitutional democratic political system. . . . [Such a] revolution would be necessary even if the monarch were a Han.

As for the Principle of the People's Livelihood . . . , we must try to improve the economic structures of society so as to preclude a social revolution in the future. . . . As civilization advanced, people relied less on physical labor and more on natural forces, since electricity and steam could accomplish things a thousand times faster than physical strength. . . . [N]ow with the development of natural forces that human labor cannot match, agriculture and industry have fallen completely into the hands of capitalists. Unable to compete, the poor have naturally been reduced to destitution. . . . [E]very informed person knows that a social revolution is inevitable in Europe and America.

Indeed this constitutes a lesson for China. . . . Civilization [advanced industrial capitalist countries] yields both good and bad fruits, and we should embrace the good and reject the bad. In Europe and America the rich monopolize the good fruits of civilization, while the poor suffer from its evil fruits. . . .

With respect to a solution . . . the procedure I most favor is land valuation. For example, if a landlord has land worth 1000 dollars, its price can be set at 1000 or even 2000 dollars. Perhaps in the future, after communications have been developed, the value of his land will rise to 10,000 dollars; the owner should receive 2000, which entails a profit and no loss, and the 8000 increment will go to the state. Such an arrangement will greatly benefit both the state and the people's livelihood. Naturally it will also eliminate the shortcomings that have permitted a few people to monopolize wealth. . . .

As to the future constitution I propose that we introduce a new principle, that of the "five separate powers." Under this system there will be two other powers in addition to the [executive, legislative, and judicial]. One is the examination power. . . . American officials are either elected or appointed. Formerly there were no civil service examinations, which led to serious shortcomings. . . . With respect to elections, those endowed with eloquence ingratiated themselves with the public and won elections, while those who had learning and ideals but lacked eloquence were ignored. Consequently members of America's House of Representatives have often been foolish and ignorant people who have made its history quite ridiculous. . . . Therefore the future constitution of the Republic of China must provide for an independent branch expressly responsible for civil service examinations. Furthermore all officials, however high their rank, must undergo examinations in order to determine their qualifications.

The other power is the supervisory power, responsible for monitoring matters involving impeachment. . . . Since ancient times, China had a supervisory organization, the Censorate, to monitor the traditional social order.

Source: Julie Lee Wei et al., *Prescriptions for Saving China: Selected Writings of Sun Yat-sen* (Stanford, CA: Hoover Institution Press, 1994), 41–50.

DOING HISTORY

Changing China

1. **Defining obstacles to change:** What hindrances to China's effective transformation are stated or implied in these documents? Do their authors perceive any positive qualities in Chinese civilization that might facilitate the country's transformation?

2. **Assessing goals:** "China as a culture and a political system must be destroyed in order to preserve China as a nation." To what extent would the authors of these documents have agreed or disagreed with this statement?

3. **Identifying differences:** Imagine a conversation among the authors of these documents. What points of agreement might they find? What conflicts would likely arise among them?

4. **Considering "westernization" and "modernization":** To what extent do these proposals represent plans to "westernize" China? Or might they rather be considered "modernizing" efforts? What is the difference between the two concepts?

Multiple-Choice Questions

Use the quote and photograph on page 803, along with your knowledge of world history, to answer questions 1–3.

1. To which of these processes do the documents refer?
   a. Missionary efforts by Europeans in Africa
   b. Exploration of African territory by Europeans
   c. Exploitation of African workers by Europeans
   d. African resistance movements against European colonization

2. The labor system described in the documents most closely resembles which of these labor systems in world history?
   a. Serfdom in the Russian Empire
   b. The *mita* system in the Inca Empire
   c. Indentured servitude in British North American colonies

3. Some Europeans justified coerced labor systems in their African and Asian colonies by citing
   a. Darwin's nineteenth-century theories on evolution.
   b. Marx's nineteenth-century theories on economics.
   c. Voltaire's eighteenth-century theories on government.
   d. Catherine the Great's eighteenth-century theories on westernization.

Short-Answer Question

Question 4 refers to the passages below.

Attitudes to India changed markedly after the subcontinent had fallen into British hands. Before this, travelers found much to admire in technologies ranging from agriculture to metallurgy. After 1803, however, the arrogance of conquest was reinforced by the rapid development of British industry.... India was then made to appear rather primitive, and the idea grew that its proper role was to provide raw materials for western industry, including raw cotton and indigo dye, and to function as a market for British goods.... Given an independent and more prosperous India, it is difficult not to believe that a response to British industrialization might well have taken the form of a spread of skill and innovation.

Arnold Pacey, historian, *Technology in World Civilization*, 1990.

[U]nusual events and discoveries...led to unexpected changes in Europe's approach to science. By the mid-1600s...European philosophers and scientists found themselves in a world where the authority of ancient texts was clearly no longer a secure foundation for knowledge.... Just when Europeans...put forth their alternative ideas, the ... Mughal and Chinese Empires were focused on internal concerns, seeking to recover from internal rebellions by closing off outside influences and strengthening traditional orthodox beliefs.... [T]he Europeans, more than any other major civilization, suddenly found that the classical tradition...had to be escaped if they were going to understand the true nature of their world and their universe.... European thinkers... turned away from ... tradition and religion ... to seek new systems of knowledge ... [in] rationalism and empiricism.

Jack Goldstone, historian, *Why Europe?*, 2009.

4. Answer parts A, B, and C

    A. Briefly explain ONE specific historical difference between Pacey's and Goldstone's interpretations.

    B. Briefly explain how ONE specific historical event or development from the period 1550–1850 that is not explicitly mentioned in the excerpts could be used to support Pacey's interpretation.

    C. Briefly explain how ONE specific historical event or development from the period 1550–1850 that is not explicitly mentioned in the excerpts could be used to support Goldstone's interpretation.

Document-Based Question

Directions: Question 5 refers to the following documents. You will likely need to flip back and forth between these documents to answer the question adequately. Use scrap pieces of paper or sticky notes to tab these documents. When answering the question, refer to the "Advice for Responding to a DBQ" on the inside of the back cover.

5. Using the following documents from this textbook and your knowledge of world history, analyze responses to the effects of the Industrial Revolution in the nineteenth and early twentieth centuries.

DOCUMENT	PAGE	DOCUMENT NAME
1	750	The Urban Poor of Industrial Britain
2	756	European Migration in the Industrial Age
3	758–59	The English Luddites and Machine Breaking
4	767	The Industrial Revolution and the Global Divide
5	777–79	Karl Marx and Friedrich Engels, *The Communist Manifesto*
6	789	Cecil Rhodes, British imperialist, letter to a friend
7	858	Japan's Modernization

Long-Essay Question

When answering the following question, refer to the "Advice for Responding to an LEQ" on the inside of the back cover.

6. Compare and contrast settler colonialism and economic imperialism in the period from 1750 to 1900, analyzing reasons for the similarities and differences between settler colonialism and economic imperialism.

PART SIX

THE MOST RECENT CENTURY

1900–present

1778 1943

AMERICANS
will always fight for liberty

Contents

SINCE WORLD WAR I: A NEW PERIOD IN WORLD HISTORY?

Dividing up time into coherent segments—periods, eras, ages—is the way historians mark major changes in the lives of individuals, local communities, social groups, nations, and civilizations and also in the larger story of humankind as a whole. Because all such divisions are artificial, imposed by scholars on a continuously flowing stream of events, they are endlessly controversial and never more so than in the case of the twentieth century. To many historians, that century, and a new era in the human journey, began in 1914 with the outbreak of World War I. That terrible conflict, after all, represented a fratricidal civil war within Western civilization, triggered the Russian Revolution and the beginning of world communism, and stimulated many in the colonial world to work for their own independence. And the way it ended set the stage for an even more terrible struggle in World War II.

But does the century since 1914 represent a separate phase of world history? Granting it that status has become conventional in many world history textbooks, including this one, but there are reasons to wonder whether future generations will agree. One problem, of course, lies in the brevity of this period—only 100 years, compared to the many centuries or millennia that define earlier eras. It is interesting to notice that our time periods get progressively shorter as we approach the present. Perhaps this is because an immense overload of information about the most recent century makes it difficult to distinguish what will prove of lasting significance and what will later seem of only passing importance. Furthermore, because we are so close to the events we study and obviously ignorant of the future, we cannot know if or when this most recent period of world history will end. Or, as some have argued, has it ended already, perhaps with the collapse of the Soviet Union in 1991, with the attacks of September 11, 2001, or with the global economic crisis beginning in 2008? If so, are we now in yet another phase of historical development?

Like all other historical periods, this most recent century both carried on from the past and developed distinctive characteristics as well. Whether that combination of the old and new merits the designation of a separate era in world history will likely be debated for a long time to come. For our purposes, it will be enough to highlight both its continuities with the past and the sharp changes that the last 100 years have witnessed.

One World (p. 1022)

Image created by Reto Stockli, Nazmi El Saleous, and Marit Jentoft-Nilsen, NASA GSFC

Consider, for example, the world wars that played such an important role in the first half of the century. Featured in Chapter 20, they grew out of Europeans' persistent inability to embody their civilization within a single state or empire, as China had long done. They also represent a further stage of European rivalries around the globe that had been going on for four centuries. Nonetheless, the world wars of the twentieth century were also new in the extent to which whole populations were mobilized to fight them and in the enormity of the destruction that they caused. During World War II, for example, Hitler's attempted extermination of the Jews in the Holocaust and the United States' dropping of atomic bombs on Japanese cities marked something new in the history of human conflict.

The communist phenomenon, examined in Chapter 21, provides another illustration of the blending of old and new. The Russian (1917) and Chinese (1949) revolutions, both of which were enormous social upheavals, brought to power regimes committed to remaking their societies from top to bottom along socialist lines. They were the first large-scale attempts in modern world history to undertake such a gigantic task, and in doing so they broke sharply with the capitalist democratic model of the West. They also created a new and global division of humankind, expressed most dramatically in the cold war between the communist East and the capitalist West. On the other hand, the communist experience also drew much from the past. The great revolutions of the twentieth century derived from long-standing conflicts within Russian and Chinese societies, particularly between impoverished and exploited peasants and dominant landlord classes. The ideology of those communist governments came from the thinking of the nineteenth-century German intellectual Karl Marx. Their intentions, like those of their capitalist enemies, were modernization and industrialization. They simply claimed to do it better—more rapidly and more justly.

Another distinguishing feature of the twentieth century lay in the disintegration of its great empires—the Austro-Hungarian, Ottoman, and Russian/Soviet empires and especially the European empires that had encompassed so much of Asia and Africa. In their wake, dozens of new nation-states emerged, fundamentally reshaping the world of this most recent century. Examined in Chapter 22, this enormous process is, at one level, simply the latest turn of the wheel in the endless rise and fall of empires, dating back to the ancient Akkadian Empire, over 4,000 years ago. But in the twentieth century, something new occurred, for the very idea of empire was rendered illegitimate, much as slavery lost its international acceptance in the nineteenth century. The superpowers of the mid-twentieth century—the Soviet Union and the United States—both claimed an anticolonial ideology, even as both of them constructed their own "empires" of a different kind. By the beginning of the twenty-first century, some 200 nation-states, many of them in the Global South and each claiming sovereignty and legal equality with all the others, provided a distinctly new political order for the planet.

The less visible underlying processes of the twentieth century, just like the more dramatic wars, revolutions, and political upheavals, also had roots in the past as well as new expressions in the new century. Feminism, for example, explored in Chapter 23, had taken root in the West during the nineteenth century but became global in the twentieth, challenging women's subordination more extensively than ever before. Perhaps the most fundamental process of the past century has been explosive population growth, as human numbers more than quadrupled since 1900, leaving the planet with over 7.2 billion people by 2014. This was an absolutely unprecedented rate of growth that conditioned practically every other feature of the century's history. Still, this new element of twentieth-century world history built on earlier achievements, most notably the increased food supply deriving from the global spread of American crops such as corn and potatoes. Improvements in medicine and sanitation, which grew out of the earlier Scientific and Industrial Revolutions, likewise drove down death rates and thus spurred population growth.

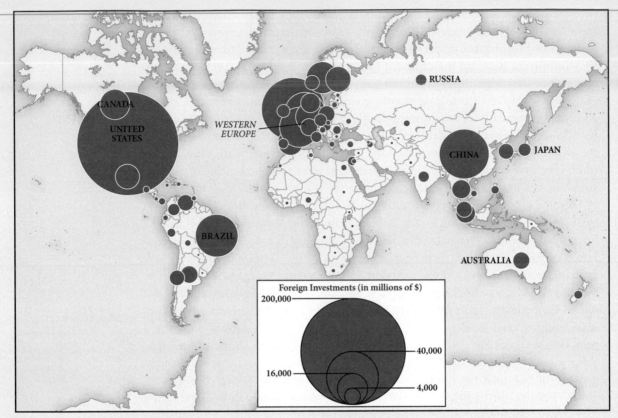

Globalization in Action: Foreign Direct Investment in the Late Twentieth Century (p. 1027)

While global population increased fourfold in the twentieth century, industrial output grew fortyfold. Despite large variations over time and place, this unprecedented economic growth was associated with a cascading rate of scientific and technological innovation as well as with the extension of industrial production to many regions of the world. This too was a wholly novel feature of twentieth-century world history and, combined with population growth, resulted in an extraordinary and mounting human impact on the environment. Historian J. R. McNeill wrote, "This is the first time in human history that we have altered ecosystems with such intensity, on such a scale, and with such speed. . . . The human race, without intending anything of the sort, has undertaken a gigantic uncontrolled experiment on the earth."[1] By the late twentieth century, that experiment had taken humankind well into what many scientists have been calling the Anthropocene, the "age of man," in which human activity is leaving an enduring and global mark on the geological, atmospheric, and biological history of the planet itself. From a longer-term perspective, of course, these developments represent a continued unfolding of the Scientific and Industrial Revolutions. Both began in Europe, but in the twentieth century they largely lost their unique association with the West as they took hold in many cultures. Furthermore, the human impact on the earth and other living creatures has a history dating back to the extinction of some large mammals at the hands of Paleolithic hunters, although the scope and extent of that impact during the past century is without precedent.

Much the same might be said about that other grand process of contemporary world history—globalization, which is the focus of Chapter 23. It too has a genealogy reaching deep into the past, reflected in the Silk Road trading network; Indian Ocean and trans-Saharan commerce; the spread of Buddhism, Christianity, and Islam; and the Columbian exchange. But the most recent century deepened and extended the connections among the distinct peoples, nations, and regions of the world in ways unparalleled in earlier times. A few strokes on a keyboard can send money racing around the planet; radio, television, and the Internet link the world in an unprecedented network of communication; far more people than ever before produce for and depend on the world market; and global inequalities increasingly surface as sources of international conflict. For good or ill, we live—all of us—in a new phase of an ancient process.

The four chapters of Part Six explore these global themes that have so decisively shaped the history of the past century. Perhaps there is enough that is new about that century to treat it, tentatively, as a distinct era in human history, but only what happens next will determine how this period will be understood by later generations. Will it be regarded as the beginning of the end of the modern age, as human demands on the earth prove unsustainable? Or will it be seen as the midpoint of an ongoing process that extends a full modernity to the entire planet? Will recognition of our common fate as human beings generate shared values, a culture of tolerance, and an easing of international tensions? Or will global inequalities and rivalry over diminishing resources foster even greater and more dangerous conflicts? Like all of our ancestors, every one of them, we too live in a fog when contemplating our futures and see more clearly only in retrospect. In this strange way, our future will shape the telling of the past, even as the past shapes the living of the future.

Landmarks in World History (ca. 1900–present)

	1910	1920	1930	1940	1950	1960

THE WESTERN/DEVELOPED WORLD

1914–1918
World War I

1929
Great Depression begins

1933
Nazis come to
power in Germany

1937
Japan invades China; start
of World War II in Asia

1939–1945
World War II;
Holocaust in Europe

1945
U.S. drops atomic
bombs on Hiroshima
and Nagasaki

1957
European Economic
Community
established

1962
Rachel Carson's
Silent Spring
launches
environmental
movement

THE COMMUNIST WORLD

1917
Russian Revolution

1921
Founding
of Chinese
Communist
Party

1929–1953
Stalin era in Soviet Union

1945–1950
Communist takeover
in Eastern Europe

1949
Communist triumph in
Chinese revolution

1950–1953
Korean War

1959–1962
Cuban Revolution;
Cuban missile crisis

THE GLOBAL SOUTH / DEVELOPING WORLD

1910–1920
Mexican Revolution

1923–1938
Turkey's secular modernization;
Kemal Atatürk

1928
Muslim Brotherhood
established in Egypt

1947–1949
Independence of
India, Pakistan,
Israel, Indonesia

1957–1975
African independence
achieved

THE WHOLE WORLD (MARKERS OF GLOBALIZATION)

1920–1946
League of Nations

1945
Founding of United
Nations, World Bank, and
International Monetary Fund

1960
Organization
of Petroleum
Exporting Countries
established

1946–1991
Cold war

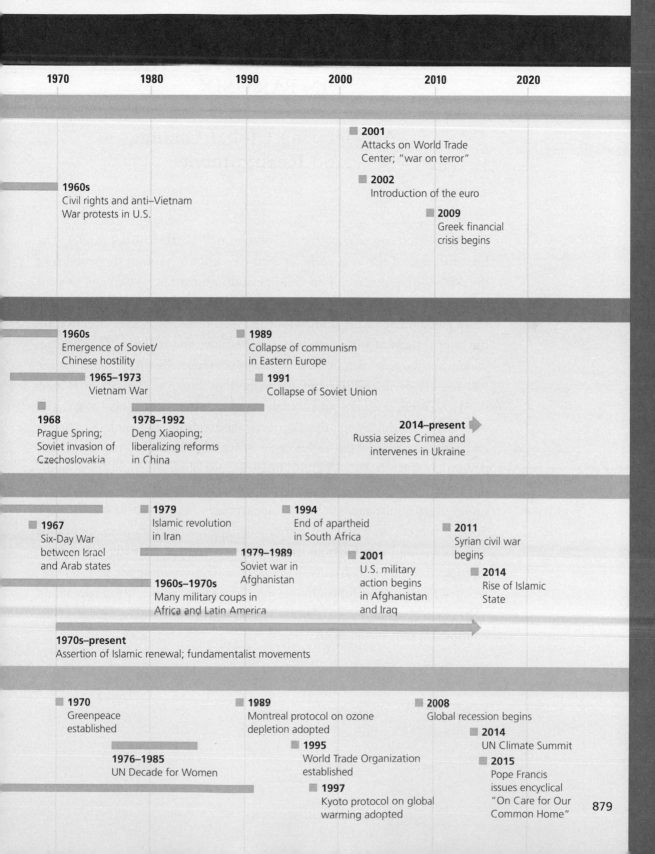

1970　　1980　　1990　　2000　　2010　　2020

2001
Attacks on World Trade
Center; "war on terror"

2002
Introduction of the euro

2009
Greek financial
crisis begins

1960s
Civil rights and anti–Vietnam
War protests in U.S.

1960s
Emergence of Soviet/
Chinese hostility

1965–1973
Vietnam War

1968
Prague Spring;
Soviet invasion of
Czechoslovakia

1978–1992
Deng Xiaoping;
liberalizing reforms
in China

1989
Collapse of communism
in Eastern Europe

1991
Collapse of Soviet Union

2014–present
Russia seizes Crimea and
intervenes in Ukraine

1967
Six-Day War
between Israel
and Arab states

1979
Islamic revolution
in Iran

1979–1989
Soviet war in
Afghanistan

1960s–1970s
Many military coups in
Africa and Latin America

1994
End of apartheid
in South Africa

2001
U.S. military
action begins
in Afghanistan
and Iraq

2011
Syrian civil war
begins

2014
Rise of Islamic
State

1970s–present
Assertion of Islamic renewal; fundamentalist movements

1970
Greenpeace
established

1976–1985
UN Decade for Women

1989
Montreal protocol on ozone
depletion adopted

1995
World Trade Organization
established

1997
Kyoto protocol on global
warming adopted

2008
Global recession begins

2014
UN Climate Summit

2015
Pope Francis
issues encyclical
"On Care for Our
Common Home"

879

UNDERSTANDING AP® THEMES
IN PART SIX

Accelerating Global Change
and Realignment

Congratulations on nearing the end of your AP® World History studies. The final chapters of this text make up Part Six and correspond to Period 6 of the AP® course outline. This time period constitutes 20 percent of your AP® exam.

In every phase of the human journey, world history focuses attention on the intersections of various peoples, civilizations, and societies. That process, widely known now as globalization, has been especially prominent over the past century or so and is therefore the guiding theme of Part Six of *Ways of the World*. Wars, both hot and cold, have taken shape on a global stage. The emergence of dozens of new nations, arising from the end of empires, emphatically changed the architecture of world politics. Modern economic development has become a global quest; industrialization and its profoundly disruptive environmental impact likewise operated globally even as the economies of particular nations became inextricably connected to one another. Social, cultural, and political movements such as communism, feminism, nationalism, and religious fundamentalism assumed worldwide dimensions, crossing national or civilizational boundaries. To paraphrase the seventeenth-century English poet John Donne, more than ever before in human affairs, "No man or woman is an island, entire of itself; everyone is a piece of the continent, a part of the main."

Environment	Cultures	State Building	Economies	Social Structures
Early environmental movements in the 19th and early 20th centuries	Fascist ideology	World Wars I and II	Great Depression in • Europe • United States • The colonies • Latin America • Japan	Social outcomes of world wars in the West
Entering the Anthropocene era: global environmental transformations in the 20th century	Anti-Semitism and the Holocaust	Authoritarian states: comparing Italy, Germany, and Japan		Class, gender, and fascism
	Japanese nationalist ideology	League of Nations and United Nations	Fascist economic policies	Class and gender issues in prewar Japan
Nuclear weapons and the environment	Communism as ideology	Revolutions: comparing Russia and China	Marshall Plan; recovery of Europe	Social transformation in communist revolutions
Environmental issues after collapse of USSR	Islam and modernity: westernization in Turkey and Islamic renewal in Iran	Constructing the Soviet state	Communist industrial development	Urbanization and elite privilege in the USSR
Climate change / global warming: origins and outcomes	Religion and politics in India	The cold war	Collectivization of agriculture in USSR and China	Effects of bureaucracy and inequality in Mao's China
	Critique of capitalist globalization emerges	Economic reforms in communist China	Muslim Brotherhood: goals and outcomes	Communist feminism
Second-wave environmentalism • In the West • Role of Rachel Carson • In the communist world • In the Global South • North/South conflict about environmental issues	Global culture of liberation	End of communism in Eastern Europe	Economic development in the Global South: problems, policies, and varying outcomes	Women and Islam: ex.. Turkey, Iran, Morocco, Pakistan
	Western feminism	Collapse of the Soviet Union		Searching for enemies in USSR and China
	Feminism in the Global South	Decolonization in Asia and Africa: comparing India and South Africa	Economic globalization since the 1980s: growth, instability, and inequality	Global population growth and patterns of migration
	Religious fundamentalism: Christian, Hindu, and Islamic	Political variations in the Global South • Democracy in India • Military rule in Africa and Latin America • Communist states in China, Vietnam, Cuba	Globalization of industrialization in the 20th century	Ethnicity and political conflict in the developing countries
	Islamic radicalism: growth, expressions, impact		Debating an American empire	
	Religious alternatives to fundamentalism	Globalization of democracy in the late 20th century		

1778 1943

AMERICANS
will <u>always</u> fight for liberty

CHAPTER 20

Collapse at the Center

World War, Depression, and the Rebalancing of Global Power

1900–1970s

"I was told that I was fighting a war that would end all wars, but that wasn't the case." Spoken a few years before his death, these were the thoughts of Alfred Anderson, a World War I veteran who died in Scotland in November 2005, at the age of 109. He was apparently the last survivor of the famous Christmas truce of 1914, when British and German soldiers, enemies on the battlefield of that war, briefly mingled, exchanged gifts, and played football in the no-man's-land that lay between their entrenchments in Belgium. He had been especially dismayed when in 2003 his own unit, the famous Black Watch regiment, was ordered into Iraq along with other British forces.[1] Despite his disappointment at the many conflicts that followed World War I, Anderson's own lifetime had witnessed the fulfillment of the promise of the Christmas truce. By the time he died, the major European nations had put aside their centuries-long hostilities, and war between Britain and Germany, which had erupted twice in the twentieth century, seemed unthinkable.

The "Great War," which came to be called the First World War or World War I (1914–1918), effectively launched the twentieth century, considered as a new phase of world history. That bitter conflict — essentially a European civil war with a global reach — provoked the Russian Revolution and the beginnings of world communism. It was followed by the economic meltdown of the Great Depression, by the rise of Nazi Germany and the horror of the Holocaust, and by World War II, an even bloodier and more destructive struggle that encompassed much of the world. During those three decades, Western Europe—for more than a century

The United States and World War II The Second World War and its aftermath marked the decisive emergence of the United States as a global superpower. In this official 1943 poster, U.S. soldiers march forward to "fight for liberty" against fascism while casting a sideways glance for inspiration at the ragged colonial militiamen of their Revolutionary War.

the dominant and dominating center of the modern "world system"—largely self-destructed, in a process with profound and long-term implications far beyond Europe itself. By 1945, an outside observer might well have thought that Western civilization, which for several centuries was in the ascendancy on the global stage, had damaged itself beyond repair. Certainly, the subsequent emergence of the United States and the Soviet Union as rival superpowers marked a very different balance of global power.

In the second half of the century, however, European civilization proved resilient. Western Europe recovered remarkably from the devastation of war, rebuilt its industrial economy, and set aside its war-prone nationalist passions in a loose European Union. But as Europe revived after 1945, it lost both its overseas colonial possessions and its position as the political, economic, and military core of Western civilization. That role now passed across the Atlantic to the United States, marking a major change in the historical development of the West. The offspring now overshadowed its parent.

The First World War: European Civilization in Crisis, 1914–1918

Since 1500, Europe had assumed an increasingly prominent position on the global stage, driven by its growing military capacity and the marvels of its Scientific and Industrial Revolutions. By 1900, Europeans, or people with European ancestry, largely controlled the world's other peoples through their formal empires, their informal influence, or the weight of their numbers (see Map 20.1). That unique situation provided the foundation for Europeans' pride, self-confidence, and sense of superiority. Few could have imagined that this "proud tower" of European dominance would lie shattered less than a half century later. The starting point in that unraveling was the First World War.

An Accident Waiting to Happen

Europe's modern transformation and its global ascendancy were certainly not accompanied by a growing unity or stability among its own peoples—quite the opposite. The most obvious division was among its competing states, a long-standing feature of European political life. Those historical rivalries further sharpened as both Italy and Germany joined their fragmented territories into two major new powers around 1870. The arrival on the international scene of a powerful and rapidly industrializing Germany, seeking its "place in the sun," was a disruptive new element in European political life, especially for the more established powers, such as Britain, France, and Russia. Since the defeat of Napoleon in 1815, a fragile and fluctuating balance of power had generally maintained the peace among Europe's

A MAP OF TIME

1914–1918	World War I
1917	Bolshevik Revolution in Russia; United States enters World War I
1919	Treaty of Versailles ending World War I; founding of Nazi Party
1920	Treaty of Sèvres, dissolving the Ottoman Empire
1922	Mussolini comes to power in Italy
1929	Beginning of Great Depression
1933	Hitler assumes power in Germany
1937–1938	Japan invades China, beginning World War II in Asia; Rape of Nanjing
1939	Germany invades Poland, beginning World War II in Europe
1939–1945	World War II; the Holocaust
1941	Japanese attack on Pearl Harbor
1945	Atomic bombing of Hiroshima and Nagasaki; United Nations created
1945–1952	U.S. occupation of Japan
1946–1991	Cold war
1948–1952	Marshall Plan for Europe
1957	European Economic Community established
1994	European Union established
2002	Introduction of the euro

major countries. By the early twentieth century, that balance of power was expressed in two rival alliances, the Triple Alliance of Germany, Italy, and the Austro-Hungarian Empire and the Triple Entente of Russia, France, and Britain. Those commitments, undertaken in the interests of national security, transformed a relatively minor incident in the Balkans into a conflagration that consumed almost all of Europe.

That incident occurred on June 28, 1914, when a Serbian nationalist assassinated the heir to the Austro-Hungarian throne, Archduke Franz Ferdinand. To the rulers of Austria-Hungary, the surging nationalism of Serbian Slavs was a mortal threat to the cohesion of their fragile multinational empire, which included other Slavic peoples as well. Thus they determined to crush it. But behind Austria-Hungary lay its far more powerful ally, Germany, and behind tiny Serbia lay Russia, with its self-proclaimed mission of protecting other Slavic peoples. Allied to Russia were

Map 20.1   The World in 1914

A map of the world in 1914 shows an unprecedented situation in which one people—Europeans or those of European descent—exercised enormous control and influence over virtually the entire planet.

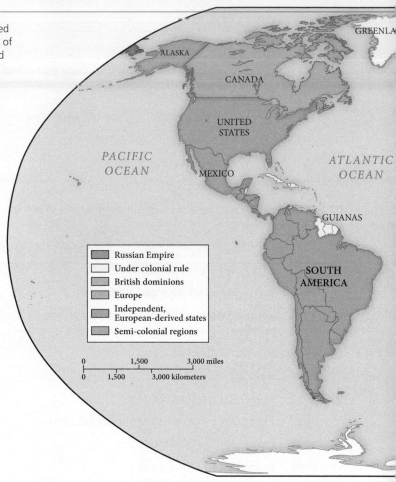

Russian Empire
Under colonial rule
British dominions
Europe
Independent, European-derived states
Semi-colonial regions

Guided Reading Question

■ EXPLANATION

What aspects of Europe's nineteenth-century history contributed to the First World War?

AP® EXAM TIP

Keep a record of common factors that led to the three twentieth-century global wars.

the French and the British. Thus a system of alliances intended to keep the peace created obligations that drew the Great Powers of Europe into a general war by early August 1914 (see Map 20.2).

The outbreak of that war was something of an accident, in that none of the major states planned or predicted the archduke's assassination or deliberately sought a prolonged conflict, but the system of rigid alliances made Europe vulnerable to that kind of accident. Moreover, behind those alliances lay other factors that contributed to the eruption of war and shaped its character. One of them was a mounting popular nationalism (see Chapter 18, pages 790–92). Slavic nationalism and Austro-Hungarian opposition to it certainly lay at the heart of the war's beginning. More importantly, the rulers of the major countries of Europe saw the world as an arena of conflict and competition among rival nation-states. The Great Powers of Europe competed intensely for colonies, spheres of influence, and superiority in armaments. Schools, mass media, and military service had convinced millions of

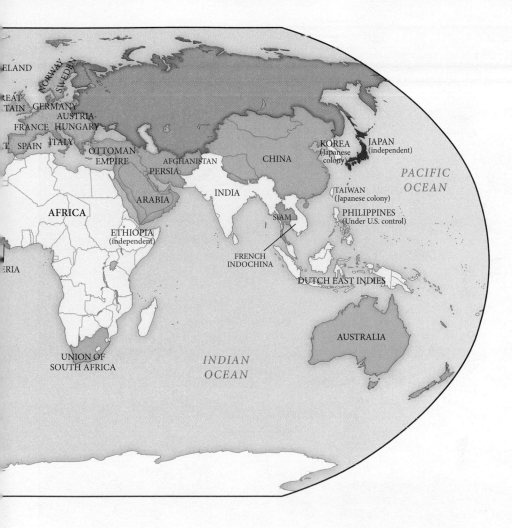

ordinary Europeans that their national identities were profoundly and personally meaningful. The public pressure of these competing nationalisms allowed states-men little room for compromise and ensured widespread popular support, at least initially, for the decision to go to war. Many men rushed to recruiting offices, fear-ing that the war might end before they could enlist. Celebratory parades sent them off to the front. British women were encouraged to present a white feather, a sym-bol of cowardice, to men not in uniform, thus affirming a warrior understanding of masculinity. For conservative governments, the prospect of war was a welcome occasion for national unity in the face of the mounting class- and gender-based conflicts in European societies.

Also contributing to the war was an industrialized militarism. Europe's armed rivalries had long ensured that military men enjoyed great social prestige, and most heads of state wore uniforms in public. All the Great Powers had substantial standing armies and, except for Britain, relied on conscription (compulsory military service)

Map 20.2   Europe on the Eve of World War I

Despite many elements of common culture, Europe in 1914 was a powder keg, with its major states armed to the teeth and divided into two rival alliances. In the early stages of the war, Italy changed sides to join the French, British, and Russians.

to staff them. One expression of the quickening rivalry among these states was a mounting arms race in naval warships, particularly between Germany and Britain. Furthermore, each of the major states had developed elaborate "war plans" that spelled out in great detail the movement of men and materials that should occur immediately upon the outbreak of war. Such plans created a hair-trigger mentality since each country had an incentive to strike first so that its particular strategy could be implemented on schedule and without interruption or surprise. The rapid industrialization of warfare had generated an array of novel weapons, including submarines, tanks, airplanes, poison gas, machine guns, and barbed wire. This new military technology contributed to the staggering casualties of the war, including some 10 million deaths, the vast majority male; perhaps twice that number were wounded, crippled, or disfigured. For countless women, as a result, there would be no husbands or children.

Europe's imperial reach around the world likewise shaped the scope and conduct of the war. It funneled colonial troops and laborers by the hundreds of thousands into the war effort, with men from Africa, India, China, Southeast Asia, Australia, New Zealand, Canada, and South Africa taking part in the conflict. Battles raged in Africa and the South Pacific as British and French forces sought to seize German colonies abroad. Japan, allied with Britain, took various German possessions in China and the Pacific and made heavy demands on China itself. The Ottoman Empire, which entered the conflict on the side of Germany, became the site of intense military actions and witnessed an Arab revolt against Ottoman control. Finally, the United States, after initially seeking to avoid involvement in European quarrels, joined the war in 1917 when German submarines threatened American shipping. Some 2 million Americans took part in the first U.S. military action on European soil and helped turn the tide in favor of the British and French. Thus the war, though centered in Europe, had global dimensions and certainly merited its title as a "world war."

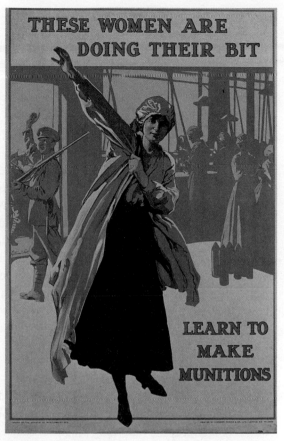

Women and the Great War

World War I temporarily brought a halt to the women's suffrage movement as well as to women's activities on behalf of international peace. Most women on both sides actively supported their countries' war efforts, as suggested by this British wartime poster, inviting women to work in the munitions industry. (Eileen Tweedy/The Art Archive at Art Resource, NY)

Legacies of the Great War

The Great War shattered almost every expectation. Most Europeans believed in the late summer of 1914 that "the boys will be home by Christmas," but instead the war ground relentlessly on for more than four years before ending in a German defeat in November 1918. At the beginning, most military experts expected a war of movement and attack, but armies on the western front soon became bogged down in a war of attrition; combatants engaging in trench warfare experienced enormous casualties while gaining or losing only a few yards of muddy, blood-soaked ground. Extended battles lasting months—such as those at Verdun and the Somme in France—generated casualties of a million or more each, as the destructive potential of industrialized warfare made itself tragically felt. Moreover, everywhere the conflict became a "total war," requiring the mobilization of each country's entire population. Thus the authority of governments expanded greatly. The German state, for example, assumed such control over the economy that its policies became known as "war socialism." Vast propaganda campaigns sought to arouse citizens by depicting a cruel and inhuman enemy who killed innocent children and violated women. Labor unions agreed to suspend strikes and accept sacrifices for the common good, while women, replacing the men who had left the factories for the battlefront, temporarily abandoned the struggle for the vote.

No less surprising were the longer-term outcomes of the war. In the European cockpit of that conflict, unprecedented casualties, particularly among elite and well-educated groups, and physical destruction, especially in France, led to a widespread disillusionment among intellectuals with their own civilization. The war seemed to mock the Enlightenment values of progress, tolerance, and rationality. Who could believe any longer that the West was superior or that its vaunted science and technology were unquestionably good things? In the most famous novel to emerge from the war, the German veteran Erich Maria Remarque's *All Quiet on the Western Front*, one soldier expressed what many no doubt felt: "It must all be lies and of no account when the culture of a thousand years could not prevent this stream of blood being poured out."

The aftermath of war also brought substantial social and cultural changes to ordinary Europeans and Americans. Integrating millions of returning veterans into civilian life was no easy task, for they had experienced horrors almost beyond imagination. Governments sought to accommodate them, in Britain for example, with housing programs called "homes for heroes" emphasizing traditional family values. Women were urged to leave factory work and return to their homes, where they would not compete for "men's jobs." French authorities proclaimed Mother's Day as a new holiday, designed to encourage childbearing and thus replace the millions lost in the war.

Nonetheless, the war had loosened the hold of tradition in various ways. Enormous casualties promoted social mobility, allowing the less exalted to move into positions previously dominated by the upper classes. As the war ended, suffrage movements revived and women received the right to vote in a number of countries—Britain, the United States, Germany, the Soviet Union, Hungary, and Poland—in part perhaps because of the sacrifices they had made during the conflict. Young middle-class women, sometimes known as "flappers," began to flout convention by smoking, dancing, appearing at nightclubs, drinking hard liquor, cutting their hair short, wearing revealing clothing, and generally expressing a more open sexuality. A new consumerism encouraged those who could to acquire cars, washing machines, vacuum cleaners, electric irons, gas ovens, and other newly available products. Radio and the movies now became vehicles of popular culture, transmitting American jazz to Europe and turning Hollywood stars into international celebrities.

Guided Reading Question

■ CHANGE

In what ways did World War I mark new departures in the history of the twentieth century?

AP® EXAM TIP

It is important to remember that the causes and effects of wars are more important than the battles.

Map 20.3   Europe and the Middle East after World War I

The Great War brought into existence a number of new states that were carved out of the old German, Austro-Hungarian, Russian, and Ottoman empires. Turkey and the new states in Europe were independent, but those in the Middle East—Syria, Palestine, Iraq, and Transjordan—were administered by Britain or France as mandates of the League of Nations.

The war also transformed international political life. From the collapse of the German, Russian, and Austro-Hungarian empires emerged a new map of Central Europe with an independent Poland, Czechoslovakia, Hungary, and Yugoslavia as well as other newly independent nations (see Map 20.3). Such new states were based on the principle of "national self-determination," a concept championed by

AP® EXAM TIP

Refer back to the changes seen in this post–World War I map when you study the political causes of World War II.

U.S. president Woodrow Wilson, but each of them also contained dissatisfied ethnic minorities, who claimed the same principle. In Russia, the strains of war triggered a vast revolutionary upheaval that brought the radical Bolsheviks to power
in 1917 and took Russia out of the war. Thus was launched world communism,
which was to play such a prominent role in the history of the twentieth century
(see Chapter 21).

The Treaty of Versailles, which formally concluded the war in 1919, proved in
retrospect to have established conditions that contributed to a second world war
only twenty years later. In that treaty, Germany lost its colonial empire and 15
percent of its European territory, was required to pay heavy reparations to the winners, had its military forces severely restricted, and was required to accept sole
responsibility for the outbreak of the war. All of this created immense resentment
in Germany. One of the country's many demobilized and disillusioned soldiers
declared in 1922: "It cannot be that two million Germans should have fallen in
vain. . . . No, we do not pardon, we demand—vengeance."[2] His name was Adolf
Hitler, and within two decades he had begun to exact that vengeance.

The Great War generated profound changes in the world beyond Europe as
well. During the conflict, Ottoman authorities, suspecting that some of their Armenian subjects were collaborating with the Russian enemy, massacred or deported
an estimated 1 million Armenians. Although the term "genocide" had not yet been
invented, some historians have applied it to those atrocities, arguing that they
established a precedent on which the Nazis later built. The war also brought a final
end to a declining Ottoman Empire, creating the modern map of the Middle East,
with the new states of Turkey, Syria, Iraq, Transjordan, and Palestine. Thus Arabs
emerged from Turkish rule, but many of them were governed for a time by the
British or French, as "mandates" of the League of Nations (see Map 20.3). Conflicting British promises to both Arabs and Jews regarding Palestine set the stage for
an enduring struggle over that ancient and holy land. Although Latin American
countries remained bystanders in the war, many of them benefited from the growing demand for their primary products such as Chilean nitrates, used in explosives.
But the sharp drop in nitrate exports after the war ended brought to Chile mass
unemployment, urban riots, bloody strikes, and some appeal for the newly established Chilean Communist Party.

In the world of European colonies, the war echoed loudly. Millions of Asian
and African men had watched Europeans butcher one another without mercy, had
gained new military skills and political awareness, and returned home with less
respect for their rulers and with expectations for better treatment as a reward for
their service. To gain Indian support for the war, the British had publicly promised to put that colony on the road to self-government, an announcement that set
the stage for the independence struggle that followed. In East Asia, Japan emerged
strengthened from the war, with European support for its claim to take over German territory and privileges in China. That news enraged Chinese nationalists and
among a few sparked an interest in Soviet-style communism, for only the new

communist rulers of Russia seemed willing to end the imperialist penetration of China.

Finally, the First World War brought the United States to center stage as a global power. Its manpower had contributed much to the defeat of Germany, and its financial resources turned the United States from a debtor nation into Europe's creditor. When the American president Woodrow Wilson arrived in Paris for the peace conference in 1919, he was greeted with an almost religious enthusiasm. His famous Fourteen Points seemed to herald a new kind of international life, one based on moral principles rather than secret deals and imperialist machinations. Particularly appealing to many was his idea for the League of Nations, a new international peacekeeping organization committed to the principle of "collective security" and intended to avoid any repetition of the horrors that had just ended. Wilson's idealistic vision largely failed, however. Germany was treated more harshly than he had wished. And in his own country, the U.S. Senate refused to join the League, on which Wilson had pinned his hopes for a lasting peace. Its opponents feared that Americans would be forced to bow to "the will of other nations." That refusal seriously weakened the League of Nations as a vehicle for a new international order.

Capitalism Unraveling: The Great Depression

Far and away the most influential change of the postwar decades lay in the Great Depression. If World War I represented the political collapse of Europe, this catastrophic downturn suggested that Western capitalism was likewise failing. During the nineteenth century, that economic system had spurred the most substantial economic growth in world history and had raised the living standards of millions, but to many people it was a troubling system. Its very success generated an individualistic materialism that seemed to conflict with older values of community and spiritual life. To socialists and many others, its immense social inequalities were unacceptable. Furthermore, its evident instability—with cycles of boom and bust, expansion and recession—generated profound anxiety and threatened the livelihood of both industrial workers and those who had gained a modest toehold in the middle class.

Never had the flaws of capitalism been so evident or so devastating as during the decade that followed the outbreak of the Great Depression in 1929. All across the Euro-American heartland of the capitalist world, this vaunted economic system seemed to unravel. For the rich, it meant contracting stock prices that wiped out paper fortunes almost overnight. On the day that the American stock market initially crashed (October 24, 1929), eleven Wall Street financiers committed suicide, some jumping out of skyscrapers. Banks closed, and many people lost their life savings. Investment dried up, world trade dropped by 62 percent within a few years, and businesses contracted when they were unable to sell their products. For ordinary people, the worst feature of the Great Depression was the loss of work.

AP® EXAM TIP

Political responses to the Great Depression around the world are "must know" information for the AP® exam.

Guided Reading Question

■ CONNECTION
In what ways was the Great Depression a global phenomenon?

SNAPSHOT   Comparing the Impact of the Depression

As industrial production dropped during the Depression, unemployment soared.[3] Yet the larger Western capitalist countries differed considerably in the duration and extent of this unemployment. Note especially the differences between Germany and the United States. How might you account for this difference?

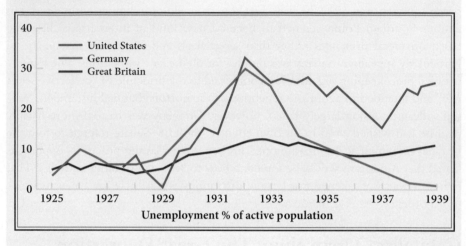

Unemployment soared everywhere, and in both Germany and the United States it reached 30 percent or more by 1932. (See Snapshot, above.) Beggars, soup kitchens, breadlines, shantytowns, and vacant factories came to symbolize the human reality of this economic disaster.

Explaining its onset, its spread from America to Europe and beyond, and its continuation for a decade has been a complicated task for historians. Part of the story lies in the United States' booming economy during the 1920s. In a country physically untouched by the Great War, wartime demand had greatly stimulated agricultural and industrial capacity. By the end of the 1920s, its farms and factories were producing more goods than could be sold because a highly unequal distribution of income meant that many people could not afford to buy the products that American factories were churning out. Nor were major European countries able to purchase those goods. Germany and Austria had to make huge reparation payments and were able to do so only with extensive U.S. loans. Britain and France, which were much indebted to the United States, depended on those reparations to repay their loans. Furthermore, Europeans generally had recovered enough to begin producing some of their own goods, and their expanding production further reduced the demand for American products. Meanwhile, a speculative stock market frenzy had driven up stock prices to an unsustainable level. When that bubble burst in late 1929, this intricately connected and fragile economic network across the Atlantic collapsed like a house of cards.

Much as Europe's worldwide empires had globalized the Great War, its economic linkages globalized the Great Depression. Countries or colonies tied to exporting one or two products were especially hard-hit. Colonial Southeast Asia, the world's major rubber-producing region, saw the demand for its primary export drop dramatically as automobile sales in Europe and the United States were cut in half. In Britain's West African colony of the Gold Coast (present-day Ghana), farmers who had staked their economic lives on producing cocoa for the world market were badly hurt by the collapse of commodity prices. Latin American countries, whose economies were based on the export of agricultural products and raw materials, were also vulnerable to major fluctuations in the world market. The region as a whole saw the value of its exports cut by half during the Great Depression. In an effort to maintain the price of coffee, Brazil destroyed enough of its crop to have supplied the world for a year. Such conditions led to widespread unemployment and social tensions.

Those tensions of the Depression era often found political expression in Latin America in the form of a military takeover of the state. Such governments sought to steer their countries away from an earlier dependence on exports toward a policy of generating their own industries. Known as import substitution industrialization, such policies hoped to achieve greater economic independence by manufacturing for the domestic market goods that had previously been imported. These efforts were accompanied by more authoritarian and intrusive governments that played a greater role in the economy by enacting tariffs, setting up state-run industries, and favoring local businesses. They often adopted a highly nationalist and populist posture as they sought to extricate themselves from economic domination by the United States and Europe and to respond to the growing urban classes of workers and entrepreneurs.

In Brazil, for example, the Depression discredited the established export elites such as coffee growers and led to the dictatorship of Getúlio Vargas (r. 1930–1945). Supported by the military, his government took steps to modernize the urban industrial sector of the economy, including a state enterprise to manufacture trucks and airplane engines and regulations that gave the state considerable power over both unions and employers. But little was done to alleviate rural poverty. In Mexico, the Depression opened the way to a revival of the principles of the Mexican Revolution under the leadership of Lázaro Cárdenas (r. 1934–1940). He pushed land reform, favored Mexican workers against foreign interests, and nationalized an oil industry dominated by American capital.

These were but two cases of the many political and economic changes stimulated in Latin America by the Great Depression. Many of those changes—the growing role of the army in politics; authoritarian, populist, and interventionist governments; import substitution industrialization; and the assumption that governments should improve economic life—persisted in the decades that followed.

The Great Depression also sharply challenged the governments of industrialized capitalist countries, which generally had believed that the economy would regulate

Contrasts of the Great Depression

This 1937 *Life* magazine image by famed photographer Margaret Bourke-White shows black victims of a flood in Louisville, Kentucky, standing in a breadline during the Depression while behind them rises a billboard of a happy and prosperous white family. (Margaret Bourke-White/Time & Life Pictures/Getty Images)

itself through the market. The market's apparent failure to self-correct led many people to look twice at the Soviet Union, the communist state that grew out of the Russian Revolution and encompassed much of the territory of the old Russian Empire (see Chapter 13, pages 572–77). There, the dispossession of the propertied classes and a state-controlled economy had generated an impressive economic growth with almost no unemployment in the 1930s, even as the capitalist world was reeling. No Western country opted for the dictatorial and draconian socialism of the Soviet Union, but in Britain, France, and Scandinavia the Depression energized a "democratic socialism" that sought greater regulation of the economy and a more equal distribution of wealth through peaceful means and electoral politics.

The United States' response to the Great Depression came in the form of President Franklin Roosevelt's New Deal (1933–1942), an experimental combination of reforms seeking to restart economic growth and to prevent similar calamities in the future. These measures reflected the thinking of John Maynard Keynes, a prominent British economist who argued that government actions and spending programs could moderate the recessions and depressions to which capitalist economies were prone. Although this represented a departure from standard economic thinking, none of it was really "socialist," even if some of the New Deal's opponents labeled it as such. Keynes's ideas became capitalist economic orthodoxy in the postwar era.

Nonetheless, Roosevelt's efforts permanently altered the relationship among government, the private economy, and individual citizens. Through immediate programs of public spending (for dams, highways, bridges, and parks), the New Deal sought to prime the pump of the economy and thus reduce unemployment. The New Deal's longer-term reforms, such as the Social Security system, the minimum wage, and various relief and welfare programs, attempted to create a modest economic safety net to sustain the poor, the unemployed, and the elderly. By supporting labor unions, the New Deal strengthened workers in their struggles with business owners or managers. Subsidies for farmers gave rise to a permanent agribusiness that encouraged continued production even as prices fell. Finally, a mounting number of government agencies marked a new degree of federal regulation and supervision of the economy.

Ultimately, none of the New Deal's programs worked very well to end the Great Depression. Not until the massive government spending required by World War II kicked in did that economic disaster abate in the United States. The most successful efforts to cope with the Depression came from unlikely places—Nazi Germany and an increasingly militaristic Japan.

Democracy Denied: Comparing Italy, Germany, and Japan

Despite the victory of the democratic powers in World War I—Britain, France, and the United States—their democratic political ideals and their cultural values celebrating individual freedom came under sharp attack in the aftermath of that bloody conflict. One challenge derived from communism, which was initiated in the Russian Revolution of 1917 and expressed most fully in the cold war during the second half of the twentieth century (see Chapter 21). In the 1920s and 1930s, however, the more immediate challenge to the victors in the Great War came from highly authoritarian, intensely nationalistic, territorially aggressive, and ferociously anticommunist regimes, particularly those that took shape in Italy, Germany, and Japan. (See Working with Evidence: Ideologies of the Axis Powers, page 922, for the ideas underlying these regimes.) Such common features of these three countries drew them together by 1936–1937 in a political alliance directed against the Soviet Union and international communism. In 1940, they solidified their relationship in a formal military alliance, creating the so-called Axis powers. Within this alliance, Germany and Japan clearly stand out, though in quite different ways, in terms of their impact on the larger patterns of world history, for it was their efforts to "establish and maintain a new order of things," as the Axis Pact put it, that generated the Second World War both in East Asia and in Europe.

The Fascist Alternative in Europe

Between 1919 and 1945, a new political ideology, known as fascism, found expression across much of Europe. At the level of ideas, fascism was intensely nationalistic, seeking to revitalize and purify the nation and to mobilize its people for some grand task. Its spokesmen praised violence against enemies as a renewing force in society, celebrated action rather than reflection, and placed their faith in a charismatic leader. Fascists also bitterly condemned individualism, liberalism, feminism, parliamentary democracy, and communism, all of which, they argued, divided and weakened the nation. In their determination to overthrow existing regimes, they were revolutionary; in their embrace of traditional values and their opposition to much of modern life, however, they were conservative or reactionary.

Such ideas appealed to aggrieved people all across the social spectrum. In the devastation that followed the First World War, the numbers of such people grew substantially. In the aftermath of the Russian Revolution of 1917, some among the middle and upper classes felt the rise of socialism and communism as a dire threat; small-scale merchants, artisans, and farmers feared the loss of their independence to either big business or socialist revolution; demobilized soldiers had few prospects and nursed many resentments; and intellectuals were appalled by the materialism and artificiality of modern life. Such people had lost faith in the capacity of liberal democracy and capitalism to create a good society and to protect their interests. Some among them proved a receptive audience for the message of fascism.

Small fascist movements appeared in many Western European countries, including France, Great Britain, and the Netherlands, but they had little political impact. More substantial movements took shape in Austria, Hungary, and Romania. In Spain, the rise of a fascist movement led to a bitter civil war (1936–1939) and a dictatorial regime that lasted into the 1970s. Conservative and authoritarian regimes or social movements in Latin America sometimes adopted the trappings of fascism—one-man rule, state-controlled parties, youth organizations or militias, a rhetoric of national renewal, anti-Semitic measures—though without implementing its more revolutionary features. But in Italy and Germany, such movements achieved prolonged power in major states, with devastating consequences for Europe and the world.

The fascist alternative took shape first in Italy. That nation had become a unified state only in 1870 and had not yet developed a modern and thoroughly democratic culture. In the early twentieth century, conservative landlords still dominated much of the countryside. Northern Italy, however, had begun to industrialize in the late nineteenth century, generating the characteristic tension between an industrial working class and a substantial middle class. The First World War gave rise to resentful veterans, many of them unemployed, and to patriots who believed that Italy had not gained the territory it deserved from the Treaty of Versailles. During the serious economic downturn after World War I, trade unions, peasant movements, and various communist and socialist parties threatened the established social order with a wave of strikes and land seizures.

Guided Reading Question

■ CHANGE
In what ways did fascism challenge the ideas and practices of European liberalism and democracy?

Into this setting stepped a charismatic orator and a former journalist with a socialist background, Benito Mussolini (1883–1945). With the help of a private army of disillusioned veterans and jobless men known as the Black Shirts, Mussolini swept to power in 1922, promising an alternative to both communism and ineffective democratic rule. Considerable violence accompanied Mussolini's rise to power as bands of Black Shirts destroyed the offices of socialist newspapers and attacked striking workers. Fearful of communism, big business threw its support to Mussolini, who promised order in the streets, an end to bickering party-based politics, and the maintenance of the traditional social order. That Mussolini's government allegedly made the trains run on time became evidence that these promises might be fulfilled. The symbol of this movement was the *fasces*, a bundle of birch rods bound together around an axe, which represented power and strength in unity and derived from ancient Rome. Thus fascism was born.

In Mussolini's thinking, fascism was resolutely anticommunist—he called it "the complete opposite . . . of Marxian socialism"—and equally antidemocratic. "Fascism combats the whole complex system of democratic ideology, and repudiates it," he wrote. At the core of Mussolini's fascism was his conception of the state. "Fascism conceives of the State as an absolute, in comparison with which all individuals and groups are relative, only to be conceived of in their relation to the State." To Mussolini, the state was a conscious entity with "a will and a personality," which represented the "spirit of the nation." Its expansion in war and empire building was "an essential manifestation of vitality."[4]

The Faces of European Fascism
Benito Mussolini (left) and Adolf Hitler came to symbolize fascism in Europe in the several decades between the two world wars. In this photograph from September 1937, they are reviewing German troops in Munich during Mussolini's visit to Germany, a trip that deepened the growing relationship between their two countries. (Luce/Keystone/Getty Images)

AP® EXAM TIP

Take notes on features of fascism and be prepared to compare them with those of communism when you read Chapter 21.

Mussolini promised his mass following major social reforms, though in practice he concentrated on consolidating the power of the central state. His government suspended democracy and imprisoned, deported, or sometimes executed opponents. Italy's fascist regime also disbanded independent labor unions and peasant groups as well as all opposing political parties. In economic life, a "corporate state" took shape, at least in theory, in which workers, employers, and various professional groups were organized into "corporations" that were supposed to settle their disagreements and determine economic policy under the supervision of the state.

Culturally, fascists invoked various aspects of traditional Italian life. Though personally an atheist, Mussolini embraced the Catholic culture of Italy in a series of agreements with the Church, known as the Lateran Accords of 1929, which made the Vatican a sovereign state and Catholicism Italy's national religion. In fascist propaganda, women were portrayed in highly traditional domestic terms, particularly as mothers creating new citizens for the fascist state, with no hint of equality or liberation. Nationalists were delighted when Italy invaded Ethiopia in 1935, avenging the embarrassing defeat that Italians suffered at the hands of Ethiopians in 1896. In the eyes of Mussolini and fascist believers, all of this was the beginning of a "new Roman Empire" that would revitalize Italian society and give it a global mission.

Hitler and the Nazis

Far more important in the long run was the German expression of European fascism, which took shape as the Nazi Party under the leadership of Adolf Hitler (1889–1945). In many respects, German fascism was similar to its Italian counterpart. Both expressions of fascism espoused an extreme nationalism, openly advocated the use of violence as a political tool, generated a single-party dictatorship, were led by charismatic figures, despised parliamentary democracy, hated communism, and viewed war as a positive and ennobling experience.[5] The circumstances that gave rise to the Nazi movement were likewise broadly similar to those that generated Italian fascism, although the Nazis did not achieve national power until 1933.

The end of World War I witnessed the collapse of the German imperial government, itself less than a half century old. It was left to the democratic politicians of a new government—known as the Weimar Republic—to negotiate a peace settlement with the victorious allies. Traditional elites, who had withdrawn from public life in disgrace, never explicitly took responsibility for Germany's defeat; instead they attacked the democratic politicians who had the unenviable task of signing the Treaty of Versailles and enforcing it. In this setting, some began to argue that German military forces had not really lost the war but that civilian socialists, communists, and Jews had betrayed the nation, "stabbing it in the back."

As in postwar Italy, liberal or democratic political leaders during the 1920s faced considerable hostility. Paramilitary groups of veterans known as the Freikorps assassinated hundreds of supporters of the Weimar regime. Gradually, some among the middle classes as well as conservative landowners joined in opposition to the Weimar government, as both groups were threatened by the ruinous inflation of 1923 and then the Great Depression. The German economy largely ground to a halt in the early 1930s amid massive unemployment among workers and the middle class alike. Everyone demanded decisive action from the state. Many industrial workers looked to socialists and communists for solutions; others turned to fascism. Large numbers of middle-class people deserted moderate political parties in favor of conservative and radical right-wing movements.

Guided Reading Question

■ COMPARISON
What was distinctive about the German expression of fascism? What was the basis of popular support for the Nazis?

AP® EXAM TIP

Pay close attention to causes of the rise of authoritarian governments in the early twentieth century.

This was the context in which Adolf Hitler's National Socialist, or Nazi, Party gained growing public support. Founded shortly after the end of World War I, that party under Hitler's leadership proclaimed a message of intense German nationalism cast in terms of racial superiority, bitter hatred for Jews as an alien presence, passionate opposition to communism, a determination to rescue Germany from the humiliating requirements of the Treaty of Versailles, and a willingness to decisively tackle the country's economic problems. Throughout the 1920s, the Nazis were a minor presence in German politics, gaining only 2.6 percent of the vote in the national elections of 1928. Just four years later, however, in the wake of the Depression's terrible impact and the Weimar government's inability to respond effectively, the Nazis attracted 37 percent of the vote. In 1933, Hitler was legally installed as the chancellor of the German government. Thus did the Weimar Republic, a democratic regime that never gained broad support, give way to the Third Reich.

Once in power, Hitler moved quickly to consolidate Nazi control of Germany. All other political parties were outlawed; independent labor unions were ended; thousands of opponents were arrested; and the press and radio came under state control. Far more thoroughly than Mussolini in Italy, Hitler and the Nazis established their control over German society.

By the late 1930s, Hitler apparently had the support of a considerable majority of the population, in large measure because his policies successfully brought Germany out of the Depression. The government invested heavily in projects such as superhighways, bridges, canals, and public buildings and, after 1935, in rebuilding and rearming the country's diminished military forces. These policies drove down the number of unemployed Germans from 6.2 million in 1932 to fewer than 500,000 in 1937. Two years later, Germany had a labor shortage. Erna Kranz, a teenager in the 1930s, later remembered the early years of Nazi rule: "[There was] a glimmer of hope . . . not just for the unemployed but for everybody because we all knew that we were downtrodden. . . . It was a good time . . . there was order and discipline."[6] Millions agreed with her.

Other factors as well contributed to Nazi popularity. Like Italian fascists, Hitler too appealed to rural and traditional values that many Germans feared losing as their country modernized. In Hitler's thinking and in Nazi propaganda, Jews became the symbol of the urban, capitalist, and foreign influences that were undermining traditional German culture. Thus the Nazis reflected and reinforced a broader and long-established current of anti-Semitism that had deep roots in much of Europe. In his book *Mein Kampf* (*My Struggle*), Hitler outlined his case against the Jews and his call for the racial purification of Germany in vitriolic terms. (See Working with Evidence, Source 20.1, page 922, for a statement of Hitler's thinking.)

Far more than elsewhere, this insistence on a racial revolution was a central feature of the Nazi program and differed from the racial attitudes in Italy, where Jews were a tiny minority of the population and deeply assimilated into Italian culture. Early on, Mussolini had ridiculed Nazi racism, but as Germany and Italy drew closer together, Italy too began a program of overt anti-Semitism, though nothing approaching the extremes that characterized Nazi Germany.

Nazi Hatred of the Jews
This picture served as the cover of a highly anti-Semitic book of photographs titled *The Eternal Jew*, published by the Nazis in 1937. It effectively summed up many of the themes of the Nazi case against the Jews, showing them as ugly and sub-human, as the instigators of communism (the hammer and sickle on a map of Russia), as greedy capitalists (coins in one hand), and as seeking to dominate the world (the whip). (akg-images)

AP® EXAM TIP
You should be able to cite examples of repression of minority groups in the twentieth century, like that of Jews in Europe.

Upon coming to power, Hitler implemented policies that increasingly restricted Jewish life. Soon Jews were excluded from universities, professional organizations, and civil employment. In 1935, the Nuremberg Laws ended German citizenship for Jews and forbade marriage or sexual relations between Jews and Germans. On the night of November 9, 1938, known as Kristallnacht, persecution gave way to terror when Nazis smashed and looted Jewish shops. Such actions made clear the Nazis' determination to rid Germany of its Jewish population, thus putting into effect the most radical element of Hitler's program. (See Zooming In: Etty Hillesum, page 902.) Still, it was not yet apparent that this "racial revolution" would mean the mass killing of Europe's Jews. That horrendous development emerged only in the context of World War II.

Beyond race, gender too figured prominently in Nazi thought and policies. Deeply antifeminist and resentful of the liberating changes that modern life had brought to European women, Nazis wanted to limit women largely to the home, removing them from the paid workforce. To Hitler, the state was the natural domain of men, while the home was the realm of women. "Woman in the workplace is an oppressed and tormented being," declared a Nazi publication.[7] Concerned about declining birthrates, Italy and Germany alike promoted a cult of motherhood, glorifying and rewarding women who produced children for the state. Accordingly, fascist regimes in both countries generally opposed abortion, contraception, family planning, and sex education, all of which were associated with feminist thinking.

Yet such an outlook did not necessarily coincide with conservative or puritanical sexual attitudes. In Germany, a state-sponsored system of brothels was initiated in the mid-1930s, for it was assumed that virile men would be promiscuous and that soldiers required a sexual outlet, if they were to contribute to the nation's military strength. Because of this "need," Nazi policy exempted condoms from the ban on birth control. Heinrich Himmler, a leading Nazi official, also openly encouraged illegitimate births among Aryans to augment the nation's numbers. Thus Nazi rhetoric about the chaste Aryan family was trumped—or supplemented—by a desire to use sexuality to advance the cause of the nation.

Also sustaining Nazi rule were massive torchlight ceremonies celebrating the superiority of the German race and its folk culture. In these settings, Hitler was the mystical leader, the Führer, a mesmerizing orator who would lead Germany to national greatness and individual Germans to personal fulfillment.

If World War I and the Great Depression brought about the political and economic collapse of Europe, the Nazi phenomenon represented a moral collapse within the West, deriving from a highly selective incorporation of earlier strands of European culture. On the one hand, the Nazis actively rejected some of the values—rationalism, tolerance, democracy, human equality—that for many people had defined the core of Western civilization since the Enlightenment. On the other hand, they claimed the legacy of modern science, particularly in their concern to classify and rank various human groups. Thus they drew heavily on the "scientific racism" of the late nineteenth century and its expression in phrenology, which linked the size and shape of the skull to human behavior and personality (see Chapter 18, pages 791–92). Moreover, in their effort to purify German society, the Nazis reflected the Enlightenment confidence in the perfectibility of humankind and in the social engineering necessary to achieve it.

Japanese Authoritarianism

In various ways, the modern history of Japan paralleled that of Italy and Germany. All three were newcomers to great power status, with Japan joining the club of industrializing and empire-building states only in the late nineteenth century as its sole Asian member (see Chapter 19, pages 855–60). Like Italy and Germany, Japan had a rather limited experience with democratic politics, for its elected parliament was constrained by a very small electorate (only 1.5 million men in 1917) and by the exalted position of a semi-divine emperor and his small coterie of elite advisers. During the 1930s, Japan too moved toward authoritarian government and a denial of democracy at home, even as it launched an aggressive program of territorial expansion in East Asia.

Despite these broad similarities, Japan's history in the first half of the twentieth century was clearly distinctive. In sharp contrast to Italy and Germany, Japan participated only minimally in World War I, and it experienced considerable economic growth as other industrialized countries were consumed by the European conflict. At the peace conference ending that war, Japan was seated as an equal participant, allied with the winning side of democratic countries such as Britain, France, and the United States.

During the 1920s, Japan seemed to be moving toward more democratic politics and Western cultural values. Universal male suffrage was achieved in 1925; cabinets led by leaders of the major parties, rather than bureaucrats or imperial favorites, governed the country; and a two-party system began to emerge. Supporters of these developments generally embraced the dignity of the individual, free expression of ideas, and greater gender equality. Education expanded; an urban

Guided Reading Question

■ COMPARISON

How did Japan's experience during the 1920s and 1930s resemble that of Germany, and how did it differ?

Etty Hillesum,
Witness to the Holocaust

Not often can historians penetrate the inner worlds of the people they study. But in the letters and diary of Etty Hillesum, a young Dutch Jewish woman caught up in the Nazi occupation of her country during the early 1940s, we can catch a glimpse of her expanding interior life even as her external circumstances contracted sharply amid the unfolding of the Holocaust.[8]

Born in 1914, Etty was the daughter of a Dutch academic father and a Russian-born mother. She attended university, tutored students in the Russian language, and hoped to become a writer. The Nazi invasion of the Netherlands in May 1940 found Etty living in Amsterdam with five other people. There she experienced and described Nazi rule and its mounting impact on Jews. "More arrests, more terror, concentration camps; the arbitrary dragging off of fathers, sisters, brothers," she wrote in June 1941. Soon Amsterdam's Jews were required to wear identifying yellow stars and were forbidden from walking on certain streets, riding the tram, visiting particular shops, or eating in cafés. Signs reading "No Admittance to Jews" sprang up across the city.

Etty Hillesum.

Etty initially reacted to these events with hatred and depression. She wrote, "I am suddenly beside myself with anger, cursing and swearing at the Germans," and was even upset with a German woman living in her house who had no connections whatever with the Nazis. "They are out to destroy us completely," she wrote on July 3, 1942. "Today I am filled with despair." Over time, however, her perspective changed. "I really see no other solution than to turn inward and to root out all the rottenness there." One day, with the "sound of fire, shooting, bombs" raging outside, Etty listened to a Bach recording and wrote: "I know and share the many sorrows a human being can experience, but I do not cling to them; they pass through me, like life itself, as a broad eternal stream . . . and life continues. . . . If you have given sorrow the space that its gentle origins demand, then you may say that life is beautiful and so rich . . . that it makes you want to believe in God."

photo: Etty Hillesum. Collection Jewish Historical Museum, Amsterdam

consumer society developed; middle-class women entered new professions; young women known as *moga* (modern girls) sported short hair and short skirts, while dancing with *mobo* (modern boys) at jazz clubs and cabarets. To such people, the Japanese were becoming world citizens and their country was becoming "a province of the world" as they participated increasingly in a cosmopolitan and international culture.

In this environment, the accumulated tensions of Japan's modernizing and industrializing processes found expression. "Rice riots" in 1918 brought more than a million people into the streets of urban Japan to protest the rising price of that essential staple. Union membership tripled in the 1920s as some factory workers began to think in terms of entitlements and workers' rights rather than the benevo-

Meanwhile, Etty had fallen deeply in love with her fifty-five-year-old German Jewish therapist, Julius Spier. She worried that she was becoming overly dependent on a man, particularly since she was already sleeping with another man in whose house she lived. Yet Spier had become her spiritual companion and mentor as well as her lover. When he died in September 1942, she was devastated but determined to go on. "You were the mediator between God and me," she wrote of Spier, "and now you have gone and my path leads straight to God."

Eventually, Etty found herself in Westerbork, a transit camp for Dutch Jews awaiting transport to the east and almost certain death. Friends had offered to hide her, but Etty insisted on voluntarily entering the camp, where she operated as an unofficial social worker and sought to become the "thinking heart of the barracks." In the camp, panic erupted regularly as new waves of Jews were transported east. Babies screamed as they were awakened to board the trains. "The misery here is really indescribable," she wrote in mid-1943. "People live in those big barracks like so many rats in a sewer."

Even there, however, Etty's emerging inner life found expression. "Late at night . . . ," she wrote, "I often walk with a spring in my step along the barbed wire. And then time and again, it soars straight from my heart . . . the feeling that life is glorious and magnificent and that one day we shall be building a whole new world. Against every new outrage and every fresh horror, we shall put up one more piece of love and goodness, drawing strength from within ourselves. We may suffer, but we must not succumb."

Etty's transport came on September 7, 1943, when she, her parents, and a brother boarded a train for Auschwitz. Her parents were gassed immediately upon arrival, and Etty followed on November 30. Her last known writing was a postcard tossed from the train as it departed Westerbork. It read in part: "I am sitting on my rucksack in the middle of a full freight car. Father, mother, and Mischa [her brother] are a few cars behind. . . . We left the camp singing."

Etty Hillesum's public life, like that of most people, left little outward mark on the world she briefly inhabited, except for the small circle of her friends and family. But the record of her inner life, miraculously preserved, remains among the greatest spiritual testaments to emerge from the horrors of the Nazi era, a tribute to the possibilities of human transformation, even amid the most horrendous of circumstances.

Questions: In what ways did Etty experience the Nazi phenomenon? How might you assess Etty's interior response to the Nazis? Was it a "triumph of the human spirit" or an evasion of the responsibility to resist evil more directly?

favor of their employers. In rural areas, tenant unions multiplied, and disputes with landowners increased amid demands for a reduction in rents. A mounting women's movement advocated a variety of feminist issues, including suffrage and the end of legalized prostitution. "All the sleeping women are now awake and moving," declared Yosano Akiko, a well-known poet, feminist, and social critic. Within the political arena, a number of "proletarian parties"—the Labor Farmer Party, the Socialist People's Party, and a small Japan Communist Party—promised radical change, what one of them referred to as "the political, economic and social emancipation of the proletarian class."[9]

For many people in established elite circles—bureaucrats, landowners, industrialists, military officials—all of this was both appalling and alarming, suggesting

Japanese Women Modeling Swimsuits
This photo from around 1930 shows young Japanese women in Western swimwear and clothing during a fashion show in Tokyo. (ullstein bild/The Granger Collection, NYC—All rights reserved)

AP® EXAM TIP

Look at this photo and recall learning about the social changes brought on by the Meiji Restoration in Chapter 19.

echoes of the Russian Revolution of 1917. A number of political activists were arrested, and a few were killed. A Peace Preservation Law, enacted in 1925, promised long prison sentences, or even the death penalty, to anyone who organized against the existing imperial system of government or private property.

As in Germany, however, it was the impact of the Great Depression that paved the way for harsher and more authoritarian action. That worldwide economic catastrophe hit Japan hard. The shrinking world demand for silk impoverished millions of rural dwellers who raised silkworms. Japan's exports fell by half between 1929 and 1931, leaving a million or more urban workers unemployed. Many young workers returned to their rural villages only to find food scarce, families forced to sell their daughters to urban brothels, and neighbors unable to offer the customary money for the funerals of their friends. In these desperate circumstances, many began to doubt the ability of parliamentary democracy and capitalism to address Japan's "national emergency." Politicians and business leaders alike were widely regarded as privileged, self-centered, and heedless of the larger interests of the nation.

Such conditions energized a growing movement in Japanese political life known as Radical Nationalism or the Revolutionary Right. Expressed in dozens of small groups, it was especially appealing to younger army officers. The movement's many separate organizations shared an extreme nationalism, hostility to parliamentary democracy, a commitment to elite leadership focused around an exalted emperor, and dedication to foreign expansion. The manifesto of one of those organizations, the Cherry Blossom Society, expressed these sentiments clearly in 1930:

> As we observe recent social trends, top leaders engage in immoral conduct, political parties are corrupt, capitalists and aristocrats have no understanding of the masses, farming villages are devastated, unemployment and depression are serious. . . . The rulers neglect the long term interests of the nation, strive to win only the pleasure of foreign powers and possess no enthusiasm for external expansion. . . . The people are with us in craving the appearance of a vigorous and clean government that is truly based upon the masses, and is genuinely centered around the Emperor.[10]

Members of such organizations managed to assassinate a number of public officials and prominent individuals, in the hope of provoking a return to direct rule by the emperor, and in 1936 a group of junior officers attempted a military takeover of the government, which was quickly suppressed. In sharp contrast to developments in Italy and Germany, however, no right-wing party gained wide popular support, nor was any such party able to seize power in Japan. Although individuals and small groups sometimes espoused ideas similar to those of European fascists, no major fascist party emerged. Nor did Japan produce any charismatic leader on the order of Mussolini or Hitler. People arrested for political offenses were neither criminalized nor exterminated, as in Germany, but instead were subjected to a process of "resocialization" that brought the vast majority of them to renounce their "errors" and return to the "Japanese way." Japan's established institutions of government were sufficiently strong, and traditional notions of the nation as a family headed by the emperor were sufficiently intact, to prevent the development of a widespread fascist movement able to take control of the country.

In the 1930s, though, Japanese public life clearly changed in ways that reflected the growth of right-wing nationalist thinking. Parties and the parliament continued to operate, and elections were held, but major cabinet positions now went to prominent bureaucrats or military figures rather than to party leaders. The military in particular came to exercise a more dominant role in Japanese political life, although military men had to negotiate with business and bureaucratic elites as well as party leaders. Censorship limited the possibilities of free expression, and a single news agency was granted the right to distribute all national and most international news to the country's newspapers and radio stations. An Industrial Patriotic Federation replaced independent trade unions with factory-based "discussion councils" to resolve local disputes between workers and managers.

Established authorities also adopted many of the ideological themes of these radical right-wing groups. In 1937, the Ministry of Education issued a new textbook, *Cardinal Principles of the National Entity of Japan*, for use in all Japanese schools.

(See Working with Evidence, Source 20.2, page 925.) That document proclaimed the Japanese to be "intrinsically quite different from the so-called citizens of the Occidental [Western] countries." Those nations were "conglomerations of separate individuals" with "no deep foundation between ruler and citizen to unite them." In Japan, by contrast, an emperor of divine origin related to his subjects as a father to his children. It was a natural, not a contractual, relationship, expressed most fully in the "sacrifice of the life of a subject for the Emperor." In addition to studying this text, students were now required to engage in more physical training, in which Japanese martial arts replaced baseball in the physical education curriculum.

The erosion of democracy and the rise of the military in Japanese political life reflected long-standing Japanese respect for the military values of the ancient samurai warrior class as well as the relatively independent position of the military in Japan's Meiji constitution. The state's success in quickly bringing the country out of the Depression likewise fostered popular support. As in Nazi Germany, state-financed credit, large-scale spending on armaments, and public works projects enabled Japan to emerge from the Depression more rapidly and more fully than major Western countries. "By the end of 1937," noted one Japanese laborer, "everybody in the country was working."[11] By the mid-1930s, the government increasingly assumed a supervisory or managerial role in economic affairs that included subsidies to strategic industries; profit ceilings on major corporations; caps on wages, prices, and rents; and a measure of central planning. Private property, however, was retained, and the huge industrial enterprises called *zaibatsu* continued to dominate the economic landscape.

Although Japan during the 1930s shared some common features with fascist Italy and Nazi Germany, it remained, at least internally, a less repressive and more pluralistic society than either of those European states. Japanese intellectuals and writers had to contend with government censorship, but they retained some influence in the country. Generals and admirals exercised great political authority as the role of an elected parliament declined, but they did not govern alone. Political prisoners were few and were not subjected to execution or deportation as in European fascist states. Japanese conceptions of their racial purity and uniqueness were directed largely against foreigners rather than an internal minority. Nevertheless, like Germany and Italy, Japan developed extensive imperial ambitions. Those projects of conquest and empire building collided with the interests of established world powers such as the United States and Britain, launching a second, and even more terrible, global war.

A Second World War, 1937–1945

World War II, even more than the Great War, was a genuinely global conflict with independent origins in both Asia and Europe. Their common feature lay in dissatisfied states in both continents that sought to fundamentally alter the international arrangements that had emerged from World War I. Many Japanese, like their counterparts in Italy and Germany, felt stymied by Britain and the United States as they sought empires that they regarded as essential for their national greatness and economic well-being.

The Road to War in Asia

World War II began in Asia before it occurred in Europe. In the late 1920s and the 1930s, Japanese imperial ambitions mounted as the military became more powerful in Japan's political life and as an earlier cultural cosmopolitanism gave way to more nationalist sentiments. An initial problem was the rise of Chinese nationalism, which seemed to threaten Japan's sphere of influence in Manchuria, acquired after the Russo-Japanese War of 1904–1905. Acting independently of civilian authorities in Tokyo, units of the Japanese military seized control of Manchuria in 1931 and established a puppet state called Manchukuo. This action infuriated Western powers, prompting Japan to withdraw from the League of Nations, to break politically with its Western allies, and in 1936 to align more closely with Germany and Italy. By that time, relations with an increasingly nationalist China had deteriorated further, leading to a full-scale attack on heartland China in 1937 and escalating a bitter conflict that would last another eight years. World War II in Asia had begun (see Map 20.4).

As Japan's war against China unfolded, the view of the world held by Japanese authorities and many ordinary people hardened. Increasingly, they felt isolated, surrounded, and threatened. A series of international agreements in the early 1920s that had granted Japan a less robust naval force than Britain or the United States, as well as anti-Japanese immigration policies in the United States, convinced some Japanese that racism prevented the West from acknowledging Japan as an equal power. Furthermore, Japan was quite dependent on foreign, especially American, sources of strategic goods. By the late 1930s, some 73 percent of Japan's scrap iron, 60 percent of its imported machine tools, 80 percent of its oil, and about half of its copper came from the United States, which was becoming increasingly hostile to Japanese ambitions in Asia. Moreover, Western imperialist powers—the British, French, and Dutch—controlled resource-rich colonies in Southeast Asia. Finally, the Soviet Union, proclaiming an alien communist ideology, loomed large in northern Asia. To growing numbers of Japanese, their national survival was at stake.

Thus, in 1940–1941, Japan extended its military operations to the French, British, Dutch, and American colonies of Southeast Asia—Malaya, Burma, Indonesia, Indochina, and the Philippines—in an effort to acquire the resources that would free it from dependence on the West. In carving out this Pacific empire, the Japanese presented themselves as liberators and modernizers, creating an "Asia for Asians" and freeing their continent from European and American dominance. Experience soon showed that Japan was far more concerned with Asia's resources than with its liberation and that Japanese rule exceeded in brutality even that of the Europeans.

Guided Reading Question

■ COMPARISON

In what ways were the origins of World War II in Asia and in Europe similar to each other? How were they different?

Map 20.4   World War II in Asia and the Pacific

Japanese aggression temporarily dislodged the British, French, Dutch, and Americans from their colonial possessions in Asia, while inflicting vast devastation on China. Much of the American counterattack involved "island hopping" across the Pacific until the dropping of the atomic bombs on Hiroshima and Nagasaki finally prompted the Japanese surrender in August 1945.

A decisive step in the development of World War II in Asia lay in the Japanese attack on the United States at Pearl Harbor in Hawaii in December 1941. Japanese authorities undertook that attack with reluctance and only after negotiations to end American hostility to Japan's empire-building enterprise proved fruitless and an American oil embargo was imposed on Japan in July 1941. American opinion in the 1930s increasingly saw Japan as aggressive, oppressive, and a threat to U.S. economic interests in Asia. In the face of this hostility, Japan's leaders felt that the alternatives for their country boiled down to either an acceptance of American terms, which they feared would reduce Japan to a second- or third-rank power, or a war with an uncertain outcome. Given those choices, the decision for war was made more with foreboding than with enthusiasm. A leading Japanese admiral made the case for war in this way in late 1941: "The government has decided that if there were no war the fate of the nation is sealed. Even if there is a war, the country may be ruined. Nevertheless a nation that does not fight in this plight has lost its spirit and is doomed."[12]

As a consequence of the attack on Pearl Harbor, the United States entered the war in the Pacific, beginning a long and bloody struggle that ended only with the use of atomic bombs against Hiroshima and Nagasaki in 1945. The Pearl Harbor action also joined the Asian theater of the war and the ongoing conflict in Europe into a single global struggle that pitted Germany, Italy, and Japan (the Axis powers) against the United States, Britain, and the Soviet Union (the Allies).

The Road to War in Europe

If Japan was the dissatisfied power in Asia, Nazi Germany clearly occupied that role in Europe. As a consequence of their defeat in World War I and the harsh terms of the Treaty of Versailles, many Germans harbored deep resentments about their country's position in the international arena. Taking advantage of those resentments, the Nazis pledged to rectify the treaty's perceived injustices. Thus, to most historians, the origins of World War II in Europe lie squarely in German aggression, although scholars acknowledge that events took many twists and turns and that German aggression was encouraged by the initial unwillingness of Britain, France, or the Soviet Union to confront it forcefully. If World War I was accidental and unintended, World War II was deliberate and planned—perhaps even desired—by the German leadership and by Hitler in particular.

War was central to the Nazi agenda in several ways. Nazism was born out of World War I, the hated treaty that ended it, and the disillusioned ex-soldiers who emerged from it. Furthermore, the celebration of war as a means of ennobling humanity and enabling the rise of superior peoples was at the core of Nazi ideology. "Whoever would live must fight," Hitler declared. "Only in force lies the right of possession." He consistently stressed the importance for Germany of gaining *lebensraum* (living space) in the east, in the lands of Slavic Poland and Russia. Inevitably, this required war.

Slowly at first and then more aggressively, Hitler prepared the country for war as he also pursued territorial expansion. A major rearmament program began in 1935. The next year, German forces entered the Rhineland, which the Treaty of Versailles had ordered demilitarized. In 1938, Germany annexed Austria and the German-speaking parts of Czechoslovakia. At a famous conference in Munich in that year, the British and the French gave these actions their reluctant blessing, hoping that this "appeasement" of Hitler could satisfy his demands and prevent all-out war. But it did not. On September 1, 1939, Germany unleashed a devastating attack on Poland, triggering the Second World War in Europe, as Britain and France declared war on Germany. Quickly defeating France, the Germans launched a destructive air war against Britain and in 1941 turned their war machine loose on the Soviet Union. By then, most of Europe was under Nazi control (see Map 20.5).

Although Germany was central to both world wars, the second one was quite different from the first. It was not welcomed with the kind of mass enthusiasm across Europe that had accompanied the opening of World War I in 1914. The bitter experience of the Great War suggested to most people that only suffering lay ahead. The conduct of the two wars likewise differed. The first war had quickly bogged down in trench warfare that emphasized defense, whereas in the second war the German tactic of *blitzkrieg* (lightning war) coordinated the rapid movement of infantry, tanks, and airpower over very large areas.

Such military tactics were initially successful and allowed German forces, aided by their Italian allies, to sweep over Europe, the western Soviet Union, and North Africa. The tide began to turn in 1942 when the Soviet Union absorbed the German onslaught and then began to counterattack, slowly and painfully moving westward toward the German heartland. The United States, with its enormous material and human resources, fully joined the struggle against Germany in 1942 and led the invasion of northern France in 1944, opening a long-awaited second front in the struggle against Hitler's Germany. Years of bitter fighting ensued before these two huge military movements ensured German defeat in May 1945.

AP® EXAM TIP

You should know the effects of technology on twentieth-century warfare casualties.

Guided Reading Question

■ COMPARISON
How did World War II differ from World War I?

The Outcomes of Global Conflict

The Second World War was the most destructive conflict in world history, with total deaths estimated at around 60 million, some six times that of World War I. More than half of those casualties were civilians. Partly responsible for this horrendous toll were the new technologies of warfare—heavy bombers, jet fighters, missiles, and atomic weapons. Equally significant, though, was the almost complete blurring of the traditional line between civilian and military targets, as entire cities and whole populations came to be defined as the enemy.

Nowhere was that blurring more complete than in the Soviet Union, which accounted for more than 40 percent of the total deaths in the war—probably around 25 million, with an equal number made homeless and thousands of towns, villages, and industrial enterprises destroyed. German actions fulfilled Hitler's instructions to

Map 20.5   World War II in Europe and Africa

For a brief moment during World War II, Nazi Germany came close to bringing all of Europe and North Africa under its rule. Then in late 1942, the Allies began a series of counterattacks that led to German surrender in May 1945.

Hiroshima

"If the radiance of a thousand suns were to burst at once into the sky. That would be the splendor of the Mighty One."[13] This passage from the Bhagavad Gita, an ancient Hindu sacred text, occurred to J. Robert Oppenheimer, a leading scientist behind the American push to create a nuclear bomb, as he watched the first successful test of a nuclear weapon in the desert south of Santa Fe, New Mexico, on the evening of July 16, 1945. Years later, he recalled that another verse from the same sacred text had also entered his mind: "I am become Death, the Destroyer of Worlds." And so the atomic age was born amid Oppenheimer's thoughts of divine splendor and divine destruction.

Several weeks later, the whole world became aware of this new era when American forces destroyed the Japanese cities of Hiroshima and Nagasaki with nuclear

A mother and child, victims of Hiroshima, on the floor of a makeshift hospital, two months after the attack.

bombs. The U.S. government decided to use this powerful new weapon partially to hasten the end of World War II, but also to strengthen the United States' position in relation to the Soviet Union in the postwar world. Whether the bomb was necessary to force Japan to surrender is a question of some historical debate. What is not in dispute was the horrific destruction and human suffering wrought by the two bombs. The centers of both cities were flattened, and as many as 80,000 inhabitants of Hiroshima and 40,000 of Nagasaki perished almost instantly from the force and intense heat of the explosions.

The harrowing accounts of survivors offer some sense of the suffering that followed. Iwao Nakamura, photo: Associated Press

his leading generals: "The war against Russia will be such that it cannot be conducted in a knightly fashion; the struggle is one of ideologies and racial differences and will have to be conducted with unprecedented, unmerciful, and unrelenting harshness. . . . German soldiers guilty of breaking international law . . . will be excused."[14]

In China as well, perhaps 15 million people died and uncounted numbers became refugees as a result of prolonged Chinese resistance and the shattering Japanese response, including the killing of every person and every animal in many villages. Within a few months, during the infamous Rape of Nanjing in 1937–1938, some 200,000 to 300,000 Chinese civilians were killed and often mutilated, and countless women were sexually assaulted. Indiscriminate German bombing of British cities and the Allied firebombing of Japanese and German cities likewise reflected the new morality of total war, as did the dropping of atomic bombs on Hiroshima a schoolboy in Hiroshima who lived through the attack, recalled "old people pleading for water, tiny children seeking help, students unconsciously calling for their parents." He remembered that "there was a mother prostrate on the ground, moaning with pain but with one arm still tightly embracing her dead baby."[15] But for many of these survivors, the suffering had only begun. It is estimated that by 1950 as many as 200,000 additional victims had succumbed to their injuries, especially burns and the terrible effects of radiation. Cancer and genetic deformations caused by exposure to radiation continue to affect survivors and their descendants today.

Human suffering on a massive scale was a defining feature of total war during the first half of the twentieth century. In this sense, the atomic bomb was just the latest development in an arms race that drew on advances in manufacturing, technology, and science to create ever more horrific weapons of mass destruction. But no other weapon from that period was as revolutionary as the atomic bomb, which made use of recent discoveries in theoretical physics to harness the fundamental forces of the universe for war. The subsequent development of those weapons has cast an enormous shadow on the world ever since.

That shadow lay in a capacity for destruction previously associated only with an apocalypse of divine origin. Now human beings have acquired that capacity. A single bomb in a single instant can obliterate any major city in the world, and the detonation of even a small fraction of the weapons in existence today would reduce much of the world to radioactive rubble and social chaos. The destructive power of nuclear weapons has led responsible scientists to contemplate the possible extinction of our species—by our own hands. It is hardly surprising that the ongoing threat of nuclear war has led many survivors of the Hiroshima and Nagasaki bombings to push for a world free of nuclear weapons by highlighting the human suffering that they cause. In a speech to a United Nations Special Session on Disarmament in 1982, Senji Yamaguchi, a survivor of the Nagasaki bombing, pleaded, "Please look closely at my [burnt] face and hands. . . . We, atomic bomb survivors, are calling out. I continue calling out as long as I am alive: no more Hiroshima, no more Nagasaki, no more war, no more [victims of nuclear attacks]."[16]

Question: How might you define both the short- and long-term outcomes of the Hiroshima bombing?

and Nagasaki, which in a single instant vaporized tens of thousands of people. This was total war with a scale, intensity, and indiscriminate brutality that exceeded even the horrors of World War I. (See Zooming In: Hiroshima, above.)

A further dimension of total war lay in governments' efforts to mobilize their economies, their people, and their propaganda machines even more extensively than before. Colonial resources were harnessed once again. The British in particular made extensive use of colonial troops and laborers from India and Africa. Japan compelled several hundred thousand women from Korea, China, and elsewhere to serve the sexual needs of Japanese troops as so-called comfort women, who often accommodated twenty to thirty men a day.

As in World War I, though on a much larger scale, the needs of the war drew huge numbers of women into both industry and the military. In the United States, "Rosie the Riveter" represented those women who now took on heavy industrial

AP® EXAM TIP

The twentieth century concept of "total war," including its effect on women's roles, is an important one in the AP® course.

jobs, which previously had been reserved for men. In the Soviet Union, women constituted more than half of the industrial workforce by 1945 and almost completely dominated agricultural production. Soviet women also participated actively in combat, with some 100,000 of them winning military honors. A much smaller percentage of German and Japanese women were mobilized for factory work, but a Greater Japan Women's Society enrolled some 19 million members, who did volunteer work and promised to lay aside their gold jewelry and abandon extravagant weddings. As always, war heightened the prestige of masculinity, and given the immense sacrifices that men had made, few women were inclined to directly challenge the practices of patriarchy immediately following the war.

But, while women had largely escaped death and injury in the First World War, neither women nor children were able to do so amid the indiscriminate slaughter of World War II. Urban bombing, blockades, mass murder, starvation, concentration camps—all of this affected men, women, and children alike. But women were almost exclusively the victims of the widespread rape that accompanied World War II—Japanese soldiers against Chinese women, Soviet troops against German women, among others. A prominent American observer commented in 1945 on the pervasive victimization of European women: "Europe is now a place where woman has lost her perennial fight for decency because the indecent alone live."[17]

Among the most haunting outcomes of the war was the Holocaust. The outbreak of that war closed off certain possibilities, such as forced emigration, for implementing the Nazi dream of ridding Germany of its Jewish population. It also brought millions of additional Jews in Poland and the Soviet Union under German control and triggered among Hitler's enthusiastic subordinates various schemes for a "final solution" to the Jewish question. From this emerged the death camps that included Auschwitz, Dachau, and Bergen-Belsen. Altogether, some 6 million Jews perished in a technologically sophisticated form of mass murder that set a new standard for human depravity. Millions more whom the Nazis deemed inferior, undesirable, or dangerous—Russians, Poles, and other Slavs; Gypsies, or the Roma; mentally or physically handicapped people; homosexuals; communists; and Jehovah's Witnesses—likewise perished in Germany's efforts at racial purification. (For the personal story of a Holocaust victim, see Zooming In: Etty Hillesum, page 902.)

Although the Holocaust was concentrated in Germany, its significance in twentieth-century world history has been huge. It has haunted postwar Germany in particular and the Western world in general. How could such a thing have occurred in a Europe bearing the legacy of both Christianity and the Enlightenment? More specifically, it sent many of Europe's remaining Jews fleeing to Israel and gave urgency to the establishment of a modern Jewish nation in the ancient Jewish homeland. That action outraged many Arabs, some of whom were displaced by the arrival of the Jews, and has fostered an enduring conflict in the Middle East. Furthermore, the Holocaust defined a new category of crimes against humanity—genocide, the attempted elimination of entire peoples. Universal condemnation of the Holocaust, however, did not end the practice, as cases of mass slaughter in Cambodia, Rwanda, Bosnia, and Sudan have demonstrated.

On an even larger scale than World War I, this second global conflict rearranged the architecture of world politics. As the war ended, Europe was impoverished, its industrial infrastructure was shattered, many of its great cities were in ruins, and millions of its people were homeless or displaced. Within a few years, this much-weakened Europe was effectively divided, with its western half operating under an American security umbrella and its eastern half subject to Soviet control. It was clear that Europe's dominance in world affairs was finished.

Over the next two decades, Europe's greatly diminished role in the world registered internationally as its Asian and African colonies achieved independence. Not only had the war weakened both the will and the ability of European powers to hold on to their colonies, but it had also emboldened nationalist and anticolonial movements everywhere (see Chapter 22). Japanese victories in Southeast Asia had certainly damaged European prestige, for British, Dutch, and American military forces fell to Japanese conquerors, sometimes in a matter of weeks. Japanese authorities staged long and brutal marches of Western prisoners of war, partly to drive home to local people that the era of Western domination was over. Furthermore, tens of thousands of Africans had fought for the British or the French, had seen white people die, had enjoyed the company of white women, and had returned home with very different ideas about white superiority and the permanence of colonial rule. Colonial subjects everywhere were very much aware that U.S. president Franklin Roosevelt and British prime minister Winston Churchill had solemnly declared in 1941: "We respect the right of all peoples to choose the form of government under which they will live." Many asked whether those principles should not apply to people in the colonial world as well as to Europeans.

A further outcome of World War II lay in the consolidation and extension of the communist world. The Soviet victory over the Nazis, though bought at an unimaginable cost in blood and treasure, gave immense credibility to that communist regime and to its leader, Joseph Stalin. In the decades that followed, Soviet authorities nurtured a virtual cult of the war: memorials were everywhere; wedding parties made pilgrimages to them, and brides left their bouquets behind; May 9, Victory Day, saw elaborately orchestrated celebrations; veterans were honored and granted modest privileges. Furthermore, communist parties, largely dominated by the Soviet Union and supported by its armed forces, took power all across Eastern Europe, pushing the communist frontier deep into the European heartland. Even more important was a communist takeover in China in 1949. The Second World War allowed the Chinese Communist Party to gain support and credibility by leading the struggle against Japan. By 1950, the communist world seemed to many in the West very much on the offensive (see Chapter 21).

The horrors of two world wars within a single generation prompted a renewed interest in international efforts to maintain the peace in a world of competing and sovereign states. The chief outcome was the United Nations (UN), established in 1945 as a successor to the moribund League of Nations. As a political body dependent on agreement among its most powerful members, the UN proved more effective as a forum for international opinion than as a means of resolving the major

AP® EXAM TIP
Note that Europe's colonial power was greatly diminished after World War II.

AP® EXAM TIP
You must know examples of international peace-keeping movements in the twentieth century, like the United Nations.

conflicts of the postwar world, particularly the Soviet/American hostility during the cold war decades. Further evidence for a growing internationalism lay in the creation in late 1945 of the World Bank and International Monetary Fund, whose purpose was to regulate the global economy, prevent another depression, and stimulate economic growth, especially in the poorer nations.

What these initiatives shared was the dominant presence of the United States.

PRACTICING AP® HISTORICAL THINKING

Is it more useful to view the two world wars as separate and distinct conflicts or as a single briefly interrupted phenomenon?

Unlike the aftermath of World War I, when an isolationist United States substantially withdrew from world affairs, the half century following the end of World War II witnessed the emergence of the United States as a global superpower. This was one of the major outcomes of the Second World War and a chief reason for the remarkable recovery of a badly damaged and discredited Western civilization.

The Recovery of Europe

The tragedies that afflicted Europe in the first half of the twentieth century—fratricidal war, economic collapse, the Holocaust—were wholly self-inflicted, and yet despite the sorry and desperate state of heartland Europe in 1945, that civilization had not permanently collapsed. In the twentieth century's second half, Europeans rebuilt their industrial economies and revived their democratic political systems, while the United States, a European offshoot, assumed a dominant and often-dominating role both within Western civilization and in the world at large.

Three factors help to explain this astonishing recovery. One is the apparent resiliency of an industrial society, once it has been established. The knowledge, skills, and habits of mind that enabled industrial societies to operate effectively remained intact, even if the physical infrastructure had been substantially destroyed. Thus even the most terribly damaged countries—Germany, the Soviet Union, and Japan—had largely recovered, both economically and demographically, within a quarter of a century. A second factor lay in the ability of the major Western European countries to integrate their recovering economies. After centuries of military conflict climaxed by the horrors of the two world wars, the major Western European powers were at last willing to put aside some of their prickly nationalism in return for enduring peace and common prosperity.

Guided Reading Question

■ CHANGE
How was Europe able to recover from the devastation of war?

A third contribution to European recovery derives from the fact that Europe had long ago spawned an overseas extension of its own civilization in what became the United States. In the twentieth century, that country served as a reservoir of military manpower, economic resources, and political leadership for the West as a whole. By 1945, the center of gravity within Western civilization had shifted decisively and had relocated across the Atlantic. With Europe diminished, divided, and on the defensive against the communist threat, leadership of the Western world passed, almost by default, to the United States. It was the only major country physically untouched by the war. Its economy had demonstrated enormous productivity during that struggle and by 1945 was generating fully 50 percent of total world production. Its overall military strength was unmatched, and it was briefly in sole possession of the atomic bomb, the most powerful weapon ever constructed. Thus the United States became the new heartland of the West as well as a global superpower. In 1941, the publisher Henry Luce had proclaimed the twentieth century as "the American century." As the Second World War ended, that prediction seemed to be coming true.

An early indication of the United States' intention to exercise global leadership took shape in its efforts to rebuild and reshape shattered European economies. Known as the Marshall Plan, that effort funneled into Europe some $12 billion, at the time a very large amount, together with numerous advisers and technicians. It was motivated by some combination of genuine humanitarian concern, a desire to prevent a new depression by creating overseas customers for American industrial goods, and an interest in undermining the growing appeal of European communist parties. This economic recovery plan was successful beyond anyone's expectations. Between 1948 and the early 1970s, Western European economies grew rapidly, generating a widespread prosperity and improving living standards. At the same time, Western Europe became both a major customer for American goods and a major competitor in global markets.

The Marshall Plan also required its European recipients to cooperate with one another. After decades of conflict and destruction almost beyond description, many Europeans were eager to do so. That process began in 1951 when Italy, France, West Germany, Belgium, the Netherlands, and Luxembourg created the European Coal and Steel Community to jointly manage the production of these critical items. In 1957, these six countries deepened their level of cooperation by establishing the European Economic Community (EEC), more widely known as the Common Market, whose members reduced their tariffs and developed common trade policies. Over the next half century, the EEC expanded its membership to include almost all of Europe, including many former communist states. In 1994, the EEC was renamed the European Union, and in 2002 twelve of its members, later increased to seventeen, adopted a common currency, the euro (see Map 20.6). All of this sustained Europe's remarkable economic recovery and expressed a larger European identity, although it certainly did not erase deeply rooted national loyalties or lead, as some had hoped, to a political union, a United States of Europe. Nor did it generate persistent economic stability as the European financial crisis beginning in 2010 called into question the viability of the euro zone and perhaps of the European Union as well. In elections to the European Parliament in 2014, parties skeptical of or outright opposed to the European Union won almost 20 percent of the seats in the body.

Beyond economic assistance, the American commitment to Europe soon came to include political and military security against the distant possibility of renewed German aggression and the more immediate communist threat from the Soviet Union. Without that security, economic recovery was unlikely to continue. Thus

AP® EXAM TIP

It's important to note that the European Union is a rare example in history of unity on the European continent.

Map 20.6   The Growth of European Integration

During the second half of the twentieth century, Europeans gradually put aside their bitter rivalries and entered into various forms of economic cooperation with one another, although these efforts fell short of complete political union. This map illustrates the growth of what is now called the European Union (EU). Notice the eastward expansion of the EU following the collapse of communism in Eastern Europe and the Soviet Union.

AP® EXAM TIP

NATO is an important example of a military alliance in the twentieth century.

was born the military and political alliance known as the North Atlantic Treaty Organization (NATO) in 1949. It committed the United States and its nuclear arsenal to the defense of Europe against the Soviet Union, and it firmly anchored West Germany within the Western alliance. Thus, as Western Europe revived economically, it did so under the umbrella of U.S. political and military leadership, which Europeans generally welcomed. It was perhaps an imperial relationship, but to historian John Gaddis, it was "an empire by invitation" rather than by imposition.[18]

A parallel process in Japan, which was under American occupation between 1945 and 1952, likewise revived that country's devastated but already industrialized economy. In the two decades following the occupation, Japan's economy grew at the remarkable rate of 10 percent a year, and the nation became an economic giant on the world stage. This "economic miracle" received a substantial boost from some $2 billion in American aid during the occupation and even more from U.S. military purchases in Japan during the Korean War (1950–1953). Furthermore, the democratic constitution imposed on Japan by American occupation authorities required that "land, sea, and air forces, as well as other war potential, will never be maintained." This meant that Japan, even more so than Europe, depended on the United States for its military security. Because it spent only about 1 percent of its gross national product on defense, more was available for productive investment.

The world had changed dramatically during the first seventy years of the twentieth century. That century began with a Europe of rival nations as clearly the dominant imperial center of a global network. But European civilization substantially self-destructed in the first half of the century, though it revived during the second half in a changed form—without its Afro-Asian colonies and with new leadership in the United States. Accompanying this process and intersecting with it was another major theme of twentieth-century world history—the rise and fall of world communism, which is the focus of the next chapter.

AP® EXAM TIP

You need to know contrasts between the economic outcomes of World War I and World War II.

REFLECTIONS

War and Remembrance: Learning from History

When asked about the value of studying history, most students respond with some version of the Spanish-born philosopher George Santayana's famous dictum: "Those who cannot remember the past are condemned to repeat it." At one level, this notion of learning from the "lessons of history" has much to recommend it, for there is, after all, little else except the past on which we can base our actions in the present. And yet historians in general are notably cautious about drawing particular lessons from the past and applying them to present circumstances.

For one thing, the historical record is sufficiently rich and complex to allow many people to draw quite different lessons from it. The world wars of the twentieth century represent a case in point, as writer Adam Gopnik has pointed out:

> The First World War teaches that territorial compromise is better than full-scale war, that an "honor-bound" allegiance of the great powers to small nations is a recipe for mass killing, and that it is crazy to let the blind mechanism of armies and alliances trump common sense. The Second teaches that searching for an accommodation with tyranny by selling out small nations only encourages the tyrant, that refusing to fight now leads to a worse fight later on. . . . The First teaches us never to rush into a fight, the Second never to back down from a bully.[19]

Did the lessons of the First World War lead Americans to ignore the rise of fascism until the country was directly threatened by Japanese attack? Did the lessons of World War II contribute to unnecessary wars in Vietnam and more recently in Iraq? There are no easy answers to such questions, for the lessons of history are many, varied, and changing.

Behind any such lesson is the common assumption that history repeats itself. This too is a notion to which historians bring considerable skepticism. They are generally more impressed with the complexity and particularity of major events such as wars than with their common features. Here is a further basis for caution in easily drawing lessons from the past.

But the wars of the past century perhaps share one broad similarity: all of them led to unexpected consequences. Few people expected the duration and carnage of World War I. The Holocaust was unimaginable when Hitler took power in 1933 or even at the outbreak of the Second World War in 1939. Who would have expected an American defeat at the hands of the Vietnamese? And the invasion of Iraq in 2003 generated a long list of surprises for the United States, including the absence of weapons of mass destruction and a prolonged insurgency. History repeats itself most certainly only in its unexpectedness.

Chapter Review

What's the Significance?

World War I, 882–91

Treaty of Versailles, 890

Woodrow Wilson / Fourteen Points, 891

Great Depression, 891–95

New Deal, 894–95

fascism, 896–98

Mussolini, 897–98

Nazi Germany, 898–901

Hitler, 899–900

Etty Hillesum, 902–3

Revolutionary Right (Japan), 904–5

World War II in Asia, 907–9

World War II in Europe, 909–10

total war, 910–13

Hiroshima, 912–13

Holocaust, 914

Marshall Plan, 917

European Economic Community, 917

NATO, 918

Big Picture Questions

1. What explains the disasters that befell Europe in the first half of the twentieth century?
2. To what extent did the two world wars settle the issues that caused them? What legacies to the future did they leave?
3. In what ways did Europe's internal conflicts between 1914 and 1945 have global implications?
4. **Looking Back:** In what ways were the major phenomena of the first half of the twentieth century — world wars, the Great Depression, fascism, the Holocaust, the emergence of the United States as a global power — rooted in earlier times?

Next Steps: For Further Study

Michael Burleigh, *The Third Reich: A New History* (2001). A fresh and thorough look at the Nazi era in Germany's history.

John Keegan, *The Second World War* (2005). A comprehensive account by a well-known scholar.

Bernd Martin, *Japan and Germany in the Modern World* (1995). A comparative study of these two countries' modern history and the relationship between them.

Mark Mazower, *Dark Continent* (2000). A history of Europe in the twentieth century that views the era as a struggle among liberal democracy, fascism, and communism.

Michael S. Nieberg, *Fighting the Great War: A Global History* (2006). An exploration of the origins and conduct of World War I.

Dietman Rothermund, *The Global Impact of the Great Depression, 1929–1939* (1996). An examination of the origins of the Depression in America and Europe and its impact in Asia, Africa, and Latin America.

First World War.com, http://www.firstworldwar.com. A Web site rich with articles, documents, photos, diaries, and more that illustrate the history of World War I.

"The Holocaust," http://www.jewishvirtuallibrary.org/jsource/holo.html. A wealth of essays, maps, photographs, and timelines that explores the Holocaust and the context in which it arose.

Ideologies of the Axis Powers

Even more than the Great War of 1914–1918, the Second World War was a conflict of ideas and ideologies as well as a struggle of nations and armies. The ideas of the losing side in that war, repellant as they were to their enemies, had for a time attracted considerable support. Described variously as fascist, authoritarian, right-wing, or radically nationalist, the ideologies of the Axis powers differed in tone and emphasis. But they shared a repudiation of mainstream Western liberalism and democracy, as well as an intense hatred of Marxist communism. The documents that follow provide a taste of this thinking as it took shape in Germany and Japan.

Source 20.1
Hitler on Nazism

Adolf Hitler published his political views well before he came to power. Born in Austria, Hitler absorbed a radical form of German nationalism, which he retained as a profoundly disillusioned veteran of World War I. In 1919, he joined a very small extremist group called the German Workers Party, where he rose quickly to a dominant role based on his powerful oratorical abilities. Inspired by Mussolini's recent victory in Italy, Hitler launched in 1923 an unsuccessful armed uprising in Munich for which he was arrested and imprisoned. During his brief stay in prison (less than a year), he wrote *Mein Kampf* (*My Struggle*), part autobiography and part an exposition of his political and social philosophy. Armed with these ideas, Hitler assumed the leadership of Germany in 1933 (see pages 898–901).

■ What larger patterns in European thinking do Hitler's ideas reflect, and what elements of European thought does he reject? Consider in particular his use of social Darwinism, then an idea with wide popularity in Europe.

■ How does Hitler distinguish between Aryans and Jews? How does he understand the role of race in human affairs?

■ What kind of political system does Hitler advocate?

■ What goals for Germany—both domestic and foreign—did Hitler set forth in *Mein Kampf*?

■ What aspects of Hitler's thinking might have had wide appeal in Germany during the 1930s?

ADOLF HITLER

Mein Kampf (My Struggle)

1925–1926

Nation and Race

There are some truths which are so obvious that for this very reason they are not seen or at least not recognized by ordinary people. . . . Every animal mates only with a member of the same species. . . . Any crossing of two beings not at exactly the same level produces a medium between the level of the two parents. . . . Such mating is contrary to the will of Nature for a higher breeding of all life. . . . The stronger must dominate and not blend with the weaker, thus sacrificing his own greatness. Only the born weakling can view this as cruel . . . , for if this law did not prevail, any conceivable higher development of organic living beings would be unthinkable.

In the struggle for daily bread all those who are weak and sickly or less determined succumb, while the struggle of the males for the female grants the right or opportunity to propagate only to the healthiest. . . . No more than Nature desires the mating of weaker with stronger individuals, even less does she desire the blending of a higher with a lower race, since, if she did, her whole work of higher breeding, over perhaps hundreds of thousands of years, might be ruined with one blow. . . . All great cultures of the past perished only because the originally creative race died out from blood poisoning.

Those who want to live, let them fight, and those who do not want to fight in this world of eternal struggle do not deserve to live. . . .

All the human culture, all the results of art, science, and technology that we see before us today, are almost exclusively the creative product of the Aryan. . . . [H]e alone was the founder of all higher humanity, therefore representing the prototype of all that we understand by the word "man." He is the Prometheus of mankind from whose bright forehead the divine spark of genius has sprung at all times. . . .

All who are not of good race in this world are chaff.

The mightiest counterpart to the Aryan is represented by the Jew. . . . Since the Jew . . . was never in possession of a culture of his own, the foundations of his intellectual work were always provided by others. His intellect at all times developed through the cultural world surrounding him. . . .

He lacks completely the most essential requirement for a cultured people, the idealistic attitude. In the Jewish people the will to self-sacrifice does not go beyond the individual's naked instinct of self-preservation. Their apparently great sense of solidarity is based on the very primitive herd instinct that is seen in many other living creatures in this world. . . . [T]he Jew is led by nothing but the naked egoism of the individual.

With satanic joy in his face, the black-haired Jewish youth lurks in wait for the unsuspecting girl whom he defiles with his blood, thus stealing her from her people. With every means he tries to destroy the racial foundations of the people he has set out to subjugate. . . . And so he tries systematically to lower the racial level by a continuous poisoning of individuals. And in politics he begins to replace the idea of democracy by the dictatorship of the proletariat. In the organized mass of Marxism he has found the weapon which lets him . . . subjugate and govern the peoples with a dictatorial and brutal fist.

In economics he undermines the states until the social enterprises which have become unprofitable are taken from the state and subjected to his financial control.

In the political field he refuses the state the means for its self-preservation, destroys the foundations of all national self-maintenance and defense, destroys faith in the leadership, scoffs at its history and past, and drags everything that is truly great into the gutter.

Culturally he contaminates art, literature, the theater, makes a mockery of natural feeling, overthrows all concepts of beauty and sublimity, of the noble and the good, and instead drags men down into the sphere of his own base nature. Religion is ridiculed, ethics and morality represented as outmoded, until the last props of a nation in its struggle for existence in this world have fallen.

If we pass all the causes of the German collapse [defeat in World War I] in review, the ultimate and most decisive remains the failure to recognize the racial problem and especially the Jewish menace. . . . The lost purity of the blood alone destroys inner happiness forever, plunges man into the abyss for all time, and the consequences can never more be eliminated from body and spirit. . . . All really significant symptoms of decay of the pre–War period can in the last analysis be reduced to racial causes.

The State

The State is only a means to an end. . . . Above all, it must preserve the existence of the race. . . . We, as Aryans, can consider the State only as the living organism of a people, an organism which does not merely maintain the existence of a people, but functions in such a way as to lead its people to a position of supreme liberty by the progressive development of the intellectual and cultural faculties.

We National Socialists know that in holding these views we take up a revolutionary stand in the world of today and that we are branded as revolutionaries. . . .

As a State the German Reich shall include all Germans. Its task is not only to gather in and foster the most valuable sections of our people but to lead them slowly and surely to a dominant position in the world. . . . It will be the task of the People's State to make the race the centre of the life of the community. It must make sure that the purity of the racial strain will be preserved. . . . Those who are physically and mentally unhealthy and unfit must not perpetuate their own suffering in the bodies of their children. . . .

One thing is certain: our world is facing a great revolution. The only question is whether the outcome will be propitious for the Aryan portion of mankind or whether the everlasting Jew will profit by it. By educating the young generation along the right lines, the People's State will have to see to it that a generation of mankind is formed which will be adequate to this supreme combat that will decide the destinies of the world. . . .

[T]he People's State must mercilessly expurgate . . . the parliamentarian principle, according to which decisive power through the majority vote is invested in the multitude. Personal responsibility must be substituted in its stead. . . . The best constitution and the best form of government is that which makes it quite natural for the best brains to reach a position of dominant importance and influence in the community. . . . Genius of an extraordinary stamp is not to be judged by normal standards whereby we judge other men.

There are no decisions made by the majority vote, but only by responsible persons. And the word "council" is once more restored to its original meaning. Every man in a position of responsibility will have councilors at his side, but the decision is made by that individual person alone. . . .

[T]he principle of parliamentarian democracy, whereby decisions are enacted through the majority vote, has not always ruled the world. On the contrary, we find it prevalent only during short periods of history, and those have always been periods of decline in nations and States. . . .

Eastern Orientation or Eastern Policy

[W]e National Socialists must hold unflinchingly to our aim in foreign policy, namely, to secure for the German people the land and soil to which they are entitled on this earth. . . . If we speak of soil in Europe today, we can primarily have in mind only Russia and her vassal border states. . . .

The National Socialist movement must strive to eliminate the disproportion between our population and our area—viewing this latter as a source of food as well as a basis for power politics—between our historical past and the hopelessness of our present impotence. And in this it must remain aware that we, as guardians of the highest humanity on this earth, are bound by the highest obligation, and the more it strives to bring the German people to racial awareness . . . , the more it will be able to meet this obligation. . . .

State boundaries are made by man and changed by man. . . . And in this case, right lies in this strength alone. . . . Just as our ancestors did not receive the soil on which we live today as a gift from Heaven, but had to fight for it at the risk of their lives, in the future no folkish grace will win soil for us . . . but only the might of a victorious sword. . . .

Never forget that the most sacred right on this earth is a man's right to have earth to till with his own hands, and the most sacred sacrifice the blood that a man sheds for this earth.

Source: Adolf Hitler, *Mein Kampf*, translated by Ralph Manheim (Boston: Houghton Mifflin, 1943).

Source 20.2
The Japanese Way

In the Japanese language, the word *kokutai* is an evocative term that refers to the national essence or the fundamental character of the Japanese nation and people. Drawing both on long-established understandings and on recently developed nationalist ideas, the Ministry of Education in 1937 published a small volume, widely distributed in schools and homes throughout the country, titled *Kokutai No Hongi* (*Cardinal Principles of the National Entity of Japan*). That text, excerpted in Source 20.2, defined the uniqueness of Japan and articulated the philosophical foundation of its authoritarian regime. (See pages 901–6 for the background to this document.) When the Americans occupied a defeated and devastated Japan in 1945, they forbade the further distribution of the book.

- According to *Cardinal Principles*, what was *kokutai*? How did the document define the national essence of Japan? How did its authors compare Japan to the West?

- What was the ideal role of the individual in Japanese society?

- To whom might these ideas have been attractive? Why?

- How might this document have been used to justify Japan's military and territorial expansion?

- Why do you think the American occupation authorities banned the document?

Cardinal Principles of the National Entity of Japan
1937

The various ideological and social evils of present-day Japan are the result of ignoring the fundamental and running after the trivial, of lack of judgment, and a failure to digest things thoroughly; and this is due to the fact that since the days of *Meiji* so many aspects of European and American culture, systems, and learning, have been imported, and that, too rapidly. As a matter of fact, the foreign ideologies imported into our country are in the main ideologies of the [European] Enlightenment that have come down from the eighteenth century, or extensions of them. The views of the world and of life that form the basis of these ideologies . . . lay the highest value on, and assert the liberty and equality of, individuals. . . .

We have already witnessed the boundless Imperial virtues. Wherever this Imperial virtue of compassion radiates, the Way for the subjects naturally becomes clear. The Way of the subjects exists where the entire nation serves the Emperor united in mind. . . . That is, we by nature serve the Emperor and walk the Way of the Empire. . . .

We subjects are intrinsically quite different from the so-called citizens of the Occidental [Western] countries. . . .

When citizens who are conglomerations of separate individuals independent of each other give support to a ruler, . . . there exists no deep foundation between ruler and citizen to unite them. However, the relationship between the Emperor and his subjects arises from the same fountainhead, and has prospered ever since the founding of the nation as one in essence. . . .

Our country is established with the Emperor. . . . For this reason, to serve the Emperor and to receive the Emperor's great august Will as one's own is the rationale of making our historical "life" live in the present. . . .

Loyalty means to reverence the Emperor as [our] pivot and to follow him implicitly. . . . Hence, offering our lives for the sake of the Emperor does not mean so-called self-sacrifice, but the casting aside of our little selves to live under his august grace and the enhancing of the genuine life of the people of a State. . . . An individual is an existence belonging to the State and her history, which forms the basis of his origin, and is fundamentally one body with it. . . .

We must sweep aside the corruption of the spirit and the clouding of knowledge that arises from setting up one's "self" and from being taken up with one's "self" and return to a pure and clear state of mind that belongs intrinsically to us as subjects, and thereby fathom the great principle loyalty. . . .

Indeed, loyalty is our fundamental Way as subject, and is the basis of our national morality. Through loyalty are we become Japanese subjects; in loyalty do we obtain life and herein do we find the source of all morality. . . .

In our country filial piety is a Way of the highest importance. Filial piety originates with one's family as its basis, and in its larger sense has the nation for its foundation. . . .

Our country is a great family nation, and the Imperial Household is the head family of the subjects and the nucleus of national life. The subjects revere the Imperial Household, which is the head family, with the tender esteem they have for their ancestors; and the Emperor loves his subjects as his very own. . . .

When we trace the marks of the facts of the founding of our country and the progress of our history, what we always find there is the spirit of harmony. . . . The spirit of harmony is built upon the concord of all things. When people determinedly count themselves as masters and assert their egos, there is nothing but contradictions and the setting of one against the other; and harmony is not begotten. . . . That is, a society of individualism is one of the clashes between [masses of] people . . . and all history may be looked upon as one of class wars. . . .

And this, this harmony is clearly seen in our nation's martial spirit. Our nation is one that holds bushido [the way of the warrior/samurai] in high regard, and there are shrines deifying warlike spirits. . . . Bushido may be cited as showing an outstanding characteristic of our national morality. . . . That is to say, though a sense of obligation binds master and servant, this has developed in a spirit of self-effacement and meeting death with a perfect calmness. In this, it was not that death was made light of so much as that man tempered himself to death and in a true sense regarded it with esteem. In effect, man tried to fulfill true life by the way of death. . . .

To put it in a nutshell, while the strong points of Occidental learning and concepts lie in their analytical and intellectual qualities, the characteristics of Oriental learning and concepts lie in their intuitive and aesthetic qualities. These are natural tendencies that arise through racial and historical differences; and when we compare them with our national spirits, concepts, or mode of living, we cannot help recognizing further great and fundamental differences. Our nation has in the past imported, assimilated, and sublimated Chinese and Indian ideologies, and has therewith supported the Imperial Way, making possible the establishment of an original culture based on her national polity. . . .

Since the *Meiji* restoration our nation has adapted the good elements of the advanced education seen among European and American nations, and has exerted efforts to set up an educational system and materials for teaching. The nation has also assimilated on a wide scale the scholarship of the West, not only in the fields of natural science, but of the mental sciences, and has thus striven to see progress made in our scholastic pursuits and to make education more popular. . . .

However, at the same time, through the infiltration of individualistic concepts, both scholastic pursuits and education have tended to be taken up with a world in which the intellect alone mattered. . . .

In order to correct these tendencies, the only course open to us is to clarify the true nature of our national polity, which is at the very source of our education, and to strive to clear up individualistic and abstract ideas.

Source: J. O. Gauntlett, trans., and R. K. Hall, ed., *Kokutai No Hongi* (*Cardinal Principles of the National Entity of Japan*) (Cambridge, MA: Harvard University Press, 1949), 53–183.

DOING HISTORY

Ideologies of the Axis Powers

1. **Making comparisons:** What aspects of the Japanese document might Hitler have viewed with sympathy, and what parts of it might he have found distasteful or offensive?

2. **Criticizing the West:** In what ways did Hitler and the authors of *Cardinal Principles* find fault with mainstream Western societies and their political and social values?

3. **Considering ideas and circumstances:** From what sources did the ideas expressed in these documents arise? What kinds of people would have found them attractive, and why?

4. **Considering ideas and action:** To what extent did the ideas articulated in these documents find expression in particular actions or policies of political authorities?

5. **Noticing continuity and change:** To what extent were the ideas in these documents new and revolutionary? In what respects did they draw on long-standing traditions in their societies? In what ways did they embrace modern life, and what aspects of it did they reject? Have these ideas been completely discredited, or do they retain some resonance in contemporary political discourse?

ЛЕНИН –
ЖИЛ,
ЛЕНИН –
ЖИВ,
ЛЕНИН –
БУДЕТ ЖИТЬ!

ВЛ. МАЯКОВСКИЙ.

CHAPTER 21

Revolution, Socialism, and Global Conflict

The Rise and Fall of World Communism
1917–present

An upstanding Soviet citizen entered a medical clinic one day and asked to see an ear-and-eye doctor. Asked about his problem, the man replied, "Well, I keep hearing one thing and seeing another."

A Frenchman, an Englishman, and a Soviet Russian are admiring a painting of Adam and Eve in the Garden of Eden. The Frenchman says, "They must be French; they're naked and they're eating fruit." The Englishman says, "Clearly, they're English; observe how politely the woman is offering fruit to the man." The Russian replies, "No, they are Russian communists, of course. They have no house, nothing to wear, little to eat, and they think they are in Paradise."

These are two of an endless array of jokes that had long circulated in the Soviet Union as a means of expressing in private what could not be said in public. A major theme of those jokes involved the hypocrisy of a communist system that promised equality and abundance for all but delivered a dismal and uncertain economic life for the many and great privileges for the few. The growing disbelief in the ability or willingness of the communist regime to provide a decent life for its people was certainly an important factor in the collapse of the Soviet Union in 1991 and the end of communism in the land of its birth. Amid that disillusionment, it was hard to remember that earlier in the century communism had been greeted with enthusiasm by many people—in Russia, China, Cuba, Vietnam, and elsewhere—as a promise of liberation from inequality, oppression, exploitation, and backwardness.

Lenin   Vladimir Ulyanov, better known as Lenin, was the Bolshevik leader of the Russian Revolution. He became the iconic symbol of world communism and in his own country was the focus of a semi-religious cult. This widely distributed Soviet propaganda poster reads, "Lenin lived; Lenin lives; Lenin will live."

Communism was a phenomenon of enormous significance in the world of the twentieth century. Communist regimes came to power almost everywhere in the tumultuous wake of war, revolution, or both. Once established, those regimes set about a thorough and revolutionary transformation of their societies— "building socialism," as they so often put it. Internationally, world communism posed a profound military and political/ideological threat to the Western world of capitalism and democracy, particularly during the decades of the cold war from the late 1940s through 1991. That struggle divided continents, countries, and cities into communist and noncommunist halves. It also prompted a global rivalry between the United States and the Soviet Union (USSR) for influence in the Global South. Most hauntingly, it spawned an arms race in horrendously destructive nuclear weapons that sent schoolchildren scrambling under their desks during air raid drills, while sober scientists speculated about the possible extinction of human life, and perhaps all life, in the event of a major war.

Then, to the amazement of everyone, it was over, more with a whimper than a bang. The last two decades of the twentieth century witnessed the collapse of communist regimes or the abandonment of communist principles practically everywhere. The great global struggle of capitalism and communism, embodied in the United States and the Soviet Union, was resolved in favor of the former far more quickly and much more peacefully than anyone had imagined possible.

SEEKING THE MAIN POINT

What was the appeal of communism, both in terms of its promises and its achievements? To what extent did promises match achievements?

AP® EXAM TIP

Look back at Marx's theories in Chapter 17 and note their twentieth-century outcomes. Also remember that the rise, fall, and features of communism are some of the most important developments in the twentieth century.

Guided Reading Question

■ DESCRIPTION
When and where did communism exercise influence during the twentieth century?

Global Communism

Modern communism found its political and philosophical roots in nineteenth-century European socialism, inspired by the teachings of Karl Marx. Although most European socialists came to believe that they could achieve their goals peacefully and through the democratic process, those who defined themselves as communists in the twentieth century disdained such reformism and advocated uncompromising revolution as the only possible route to a socialist future. Russia, later called the Soviet Union, was the first country to experience such a revolution. Other movements that later identified or allied with the Soviet Union likewise defined themselves as communist. In Marxist theory, communism also referred to a final stage of historical development when social equality and collective living would be most fully developed, largely without private property. Socialism was an intermediate stage along the way to that final goal.

By the 1970s, almost one-third of the world's population lived in societies governed by communist regimes. By far the most significant were the Soviet Union, the world's largest country in size, and China, the world's largest country in population. But Mongolia had come under communist rule in 1924 as a spillover of the Russian Revolution. Communist regimes came to power in Eastern Europe in the wake of World War II and the extension of the Soviet military presence there. Fol-

A MAP OF TIME

Year	Event
1917	Russian Revolution
1921	Founding of Chinese Communist Party
1929–1953	Stalin in power in Soviet Union
1934–1935	Long March in China
1945–1950	Imposition of communist regimes in Eastern Europe
1949	Communist triumph in China
1950–1953	Korean War
1958–1961	China's Great Leap Forward and massive famine
1959	Cuban Revolution
1962	Cuban missile crisis
1965–1973	U.S.-Vietnam war
1966–1976	China's Cultural Revolution
1968	Prague Spring: communist reform movement in Czechoslovakia
1975–1979	Genocide in communist Cambodia
1976–early 1990s	Deng Xiaoping and beginnings of communist reforms in China
1979	Soviet invasion of Afghanistan
1985–1991	Gorbachev reforms in USSR
1989	Collapse of communist regimes in Eastern Europe
1991	Disintegration of Soviet Union
1990s	Economic contraction in the former Soviet Union and economic expansion in China
2007–2009	Communist North Korea acquires nuclear weapons
2008	Fidel Castro steps down as leader of communist Cuba
2014	United States proposes to restore diplomatic relations with Cuba

lowing Japan's defeat in World War II, its Korean colony was partitioned, with the northern half coming under Soviet and therefore communist control. In Vietnam, a much more locally based communist movement, under the leadership of Ho Chi Minh, embodied both a socialist vision and Vietnamese nationalism as it battled Japanese, French, and later American invaders and established communist control first in the northern half of the country and after 1975 throughout the whole country. The victory of the Vietnamese communists spilled over into neighboring Laos and Cambodia, where communist parties took power in the mid-1970s. In Latin America, Fidel Castro led a revolutionary nationalist movement against a repressive, American-backed government in Cuba. On coming to power in 1959, Castro moved toward communism and an alliance with the Soviet Union. Finally, a shaky communist regime took power in Afghanistan in 1979, propped up briefly by massive Soviet military support. None of these countries had achieved the kind of advanced industrial capitalism that Karl Marx had viewed as a prerequisite for revolution and socialism. Indeed, in one of history's strange twists, the communist revolutions of the twentieth century took place in largely agrarian societies. (See Map 21.3, page 950, for a global view of the communist world in the 1970s, the period of its greatest extent.)

In addition to those countries where communist governments controlled state power, communist movements took root in still other places, where they exercised various degrees of influence. In the aftermath of World War II, communist parties played important political roles in Greece, France, and Italy. In the 1950s, a small communist party in the United States became the focus of an intense wave of fear and political repression known as McCarthyism. Revolutionary communist movements threatened established governments in the Philippines, Malaysia, Indonesia, Bolivia, Peru, and elsewhere, sometimes provoking brutal crackdowns by those governments. A number of African states in the 1970s proclaimed themselves Marxist for a time and aligned with the Soviet Union in international affairs. All of this was likewise part of global communism.

These differing expressions of communism were linked to one another in various ways. They shared a common ideology derived from European Marxism, although it was substantially modified in many places. That ideology minimized the claims of national loyalty and looked forward to an international revolutionary movement of the lower classes and a worldwide socialist federation. The Russian Revolution of 1917 served as an inspiration and an example to aspiring revolutionaries elsewhere, and the new Soviet Communist Party and government provided them aid and advice. Through an organization called Comintern (Communist International), Soviet authorities also sought to control their policies and actions.

During the cold war decades, the Warsaw Pact brought the Soviet Union and Eastern European communist states together in a military alliance designed to counter the threat from the Western capitalist countries of the NATO alliance. A parallel organization called the Council on Mutual Economic Assistance tied Eastern European economies tightly to the economy of the Soviet Union. A Treaty of Friendship between the Soviet Union and China in 1950 joined the two communist giants in an alliance that caused many in the West to view communism as a unified international movement aimed at their destruction. Nevertheless, rivalry, outright hostility, and on occasion military conflict marked the communist world as much as or more than solidarity and cooperation. Eastern European nations' resentment of their Soviet overlords boiled over in periodic rebellions, even as the Soviet Union and China came close to war in the late 1960s.

Although the globalization of communism found expression primarily in the second half of the twentieth century, that process began with two quite distinct and different revolutionary upheavals—one in Russia and the other in China—in the first half of the century.

Revolutions as a Path to Communism

Communist movements of the twentieth century quite self-consciously drew on the mystique of the earlier French Revolution, which suggested that new and better worlds could be constructed by human actions. Like their French predecessors, communist revolutionaries ousted old ruling classes and dispossessed landed aristocracies. Those twentieth-century upheavals also involved vast peasant upheavals in the countryside and an educated leadership with roots in the cities. All three revolutions—French, Russian, and Chinese—found their vision of the good society in a modernizing future, not in some nostalgic vision of the past. Communists also worried lest their revolutions end up in a military dictatorship like that of Napoleon following the French Revolution.

But the communist revolutions were distinctive as well. They were made by highly organized parties guided by a Marxist ideology, were committed to an industrial future, pursued economic as well as political equality, and sought the abolition of private property. In doing so, they mobilized, celebrated, and claimed to act on behalf of society's lower classes—exploited urban workers and impoverished rural peasants. The middle classes, who were the chief beneficiaries of the French Revolution, numbered among the many victims of the communist upheavals. And unlike the French or American revolutionaries, communists also carried an explicit message of gender equality. The Russian and Chinese revolutions shared these general features, but in other respects they differed sharply from each other.

Russia: Revolution in a Single Year

In Russia, communists came to power on the back of a revolutionary upheaval that took place within a single year, 1917. The immense pressures of World War I, which was going very badly for the Russians, represented the catalyst for that revolution as the accumulated tensions of Russian society exploded. Much exploited and suffering from wartime shortages, workers—men and women alike—took to the streets to express their outrage at the incompetence and privileges of the elites. In St. Petersburg, some 100,000 wives of soldiers demonstrated for bread and peace. Activists from various parties, many of them socialist, recruited members, organized demonstrations, published newspapers, and plotted revolution. By February 1917, Tsar Nicholas II had lost almost all support and was forced to abdicate the throne, thus ending the Romanov dynasty, which had ruled Russia for more than three centuries.

AP® EXAM TIP

Take notes on these comparisons of the French, Russian, and Chinese revolutions.

Guided Reading Question

■ COMPARISON

Identify the major differences between the Russian and Chinese revolutions.

AP® EXAM TIP

Return to Chapter 3 and compare the causes of the fall of the Russian Empire with those of the Han and Roman empires.

Map 21.1   Russia in 1917

In 1917 during the First World War, the world's largest state, bridging both Europe and Asia, exploded in revolution. The Russian Revolution brought to power the twentieth century's first communist government and launched an international communist movement that eventually incorporated about one-third of the world's people.

That historic event opened the door for a massive social upheaval. Ordinary soldiers, seeking an end to a terrible war and despising their upper-class officers, deserted in substantial numbers. In major industrial centers such as St. Petersburg and Moscow, new trade unions arose to defend workers' interests, and some workers seized control of their factories. Grassroots organizations of workers and soldiers, known as soviets, emerged to speak for ordinary people. Peasants, many of whom had been serfs only a generation or two earlier, seized landlords' estates, burned their manor houses, and redistributed the land among themselves. Non-Russian nationalists in Ukraine, Poland, Muslim Central Asia, and the Baltic region demanded greater autonomy or even independence (see Map 21.1).

This was social revolution, and it quickly demonstrated the inadequacy of the Provisional Government, which had come to power after the tsar abdicated. Consisting of middle-class politicians and some moderate socialist leaders, that government was divided and ineffectual, unable or unwilling to meet the demands of

Russia's revolutionary masses. It was also unwilling to take Russia out of the war, as many were now demanding. Impatience and outrage against the Provisional Government provided an opening for more radical groups. The most effective were the Bolsheviks (BOHL-shih-vehks), a small socialist party with a determined and charismatic leader, Vladimir Ilyich Ulyanov, more commonly known as Lenin. He had long believed that Russia, despite its industrial backwardness, was none-theless ready for a socialist revolution that would, he expected, spark further revo-lutions in the more developed countries of Europe. Thus backward Russia would be a catalyst for a more general socialist breakthrough. It was a striking revision of Marxist thinking to accommodate the conditions of a largely agrarian Russian society.

In the desperate circumstances of 1917, his party's message—an end to the war, land for the peasants, workers' control of factories, self-determination for non-Russian nationalities—resonated with an increasingly rebellious public mood, par-ticularly in the major cities. On the basis of this program, the Bolsheviks—claiming to act on behalf of the highly popular soviets—seized power in late October during an overnight coup in the capital city of St. Petersburg.

Taking or claiming power was one thing; holding on to it was another. A three-year civil war followed in which the Bolsheviks, now officially calling their party "communist," battled an assortment of enemies—tsarist officials, landlords, dis-affected socialists, and regional nationalist forces, as well as troops from the United States, Britain, France, and Japan, all of which were eager to crush the fledgling communist regime. Remarkably, the Bolsheviks held on and by 1921 had stag-gered to victory over their divided and uncoordinated opponents. That remarkable victory was assisted by the Bolsheviks' willingness to sign a separate peace treaty with Germany, thus taking Russia out of World War I in early 1918, but at a great, though temporary, loss of Russian territory.

During the civil war (1918–1921), the Bolsheviks harshly regimented the econ-omy, seized grain from angry peasants, suppressed nationalist rebellions, and perpe-trated bloody atrocities, as did their enemies as well. But they also integrated many lower-class men into the Red Army, as Bolshevik military forces were known, and into new local governments, providing them a fresh avenue of social mobility. By battling foreign troops, the Bolsheviks claimed to be defending Russia from impe-rialists and protecting the downtrodden masses from their exploiters. The civil war exaggerated even further the Bolsheviks' authoritarian tendencies and their inclina-tion to use force. Shortly after that war ended, they renamed their country the Union of Soviet Socialist Republics (USSR or Soviet Union) and set about its transformation.

For the next twenty-five years, the Soviet Union remained a communist island in a capitalist sea. The next major extension of communist control occurred in Eastern Europe in the aftermath of World War II, but it took place quite differently than in Russia. That war ended with Soviet military forces occupying much of Eastern Europe. Stalin, the USSR's longtime leader, determined that Soviet security

Guided Reading Question

■ CHANGE

Why were the Bolsheviks able to ride the Russian Revolution to power?

The Russian Civil War through Bolshevik Eyes
This Bolshevik poster from 1921, titled "Electrification and Counterrevolution," presents a communist view of the civil war that followed the Russian Revolution. It shows a worker bringing electricity and more generally the light of modernity and progress to a backward country, while depicting their opponents, which include a priest, a general, and a businessman, as seeking to extinguish that light. (The New York Public Library/Art Resource, NY)

required "friendly" governments in the region to permanently end the threat of invasion from the West. When the Marshall Plan seemed to suggest American efforts to incorporate Eastern Europe into a Western economic network, Stalin acted to install fully communist governments, loyal to himself, in Poland, East Germany, Czechoslovakia, Hungary, Romania, and Bulgaria. Backed by the pressure and presence of the Soviet army, communism was largely imposed on Eastern Europe from outside rather than growing out of a domestic revolution, as had happened in Russia itself.

Local communist parties, however, had some domestic support, deriving from their role in the resistance against the Nazis and their policies of land reform. In Hungary and Poland, for example, communist pressures led to the redistribution of much land to poor or landless peasants, and in free elections in Czechoslovakia in 1946 communists received 38 percent of the vote. The situation in Yugoslavia differed sharply from that of the rest of Eastern Europe. There a genuinely popular communist movement had played a leading role in the struggle against Nazi occupation and came to power on its own with little Soviet help. Its leader, Josef Broz, known as Tito, openly defied Soviet efforts to control Yugoslav communism. He proclaimed, "Our goal is that everyone should be master in his own house."[1]

China: A Prolonged Revolutionary Struggle

Communism triumphed in the ancient land of China in 1949, about thirty years after the Russian Revolution, likewise on the heels of war and domestic upheaval. But that revolution, which was a struggle of decades rather than a single year, was far different from its earlier Russian counterpart. The Chinese imperial system had collapsed in 1911, under the pressure of foreign imperialism, its own inadequacies, and mounting internal opposition (see Chapter 19, pages 834–44). Unlike in Russia, where intellectuals had been discussing socialism for half a century or more before the revolution, in China the ideas of Karl Marx were barely known in the early twentieth century. Not until 1921 was a small Chinese Communist Party (CCP) founded, aimed initially at organizing the country's minuscule urban working class.

Over the next twenty-eight years, that small party, with an initial membership of only sixty people, grew enormously, transformed its strategy, found a charismatic leader in Mao Zedong, engaged in an epic struggle with its opponents, fought the Japanese heroically, and in 1949 emerged victorious as the rulers of China. That victory was all the more surprising because the CCP faced a far more formidable foe than the weak Provisional Government over which the Bolsheviks had triumphed in Russia. That opponent was the Guomindang (GWOH-mihn-dahng) (Nationalist Party), which governed China after 1928. Led by a military officer, Chiang Kai-shek, that party promoted a measure of modern development (railroads, light industry, banking, airline services) in the decade that followed. However, the impact of these achievements was limited largely to the cities, leaving the rural areas, where most people lived, still impoverished. The Guomindang's base of support was also narrow, deriving from urban elites, rural landlords, and Western powers.

Chased out of China's cities in a wave of Guomindang-inspired anticommunist terror in 1927, the CCP groped its way toward a new revolutionary strategy, quite at odds with both classical Marxism and Russian practice. Whereas the Bolsheviks had found their primary audience among workers in Russia's major cities, Chinese communists increasingly looked to the country's peasant villages for support. Thus European Marxism was adapted once again, this time to fit the situation of a mostly peasant China. Still, it was no easy sell. Chinese peasants did not rise up spontaneously against their landlords, as Russian peasants had. However, years of guerrilla warfare, experiments with land reform in areas under communist control, and

the creation of a communist military force to protect liberated areas slowly gained for the CCP a growing measure of respect and support among China's peasants. In the process, Mao Zedong, the son of a prosperous Chinese peasant family and a professional revolutionary since the early 1920s, emerged as the party's leader.

To recruit women for the revolution, communists drew on a theoretical commitment to the liberation of women and in the areas under communist control established a Marriage Law that outlawed arranged or "purchased" marriages, made divorce easier, and gave women the right to vote and own property. Early experiments with land reform offered equal shares to men and women alike. Women's associations enrolled

Guided Reading Question

■ CHANGE
What was the appeal of communism in China before 1949?

AP® EXAM TIP

You need to know ways that communism in China differed from communism in Russia.

Mao Zedong and the Long March
An early member of China's then-minuscule Communist Party, Mao rose to a position of dominant leadership during the Long March of 1934–1935, when beleaguered communists from southeastern China trekked to a new base area in the north. This photograph shows Mao on his horse during that epic journey of some 6,000 miles. (© Collection A. Fox/Magnum Photos)

AP® EXAM TIP

You should know how the communist revolutions in Russia and China affected women's roles in society and politics.

hundreds of thousands of women and promoted literacy, fostered discussions of women's issues, and encouraged handicraft production, such as making the clothing, blankets, and shoes that were so essential for the revolutionary forces. But resistance to such radical measures from more traditional rural villagers, especially the male peasants and soldiers on whom the communists depended, persuaded the communists to modify these measures. Women were not permitted to seek divorce from men on active military duty. Women's land deeds were often given to male family heads and were regarded as family property. Female party members found themselves limited to work with women or children.

It was Japan's brutal invasion of China that gave the CCP a decisive opening, for that attack destroyed Guomindang control over much of the country and forced it to retreat to the interior, where it became even more dependent on conservative landlords. The CCP, by contrast, grew from just 40,000 members in 1937 to more than 1.2 million in 1945, while the communist-led People's Liberation Army mushroomed to 900,000 men, supported by an additional 2 million militia troops (see Map 21.2). Much of this growing support derived from the vigor with which the CCP waged war against the Japanese invaders. Using guerrilla warfare techniques learned in the struggle against the Guomindang, communist forces established themselves behind enemy lines and, despite periodic setbacks, offered a measure of security to many Chinese faced with Japanese atrocities. The Guomindang, by contrast, sometimes seemed to be more interested in eliminating the communists than in actively fighting the Japanese. Furthermore, in the areas it controlled, the CCP reduced rents, taxes, and interest payments for peasants; established literacy programs for adults; and mobilized women for the struggle. As the war drew to a close, more radical action followed. Teams of activists encouraged poor peasants to "speak bitterness" in public meetings, to "struggle" with landlords, and to "settle accounts" with them.

Thus the CCP frontally addressed both of China's major problems—foreign imperialism and peasant exploitation. It expressed Chinese nationalism as well as a demand for radical social change. It gained a reputation for honesty that contrasted sharply with the massive corruption of Guomindang officials. It put down deep roots among the peasantry in a way that the Bolsheviks never did. And whereas the Bolsheviks gained support by urging Russian withdrawal from the highly unpopular First World War, the CCP won support by aggressively pursuing the struggle against Japanese invaders during World War II. In 1949, four years after the war's end, the Chinese communists swept to victory over the Guomindang, many of whose followers fled to Taiwan. Mao Zedong announced triumphantly in Beijing's Tiananmen Square that "the Chinese people have stood up."

Building Socialism

Once they came to power, communist parties everywhere set about the construction of socialist societies. In the Soviet Union, this massive undertaking occurred under the leadership of Joseph Stalin in the 1920s and 1930s. The corresponding

Map 21.2 The Rise of Communism in China

Communism arose in China at the same time as the country was engaged in a terrible war with Japan and in the context of a civil war with Guomindang forces.

Map legend:
- Communist base areas before 1934
- Yanan base area, 1936–1947
- Japanese conquests by 1938
- ← Long March, 1934–1935

Jianxsi Soviet under Mao Zedong, 1929–1934

Chinese effort took place during the 1950s and 1960s with Mao Zedong at the helm.

To communist regimes, building socialism meant first of all the modernization and industrialization of their backward societies. They sought, however, a distinctly socialist modernity. This involved a frontal attack on long-standing inequalities of class and gender, an effort to prevent the making of new inequalities as the process of modern development unfolded, and the promotion of cultural values of selfless-ness and collectivism that could support a socialist society.

Those imperatives generated a political system thoroughly dominated by the Communist Party. Top-ranking party members enjoyed various privileges but were expected to be exemplars of socialism in the making by being disciplined, selfless, and utterly loyal to their country's Marxist ideology. The party itself penetrated society in ways that Western scholars called "totalitarian," for other parties were forbidden, the state controlled almost the entire economy, and political authorities ensured that the arts, education, and the media conformed to approved ways of thinking. Mass organizations for women, workers, students, and various professional groups operated under party control, with none of the independence that characterized civil society in the West.

In undertaking these tasks, the Soviet Union and China started from different places, most notably their international positions. In 1917, Russian Bolsheviks faced a hostile capitalist world alone, while Chinese communists, coming to power over thirty years later, had an established Soviet Union as a friendly northern neighbor and ally. Furthermore, Chinese revolutionaries had actually governed parts of their huge country for decades, gaining experience that the new Soviet rulers had altogether lacked, since they had come to power so quickly. And the Chinese communists were firmly rooted in the rural areas and among the country's vast peasant population, while their Russian counterparts had found their support mainly in the cities.

If these comparisons generally favored China in its efforts to "build socialism," in economic terms that country faced even more daunting prospects than did the Soviet Union. Its population was far greater, its industrial base far smaller, and the availability of new agricultural land far more limited than in the Soviet Union. Likewise, in China fewer people were literate, and the education system and transportation network were much less developed. Even more than the Soviets, Chinese communists had to build a modern society from the ground up.

Communist Feminism

Among the earliest and most revolutionary actions of these new communist regimes were efforts at liberating and mobilizing women. Communist countries in fact pioneered forms of women's liberation that only later were adopted in the West. This communist feminism was largely state directed, with the initiative coming from the top rather than bubbling up from grassroots movements as in the West. In the Soviet Union, where a small women's movement had taken shape in pre–World War I Russia, the new communist government almost immediately issued a series of laws and decrees regarding women. These measures declared full legal and political equality for women; marriage became a civil procedure among freely consenting adults; divorce was legalized and made easier, as was abortion; illegitimacy was abolished; women no longer had to take their husbands' surnames; pregnancy leave for employed women was mandated; and women were actively mobilized as workers in the country's drive to industrialization. Addressing a Congress of Women Workers and Peasants, Lenin declared: "Root out old habits. Every cook must learn to rule the state."[2]

In 1919, the party set up a special organization called Zhenotdel (zhen-ut-DEL) (Women's Department), whose radical leaders, all women, pushed a decidedly feminist agenda during the 1920s. They organized numerous conferences for women, trained women to run day-care centers and medical clinics, published newspapers and magazines aimed at a female audience, provided literacy and prenatal classes, and encouraged Muslim women to take off their veils. Alexandra Rodionova, a former streetcar conductor who had played an active role in the revolution, recalled the impact of participation in Zhenotdel: "This former illiterate working girl had been transformed into a person, powerful with the knowledge of her own rights, a consciousness of responsibility for everything happening in the country."[3] Much of this agenda encountered opposition from male communist officials and from ordinary people as well, and Stalin abolished Zhenotdel in 1930. While it lasted, though, it was a remarkable experiment in women's liberation by means of state action, animated by an almost utopian sense of new possibilities set loose by the revolution.

Guided Reading Question

■ CHANGE
What changes did communist regimes bring to the lives of women?

Similar policies took shape in communist China. The Marriage Law of 1950 was a direct attack on patriarchal and Confucian traditions. It decreed free choice in marriage, relatively easy divorce, the end of concubinage and child marriage, permission for widows to remarry, and equal property rights for women. A short but intense campaign by the CCP in the early 1950s sought to implement these changes, often against strenuous opposition. The party also launched a Women's Federation, a mass organization that enrolled millions of women. Its leaders, however, were far less radical than the Bolshevik feminists who led Zhenotdel in the 1920s. In China, there was little talk of "free love" or the "withering away of the family," as there had been in the USSR. Nevertheless, like their Soviet counterparts, Chinese women became much more actively involved in production outside the home. By 1978, 50 percent of agricultural workers and 38 percent of nonagricultural laborers were female. "Women can do anything" became a famous party slogan in the 1960s. (See Working with Evidence, Source 21.3, page 971.)

Mobilizing Women for Communism
As the Soviet Union mobilized for rapid economic development in the 1930s, women entered the workforce in great numbers. Here two young women are mastering the skills of driving a tractor on one of the large collective farms that replaced the country's private agriculture. (Sovoto/UIG via Getty Images)

Still, communist-style women's liberation had definite limits. Fearing that the "woman question" would detract from his emphasis on industrial production, Stalin declared it "solved" in 1930. Little direct discussion of women's issues was permitted in the several decades that followed. In neither the Soviet Union nor China did the Communist Party undertake a direct attack on male domination within the family. Thus the double burden of housework and child care plus paid employment continued to afflict most women. Moreover, women appeared only very rarely in the top political leadership of either country.

Socialism in the Countryside

AP® EXAM TIP

You must remember that most revolutions since the French Revolution have promised some type of land reform.

In their efforts to build socialism, both the Soviet Union and China first expropriated landlords' estates and redistributed that land on a much more equitable basis to the peasantry. Such actions, although clearly revolutionary, were not socialist, for peasants initially received their land as private property. In Russia, the peasants had spontaneously redistributed the land among themselves, and the victorious Bolsheviks merely ratified their actions. In China after 1949, land reform was a more prolonged and difficult process. Hastily trained teams were dispatched to the newly liberated areas, where they mobilized the poorer peasants in thousands of separate villages to confront and humiliate the landlords or the more wealthy peasants. Their land, animals, tools, houses, and money were then redistributed to the poorer members of the village. In these villages, land reform teams encountered the age-old deference that peasants traditionally had rendered to their social superiors. One young woman activist described the confrontational meetings intended to break this ancient pattern:

> "Speak bitterness meetings," as they were called, would help [the peasants] to understand how things really had been in the old days, to realize that their lives were not blindly ordained by fate . . . and that far from owing anything to the feudal landlords, it was the feudal landlords who owed them a debt of suffering beyond all reckoning.[4]

It was, as Mao Zedong put it, "not a dinner party." Approximately 1 to 2 million landlords were killed in the process, which was largely over by 1952.

Guided Reading Question

■ COMPARISON
How did the collectivization of agriculture differ between the USSR and China?

A second and more distinctly socialist stage of rural reform sought to end private property in land by collectivizing agriculture. In China, despite brief resistance from richer peasants, collectivization during the 1950s was a generally peaceful process, owing much to the close relationship between the Chinese Communist Party and the peasantry, which had been established during three decades of struggle. This contrasted markedly with the earlier experience of the Soviet Union from 1928 to 1933, when peasants were forced into collective farms and violence was extensive. Russian peasants slaughtered and consumed hundreds of thousands of animals rather than surrender them to the collectives. Stalin singled out the richer peasants, known as *kulaks* (koo-LAHKS), for exclusion from the new collective farms. Some were killed, and many others were deported to remote areas of the country. With little support or experience in the countryside, Soviet communists, who came mostly from the cities, were viewed as intrusive outsiders in Russian peasant villages. A terrible famine ensued, with some 5 million deaths from starvation or malnutrition. China, however, pushed collectivization even further than the Soviet Union did, particularly in huge "people's communes" during the Great Leap Forward in the late 1950s. It was an effort to mobilize China's enormous population for rapid development and at the same time to move toward a more fully communist society with an even greater degree of social equality and collective living. (See Working with Evidence, Source 21.2, page 969, for more on communes.) Administrative chaos, disruption of marketing networks, and bad weather combined to produce a massive famine that killed an amazing 20 million people or more between 1959 and 1962, dwarfing even the earlier Soviet famine.

Communism and Industrial Development

Both the Soviet Union and China defined industrialization as a fundamental task of their regimes. That process was necessary to end humiliating backwardness and poverty, to provide the economic basis for socialism, and to create the military strength that would enable their revolutions to survive in a hostile world. Though strongly anticapitalist, communists everywhere were ardent modernizers.

When the Chinese communists began their active industrialization efforts in the early 1950s, they largely followed the model pioneered by the Soviet Union in the late 1920s and the 1930s. That model involved state ownership of property, centralized planning embodied in successive five-year plans, priority to heavy industry, massive mobilization of the nation's human and material resources, and intrusive Communist Party control of the entire process. Both countries experienced major—indeed unprecedented—economic growth. The Soviet Union constructed the foundations of an industrial society in the 1930s that proved itself in the victory over Nazi Germany in World War II and that by the 1960s and 1970s had generated substantially improved standards of living. China also quickly expanded its output. (See Snapshot, page 944.) In addition, both countries achieved massive improvements in their literacy rates and educational opportunities, allowing far greater social mobility for millions of people than ever before. In both countries, industrialization fostered a similar set of social outcomes: rapid urbanization, exploitation of the countryside to provide resources for modern industry in the cities, and the growth of a privileged bureaucratic and technological elite intent on pursuing their own careers and passing on their new status to their children.

Perhaps the chief difference in the industrial histories of the Soviet Union and China lies in the leadership's response to these social outcomes. In the Soviet Union under Stalin and his successors, they were largely accepted. Industrialization was centered in large urban areas, which pulled from the countryside the most ambitious and talented people. A highly privileged group of state and party leaders emerged in the Stalin era and largely remained the unchallenged ruling class of the country until the 1980s. Even in the 1930s, the outlines of a conservative society, which had discarded much of its revolutionary legacy, were apparent. Stalin himself

AP® EXAM TIP

Take notes on these features of communist-led planned economies.

Guided Reading Question

■ CHANGE
What were the achievements of communist efforts at industrialization? What problems did these achievements generate?

SNAPSHOT China under Mao, 1949–1976

The following table reveals some of the achievements, limitations, and tragedies of China's communist experience during the era of Mao Zedong.[5]

Steel production	from 1.3 million to 23 million tons
Coal production	from 66 million to 448 million tons
Electric power generation	from 7 million to 133 billion kilowatt-hours
Fertilizer production	from 0.2 million to 28 million tons
Cement production	from 3 million to 49 million tons
Industrial workers	from 3 million to 50 million
Scientists and technicians	from 50,000 to 5 million
"Barefoot doctors" posted to countryside	1 million
Annual growth rate of industrial output	11 percent
Annual growth rate of agricultural output	2.3 percent
Total population	from 542 million to 1 billion
Average population growth rate per year	2 percent
Per capita consumption of rural dwellers	from 62 to 124 yuan annually
Per capita consumption of urban dwellers	from 148 to 324 yuan
Overall life expectancy	from 35 to 65 years
Counterrevolutionaries killed (1949–1952)	between 1 million and 3 million
People labeled "rightists" in 1957	550,000
Deaths from famine during Great Leap Forward	20 million or more
Deaths during Cultural Revolution	500,000
Officials sent down to rural labor camps during Cultural Revolution	3 million or more
Urban youth sent down to countryside	17 million (1967–1976)

endorsed Russian patriotism, traditional family values, individual competition, and substantial differences in wages to stimulate production, as an earlier commitment to egalitarianism was substantially abandoned. Increasingly the invocation of revolutionary values was devoid of real content, and by the 1970s the perception of official hypocrisy was widespread.

The unique feature of Chinese history under Mao Zedong's leadership was a recurrent effort to combat these perhaps inevitable tendencies of any industrializing process and to revive and preserve the revolutionary spirit, which had animated the

Communist Party during its long struggle for power. By the mid-1950s, Mao and some of his followers had become persuaded that the Soviet model of industrialization was leading China away from socialism and toward new forms of inequality, toward individualistic and careerist values, and toward an urban bias that privileged the cities at the expense of the countryside. The Great Leap Forward of 1958–1960 marked Mao's first response to these distortions of Chinese socialism. It promoted small-scale industrialization in the rural areas rather than focusing wholly on large enterprises in the cities; it tried to foster widespread and practical technological education for all rather than relying on a small elite of highly trained technical experts; and it envisaged an immediate transition to full communism in the "people's communes" rather than waiting for industrial development to provide the material basis for that transition. The massive famine that followed temporarily discredited Mao's radicalism.

Nonetheless, in the mid-1960s Mao launched yet another campaign—the Great Proletarian Cultural Revolution—to combat the capitalist tendencies that he believed had penetrated even the highest ranks of the Communist Party itself. The Cultural Revolution also involved new policies to bring health care and education to the countryside and to reinvigorate earlier efforts at rural industrialization under local rather than central control. In these ways, Mao struggled, though without great success, to overcome the inequalities associated with China's modern development and to create a model of socialist modernity quite distinct from that of the Soviet Union.

The Cultural Revolution also rejected feminism, any specific concern with women's issues, and much that was feminine. A popular slogan stated: "The times have changed; men and women are the same." Yet the supposedly gender-neutral model seemed strikingly masculine. Women cut their hair short, wore army clothes, and learned to curse; they were depicted in propaganda posters as "iron girls," strong, muscular, and performing heavy traditionally male work. (See Working with Evidence, Source 21.3, page 971.) Art, literature, ballet, and opera cast them as militant revolutionary participants. And yet, factory managers continued to prefer women workers because of their alleged patience and manual dexterity. Young women sent to the countryside to work with peasants found themselves subject to

The Great Leap Forward
This Chinese poster from 1960 celebrates both the agricultural and industrial efforts of the Great Leap Forward. The caption reads: "Start the movement to increase production and practice thrift, with foodstuffs and steel at the center, with great force!" The great famine that accompanied this "great leap" belied the optimistic outlook of the poster. (Stefan R. Landsberger Collections/ International Institute of Social History, Amsterdam/www.chineseposters.net)

sexual abuse by male officials. Thus strenuous Maoist efforts to eliminate differences between classes, between urban and rural life, and between men and women largely failed.

A final commonality among communist industrializers lay in their great confidence in both human rationality and the centralized planning embodied in huge projects—enormous factories, large collective farms, gigantic dams. Soviet officials saw the environment as an enemy, spoke about "the struggle against nature," and looked forward to "a profound rearrangement of the entire living world."[6] This attitude, no less than capitalist assumptions, led to immense environmental devastation and a very difficult legacy for postcommunist regimes. In the Soviet Union, for example, huge industrial complexes such as Magnitogorsk concentrated air and water pollution. A scheme to bring millions of acres of semi-arid land under cultivation in Central Asia depleted and eroded the fragile soil. Diverting the waters of several rivers feeding the Aral Sea for irrigating cotton fields reduced the size of that huge inland sea by 90 percent. By the late 1980s, such environmental heedlessness meant that about half of the cultivated land in the country was endangered by erosion, salinization, or swamping; some 30 percent of food products were contaminated by pesticides or herbicides; 75 percent of the surface water was severely polluted; and 70 million people lived in cities with air pollution five or more times the acceptable level.[7] But nothing brought Soviet environmental problems to public attention more dramatically than the explosion of a nuclear reactor at Chernobyl in 1986. It scattered highly radioactive material over parts of Ukraine and Belorussia, while the cloud from the explosion swept across parts of Eastern Europe and Scandinavia, terrifying millions even much farther away.

The Search for Enemies

Despite their totalitarian tendencies, the communist societies of the Soviet Union and China were laced with conflict. Under both Stalin and Mao, those conflicts erupted in a search for enemies that disfigured both societies. An elastic concept of "enemy" came to include not only surviving remnants from the prerevolutionary elites but also, and more surprisingly, high-ranking members and longtime supporters of the Communist Party who allegedly had been corrupted by bourgeois ideas. Refracted through the lens of Marxist thinking, these people became class enemies who had betrayed the revolution and were engaged in a vast conspiracy, often linked to foreign imperialists, to subvert the socialist enterprise and restore capitalism. In the rhetoric of the leadership, the class struggle continued and even intensified as the triumph of socialism drew closer.

In the Soviet Union, that process culminated in the Terror, or the Great Purges, of the late 1930s, which enveloped tens of thousands of prominent communists, including virtually all of Lenin's top associates, and millions of more ordinary people. (See Zooming In: Anna Dubova, page 948, for an individual experience of the Terror.) Based on suspicious associations in the past, denunciations by colleagues,

AP® EXAM TIP

Compare ways the French (in Chapter 16), Russian, and Chinese revolutions attacked perceived "enemies" to chart how revolutions deal with opposition.

Guided Reading Question

■ EXPLANATION
Why did communist regimes generate terror and violence on such a massive scale?

connections to foreign countries, or simply bad luck, such people were arrested, usually in the dead of night, and then tried and sentenced either to death or to long years in harsh and remote labor camps known as the gulag. A series of show trials publicized the menace that these "enemies of the people" allegedly posed to the country and its revolution. Close to 1 million people were executed between 1936 and 1941. An additional 4 or 5 million were sent to the gulag, where they were forced to work in horrendous conditions and died in appalling numbers. Victimizers too were numerous: the Terror consumed the energies of a huge corps of officials, investigators, interrogators, informers, guards, and executioners, many of whom were themselves arrested, exiled, or executed in the course of the purges.

In the Soviet Union, the search for enemies occurred under the clear control of the state. In China, however, it became a much more public process, escaping the control of the leadership, particularly during the most violent years of the Cultural Revolution (1966–1969). Mao had become convinced that many within the Communist Party had been seduced by capitalist values of self-seeking and materialism and were no longer animated by the idealistic revolutionary vision of earlier times. Therefore, he called for rebellion, against the Communist Party itself. Millions of young people responded, and, organized as Red Guards, they set out to rid China of those who were "taking the capitalist road." Following gigantic and ecstatic rallies in Beijing, they fanned out across the country and attacked local party and government officials, teachers, intellectuals, factory managers, and others they defined as enemies. (See Working with Evidence, Sources 21.1 and 21.4, pages 968 and 972.) Rival revolutionary groups soon began fighting with one another, violence erupted throughout the country, and civil war threatened China. Mao was forced to call in the military to restore order and Communist Party control. Both the Soviet Terror and the Chinese Cultural Revolution badly discredited the very idea of socialism and contributed to the ultimate collapse of the communist experiment at the end of the century.

> **PRACTICING AP® HISTORICAL THINKING**
>
> How did the Soviet Union and China differ in terms of the revolutions that brought communists to power and in the construction of socialist societies? What commonalities are also apparent?

East versus West: A Global Divide and a Cold War

Not only did communist regimes bring revolutionary changes to the societies they governed, but their very existence launched a global conflict that restructured international relations and touched the lives of almost everyone, particularly in the twentieth century's second half. That rift began soon after the Russian Revolution when the new communist government became the source of fear and loathing to many in the Western capitalist world. The common threat of Nazi Germany temporarily made unlikely allies of the Soviet Union, Britain, and the United States, but a few years after World War II ended, that division erupted again in what became known as the cold war. Underlying that conflict were the geopolitical and ideological realities of the postwar world. The Soviet Union and the United States

Anna Dubova, a Russian Peasant Girl and Urban Woman

Born into a large peasant family near Smolensk in western Russia in 1916, Anna Dubova lived through the entire communist experience of her country.[8] Hers was a life that illustrates the complexities that ordinary individuals faced as they sought to navigate the communist system.

Anna was one of fourteen children, of whom seven survived. Her family was dominated by a strict, hardworking, and highly religious father, who was choirmaster of the local church. Anna's father was suspicious of the communists when they came to power the year after Anna's birth, but her grandmother was more forthright. "We have a new tsar," she declared. "The forces of the Antichrist have triumphed." Nonetheless, her father accepted an appointment in 1922 as chairman of the village soviet, the new communist organ of local government. During the 1920s, the village and Anna's family flourished under Lenin's New Economic Policy, which briefly permitted a considerable measure of private enterprise and profit making. Her father even opened a small shop in the village where he sold goods purchased in the city.

A 1941 image of a woman factory worker in Moscow.

By 1928, however, everything changed as the Soviet regime, now under Joseph Stalin's leadership, abruptly moved to collectivize agriculture and root out *kulaks*, supposedly wealthy peasants who were thought to bear the germ of a hated capitalism. Because of her father's shop, the family was labeled as kulak and their property was confiscated. "I remember so well how Mama sat and cried when they took away the cow," Anna recalled years later. The family forestalled their expected deportation to the far north of the Soviet Union only by promising Anna, then just thirteen, in marriage to the local Communist Party secretary. The marriage never took place, however, and the family was forced to leave. Later, Anna was permitted to join her older sister in Moscow, but approval for that much-coveted move came at a very high price. Anna recalled, "I had to write out an official statement that I renounced my parents, that I no longer had any ties with them."

were now the world's major political/military powers, replacing the shattered and diminished states of Western Europe, but they represented sharply opposed views of history, society, politics, and international relations. Conflict, in retrospect, seemed almost inevitable.

Military Conflict and the Cold War

The initial arena of the cold war was Eastern Europe, where Soviet insistence on security and control clashed with American and British desires for open and democratic societies with ties to the capitalist world economy. What resulted were rival

Thus Anna, a rural teenager, joined millions of other peasants who flocked to the city to pursue new opportunities that became available as the Soviet Union launched its industrialization drive. In Moscow, she gained a basic education, a vocation in cake decorating, which she enjoyed, and a brief stint as a mechanic and chauffeur, which she detested. All the while the shadow of her kulak label followed her. Had it been discovered, she could have lost her job and her permission to live in Moscow. And so she married a party activist from a poor peasant family, she explained years later, "just so I could cover up my background." Her husband drank heavily, leaving her with a daughter when he went off to war in 1941.

In the Soviet Union, the late 1930s witnessed the Terror when millions of alleged "enemies of the people" were arrested and hauled off to execution or labor camps. Anna recalled what it was like: "You'd come home and they'd say, Yesterday they took away Uncle Lesha. . . . You'd go to see a girlfriend, they'd say, We have an empty room now; they've exiled Andreitsev." Like most people not directly involved, Anna believed in the guilt of these people. And she feared that she herself might be mistakenly accused, for those with a kulak label were particular targets of the search for enemies. "I was only afraid," she remembered, "that I would be raped in prison."

Beyond her kulak background, Anna also felt compelled to hide a deep religious sensibility derived from her childhood. She remembered the disappearance of the village priest, the looting of the churches, and the destruction of icons. And so she never entered a church or prayed in front of others. But she wore a cross under her clothing. "I never stopped [believing]," she recalled. "But I concealed it. Deep down . . . I believed." Nor did she ever seek to join the Communist Party, though it may well have advanced her career prospects and standard of living. Perhaps she feared that the investigations accompanying party membership would have disclosed her compromising social and religious background.

In the decades following World War II and especially after Stalin's death in 1953, Anna's life seemed to stabilize. She entered into a thirty-year relationship with a man and found satisfying work in a construction design office, though the lack of higher education and party connections prevented her from moving into higher-paid jobs. Looking back on her life, she regretted the communist intrusion, particularly in its Stalinist phase, into what she remembered as a happy childhood. She had come to value, perhaps nostalgically, the life of a peasant over that of an urban worker. She reflected, "[As a peasant,] I would have lived on the fruits of my labor. . . . [Instead,] I've lived someone else's life."

Question: In what ways did communism shape Anna's life, and in what respects was she able to construct her own life within that system?

---

military alliances (NATO and the Warsaw Pact), a largely voluntary American sphere of influence in Western Europe, and an imposed Soviet sphere in Eastern Europe. The heavily fortified border between Eastern and Western Europe came to be known as the Iron Curtain. Thus Europe was bitterly divided. But although tensions flared across this dividing line, particularly in Berlin, no shooting war occurred between the two sides (see Map 21.3).

By contrast, the extension of communism into Asia—China, Korea, and Vietnam—globalized the cold war and occasioned its most destructive and prolonged "hot wars." A North Korean invasion of South Korea in 1950 led to both Chinese and American involvement in a bitter three-year war (1950–1953), which ended in

Guided Reading Question

■ CONNECTION

In what different ways was the cold war expressed?

Map 21.3   The Global Cold War

The cold war witnessed a sharp division between the communist world and the Western democratic world. It also divided the continent of Europe; the countries of China, Korea, Vietnam, and Germany; and the city of Berlin. In many places, it also sparked crises that brought the nuclear-armed superpowers of the United States and the USSR to the brink of war, although in every case they managed to avoid direct military conflict between themselves. Many countries in Africa and Asia claimed membership in a Non-Aligned Movement, which sought to avoid entanglements in cold war conflicts.

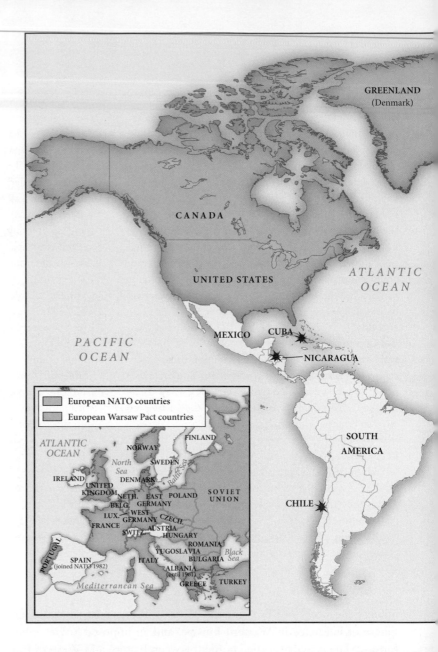

an essential standoff that left the Korean peninsula still divided in the early twenty-first century. Likewise in Vietnam, military efforts by South Vietnamese communists and the already-communist North Vietnamese government to unify their country prompted massive American intervention in the 1960s. To American authorities, a communist victory opened the door to further communist expansion in Asia and beyond. Armed and supported by the Soviets and Chinese and willing to endure enormous losses, the Vietnamese communists bested the Americans, who were

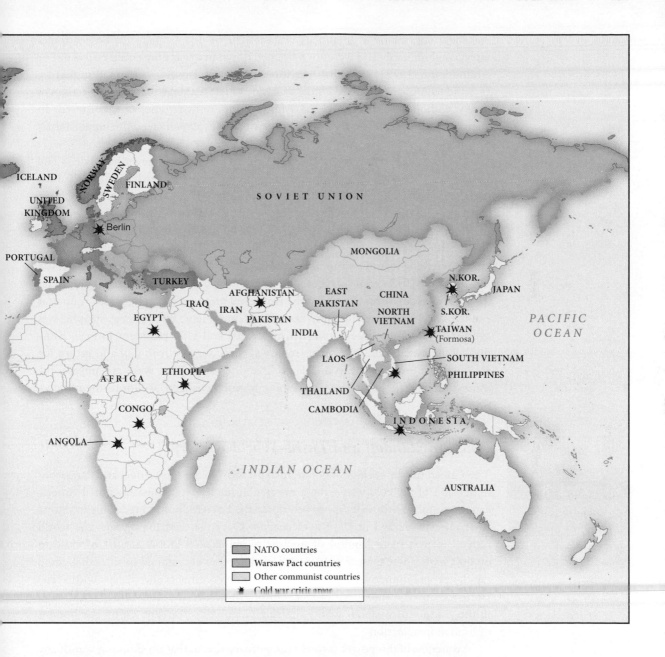

NATO countries
Warsaw Pact countries
Other communist countries
Cold war crisis areas

hobbled by growing protest at home. The Vietnamese united their country under communist control by 1975.

A third major military conflict of the cold war era occurred in Afghanistan, where a Marxist party had taken power in 1978. Soviet leaders were delighted at this extension of communism on their southern border, but radical land reforms and efforts to liberate Afghan women soon alienated much of this conservative Muslim country and led to a mounting opposition movement. Fearing the overthrow of a new communist state and its replacement by Islamic radicals, Soviet forces intervened militarily and were soon bogged down in a war they could not win. For a full decade (1979–1989), that war was a "bleeding wound," sustained in part by U.S. aid to Afghan guerrillas. Under widespread international pressure, Soviet forces finally withdrew in 1989, and the Afghan communist regime soon collapsed. In Vietnam and Afghanistan, both superpowers painfully experienced the limits of their power.

The most haunting battle of the cold war era was one that never happened. The setting was Cuba, where a communist regime under the leadership of Fidel Castro had emerged by the early 1960s. (See Zooming In: The Cuban Revolution, page 954.) Intense American hostility to this nearby outpost of communism prompted the Soviet leader Nikita Khrushchev (KROOSH-chef), who had risen to power after Stalin's death in 1953, to secretly deploy nuclear-tipped Soviet missiles to Cuba, believing that this would deter further U.S. action against Castro. When the missiles were discovered in October 1962, the world held its breath for thirteen days as American forces blockaded the island and prepared for an invasion. A nuclear exchange between the superpowers seemed imminent, but that catastrophe was averted by a compromise between Khrushchev and U.S. president John F. Kennedy. Under its terms, the Soviets removed their missiles from Cuba in return for an American promise not to invade the island. That promise was kept and a communist regime still persists in Cuba, though much changed, well into the twenty-first century.

Nuclear Standoff and Third-World Rivalry

AP® EXAM TIP

Cold war tensions around the globe are an important subject in the AP® course.

The Cuban missile crisis gave concrete expression to the most novel and dangerous dimension of the cold war—the arms race in nuclear weapons. An initial American monopoly on those weapons prompted the Soviet Union to redouble its efforts to acquire them, and in 1949 it succeeded. Over the next forty years, the world moved from a mere handful of nuclear weapons to a global arsenal of close to 60,000 warheads. Delivery systems included bomber aircraft and missiles that could rapidly propel numerous warheads across whole continents and oceans with accuracies measured in hundreds of feet. During those decades, the entire world lived in the shadow of weapons whose destructive power is scarcely within the bounds of human imagination.

Awareness of this power is surely the primary reason that no shooting war of any kind occurred between the two superpowers. In the two world wars, the participants had been greatly surprised by the destructiveness of modern weapons. During the cold war, however, the leaders of the two superpowers knew beyond any doubt that a nuclear war would produce only losers and utter catastrophe. Already in 1949, Stalin had observed that "atomic weapons can hardly be used without spelling the end of the world."[9] Particularly after the frightening Cuban missile crisis of 1962, both sides carefully avoided further nuclear provocation, even while con-

The Hydrogen Bomb
During the 1950s and early 1960s, tests in the atmosphere of ever larger and more sophisticated hydrogen bombs made images of enormous fireballs and mushroom-shaped clouds the universal symbol of these weapons, which were immensely more powerful than the atomic bombs dropped on Japan. The American test pictured here took place in 1957. (Photo courtesy of National Nuclear Security Administration/Nevada Site Office)

tinuing the buildup of their respective arsenals. Moreover, because they feared that a conventional war would escalate to the nuclear level, they implicitly agreed to sidestep any direct military confrontation at all.

Still, opportunities for conflict abounded as the U.S.-Soviet rivalry spanned the globe. Using military and economic aid, educational opportunities, political pressure, and covert action, both sides courted countries emerging from colonial rule. Cold war fears of communist penetration prompted U.S. intervention, sometimes openly and often secretly, in Iran, the Philippines, Guatemala, El Salvador, Chile, the Congo, and elsewhere. In the process, the United States frequently supported anticommunist but corrupt and authoritarian regimes. However, neither superpower was able to completely dominate its supposed allies, many of whom resisted the role of pawns in superpower rivalries. Some countries, such as India, took a posture of nonalignment in the cold war, while others tried to play off the superpowers against each other. Indonesia received large amounts of Soviet and Eastern European aid, but that did not prevent it from destroying the Indonesian Communist Party in 1965, killing half a million suspected communists in the process. When the Americans refused to assist Egypt in building the Aswan Dam in the mid-1950s, that country developed a close relationship with the Soviet Union. Later, in 1972, Egypt expelled 21,000 Soviet advisers and again aligned more clearly with the United States.

The Cuban Revolution

"You Americans must realize what Cuba means to us old Bolsheviks," declared a high-ranking Soviet official, Anastas Mikoyan, in 1960. "We have been waiting all our lives for a country to go communist without the Red Army. It has happened in Cuba, and it makes us feel like boys again."[10] The triumph of the Cuban revolutionaries must have been exhilarating for communists everywhere because it occurred in such an unlikely place. Located just 90 miles from Florida, Cuba had been a virtual protectorate of the United States in the decades following its independence from Spain in 1902. Moreover, U.S. companies had long exerted considerable influence over the weak and corrupt Cuban government and dominated key sectors of the economy, including sugar, the island's most important export. Nonetheless, Fidel Castro, son of a wealthy sugar plantation owner, led a successful popular insurrection that transformed Cuba into a Marxist socialist state just off the southern coast of the United States.

The armed revolt began disastrously. In 1953, the Cuban army defeated Castro and 123 of his supporters

Fidel Castro fighting in the mountains of Cuba in 1957.

when they attacked two army barracks in what was their first major military operation. Castro himself was captured, sentenced to jail, and then released into exile. However, fortunes shifted in 1956, when Castro slipped back into Cuba and succeeded in bringing together many opponents of the current regime in an armed nationalist insurgency dedicated to radical economic and social reform. Upon seizing power in 1959, Castro and his government acted decisively to implement their revolutionary agenda. Within a year, they had effectively redistributed 15 percent of the nation's wealth by granting land to the poor, increasing wages, and lowering rents. In the following year, the new government nationalized the property of both wealthy Cubans and U.S. corporations. Many Cubans, particularly among the elite, fled into exile. "The revolution," declared Castro, "is the dictatorship of the exploited against the exploiters."[11]

The Cold War and the Superpowers

World War II and the cold war provided the context for the emergence of the United States as a global superpower, playing a role that has often been compared to that of Great Britain in the nineteenth century. Much of that effort was driven by the perceived demands of the cold war, during which the United States spearheaded the Western effort to contain a worldwide communist movement that seemed to be advancing. By 1970, one writer observed, "the United States had more than 1,000,000 soldiers in 30 countries, was a member of four regional defense alliances and an active participant in a fifth, had mutual defense treaties with 42 nations, was

Economic and political pressure from the United States followed, culminating in the Bay of Pigs, a failed invasion of the island in 1961 by Cuban exiles with covert support from the U.S. government. American hostility pushed the revolutionary nationalist Castro closer to the Soviet Union, and gradually he began to think of himself and his revolution as Marxist. In response to Cuban pleas for support against American aggression, the Soviet premier Khrushchev deployed nuclear missiles on the island, sparking the Cuban missile crisis. While the compromise reached between the two superpowers resulted in the withdrawal of the missiles, it did include assurances from the United States that it would not attack Cuba.

In the decades that followed, Cuba sought to export its brand of revolution beyond its borders, especially in Latin America and Africa. Che Guevara, an Argentine who had fought in the Cuban Revolution, declared, "Our revolution is endangering all American possessions in Latin America. We are telling these countries to make their own revolution."[12] Cuba supported revolutionary movements in many regions; however, none succeeded in creating a lasting Cuban-style regime.

The legacy of the Cuban Revolution has been mixed. The new government devoted considerable resources to improving health and education on the island. By the mid-1980s, Cuba possessed both the highest literacy rate and the lowest infant mortality rate in Latin America,

Over the same period, life expectancy increased from fifty-eight to seventy-three years, putting Cuba on a par with the United States. Living standards for most improved as well. Indeed, Cuba became a model for development in other Latin American countries.

However, earlier promises to establish a truly democratic system never materialized. Castro declared in 1959 that elections were unneeded because "this democracy . . . has found its expression, directly, in the intimate union and identification of the government with the people."[13] The state placed limits on free expression and arrested opponents or forced them into exile. Cuba has also failed to achieve the economic development originally envisioned at the time of the revolution. Sugar remains its chief export crop, and by the 1980s Cuba had become almost as economically dependent on the Soviet Union as it had been upon the United States. Desperate consequences followed when the Cuban economy shrank by a third following the collapse of the Soviet Union.

Like communist experiments in the Soviet Union and China, Cuba experienced real improvements in living standards, especially for the poor, but these gains were accompanied by sharp restraints on personal freedoms and mixed results in the economy. Such have been the ambivalent outcomes of many revolutionary upheavals.

Question: Compare the Cuban Revolution to those in Russia and China. What are the similarities and differences?

a member of 53 international organizations, and was furnishing military or economic aid to nearly 100 nations across the face of the globe."[14]

The need for quick and often secret decision making gave rise in the United States to a strong or "imperial" presidency and a "national security state," in which defense and intelligence agencies acquired great power within the government and were often unaccountable to Congress. This served to strengthen the influence of what U.S. president Dwight Eisenhower (r. 1953–1961) called the "military-industrial complex," a coalition of the armed services, military research laboratories, and private defense industries that both stimulated and benefited from increased military spending and cold war tensions.

Guided Reading Question

■ CONNECTION

In what ways did the United States play a global role after World War II?

AP® EXAM TIP

Pay attention to the rise of multinational corporations (MNCs) after World War II here and in Chapters 22 and 23.

Sustaining this immense military effort was a flourishing U.S. economy and an increasingly middle-class society. The United States was the only major industrial country to escape the physical devastation of war on its own soil. As World War II ended with Europe, the Soviet Union, and Japan in ruins, the United States was clearly the world's most productive economy. "The whole world is hungry for American goods," wrote one American economist in 1945.[15] Beyond their goods, Americans sent their capital abroad in growing amounts—from $19 billion in 1950 to $81 billion in 1965. Huge American firms such as General Motors, Ford, Mobil, Sears, General Electric, and Westinghouse established factories, offices, and subsidiaries in many countries and sold their goods locally. The U.S. dollar replaced the British pound as the most trusted international currency.

Accompanying the United States' political and economic penetration of the world was its popular culture. In musical terms, first jazz, then rock and roll, and most recently rap have found receptive audiences abroad, particularly among the young. By the 1990s, American movies took about 70 percent of the market in Europe, and in 2012 some 33,000 McDonald's restaurants in 119 countries served 68 million customers every day. Various American brand names—Marlboro, Coca-Cola, Jeep, Spam, Nike, Kodak—became common points of reference around the world. English became a global language, while American slang terms—"groovy," "crazy," "cool"—were integrated into many of the world's languages.

On the communist side, the cold war was accompanied by considerable turmoil both within and among the various communist states. Joseph Stalin, Soviet dictator and acknowledged leader of the communist world in general, died in 1953 as that global conflict was mounting. His successor, Nikita Khrushchev, stunned his country and communists everywhere with a lengthy speech delivered to a party congress in 1956 in which he presented a devastating account of Stalin's crimes, particularly those against party members. These revelations shocked many of the party faithful, for Stalin had been viewed as the "genius of all time." Now he was presented as a criminal.

Guided Reading Question

■ DESCRIPTION
What were the strengths and weaknesses of the communist world by the 1970s?

In the Soviet Union, the superpower of the communist world, the cold war justified a continuing emphasis on military and defense industries after World War II and gave rise to a Soviet version of the military-industrial complex. Soviet citizens, even more than Americans, were subject to incessant government propaganda that glorified their system and vilified that of their American opponents.

As the communist world expanded, so too did divisions and conflicts among its various countries. Many in the West had initially viewed world communism as a monolithic force whose disciplined members meekly followed Soviet dictates in cold war solidarity against the West. And Marxists everywhere contended that revolutionary socialism would erode national loyalties as the "workers of the world" united in common opposition to global capitalism. Nonetheless, the communist world experienced far more bitter and divisive conflict than did the Western alliance, which was composed of supposedly warlike, greedy, and highly competitive nations.

Czechoslovakia, 1968
In August 1968, Soviet forces invaded Czechoslovakia, where a popular reform movement proclaiming "socialism with a human face" threatened to erode established communist control. The Soviet troops that crushed this so-called Prague Spring were greeted by thousands of peaceful street demonstrators begging them to go home. (Libor Hajsky/CTK/AP Photo)

In Eastern Europe, Yugoslav leaders early on had rejected Soviet domination of their internal affairs and charted their own independent road to socialism. Fearing that reform might lead to contagious defections from the communist bloc, Soviet forces actually invaded their supposed allies in Hungary (1956–1957) and Czechoslovakia (1968) to crush such movements. In the early 1980s, Poland was seriously threatened with a similar action. The brutal suppression of these reform movements gave credibility to Western perceptions of the cold war as a struggle between tyranny and freedom and badly tarnished the image of Soviet communism as a reasonable alternative to capitalism.

Even more startling, the two communist giants, the Soviet Union and China, found themselves sharply opposed, owing to territorial disputes, ideological differences, and rivalry for communist leadership. The Chinese bitterly criticized Khrushchev for backing down in the Cuban missile crisis, while to the Soviet leadership, Mao was insanely indifferent to the possible consequences of a nuclear war. In 1960, the Soviet Union backed away from an earlier promise to provide China with the prototype of an atomic bomb and abruptly withdrew all Soviet advisers and technicians, who had been assisting Chinese development. By the late 1960s, China on its own had developed a modest nuclear capability, and the two countries were at the brink of war, with the Soviet Union hinting at a possible nuclear strike on Chinese military targets. Their enmity certainly benefited the United States, which in the 1970s was able to pursue a "triangular diplomacy," easing tensions and simultaneously signing arms control agreements with the USSR and opening a formal relationship with China. Beyond this central conflict, a communist China in fact went to war against a communist Vietnam in 1979, while Vietnam invaded a communist Cambodia in the late 1970s. Nationalism, in short, proved more powerful than communist solidarity, even in the face of cold war hostilities with the West.

Despite its many internal conflicts, world communism remained a powerful global presence during the 1970s, achieving its greatest territorial reach. China was emerging from the chaos of the Cultural Revolution. The Soviet Union had matched U.S. military might; in response, the Americans launched a major buildup of their own military forces in the early 1980s. Despite American hostility, Cuba remained a communist outpost in the Western Hemisphere, with impressive achievements in education and health care for its people. Communism triumphed in Vietnam, dealing a major setback to the United States. A number of African countries affirmed their commitment to Marxism. Few people anywhere expected that within two decades most of the twentieth century's experiment with communism would be over.

Paths to the End of Communism

More rapidly than its beginning, and far more peacefully, the communist era came to an end during the last twenty years of the twentieth century. It was a drama in three acts. Act One began in China during the late 1970s, following the death of its towering revolutionary leader Mao Zedong in 1976. Over the next several decades, the CCP gradually abandoned almost everything that had been associated with Maoist communism, even as the party retained its political control of the country. Act Two took place in Eastern Europe in the "miracle year" of 1989, when popular movements toppled despised communist governments one after another all across the region. The climactic Act Three in this "end of communism" drama occurred in 1991 in the Soviet Union, where the entire "play" had opened seventy-four years earlier. There the reformist leader Mikhail Gorbachev (GORE-beh-CHOF) had come to power in 1985 intending to revive and save Soviet socialism from its accumulated dysfunctions. Those efforts, however, only exacerbated the country's many difficulties and led to the political disintegration of the Soviet Union on December 25, 1991. The curtain had fallen on the communist era and on the cold war as well.

Behind these separate stories lay two general failures of the communist experiment, measured both by their own standards and by those of the larger world. The first was economic. Despite their early successes, communist economies by the late 1970s showed no signs of catching up to the more advanced capitalist countries.

AP® EXAM TIP

Make a list of the major steps toward the fall of global communism, beginning in the late 1960s.

Guided Reading Question

■ CHANGE

What explains the rapid end of the communist era?

The highly regimented Soviet economy in particular was largely stagnant, its citizens were forced to stand in long lines for consumer goods and complained endlessly about their poor quality and declining availability. This was enormously embarrassing, for it had been the proud boast of communist leaders everywhere that they had found a better route to modern prosperity than their capitalist rivals had. Furthermore, these comparisons were increasingly well known, thanks to the global information revolution. This failure had security implications as well, for economic growth, even more than military capacity, was the measure of state power as the twentieth century approached its end.

The second failure was moral. The horrors of Stalin's Terror and the gulag, of Mao's Cultural Revolution, of something approaching genocide in communist Cambodia—all of this wore away at communist claims to moral superiority over capitalism. Moreover, this erosion occurred as global political culture more widely embraced democracy and human rights as the universal legacy of humankind, rather than the exclusive possession of the capitalist West. In both economic and moral terms, the communist path to the modern world was increasingly seen as a road to nowhere.

Communist leaders were not ignorant of these problems, and they moved aggressively to address them, particularly in China and the Soviet Union. But their approach to doing so varied greatly, as did the outcomes of those efforts. Thus, much as the Russian and Chinese revolutions differed and their approaches to building socialism diverged, so too did these communist giants chart distinct paths during the final years of the communist experiment.

China: Abandoning Communism and Maintaining the Party

As the dust settled from the political shakeout following Mao's death in 1976, Deng Xiaoping (dung shee-yao-ping) emerged as China's "paramount leader," committed to ending the periodic upheavals of the Maoist era while fostering political stability and economic growth. Soon previously banned plays, operas, films, and translations of Western classics reappeared, and a "literature of the wounded" exposed the sufferings of the Cultural Revolution. Some 100,000 political prisoners, many of them high-ranking communists, were released and restored to important positions. A party evaluation of Mao severely criticized his mistakes during the Great Leap Forward and the Cultural Revolution, while praising his role as a revolutionary leader.

Even more dramatic were Deng's economic reforms. In the rural areas, these reforms included a rapid dismantling of the country's system of collectivized farming and a return to something close to small-scale private agriculture. Impoverished Chinese peasants eagerly embraced these new opportunities and pushed them even further than the government had intended. Industrial reform proceeded more gradually. Managers of state enterprises were given greater authority and encouraged to act like private owners, making many of their own decisions and seeking profits.

AP® EXAM TIP

Take notes on factors that led to more economic freedom in communist China starting in the late twentieth century.

China opened itself to the world economy and welcomed foreign investment in special enterprise zones along the coast, where foreign capitalists received tax breaks and other inducements. Local governments and private entrepreneurs joined forces in thousands of flourishing "township and village enterprises" that produced food, clothing, building materials, and much more.

The outcome of these reforms was stunning economic growth and a new prosperity for millions. Better diets, lower mortality rates, declining poverty, massive urban construction, and surging exports—all of this accompanied China's rejoining of the world economy and contributed to a much-improved material life for millions of its citizens. To many observers, China was the emerging economic giant of the twenty-first century. On the other hand, the country's burgeoning economy also generated massive corruption among Chinese officials, sharp inequalities between the coast and the interior, a huge problem of urban overcrowding, terrible pollution in major cities, and periodic inflation as the state loosened its controls over the economy. Urban vices such as street crime, prostitution, gambling, drug addiction, and a criminal underworld, which had been largely eliminated after 1949, surfaced again in China's booming cities. Nonetheless, something remarkable had occurred in China: an essentially capitalist economy had been restored, and by none other than the Communist Party itself. Mao's worst fears had been realized, as China "took the capitalist road."

Although the party was willing to largely abandon communist economic policies, it was adamantly unwilling to relinquish its political monopoly or to promote democracy at the national level. "Talk about democracy in the abstract," Deng Xiaoping declared, "will inevitably lead to the unchecked spread of ultrademocracy and anarchism, to the complete disruption of political stability, and to the total failure of our modernization program. . . . China will once again be plunged into chaos, division, retrogression, and darkness."[16] Such attitudes associated democracy with the chaos and uncontrolled mass action of the Cultural Revolution. Thus, when a democracy movement spearheaded by university and secondary school students surfaced in the late 1980s, Deng ordered the brutal crushing of its brazen demonstration in Beijing's Tiananmen Square before the television cameras of the world.

After Communism in China
Although the Communist Party still governed China in the early twenty-first century, communist values of selflessness, community, and simplicity had been substantially replaced for many by Western-style consumerism. This New Year's Good Luck poster from 1993 illustrates the new interest in material wealth in the form of American dollars and the return of older Chinese cultural patterns represented by the traditional gods of wealth, happiness, and longevity. The caption reads: "The gods of wealth enter the home from everywhere." (Zhejianq People's Art Publishing House/Stefan R. Landsberger Collections/International Institute of Social History, Amsterdam/www.chineseposters.net)

China entered the new millennium as a rapidly growing economic power with an essentially capitalist economy presided over by an intact and powerful Communist Party. Culturally, some combination of nationalism, consumerism, and a renewed respect for ancient traditions had replaced the collectivist and socialist values of the Maoist era. It was a strange and troubled hybrid.

The Soviet Union: The Collapse of Communism and Country

By the mid-1980s, the reformist wing of the Soviet Communist Party, long squelched by an aging conservative establishment, had won the top position in the party as Mikhail Gorbachev assumed the role of general secretary. Like Deng Xiaoping in China, Gorbachev was committed to aggressively tackling the country's many problems—economic stagnation, a flourishing black market, public apathy, and cynicism about the party. His economic program, launched in 1987 and known as *perestroika* (per-uh-STROI-kuh) (restructuring), paralleled aspects of the Chinese approach by freeing state enterprises from the heavy hand of government regulation, permitting small-scale private businesses called cooperatives, offering opportunities for private farming, and cautiously welcoming foreign investment in joint enterprises.

But in cultural and political affairs, Gorbachev moved far beyond Chinese reforms. His policy of *glasnost* (GLAHS-nohst) (openness) now permitted an unprecedented range of cultural and intellectual freedoms. In the late 1980s, glasnost hit the Soviet Union like a bomb. Newspapers and TV exposed social pathologies—crime, prostitution, child abuse, suicide, corruption, and homelessness—that previously had been presented solely as the product of capitalism. Films broke the ban on nudity and explicit sex. TV reporters climbed the wall of a secluded villa to film the luxurious homes of the party elite. Soviet history was also reexamined as revelations of Stalin's crimes poured out of the media. The Bible and the Quran became more widely available, atheistic propaganda largely ceased, and thousands of churches and mosques were returned to believers and opened for worship. Plays, poems, films, and novels that had long been buried "in the drawer" were now released to a public that virtually devoured them. "Like an excited boy reads a note from his girl," wrote one poet, "that's how we read the papers today."[17] And beyond glasnost lay democratization and a new parliament with real powers, chosen in competitive elections. When those elections occurred in 1989, dozens of leading communists were rejected at the polls. In foreign affairs, Gorbachev moved to end the cold war by making unilateral cuts in Soviet military forces, engaging in arms control negotiations with the United States, and refusing to intervene as communist governments in Eastern Europe were overthrown.

But almost nothing worked out as Gorbachev had anticipated. Far from strengthening socialism and reviving a stagnant Soviet Union, the reforms led to its further weakening and collapse. In a dramatic contrast with China's booming economy,

AP® EXAM TIP

You need to know examples of resistance to authoritarian governments in the twentieth century.

Guided Reading Question

■ COMPARISON

How did the end of communism in the Soviet Union differ from communism's demise in China?

the Soviet Union's planned economy spun into a sharp decline as it was dismantled before a functioning market-based system could emerge. Inflation mounted; consumer goods were in short supply, and ration coupons reappeared; many feared the loss of their jobs. Unlike Chinese peasants, few Soviet farmers were willing to risk the jump into private farming, and few foreign investors found the Soviet Union a tempting place to do business.

Furthermore, the new freedoms provoked demands that went far beyond what Gorbachev had intended. A democracy movement of unofficial groups and parties now sprang to life, many of them seeking a full multiparty democracy and a market-based economy. They were joined by independent labor unions, which actually went on strike, something unheard of in the "workers' state." Most corrosively, a multitude of nationalist movements used the new freedoms to insist on greater autonomy, or even independence, from the Soviet Union. Environmental issues were prominent in many of these movements. Their leaders argued that centralized decision making in Moscow treated the non-Russian areas as colonies to be exploited and was responsible for numerous environmental outrages. Activists in the Baltic region, for example, protested phosphorite mining in Estonia, a proposed nuclear reactor in Lithuania, and the construction of a massive hydroelectric station in Latvia. The Chernobyl explosion and the government's initial reluctance to fully disclose what happened only added fuel to these growing anti-Soviet movements. In the face of these mounting demands, Gorbachev resolutely refused to use force to crush the protesters, another sharp contrast with the Chinese experience.

Events in Eastern Europe now intersected with those in the Soviet Union. Gorbachev's reforms had lit a fuse in these Soviet satellites, where communism had been imposed and maintained from outside. If the USSR could practice glasnost and hold competitive elections, why couldn't Eastern Europe do so as well? This was the background for the "miracle year" of 1989. Massive demonstrations, last-minute efforts at reforms, the breaching of the Berlin Wall, the surfacing of new political groups—all of this and more quickly overwhelmed the highly unpopular communist regimes of Poland, Hungary, East Germany, Bulgaria, Czechoslovakia, and Romania, which were quickly swept away. This success then emboldened nationalists and democrats in the Soviet Union. If communism had been overthrown in Eastern Europe, perhaps it could be overthrown in the USSR as well. Soviet conservatives and patriots, however, were outraged. To them, Gorbachev had stood idly by while the political gains of World War II, for which the Soviet Union had paid in rivers of blood, vanished before their eyes. It was nothing less than treason.

A brief and unsuccessful attempt to restore the old order through a military coup in August 1991 triggered the end of the Soviet Union and its communist regime. From the wreckage emerged fifteen new and independent states, following the internal political divisions of the USSR (see Map 21.4). Arguably, the collapse of the Soviet Union was due less to its multiple problems and more to the unexpected consequences of Gorbachev's efforts to address them.

The Soviet collapse represented a unique phenomenon in the world of the late twentieth century. Simultaneously, the world's largest state and its last territorial

AP® EXAM TIP

Compare the internal and external forces that led to the fall of the USSR with those that led to the fall of earlier empires.

Map 21.4   The Collapse of the Soviet Empire

Soviet control over its Eastern European dependencies vanished as those countries threw off their communist governments in 1989. Then, in 1991, the Soviet Union itself disintegrated into fifteen separate states, none of them governed by communist parties.

empire vanished; the world's first Communist Party disintegrated; a powerful command economy broke down; an official socialist ideology was repudiated; and a forty-five-year global struggle between the East and the West ended. In Europe, Germany was reunited, and a number of former communist states joined NATO and the European Union, ending the division of the continent. At least for the moment, capitalism and democracy seemed to triumph over socialism and authoritarian governments. In many places, the end of communism allowed simmering ethnic tensions to explode into open conflict. Beyond the disintegration of the Soviet Union, both Yugoslavia and Czechoslovakia fragmented, the former amid terrible violence and the latter peacefully. Chechens in Russia, Abkhazians in Georgia, Russians in the Baltic states and Ukraine, Tibetans and Uighurs in China—all of these minorities found themselves in opposition to the states in which they lived.

As the twenty-first century dawned, the communist world had shrunk considerably from its high point just three decades earlier. In the Soviet Union and Eastern Europe, communism had disappeared entirely as the governing authority and dominant ideology. In the immediate aftermath of the Soviet collapse, Russia quickly and haphazardly privatized many of its state-owned firms, vastly enriching their new and well-connected owners, who came to be called the "oligarchs." The result was cata-strophic as the country experienced a sharply contracting economy, widespread pov-erty and inequality, and declining life expectancy. Not until 2006 did its economy recover to the level of 1991. Even then, much of Russia's subsequent economic growth depended substantially on the export of oil and gas, rather than on competi-tive manufacturing. Russia's military intervention in Ukraine in 2014 prompted Western economic sanctions, which, together with the sharply declining price of oil on the world market, resulted in a major downturn in Russian economic life, at least temporarily. Some twenty-five years after the collapse of the Soviet Union, the continuing weakness and vulnerability of the Russian economy were evident.

Elsewhere, China had largely abandoned its communist economic policies as a market economy took shape, spurring remarkable economic growth. Like China, Vietnam and Laos remained officially communist, even while they pursued Chinese-style reforms, though more cautiously. Even Cuba, which was beset by economic crisis in the 1990s following the end of massive Soviet subsidies, began after 2008 to allow small businesses, private food markets, the buying and selling of cars, the sale of computers and cell phones, and luxury hotels for tourists, while still harshly suppressing opposition political groups. A growing cultural openness allowed films highly critical of Cuban society to be produced and shown publicly, including one, *Juan of the Dead*, that portrayed Cuba in 2010 as a country of dazed zombies. And in late 2014, after more than five decades of efforts to isolate a communist-ruled Cuba from the larger international arena, the United States finally began to reopen diplomatic relations with this Caribbean nation.

An impoverished North Korea remained the most unreformed and repressive of the remaining communist countries and the only major flashpoint of cold war–era conflicts. Its small nuclear arsenal controlled by an unpredictable leadership made it a cause of great concern in the region and beyond. And its alleged ability to hack into Sony Pictures computers in late 2014 to protest an unflattering film portrayal of the North Korean leader illustrated the intersection of popular culture, a world linked by the Internet, and global political conflicts.

But as a primary source of international tensions or as a compelling path to modernity and social justice, communism was effectively dead. The brief commu-nist era in world history had ended. However, the rivalries of the Great Powers had certainly not ended, as Russia and China alike continued to challenge American global dominance. Russian president Vladimir Putin deeply resented the loss of his country's international stature after the breakup of the Soviet Union and what he regarded as U.S. efforts to intrude upon Russia's legitimate interests. By 2014 issues involving the eastward expansion of NATO and the Russian intervention in Ukraine had brought the relationship between Russia and the West to something resembling cold war–era hostility. And the rising economic and military power of China gen-erated many tensions in its relationship with the United States in East Asia and the Pacific world. The demise of communism, in short, did not bring about a golden age of international harmony, as the geopolitical and economic competition of major nation-states persisted.

REFLECTIONS

To Judge or Not to Judge

Should historians or students of history make moral judgments about the people and events they study? On the one hand, some would argue, scholars do well to act as detached and objective observers of the human experience. The task is to describe what happened and to explain why things turned out as they did. Whether we approve or condemn the outcomes of the historical process is, in this view, beside the point. On the other hand, all of us, scholars and students alike, stand somewhere. We are members of particular cultures; we have values and outlooks on the world that inevitably affect the way we think about the past. Perhaps it is better to recognize and acknowledge these realities than to pretend to some unattainable objectivity that places us above it all. Furthermore, making judgments is a way of caring about the past, of affirming our continuing relationship with those who have gone before us.

The question of making judgments arises strongly in any examination of the communist phenomenon. In a United States lacking a major socialist tradition, sometimes saying anything positive about communism or even noting its appeal to millions of people has brought charges of whitewashing its crimes. Within the communist world, even modest criticism was usually regarded as counterrevolutionary and was largely forbidden and harshly punished. Certainly, few observers were neutral in their assessment of the communist experiment.

Were the Russian and Chinese revolutions a blow for human freedom and a cry for justice on the part of oppressed people, or did they simply replace one tyranny with another? Was Stalinism a successful effort to industrialize a backward country or a ferocious assault on its moral and social fabric? Did Chinese reforms of the late twentieth century represent a return to sensible policies of modernization, a continued denial of basic democratic rights, or an opening to capitalist inequalities, corruption, and acquisitiveness? Passionate debate continues on all of these questions.

Communism, like many human projects, has been an ambiguous enterprise. On the one hand, communism brought hope to millions by addressing the manifest injustices of the past; by providing new opportunities for women, workers, and peasants; by promoting rapid industrial development; and by ending Western domination. On the other hand, communism was responsible for mountains of crimes—millions killed and wrongly imprisoned; massive famines partly caused by radical policies; human rights violated on an enormous scale; lives uprooted and distorted by efforts to achieve the impossible.

Studying communism challenges our inclination to want definitive answers and clear moral judgments. Can we hold contradictory elements in some kind of tension? Can we affirm our own values while acknowledging the ambiguities of life, both past and present? Doing so is arguably among the essential tasks of growing up and achieving a measure of intellectual maturity. In that undertaking, history can be helpful.

Chapter Review

What's the Significance?

Russian Revolution (1917), 933–36

Bolsheviks/Lenin, 935

Guomindang, 937–38

Mao Zedong, 937–38

Chinese Revolution, 938

Stalin, 938; 941–44

building socialism, 938–40

Zhenotdel, 941

collectivization, 942–43

Cultural Revolution, 945–46

Great Purges/Terror, 946–47

Anna Dubova, 948–49

Cuban Revolution / missile crisis, 952

Nikita Khrushchev, 952–56

Deng Xiaoping, 959–60

perestroika/glasnost, 961

Mikhail Gorbachev, 961–62

Big Picture Questions

1. Why did the communist experiment, which was committed to equality, abundance, and a humane socialism, generate failed economies and oppressive, brutal, and totalitarian regimes?
2. In what ways did communism have a global impact beyond those countries that were governed by communist parties?
3. What was the global significance of the cold war?
4. "The end of communism was as revolutionary as its beginning." Do you agree with this statement?
5. **Looking Back:** What was distinctive about twentieth-century communist industrialization and modernization compared to the same processes in the West a century earlier?

Next Steps: For Further Study

Archie Brown, *The Rise and Fall of Communism* (2009). A global overview of the communist phenomenon in the twentieth century by a respected scholar.

Jung Chang, *Wild Swans* (2004). A compelling view of twentieth-century Chinese history through the eyes of three generations of women in a single family.

Timothy Check, *Mao Zedong and China's Revolutions* (2002). A collection of documents about the Chinese Revolution and a fine introduction to the life of Mao.

John L. Gaddis, *The Cold War: A New History* (2005). An overview by one of the most highly regarded historians of the cold war.

Peter Kenez, *A History of the Soviet Union from the Beginning to the End* (1999). A thoughtful overview of the entire Soviet experience.

Robert Strayer, *The Communist Experiment* (2007). A comparative study of Soviet and Chinese communism.

"Mao Zedong Internet Archive," http://www.marxists.org/reference/archive/mao. A Web site offering the translated writings of Mao, including poetry and some images.

"Soviet Archives Exhibit," http://www.ibiblio.org/expo/soviet.exhibit/entrance.html. A rich Web site from the Library of Congress, focusing on the operation of the Soviet system and relations with the United States.

WORKING WITH EVIDENCE

Poster Art in Mao's China

" I wanted to be the girl in the poster when I was growing up. Every day I dressed up like that girl in a white cotton shirt with a red scarf around my neck, and I braided my hair in the same way. I liked the fact that she was surrounded by revolutionary martyrs whom I was taught to worship since kindergarten."[18] As things turned out, this young girl, Anchee Min, did become the subject of one of the many thousands of propaganda posters with which the Chinese communist government flooded the country during the thirty years or so following the Chinese Revolution of 1949.

In China, as in other communist countries, art served the state and the Communist Party. Nowhere was this more apparent than in these propaganda posters, which were found in homes, schools, workplaces, railway stations, and elsewhere. The artists who created these images were under the strict control of Communist Party officials and were expected to use their skills to depict the party's leaders and achievements favorably, even grandly. They were among the "engineers of the human soul" who were reshaping the consciousness of individuals and remaking their entire society. One young man, born in 1951, testified to the effectiveness of these posters. "They . . . were my signposts through life. They made sure we did not make mistakes. . . . My life is reflected in them."[19]

The posters that follow illustrate the kind of society and people that the communist leadership sought to create during the years that Mao Zedong ruled the country (1949–1976). The realities behind these images, of course, were often far different.

Coming to power in 1949, Chinese Communist Party leaders recognized that their enemies were by no means totally defeated. A persistent theme throughout the years of Mao's rule was an effort to eliminate those enemies or convert them to the communist cause. Spies, imperialist sympathizers, those infected with "bourgeois values" such as materialism and individualism, landowners or capitalists yearning for the old life—all of these had to be identified and confronted. So too were many "enemies" within the Communist Party itself, people who were suspected of opposition to the radical policies of Mao. Some of these alleged enemies were killed, others imprisoned, and still others—millions of them—were subjected to endless self-criticism sessions or sent down to remote rural areas to "learn from the peasants." This need to demolish the old society and old values is reflected in Source 21.1, a poster from 1967, the height of the Cultural Revolution (see pages 945–47). Its caption reads: "Destroy the Old World; Establish the New World."

- Notice the various items beneath this young revolutionary's feet. What do they represent to the ardent revolutionaries seeking to "destroy the old world"? What groups of people were most likely to be affected by such efforts?

- What elements of a new order are being constructed in this image?

- How does the artist distinguish visually between the old and the new? Note the use of colors and the size of various figures and objects in the poster.

Source 21.1 Smashing the Old Society

The centerpiece of Mao's plans for the vast Chinese countryside lay in the "people's communes." Established during the Great Leap Forward in the late 1950s, these were huge political and economic units intended to work the land more efficiently and collectively, to undertake large-scale projects such as building dams and irrigation systems, to create small-scale industries in rural areas, and to promote local self-reliance. The leaders who created the communes also sought to move China more rapidly toward genuine communism by eliminating virtually every form of private property and emphasizing social equality and shared living. Commune members ate together in large dining halls, and children were cared for during the day in collective nurseries rather than by their own families. Source 21.2, a poster created in 1958 under the title "The People's Communes Are Good," shows a highly idealized image of one such commune. See also the celebratory poster on page 945.

The actual outcomes of the commune movement departed radically from its idealistic goals. Economic disruption occasioned by the creation of

Source 21.2 Building the New Society: The People's Commune

Shanghai Educational Publishing House/Stefan R. Landsberger Collections/International Institute of Social History, Amsterdam/www.chineseposters.net

communes contributed a great deal to the enormous famines of the late 1950s and early 1960s, in which many millions perished. Furthermore, efforts to involve the peasants in iron and steel production through the creation of much-heralded "backyard furnaces," illustrated in Source 21.2, proved a failure. Most of the metal produced in these primitive facilities was of poor quality and essentially unusable. Such efforts further impoverished the rural areas as peasants were encouraged to contribute their pots, pans, and anything made of iron to the smelting furnaces.

- What appealing features of commune life and a communist future are illustrated in this poster and the poster on page 945? Notice the communal facilities for eating and washing clothes as well as the drill practice of a "people's militia" unit at the bottom of Source 21.2.

- One of Mao's chief goals was to overcome the sharp division between industrial cities and the agricultural countryside. How is this effort illustrated in these posters?

Among the core values of Maoist communism were human mastery over the natural order, rapid industrialization, and the liberation of women from ancient limitations and oppressions in order to mobilize them for the task of building socialism. Source 21.3, a 1975 poster, illustrates these values. Its caption reads: "Women Can Hold Up Half the Sky; Surely the Face of Nature Can Be Transformed."

- In what ways does this poster reflect Chinese communism's core values?

- How is the young woman in this image portrayed? What does the expression on her face convey? Notice her clothing and the shape of her forearms, and the general absence of a feminine figure. Why do you think she is portrayed in this largely sexless fashion? What does this suggest about the communist attitude toward sexuality?

- What does this image suggest about how the party sought to realize gender equality? What is the significance of the work the young woman is doing?

- Notice the lights that illuminate a nighttime work scene. What does this suggest about attitudes toward work and production?

A central feature of Chinese communism, especially during the Cultural Revolution of 1966–1976, was the growing veneration, even adoration, of Chairman Mao. Portraits, statues, busts, and Mao badges proliferated. Everyone was expected to read repeatedly the "Red Treasured Book," which offered a selection of quotations from Mao's writings, believed to facilitate solutions to almost all problems, both public and private. Many families erected "tablets of loyalty" to Mao, much like those previously devoted to ancestors.

Source 21.3 Women, Nature, and Industrialization

我們心中最紅最紅的紅太陽毛主席和我們在一起

Source 21.4 The Cult of Mao

People made pilgrimages to "sacred shrines" associated with key events in his life. Schoolchildren began the day by chanting, "May Chairman Mao live ten thousand times ten thousand years."

And Mao was the centerpiece of endless posters. Source 21.4, a poster created in 1968, portrays a familiar scene from the Cultural Revolution. Millions of young people, organized as Red Guards and committed to revolutionary action, flocked to Beijing, where enormous and ecstatic rallies allowed them to catch a glimpse of their beloved leader and to unite with him in the grand task of creating communism in China. The poster's caption reads: "The reddest, reddest, red sun in our heart, Chairman Mao, and us together."

■ What relationship between Mao and his young followers does the poster suggest? Why might some scholars have seen a quasi-religious dimension to that relationship?

■ How do you understand the significance of the "Red Treasured Book" of quotations from Mao, which the young people are waving?

■ How might you account for the unbridled enthusiasm expressed by the Red Guards? In this case, the poster portrays the realities of these rallies with considerable accuracy. Can you think of other comparable cases of such mass enthusiasm?

DOING HISTORY

Poster Art in Mao's China

1. **Reading communist intentions:** Based on these visual sources, how would you describe the kind of society that the Chinese Communist Party sought to create in China during Mao's lifetime?

2. **Distinguishing image and reality:** Based on the narrative of this chapter and especially on what happened after Mao's death, assess the realities that lay behind these visual sources. To what extent do the posters accurately represent the successes of Maoist communism? What insights do they shed on its failures?

3. **Defining audience and appeal:** To whom do you think these posters were directed? What appeal might they have for the intended audience?

4. **Noticing change:** How could you use these posters to define the dramatic changes that transformed China since 1949? How might a traditional Chinese official from the nineteenth century respond to them?

5. **Assessing posters as evidence:** What are the strengths and limitations of poster art for understanding Chinese communism under Mao?

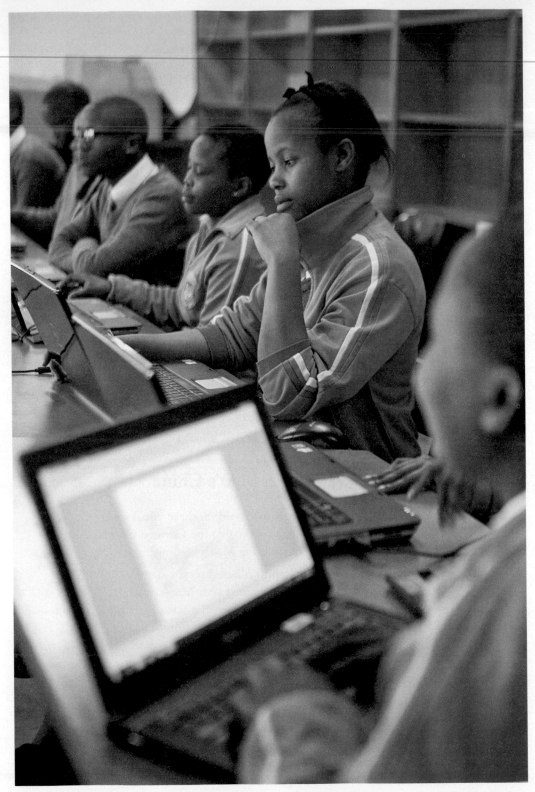

CHAPTER 22

The End of Empire

The Global South on the Global Stage
1900–present

"During my lifetime I have dedicated myself to this struggle of the African people. I have fought against white domination, and I have fought against black domination. I have cherished the ideal of a democratic and free society in which all persons live together in harmony and with equal opportunity. It is an ideal which I hope to live for and to achieve. But, if need be, it is an ideal for which I am prepared to die."[1]

Nelson Mandela, South Africa's nationalist leader, first uttered these words in 1964 at his trial for treason, sabotage, and conspiracy to overthrow the apartheid government of his country. Convicted of those charges, he spent the next twenty-seven years in prison, sometimes working at hard labor in a stone quarry. Often the floor was his bed, and a bucket was his toilet. For many years, he was allowed one visitor a year for thirty minutes and permitted to write and receive one letter every six months. When he was finally released from prison in 1990 under growing domestic and international pressure, he concluded his first speech as a free person with the words originally spoken at his trial. Four years later, in 1994, South Africa held its first election in which blacks and whites alike were able to vote. The outcome of that election made Mandela the country's first black African president, and it linked South Africa to dozens of other countries all across Africa, Asia, and Oceania that had thrown off European rule or the control of white settlers during the second half of the twentieth century.

Variously called decolonization or the struggle for independence, that process carried an immense significance for the history of the twentieth century. It marked a dramatic change in

---

Independence and Development In the eyes of most Asians and Africans, the struggle for national independence from European colonial rule was but a prelude to and prerequisite for the even greater struggle for modern development, symbolized here by a photo from 2012 showing South African high school students in a computer-education classroom.

the world's political architecture, as nation-states triumphed over the empires that had structured much of the world's political life in the nineteenth and early twentieth centuries. It mobilized millions of people, thrusting them into political activity and sometimes into violence and warfare. Decolonization signaled the declining legitimacy of both empire and race as a credible basis for political or social life. It promised not only national freedom but also personal dignity, abundance, and opportunity.

What followed in the decades after independence was equally significant. Political, economic, and cultural experiments proliferated across these newly independent nations, which faced enormous challenges: the legacies of empire; their own deep divisions of language, ethnicity, religion, and class; their rapidly growing numbers; the competing demands of the capitalist West and the communist East; and the difficult tasks of simultaneously building modern economies, stable politics, and coherent nations. And they confronted all of these in a world still shaped by the powerful economies and armies of the wealthy, already-industrialized nations. The emergence of these new nations onto the world stage as independent and assertive actors has been a distinguishing feature of world history in this most recent century.

> **SEEKING THE MAIN POINT**
>
> In what ways did the experience of the "Global South" during the past century register on the larger stage of world history?

Toward Freedom: Struggles for Independence

In 1900, European colonial empires in Africa, Asia, the Caribbean region, and Pacific Oceania appeared as enduring features of the world's political landscape. Well before the end of the twentieth century, they were gone. The first major breakthroughs occurred in Asia and the Middle East in the late 1940s, when the Philippines, India, Pakistan, Burma, Indonesia, Syria, Iraq, Jordan, and Israel achieved independence. The period from the mid-1950s through the mid-1970s was an age of African independence as colony after colony, more than fifty in total, emerged into what was then seen as the bright light of freedom. During the 1970s, many of the island societies of Pacific Oceania—Samoa, Fiji, Tonga, the Solomon Islands, Kiribati—joined the ranks of independent states, almost entirely peacefully and without much struggle as the various colonial powers willingly abandoned their right to rule. Hawaiians, however, sought incorporation as a state within the United States, rather than independence, attracting opposition from some American conservatives who were not easily persuaded that this multiethnic society was genuinely American. Finally, a number of Caribbean societies—the Bahamas, Barbados, Belize, Jamaica, Trinidad, and Tobago—achieved independence during the 1960s and 70s, informed by a growing awareness of a distinctive Caribbean culture. Cuba, although formally independent since 1902, dramatically declared its rejection of American control in its revolutionary upheaval in 1959. Efforts to join a number of former British colonies into a Federation of the West Indies failed, and by 1983 the Caribbean region hosted sixteen separate independent states.

A MAP OF TIME

1915	Gandhi returns to India from South Africa
1923–1938	Turkey's secular modernization initiated under Kemal Atatürk
1928	Muslim Brotherhood established in Egypt
1947	Independence of India/Pakistan
1948	Establishment of state of Israel; apartheid formally established in South Africa
1949	Independence of Indonesia; communist victory in China
1955	Bandung Conference of nonaligned nations
1957–1975	Independence of African countries
1959	Cuban Revolution
1960–1970s	Wave of military coups in Africa and Latin America
1973	OPEC oil embargo
1979	Revolution in Iran
1980s–1990s	Growth of democratic movements and governments in Africa and Latin America
1988–1989	Founding of al-Qaeda
1994	End of apartheid in South Africa; genocide in Rwanda
2011	Arab Spring in the Middle East
2013	Turkish young people in Istanbul protest the Islamist and authoritarian trends of the government
2013	Iran elects a moderate president, raising hopes of agreement with the West on its nuclear program
2014	Radical Islamist organization Boko Haram captures over 200 schoolgirls in northern Nigeria
2015	Radical French Muslims in Paris attack a satirical magazine that had lampooned the Prophet Muhammad

The End of Empire in World History

At one level, this vast process was but the latest case of imperial dissolution, a fate that had overtaken earlier empires, including those of the Assyrians, Romans, Arabs, and Mongols. But never before had the end of empire been so associated with the mobilization of the masses around a nationalist ideology. Nor had these earlier cases generated a plethora of nation-states, each claiming an equal place in a world of nation-states. More comparable perhaps was that first decolonization, in

AP® EXAM TIP

Take notes on these examples of continuities in empire collapse in world history.

which the European colonies in the Americas threw off British, French, Spanish, or Portuguese rule during the late eighteenth and early nineteenth centuries (see Chapter 16). Like their earlier counterparts, the new nations of the twentieth century claimed an international status equivalent to that of their former rulers. In the Americas, however, many of the colonized people were themselves of European origin, sharing much of their culture with their colonial rulers. In that respect, the freedom struggles of the twentieth century were very different, for they not only asserted political independence but also affirmed the vitality of their cultures, which had been submerged and denigrated during the colonial era. In Oceania, for example, the idea of a "Pacific Way" sought to articulate a style of political action in keeping with what were held to be "traditional" principles—decision making by consensus and resolving differences in a fashion that left no one feeling defeated.

Guided Reading Question

....

■ COMPARISON
What was distinctive about the end of Europe's African and Asian empires compared to other cases of imperial disintegration?

The twentieth century witnessed the demise of many empires. The Austrian and Ottoman empires collapsed following World War I, giving rise to a number of new states in Europe and the Middle East. The Russian Empire also unraveled, although it was soon reassembled under the auspices of the Soviet Union. World War II ended the German and Japanese empires. African and Asian movements for independence shared with these other end-of-empire stories the ideal of national self-determination. This novel idea—that humankind was naturally divided into distinct peoples or nations, each of which deserved an independent state of its own—was loudly proclaimed by the winning side of both world wars. It gained a global acceptance, particularly in the colonial world, during the twentieth century and rendered empire illegitimate in the eyes of growing numbers of people.

Empires without territory, such as the powerful influence that the United States exercised in Latin America, likewise came under attack from highly nationalist governments. An intrusive U.S. presence was certainly one factor stimulating the Mexican Revolution, which began in 1910. One of the outcomes of that upheaval was the nationalization in 1937 of Mexico's oil industry, much of which was owned by American and British investors. Similar actions accompanied Cuba's revolution of 1959 and also occurred in other places throughout Latin America and elsewhere. National self-determination and freedom from Soviet control likewise lay behind the Eastern European revolutions of 1989. The disintegration of the Soviet Union itself in 1991 brought to an inglorious end the last of the major territorial empires of the twentieth century and led to the birth of fifteen new national states. Although the winning of political independence for Europe's African and Asian colonies was perhaps the most spectacular challenge to empire in the twentieth century, that process was part of a larger pattern in modern world history (see Map 22.1).

Explaining African and Asian Independence

As the twentieth century closed, the end of European empires seemed an almost inevitable phenomenon, for colonial rule had lost any credibility as a form of political order. What could be more natural than for people to seek to rule themselves?

Yet at the beginning of the century, few observers were predicting the collapse of these empires, and the idea that "the only legitimate government is national self-government" was not nearly so widespread as it subsequently became. This situation has presented historians with a problem of explanation—how to account for the fall of European colonial empires and the emergence of dozens of new nation-states.

One approach to explaining the end of colonial empires focuses attention on fundamental contradictions in the entire colonial enterprise. The rhetoric of Christianity, Enlightenment thought, and material progress sat awkwardly with the realities of colonial racism, exploitation, and poverty. The increasingly democratic values of European states ran counter to the essential dictatorship of colonial rule. The ideal of national self-determination was profoundly at odds with the possession of colonies that were denied any opportunity to express their own national character. The enormously powerful force of nationalism, having earlier driven the process of European empire building, now played a major role in its disintegration. Colonial rule, in this argument, dug its own grave because its practice ran counter to established European values.

But why did this "fatal flaw" of European colonial rule lead to independence in the post–World War II decades rather than earlier or later? In explaining the timing of the end of empire, historians frequently use the notion of "conjuncture," the coming together of several separate developments at a particular time. At the international level, the world wars had weakened Europe, while discrediting any sense of European moral superiority. Both the United States and the Soviet Union, the new global superpowers, generally opposed the older European colonial empires, even as they created empire-like international relationships of their own. Meanwhile, the United Nations provided a prestigious platform from which to conduct anticolonial agitation. All of this contributed to the global illegitimacy of empire, a novel and stunning transformation of social values that was enormously encouraging to anticolonial movements everywhere.

At the same time, social and economic circumstances within the colonies themselves generated the human raw material for anticolonial movements. By the early twentieth century in Asia and the mid-twentieth century in Africa, a second or third generation of Western-educated elites, largely male, had arisen throughout the colonial world. These young men were thoroughly familiar with European culture; they were deeply aware of the gap between its values and its practices; they no longer viewed colonial rule as a vehicle for their peoples' progress as their fathers had; and they increasingly insisted on immediate independence. Moreover, growing numbers of ordinary people—women and men alike—were receptive to this message. Veterans of the world wars, young people with some education but no jobs commensurate with their expectations; a small class of urban workers who were increasingly aware of their exploitation; small-scale female traders resentful of European privileges; rural dwellers who had lost land or suffered from forced labor; impoverished and insecure newcomers to the cities—all of these groups had reason to believe that independence held great promise.

Guided Reading Question

■ CHANGE

What international circumstances and social changes contributed to the end of colonial empires?

Map 22.1
The End of Empire in Africa and Asia

In the second half of the twentieth century, under pressure from nationalist movements, Europe's Asian and African empires dissolved into dozens of new independent states.

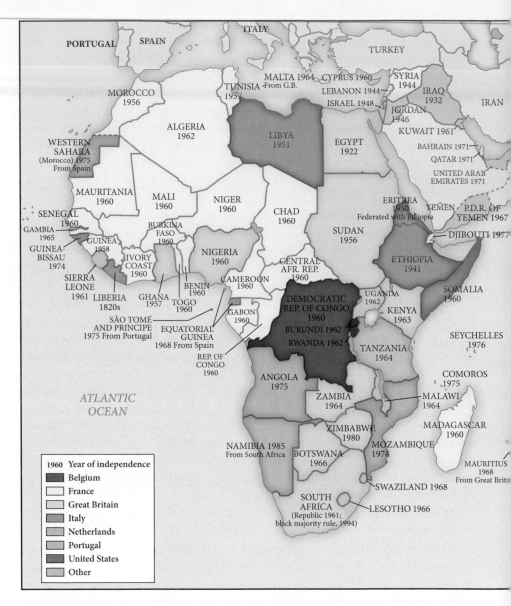

PORTUGAL SPAIN ITALY TURKEY

MOROCCO 1956
MALTA 1964 From G.B.
CYPRUS 1960
SYRIA 1944
TUNISIA 1956
LEBANON 1944
ISRAEL 1948
IRAQ 1932
IRAN
JORDAN 1946
KUWAIT 1961
ALGERIA 1962
LIBYA 1951
EGYPT 1922
BAHRAIN 1971
QATAR 1971
UNITED ARAB EMIRATES 1971
WESTERN SAHARA (Morocco) 1975 From Spain
MAURITANIA 1960
MALI 1960
NIGER 1960
CHAD 1960
SUDAN 1956
ERITREA 1950 Federated with Ethiopia
YEMEN
P.D.R. OF YEMEN 1967
DJIBOUTI 1977
SENEGAL 1960
GAMBIA 1965
GUINEA-BISSAU 1974
GUINEA 1958
BURKINA FASO 1960
NIGERIA 1960
CENTRAL AFR. REP. 1960
ETHIOPIA 1941
SOMALIA 1960
SIERRA LEONE 1961
IVORY COAST 1960
GHANA 1957
BENIN 1960
TOGO 1960
CAMEROON 1960
UGANDA 1962
KENYA 1963
SEYCHELLES 1976
LIBERIA 1820s
GABON 1960
DEMOCRATIC REP. OF CONGO 1960
BURUNDI 1962
RWANDA 1962
SÃO TOMÉ AND PRINCIPE 1975 From Portugal
EQUATORIAL GUINEA 1968 From Spain
REP. OF CONGO 1960
TANZANIA 1964
ANGOLA 1975
ZAMBIA 1964
COMOROS 1975
MALAWI 1964
MADAGASCAR 1960
ATLANTIC OCEAN
ZIMBABWE 1980
MOZAMBIQUE 1974
NAMIBIA 1985 From South Africa
BOTSWANA 1966
MAURITIUS 1968 From Great Britain
SWAZILAND 1968
SOUTH AFRICA (Republic 1961; black majority rule, 1994)
LESOTHO 1966

1960	Year of independence
	Belgium
	France
	Great Britain
	Italy
	Netherlands
	Portugal
	United States
	Other

Such pressures increasingly placed colonial rulers on the defensive. As the twentieth century wore on, these colonial rulers began to plan—tentatively at first—for a new political relationship with their Asian and African subjects. The colonies had been integrated into a global economic network, and local elites were largely committed to maintaining those links. In these circumstances, Europeans could imagine retaining profitable economic interests in Asia, Africa, and Oceania without the expense and trouble of formal colonial governments. Deliberate planning for decolonization included gradual political reforms; investments in railroads, ports, and

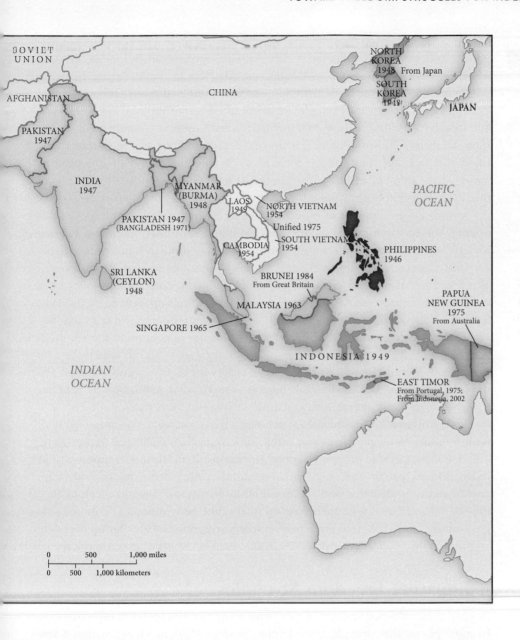

telegraph lines; the holding of elections; and the writing of constitutions. To some observers, it seemed as if independence was granted by colonial rulers rather than gained or seized by nationalist movements.

But these reforms, and independence itself, occurred only under considerable pressure from mounting nationalist movements. Creating such movements was no easy task. Leaders, drawn everywhere from the ranks of the educated few and almost always male, organized political parties, recruited members, plotted strategy, developed an ideology, and negotiated with one another and with the colonial state. The

AP® EXAM TIP

Make a list of similarities in the educational and social backgrounds of leaders of independence movements in Asia and Africa in the twentieth century.

Guided Reading Question

■ DESCRIPTION

What obstacles confronted the leaders of movements for independence?

most prominent among them became the "fathers" of their new countries as independence dawned—Gandhi and Nehru in India, Sukarno in Indonesia, Ho Chi Minh in Vietnam, Nkrumah in Ghana, and Mandela in South Africa. In places where colonial rule was particularly intransigent—settler-dominated colonies and Portuguese territories, for example—leaders also directed military operations and administered liberated areas. While such movements drew on memories of earlier, more localized forms of resistance, nationalist leaders did not seek to restore a vanished past. Rather, they looked forward to joining the world of independent nation-states, to membership in the United Nations, and to the wealth and power that modern technology promised.

A further common task of the nationalist leadership was to recruit a mass following, and to varying degrees, they did. Millions of ordinary men and women joined Gandhi's nonviolent campaigns in India; tens of thousands of freedom fighters waged guerrilla warfare in Algeria, Kenya, Mozambique, and Zimbabwe; in West Africa workers went on strike and market women joined political parties, as did students, farmers, and the unemployed. The relationship between nationalist leaders and their followers was frequently fraught with tension. One such Indonesian leader, educated in Holland, spoke of his difficulty in relating to the common people: "Why am I vexed by the things that fill their lives, and to which they are so attached? Why are the things that contain beauty for them . . . only senseless and displeasing for me? We intellectuals here are much closer to Europe or America than we are to the primitive Islamic culture of Java and Sumatra."[2]

Thus struggles for independence were rarely if ever cohesive movements of uniformly oppressed people. More often, they were fragile alliances representing different classes, ethnic groups, religions, or regions. Beneath the common goal of independence, people struggled with one another over questions of leadership, power, strategy, ideology, and the distribution of material benefits, even as they fought and negotiated with their colonial rulers. The very notion of "national self-government" posed obvious but often-contentious questions: What group of people constituted the "nation" that deserved to rule itself? And who should speak for it?

Comparing Freedom Struggles

Beyond these common features of most nationalist movements lay many variations. In some places, that struggle, once begun, produced independence within a few years, four in the case of the Belgian Congo. Elsewhere it was measured in many decades. Nationalism surfaced in Vietnam in the early 1900s, but the country achieved full political independence only in the mid-1970s, having fought French colonial rulers, Japanese invaders during World War II, and U.S. military forces in the 1960s and 1970s, as well as Chinese forces during a brief war in 1979. Tactics too varied considerably. In many places, West Africa for example, nationalists relied on peaceful political pressure—demonstrations, strikes, mass mobilization, and negotiations—to achieve independence. Elsewhere armed struggle was required.

Eight years of bitter guerrilla warfare preceded Algerian independence from France in 1962.

While all nationalist movements sought political independence for modern states, their ideologies and outlooks also differed. Many in India and the Islamic world viewed their new nations through the prism of religion, while elsewhere more secular outlooks prevailed. In Indonesia, an early nationalist organization, the Islamic Union, appealed on the basis of religion, while later groups espoused Marxism. Indonesia's primary nationalist leader, Sukarno, sought to embrace and reconcile these various outlooks. "What is Sukarno?" he asked. "A nationalist? An Islamist? A Marxist? . . . Sukarno is a mixture of all these isms."[3] Nationalist movements led by communist parties, such as those in Vietnam and China, sought major social transformations as well as freedom from foreign rule, while those in most of Africa focused on ending racial discrimination and achieving political independence with little concern about emerging patterns of domestic class inequality.

Two of the most extended freedom struggles—in India and South Africa—illustrate both the variations and the complexity of this process, which was so central to twentieth-century world history. India was among the first colonies to achieve independence and provided both a model and an inspiration to others, whereas South Africa, though not formally a colony, was among the last to throw off political domination by whites.

The Case of India: Ending British Rule

Surrounded by the Himalayas and the Indian Ocean, the South Asian peninsula, commonly known as India, enjoyed a certain geographic unity. But before the twentieth century, few of its people thought of themselves as "Indians." Cultural identities were primarily local and infinitely varied, rooted in differences of family, caste, village, language, region, tribe, and religious practice. In earlier centuries—during the Mauryan, Gupta, and Mughal empires, for example—large areas of the subcontinent had been temporarily enclosed within a single political system, but always these were imperial overlays, constructed on top of enormously diverse Indian societies.

So too was British colonial rule, but the British differed from earlier invaders in ways that promoted a growing sense of Indian identity. Unlike previous foreign rulers, the British never assimilated into Indian society because their acute sense of racial and cultural distinctiveness kept them apart. This served to intensify Indians' awareness of their collective difference from their alien rulers. Furthermore, British railroads, telegraph lines, postal services, administrative networks, newspapers, and schools as well as the English language bound India's many regions and peoples together more firmly than ever before and facilitated communication, especially among those with a modern education. Early nineteenth-century cultural nationalists, seeking to renew and reform Hinduism, registered this sense of India as a cultural unit.

AP® EXAM TIP

You should know the features of India's independence movement for the AP® exam.

Guided Reading Question

■ CHANGE
How did India's nationalist movement change over time?

The most important political expression of an all-Indian identity took shape in the Indian National Congress (INC), often called the Congress Party, which was established in 1885. This was an association of English-educated Indians—lawyers, journalists, teachers, businessmen—drawn overwhelmingly from regionally prominent high-caste Hindu families. It represented the beginning of a new kind of political protest, quite different from the rebellions, banditry, and refusal to pay taxes that had periodically erupted in the rural areas of colonial India. The INC was largely an urban phenomenon and quite moderate in its demands. Initially, its well-educated members did not seek to overthrow British rule; rather they hoped to gain greater inclusion within the political, military, and business life of British India. From such positions of influence, they argued, they could better protect the interests of India than could their foreign-born rulers. The British mocked their claim to speak for ordinary Indians, referring to them as "babus," a derogatory term that implied a semi-literate "native" with only a thin veneer of modern culture.

As an elite organization, the INC had difficulty gaining a mass following among India's vast peasant population. That began to change in the aftermath of World War I. To attract Indian support for the war effort, the British in 1917 had promised "the gradual development of self-governing institutions," a commitment that energized nationalist politicians to demand more rapid political change. Furthermore, British attacks on the Islamic Ottoman Empire antagonized India's Muslims. The end of the war was followed by a massive influenza epidemic, which cost the lives of millions of Indians. Finally, a series of violent repressive British actions antagonized many. This was the context in which Mohandas Gandhi (1869–1948) arrived on the Indian political scene and soon transformed it.

Gandhi was born in the province of Gujarat in western India to a pious Hindu family of the Vaisya, or business, caste. He was married at the age of thirteen, had only a mediocre record as a student, and eagerly embraced an opportunity to study law in England when he was eighteen. He returned as a shy and not very successful lawyer, and in 1893 he accepted a job with an Indian firm in South Africa, where a substantial number of Indians had migrated as indentured laborers during the nineteenth century. While in South Africa, Gandhi personally experienced overt racism for the first time and soon became involved in organizing Indians, mostly Muslims, to protest that country's policies of racial segregation. He also developed a concept of India that included Hindus and Muslims alike and pioneered strategies

Mahatma Gandhi
The most widely recognized and admired figure in the global struggle against colonial rule was India's Mahatma Gandhi. In this famous photograph, he is sitting cross-legged on the floor, clothed in a traditional Indian garment called a dhoti, while nearby stands a spinning wheel, symbolizing the independent and nonindustrial India that Gandhi sought. (Margaret Bourke-White/Time Life Pictures/Getty Images)

of resistance that he would later apply in India itself. His emerging political philosophy, known as *satyagraha* (truth force), was a confrontational, though nonviolent, approach to political action. Gandhi argued:

> Non-violence means conscious suffering. It does not mean meek submission to the will of the evil-doer, but it means the pitting of one's whole soul against the will of the tyrant. . . . It is possible for a single individual to defy the whole might of an unjust empire to save his honour, his religion, his soul.[4]

Returning to India in 1915, Gandhi quickly rose within the leadership ranks of the INC. During the 1920s and 1930s, he applied his approach in periodic mass campaigns that drew support from an extraordinarily wide spectrum of Indians — peasants and the urban poor, intellectuals and artisans, capitalists and socialists, Hindus and Muslims. The British responded with periodic repression as well as concessions that allowed a greater Indian role in political life. Gandhi's conduct and actions — his simple and unpretentious lifestyle, his support of Muslims, his frequent reference to Hindu religious themes — appealed widely in India and transformed the INC into a mass organization. To many ordinary people, Gandhi possessed magical powers and produced miraculous events. He was the Mahatma, the Great Soul.

His was a radicalism of a different kind. He did not call for social revolution but sought the moral transformation of individuals. He worked to raise the status of India's untouchables, the lowest and most ritually polluting groups within the caste hierarchy, but he launched no attack on caste in general and accepted support from businessmen and their socialist critics alike. His critique of India's situation went far beyond colonial rule. "India is being ground down," he wrote in 1909, "not under the English heel, but under that of modern civilization" — its competitiveness, its materialism, its warlike tendencies, its abandonment of religion.[5] Almost alone among nationalist leaders in India or elsewhere, Gandhi opposed a modern industrial future for his country, seeking instead a society of harmonious self-sufficient villages drawing on ancient Indian principles of duty and morality.

Gandhi also embraced efforts to mobilize women for the struggle against Britain and to elevate their standing in marriage and society. While asserting the spiritual and mental equality of women and men, he regarded women as uniquely endowed with a capacity for virtue, self-sacrifice, and endurance and thus particularly well suited for nonviolent protest. They could also contribute by spinning and weaving their families' clothing, while boycotting British textiles. But Gandhi never completely broke with older Indian conceptions of gender roles. He wrote, "The duty of motherhood . . . requires qualities which man need not possess. She is passive, he is active. She is essentially mistress of the house. He is the bread-winner."[6] Hundreds of thousands of women responded to Gandhi's call for participation in the independence struggle, marching, demonstrating, boycotting, and spinning. The moral and religious context in which he cast his appeal allowed them to do so without directly challenging traditional gender roles.

Guided Reading Question

■ CHANGE

What was the role of Gandhi in India's struggle for independence?

Gandhi and the INC leadership had to contend with a wide range of movements, parties, and approaches whose very diversity tore at the national unity that they so ardently sought. Whereas Gandhi rejected modern industrialization, his own chief lieutenant, Jawaharlal Nehru, thoroughly embraced science, technology, and industry as essential to India's future. And not everyone accepted Gandhi's nonviolence and his inclusive definition of India. A militant Hindu organization preached hatred of Muslims and viewed India as an essentially Hindu nation. Some in the Congress Party believed that efforts to improve the position of women or untouchables were a distraction from the chief task of gaining independence. Whether to participate in British-sponsored legislative bodies without complete independence also became a divisive issue. Furthermore, a number of smaller parties advocated on behalf of particular regions or castes. India's nationalist movement, in short, was beset by division and controversy.

By far the most serious threat to a unified movement derived from the growing divide between the country's Hindu and Muslim populations. As early as 1906, the formation of an All-India Muslim League contradicted the Congress Party's claim to speak for all Indians. As the British allowed more elected Indian representatives on local councils, the League demanded separate electorates, with a fixed number of seats for Muslims. As Muslims were a distinct minority within India, some of them feared that their voice could be swamped by a numerically dominant Hindu population, despite Gandhi's inclusive sensibility. Some Hindu politicians confirmed those fears when they cast the nationalist struggle in Hindu religious terms, hailing their country, for example, as a goddess, Bande Mataram (Mother India). When the 1937 elections gave the Congress Party control of many provincial governments, some of those governments began to enforce the teaching of Hindi in schools, rather than Urdu, which is written in a Persian script and favored by Muslims. This policy, as well as Hindu efforts to protect cows from slaughter, antagonized Muslims.

As the movement for independence gained ground, the Muslim League and its leader, Muhammad Ali Jinnah (JIN-uh), argued that those parts of India that had a Muslim majority should have a separate political status. They called it Pakistan, meaning "land of the pure." In this view, India was not a single nation, as Gandhi had long argued. Jinnah put his case succinctly:

> The Muslims and Hindus belong to two different religious philosophies, social customs, and literatures. They neither intermarry nor interdine [eat] together and, indeed, they belong to two different civilizations.[7]

With great reluctance and amid mounting violence, Gandhi and the Congress Party finally agreed to partition as the British declared their intention to leave India after World War II (see Map 22.2).

Thus colonial India became independent in 1947 as two countries—a Muslim Pakistan, itself divided into two wings 1,000 miles apart, and a mostly Hindu India governed by a secular state. Dividing colonial India in this fashion was horrendously

Guided Reading Question

■ DESCRIPTION
What conflicts and differences divided India's nationalist movement?

AP® EXAM TIP

You need to know the definition of "partition" in relation to the dividing of India after its independence.

Map 22.2   **The Partition of British South Asia**

The independence of British India witnessed the violent partition of the subcontinent into a largely Hindu India and a Muslim Pakistan. Later, in 1971, East Pakistan established itself as the separate state of Bangladesh.

painful. A million people or more died in the communal violence that accompanied partition, and some 12 million refugees moved from one country to the other to join their religious compatriots. Gandhi himself, desperately trying to stem the mounting tide of violence in India's villages, refused to attend the independence celebrations. Only a year after independence, he was assassinated by a Hindu extremist. The great triumph of independence, secured from the powerful British Empire, was overshadowed by the great tragedy of the violence of partition. (See Zooming In: Abdul Ghaffar Khan, page 988.)

The Case of South Africa: Ending Apartheid

The setting for South Africa's freedom struggle was very different from that of India. In the twentieth century, that struggle was not waged against an occupying European colonial power, for South Africa had in fact been independent of Great Britain since 1910. Independence, however, had been granted to a government wholly controlled by a white settler minority, which represented less than 20 percent of the total population. The country's black African majority had no political rights whatsoever within the central state. Black South Africans' struggle therefore was against this internal opponent rather than against a distant colonial authority, as in India. Economically, the most prominent whites were of British descent. They or their forebears had come to South Africa during the nineteenth century, when Great Britain was the ruling colonial power. But the politically dominant section of the white community, known as Boers or Afrikaners, was descended from the early Dutch settlers, who had arrived in the mid-seventeenth century. The term "Afrikaner" reflected their image of themselves as "white Africans," permanent residents of the continent rather than colonial intruders. They had unsuccessfully sought independence from a British-ruled South Africa in a bitter struggle (the Boer War, 1899–1902), and a sense of difference and antagonism lingered. Despite continuing

AP® EXAM TIP

You may need to know the features of apartheid in South Africa, and Mandela's role in ending that policy.

Abdul Ghaffar Khan, Muslim Pacifist

Born in 1890 in the Northwest Frontier Province of colonial India, Abdul Ghaffar Khan hailed from a well-to-do landowning family among the Muslim Pathan people, widely known for their tribal conflicts. Abdul Khan himself described his people as "inclined to be violent, . . . always ready to inflict harm and injury on their own brethren."[8] So it is all the more remarkable that a widespread movement of Islamic nonviolent

Abdul Ghaffar Khan (left) with Gandhi (on the right).

resistance to British rule emerged among the Pathan people during the 1930s and 1940s, with Abdul Khan as its leader.

As a boy, Khan attended a British mission school, which he credited with instilling in him a sense of service to his people. He later turned down a chance to enter an elite military unit of the Indian army when he learned that he would be required to defer to British officers junior to him in rank. His mother opposed his own plan to study in an English university, and so he turned instead to the "service of God and humanity." In practice, this initially meant social reform and educational advancement within Pathan villages, but in the increasingly nationalist environment of early twentieth-century

India, it soon meant anticolonial politics as well.

Deeply impressed with Gandhi's message of nonviolent protest, in 1929 Abdul Khan established the Khudai Khidmatgar, or "Servants of God," movement in his home region. Committed to nonviolence, social reform, the unity of the Pathan people, and the independence of India, the Khudai Khidmatgar soon became affiliated with the Indian National Congress, led by Gandhi, which was the leading nationalist organization in the country. During the 1930s and early 1940s, Abdul Khan's movement gained a substantial following in the Frontier Province, becoming the dominant political force in the area. Moreover, it largely adhered to its nonviolent creed in the face of severe British oppression and even massacres. In the process, Abdul Khan acquired a prominent place beside Gandhi in the Congress Party and an almost legendary status in his own Frontier region. His imposing six-foot-three stature, his constant touring of Pathan villages, his obvious commitment to Islam, his frequent imprison-

photo: © Hulton-Deutsch Collection/Corbis

Guided Reading Question

■ COMPARISON

Why was African rule in South Africa delayed until 1994, when it had occurred decades earlier elsewhere in the colonial world?

hostility between white South Africans of British and Afrikaner background, both felt that their way of life and standard of living were jeopardized by any move toward black African majority rule. The intransigence of this sizable and threatened settler community helps explain why African rule was delayed until 1994, while India, lacking any such community, had achieved independence almost a half century earlier.

Unlike a predominantly agrarian India, South Africa by the early twentieth century had developed a mature industrial economy, based initially in gold and diamond mining, but by midcentury including secondary industries such as steel, chemicals, automobile manufacturing, rubber processing, and heavy engineering.

ment by the British — all of this fostered a saintly image of the Pathan leader. The wells he drank from were thought to cure diseases. He became Badshah Khan (the king of khans) or the Frontier Gandhi.

It was a remarkable achievement. Gandhi's close associate Jawaharlal Nehru later wrote that both he and Gandhi were astonished that "Abdul Gaffar Khan made his turbulent and quarrelsome people accept peaceful methods of political action, involving enormous suffering."[9] In large measure, this had happened because Abdul Khan was able to root nonviolence in both Islam and Pathan culture. In fact, he had come to nonviolence well before meeting Gandhi, seeing it as necessary for overcoming the incessant feuding of his Pathan people. The Prophet Muhammad's mission, he declared, was "to free the oppressed, to feed the poor, and to clothe the naked."[10] Nonviolent struggle was a form of jihad, or Islamic holy war, and the suffering it generated was a kind of martyrdom. Furthermore, he linked nonviolent struggle to Pathan male virtues of honor, bravery, and strength.

By the mid-1940s, however, Pathan Muslims increasingly favored a separate state (Pakistan) rather than an alliance with Hindus in a unified India, as Gandhi and Abdul Khan so fervently hoped for. Abdul Khan's political critics stigmatized him as "Hindu," while many orthodox Islamic scholars viewed his more inclusive and nonviolent view of Islam as a challenge to their authority and their understanding of the faith. When the Congress finally and reluctantly accepted the partition of India into two states, Abdul Khan felt betrayed. "You have thrown us to the wolves," he said.

Despite his deep disappointment about partition and the immense violence that accompanied it, Abdul Khan declared his allegiance to Pakistan. But neither he nor his Servants of God followers could gain the trust of the new Pakistani authorities, who refused to recognize their role as freedom fighters in the struggle against colonial rule. His long opposition to the creation of Pakistan made his patriotism suspect; his advocacy of Pathan unity raised fears that he was fostering the secession of that region; and his political liberalism and criticism of Pakistani military governments generated suspicions that he was a communist. Thus he was repeatedly imprisoned in Pakistan and in conditions far worse than he had experienced in British jails. He viewed Pakistan as a British effort at divide and rule, "so that the Hindus and the Muslims might forever be at war and forget that they were brothers."[11]

Until his death in 1988 at the age of ninety-eight, he held firmly to his Islam-based nonviolent beliefs. But like Gandhi, he was far more widely admired than he was imitated.

Questions: Why do you think Abdul Khan is generally unknown? Where does he fit in the larger history of the twentieth century?

Particularly since the 1960s, the economy benefited from extensive foreign investment and loans. Almost all black Africans were involved in this complex modern economy, working in urban industries or mines, providing labor for white-owned farms, or receiving payments from relatives who did. The extreme dependence of most Africans on the white-controlled economy rendered individuals highly vulnerable to repressive action, but collectively the threat to withdraw their essential labor also gave them a powerful weapon.

A further unique feature of the South African situation was the overwhelming prominence of race, expressed since 1948 in the official policy of apartheid, which attempted to separate blacks from whites in every conceivable way while retaining

Africans' labor power in the white-controlled economy. An enormous apparatus of repression enforced that system. Rigid "pass laws" monitored and tried to control the movement of Africans into the cities, where they were subjected to extreme forms of social segregation. In the rural areas, a series of impoverished and over-crowded "native reserves," or Bantustans, served as ethnic homelands that kept Africans divided along tribal lines. Even though racism was present in colonial India, nothing of this magnitude developed there.

As in India, various forms of opposition—resistance to conquest, rural rebel-lions, urban strikes, and independent churches—arose to contest the manifest injustices of South African life. There too an elite-led political party provided an organizational umbrella for many of the South African resistance efforts in the twentieth century. Established in 1912, the African National Congress (ANC), like its Indian predecessor, was led by male, educated, professional, and middle-class Africans who sought not to overthrow the existing order, but to be accepted as "civilized men" within it. They appealed to the liberal, humane, and Christian values that white society claimed. For four decades, its leaders pursued peaceful and moderate protest—petitions, multiracial conferences, delegations appealing to the authorities—even as racially based segregationist policies were implemented one after another.

Women were denied full membership in the ANC until 1943 and were restricted to providing catering and entertainment services for the men. But they took action in other arenas. In 1913, they organized a successful protest against carrying passes, an issue that endured through much of the twentieth century. Rural women in the 1920s used church-based networks to organize boycotts of local shops and schools. Women were likewise prominent in trade union protests, including wage demands for domestic servants and washerwomen. By 1948, when the Afrikaner-led National Party came to power on a platform of apartheid, it was clear that peaceful protest, whether organized by men or by women, had produced no meaningful movement toward racial equality.

During the 1950s, a new and younger generation of the ANC leadership, which now included Nelson Mandela, broadened its base of support and launched non-violent civil disobedience—boycotts, strikes, demonstrations, and the burning of the hated passes that all Africans were required to carry. All of these actions were similar to and inspired by the tactics that Gandhi had pioneered in South Africa and used in India twenty to thirty years earlier. The government of South Africa responded with tremendous repression, including the shooting of sixty-nine unarmed demon-strators at Sharpville in 1960, the banning of the ANC, and the imprisonment of its leadership, including Nelson Mandela.

At this point, the freedom struggle in South Africa took a different direction than it had in India. Its major political parties were now illegal. Underground nationalist leaders turned to armed struggle, authorizing selected acts of sabotage and assassina-tion, while preparing for guerrilla warfare in camps outside the country. Active

Guided Reading Question

■ CHANGE

How did South Africa's struggle against white dom-ination change over time?

opposition within South Africa was now primarily expressed by student groups that were part of the Black Consciousness movement, an effort to foster pride, unity, and political awareness among the country's African majority, with a particular emphasis on mobilizing women for the struggle. Such young people were at the center of an explosion of protest in 1976 in a sprawling, segregated, impoverished black neighborhood called Soweto, outside Johannesburg, in which hundreds were killed. The initial trigger for the uprising was the government's decision to enforce education for Africans in the hated language of the white Afrikaners rather than English. However, the momentum of the Soweto rebellion persisted, and by the mid-1980s spreading urban violence and the radicalization of urban young people had forced the government to declare a state of emergency. Furthermore, South Africa's black labor movement, legalized only in 1979, became increasingly active and political. In June 1986, to commemorate the tenth anniversary of the Soweto uprising, the Congress of South African Trade Unions orchestrated a general strike involving some 2 million workers.

Beyond this growing internal pressure, South Africa faced mounting international

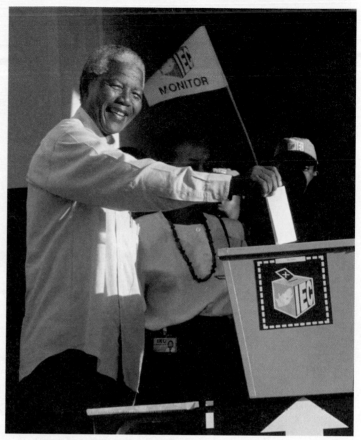

Nelson Mandela
In April 1994, the long struggle against apartheid and white domination in South Africa came to an end in the country's first democratic and nonracial election. The symbol of that triumph was Nelson Mandela, long a political prisoner, head of the African National Congress, and the country's first black African president. He is shown here voting in that historic election. (© Peter Turnley/Corbis)

demands to end apartheid as well. Exclusion from most international sporting events, including the Olympics; the refusal of many artists and entertainers to perform in South Africa; economic boycotts; the withdrawal of private investment funds—all of this isolated South Africa from a Western world in which its white rulers claimed membership. None of this had any parallel in India.

The combination of these internal and external pressures persuaded many white South Africans by the late 1980s that discussion with African nationalist leaders was the only alternative to a massive, bloody, and futile struggle to preserve white privileges. The outcome was the abandonment of key apartheid policies, the release of Nelson Mandela from prison, the legalization of the ANC, and a prolonged process of negotiations that in 1994 resulted in national elections, which brought the ANC

Map 22.3   South Africa after Apartheid

Under apartheid, all black Africans were officially designated as residents of small, scattered, impoverished Bantustans, shown on the inset map. Many of these people, of course, actually lived in white South Africa, where they worked. The main map shows the new internal organization of the country as it emerged after 1994, with the Bantustans abolished and the country divided into nine provinces. Lesotho and Swaziland had been British protectorates during the colonial era and subsequently became separate independent countries, although surrounded by South African territory.

to power. To the surprise of almost everyone, the long nightmare of South African apartheid came to an end without a racial bloodbath (see Map 22.3).

As in India, the South African nationalist movement was divided and conflicted. Unlike in India, though, these divisions did not occur along religious lines. Rather, it was race, ethnicity, and ideology that generated dissension and sometimes violence. Whereas the ANC generally favored a broad alliance of everyone opposed to apartheid (black Africans, Indians, "coloreds" or mixed-race people, and sympathetic whites), a smaller group known as the Pan Africanist Congress rejected cooperation with other racial groups and limited its membership to black Africans. During the urban uprisings of the 1970s and 1980s, young people supporting the Black Consciousness movements and those following Mandela and the ANC waged war against each other in the townships of South African cities. Perhaps most threatening to the unity of the nationalist struggle were the separatist tendencies of the Zulu-based Inkatha Freedom Party. Its leader, Gatsha Buthelezi, had cooperated with the apartheid state and even received funding from it. As negotiations for a transition to African rule unfolded in the early 1990s, considerable violence between Inkatha followers, mostly Zulu migrant workers, and ANC supporters broke out in a number of cities. None of this, however, approached the massive killing of Hindus and Muslims that accompanied the partition of India. South Africa, unlike India, acquired its political freedom as an intact and unified state.

> **PRACTICING AP® HISTORICAL THINKING**
>
> How and why did the anticolonial struggles in India and South Africa differ?

Experiments with Freedom

Africa's first modern nationalist hero, Kwame Nkrumah (KWAH-may ehn-KROO-mah) of Ghana, paraphrased a biblical quotation when he urged his followers, "Seek ye first the political kingdom and all these other things will be added unto you." But would winning the political kingdom of independence or freedom from European rule really produce "all these other things"—release from state oppression, industrial growth, economic development, reasonably unified nations, and a better life for all? That was the central question confronting the new nations emerging from colonial rule. They were joined in that quest by already independent but nonindustrialized countries and regions such as China, Thailand, Ethiopia, Iran, Turkey, and Central and South America. Together they formed the bloc of nations known variously as the third world, the developing countries, or the Global South. Those countries accounted for about 90 percent of the fourfold increase in human numbers that the world experienced during the twentieth century. Between 1950 and 2000, the populations of Asia and Africa alone grew from 64 percent of the world's total to 70 percent, with an estimated increase to 79 percent by 2050. (See Snapshot: World Population Growth, page 994.) That immense surge in global population, at one level a great triumph for the human species, also underlay many of the difficulties these nations faced as they conducted their various experiments with freedom.

Almost everywhere, the moment of independence generated something close to euphoria. Having emerged from the long night of colonial rule, free peoples had the opportunity to build anew. The developing countries would be laboratories for fresh approaches to creating modern states, nations, cultures, and economies. In the decades that followed, experiments with freedom multiplied, but the early optimism was soon tempered by the difficulties and disappointments of those tasks.

> **AP® EXAM TIP**
>
> Pay attention to examples of struggles faced by emerging independent countries in the twentieth century.

SNAPSHOT   World Population Growth, 1950–2011

The great bulk of the world's population growth in the second half of the twentieth century
occurred in the developing countries of Asia, Africa, the Middle East, and Latin America.[12]

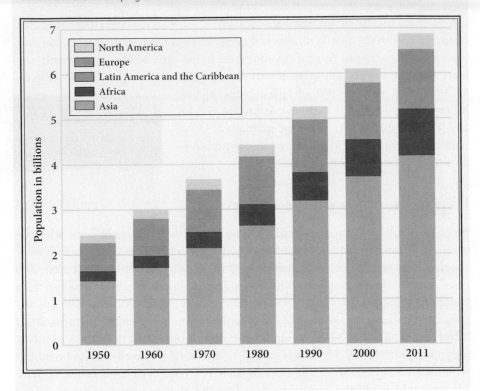

Experiments in Political Order:
Party, Army, and the Fate of Democracy

All across the developing world, efforts to create political order had to contend with
a set of common conditions. Populations were exploding, and expectations for independence ran very high, often exceeding the available resources. Many developing
countries were culturally very diverse, with little loyalty to a central state. Nonetheless, public employment mushroomed as the state assumed greater responsibility
for economic development. In conditions of widespread poverty and weak private
economies, groups and individuals sought to capture the state, or parts of it, both
for the salaries and status it offered and for the opportunities for private enrichment
that public office provided.

   This was the formidable setting in which developing countries had to hammer
out new political systems. The range of that effort was immense: Communist Party
control in China, Vietnam, and Cuba; multiparty democracy in India and South

Africa; one party democracy in Mexico, Tanzania, and Senegal; military regimes for a time in much of Latin America, Africa, and the Middle East; personal dictatorships in Uganda and the Philippines. In many places, one kind of political system followed another in kaleidoscopic succession.

As colonial rule drew to a close, European authorities in many places attempted to transplant democratic institutions to colonies they had long governed with such a heavy and authoritarian hand. They established legislatures, permitted elections, allowed political parties to operate, and in general anticipated the development of constitutional, parliamentary, multiparty democracies similar to their own.

It was in India that such a political system established its deepest roots. There Western-style democracy, including regular elections, multiple parties, civil liberties, and peaceful changes in government, has been practiced almost continuously since independence. What made this remarkable democratic continuity possible?

The struggle for independence in India had been a prolonged affair, thus providing time for an Indian political leadership to sort itself out. Furthermore, the British began to hand over power in a gradual way well before complete independence was granted in 1947. Thus a far larger number of Indians had useful administrative or technical skills than was the case elsewhere. In sharp contrast to most African countries, for example, the nationalist movement in India was embodied in a single national party (the Congress Party), which encompassed a wide variety of other parties and interest groups. Its leaders, Gandhi and Nehru in particular, were genuinely committed to democratic practice, which, some have argued, allowed elites from the many and varied groups of Indian society to find a place in the political system. Even the tragic and painful partition of colonial India into two countries minimized a major source of internal discord as independent India was born. Moreover, Indian statehood could be built on common cultural and political traditions that were far more deeply rooted than in many former colonies.

Elsewhere in the colonial world, democracy proved a far more fragile transplant. Among the new states of Africa, for example, few retained their democratic institutions beyond the initial post-independence decade. Many of the apparently popular political parties that had led the struggle for independence lost mass support and were swept away by military coups. When the army took power in Ghana in 1966, no one lifted a finger to defend the party that had led the country to independence only nine years earlier. Other states evolved into one-party systems, and still others degenerated into personal tyrannies or dictatorships. Freedom from colonial rule certainly did not automatically generate the internal political freedoms associated with democracy.

Africans sometimes suggested that their traditional cultures, based on communal rather than individualistic values and concerned with achieving consensus rather than majority rule, were not compatible with the competitiveness of party politics. Others argued that Western-style democracy was simply inadequate for the tasks of development confronting the new states. Creating national unity was surely more difficult when competing political parties identified primarily with particular ethnic

Guided Reading Question

■ CHANGE

What led to the erosion of democracy and the establishment of military government in much of Africa and Latin America?

or "tribal" groups, as was frequently the case in Africa. Certainly Europe did not begin its modernizing process with such a system. Why, many Africans asked, should they be expected to do so?

The economic disappointments of independence also contributed to the erosion of support for democracy. By almost any measure, African economic performance since independence has been the poorest in the developing world. As a result, college and high school graduates were unable to find the white-collar careers they expected; urban migrants had little opportunity for work; farmers received low prices for their cash crops; consumers resented shortages and inflation; and millions of impoverished and malnourished peasants lived on the brink of starvation. These were people for whom independence was unable to fulfill even the most minimal of expectations, let alone the grandiose visions of a better life that so many had embraced in the early 1960s. Since modern governments everywhere staked their legitimacy on economic performance, it is little wonder that many Africans became disaffected and withdrew their support from governments they had enthusiastically endorsed only a few years earlier. Further resentments arose from the privileges of the relatively well-educated elite who had found high-paying jobs in the growing bureaucracies of the newly independent states. Such grievances often found expression in ethnic conflict, as Africa's immense cultural diversity became intensely politicized. An ethnically based civil war in Nigeria during the late 1960s cost the lives of millions, while in the mid-1990s ethnic hatred led Rwanda into the realm of genocide. (See Zooming In: Mozambique, page 998.)

These economic disappointments, class resentments, and ethnic conflicts provided the context for numerous military takeovers. By the early 1980s, the military had intervened in at least thirty of Africa's forty-six independent states and actively governed more than half of them. In doing so, they swept aside the old political parties and constitutions and vowed to begin anew, while promising to return power to civilians and restore democracy at some point in the future.

A similar wave of military interventions swept over Latin America during the 1960s and 1970s, leaving Brazil, Argentina, Peru, Chile, Uruguay, Bolivia, the Dominican Republic, and other countries governed at times by their armed forces. However, the circumstances in Latin America were quite different from those in Africa. While military rule was something new and unexpected in Africa, Latin American armed forces had long intervened in political life. The region had also largely escaped the bitter ethnic conflicts that afflicted so many African states, though its class antagonisms were more clearly defined and expressed. Furthermore, Latin American societies in general were far more modernized and urbanized than those of Africa. And while newly independent African states remained linked to their former European rulers, long-independent Latin American states lived in the shadow of a dominant United States. "Poor Mexico," bemoaned Porfirio Díaz, that country's dictator before the Mexican Revolution, "so far from God and so close to the United States."

But beneath the changes in political regimes in Latin America lay the more deeply rooted transformations of the twentieth century: population growth and

AP® EXAM TIP

Take notes comparing post-independence conditions in Africa and Latin America.

large-scale migration from rural areas to the urban slums of big cities; industrial development and trade union activism; rural poverty and sharp divisions between rich and poor; resentment against American economic and political power; and the influence of ideas deriving from European socialism, the American New Deal, the Mexican Revolution, and Christian "liberation theology." All of this pushed Latin American politics away from the elitist orientation that had largely prevailed since independence toward concerns with economic development, social reform, mass participation, nationalism, and anti-imperialism.

These issues found expression in a wide range of political movements and government programs. Early in the century, the revolution in Mexico and a peaceful program of radical state-directed social reforms in Uruguay were early examples of the new politics. During the 1930s, the Aprista movement in Peru blended ideas of Latin American uniqueness, democratic socialism, the full integration of indigenous peoples into society, and anti-imperialism into a political outlook that had appeal in many parts of the continent. The "social justice" program of Juan Perón in Argentina between 1945 and 1955 enacted a large body of social and labor legislation, aimed largely at the mass of long-ignored and marginalized urban workers. A broadly similar program took shape in Brazil under the leadership of Getúlio Vargas. The Cuban Revolution of 1959 likewise gave expression to these ideas

Slums and Skyscrapers
The enormous disparities that have accompanied modern economic development in Latin America and elsewhere are illustrated in this photograph from São Paulo, Brazil. (© Florian Kopp/Image BROKER/age fotostock)

and sought to export them to the rest of Latin America. The 1960s and later years witnessed guerrilla warfare in Peru, Bolivia, and Colombia and short-lived left-wing governments in Guatemala, Brazil, and Nicaragua.

Chile illustrated both these new political directions and the fears they generated. In 1970, Chileans narrowly elected to the presidency a Marxist politician, Salvador Allende, who soon launched an ambitious program to achieve a peaceful transition to socialism. In an effort to redistribute wealth, he ordered prices frozen and wages raised. Nationalization of major industries followed—including copper, coal, steel, and many banks—without compensation to their former owners, many of whom were foreign corporations. In rural areas, land reform programs soon seized large estates, redistributing them to small farmers. And Allende warmly welcomed Fidel Castro for a month-long visit in 1971. It was an audacious effort to achieve genuinely revolutionary change by legal and peaceful means.

Mozambique: Civil War and Reconciliation

In the decades after independence, many Asian and African countries experienced bitter civil wars—Nigeria, Rwanda, Somalia, Sri Lanka, Cambodia, and Burma among others. As their conflicts ended, these countries have faced the issue of reconciliation among former enemies who often hated, despised, and feared one another. Such has been the case in Mozambique, a

The *Tree of Life* in Mozambique in 2005.

Portuguese colony in southeastern Africa, which achieved its independence in 1975, after a ten-year armed struggle led by a party called the Front for the Liberation of Mozambique (FRELIMO).

Mozambique's newly independent government, controlled by FRELIMO, came to power in a single-party Marxist-oriented state with strong support from the communist world. Some of its policies—a socialist agenda, dismissal of many traditional chiefs, imprisonment of opponents in "reeducation" camps, forced resettlement of scattered farmers in communal villages—soon antagonized many people. Opposition came together as the Mozambique National Resistance (RENAMO) and found support from the threatened white-ruled regimes in neighboring Rhodesia and South Africa. As weapons from many sources flowed into the country, a terrible civil war erupted in 1977, lasting fifteen years. Alto-

gether, 1 million or more people were killed and another 5 million were displaced, accounting for nearly half the country's population. On both sides, it was a brutal conflict, with RENAMO especially employing systematic mass killings, rape, and mutilation as a tactic of war. By the end of the 1980s, the military stalemate in Mozambique, coupled with the collapse of white rule in southern Africa and the abandonment of communism in the Soviet Union and China, provided conditions for negotiations, an end to the fighting, and finally a new constitution. In the early 1990s, Mozambique emerged as a democratic, multi-party, market-oriented democracy, and since then the nation has held regular elections every five years.

RENAMO supporters have participated in those elections, and some of their fighters have been integrated into Mozambique's military forces. But the Mozambican government has not initiated any large-scale process to deal with the enormous abuse and trauma that so many people experienced. State authorities authorized a general amnesty for all crimes committed during the civil war, but they expressed no official recognition of the suffering

photo: David Rose/Panos Pictures

But internal opposition mounted—from the bureaucracy, military officers, church hierarchy, and wealthy business and landlord elites as well as various small-business and middle-class elements, climaxing in a huge strike in late 1972. Furthermore, the U.S. government, which had long armed, funded, and trained military forces throughout Latin America, actively opposed the Allende regime, as did U.S. corporations. A CIA document declared, "It is firm and continuing policy that Allende be overthrown by a coup."[13] And in September 1973, he was. What followed was an extraordinarily repressive military regime, headed by General Augusto Pinochet, which lasted until the restoration of democracy in 1988.

involved or compassion for the victims. Nothing similar to South Africa's Truth and Reconciliation Commission emerged in Mozambique. The government, Christian churches, and local chiefs alike urged forgiveness without revenge, but offered little to deal with the emotional scars and social conflicts that the civil war had generated. It was, critics charged, "reconciliation without truth." Indirectly, however, by acknowledging the legitimacy of customary institutions and practices, which FRELIMO had earlier tried to destroy, the government made it possible for local initiatives to operate within a traditional setting.

One of these initiatives involved the spirits of dead soldiers, known as *gamba*, who returned to possess particular individuals. Traditional healers created rituals designed to appease these spirits. Such ceremonies brought alienated people together, reminded them of the violence of the civil war, elicited confessions of wrongdoing, and set appropriate compensations. In these encounters, local people, whose families and communities were often torn apart by the war, found a way to confront the past and to experience some reconciliation within a culturally familiar setting.

Yet another remarkable private initiative of reconciliation with the past involved young people, many of whom had been forced to participate in the civil war as teenagers. In partnership with the Christian Council of Mozambique, they created a "transforming weapons into tools" project, which sought to collect and destroy some of the millions of weapons left over from the civil war. Animated by the biblical "swords into plowshares" notion, this project invited people to exchange their weapons for tools, such as sewing machines, hoes, plows, bicycles, and construction material. Hundreds of thousands of weapons, perhaps millions, were turned in. One village that recovered a very large number of weapons received a tractor in return. The weapons were then taken apart and turned over to Mozambican artists, who fashioned them into remarkable sculptures—chairs, trees, animals, musical instruments, bicycles, human figures, and more.

Among the most memorable of those sculptures was a *Tree of Life*, some ten feet tall and weighing 1,000 pounds, accompanied by birds and animals, all made from pieces of dismantled weapons. The symbolism of weapons transformed into objects of comfort or inspiration allowed people to confront the past, while evoking some sense of hope and possibility from the tragedy of the civil war. There was irony too in this project. The *Tree of Life* was commissioned by and displayed in the British Museum, thus returning to Europe some of the weapons that originated in Europe to fuel the civil war in Mozambique.

Questions: What common features do these various reconciliation efforts share, and how do they differ? What possible responses to them can you imagine?

Chile's return to democratic practice was a small part of a remarkable late twentieth-century political reversal, a globalization of democracy that brought popular movements, multiparty elections, and new constitutions to many countries all around the world. This included the end of military and autocratic rule in Spain, Portugal, and Greece as well as the stunning rise of democratic movements, parties, and institutions amid the collapse of communism in the Soviet Union and Eastern Europe. But the most extensive expression of this global reemergence of democracy lay in the developing countries. By 2000, almost all Latin American countries had abandoned their military-controlled regimes and returned to some form of democratic governance. So too did most African states previously ruled by soldiers, dictators, or single parties. In Asia, authoritarian regimes, some long established, gave way to more pluralistic and participatory political systems in South Korea, Taiwan, Thailand, the Philippines, Iraq, and Indonesia. And in 2011, mass movements in various Arab countries—Tunisia, Egypt, Libya, Syria, Bahrain, Yemen—had challenged or ended the hold of entrenched, corrupt, and autocratic rulers, while proclaiming their commitment to democracy, human dignity, and honest government. What might explain this global pattern and its expression in the Global South in particular?

One factor surely was the untethering of the ideas of democracy and human rights from their Western origins. By the final quarter of the twentieth century, democracy was increasingly viewed as a universal political principle to which all could aspire rather than an alien and imposed system deriving from the West. Democracy, like communism, feminism, modern science, and Christianity, was a Western import that took root and substantially lost its association with the West. It was therefore increasingly available as a vehicle for social protest in the rest of the world.

Perhaps the most important internal factor favoring a revival of democracy lay in the apparent failure of authoritarian governments to remedy disastrous economic situations, to raise standards of living, to provide jobs for the young, and to curb pervasive corruption. The oppressive and sometimes-brutal behavior of repressive governments humiliated and outraged many. Furthermore, the growth of civil society with its numerous voluntary groups provided a social foundation, independent of the state, for demanding change. Disaffected students, professionals, urban workers, religious organizations, women's groups, and more joined in a variety of grassroots movements, some of them mobilized through social media, to insist on democratic change as a means to a better life. Such movements found encouragement in the demands for democracy that accompanied the South African struggle against apartheid and the collapse of Soviet and Eastern European communism. And the end of the cold war reduced the willingness of the major industrial powers to underwrite their authoritarian client states.

But the consolidation of democratic practice was an uncertain and highly variable process. Some elected leaders, such as Hugo Chávez in Venezuela and Vladimir Putin in Russia, turned authoritarian once in office. Even where parliaments existed, they were often quite circumscribed in their powers. Outright electoral fraud tainted democratic institutions in many places, while established elites and oligarchies found it possible to exercise considerable influence even in formal democracies, and not only in the Global South. Chinese authorities brutally crushed a democratic movement in 1989. The Algerian military sponsored elections in 1992 and then abruptly canceled them when an Islamic party seemed poised to win. And the political future of the Arab Spring remained highly uncertain, as a military strongman became a civilian politician and returned to power in Egypt in 2014. Nonetheless, this worldwide revival of democracy represented the globalization of what had been a Western idea and the continuation of the political experiments that had begun with independence.

Experiments in Economic Development: Changing Priorities, Varying Outcomes

At the top of the agenda everywhere in the Global South was economic development, a process that meant growth or increasing production as well as distributing the fruits of that growth to raise living standards. This quest for development, now operating all across the planet, represented the universal acceptance of beliefs unheard of not many centuries earlier—that poverty was no longer inevitable and that it was possible to deliberately improve the material conditions of life for everyone. Economic development was a central promise of all independence struggles, and it was increasingly the standard by which people measured and granted legitimacy to their governments.

Achieving economic development, however, was no easy or automatic task. It took place in societies sharply divided by class, religion, ethnic group, and gender and in the face of explosive population growth. In many places, colonial rule had provided only the most slender foundations for modern development, as new nations often came to independence with low rates of literacy, few people with managerial experience, a weak private economy, and transportation systems oriented to export rather than national integration. Furthermore, the entire effort occurred in a world split by rival superpowers and economically dominated by the powerful capitalist economies of the West. Despite their political independence, most developing countries had little leverage in negotiations with the wealthy nations of the Global North and their immense transnational corporations. It was hardly an auspicious environment in which to seek a fundamental economic transformation.

Beyond these difficulties lay the question of what strategies to pursue. The academic field of "development economics" was new; its experts disagreed and often changed their minds; and conflicting political pressures, both internal and international, only added to the confusion. All of this resulted in considerable controversy, changing policies, and much experimentation.

One fundamental issue lay in the role of the state. All across the developing world and particularly in newly independent nations, most people expected that state authorities would take major responsibility for spurring the economic development of their countries. After all, the private economy was weakly developed; few entrepreneurs had substantial funds to invest; the example of rapid Soviet industrialization under state direction was hopeful; and state control held the promise of protecting vulnerable economies from the ravages of international capitalism. Some state-directed economies had real successes. China launched a major industrialization effort and massive land reform under the leadership of the Communist Party. A communist Cuba, even while remaining dependent on its sugar production, wiped out illiteracy and provided basic health care to its entire population, raising life expectancy to seventy-six years by 1992, equivalent to that of the United States. Elsewhere as well—in Turkey, India, South Korea, and much of Africa—the state provided tariffs, licenses, loans, subsidies, and overall planning, while most productive property was owned privately.

AP® EXAM TIP

Make sure you can identify regions in the "Global South" and their significance in the second half of the twentieth century.

Guided Reading Question

■ CHANGE
What obstacles impeded the economic development of third-world countries?

Guided Reading Question

■ CHANGE
How and why did thinking about strategies for economic development change over time?

AP® EXAM TIP

You need to know examples of international organizations that promoted free market economies, like the World Bank.

Yet in the last three decades of the twentieth century, an earlier consensus in favor of state direction largely collapsed, replaced by a growing dependence on the market to generate economic development. This was most apparent in the abandonment of much communist planning in China and the return to private farming (see Chapter 21, pages 959–60). India and many Latin American and African states privatized their state-run industries and substantially reduced the role of the state in economic affairs. In part, this sharp change in economic policies reflected the failure, mismanagement, and corruption of many state-run enterprises, but it was also influenced by the collapse in the Soviet Union of the world's first state-dominated economy. Western pressures, exercised through international organizations such as the World Bank, likewise pushed developing countries in a capitalist direction. In China and India, the new approach generated rapid economic growth, but also growing inequalities and social conflict. But as the new millennium dawned, a number of developing countries once again asserted a more prominent role for the state in their quests for economic development and social justice. In China, Russia, Brazil, Saudi Arabia, Mexico, India, and elsewhere, state-owned companies currently buy and sell shares on the stock market, seeking profits in an economic system that has been called "state capitalism." Thus the search for an appropriate balance between state action and market forces in the management of modern economies continues.

A related issue involved the most appropriate posture for developing countries to adopt toward the world market as they sought to industrialize. Should they try to shield themselves from the influences of international capitalism, or were they better off vigorously engaging with the global economy? In the aftermath of the Great Depression of the 1930s, many Latin American countries followed the first path. Their traditional reliance on exporting agricultural products and raw materials had largely collapsed as the world economy sharply contracted (see Chapter 20, page 893). So they chose an alternative approach, known as import substitution industrialization, intended to reduce their dependence on the uncertain global marketplace by processing their own raw materials and manufacturing their own consumer goods behind high tariff barriers if necessary.

Brazil, for example, largely followed such policies from the 1930s through the late 1970s with some success. Between 1968 and 1974, the country experienced rapid industrial growth, dubbed the "Brazilian miracle." By the early 1980s, the country produced about 90 percent of its own consumer goods. But Brazil's industrialization was also accompanied by massive investment by foreign corporations, by the accumulation of a huge national debt to foreign lenders, by periodic bouts of inflation, and by very high levels of social inequality and poverty. Brazil's military president famously remarked in 1971: "The economy is doing fine but the people are doing badly."

The classic contrast to Latin American approaches to industrial development lay in East Asia, where South Korea, Taiwan, Hong Kong, and Singapore chose a different strategy. Rather than focusing on industrial production for domestic consumption, they chose to specialize in particular products for an export market textiles, electronic goods, and automobiles, for example. Many of these industries were labor-intensive, drawing large numbers of women into the workforce, though at very low wages. Initiated in the 1960s, this export-led industrialization strategy generated rapid economic growth, propelling these countries into the ranks of the industrialized world by the end of the century. In the 1980s and 1990s, Brazil too entered the world market more vigorously, developing export industries in automobiles, steel, aircraft, computers, and more.

Other issues as well inspired debate. In many places, an early emphasis on city-based industrial development, stirred by visions of a rapid transition to modernity, led to a neglect or exploitation of rural areas and agriculture. This "urban bias" subsequently came in for much criticism and some adjustment in spending priorities. (See Snapshot: Global Urbanization, page 1004.) A growing recognition of the role of women in agriculture led to charges of "male bias" in development planning and to mounting efforts to assist women farmers directly. Women were also central to many governments' increased interest in curtailing population growth. Women's access to birth control, education, and employment, it turned out, provided powerful incentives to limit family size. Another debate pitted the advocates of capital- and technology-driven projects (dams and factories, for example) against those who favored investment in "human capital," such as education, technical training, health care, and nutrition. The benefits and drawbacks of foreign aid, investment, and trade have likewise been contentious issues.

Economic development was never simply a matter of technical expertise or deciding among competing theories. Every decision was political, involving winners and losers in terms of power, advantage, and wealth. Where to locate schools, roads, factories, and clinics, for example, provoked endless controversies, some of them expressed in terms of regional or ethnic rivalries. It was an experimental process, and the stakes were high.

The results of those experiments have varied considerably. (See Snapshot, Chapter 23, page 1031, for global variations in economic development.) East Asian countries in general have had the strongest record of economic growth. South Korea, Taiwan, Singapore, and Hong Kong were dubbed "newly industrialized countries," and China boasted the most rapid economic growth in the world by the end of the twentieth century, replacing Japan as the world's second-largest economy. In the 1990s, Asia's other giant, India, opened itself more fully to the world market and launched rapid economic growth with a powerful high-tech sector and an expanding middle class. Oil-producing countries reaped a bonanza when they were able to demand much higher prices for that essential commodity in the 1970s and later. By 2008, Brazil ranked as the eighth-largest economy in the world with a rapidly growing industrial sector, while Turkey and Indonesia numbered in the top twenty. Limited principally to Europe, North America, and Japan in the nineteenth century, industrialization had become a global phenomenon by the early twenty-first.

AP® EXAM TIP

You should know that these East Asian economies are known as the "Asian Tigers."

SNAPSHOT   Global Urbanization, 1950–2014

In 1950, 29.6 percent of the world's population lived in urban areas, while by 2014 that figure had risen to 54 percent. This chart highlights the top twenty cities in terms of their population in those two years.[14] What changes can you identify in the size of those cities and in their geographic distribution?

	1950			2014		
Rank	City	Country	Population in millions	City	Country	Population in millions
1	New York City	USA	12.3	Tokyo	Japan	37.8
2	Tokyo	Japan	11.3	Delhi	India	24.9
3	London	UK	8.4	Shanghai	China	23.0
4	Paris	France	6.5	Mexico City	Mexico	20.84
5	Moscow	USSR	5.6	São Paulo	Brazil	20.83
6	Buenos Aires	Argentina	5.1	Mumbai	India	20.7
7	Chicago	USA	5.0	Osaka	Japan	20.1
8	Calcutta	India	4.5	Beijing	China	19.5
9	Shanghai	China	4.3	New York/Newark	USA	18.6
10	Osaka	Japan	4.2	Cairo	Egypt	18.4
11	Los Angeles	USA	4.0	Dhaka	Bangladesh	17.0
12	Berlin	Germany	3.3	Karachi	Pakistan	16.1
13	Philadelphia	USA	3.1	Buenos Aires	Argentina	15.0
14	Rio de Janeiro	Brazil	2.95	Calcutta	India	14.8
15	Leningrad/St. Petersburg	USSR	2.9	Istanbul	Turkey	14.0
16	Mexico City	Mexico	2.88	Chongqing	China	12.9
17	Bombay/Mumbai	India	2.86	Rio de Janeiro	Brazil	12.8
18	Detroit	USA	2.77	Manila	Philippines	12.76
19	Boston	USA	2.55	Lagos	Nigeria	12.6
20	Cairo	Egypt	2.5	Los Angeles area	USA	12.3

AP® EXAM TIP

Pay attention to the examples of continuities and changes in city populations in the Snapshot above.

Elsewhere, the story was very different. In most of Africa, much of the Arab world, and parts of Asia—regions representing about one-third of the world's population—there was little sign of catching up, and there had been frequent examples of declining standards of living since the end of the 1960s. Between 1980 and 2000, the average income in forty-three of Africa's poorest countries dropped by 25 percent, pushing living standards for many below what they had been at independence.

But in the early twenty-first century, a number of African countries began to experience encouraging economic growth, an expanding middle class with some money to spend, and more international investment. Some observers began to speak about "Africa rising."

Scholars and politicians alike argue about the reasons for such sharp differences in economic performance. Variations in factors such as geography and natural resources, colonial experiences, regional cultures, the degree of political stability and social equality, state economic policies, population growth rates, and forms of involvement with the world economy—all of these have been invoked to explain the widely diverging trajectories among developing countries.

Microloans
Bangladesh's Grameen Bank pioneered an innovative approach to economic development by offering modest loans to poor people, enabling them to start small businesses. Here a group of women who received such loans meet in early 2004 to make an installment payment to an officer of the bank. (Rafiqur Rahman/Reuters/Landov)

Experiments with Culture: The Role of Islam in Turkey and Iran

The quest for economic development represented the embrace of an emerging global culture of modernity with its scientific outlook, its technological achievements, and its focus on material values. Developing countries were also exposed to the changing culture of the West, including feminism, rock and rap, sexual permissiveness, consumerism, and democracy. But the peoples of the Global South had inherited cultural patterns from the more distant past as well. A common issue all across the developing world involved the uneasy relationship between these older traditions and the more recent outlooks associated with modernity and the West. How should traditional African "medicine men" relate to modern hospitals? What happens to Confucian based family values when confronted with the urban and commercial growth of recent Chinese history? Such tensions provided the raw material for a series of cultural experiments in the twentieth century, and nowhere were they more consequential than in the Islamic world. No single answer emerged to the question of how Islam and modernity should relate to each other, but the experiences of Turkey and Iran illustrate two quite different approaches to this fundamental issue (see Map 22.4). (See Working with Evidence: Contending for Islam, page 1012, for more on this topic.)

In the aftermath of World War I, modern Turkey emerged from the ashes of the Ottoman Empire, led by an energetic general, Mustafa Kemal Atatürk

Guided Reading Question

■ COMPARISON
In what ways did cultural revolutions in Turkey and Iran reflect different understandings of the role of Islam in modern societies?

Map 22.4   Iran, Turkey, and the Middle East

Among the great contrasts of a very diverse Middle East has been between Turkey, the most secular and Western-oriented country of the region, and Iran, home to the most sustained Islamic revolution in the area.

AP® EXAM TIP

Pay attention to the philosophical disagreements among Islamic leaders in the twentieth century.

(ATT-a-turk) (1881–1938), who fought off British, French, Italian, and Greek efforts to dismember what was left of the old empire. Often compared to Peter the Great in Russia (see Chapter 13, page 576), Atatürk then sought to transform his country into a modern, secular, and national state. Such ambitions were not entirely new, for they built upon the efforts of nineteenth-century Ottoman reformers, who, like Atatürk, greatly admired European Enlightenment thinking and sought to bring its benefits to their country.

To Atatürk and his followers, to become modern meant "to enter European civilization completely." They believed that this required totally removing Islam from public life and relegating it to the personal and private realm. Atatürk argued, "Islam will be elevated, if it will cease to be a political instrument." In fact, he sought to broaden access to the religion by translating the Quran into Turkish and issuing the call to prayer in Turkish rather than Arabic.

Atatürk largely ended, however, the direct political role of Islam. The old sultan, or ruler, of the Ottoman Empire, whose position had long been sanctified by Islamic tradition, was deposed as Turkey became a republic. Furthermore, the caliphate, by which Ottoman sultans had claimed leadership of the entire Islamic world, was abolished, although in fact it had atrophied to the point of having almost no real authority outside of Turkey. All Sufi organizations, sacred tombs, and religious schools were closed and outlawed, and a number of religious titles abolished. Islamic courts were likewise dissolved, while secular law codes, modeled on those of Europe, replaced the *sharia*. In history textbooks, pre-Islamic Turkish culture was celebrated as the foundation for all ancient civilizations. The Arabic script in which the Turkish language had long been written was exchanged for a new Western-style alphabet that made literacy much easier but rendered centuries of Ottoman culture inaccessible to these newly literate people. (See Working with Evidence, Source 22.1, page 1012, for an example of Atatürk's thinking.)

The most visible symbols of Atatürk's revolutionary program occurred in the realm of dress. Turkish men were ordered to abandon the traditional headdress known as the fez and to wear brimmed hats. Atatürk proclaimed:

A civilized, international dress is worthy and appropriate for our nation, and we will wear it. Boots or shoes on our feet, trousers on our legs, shirt and tie, jacket and waistcoat—and of course, to complete these, a cover with a brim on our heads.[15]

Although women were not forbidden to wear the veil, many elite women abandoned it and set the tone for feminine fashion in Turkey.

In Atatürk's view, the emancipation of women was a cornerstone of the new Turkey. In a much-quoted speech, he declared:

> If henceforward the women do not share in the social life of the nation, we shall never attain to our full development. We shall remain irremediably backward, incapable of treating on equal terms with the civilizations of the West.[16]

Thus polygamy was abolished; women were granted equal rights in divorce, inheritance, and child custody; and in 1934 Turkish women gained the right to vote and hold public office, a full decade before French women gained that right. Public beaches were now opened to women as well. As in the early Soviet Union, this was a state-directed feminism, responsive to Atatürk's views, rather than reflecting popular demands from women themselves.

These reforms represented a "cultural revolution" unique in the Islamic world of the time, and they were imposed against considerable opposition. After Atatürk's death in 1938, some of them were diluted or rescinded. The call to prayer returned to the traditional Arabic in 1950, and various political groups urged a greater role for Islam in the public arena. Since 2002, a moderate Islamic party has governed the country, while the political role of the military, long the chief defender of Turkish secularism, has diminished. By 2010, an earlier prohibition on women wearing headscarves in universities had largely ended. Nevertheless, the secularism of Atatürk persisted for many Turks and provided a major element in large-scale protests against the government in 2013. But elsewhere in the Islamic world, other solutions to the question of Islam and modernity took shape.

A very different answer emerged in Iran in the final quarter of the twentieth century. That country seemed an unlikely place for an Islamic revolution. Under the government of Shah Mohammad Reza Pahlavi (r. 1941–1979), Iran had undertaken what many saw as a quite successful and largely secular modernization effort. The country had great wealth in oil, a powerful military, a well-educated elite, and a solid alliance with the United States. Furthermore, the shah's so-called White Revolution, intended to promote the country's modernization, had redistributed land to many of Iran's impoverished peasants, granted women the right to vote, invested substantially in rural health care and education, initiated a number of industrial projects, and offered workers a

Westernization in Turkey
Mustafa Kemal Atatürk, the founder of modern Turkey, often appeared in public in elegant European dress, symbolizing for his people a sharp break with traditional Islamic ways of living. Here he is dancing with his adopted daughter at her high-society wedding in 1929. (Hulton Archive/Getty Images)

share in the profits of those industries. But beneath the surface of apparent success, discontent and resentment were brewing. Traditional small-scale merchants felt threatened by an explosion of imported Western goods and by competition from large businesses. Religious leaders, the *ulama*, were offended by state control of religious institutions and by secular education programs that bypassed Islamic schools. Educated professionals found Iran's reliance on the West disturbing. Rural migrants to the country's growing cities, especially Tehran, faced rising costs and uncertain employment.

A repressive and often-brutal government allowed little outlet for such grievances. Thus opposition to the shah's regime came to center on the country's many mosques, where Iran's Shia religious leaders invoked memories of earlier persecution and martyrdom as they mobilized that opposition and called for the shah's removal. The emerging leader of that movement was the high-ranking Shia cleric Ayatollah Ruhollah Khomeini (ko-MAY-nee) (1902–1989), who in 1979 returned from long exile in Paris to great acclaim. By then, massive urban demonstrations, strikes, and defections from the military had eroded support for the shah, who abdicated the throne and left the country.

What followed was also a cultural revolution, but one that moved in precisely the opposite direction from that of Atatürk's Turkey—toward, rather than away from, the Islamization of public life. The new government defined itself as an Islamic republic, with an elected parliament and a constitution, but in practice conservative Islamic clerics, headed by Khomeini, exercised dominant power. A Council of Guardians, composed of leading legal scholars, was empowered to interpret the constitution, to supervise elections, and to review legislation—all designed to ensure compatibility with a particular vision of Islam. Opposition to the new regime was harshly crushed, with some 1,800 executions in 1981 alone for those regarded as "waging war against God."[17]

Khomeini believed that the purpose of government was to apply the law of Allah as expressed in the sharia. Thus all judges now had to be competent in Islamic law, and those lacking that qualification were dismissed. The secular law codes under which the shah's government had operated were discarded in favor of those based solely on Islamic precedents. Islamization likewise profoundly affected the domain of education and culture. In June 1980, the new government closed some 200 universities and colleges for two years while textbooks, curricula, and faculty were "purified" of un-Islamic influences. Elementary and secondary schools, largely secular under the shah, now gave priority to religious instruction and the teaching of Arabic, even as about 40,000 teachers lost their jobs for lack of sufficient Islamic piety. Pre-Islamic Persian literature and history were now out of favor, while the history of Islam and Iran's revolution predominated in schools and the mass media. Western loan words were purged from the Farsi language and replaced by their Arabic equivalents.

As in Turkey, the role of women became a touchstone of this Islamic cultural revolution. By 1983, all women were required to wear the modest head-to-toe cov-

Women and the Iranian Revolution
One of the goals of Iran's Islamic revolution was to enforce a more modest and traditional dress code for the country's women. In this photo from 2004, a woman clad in a *chador* and talking on her cell phone walks past a poster of Ayatollah Khomeini, who led that revolution in 1979. (AP Images)

ering known as hijab, a regulation enforced by roving groups of militants, or "revolutionary guards." Those found with "bad hijab" were subject to harassment and sometimes lashings or imprisonment. Sexual segregation was imposed in schools, parks, beaches, and public transportation. The legal age of marriage for girls, set at eighteen under the shah, was reduced to nine with parental consent and thirteen, later raised to fifteen, without it. Married women could no longer file for divorce or attend school. Yet, despite such restrictions, many women supported the revolution and over the next several decades found far greater opportunities for employment and higher education than before. By the early twenty-first century, almost 60 percent of university students were women. And women's right to vote remained intact.

While Atatürk's cultural revolution of westernization and secularism was largely an internal affair with little interest in extending the Turkish model abroad, Khomeini clearly sought to export Iran's Islamic revolution. He openly called for the replacement of insufficiently Islamic regimes in the Middle East and offered training and support for their opponents. In Lebanon, Syria, Bahrain, Saudi Arabia, Iraq, and elsewhere, Khomeini appealed to Shia minorities and other disaffected people, and Iran became a model to which many Islamic radicals looked. An eight-year war with Saddam Hussein's highly secularized Iraq (1980–1988) was one of the outcomes and generated enormous casualties. That conflict reflected the differences between Arabs and Persians, between Sunni and Shia versions of Islam, and between a secular Iraqi regime and Khomeini's revolutionary Islamic government.

After Khomeini's death in 1989, some elements of this revolution eased a bit. For a time, enforcement of women's dress code was not so stringent, and a more moderate government came to power in 1997, raising hopes for a loosening of strict

Islamic regulations. By 2005, however, more conservative elements were back in control and a new crackdown on women's clothing soon surfaced. A heavily disputed election in 2009 revealed substantial opposition to the country's rigid Islamic regime, and a more moderate leadership returned to power in 2013. Iran's ongoing Islamic revolution, however, did not mean the abandonment of economic modernity. The country's oil revenues continued to fund its development, and by the early twenty-first century Iran was actively pursuing nuclear power and perhaps nuclear weapons, in defiance of Western opposition to these policies.

REFLECTIONS

History in the Middle of the Stream

Historians are usually more at ease telling stories that have clear endings, such as those that describe ancient Egyptian civilization, Chinese maritime voyages, the collapse of the Aztec Empire, or the French Revolution. There is a finality to these stories and a distance from them that makes it easier for historians to assume the posture of detached observers, even if their understandings of those events change over time. Finality, distance, and detachment are harder to come by when historians are describing the events of the past century, for many of its processes are clearly not over. The United States' role as a global superpower and its wars in Iraq and Afghanistan, the fate of democracy in Latin America and the Arab world, the rise of China and India as economic giants, the position of Islam in Turkey and Iran—all of these are unfinished stories, their outcomes unknown and unknowable. In dealing with such matters, historians write from the middle of the stream, often uncomfortably, rather than from the banks, where they might feel more at ease.

In part, that discomfort arises from questions about the future that such issues inevitably raise. Can the spread of nuclear weapons be halted? Will democracy flourish globally? Are Islamic and Christian civilizations headed for a global clash? Can African countries replicate the economic growth experience of India and China? Historians in particular are uneasy about responding to such questions because they are so aware of the unexpectedness and surprising quality of the historical process. Yet those questions about the future are legitimate and important, for as the nineteenth-century Danish philosopher Søren Kierkegaard remarked, "Life can only be understood backward, but it is lived forward." History, after all, is the only guide we have to the possible shape of that future. So, like everyone before us, we stumble on, both individually and collectively, largely in the dark, using analogies from the past as we make our way ahead.

These vast uncertainties about the future provide a useful reminder that although we know the outcomes of earlier human stories—the Asian and African struggles for independence, for example—those who lived that history did not. Such awareness can perhaps engender in us a measure of humility and greater sympathy with those whose lives we study. However we may differ from our ancestors across time and place, we share with them an immense ignorance about what the future holds.

Chapter Review

What's the Significance?

Big Picture Questions

1. In what ways did the colonial experience and the struggle for independence shape the agenda of developing countries in the second half of the twentieth century?
2. How would you compare the historical experiences of India and China in the twentieth century?
3. From the viewpoint of the early twenty-first century (2000–2015), to what extent had the goals of nationalist or independence movements been achieved?
4. **Looking Back:** To what extent did the struggle for independence and the postcolonial experience of African and Asian peoples in the twentieth century parallel or diverge from that of the earlier "new nations" in the Americas in the eighteenth and nineteenth centuries?

Next Steps: For Further Study

Chinua Achebe, *Anthills of the Savannah* (1989). A brilliant fictional account of post-independence Nigeria by that country's foremost novelist.

Frederick Cooper, *Africa since 1940* (2002). A readable overview of the coming of independence and efforts at development by a leading historian of Africa.

Ramachandra Guha, *India after Gandhi: The History of the World's Largest Democracy* (2007). A thoughtful account of India's first six decades of independence.

John Isbister, *Promises Not Kept* (2006). A well-regarded consideration of the obstacles to and struggles for development in the Global South.

Nelson Mandela, *Long Walk to Freedom: The Autobiography of Nelson Mandela* (1995). Mandela's account of his own amazing life as nationalist leader and South African statesman.

W. David McIntyre, *British Decolonization, 1946–1997* (1998). A global history of the demise of the British Empire.

Complete Site on Mahatma Gandhi, http://www.mkgandhi.org. A wealth of resources for exploring the life of Gandhi.

"Stunning Economic Growth in China," http://abcnews.go.com/WNT/video/stunning-economic-growth-china-12155618. A brief video from ABC News that explores the reasons for China's rapid economic growth in recent decades.

Contending for Islam

Over the past century, the growing intrusion of the West and of modern secular culture into the Islamic world has prompted acute and highly visible debate among Muslims. Which ideas and influences flowing from the West could Muslims safely utilize, and which should they decisively reject? Are women's rights and democracy compatible with Islam? To what extent should Islam find expression in public life as well as in private religious practice? The documents that follow show something of these controversies while illustrating sharp variations in the understanding of Islam.

Source 22.1

A Secular State for an Islamic Society

Modern Turkey emerged from the ashes of the Ottoman Empire after World War I and adopted a distinctive path of modernization, westernization, and secularism under the leadership of Mustafa Kemal Atatürk (see pages 1005–7). Such policies sought to remove Islam from any significant role in public life, restricting it to the realm of personal devotion, and included abolition of the caliphate, by which Ottoman rulers had claimed leadership of the entire Islamic world. In a speech delivered in 1927, Atatürk explained and justified these policies, which went against the grain of much Islamic thinking.

- On what grounds did Atatürk justify the abolition of the caliphate?

- What additional actions did he take to remove Islam from a public or political role in the new Turkish state?

- What can you infer about Atatürk's view of Islam?

- How did Atatürk's conception of a Turkish state differ from that of Ottoman authorities? In what ways did he build upon Ottoman reforms of the nineteenth century? (See Chapter 19, pages 846–49.)

Mustafa Kemal Ataturk

Speech to the General Congress of the Republican Party

1927

[Our Ottoman rulers] hoped to unite the entire Islamic world in one body, to lead it and to govern it. For this purpose, [they] assumed the title of Caliph [successor to the Prophet Muhammad]. . . . It is an unrealizable aim to attempt to unite in one tribe the various races existing on the earth, thereby abolishing all boundaries. . . .

If the Caliph and the Caliphate were to be invested with a dignity embracing the whole of Islam . . . , a crushing burden would be imposed on Turkey. . . . [Furthermore], will Persia or Afghanistan, which are [Muslim] states, recognize the authority of the Caliph in a single matter? No, and this is quite justifiable, because it would be in contradiction to the independence of the state, to the sovereignty of the people.

[The current constitution] laid down as the first duty of the Grand National Assembly that "the prescriptions of the Shari'a [Islamic law] should be put into force. . . ." [But] if a state, having among its subjects elements professing different religions and being compelled to act justly and impartially toward all of them . . . , it is obliged to respect freedom of opinion and conscience. . . . The Muslim religion includes freedom of religious opinion. . . . Will not every grown-up person in the new Turkish state be free to select his own religion? . . . When the first favorable opportunity arises, the nation must act to eliminate these superfluities [the enforcement of sharia] from our Constitution. . . .

Under the mask of respect for religious ideas and dogmas, the new Party [in opposition to Atatürk's reformist plans] addressed itself to the people in the following words: "We want the re-establishment of the Caliphate; we are satisfied with the religious law; we shall protect the Medressas [Islamic schools], the Tekkes [places for Sufi worship], the pious institutions, the Softahs [students in religious schools], the Sheikhs [Sufi masters], and their disciples. . . . The party of Mustapha Kemal, having abolished the Caliphate, is breaking Islam into ruins; they will make you into unbelievers . . . they will make you wear hats." Can anyone pretend that the style of propaganda used by the Party was not full of these reactionary appeals? . . .

Gentlemen, it was necessary to abolish the fez [a distinctive Turkish hat with no brim], which sat on our heads as a sign of ignorance, of fanaticism, of hatred to progress and civilization, and to adopt in its place the hat, the customary headdress of the whole civilized world, thus showing that no difference existed in the manner of thought between the Turkish nation and the whole family of civilized mankind. . . . [Thus] there took place the closing of the Tekkes, of the convents, and of the mausoleums, as well as the abolition of all sects and all kinds of [religious] titles. . . .

Could a civilized nation tolerate a mass of people who let themselves be led by the nose by a herd of Sheikhs, Dedes, Seids, Tschelebis, Babas, and Emirs [various religious titles]? . . . Would not one therewith have committed the greatest, most irreparable error to the cause of progress and awakening?

Source: *A Speech Delivered by Ghazi Mustapha Kemal, October 1927* (Leipzig: K. F. Koehler, 1929), 377–79, 591–93, 595–98, 717, 721–22.

Source 22.2

Toward an Islamic Society

Even as Kemal Atatürk was seeking to remove Islam from the public life of Turkey, a newly formed Muslim organization in Egypt was strongly advocating precisely the opposite course of action. Founded in 1928 by impoverished schoolteacher Hassan al-Banna (1906–1949), the Muslim Brotherhood argued in favor of "government that will act in conformity to the law and Islamic principles." As the earliest mass movement in the Islamic world advocating such ideas, the Brotherhood soon attracted a substantial following, including many poor urban residents recently arrived from the countryside. Long a major presence in Egyptian political life, the Brotherhood has frequently come into conflict with state authorities. In 1936, it published a pamphlet, addressed to Egyptian and other Arab political leaders, which spelled out its views about the direction toward which a proper Islamic society should move.

- How does this document define the purposes of government?
- How does the Muslim Brotherhood understand the role of Islam in public life?
- To what extent was this document anti-Western in its orientation?
- How might Kemal Atatürk respond to these views?

THE MUSLIM BROTHERHOOD

Toward the Light

1936

After having studied the ideals which ought to inspire a renascent nation on the spiritual level, we wish to offer, in conclusion, some practical suggestions. . . . The following are the chapter headings for a reform based upon the true spirit of Islam:

I. In the political, judicial, and administrative fields:

1st. To prohibit political parties and to direct the forces of the nation toward the formation of a united front;

2nd. To reform the law in such a way that it will be entirely in accordance with Islamic legal practice;

3rd. To build up the army, to increase the number of youth groups; to instill in youth the spirit of holy struggle, faith, and self-sacrifice;

4th. To strengthen the ties among Islamic countries and more particularly among Arab countries which is a necessary step toward serious examination of the question of the defunct Caliphate;

5th. To propagate an Islamic spirit within the civil administration so that all officials will understand the need for applying the teachings of Islam;

6th. To supervise the personal conduct of officials because the private life and the administrative life of these officials forms an indivisible whole; . . .

9th. Government will act in conformity to the law and to Islamic principles; . . . The scheduling of government services ought to take account of the hours set aside for prayer. . . .

II. In the fields of social and everyday practical life:

1st. . . . [T]o strongly condemn attacks upon public mores and morality;

2nd. To find a solution for the problems of women, a solution that will allow her to progress and which will protect her while conforming to Islamic principles. This very important social question should not be ignored because it has become the subject of polemics and of more or less unsupported and exaggerated opinion;

3rd. To root out clandestine or public prostitution and to consider fornication as a reprehensible crime the authors of which should be punished;

4th. To prohibit all games of chance (gaming, lotteries, races, golf);

5th. To stop the use of alcohol and intoxicants—these obliterate the painful consequences of people's evil deeds;

6th. To . . . educate women, to provide quality education for female teachers, school pupils, students, and doctors;

7th. To prepare instructional programs for girls; to develop an educational program for girls different than the one for boys;

8th. Male students should not be mixed with female students—any relationship between unmarried men and women is considered to be wrong until it is approved;

9th. To encourage marriage and procreation—to develop legislation to safeguard the family and to solve marriage problems;

10th. To close dance halls; to forbid dancing;

11th. To censor theater productions and films; to be severe in approving films;

12th. To supervise and approve music;

13th. To approve programs, songs, and subjects before they are released, to use radio to encourage national education;

14th. To confiscate malicious articles and books as well as magazines displaying a grotesque character or spreading frivolity;

15th. To carefully organize vacation centers;

16th. To change the hours when public cafes are opened or closed, to watch the activities of those who habituate them—to direct these people towards wholesome pursuits, to prevent people from spending too much time in these cafes;

17th. To use the cafes as centers to teach reading and writing to illiterates, to seek help in this task from primary school teachers and students;

18th. To combat the bad practices which are prejudicial to the economy and to the morale of the nation, to direct the people toward good customs and praiseworthy projects such as marriage, orphanages, births, and festivals.

19th. To bring to trial those who break the laws of Islam, who do not fast, who do not pray, and who insult religion;

20th. To transfer village primary schools to the mosque. . . .

21st. Religious teaching should constitute the essential subject matter to be taught in all educational establishments and faculties;

22nd. To memorize the Quran in state schools . . . in every school students should learn part of the Quran;

24th. . . . Support for teaching the Arabic language in all grades—absolute priority to be given to Arabic over foreign languages;

25th. To study the history of Islam, the nation, and Muslim civilization;

26th. To study the best way to allow people to dress . . . in an identical manner;

27th. To combat foreign customs (in the realm of vocabulary, customs, dress, nursing) and to Egyptianize all of these (one finds these customs among the well-to-do members of society);

28th. To orient journalism toward wholesome things, to encourage writers and authors, who should study specifically Muslim and Oriental subjects;

29th. To safeguard public health through every kind of publicity—increasing the number of hospitals, doctors, and out-patient clinics;

30th. To call particular attention to the problems of village life (administration, hygiene, water supply, education, recreation, morality).

III. The economic field:

1st. Organization of the zakat tax [an obligatory payment to support the poor] according to Islamic precepts, using zakat proceeds for welfare projects such as aiding the indigent, the poor, orphans; the zakat should also be used to strengthen the army;

2nd. To prevent the practice of usury, to direct banks to implement this policy; the government should provide an example by giving up the interest fixed by banks for servicing a personal loan or an industrial loan, etc.;

3rd. To facilitate and to increase the number of economic enterprises and to employ the jobless, to employ for the nation's benefit the skills possessed by the foreigners in these enterprises;

4th. To protect workers against monopoly companies, to require these companies to obey the law, the public should share in all profits;

5th. Aid for low-ranking employees and enlargement of their pay, lowering the income of high-ranking employees; . . .

7th. To encourage agricultural and industrial works, to improve the situation of the peasants and industrial workers;

8th. To give special attention to the technical and social needs of the workers, to raise their level of life and aid their class;

9th. Utilization of certain natural resources (unworked land, neglected mines, etc.). . . .

Source: Hasan al-Banna, "Towards the Light," in Robert Langdon, *The Emergence of the Middle East* (Van Nostrand, 1970).

Source 22.3
Progressive Islam

By the late twentieth century, the most widely publicized face of Islam, at least in the West, derived from groups sympathetic to the views of the Muslim Brotherhood, though these groups often expressed themselves in a more militant and aggressive fashion than the Brotherhood did. The Iranian revolution of 1979, for example, brought to power an Islamist government able to infuse public life with "the spirit of Islam," as they understood it, purging those who disagreed with their interpretation of the faith. In Saudi Arabia, Afghanistan, and elsewhere in the Islamic world, governments sought to implement various aspects of the Muslim Brotherhood's Islamist agenda, sometimes brutally. And social movements in other places, such as al-Qaeda, the Islamic State in Iraq and Syria, and Boko Haram in northern Nigeria, looked forward to the creation of societies governed by the sharia, or Islamic law, and were willing to undertake violent action to achieve those goals.

But these were not the only voices speaking in the name of Islam. All across the Islamic world, others argued that Muslims could retain their distinctive religious sensibility while embracing democracy, women's rights, technological progress, freedom of thought, and religious pluralism. Such thinkers were following in the tradition of nineteenth-century Islamic modernism (see Chapter 19, pages 847–49), even as they recalled earlier centuries of Islamic intellectual and scientific achievement and religious tolerance. That viewpoint was expressed in a pamphlet composed by a leading American Muslim scholar, translator, and Sufi teacher, Sheikh Kabir Helminski, in 2009.

- Against what charges does Sheikh Kabir seek to defend Islam? How does this document reflect the experience of 9/11?

- In what ways are Sheikh Kabir's views critical of radical, or "fundamentalist," ideas and practices?

- How does this document articulate the major features of a more progressive or liberal Islam? What kinds of arguments does Sheikh Kabir employ to make his case?

- To whom might these arguments appeal? What obstacles do they face in being heard within the Islamic world?

- How might Hassan al-Banna or Kemal Atatürk respond to these views?

Kabir Helminski
Islam and Human Values
2009

If the word "Islam" gives rise to fear or mistrust today, it is urgent that American Muslims clarify what we believe Islam stands for in order to dispel the idea that there is a fundamental conflict between the best values of Western civilization and the essential values of Islam. . . .

Islamic civilization, which developed out of the revelation of the Qur'an in the seventh century, affirms the truth of previous revelations, affirms religious pluralism, cultural diversity, and human rights, and recognizes the value of reason and individual conscience. . . .

[One issue] is the problem of violence. . . . Thousands of Muslim institutions and leaders, the great majority of the world's billion or more Muslims, have unequivocally condemned the hateful and violent ideologies that kill innocents and violate the dignity of all humanity. . . .

Islamic civilizations have a long history of encouraging religious tolerance and guaranteeing the rights of religious minorities. The reason for this is that the Qur'an explicitly acknowledges that the diversity of religions is part of the Divine Plan and no religion has a monopoly on truth or virtue. . . .

Jerusalem, under almost continuous Islamic rule for nearly fourteen centuries, has been a place where Christians and Jews have lived side by side with Muslims, their holy sites and religious freedom preserved. Medieval Spain also created a high level of civilization as a multi-cultural society under Islamic rule for several centuries. The Ottoman Empire, the longest lived in history, for the more than six centuries of its existence encouraged ethnic and religious minorities to participate in and contribute to society. It was the Ottoman sultan who gave sanctuary to the Jews expelled from Catholic Spain. India was governed for centuries by Muslims, even while the majority of its people practiced Hinduism. . . .

[T]he acceptance of Islam must be an act of free will. Conversion by any kind of coercion was universally condemned by Islamic scholars. . . .

There are many verses in the Qur'an that affirm the actuality and even the necessity of diversity in ways of life and religious belief: [For example,] O mankind, truly We [God] have created you male and female, and have made you nations and tribes that ye may know one another [Surah 49:13]. . . .

In general, war is forbidden in Islam, except in cases of self-defense in response to explicit aggression. If there is a situation where injustice is being perpetrated or if the community is being invaded, then on a temporary basis permission is given to defend oneself. This principle is explained in the following verses: *And fight in God's cause against those who war against you, but do not commit aggression—for, verily, God does not love aggressors* [Surah 2:190].

[I]n recent decades . . . an intolerant ideology has been unleashed. A small minority of the world's one and a half billion Muslims has misconstrued the teachings of Islam to justify their misguided and immoral actions. It is most critical at this time for Muslims to condemn such extreme ideologies and their manifestations. It is equally important that non-Muslims understand that this ideology violates the fundamental moral principles of Islam and is repugnant to the vast majority of Muslims in the world. . . . So-called "suicide-bombers" did not appear until the mid-1990s. Such strategies have no precedent in Islamic history. The Qur'an says quite explicitly: *Do not kill yourselves* [4:29]. . . .

Muslims living in pluralistic societies have no religious reasons to oppose the laws of their own societies as long as they are just, but rather are encouraged to uphold the duly constituted laws of their own societies. . . . Islam and democracy are compatible and can coexist because Islam organizes humanity on the basis of the rule of law and human dignity.

The first four successors to the Prophet Muhammad were chosen by the community through consultation, i.e., a representative democracy. The only principle of political governance expressed in the Qur'an is the principle of Consultation (Shura), which holds that communities will "*rule themselves by means of mutual consultation*" [Surah 42:38].

Following the principles of the Qur'an, Muslims are encouraged to cooperate for the well-being of all. The Qur'an emphasizes three qualities above all others: peace, compassion, and mercy. The standard greeting in Islam is "As-Salam alay-kum (Peace be with you)."

An American Muslim scholar, Abdul Aziz Sachedina, expresses it this way: "Islam does not encourage turning God into a political statement since humans cannot possess God. . . ."

[T]here is nothing in the Qur'an that essentially contradicts reason or science. . . . Repeatedly the Qur'an urges human beings to "reflect" and "use their intelligence."

Islam is not an alien religion. It does not claim a monopoly on virtue or truth. It follows in the way of previous spiritual traditions that recognized One Spirit operating within nature and human life. It continues on the Way of the great Prophets and Messengers of all sacred traditions.

Source: Selections from Kabir Helminski, *Islam and Human Values*, unpublished pamphlet, 2009.

Source 22.4

Islam and Women's Dress

Among the contested issues in the Islamic world, none have been more prominent than those involving the lives—and the bodies—of women. Within this controversy, matters of dress have loomed large. The Iranian revolution sought to impose hijab on its women (see pages 1008–10), while the French government sought to prevent its Muslim women from covering up. In early 2014, billboard advertisements showing women's bodies in Istanbul, Turkey, were sprayed with black paint, and next to one of them was scrawled, "Do not commit indecency." In response, a prominent and outspoken writer and scholar, Elif Shafak, declared that "uncovered Turkish women are feeling uncomfortable and unwanted in their own country."[18] The sources that follow present two diverging views on the question of women's dress, the first from a young Afghan woman named Emaan, who is a writer and poet, and the second from a British Muslim woman of Pakistani background, Saira Khan, who is a TV personality in Britain.

- How might you summarize the debate between these points of view? Are there areas of agreement as well as those of difference?

- What kinds of evidence or arguments do Emaan and Saira Khan use to make their cases? How do they use the Quran to support both sides of the debate?

- What larger issues or principles are at stake in this controversy?

EMAAN
Hijab: The Beauty of Muslim Women
2010

*H*ijab means "being covered." Islam requires Muslim women to cover themselves in public and in the presence of a person who is not *mahram* (people or family who are allowed to see women without cover). . . .

Proper *hijab* (concealment for the Muslim woman) dictates that the entire body must be covered, although the face and hands should be exposed. As Prophet Muhammad . . . said, "If the woman reaches the age of puberty, no part of her body should be seen but this, and he pointed to his face and hand."

Hijab has three roles that should be considered by Muslim women: it should be not form fitted, it should not be transparent, and it should not be attractive.

Hijab has many benefits for Muslim women as well as for the society that they live in. A Muslim woman is allowed to show her beauty only to her husband, to her family and to her women friends. It's considered a way of preventing attraction. Because when a woman shows her beauty in public it attracts the attention of men and it can lead men to act inappropriately.

The *hijab* also promotes more respect from a husband to a Muslim woman, as he sees his wife being faithful only to him and he is then convinced to be faithful only to his wife.

The *Qur'an* also emphasizes that the *hijab* is a way of keeping society . . . from abusing women. It's mentioned in the *Qur'an*: "Tell believing women to avert their glances and guard their private parts and not to display their charms except what (normally) appears of them. They should draw their coverings over their bosoms and not show their charms except to their husbands" (24:30–31).

In the western world, Muslim women are seen as oppressed and passive. Most think that Muslim women's rights are violated according to Islamic law. Wearing a *hijab* doesn't make a woman passive because scarves cover the heads, not the minds, of Muslim women. . . .

Islam respects women and does not allow them to be used as objects in public or through the media. Most people are concerned about women being used as sex objects, as in the western world today. But *hijab* saves Muslim women from this contemporary concern. *Hijab* equalizes all women and avoids concerns of artifice among women.

In contrast, it lets women focus on their spiritual, intellectual, and professional development and work comfortably in public spaces without being worried about their looks or concerned about the men around them.

Hijab has given the Muslim women freedom from constant attention to their physical parts, because their appearance is not subjected to public scrutiny. Their beauty, or perhaps lack of it, has been removed from the realm of what can legitimately be discussed.

Islam did not introduce wearing the burqa, veiling, and covering the face; it existed in previous cultures in India and the Arab world. . . . Islam does not oblige women to wear a burqa or veil. The wearing of the burqa or veil is a cultural custom, not an Islamic mandate. . . . Most of the restrictions are not from Islam, but rather from cultural customs sometimes wrongly justified under an Islamic banner.

I, as a Muslim woman, feel very comfortable wearing the *hijab*. For me the *hijab* means religious devotion, discipline, reflection, respect, freedom, and modernity. I am pro-democracy because for me democracy means having choices in how to live our lives. I also support and promote mutual respect between Muslim and non-Muslim women. I want the world to treat Muslim women with the same respect they treat other women, from other religions and cultures who wear headscarves such as Hindu women, Jewish women, Greek women, and Catholic nuns. The assumption that wearing a *hijab* is oppressive should change from an oppressive idea to a liberating one.

Source: Emaan, "Hijab: The Beauty of Muslim Women," Afghan Women's Writing Project, June 29, 2010, http://awwproject .org/2010/06/hijab-the-beauty-of-muslim-women/.

Saira Khan
Why I, as a British Muslim Woman, Want the Burkha Banned from Our Streets
2009

Shopping in Harrods last week, I came across a group of women wearing black burkhas, browsing the latest designs in the fashion department. The irony of the situation was almost laughable. Here was a group of affluent women window shopping for designs that they would never once be able to wear in public. Yet it's a sight that's becoming more and more commonplace. In hardline Muslim communities right across Britain, the burkha and hijab—the Muslim headscarf—are becoming the norm. . . .

And yet, as a British Muslim woman, I abhor the practice and am calling on the Government to follow the lead of French President Nicolas Sarkozy and ban the burkha in our country.

The veil is simply a tool of oppression which is being used to alienate and control women under the guise of religious freedom.

My parents moved here from Kashmir in the 1960s. They brought with them their faith and their traditions, but they also understood that they were starting a new life in a country where Islam was not the main religion. My mother has always worn traditional Kashmiri clothes. . . . When she found work in England, she adapted her dress without making a fuss. She is still very much a traditional Muslim woman, but she swims in a normal swimming costume and jogs in a tracksuit. . . .

I have read the Koran. Nowhere in the Koran does it state that a woman's face and body must be covered in a layer of heavy black cloth. Instead, Muslim women should dress modestly, covering their arms and legs. Many of my adult British Muslim friends cover their heads with a headscarf— and I have no problem with that. The burkha is an entirely different matter. It is an imported Saudi Arabian tradition, and the growing number of women veiling their faces in Britain is a sign of creeping radicalisation, which is not just regressive, it is oppressive and downright dangerous. . . . It sends out a clear message: "I do not want to be part of your society."

Every time the burkha is debated, Muslim fundamentalists bring out all these women who say:

"It's my choice to wear this." Perhaps so—but what pressures have been brought to bear on them? The reality, surely, is that a lot of women are not free to choose.

And behind the closed doors of some Muslim houses, countless young women are told to wear the *hijab* and the veil. These are the girls who are hidden away, they are not allowed to go to university or choose who they marry. In many cases, they are kept down by the threat of violence.

The burkha is the ultimate visual symbol of female oppression. It is the weapon of radical Muslim men who want to see Sharia law on Britain's streets, and would love women to be hidden, unseen and unheard. It is totally out of place in a civilised country.

[French] President Sarkozy is absolutely right to say: "If you want to live here, live like us."

It is time for ministers and ordinary British Muslims to say, "Enough is enough." For the sake of women and children, the Government must ban the wearing of the hijab in school and the burkha in public places.

Two years ago, I wore a burkha for the first time for a television programme. It was the most horrid experience. It restricted the way I walked, what I saw, and how I interacted with the world. It took away my personality. I felt alienated and like a freak. It was hot and uncomfortable, and I was unable to see behind me, exchange a smile with people, or shake hands.

If I had been forced to wear a veil, I would certainly not be free to write this article. Nor would I have run a marathon, become an aerobics teacher or set up a business.

Source: Saira Khan, "Why I, as a British Muslim Woman, Want the Burkha Banned from Our Streets," *Daily Mail*, June 24, 2009, http://www.dailymail.co.uk/debate/article-1195052/Why-I-British-Muslim-woman-want-burkha-banned-streets.html.

DOING HISTORY

Contending for Islam

1. **Understanding the issues:** What are the core concerns that divide the writers of these documents?

2. **Comparing Islamic modernists:** How do you think Kemal Atatürk would have responded to later Islamic modernists such as Sheikh Kabir and perhaps Saira Khan?

3. **Imagining a conversation:** What issues might arise in a conversation among the five authors represented here? Can you identify any areas of agreement? On which points would they probably never agree?

4. **Explaining variations:** What personal or historical circumstances might help to account for the very different understandings of Islam that are reflected in these documents?

Image created by Reto Stockli, Nazmi El Saleous, and Marit Jentoft-Nilsen, NASA GSFC

CHAPTER 23

Capitalism and Culture

The Acceleration of Globalization since 1945

Memey, a young uneducated woman from Java in Indonesia, was in a very difficult situation early in the twenty-first century. Her husband had died, leaving her in poverty with a young child. When she heard from a neighbor about waitressing opportunities in Malaysia, she saw a way of providing for her son. So she entered Malaysia illegally and was met by a contact person, who took her shopping for clothes and makeup. "After dinner," she later recalled, "a man came for me and took me to a hotel room nearby to start work. That was when it finally dawned on me that it was not a waitressing job. I was being made to work as a sex worker." Witnessing other women severely beaten or threatened, Memey was afraid to run away. After about four months in this situation, she was able to escape with the help of a sympathetic client, returning to Indonesia with bitter memories and an HIV infection. Subsequently she found work with an organization devoted to helping other women in her position.[1]

Memey was but one of millions of women victimized by international networks of sex trafficking. Those networks represented one dark and tragic thread in a vast web of political relationships, economic transactions, cultural influences, and the movement of people across international borders that linked the world's separate countries and regions, binding them together more tightly, but also more contentiously. By the 1990s, this process of accelerating engagement among distant peoples was widely known as globalization. Debating the pros and cons of this encompassing pattern of interaction and exchange has been central to global discourse over the past half century or more. More importantly, it has

---

One World   This NASA photograph, showing both the earth and the moon, reveals none of the national, ethnic, religious, or linguistic boundaries that have long divided humankind. Such pictures have both reflected and helped create a new planetary consciousness among growing numbers of people.

been central to the lives of billions of individuals, like Memey, and to the societies they inhabit.

Although the term was relatively new, the process was not. From the viewpoint of world history, the genealogy of globalization reached far into the past. The Arab, Mongol, Russian, Chinese, and Ottoman empires; the Silk Road, Indian Ocean, and trans-Saharan trade routes; the spread of Buddhism, Christianity, and especially Islam—all of these connections had long linked the societies of the Eastern Hemisphere, bringing new rulers, religions, products, diseases, and technologies to many of its peoples. Later, in the centuries after 1500, European maritime voyages and colonizing efforts launched the Columbian exchange, incorporating the Western Hemisphere and inner Africa firmly and permanently into a genuinely global network of communication, exchange, and often exploitation. During the nineteenth century, as the Industrial Revolution took hold and Western nations began a new round of empire building in Asia and Africa, that global network tightened further, and its role as generator of social and cultural change only increased.

These were the foundations on which twentieth-century globalization was built. A number of prominent developments of the past century, explored in the previous three chapters, operated on a global scale: the world wars, the Great Depression, communism, the cold war, the end of empire, and the growing prominence of developing countries. But global interaction quickened its pace and deepened its impact after World War II. From the immense range of interactions that make up modern globalization, this chapter focuses on four major processes: the transformation of the world economy, the emergence of global feminism, the response of world religions to modernity, and the growing awareness of humankind's enormous impact on the environment.

SEEKING THE MAIN POINT

To what extent has globalization fostered converging values and common interests among the world's peoples? In what ways has it generated new conflicts among them?

The Transformation of the World Economy

When most people speak of globalization, they are referring to the immense acceleration in international economic transactions that took place in the second half of the twentieth century and continued into the twenty-first. Many have come to see this process as almost natural, certainly inevitable, and practically unstoppable. Yet the first half of the twentieth century, particularly the decades between the two world wars, witnessed a deep contraction of global economic linkages as the aftermath of World War I and then the Great Depression wreaked havoc on the world economy. International trade, investment, and labor migration dropped sharply as major states turned inward, favoring high tariffs and economic autonomy in the face of a global economic collapse.

The aftermath of World War II was very different. The capitalist victors in that conflict, led by the United States, were determined to avoid any return to such Depression-era conditions. At a conference in Bretton Woods, New Hampshire, in

Guided Reading
Question

■ CHANGE
What factors contributed to economic globalization in the second half of the twentieth century?

A MAP OF TIME

1919–1946	League of Nations
1945	United Nations, World Bank, and International Monetary Fund established
1960	Organization of Petroleum Exporting Countries founded
1962	Rachel Carson publishes *Silent Spring*
1963	Betty Friedan publishes *The Feminine Mystique*
1967	Six-day Arab-Israeli war
1970	Greenpeace established
1973–1974	Arab members of OPEC place an embargo on oil exports to the West
1979	Convention on the Elimination of All Forms of Discrimination against Women adopted by UN; Iranian revolution
1982	Law of the Sea Convention establishes international agreement about the uses of the world's oceans
1994	North American Free Trade Agreement (NAFTA) enacted
1995	World Trade Organization created
1997	Kyoto protocol on global warming introduced
2001	September 11 attacks on World Trade Center and Pentagon
2008	Global economic crisis begins
2011	Osama bin Laden killed
2013–2014	The Islamic State, a radical jihadist organization, proclaims a new caliphate in parts of Syria and Iraq
2014	Tunisia's new constitution enshrines many rights of women; World Bank declares China the world's largest economy; People's Climate March in conjunction with the UN-sponsored Leaders Climate Summit

1944, they forged a set of agreements and institutions (the World Bank and the International Monetary Fund [IMF]) that laid the foundation for postwar globalization. This "Bretton Woods system" negotiated the rules for commercial and financial dealings among the major capitalist countries, while promoting relatively free trade, stable currency values linked to the U.S. dollar, and high levels of capital investment.

Technology also contributed to the acceleration of economic globalization. Containerized shipping, huge oil tankers, and air express services dramatically lowered

AP® EXAM TIP

The World Bank and International Monetary Fund are important examples of institutions that promoted free trade in the second half of the twentieth century.

transportation costs, while fiber-optic cables and later the Internet provided the communication infrastructure for global economic interaction. In the developing countries, population growth, especially when tied to growing economies and modernizing societies, further fueled globalization as dozens of new nations entered the world economy.

The kind of economic globalization taking shape in the 1970s and later was widely known as neoliberalism. Major capitalist countries such as the United States and Great Britain abandoned many earlier political controls on economic activity as their leaders and businesspeople increasingly viewed the entire world as a single market. This approach to the world economy favored the reduction of tariffs, the free global movement of capital, a mobile and temporary workforce, the privatization of many state-run enterprises, the curtailing of government efforts to regulate the economy, and both tax and spending cuts. Powerful international lending agencies such as the World Bank and the IMF imposed such free market and pro-business conditions on many poor countries if they were to qualify for much-needed loans. The collapse of the state-controlled economies of the communist world only furthered such unrestricted global capitalism. In this view, the market, operating both globally and within nations, was the most effective means of generating the holy grail of economic growth. As communism collapsed by the end of the twentieth century, "capitalism was global and the globe was capitalist."[2]

Reglobalization

These conditions provided the foundations for a dramatic quickening of global economic transactions after World War II, a "reglobalization" of the world economy following the contractions of the 1930s. This immensely significant process was expressed in the accelerating circulation of goods, capital, and people.

World trade, for example, skyrocketed from a value of some $57 billion in 1947 to about $18.3 trillion in 2012. Department stores and supermarkets around the world stocked their shelves with goods from every part of the globe. Twinings of London marketed its 120 blends of tea in more than 100 countries, and the Australian-based Kiwi shoe polish was sold in 180 countries. In 2005, about 70 percent of Walmart products reportedly included components from China. And the following year, Toyota replaced General Motors as the world's largest automaker, with manufacturing facilities in at least eighteen countries.

Money as well as goods achieved an amazing global mobility in three ways. The first was "foreign direct investment," whereby a firm in, say, the United States opens a factory in China or Mexico (see Map 23.1). Such investment exploded after 1960 as companies in rich countries sought to take advantage of cheap labor, tax breaks, and looser environmental regulations in developing countries. A second form of money in motion has been the short-term movement of capital, in which investors annually spent trillions of dollars purchasing foreign currencies or stocks likely to increase in value and often sold them quickly thereafter, with unsettling conse-

Guided Reading Question

■ CONNECTION
In what ways has economic globalization more closely linked the world's peoples?

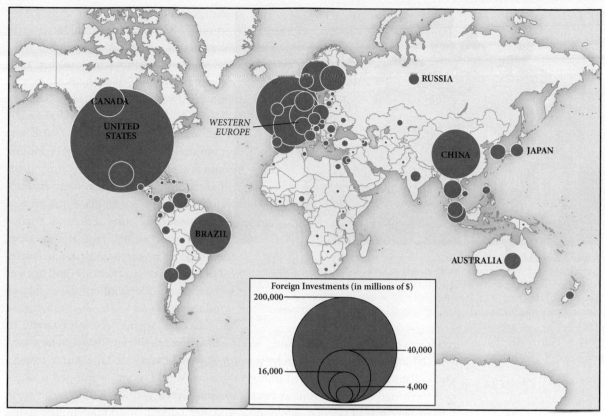

Map 23.1   Globalization in Action: Foreign Direct Investment in the Late Twentieth Century

Investment across national borders has been a major expression of globalization. This map shows the global distribution of investment inflows as of 1998. Notice which countries or regions were receiving the most investment from abroad and which received the least. How might you account for this pattern? Keep in mind that some regions, such as the United States, Western Europe, and Japan, were major sources of such investment as well as recipients of it.

quences. A third form of money movement involved the personal funds of individuals. By the end of the twentieth century, international credit cards had taken hold almost everywhere, allowing for easy transfer of money across national borders. In 2012, MasterCard was accepted at some 33 million businesses in 220 countries or territories.

Central to the acceleration of economic globalization have been huge global businesses known as transnational corporations (TNCs), which produce goods or deliver services simultaneously in many countries. For example, Mattel Corporation produced Barbie, that quintessentially American doll, in factories located in Indonesia, Malaysia, and China, using molds from the United States, plastic and hair from Taiwan and Japan, and cotton cloth from China. From distribution centers in Hong Kong, more than a billion Barbies were sold in 150 countries by 1999.

AP® EXAM TIP

You need to know examples of twentieth-century multinational corporations (MNCs), like those named here.

A World Economy
Indian-based call centers that serve North American or European companies and customers have become a common experience of globalization for many. Here employees in one such call center in Patna, a major city in northeastern India, undergo voice training in order to communicate more effectively with their English-speaking callers. (Indiapicture/Alamy)

Burgeoning in number since the 1960s, those TNCs, such as Royal Dutch Shell, Sony, and General Motors, often were of such an enormous size and had such economic clout that their assets and power dwarfed that of many countries. By 2000, 51 of the world's 100 largest economic units were in fact TNCs, not countries. In the permissive economic climate of recent decades, such firms have been able to move their facilities quickly from place to place in search of the lowest labor costs or the least restrictive environmental regulations. During one five-year period, for example, Nike closed twenty factories and opened thirty-five others, often thousands of miles apart.

Accompanying the movement of goods and capital in the globalizing world of the twentieth century were new patterns of human migration, driven by war, revolution, poverty, and the end of empire. The collapse of the Ottoman Empire following World War I witnessed a large-scale exchange of populations as over a million Greek Orthodox Christians from Turkey relocated to Greece, while some 400,000 Turkish-speaking Muslims living in Greece moved in the other direction. Fleeing anti-Semitism, fascism, and the Holocaust, Jews emigrated to what is now Israel in large numbers, generating in the process a flow of Palestinian refugees to settlements in neighboring countries. Political repression and forced labor in the Soviet Union pushed millions into the camps of the gulag, primarily in Siberia. In South Africa, an industrializing economy and apartheid policies drew millions of male workers from the countryside into mines and factories, often under horrific conditions. In the early twenty-first century, over a million Chinese have migrated to Africa, where Chinese trade and investment have mounted.

But perhaps the most significant pattern of global migration since the 1960s has featured a vast movement of people from the developing countries of Asia, Africa, and Latin America to the industrialized world of Europe and North America. Pakistanis, Indians, and West Indians moved to Great Britain; Algerians and West Africans to France; Turks and Kurds to Germany; Filipinos, Koreans, Cubans, Mexicans, and Haitians to the United States. A considerable majority of these people have been dubbed "labor migrants." Most moved, often illegally and with few skills, to escape poverty in their own lands, drawn by an awareness of Western prosperity and a belief that a better future awaited them in the developed countries. By 2003, some 4 million Filipino domestic workers were employed in 130 coun-

AP® EXAM TIP

Human migration remains an important continuity in AP® World History, even into the twenty-first century. Pay attention to these examples.

tries. Young women by the hundreds of thousands from poor countries have been recruited as sex workers in wealthier nations, sometimes in conditions approaching slavery. Smaller numbers of highly skilled and university-trained people, such as doctors and computer scientists, came in search of professional opportunities less available in their own countries. All of this represented a kind of reverse "development aid"—as either cheap labor or intellectual resources—from poor countries to rich. Still other peoples moved as refugees, fleeing violence or political oppression in places such as Vietnam, Cambodia, Sudan, Uganda, Cuba, and Haiti.

Many of those people in motion were headed for the United States, drawn by its reputation for wealth and opportunity. In the forty years between 1971 and 2010, almost 20 million immigrants arrived in the United States legally, and millions more entered illegally, the vast majority of both from the Latin American/Caribbean region and from Asia. Mexicans have been by far the largest group of immigrants to the United States, and many have arrived without legal documentation, an estimated 6.65 million during the first decade of the twenty-first century alone. Often their journeys north have been dangerous as they confronted long treks through burning deserts, sought to evade American immigration authorities, and depended on the expensive and sometimes unreliable "coyotes" who facilitated the smuggling of people across the border. Once in the United States, many of these immigrants provided inexpensive manual labor in fields, factories, and homes of the well-to-do, even as the money they sent back to their families in Mexico represented that nation's largest source of foreign exchange. The presence of migrants from the Global South has prompted considerable cultural and political conflict in both the United States and Europe, illustrated by a prolonged controversy about the wearing of headscarves by Muslim girls in French public schools.

Growth, Instability, and Inequality

The impact of these tightening economic links has provoked enormous debate and controversy. Amid the swirl of contending opinion, one thing seemed reasonably clear: economic globalization accompanied, and arguably helped generate, the most remarkable spurt of economic growth in world history. On a global level, total world output grew from a value of $7 trillion in 1950 to $73 trillion in 2009 and on a per capita basis from $2,652 to $10,728.[3] This represents an immense, rapid, and unprecedented creation of wealth with a demonstrable impact on human welfare. Life expectancies expanded almost everywhere, infant mortality declined, and literacy increased. The UN Human Development Report in 1997 concluded that "in the past 50 years, poverty has fallen more than in the previous 500."[4]

Far more problematic have been the instability of this emerging world economy and the distribution of the wealth it has generated. Amid overall economic growth, periodic crises and setbacks have shaped recent world history. Soaring oil prices contributed to a severe stock market crash in 1973–1974 and great hardship for many developing countries. Inability to repay mounting debts triggered a major

Guided Reading Question

■ CONNECTION

What new or sharper divisions has economic globalization generated?

financial crisis in Latin America during the 1980s and resulted in a "lost decade" in terms of economic development. Another financial crisis in Asia during the late 1990s resulted in the collapse of many businesses, widespread unemployment, and political upheaval in Indonesia and Thailand.

But nothing since the Great Depression more clearly illustrated the unsettling consequences of global connectedness in the absence of global regulation than the worldwide economic contraction that began in 2008. An inflated housing market—or "bubble"—in the United States collapsed, triggering millions of home fore-closures, growing unemployment, the tightening of credit, and declining consumer spending. Soon this crisis rippled around the world. Iceland's rapidly growing econ-omy collapsed almost overnight as three major banks failed, the country's stock market dropped by 80 percent, and its currency lost more than 70 percent of its value—all in a single week. In Africa, reduced demand for exports threatened to halt a promising decade of economic progress. In Sierra Leone, for example, some 90 percent of the country's diamond-mine workers lost their jobs. The slowing of China's booming economy led to unemployment for one in seven of the country's urban migrants, forcing them to return to already-overcrowded rural areas. Impov-erished Central American and Caribbean families, dependent on money sent home by family members working abroad, suffered further as those remittances dropped sharply. Contracting economies contributed to debt crises in Greece, Italy, and Spain and threatened to unravel European economic integration. Calls for both protectionism and greater regulation suggested that the wide-open capitalist world economy of recent decades was perhaps not as inevitable as some had thought. Whatever the overall benefits of the modern global system, economic stability and steady progress were not among them.

Nor was equality. As Europe's Industrial Revolution began to take hold in the early nineteenth century, a wholly new division appeared within the human com-munity—between the rich industrialized countries, primarily in Europe and North America, and everyone else. In 1820, the ratio between the income of the top and bottom 20 percent of the world's population was three to one. By 1991, it was eighty-six to one.[5] The accelerated economic globalization of the twentieth cen-tury did not create this global rift, but it arguably has worsened the North/South gap and certainly has not greatly diminished it. Even the well-known capitalist financier and investor George Soros, a billionaire many times over, acknowledged this reality in 2000: "The global capitalist system has produced a very uneven play-ing field. The gap between the rich and the poor is getting wider."[6] That gap has been evident, often tragically, in great disparities in incomes, medical care, avail-ability of clean drinking water, educational and employment opportunities, access to the Internet, and dozens of other ways. It has shaped the life chances of practi-cally everyone. (See Snapshot, opposite.)

These disparities were the foundations for a new kind of global conflict. As the East/West division of capitalism and communism faded, differences between the rich nations of the Global North and the developing countries of the Global South

AP® EXAM TIP

Take notes on these long-term effects of the Industrial Revolution.

SNAPSHOT   Global Development and Inequality, 2011

This table shows thirteen commonly used indicators of "development" and their variations in 2011 across four major groups of countries defined by average level of per capita income.[7] In which areas has the Global South most nearly caught up with the Global North?

Gross National Income per Capita with Sample Countries	Low Income: $995 or Less (Congo, Kenya, Ethiopia, Afghanistan, Myanmar)	Lower Middle Income: $996– $3,945 (India, China, Egypt, Algeria, Indonesia, Nigeria)	Upper Middle Income: $3,946– $12,195 (Mexico, Brazil, Turkey, Russia, Iran)	Upper Income: $12,196 or More (USA, Western Europe, Japan, South Korea, Australia)
Life expectancy M/F in years	58/60	66/70	68/75	77/83
Deaths under age 5 per 1,000 live births	120	60	24	7
Deaths from infectious disease: %	36	14	11	7
Access to toilets: %	35	50	84	99
Years of education	7.9	10.3	13.8	14.5
Literacy rate: %	66	80	93	99
Population growth: % annual	2.27	1.27	.96	.39
Urban population: %	27	41	74	78
Cell phones per 100 people	22	47	92	106
Internet users per 100 people	2.3	13.7	29.9	68.3
Personal computers per 100 people	1.2	4.3	11.9	60.4
Cars per 1,000 people	5.8	20.3	125.2	435.1
Carbon dioxide emissions: metric tons per capita	1	3	5	13

assumed greater prominence in world affairs. Highly contentious issues have included the rules for world trade, availability of and terms for foreign aid, representation in international economic organizations, the mounting problem of indebtedness, and environmental and labor standards. Such matters surfaced repeatedly in international negotiations during the second half of the twentieth century and into the twenty-first. In the 1970s, for example, a large group of developing countries joined together to demand a "new international economic order" that was more favorable to the poor countries. Not much success attended this effort. More recently, developing countries have contested protectionist restrictions on their agricultural exports imposed by rich countries seeking to protect their own politically powerful farmers.

Beyond active resistance by the rich nations, a further obstacle to reforming the world economy in favor of the poor lay in growing disparities among the developing countries themselves. The oil-rich economies of the Middle East had little in common with the banana-producing countries of Central America. The rapidly industrializing states of China, India, and South Korea had quite different economic agendas than impoverished African countries. Such disparities made common action difficult to achieve.

Economic globalization has contributed to inequalities not only at the global level and among developing countries but also within individual nations, rich and poor alike. In the United States, for example, a shifting global division of labor required the American economy to shed millions of manufacturing jobs. With recent U.S. factory wages far higher than those of China, many companies moved their manufacturing operations offshore to Asia or Latin America. This left many relatively unskilled American workers in the lurch, forcing them to work in the low-wage service sector, even as other Americans were growing prosperous in emerging high-tech industries. Even some highly skilled work, such as computer programming, was outsourced to lower-wage sites in India, Ireland, Russia, and elsewhere. Mounting income inequality and the erosion of the country's middle class became major issues in American political debate.

Globalization divided Mexico as well. The northern part of the country, with close business and manufacturing ties to the United States, grew much more prosperous than the south, which was a largely rural agricultural area and had a far more slowly growing economy. Beginning in 1994, southern resentment boiled over in the Chiapas rebellion, which featured a strong anti-globalization platform. Its leader, known as Subcomandante Marcos, referred to globalization as a "process to eliminate that multitude of people who are not useful to the powerful."[8] China's rapid economic growth likewise fostered mounting inequality between its rural households and those in its burgeoning cities, where income by 2000 was three times that of the countryside. Economic globalization may have brought people together as never before, but it also divided them sharply.

The hardships and grievances of those left behind or threatened by the march toward economic integration have fueled a growing popular movement aimed at criticizing and counteracting globalization. Known variously as an anti-globalization, alternative globalization, or global justice movement, it emerged in the 1990s as an international coalition of political activists, concerned scholars and students, trade unions, women's and religious organizations, environmental groups, and others, hailing from rich and poor countries alike. Thus opposition to neoliberal globalization was itself global in scope. Though reflecting a variety of viewpoints, that opposition largely agreed that free trade and market driven corporate globalization had lowered labor standards, fostered ecological degradation, prevented poor countries from protecting themselves against financial speculators, ignored local cultures, disregarded human rights, and enhanced global inequality, while favoring the interests of large corporations and the rich countries.

This movement appeared dramatically on the world's radar screen in late 1999 in Seattle at a meeting of the World Trade Organization (WTO). An international body representing 149 nations and charged with negotiating the rules for global commerce and promoting free trade, the WTO had become a major target of globalization critics. "The central idea of the WTO," argued one such critic, "is that *free trade*—actually the values and interests of global corporations—should supersede all other values."[9] Tens of thousands of protesters—academics, activists, farmers, labor union leaders from all over the world—descended on Seattle in what became a violent, chaotic, and much-publicized protest. At the city's harbor, protest organizers created a Seattle Tea Party around the slogan "No globalization without representation," echoing the Boston Tea Party of 1773. Subsequent meetings of the WTO and other high-level international economic gatherings were likewise greeted with large-scale protests and a heavy police presence. In 2001, alternative globalization activists created the World Social Forum, an annual gathering to coordinate strategy, exchange ideas, and share experiences, under the slogan "Another world is possible." It was an effort to demonstrate that neoliberal globalization was not inevitable and that the processes of a globalized economy could and should be regulated and subjected to public accountability. (See Working with Evidence, Source 23.3, page 1068.)

Globalization and an American Empire

For many people, opposition to this kind of globalization also expressed resistance to mounting American power and influence in the world. An "American Empire," some have argued, is the face of globalization (see Map 23.2), but scholars, commentators, and politicians have disagreed about how best to describe the United States' role in the postwar world. Certainly it has not been a colonial territorial empire such as that of the British or the French in the nineteenth century. Seeking to distinguish themselves from Europeans, Americans generally have vigorously denied that they have an empire at all.

In some ways, the U.S. global presence might be seen as an "informal empire," similar to the ones that Europeans exercised in China and the Middle East during the nineteenth century. In both cases, dominant powers sought to use economic penetration, political pressure, and periodic military action to create societies and governments compatible with their values and interests, but without directly governing large populations for long periods. In its economic dimension, American dominance has been termed an "empire of production," which uses its immense wealth to entice or intimidate potential collaborators.[10] Some scholars have emphasized the

AP® EXAM TIP

Make a chart showing ways that the United States acted as a traditional empire and ways that it did not.

U.S. Bases and Interventions Abroad: The Political/Military Face of the American Empire

Countries housing U.S. military bases in the early 21st century

• U.S. military/CIA interventions since 1950

Global McDonald's: The Economic/Cultural Face of the American Empire

Global McDonald's Restaurants by Country, 2003

1–19
20–99
100–499
500–999
1,000–1,999
2,000–9,999
10,000 +

Map 23.2   Two Faces of an "American Empire"

Those who argue that the United States constructed an empire in the second half of the twentieth century point both to its political/military alliances and interventions around the world and to U.S. economic and cultural penetration of many countries. The distribution of U.S. military bases, a partial indication of its open and covert interventions, and the location of McDonald's restaurants indicate something of the scope of America's global presence in the early twenty-first century.

United States' frequent use of force around the world, while others have focused attention on the "soft power" of its cultural attractiveness, its political and cultural freedoms, the economic benefits of cooperation, and the general willingness of many to follow the American lead voluntarily.

With the collapse of the Soviet Union and the end of the cold war by the early 1990s, U.S. military dominance was unchecked by any equivalent power. When the United States was attacked by Islamic militants on September 11, 2001, that power was unleashed first against Afghanistan (2001), which had sheltered the al-Qaeda instigators of that attack, and then against Iraq (2003), where Saddam Hussein allegedly had been developing weapons of mass destruction. In the absence of the Soviet Union, the United States could act unilaterally without fear of triggering a conflict with another major power. Although the Afghan and Iraqi regimes were quickly defeated, establishing a lasting peace and rebuilding badly damaged Muslim countries have proved difficult tasks. Thus, within a decade of the Soviet collapse, the United States found itself in yet another global struggle, an effort to contain or eliminate Islamic "terrorism."

Since the 1980s, as its relative military strength has peaked, the United States has faced growing international economic competition. The recovery of Europe and Japan and the emergent industrialization of South Korea, Taiwan, China, and India substantially reduced the United States' share of overall world production from about 50 percent in 1945 to 20 percent in the 1980s. By 2008 the United States accounted for just 8.1 percent of world merchandise exports. Accompanying this relative decline was a sharp reversal of the country's trade balance as U.S. imports greatly exceeded its exports. In 2014 the World Bank reported that China had overtaken the United States as the world's largest economy, even as it held much of the mounting American national debt.

However it might be defined, the exercise of American power, like that of many empires, was resisted abroad and contested at home. In Korea, Vietnam, Cuba, Iraq, Afghanistan, and elsewhere, armed struggle against U.S. intervention was both costly and painful. During the cold war, the governments of India, Egypt, and Ethiopia sought to diminish American influence in their affairs by turning to the Soviet Union or playing off the two superpowers against each other. Even France, resenting U.S. domination, withdrew from the military structure of NATO in 1967 and expelled all foreign-controlled troops from the country. In 2014, Russia strongly expressed its opposition to Western efforts to incorporate former Soviet territories or dependencies into NATO or the European Union by seizing Crimea and pressuring Ukraine to remain within the Russian sphere of influence. Many intellectuals, fearing the erosion of their own cultures in the face of well-financed American media around the world, have decried American "cultural imperialism." By the early twenty-first century, the United States' international policies—such as its refusal to accept the jurisdiction of the International Criminal Court; its refusal to ratify the Kyoto protocol on global warming; its doctrine of preemptive war, which was exercised in Iraq; and its apparent use of torture—had generated widespread opposition.

Within the United States as well, the global exercise of American power generated controversy. The Vietnam War, for example, divided the United States more sharply than at any time since the Civil War. It split families and friendships, churches and political parties. The war provided a platform for a growing number of critics, both at home and abroad, who had come to resent American cultural and economic dominance in the post-1945 world. It stimulated a new sense of activism among students in the nation's colleges and universities. Many of them came to see America itself as an imperialist power. A similar set of issues, protests, and controversies followed the American invasion of Iraq in 2003.

The Globalization of Liberation: Focus on Feminism

AP® EXAM TIP

You must know features of the rise of women's rights in many countries since the early nineteenth century.

More than goods, money, and people traversed the planet during the most recent century. So too did ideas, and none was more powerful than that of liberation. Communism promised workers and peasants liberation from capitalist oppression. Nationalism offered subject peoples liberation from imperialism. Advocates of democracy sought liberation from authoritarian governments.

The 1960s in particular witnessed an unusual convergence of protest movements around the world, suggesting the emergence of a global culture of liberation. Within the United States, several such movements—the civil rights demands of African Americans and Hispanic Americans; the youthful counterculture of rock music, sex, and drugs; the prolonged and highly divisive protests against the war in Vietnam—gave the 1960s a distinctive place in the country's recent history. Across the Atlantic, swelling protests against unresponsive bureaucracy, consumerism, and middle-class values likewise erupted, most notably in France in 1968. There a student-led movement protesting conditions in universities attracted the support of many middle-class people, who were horrified at the brutality of the police, and stimulated an enormous strike among some 9 million workers. France seemed on the edge of another revolution. Related but smaller-scale movements took place in Germany, Italy, Japan, Mexico, Argentina, and elsewhere.

The communist world too was rocked by protest. In 1968, a new Communist Party leadership in Czechoslovakia, led by Alexander Dubcek, initiated a sweeping series of reforms aimed at creating "socialism with a human face." Censorship ended, generating an explosion of free expression in what had been a highly repressive regime; unofficial political clubs emerged publicly; victims of earlier repression were rehabilitated; secret ballots for party elections were put in place. To the conservative leaders of the Soviet Union, this "Prague Spring" seemed to challenge communist rule itself, and they sent troops and tanks to crush it. Across the world in communist China, another kind of protest was taking shape in that country's Cultural Revolution (see Chapter 21, page 945).

In the developing countries, a substantial number of political leaders, activists, scholars, and students developed the notion of a "third world." Their countries, many only recently free from colonial rule, would offer an alternative to both a decrepit Western capitalism and a repressive Soviet communism. They claimed to pioneer new forms of economic development, of grassroots democracy, and of cultural renewal. By the late 1960s, the icon of this third-world ideology was Che Guevara, the Argentine-born revolutionary who had embraced the Cuban Revolution and subsequently attempted to replicate its experience of liberation through guerrilla warfare in parts of Africa and Latin America. Various aspects of his life story—his fervent anti-imperialism, cast as a global struggle; his self-sacrificing lifestyle; his death in 1967 at the hands of the Bolivian military, trained and backed by the American CIA—made him a heroic figure to third-world revolutionaries. He was popular as well among Western radicals, who were disgusted with the complacency and materialism of their own societies.

Che Guevara

In life, Che was an uncompromising but failed revolutionary, while in death he became an inspiration to third-world liberation movements and a symbol of radicalism to many in the West. His image appeared widely on T-shirts and posters, and in Cuba itself a government-sponsored cult featured schoolchildren chanting each morning "We will be like Che." This billboard image of Che was erected in Havana in 1988. (© Tim Page/Corbis)

No expression of this global culture of liberation held a more profound potential for change than feminism, for it represented a rethinking of the most fundamental and personal of all human relationships—that between women and men. Feminism had begun in the West in the nineteenth century with a primary focus on suffrage and in several countries had achieved the status of a mass movement by the outbreak of World War I (see Chapter 16, pages 723–27). The twentieth century, however, witnessed the globalization of feminism as organized efforts to address the concerns of women took shape across the world. Communist governments—in the Soviet Union, China, and Cuba, for example—mounted vigorous efforts to gain the support of women and to bring them into the workforce by attacking major elements of older patriarchies (see Chapter 21, pages 940–42). But feminism took hold in many cultural and political settings, where women confronted different issues, adopted different strategies, and experienced a range of outcomes.

Feminism in the West

In the West, organized feminism had lost momentum by the end of the 1920s, when many countries in Western Europe and North America had achieved women's suffrage. When it revived in the 1960s in both Western Europe and the United States, it did so with a quite different agenda. In France, for example, the writer and philosopher Simone de Beauvoir in 1949 had published *The Second Sex*, a book arguing that women had historically been defined as "other," or deviant from the "normal" male sex. The book soon became a central statement of a reviving women's movement. French feminists staged a counter–Mother's Day parade under the slogan "Celebrated one day; exploited all year." To highlight their demand to control their own bodies, some 343 women signed a published manifesto stating that they had undergone an abortion, which was then illegal in France.

Across the Atlantic, millions of American women responded to Betty Friedan's book *The Feminine Mystique* (1963), which disclosed the identity crisis of educated women, unfulfilled by marriage and motherhood. Some adherents of this second-wave feminism took up the equal rights agenda of their nineteenth-century predecessors, but with an emphasis now on employment and education rather than voting rights. A more radical expression of American feminism, widely known as "women's liberation," took broader aim at patriarchy as a system of domination, similar to those of race and class. One manifesto from 1969 declared:

> We are exploited as sex objects, breeders, domestic servants, and cheap labor. We are considered inferior beings, whose only purpose is to enhance men's lives. . . . Because we live so intimately with our oppressors, we have been kept from seeing our personal suffering as a political condition.[11]

Thus liberation for women meant becoming aware of their own oppression, a process that took place in thousands of consciousness-raising groups across the country. Many such women advocated direct action rather than the political lobbying favored by equal rights feminists. They challenged the Miss America contest of 1968 by tossing stink bombs in the hall, crowning a live sheep as their Miss America, and disposing of girdles, bras, high-heeled shoes, tweezers, and other "instruments of oppression" in a Freedom Trashcan. They also brought into open discussion issues involving sexuality, insisting that free love, lesbianism, and celibacy should be accorded the same respect as heterosexual marriage.

Yet another strand of Western feminism emerged from women of color. For many of them, the concerns of white, usually middle-class, feminists were hardly relevant to their oppression. Black women had always worked outside the home and so felt little need to be liberated from the chains of homemaking. Whereas white women might find the family oppressive, African American women viewed it as a secure base from which to resist racism. Solidarity with black men, rather than separation from them, was essential in confronting a racist America. Viewing mainstream feminism as "a family quarrel between White women and White men," many women of African descent in the United States and Britain established their own organizations, with a focus on racism and poverty.[12]

Feminism in the Global South

As women mobilized outside of the Western world during the twentieth century, they faced very different situations than did white women in the United States and Europe. For much of Asia, Africa, and Latin America, the predominant issues—

Guided Reading Question

■ COMPARISON

What distinguished feminism in the industrialized countries from that in the Global South?

colonialism, racism, national independence, poverty, development, political oppression, and sometimes revolution—were not directly related to gender. Women were affected by and engaged with all of these efforts and were welcomed by nationalist and communist leaders, mostly men, who needed their support. But once independence or the revolution was achieved, the women who had joined those movements often were relegated to marginal positions.

The different conditions within developing countries sometimes generated sharp criticism of Western feminism. To many African feminists in the 1970s and later, the concerns of their American or European sisters were too individualistic, too focused on sexuality, and insufficiently concerned with issues of motherhood, marriage, and poverty to be of much use. Furthermore, they resented Western feminists' insistent interest in cultural matters such as female genital mutilation and polygamy, which sometimes echoed the concerns of colonial-era missionaries and administrators. Western feminism could easily be seen as a new form of cultural imperialism. Moreover, many African governments and many African men defined feminism of any kind as "un-African" and associated with a hated colonialism.

Women's movements in the Global South took shape around a wide range of issues, not all of which were explicitly gender based. In the East African country of Kenya, a major form of mobilization was the women's group movement. Some 27,000 small associations of women, an outgrowth of traditional self-help groups, had a combined membership of more than a million by the late 1980s. Members provided support for one another during times of need, such as weddings, births, and funerals, and took on community projects, such as building water cisterns, schools, and dispensaries. In one province, for example, women's groups focused on providing permanent iron roofing for homes. Some groups became revolving loan societies or bought land or businesses. One woman testified to the sense of empowerment she derived from membership in her group:

> I am a free woman. I bought this piece of land through my group. I can lie on it, work on it, keep goats or cows. What more do I want? My husband cannot sell it. It is mine.[13]

Elsewhere, other issues and approaches predominated. In the North African Islamic kingdom of Morocco, a more centrally directed and nationally focused feminist movement targeted the country's Family Law Code, which still defined women as minors. In 2004, a long campaign by Morocco's feminist movement, often with the help of supportive men and a liberal king, resulted in a new Family Law Code, which recognized women as equals to their husbands and allowed them to initiate divorce and to claim child custody, all of which had previously been denied.

In Chile, a women's movement emerged as part of a national struggle against the military dictatorship of General Augusto Pinochet, who ruled the country from 1973 to 1990. Because they were largely regarded as "invisible" in the public sphere, women were able to organize extensively, despite the repression of the Pinochet regime. From this explosion of organizing activity emerged a women's movement that crossed class lines and party affiliations. Human rights activists, most of them women, called attention to the widespread use of torture and to the "disappear-ance" of thousands of opponents of the regime, while demanding the restoration of democracy. Poor urban women by the tens of thousands organized soup kitchens, craft workshops, and shopping collectives, all aimed at the economic survival of their families. Smaller numbers of middle-class women brought more distinctly feminist perspectives to the movement and argued pointedly for "democracy in the country and in the home." This diverse women's movement was an important part of the larger national protest that returned Chile to democratic government in 1990.

International Feminism

Perhaps the most impressive achievement of feminism in the twentieth century was its ability to project the "woman question" as a global issue and to gain interna-tional recognition for the view that "women's rights are human rights." Like slav-ery and empire before it, patriarchy lost at least some of its legitimacy during this most recent century, although clearly it has not been vanquished.

Feminism registered as a global issue when the United Nations (UN), under pressure from women activists, declared 1975 as International Women's Year and the next ten years as the Decade for Women. The UN also sponsored a series of World Conferences on Women over the next twenty years. By 2006, 183 nations, though not the United States, had ratified a UN Convention on the Elimination of All Forms of Discrimination against Women, which committed them to promote women's legal equality, to end discrimination, to actively encourage women's development, and to protect women's human rights. Clearly, this international attention to women's issues was encouraging to feminists operating in their own countries and in many places stimulated both research and action.

This growing international spotlight on women's issues also revealed sharp divi-sions within global feminism. One issue was determining who had the right to speak on behalf of women at international gatherings—the official delegates of male-dominated governments or the often more radical unofficial participants rep-resenting various nongovernmental organizations. North/South conflicts also sur-faced at these international conferences. In preparing for the Mexico City gathering in 1975, the United States attempted to limit the agenda to matters of political and civil rights for women, whereas delegates from third-world and communist coun-tries wanted to include issues of economic justice, decolonization, and disarma-ment. Feminists from the South resented the dominance and contested the ideas of their Northern sisters. One African group highlighted the differences:

> While patriarchal views and structures oppress women all over the world, women
> are also members of classes and countries that dominate others and enjoy privi-
> leges in terms of access to resources. Hence, contrary to the best intentions of
> "sisterhood," not all women share identical interests.[14]

An Aspect of Brazilian Feminism
Protesting macho culture and violence against women, demonstrations in São Paulo, Brazil, began in 2011, challenging the assumption that female victims of rape were responsible for those attacks because of how they dressed. Participants marched as "sluts," wearing sexually provocative clothing, while urging the "transformation of the world by feminism." The "slutwalk" shown here took place in São Paulo in mid-2014. (© Aaron Cadena Ovalle/epa/Corbis)

Nor did all third-world groups have identical views. Some Muslim delegates at the Beijing Conference in 1995 opposed a call for equal inheritance for women because Islamic law required that sons receive twice the amount that daughters inherit. In contrast, Africans, especially in non-Muslim countries, were aware of how many children had been orphaned by AIDS and felt that girls' chances for survival depended on equal inheritance.

Finally, beyond such divisions within international feminism lay a global backlash among those who felt that its radical agenda had undermined family life, the proper relationship of men and women, and civilization generally. To Phyllis Schlafly, a prominent American opponent of the Equal Rights Amendment, feminism was a "disease" that brought in its wake "fear, sickness, pain, anger, hatred, danger, violence, and all manner of ugliness."[15] In the Islamic world, Western-style feminism, with its claims of gender equality and open sexuality, was highly offensive to many and fueled movements of religious revivalism that invited or compelled women to wear the veil and sometimes to lead highly restricted lives. The Vatican, some Catholic and Muslim countries, and at times the U.S. government took strong exception to aspects of global feminism, particularly its emphasis on reproductive rights, including access to abortion and birth control. Thus feminism was global as the twenty-first century dawned, but it was very diverse and much contested.

Religion and Global Modernity

Beyond liberation and feminism, a further dimension of cultural globalization took shape in the challenge that modernity presented to the world's religions. To the most "advanced" thinkers of the past several hundred years—Enlightenment writers in the eighteenth century, Karl Marx in the nineteenth, and many academics and secular-minded intellectuals in the twentieth—religion was headed for extinction in the face of modernity, science, communism, or globalization. In some places—Britain, France, the Netherlands, and the Soviet Union, for example—religious belief and practice had declined sharply. Moreover, the spread of a scientific culture around the world persuaded small minorities everywhere, often among the most highly educated, that the only realities worth considering were those that could be measured with the techniques of science. To such people, all else was superstition, born of ignorance. Nevertheless, the far more prominent trends of the last century have been those that involved the further spread of major world religions, their resurgence in new forms, their opposition to elements of a secular and global modernity, and their political role as a source of community identity and conflict. Contrary to earlier expectations, religion has played an unexpectedly powerful role in this most recent century.

Buddhism, Christianity, and Islam had long functioned as transregional cultures, spreading far beyond their places of origin. That process continued in the twentieth century. Buddhist ideas and practices such as meditation found a warm reception in the West, as did yoga, originally a mind-body practice of Indian origin. Christianity of various kinds spread widely in non-Muslim Africa and South Korea and less extensively in parts of India. By the end of the twentieth century, it was growing even in China, where perhaps 7 to 8 percent of China's population—some 84 to 96 million people—claimed allegiance to the faith. No longer a primarily European or North American religion, Christianity by the early twenty-first century found some 62 percent of its adherents in Asia, Africa, Oceania, and Latin America. In some instances, missionaries from those regions have set about the "re-evangelization" of Europe and North America. Moreover, millions of migrants from the Islamic world have planted their religion solidly in the West. In the United States, for example, a substantial number of African Americans and smaller numbers of European Americans engage in Islamic practice. For several decades, the writings of the thirteenth-century Islamic Sufi poet Rumi have been best sellers in the United States. Religious exchange, in short, has been a two-way street, not simply a transmission of Western ideas to the rest of the world. More than ever before, religious pluralism characterizes many of the world's societies, confronting people with the need to make choices in a domain of life previously regarded as given and fixed.

Fundamentalism on a Global Scale

Religious vitality in the twentieth century was expressed not only in the spread of particular traditions to new areas but also in the vigorous response of those traditions to the modernizing and globalizing world in which they found themselves. One such response has been widely called "fundamentalism," a militant piety—defensive, assertive, and exclusive—that took shape to some extent in every major religious tradition. Many features of the modern world, after all, appeared threatening to established religion. The scientific and secular focus of global modernity challenged the core beliefs of religion, with its focus on an unseen realm of reality. Furthermore, the social upheavals connected with capitalism, industrialization, and globalization thoroughly upset customary class, family, and gender relationships that had long been sanctified by religious tradition. Nation-states, often associated with particular religions, were likewise undermined by the operation of a global economy and challenged by the spread of alien cultures. In much of the world, these disruptions came at the hands of foreigners, usually Westerners, in the form of military defeat, colonial rule, economic dependency, and cultural intrusion.

AP® EXAM TIP

Take notes on these reasons for resistance to changes within and among religions in the twentieth century.

To such threats, fundamentalism represented a religious response, characterized by one scholar as "embattled forms of spirituality . . . experienced as a cosmic war between the forces of good and evil."[16] Although fundamentalisms everywhere looked to the past for ideals and models, their rejection of modernity was selective, not wholesale. What they sought was an alternative modernity, infused with particular religious values. Most, in fact, made active use of modern technology to communicate their message and certainly sought the potential prosperity associated with modern life. Extensive educational and propaganda efforts, political mobilization of their followers, social welfare programs, and sometimes violence ("terrorism" to their opponents) were among the means that fundamentalists employed.

Guided Reading Question

■ CHANGE
In what respect did the various religious fundamentalisms of the twentieth century express hostility to global modernity?

The term "fundamentalism" derived from the United States, where religious conservatives in the early twentieth century were outraged by critical and "scientific" approaches to the Bible, by Darwinian evolution, and by liberal versions of Christianity that accommodated these heresies. They called for a return to the "fundamentals" of the faith, which included a belief in the literal truthfulness of the scriptures, in the virgin birth and physical resurrection of Jesus, and in miracles. After World War II, American Protestant fundamentalism came to oppose political liberalism and "big government," the sexual revolution of the 1960s, homosexuality and abortion rights, and secular humanism generally. Many fundamentalists saw the United States on the edge of an abyss. For one major spokesman, Francis Schaeffer (1912–1984), the West was about to enter "an electronic dark age, in which the new pagan hordes, with all the power of technology at their command, are on the verge of obliterating the last strongholds of civilized humanity." He declared, "A vision of darkness lies before us. As we leave the shores of Christian Western man behind, only a dark and turbulent sea of despair stretches endlessly ahead . . . unless we fight."[17]

And fight they did! At first, fundamentalists sought to separate themselves from the secular world in their own churches and schools, but from the 1970s on, they entered the political arena as the "religious right," determined to return America to a "godly path." "We have enough votes to run this country," declared Pat Robertson, a major fundamentalist evangelist and broadcaster who ran for president in 1988. Conservative Christians, no longer willing to restrict their attention to personal salvation, had emerged as a significant force in American political life well before the end of the century.

In the very different setting of independent India, another fundamentalist movement—known as Hindutva (Hindu nationalism)—took shape during the 1980s, although the concept had appeared as early as 1923 and Gandhi's assassination in 1948 had occurred at the hands of men in that movement. Like American fundamentalism, it represented a politicization of religion within a democratic context. To its advocates, India was, and always had been, an essentially Hindu land, even though it had been overwhelmed in recent centuries by Muslim invaders, then by the Christian British, and most recently by the secular state of the post-independence decades. The leaders of modern India, they argued, and particularly its first prime minister, Jawaharlal Nehru, were "the self-proclaimed secularists who . . . seek to remake India in the Western image," while repudiating its basically Hindu religious character. The Hindutva movement took political shape in an increasingly popular party called the Bharatiya Janata Party (BJP), with much of its support coming from urban middle-class or upper-caste people who resented the state's efforts to cater to the interests of Muslims, Sikhs, and the lower castes. Muslims in particular were defined as outsiders, potentially more loyal to a Muslim Pakistan than to India. The BJP became a major political force in India during the 1980s, winning a number of elections and promoting a distinctly Hindu identity in education, culture, and religion. Its sweeping victory in national elections in 2014 raised questions about how its Hindu nationalism would fare in twenty-first-century India.

Creating Islamic Societies: Resistance and Renewal in the World of Islam

The most prominent of the late twentieth-century fundamentalisms was surely that of Islam. Expressed in many and various ways, it was an effort among growing numbers of Muslims to renew and reform the practice of Islam and to create a new religious/political order centered on a particular understanding of their faith. Earlier renewal movements, such as the eighteenth-century Wahhabis (see pages 660–61) focused largely on the internal problems of Muslim societies, while those of the twentieth century responded as well to the external pressures of colonial rule, Western imperialism, and secular modernity.

Emerging strongly in the last quarter of the twentieth century, Islamic renewal movements gained strength from the enormous disappointments that had accumu-

Guided Reading Question

■ CHANGE
From what sources did Islamic renewal movements derive?

lated in the Muslim world by the 1970s. Conquest and colonial rule; awareness of the huge technological and economic gap between Islamic and European civilizations; the disappearance of the Ottoman Empire, long the chief Islamic state; elite enchantment with Western culture; the retreat of Islam for many to the realm of private life — all of this had sapped the cultural self-confidence of many Muslims by the mid-twentieth century. Political independence for former colonies certainly represented a victory for Islamic societies, but it had given rise to major states — Egypt, Pakistan, Indonesia, Iraq, Algeria, and others — that pursued essentially Western and secular policies of nationalism, socialism, and economic development, often with only lip service to an Islamic identity.

Even worse, these policies were not very successful. A number of endemic problems — vastly overcrowded cities with few services, widespread unemployment, pervasive corruption, slow economic growth, a mounting gap between the rich and poor — flew in the face of the great expectations that had accompanied the struggle against European domination. Despite formal independence, foreign intrusion still persisted. Israel, widely regarded as an outpost of the West, had been reestablished as a Jewish state in the very center of the Islamic world in 1948. In 1967, Israel inflicted a devastating defeat on Arab forces in the Six-Day War and seized various Arab territories, including the holy city of Jerusalem. Furthermore, broader signs of Western cultural penetration persisted — secular schools, alcohol, Barbie dolls, European and American movies, scantily clad women. (For more on Muslim views on Barbie dolls, see Zooming In: Barbie and Her Competitors in the Muslim World, page 1046.) The largely secular leader of independent Tunisia, Habib Bourguiba, argued against the veil for women as well as polygamy for men and discouraged his people from fasting during Ramadan. In 1960, he was shown on television drinking orange juice during the sacred month to the outrage of many traditional Muslims.

This was the context in which the idea of an Islamic alternative to Western models of modernity began to take hold more broadly, although its origins go back to the Young Ottomans of the 1860s. The intellectual and political foundations of this Islamic renewal had been established earlier in the century. Its leading figures, such as the Indian Mawlana Mawdudi and the Egyptian Sayyid Qutb, insisted that the Quran and the sharia (Islamic law) provided a guide for all of life — political, economic, and spiritual — and a blueprint for a distinctly Islamic modernity not dependent on Western ideas. It was the departure from Islamic principles, they argued, that had led the Islamic world into decline and subordination to the West, and only a return to the "straight path of Islam" would ensure a revival of Muslim societies. That effort to return to Islamic principles was labeled *jihad*, an ancient and evocative religious term that refers to "struggle" or "striving" to please God. In its twentieth-century political expression, jihad included the defense of an authentic Islam against Western aggression and vigorous efforts to achieve the Islamization of social and political life within Muslim countries. It was a posture that would enable Muslims to resist the seductive but poisonous culture of the West. Sayyid Qutb had

Barbie and Her Competitors in the Muslim World

"I think every Barbie doll is more harmful than an American missile," declared Iranian toy seller Masoumeh Rahimi in 2002. To Rahimi, Barbie's revealing clothing, her shapely appearance, and her close association with Ken, her longtime unmarried companion, were "foreign to Iran's culture." Thus Rahimi warmly welcomed the arrival in 2002 of Sara and Dara, Iranian Muslim dolls meant to counteract the negative influence of Barbie, who had long dominated Iran's toy market. Created by the Iranian government, Sara and her brother, Dara, represented eight-year-old twins and were intended to replace Barbie and Ken, the sale of which the authorities had officially banned in the mid-1990s because they represented a "Trojan horse" for Western values. Sara came complete with a headscarf to cover her hair in modest Muslim fashion and a full-length white chador enveloping her from head to toe. She and her brother were described as helping each other solve problems,

A Syrian girl examining Fulla dolls at a toy store in Damascus in 2005.

while looking to their loving parents for guidance, hardly the message that Barbie and Ken conveyed.[18]

In 2003, a toy company based in Syria introduced Fulla, a doll depicting a young Muslim woman about the same age as Barbie, perhaps a grown-up version of Sara. Dressed modestly in a manner that reflected the norms of each national market, Fulla was described by her creator as representing "Muslim values." Unlike Barbie, with her boyfriend and a remarkable range of careers, including astronaut and president of the United States, Fulla was modeled on the ideal traditional Arab woman. She interacted with male family members rather than a boyfriend and was depicted only as a teacher or a doctor, both respected professions for women in the Islamic world. But she did share an eye for fashion with Barbie. Underneath her

photo: © Khaled Al-Hariri/Reuters/Landov

witnessed that culture during a visit to the United States in the late 1940s and was appalled by what he saw:

> Look at this capitalism with its monopolies, its usury . . . at this individual freedom, devoid of human sympathy and responsibility for relatives except under force of law; at this materialistic attitude which deadens the spirit; at this behavior like animals which you call "free mixing of the sexes"; at this vulgarity which you call "emancipation of women"; at this evil and fanatical racial discrimination.[19]

By the 1970s, ideas and organizations favoring the Islamization of public life echoed widely across the Islamic world and found expression in many ways. At the level of personal practice, many people became more religiously observant, attending mosque, praying regularly, and fasting. Substantial numbers of women, many

Guided Reading Question

■ COMPARISON

In what different ways did Islamic renewal express itself?

modest outer dress, Fulla wore stylish clothing, although it was less revealing than that of her American counterpart, and, like Barbie, she chose from an extensive wardrobe, sold separately of course. "This isn't just about putting the hijab [a headscarf covering a woman's hair and chest] on a Barbie doll," Fawaz Abidin, the Fulla brand manager, noted. "You have to create a character that parents and children want to relate to."[20]

Fulla proved far more popular than Sara among Muslim girls, becoming one of the best-selling dolls in the Muslim world. In part, the adoption by Fulla's creators of Western marketing techniques, similar to those that had been used to promote Barbie for decades, lay behind the doll's remarkable success. Fulla-themed magazines appeared on newsstands, and commercials advertising Fulla dolls and their accessories permeated children's television stations in the Muslim world. "When you take Fulla out of the house, don't forget her new spring abaya [a long, robe-like full-body covering]!" admonished one advertisement. Fulla's image was used to market an endless number of other licensed products, including branded stationery, backpacks, prayer rugs, bikes, and breakfast cereals, all in trademark "Fulla pink." In this respect, Fulla and Barbie shared a great deal. Despite Fulla's success, Barbie has continued to enjoy a loyal following in the region, in part because of her exotic qualities. "All my friends have Fulla now, but I still like Barbie the best," one ten-year-old Saudi girl stated. "She has blonde hair and cool clothes. Every single girl in Saudi looks like Fulla. . . . What's so special about that?"

The widespread availability of Barbie in the Muslim world provides one small example of the power of global commerce in the world of the early twenty-first century. But Sara and Fulla illustrate resistance to the cultural values associated with this American product. Still, Sara, Fulla, and Barbie had something in common: nearly all were manufactured in East Asian factories. Indeed, the same factories frequently manufactured the rival dolls. This triangular relationship of the United States, the Muslim world, and East Asia symbolized the growing integration of world economies and cultures as well as the divergences and conflicts that this process has generated. These linked but contrasting patterns involve much more than dolls in the early twenty-first century, for they define major features of the world we all share.

Questions: What can Barbie, Sara, and Fulla tell us about the globalized world of the twenty-first century? What different values and sensibilities do they convey?

of them young, urban, and well educated, adopted modest Islamic dress and the veil quite voluntarily. Participation in Sufi mystical practices increased in some places. Furthermore, many governments sought to anchor themselves in Islamic rhetoric and practice. During the 1970s, President Anwar Sadat of Egypt claimed the title of "Believer-President," referred frequently to the Quran, and proudly displayed his "prayer mark," a callus on his forehead caused by touching his head to the ground in prayer. Under pressure from Islamic activists, the government of Sudan in the 1980s adopted Quranic punishments for various crimes (such as amputating the hand of a thief) and announced a total ban on alcohol, dramatically dumping thousands of bottles of beer and wine into the Nile.

All over the Muslim world, from North Africa to Indonesia (see Map 23.3), Islamic renewal movements spawned organizations that operated legally to provide social services—schools, clinics, youth centers, legal-aid societies, financial

Map 23.3   The Islamic World in the Early Twenty-First Century

An Islamic world of well over a billion people incorporated much of the Afro-Asian landmass but was divided among many nations and along linguistic and ethnic lines as well. The long-term split between the majority Sunnis and the minority Shias also sharpened in the new millennium.

institutions, publishing houses—that the state offered inadequately or not at all. Islamic activists took leadership roles in unions and professional organizations of teachers, journalists, engineers, doctors, and lawyers. Such people embraced modern science and technology but sought to embed these elements of modernity within a distinctly Islamic culture. Some served in official government positions or entered political life and contested elections where it was possible to do so. The Algerian Islamic Salvation Front was poised to win elections in 1992, when a frightened military government intervened to cancel the elections, an action that plunged the country into a decade of bitter civil war. Egypt's Muslim Brotherhood did come to power peacefully in 2012, but was removed by the military a year later amid widespread protests against its policies.

Movements embracing another face of religious renewal, however, sought the forcible overthrow of what they saw as compromised regimes in the Islamic world, most successfully in Iran in 1979 (see Chapter 22, pages 1007–10), but also in Afghanistan (1996), northern Nigeria (2009–2015), and parts of Syria and Iraq (2013–2015). Here Islamic movements succeeded in seizing state power or controlling certain territories and began to implement, sometimes brutally, a program of Islamization based on the sharia. Elsewhere military governments in Pakistan and Sudan likewise introduced elements of sharia-based law. Hoping to spark an Islamic revolution, the Egyptian Islamic Jihad organization assassinated President Sadat in 1981, following Sadat's brutal crackdown on both Islamic and secular opposition groups. One of the leaders of Islamic Jihad explained:

> We have to establish the Rule of God's Religion in our own country first, and to make the Word of God supreme. . . . There is no doubt that the first battlefield for jihad is the extermination of these infidel leaders and to replace them by a complete Islamic Order.[21]

Islamic revolutionaries also took aim at hostile foreign powers. Hamas in Palestine and Hezbollah in Lebanon, supported by the Islamic regime in Iran, targeted Israel with popular uprisings, suicide bombings, and rocket attacks in response to the Israeli occupation of Arab lands. For some, Israel's very existence was illegitimate. The Soviet invasion of Afghanistan in 1979 prompted widespread opposition aimed at liberating that country from atheistic communism and creating an Islamic state. Sympathetic Arabs from the Middle East and other Muslims flocked to the aid of their Afghan compatriots.

Among them was the young Osama bin Laden, a wealthy Saudi Arab, who created an organization, al-Qaeda (meaning "the base" in Arabic), to funnel fighters and funds to the Afghan resistance. At the time, bin Laden and the Americans were on the same side, both opposing Soviet expansion into Afghanistan, but they soon parted ways. Returning to his home in Saudi Arabia, bin Laden became disillusioned and radicalized when the government of his country allowed the stationing of "infidel" U.S. troops in Islam's holy land, where the faith had begun, during and after the first American war against Iraq in 1991. By the mid-1990s, he had found a safe haven in Taliban-ruled Afghanistan, from which he and other leaders of al-Qaeda planned their attack on the World Trade Center and other targets in the United States on September 11, 2001. Although they had no standing as Muslim clerics, in 1998 they had issued a *fatwa* (religious edict) declaring war on America:

> For over seven years the United States has been occupying the lands of Islam in the holiest of places, the Arabian Peninsula, plundering its riches, dictating to its rulers, humiliating its people, terrorizing its neighbors, and turning its bases in the Peninsula into a spearhead through which to fight the neighboring Muslim peoples. . . . The ruling to kill the Americans and their allies—civilians and military—is an individual duty for every Muslim who can do it in any country in which it is possible to do it, in order to liberate the al-Aqsa Mosque in Jerusalem and the holy mosque [in Mecca] from their grip, and in order for their armies to move out of all the lands of Islam, defeated and unable to threaten any Muslim.[22]

AP® EXAM TIP

You should know examples of twentieth-century nationalist movements with religious roots.

Hamas in Action

The Palestinian militant organization Hamas, founded in 1987 as an offshoot of Egypt's Muslim Brotherhood, illustrates two dimensions of Islamic radicalism. On the one hand, Hamas repeatedly sent suicide bombers to target Israeli civilians and sought the elimination of the Israeli state. A group of would-be suicide bombers are shown here in white robes during the funeral of colleagues killed by Israeli security forces in late 2003. On the other hand, Hamas ran a network of social services, providing schools, clinics, orphanages, summer camps, soup kitchens, and libraries for Palestinians. The classroom pictured here from 2006 was part of a school founded by Hamas. (left: Andrea Comas/ Reuters/Landov; right: Abid Katib/Getty Images)

Elsewhere as well—in East Africa, Indonesia, Great Britain, Spain, France, Saudi Arabia, and Yemen—al-Qaeda or groups associated with it launched scattered attacks on Western interests. At the international level, the great enemy was not Christianity itself or even Western civilization, but irreligious Western-style modernity, U.S. imperialism, and the American-led economic globalization so aptly symbolized by the World Trade Center. Ironically, al-Qaeda itself was a modern and global organization, many of whose members were highly educated professionals from a variety of countries.

Despite this focus on the West, the violent struggles undertaken by politicized Islamic activists were directed as much against elements within the Islamic world as they were against the external enemy. Broadly known as Salafis, these activists and their supporters sought to follow what they understood to be the example of the *salaf*, or "ancestors," men of Muhammad's time and shortly thereafter. Their understanding of Islam, heavily influenced by Wahhabi ideas (see pages 660–61), was in various ways quite novel and at odds with classical Islamic practice. It was highly literal and dogmatic in its understanding of the Quran, legalistic in its effort to regulate the minute details of daily life, deeply opposed to any "innovation" in religious practice, inclined to define those who disagreed with them as "non-Muslims," and drawn to violent jihad as a legitimate part of Islamic life. It was also deeply skeptical about the interior spiritual emphasis of Sufism, which had informed so much of earlier Islamic culture. The spread of Salafi Islam owed much to massive financial backing from oil-rich Saudi Arabia, which funded Wahhabi/Salafi mosques and schools across the Islamic world and in the West as well.

Religious Alternatives to Fundamentalism

Militant revolutionary fundamentalism has certainly not been the only religious response to modernity and globalization within the Islamic world. Many who shared a desire to embed Islamic values more centrally in their societies have acted peacefully and within established political structures. In Turkey, Egypt, Jordan, Iraq, Palestine, Morocco, Tunisia, and Lebanon, Islamic parties with various agendas made impressive electoral showings in the 1990s and the early twenty-first century. Considerable debate among Muslims has raised questions about the proper role of the state, the difference between the eternal law of God (sharia) and the human interpretations of it, the rights of women, the possibility of democracy, and many other issues. (See Working with Evidence: Contending for Islam, Chapter 22, page 1012.) Some Muslim intellectuals and political leaders have called for a dialogue between civilizations; others have argued that traditions can change in the face of modern realities without losing their distinctive Islamic character. In 1996, Anwar Ibrahim, a major political and intellectual figure in Malaysia, insisted:

> [Southeast Asian Muslims] would rather strive to improve the welfare of the women and children in their midst than spend their days elaborately defining the nature and institutions of the ideal Islamic state. They do not believe it makes one less of a Muslim to promote economic growth, to master the information revolution, and to demand justice for women.[23]

In Turkey, a movement inspired by the teachings of Fethullah Gulen, a Turkish Muslim scholar and preacher, has sought to apply the principles of Islamic spirituality and Sufi piety to the problems of modern society. Gaining a mass following in the 1990s and later, the Gulen movement has advocated interfaith and cross-cultural dialogue, multiparty democracy, nonviolence, and modern scientifically based education for girls and boys alike. Operating through schools, universities, conferences, newspapers, radio and TV stations, and various charities, it has a presence in more than 100 countries around the world. Claiming to be "faith based but not faith limited," the movement rejects the "fundamentalist" label even as it has challenged a wholly secular outlook on public life. And in 2004–2005, a gathering in Jordan of scholars from all major schools of Islamic thought issued the "Amman Message," which called for Islamic unity, condemned terrorism, forbade Muslims from declaring one another as "apostate" or nonbelievers, and emphasized the commonalities shared by Muslims, Christians, and Jews.

Within other religious traditions as well, believers found various ways of responding to global modernity. A number of liberal and mainstream Christian groups spoke to the ethical issues arising from economic globalization. Many Christian organizations, for example, were active in agitating for debt relief for poor countries. Pope John Paul II (r. 1978–2005) voiced his concern about "the growing distance between rich and poor, [and] unfair competition which puts the poor nations in a situation of ever-increasing inferiority." Pope Francis (r. 2013–), the first pontiff from Latin America, sought even more emphatically to direct the attention of

Catholics toward the poor, the marginalized, and the suffering people of the world. Adherents of "liberation theology," particularly in Latin America, sought a Christian basis for action in the areas of social justice, poverty, and human rights, while viewing Jesus as liberator as well as savior.

In Asia, a growing movement known as "socially engaged Buddhism" addressed the needs of the poor through social reform, educational programs, health services, and peacemaking action during times of conflict and war. A leading proponent of this approach was the Buddhist monk Maha Ghosananda. In the late 1970s, when Cambodia had been ravaged by the "killing fields" of the Khmer Rouge communist regime, he repeatedly visited the squalid refugee camps to which so many Cambodians had fled. There he led religious services, and later peace marches, endlessly reciting an ancient Buddhist chant: "Hatred never ceases by hatred, but by love alone is healed. This is an ancient and eternal law." In short, religious responses to global modernity were articulated in many voices.

PRACTICING AP® HISTORICAL THINKING

How might you compare feminism and fundamentalism as global movements? In what ways did they challenge earlier values and expectations? To what extent were they in conflict with one another?

Experiencing the Anthropocene Era: Environment and Environmentalism

Even as world religions, fundamentalist and otherwise, challenged global modernity on cultural or spiritual grounds, burgeoning environmental movements in the 1960s and later also did so with an eye to the human impact on the earth and its many living creatures, including ourselves. Among the distinctive features of the twentieth century, none has been more pronounced than humankind's growing ability to alter the natural order and the mounting awareness of this phenomenon. When the wars, revolutions, and empires of this most recent century have faded from memory, environmental transformation and environmental consciousness may well seem to future generations the decisive feature of that century. Already, many scientists and other scholars have begun to refer to the current era, since at least the advent of the Industrial Revolution, as the Anthropocene, or the "age of man." That informal term has called attention to the lasting impact of human activity on the planet.[24] Species extinctions, increases of carbon dioxide in the atmosphere, the depletion of groundwater reserves, the enlargement of deserts, dead zones in the oceans, transformation of the landscape as wetlands shrink and urban centers grow—these and other environmental changes, all of them generated by human actions, will be apparent to our descendants thousands of years in the future, should they be around to reflect on them.

AP® EXAM TIP

Relationships between humans and the environment are always "must know" information for success on the AP® exam.

The Global Environment Transformed

Underlying the environmental changes of the twentieth century were three factors that vastly magnified the human impact on earth's ecological systems far beyond anything previously known.[25] One was the explosion of human numbers, an unprecedented quadrupling of the world's population in a single century, leaving the world of 2014 with about 7.2 billion people compared to about 1.6 billion in 1900. It was a demographic revolution born of medical and sanitation advances that dramatically lowered death rates and Green Revolution technologies such as genetically modified seeds and fertilizers that substantially increased world food supplies.

This vast enlargement of the human population meant more consumption and thus more demands on the earth's resources. It also fostered massive urbanization and global migration, even as it contributed to many political and social upheavals, especially in the second half of the century. By the end of the century, the rate of global population growth had begun to slow. From a peak of over 2 percent per year in the 1960s, it had dropped to 1.14 percent by 2014. This transition had occurred first in the more developed countries, where birth control measures were widely available, women were educated and pursuing careers, and large families were economically burdensome. This pattern began to take hold in developing countries as well, assisted by vigorous family-planning programs in many places, the most dramatic of which was China's famous "one-child family" policy. Experts predict that the modern population explosion will level off by the mid-twenty-first century at some 9 to 12 billion people, although whether the world economy and its resource base can support these enormously enhanced numbers remains an open question.

A second cause of environmental stress lay in the amazing new ability of humankind to tap the energy potential of fossil fuels—coal in the nineteenth century and oil in the twentieth. These fuels drove the industrialization process everywhere, with coal providing the major source for electricity generation and oil giving rise to the immense automobile industry. Hydroelectricity, natural gas, solar power, and nuclear power added to the energy resources available to our species.

These new sources of energy made possible a third contribution to environmental transformation—phenomenal economic growth—as modern science and technology immensely increased the production of goods and services. Between the 1890s and the 1990s, global industrial output grew by a factor of forty, although very unevenly across the planet. But almost everywhere—in capitalist, communist, and developing countries alike—the idea of economic growth or "development" as something possible and desirable took hold as a novel element of global culture.

These three factors were the foundations for the immense environmental transformations of this most recent century. Human activity had always altered the natural order, usually on a local basis, but now the scale of that impact assumed global and perhaps even geological proportions. The growing numbers of the poor and the growing consumption of the rich led to the doubling of cropland; a corresponding contraction of the world's forests, wetlands, and grasslands; and dramatic increases in the rate of erosion. Huge urban complexes have transformed the landscape in many places. With diminished habitats, numerous species of plants and animals either disappeared or were threatened with extinction at a rate many times greater than the background level. Certainly, massive species extinctions have occurred much earlier in the history of the planet (the dinosaurs, for example), but this wave of extinctions is happening at the hands of humankind. The human

AP® EXAM TIP

Make a list of causes and effects of sky-rocketing human population since around 1900.

Guided Reading Question

■ CHANGE
How can we explain the dramatic increase in the human impact on the environment in the twentieth century?

remaking of the ecosystem has also greatly increased the presence of plants and animals that have benefited from human activity—cattle, pigs, chickens, rats, wheat, corn, and dandelions. By some estimates, 90 percent of all plant activity now occurs in environments shaped by human action.

The global spread of modern industry, heavily dependent on fossil fuels, generated dramatic changes in the air, water, soil, and atmosphere with profound impacts on human life. China's spectacular economic growth since the 1980s, fueled largely by coal, has resulted in the equally spectacular pall of air pollution in its major cities. In 2004, the World Bank reported that twelve of the world's twenty most polluted cities were in China. Degradation of the world's rivers, seas, and oceans has also mounted as pesticides, herbicides, chemical fertilizers, detergents, oil, sewage, industrial waste, and plastics have made their way from land to water. By the 1960s, Lake Erie in the United States was widely reported as "dead." The Great Pacific Garbage Patch, an area of about 7 million square miles in the North Pacific, has trapped an enormous quantity of marine debris, mostly plastics, endangering oceanic food webs and proving deadly to creatures of the sea, which ingest or become entangled in this human garbage. Industrial pollution in the Soviet Union rendered about half of the country's rivers severely polluted by the late 1980s, while fully 20 percent of its population lived in regions defined as "ecological disasters." In addition, the release of chemicals known as chlorofluorocarbons thinned the ozone layer, which protects the earth from excessive ultraviolet radiation.

The most critical and intractable environmental challenge of recent decades has been global warming. Scientists became concerned about this phenomenon in the 1970s, although their research drew on earlier studies dating to the nineteenth century. By the end of the twentieth century, a worldwide scientific consensus had emerged that a dangerously warming climate was well under way, driven by human actions. Particularly responsible for this global warming has been the vastly increased burning of fossil fuels, which release heat-trapping greenhouse gases such as carbon dioxide into the atmosphere, as well as by the loss of trees that would otherwise remove the carbon dioxide from the air. By 2014, carbon dioxide concentration in the atmosphere, which had been roughly 275 ppm (parts per million) before the Industrial Revolution, had risen to 400 ppm, well above the level of 350 ppm that is generally considered "safe." Scientists have associated this global warming with all manner of environmental changes, both current and projected: the melting of glaciers and the rising of sea levels; extreme weather events such as floods, droughts, hurricanes, and typhoons; increased acidification of the oceans; decreased crop yields; disruptions of ecosystems and the extinction of many species. All of this has varied and will continue to vary substantially from region to region, but serious observers have begun to speak about the possibility of "a crisis that threatens our survival as a species."[26]

Beyond these weather- and climate-related changes, global warming has interacted with a variety of social conditions—poverty, inequality, oppression—to generate or exacerbate conflict and upheaval. Syria's bitter civil war, which has killed over 200,000 people and displaced or made refugees of many millions more since 2011, followed on the heels of a severe and prolonged drought and related crop failures. More broadly, in 2010 and 2011 extreme weather conditions characteristic of global warming—droughts, dust storms, fires, heavy rainfall—afflicted many grain-producing regions of the world, including Canada, Russia, China, Argentina, and Australia, causing a sharp spike in grain prices on the world market. The Middle East and North Africa, heavily dependent on grain imports, experienced sharply rising food prices, arguably aggravating social unrest and contributing to the political protests of the Arab Spring. Even the American military has taken climate change seriously. A 2007 report by a number of senior retired officers concluded that "climate change poses a serious threat to America's national security . . . [and] acts as a threat multiplier for instability in some of the most volatile regions of the world."[27]

Green and Global

Modern environmentalism, with its awareness of ecological damage and a desire to counteract it, dates to the late eighteenth or early nineteenth century.[28] One strand in this "first-wave environmentalism" lay in a direct response to early industrialization. Romantic poets such as William Blake and William Wordsworth denounced the industrial era's "dark satanic mills," which threatened the "green and pleasant land" of an earlier England. In opposing the extension of railroads, the British writer John Ruskin in 1876 declared, "The frenzy of avarice is daily drowning our sailors, suffocating our miners, poisoning our children and blasting the cultivable surface of England into a treeless waste of ashes."[29] Mahatma Gandhi came into contact with this strand of thinking during his time in England during the late 1880s. "God forbid," he later wrote, "that India should ever take to industrialism after the manner of the West." Another element in early environmentalism, especially prominent in the United States and Germany, derived from a concern with deforestation, drought, and desertification as pioneering settlers, lumbermen, miners, and the owners of colonial plantations inflicted terrible damage on the woodlands and pasturelands of the world. Articulated primarily by men of science, often those working in the colonial world, this approach sought to mobilize scientific expertise and state control to manage, contain, and tame modern assaults on the environment.

Protecting remaining wilderness areas was yet another aspect of early environmentalism. The first international environmental conference, held in London in 1900, aimed at preserving African wildlife from voracious European hunters. In the United States, it was the opening of the west to European settlers that threatened the natural order. "With no eye to the future," wrote naturalist John Muir in 1897, "these pious destroyers waged interminable forest wars . . . , spreading ruthless devastation ever wider and further." Muir understood the economic rationale for preserving the wilderness, but for him it also held spiritual significance. "Wilderness is

> **AP® EXAM TIP**
>
> You should know causes and features of the late twentieth-century environmental movement.

a necessity . . . not only as fountains of timber and irrigating rivers, but as fountains of life."[30] This kind of sensibility found expression in the American national parks, the first of which, Yellowstone, was established in 1872.

These early examples of environmental awareness were distinctly limited, largely a product of literary figures, scientists, and some government officials. None of them attracted a mass following or provoked a global response. But "second-wave environmentalism," beginning in the 1960s, did both of these things, even as it found expression in many quite different ways.

This new phase of environmentalism is most often associated with the publication in 1962 of Rachel Carson's *Silent Spring*, exposing the chemical contamination of the environment with a particular emphasis on the use of pesticides. The book struck a chord with millions, triggering environmental movements on both sides of the Atlantic. (See Zooming In: Rachel Carson, page 1058.) Ten years later, the Club of Rome, a global think tank, issued a report called *Limits to Growth*, which warned of resource exhaustion and the collapse of industrial society in the face of unrelenting economic and population growth. Soon a mounting wave of environmental books, articles, treatises, and conferences emerged in Europe and North America, pushing back in various ways against the postwar emphasis on "development" and unending economic growth. That sensibility was aptly captured in the title of a best-selling book by British economist E. F. Schumacher in 1973: *Small Is Beautiful*.

Guided Reading Question

■ COMPARISON
What differences emerged between environmentalism in the Global North and that in the Global South?

But what most clearly distinguished second-wave environmentalism was widespread grassroots involvement and activism. By the late 1990s, millions of people in North America, Europe, Japan, Australia, and New Zealand had joined one of the rapidly proliferating environmental organizations, many of them local. The issues addressed in these burgeoning movements were many and various: pollution, resource depletion, toxic waste, protecting wildlife habitats, nuclear power and nuclear testing, limiting development, and, increasingly at the top of the agenda in the twenty-first century, climate change. Beyond particular issues, proponents of "deep ecology" put forward an understanding of the world in which human beings were no longer at the center but occupied a place of equivalence with other species. Those supporting an "environmental justice" outlook were more concerned with the unequal impact of environmental problems on the poor, minorities, and developing countries.

The tactics of these movements were as varied as the issues they addressed. Much attention was given to public education and lobbying governments and corporations, often through highly organized and professionally run organizations. In Germany, New Zealand, and Australia, environmentalists created Green parties, which contested elections and on occasion shared power. Teach-ins, demonstrations, street protests, and various local actions also played a role in the strategies of environmental activists.

In the communist world, environmentalism was constrained by highly authoritarian states, which were committed to large-scale development. In the late 1980s, the Chinese government, for example, sharply repressed groups critical of the enormous Three Gorges Dam project across the Yangzi River. By the early twenty-first century, however, a grassroots environmental movement had taken root in China, expressed in hundreds of private groups and state-sponsored organizations. Many of these sought to ground their activism in Buddhist or Daoist traditions that stressed the harmony of humankind and the natural order. The Chinese state itself has enacted a large body of environmental laws and regulations.[31] In the Soviet Union during the 1970s and later, environmentalists were able to voice their concerns about the shrinking of the Aral Sea, pollution threats to Lake Baikal in Siberia, and poor air quality in many cities. After the nuclear disaster at Chernobyl in 1986, Gorbachev's policy of *glasnost* allowed greater freedom of expression as environmentalist concerns became part of a broader challenge to communism and Russian domination (see Chapter 21, pages 961–62).

Quite quickly, during the 1970s and 1980s, environmentalism also took root in the Global South, where it frequently assumed a distinctive character compared to the more industrialized countries. It was more locally based and had fewer large national organizations than in the West; it involved more poor people in direct actions; it was less engaged in political lobbying and corporate strategies; it was more concerned with issues of food security, health, and basic survival than with the rights of nature or wilderness protection; and it was more closely connected to movements for social justice.[32] Thus, whereas Western environmentalists defended forests where few people lived, the Chikpo, or "tree-hugging," movement in India sought to protect the livelihood of farmers, artisans, and herders living in areas subject to extensive deforestation. A massive movement to prevent or limit the damming of India's Narmada River derived from the displacement of local people; similar anti-dam protests in the American Northwest were more concerned with protecting salmon runs.

In the Global South, this "environmentalism of the poor" took shape in various ways, often in opposition to the gigantic development projects of national governments. Residents of the Brazilian Amazon basin, facing the loss of their livelihood to lumbering interests, ranchers, and government road-building projects, joined hands and directly confronted workers sent to cut down trees with their chainsaws. When the Thai government sought to create huge eucalyptus plantations, largely to supply Japanese-owned paper mills, Buddhist teachers, known as "ecology monks," mobilized peasants to put their case to public officials. In the Philippines, coalitions of numerous local groups—representing various religious, women's, human rights, indigenous peoples', peasant, and political organizations—mobilized large-scale grassroots movements against foreign-owned mining companies. And in Kenya, the Green Belt Movement organized groups of village women to plant millions of trees intended to forestall the growth of deserts and protect the soil.

By the early twenty-first century, environmentalism had become a matter of global concern and had prompted change at many levels. National governments acted to curtail pollution and to foster the use of renewable energy sources. By

Rachel Carson, Pioneer of Environmentalism

"Over increasingly large areas of the United States, spring now comes unheralded by the return of the birds, and the early mornings are strangely silent."[33] This was the appalling vision that inspired *Silent Spring*, a book that effectively launched the American environmental movement in 1962 with its devastating critique of unregulated pesticide use. Its author, Rachel Carson, was born in 1907 on a farm near Pittsburgh. Her childhood interest in nature led to college and graduate studies in biology and then a career as a marine biologist with the U.S. Department of Fisheries, where she was only the second woman hired for such a position. She was also finding her voice as a writer, penning three well-received books on the ecology of the sea.

Rachel Carson.

Through this work, Carson gained an acute awareness of the intricate and interdependent web of life, but she assumed that "much of nature was forever beyond the tampering hand of man." However, the advent of the atomic age, with the dramatic bombings of Hiroshima and Nagasaki in 1945, shook her confidence that nature was immune to human action, and she began to question the widely held assumption that science always held positive outcomes for human welfare. That skepticism gradually took shape around the issue of pesticides and other toxins deliberately introduced into the environment in the name of progress. In 1958, a letter from a friend describing the death of birds in her yard following aerial spraying for mosquito control prompted Carson to take on a project that became *Silent Spring*. Initially she called it "Man against the Earth."

From government agencies, independent scientists, public health specialists, and her own network of contacts, Carson began to assemble data about the impact of pesticides on natural ecosystems and human health. While she never called for their complete elimination, she argued for much greater care and sensitivity to the environment in employing chemical pesticides. She further urged natural biotic agents as a preferable alternative for pest control. The book also criticized the government regulatory agencies for their negligent oversight and scientific specialists for their "fanatical zeal" to create "a chemically sterile insect-free world." Chemical

photo: Erich Hartmann/Magnum Photos

2014, Germany was edging up on getting 30 percent of its energy from such sources, most of it from solar and wind, while Brazil and Canada received 82 percent and 62 percent respectively from renewables, primarily hydropower. Furthermore, some 6,000 national parks in over 100 countries served to protect wildlife and natural beauty. In addition to governments, many businesses found it useful to become more clearly "green." Reforestation programs were accordingly under way in China, Honduras, Kenya, and elsewhere. In recent years, international agreements have come close to eliminating the introduction of ozone-depleting substances into the atmosphere. And millions of individuals have altered their way companies, she wrote, gave out only "little tranquilizing pills of half-truth" when confronted with evidence of their products' harmful results. While she worked hard to ensure the book's scientific credentials, it was a passionate work, fueled by Carson's "anger at the senseless brutish things that were being done." It was also a book written under growing personal difficulties. Her mother, for whom she had long been a caretaker, died in 1958, while Carson's own health too deteriorated as cancer and other ailments took their toll.

When *Silent Spring* was finally published in 1962, the book provoked a firestorm of criticism. Velsicol, a major chemical company, threatened a lawsuit to prevent its publication. Critics declared that following her prescriptions would mean "the end of all human progress," even a "return to the Dark Ages [when] insects and diseases and vermin would once again inherit the earth." Some of the attacks were more personal. Rachel Carson had never married, and Ezra Taft Benson, a former secretary of agriculture, wondered "why a spinster with no children was so concerned about genetics," while opining that she was "probably a communist." It was the height of the cold war era, and challenges to government agencies and corporate capitalism were often deemed "un-American" and "sinister."

Carson evoked such a backlash because she had called into question the whole idea of science as progress, so central to Western culture since the Enlightenment. Humankind had acquired the power to "alter the very nature of the [earth's] life," she declared. The book ended with a dire warning: "It is our alarming misfortune that so primitive a science has armed itself with the most modern and terrible weapons, and that in turning them against the insects, it has also turned them against the earth."

But Carson also had a growing number of enthusiastic supporters. Before she died in 1964, she witnessed the vindication of much of her work. Honors and awards poured in; she more than held her own against her critics in a CBS News program devoted to her book; and a presidential Science Advisory Committee cited Carson's work while recommending the "orderly reduction of persistent pesticides." Following her death, a range of policy changes reflected her work, including the creation of the Environmental Protection Agency in 1970 and the banning of the insecticide DDT in 1973. *Silent Spring* also motivated many to join the growing array of environmentalist groups.

Approaching her death, Carson applied her ecological understanding of the world to herself as well. In a letter to her best friend not long before she died, she recalled seeing some monarch butterflies leaving on a journey from which they would not return. And then she added: "When the intangible cycle has run its course, it is a natural and not unhappy thing that a life comes to an end."

Question: In what larger contexts might we understand Rachel Carson and the book that gained her such attention?

of life, agreeing to recycle, to install solar panels, to buy fuel-efficient cars, to shop in local markets, and to forgo the use of plastic bags.

But will these piecemeal efforts be enough to avoid the catastrophes that scientists predict will occur if global warming continues unchecked? Effective action on climate change, surely the most critical issue of the twenty-first century, has been difficult, partly because it would require some adjustment for citizens and corporations in the Global North and for elites everywhere. Furthermore, large-scale international agreement on global warming has come up against sharp conflicts between the Global North and South. Both activists and governments in the developing

Environmentalism in Action
These South Korean environmental activists are wearing death masks and holding crosses representing various countries during an antinuclear protest in Seoul in 1996, exactly ten years after a large-scale nuclear accident at Chernobyl in the Soviet Union. The lead protester holds a placard reading "Don't forget Chernobyl!" (Yun Jai-hyoung/AP Photo)

countries have often felt that Northern initiatives to address atmospheric pollution and global warming would curtail their industrial development, leaving the North/South gap intact. "The threat to the atmospheric commons has been building over centuries," argued Indian environmentalist Vandana Shiva, "mainly because of industrial activity in the North. Yet . . . the North refuses to assume extra responsibility for cleaning up the atmosphere. No wonder the Third World cries foul when it is asked to share the costs." A Malaysian official put the dispute succinctly: "The developed countries don't want to give up their extravagant lifestyles, but plan to curtail our development."[34] Western governments argued that newly industrializing countries such as China and India must also agree to specific limits on their growing emissions if further global warming is to be prevented. Such deep disagreements between industrialized and developing countries have contributed to the failure of global efforts to reduce greenhouse gas emissions. But negotiations continue regarding a climate change treaty that would be legally binding on all parties or at least voluntarily accepted by them. Beyond such efforts to limit greenhouse gas emissions, more exotic solutions have also surfaced such as capturing and burying carbon emissions or injecting light-reflecting sulfur particles into the atmosphere.

More than any other widespread movement, global environmentalism came to symbolize "one world" thinking, a focus on the common plight of humankind across the artificial boundaries of nation-states. It also marked a challenge to modernity itself, particularly its consuming commitment to endless growth. The ideas of sustainability and restraint, certainly not prominent in any list of modern values, entered global discourse and marked the beginnings of a new environmental ethic. This change in thinking, although limited, was perhaps the most significant achievement of global environmentalism.

REFLECTIONS

Pondering the Past: Limitations and Possibilities

All of us engaged in the study of world history describe global changes, make global comparisons, assess connections among distant peoples, and explain, as best we can, and sometimes amid intense controversy, why things turned out as they did. But to put it mildly, these are not easy tasks, and the entire enterprise is subject to various challenges and to some outright limitations. One challenge derives from the limitations of our sources. We simply lack information about much that we would like to uncover. Who wouldn't like to know more about the thinking of our distant ancestors, the life of the Buddha or Jesus, or what was in the mind of Stalin during the upheavals of the 1930s? When written records are not available, scholars depend largely on material remains as they seek to reconstruct the past. Even when written sources are more plentiful, these materials often reflect the narrow experience of elites, leaving few sources available to assist in understanding the lives of women, peasants, slaves, and other marginalized groups.

Another challenge for students of world history lies in the particularities of time and place. In seeking to understand the past, we all start from somewhere specific — our own time and our own culture. Whether we are insiders or outsiders to the societies we explore, all of us operate within a set of assumptions and values that shape our understanding of the past. Views of Columbus in 1992, the 500th anniversary of his arrival in the Americas, differed greatly from what they had been a century earlier. Many in his Italian homeland no doubt view him differently than do Native Americans. The absence of women, until quite recently, from many historical accounts owes something to the fact that most writers of history were men. In these differences of time, place, gender, and position in society lies the source of much of the controversy that attends the study of history. It makes finality and objectivity difficult to achieve.

A further limitation derives from the unalterable "otherness" of every person. This is not so much a matter of ignorance as of mystery. Most of us have some

AP® EXAM TIP

Carefully read the author's final thoughts about the meaning of history as a starting point for your upcoming AP® exam reviews.

difficulty understanding ourselves and those with whom we are on intimate terms in any full and final fashion. It is not so much that we lack information, but that we run up against what Elizabeth Cady Stanton famously called the "solitude of the self," which "no eye nor touch of man or angel has ever pierced." This profound individuality, this essential singularity, of every person makes it difficult to penetrate the inner recesses of human motivation, which are among the major drivers of the historical process.

Despite the challenges and limitations, as historians and students of history, we persist in the task, seeking what knowledge we can achieve, what insights we can gain, what perspective on our own lives we can generate. In doing so, historians have pioneered creative techniques for obtaining data—from DNA analysis to critical reading of ancient texts. We also make concerted efforts to identify our own assumptions and outlooks and, so far as is humanly possible, to set them aside as we seek to grasp the worlds of other times and places. We have at our disposal the marvelous human capacity of informed imagination: the ability to empathize with others based on our common humanity and our knowledge of their particular circumstances.

But historical understanding is always incomplete, relative, and subject to change. Nonetheless, the achievements of the historical enterprise are impressive and enormously enriching. Our subject—world history—makes us witnesses to the broad contours of the human journey and provides a context in which our individual lives can find a place and, perhaps, a measure of meaning. It serves to open us to and inform us about the wider world that shapes our daily experience. If we base our understanding of life only on what we personally experience in our own lives, we render ourselves both impoverished and ineffective.

World history opens a marvelous window into the unfamiliar. It confronts us with the "ways of the world," the whole panorama of human achievement, tragedy, and sensibility. It allows us some modest entry into the lives of people far removed from us in time and place. And it offers us company for the journey of our own lives. Pondering the global past with a receptive heart and an open mind can assist us in enlarging and deepening our sense of self. In exposing us to the wider experience of "all under Heaven," as the Chinese put it, world history can aid us in becoming wiser and more mature persons. That is among the many gifts that the study of the global past, despite its various challenges and limitations, offers to us all.

Chapter Review

What's the Significance?

Big Picture Questions

1. In what ways did the Global North/South divide find expression in the past century?
2. What have been the benefits and drawbacks of globalization since 1945?
3. Do the years since 1914 confirm or undermine Enlightenment predictions about the future of humankind?
4. "The most recent century marks the end of the era of Western dominance in world history." What evidence might support this statement? What evidence might contradict it?
5. To what extent did the various liberation movements of the past century — communism, nationalism, democracy, feminism, internationalism — achieve their goals?
6. **Looking Back:** To what extent did the processes discussed in this chapter (globalization, feminism, fundamentalism, environmentalism) have roots in the more distant past? In what respects did they represent something new in the past century?

Next Steps: For Further Study

Karen Armstrong, *The Battle for God* (2000). A comparison of Christian, Jewish, and Islamic fundamentalism in historical perspective.

Nayan Chanda, *Bound Together: How Traders, Preachers, Adventurers, and Warriors Shaped Globalization* (2007). An engaging, sometimes humorous, long-term view of the globalization process.

Jeffry A. Frieden, *Global Capitalism: Its Fall and Rise in the Twentieth Century* (2006). A thorough, thoughtful, and balanced history of economic globalization.

Michael Hunt, *The World Transformed* (2004). A thoughtful global history of the second half of the twentieth century.

J. R. McNeill, *Something New under the Sun: An Environmental History of the Twentieth-Century World* (2001). A much-acclaimed global account of the rapidly mounting human impact on the environment during the most recent century.

Bonnie G. Smith, ed., *Global Feminisms since 1945* (2000). A series of essays about feminist movements around the world.

"Globalization," https://www.youtube.com/watch?v=3oTLyPPrZE4. A brief eight-minute animated primer on the causes and consequences of globalization.

"No Job for a Woman," http://www.iwm.org.uk/upload/package/30/women/index.htm. A Web site illustrating the impact of war on the lives of women in the twentieth century.

WORKING WITH EVIDENCE

Faces of Globalization

Not many people in the world of the early twenty-first century remain untouched by globalization. For most of humankind, the pervasive processes of interaction among distant peoples has shaped the clothing we wear, the foods we eat, the products we consume, the ways we work, the music we listen to, the religions we practice, and the identities we assume. Such interactions are, in fact, difficult to avoid. The images that follow offer just a few reminders of the many dimensions of this immense process and provide grist for the mill of our reflection upon them.

Among the common experiences of globalization for some people living in Asia, Africa, or Latin America has been that of working in foreign-owned production facilities. Companies in wealthier countries have often found it advantageous to build such facilities in places where labor is less expensive or environmental regulations are less restrictive. China, Vietnam, Indonesia, Bangladesh, the Philippines, Mexico, Brazil, and various African states are among the countries that have hosted foreign-owned manufacturing operations. The worst of them—in terms of child labor, low pay, few benefits, and dangerous working conditions—have been called "sweatshops." Such abuses have generated an international movement challenging those conditions. Source 23.1 illustrates an interesting twist on this common feature of a globalized world economy—a Chinese-owned company producing Western-style blue jeans in Lesotho, a small country in southern Africa. The photo on page 1028 shows a parallel phenomenon—the outsourcing of services such as call centers as well as manufacturing.

- Why might China, itself the site of many foreign-owned factories, place such a factory in Africa? What does this suggest about the changing position of China in the world economy? What is the significance of the blue jeans for an understanding of contemporary globalization?

- Does this photograph conform to your image of a sweatshop? Why might many developing countries accept foreign-owned production facilities, despite the criticisms of the working conditions in them?

- Why do you think most of the workers in this photo are women? How might you imagine their motivations for seeking this kind of work? Keep in mind that the unemployment rate in Lesotho in the early twenty-first century was 45 percent.

brianafrica/Alamy

Source 23.1 Globalization and Work

■ What differences can you observe between the workers in this assembly
factory and those in the Indian call center shown on page 1028? Do you
imagine that workers in either setting consider themselves fortunate or
exploited?

If globalization offered employment opportunities—albeit in often-
wretched conditions—to some people in the developing countries, it also
promoted a worldwide culture of consumerism. That culture placed the accumulation of material goods, many of them of Western origin, above older
values of spiritual attainment or social responsibility. Nowhere has this culture of consumerism been more prominent than in China, where the fading
of Maoist communism, the country's massive economic growth, and its new
openness to the wider world combined to generate an unabashed materialism
in the late twentieth and early twenty-first centuries. A popular slogan suggested that life in modern China required the "eight bigs": color TV, refrig-
erator, stereo, camera, motorcycle, a suite of furniture, washing machine, and
an electric fan. Source 23.2 illustrates this culture of consumerism as well as
one of the "eight bigs" in a poster from the post-Mao era. The poster on page
960 in Chapter 21 provides further illustration of Chinese consumerism.

Source 23.2 Globalization and Consumerism

- In what ways might these images be used to illustrate westernization, modernization, globalization, and consumerism?

- How might the young people on the motorcycle understand their own behavior? Do you think they are conscious of behaving in Western ways, or have these ways become Chinese?

- What is the significance of a Chinese couple riding a Suzuki motorcycle, a Japanese product probably manufactured in China under a license agreement?

- Beyond consumerism, how does this poster reflect changes in relationships between men and women in China after Mao? Is this yet another face of globalization, or does it remain a distinctly Western phenomenon?

- How might these images be read as a celebration of Chinese success? How might they be used to criticize contemporary Chinese society?

During the last several decades of the twentieth century, the process of economic globalization spawned various movements of resistance and criticism (see pages 1032–33). In dozens of developing countries, protesters demonstrated or rioted against government policies that removed subsidies, raised prices on essential products, froze salaries, or cut back on social services. Because such policies were often required by the World Bank or the International Monetary Fund as a condition for receiving much-needed loans, protesters often directed their anger at these international financial institutions. Activists in developed and developing countries alike have mounted large-scale protests against what they see as the abuses of unregulated corporate power operating in the world economy.

Source 23.3 shows one such activist in São Paulo, Brazil, during a demonstration in 2013, part of a series of marches and protests against the biotech giant Monsanto that were held in many countries around the world. The sign reads: "A better world according to Monsanto is a world with more cancer." A major producer of herbicides and genetically modified foods, Monsanto had also earlier in its history manufactured a number of highly controversial chemicals such as DDT, PCBs, Agent Orange, and bovine growth hormones. Its insistence on patent rights to some of its products has also generated contentious debate.

- What do the slogans and symbolism of this image reveal about the criticisms of corporate globalization? What political message does it convey?

- To what groups of people might such images be most compelling? How might Monsanto respond to such protesters?

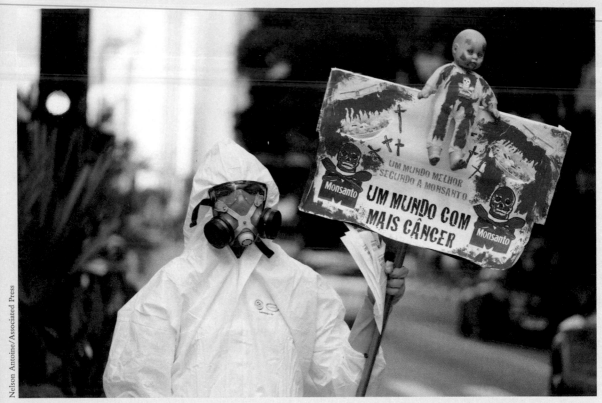

Source 23.3 Globalization and Protest

Among the many faces of globalization, none has grown more rapidly than Internet usage. In 1995, there were about 16 million users of the Internet, representing 0.4 percent of the world's population. By 2014, that number had swelled to almost 3 billion people, or 41 percent of the world's population. That kind of connectivity had profound implications for business, education, religion, social relationships, and politics. Source 23.4 shows a scene from the Arab Spring uprising in Cairo, Egypt, in early 2011 and illustrates the role of Internet-based social media such as Facebook and Twitter in mobilizing support during such protests. The sign around the young man's neck reads: "The age of fear has come to an end." It referred to the regime of longtime dictatorial ruler Hosni Mubarak, which was eventually overthrown in the uprising.

■ How do you think this young man would describe Facebook? How might he see it in relationship to the injustice and fear to which his signs refer?

■ How does his understanding and use of Facebook compare to yours?

Khaled Desouki/AFL/Getty Images

Source 23.4 Globalization and Social Media

- What capacities of the Internet and social media have made them such powerful political tools?

- In what other ways has the Internet transformed life on the planet and your own life?

Beyond politics and economics, globalization has had cultural dimensions as well. Various linguistic, religious, culinary, and artistic traditions have spread globally. Among them is yoga, a mind/body practice from India that has become a part of global culture. Source 23.5 shows a yoga class in a treatment program for teenagers facing homicide and robbery charges in a Mexico City prison in 2013. The instructor is a thirty-eight-year-old former drug dealer.

- Why might yoga be a helpful tool in dealing with young people charged with serious crimes?

- What does the use of yoga in a Mexican prison tell us about the globalization process and the assimilation of foreign practices?

Omar Torres/AFP/Getty Images

Source 23.5 Globalization and Culture

■ The physical postures of yoga were long associated with and often a preparation for spiritual practices such as meditation, leading to a sense of union with the Divine. In what respects has yoga lost its original spiritual function as it has become assimilated into the cultures of many countries?

■ What other cultural patterns from beyond the West have found a place in European and North American life as globalization has unfolded?

Source 23.6, a composite satellite photograph of the world at night taken in late 2000, reflects three aspects of the globalization process. The first is the growing consciousness of the earth as a single place, the common home of humankind. Such thinking has been fostered by and expressed in those many remarkable images of the earth taken from space or from the moon (see the photo on page 1022). In such photographs, no artificial boundaries of state or nation are visible, just a solitary planet cast against the immeasurable vastness of space. Second, this photograph shows the globalization of electricity, a central feature of modern life, which has taken place since the late nineteenth century. Third, and finally, the relative levels of electrification depicted in this image reflect the sharp variations in modern development across the planet as the twenty-first century dawned.

■ To what extent has your thinking about the earth and its inhabitants been shaped by images such as this?

■ Based on the electrification evident in this photo, what does this image show about the economic divisions of the world in the early twenty-first century?

■ Does this image support or contradict the Snapshot on page 1031? What features of this image might you find surprising?

NASA/GSFC Digital Archive

Source 23.6 Globalization: One World or Many?

Faces of Globalization

1. **Defining differences:** Based on these images and the text of Chapter 23, in what different ways have various groups of people experienced globalization since the end of World War II?

2. **Noticing change:** Based on these images as well as those in the text of Chapter 23, in what respects does contemporary globalization differ from that of earlier times? What continuities might you observe? Consider in particular the question of who is influencing whom. Does recent globalization represent largely the impact of the West on the rest of the world, or is it more of a two-way street?

3. **Making assessments:** Opinions about contemporary globalization depend heavily on the position of observers—their class, gender, or national locations. How might you illustrate this statement using the images in this chapter?

4. **Seeking further evidence:** What images might you choose to illustrate visually the various faces of contemporary globalization? What images can you imagine that might be relevant fifty or a hundred years from now?

Multiple-Choice Questions

Use the chart on page 892 and your knowledge of world history to answer questions 1–3.

1. According to the chart, which of the following would be the best date to set the beginning of the global Great Depression?
   a. 1926, when Germany's unemployment rate increased
   b. 1929, when Germany, Great Britain, and the United States saw increases in unemployment
   c. 1932, when unemployment peaked in Germany, Great Britain, and the United States
   d. 1938, when unemployment rose in Great Britain and the United States

2. Which answer below best explains the rapid decrease in Germany's unemployment rate after 1933?
   a. Germany's communist government began its first five-year plan in 1933, investing in sweeping agricultural programs.
   b. Massive foreign aid from the United States revived Germany's economy.
   c. The National Socialist government in Germany began public building projects and increased military spending.
   d. The Weimar government sent all workers from Germany's African and Asian colonies back to their homelands, freeing up jobs for German-born citizens.

3. Which of the following is the most likely explanation for why Great Britain appeared to be less affected by the Great Depression than either Germany or the United States?
   a. Because of its colonies, Great Britain was more able to be self-sufficient in the global economy.
   b. Because it lost millions of men in World War I, Britain's unemployment rate stayed artificially low.
   c. Great Britain experienced a boom-and-bust cycle that was less intense than that of Germany and the United States.
   d. Because its share of the global economy was twice that of the United States and Germany, Great Britain was able to maintain a low unemployment rate.

Short-Answer Question

4. Answer parts A, B, and C.

  A. Briefly explain ONE specific historical example of how a change in state economic policies of the Soviet Union influenced another nation's economic policies in the period 1920–1990.

  B. Briefly explain a SECOND specific historical example of how a change in state economic policies of the Soviet Union influenced the economic policies of a nation other than the one discussed in part A in the period 1920–1990.

  C. Briefly explain ONE specific historical example of how continuity in state economic policies of the Soviet Union influenced another nation's economic policies in the period 1920–1990.

Document-Based Question

Directions: Question 5 refers to the following documents. You will likely need to flip back and forth between these documents to answer the question adequately. Use scrap pieces of paper or sticky notes to tab these documents. When answering the question, refer to the "Advice for Responding to a DBQ" on the inside of the back cover.

5. Using the following documents from this textbook and your knowledge of world history, analyze political, social, and economic themes related to the global wars of the twentieth century: World War I, World War II, and the cold war.

DOCUMENT	PAGE	DOCUMENT NAME
1	880	Military recruiting poster
2	887	Women and the Great War
3	923–25	Adolf Hitler, *Mein Kampf*
4	925–27	*Cardinal Principles of the National Entity of Japan*
5	954–55	The Cuban Revolution

Long-Essay Question

When answering the following question, refer to the "Advice for Responding to an LEQ" on the inside of the back cover.

6. Evaluate the extent to which World War II (1937–1945) marked a turning point in colonialism, analyzing what changed and what stayed the same from the period before the war to the period during and after it.

Notes

Prologue

1. Adapted from Carl Sagan, *The Dragons of Eden* (New York: Random House, 1977), 13–17.
2. See David Christian, *Maps of Time* (Berkeley: University of California Press, 2004).
3. Voltaire, *Treatise on Toleration*, chap. 22.
4. See David Christian, "World History in Context," *Journal of World History* 14, no. 4 (December 2003): 437–58.

Chapter 1

1. Richard Rainsford, "What Chance, the Survival Prospects of East Africa's Last Hunting and Gathering Tribe the Hadzabe, in a Gameless Environment?," Information about Northern Tanzania, March 1997, http://www.ntz.info/gen/n00757.html.
2. What follows comes from Sally McBreatry and Alison S. Brooks, "The Revolution That Wasn't: A New Interpretation of the Origin of Modern Human Behavior," *Journal of Human Evolution* 39 (2000): 453–563.
3. Fred Spier, *Big History and the Future of Humanity* (West Sussex: Wiley-Blackwell, 2011), 132; David Christian, *Maps of Time* (Berkeley: University of California Press, 2004), 143.
4. Richard B. Lee, *The Dobe Ju/'hoansi* (New York: Harcourt Brace, 1993), 58.
5. J. C. Beaglehole, *The Journals of Captain James Cook* (Cambridge: Hakluyt Society, 1968), 1:399.
6. Inga Clendinnen, *Dancing with Strangers* (Cambridge: Cambridge University Press, 2005), 159–67.
7. Steven Pinker, *The Better Angels of Our Nature* (New York: Viking, 2011), 47–52.
8. Marshall Sahlins, *Stone Age Economics* (London: Tavistock, 1972), 1–39.
9. Christopher Ehret, *The Civilizations of Africa* (Charlottesville: University of Virginia Press, 2002), chap. 2.
10. Marija Gimbutas, *The Language of the Goddess* (San Francisco: HarperCollins, 1989), 316–18.
11. Derived from Christian, *Maps of Time*, 208.
12. Neil Roberts, *The Holocene: An Environmental History* (Oxford: Blackwell, 1998), 116.
13. Nina V. Federoff, "Prehistoric GM Corn," *Science* 302 (November 2003): 1158.
14. Theodora Kroeber, *Ishi in Two Worlds* (Berkeley: University of California Press, 1961), 229. See also Karl Kroeber and Clifton Kroeber, *Ishi in Three Centuries* (Lincoln: University of Nebraska Press, 2003).
15. Andrew Sherrat, "The Secondary Exploitation of Animals in the Old World," *World Archeology* 15, no. 1 (1983): 90–104.
16. Tom Standage, *A History of the World in Six Glasses* (New York: Walker and Company, 2005), chaps. 1, 2; Li Zhengping, *Chinese Wine* (Cambridge: Cambridge University Press, 2011), 1–3.
17. Anatoly M. Khazanov, *Nomads and the Outside World* (Madison: University of Wisconsin Press, 1994), 15.
18. Ian Hodder, "Women and Men at Catalhoyuk," *Scientific American* 15, no. 1 (2005): 35–41.
19. Marija Gimbutas, *The Language of the Goddess* (New York: Harper and Row, 1989), xix.
20. "Cultural Information," Jinta Desert Art, accessed October 14, 2014, http://www.jintaart.com.au/culinfo.html.

Chapter 2

1. Bryan Nelson, "Becoming One with Nature," Mother Nature Network, http://www.mnn.com/earth-matters/wilderness-resources/photos/7-people-who-gave-up-on-civilization-to-live-in-the-wild-0.
2. Charles C. Mann, *1491: New Revelations of the Americas before Columbus* (New York: Alfred A. Knopf, 2005), 174–91.
3. Jonathan Mark Kenoyer, *Ancient Cities of the Indus Valley Civilization* (Oxford: Oxford University Press, 1998), 83–84.
4. David Christian, *A History of Russia, Central Asia and Mongolia* (Oxford: Blackwell, 1998), 114.
5. Robert Carneiro, "A Theory of the Origin of the State," *Science* 169 (1970): 733–38.
6. Susan Pollock, *Ancient Mesopotamia* (Cambridge: Cambridge University Press, 1999), 48.
7. *The Epic of Gilgamesh*, translated and edited by Benjamin R. Foster (New York: W. W. Norton, 2001), 10, tablet 1: 226–32.

8. James Legge, trans., *The Chinese Classics* (London: Henry Frowde, 1893), 4:171–72.

9. Margaret Ehrenberg, *Women in Prehistory* (London: British Museum, 1989), 107.

10. Sherry Ortner, "Is Female to Male as Nature Is to Culture?," in *Women, Culture, and Society*, edited by Michelle Rosaldo and Louise Lamphere (Stanford, CA: Stanford University Press, 1974), 67–88.

11. Gerda Lerner, *The Creation of Patriarchy* (New York: Oxford University Press, 1986), 70.

12. Miriam Lichtheim, *Ancient Egyptian Literature* (Berkeley: University of California Press, 1975), 2:168–75.

13. Steven Pinker, *The Better Angels of Our Nature* (New York: Viking, 2011), chaps. 2, 3.

14. Hammurabi, *The Code of Hammurabi King of Babylon . . .* by Robert Francis Harper (Chicago: University of Chicago Press, 1904), http://oll.libertyfund.org/titles /1276#Harper_0762_26.

15. Adolf Erman, *The Literature of the Ancient Egyptians*, translated by Aylward M. Blackman (London: Methuen, 1927), 136–37.

16. Henri Frankfort et al., *Before Philosophy: The Intellectual Adventure of Ancient Man* (Baltimore: Penguin Books, 1963), 39, 138.

17. Quoted in Peter Stearns et al., *World Civilizations* (New York: Longman, 1996), 1:30.

18. See Clive Ponting, *A Green History of the World* (New York: St. Martin's Press, 1991), chap. 5.

19. K. J. W. Oosthoek, "The Role of Wood in World History," Environmental History Resources, 1998, http://www .eh-resources.org/wood.html#_ednrefl.

20. Pascal Vernus, *Affairs and Scandals in Ancient Egypt* (Ithaca, NY: Cornell University Press, 2003), 70–86; Toby Wilkinson, *Lives of the Ancient Egyptians* (London: Thames and Hudson, 2007), 259–61.

21. James B. Pritchard, ed., *Ancient Near Eastern Texts Relating to the Old Testament* (Princeton, NJ: Princeton University Press, 1969), 647–48.

22. Lichtheim, *Ancient Egyptian Literature*, 1:25–27.

23. M. J. Rowlands et al., eds., *Center and Periphery in the Ancient World* (Cambridge: Cambridge University Press, 1987), 59.

24. Marvin Harris, ed., *Cannibals and Kings* (New York: Vintage, 1978), 102.

25. Jonathan M. Kenoyer, *Ancient Cities of the Indus Valley Civilization* (Karachi: Oxford University Press, 1998), 84.

26. Ibid., 100.

27. Gregory L. Possehl, *The Indus Civilization: A Contemporary Perspective* (Walnut Creek, CA: AltaMira Press, 2002), 114.

Part Two

1. Data from Stephen K. Sanderson, *Social Transformation* (Oxford: Blackwell, 1995), 103.

2. Colin Ronan and Joseph Needham, *The Shorter Science and Civilization in China* (Cambridge: Cambridge University Press, 1978), 58.

3. William H. McNeill, *Plagues and Peoples* (New York: Doubleday, 1977), 94.

Chapter 3

1. Cullen Murphy, *Are We Rome? The Fall of an Empire and the Fate of America* (Boston: Houghton Mifflin, 2007).

2. J. M. Cook, *The Persian Empire* (London: J. M. Dent & Sons, 1983), 76.

3. George Rawlinson, trans., *The Histories of Herodotus* (London: Dent, 1910), 1:131–40.

4. Erich F. Schmidt, *Persepolis I: Structures, Reliefs, Inscriptions*, OIP 68 (Chicago: University of Chicago Press, 1953), 63.

5. Quoted in Anthony N. Penna, *The Human Footprint* (Oxford: Wiley-Blackwell, 2010), 151.

6. Quoted in Thomas R. Martin, *Ancient Greece from Prehistoric to Hellenistic Times* (New Haven, CT: Yale University Press, 1996), 86.

7. Christian Meier, *Athens* (New York: Metropolitan Books, 1993), 93.

8. Arrian, *The Campaigns of Alexander*, translated by Aubrey de Selincourt, revised by J. R. Hamilton (London: Penguin, 1971), 395–96.

9. Stanley Burstein, *The Hellenistic Period in World History* (Washington, DC: American Historical Association, 1996), 12.

10. Norman F. Cantor, *Antiquity* (New York: HarperCollins, 2003), 25.

11. Paul Halsall, "Early Western Civilization under the Sign of Gender," in *A Companion to Gender History*, edited by Teresa A. Meade and Merry E. Wiesner-Hanks (London: Blackwell, 2004), 293–94.

12. Aelius Aristides, *The Complete Works*, vol. 2, translated by P. Charles A. Behr (Leiden: E. J. Brill, 1986), 73–97.

13. Keith W. Taylor, *The Birth of Vietnam* (Berkeley: University of California Press, 1983), 334.

14. See Robert Marks, *China: Its Environment and History* (Lanham, MD: Rowman and Littlefield, 2012), chap. 3.

15. Craig Benjamin, "The Kushans in World History," *World History Bulletin* 25, no. 1 (Spring 2009): 30. This feature is derived largely from this article.

16. S. A. M. Adshead, *China in World History* (London: Macmillan Press, 1988), 4–21.

17. See Padma Manian, "Harappans and Aryans: Old and New Perspectives on Ancient Indian History," *History Teacher* 32, no. 1 (1998): 17–32.

18. Roger Boesche, *The First Great Political Realist: Kautilya and His Arthashastra* (Lanham, MD: Lexington Books, 2002), 17.

19. Stanley Wolpert, *A New History of India* (New York: Oxford University Press, 1993), 90.

20. Zhengyuan Fu, *Autocratic Tradition and Chinese Politics* (New York: Cambridge University Press, 1993), 188.

Chapter 4

1. "Birthday of Confucius . . . ," China View, September 28, 2009, http://news.xinhuanet.com/english/2009-09/28/content_12123115.htm.

2. S. N. Eisenstadt, ed., *The Origins and Diversity of Axial Age Civilizations* (Albany: SUNY Press, 1986), 1–4; Karen Armstrong, *The Great Transformation* (New York: Alfred A. Knopf, 2006).

3. Quoted in Arthur Waley, *Three Ways of Thought in Ancient China* (Garden City, NY: Doubleday, 1956), 159–60.

4. Nancy Lee Swann, trans., *Pan Chao: Foremost Woman Scholar of China* (New York: Century, 1932), 111–14.

5. Kam Louie and Morris Low, *Asian Masculinities* (London: Routledge, 2003), 3–6.

6. Quoted in Huston Smith, *The Illustrated World's Religions* (San Francisco: HarperCollins, 1994), 123.

7. Robert Marks, *China: Its Environment and History* (Lanham, MD: Rowman and Littlefield, 2012), 94–95.

8. Sam Hamill, trans., in *The Enlightened Heart*, edited by Stephen Mitchell (New York: Harper and Row, 1989), 32.

9. Lao-tzu, *Tao Te Ching,* translated by James Legge, in *Sacred Books of the East*, vol. 39 (Oxford: The Clarendon Press, 1891), 122.

10. Catherine Clay et al., *Envisioning Women in World History* (New York: McGraw-Hill, 2009), 1:67–77.

11. Quoted in Karen Andrews, "Women in Theravada Buddhism," Institute of Buddhist Studies, accessed February 19, 2012, http://www.enabling.org/ia/vipassana/Archive/A/Andrews/womenTheraBudAndrews.html.

12. Li Rongxi, trans., *A Biography of the Tripitaka Master of the Great Ci'en Monastery of the Great Tang Dynasty* (Berkeley, CA: Numata Center for Buddhist Translation, 1995), 89–90, 94–95.

13. Quoted in "Seminar on Nalanda Tradition of Buddhism in Asia as Inaugurated by His Holiness the Dalai Lama," His Holiness, the 14th Dalai Lama of Tibet, November 14, 2013, http://www.dalailama.com/news/post/1029-seminar-on-nalanda-tradition-of-buddhism-in-asia-inaugurated-by-his-holiness-the-dalai-lama.

14. A. L. Basham, *The Wonder That Was India* (London: Sidgwick and Jackson, 1967), 309.

15. S. A. Nigosian, *The Zoroastrian Faith: Tradition and Modern Research* (Montreal: McGill–Queen's University Press, 1993), 95–97.

16. Isaiah 1:11–17.

17. Plato, *Apologia*, translated by Benjamin Jowett (1891).

18. Hippocrates, *On the Sacred Disease*, translated by Francis Adams, Internet Classics Archive, accessed February 2, 2012, http://classics.mit.edu/Hippocrates/sacred.html.

19. Thanissaro Bhikkhu, trans., "Karaniya Metta Sutta: Good Will," 2004, http://www.accesstoinsight.org/tipitaka/kn/snp/snp.1.08.than.html.

20. Matthew 5:43–44.

21. See Marcus Borg, ed., *Jesus and Buddha: The Parallel Sayings* (Berkeley, CA: Ulysses Press, 1997).

22. Galatians 3:28.

23. Cynthia Bourgeault, *The Meaning of Mary Magdalene* (Boston: Shambala, 2010).

24. Ephesians 5:22–23; 1 Corinthians 14:35.

25. Peter Brown, *The Rise of Western Christendom* (London: Blackwell, 2003), 69–71.

26. "The Martyrdom of Saints Perpetua and Felicitas," *Frontline*, "From Jesus to Christ," PBS, April 1998, http://www.pbs.org/wgbh/pages/frontline/shows/religion/maps/primary/perpetua.html.

27. Robert Sider, "Early Christians in North Africa," *Coptic Church Review* 19, no. 3 (1998): 2.

28. Quoted in Mary Ann Rossi, "Priesthood, Precedent, and Prejudice: On Recovering the Women Priests of Early Christianity," *Journal of Feminist Studies* 7, no. 1 (1991): 73–94.

29. Chai-Shin Yu, *Early Buddhism and Christianity* (Delhi: Motilal Banarsidass, 1981), 211.

30. "Footprints of the Buddha," Internet Sacred Text Archive, accessed February 2, 2012, http://www.sacred-texts.com/shi/igj/igj09.htm.

Chapter 5

1. Quoted in Lydia Polgreen, "Business Class Rises in Ashes of Caste System," *New York Times*, September 10, 2010.

2. Po Chu-I, "After Passing the Examination," in *More Translations from the Chinese*, by Arthur Waley (New York: Alfred A. Knopf, 1919), 37.

3. Quoted in Michael Lowe, *Everyday Life in Early Imperial China* (New York: Dorset, 1968), 38.

4. "Ge Hong's Autobiography," in *Chinese Civilization*, 2nd ed., edited by Patricia Buckley Ebrey (New York: Free Press, 1993), 91–96; Keith Knapp, "Ge Hong," *Internet Encyclopedia of Philosophy*, 2005, http://www.iep.utm.edu/gehong/.

5. Robert Ford Campany, *To Live as Long as Heaven and Earth* (Berkeley: University of California Press, 2002), 91–96.

6. Li Shen, "Old Style," Selected Poems from T'ang Dynasty, accessed May 15, 2014, http://www.shigeku .org/xlib/lingshidao/hanshi/tang1.htm.

7. Orlando Patterson, *Slavery and Social Death* (Cambridge, MA: Harvard University Press, 1982).

8. A. L. Basham, *The Wonder That Was India* (London: Sidgwick and Jackson, 1967), 152.

9. Sarah Pomeroy et al., *Ancient Greece* (New York: Oxford University Press, 1999), 63, 239.

10. R. Zelnick-Abramovitz, *Not Wholly Free* (Leiden: Brill, 2005), 337, 343.

11. Keith Bradley, *Slavery and Society at Rome* (Cambridge: Cambridge University Press, 1994), 30.

12. 1 Peter 2:18.

13. Milton Meltzer, *Slavery: A World History* (New York: Da Capo Press, 1993), 189.

14. Quoted in Brent D. Shaw, *Spartacus and the Slave Wars: A Brief History with Documents* (Boston: Bedford/St. Martin's, 2001), 145.

15. Quoted ibid., 143.

16. Judith Bennett, *History Matters: Patriarchy and the Challenge of Feminism* (Philadelphia: University of Pennsylvania Press, 2006), chap. 4.

17. Quoted in Bret Hinsch, *Women in Early Imperial China* (Oxford: Rowman and Littlefield, 2002), 155.

18. Nancy Lee Swann, trans., *Pan Chao: Foremost Woman Scholar of China* (New York: Century, 1932), 111–14.

19. Quoted in Valerie Hansen, *The Open Empire* (New York: Norton, 2000), 183–84; see also Thomas Barfield, *The Perilous Frontier* (Cambridge: Blackwell, 1989), 140.

20. Aristotle, *Politica*, translated by H. Rackham, Loeb Classical Library, no. 264 (Cambridge, MA: Harvard University Press, 1932), 1254b10–14.

21. Quoted in Pomeroy et al., *Ancient Greece*, 146.

22. Quoted in "The Destruction of Pompeii, 79 AD," EyeWitness to History, 1999, www.eyewitnesstohistory .com/pompeii.htm.

23. August Mau, *Pompeii: Its Life and Art* (New Rochelle, NY: Caratzas Bros., 1982), 16.

24. "Graffiti from Pompeii," Pompeiana.org, accessed February 2, 2012, http://www.pompeiana.org/Resources /Ancient/Graffiti%20from%20Pompeii.htm.

Chapter 6

1. Quoted in "Morales Becomes Head of a Pluri-national State Blessed by Aymara Gods," *MercoPress*, January 22, 2010, http://en.mercopress.com/2010/01/22/morales -becomes-head-of-a-pluri-national-state-blessed-by -aymara-gods.

2. Population figures through 1750 are taken from Paul Adams et al., *Experiencing World History* (New York: New York University Press, 2000), 334; 2013 figures derive from "World Population by Region," Worldometers, accessed November 19, 2014, http://www.worldometers .info/world-population/#region.

3. "The Stela of Piye," accessed February 3, 2012, http:// wysinger.homestead.com/piyevictorystela.html.

4. Toby Wilkinson, *Lives of the Ancient Egyptians* (London: Thames and Hudson, 2007), 287.

5. Roderick J. McIntosh, *Ancient Middle Niger* (Cambridge: Cambridge University Press, 2005), 10.

6. Roderick J. McIntosh, *The Peoples of the Middle Niger* (Oxford: Blackwell, 1998), 1776.

7. Richard E. W. Adams, *Ancient Civilizations of the New World* (Boulder, CO: Westview Press, 1997), 53–56; T. Patrick Culbert, "The New Maya," *Archeology* 51, no. 5 (1998): 47–51.

8. Esther Pasztory, *Teotihuacán: An Experiment in Living* (Norman: University of Oklahoma Press, 1997), 193.

9. George L. Cowgill, "The Central Mexican Highlands . . . ," in *The Cambridge History of the Native Peoples of the Americas*, vol. 2, pt. 1, "Mesoamerica," edited by Richard E. W. Adams and Murdo J. MacLeod (Cambridge: Cambridge University Press, 2000), 289.

10. Gordon F. McEwan, *The Inca: New Perspectives* (New York: W. W. Norton, 2008), 39–41.

11. Scott Norris, "Mummy of Tattooed Woman Discovered in Peru Pyramid," *National Geographic News*, May 16, 2006, http://news.nationalgeographic.com/news/2006 /05/mummy-peru.html.

12. Christopher Ehret, *The Civilizations of Africa* (Charlottes- ville: University of Virginia Press, 2002), 175.

13. David Schoenbrun, "Gendered Themes in Early African History," in *A Companion to Gender History*, edited by Teresa Meade and Merry Wiesner-Hanks (Oxford: Blackwell, 2004), 253–56.

14. See Jan Vansina, *Paths in the Rainforest* (Madison: University of Wisconsin Press, 1990), 95–99.

15. Much of this section draws on Brian M. Fagan, *Ancient North America* (London: Thames and Hudson, 2005), chaps. 14, 15. The quote is from page 345.

16. David Hurst Thomas, *Exploring Ancient Native America* (New York: Routledge, 1999), 137–42.

17. Fagan, *Ancient North America*, 475.

18. Quoted in Lynda Norene Shaffer, *Native Americans before 1492* (Armonk, NY: M. E. Sharpe, 1992), 70.

19. Steven R. Fischer, *A History of the Pacific Islands* (New York: Palgrave Macmillan, 2013), 37. This section draws heavily on Fischer, chaps. 1, 2; Ian Campbell, *Worlds Apart* (Cambridge: Cambridge University Press,

2011), chaps. 1, 2; and Matt K. Matsuda, *Pacific Worlds* (Cambridge: Cambridge University Press, 2012), chaps. 1, 2.

20. Campbell, *Worlds Apart*, 48.

21. Terry L. Hunt, "Rethinking the Fall of Easter Island," *American Scientist* 94, no. 5 (September/October 2006), 412–19.

22. See Stanley Burstein, *Ancient African Civilizations: Kush and Axum* (Princeton, NJ: Markus Weiner, 1998), 14–20. I am grateful to Professor Burstein and this book for references to many of the documents in this section.

Part Three

1. Marshall G. S. Hodgson, *The Venture of Islam* (Chicago: University of Chicago Press, 1974), 1:71.

Chapter 7

1. Nayan Chanda, *Bound Together* (New Haven, CT: Yale University Press, 2007), 35–36.

2. William J. Bernstein, *A Splendid Exchange* (New York: Grove Press, 2008), 58–66; Proverbs 7:17–18.

3. Quoted in Patricia Buckley Ebrey, *The Inner Quarters* (Berkeley: University of California Press, 1993), 150.

4. Seneca the Younger, *Declamations*, vol. 1.

5. Liu Xinru, "Silks and Religion in Eurasia, A.D. 600–1200," *Journal of World History* 6, no. 1 (1995): 25–48.

6. Boccaccio, *The Decameron*, translated by M. Rigg (London: David Campbell, 1921), 1:5–11.

7. Kenneth McPherson, *The Indian Ocean* (Oxford: Oxford University Press, 1993), 15.

8. Janet L. Abu-Lughod, *Before European Hegemony* (Oxford: Oxford University Press, 1989), 269.

9. Quoted in Stanley M. Burstein, "State Formation in Ancient Northeast Africa and the Indian Ocean Trade," History Cooperative Conference Proceedings, 2001, http://webdoc.sub.gwdg.de/ebook/p/2005/history_cooperative/www.historycooperative.org/proceedings/interactions/burstein.html.

10. McPherson, *Indian Ocean*, 97.

11. This section draws heavily on Craig A. Lockard, *Southeast Asia in World History* (Oxford: Oxford University Press, 2009), chaps. 2, 3. See also Victor Lieberman, *Strange Parallels* (Cambridge: Cambridge University Press, 2009), chaps. 1, 7.

12. Kenneth R. Hall, *Maritime Trade and State Development in Early Southeast Asia* (Honolulu: University of Hawaii Press, 1985), 101.

13. M. C. Horton and T. R. Burton, "Indian Metalwork in East Africa: The Bronze Lion Statuette from Shanga," *Antiquities* 62 (1988): 22.

14. Ross Dunn, *The Adventures of Ibn Battuta* (Berkeley: University of California Press, 1986), 124.

15. Christopher Ehret, *The Civilizations of Africa* (Charlottesville: University of Virginia Press, 2002), 255.

16. Richard W. Bulliet, *The Camel and the Wheel* (New York: Columbia University Press, 1990), 8. This feature largely derives from this book.

17. Nehemia Levtzion and Jay Spaulding, eds., *Medieval West Africa: Views from Arab Scholars and Merchants* (Princeton, NJ: Marcus Wiener, 2003), 5.

18. David Schoenbrun, "Gendered Themes in Early African History," in *A Companion to Gender History*, edited by Teresa Meade and Merry Wiesner-Hanks (Oxford: Blackwell, 2004), 263.

19. Quoted in John Iliffe, *Africans: The History of a Continent* (Cambridge: Cambridge University Press, 1995), 75–76.

20. "The Saga of Eric the Red" and "The Saga of Thorfinn Karlsefne" in *The Norse Discovery of America*, translated by Arthur Reeves et al. (London: Norroena Society, 1906), http://www.sacred-texts.com/neu/nda/index.htm.

21. J. R. McNeill and William McNeill, *The Human Web* (New York: W. W. Norton, 2003), 160.

22. Caroline Roullier et al., "Historical Collections Reveal Patterns of Diffusion of Sweet Potato in Oceania . . . ," *Proceedings of the National Academy of Sciences*, January 22, 2013, http://www.pnas.org/content/110/6/2205.full.

23. Li Rongxi, trans., *A Biography of the Tripitaka Master of the Great Ci'en Monastery of the Great Tang Dynasty* (Berkeley, CA: Numata Center for Buddhist Translation, 1995), 31.

Chapter 8

1. *Guardian*, June 15, 2006.

2. Quoted in Mark Elvin, *The Retreat of the Elephants* (New Haven, CT: Yale University Press, 2004), 19.

3. Mark Elvin, *The Pattern of the Chinese Past* (London: Eyre Methuen, 1973), 55.

4. Samuel Adshead, *Tang China: The Rise of the East in World History* (New York: Palgrave, 2004), 30.

5. William McNeill, *The Pursuit of Power* (Chicago: University of Chicago Press, 1984), 50.

6. See "The Attractions of the Capital," in *Chinese Civilization: A Sourcebook*, edited by Patricia Buckley Ebrey (New York: Free Press, 1993), 178–85.

7. Marco Polo, *The Travels of Marco Polo*, translated by Henry Yule (Toronto: General, 1993), 2:185.

8. Jack Kelly, *Gunpowder: Alchemy, Bombards, and Pyrotechnics: The History of the Explosive That Changed the World* (New York: Basic Books, 2005), 4. Much of this feature is derived from this book.

9. John K. Fairbank, *China: A New History* (Cambridge, MA: Harvard University Press, 1992), 89.

10. J. R. McNeill and William H. McNeill, *The Human Web* (New York: W. W. Norton, 2003), 123.

11. Quoted in Francesca Bray, *Technology and Gender: Fabrics of Power in Late Imperial China* (Berkeley: University of California Press, 1997), 116.

12. Patricia Buckley Ebrey, *The Inner Quarters* (Berkeley: University of California Press, 1993), 207.

13. Ibid., 37–43.

14. Ibid., 6.

15. Quoted in Thomas J. Barfield, "Steppe Empires, China, and the Silk Route," in *Nomads in the Sedentary World*, edited by Anatoly M. Khazanov and Andre Wink (Richmond: Kurzon Press, 2001), 237.

16. Quoted in Edward H. Shafer, *The Golden Peaches of Samarkand* (Berkeley: University of California Press, 1963), 28.

17. Susan Mann, "Women in East Asia," in *Women's History in Global Perspective*, edited by Bonnie Smith (Urbana: University of Illinois Press, 2005), 2:53–56.

18. Quoted in McNeill, *Pursuit of Power*, 40.

19. John K. Fairbank et al., *East Asia: Tradition and Transformation* (Boston: Houghton Mifflin, 1978), 353.

20. Quoted in Jane Hirshfield, trans., *The Ink Dark Moon* (New York: Vintage Books, 1990), xiii.

21. Edwin A. Cranston, trans., *The Izumi Shikibu Diary* (Cambridge, MA: Harvard University Press, 1969), 11.

22. Hirshfield, *Ink Dark Moon*, 94, 148.

23. Quoted in Earl Miner, *Japanese Poetic Diaries* (Berkeley: University of California Press, 1969), 33.

24. Cranston, *Izumi Shikibu Diary*, 18, 206.

25. Hirshfield, *Ink Dark Moon*, 49, 65, 96, 139.

26. Chieko Irie Mulhern, ed., *Japanese Women Writers* (Westport, CT: Greenwood Press, 1994), 155.

27. Arnold Pacey, *Technology in World Civilization* (Cambridge, MA: MIT Press, 1991), 50–53.

28. Compiled from Joseph Needham, *Science and Civilization in China* (Cambridge: Cambridge University Press, 1965), 1:242; and Robert Temple, *The Genius of China* (New York: Simon and Schuster, 1986).

29. McNeill, *Pursuit of Power*, 24–25.

30. Quoted in Arthur F. Wright, *Studies in Chinese Buddhism* (New Haven, CT: Yale University Press, 1990), 16.

31. Arthur F. Wright, *Buddhism in Chinese History* (Stanford, CA: Stanford University Press, 1959), 36–39.

32. Quoted ibid., 67.

33. Quoted in Eric Zurcher, *The Buddhist Conquest of China* (Leiden: E. J. Brill, 1959), 1:262.

34. Quoted in Robert Marks, *China: Its Environment and History* (Lanham, MD: Rowman and Littlefield, 2012), location 2963-64.

35. Edwin O. Reischauer, *Ennin's Travels in Tang China* (New York: Ronald Press, 1955), 221–24.

36. Quoted in "Jake Holman's Selection of Favourite Chinese Poems," China History Forum, accessed

October 17, 2014, http://www.chinahistoryforum.com/index.php?showtopic=17789&st=30&start=30.

Chapter 9

1. "Religion in Sierra Leone," *The Economist*, May 31, 2014.

2. Reza Aslan, *No God but God* (New York: Random House, 2005), 14.

3. Quoted in Karen Armstrong, *A History of God* (New York: Ballantine Books, 1993), 146.

4. Quran 1:5 and 41:53.

5. Ibid., 3:110.

6. Ibid., 9:71.

7. "Prophet Muhammad's Farewell Sermon," IslamiCity, accessed November 28, 2014, http://www.islamicity.com/articles/Articles.asp?ref=ic0107-322.

8. Quoted in Fred M. Donner, *Muhammad and the Believers* (Cambridge, MA: Harvard University Press, 2010), 114. The preceding section draws on chapter 3.

9. Richard Bulliet, *Conversion to Islam in the Medieval Period* (Cambridge, MA: Harvard University Press, 1979), 33.

10. Quoted in Bertold Spuler, *The Muslim World*, vol. 1, *The Age of the Caliph* (Leiden: E. J. Brill, 1960), 29.

11. Bernard Lewis, *Islam and the West* (New York: Oxford University Press, 1993), 157.

12. Quoted in Patricia Crone, "The Rise of Islam in the World," in *Cambridge Illustrated History of the Islamic World*, edited by Francis Robinson (Cambridge: Cambridge University Press, 1996), 14.

13. Many of these stories are summarized from accounts in Imam Jamal Rahman, *Sacred Laughter of the Sufis* (Woodstock, VT: Skylight Paths, 2014).

14. Aslan, *No God but God*, 201.

15. Quran 33:35.

16. Ibid., 4:34.

17. Quoted in Judith Tucker, "Gender and Islamic History," in *Islamic and European Expansion*, edited by Michael Adas (Philadelphia: Temple University Press, 1993), 46.

18. Nikki R. Keddie, "Women in the Middle East since the Rise of Islam," in *Women's History in Global Perspective*, edited by Bonnie G. Smith (Urbana: University of Illinois Press, 2005), 74–75.

19. Ria Kloppenborg and Wouter Hanegraaf, eds., *Female Stereotypes in Religious Traditions* (Leiden: E. J. Brill, 1995), 111.

20. Quoted in William T. de Bary, ed., *Sources of Indian Tradition* (New York: Columbia University Press, 1958), 2:355–57.

21. Quoted in Keddie, "Women in the Middle East," 81.

22. Ross Dunn, *The Adventures of Ibn Battuta* (Berkeley: University of California Press, 1986), 300.

23. Jane I. Smith, "Islam and Christendom," in *The Oxford History of Islam*, edited by John L. Esposito (Oxford: Oxford University Press, 1999), 317–21.

24. Al-Umari, "The Kingdoms of the Muslim Sudan," in *Medieval West Africa*, edited by Nehemia Levtzion and Jay Spaulding (Princeton, NJ: Markus Weiner, 2003), 60.

25. Marq de Villieres and Sheila Hirtle, *Timbuktu* (New York: Walker, 2007), 77.

26. Al-Umari, "Kingdoms of the Muslim Sudan," 59.

27. Ibid.

28. Richard Eaton, "Islamic History as Global History," in Adas, *Islamic and European Expansion*, 12.

29. Francis Robinson, "Knowledge, Its Transmission and the Making of Muslim Societies," in Robinson, *Cambridge Illustrated History of the Islamic World*, 230.

30. Ibid., 215.

31. Lohoucine Ouzgan, ed., *Islamic Masculinities* (London: Zed Books, 2006), 57–59.

32. Oleg Grabar, *Mostly Miniatures: An Introduction to Persian Painting* (Princeton, NJ: Princeton University Press, 2000), 2.

33. Biographical details about the life of Muhammad derive largely from Karen Armstrong, *Muhammad: A Biography of the Prophet* (New York: HarperCollins, 1992).

Chapter 10

1. Louisa Lim, "In the Land of Mao, a Rising Tide of Christianity," *All Things Considered*, NPR, July 19, 2010, http://www.npr.org/templates/story/story.php?storyId=128546334.

2. This section relies heavily on Diarmaid MacCulloch, *Christianity: The First Three Thousand Years* (New York: Viking, 2010), chap. 8.

3. Oleg Grabar, "The Umayyad Dome of the Rock in Jerusalem," in *Late Antique and Medieval Art of the Mediterranean World*, edited by Eva R. Hoffman (London: John Wiley and Sons, 2007), 166.

4. Quoted in Roger Boase, ed., *Islam and Global Dialogue* (Burlington, VT: Ashgate, 2005), 95.

5. Quoted in Ray Riegert and Thomas Moore, eds., *The Lost Sutras of Jesus* (Berkeley, CA: Ulysses Press, 2006), 103.

6. Leonora Neville, *Authority in Byzantine Provincial Society, 950–1100* (Cambridge: Cambridge University Press, 2004), 2.

7. Quoted in Deno John Geanakoplos, *Byzantium: Church, Society, and Civilization Seen through Contemporary Eyes* (Chicago: University of Chicago Press, 1984), 389.

8. Quoted ibid., 143.

9. Quoted in A. A. Vasiliev, *History of the Byzantine Empire* (Madison: University of Wisconsin Press, 1978), 79–80.

10. Quoted in Geanakoplos, *Byzantium*, 362.

11. Quoted ibid., 369.

12. "Russian Primary Chronicle," in Daniel H. Kaiser and Gary Marker, *Reinterpreting Russian History* (Oxford: Oxford University Press, 1994), 63–67.

13. Quoted in Patrick J. Geary, *Before France and Germany* (New York: Oxford University Press, 1988), 79.

14. Quoted in Stephen Williams, *Diocletian and the Roman Recovery* (London: Routledge, 1996), 218.

15. Peter Brown, *The Rise of Western Christendom* (London: Blackwell, 1996), 305.

16. Quoted in John M. Hobson, *The Eastern Origins of Western Civilization* (New York: Cambridge University Press, 2004), 113.

17. Clive Ponting, *A Green History of the World* (New York: St. Martin's, 1991), 121–23.

18. Quoted in Richard C. Hoffman, "Economic Development and Aquatic Ecosystems in Medieval Europe," *American Historical Review* 101, no. 3 (1996): 648.

19. Judith M. Bennett, *A Medieval Life* (Boston: McGraw-Hill, 1998).

20. Bonnie Anderson and Judith Zinsser, *A History of Their Own* (Oxford: Oxford University Press, 2000), 1:210.

21. Ibid., 1:393–94.

22. Christopher Tyerman, *Fighting for Christendom: Holy Wars and the Crusades* (Oxford: Oxford University Press, 2004), 16.

23. Quoted in Elizabeth Hallam, *Chronicles of the Crusades* (New York: Welcome Rain, 2000), 127.

24. Quoted in Peter Watson, *Ideas* (New York: Harper, 2006), 319.

25. Quoted in Jean Gimple, *The Medieval Machine* (New York: Holt, 1976), 178.

26. Quoted in Stuart B. Schwartz, ed., *Victors and Vanquished* (Boston: Bedford/St. Martin's, 2000), 147.

27. Quoted in Carlo Cipolla, *Before the Industrial Revolution* (New York: Norton, 1976), 207.

28. Quoted in S. Lilley, *Men, Machines, and History* (New York: International, 1965), 62.

29. See Toby Huff, *The Rise of Early Modern Science* (Cambridge: Cambridge University Press, 1993).

30. Quoted in Edward Grant, *Science and Religion from Aristotle to Copernicus* (Westport, CT: Greenwood Press, 2004), 158.

31. Quoted in L. Thorndike, *A History of Magic and Experimental Science* (New York: Columbia University Press, 1923), 2:58.

32. Quoted in Edward Grant, *God and Reason in the Middle Ages* (Cambridge: Cambridge University Press, 2001), 70.

33. Quoted in Grant, *Science and Religion*, 228–29.

34. Marcia L. Colish, *Medieval Foundations of the Western Intellectual Tradition* (New Haven, CT: Yale University Press, 1997), 128.

Chapter 11

1. All data derived from Thomas J. Barfield, "Pastoral Nomadic Societies," in *Berkshire Encyclopedia of World History* (Great Barrington, MA: Berkshire, 2005), 4:1432–37.
2. Giovanni Carpini, *The Story of the Mongols*, translated by Erik Hildinger (Boston: Braden, 1996), 54.
3. Quoted in Peter B. Golden, "Nomads and Sedentary Societies in Eurasia," in *Agricultural and Pastoral Societies in Ancient and Classical History*, edited by Michael Adas (Philadelphia: Temple University Press, 2001), 73.
4. Anatoly Khazanov, "The Spread of World Religions in Medieval Nomadic Societies of the Eurasian Steppes," in *Nomadic Diplomacy, Destruction and Religion from the Pacific to the Adriatic*, edited by Michael Gervers and Wayne Schlepp (Toronto: Joint Center for Asia Pacific Studies, 1994), 11.
5. Quoted in J. Otto Maenchen-Helfer, *The World of the Huns* (Berkeley: University of California Press, 1973), 14.
6. Carter Finley, *The Turks in World History* (Oxford: Oxford University Press, 2005), 28–37.
7. Ibid., 40.
8. David Christian, *A History of Russia, Central Asia, and Mongolia* (London: Blackwell, 1998), 1:385.
9. Quoted ibid., 389.
10. Jack Weatherford, *Genghis Khan and the Making of the Modern World* (New York: Crown, 2004), 86.
11. Chinggis Khan, "Letter to Changchun," in E. Bretschneider, *Mediaeval Researches from Eastern Asiatic Sources*, vol. 1 (London: Kegan, Paul, Trench, Trübner, 1875), 37–39.
12. Thomas T. Allsen, *Mongol Imperialism* (Berkeley: University of California Press, 1987), 6.
13. Chinggis Khan, "Letter to Changchun," 38.
14. Stephen Turnbull, *The Mongol Invasions of Japan, 1274 and 1281* (Oxford: Osprey Publishing, 2010). This feature is derived largely from this book.
15. Quoted in Weatherford, *Genghis Khan*, 111.
16. Thomas J. Barfield, *The Nomadic Alternative* (Englewood Cliffs, NJ: Prentice Hall, 1993), 166.
17. Quoted in Christian, *History of Russia*, 1:425.
18. Quoted in David Morgan, *Medieval Persia* (London: Longman, 1988), 79.
19. Morgan, *Medieval Persia*, 82.
20. Guity Nashat, "Women in the Middle East," in *A Companion to Gender History*, edited by Teresa A. Meade and Merry E. Wiesner-Hanks (London: Blackwell, 2004), 243.
21. This feature is based on Jack Weatherford, *The Secret History of the Mongol Queens* (New York: Random House, 2010), 116–26, 274.
22. Charles J. Halperin, *Russia and the Golden Horde* (Bloomington: Indiana University Press, 1985), 126.
23. Charles H. Halperin, "Russia in the Mongol Empire in Comparative Perspective," *Harvard Journal of Asiatic Studies* 43, no. 1 (1983). 261.
24. Quoted in Christopher Dawson, *Mission to Asia* (New York: Harper and Row, 1966), 83–84.
25. Thomas Allsen, *Culture and Conquest in Mongol Eurasia* (Cambridge: Cambridge University Press, 2001), 211.
26. Quoted ibid., 121.
27. John Aberth, *The First Horseman: Disease in Human History* (Upper Saddle River, NJ: Pearson/Prentice Hall, 2007), 18.
28. Quoted in John Aberth, *The Black Death: The Great Mortality of 1348–1350* (Boston: Bedford/St. Martin's, 2005), 84–85.
29. Michael Dols, *The Black Death in the Middle East* (Princeton, NJ: Princeton University Press, 1977), 212, 223.
30. Quoted in John Aberth, *A Knight at the Movies: Medieval History on Film* (New York: Routledge, 2003), 225.
31. Quoted in Aberth, *Black Death*, 72.
32. Quoted in Dols, *Black Death in the Middle East*, 67.
33. Andre Gunder Frank, *ReOrient: Global Economy in the Asian Age* (Berkeley: University of California Press, 1998), 256.
34. Arnold Pacey, *Technology in World Civilization* (Cambridge, MA: MIT Press, 1990), 62.
35. Quoted in Golden, "Nomads and Sedentary Societies," 72–73.
36. Quoted in Gregory Guzman, "Were the Barbarians a Negative or Positive Factor in Ancient and Medieval History?" *Historian* 50 (August 1988): 558–72.
37. Quoted in Barfield, *Nomadic Alternative*, 3.

Chapter 12

1. Winona LaDuke, "We Are Still Here: The 500 Year Celebration," *Sojourners*, October 1991.
2. Brian Fagan, *Ancient North America* (London: Thames and Hudson, 2005), 503.
3. Quoted in Charles C. Mann, *1491: New Revelations of the Americas before Columbus* (New York: Alfred A. Knopf, 2005), 334.
4. Edward Dreyer, *Zheng He* (New York: Pearson Longman, 2007).
5. Louise Levanthes, *When China Ruled the Seas* (New York: Simon and Schuster, 1994), 175.
6. Niccolò Machiavelli, *The Prince* (New York: New American Library, 1952), 90, 94.
7. Christine de Pisan, *The Book of the City of Ladies*, translated by Rosalind Brown-Grant (New York: Penguin Books, 1999), pt. 1, p. 1.

8. Frank Viviano, "China's Great Armada," *National Geographic*, July 2005, 34.

9. Quoted in John J. Saunders, ed., *The Muslim World on the Eve of Europe's Expansion* (Englewood Cliffs, NJ: Prentice Hall, 1966), 41–43.

10. Quoted in C. R. N. Routh, *They Saw It Happen in Europe, 1450–1650* (Blackwell, 1965), 386.

11. Leo Africanus, *History and Description of Africa* (London: Hakluyt Society, 1896), 824–25.

12. Quoted in Craig A. Lockhard, *Southeast Asia in World History* (Oxford: Oxford University Press, 2009), 67.

13. Quoted in Patricia Risso, *Merchants and Faith* (Boulder, CO: Westview Press, 1995), 49.

14. Quoted in Stuart B. Schwartz, ed., *Victors and Vanquished* (Boston: Bedford/St. Martin's, 2000), 8.

15. Quoted in Michael E. Smith, *The Aztecs* (London: Blackwell, 2003), 108.

16. Smith, *Aztecs*, 220.

17. Quoted in Miguel Leon-Portilla, *Aztec Thought and Culture*, translated from the Spanish by Jack Emory Davis (Norman: University of Oklahoma Press, 1963), 7.

18. For a summary of this practice among the Aztecs and Incas, see Karen Vieira Powers, *Women in the Crucible of Conquest* (Albuquerque: University of New Mexico Press, 2005), chap. 1.

19. Ibid., 25.

20. Louise Burkhart, "Mexica Women on the Home Front," in *Indian Women of Early Mexico*, edited by Susan Schroeder et al. (Norman: University of Oklahoma Press, 1997), 25–54.

21. The "web" metaphor is derived from J. R. McNeill and William H. McNeill, *The Human Web* (New York: W. W. Norton, 2003).

22. Graph from David Christian, *Map of Time* (Berkeley: University of California Press, 2004), 343.

23. Quoted in Rosamund E. Mack, *Bazaar to Piazza* (Berkeley: University of California Press, 2002), 1.

24. This and all subsequent quotes come from Jerry Brotton, *The Renaissance Bazaar* (Oxford: Oxford University Press, 2002).

Part Four

1. Victor Lieberman, *Strange Parallels*, vol. 2 (Cambridge: Cambridge University Press, 2009).

Chapter 13

1. See Kevin Meerschaert, "U.S. Sen. Nelson Says Putin Wants to Rebuild Russian Empire," WJCT News, March 17, 2014, http://news.wjct.org/post/us-sen-nelson -says-putin-wants-rebuild-russian-empire; and Asli Aydintasbas, "Rebuilding the Turkish Empire: Fantasy or Reality?" *Advancing a Free Society*, April 17, 2013, http://www.hoover.org/research/rebuilding-turkish -empire-fantasy-or-reality.

2. Quoted in Thomas E. Skidmore and Peter H. Smith, *Modern Latin America* (New York: Oxford University Press, 2001), 15.

3. George Raudzens, ed., *Technology, Disease, and Colonial Conquest* (Boston: Brill Academic, 2003), xiv.

4. A major source for the life of Doña Marina is Bernal Díaz, *The Conquest of New Spain*, translated by J. M. Cohen (Baltimore: Penguin Books, 1963).

5. Charles C. Mann, *1493: Uncovering the New World Columbus Created* (New York: Alfred A. Knopf, 2011), 12.

6. Quoted in Noble David Cook, *Born to Die: Disease and the New World Conquest* (Cambridge: Cambridge University Press, 1998), 202.

7. Quoted ibid., 206.

8. Quoted in Charles C. Mann, *1491: New Revelations of the Americas before Columbus* (New York: Alfred A. Knopf, 2005), 56.

9. Geoffrey Parker, *Global Crisis* (New Haven, CT: Yale University Press, 2013), chap. 15.

10. Quoted in Mann, *1493*, 165.

11. Felipe Fernandez-Armesto, "Empires in Their Global Context," in *The Atlantic in Global History*, edited by Jorge Canizares-Esguerra and Erik R. Seeman (Upper Saddle River, NJ: Prentice Hall, 2007), 105.

12. Quoted in Alejandro Lugo, *Fragmented Lives; Assembled Parts* (Austin: University of Texas Press, 2008), 53.

13. Quoted in Anthony Padgen, "Identity Formation in Spanish America," in *Colonial Identity in the Atlantic World, 1500–1800*, edited by Nicholas Canny and Anthony Padgen (Princeton, NJ: Princeton University Press, 1987), 56.

14. Colin M. MacLachlan and Jaime E. Rodriguez, *The Forging of the Cosmic Race* (Berkeley: University of California Press, 1990), 244–45.

15. Ann Twinam, "Women and Gender in Colonial Latin America," in *Women's History in Global Perspective*, edited by Bonnie G. Smith (Urbana: University of Illinois Press, 2005), 2:195.

16. Quoted in James Lockhart and Stuart B. Schwartz, *Early Latin America* (Cambridge: Cambridge University Press, 1983), 206.

17. Mary Prince, *The History of Mary Prince* (1831; Project Gutenberg, 2006), http://www.gutenberg.org/ebooks /17851.

18. Derived from Skidmore and Smith, *Modern Latin America*, 25.

19. Kevin Reilly et al., eds., *Racism: A Global Reader* (Armonk, NY: M. E. Sharpe, 2003), 136–37.

20. Felipe Fernandez-Armesto, *The Americas: A Hemispheric History* (New York: Modern Library, 2003), 58–59.

21. Benjamin Wadsworth, *The Well-Ordered Family* (1712), 39.

22. Willard Sutherland, *Taming the Wild Fields: Colonization and Empire on the Russian Steppe* (Ithaca, NY: Cornell University Press, 2004), 223–24.

23. Quoted in Michael Khodarkovsky, *Russia's Steppe Frontier* (Bloomington: Indiana University Press, 2002), 216.

24. Andreas Kappeler, *The Russian Empire* (New York: Longman, 2001), 115–17, 397–99.

25. Khodarkovsky, *Russia's Steppe Frontier*, 222.

26. Geoffrey Hosking, "The Freudian Frontier," *Times Literary Supplement*, March 10, 1995, 27.

27. Peter Perdue, *China Marches West: The Qing Conquest of Central Eurasia* (Cambridge, MA: Harvard University Press, 2005), 10–11.

28. Quoted in Stephen F. Dale, "The Islamic World in the Age of European Expansion," in *The Cambridge Illustrated History of the Islamic World*, edited by Francis Robinson (Cambridge: Cambridge University Press, 1996), 80.

29. Quoted in P. Lewis, *Pirs, Shrines, and Pakistani Islam* (Rawalpindi, Pakistan: Christian Study Centre, 1985), 84.

30. Quoted in Stanley Wolpert, *A New History of India* (New York: Oxford University Press, 1993), 160.

31. Lewis Melville, *Lady Mary Wortley Montagu: Her Life and Letters* (Whitefish, MT: Kessinger, 2004), 88.

32. Jane I. Smith, "Islam and Christendom," in *The Oxford History of Islam*, edited by John Esposito (Oxford: Oxford University Press, 1999), 342.

33. Charles Thornton Forester and F. H. Blackburne Daniell, *The Life and Letters of Ogier Ghiselin de Busbecq* (London: C. Kegan Paul, 1881), 1:405–6.

34. Caroline Finkel, *Osman's Dream: The History of the Ottoman Empire* (New York: Basic Books, 2007), 231–33.

35. Jean Bodin, "The Rise and Fall of Commonwealths," chap. 7, Constitution Society, accessed February 21, 2012, http://www.constitution.org/bodin/bodin_4.htm.

36. Speros Vryonis, "Isidore Glabas and the Turkish Devshirme," *Speculum* 31, no. 3 (1956): 436–37.

37. Kathryn Hain, "Devshirme Is a Contested Practice," *Utah Historical Review* 2 (2012): 175.

Chapter 14

1. Jacob Wheeler, "From Slave Post to Museum," *Christian Science Monitor*, December 31, 2002.

2. M. N. Pearson, ed., *Spices in the Indian Ocean World* (Aldershot: Valorium, 1996), xv.

3. Quoted in Paul Lunde, "The Coming of the Portuguese," *Saudi Aramco World*, July/August 2005, 56.

4. Quoted in Patricio N. Abinales and Donna J. Amoroso, *State and Society in the Philippines* (Lanham, MD: Rowman and Littlefield, 2005), 50.

5. Quoted in Craig A. Lockard, *Southeast Asia in World History* (Oxford: Oxford University Press, 2009), 85.

6. Anthony Reid, *Southeast Asia in the Age of Commerce, 1450–1680* (New Haven, CT: Yale University Press, 1993), 2:274, 290.

7. Tonio Andrade, *How Taiwan Became Chinese* (New York: Columbia University Press, 2008).

8. Anthony Reid, *Charting the Shape of Early Modern Southeast Asia* (Chiang Mai: Silkworm Books, 1999), 227.

9. Quoted in Adam Clulow, "Like Lambs in Japan and Devils outside Their Land: Diplomacy, Violence, and Japanese Merchants in Southeast Asia," *Journal of World History* 24, no. 2 (2013): 343.

10. Kenneth Pomeranz and Steven Topic, *The World That Trade Created* (Armonk, NY: M. E. Sharpe, 2006), 28.

11. Makrand Mehta, *Indian Merchants and Entrepreneurs in Historical Perspective* (Delhi: Academic Foundation, 1991), chap. 4.

12. Andre Gunder Frank, *ReOrient: Global Economy in the Asian Age* (Berkeley: University of California Press, 1998), 131.

13. Quoted in Richard von Glahn, "Myth and Reality of China's Seventeenth Century Monetary Crisis," *Journal of Economic History* 56, no. 2 (1996): 132.

14. Dennis O. Flynn and Arturo Giraldez, "Born with a 'Silver Spoon,'" *Journal of World History* 6, no. 2 (1995): 210.

15. Quoted in John Hemming, *The Conquest of the Incas* (New York: Harcourt, 1970), 372.

16. Quoted in Mark Elvin, *The Retreat of the Elephant* (New Haven, CT: Yale University Press, 2004), 37.

17. Quoted in Robert Marks, *The Origins of the Modern World* (Lanham, MD: Rowman and Littlefield, 2002), 81.

18. See John Richards, *The Endless Frontier* (Berkeley: University of California Press, 2003), pt. 4. Much of this section is drawn from this source.

19. Quoted in Elspeth M. Veale, *The English Fur Trade in the Later Middle Ages* (Oxford: Clarendon Press, 1966), 141.

20. Quoted in Herbert Milton Sylvester, *Indian Wars of New England* (Cleveland, 1910), 1:386.

21. Quoted in Richards, *Endless Frontier*, 499.

22. Richards, *Endless Frontier*, 504.

23. Quoted in "Fur Trader," The Iroquois Confederacy, Portland State University Graduate School of Education, October 1, 2001, http://www.iroquoisdemocracy.pdx.edu/html/furtrader.htm.

24. Pamela McVay, *Envisioning Women in World History* (New York: McGraw-Hill, 2009), 86.

25. These figures derive from the Trans-Atlantic Slave Trade Database, accessed December 11, 2014, http://www.slavevoyages.org/tast/assessment/estimates.faces.

26. Quoted in Charles E. Curran, *Change in Official Catholic Moral Teaching* (Mahwah, NJ: Paulist Press, 2003), 67.

27. David Brion Davis, *Challenging the Boundaries of Slavery* (Cambridge, MA: Harvard University Press, 2003), 13.

28. Quoted in Bernard Lewis, *Race and Slavery in the Middle East* (New York: Oxford University Press, 1990), 52–53.

29. Audrey Smedley, *Race in North America* (Boulder, CO: Westview Press, 1993), 57.

30. Kevin Reilly et al., eds., *Racism: A Global Reader* (Armonk, NY: M. E. Sharpe, 2003), 131.

31. Quoted in Donald R. Wright, *The World and a Very Small Place in Africa* (Armonk, NY: M. E. Sharpe, 1997), 109–10.

32. John Thornton, *Africa and Africans in the Making of the Atlantic World* (Cambridge: Cambridge University Press, 1998), 72.

33. Thomas Phillips, "A Journal of a Voyage Made in the Hannibal of London in 1694," in *Documents Illustrative of the History of the Slave Trade to America*, edited by Elizabeth Donnan (Washington, DC: Carnegie Institute, 1930), 399–410.

34. Erik Gilbert and Jonathan T. Reynolds, *Africa in World History* (Upper Saddle River, NJ: Pearson Educational, 2004), 160.

35. Trans-Atlantic Slave Trade Database, accessed December 11, 2014, http://www.slavevoyages.org/tast/assessment/estimates.faces.

36. Paul Adams et al., *Experiencing World History* (New York: New York University Press, 2000), 334.

37. Anne Bailey, *African Voices in the Atlantic Slave Trade* (Boston: Beacon Press, 2005), 153–54.

38. This account is based largely on Thomas Bluett, *Some Memoirs of the Life of Job . . .* (London, 1734), http://docsouth.unc.edu/neh/bluett/bluett.html/; and James T. Campbell, *Middle Passages* (New York: Penguin Books, 2007), 1–14.

39. Francis Moore, *Travels into the Inland Parts of Africa* (London, 1755), 146–47.

40. Erik Gilbert and Jonathan Reynolds, *Trading Tastes: Commodity and Cultural Exchange to 1750* (Upper Saddle River, NJ: Pearson/Prentice Hall, 2006), 9.

41. Quoted in Alex Szogyi, ed., *Chocolate: Food of the Gods* (Santa Barbara, CA: Greenwood Press, 1997), 166.

42. James Grehan, "Smoking and 'Early Modern' Sociability: The Great Tobacco Debate in the Ottoman Middle East (Seventeenth to Eighteenth Centuries)," *American Historical Review* 111, no. 5 (2006): 1352–77.

Chapter 15

1. Andrew Rice, "Mission from Africa," *New York Times Magazine*, April 8, 2009; "African Missionaries Take Religion to the West," *Church Shift*, August 7, 2006, http://www.churchshift.org/in-the-press/70-african-missionaries-take-religion-to-the-west.

2. Quoted in http://frontline-org-za.win03.glodns.net/articles/thereformation_lectures.htm (accessed December 18, 2014).

3. Glenn J. Ames, *Vasco da Gama: Renaissance Crusader* (New York: Pearson/Longman, 2005), 50.

4. Cecil Jane, ed. and trans., *Selected Documents Illustrating the Four Voyages of Columbus* (London: Hakluyt Society, 1930–1933), 2:2–18.

5. Nancy E. van Deusen, "Úrsula de Jesús," in *The Human Tradition in Colonial Latin America*, edited by Kenneth J. Andrien (Wilmington, DE: Scholarly Resources, 2002), 88–103; Úrsula de Jesús, *The Souls of Purgatory: The Spiritual Diary of a Seventeenth-Century Afro-Peruvian Mystic*, edited and with a scholarly introduction by Nancy E. van Deusen (Albuquerque: University of New Mexico Press, 2004).

6. Quoted in Marysa Navarro et al., *Women in Latin America and the Caribbean* (Bloomington: Indiana University Press, 1999), 37.

7. Quoted in James Rinehart, *Apocalyptic Faith and Political Violence* (New York: Palgrave Macmillan, 2006), 42.

8. Quoted in Nicolas Griffiths, *The Cross and the Serpent* (Norman: University of Oklahoma Press, 1996), 263.

9. Quoted in Joanna Waley-Cohen, *The Sextants of Beijing* (New York: W. W. Norton, 1999), 76–77.

10. Richard M. Eaton, "Islamic History as Global History," in *Islamic and European Expansion*, edited by Michael Adas (Philadelphia: Temple University Press, 1993), 25.

11. Patricia Buckley Ebrey, ed. and trans., *Chinese Civilization: A Sourcebook* (New York: Free Press, 1993), 257.

12. Robert Bly and Jane Hirshfield, trans., *Mirabai: Ecstatic Poems* (Boston: Beacon Press, 2004), ix–xi.

13. Quoted in Steven Shapin, *The Scientific Revolution* (Chicago: University of Chicago Press, 1996), 66.

14. This section draws heavily on Toby E. Huff, *The Rise of Early Modern Science* (Cambridge: Cambridge University Press, 2004), 47, 52, 76.

15. Ibid., 87, 288.

16. Jerome Cardano, *The Book of My Life*, translated by Jean Stoner (London: J. M. Dent, 1931), 189.

17. Quoted in Shapin, *Scientific Revolution*, 28.

18. Quoted ibid., 61.

19. Quoted in Andrew Lossky, *The Seventeenth Century: Sources in Western Civilization* (New York: Free Press, 1967), 72.

20. Quoted in Shapin, *Scientific Revolution*, 33.

21. For this observation, see Clifford R. Backman, *The Cultures of the West: A History* (Oxford: Oxford University Press, 2013), 473.

22. Pope John Paul II, "Faith Can Never Conflict with Reason," *L'Osservatore Romano*, November 4, 1992.

23. Quoted in Lossky, *Seventeenth Century*, 88.

24. Quoted in Shapin, *Scientific Revolution*, 68.

25. David C. Lindberg and Ronald L. Numbers, "Beyond War and Peace: A Reappraisal of the Encounter between Christianity and Science," *Perspectives on Science and Christian Faith* 39, no. 3 (1987): 140–49.

26. H. S. Thayer, ed., *Newton's Philosophy of Nature: Selections from His Writings* (New York: Hafner Library of Classics, 1953), 42.

27. Immanuel Kant, "What Is Enlightenment?" translated by Peter Gay, in *Introduction to Contemporary Civilization in the West* (New York: Columbia University Press, 1954), 1071.

28. Voltaire, *A Treatise on Toleration* (1763), chap. 22, http://www.constitution.org/volt/tolerance.htm.

29. Quoted in Margaret C. Jacob, *The Enlightenment* (Boston: Bedford/St. Martin's, 2001), 103.

30. Quoted in Karen Offen, *European Feminisms, 1700–1950* (Stanford, CA: Stanford University Press, 2000), 39.

31. Quoted in Toby E. Huff, *Intellectual Curiosity and the Scientific Revolution* (Cambridge: Cambridge University Press, 2010), 48.

32. Quoted in Jonathan Spence, *The Search for Modern China* (New York: W. W. Norton, 1999), 104.

33. Waley-Cohen, *Sextants of Beijing*, 105–14.

34. Benjamin A. Elman, *On Their Own Terms: Science in China, 1550–1900* (Cambridge, MA: Harvard University Press, 2005).

35. Quoted in David R. Ringrose, *Expansion and Global Interaction, 1200–1700* (New York: Longman, 2001), 188.

36. Quoted in Sergiusz Michalski, *The Reformation and the Visual Arts* (New York: Routledge, 1993), 7.

37. Quoted in Angela Vanhaelen, "Iconoclasm and the Creation of Images in Emanuel de Witte's *Old Church in Amsterdam*," *Art Bulletin*, June 2005, 5.

38. David Brett, *The Plain Style* (Cambridge: Letterworth Press, 2004), 61–62.

39. Gauvin Alexander Bailey, *Art on the Jesuit Missions in Asia and Latin America* (Toronto: University of Toronto Press, 1999), 102–4.

40. John W. O'Malley et al., *The Jesuits* (Toronto: University of Toronto Press, 1999), 381.

Part Five

1. Quoted in Ross Dunn, *The New World History* (Boston: Bedford/St. Martin's, 2000), 17.

2. William H. McNeill, "*The Rise of the West* after 25 Years," *Journal of World History* 1, no. 1 (1990): 7.

Chapter 16

1. Quoted in Keith M. Baker, "A World Transformed," *Wilson Quarterly* (Summer 1989): 37.

2. Quoted in Thomas Benjamin et al., *The Atlantic World in the Age of Empire* (Boston: Houghton Mifflin, 2001), 205.

3. Jack P. Greene, "The American Revolution," *American Historical Review* 105, no. 1 (2000): 96–97.

4. Quoted ibid., 102.

5. Quoted in Susan Dunn, *Sister Revolutions* (New York: Faber and Faber, 1999), 11, 12.

6. Quoted ibid., 9.

7. Quoted in Lynn Hunt et al., *The Making of the West* (Boston: Bedford/St. Martin's, 2003), 625.

8. Lynn Hunt, ed., *The French Revolution and Human Rights* (Boston: Bedford, 1996), 123.

9. Bonnie S. Anderson and Judith P. Zinsser, *A History of Their Own* (New York: Harper and Row, 1988), 283.

10. Hunt, *French Revolution*, 29.

11. From James Leith, "Music for Mass Persuasion during the Terror," copyright James A. Leith, Queen's University Kingston.

12. Franklin W. Knight, "The Haitian Revolution," *American Historical Review* 105, no. 1 (2000): 103.

13. Quoted in David P. Geggus, *Haitian Revolutionary Studies* (Bloomington: Indiana University Press, 2002), 27.

14. John C. Chasteen, *Born in Blood and Fire* (New York: W. W. Norton, 2006), 103.

15. Peter Winn, *Americas: The Changing Face of Latin America and the Caribbean* (Berkeley: University of California Press, 2006), 83.

16. Quoted in Thomas E. Skidmore and Peter H. Smith, *Modern Latin America* (New York: Oxford University Press, 2001), 33.

17. Quoted in David Armitage and Sanjay Subrahmanyam, eds., *The Age of Revolutions in Global Context, c. 1760–1840* (New York: Palgrave Macmillan, 2010), xxiii.

18. James Walvin, "The Public Campaign in England against Slavery," in *The Abolition of the Atlantic Slave Trade*, edited by David Eltis and James Walvin (Madison: University of Wisconsin Press, 1981), 76.

19. Michael Craton, "Slave Revolts and the End of Slavery," in *The Atlantic Slave Trade*, edited by David Northrup (Boston: Houghton Mifflin, 2002), 200.

20. Ludmilla A. Trigos, *The Decembrist Myth in Russian Culture* (New York: Palgrave Macmillan, 2009), xv–xxiii.

21. Joseph Dupuis, *Journal of a Residence in Ashantee* (London: Henry Colburn, 1824), 162–64.

22. Eric Foner, *Nothing but Freedom* (Baton Rouge: Louisiana State University Press, 1983).

23. Quoted in Daniel Moran and Arthur Waldron, eds., *The People in Arms: Military Myth and National Mobilization since the French Revolution* (Cambridge: Cambridge University Press, 2003), 14.

24. Barbara Winslow, "Feminist Movements: Gender and Sexual Equality," in *A Companion to Gender History*, edited by Teresa A. Meade and Merry E. Wiesner-Hanks (London: Blackwell, 2004), 186.

25. Quoted in Claire G. Moses, *French Feminism in the Nineteenth Century* (Albany: SUNY Press, 1984), 135.

26. Raden Adjeng Kartini, *Letters of a Javanese Princess* (New York: W. W. Norton, 1964). Unless otherwise noted, all quotes come from this source.

27. Quoted in Jooste Cote, "Raden Ajeng Kartini," in *Gender, Colonialism and Education*, edited by Joyce Goodman and Jayne Martin (London: Woburn Press, 2002), 204.

Chapter 17

1. R. K. Prabhu and U. R. Rao, eds., *The Mind of Mahatma Gandhi* (Ahmedabad, India: Navjeevan Trust, 1960); Mahatma Gandhi's Writings, Philosophy, Audio, Video & Photographs, under "The Curse of Industrialization," http://www.mkgandhi.org/momgandhi/chap49.htm.

2. Edmund Burke III and Kenneth Pomeranz, eds., *The Environment and World History* (Berkeley: University of California Press, 2009), 41.

3. Gregory T. Cushman, *Guano and the Opening of the Pacific World* (Cambridge: Cambridge University Press, 2013), chaps. 1–3.

4. Ricardo Duchesne, *The Uniqueness of Western Civilization* (Leiden: Brill, 2011).

5. Joel Mokyr, *The Lever of Riches* (New York: Oxford University Press, 1990), 40–44.

6. Lynda Shaffer, "Southernization," *Journal of World History* 5, no. 1 (1994): 1–21.

7. Kenneth Pomeranz, *The Great Divergence* (Princeton, NJ: Princeton University Press, 2000). See also Jack Goldstone, *Why Europe? The Rise of the West in World History, 1500–1850* (Boston: McGraw-Hill, 2009).

8. Pier Vries, "Are Coal and Colonies Really Crucial?" *Journal of World History* 12, no. 2 (2001): 411.

9. E. L. Jones, *The European Miracle* (Cambridge: Cambridge University Press, 1981), 119.

10. David Christian, *Maps of Time* (Berkeley: University of California Press, 2004), 390.

11. Quoted in Mokyr, *Lever of Riches*, 188.

12. Quoted in Prasannan Parthansaranthi, "Rethinking Wages and Competitiveness in the Eighteenth Century," *Past and Present* 158 (February 1998): 79.

13. Maxine Berg, *Luxury and Pleasure in Eighteenth-Century Britain* (Oxford: Oxford University Press, 2005), 79–84.

14. Peter Stearns, *The Industrial Revolution in World History* (Boulder, CO: Westview Press, 1998), 36.

15. Goldstone, *Why Europe?* chap. 8.

16. Eric Hopkins, *Industrialization and Society* (London: Routledge, 2000), 2.

17. Mokyr, *Lever of Riches*, 81.

18. Eric Hobsbawm, *Industry and Empire* (New York: New Press, 1999), 58. This section draws heavily on Hobsbawm's celebrated account of British industrialization.

19. Samuel Smiles, *Thrift* (London: John Murray, 1875), 30–40.

20. Quoted in Bonnie S. Anderson and Judith P. Zinsser, *A History of Their Own* (New York: Harper and Row, 1988), 2:131.

21. Hobsbawm, *Industry and Empire*, 65.

22. Peter Stearns and John H. Hinshaw, *Companion to the Industrial Revolution* (Santa Barbara, CA: ABC-CLIO, 1996), 150.

23. Quoted in Herbert Vere Evatt, *The Tolpuddle Martyrs* (Sydney: Sydney University Press, 2009), 49.

24. Ellen Johnston, *Autobiography, Poems, and Songs* (Glasgow: William Love, 1867; Google Books, 2006), http://books.google.com/books/about/Autobiography_poems_and_songs.html?id=QUwCAAAAQAAJ.

25. Hobsbawm, *Industry and Empire*, 171.

26. Dirk Hoeder, *Cultures in Contact* (Durham, NC: Duke University Press, 2002), 331–32.

27. Carl Guarneri, *America in the World* (Boston: McGraw-Hill, 2007), 180.

28. Much of this feature draws from E. P. Thompson, *The Making of the English Working Class* (New York: Vintage Books, 1966).

29. Quoted in Hoeder, *Cultures in Contact*, 318.

30. Derived from Paul Kennedy, *The Rise and Fall of the Great Powers* (New York: Random House, 1987), 149.

31. John Charles Chasteen, *Born in Blood and Fire* (New York: W. W. Norton, 2006), 181.

32. Peter Bakewell, *A History of Latin America* (Oxford: Blackwell, 1997), 425.

33. Michael Adas, *Machines as the Measure of Men* (Ithaca, NY: Cornell University Press, 1990).

Chapter 18

1. Quoted in Robert Strayer, *The Making of Mission Communities in East Africa* (London: Heinemann, 1978), 89.

2. Quoted in Heinz Gollwitzer, *Europe in the Age of Imperialism* (London: Thames and Hudson, 1969), 136.

3. Quoted in Steven Roger Fischer, *A History of the Pacific Islands* (New York: Palgrave Macmillan, 2013), 112.

4. Charles Griffith, *The Present State and Prospects of the Port Phillips District . . .* (Dublin: William Curry and Company, 1845), 169.

5. Robert Knox, *Races of Man* (Philadelphia: Lea and Blanchard, 1850), v.

6. Quoted in Ralph Austen, ed., *Modern Imperialism* (Lexington, MA: D. C. Heath, 1969), 70–73.

7. Quoted in Julian Burger, "Echoes of History," *New Internationalist*, August 1988, http://www.newint.org /issue186/echoes.htm.

8. Quoted in John Iliffe, *Africans: The History of a Continent* (Cambridge: Cambridge University Press, 1995), 191.

9. Quoted in Nicholas Tarling, "The Establishment of Colonial Regimes," in *The Cambridge History of Southeast Asia*, edited by Nicholas Tarling (Cambridge: Cambridge University Press, 1992), 2:76.

10. R. Meinertzhagen, *Kenya Diary* (London: Oliver and Boyd, 1957), 51–52.

11. Quoted in Neil Jamieson, *Understanding Vietnam* (Berkeley: University of California Press, 1993), 49–57.

12. Mrinalini Sinha, *Colonial Masculinity* (Manchester: Manchester University Press, 1995), 35; Jane Burbank and Frederick Cooper, *Empires in World History* (Princeton, NJ: Princeton University Press, 2010), 308–9.

13. Nupur Chaudhuri, "Clash of Cultures," in *A Companion to Gender History*, edited by Teresa A. Meade and Merry E. Wiesner-Hanks (London: Blackwell, 2004), 437.

14. Quoted in Donald R. Wright, *The World and a Very Small Place in Africa* (Armonk, NY: M. E. Sharpe, 2004), 170.

15. Quoted in Scott B. Cook, *Colonial Encounters in the Age of High Imperialism* (New York: HarperCollins, 1996), 53.

16. Craig Timberg and Daniel Halperin, *Tinderbox* (New York: Penguin Press, 2012), 52.

17. D. R. SarDesai, *Southeast Asia: Past and Present* (Boulder, CO: Westview Press, 1997), 95–98.

18. Quoted in G. C. K. Gwassa and John Iliffe, *Records of the Maji Maji Rising* (Nairobi: East African, 1967), 1:4–5.

19. Iliffe, *Africans*, 216.

20. Derived from Adam McKeown, "Global Migration, 1846–1940," *Journal of World History* 15, no. 2 (2004): 156.

21. Quoted in Basil Davidson, *Modern Africa* (London: Longman, 1983), 79, 81.

22. This section draws heavily on Margaret Jean Hay and Sharon Stichter, eds., *African Women South of the Sahara* (London: Longman, 1984), especially chaps. 1–5.

23. Jean Davison, *Voices from Mutira* (Boulder, CO: Lynne Reinner, 1996), 51–74.

24. Quoted in Robert A. Levine, "Sex Roles and Economic Change in Africa," in *Black Africa*, edited by John Middleton (London: Macmillan, 1970), 178.

25. Quoted in Mike Davis, *Late Victorian Holocausts* (London: Verso, 2001), 37.

26. Josiah Kariuki, *Mau Mau Detainee* (London: Oxford University Press, 1963), 5.

27. Quoted in Harry Benda and John Larkin, *The World of Southeast Asia* (New York: Harper and Row, 1967), 182–85.

28. Quoted in William Theodore de Bary, *Sources of Indian Tradition* (New York: Columbia University Press, 1958), 619.

29. Quoted in Edward W. Smith, *Aggrey of Africa* (London: SCM Press, 1929).

30. Strayer, *Making of Mission Communities*, 78–82, 136–39.

31. Unless otherwise noted, this essay and all the quotes derive from Philip Goldberg, *American Vedas* (New York: Harmony Books, 2010), 47–66; and Diana L. Eck, *A New Religious America* (New York: HarperCollins, 2001), 94–104.

32. Quoted in William Theodore de Bary, *Sources of Indian Tradition* (New York: Columbia University Press, 1958), 652.

33. C. A. Bayly, *The Birth of the Modern World* (Oxford: Blackwell, 2004), 343.

34. Nirad Chaudhuri, *Autobiography of an Unknown Indian* (London: John Farquharson, 1968), 229.

35. Edward Blyden, *Christianity, Islam, and the Negro Race* (Edinburgh: Edinburgh University Press, 1967), 124.

36. John Iliffe, *A Modern History of Tanganyika* (Cambridge: Cambridge University Press, 1979), 324.

Chapter 19

1. "Full Text of Hu Jintao's Speech," July 1, 2011, http:// cpcchina.chinadaily.com.cn/news/2011-07/01/content _12819337.htm. Accessed December 31, 2014.

2. Dun J. Li, ed., *China in Transition, 1517–1911* (New York: Van Nostrand Reinhold, 1969), 112.

3. Quoted in Jonathan D. Spence, *The Search for Modern China* (New York: W. W. Norton, 1999), 169.

4. Quoted in Vincent Shih, *The Taiping Ideology: Its Sources, Interpretations, and Influences* (Seattle: University of Washington Press, 1967), 73.

5. Barbara Hodgson, *Opium: A Portrait of the Heavenly Demon* (San Francisco: Chronicle Books, 1999), 32.

6. Hsin-Pao Chang, ed., *Commissioner Lin and the Opium War* (New York: W. W. Norton, 1970), 226–27.

7. This account of Lin Zexu draws from Spence, *Search for Modern China*; and Arthur Waley, *The Opium War through Chinese Eyes* (London: George Allen and Unwin, 1968).

8. Quoted in Teng Ssu and John K. Fairbanks, eds. and trans., *China's Response to the West* (New York: Atheneum, 1963), 69.

9. Quoted in Magali Morsy, *North Africa: 1800–1900* (London: Longman, 1984), 79.

10. Quoted in M. Sukru Hanioglu, *The Young Turks in Opposition* (New York: Oxford University Press, 1995), 17.

11. Marius B. Jansen, *The Making of Modern Japan* (Cambridge, MA: Harvard University Press, 2002), 33.

12. Quoted in Carol Gluck, "Themes in Japanese History," in *Asia in Western and World History*, edited by Ainslie T. Embree and Carol Gluck (Armonk, NY: M. E. Sharpe, 1997), 754.

13. Quoted in S. Hanley and K. Yamamura, *Economic and Demographic Change in Pre-Industrial Japan* (Princeton, NJ: Princeton University Press, 1977), 88–90.

14. Quoted in Harold Bolitho, "The Tempo Crisis," in *The Cambridge History of Japan*, vol. 5, *The Nineteenth Century*, edited by Marius B. Jansen (Cambridge: Cambridge University Press, 1989), 230.

15. Kenneth Henshall, *A History of Japan* (New York: Palgrave, 2004), 67.

16. Quoted in James L. McClain, *Japan: A Modern History* (New York: W. W. Norton, 2002), 177.

17. Quoted in Renée Worringer, *Ottomans Imagining Japan* (New York: Palgrave Macmillan, 2014), 59.

18. Quoted in Ono Kazuko, *Chinese Women in a Century of Revolution* (Stanford: Stanford University Press, 1989), 60.

19. Quoted in Jonathan D. Spence, *The Gate of Heavenly Peace* (New York: Penguin Books, 1981), 85.

20. Quoted in Charlotte Beahan, "Feminism and Nationalism in the Chinese Women's Press, 1902–1911," *Modern China* 1, no. 4 (1975): 384.

21. Quoted in J. A. Mangan and Fan Hong, eds., *Freeing the Female Body: Inspirational Icons* (London: Frank Cass Publishers, 2001), 45.

Part Six

1. J. R. McNeill, *Something New under the Sun* (New York: W. W. Norton, 2000), 3–4.

Chapter 20

1. John Innes, "Scotland's Oldest Man Turns 107," *Scotsman*, June 25, 2003, http://www.aftermathww1.com/oldestscot.asp; Associated Press, "One of Last British WWI Veterans Dies at 109," NBC News.com, November 21, 2005, http://www.nbcnews.com/id/10138446/.

2. Quoted in John Keegan, *The First World War* (New York: Vintage Books, 1998), 3.

3. Adapted from Lynn Hunt et al., *The Making of the West: Peoples and Cultures* (Boston: Bedford/St. Martin's, 2001), 1024.

4. Benito Mussolini, *The Political and Social Doctrine of Fascism*, translated by Jane Soames (London: Leonard and Virginia Woolf at the Hogarth Press, 1933).

5. Stanley Payne, *History of Fascism, 1914–1945* (Madison: University of Wisconsin Press, 1995), 208.

6. Quoted in Laurence Rees, *The Nazis: A Warning from History* (New York: New Press, 1997), 62.

7. Quoted in Claudia Koonz, *Mothers in the Fatherland* (New York: St. Martin's Press, 1987), 75.

8. Klaas A. D. Smelik, ed., *Etty: The Letters and Diaries of Etty Hillesum* (Grand Rapids: Erdmans, 2002).

9. Quoted in James L. McClain, *Japan: A Modern History* (New York: W. W. Norton, 2002), 378.

10. Quoted ibid., 414.

11. Quoted in Marius B. Jansen, *The Making of Modern Japan* (Cambridge, MA: Harvard University Press, 2000), 607.

12. Quoted ibid., 639.

13. Robert Jungk, *Brighter Than a Thousand Suns: A Personal History of the Atomic Scientists* (New York: Harcourt Brace, 1958), 201.

14. Quoted in John Keegan, *The Second World War* (New York: Viking Penguin, 1989), 186.

15. Merry E. Wiesner et al., *Discovering the Global Past*, 3rd ed. (Boston: Houghton Mifflin, 2007), 422.

16. Quoted in Kyosuke Yamamoto, "Drafts Show A-Bomb Survivor Bridged Differences in Anti-nuke Speech at U.N.," *Asahi Shimbun*, December 21, 2013, http://ajw.asahi.com/article/behind_news/social_affairs/AJ201312310065.

17. Quoted in Ralph F. Keeling, *Gruesome Harvest* (Chicago: Institute of American Economics, 1947), 60.

18. John Lewis Gaddis, *We Now Know: Rethinking Cold War History* (Oxford: Oxford University Press, 1997), 52.

19. Adam Gopnik, "The Big One: Historians Rethink the War to End All Wars," *New Yorker*, August 23, 2004, 78.

Chapter 21

1. Quoted in Ronald Suny, *The Soviet Experiment* (Oxford: Oxford University Press, 1998), 357.

2. Quoted in Bonnie S. Anderson and Judith P. Zinsser, *A History of Their Own* (New York: Harper and Row, 1988), 2:299.

3. Quoted in William M. Mandel, *Soviet Women* (Garden City, NJ: Doubleday, 1975), 44.

4. Yuan-tsung Chen, *The Dragon's Village* (New York: Penguin Books, 1980), 85.

5. Such figures are often highly controversial. See Maurice Meisner, *Mao's China and After* (New York: Free Press, 1999), 413–25; and Roderick MacFarquhar, ed., *The Politics of China* (Cambridge: Cambridge University Press, 1997), 243–45.

6. Douglas Weiner, "The Predatory Tribute-Taking State," in *The Environment and World History*, edited by Edmund Burke III and Kenneth Pomeranz (Berkeley: University of California Press, 2009), 284–90.

7. Richard F. Kaufman and John P. Hardt, eds., *The Former Soviet Union in Transition* (Armonk, NY: M. E. Sharpe, 1993), 580–83.

8. Barbara Engel and Anastasia Posadskaya-Vanderbeck, eds., *A Revolution of Their Own* (Boulder, CO: Westview Press, 1998), 17–46.

9. Quoted in John L. Gaddis, *The Cold War: A New History* (New York: Penguin Press, 2005), 57.

10. Quoted in Dean Rusk, *As I Saw It* (New York: Norton, 1990), 245.

11. Quoted in Frank Mankiewicz and Kirby Jones, *With Fidel: A Portrait of Castro and Cuba* (New York: Ballantine Books, 1976), 83.

12. Quoted in Paul Mason, *Cuba* (New York: Marshall Cavendish, 2010), 14.

13. Quoted in Peter Roman, *People's Power: Cuba's Experience with Representative Government* (Lanham, MD: Rowman and Littlefield, 2003), 63.

14. Ronald Steel, *Pax Americana* (New York: Viking Press, 1970), 254.

15. Quoted in Donald W. White, *The American Century* (New Haven, CT: Yale University Press, 1996), 164.

16. Deng Xiaoping, "The Necessity of Upholding the Four Cardinal Principles in the Drive for the Four Modernizations," in *Major Documents of the People's Republic of China* (Beijing: Foreign Language Press, 1991), 54.

17. Quoted in Abraham Brumberg, *Chronicle of a Revolution* (New York: Pantheon Books, 1990), 225–26.

18. Anchee Min et al., *Chinese Propaganda Posters* (Köln: Taschen, 2003), 5.

19. Quoted ibid., 10.

Chapter 22

1. Nelson Mandela, "Statement from the Dock . . . in the Rivonia Trial," African National Congress, April 20, 1964, http://www.anc.org.za/show.php?id=3430&t=Famous Speeches.

2. Quoted in Craig A. Lockard, *Southeast Asia in World History* (Oxford: Oxford University Press, 2009), 138–39.

3. Quoted in J. D. Legge, *Sukarno: A Political Biography* (New York: Praeger, 1972), 341.

4. Quoted in Jim Masselos, *Nationalism on the Indian Subcontinent* (Melbourne: Nelson, 1972), 122.

5. Mahatma Gandhi, *Indian Home Rule* (Auckland, New Zealand: The Floating Press, 2014), 35.

6. Quoted in Bidyut Chakrabarty, *Social and Political Thought of Mahatma Gandhi* (New York: Routledge, 2006), 139.

7. Quoted in Stanley Wolpert, *A New History of India* (Oxford: Oxford University Press, 1993), 331.

8. Badshah Khan, *My Life and Struggle* (Delhi: Hind Pocket Books, 1969), 96–97.

9. Jawaharlal Nehru, *The Discovery of India* (New York: John Day Co., 1946), 486.

10. Quoted in M. S. Korejo, *The Frontier Gandhi* (New York: Oxford University Press, 1993), 25.

11. Khan, *My Life*, 209–10.

12. Adapted and updated from Lynn Hunt et al., *The Making of the West: Peoples and Cultures* (Boston: Bedford/St. Martin's, 2009), 968; and Population Reference Bureau, *World Population Data Sheet, 2011*, http://www.prb.org/pdf11/2011population-data-sheet_eng.pdf.

13. Quoted in Paul E. Sigmund, *The Overthrow of Allende and the Politics of Chile* (Pittsburgh: University of Pittsburgh Press, 1977), 122.

14. 1950 data from United Nations, "World Urbanization Prospects, the 2011 Revision," Figure 11a; 2014 data from United Nations, Department of Economic and Social Affairs, Population Division (2014), *World Urbanization Prospects: The 2014 Revision, Highlights*, Table II, p. 26, http://esa.un.org/unpd/wup/Highlights/WUP2014-Highlights.pdf.

15. Quoted in Bernard Lewis, *The Emergence of Modern Turkey* (London: Oxford University Press, 1968), 268–69.

16. Quoted in Patrick B. Kinross, *Ataturk: A Biography of Mustafa Kemal* (New York: Morrow, 1965), 390.

17. Sandra Mackey, *The Iranians* (New York: Penguin, 1998), 306.

18. Elif Shafak, "Turkey's Culture Wars," *New York Times*, July 23, 2014.

Chapter 23

1. "Put Yourself in My Shoes: A Human Trafficking Victim Speaks Out," United Nations Office on Drugs and Crime, November 28, 2012, http://www.unodc.org/unodc/en/frontpage/2012/November/put-yourself-in-my-in-my-shoes-a-human-trafficking-victim-speaks-out.html.

2. Jeffry A. Frieden, *Global Capitalism: Its Fall and Rise in the Twentieth Century* (New York: W. W. Norton, 2006), 476.

3. Lester R. Brown, "Gross World Product, 1950–2009," in *World on the Edge* (New York: W. W. Norton, 2011; Earth Policy Institute), http://www.earth-policy.org/books/wote/wote_data.

4. United Nations, *Human Development Report 1997*, 2, http://hdr.undp.org/en/content/human-development-report-1997.

5. Michael Hunt, *The World Transformed* (Boston: Bedford/St. Martin's, 2004), 442.

6. Quoted in Frieden, *Global Capitalism*, 408.

7. "Map Supplement," *National Geographic* (Washington, DC: National Geographic Society, March 2011).

8. Quoted in Manfred B. Steger, *Globalization: A Very Short Introduction* (Oxford: Oxford University Press, 2003), 122.

9. Quoted in Frieden, *Global Capitalism*, 459.

10. Charles S. Maier, *Among Empires: American Ascendancy and Its Predecessors* (Cambridge, MA. Harvard University Press, 2006), chap. 5.

11. Quoted in Sarah Shaver Hughes and Brady Hughes, *Women in World History* (Armonk, NY: M. E. Sharpe, 1997), 2:268.

12. Susan Kent, "Worlds of Feminism," in *Women's History in Global Perspective*, edited by Bonnie G. Smith (Urbana: University of Illinois Press, 2004), 1:305–6.

13. Quoted in Wilhelmina Oduol and Wanjiku Mukabi Kabira, "The Mother of Warriors and Her Daughters: The Women's Movement in Kenya," in *Global Feminisms since 1945*, edited by Bonnie G. Smith (London: Routledge, 2000), 111.

14. Quoted in Mary E. Hawkesworth, *Globalization and Feminist Activism* (New York: Rowman and Littlefield, 2006), 124.

15. Phyllis Schlafly, *The Power of the Christian Woman* (Cincinnati: Standard, 1981), 117.

16. Karen Armstrong, *The Battle for God* (New York: Alfred A. Knopf, 2000), xi.

17. Quoted ibid., 273.

18. "Muslim Dolls Tackle 'Wanton Barbie,'" BBC News, March 5, 2002, http://news.bbc.co.uk/2/hi/middle _east/1856558.stm.

19. Quoted in John Esposito, *Unholy War* (Oxford: Oxford University Press, 2002), 57.

20. Quoted in Katherine Zoepf, "Barbie Pushed Aside in Mideast Cultural Shift. Little Girls Obsessed with Fulla in Scarf," *International Herald Tribune*, September 22, 2005, 2. The passages concerning Fulla are largely drawn from this article.

21. Quoted in Esposito, *Unholy War*, 63.

22. "Al Qaeda's Second Fatwah," PBS News Hour, February 23, 1998, http://www.pbs.org/newshour /updates/military-jan-june98-fatwa_1998/.

23. Anwar Ibrahim, "The Ardent Moderates," *Time*, September 23, 1996, 24.

24. Jan Zalasiewicz et al., "The New World of the Anthropocene," *Environmental Science and Technology* 44, no. 7 (2010): 2228–31.

25. See J. R. McNeill, *Something New under the Sun: An Environmental History of the Twentieth-Century World* (New York: W. W. Norton, 2001).

26. Naomi Klein, *This Changes Everything* (New York: Simon and Schuster, 2014), 2.

27. Center for Naval Analysis, *National Security and the Threat of Climate Change*, 2007, 6, http://www.cna.org/reports /climate.

28. This section on environmentalism draws heavily on Ramachandra Guha, *Environmentalism: A Global History* (New York: Longman, 2000).

29. Quoted ibid., 14.

30. Quoted ibid., 50, 53.

31. Guobin Yang, "Global Environmentalism Hits China," *Yale Global Online*, February 4, 2004, http://yaleglobal .yale.edu/content/global-environmentalism-hits -china.

32. Timothy Doyle, *Environmental Movements in Minority and Majority Worlds: A Global Perspective* (New Brunswick, NJ: Rutgers University Press, 2005).

33. Rachel Carson, *Silent Spring* (Boston: Houghton Mifflin, 1962), 103. In addition to Carson's book, this account of her life draws on Mark Hamilton Lytle, *The Gentle Subversive: Rachel Carson, "Silent Spring," and the Rise of the Environmental Movement* (New York: Oxford University Press, 2007), and Arlene R. Quaratiello, *Rachel Carson: A Biography* (Westport, CT: Greenwood Press, 2004).

34. Quoted in Shiraz Sidhva, "Saving the Planet: Imperialism in a Green Garb," *UNESCO Courier*, April 2001, 41–43.

Acknowledgments

Chapter 1

Document 1.3: Excerpts from pp. 145–48 from *Time Before Morning: Art and Myth of the Australian Aborigines* by Louis A. Allen. Copyright © 1975 by Louis A. Allen. Reprinted by permission of HarperCollins Publishers.

Document 1.4: Excerpts from pp. 215–19 from *Time Before Morning: Art and Myth of the Australian Aborigines* by Louis A. Allen. Copyright © 1975 by Louis A. Allen. Reprinted by permission of HarperCollins Publishers.

Chapter 2

"Come then, Enkidu" from *The Epic of Gilgamesh,* translated by Benjamin R. Foster. Copyright © 2001 by W. W. Norton & Company. Used by permission of W. W. Norton & Company, Inc.

"Now the scribe" from *Ancient Egyptian Literature: The New Kingdom* by Miriam Lichtheim. Reproduced with permission of University of California Press in the format Republish in a book via Copyright Clearance Center.

"He has come unto us" from Adolf Erman, *The Literature of the Ancient Egyptians,* translated by Aylward M. Blackman. Copyright © 1927 Methuen. Reproduced by permission of Taylor & Francis Books UK.

"In those days" from James B. Pritchard, editor, *Ancient Near Eastern Texts Relating to the Old Testament — Third Edition with Supplement.* © 1950, 1955, 1969 Princeton University Press. Reprinted by permission of Princeton University Press.

Chapter 8

"A tumbled confusion" from Mark Elvin, *The Retreat of the Elephants* (New Haven, CT: Yale University Press, 2004). Copyright © 2004 by Mark Elvin. Used by permission of Yale University press.

"Ever since the Western horsemen" from Edward A. Schafer, *The Golden Peaches of Samarkand: A Study of T'ang Exotics.* Reproduced with permission of UNIVERSITY OF CALIFORNIA PRESS in the format Republish in a book via Copyright Clearance Center.

"From utter darkness" from *Japanese Women Writers: A Biocritical Sourcebook,* by HIEKO IRIE MULHERN. Reproduced with permission of GREENWOOD PRESS, in the format Republish in a book via Copyright Clearance Center.

Chapter 10

Document 10.5: From *Popular Religion in Saxon England: Elf Charms in Context,* by Karen Louise Jolly (Chapel Hill: University of North Carolina Press, 1996). Copyright © 1996 by the University of North Carolina Press. Used by permission of the publisher, www.uncpress.unc.edu.

Chapter 11

Document 11.1: Excerpt from *The Secret History of the Mongols: The Origins of Chingis Khan.* An adaptation by Paul Kahn (San Francisco: North Point Press, 1984). Copyright © 1984 by Paul Kahn. Reprinted by permission of the author.

Chapter 12

"Truly do we live on earth" from AZTEC THOUGHT AND CULTURE: A STUDY OF THE ANCIENT NAHUATL MIND by MIGUEL LEON PORTILLA. Reproduced with permission of UNIVERSITY OF OKLAHOMA PRESS in the format Republish in a book via Copyright Clearance Center.

Chapter 13

Document 13.3: *Memoirs,* from *Louis XIV* by Robert Campbell, Pearson Education Limited. © Longman Group UK Limited 1993. Used by permission of Taylor & Francis Books UK.

Document 13.4: *The Incas of Pedro de Cieza de León* by PEDRO DE CIEZA DE LEÓN. Reproduced with permission of UNIVERSITY OF OKLAHOMA PRESS in the format Republish in a book via Copyright Clearance Center.

Chapter 15

"What I was paid" from *Mirabai,* translated by Robert Bly and Jane Hirschfield. Copyright © by Robert Bly and Jane Hirschfield. Reprinted by permission of Beacon Press, Boston.

Chapter 18

"Fine wine but no good friends" from Neil L. Jamieson, *Understanding Vietnam,* © 1995 by the Regents of the University of California, Published by the University of California Press. Used by permission of the University of California Press.

Chapter 19

Document 19.1: From *Sources of Chinese Tradition: From 1600 Through the Twentieth Century,* compiled by Wm. Theodore de Bary and Richard Lufrano. Copyright © 2000 by Columbia University Press. Reprinted with the permission of the publisher.

Chapter 20

Etty Hillesum material from Collection Jewish Historical Museum, Amsterdam. Used by permission of the Etty Hillesum Research Centre.

Document 20.1: Adolf Hitler, *Mein Kampf,* translated by Ralph Manheim (Boston: Houghton Mifflin, 1943). Published also by Hutchinson. Used by permission of Houghton Mifflin Harcourt and Random House Group Limited.

Document 20.2: Reprinted by permission of the publisher from *Kokutai No Hongi: Cardinal Principles of the National Entity of Japan*, translated by John Owen Gauntlett, and edited with an introduction by Robert King Hall, pp. 52, 79, 80, 81, 82, 83, 87, 89–90, 93, 94, 144–145, 178, 181–182, Cambridge, Mass.: Harvard University Press. Copyright © 1949 by the President and Fellows of Harvard College. Copyright © renewed 1977 by Robert King Hall.

Chapter 22

Document 22.4a: From Afghan Women's Writing Project: http:// awwproject.org/2010/06/hijab-the-beauty-of-muslim-women/. Used by permission.

Document 22.4b: From *Daily Mail*, June 24, 2009. Online: http:// www.dailymail.co.uk/debate/article-1195052/Why-I-British -Muslim-woman-want-burkha-banned-streets.html. Used by permission.

Index

power (authority). *See* authority
(power); kings and kingdoms;
political entries; specific countries
power (energy)
European sources of, 440
solar, 1058
power loom, 740
Prague Spring (Czechoslovakia),
957*(i)*, 1036
pre-Columbian Americas, 241–242,
522–529, 523*(m)*, 557–558
Prester John (mythical monarch),
603
Prince, Mary (Caribbean slave),
568
Prince, The (Machiavelli), 511–512
printing
China and, 326, 328, 329, 346, 348
Islam and, 346
privatization, globalization and, 1026
production
American empire of, 1033–1035
European innovation in, 440
Great Depression and, 892
products. *See also* trade; specific
goods
in American trade, 308
Silk Roads trade of, 284, 285–288
professions, European women in, 431
progress
Condorcet on, 673
Enlightenment belief in, 673
spread of agriculture and, 37
Progressives (U.S.), 762
proletariat, 778
Promised Land, 167
promissory notes, in China, 330
propaganda
Nazi, 899
in World War I, 888
writing as, 77–79
property ownership
by gender, 73, 75, 120, 212, 332, 339,
344
in Ottoman Empire, 582–583
in Spanish colonies, 567
prophets
Jewish (Hebrew), 148, 151*(t)*
Muhammad as, 367–368, 367*(i)*,
399–405
prosperity. *See* economy; wealth

protectionism, debt crisis and, 1030
protest(s). *See also* revolts and
rebellions; revolution(s); specific
protests
in 1960s, 1036
in Eastern Europe, 962
against globalization, 1033, 1067,
1068
social, 751–755
Protestantism. *See also* Christianity;
Protestant Reformation
Catholic differences with, 647*(t)*,
649
churches of, 649, 679–681, 680*(v)*
fundamentalism of, 1043
Protestant Reformation, 529, 645–
650, 648*(m)*. *See also*
Protestantism
Provisional Government (Russia),
934–935
Prussia, Poland and, 722*(i)*
psychology, Freud and, 675
Ptolemaic empire (Egypt), 116
Ptolemy (astronomer/
mathematician), 667
public health, in Latin America, 770
public works
in Chinese and Roman empires,
123
in Germany, 899
in Great Depression, 895
in Japan, 906
Pueblo Bonito, 256
pueblo peoples. *See* Ancestral Pueblo
people
Puerto Rico, United States and, 772
Punic Wars, 118
punishment
in Charlemagne's *Capitulary,* 451
in China, 122, 150, 197, 836, 841
Congo mutilation as, 803*(i)*
of European peasants, 731
in Gupta Empire, 133
in Mesopotamia, 71, 75
in Quran, 381, 382, 1047
of slaves in Americas, 568
in Zoroastrianism, 165
Punjab, Islam in, 384
Punt, 86
Pure Land Buddhism, 351
purges, in Soviet Union, 946–947

Puritans, 571, 652
Purusha (Indian god), 200, 201*(t)*
Putin, Vladimir (Russian president),
964, 1000
Pwa Saw (Pagan queen), 299
Pygmy people. *See* Batwa (Pygmy)
people
pyramids
in Egypt, 81, 83
Mesoamerican, 79, 80
in Teotihuacán, 70, 245, 245*(i)*
ziggurats as, 69
Pythagoras (Greek philosopher),
169

Qadiriya order (Sufi), 392
Qatar, 980*(m)*
Qianlong (Chinese emperor), 834
Qin dynasty (China), 122, 150
Qing dynasty (Manchu dynasty,
China), 658–659, 662
Chinese Empire under, 554, 577–
580, 579*(m)*
opposition to Han Chinese, 836,
843, 846
reforms in, 843–844, 863, 869
Taiping Uprising and, 836, 837
Western imperialism and, 841
Qin Shihuangdi (Chinese emperor),
122, 135, 150
Qiu Jin (Chinese revolutionary
woman), 843, 867, 868–869*(d)*
Quakers, 571, 649, 674, 715, 715*(i)*
women and, 648
quantum theory (physics), 675
Quechua language, 526
queen(s). *See also* specific rulers
in Egypt, 75
in Meroë, 234
Queen Mother of the West (deity),
331
quipu (counting device), 64, 78*(t)*,
309, 526
Quran (Koran), 367, 368
on creation, 168
laws based on, 377
as life guide, 1045
Muhammad's revelations in, 400
qualities valued in, 1018*(d)*
Sadat and, 1047
Salafis and, 1050

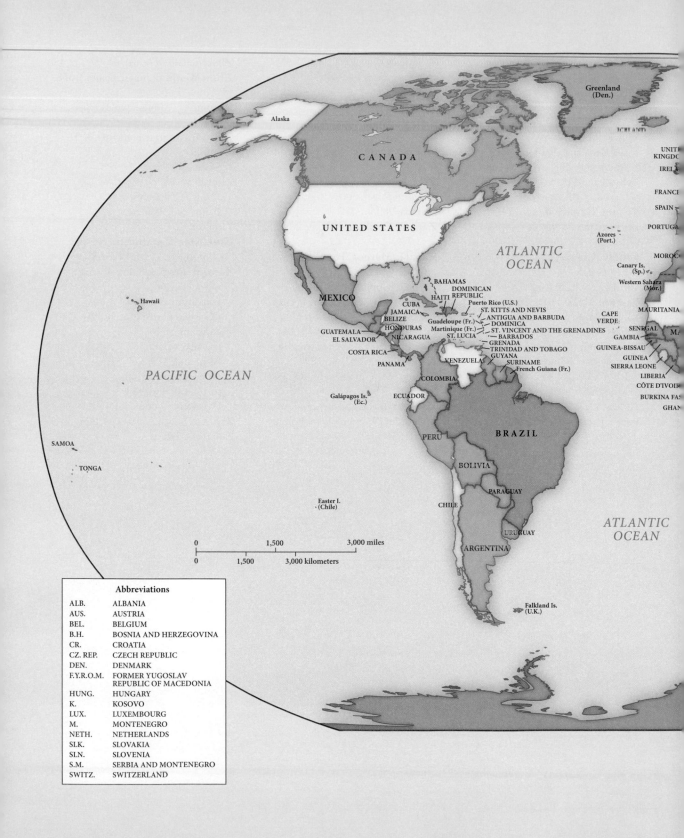

Greenland
(Den.)

ICELAND

Alaska

CANADA

UNITED
KINGDO

IRELA

FRANCE

UNITED STATES

ATLANTIC
OCEAN

SPAIN

PORTUGA

Azores
(Port.)

MOROC

Hawaii

MEXICO

BAHAMAS
DOMINICAN
REPUBLIC
CUBA   HAITI
JAMAICA
BELIZE
HONDURAS
GUATEMALA
EL SALVADOR   NICARAGUA

Puerto Rico (U.S.)
ST. KITTS AND NEVIS
ANTIGUA AND BARBUDA
Guadeloupe (Fr.)   DOMINICA
Martinique (Fr.)   ST. VINCENT AND THE GRENADINES
ST. LUCIA   BARBADOS
GRENADA
TRINIDAD AND TOBAGO
GUYANA

Canary Is.
(Sp.)

Western Sahara
(Mor.)

CAPE
VERDE

MAURITANIA

SENEGAL
GAMBIA
GUINEA-BISSAU
GUINEA
SIERRA LEONE
LIBERIA
CÔTE D'IVOIR
BURKINA FAS
GHAN

M

COSTA RICA

PANAMA

VENEZUELA

SURINAME
French Guiana (Fr.)

COLOMBIA

PACIFIC OCEAN

Galápagos Is.
(Ec.)

ECUADOR

PERU

BRAZIL

BOLIVIA

SAMOA

TONGA

Easter I.
(Chile)

CHILE

PARAGUAY

URUGUAY

ATLANTIC
OCEAN

ARGENTINA

0		1,500		3,000 miles
0	1,500	3,000 kilometers		

Falkland Is.
(U.K.)

Abbreviations	
ALB.	ALBANIA
AUS.	AUSTRIA
BEL.	BELGIUM
B.H.	BOSNIA AND HERZEGOVINA
CR.	CROATIA
CZ. REP.	CZECH REPUBLIC
DEN.	DENMARK
F.Y.R.O.M.	FORMER YUGOSLAV REPUBLIC OF MACEDONIA
HUNG.	HUNGARY
K.	KOSOVO
LUX.	LUXEMBOURG
M.	MONTENEGRO
NETH.	NETHERLANDS
SLK.	SLOVAKIA
SLN.	SLOVENIA
S.M.	SERBIA AND MONTENEGRO
SWITZ.	SWITZERLAND

ARCTIC   OCEAN

SWEDEN
FINLAND
ESTONIA
LATVIA
LITHUANIA
POLAND BELARUS
RMANY
UX. CZ. REP.
AUS. SLK.
IN. HUNG.
CRO.
B.H.
ITALY S.
ALB. M.FYROM.
GREECE
TUNISIA
MALTA

RUSSIAN FEDERATION

KAZAKHSTAN

UKRAINE
MOLDOVA
ROMANIA
BULGARIA
GEORGIA
ARMENIA
TURKEY
AZERBAIJAN
CYPRUS
ISRAEL
LEBANON
SYRIA
Gaza Strip
West Bank
JORDAN
KUWAIT
IRAQ
IRAN
BAHRAIN
QATAR
UNITED ARAB
EMIRATES
OMAN

UZBEKISTAN
KYRGYZSTAN
TURKMENISTAN
TAJIKISTAN
AFGHANISTAN
PAKISTAN

MONGOLIA

CHINA

N. KOREA
S. KOREA

JAPAN

PACIFIC OCEAN

TAIWAN

LIBYA
EGYPT

SAUDI ARABIA

YEMEN

NEPAL
BHUTAN
BANGLADESH
INDIA
MYANMAR
(BURMA)
THAILAND
LAOS
VIETNAM
CAMBODIA

PHILIPPINES

Mariana Is.
(U.S.)
Guam
(U.S.)

MARSHALL
IS.

IGER
CHAD
SUDAN
ERITREA
DJIBOUTI

SOUTH
SUDAN
ETHIOPIA
SOMALIA

MALDIVES

SRI
LANKA

BRUNEI
MALAYSIA

PALAU

FEDERATED STATES
OF MICRONESIA

NAURU
KIRIBATI

ERIA
NIN
O
AMEROON
GABON
RWANDA
UGANDA
KENYA
DEM. REP. OF
THE CONGO
BURUNDI
TANZANIA
CENTRAL
AFRICAN REP.

SINGAPORE

INDONESIA

PAPUA
NEW
GUINEA

SOLOMON
IS.

TUVALU

O
MÉ
NCIPE

COMOROS
SEYCHELLES

INDIAN OCEAN

EAST
TIMOR

VANUATU
FIJI

ANGOLA
ZAMBIA
MALAWI
ZIMBABWE
MADAGASCAR

New Caledonia
(Fr.)

NAMIBIA
BOTSWANA

MAURITIUS

AUSTRALIA

MOZAMBIQUE
SWAZILAND
SOUTH
AFRICA
LESOTHO

NEW
ZEALAND

Tasmania
(Aust.)

ANTARCTICA

ROCKY MTS.

APPALACHIAN MTS.

Mississippi R.

ATLANTIC
OCEAN

Tropic of Cancer

Gulf of
Mexico

PACIFIC OCEAN

Equator

Amazon R.

A
N
D
E
S

M
T
S

Tropic of Capricorn

ATLANTIC
OCEAN

URAL MTS.

Volga R.

Ob R.

L P S

Mediterranean Sea

SYRIAN
DESERT

GOBI

Yellow R.

HIMALAYA MTS.

Ganges

Yangzi R.

A R A

Nile R.

Tropic of Cancer

Arabian
Sea

Bay of
Bengal

South
China
Sea

PACIFIC OCEAN

Congo R.

Equator

INDIAN OCEAN

Zambezi R.

KALAHARI
DESERT

Tropic of Capricorn

Vegetation Zones

Tundra
Northern forest
Temperate forest
Temperate grassland
Desert and dry shrub
Mediterranean shrub
Mountain grassland
Tropical grassland and savanna
Tropical forest
Permanent ice cover